Ordnance Survey

STREET ATLAS
West Yorkshire

Contents

III *Key to map symbols*

IV-V *Key to map pages*

VI-VII *Route planning*

VIII *Administrative and post code boundaries*

1 *Street maps*

201 *Extra-large-scale maps of town centres*

- 201 *Bradford*
- 202 *Halifax*
- 204 *Leeds*
- 216 *Wakefield*

217 *Index of hospitals, industrial estates, railway stations, schools, shopping centres, street names and universities*

PHILIP'S

First edition published 1996
Second edition published 1999 by

Ordnance Survey® and George Philip Ltd, a division of Octopus Publishing Group Ltd
Romsey Road, Maybush, Southampton, SO16 4GU
2-4 Heron Quays, London, E14 4JP

ISBN 0-540-07671 6 (hardback)
ISBN 0-540-07672 4 (spiral)

To the best of the Publishers' knowledge, the information in this atlas was correct at the time of going to press. No responsibility can be accepted for any errors or their consequences.

The representation in this atlas of a road, track or path is no evidence of the existence of a right of way.

The mapping between pages 1 and 216 (inclusive) in this atlas is derived from Ordnance Survey® OSCAR® and Land-Line® data and Landranger® mapping.

Ordnance Survey, OSCAR, Land-line and Landranger are registered trade marks of Ordnance Survey, the national mapping agency of Great Britain.

Printed and bound in Spain by Cayfosa

Digital Data

The exceptionally high-quality mapping found in this book is available as digital data in TIFF format, which is easily convertible to other bit-mapped (raster) image formats.

The index is also available in digital form as a standard database table. It contains all the details found in the printed index together with the National Grid reference for the map square in which each entry is named and feature codes for places of interest in eight categories such as education and health.

For further information and to discuss your requirements, please contact the Ordnance Survey Solutions Centre on 01703 792929.

22a	**Motorway** (with junction number)
	Primary route (dual carriageway and single)
	A road (dual carriageway and single)
	B road (dual carriageway and single)
	Minor road (dual carriageway and single)
	Other minor road (dual carriageway and single)
	Road under construction
	Pedestrianised area
DY7	**Postcode boundaries**
	County and Unitary Authority boundaries
	Railway
	Tramway, miniature railway
	Rural track, private road or narrow road in urban area
	Gate or obstruction to traffic (restrictions may not apply at all times or to all vehicles)
	Path, bridleway, byway open to all traffic, road used as a public path

The representation in this atlas of a road, track or path is no evidence of the existence of a right of way

126 94	**Adjoining page indicators**
164	**The map area within the pink band is shown at a larger scale on the page indicated by the red block and arrow**

Acad	**Academy**	Meml	**Memorial**
Crem	**Crematorium**	Mon	**Monument**
Cemy	**Cemetery**	Mus	**Museum**
C Ctr	**Civic Centre**	Obsy	**Observatory**
CH	**Club House**	Pal	**Royal Palace**
Coll	**College**	PH	**Public House**
Ent	**Enterprise**	Recn Gd	**Recreation Ground**
Ex H	**Exhibition Hall**	Resr	**Reservoir**
Ind Est	**Industrial Estate**	Ret Pk	**Retail Park**
Inst	**Institute**	Sch	**School**
Ct	**Law Court**	Sh Ctr	**Shopping Centre**
L Ctr	**Leisure Centre**	TH	**Town Hall/House**
LC	**Level Crossing**	Trad Est	**Trading Estate**
Liby	**Library**	Univ	**University**
Mkt	**Market**	YH	**Youth Hostel**

Walsall	**Railway station**
U	**Glasgow Underground station**
	Midland Metro
M	**Metrolink station**
	London Underground station
D	**Docklands Light Railway station**
M	**Tyne and Wear Metro**
	Private railway station
	Bus, coach station
	Ambulance station
	Coastguard station
	Fire station
	Police station
	Accident and Emergency entrance to hospital
H	**Hospital**
+	**Church, place of worship**
i	**Information Centre** (open all year)
P P&R	**Parking, Park and Ride**
PO	**Post Office**
Prim Sch	**Important buildings, schools, colleges, universities and hospitals**
River Medway	**Water name**
	Stream
	River or canal (minor and major)
	Water
	Tidal water
	Woods
	Houses
House	**Non-Roman antiquity**
VILLA	**Roman antiquity**

■ The dark grey border on the inside edge of some pages indicates that the mapping does not continue onto the adjacent page ■ The small numbers around the edges of the maps identify the 1 kilometre National Grid lines

The scale of the maps is 5.52 cm to 1 km ($3\frac{1}{2}$ inches to 1 mile)

0 — 1/4 — 1/2 — 3/4 — 1 mile
0 — 250 m — 500 m — 750 m — 1 kilometre

The scale of the maps on pages numbered in red is 11.04 cm to 1 km (7 inches to 1 mile)

0 — 220 yards — 440 yards — 660 yards — 1/2 mile
0 — 125m — 250m — 375m — 1/2 kilometre

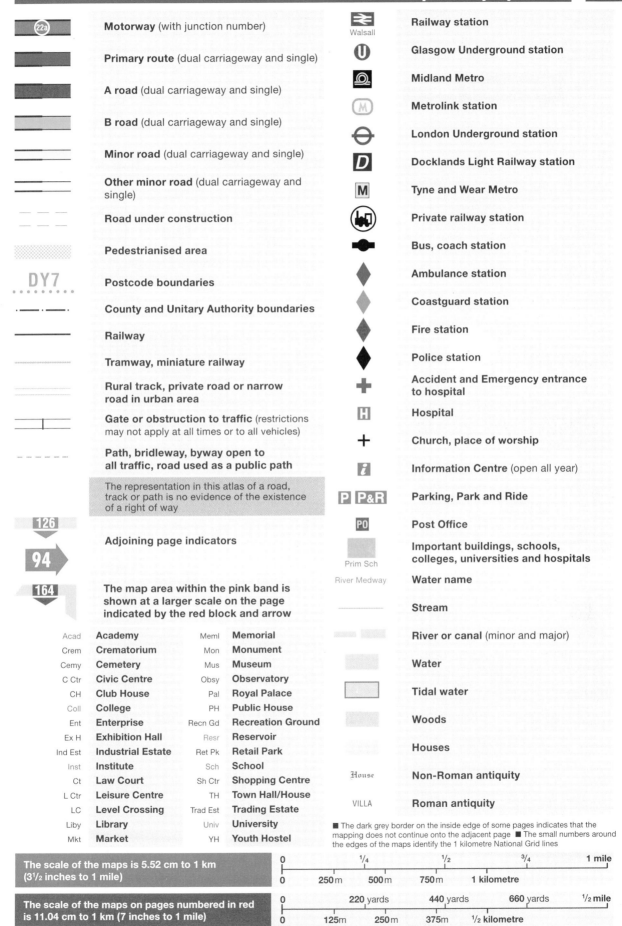

Key to map pages

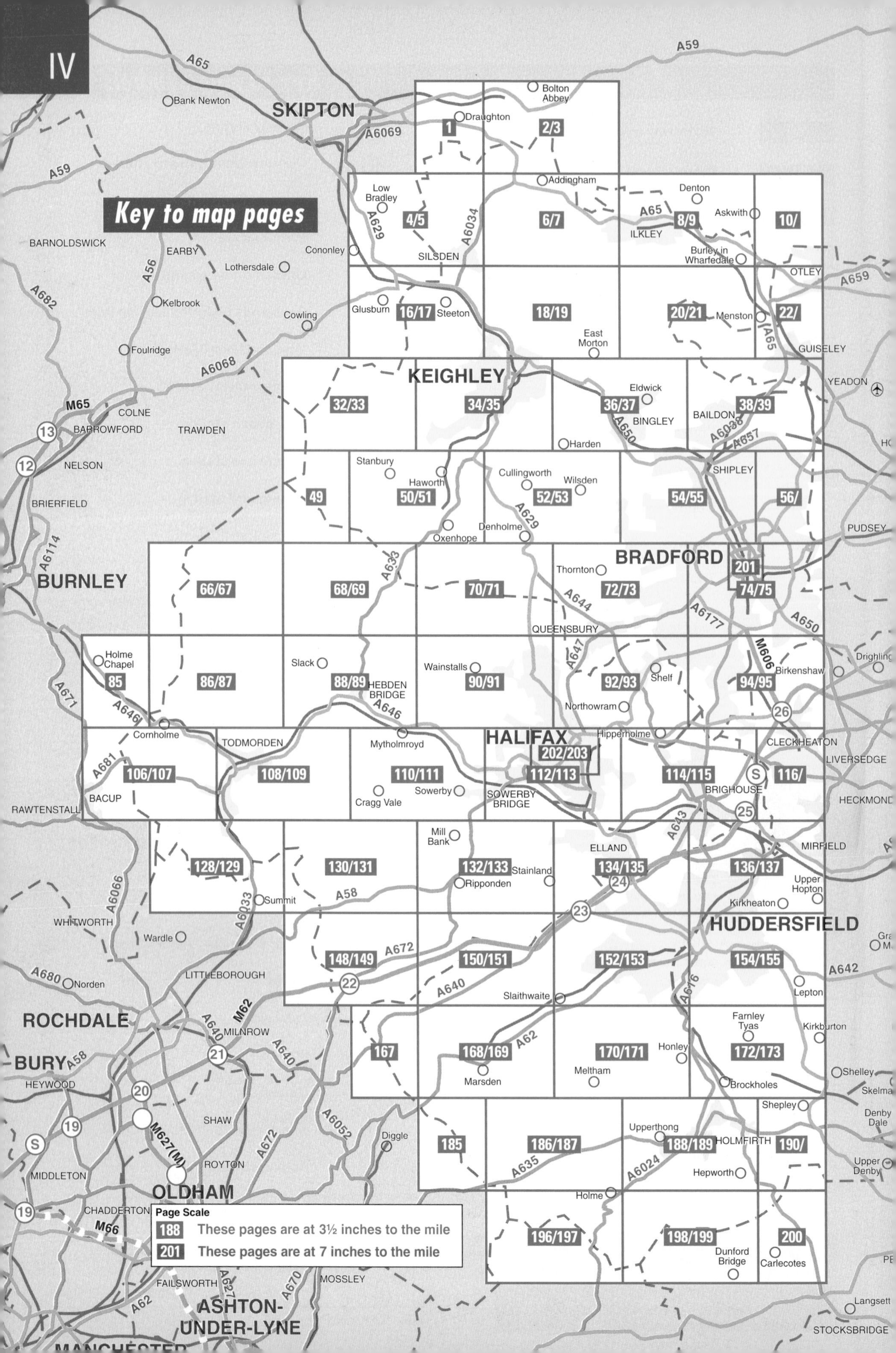

Page Scale

188 These pages are at 3½ inches to the mile

201 These pages are at 7 inches to the mile

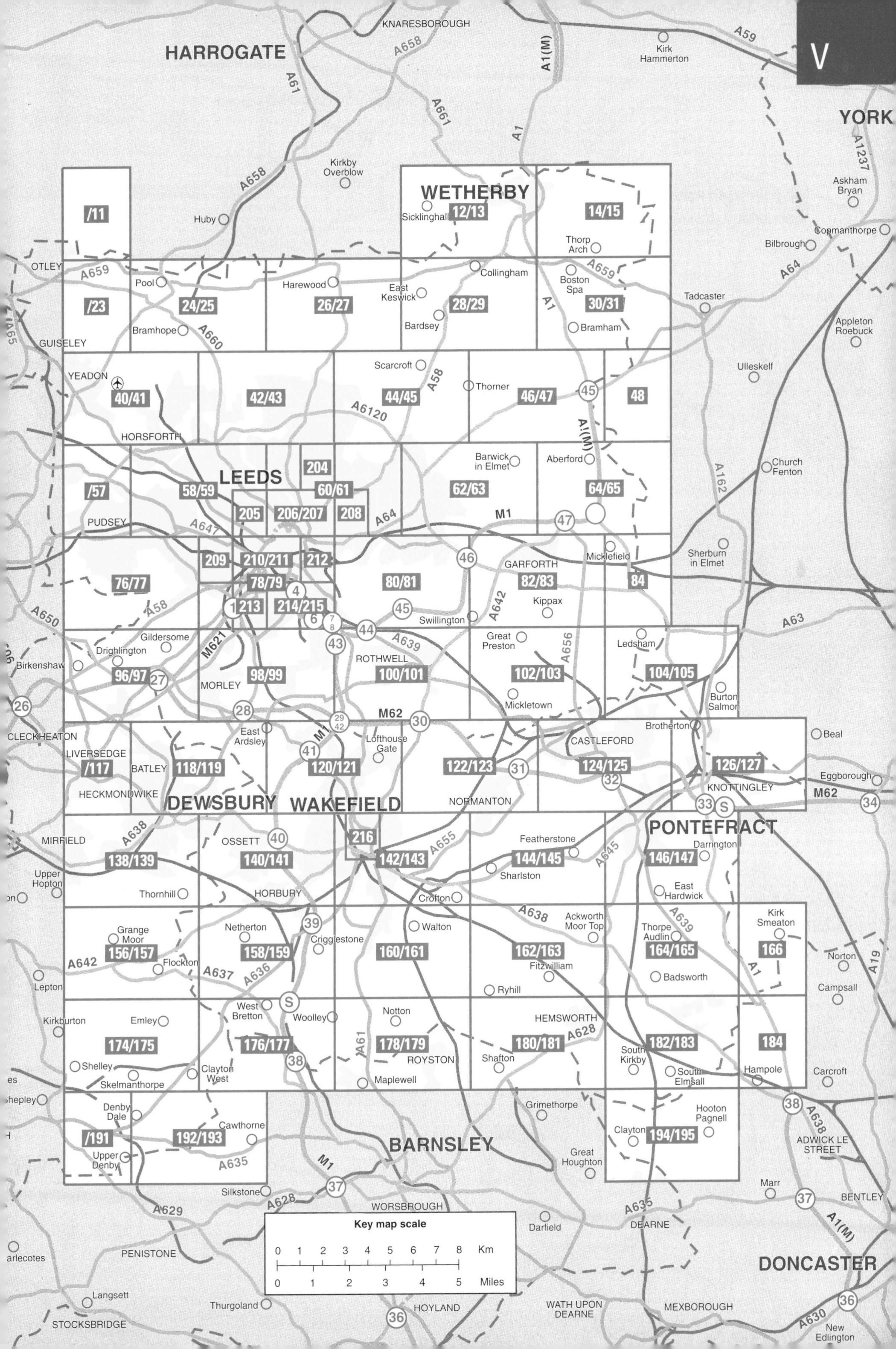
KNARESBOROUGH
HARROGATE
A658
A61
A1(M)
A59
Kirk Hammerton
A661
A1
YORK
A1237
Kirkby Overblow
A658
Huby
WETHERBY
Sicklinghall
/11
12/13
14/15
Thorp Arch
Askham Bryan
Copmanthorpe
Bilbrough
OTLEY
A659
Pool
Harewood
East Keswick
Collingham
Boston Spa
A659
A64
Tadcaster
/23
24/25
26/27
28/29
30/31
A1
Bramhope
A660
Bardsey
Bramham
Appleton Roebuck
GUISELEY
A65
YEADON
Scarcroft
A58
Thorner
Ulleskelf
40/41
42/43
44/45
46/47
45
48
A6120
HORSFORTH
A1(M)
LEEDS
204
Barwick in Elmet
Aberford
Church Fenton
/57
58/59
60/61
62/63
64/65
A162
PUDSEY
A647
205
206/207
208
A64
M1
47
209
210/211
212
46
Micklefield
GARFORTH
Sherburn in Elmet
76/77
78/79
80/81
82/83
84
A58
4
A642
Kippax
A650
1
213
214/215
45
6
7
8
44
Swillington
A63
Gildersome
M621
43
A639
Great Preston
A656
Ledsham
Drighlington
Birkenshaw
ROTHWELL
96/97
27
98/99
100/101
102/103
104/105
MORLEY
Burton Salmon
26
28
M62
29
42
30
Mickletown
CLECKHEATON
East Ardsley
Lofthouse Gate
Brotherton
Beal
LIVERSEDGE
CASTLEFORD
/117
BATLEY
118/119
41
M1
120/121
122/123
31
124/125
32
126/127
Eggborough
HECKMONDWIKE
NORMANTON
KNOTTINGLEY
M62
DEWSBURY
WAKEFIELD
33
S
34
A638
PONTEFRACT
MIRFIELD
OSSETT
40
216
A655
Featherstone
Darrington
138/139
140/141
142/143
144/145
146/147
Upper Hopton
A645
Sharlston
Thornhill
HORBURY
East Hardwick
Crofton
A638
Ackworth Moor Top
A639
Kirk Smeaton
Grange Moor
Netherton
39
Walton
Thorpe Audlin
Crigglestone
156/157
158/159
160/161
162/163
164/165
166
Norton
A642
Flockton
A637
A636
Fitzwilliam
A1
A19
Lepton
Badsworth
Campsall
Ryhill
West Bretton
S
Notton
Kirkburton
Emley
Woolley
HEMSWORTH
A628
174/175
176/177
178/179
180/181
182/183
184
A61
South Kirkby
Shelley
38
ROYSTON
Shafton
South Elmsall
Hampole
Carcroft
Clayton West
Skelmanthorpe
Maplewell
Shepley
Denby Dale
Grimethorpe
Hooton Pagnell
38
A638
Cawthorne
Clayton
/191
192/193
194/195
ADWICK LE STREET
BARNSLEY
Upper Denby
A635
M1
Great Houghton
Silkstone
37
Marr
A629
A628
WORSBROUGH
A635
37
BENTLEY
Darfield
DEARNE
A1(M)
PENISTONE
DONCASTER
Key map scale
0 1 2 3 4 5 6 7 8 Km
0 1 2 3 4 5 Miles
Langsett
Thurgoland
WATH UPON DEARNE
MEXBOROUGH
36
HOYLAND
36
A630
STOCKSBRIDGE
New Edlington

Route planning

VII
Forest Moor
A59
HARROGATE
KNARESBOROUGH
Goldsborough
Whixley
Green Hammerton
Moor Monkton
Kirk Hammerton
Poppleton
Marston Moor
Cattal
Hunsingore
Tockwith 1644
Hessay
Knapton
Rufforth
A1(M)
A661
A658
A61
A1
Fewston
Beaver Dyke Resrs
Scargill Resr
Bland Hill
Beckwithshaw
Swinsty Resr
Jack Hill
838
Little Ribston
North Deighton
Follifoot
Pannal
Castle Spofforth
Kirk Deighton
Bickerton
Long Marston
Hutton Wandesley
B1224
A1237
North Rigton
522
Kirkby Overblow
Lindley Wood Resr
Bilton in Ainsty
Angram
Askham Bryan
Askham Richard
Bilbrough
WETHERBY
Askwith
Weston
Farnley
OTLEY
Stainburn
Huby
Weeton Sta
Leathley
Weeton
Sicklinghall
Linton
Collingham
Walton
Trading Estate
Healaugh
Wighill
Catterton
Copmanthorpe
A660
A659
Pool
Harewood
East Keswick
Thornhurst
Boston Spa
Thorp Arch
Newton Kyme
Clifford
Bramham
Colton
Arthington
Bramhope
Eccup
Bardsey
Tadcaster
Appleton Roebuck
GUISELEY
YEADON
Rawdon
Leeds Bradford International Airport
Eccup Resr
Scarcroft
A58
Stutton
River Wharfe
Bolton Percy
Ulleskelf
Esholt
Tinshill
Thorner
Cock Beck
Towton
Ryther
HORSFORTH
A6120
Shadwell
Chapel Allerton
Barwick in Elmet
Aberford
1461
A162
Calverley
Farsley
A660
Roundhay
A64
Scholes
B1217
Saxton
Barkston Ash
Church Fenton
Headingley
Pendas Fields
Little Fenton
Biggin
PUDSEY
A647
A63
GARFORTH
A642
Newthorpe
Sherburn in Elmet
B1222
A6177
New Farnley
LEEDS
Temple Newsam
M1
Micklefield
South Milford
Hambleton
Monk Fryston
Beeston
Swillington
Kippax
Ledsham
Lumby
A650
Gildersome
M621
Drighlington
A62
River Aire
A639
Great Preston
Ledston
Hillam
Gateforth
Birkenshaw
Churwell
A653
Woodlesford
Oulton
Fairburn
Burton Salmon
Birkin
MORLEY
Middleton
A654
ROTHWELL
Carlton
Allerton Bywater
New Fryston
West Haddlesey
Birstall
Smithies
M62
Tingley
East Ardsley
Methley
Mickletown
CASTLEFORD
Brotherton
Beal
Kellington
Gomersal
BATLEY
B6124
Lofthouse Gate
Stanley
Outwood
Canal
Whitwood
Ferrybridge
A645
Eggborough
HECKMONDWIKE
Kirkhamgate
Altofts
KNOTTINGLEY
Robertown
DEWSBURY
A638
NORMANTON
Ackton
WAKEFIELD
FEATHERSTONE
PONTEFRACT
Cridling Stubbs
Whitley
Ravensthorpe
Warmfield
Purston Jaglin
Darrington
MIRFIELD
OSSETT
Sharlston
East Hardwick
Upper Hopton
Thornhill Edge
HORBURY
A655
Womersley
Kirkheaton
Middlestow
A628
High Ackworth
Wentbridge
West Hardwick
Crofton
Little Smeaton
Walden Stubbs
Grange Moor
Netherton
Crigglestone
Walton
Ackworth Moor Top
Kirk Smeaton
Lepton
A642
Fitzwilliam
Thorpe Audlin
Wintersett
Ryhill
262
Norton
Flockton
A637
A636
Highburton
Emley
West Bretton
Woolley
Badsworth
Kinsley
South Hiendley
Upton
231
Campsall
Burghwallis
Kirkburton
Notton
HEMSWORTH
South Elmsall
A19
Shelley
Skelmanthorpe
Clayton West
High Hoyland
Darton
ROYSTON
Carlton
Shafton
Brierley
Skellow
Carcroft
Staincross
A637
R Dearne
Grimethorpe
South Kirkby
Hooton Pagnell
Hampole
Clayton
Denby Dale
Cawthorne
A635
BARNSLEY
Cudworth
Great Houghton
Brodsworth
ADWICK LE STREET
Toll Bar
Ingbirchworth Resr
Upper Denby
Ingbirchworth
Silkstone
Gawber
Priory
A633
Darfield
Thurnscoe
Hickleton
Hoylandswaine
A628
WORSBROUGH
Ardsley
DEARNE
A635
Marr
BENTLEY
Thurlstone
A629
Billingley
Goldthorpe
Bolton upon Dearne
Barnburgh
Sprotbrough
High Melton
PENISTONE
River Dearne
Adwick upon Dearne
Warmsworth
A628
Langsett
Oxspring
Thurgoland
WATH UPON DEARNE
MEXBOROUGH
Cadeby
Route map scale
0 1 2 3 4 5 6 7 8 Km
0 1 2 3 4 5 Miles

Major administrative and post code boundaries

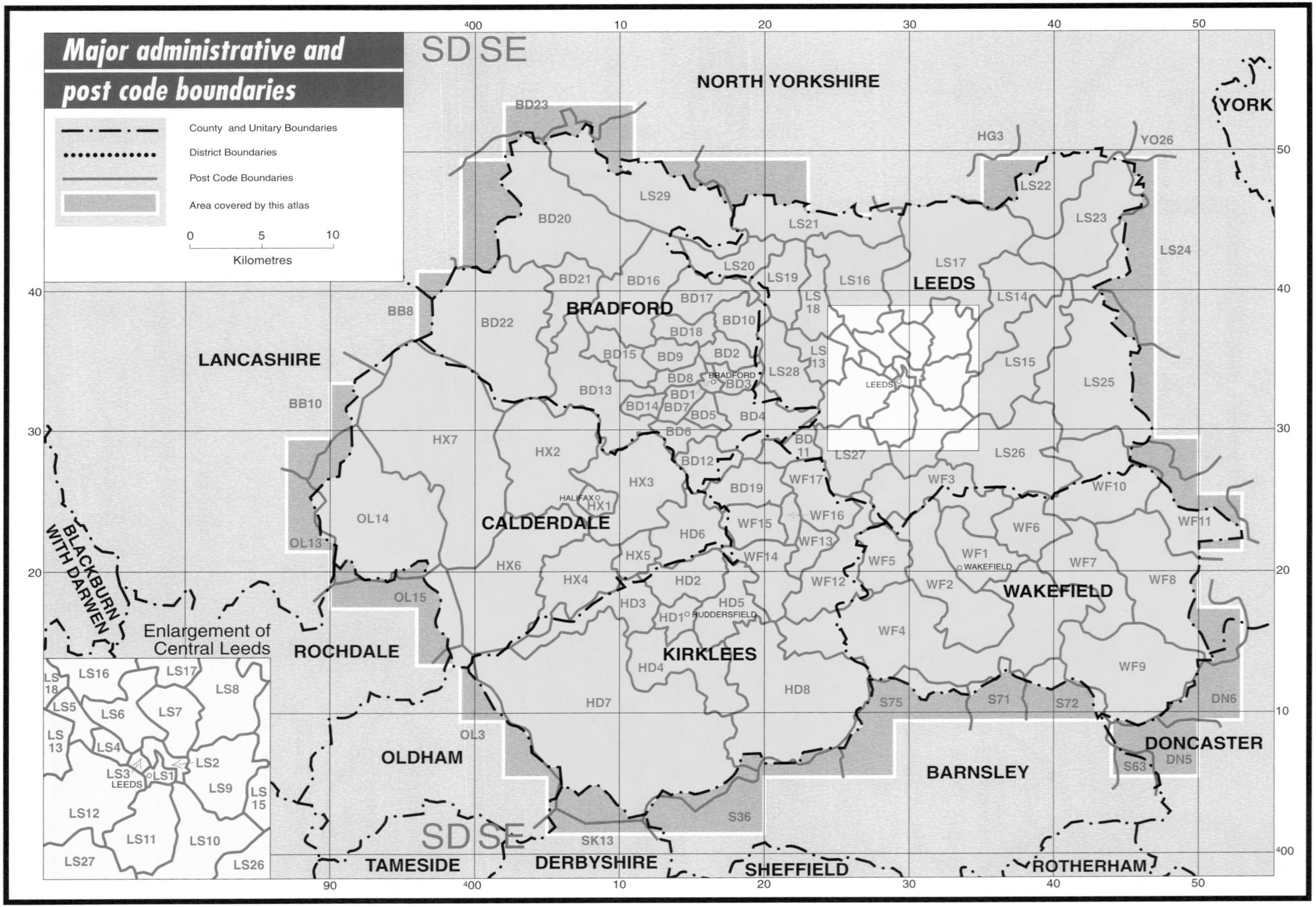

2

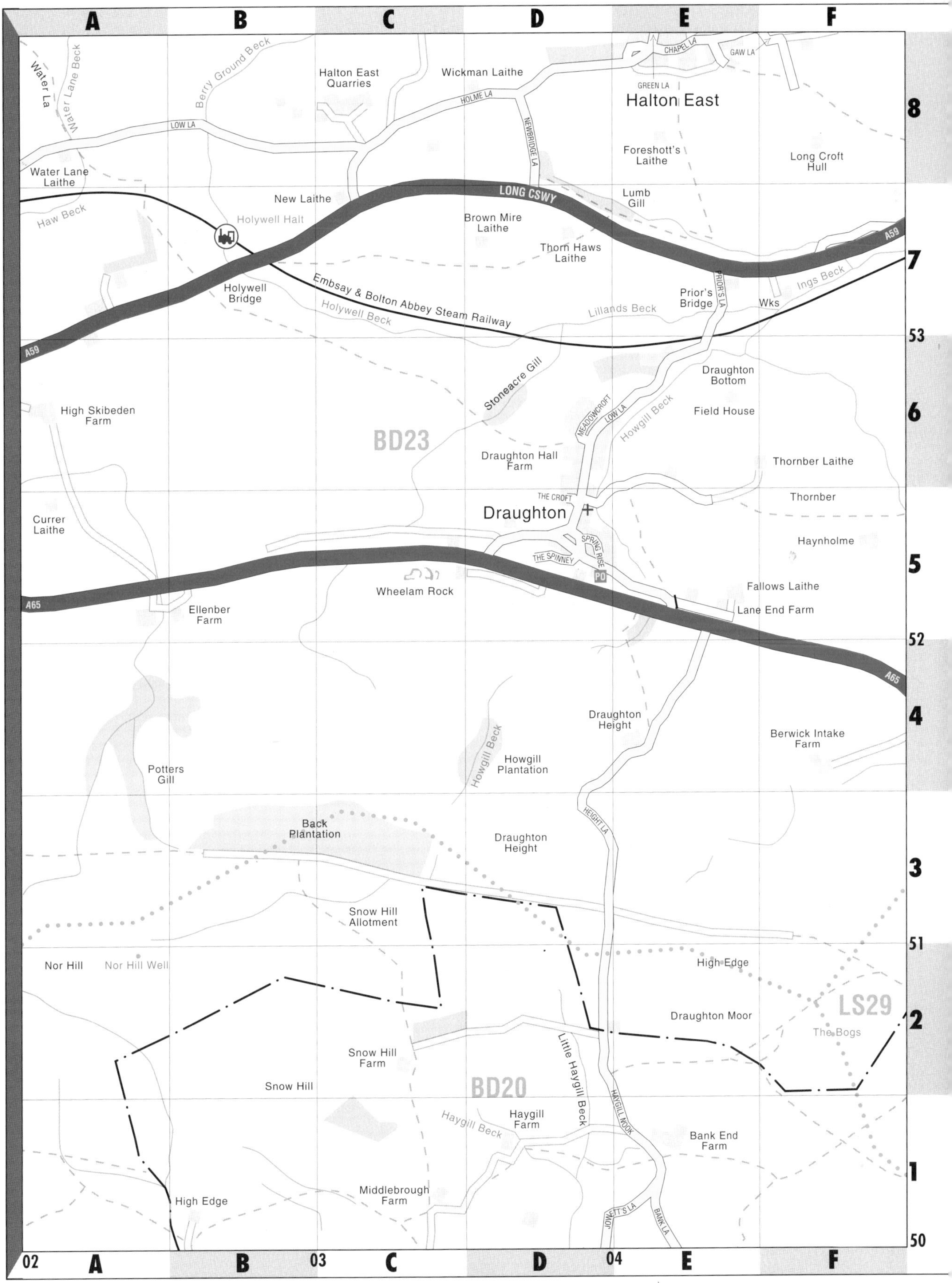
A
B
C
D
E
F
Water La
Water Lane Beck
Berry Ground Beck
Halton East Quarries
Wickman Laithe
CHAPEL LA
GAW LA
GREEN LA
Halton East
HOLME LA
LOW LA
NEWBRIDGE LA
8
Foreshott's Laithe
Long Croft Hull
Water Lane Laithe
New Laithe
LONG CSWY
Lumb Gill
Haw Beck
Holywell Halt
Brown Mire Laithe
Thorn Haws Laithe
A59
7
Embsay & Bolton Abbey Steam Railway
Holywell Bridge
Holywell Beck
Lillands Beck
Prior's Bridge
PRIOR'S LA
Wks
Ings Beck
A59
53
Draughton Bottom
Stoneacre Gill
MEADOWCROFT
LOW LA
Howgill Beck
Field House
High Skibeden Farm
6
BD23
Draughton Hall Farm
Thornber Laithe
THE CROFT
Thornber
Currer Laithe
Draughton
SPRING RISE
Haynholme
THE SPINNEY
PO
5
Wheelam Rock
Fallows Laithe
A65
Ellenber Farm
Lane End Farm
52
A65
4
Draughton Height
Berwick Intake Farm
Howgill Beck
Howgill Plantation
Potters Gill
HEIGHT LA
Back Plantation
Draughton Height
3
Snow Hill Allotment
51
Nor Hill
Nor Hill Well
High Edge
Draughton Moor
LS29
The Bogs
2
Little Haygill Beck
Snow Hill Farm
Snow Hill
BD20
HAYGILL NOOK
Haygill Beck
Haygill Farm
Bank End Farm
1
Middlebrough Farm
High Edge
JOWETT'S LA
BANK LA
50
02
03
04
A
B
C
D
E
F

5
2

1

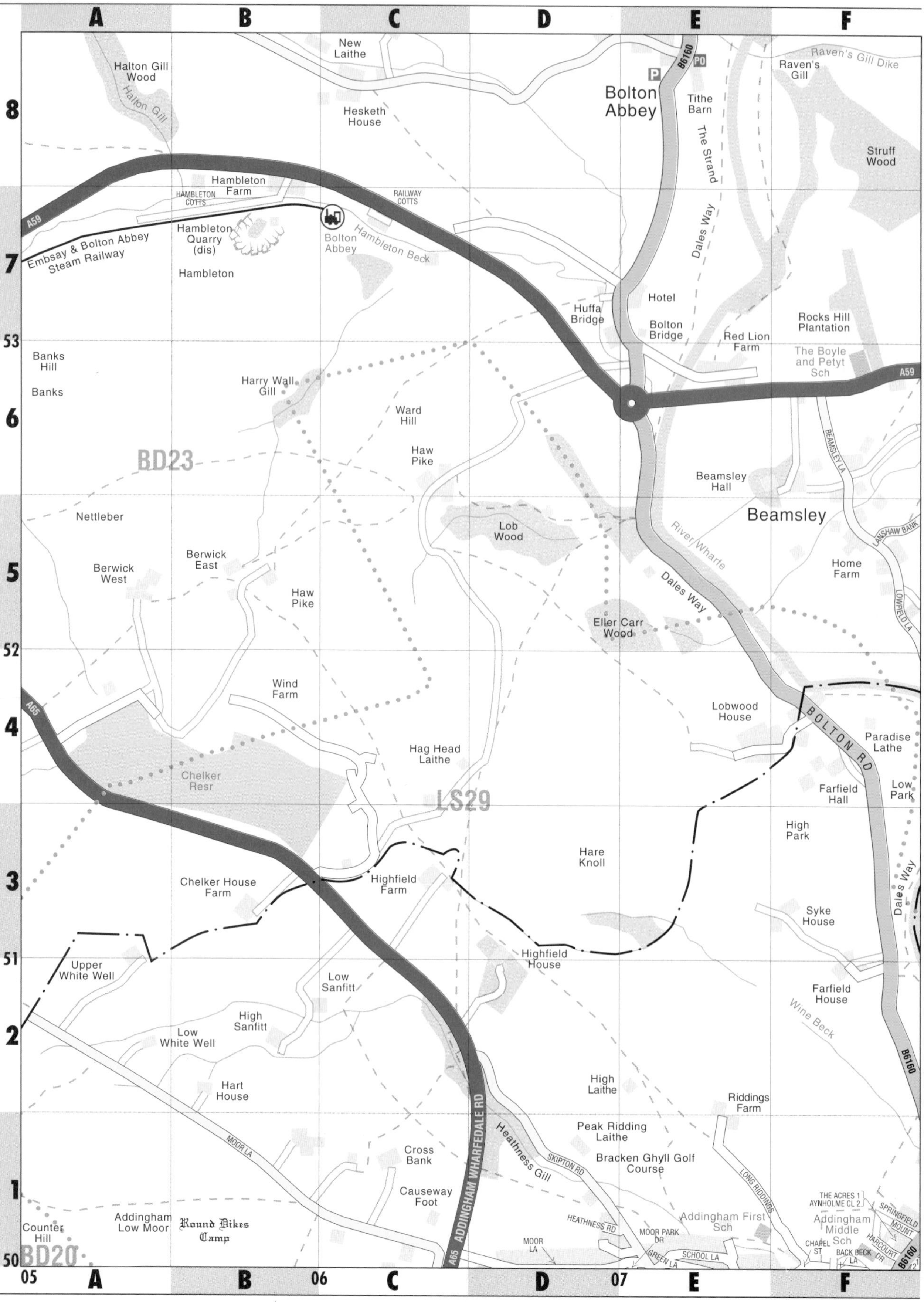
A
B
C
D
E
F
8
7
53
6
5
52
4
3
51
2
1
50
05
06
07
New Laithe
Halton Gill Wood
Halton Gill
Hesketh House
Bolton Abbey
B6160
PO
P
Tithe Barn
The Strand
Raven's Gill Dike
Raven's Gill
Struff Wood
Hambleton Farm
HAMBLETON COTTS
RAILWAY COTTS
A59
Hambleton Quarry (dis)
Embsay & Bolton Abbey Steam Railway
Bolton Abbey
Hambleton Beck
Hambleton
Dales Way
Hotel
Huffa Bridge
Bolton Bridge
Red Lion Farm
Rocks Hill Plantation
The Boyle and Petyt Sch
Banks Hill
Banks
Harry Wall Gill
Ward Hill
Haw Pike
BD23
BEAMSLEY LA
Beamsley Hall
Beamsley
Nettleber
Lob Wood
River Wharfe
LANSHAW BANK
Berwick East
Berwick West
Haw Pike
Home Farm
Dales Way
LOWFIELD LA
Eller Carr Wood
Wind Farm
A65
Lobwood House
BOLTON RD
Paradise Lathe
Hag Head Laithe
Chelker Resr
Farfield Hall
Low Park
LS29
High Park
Hare Knoll
Chelker House Farm
Highfield Farm
Dales Way
Syke House
Highfield House
Upper White Well
Low Sanfitt
Farfield House
Wine Beck
High Sanfitt
Low White Well
Hart House
High Laithe
Riddings Farm
B6160
Peak Ridding Laithe
Heathness Gill
MOOR LA
Cross Bank
SKIPTON RD
Bracken Ghyll Golf Course
ADDINGHAM WHARFEDALE RD
LONG RIDDINGS
Causeway Foot
THE ACRES 1
AYNHOLME CL 2
SPRINGFIELD MOUNT
Addingham Low Moor
Round Dikes Camp
HEATHNESS RD
Addingham First Sch
Addingham Middle Sch
Counter Hill
MOOR LA
MOOR PARK DR
GREEN LA
SCHOOL LA
CHAPEL ST
BACK BECK LA
HARCOURT DR
BD20

1

6

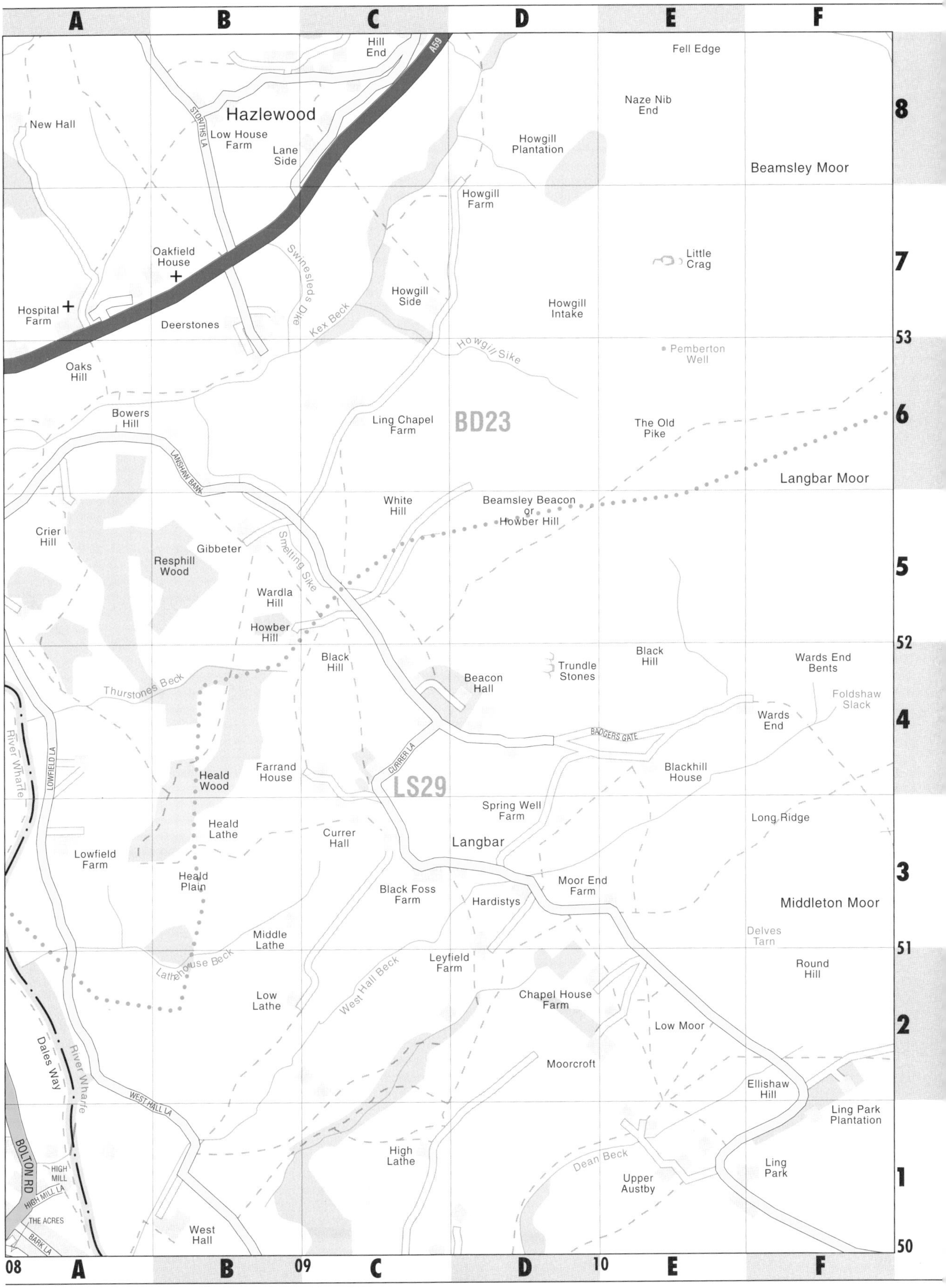
A
B
C
D
E
F
Hill End
A59
Fell Edge
8
New Hall
Hazlewood
STORITHS LA
Low House Farm
Lane Side
Naze Nib End
Howgill Plantation
Beamsley Moor
Howgill Farm
Little Crag
7
Oakfield House
Swinesleds Dike
Hospital Farm
Howgill Side
Howgill Intake
Kex Beck
Deerstones
53
Pemberton Well
Howgill Sike
Oaks Hill
Bowers Hill
Ling Chapel Farm
BD23
The Old Pike
6
LANSHAW BANK
Langbar Moor
White Hill
Beamsley Beacon or Howber Hill
Crier Hill
Gibbeter
Resphill Wood
Smelting Sike
5
Wardla Hill
Howber Hill
52
Black Hill
Black Hill
Wards End Bents
Trundle Stones
Thurstones Beck
Beacon Hall
Foldshaw Slack
Wards End
4
BADGERS GATE
River Wharfe
LOWFIELD LA
CURRER LA
Heald Wood
Farrand House
Blackhill House
LS29
Spring Well Farm
Heald Lathe
Long Ridge
Currer Hall
Langbar
Lowfield Farm
3
Heald Plain
Moor End Farm
Black Foss Farm
Hardistys
Middleton Moor
Delves Tarn
Middle Lathe
51
Lathehouse Beck
Leyfield Farm
Round Hill
West Hall Beck
Chapel House Farm
Low Lathe
Low Moor
2
Dales Way
River Wharfe
Moorcroft
Ellishaw Hill
WEST HALL LA
Ling Park Plantation
BOLTON RD
High Lathe
Dean Beck
HIGH MILL
HIGH MILL LA
Upper Austby
Ling Park
1
THE ACRES
BARK LA
West Hall
50
08
09
10

7

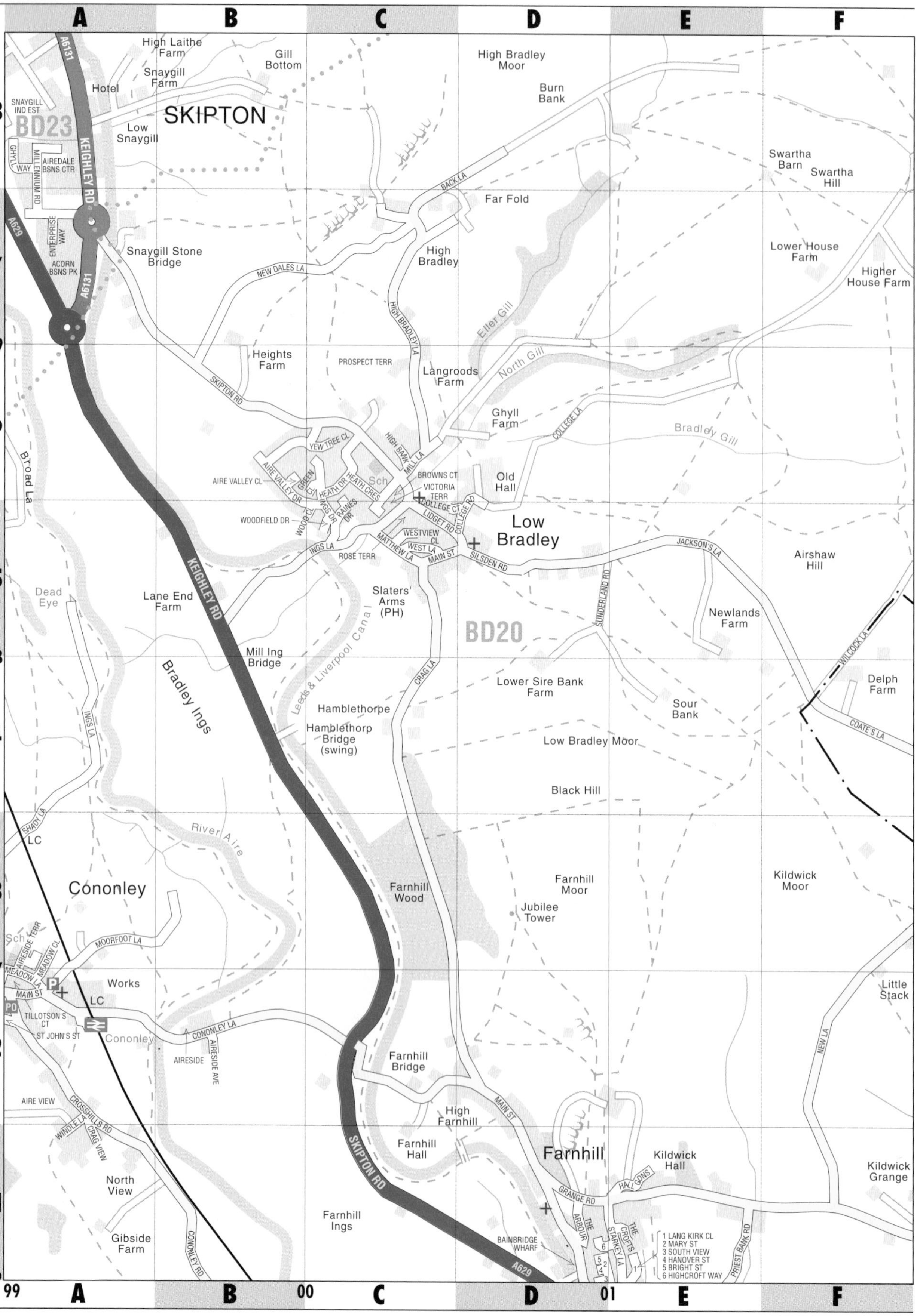
A
B
C
D
E
F
8
7
6
5
4
3
2
1
49
48
47
46
99
00
01
High Laithe Farm
Gill Bottom
Snaygill Farm
Hotel
SNAYGILL IND EST
BD23
SKIPTON
Low Snaygill
A6131
KEIGHLEY RD
GHYLL WAY
MILLENNIUM RD
AIREDALE BSNS CTR
ENTERPRISE WAY
ACORN BSNS PK
A629
Snaygill Stone Bridge
High Bradley Moor
Burn Bank
BACK LA
Far Fold
High Bradley
NEW DALES LA
Swartha Barn
Swartha Hill
Lower House Farm
Higher House Farm
Eller Gill
HIGH BRADLEY LA
Heights Farm
PROSPECT TERR
Langroods Farm
North Gill
SKIPTON RD
Ghyll Farm
COLLEGE LA
Bradley Gill
YEW TREE CL
HIGH BANK
MILL LA
AIRE VALLEY CL
AIRE VALLEY DR
GREEN CL
HEATH DR
HEATH CRES
Sch
BROWNS CT
VICTORIA TERR
Old Hall
COLLEGE CT
COLLEGE RD
LIDGET RD
WOODFIELD DR
WOOD CL
INGS DR
RAINES DR
Low Bradley
WESTVIEW CL
WEST LA
INGS LA
ROSE TERR
MATTHEW LA
MAIN ST
SILSDEN RD
JACKSON'S LA
Airshaw Hill
Dead Eye
Broad La
Lane End Farm
Slaters' Arms (PH)
SUNDERLAND RD
Newlands Farm
BD20
Mill Ing Bridge
Leeds & Liverpool Canal
CRAG LA
WILCOCK LA
Lower Sire Bank Farm
Delph Farm
Bradley Ings
INGS LA
Hamblethorpe
Sour Bank
Hamblethorp Bridge (swing)
Low Bradley Moor
COATE'S LA
Black Hill
SHADY LA
LC
River Aire
Farnhill Wood
Farnhill Moor
Kildwick Moor
Cononley
Jubilee Tower
Sch
AIRESIDE TERR
MEADOW CL
MOORFOOT LA
MEADOW LA
P
Works
Little Stack
MAIN ST
LC
PO
TILLOTSON'S CT
ST JOHN'S ST
Cononley
CONONLEY LA
AIRESIDE
AIRESIDE AVE
Farnhill Bridge
NEW LA
AIRE VIEW
CROSSHILLS RD
WINDLE LA
CRAG VIEW
High Farnhill
MAIN ST
SKIPTON RD
Farnhill Hall
Farnhill
Kildwick Hall
HALL GDNS
Kildwick Grange
North View
GRANGE RD
Farnhill Ings
THE ARBOUR
THE CROFTS
STARKEY LA
PRIEST BANK RD
Gibside Farm
CONONLEY RD
BAINBRIDGE WHARF
A629
1 LANG KIRK CL
2 MARY ST
3 SOUTH VIEW
4 HANOVER ST
5 BRIGHT ST
6 HIGHCROFT WAY

1
6

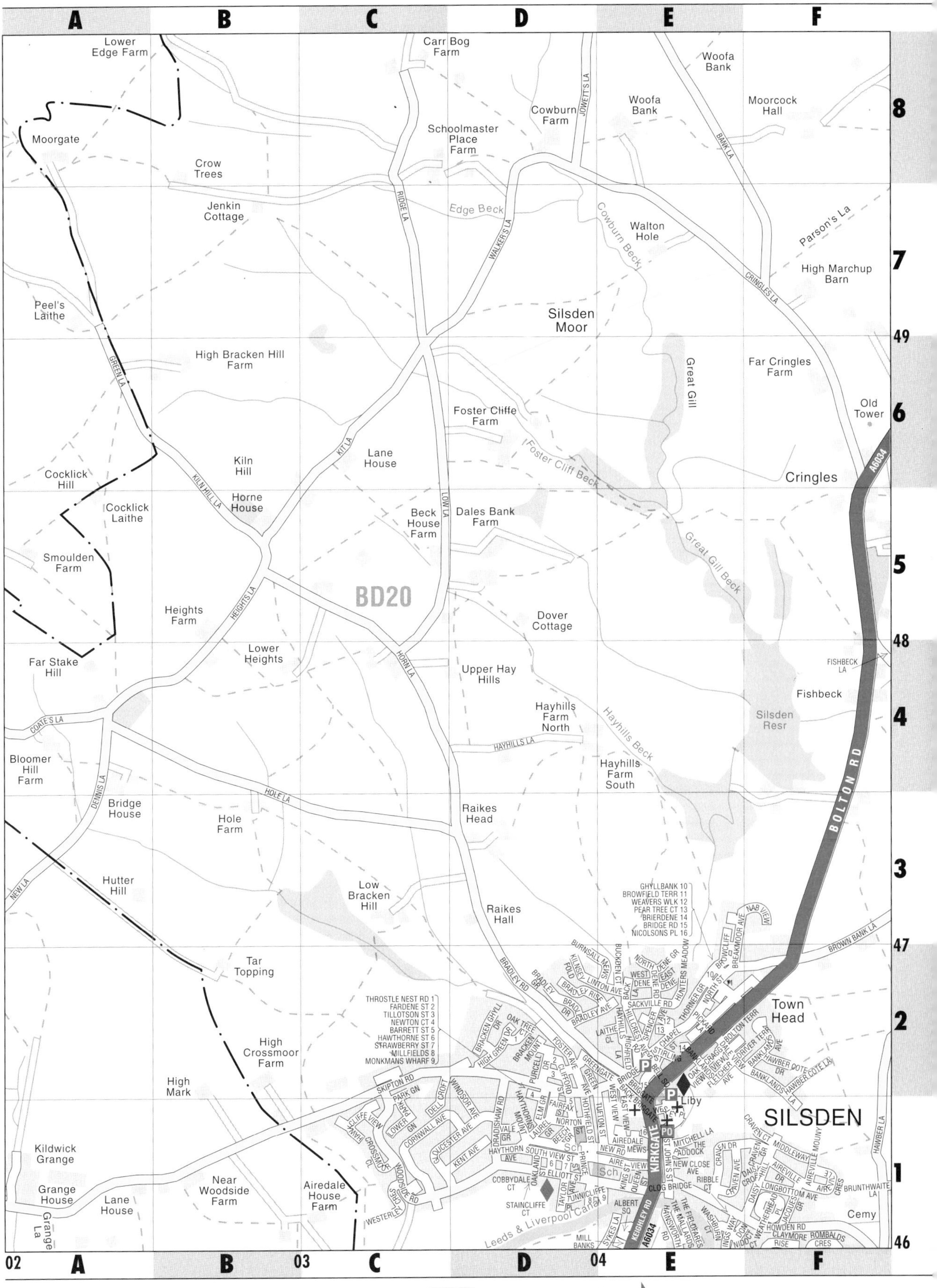
A
B
C
D
E
F
Lower Edge Farm
Carr Bog Farm
Woofa Bank
Moorgate
Crow Trees
Schoolmaster Place Farm
Cowburn Farm
JOWETT'S LA
Woofa Bank
Moorcock Hall
BANK LA
Jenkin Cottage
RIDGE LA
Edge Beck
WALKER'S LA
Cowburn Beck
Walton Hole
Parson's La
CRINGLES LA
High Marchup Barn
Peel's Laithe
Silsden Moor
GREEN LA
High Bracken Hill Farm
Great Gill
Far Cringles Farm
Old Tower
Foster Cliffe Farm
KIT LA
Lane House
Foster Cliff Beck
Kiln Hill
Cocklick Hill
KILNHILL LA
Cringles
A6034
Cocklick Laithe
Horne House
LOW LA
Beck House Farm
Dales Bank Farm
Smoulden Farm
Great Gill Beck
BD20
HEIGHTS LA
Heights Farm
Dover Cottage
Far Stake Hill
Lower Heights
HORN LA
Upper Hay Hills
FISHBECK LA
Fishbeck
Hayhills Farm North
Hayhills Beck
Silsden Resr
COATE'S LA
HAYHILLS LA
Bloomer Hill Farm
DENNIS LA
Hayhills Farm South
BOLTON RD
Bridge House
HOLE LA
Hole Farm
Raikes Head
Hutter Hill
NEW LA
Low Bracken Hill
Raikes Hall
GHYLLBANK 10
BROWFIELD TERR 11
WEAVERS WLK 12
PEAR TREE CT 13
BRIERDENE 14
BRIDGE RD 15
NICOLSONS PL 16
BROWN BANK LA
Tar Topping
BRADLEY RD
Town Head
THROSTLE NEST RD 1
FARDENE ST 2
TILLOTSON ST 3
NEWTON CT 4
BARRETT ST 5
HAWTHORNE ST 6
STRAWBERRY ST 7
MILLFIELDS 8
MONKMANS WHARF 9
High Crossmoor Farm
KIRKGATE
Liby
High Mark
SKIPTON RD
SILSDEN
HAWBER LA
Kildwick Grange
Grange House
Lane House
Near Woodside Farm
Airedale House Farm
Grange La
KEIGHLEY RD
CLOG BRIDGE
Leeds & Liverpool Canal
Cemy
BRUNTHWAITE LA
CLAYMORE
ROMBALDS CRES
HOWDEN RD
8
7
49
6
5
48
4
3
47
2
1
46
02
03
04

17
6

A · B · C · D · E · F

8
7
49
6

5
48
4

3
47
2

1
46

05 · A · B · 06 · C · D · 07 · E · F

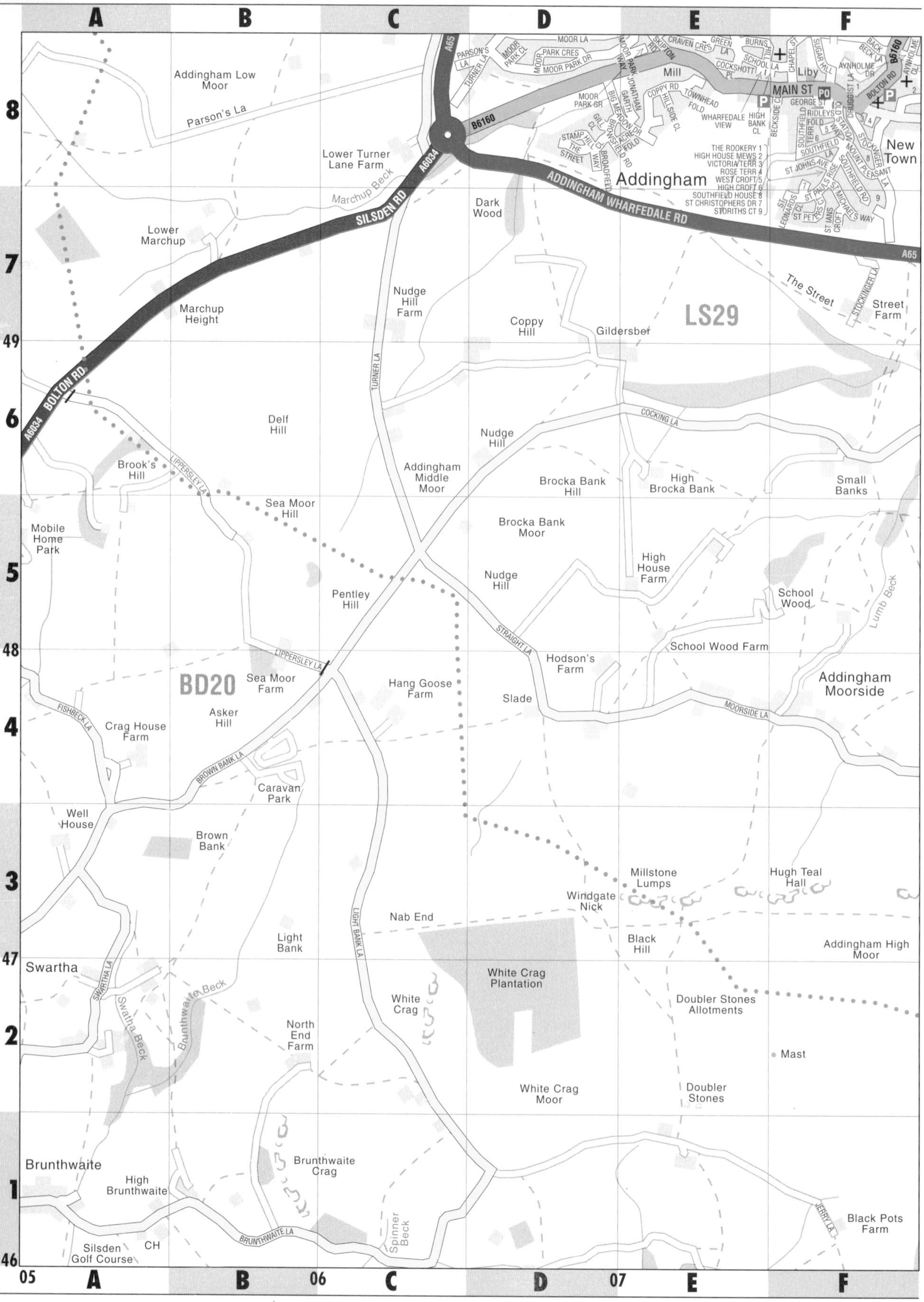

Addingham Low
Moor

Parson's La

Lower Turner
Lane Farm

Marchup Beck

SILSDEN RD

A6034

B6160

MOOR PARK CL
MOOR PARK CRES
MOOR PARK DR
PARSON'S LA
TURNER LA

Dark
Wood

ADDINGHAM WHARFEDALE RD

Mill

CRAVEN CRES
SKIPTON RD
BURNS LA
GREEN LA
COCKSHOTT LA
SCHOOL LA
CHAPEL ST

Liby
MAIN ST PO

SUGAR HILL
AYNHOLME DR
BOLTON RD
B6160
AYNHOLME CL
BACK BECK LA

New
Town

THE ROOKERY 1
HIGH HOUSE MEWS 2
VICTORIA TERR 3
ROSE TERR 4
WEST CROFT 5
HIGH CROFT 6
SOUTHFIELD HOUSE 8
ST CHRISTOPHERS DR 7
STORITHS CT 9

Addingham

Coppy
Hill

Gildersber

LS29

The Street

STOCKINGER LA

Street
Farm

Lower
Marchup

Marchup
Height

Nudge Hill
Farm

TURNER LA

Nudge
Hill

COCKING LA

Brocka Bank
Hill

High
Brocka Bank

Small
Banks

A6034 BOLTON RD

Delf
Hill

Brook's
Hill

LIPPERSLEY LA

Sea Moor
Hill

Addingham
Middle
Moor

Brocka Bank
Moor

High
House
Farm

School
Wood

Lumb Beck

Mobile
Home
Park

Pentley
Hill

Nudge
Hill

STRAIGHT LA

School Wood Farm

Addingham
Moorside

BD20

LIPPERSLEY LA

Sea Moor
Farm

Hang Goose
Farm

Hodson's
Farm

FISHBECK LA

Crag House
Farm

Asker
Hill

Slade

MOORSIDE LA

Well
House

BROWN BANK LA

Caravan
Park

Brown
Bank

Millstone
Lumps

Windgate
Nick

Hugh Teal
Hall

Nab End

Black
Hill

Addingham High
Moor

Swartha

SWARTHA LA

SWATHA BECK

BRUNTHWAITE BECK

Light
Bank

LIGHT BANK LA

White Crag
Plantation

Doubler Stones
Allotments

North
End
Farm

White
Crag

Mast

Brunthwaite

High
Brunthwaite

Brunthwaite
Crag

Spinner Beck

White Crag
Moor

Doubler
Stones

JERRY LA

Black Pots
Farm

Silsden
Golf Course

CH

BRUNTHWAITE LA

3
8
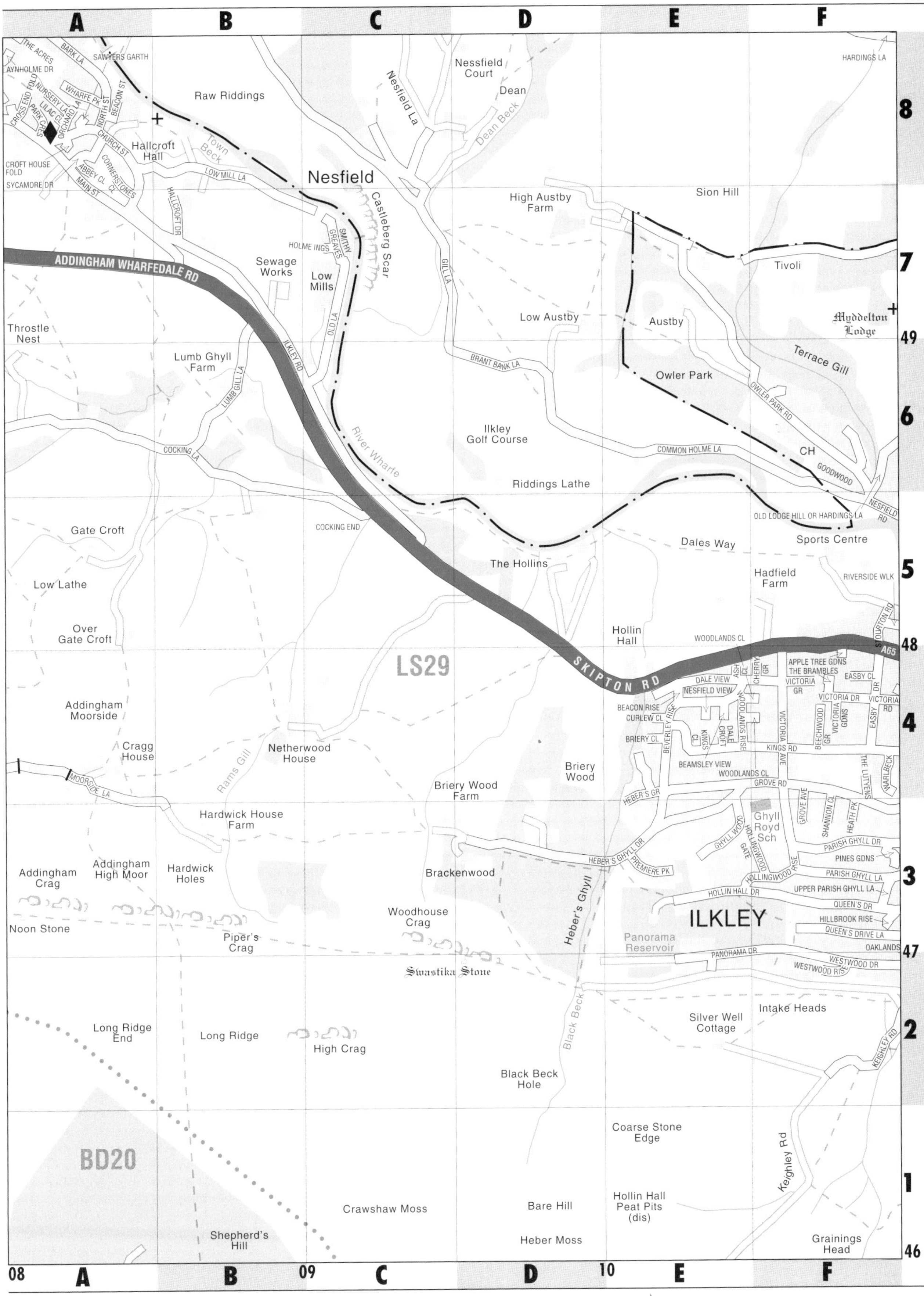
A
B
C
D
E
F
8
7
49
6
5
48
4
3
47
2
1
46
08
09
10
THE ACRES
BARK LA
SAWYERS GARTH
AYNHOLME DR
WHARFE PK
NURSERY LA
CROSS END FOLD
LILAC CL
PARK CR
ORCHARD LA
NORTH ST
BEACON ST
CHURCH ST
CROFT HOUSE FOLD
SYCAMORE DR
ABBEY CL
MAIN ST
CORNERSTONES
Hallcroft Hall
Town Beck
LOW MILL LA
HALLCROFT DR
Raw Riddings
Nesfield Court
Dean
Nesfield La
Dean Beck
Nesfield
Castleberg Scar
SMITHY GREAVES
HOLME INGS
Sewage Works
Low Mills
GILL LA
High Austby Farm
Sion Hill
Tivoli
HARDINGS LA
ADDINGHAM WHARFEDALE RD
Throstle Nest
OLD LA
Lumb Ghyll Farm
LUMB GILL LA
ILKLEY RD
Low Austby
Austby
Myddelton Lodge
BRANT BANK LA
Owler Park
Terrace Gill
OWLER PARK RD
River Wharfe
Ilkley Golf Course
COCKING LA
COMMON HOLME LA
CH
GOODWOOD
Riddings Lathe
NESFIELD RD
OLD LODGE HILL OR HARDINGS LA
COCKING END
Gate Croft
Dales Way
Sports Centre
The Hollins
Low Lathe
Hadfield Farm
RIVERSIDE WLK
Over Gate Croft
Hollin Hall
WOODLANDS CL
STOURTON RD
A65
LS29
SKIPTON RD
APPLE TREE GDNS
THE BRAMBLES
EASBY CL
DALE VIEW
ASH CL
CHERRY GR
VICTORIA GR
NESFIELD VIEW
VICTORIA DR
VICTORIA RD
Addingham Moorside
BEACON RISE
CURLEW CL
BEVERLEY RISE
WOODLANDS RISE
BEECHWOOD GR
VICTORIA GDNS
EASBY DR
BRIERY CL
KINGS CL
DALE CROFT
KINGS RD
VICTORIA AVE
Cragg House
Netherwood House
Briery Wood
BEAMSLEY VIEW
WOODLANDS CL
Rams Gill
GROVE RD
THE LUTYENS
NARLBECK
Briery Wood Farm
HEBER'S GR
MOORSIDE LA
Hardwick House Farm
Ghyll Royd Sch
GROVE AVE
SHANNON CL
HEATH PK
GHYLL WOOD
HOLLINGWOOD GATE
PARISH GHYLL DR
PINES GDNS
HEBER'S GHYLL DR
PREMIERE PK
HOLLINGWOOD RISE
PARISH GHYLL LA
Addingham Crag
Addingham High Moor
Hardwick Holes
Brackenwood
HOLLIN HALL DR
UPPER PARISH GHYLL LA
Heber's Ghyll
QUEEN'S DR
Noon Stone
Woodhouse Crag
ILKLEY
HILLBROOK RISE
QUEEN'S DRIVE LA
Piper's Crag
Panorama Reservoir
OAKLANDS
PANORAMA DR
WESTWOOD DR
WESTWOOD RISE
Swastika Stone
Black Beck
Intake Heads
Silver Well Cottage
KEIGHLEY RD
Long Ridge End
Long Ridge
High Crag
Black Beck Hole
Coarse Stone Edge
BD20
Keighley Rd
Crawshaw Moss
Bare Hill
Hollin Hall Peat Pits (dis)
Shepherd's Hill
Heber Moss
Grainings Head
19
8

7

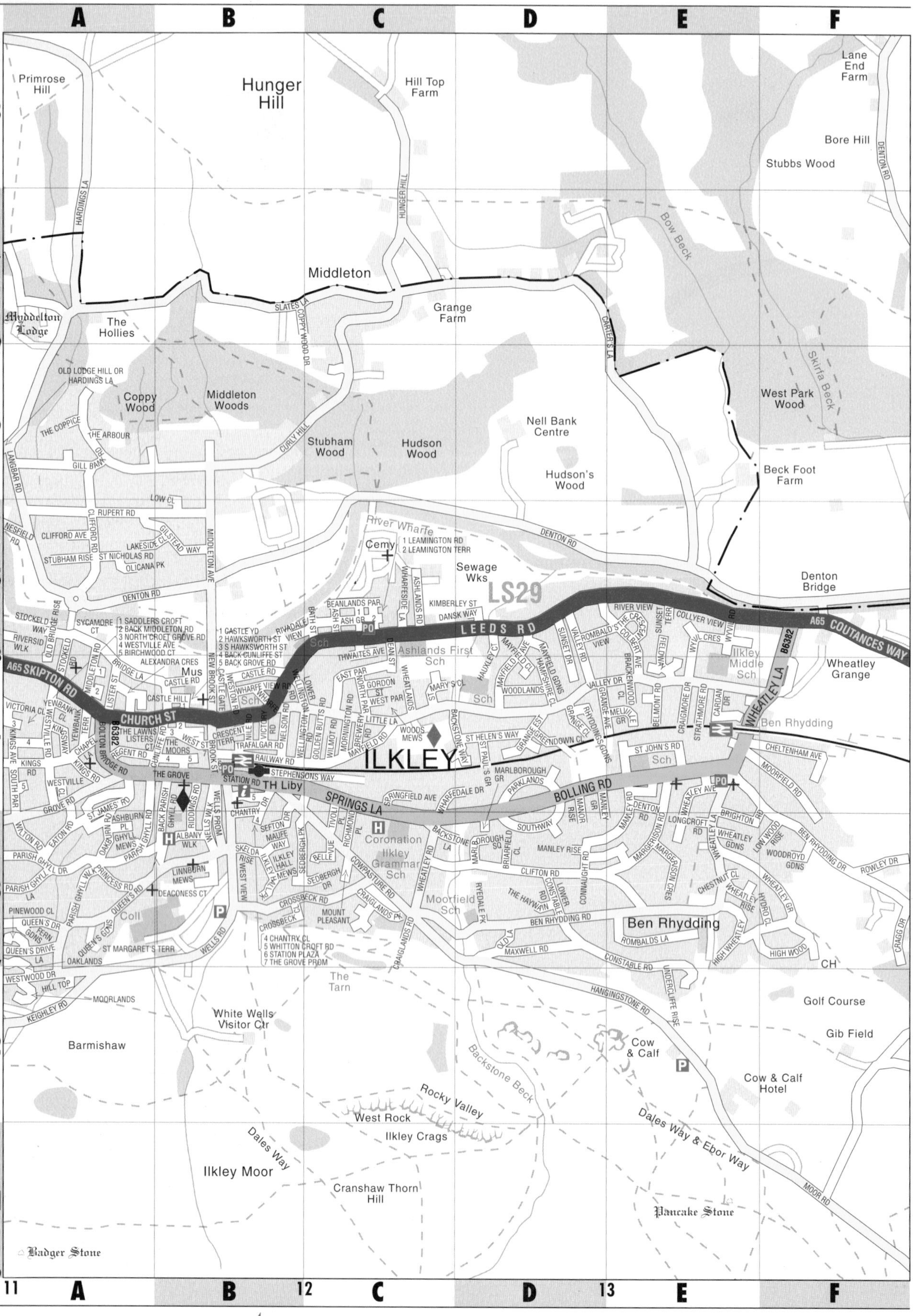
A
B
C
D
E
F
8
7
49
6
5
48
4
3
47
2
1
46
11
12
13
Primrose Hill
Hunger Hill
Hill Top Farm
Lane End Farm
Bore Hill
Stubbs Wood
Bow Beck
Middleton
Grange Farm
Myddelton Lodge
The Hollies
OLD LODGE HILL OR HARDINGS LA
HARDINGS LA
SLATES LA
COPPY WOOD DR
HUNGER HILL
CARTER'S LA
Coppy Wood
Middleton Woods
West Park Wood
Skirfa Beck
THE COPPICE
THE ARBOUR
CURLY HILL
Stubham Wood
Hudson Wood
Nell Bank Centre
Hudson's Wood
Beck Foot Farm
LANGBAR RD
GILL BANK
LOW CL
RUPERT RD
River Wharfe
DENTON RD
NESFIELD RD
CLIFFORD AVE
CLIFFORD RD
LAKESIDE CL
GILSTEAD WAY
STUBHAM RISE
ST NICHOLAS RD
OLICANA PK
MIDDLETON AVE
Cemy
1 LEAMINGTON RD
2 LEAMINGTON TERR
Sewage Wks
LS29
Denton Bridge
DENTON RD
STOCKELD WAY
OLD BRIDGE RISE
SYCAMORE CT
1 SADDLERS CROFT
2 BACK MIDDLETON RD
3 NORTH CROFT GROVE RD
4 WESTVILLE AVE
5 BIRCHWOOD CT
ALEXANDRA CRES
RIVERSIDE WLK
1 CASTLE YD
2 HAWKSWORTH ST
3 S HAWKSWORTH ST
4 BACK CUNLIFFE ST
5 BACK GROVE RD
RIVADALE VIEW
BEANLANDS PAR
ASH GR
KIMBERLEY ST
DANSK WAY
LEEDS RD
RIVER VIEW
COLLYER VIEW
A65 COUTANCES WAY
B6382
A65 SKIPTON RD
Mus
CASTLE RD
CASTLE HILL
CHURCH ST
Sch
Ashlands First Sch
THWAITES AVE
EAST PAR
GORDON ST
WEST PAR
LITTLE LA
WOODS MEWS
ST MARY'S CL
WOODLANDS
Ilkley Middle Sch
WHEATLEY LA
Wheatley Grange
Ben Rhydding
ILKLEY
VICTORIA CL
BOLTON BRIDGE RD
THE LAWNS
LISTERS CT
REGENT RD
THE MOORS
WEST ST
CRESCENT TERR
TRAFALGAR RD
RAILWAY RD
STEPHENSONS WAY
ST HELEN'S WAY
GREENDOWN CL
ST JOHN'S RD
CHELTENHAM AVE
MOORFIELD RD
KINGS RD
KINGS AVE
SOUTH PAR
WESTVILLE CL
THE GROVE
STATION RD
TH Liby
SPRINGS LA
SPRINGFIELD AVE
WHARFEDALE DR
MARLBOROUGH GR
PARKLANDS
BOLLING RD
WHEATLEY AVE
GROVE RD
ST JAMES' RD
ASHBURN PL
CHANTRY DR
SOUTHWAY
BRIGHTON RD
WYLTON RD
EATON RD
GHYLL MEWS
ALBANY WLK
SEFTON DR
MAUFE WAY
Coronation
Ilkley Grammar Sch
MARLBOROUGH SQ
MANLEY RISE
WHEATLEY GDNS
WOODROYD GDNS
BEN RHYDDING DR
ROWLEY DR
PARISH GHYLL DR
LINNBURN MEWS
ILKLEY HALL MEWS
BELLE VUE
SEDBERGH DR
COWPASTURE RD
CLIFTON RD
CHESTNUT CL
PRINCESS RD
DEACONESS CT
CROSSBECK RD
Moorfield Sch
THE HAYWAIN
PINEWOOD CL
QUEEN'S RD
Coll
MOUNT PLEASANT
CRAIGLANDS PK
BEN RHYDDING RD
Ben Rhydding
ROMBALDS LA
QUEEN'S DR
FERN GDNS
QUEEN'S DRIVE LA
ST MARGARET'S TERR
WELLS RD
4 CHANTRY CL
5 WHITTON CROFT RD
6 STATION PLAZA
7 THE GROVE PROM
MAXWELL RD
HIGH WOOD
CRAGG DR
OAKLANDS
WESTWOOD DR
HILL TOP
MOORLANDS
KEIGHLEY RD
CONSTABLE RD
CH
HANGINGSTONE RD
UNDERCLIFFE RISE
The Tarn
White Wells Visitor Ctr
Golf Course
Barmishaw
Cow & Calf
Gib Field
Backstone Beck
Cow & Calf Hotel
Rocky Valley
West Rock
Ilkley Crags
Dales Way
Dales Way & Ebor Way
Ilkley Moor
Cranshaw Thorn Hill
MOOR RD
Pancake Stone
Badger Stone

7
20

10

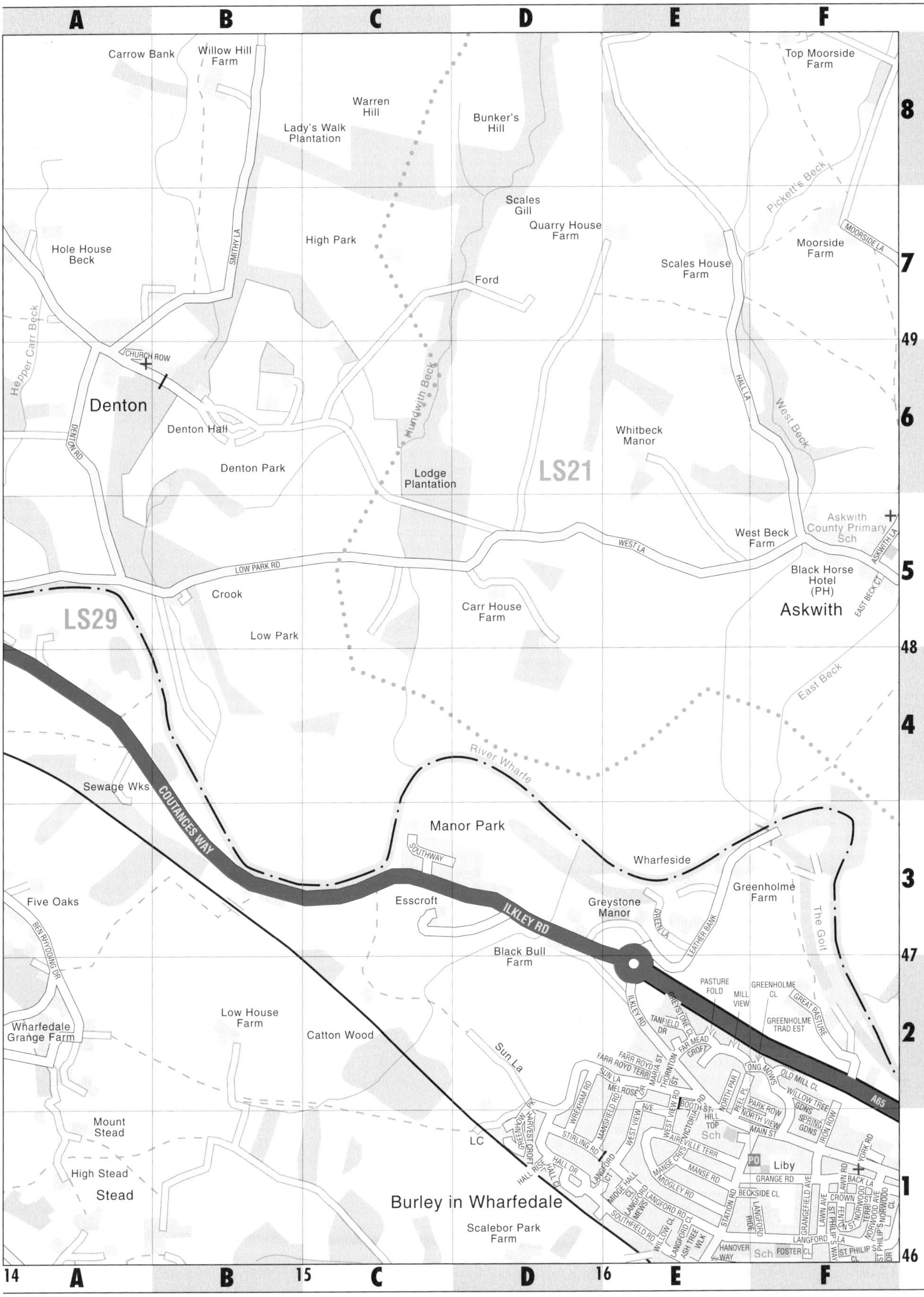
A
B
C
D
E
F
8
7
49
6
5
48
4
3
47
2
1
46
14
15
16
Carrow Bank
Willow Hill Farm
Top Moorside Farm
Warren Hill
Lady's Walk Plantation
Bunker's Hill
Pickett's Beck
Scales Gill
Quarry House Farm
High Park
Hole House Beck
SMITHY LA
MOORSIDE LA
Moorside Farm
Scales House Farm
Ford
Hepper Carr Beck
CHURCH ROW
Denton
Hundwith Beck
HALL LA
West Beck
Denton Hall
DENTON RD
Whitbeck Manor
Denton Park
Lodge Plantation
LS21
Askwith County Primary Sch
West Beck Farm
WEST LA
ASKWITH LA
LOW PARK RD
Black Horse Hotel (PH)
Crook
Carr House Farm
Askwith
EAST BECK CT
LS29
Low Park
East Beck
River Wharfe
Sewage Wks
COUTANCES WAY
Manor Park
SOUTHWAY
Wharfeside
Greenholme Farm
Five Oaks
Esscroft
ILKLEY RD
Greystone Manor
GREEN LA
LEATHER BANK
The Goit
BEN RHYDDING DR
Black Bull Farm
PASTURE FOLD
MILL VIEW
GREENHOLME CL
GREAT PASTURE
GREENHOLME TRAD EST
ILKLEY RD
GREYSTONE CL
TANFIELD DR
FAR MEAD CROFT
Wharfedale Grange Farm
Low House Farm
Catton Wood
Sun La
FARR ROYD
FARR ROYD TERR
MARIA ST
THORNTON ST
SUN LA
MELROSE DR
NORTH PAR
PEEL PL
LONG MDWS
OLD MILL CL
WILLOW TREE GDNS
SPRING GDNS
IRON ROW
A65
WREKHAM RD
MANSFIELD RD
WEST VIEW AVE
WEST VIEW RD
BOOTH ST
HILL TOP
VICTORIA RD
PARK ROW
NORTH VIEW
MAIN ST
Mount Stead
GREENHOLME PK
HARVEST CROFT
LC
STIRLING RD
AIREVILLE TERR
Sch
Liby
YORK RD
High Stead
HALL DR
HALL RISE
HALL CL
LANGFORD CT
MANSE CRES
MANSE RD
GRANGE RD
BACK LA
Stead
MIDGE HALL CL
LANGFORD MEWS
MIDGLEY RD
BECKSIDE CL
CROWN ST
Burley in Wharfedale
LANGFORD RD
STATION RD
LANGFORD RIDE
GRANGEFIELD AVE
LAWN AVE
ST PHILIP'S WAY
SOUTHFIELD RD
WILLOW CL
LANGFORD CL
ASH TREE WLK
Scalebor Park Farm
HANOVER WAY
Sch
FOSTER CL
LANGFORD LA
ST PHILIP'S CL
NORWOOD AVE

21

10

9

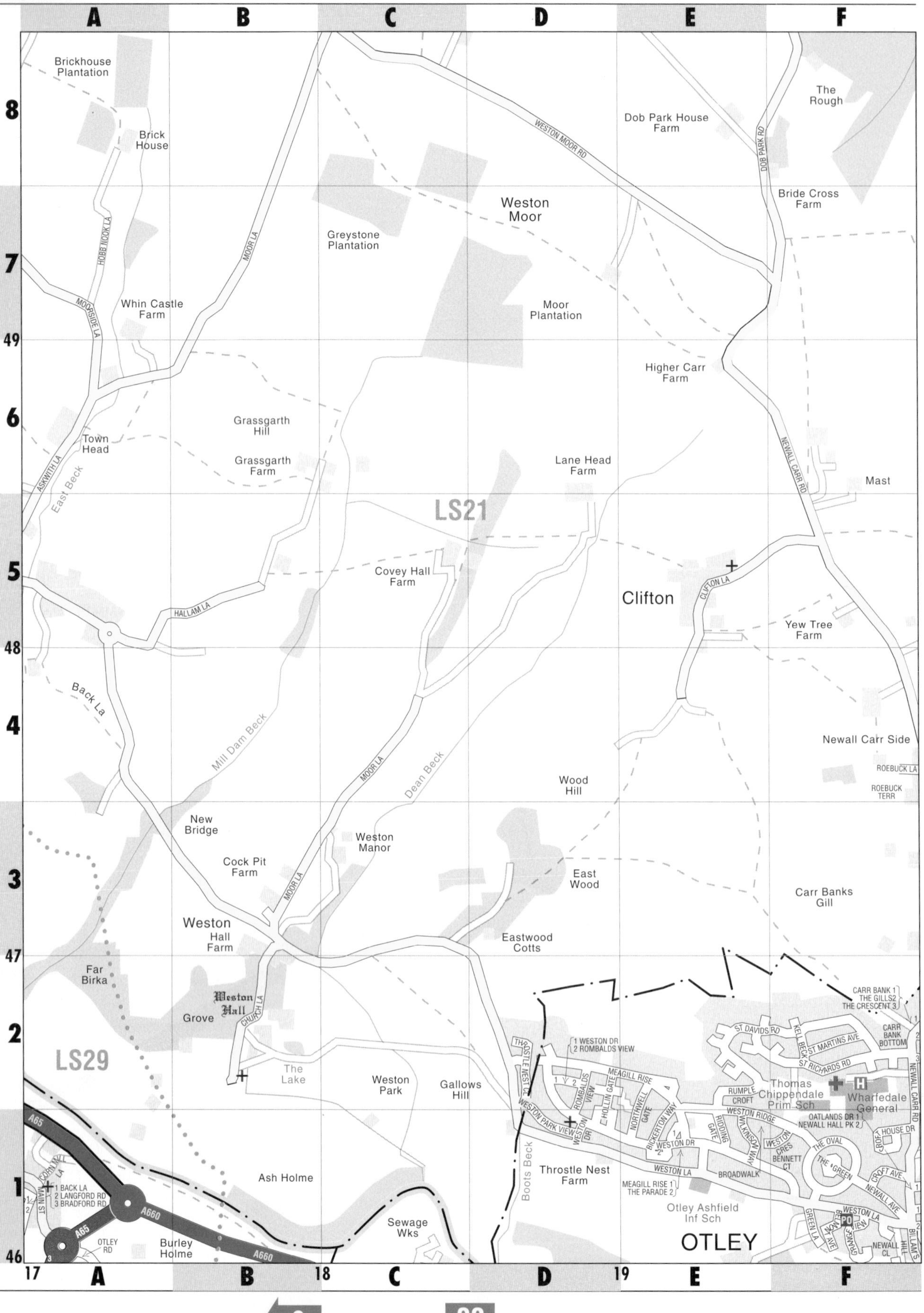

A
B
C
D
E
F
8
7
49
6
5
48
4
3
47
2
1
46
17
18
19
Brickhouse Plantation
Brick House
HOBB NOOK LA
MOOR LA
Greystone Plantation
WESTON MOOR RD
Weston Moor
Dob Park House Farm
DOB PARK RD
The Rough
Bride Cross Farm
MOORSIDE LA
Whin Castle Farm
Moor Plantation
Higher Carr Farm
Grassgarth Hill
Town Head
ASKWITH LA
East Beck
Grassgarth Farm
Lane Head Farm
NEWALL CARR RD
Mast
LS21
Covey Hall Farm
Clifton
CLIFTON LA
HALLAM LA
Yew Tree Farm
Back La
Newall Carr Side
ROEBUCK LA
ROEBUCK TERR
Mill Dam Beck
MOOR LA
Dean Beck
Wood Hill
New Bridge
Weston Manor
Cock Pit Farm
MOOR LA
East Wood
Carr Banks Gill
Weston
Hall Farm
Eastwood Cotts
Far Birka
Weston Hall
CHURCH LA
Grove
LS29
The Lake
Weston Park
Gallows Hill
CARR BANK 1
THE GILLS 2
THE CRESCENT 3
CARR BANK BOTTOM
ST DAVIDS RD
KELL BECK
ST MARTINS AVE
ST RICHARDS RD
1 WESTON DR
2 ROMBALDS VIEW
MEAGILL RISE
ROMBALDS VIEW
HOLLIN GATE
NORTHWELL GATE
RUMPLE CROFT
Thomas Chippendale Prim Sch
Wharfedale General
NEWALL CARR RD
OATLANDS DR 1
NEWALL HALL PK 2
WESTON RIDGE
RIDDING GATE
WILKINSON WAY
WESTON CRES
BENNETT CT
THE OVAL
THE GREEN
HOUSE DR
CROFT AVE
NEWALL AVE
WESTON PARK VIEW
WESTON DR
BICKERTON WAY
WESTON DR
Throstle Nest Farm
WESTON LA
BROADWALK
MEAGILL RISE 1
THE PARADE 2
Boots Beck
Otley Ashfield Inf Sch
WESTON LA
GREEN LA
GRANGE VIEW
NEWALL CL
BILLAMS HILL
PO
OTLEY
A65
CORN MILL LA
MAIN ST
1 BACK LA
2 LANGFORD RD
3 BRADFORD RD
Ash Holme
A660
A65
OTLEY RD
Burley Holme
A660
Sewage Wks

9

22

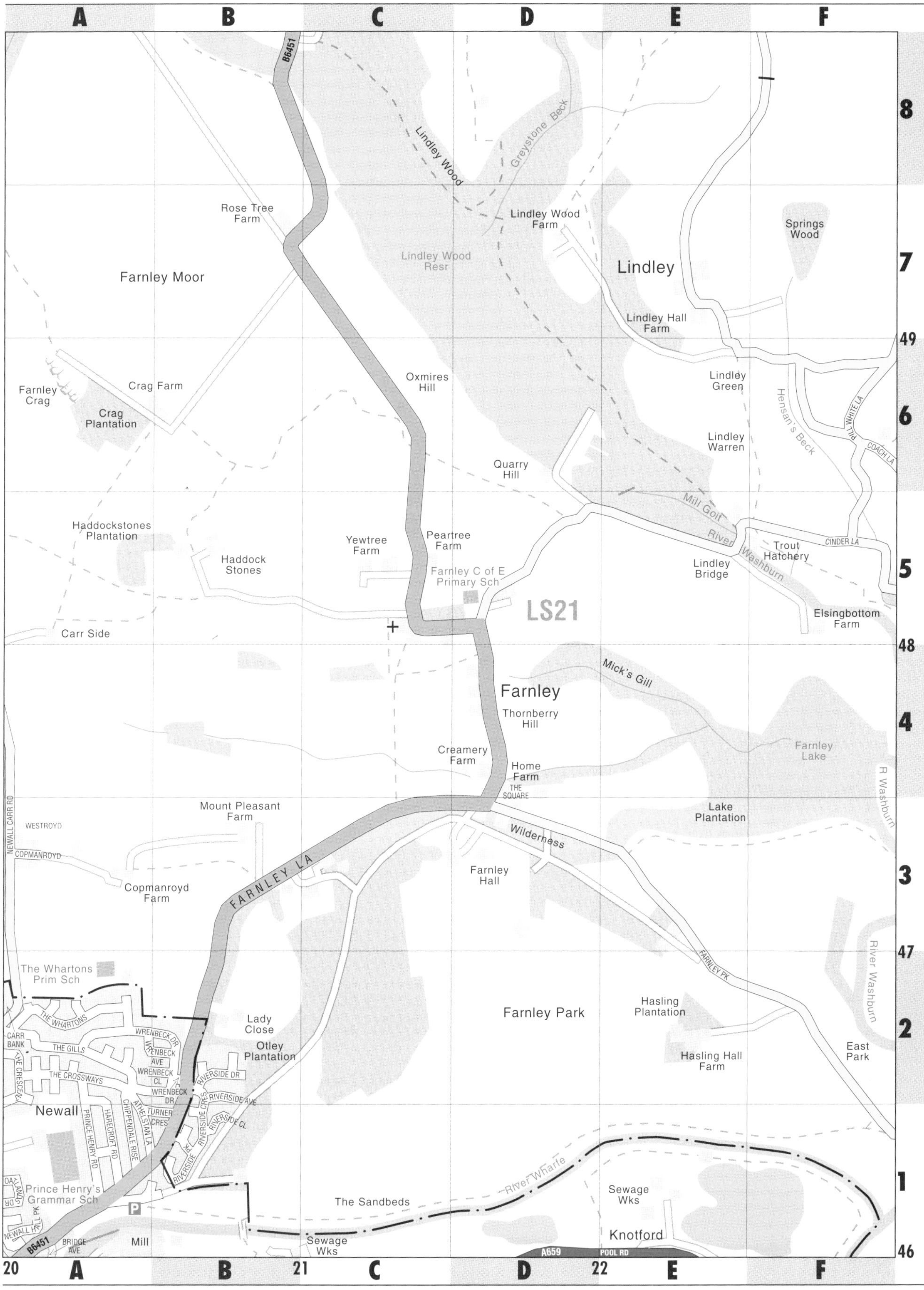

A
B
C
D
E
F
8
7
49
6
5
48
4
3
47
2
1
46
20
21
22
B6451
Lindley Wood
Greystone Beck
Rose Tree Farm
Lindley Wood Farm
Springs Wood
Lindley Wood Resr
Lindley
Farnley Moor
Lindley Hall Farm
Oxmires Hill
Lindley Green
Farnley Crag
Crag Farm
Crag Plantation
Hensan's Beck
PILL WHITE LA
COACH LA
Lindley Warren
Quarry Hill
Mill Goit
River Washburn
Haddockstones Plantation
Yewtree Farm
Peartree Farm
Trout Hatchery
CINDER LA
Haddock Stones
Farnley C of E Primary Sch
Lindley Bridge
LS21
Elsingbottom Farm
Carr Side
Mick's Gill
Farnley
Thornberry Hill
Farnley Lake
Creamery Farm
Home Farm
THE SQUARE
R Washburn
NEWALL CARR RD
Mount Pleasant Farm
Lake Plantation
WESTROYD
COPMANROYD
Wilderness
Farnley Hall
Copmanroyd Farm
FARNLEY LA
FARNLEY PK
River Washburn
The Whartons Prim Sch
THE WHARTONS
WRENBECK DR
Farnley Park
Hasling Plantation
Lady Close
CARR BANK
THE GILLS
WRENBECK AVE
Otley Plantation
East Park
Hasling Hall Farm
THE CROSSWAYS
WRENBECK CL
RIVERSIDE DR
WRENBECK DR
RIVERSIDE AVE
Newall
TURNER CRES
HARECROFT RD
PRINCE HENRY RD
CHIPPENDALE RISE
ATHELSTAN LA
RIVERSIDE CL
River Wharfe
Prince Henry's Grammar Sch
Sewage Wks
The Sandbeds
P
NEWALL HALL PK
B6451
BRIDGE AVE
Mill
Sewage Wks
Knotford
A659
POOL RD

23

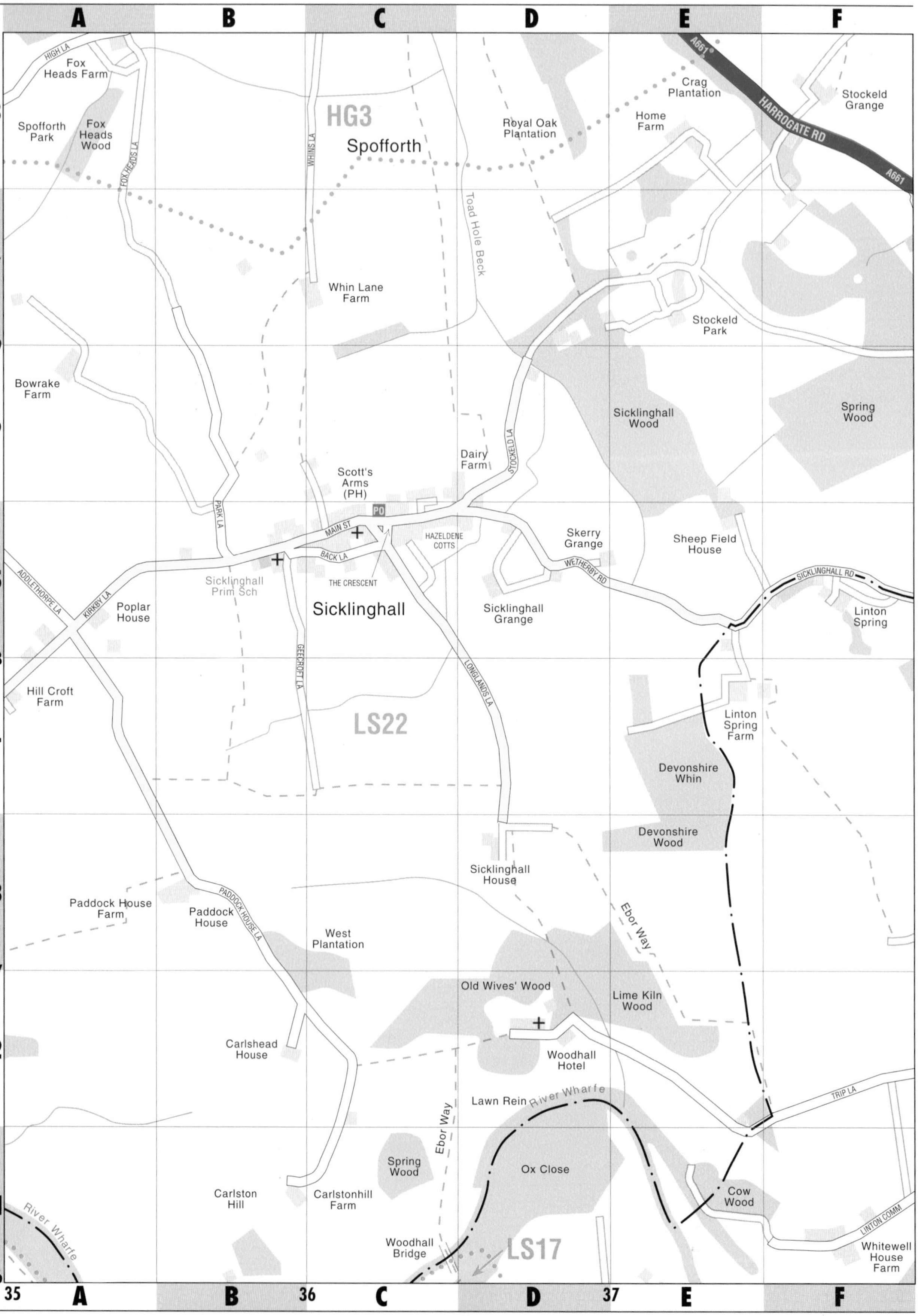
A
B
C
D
E
F
HIGH LA
Fox Heads Farm
Spofforth Park
Fox Heads Wood
FOX HEADS LA
WHINS LA
HG3
Spofforth
Royal Oak Plantation
Toad Hole Beck
Crag Plantation
Home Farm
A661
HARROGATE RD
Stockeld Grange
Whin Lane Farm
Stockeld Park
Bowrake Farm
Sicklinghall Wood
Spring Wood
Dairy Farm
STOCKELD LA
Scott's Arms (PH)
PO
PARK LA
MAIN ST
BACK LA
HAZELDENE COTTS
THE CRESCENT
Skerry Grange
WETHERBY RD
Sheep Field House
SICKLINGHALL RD
ADDLETHORPE LA
KIRKBY LA
Sicklinghall Prim Sch
Poplar House
Sicklinghall
Sicklinghall Grange
Linton Spring
GEECROFT LA
LONGLANDS LA
Hill Croft Farm
LS22
Linton Spring Farm
Devonshire Whin
Devonshire Wood
Sicklinghall House
Paddock House Farm
Paddock House
PADDOCK HOUSE LA
West Plantation
Ebor Way
Old Wives' Wood
Lime Kiln Wood
Carlshead House
Woodhall Hotel
Lawn Rein
River Wharfe
TRIP LA
Ebor Way
Spring Wood
Ox Close
Carlston Hill
Carlstonhill Farm
Cow Wood
LINTON COMM
River Wharfe
Woodhall Bridge
LS17
Whitewell House Farm
8
7
49
6
5
48
4
3
47
2
1
46
35
36
37

28

14

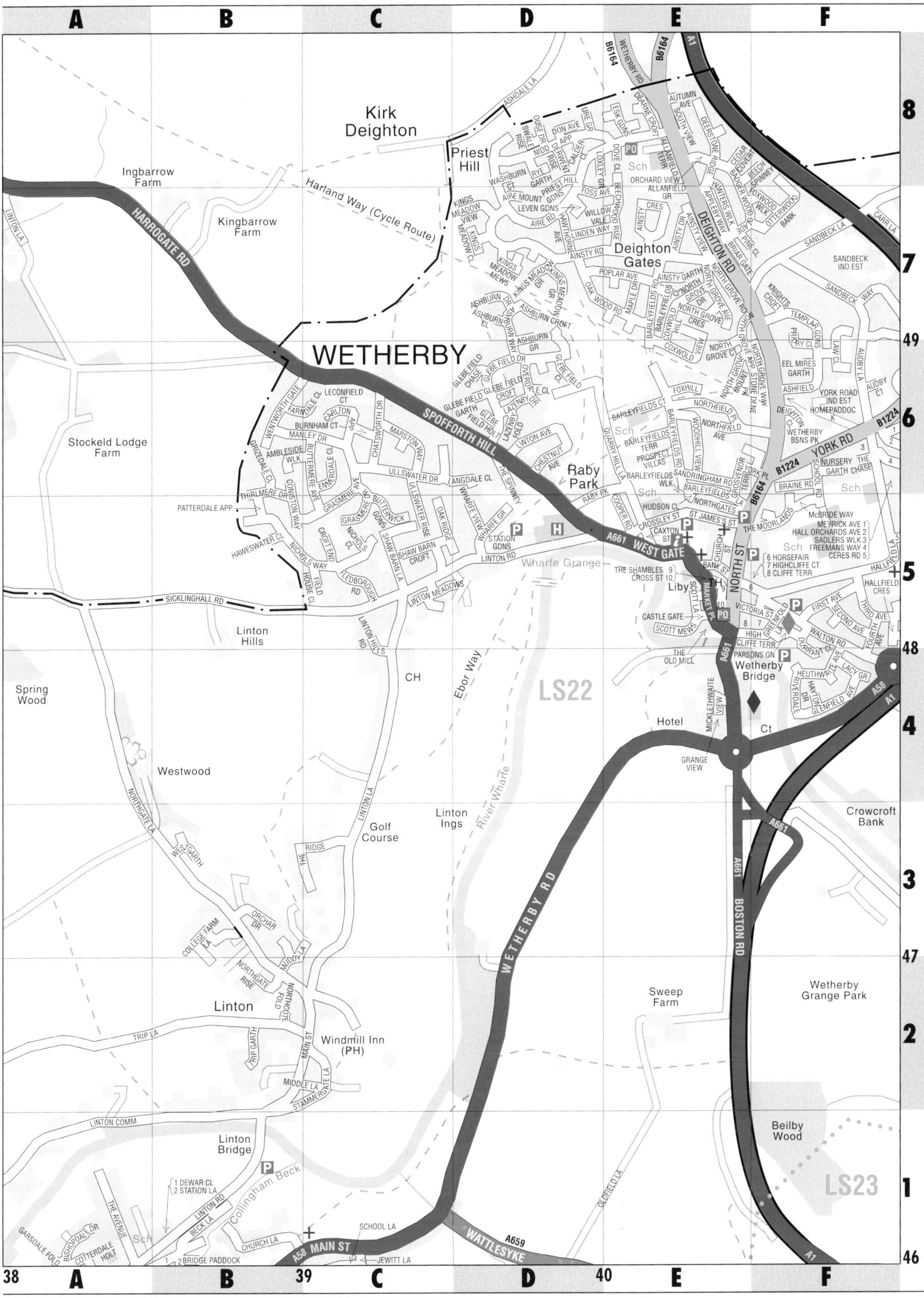
A
B
C
D
E
F
8
7
49
6
5
48
4
3
47
2
1
46
38
39
40
Kirk Deighton
Priest Hill
Ingbarrow Farm
Kingbarrow Farm
Harland Way (Cycle Route)
HARROGATE RD
LINTON LA
ASHDALE LA
B6164
WETHERBY RD
A1
DEIGHTON RD
Deighton Gates
Sch
PO
AUTUMN AVE
SOUTH VIEW
DEERSTONE RIDGE
ALLANFIELD TERR
ALLANFIELD GR
ORCHARD VIEW
DEARNE CROFT
ESK GDNS
URE GR
DON AVE
CALDER CL
DOVE CL
LOXLEY GR
FOSS AVE
BEECHWOOD RISE
AINSTY CRES
AINSTY DR
AINSTY RD
AINSTY GARTH
SWALE RISE
OUSE DR
NIDD APP
DERWENT AVE
RYE GARTH
WASHBURN CT
PRIEST HILL GDNS
AIRE MOUNT
LEVEN GDNS
AIRE RD
WILLOW VALE
LINDEN WAY
HAWTHORN AVE
POPLAR AVE
OAK WOOD RD
MAPLE DR
KINGS MEADOW VIEW
KINGS MEADOW CL
KINGS MEADOW MEWS
KINGS MEADOW DR
KINGS MEADOW GR
ASHBURN DR
ASHBURN CL
ASHBURN WAY
ASHBURN CROFT
ASHBURN GR
NORTH GROVE RD
NORTH GROVE DR
NORTH GROVE CRES
NORTH GROVE CL
NORTH GROVE AVE
NORTH GROVE WAY
NORTH GROVE MOUNT
NORTH GROVE APP
COXWOLD VIEW
COXWOLD HILL
COXWOLD WLK
BARLEYFIELDS RD
BARLEYFIELDS CL
BARLEYFIELDS CT
BARLEYFIELDS TERR
BARLEYFIELDS WLK
HUNTERS WLK
APPLEBY WAY
BADGER WOOD GLADE
CEDAR COVERT
BEECH SPINNEY
FOXWOOD WLK
OTTERWOOD BANK
PINE CL
BRIAR GATE
SANDBECK LA
SANDBECK IND EST
SANDBECK WAY
CARR LA
KNIGHTS CROFT
TEMPLAR GDNS
PRIORY CL
LAW CL
AUDBY LA
AUDBY CT
EEL MIRES GARTH
ASHFIELD
YORK ROAD IND EST
HOMEPADDOCK
DEIGHTON CL
WETHERBY BSNS PK
YORK RD
B1224
NURSERY GARTH
THE CHASE
SCHOOL RD
BRAINE RD
STONE DENE
WETHERBY
GLEBE FIELD CHASE
GLEBE FIELD DR
GLEBE FIELD GARTH
GLEBE FIELD CROFT
GLEBE FIELD HOLT
GLEBE FIELD CL
OVERDALE CL
LAZENBY FOLD
LINTON AVE
CHESTNUT AVE
FOXHILL
NORTHFIELD PL
NORTHFIELD AVE
WOODHILL VIEW
QUARRY HILL LA
PROSPECT VILLAS
SANDRINGHAM RD
GROSVENOR TERR
YORK PL
NORTHGATES
ST JAMES'S ST
THE MOORLANDS
HUDSON CL
CROSSLEY ST
CAXTON ST
COOPER RD
Raby Park
RABY PK
WENTWORTH GATE
FARNDALE CL
LECONFIELD CT
CARLTON APP
BURNHAM CT
MANLEY DR
CHATSWORTH DR
MARSTON WAY
AMBLESIDE WLK
BUTTERMERE AVE
ENNERDALE CL
GRIZEDALE CL
THIRLMERE DR
CONISTON WAY
ULLSWATER DR
ULLSWATER RISE
LANGDALE CL
GRASMERE AVE
GRASMERE DR
BUTTERWICK GDNS
SHAW BARN LA
SHAW BARN CROFT
OAK RIDGE
WHARFE VIEW
WHARFE GR
THE SPINNEY
SPOFFORTH HILL
PATTERDALE APP
HAWESWATER CL
NICHOLS WAY
NICHOLS CL
CROFT END
FLEDBOROUGH RD
HOUSE FIELD CL
STATION GDNS
LINTON RD
A661
WEST GATE
CHURCH ST
NORTH ST
BANK ST
P
H
i
TH
Liby
PO
Wharfe Grange
THE SHAMBLES 9
CROSS ST 10
SCOTT LA
MARKET PL
CASTLE GATE
SCOTT MEWS
VICTORIA ST
HIGH ST
CLIFFE TERR
PARSONS GN
GREENFOLD LA
THE OLD MILL
6 HORSEFAIR
7 HIGHCLIFFE CT
8 CLIFFE TERR
McBRIDE WAY
MEYRICK AVE 1
HALL ORCHARDS AVE 2
SADLERS WLK 3
FREEMANS WAY 4
CERES RD 5
HALLFIELD LA
HALLFIELD CRES
FIRST AVE
SECOND AVE
THIRD AVE
FOURTH AVE
WALTON RD
DURRANT CL
LACY GR
HEUTHWAITE AVE
HAYTON DR
RIVERDALE
GLENFIELD AVE
Wetherby Bridge
A58
Ct
Hotel
MICKLETHWAITE VIEW
GRANGE VIEW
SICKLINGHALL RD
LINTON MEADOWS
Linton Hills
LINTON HILLS RD
CH
Ebor Way
LS22
Stockeld Lodge Farm
Spring Wood
Westwood
NORTHGATE LA
WEST GARTH
Golf Course
LINTON LA
THE RIDGE
Linton Ings
River Wharfe
WETHERBY RD
Crowcroft Bank
BOSTON RD
ORCHARD DR
COLLEGE FARM LA
MUDDY LA
NORTHGATE RISE
NORTHCOTE FOLD
Linton
Windmill Inn (PH)
MAIN ST
TRIP LA
TRIP GARTH
MIDDLE LA
STAMMERGATE LA
Sweep Farm
Wetherby Grange Park
LINTON COMM
Linton Bridge
Collingham Beck
1 DEWAR CL
2 STATION LA
LINTON RD
BECK LA
THE AVENUE
GARSDALE FOLD
BISHOPDALE DR
COTTERDALE HOLT
1 2 BRIDGE PADDOCK
CHURCH LA
SCHOOL LA
JEWITT LA
A58 MAIN ST
WATTLESYKE
A659
OLDFIELD LA
Beilby Wood
LS23

29

14

13

A
B
C
D
E
F
8
7
49
6
5
48
4
3
47
2
1
46
41
42
43
Ingmanthorpe Park
Broad Wath
Sandbeck House
SANDBECK LA
Swinnow Hill
Moss Carrs Farm
B1224
Sandbeck Wood
Sand Beck
Cockshot Wood
Swinnow Park
YORK RD
A1
SANDBECK WAY
CARR LA
HM Young Offender Inst
Sand Bridge
Champagne Whin
THE ROWANS
Ind Est
THE BEECHES
Works
LS22
SPRINGS LA
B1224
NETHERDALE CT
Wetherby Race Course
MEYRICK AVE
HALL ORCHARDS AVE
FREEMANS WAY
MONTAGU RD
GUNTER RD
SYKE RD
CERES RD
Sykes House Farm
Stables
The Rampart
Hallfield Cemy
Springs Wood
THIRD AVE
BURREL CL
HALLFIELD CRES
MOOR LA
SPRING LA
A1
A58
WALTON RD
Park Hill Farm
SCHOOL LA
WETHERBY RD
Heuthwaite La
WATERSOLE LA
Flint Mill Grange
West Field
Ebor Way
Crowcroft Bank
LS23
WALTON CHASE
Sewage Works
FLINTMILL LA
Wray Wood
WOOD LA
Wetherby Grange
River Wharfe
Wetherby Grange Park
Whin Covert
New Springs
Middle Field
LEYS LA
WALTON RD
Hall Farm
The Leys
DEEP DALE
Hall Wood
Lady Elizabeth Hastings CE Sch
Gunter Wood
DOWKELL LA
Thorparch Hall
The Pax Inn (PH)
CHURCH CSWY
THORPE ARCH PK
PEAR TREE ACRE
THE VILLAGE
Thorp Arch
Thorparch Park
MULBERRY GARTH
LEYS LA
DEEPDALE LA
WEST AVE
WEST LA
WEST END
WEST DALE
West Park
WHINS LA

13

30

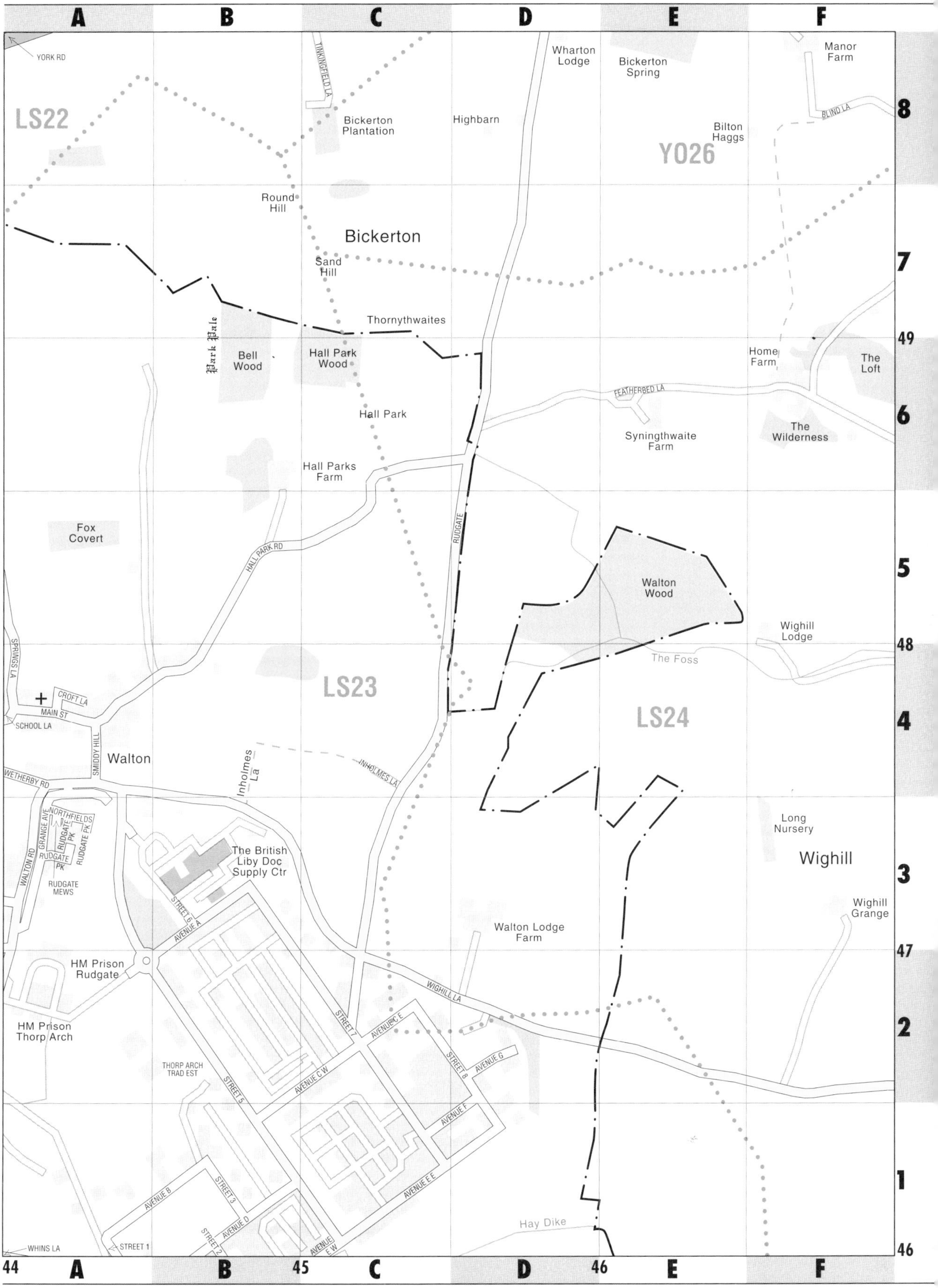
A
B
C
D
E
F
YORK RD
LS22
TINKINGFIELD LA
Bickerton Plantation
Highbarn
Wharton Lodge
Bickerton Spring
Manor Farm
BLIND LA
Bilton Haggs
YO26
Round Hill
Bickerton
Sand Hill
Thornythwaites
Park Pale
Bell Wood
Hall Park Wood
Home Farm
The Loft
FEATHERBED LA
Hall Park
Syningthwaite Farm
The Wilderness
Hall Parks Farm
RUDGATE
Fox Covert
HALL PARK RD
Walton Wood
Wighill Lodge
The Foss
SPRINGS LA
CROFT LA
MAIN ST
SCHOOL LA
LS23
LS24
SMIDDY HILL
Walton
Inholmes La
INHOLMES LA
WETHERBY RD
NORTHFIELDS
GRANGE AVE
RUDGATE PK
WALTON RD
RUDGATE MEWS
The British Liby Doc Supply Ctr
Long Nursery
Wighill
STREET 6
AVENUE A
Wighill Grange
Walton Lodge Farm
HM Prison Rudgate
WIGHILL LA
HM Prison Thorp Arch
STREET 7
AVENUE C E
STREET 8
AVENUE G
THORP ARCH TRAD EST
STREET 5
AVENUE C W
AVENUE F
AVENUE B
STREET 3
AVENUE E E
AVENUE D
STREET 2
Hay Dike
WHINS LA
STREET 1
AVENUE E W
8
7
49
6
5
48
4
3
47
2
1
46
44
45
46

31

4

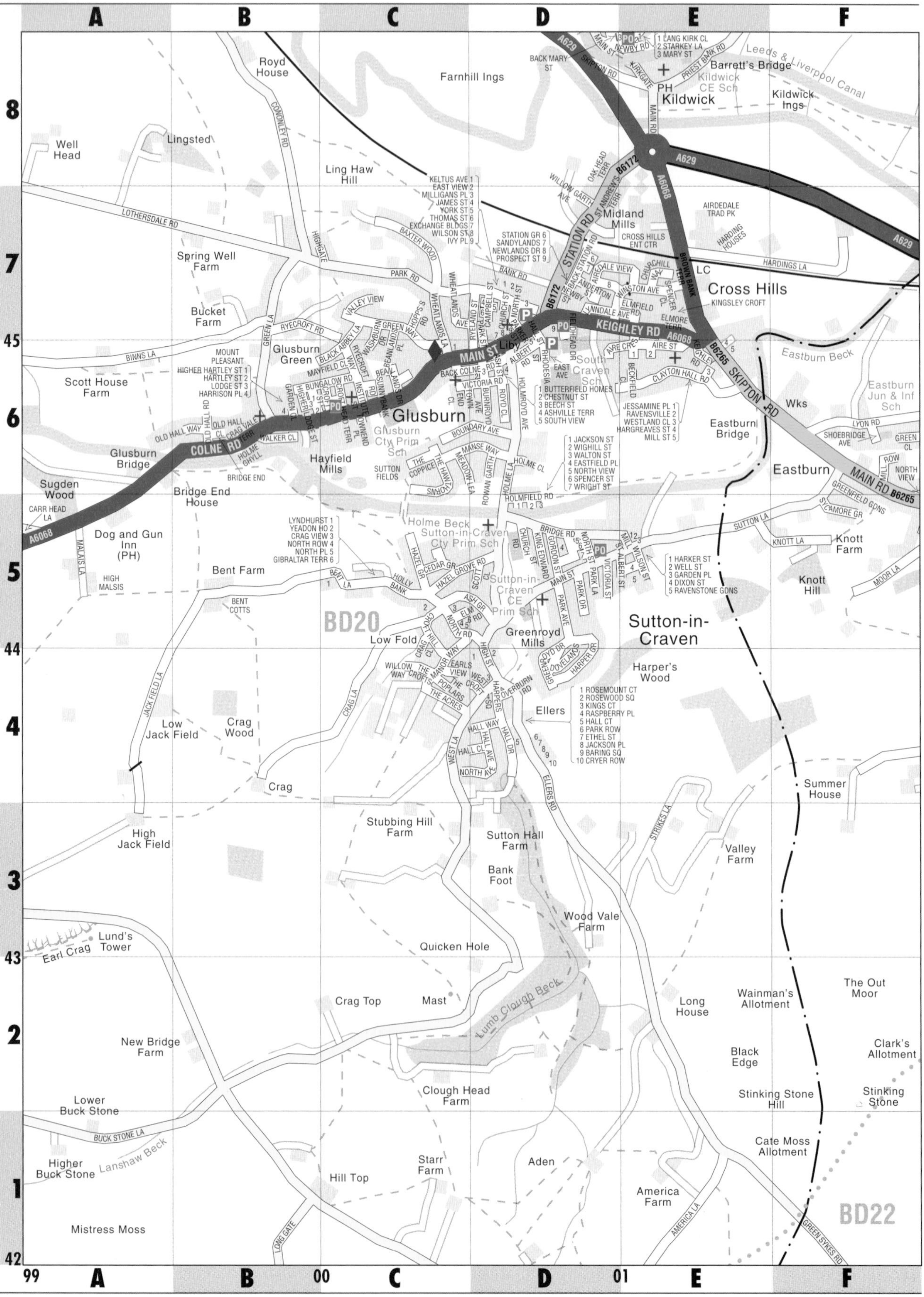
A
B
C
D
E
F
8
7
45
6
5
44
4
3
43
2
1
42
99
00
01
Royd House
Farnhill Ings
Well Head
Lingsted
Ling Haw Hill
Spring Well Farm
Bucket Farm
Scott House Farm
Glusburn Green
Glusburn
Glusburn Bridge
Hayfield Mills
Sugden Wood
Bridge End House
Dog and Gun Inn (PH)
Bent Farm
BD20
Low Fold
Low Jack Field
Crag Wood
Crag
High Jack Field
Stubbing Hill Farm
Sutton Hall Farm
Bank Foot
Wood Vale Farm
Lund's Tower
Earl Crag
Quicken Hole
Crag Top
Mast
Lumb Clough Beck
New Bridge Farm
Lower Buck Stone
Clough Head Farm
Higher Buck Stone
Lanshaw Beck
Hill Top
Starr Farm
Aden
America Farm
Mistress Moss
BD22
Kildwick
Kildwick CE Sch
Kildwick Ings
Barrett's Bridge
Leeds & Liverpool Canal
Midland Mills
Cross Hills
Eastburn Beck
Eastburn Jun & Inf Sch
Eastburn Bridge
Eastburn
Wks
Knott Farm
Knott Hill
Sutton-in-Craven
Harper's Wood
Ellers
Summer House
Valley Farm
Long House
Wainman's Allotment
The Out Moor
Black Edge
Clark's Allotment
Stinking Stone Hill
Stinking Stone
Cate Moss Allotment
Greenroyd Mills
Holme Beck
Sutton-in-Craven Cty Prim Sch
Sutton-in-Craven CE Prim Sch
Glusburn Cty Prim Sch
South Craven Sch
Liby
PO
PH
LC
A629
A6068
B6172
B6265
KEIGHLEY RD
MAIN ST
COLNE RD
SKIPTON RD
MAIN RD
STATION RD
LOTHERSDALE RD
PARK RD
BINNS LA
GREEN LA
HIGHGATE
CONONLEY RD
SUTTON LA
BUCK STONE LA
JACK FIELD LA
CRAG LA
ELLERS RD
STRIKES LA
AMERICA LA
LONG GATE
GREEN SYKES RD
HARDINGS LA
MOOR LA
KNOTT LA
MALSIS LA
CARR HEAD LA
HIGH MALSIS
BENT COTTS
BENT LA
SUTTON FIELDS
BRIDGE END
AIREDALE TRAD PK
CROSS HILLS ENT CTR
KINGSLEY CROFT
1 LANG KIRK CL
2 STARKEY LA
3 MARY ST
KELTUS AVE 1
EAST VIEW 2
MILLIGANS PL 3
JAMES ST 4
YORK ST 5
THOMAS ST 6
EXCHANGE BLDGS 7
WILSON ST 8
IVY PL 9
STATION GR 6
SANDYLANDS 7
NEWLANDS DR 8
PROSPECT ST 9
MOUNT PLEASANT
HIGHER HARTLEY ST 1
HARTLEY ST 2
LODGE ST 3
HARRISON PL 4
1 BUTTERFIELD HOMES
2 CHESTNUT ST
3 BEECH ST
4 ASHVILLE TERR
5 SOUTH VIEW
JESSAMINE PL 1
RAVENSVILLE 2
WESTLAND CL 3
HARGREAVES ST 4
MILL ST 5
1 JACKSON ST
2 WIGHILL ST
3 WALTON ST
4 EASTFIELD PL
5 NORTH VIEW
6 SPENCER ST
7 WRIGHT ST
LYNDHURST 1
YEADON HO 2
CRAG VIEW 3
NORTH ROW 4
NORTH PL 5
GIBRALTAR TERR 6
1 HARKER ST
2 WELL ST
3 GARDEN PL
4 DIXON ST
5 RAVENSTONE GDNS
1 ROSEMOUNT CT
2 ROSEWOOD SQ
3 KINGS CT
4 RASPBERRY PL
5 HALL CT
6 PARK ROW
7 ETHEL ST
8 JACKSON PL
9 BARING SQ
10 CRYER ROW

33

5
18

A
B
C
D
E
F
Grange La
Leeds & Liverpool Canal
Grange Bridge
Lane House Bridge
Woodside Bridge
Cowling Bridge
Silsden Bridge
A6034
KEIGHLEY RD
Silsden Beck
Silsden Ings
Steeton Ings
River Aire
STEETON GR
Steeton & Silsden
Hotel
STATION RD
RIVOCK AVE
SUMMERHILL LA
Airedale General
H
MAIN RD
SKIPTON RD
HAREFIELD CL
NORTH VIEW
LYON RD
GREEN CL
GREEN LA
GRANGE RD
GRANGE TERR
VINCENT AVE
HAREWOOD AVE
MOORSIDE AVE
JAMES AVE
MOOR LA
SUN ST
GRANGE VIEW
BRACKEN RD
INGS RD
WILSON AVE
HERON CL
ROBIN DR
THORNHILL RD
GAMEL VIEW
CURRER WLK
CURLEW CL
TEAL CT
ELM VIEW
STIRTON WAY
PARK HOUSE
HALSTEADS WAY
THORNHILL GR
PARKWAY
GARFORTH AVE
CLOUGH AVE
ELMSLEY ST
ST STEPHEN'S CT
ST STEPHEN'S RD
STEETON HALL GDNS
LOW FOLD
SUMMERHILL AVE
SUMMERHILL DR
EAST PAR
ASH GR
STATION VIEW
CRICKETERS WLK
PO
WILLIAMS RD
WILLIAMS DR
COPPY RD
CHAPEL RD
DALE CRES
QUEEN ST
FORGE VIEW
MILL LA
SCHOOL ST
MARKET ST
SCHOOL ST
HIGH ST
FALCON CLIFFE
DALE VIEW
BOBBIN
MILL CT
WOOD ST
SEED HILL TERR
QUARRY COTTS
1 CROFT ST
2 BEECH ST
3 DIXON CL
4 BOBBIN MILL CL
5 HILL TOP
GHYLL CL
Steeton Prim Sch
P
Steeton Manor
Coppy Farm
Currer Wood
Steeton
Hollins Bank
Hawkcliffe House
Hawkcliffe Farm
Bank House Farm
Twr
AIREBURN AVE
Steeton Beck
BARROWS LA
BD20
Moor La
HOLLINS BANK LA
A629
Whitley Head
Little Snowden
INTAKE LA
Brighton Wood
Meadow Field Farm
Great Snowden
The Hollins
SKIPTON RD B6265
Gilvatt's Allotment
White Field Farm
Hunters' Hill
Steeton Moor
REDCAR LA
Lower Redcar Farm
Moorhouse Allotment
BAR HOUSE LA
RIVOCK AVE
RIVOCK GR
FERNCLIFFE DR
HOLLINS LA
HOLLINS CL
Middle Redcar Farm
Bairstow's Allotment
Whinburn Farm
Whinburn Sch
Dam Green Top
Cockshot Dam Green
Tarn Hill
Tarn House Farm
Four Oaks Lodge
Higher Redcar
Redcar Tarn
Cutshaw Moor
GREENACRES DR
BD22
Prospect House
SHANN LA
Tarn Laddy
TARN LA
BLACK HILL LA
BRAITHWAITE EDGE RD
WESTWAY
SYKES LA
WALKER'S PL
LOW HOUSE DR
GLAISDALE CL
CROFT FIELD
CALDER WAY
DERWENT CT
CLAYMORE RISE
INGS WAY
JENNINGS CL
CHARLTON GR
ROMBALDS CRES
HEBER CL
WINDGATE
HOLDEN LA
BRINDLEY RD
TELFORD CL
WATERSIDE
LOWFIELD CRES
HAWBER LA
RIVERSIDE COTTS
BELTON RD
NIDD CT 1
THANET GARTH 2
DOBSONS WHARF 3
SWALE CT 4
AIRE CT 5
HAINSWORTH RD
KEN HOLME LA
BRUNTHWAITE BRIDGE LA
LOW LA
LOW LA
COURT YARD MEWS
Howden House Farm
8
7
45
6
5
44
4
3
43
2
1
42
02
03
04

34
18

17
6

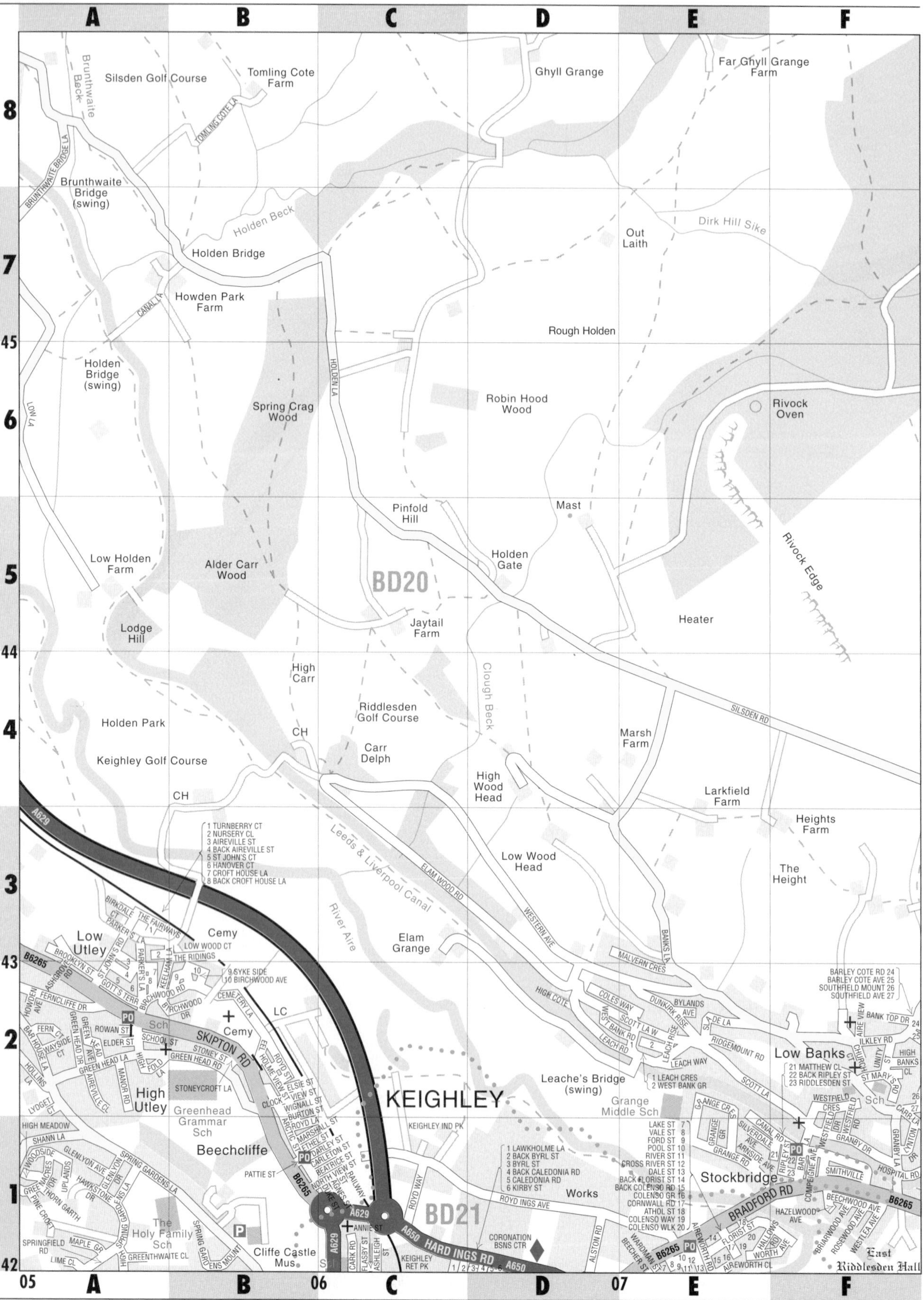
A
B
C
D
E
F
8
7
45
6
5
44
4
3
43
2
1
42
05
06
07
Silsden Golf Course
Brunthwaite Beck
Tomling Cote Farm
TOMLING COTE LA
Ghyll Grange
Far Ghyll Grange Farm
BRUNTHWAITE BRIDGE LA
Brunthwaite Bridge (swing)
Holden Beck
Holden Bridge
Dirk Hill Sike
Out Laith
CANAL LA
Howden Park Farm
Rough Holden
Holden Bridge (swing)
HOLDEN LA
LOW LA
Robin Hood Wood
Rivock Oven
Spring Crag Wood
Pinfold Hill
Mast
Rivock Edge
Low Holden Farm
Alder Carr Wood
Holden Gate
BD20
Heater
Lodge Hill
Jaytail Farm
High Carr
Clough Beck
Riddlesden Golf Course
SILSDEN RD
Holden Park
CH
Carr Delph
Marsh Farm
Keighley Golf Course
CH
High Wood Head
Larkfield Farm
A629
Heights Farm
1 TURNBERRY CT
2 NURSERY CL
3 AIREVILLE ST
4 BACK AIREVILLE ST
5 ST JOHN'S CT
6 HANOVER CT
7 CROFT HOUSE LA
8 BACK CROFT HOUSE LA
Leeds & Liverpool Canal
ELAM WOOD RD
Low Wood Head
The Height
River Aire
WESTERN AVE
Low Utley
Cemy
LOW WOOD CT
THE RIDINGS
Elam Grange
BANKS LA
MALVERN CRES
B6265
9 SYKE SIDE
10 BIRCHWOOD AVE
BARLEY COTE RD 24
BARLEY COTE AVE 25
SOUTHFIELD MOUNT 26
SOUTHFIELD AVE 27
HIGH COTE
COLES WAY
DUNKIRK RISE
BYLANDS AVE
LC
Cemy
SKIPTON RD
AIRE VIEW
BANK TOP DR
Sch
RIDGEMOUNT RD
Low Banks
21 MATTHEW CL
22 BACK RIPLEY ST
23 RIDDLESDEN ST
LEACH WAY
Leache's Bridge (swing)
1 LEACH CRES
2 WEST BANK GR
SCOTT LA
High Utley
STONEYCROFT LA
KEIGHLEY
Grange Middle Sch
Greenhead Grammar Sch
KEIGHLEY IND PK
LAKE ST 7
VALE ST 8
FORD ST 9
POOL ST 10
RIVER ST 11
CROSS RIVER ST 12
DALE ST 13
BACK FLORIST ST 14
BACK COLENSO RD 15
COLENSO GR 16
CORNWALL RD 17
ATHOL ST 18
COLENSO WAY 19
COLENSO WLK 20
Beechcliffe
1 LAWKHOLME LA
2 BACK BYRL ST
3 BYRL ST
4 BACK CALEDONIA RD
5 CALEDONIA RD
6 KIRBY ST
Stockbridge
PATTIE ST
Works
ROYD INGS AVE
BRADFORD RD
B6265
BD21
The Holy Family Sch
HARD INGS RD
A650
CORONATION BSNS CTR
Cliffe Castle Mus
KEIGHLEY RET PK
HAZELWOOD AVE
East Riddlesden Hall

17
35

7
20

A
B
C
D
E
F
8
7
45
6
5
44
4
3
43
2
1
42
08
09
10
Sike Head
Dirk Hill Sike
Bucking Hill
East Buck Stones
West Buck Stones
LS29
Cowper's Cross
Keighley Rd
Whetstone Gate
Masts
Whetstone Allotment
Thimble Stones
Brown Seaves
High Moor
Morton Moor
High Bradup
Low Bradup
ILKLEY RD
Lay Thorn Hill
Rivock
Bradup
Brass Castle
BD20
Bradup Beck
Low Moor
Sweet Well Dike
Fenny Shaw Allotment
Upwood Hall Farm
Upwood Hall
The Glen
Moorcock Farm
SILSDEN RD
Fenny Shaw Beck
Stanbury Hill
Glen Farm
Moor Side Farm
MOOR SIDE COTTS
Sunny Dale
Morton Dam
UPPER MILL ROW
Ousel Hole
BARLEY COTE RD
BARLEY COTE AVE
1 SOUTHFIELD MOUNT
2 BARLEY COTE GR
3 SOUTHFIELD WAY
4 SOUTHLANDS GR W
West Morton
STREET LA
Moorlands Farm
Botany
LAKESIDE
How Beck
SOUTHFIELD DR
FIELDEDGE LA
Dene Hole
BOTANY DR
PROVIDENCE ROW
SOUTHFIELD AVE
SOUTHLANDS RD
CARR RD
CARR LA
UPWOOD LA
GREEN END RD
SUNNYDALE PK
ALMA TERR
5 SOUTHLANDS MOUNT
6 SOUTHLANDS DR
7 SOUTHLANDS GR
8 SOUTHLANDS AVE
ALTAR DR
HOSPITAL RD
NEWLYN RD
DALESIDE RD
Bury La
East Morton
OLDSIDE CT
OTLEY RD
Riddlesden
HARTLEY'S SQ 1
THE SQUARE 2
BACK LA 3
CROFT RD 4
SUN ST
STUDLEY CL
SILK MILL DR
STEPPING STONES
BD16
Leeds & Liverpool Canal
CARR BANK
HIGHFIELD MEWS
HIGHFIELD CL
STOCKS HILL
LAYTHORP CL
TERR
MAIN RD
LITTLE LA
Green End
BRADFORD RD B6265
KINGSWAY
SOUTH VIEW
SWINE LA
CARR LA
HOWBECK AVE
HOWBECK DR
ASHWOOD DR
OTLEY MOUNT
CARR LA
HEIGHTS LA
Belle Vue Farm

36
20

19
8

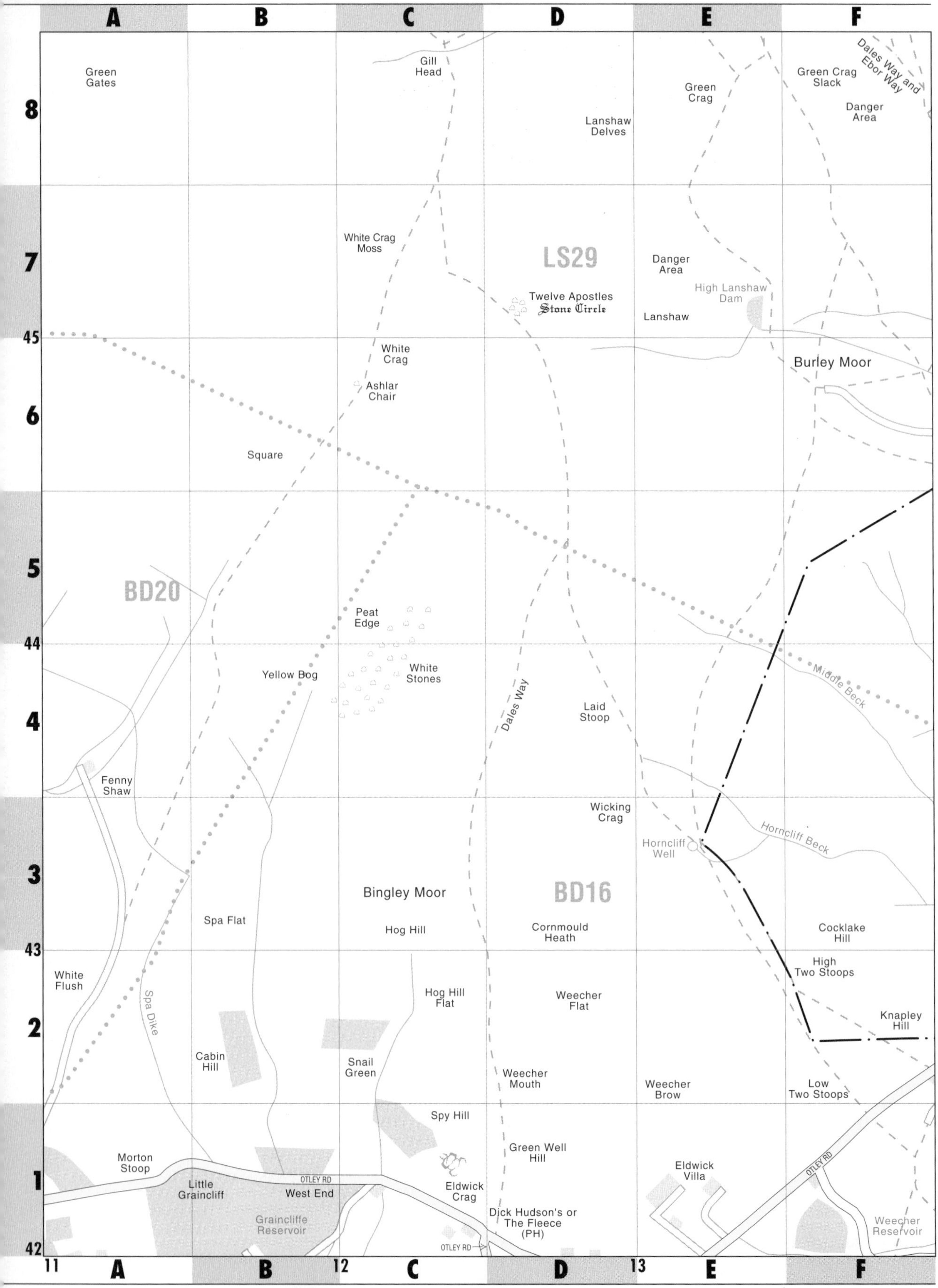
A
B
C
D
E
F
8
7
45
6
5
44
4
3
43
2
1
42
11
12
13
Green Gates
Gill Head
Green Crag
Lanshaw Delves
Green Crag Slack
Dales Way and Ebor Way
Danger Area
White Crag Moss
LS29
Danger Area
High Lanshaw Dam
Twelve Apostles
Stone Circle
Lanshaw
White Crag
Burley Moor
Ashlar Chair
Square
BD20
Peat Edge
Yellow Bog
White Stones
Dales Way
Middle Beck
Laid Stoop
Fenny Shaw
Wicking Crag
Horncliff Well
Horncliff Beck
Bingley Moor
BD16
Spa Flat
Hog Hill
Cornmould Heath
Cocklake Hill
White Flush
High Two Stoops
Spa Dike
Hog Hill Flat
Weecher Flat
Knapley Hill
Cabin Hill
Snail Green
Weecher Mouth
Weecher Brow
Low Two Stoops
Spy Hill
Green Well Hill
Morton Stoop
Eldwick Villa
OTLEY RD
Little Graincliff
West End
Eldwick Crag
Graincliffe Reservoir
Dick Hudson's or The Fleece (PH)
Weecher Reservoir

19
37

9
22

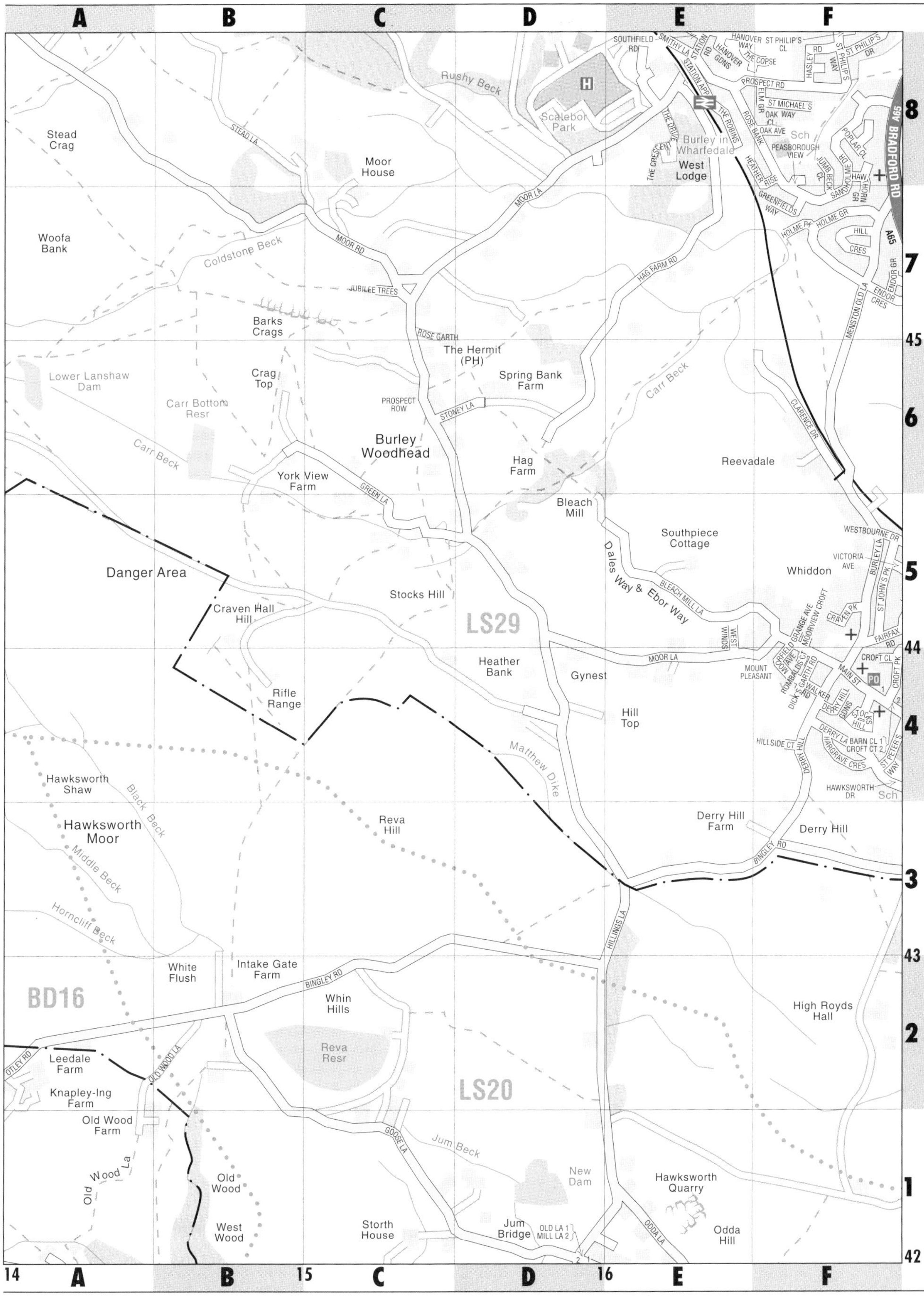
A
B
C
D
E
F
Stead Crag
Woofa Bank
Moor House
Rushy Beck
Scalebor Park
Burley in Wharfedale
West Lodge
Coldstone Beck
Barks Crags
Lower Lanshaw Dam
Carr Bottom Resr
Crag Top
The Hermit (PH)
Spring Bank Farm
Carr Beck
Burley Woodhead
Hag Farm
York View Farm
Reevadale
Bleach Mill
Southpiece Cottage
Danger Area
Dales Way & Ebor Way
Whiddon
Craven Hall Hill
Stocks Hill
LS29
Heather Bank
Gynest
Mount Pleasant
Rifle Range
Hill Top
Matthew Dike
Hawksworth Shaw
Black Beck
Hawksworth Moor
Reva Hill
Middle Beck
Derry Hill Farm
Derry Hill
Horncliff Beck
White Flush
Intake Gate Farm
BD16
Whin Hills
High Royds Hall
Leedale Farm
Reva Resr
Knapley-Ing Farm
LS20
Old Wood Farm
Jum Beck
Old Wood
New Dam
Hawksworth Quarry
West Wood
Storth House
Jum Bridge
Odda Hill
STEAD LA
MOOR RD
MOOR LA
JUBILEE TREES
ROSE GARTH
HAG FARM RD
PROSPECT ROW
STONEY LA
GREEN LA
CLARENCE DR
BLEACH MILL LA
MOOR LA
BINGLEY RD
HILLINGS LA
OTLEY RD
OLD WOOD LA
GOOSE LA
OLD LA
ODDA LA
A65 BRADFORD RD
MENSTON OLD LA
WESTBOURNE DR
SOUTHFIELD RD
SMITHY LA
STATION RD
STATION APP
THE ROBINS
HANOVER GDNS
HANOVER WAY
THE COPSE
ST PHILIP'S CL
ST PHILIP'S WAY
ST PHILIP'S DR
HASLEY RD
PROSPECT RD
ST MICHAEL'S RD
OAK WAY
OAK AVE
ROSE BANK
ELM GR
PEASBOROUGH VIEW
HEATHER RISE
GREENFIELDS WAY
HOLME PK
HOLME GR
HILL CRES
ENDOR GR
ENDOR CRES
VICTORIA AVE
BURLEY LA
ST JOHN'S PK
CRAVEN PK
FAIRFAX RD
CROFT CL
CROFT PK
MAIN ST
HILLSIDE CT
DERRY HILL
DERRY LA
BARN CL
CROFT CT
HARGRAVE CRES
ST PETER'S WAY
HAWKSWORTH DR
Sch
14
15
16
42
43
44
45
1
2
3
4
5
6
7
8

38
22

21
10

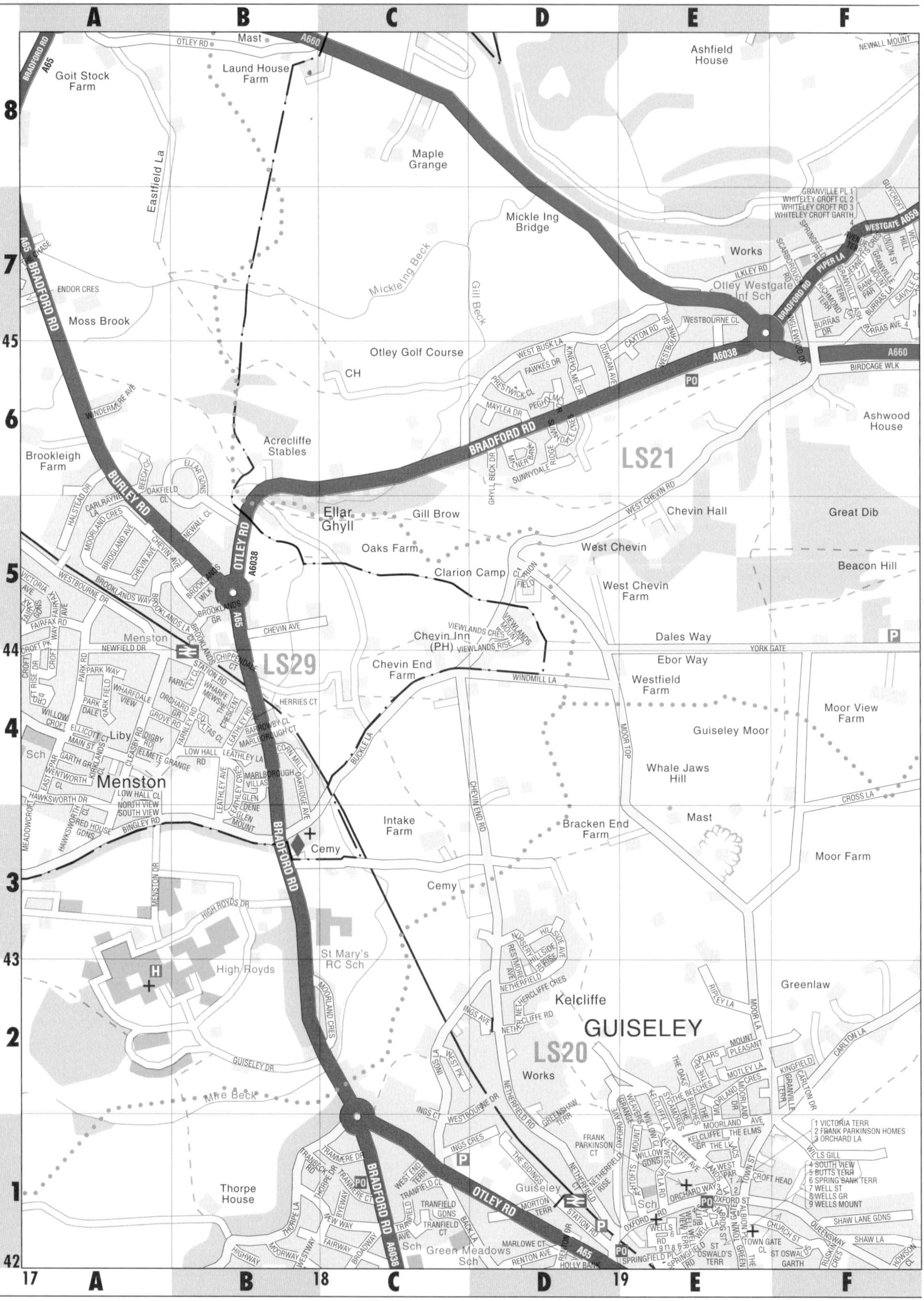
A
B
C
D
E
F
8
7
6
5
4
3
2
1
45
44
43
42
17
18
19
Mast
OTLEY RD
A660
Laund House Farm
Goit Stock Farm
Ashfield House
NEWALL MOUNT
Maple Grange
Eastfield La
Mickle Ing Bridge
Mickle Ing Beck
Gill Beck
Works
ILKLEY RD
Otley Westgate Inf Sch
WESTGATE A659
PIPER LA
GRANVILLE PL 1
WHITELEY CROFT CL 2
WHITELEY CROFT RD 3
WHITELEY CROFT GARTH 4
ENDOR CRES
Moss Brook
BRADFORD RD
A65
Otley Golf Course
CH
WESTBOURNE CL
CAXTON RD
WEST BUSK LA
FAWKES DR
PRESTWICK CL
MAYLEA DR
A6038
PO
BIRDCAGE WLK
Ashwood House
WINDERMERE AVE
Acrecliffe Stables
Brookleigh Farm
LS21
BURLEY RD
OAKFIELD CL
ELLAR GDNS
HALSTEAD DR
CARLRAYNE LA
MOORLAND CRES
BRIDGLAND AVE
NEWALL CL
CHEVIN AVE
Ellar Ghyll
Gill Brow
WEST CHEVIN RD
Chevin Hall
Great Dib
Oaks Farm
West Chevin
Beacon Hill
OTLEY RD
Clarion Camp
West Chevin Farm
VICTORIA AVE
WESTBOURNE DR
BROOKLANDS WAY
BROOKLANDS LA
FAIRFAX RD
Menston
CHEVIN AVE
VIEWLANDS CRES
Chevin Inn (PH)
VIEWLANDS RISE
Dales Way
YORK GATE
P
NEWFIELD DR
CHIPPENDALE CT
STATION RD
LS29
Ebor Way
Chevin End Farm
WINDMILL LA
Westfield Farm
PARK WAY
WHARFDALE VIEW
ORCHARD GR
HERRIES CT
Moor View Farm
MOOR TOP
Guiseley Moor
Liby
Sch
MAIN ST
LOW HALL RD
BUCKLE LA
Whale Jaws Hill
Menston
HAWKSWORTH DR
LOW HALL CL
NORTH VIEW
SOUTH VIEW
BINGLEY RD
CROSS LA
Intake Farm
Bracken End Farm
Mast
CHEVIN END RD
Cemy
Moor Farm
MEADOWCROFT
Cemy
MENSTON DR
HIGH ROYDS DR
St Mary's RC Sch
H
High Royds
MOORLAND CRES
Greenlaw
RIPLEY LA
MOOR LA
Kelcliffe
NETHERFIELD CRES
GUISELEY
LS20
CARLTON LA
Works
GUISELEY DR
Mire Beck
MOUNT PLEASANT
MOTLEY LA
KINGFIELD
CARLTON DR
WESTBOURNE DR
NETHERFIELD RD
INGS CT
INGS CRES
FRANK PARKINSON CT
1 VICTORIA TERR
2 FRANK PARKINSON HOMES
3 ORCHARD LA
WILLS GILL
4 SOUTH VIEW
5 BUTTS TERR
6 SPRING BANK TERR
7 WELL ST
8 WELLS GR
9 WELLS MOUNT
THE SIDINGS
Thorpe House
TRANMERE DR
PO
TRANFIELD CL
TRANFIELD GDNS
TRANFIELD CT
Guiseley
MORTON TERR
ORCHARD WAY
WEST PAR
CROFT HEAD
OXFORD ST
SHAW LANE GDNS
SHAW LA
THORPE LA
HIGHWAY
MOORWAY
FAIRWAY
BROADWAY
Sch
Green Meadows Sch
MARLOWE CT
RENTON AVE
HOLLY BANK
STATION RD
OXFORD RD
TOWN GATE CL
ST OSWALDS GARTH
QUEENSWAY
HOWSON CL
CHURCH ST

21
39

11
24

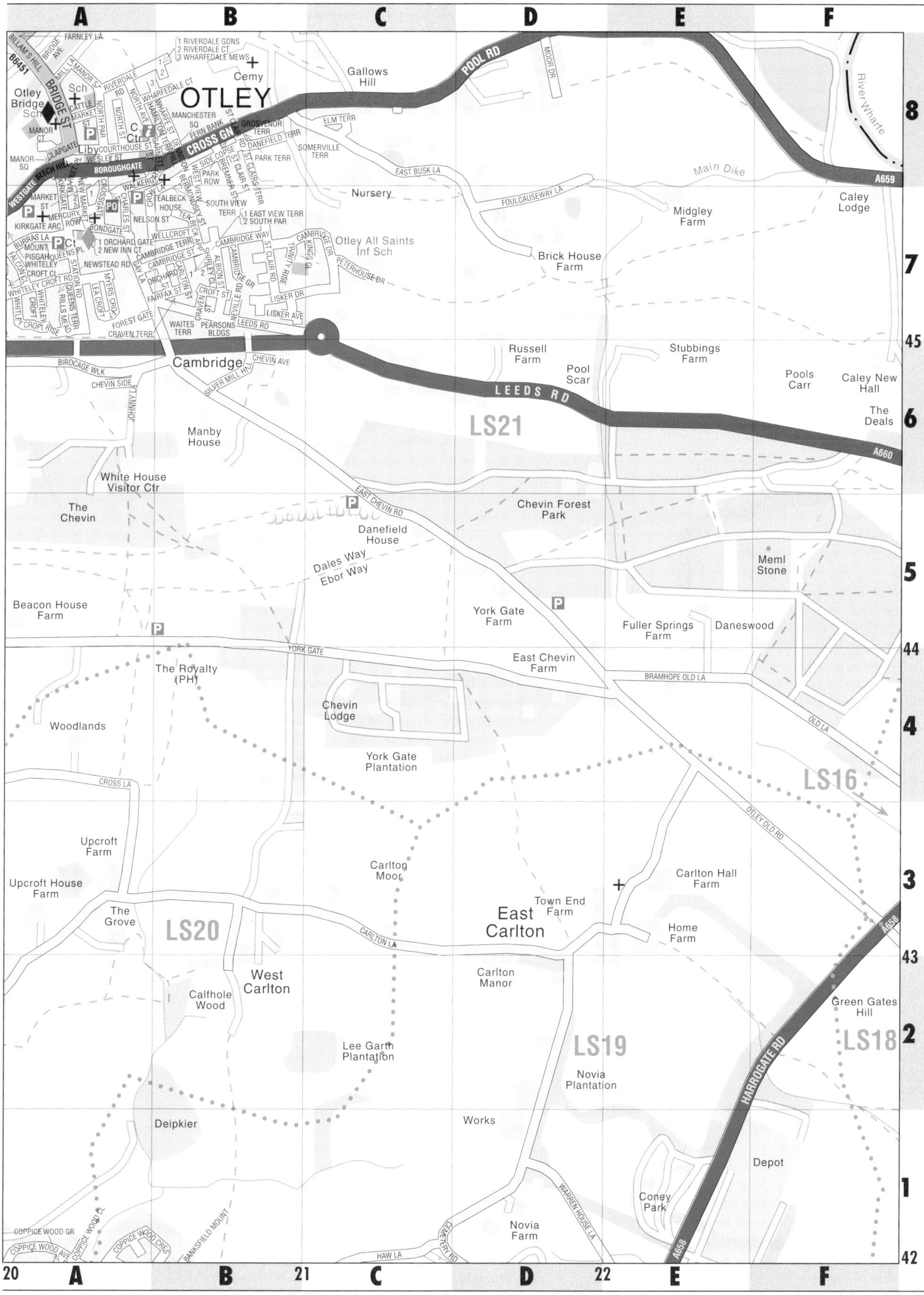
A
B
C
D
E
F
OTLEY
Otley Bridge
Sch
BRIDGE ST
B6451
BILLAM'S HILL
FARNLEY LA
MILL LA
MANOR SQ
MANOR CT
WESTGATE
BEECH HILL
BOROUGHGATE
CROSS GN
KIRKGATE ARC
MERCURY ROW
BONDGATE
Ct
Liby
C Ctr
PO
1 RIVERDALE GDNS
2 RIVERDALE CT
3 WHARFEDALE MEWS
WHARFEDALE CT
Cemy
MANCHESTER SQ
FERN BANK
GROSVENOR TERR
DANEFIELD TERR
PARK TERR
SOMERVILLE TERR
ELM TERR
EAST BUSK LA
SOUTH VIEW TERR
1 EAST VIEW TERR
2 SOUTH PAR
NELSON ST
WELLCROFT
1 ORCHARD GATE
2 NEW INN CT
NEWSTEAD RD
CAMBRIDGE WAY
CAMBRIDGE TERR
CAMBRIDGE ST
STATION RD
QUEENS TERR
WHITELEY CROFT RD
WHITELEY CROFT RISE
LEA CROFT
MYERS CROFT
FOREST GATE
CRAVEN TERR
WAITES TERR
PEARSONS BLDGS
LEEDS RD
LISKER DR
LISKER AVE
PETERHOUSE DR
Otley All Saints Inf Sch
Gallows Hill
POOL RD
MOOR DR
Nursery
FOULCAUSEWAY LA
Main Dike
Midgley Farm
Brick House Farm
River Wharfe
A659
Caley Lodge
Cambridge
BIRDCAGE WLK
CHEVIN SIDE
CHEVIN AVE
SILVER MILL HILL
JOHNNY LA
Russell Farm
Pool Scar
Stubbings Farm
Pools Carr
Caley New Hall
The Deals
LEEDS RD
LS21
A660
Manby House
White House Visitor Ctr
The Chevin
EAST CHEVIN RD
Chevin Forest Park
Danefield House
Dales Way
Ebor Way
Meml Stone
Beacon House Farm
York Gate Farm
Fuller Springs Farm
Daneswood
YORK GATE
The Royalty (PH)
East Chevin Farm
BRAMHOPE OLD LA
Chevin Lodge
Woodlands
OLD LA
York Gate Plantation
LS16
CROSS LA
OTLEY OLD RD
Upcroft Farm
Carlton Moor
Upcroft House Farm
Carlton Hall Farm
The Grove
LS20
Town End Farm
East Carlton
Home Farm
CARLTON LA
A658
West Carlton
Calfhole Wood
Carlton Manor
Green Gates Hill
HARROGATE RD
Lee Garth Plantation
LS19
LS18
Novia Plantation
Deipkier
Works
Depot
Coney Park
WARREN HOUSE LA
COPPICE WOOD GR
COPPICE WOOD AVE
COPPICE WOOD CL
COPPICE WOOD CRES
BANKSFIELD MOUNT
HAW LA
CEMETERY RD
Novia Farm
8
7
45
6
5
44
4
3
43
2
1
42
20
21
22

40
24

23

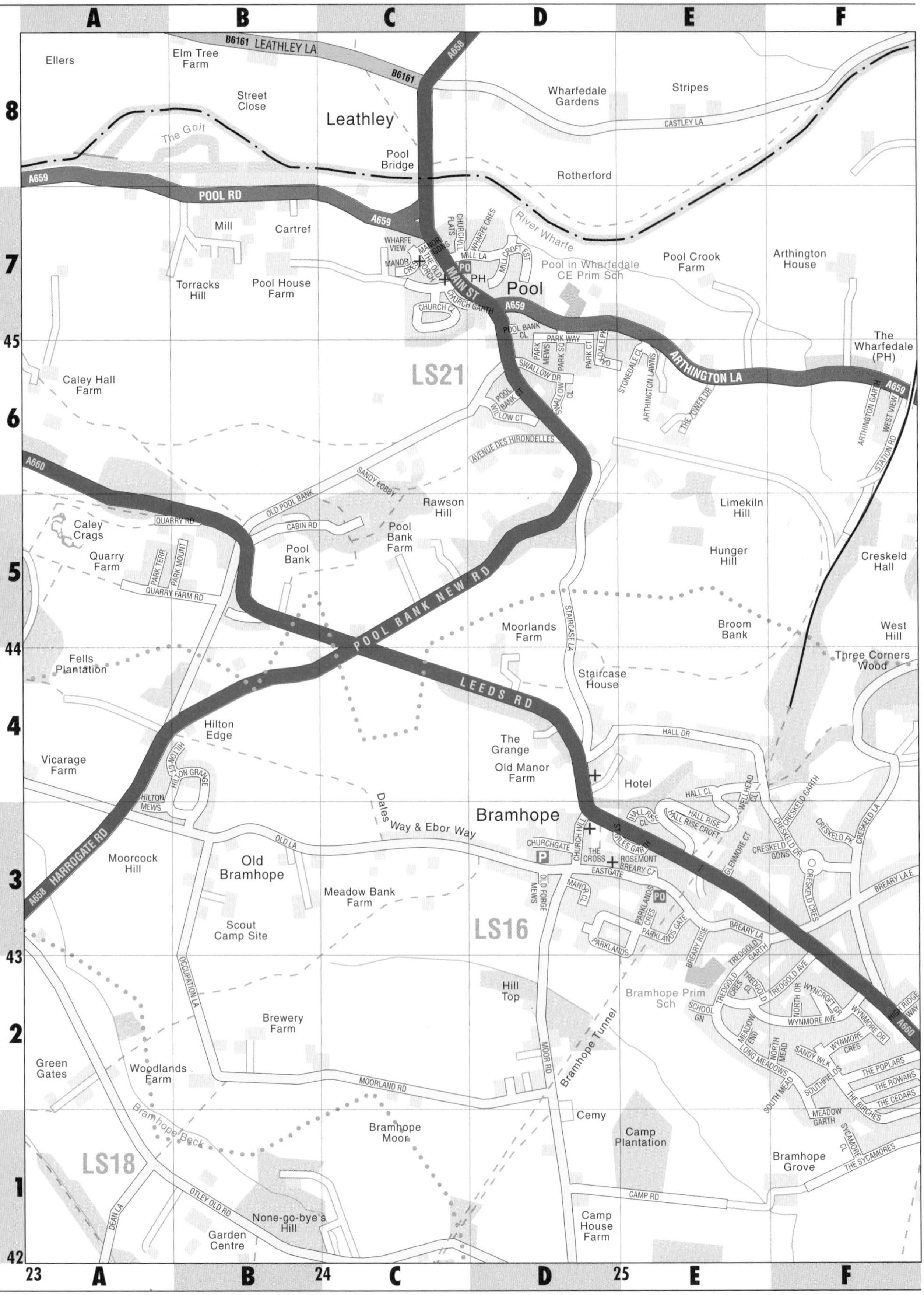
A
B
C
D
E
F
8
7
45
6
5
44
4
3
43
2
1
42
23
24
25
Ellers
Elm Tree Farm
B6161 LEATHLEY LA
B6161
A658
Street Close
Leathley
Wharfedale Gardens
Stripes
CASTLEY LA
The Goit
Pool Bridge
Rotherford
A659
POOL RD
A659
Mill
Cartref
River Wharfe
Torracks Hill
Pool House Farm
WHARFE VIEW
MANOR GDNS
CHURCHILL FLATS
WHARFE CRES
MILL LA
MILLCROFT EST
MANOR CRES
THE OLD CHURCH
MAIN ST
PO
PH
Pool
Pool in Wharfedale CE Prim Sch
Pool Crook Farm
Arthington House
CHURCH GARTH
CHURCH CL
A659
POOL BANK CL
PARK WAY
PARK MEWS
PARK SQ
PARK CT
DALE PK
STONEDALE CL
ARTHINGTON LAWNS
ARTHINGTON LA
The Wharfedale (PH)
LS21
SWALLOW DR
SWALLOW CL
POOL BANK CT
WILLOW CT
THE TOWER DR
ARTHINGTON GARTH
WEST VIEW
A659
AVENUE DES HIRONDELLES
STATION RD
A660
SANDY LOBBY
OLD POOL BANK
Rawson Hill
Limekiln Hill
Caley Crags
QUARRY RD
CABIN RD
Pool Bank Farm
Quarry Farm
PARK TERR
PARK MOUNT
Pool Bank
Hunger Hill
Creskeld Hall
QUARRY FARM RD
POOL BANK NEW RD
Moorlands Farm
STAIRCASE LA
Broom Bank
West Hill
Fells Plantation
Three Corners Wood
Staircase House
LEEDS RD
Hilton Edge
The Grange
HALL DR
Vicarage Farm
Old Manor Farm
Hotel
HILTON GRANGE
HILTON MEWS
Dales Way & Ebor Way
Bramhope
HALL CL
WELLHEAD CL
HALL RISE CL
HALL RISE
HALL RISE CROFT
CRESKELD GARTH
CRESKELD DR
CRESKELD PK
CRESKELD LA
OLD LA
CHURCHGATE
CHURCH HILL
ST GILES GARTH
GLENMORE CT
CRESKELD GDNS
CRESKELD CRES
Moorcock Hill
Old Bramhope
THE CROSS
ROSEMONT
BREARY CT
EASTGATE
BREARY LA E
HARROGATE RD
A658
Meadow Bank Farm
OLD FORGE MEWS
MANOR CL
PARKLANDS CRES
PARKLANDS GATE
Scout Camp Site
LS16
PARKLANDS
BREARY RISE
BREARY LA
TREDGOLD GARTH
OCCUPATION LA
Hill Top
Bramhope Prim Sch
TREDGOLD CRES
TREDGOLD CL
TREDGOLD AVE
WYNCROFT GR
HIGH RIDGE WAY
A660
Brewery Farm
Bramhope Tunnel
SCHOOL GN
MEADOW END
NORTH DR
WYNMORE AVE
WYNMORE DR
Green Gates
Woodlands Farm
MOOR RD
LONG MEADOWS
NORTH MEAD
SANDY WLK
WYNMORE CRES
THE POPLARS
THE ROWANS
THE CEDARS
THE BIRCHES
SOUTH MEAD
SOUTHFIELDS
MOORLAND RD
Bramhope Beck
Cemy
MEADOW GARTH
Bramhope Moor
Camp Plantation
SYCAMORE CL
LS18
Bramhope Grove
THE SYCAMORES
CAMP RD
OTLEY OLD RD
DEAN LA
None-go-bye's Hill
Garden Centre
Camp House Farm

23

41

26

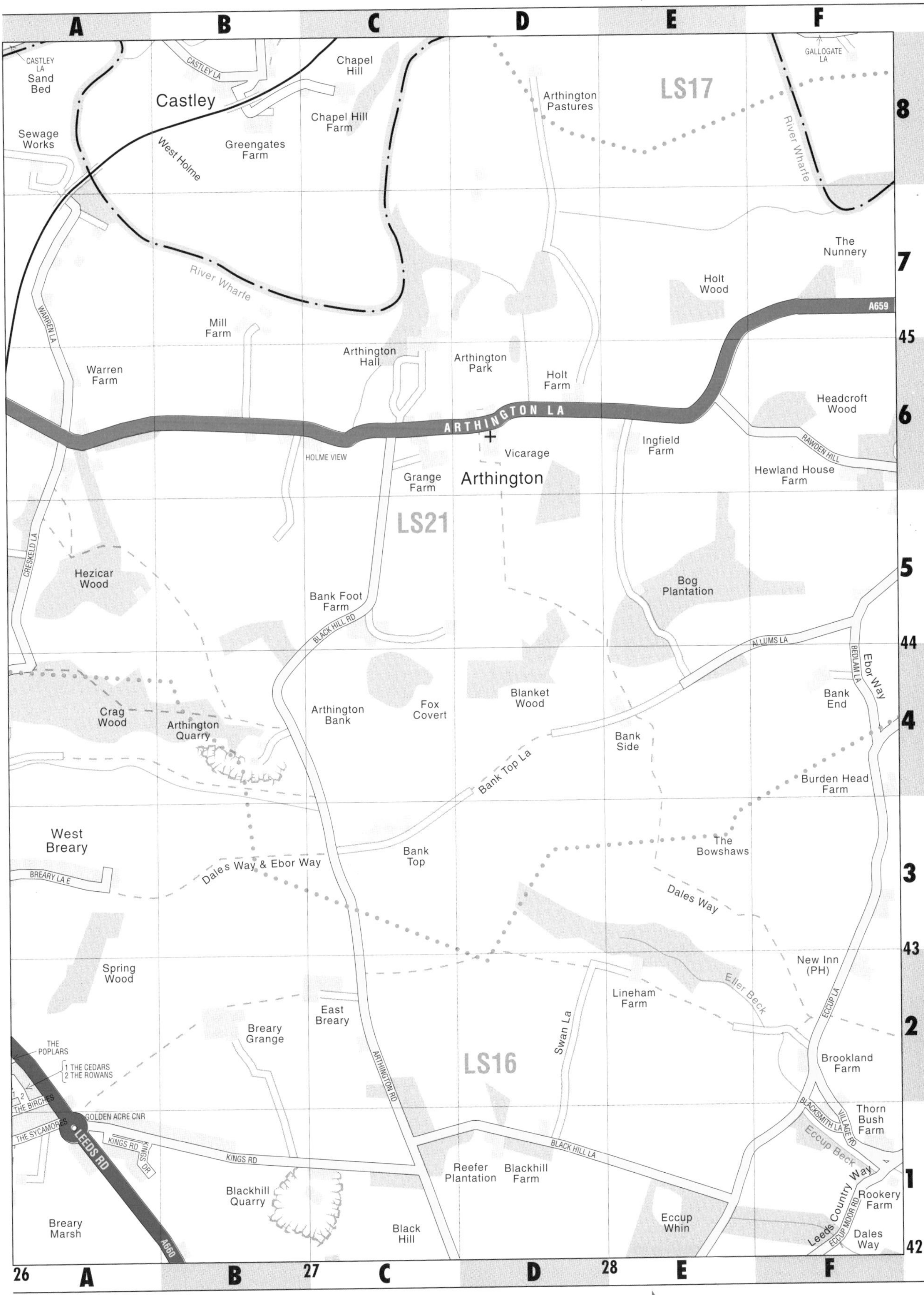

A
B
C
D
E
F
CASTLEY LA
Sand Bed
Castley
CASTLEY LA
Chapel Hill
Chapel Hill Farm
Arthington Pastures
LS17
GALLOGATE LA
Sewage Works
West Holme
Greengates Farm
River Wharfe
River Wharfe
The Nunnery
Holt Wood
WARREN LA
Mill Farm
A659
Arthington Hall
Arthington Park
Warren Farm
Holt Farm
Headcroft Wood
ARTHINGTON LA
Vicarage
Ingfield Farm
RAWDEN HILL
HOLME VIEW
Grange Farm
Arthington
Hewland House Farm
LS21
CRESKELD LA
Hezicar Wood
Bog Plantation
Bank Foot Farm
BLACK HILL RD
ALLUMS LA
BEDLAM LA
Ebor Way
Crag Wood
Arthington Quarry
Arthington Bank
Fox Covert
Blanket Wood
Bank End
Bank Side
Bank Top La
Burden Head Farm
West Breary
Bank Top
The Bowshaws
BREARY LA E
Dales Way & Ebor Way
Dales Way
Spring Wood
New Inn (PH)
Lineham Farm
Eller Beck
East Breary
Breary Grange
ECCUP LA
Swan La
THE POPLARS
1 THE CEDARS
2 THE ROWANS
THE BIRCHES
LS16
Brookland Farm
ARTHINGTON RD
GOLDEN ACRE CNR
THE SYCAMORES
LEEDS RD
KINGS RD
KINGS DR
KINGS RD
BLACK HILL LA
BLACKSMITH LA
VILLAGE RD
Thorn Bush Farm
Eccup Beck
Reefer Plantation
Blackhill Farm
Blackhill Quarry
Leeds Country Way
Rookery Farm
ECCUP MOOR RD
Breary Marsh
A660
Black Hill
Eccup Whin
Dales Way
8
7
45
6
5
44
4
3
43
2
1
42
26
A
B
27
C
D
28
E
F

42
26

25

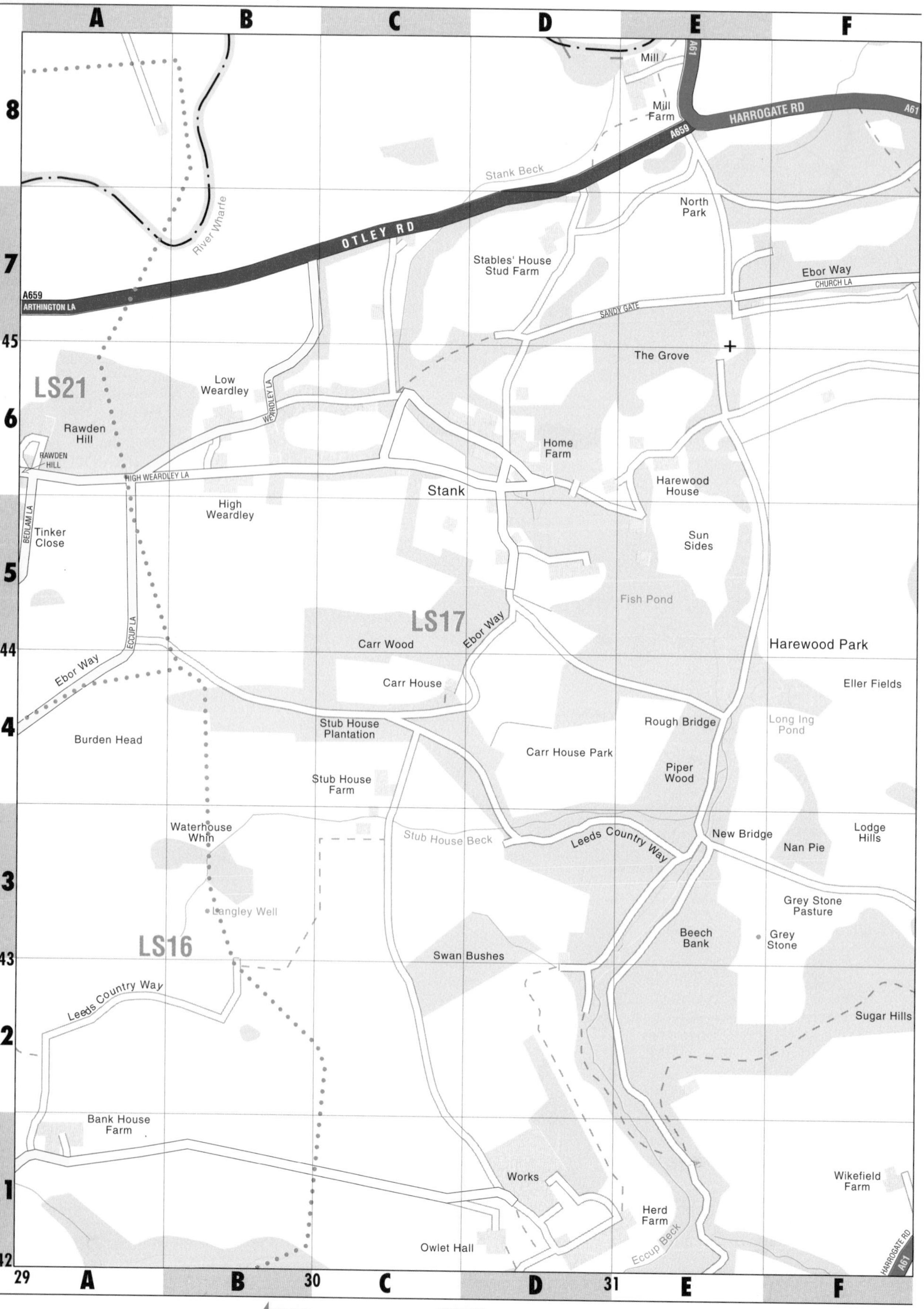
A
B
C
D
E
F
8
7
45
6
5
44
4
3
43
2
1
42
29
30
31
Mill
Mill Farm
A61
HARROGATE RD
A659
Stank Beck
North Park
OTLEY RD
River Wharfe
A659
ARTHINGTON LA
Stables' House Stud Farm
Ebor Way
CHURCH LA
SANDY GATE
The Grove
LS21
Low Weardley
WEARDLEY LA
Rawden Hill
RAWDEN HILL
HIGH WEARDLEY LA
Home Farm
Stank
Harewood House
High Weardley
BEDLAM LA
Tinker Close
Sun Sides
Fish Pond
LS17
Ebor Way
Carr Wood
Harewood Park
ECCUP LA
Ebor Way
Carr House
Eller Fields
Stub House Plantation
Rough Bridge
Long Ing Pond
Burden Head
Carr House Park
Piper Wood
Stub House Farm
Waterhouse Whin
Stub House Beck
Leeds Country Way
New Bridge
Lodge Hills
Nan Pie
Grey Stone Pasture
Langley Well
Beech Bank
Grey Stone
LS16
Swan Bushes
Leeds Country Way
Sugar Hills
Bank House Farm
Works
Wikefield Farm
Herd Farm
Owlet Hall
Eccup Beck
HARROGATE RD
A61

25

43

28

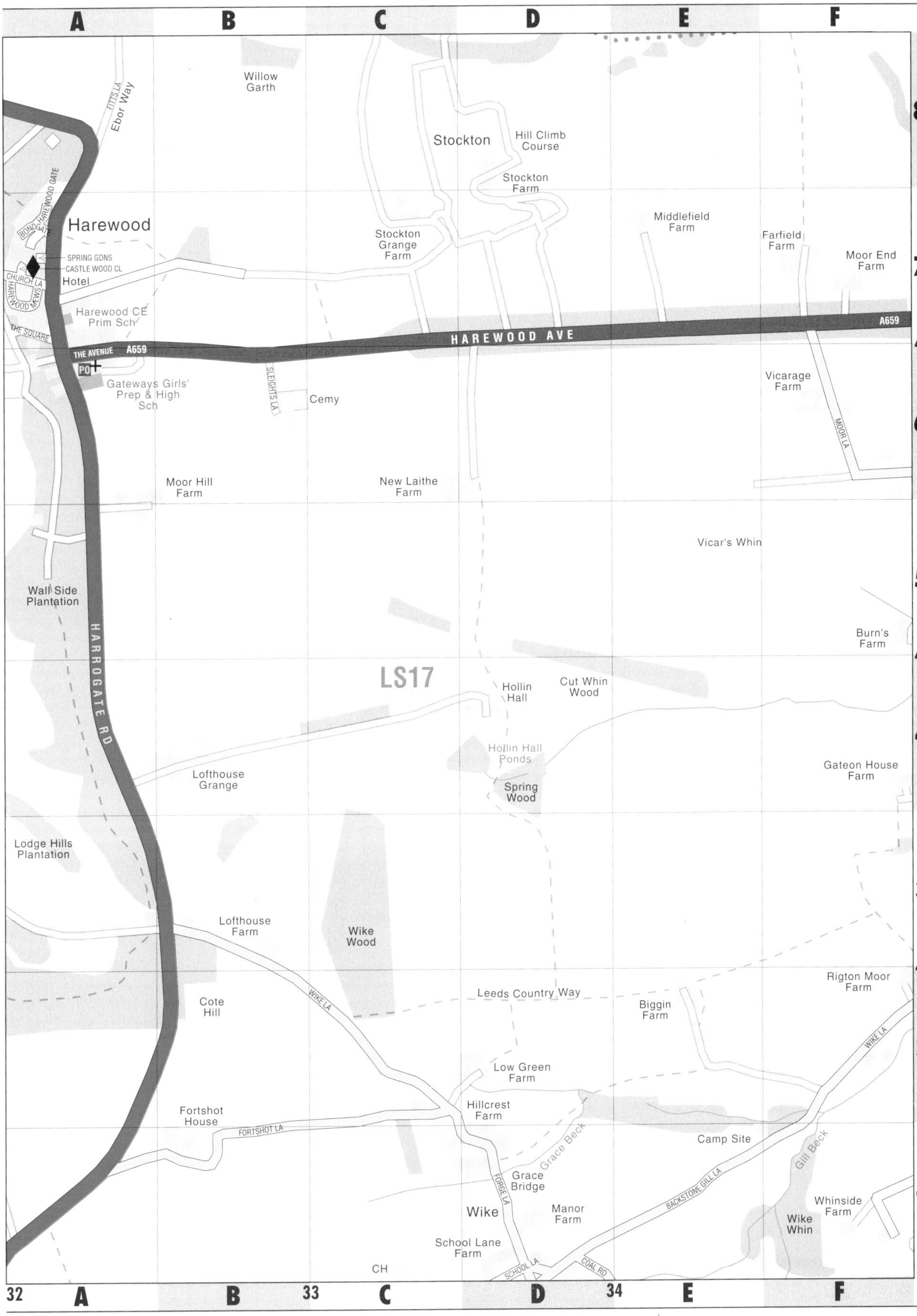

A
B
C
D
E
F
Willow Garth
FITTS LA
Ebor Way
Stockton
Hill Climb Course
Stockton Farm
HAREWOOD GATE
BONDGATE
Harewood
SPRING GDNS
CASTLE WOOD CL
CHURCH LA
HAREWOOD MEWS
Hotel
Stockton Grange Farm
Middlefield Farm
Farfield Farm
Moor End Farm
Harewood CE Prim Sch
THE SQUARE
THE AVENUE
A659
HAREWOOD AVE
PO
Gateways Girls' Prep & High Sch
SLEIGHTS LA
Cemy
Vicarage Farm
MOOR LA
Moor Hill Farm
New Laithe Farm
Vicar's Whin
Wall Side Plantation
HARROGATE RD
Burn's Farm
LS17
Hollin Hall
Cut Whin Wood
Hollin Hall Ponds
Spring Wood
Lofthouse Grange
Gateon House Farm
Lodge Hills Plantation
Lofthouse Farm
Wike Wood
Cote Hill
WIKE LA
Leeds Country Way
Biggin Farm
Rigton Moor Farm
Low Green Farm
Fortshot House
FORTSHOT LA
Hillcrest Farm
Camp Site
Grace Beck
Gill Beck
Grace Bridge
FORGE LA
Wike
Manor Farm
BACKSTONE GILL LA
Whinside Farm
Wike Whin
School Lane Farm
CH
SCHOOL LA
COAL RD
8
7
45
6
5
44
4
3
43
2
1
42
32
33
34

44
28

27
12

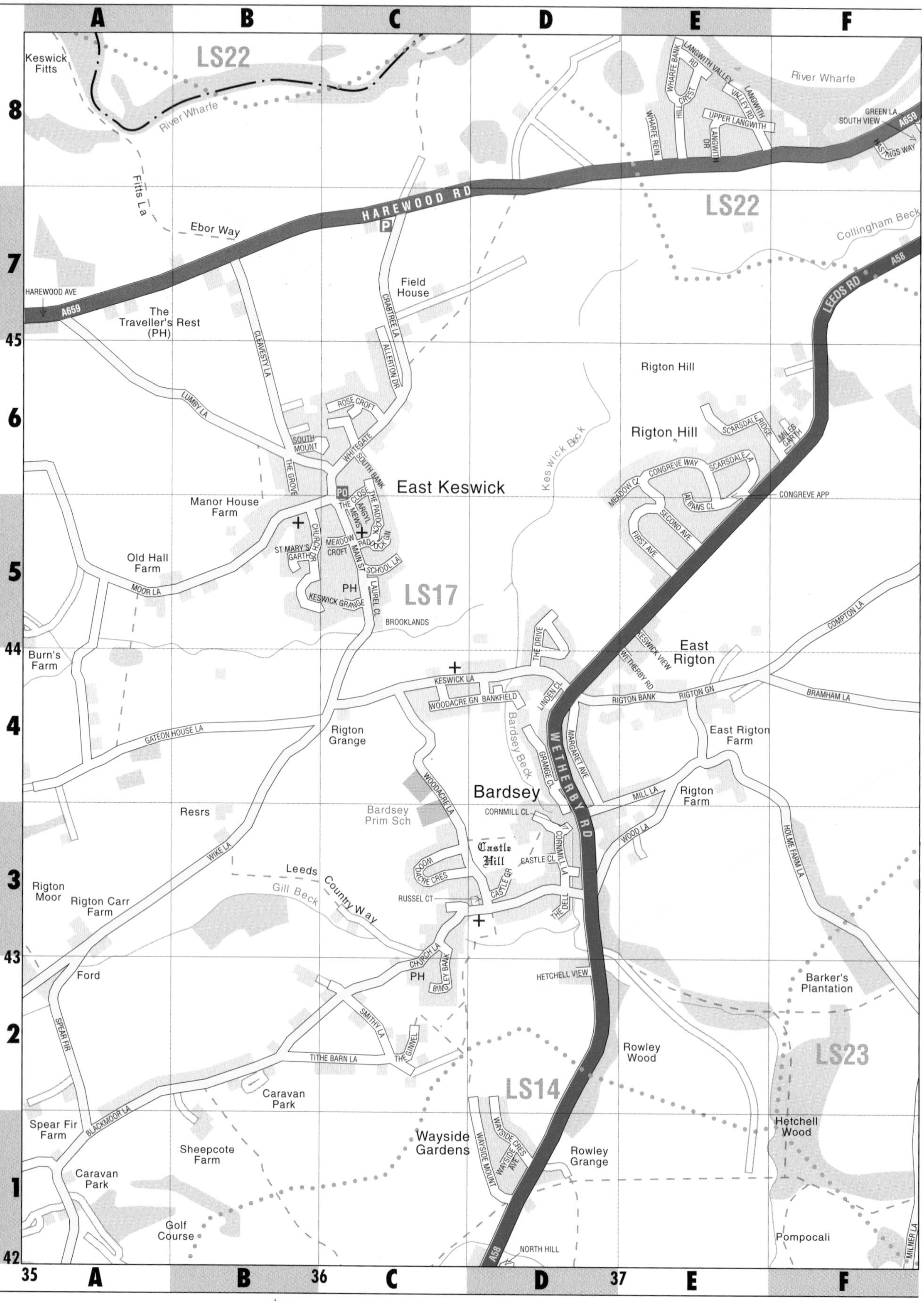
A
B
C
D
E
F
8
7
6
5
4
3
2
1
45
44
43
42
35
36
37
Keswick Fitts
LS22
River Wharfe
Fitts La
Ebor Way
HAREWOOD RD
P
LANGWITH VALLEY RD
WHARFE BANK
HILL CREST
VALLEY RD
LANGWITH
UPPER LANGWITH
LANGWITH DR
WHARFE REIN
GREEN LA
SOUTH VIEW
A659
HASTINGS WAY
LS22
Collingham Beck
LEEDS RD
A58
HAREWOOD AVE
A659
The Traveller's Rest (PH)
Field House
CRABTREE LA
ALLERTON DR
CLEAVESTY LA
Rigton Hill
LUMBY LA
ROSE CROFT
SOUTH MOUNT
WHITEGATE
SOUTH BANK
Rigton Hill
SCARSDALE RIDGE
MILLER GARTH
Keswick Beck
THE GROVE
PO
THE CLOSE
THE PADDOCK
East Keswick
CONGREVE WAY
SCARSDALE LA
MEADOW CL
ALBANS CL
CONGREVE APP
SECOND AVE
FIRST AVE
Manor House Farm
LARGYL MEWS
CHURCH DR
ST MARY'S GARTH
MEADOW CROFT
MAIN ST
PADDOCK GN
SCHOOL LA
Old Hall Farm
MOOR LA
PH
KESWICK GRANGE
LAUREL CL
LS17
BROOKLANDS
THE DRIVE
KESWICK VIEW
WETHERBY RD
East Rigton
COMPTON LA
Burn's Farm
KESWICK LA
WOODACRE GN
BANKFIELD
LINDEN CL
RIGTON BANK
RIGTON GN
BRAMHAM LA
GATEON HOUSE LA
Rigton Grange
Bardsey Beck
WETHERBY RD
MARGARET AVE
East Rigton Farm
GRANGE CL
Bardsey
MILL LA
Rigton Farm
Resrs
Bardsey Prim Sch
WOODACRE LA
CORNMILL CL
WIKE LA
Castle Hill
CORNMILL LA
CASTLE CL
WOOD LA
HOLME FARM LA
Leeds Country Way
WOODACRE CRES
CASTLE GR
Rigton Moor
Rigton Carr Farm
Gill Beck
RUSSEL CT
THE DELL
CHURCH LA
Ford
PH
BINGLEY BANK
HETCHELL VIEW
Barker's Plantation
SPEAR FIR
SMITHY LA
THE GINNEL
Rowley Wood
LS23
TITHE BARN LA
Caravan Park
LS14
Spear Fir Farm
BLACKMOOR LA
WAYSIDE CRES
WAYSIDE AVE
WAYSIDE MOUNT
Wayside Gardens
Hetchell Wood
Sheepcote Farm
Rowley Grange
Caravan Park
Golf Course
Pompocali
MILNER LA
NORTH HILL
A58

27
45

13
30

A
B
C
D
E
F
HAREWOOD RD
A659
MAIN ST
A58
PO
PH
JAMES CT
LOWER LANGWITH
THE CROFT
HIGHCROFT
LANGWITH AVE
GREEN LA
SOUTH VIEW
1 LANGWITH MEWS
2 COVERDALE GARTH
3 BISHOPDALE DR
4 COTTERDALE HOLT
5 LINTON RD
6 DEWAR CL
7 STATION LA
THE VALE
MILLBECK GN
LOWCROFT
Collingham Beck
LEEDS RD
THE CLOSE
CRABTREE HILL
CRABTREE GN
Collingham
BROOKSIDE
MILLGARTH CT
THE GARTH
GARTH AVE
SCHOOL LA
GARTH END
HOLLYBUSH GN
8 HASTINGS CT
9 ELIZABETH CT
JEWITT LA
A659
WATTLESYKE
BIRDALE FIELD LA
Collingham Fields
A1
A659
8
Cow Moor
LS22
Howcroft Wood
MOOR LA
Collingham Moor
7
Compton Grove
45
Compton La
Mast
COMPTON LA
Waver Spring Pond
Compton
6
Dalton Parlours
LS17
5
44
West Woods
4
Lund Wood
Lady Wood
Dalton Hill
BRAMHAM LA
LS23
3
Spring Wood
DALTON LA
Old Pickhill Rash
Hope Hall
43
HOLME FARM LA
THORNER LA
2
MILNER LA
Holme Farm
Wothersome
Bramham Beck
THORNER RD
Lendrick Hills
Stubbing Moor
Ragdale Plantation
Bramham Park
Stubbing Moor Plantation
Terry Lug
1
Milner Beck
KENNELS LA
42
38
39
40

46
30

29
14
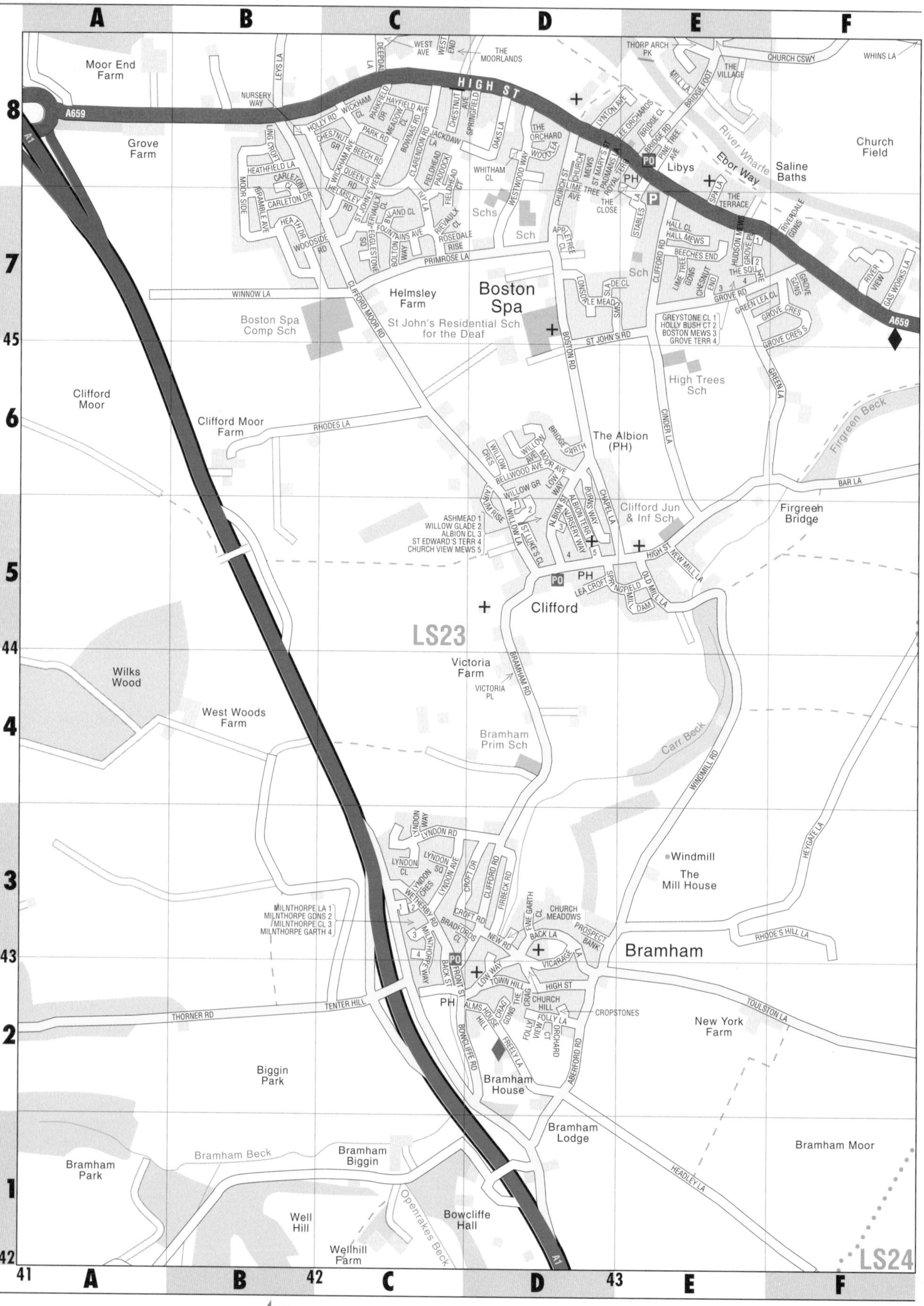
A
B
C
D
E
F
8
7
45
6
5
44
4
3
43
2
1
42
41
42
43
Moor End Farm
Grove Farm
A659
A1
HIGH ST
THE MOORLANDS
THORP ARCH PK
CHURCH CSWY
WHINS LA
THE VILLAGE
Church Field
River Wharfe
Ebor Way
Saline Baths
Libys
PH
THE TERRACE
THE CLOSE
WHITHAM CL
Schs
Sch
PRIMROSE LA
WINNOW LA
Helmsley Farm
Boston Spa
St John's Residential Sch for the Deaf
Boston Spa Comp Sch
CLIFFORD MOOR RD
BOSTON RD
ST JOHN'S RD
GREYSTONE CL 1
HOLLY BUSH CT 2
BOSTON MEWS 3
GROVE TERR 4
High Trees Sch
CINDER LA
GREEN LA
Clifford Moor
Clifford Moor Farm
RHODES LA
The Albion (PH)
Firgreen Beck
BAR LA
Firgreen Bridge
Clifford Jun & Inf Sch
ASHMEAD 1
WILLOW GLADE 2
ALBION CL 3
ST EDWARD'S TERR 4
CHURCH VIEW MEWS 5
HIGH ST
NEW MILL LA
Clifford
LS23
Wilks Wood
West Woods Farm
Victoria Farm
VICTORIA PL
BRAMHAM RD
Bramham Prim Sch
Carr Beck
WINDMILL RD
HEYGATE LA
Windmill
The Mill House
MILNTHORPE LA 1
MILNTHORPE GDNS 2
MILNTHORPE CL 3
MILNTHORPE GARTH 4
Bramham
RHODE'S HILL LA
CROPSTONES
TOULSTON LA
New York Farm
TENTER HILL
THORNER RD
Biggin Park
Bramham House
Bramham Lodge
Bramham Moor
HEADLEY LA
Bramham Beck
Bramham Biggin
Bramham Park
Well Hill
Openrakes Beck
Bowcliffe Hall
Wellhill Farm
LS24
29
47

15

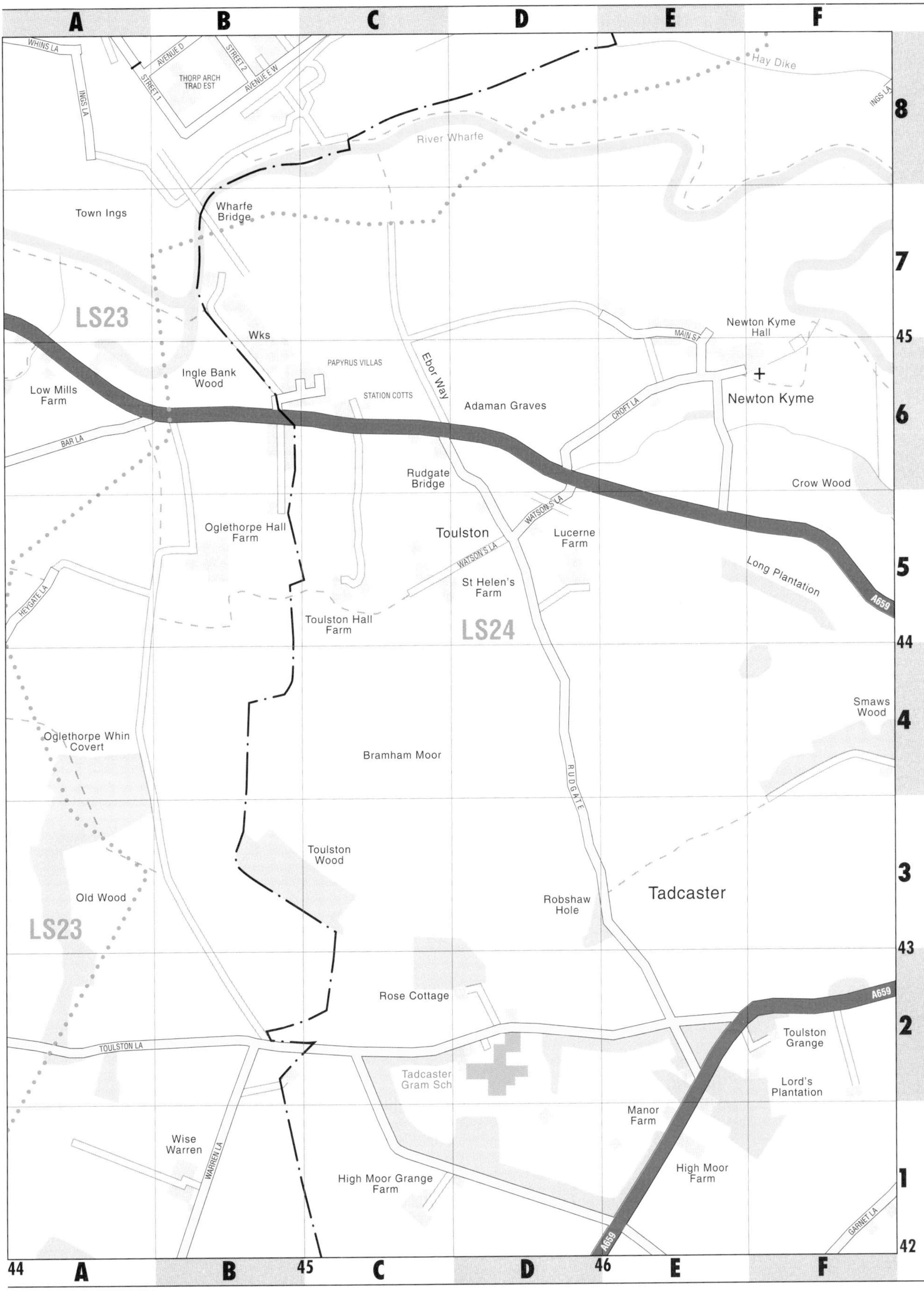
A
B
C
D
E
F
WHINS LA
AVENUE D
STREET 2
THORP ARCH
TRAD EST
STREET 1
AVENUE E W
INGS LA
Hay Dike
River Wharfe
8
Town Ings
Wharfe
Bridge
7
LS23
Wks
Newton Kyme
Hall
MAIN ST
45
Low Mills
Farm
Ingle Bank
Wood
PAPYRUS VILLAS
STATION COTTS
Ebor Way
Adaman Graves
CROFT LA
Newton Kyme
6
BAR LA
Rudgate
Bridge
Crow Wood
WATSON'S LA
Oglethorpe Hall
Farm
Toulston
Lucerne
Farm
WATSON'S LA
Long Plantation
5
HEYGATE LA
St Helen's
Farm
A659
Toulston Hall
Farm
LS24
44
Smaws
Wood
4
Oglethorpe Whin
Covert
Bramham Moor
RUDGATE
Toulston
Wood
3
Old Wood
Robshaw
Hole
Tadcaster
LS23
43
A659
Rose Cottage
2
Toulston
Grange
TOULSTON LA
Tadcaster
Gram Sch
Lord's
Plantation
Manor
Farm
Wise
Warren
WARREN LA
High Moor
Farm
1
High Moor Grange
Farm
A659
GARNET LA
42
44
A
B
45
C
D
46
E
F

48

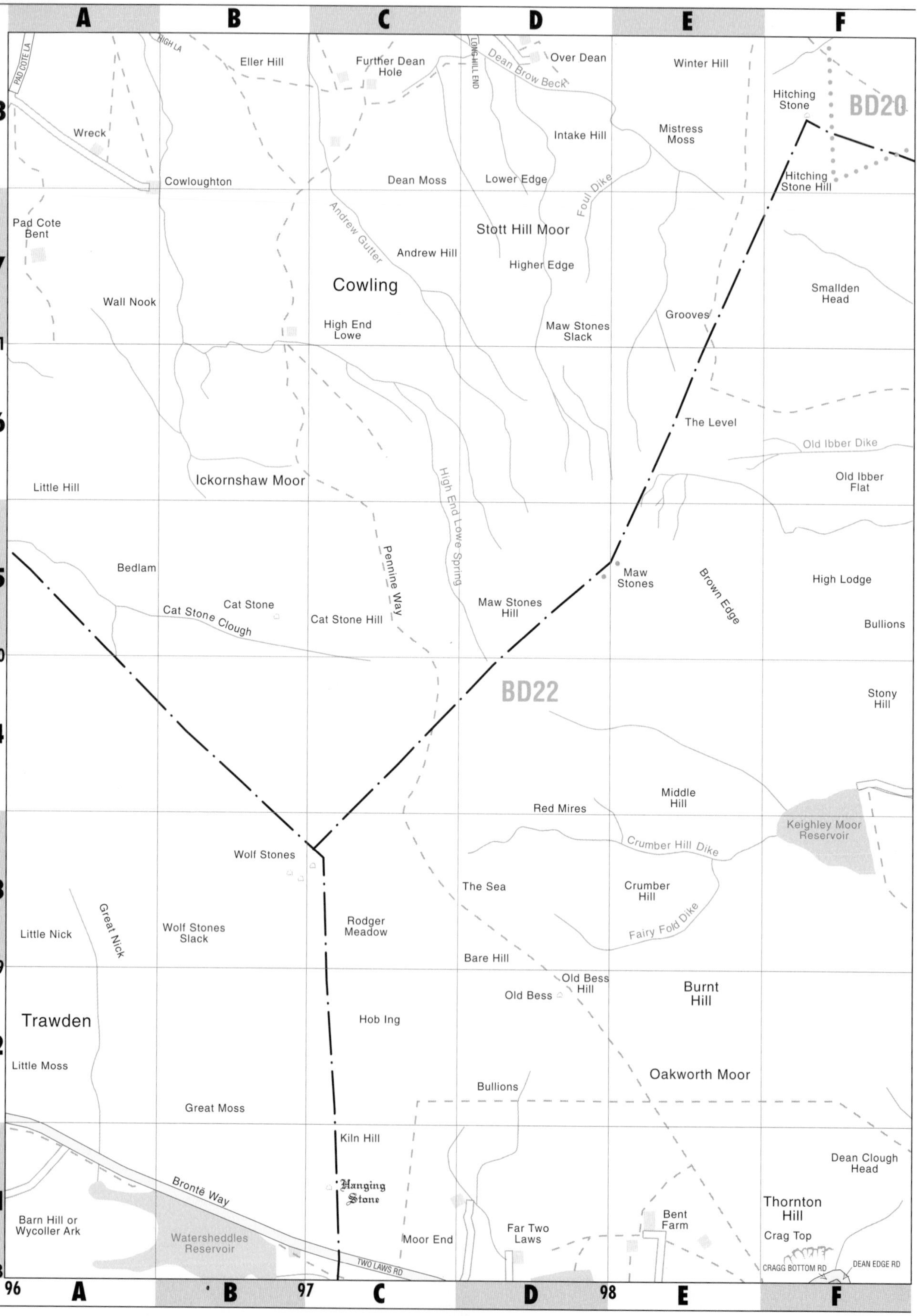
A
B
C
D
E
F
8
7
41
6
5
40
4
3
39
2
1
38
96
97
98
PAD COTE LA
HIGH LA
LONG HILL END
Eller Hill
Further Dean Hole
Over Dean
Dean Brow Beck
Winter Hill
Hitching Stone
BD20
Wreck
Intake Hill
Mistress Moss
Cowloughton
Dean Moss
Lower Edge
Foul Dike
Hitching Stone Hill
Pad Cote Bent
Andrew Gutter
Stott Hill Moor
Andrew Hill
Higher Edge
Cowling
Smallden Head
Wall Nook
High End Lowe
Maw Stones Slack
Grooves
The Level
Old Ibber Dike
Old Ibber Flat
Little Hill
Ickornshaw Moor
High End Lowe Spring
Pennine Way
Bedlam
Maw Stones
Brown Edge
High Lodge
Cat Stone
Cat Stone Clough
Cat Stone Hill
Maw Stones Hill
Bullions
BD22
Stony Hill
Middle Hill
Red Mires
Keighley Moor Reservoir
Crumber Hill Dike
Wolf Stones
The Sea
Crumber Hill
Rodger Meadow
Fairy Fold Dike
Little Nick
Great Nick
Wolf Stones Slack
Bare Hill
Old Bess Hill
Old Bess
Burnt Hill
Trawden
Hob Ing
Little Moss
Oakworth Moor
Bullions
Great Moss
Kiln Hill
Dean Clough Head
Brontë Way
Hanging Stone
Thornton Hill
Barn Hill or Wycoller Ark
Watersheddles Reservoir
Moor End
Far Two Laws
Bent Farm
Crag Top
TWO LAWS RD
CRAGG BOTTOM RD
DEAN EDGE RD

49

16
34

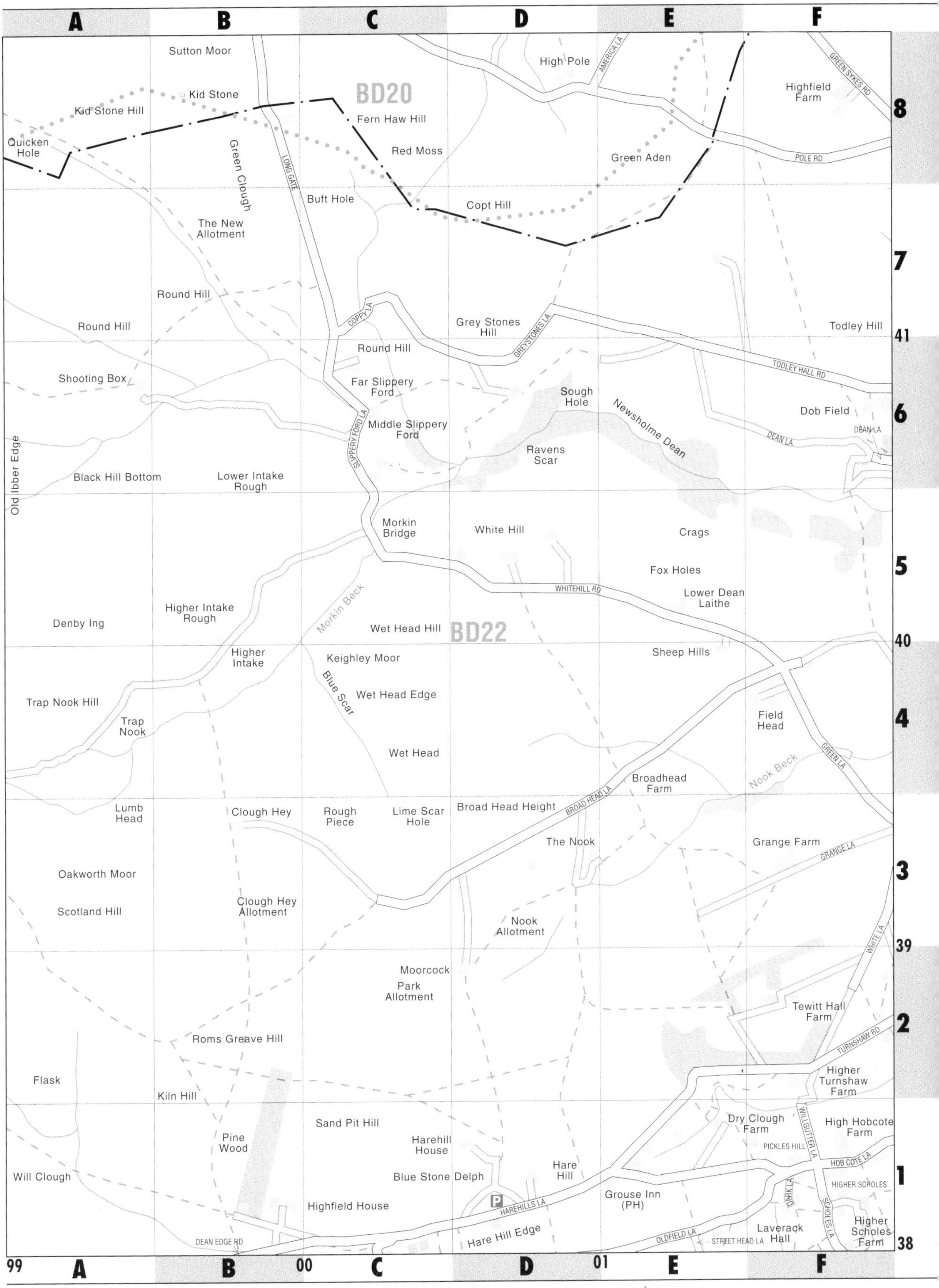
A
B
C
D
E
F
Sutton Moor
Kid Stone
Kid Stone Hill
Quicken Hole
BD20
Fern Haw Hill
High Pole
AMERICA LA
GREEN SYKES RD
Highfield Farm
8
Green Clough
LONG GATE
Red Moss
Green Aden
POLE RD
Buft Hole
Copt Hill
The New Allotment
7
Round Hill
COPPY LA
Grey Stones Hill
GREYSTONES LA
Todley Hill
Round Hill
41
Round Hill
TODLEY HALL RD
Shooting Box
Far Slippery Ford
Sough Hole
Newsholme Dean
Dob Field
6
Middle Slippery Ford
SLIPPERY FORD LA
DEAN LA
DEAN LA
Old Ibber Edge
Ravens Scar
Black Hill Bottom
Lower Intake Rough
Morkin Bridge
White Hill
Crags
5
Fox Holes
WHITEHILL RD
Lower Dean Laithe
Higher Intake Rough
Denby Ing
Morkin Beck
Wet Head Hill
BD22
40
Higher Intake
Keighley Moor
Sheep Hills
Blue Scar
Wet Head Edge
Trap Nook Hill
Trap Nook
Field Head
4
Wet Head
GREEN LA
Nook Beck
Broadhead Farm
Lumb Head
Clough Hey
Rough Piece
Lime Scar Hole
Broad Head Height
BROAD HEAD LA
The Nook
Grange Farm
GRANGE LA
Oakworth Moor
3
Scotland Hill
Clough Hey Allotment
Nook Allotment
WHITE LA
39
Moorcock
Park Allotment
Tewitt Hall Farm
2
TURNSHAW RD
Roms Greave Hill
Flask
Higher Turnshaw Farm
Kiln Hill
Sand Pit Hill
Dry Clough Farm
High Hobcote Farm
Pine Wood
Harehill House
WILLGUTTER LA
PICKLES HILL
HOB COTE LA
Will Clough
Blue Stone Delph
Hare Hill
1
HIGHER SCHOLES
P
Grouse Inn (PH)
DARK LA
SCHOLES LA
HAREHILLS LA
Highfield House
Higher Scholes Farm
Laverack Hall
DEAN EDGE RD
Hare Hill Edge
OLDFIELD LA
STREET HEAD LA
38
99
00
01

50
34

33
17

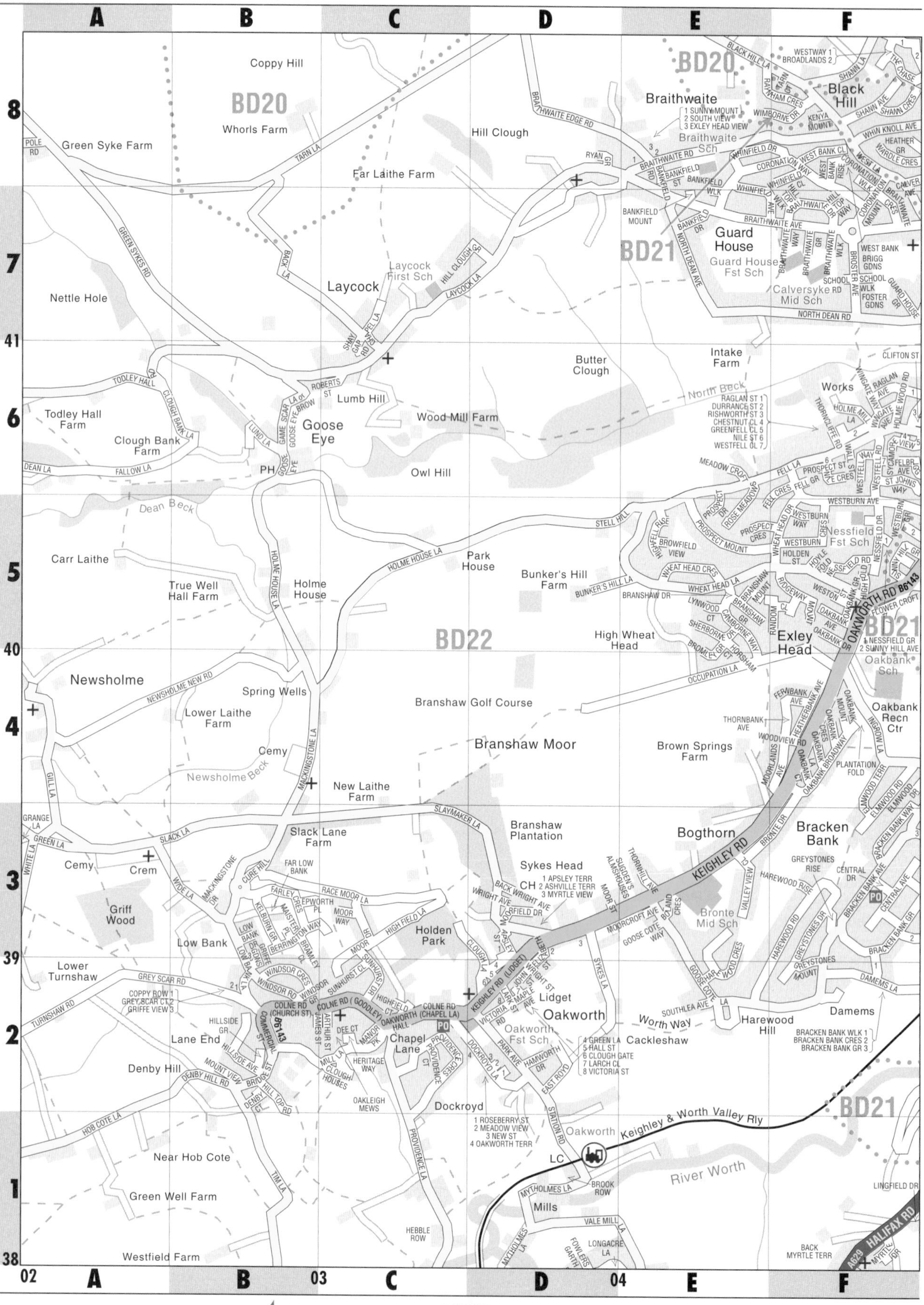
Coppy Hill
BD20
Whorls Farm
Green Syke Farm
POLE RD
TARN LA
Far Laithe Farm
Hill Clough
BRAITHWAITE EDGE RD
Braithwaite
1 SUNNY MOUNT
2 SOUTH VIEW
3 EXLEY HEAD VIEW
Braithwaite Sch
Black Hill
WESTWAY 1
BROADLANDS 2
BLACK HILL LA
RAYLEIGH CRES
WIMBORNE DR
KENYA MOUNT
SHANN LA
THE CHASE
SHANN AVE
SHANN CRES
WHIN KNOLL AVE
HEATHER GR
WARDLE CRES
BRAITHWAITE RD
BANKFIELD ST
BANKFIELD WLK
BANKFIELD MOUNT
WHINFIELD DR
CORONATION WAY
WEST BANK CL
WEST BANK RISE
BRAITHWAITE AVE
Guard House
Guard House Fst Sch
BD21
NORTH DEAN AVE
NORTH DEAN RD
WEST BANK
BRIGG GDNS
SCHOOL WLK
FOSTER GDNS
GUARD HOUSE GR
Calversyke Mid Sch
GREEN SYKES RD
BACK LA
Laycock
Laycock First Sch
HILL CLOUGH GR
LAYCOCK LA
Nettle Hole
SHAY GAP RD
CHAPEL LA
Butter Clough
Intake Farm
CLIFTON ST
TODLEY HALL RD
Todley Hall Farm
CLOUGH BANK LA
Clough Bank Farm
ROBERTS ST
Lumb Hill
GAME SCAR LA
GOOSE EYE BROW
Goose Eye
Wood Mill Farm
North Beck
Works
RAGLAN ST 1
DURRANCE ST 2
RISHWORTH ST 3
CHESTNUT CL 4
GREENFELL CL 5
NILE ST 6
WESTFELL CL 7
THORNCLIFFE RD
HOLME MILL LA
LUND LA
PH
DEAN LA
FALLOW LA
Owl Hill
MEADOW CROFT
FELL LA
PROSPECT ST
FELL GR
Dean Beck
STELL HILL
HIGHFELL RISE
BROWFIELD VIEW
PROSPECT MOUNT
ROSE MEADOWS
WESTBURN AVE
WESTBURN WAY
Nessfield Fst Sch
Carr Laithe
HOLME HOUSE LA
Park House
Holme House
True Well Hall Farm
Bunker's Hill Farm
BUNKER'S HILL LA
WHEAT HEAD CRES
WHEAT HEAD LA
BRANSHAW DR
OAKWORTH RD B6143
FLOWER CROFT
BD22
High Wheat Head
Exley Head
1 NESSFIELD GR
2 SUNNY HILL AVE
Oakbank Sch
Newsholme
NEWSHOLME NEW RD
Spring Wells
OCCUPATION LA
Lower Laithe Farm
Branshaw Golf Course
Oakbank Recn Ctr
THORNBANK AVE
Branshaw Moor
Brown Springs Farm
Cemy
Newsholme Beck
MACKINGSTONE LA
New Laithe Farm
PLANTATION FOLD
GILL LA
GRANGE LA
GREEN LA
WHITE LA
SLACK LA
Slack Lane Farm
SLAYMAKER LA
Branshaw Plantation
Bogthorn
Bracken Bank
Cemy
Crem
WIDE LA
CURE HILL
FAR LOW BANK
Sykes Head
CH
1 APSLEY TERR
2 ASHVILLE TERR
3 MYRTLE VIEW
KEIGHLEY RD
GREYSTONES RISE
CENTRAL DR
HAREWOOD RISE
Griff Wood
RACE MOOR LA
HIGH FIELD LA
Holden Park
MOORCROFT AVE
GOOSE COTE WAY
Bronte Mid Sch
Low Bank
Lower Turnshaw
GREY SCAR RD
COPPY ROW 1
GREY SCAR CT 2
GRIFFE VIEW 3
WINDSOR CRES
SUNHURST CL
KEIGHLEY RD (LIDGET)
Lidget
Oakworth
SYKES LA
HAREWOOD HILL
Damems
DAMEMS LA
TURNSHAW RD
COLNE RD (CHURCH ST)
COLNE RD (GOODLEY)
OAKWORTH HALL
COLNE RD (CHAPEL LA)
PO
Chapel Lane
Oakworth Fst Sch
Worth Way
SOUTHLEA AVE
Cackleshaw
4 GREEN LA
5 HALL ST
6 CLOUGH GATE
7 LARCH CL
8 VICTORIA ST
Harewood Hill
BRACKEN BANK WLK 1
BRACKEN BANK CRES 2
BRACKEN BANK GR 3
Lane End
HILLSIDE GR
B6143
Denby Hill
DENBY HILL RD
MOUNT VIEW
BRIDGE ST
HILL TOP RD
HERITAGE WAY
CLOUGH HOUSES
OAKLEIGH MEWS
Dockroyd
1 ROSEBERRY ST
2 MEADOW VIEW
3 NEW ST
4 OAKWORTH TERR
STATION RD
Oakworth
Keighley & Worth Valley Rly
BD21
HOB COTE LA
Near Hob Cote
TIM LA
PROVIDENCE LA
LC
River Worth
Green Well Farm
MYTHOLMES LA
BROOK ROW
Mills
VALE MILL LA
LINGFIELD DR
HEBBLE ROW
LONGACRE LA
FOWLERS GARTH
BACK MYRTLE TERR
A629 HALIFAX RD
Westfield Farm
A
B
C
D
E
F
8
7
41
6
5
40
4
3
39
2
1
38
02
03
04

A6
1 NASHVILLE TERR
2 NASHVILLE ST
3 CARLBY GR
4 NASHVILLE RD
5 BK RYDAL ST
6 CROSS RYDAL ST
7 BACK OXFORD ST
8 HARDWICK ST
9 FOURTH AVE
10 BK MANNVILLE RD
11 EXLEY ST
12 CHEYNE WLK
13 MANNVILLE ST
14 MANNVILLE WAY
15 MANNVILLE WLK
16 MANNVILLE PL
17 ARNCLIFFE GR

A7
1 BK SIMPSON ST
2 SPENCER ST
3 WATERHOUSE ST
4 TALBOT ST
5 BK SLADEN ST
6 SLADEN ST
7 BK PAGET ST
8 PAGET ST
9 BK EDENSOR RD
10 BK ADA ST
11 ADA ST
12 BK CARTMEL RD
13 THE GABLES
14 POPLAR TERR
15 NEW TOWN CT

B6
1 THIRD AVE
2 SECOND AVE
3 FIRST AVE
4 WARD ST
5 BK BALFOUR ST
6 BALFOUR ST

18

B6
7 BK HIRD ST
8 BK ACRES ST
9 ASHFIELD ST
10 CALTON ST
11 CHELSEA ST
12 KENSINGTON ST

36

B7
1 ROSEMOUNT WLK
2 ROSEMOUNT CL
3 BROOMFIELD PL
4 BROOMFIELD RD
5 BK BROOMFIELD RD
6 BK BROOMFIELD ST
7 SPENCER ST
8 WATERHOUSE ST
9 TEMPLE ROW
10 TEMPLE ST
11 KENDALL MELLOR CT
12 RECTORY ROW
13 CROSS LEEDS ST

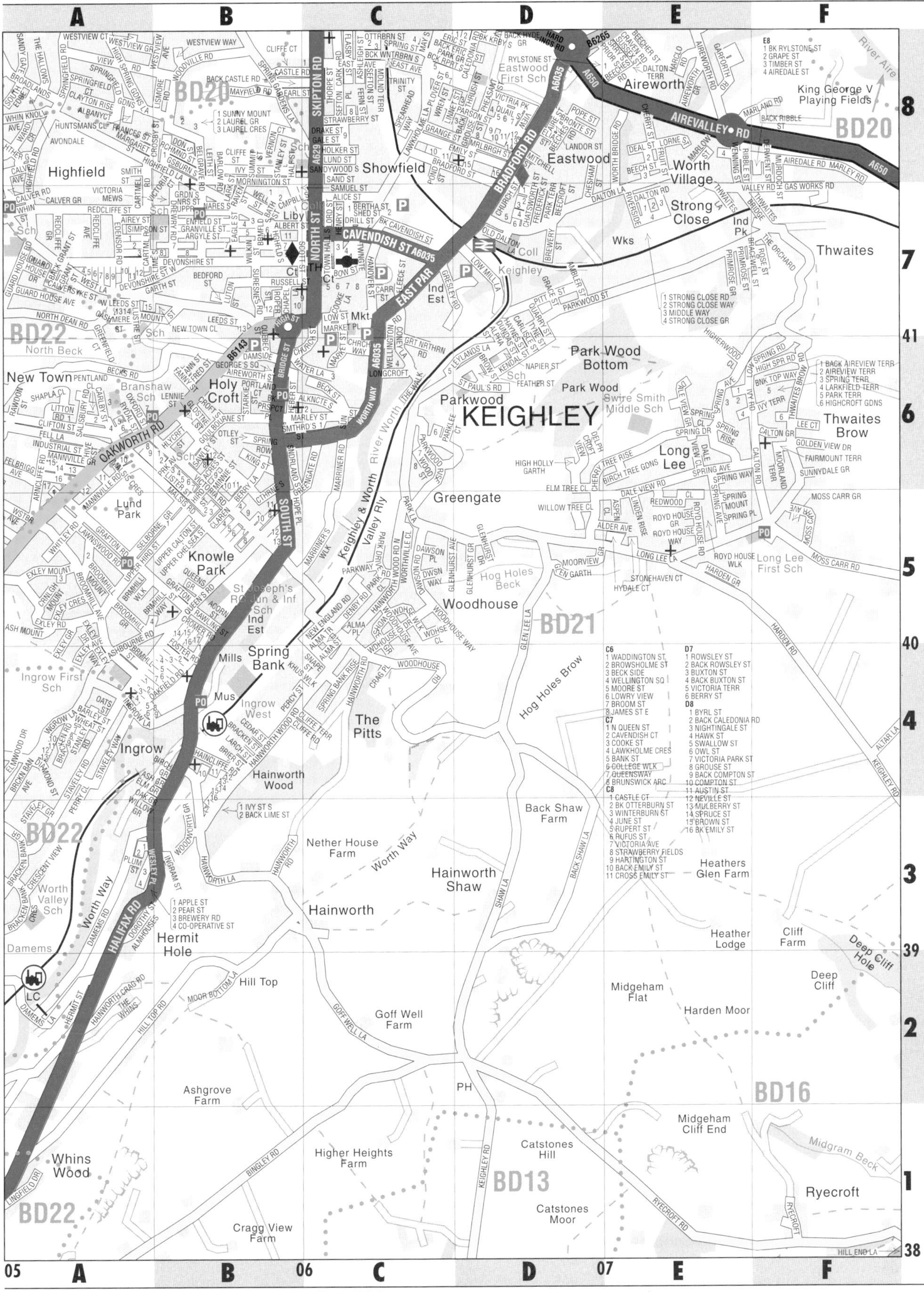

52

36

A4
1 EATON ST
2 BACK EATON ST
3 AYLESBURY ST
4 BACK AYLESBURY ST
5 MAIZE ST
6 CORN ST
7 BACK WHEAT ST
8 MALT ST
9 BACK MALT ST
10 OPAL ST
11 EMERALD ST
12 PEARL ST
13 RUBY ST

A5
1 ARNCLIFFE AVE
2 BROOMHILL DR
3 JUBILEE DR
4 BOOTHMAN WLK

B4
1 BACK CROMER GR
2 BACK FOSTER RD
3 CAISTER ST
4 BACK CAISTER ST
5 CAISTER GR
6 HEMSBY ST
7 HEMSBY GR
8 BRAN ST
9 RYE ST
10 WOODVIEW TERR
11 HAINCLIFFE PL
12 FIR ST
13 MORNING ST
14 BACK MORNING ST
15 WALNUT ST
16 BACK WALNUT ST

B5
1 KNOWLE SPRING RD
2 CALTON ST
3 CHELSEA ST
4 CHANDOS ST
5 CATHERINE ST
6 TENNYSON ST
7 RUTLAND ST
8 APSLEY ST
9 LANCASTER CT
10 BLENHEIM ST
11 BROOK ST
12 ARCADIA ST
13 PICKLES ST
14 CROMER ST
15 CROMER AVE
16 BACK CROMER AVE
17 CROMER GR

35
19

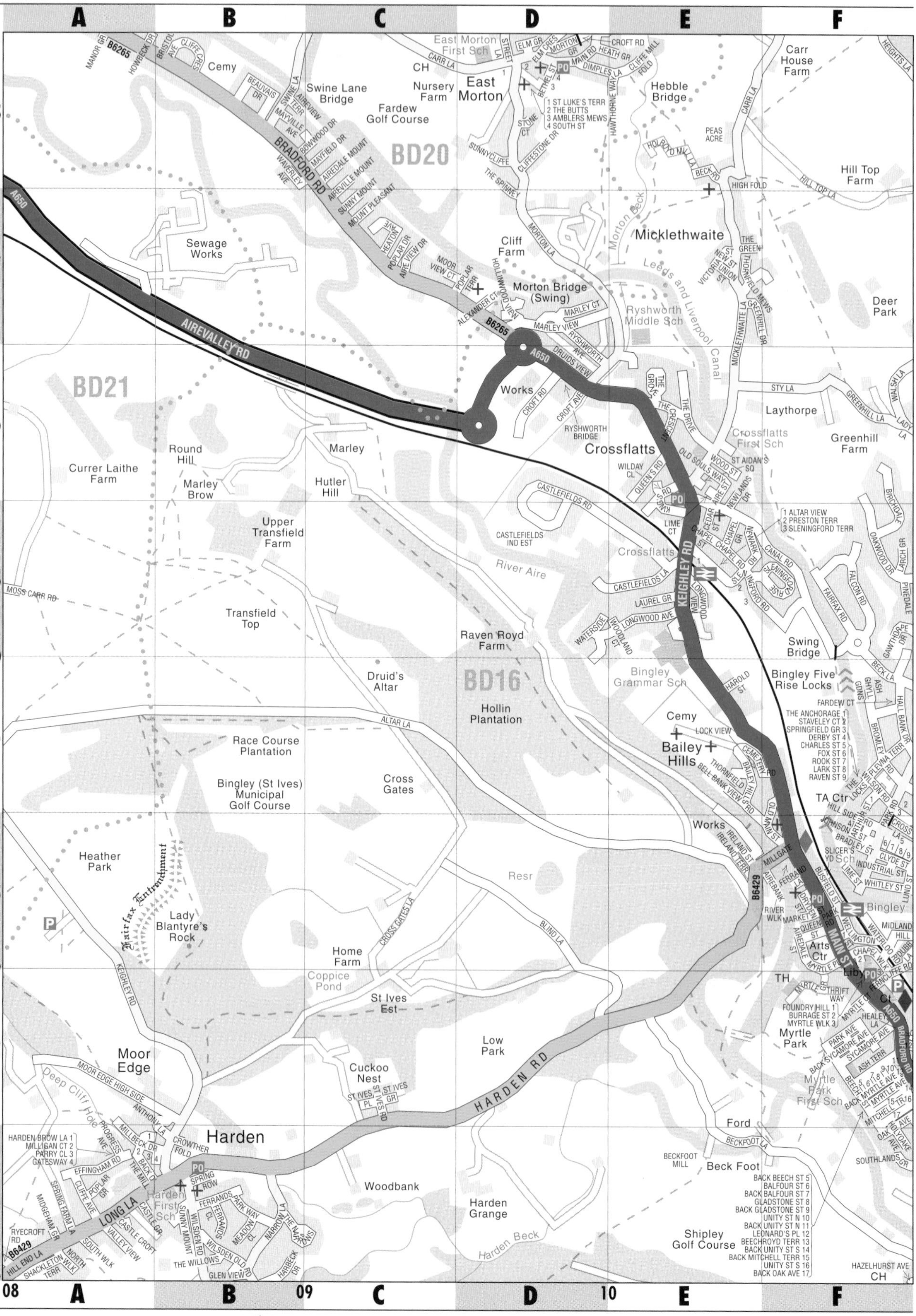
A
B
C
D
E
F
8
7
41
6
5
40
4
3
39
2
1
38
08
09
10
BD20
BD21
BD16
East Morton First Sch
East Morton
CH
Nursery Farm
Fardew Golf Course
Swine Lane Bridge
Cemy
Hebble Bridge
Carr House Farm
Hill Top Farm
Micklethwaite
Sewage Works
Cliff Farm
Morton Bridge (Swing)
Ryshworth Middle Sch
Leeds and Liverpool Canal
Deer Park
Works
Laythorpe
Crossflatts
Crossflatts First Sch
Greenhill Farm
Round Hill
Marley Brow
Marley
Hutler Hill
Currer Laithe Farm
Upper Transfield Farm
Transfield Top
Castlefields Ind Est
River Aire
Raven Royd Farm
Swing Bridge
Bingley Five Rise Locks
Bingley Grammar Sch
Druid's Altar
Hollin Plantation
Race Course Plantation
Cross Gates
Bingley (St Ives) Municipal Golf Course
Cemy
Bailey Hills
Works
TA Ctr
Heather Park
Fairfax Entrenchment
Lady Blantyre's Rock
Resr
Home Farm
Coppice Pond
St Ives Est
Bingley
Arts Ctr
Liby
TH
Ct
Low Park
Moor Edge
Cuckoo Nest
Myrtle Park
Myrtle Park First Sch
Harden
Harden First Sch
Ford
Beck Foot
Beckfoot Mill
Woodbank
Harden Grange
Harden Beck
Shipley Golf Course
Deep Cliff Hole
A650
AIREVALLEY RD
B6265
BRADFORD RD
KEIGHLEY RD
HARDEN RD
B6429
LONG LA
MAIN ST
MOSS CARR RD
ALTAR LA
BLIND LA
CROSS GATES LA
MOOR EDGE HIGH SIDE
1 ST LUKE'S TERR
2 THE BUTTS
3 AMBLERS MEWS
4 SOUTH ST
1 ALTAR VIEW
2 PRESTON TERR
3 SLENINGFORD TERR
THE ANCHORAGE 1
STAVELEY CT 2
SPRINGFIELD GR 3
DERBY ST 4
CHARLES ST 5
FOX ST 6
ROOK ST 7
LARK ST 8
RAVEN ST 9
FOUNDRY HILL 1
BURRAGE ST 2
MYRTLE WLK 3
HARDEN BROW LA 1
MILLIGAN CT 2
PARRY CL 3
GATESWAY 4
BACK BEECH ST 5
BALFOUR ST 6
BACK BALFOUR ST 7
GLADSTONE ST 8
BACK GLADSTONE ST 9
UNITY ST N 10
BACK UNITY ST N 11
LEONARD'S PL 12
BEECHROYD TERR 13
BACK UNITY ST S 14
BACK MITCHELL TERR 15
UNITY ST S 16
BACK OAK AVE 17
HAZELHURST AVE
CH

35
53

20
38

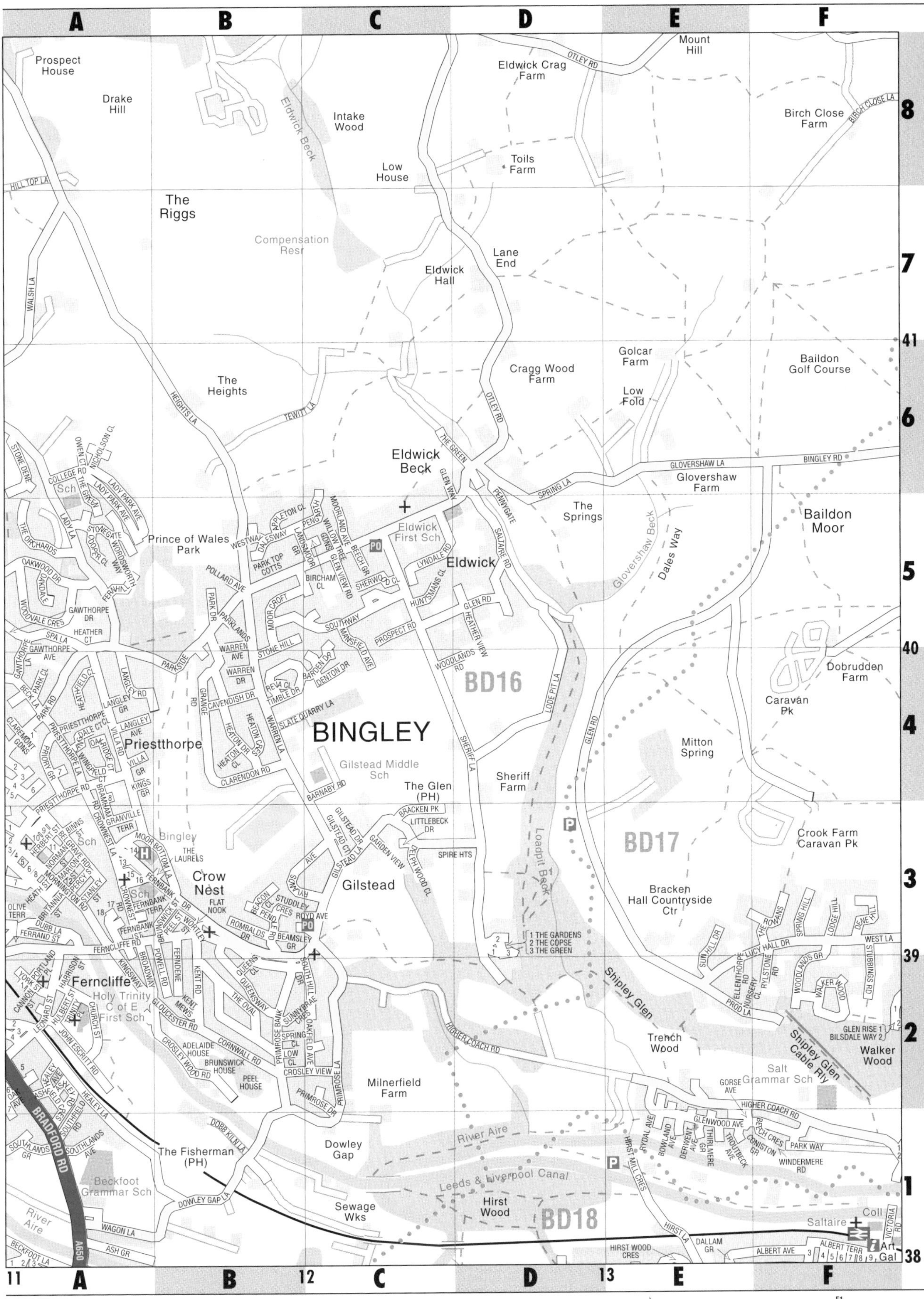

54
38

A1
1 HAZELHURST AVE
2 HAZEL BECK
3 HAZELMERE AVE

A2
1 YORK CRES
2 HEALEY LA
3 HARRIS ST
4 LEONARD'S PL
5 ASHFIELD CT
6 BACK UNITY ST S
7 OAK BANK

A3
1 CROSS LA
2 CHARLES ST
3 LYNDON TERR
4 NORFOLK ST
5 RUTLAND HO
6 KELL ST
7 WHITLEY ST
8 BARRAN ST
9 AMY ST
10 JARDINE RD
11 MYRTLE ST
12 SYDNEY ST
13 ELLEN ST
14 FERNBANK AVE
15 ELIZABETH ST
16 NETHER MOOR VIEW
17 EBRIDGE CT
18 AYRTON CRES

A4
1 MONK BARN CL
2 LEYBURN GR
3 WESTLEIGH
4 STAVELEY RD
5 STAVELEY MEWS
6 FOULDS' TERR
7 PRIORY CL
8 SCARWOOD CL

F1
1 THOMPSON LA
2 COACH RD
3 ALBERT RD
4 HERBERT ST
5 FANNY ST
6 EDWARD ST
7 AMELIA ST
8 GEORGE ST
9 WILLIAM HENRY ST

37
21

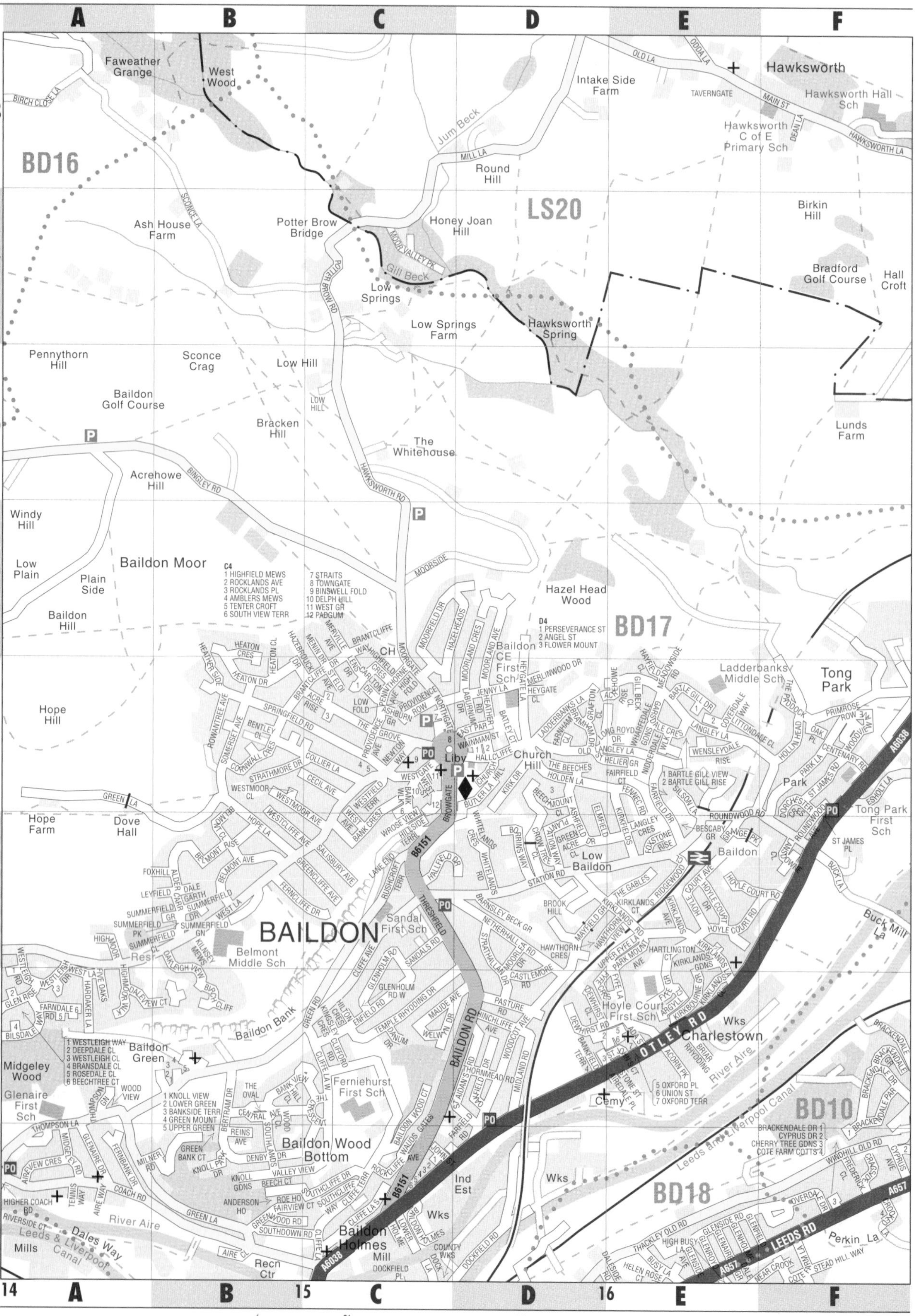

C1
1 ADELAIDE RISE
2 ALBERT ST
3 VICTORIA ST
4 WOOD ST
5 QUEEN ST
6 GEORGE ST

D2
1 IVY BANK CT
2 ROSEMONT LA
3 OAKROYD TERR
4 AIREDALE TERR

37
55

22
40

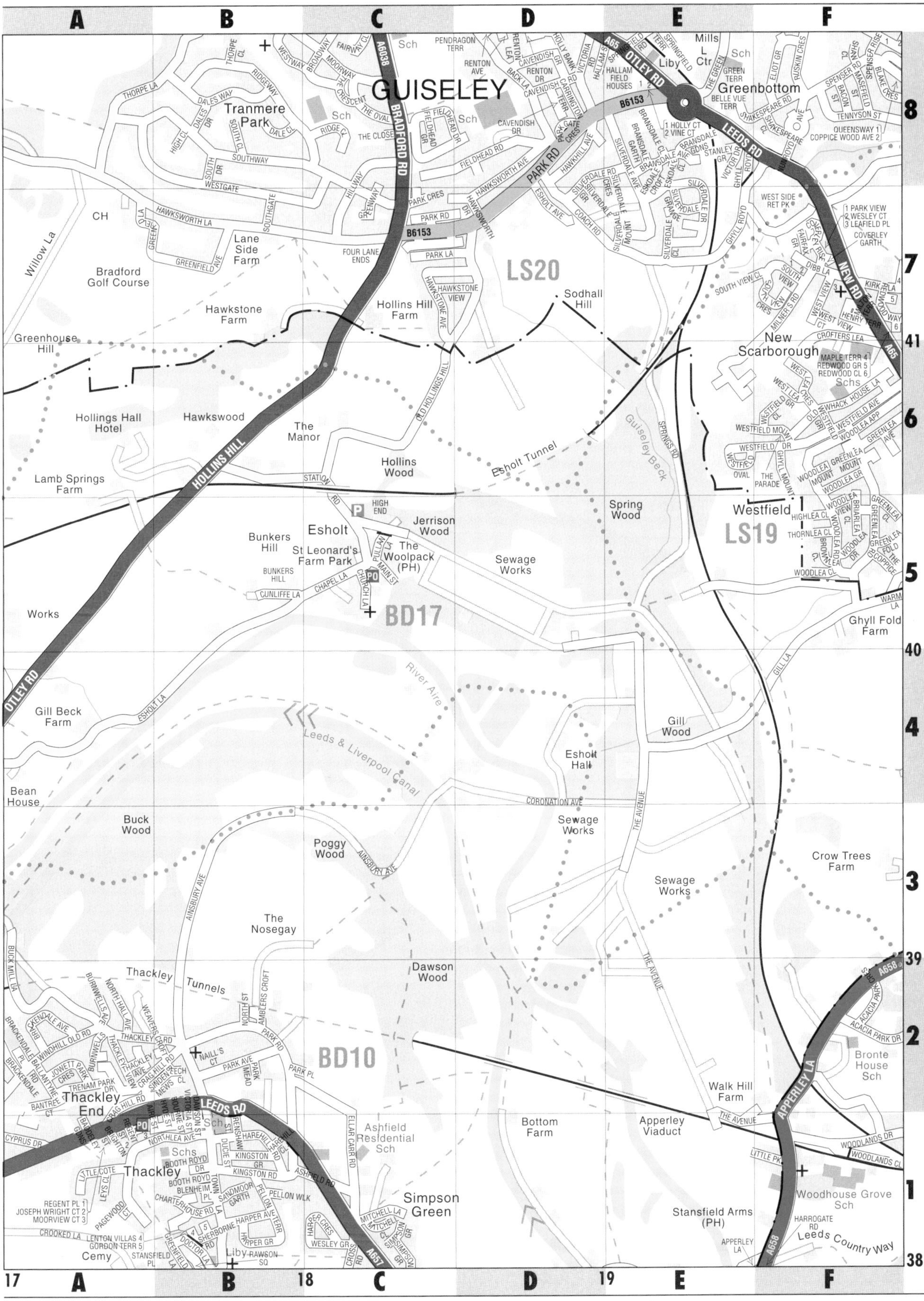
A
B
C
D
E
F
GUISELEY
Tranmere Park
Sch
Mills L Ctr
Liby
Greenbottom
BRADFORD RD
OTLEY RD
LEEDS RD
PARK RD
B6153
A6038
A65
HAWKSWORTH LA
SOUTHWAY
WESTGATE
CH
Lane Side Farm
Bradford Golf Course
Willow La
FOUR LANE ENDS
PARK LA
LS20
Sodhall Hill
Hawkstone Farm
Hollins Hill Farm
Greenhouse Hill
NEW RD
New Scarborough
Hollings Hall Hotel
Hawkswood
The Manor
Hollins Wood
Esholt Tunnel
Guiseley Beck
SPRINGS RD
Lamb Springs Farm
HOLLINS HILL
Spring Wood
Westfield
LS19
Esholt
Jerrison Wood
Bunkers Hill
St Leonard's Farm Park
The Woolpack (PH)
Sewage Works
Works
BD17
CUNLIFFE LA
CHAPEL LA
Ghyll Fold Farm
GILL LA
River Aire
OTLEY RD
Gill Beck Farm
ESHOLT LA
Leeds & Liverpool Canal
Gill Wood
Esholt Hall
Bean House
CORONATION AVE
Buck Wood
Sewage Works
Poggy Wood
AINSBURY AVE
Crow Trees Farm
Sewage Works
The Nosegay
THE AVENUE
Thackley Tunnels
Dawson Wood
A658
ACACIA PARK DR
Bronte House Sch
BD10
Walk Hill Farm
APPERLEY LA
Thackley End
LEEDS RD
Ashfield Residential Sch
Bottom Farm
Apperley Viaduct
WOODLANDS DR
Schs
Thackley
Woodhouse Grove Sch
Simpson Green
Stansfield Arms (PH)
Leeds Country Way
Cemy
A657
1
2
3
4
5
6
7
8
17
18
19
38
39
40
41

56
40

39
23

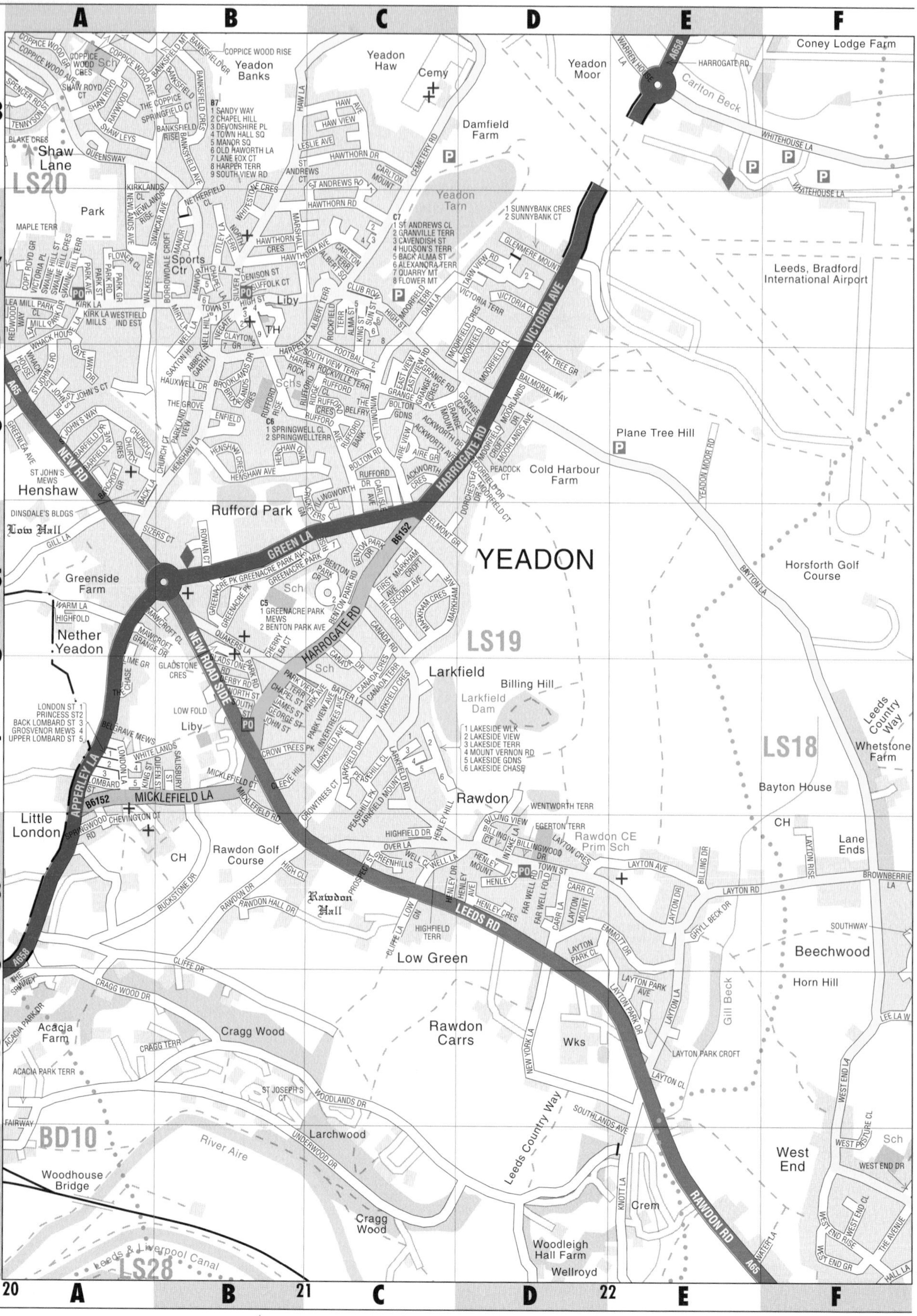
YEADON
Yeadon Banks
Yeadon Haw
Cemy
Yeadon Moor
Damfield Farm
Yeadon Tarn
Coney Lodge Farm
Leeds, Bradford International Airport
Shaw Lane
LS20
Park
Sports Ctr
Liby
TH
Henshaw
Low Hall
Rufford Park
Greenside Farm
Nether Yeadon
Plane Tree Hill
Cold Harbour Farm
Horsforth Golf Course
LS19
Larkfield
Larkfield Dam
Billing Hill
Leeds Country Way
Whetstone Farm
LS18
Bayton House
Rawdon
Little London
Rawdon Golf Course
Rawdon CE Prim Sch
Rawdon Hall
Lane Ends
Low Green
Beechwood
Horn Hill
Acacia Farm
Cragg Wood
Rawdon Carrs
Wks
Larchwood
River Aire
BD10
Woodhouse Bridge
Crem
West End
Woodleigh Hall Farm
Wellroyd
Leeds & Liverpool Canal
LS28
GREEN LA
HARROGATE RD
VICTORIA AVE
NEW RD
NEW ROAD SIDE
LEEDS RD
RAWDON RD
APPERLEY LA
MICKLEFIELD LA
B6152
A65
A658
B7
1 SANDY WAY
2 CHAPEL HILL
3 DEVONSHIRE PL
4 TOWN HALL SQ
5 MANOR SQ
6 OLD HAWORTH LA
7 LANE FOX CT
8 HARPER TERR
9 SOUTH VIEW RD
C7
1 ST ANDREWS CL
2 GRANVILLE TERR
3 CAVENDISH ST
4 HUDSON'S TERR
5 BACK ALMA ST
6 ALEXANDRA TERR
7 QUARRY MT
8 FLOWER MT
1 SUNNYBANK CRES
2 SUNNYBANK CT
C6
1 SPRINGWELL CL
2 SPRINGWELL TERR
C5
1 GREENACRE PARK MEWS
2 BENTON PARK AVE
1 LAKESIDE WLK
2 LAKESIDE VIEW
3 LAKESIDE TERR
4 MOUNT VERNON RD
5 LAKESIDE GDNS
6 LAKESIDE CHASE
LONDON ST 1
PRINCESS ST 2
BACK LOMBARD ST 3
GROSVENOR MEWS 4
UPPER LOMBARD ST 5
A B C D E F
8 7 6 5 4 3 2 1
41 40 39 38
20 21 22

39
57

24
42

Bog Plantation
Marsh Beck
None-go-bye Farm
Headlands
Marshes Plantation
Moor Side
Wrinklewood
Crag Hill
Crag House Farm
Lane End Farm
Rushes Farm
Oaks Farm
Bramhope Tunnel
LS19
Moseley Beck
Ridgeside
Kings Lea
Cookridge Hall Golf Course
Moseley Farm
Dean Grange Farm
Leeds Country Way
Cookridge
CH
Dean Grange Bungalow
Holy Trinity Prim Sch
Moseley Bottom
Holt Park
Moor Grange Farm
Scotland
Owlet Farm
Scotland Beck
Horsforth Golf Course
Moss House
Tinshill Moor
LS18
LS16
Cookridge Primary Sch
Holt Park District Ctr
Twr
Ralph Thoresby High Sch
Ling Bob
Low Farm
LEEDS
The Brownberries
Cvt
Trinity and All Saints' Coll
Tinshill Prim Sch
Tinshill
Beechwood
Westbrook Lane Prim Sch
Horsforth
Ireland Wood
Ida and Robert Arthington
Lee Lane Farm
Troy
Hill Top Farm
Cookridge
Mills
Hunger Hills
Clayton Wood
HORSFORTH
Horsforth Sch & Further Education Ctr
Woodside Quarries
Wks
Sch
Schs
Liby
A6120 RING ROAD WEST PK
1 BACK BREARY TERR
2 BREARY TERR
3 BREARY WLK
A
B
C
D
E
F
8
7
41
6
5
40
4
3
39
2
1
38
23
24
25

58
42

41
25

A
B
C
D
E
F
8
7
41
6
5
40
4
3
39
2
1
38
26
27
28
A660 LEEDS RD
OTLEY RD
Clonmore Farm
Black Hill Plantation
Leeds Country Way
Golden Acre Park & Gdns
Fish Pond Plantation
Cocker Hill Farm
Parkway Hotel
Adel Dam
ARTHINGTON RD
ECCUP LA
ECCUP MOOR RD
FIVE LANE ENDS
Golf Course
High Leas
Golf Farm
Dales Way
Headingley Golf Course
King Lane Farm
KING LA
ADEL MILL
Manor Farm
Holt Farm
Bridge House
CH
WINDERMERE DR
ALWOODLEY LA
THE DRIVE
CRESCENT VIEW
THE CRESCENT
THE VIEW
LANE END CT
LANE END CROFT
THE COURT
THE LANE
THE GROVE
GROVE RISE
ALWOODLEY CT
THE AVENUE
CRAG LA
STAIR FOOT LA
BACK CHURCH LA
CHURCH LA
KINGSLEY DR
KINGSLEY AVE
KINGSLEY RD
GAINSBRO DR
GAINSBRO AVE
HAWTHORNE GDNS
CHESTNUT WAY
CHESTNUT DR
BEECHWOOD CT
HOLT PARK CRES
HOLT PARK RD
HOLT PK GRANGE
HOLT PK GATE
HOLT PK DR
HOLT LA
HOLT FARM CL
HOLT WAY
KENWORTHY GARTH
FARRAR LA
HEATHFIELD
HOLT AVE
HOLT GDNS
HOLT CL
HOLT LANE CT
GREENFIELD CT
SADLER CL
SADLER WAY
SADLER COPSE
LS16
Adel St John the Baptist CE Prim Sch
STAIRFOOT WLK 1
EDDISON WLK 2
Adel Woods
LS17
BUCK STONE RD
BUCK STONE DR
BUCK STONE MOUNT
BUCK STONE OVAL
BUCK STONE GR
BUCK STONE RISE
BUCK STONE AVE
BUCK STONE WAY
BUCK STONE GN
BUCK STONE VIEW
EAST CAUSEWAY VALE
EAST MOOR LA
Leeds Met Univ
SPRING HILL
Adel East Moor
Adel Beck
RAYNEL GDNS
RAYNEL WAY
Ireland Wood Prim Sch
RAYNEL CL
RAYNEL DR
RAYNEL MOUNT
RAYNEL GARTH
RAYNEL GN
THE DRIVE
BROOMFIELD
WHINFIELD
THE CRESCENT
Recreation Ground
Adel
WAYLAND DR
MOOR CROFT
WOODSTOCK CL
MULBERRY RISE
MULBERRY AVE
MULBERRY GARTH
TILE LA
REDESDALE GDNS
OTTERBURN GDNS
ROTHBURY GDNS
HOLLYCROFT CT
NEW ADEL LA
NEW ADEL GDNS
NEW ADEL AVE
MAGDALENE CL
ST HELENS CROFT
ST HELENS GR
ST HELEN'S LA
ST HELENS GDNS
ST HELENS WAY
MANOR HOUSE CROFT
LAWNS HALL CL
Lawns Wood Cemetery
Leeds Crematorium
Holy Name Sch
IVESON DR
OTLEY OLD RD
THE MEADOWS
ADEL LA
ADEL PARK CT
ADEL PASTURE
ADEL PARK GDNS
OAKLANDS GR
OAKLANDS DR
OAKLANDS AVE
DUNSTARN DR
DUNSTARN LA
DUNSTARN GDNS
ADEL TOWERS CL
ADEL TOWERS CT
ADEL WOOD DR
Adel Prim Sch
1 MULBERRY VIEW
2 ADEL WOOD RD
3 ADEL WOOD PL
4 ADEL WOOD GDNS
5 OAKLANDS CL
LEEDS
Scotland Wood
Dunstarn Farm
DEANSWOOD GDNS 1
DEANSWOOD GN 2
DEANSWOOD RISE 3
DEANSWOOD HILL 4
TYNWALD DR 5
DEANSWOOD DR
BLACK MOOR RD
ADEL GRANGE CROFT 1
ADEL GRANGE MEWS 2
BEECH WLK
ALDERTON RISE 1
ALDERTON MOUNT 2
ALDERTON PL 3
ALDERTON HTS
SCOTLAND WOOD RD
ALDERTON BANK
ALDERTON CRES
IVESON APP
IVESON GARTH
IVESON RISE
IVESON LAWN
Liby
LUTTRELL GDNS
LUTTRELL CRES
LUTTRELL RD
LUTTRELL PL
LUTTRELL CL
SPENNITHORNE AVE
Iveson Prim Sch
Lawnswood
GLENDOWER PK
The Heath
Bodington Hall
OAKLEA GDNS
OAKLEA HALL CL
SMITHY MILLS LA
Bywater Farm
SCOTLAND MILL LA
University Athletic Grounds
RING RD ADEL
RING RD MEANWOOD
A6120
LAWNSWOOD GDNS
IVESON DR
PARKSTONE
PARKSTONE MOUNT
PARKSTONE GR
PARKSTONE AVE
SPEN LA
SPENNITHORNE DR
WYNFORD RISE
Ireland Wood
WYNFORD TERR
WYNFORD AVE
WYNFORD MOUNT
WYNFORD GR
THE GRANGE RD
GRANGEWOOD GDNS
GRANGEWOOD CT
WOODLANDS CT
REDVERS CL
RING RD WEST PK
LATCHMERE VIEW
LATCHMERE GDN
SPEN LA
RING RD WEETWOOD
Moorlands Sch
WEETWOOD LA
FOXHILL CT
FOXHILL GN
FOXHILL DR
FOXHILL AVE
FOXHILL CRES
Weetwood
Weetwood Hall (Hotel)
MEANWOOD GR
PARKSIDE RD
Meanwood Park
Pennyfield Sch
WOODLEA APP 1
WOODLEA CROFT 2
WOODLEA DR
WOODLEA LAWN
WOODLEA GARTH
WOODLEA GDNS
WOODLEA PL
TONGUE LA
LS6

41
59

26
44

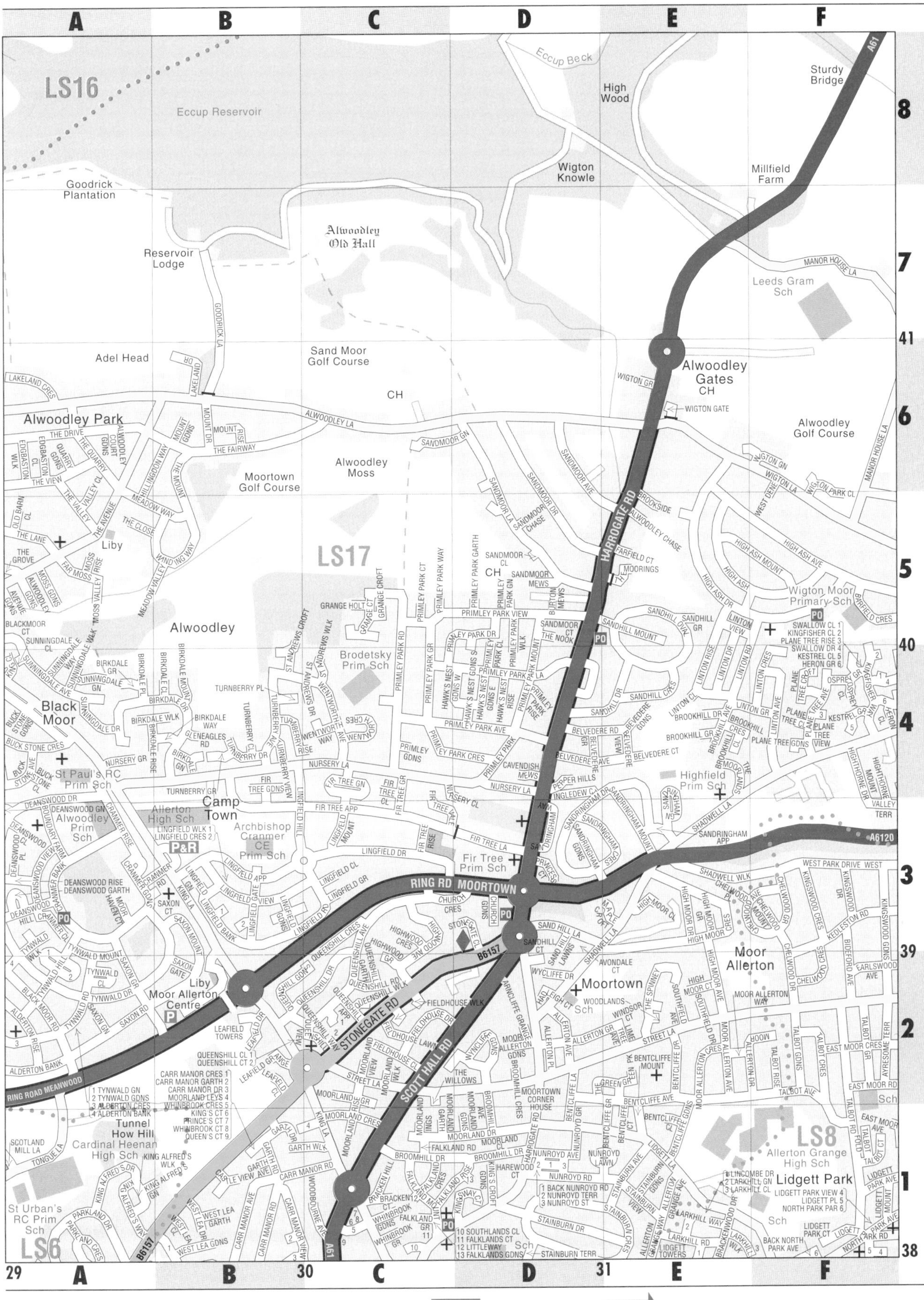
LS16
Eccup Reservoir
Eccup Beck
High Wood
Sturdy Bridge
A61
Wigton Knowle
Millfield Farm
Goodrick Plantation
Alwoodley Old Hall
Reservoir Lodge
GOODRICK LA
MANOR HOUSE LA
Leeds Gram Sch
Adel Head
Sand Moor Golf Course
Alwoodley Gates
CH
WIGTON GR
WIGTON GATE
LAKELAND CRES
ALWOODLEY LA
Alwoodley Park
Alwoodley Golf Course
THE DRIVE
THE QUARRY
THE FAIRWAY
MOUNT RISE
SANDMOOR GN
Moortown Golf Course
Alwoodley Moss
HILLINGDON WAY
MEADOW WAY
THE CLOSE
THE VALLEY
THE AVENUE
THE LANE
THE GROVE
Liby
LS17
WINDING WAY
SANDMOOR DR
SANDMOOR AVE
SANDMOOR CHASE
HARROGATE RD
BROOKSIDE
ALWOODLEY CHASE
WIGTON GN
WIGTON LA
WIGTON PARK CL
WEST DENE
HIGH ASH AVE
HIGH ASH MOUNT
HIGH ASH DR
FARFIELD CT
MOORINGS
Wigton Moor Primary Sch
BARFIELD CRES
Alwoodley
GRANGE HOLT
GRANGE CROFT
PRIMLEY PARK WAY
PRIMLEY PARK VIEW
PRIMLEY PARK DR
PRIMLEY PARK RD
PRIMLEY PARK AVE
PRIMLEY PARK CRES
SANDHILL MOUNT
SANDHILL OVAL
SANDHILL GR
SANDHILL DR
SANDHILL CRES
LINTON RISE
LINTON DR
LINTON RD
LINTON AVE
LINTON GR
Brodetsky Prim Sch
TURNBERRY PL
TURNBERRY AVE
TURNBERRY DR
BIRKDALE WLK
BIRKDALE WAY
GLENEAGLES RD
Black Moor
BUCK STONE CRES
SUNNINGDALE AVE
SUNNINGDALE DR
NURSERY GR
NURSERY LA
BELVEDERE RD
BELVEDERE AVE
BELVEDERE CT
BROOKHILL DR
BROOKHILL GR
PLANE TREE GDNS
CAVENDISH MEWS
PEPER HILLS
Highfield Prim Sch
St Paul's RC Prim Sch
TURNBERRY GR
FIR TREE GDNS
FIR TREE GN
FIR TREE APP
FIR TREE LA
Camp Town
Allerton High Sch
Archbishop Cranmer CE Prim Sch
Alwoodley Prim Sch
DEANSWOOD DR
LINGFIELD HILL
LINGFIELD DR
LINGFIELD CL
LINGFIELD GR
Fir Tree Prim Sch
SANDRINGHAM APP
SHADWELL LA
SHADWELL WLK
A6120
WEST PARK DRIVE WEST
RING RD MOORTOWN
CHURCH CRES
STONEGATE CL
SAND HILL LA
HIGH MOOR CL
HIGH MOOR CRES
KEDLESTON RD
Moor Allerton
B6157
Moortown
WYCLIFFE DR
AVONDALE CT
TYNWALD MOUNT
SAXON GATE
Liby
Moor Allerton Centre
P&R
ALDERTON RISE
ALDERTON BANK
RING ROAD MEANWOOD
LEAFIELD TOWERS
STONEGATE RD
FIELDHOUSE WLK
SCOTT HALL RD
ALLERTON AVE
ALLERTON GR
STREET LA
MOOR ALLERTON WAY
TALBOT AVE
EAST MOOR RD
THE WILLOWS
MOORTOWN CORNER HOUSE
BENTCLIFFE AVE
BENTCLIFFE MOUNT
LS8
Allerton Grange High Sch
Lidgett Park
Tunnel How Hill
Cardinal Heenan High Sch
SCOTLAND MILL LA
TONGUE LA
KING ALFRED'S WLK
CARR MANOR RD
FALKLAND RD
NUNROYD RD
STAINBURN DR
STAINBURN TERR
LARKHILL WAY
LARKHILL RD
St Urban's RC Prim Sch
LS6
WEST LEA GDNS
PARKLAND CRES
A61
8
7
6
5
4
3
2
1
41
40
39
38
A
B
C
D
E
F
29
30
31

60
44

43
27

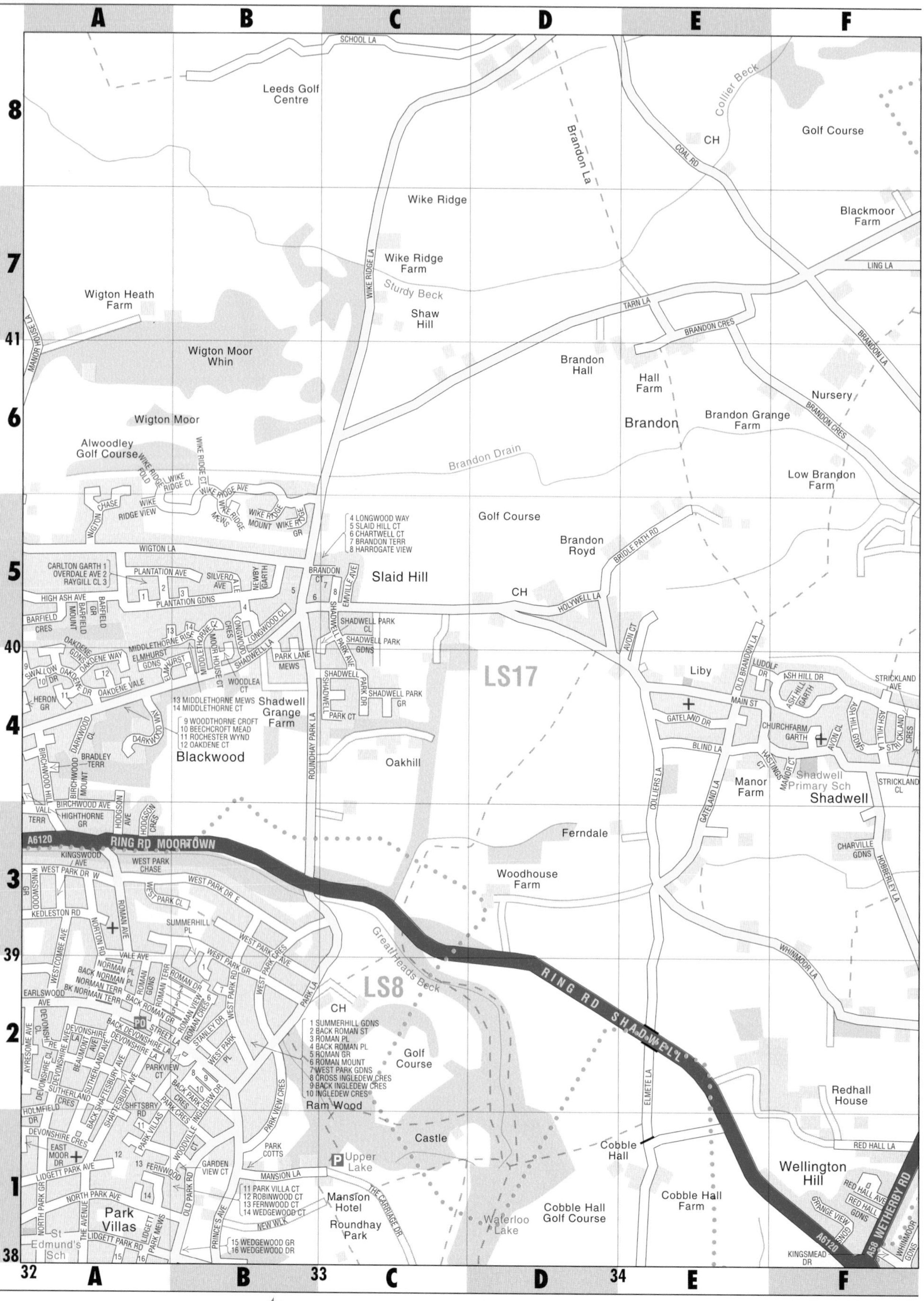
A
B
C
D
E
F
8
7
6
5
4
3
2
1
41
40
39
38
32
33
34
SCHOOL LA
Leeds Golf Centre
Collier Beck
CH
Golf Course
Brandon La
COAL RD
Wike Ridge
Blackmoor Farm
Wike Ridge Farm
WIKE RIDGE LA
Sturdy Beck
LING LA
Wigton Heath Farm
Shaw Hill
TARN LA
BRANDON CRES
MANOR HOUSE LA
Wigton Moor Whin
Brandon Hall
Hall Farm
BRANDON LA
Nursery
Wigton Moor
Brandon
Brandon Grange Farm
Alwoodley Golf Course
Brandon Drain
Low Brandon Farm
WIGTON CHASE
WIKE RIDGE VIEW
Golf Course
Brandon Royd
BRIDLE PATH RD
4 LONGWOOD WAY
5 SLAID HILL CT
6 CHARTWELL CT
7 BRANDON TERR
8 HARROGATE VIEW
WIGTON LA
CARLTON GARTH 1
OVERDALE AVE 2
RAYGILL CL 3
PLANTATION AVE
Slaid Hill
CH
HOLYWELL LA
HIGH ASH AVE
PLANTATION GDNS
SHADWELL PARK CL
SHADWELL PARK GDNS
LS17
Liby
OLD BRANDON LA
AVON CT
PARK LANE MEWS
Shadwell Grange Farm
13 MIDDLETHORNE MEWS
14 MIDDLETHORNE CT
9 WOODTHORNE CROFT
10 BEECHCROFT MEAD
11 ROCHESTER WYND
12 OAKDENE CT
SHADWELL PARK GR
PARK CT
MAIN ST
GATELAND DR
BLIND LA
CHURCHFARM GARTH
STRICKLAND AVE
Blackwood
Oakhill
ROUNDHAY PARK LA
COLLIERS LA
GATELAND LA
Manor Farm
Shadwell Primary Sch
Shadwell
STRICKLAND CL
BIRCHWOOD AVE
HIGHTHORNE GR
A6120
RING RD MOORTOWN
Ferndale
CHARVILLE GDNS
KINGSWOOD AVE
WEST PARK CHASE
WEST PARK DR W
WEST PARK DR E
Woodhouse Farm
HOBBERLEY LA
KEDLESTON RD
SUMMERHILL PL
Great Heads Beck
WHINMOOR LA
LS8
RING RD SHADWELL
CH
1 SUMMERHILL GDNS
2 BACK ROMAN ST
3 ROMAN PL
4 BACK ROMAN PL
5 ROMAN GR
6 ROMAN MOUNT
7 WEST PARK GDNS
8 CROSS INGLEDEW CRES
9 BACK INGLEDEW CRES
10 INGLEDEW CRES
Golf Course
ELMETE LA
Redhall House
Ram Wood
Castle
Cobble Hall
RED HALL LA
Upper Lake
Wellington Hill
MANSION LA
11 PARK VILLA CT
12 ROBINWOOD CT
13 FERNWOOD CT
14 WEDGEWOOD CT
Mansion Hotel
Cobble Hall Farm
Cobble Hall Golf Course
NEW WLK
Roundhay Park
Waterloo Lake
THE CARRIAGE DR
Park Villas
St Edmund's Sch
15 WEDGEWOOD GR
16 WEDGEWOOD DR
KINGSMEAD DR
A58 WETHERBY RD
A6120

43
61

28
46

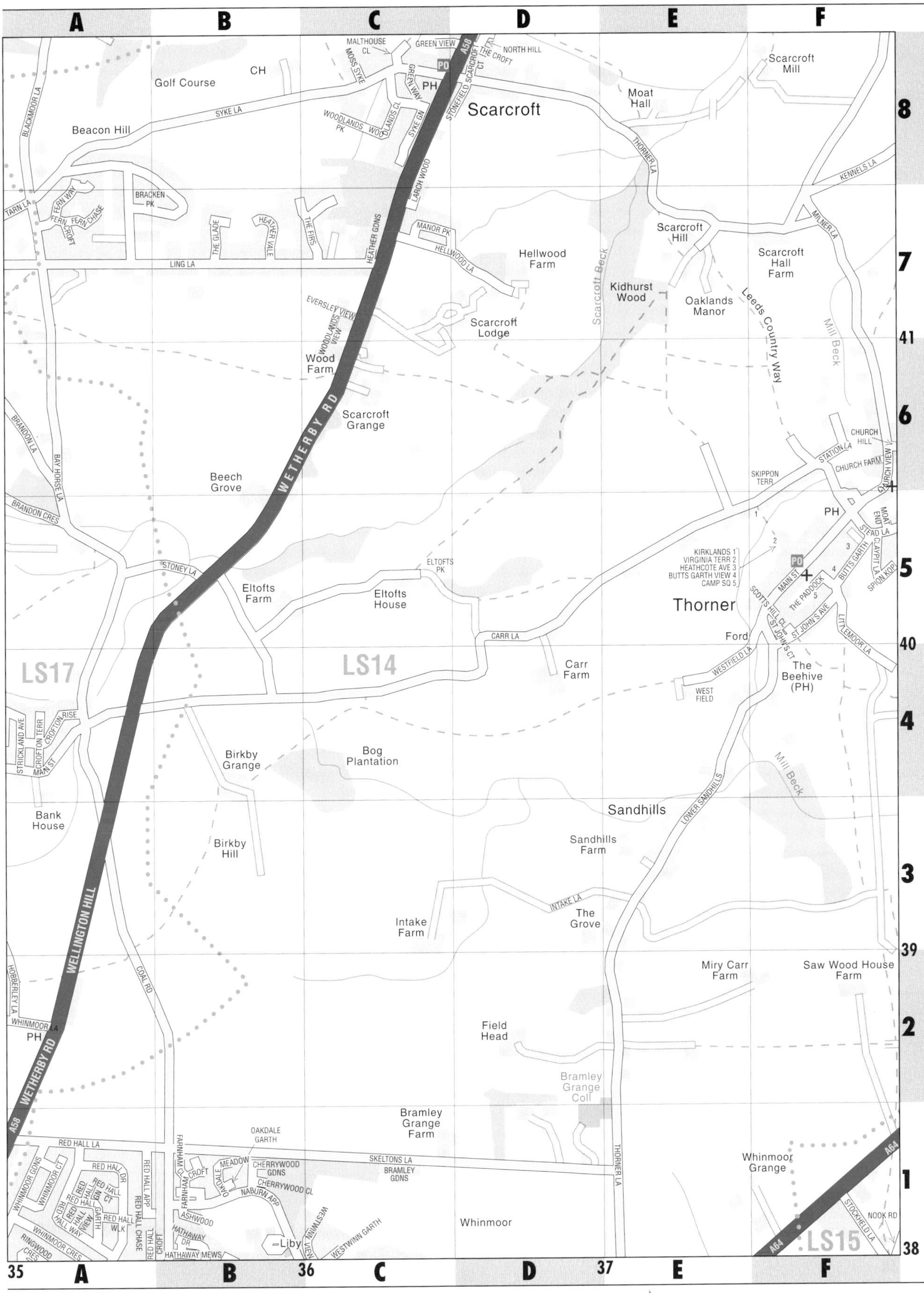
A
B
C
D
E
F
8
7
6
5
4
3
2
1
41
40
39
38
35
36
37
Golf Course
CH
Beacon Hill
BLACKMOOR LA
SYKE LA
MALTHOUSE CL
MOSS SYKE
GREEN VIEW
GREEN WAY
PO
PH
A58
SCARCROFT CT
THE CROFT
NORTH HILL
STONEFIELD
WOODLANDS PK
WOODLANDS CL
SYKE GN
Scarcroft
Moat Hall
Scarcroft Mill
THORNER LA
KENNELS LA
LARCH WOOD
TARN LA
FERN WAY
FERN CROFT
FERN CHASE
BRACKEN PK
THE GLADE
HEATHER VALE
THE FIRS
HEATHER GDNS
MANOR PK
HELLWOOD LA
LING LA
Hellwood Farm
Scarcroft Beck
Kidhurst Wood
Scarcroft Hill
Oaklands Manor
Scarcroft Hall Farm
MILNER LA
Leeds Country Way
Mill Beck
EVERSLEY VIEW
WOODLANDS VIEW
Scarcroft Lodge
Wood Farm
Scarcroft Grange
BRANDON LA
BAY HORSE LA
BRANDON CRES
Beech Grove
WETHERBY RD
CHURCH HILL
STATION LA
CHURCH FARM
CHURCH VIEW
SKIPPON TERR
PH
MOAT END
STEAD LA
CLAYPIT LA
BUTTS GARTH
SPION KOP
KIRKLANDS 1
VIRGINIA TERR 2
HEATHCOTE AVE 3
BUTTS GARTH VIEW 4
CAMP SQ 5
MAIN ST
THE PADDOCK
SCOTTS HILL CL
ST JOHN'S CT
ST JOHN'S AVE
LITTLEMOOR LA
Thorner
Ford
STONEY LA
ELTOFTS PK
Eltofts Farm
Eltofts House
CARR LA
Carr Farm
WESTFIELD LA
WEST FIELD
The Beehive (PH)
LS17
LS14
STRICKLAND AVE
CROFTON TERR
CROFTON RISE
MAIN ST
Birkby Grange
Bog Plantation
Mill Beck
Bank House
Sandhills
LOWER SANDHILLS
Birkby Hill
Sandhills Farm
Intake Farm
INTAKE LA
The Grove
WELLINGTON HILL
HOBBERLEY LA
COAL RD
Miry Carr Farm
Saw Wood House Farm
WHINMOOR LA
PH
Field Head
Bramley Grange Coll
Bramley Grange Farm
OAKDALE GARTH
RED HALL LA
SKELTONS LA
THORNER LA
Whinmoor Grange
A64
WHINMOOR GDNS
WHINMOOR CT
RED HALL DR
RED HALL GN
RED HALL CT
RED HALL GARTH
RED HALL VIEW
RED HALL WAY
RED HALL WLK
RED HALL APP
RED HALL CHASE
RED HALL CROFT
FARNHAM CL
FARNHAM CROFT
OAKDALE
MEADOW
CHERRYWOOD GDNS
CHERRYWOOD CL
BRAMLEY GDNS
NABURN APP
ASHWOOD
HATHAWAY DR
HATHAWAY MEWS
Liby
WESTWINN VIEW
WESTWINN GARTH
Whinmoor
WHINMOOR CRES
RINGWOOD CRES
STOCKHELD LA
NOOK RD
LS15

62
46

45
29

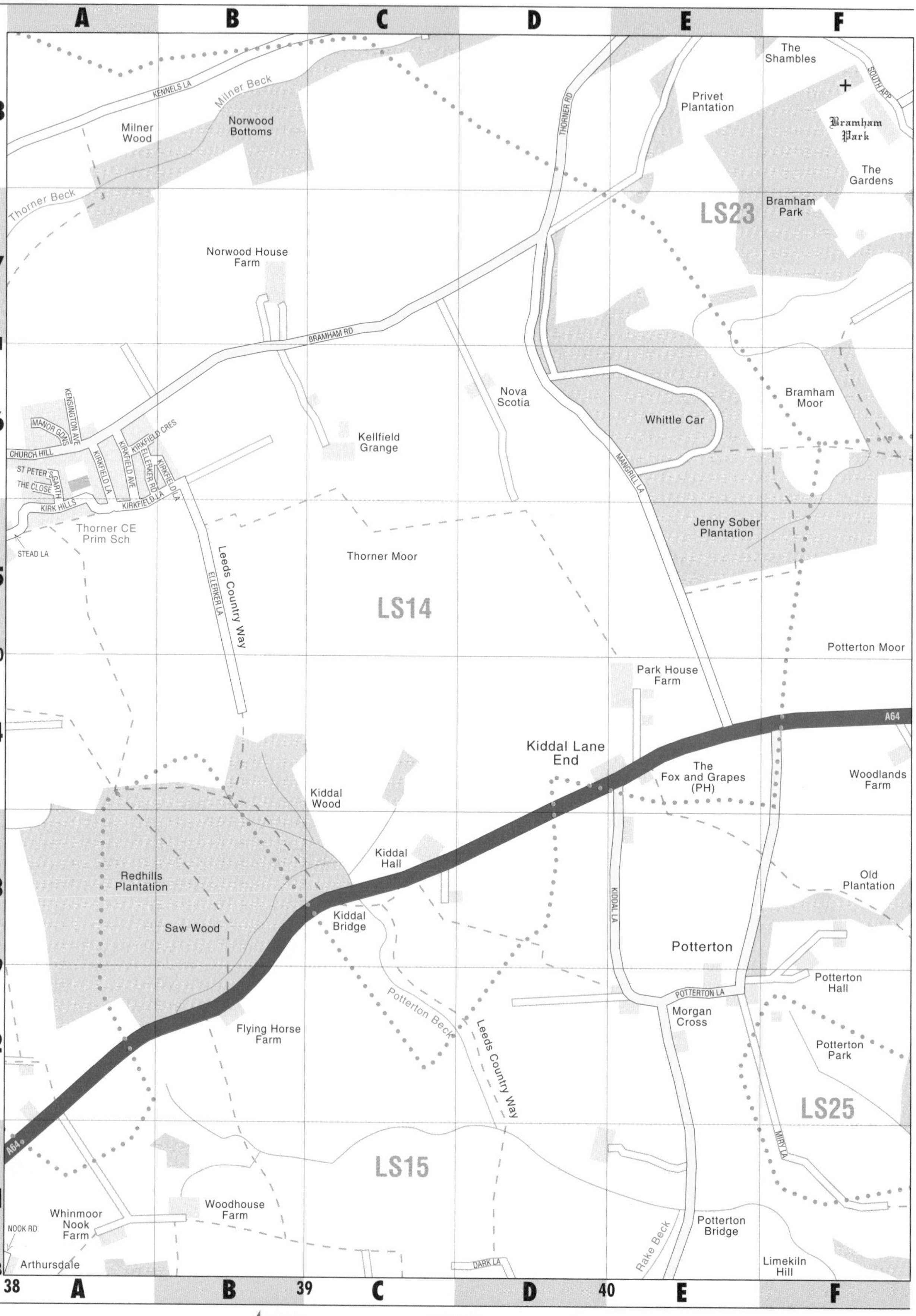
A
B
C
D
E
F
8
7
41
6
5
40
4
3
39
2
1
38
38
39
40
KENNELS LA
Milner Beck
Milner Wood
Norwood Bottoms
Thorner Beck
THORNER RD
Privet Plantation
The Shambles
SOUTH APP
Bramham Park
The Gardens
Bramham Park
LS23
Norwood House Farm
BRAMHAM RD
Nova Scotia
Whittle Car
Bramham Moor
KENSINGTON AVE
MANOR GDNS
CHURCH HILL
KIRKFIELD LA
KIRKFIELD AVE
KIRKFIELD CRES
ELLERKER RD
KIRKFIELD DR
ST PETER'S GARTH
THE CLOSE
KIRK HILLS
Kellfield Grange
MANGRILL LA
Thorner CE Prim Sch
STEAD LA
Jenny Sober Plantation
Thorner Moor
Leeds Country Way
ELLERKER LA
LS14
Potterton Moor
Park House Farm
A64
Kiddal Lane End
The Fox and Grapes (PH)
Woodlands Farm
Kiddal Wood
Kiddal Hall
Redhills Plantation
Saw Wood
Kiddal Bridge
KIDDAL LA
Old Plantation
Potterton
Potterton Hall
POTTERTON LA
Morgan Cross
Potterton Beck
Leeds Country Way
Flying Horse Farm
Potterton Park
LS25
MIRY LA
LS15
Whinmoor Nook Farm
Woodhouse Farm
NOOK RD
Arthursdale
Rake Beck
Potterton Bridge
Limekiln Hill
DARK LA

45
63

30
48

A
B
C
D
E
F
8
7
41
6
5
40
4
3
39
2
1
38
41
42
43
A1
HEADLEY LA
Paradise Farm
LS23
Dawsonfield Plantation
Rakes Wood
Bramham Park
Camp Hill
Spen Common
Open Rakes
SPEN COMMON LA
Openrakes Beck
Spen Farm
Quarry Farm
SOUTH APP
Obelisk
Black Fen
Bramham Moor
Beccamoor Wood
New Black Fen
LS24
Whitewells Bottom
A1 (M)
Crossroads Farm
A64
Blackfen Plantation
Becca Moor
45
NORTH APP
Windsor Farm
Whitewell Farm
OCCUPATION LA
Becca Lodge
Becca Moor
LS15
Cowthwaite Plain
Graystone Plain
Beccamoor Plantation
Hazel Wood
Nut Hill Farm
Nut Hill
Cowthwaite Plantation
Little Moor
Hick Wood
Mast
Birch Spring
SOUTH APP
Becca Home Farm
Black Horse Farm
Becca Hall
LS25
South Plantation
Becca Park
ABERFORD BY-PASS
Strawberry Hill
HAVERTHWAITES DR
GREYSTONE PK
Becca Low Wood
St John's
MAIN ST
Becca Banks
Cufforth House
GREYSTONES CL
LS15
Ridge Plantation
The Ridge
Cock Beck
ST JOHN'S CL
THE DALE
A1 (M)
FIELD LA

64
48

47
31

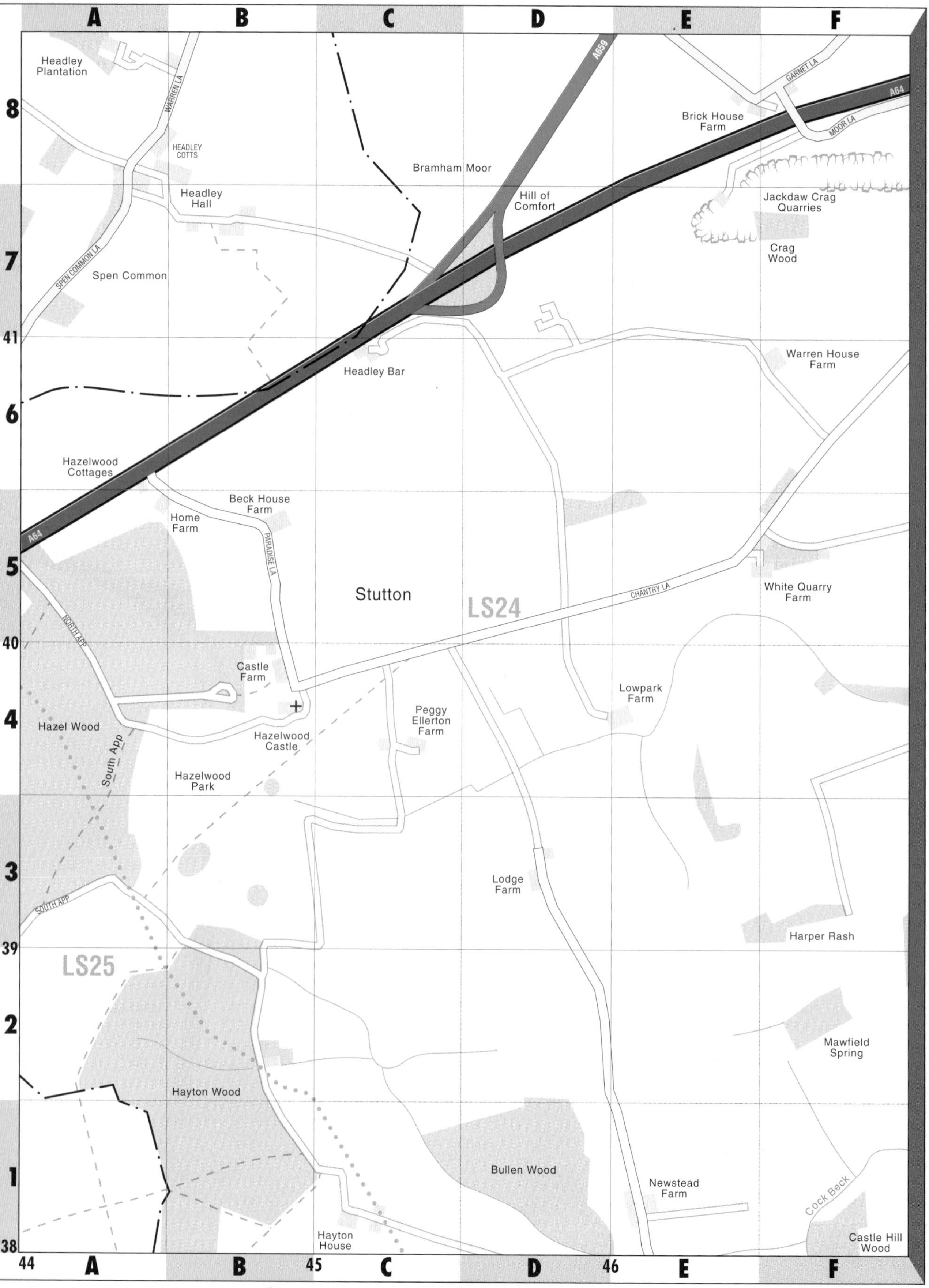
A
B
C
D
E
F
8
7
6
5
4
3
2
1
41
40
39
38
44
45
46
Headley Plantation
WARREN LA
HEADLEY COTTS
Headley Hall
SPEN COMMON LA
Spen Common
Bramham Moor
A659
Hill of Comfort
GARNET LA
Brick House Farm
A64
MOOR LA
Jackdaw Crag Quarries
Crag Wood
Headley Bar
Warren House Farm
Hazelwood Cottages
Beck House Farm
Home Farm
PARADISE LA
A64
NORTH APP
Stutton
LS24
CHANTRY LA
White Quarry Farm
Castle Farm
Hazel Wood
Hazelwood Castle
Peggy Ellerton Farm
Lowpark Farm
South App
Hazelwood Park
Lodge Farm
SOUTH APP
Harper Rash
LS25
Mawfield Spring
Hayton Wood
Bullen Wood
Newstead Farm
Cock Beck
Castle Hill Wood
Hayton House

47
65

32 50

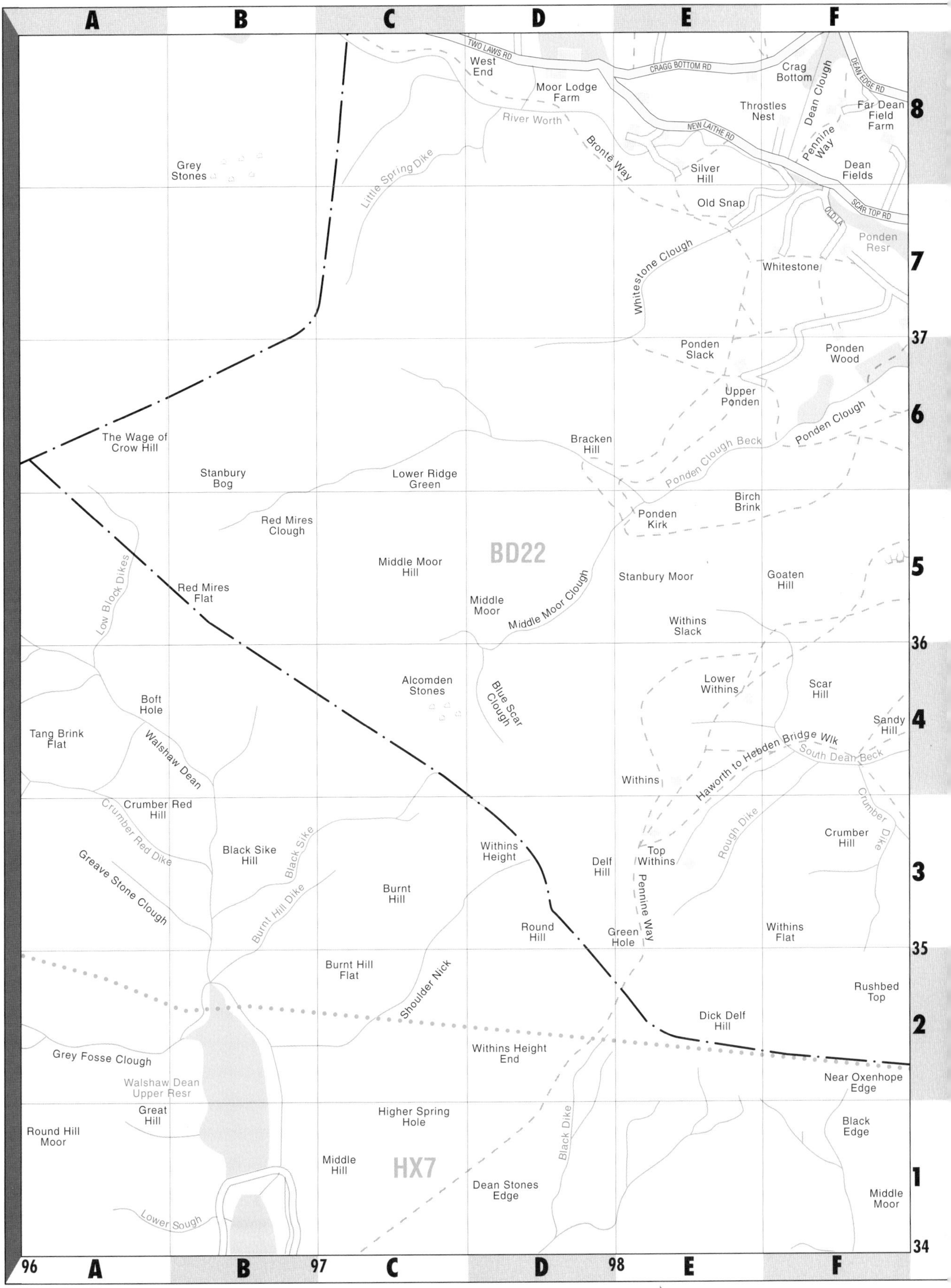
A
B
C
D
E
F
TWO LAWS RD
West End
CRAGG BOTTOM RD
Crag Bottom
DEAN EDGE RD
Moor Lodge Farm
Throstles Nest
Dean Clough
Far Dean Field Farm
8
River Worth
NEW LAITHE RD
Brontë Way
Pennine Way
Grey Stones
Little Spring Dike
Silver Hill
Dean Fields
Old Snap
SCAR TOP RD
OLD LA
Ponden Resr
Whitestone Clough
Whitestone
7
37
Ponden Slack
Ponden Wood
Upper Ponden
6
Ponden Clough
The Wage of Crow Hill
Bracken Hill
Ponden Clough Beck
Stanbury Bog
Lower Ridge Green
Birch Brink
Red Mires Clough
Ponden Kirk
BD22
Middle Moor Hill
5
Low Block Dikes
Stanbury Moor
Goaten Hill
Red Mires Flat
Middle Moor
Middle Moor Clough
Withins Slack
36
Alcomden Stones
Lower Withins
Boft Hole
Blue Scar Clough
Scar Hill
Tang Brink Flat
Walshaw Dean
Sandy Hill
4
Haworth to Hebden Bridge Wlk
South Dean Beck
Withins
Crumber Red Hill
Crumber Red Dike
Crumber Dike
Crumber Hill
Black Sike
Black Sike Hill
Greave Stone Clough
Withins Height
Rough Dike
Delf Hill
Top Withins
3
Burnt Hill
Burnt Hill Dike
Pennine Way
Round Hill
Green Hole
Withins Flat
35
Burnt Hill Flat
Shoulder Nick
Rushbed Top
Dick Delf Hill
2
Grey Fosse Clough
Withins Height End
Near Oxenhope Edge
Walshaw Dean Upper Resr
Great Hill
Higher Spring Hole
Black Edge
Round Hill Moor
Black Dike
Middle Hill
HX7
1
Dean Stones Edge
Middle Moor
Lower Sough
34
96
A
B
97
C
D
98
E
F

68 50

49
33

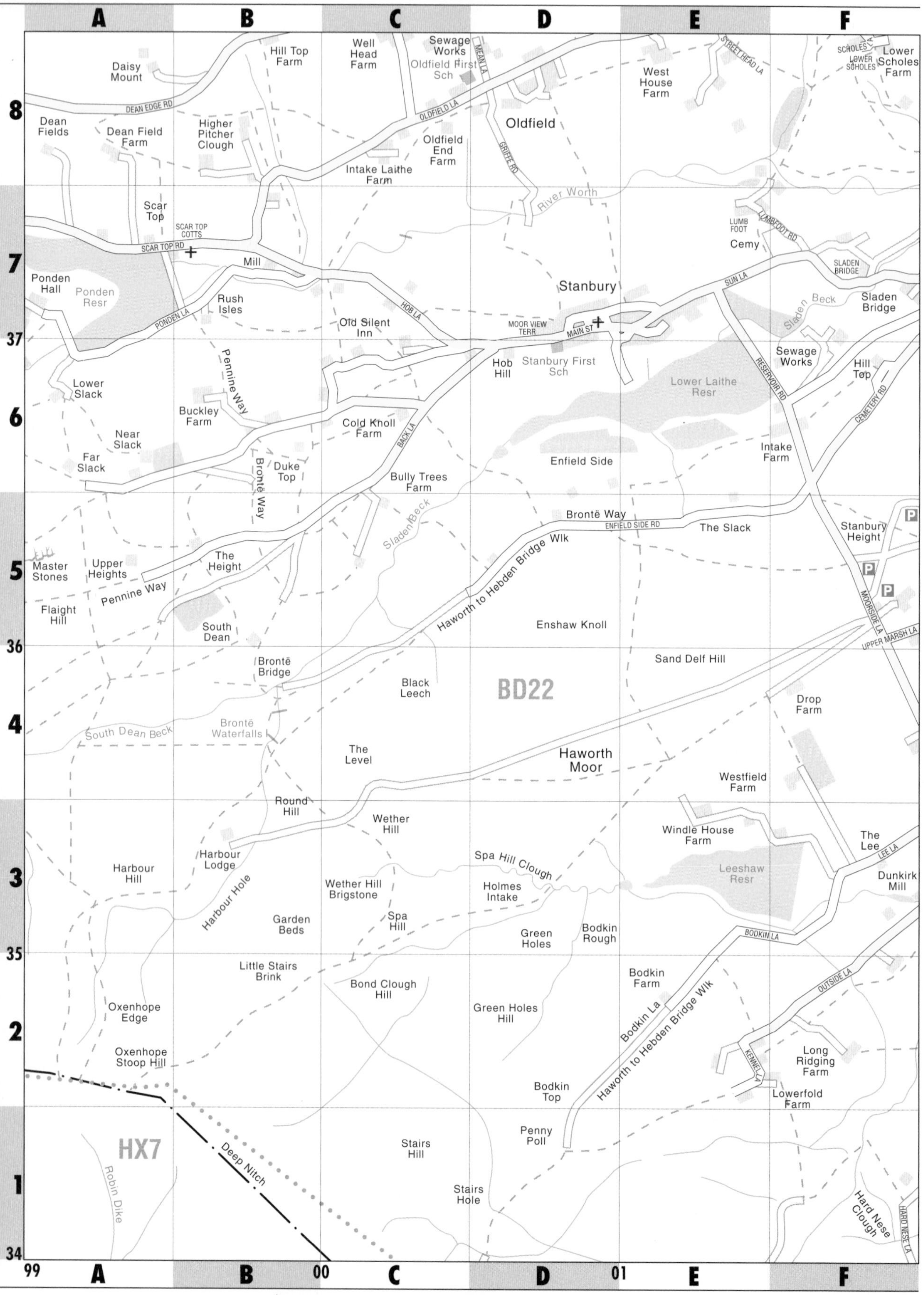
A
B
C
D
E
F
8
7
37
6
5
36
4
3
35
2
1
34
99
00
01
Daisy Mount
Hill Top Farm
Well Head Farm
Sewage Works
Oldfield First Sch
MEAN LA
West House Farm
STREET HEAD LA
SCHOLES LA
LOWER SCHOLES
Lower Scholes Farm
DEAN EDGE RD
Dean Fields
Dean Field Farm
Higher Pitcher Clough
OLDFIELD LA
Oldfield
Oldfield End Farm
GRIFFE RD
Intake Laithe Farm
River Worth
Scar Top
SCAR TOP COTTS
SCAR TOP RD
Mill
LUMB FOOT
Cemy
LUMBFOOT RD
SLADEN BRIDGE
Ponden Hall
Ponden Resr
PONDEN LA
Rush Isles
HOB LA
Stanbury
SUN LA
Sladen Beck
Sladen Bridge
Old Silent Inn
MOOR VIEW TERR
MAIN ST
Hob Hill
Stanbury First Sch
Sewage Works
Hill Top
Pennine Way
Lower Slack
Lower Laithe Resr
RESERVOIR RD
CEMETERY RD
Buckley Farm
Cold Knoll Farm
Near Slack
BACK LA
Far Slack
Duke Top
Brontë Way
Enfield Side
Intake Farm
Bully Trees Farm
Brontë Way
ENFIELD SIDE RD
The Slack
Stanbury Height
Sladen Beck
Haworth to Hebden Bridge Wlk
Master Stones
Upper Heights
The Height
P
Pennine Way
MOORSIDE LA
Flaight Hill
South Dean
Enshaw Knoll
UPPER MARSH LA
Brontë Bridge
Sand Delf Hill
Black Leech
BD22
Drop Farm
South Dean Beck
Brontë Waterfalls
The Level
Haworth Moor
Westfield Farm
Round Hill
Wether Hill
Windle House Farm
The Lee
LEE LA
Harbour Lodge
Spa Hill Clough
Harbour Hill
Leeshaw Resr
Dunkirk Mill
Harbour Hole
Wether Hill Brigstone
Holmes Intake
Garden Beds
Spa Hill
Green Holes
Bodkin Rough
BODKIN LA
Little Stairs Brink
Bond Clough Hill
Bodkin Farm
OUTSIDE LA
Oxenhope Edge
Green Holes Hill
Bodkin La
Haworth to Hebden Bridge Wlk
Oxenhope Stoop Hill
Long Ridging Farm
KENNEL LA
Bodkin Top
Lowerfold Farm
HX7
Penny Poll
Stairs Hill
Deep Nitch
Robin Dike
Stairs Hole
Hard Nese Clough
HARD NESE LA

49
69

D7
1 TYNE ST
2 OUSE ST
3 AIRE ST
4 GAS ST
5 BACK RIVER ST
6 RIVER ST
7 APSLEY ST
8 BRIGHT ST
9 THORNFIELD
10 CARLTON ST
11 DUKE ST
12 LORD ST
13 REGENT ST
14 NORMAN ST
15 FIFE ST
16 DOVE ST
17 WREN ST

E8
1 DAISY ST
2 CHERRY ST
3 THORN ST
4 LEAF ST
5 JANET ST
6 ARCTIC ST
7 LEESWORTH CT
8 DOUGLAS ST
9 NARES ST
10 GORDON ST
11 CECIL ST
12 VALLEY VIEW GDNS
13 PARK VIEW AVE
14 FRITH ST
15 RUTH ST
16 MIDGLEY ALMSHOUSES
17 RYLANDS MDW
18 COLLINS CL

34

52

F8
1 ALBERT ST
2 LORNE ST
3 SPRING ST
4 SALTAIRE
5 GALE ST
6 CANBERRA CL
7 BANCROFT ST
8 WEST VIEW ST
9 WOODVILLE GR
10 WOODVILLE TERR
11 GARDEN ST
12 MYRTLE VIEW

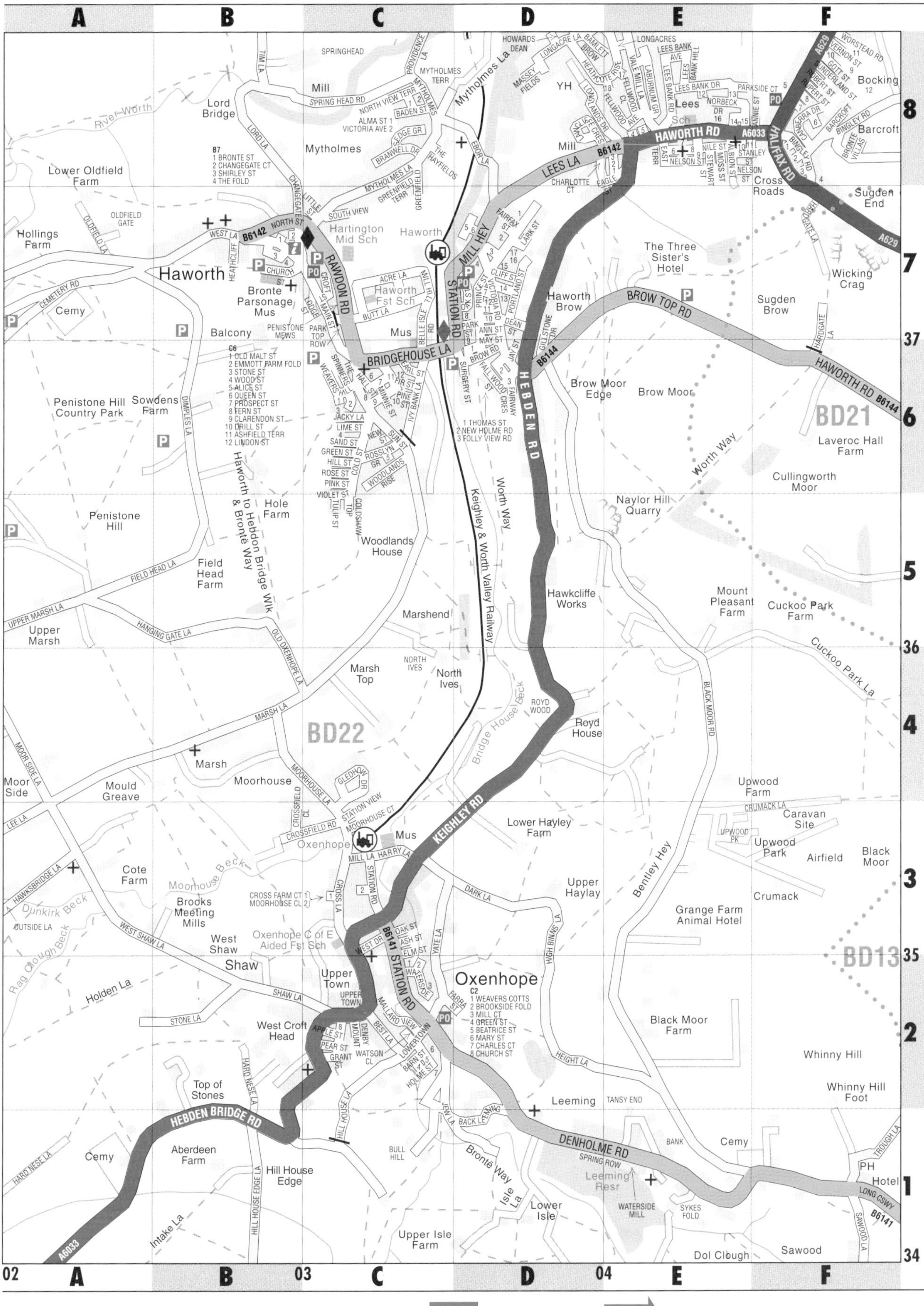

70

52

51
35

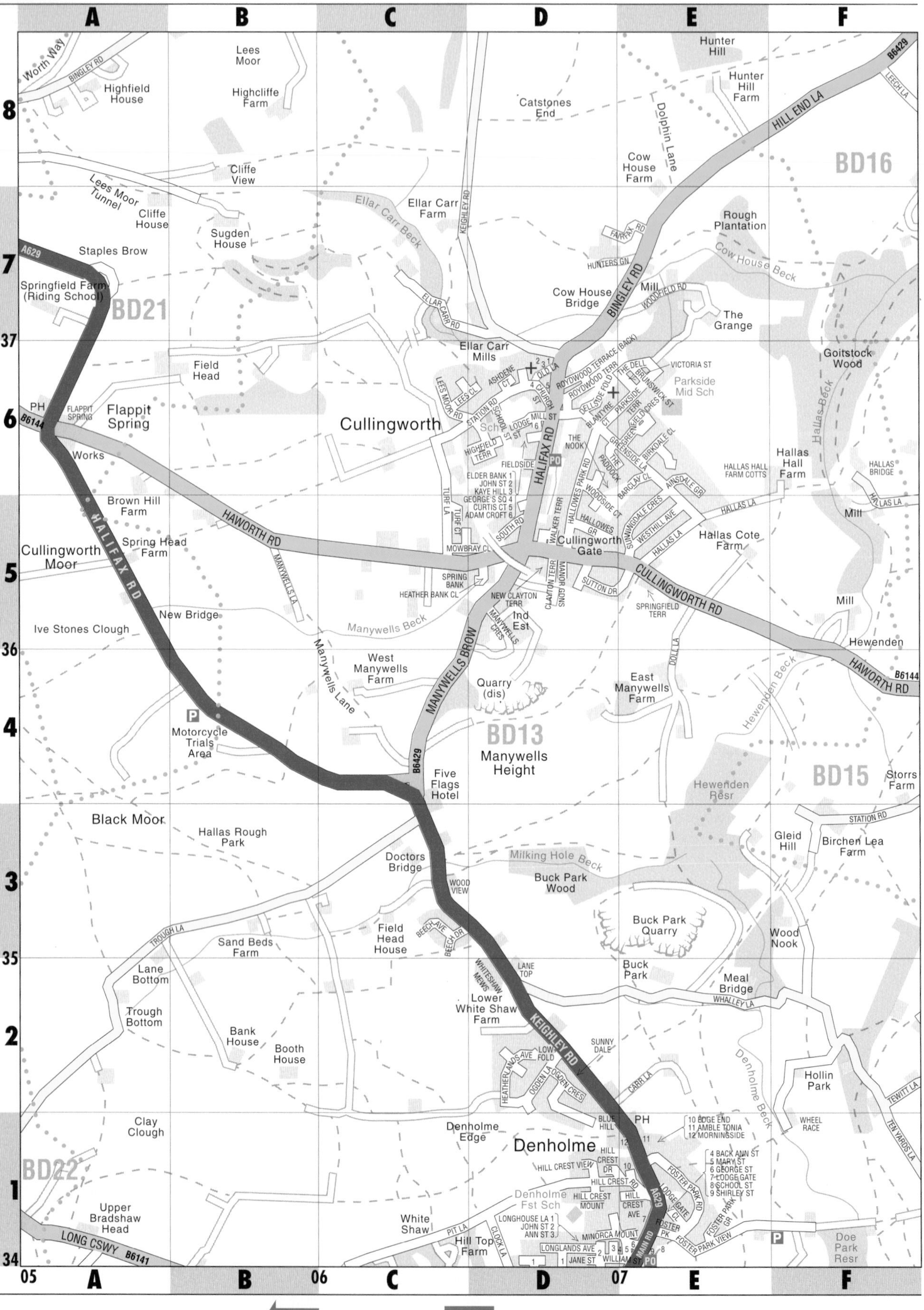
A
B
C
D
E
F
8
7
37
6
5
36
4
3
35
2
1
34
05
06
07
Worth Way
BINGLEY RD
Highfield House
Lees Moor
Highcliffe Farm
Catstones End
Hunter Hill
Hunter Hill Farm
B6429
LEECH LA
HILL END LA
Dolphin Lane
Cow House Farm
BD16
Cliffe View
Lees Moor Tunnel
Cliffe House
Sugden House
Ellar Carr Beck
Ellar Carr Farm
KEIGHLEY RD
FAIRFAX RD
Rough Plantation
Cow House Beck
A629
Staples Brow
Springfield Farm (Riding School)
BD21
HUNTERS GN
Cow House Bridge
BINGLEY RD
Mill
WOODFIELD RD
The Grange
ELLAR CARR RD
Ellar Carr Mills
Field Head
Goitstock Wood
ASHDENE CT
OLD LA
CHURCH ST
ROYDWOOD TERRACE (BACK)
ROYDWOOD TERR
THE DELL
VICTORIA ST
Parkside Mid Sch
LEES MOOR RD
LEES CL
STATION RD
SCHOOL ST
LODGE ST
MILL ST
DELLSIDE FOLD
BLANTYRE CT
PARKSIDE TERR
GREENFIELD CRES
BRUNSWICK ST
Hallas Beck
PH
FLAPPIT SPRING
Flappit Spring
B6144
Cullingworth
Sch
HIGHFIELD TERR
HALIFAX RD
THE NOOK
GREENSIDE LA
BIRKDALE CL
Works
FIELDSIDE
PO
THE PADDOCK
HALLAS HALL FARM COTTS
Hallas Hall Farm
HALLAS BRIDGE
Brown Hill Farm
ELDER BANK 1
JOHN ST 2
KAYE HILL 3
GEORGE'S SQ 4
CURTIS CT 5
ADAM CROFT 6
TURF LA
TURF CT
HALLOWES PARK RD
WOODSIDE CT
BARCLAY CL
AINSDALE GR
HALLAS LA
Mill
Spring Head Farm
HAWORTH RD
WALKER TERR
HALLOWES GR
SUNNINGDALE CRES
WESTHILL AVE
Cullingworth Moor
MANYWELLS LA
MOWBRAY CL
SOUTH RD
Cullingworth Gate
HALLAS LA
Hallas Cote Farm
HALIFAX RD
SPRING BANK
HEATHER BANK CL
CLAYTON TERR
MANOR GDNS
SUTTON DR
CULLINGWORTH RD
NEW CLAYTON TERR
SPRINGFIELD TERR
Mill
New Bridge
MANYWELLS CRES
Ind Est
Ive Stones Clough
Manywells Beck
Hewenden
HAWORTH RD
B6144
DOLL LA
Manywells Lane
West Manywells Farm
MANYWELLS BROW
Quarry (dis)
East Manywells Farm
Hewenden Beck
P
Motorcycle Trials Area
BD13
Manywells Height
B6429
Five Flags Hotel
Hewenden Resr
BD15
Storrs Farm
STATION RD
Black Moor
Hallas Rough Park
Gleid Hill
Birchen Lea Farm
Doctors Bridge
Milking Hole Beck
Buck Park Wood
WOOD VIEW
TROUGH LA
Sand Beds Farm
Field Head House
BEECH AVE
BEECH DR
Buck Park Quarry
Wood Nook
Lane Bottom
LANE TOP
WHITESHAW MEWS
Lower White Shaw Farm
Buck Park
Meal Bridge
WHALLEY LA
Trough Bottom
Bank House
Booth House
KEIGHLEY RD
SUNNY DALE
LOW FOLD
HEATHERLANDS AVE
OGDEN LA
OGDEN CRES
CARR LA
Denholme Beck
Hollin Park
TEWITT LA
WHEEL RACE
TEN YARDS LA
Clay Clough
Denholme Edge
BLUE HILL
PH
10 EDGE END
11 AMBLE TONIA
12 MORNINGSIDE
Denholme
HILL CREST DR
HILL CREST VIEW
HILL CREST RD
FOSTER PARK RD
LODGE GATE CL
4 BACK ANN ST
5 MARY ST
6 GEORGE ST
7 LODGE GATE
8 SCHOOL ST
9 SHIRLEY ST
BD22
Denholme Fst Sch
HILL CREST MOUNT
HILL CREST AVE
A629
FOSTER PARK GR
Upper Bradshaw Head
White Shaw
PIT LA
LONGHOUSE LA 1
JOHN ST 2
ANN ST 3
Hill Top Farm
CLOCK LA
MINORCA MOUNT
FOSTER PK
FOSTER PARK VIEW
P
Doe Park Resr
LONG CSWY
B6141
LONGLANDS AVE
JANE ST
WILLIAM ST
MAIN RD
PO

51
71

36
54

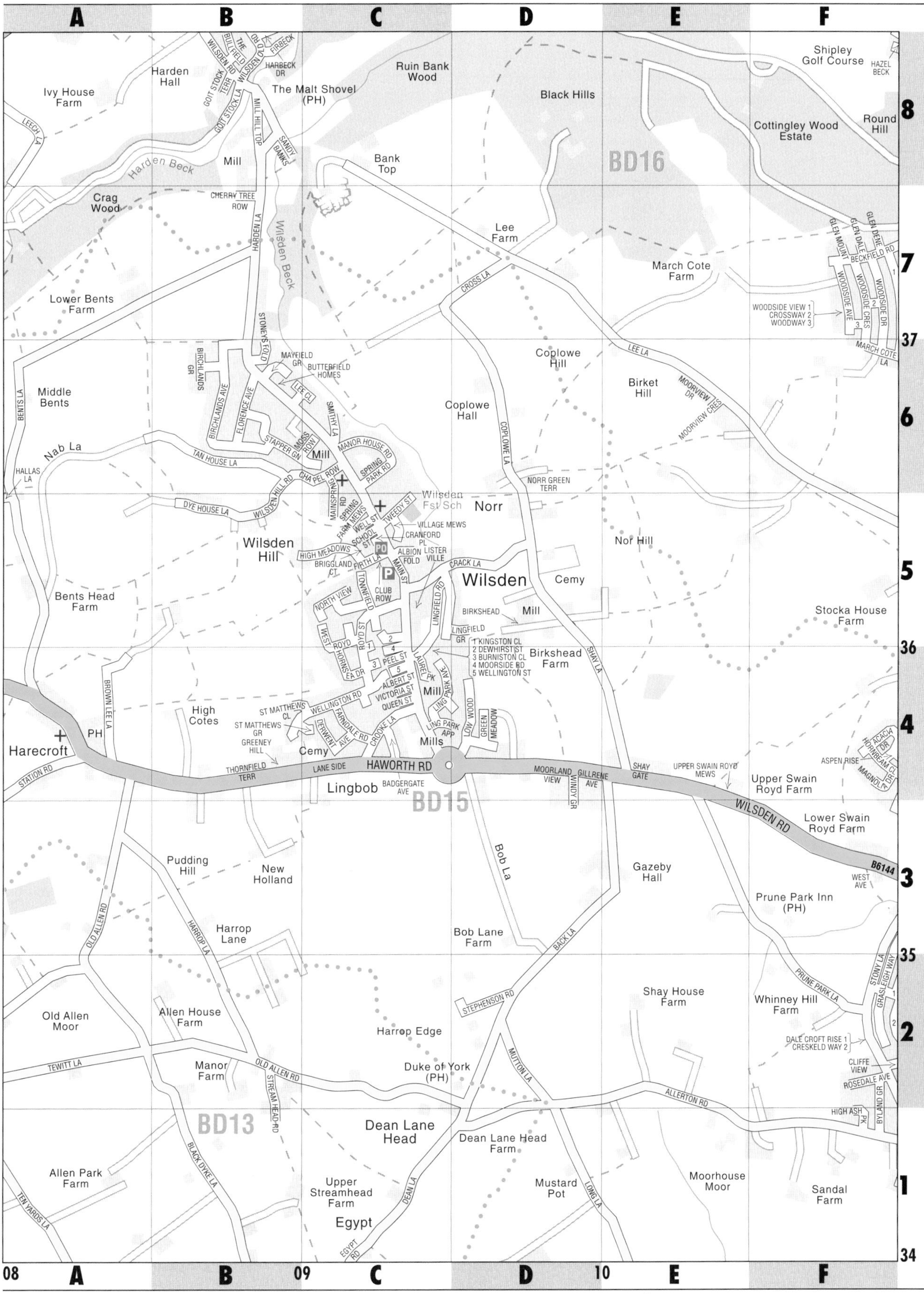
A
B
C
D
E
F
8
7
37
6
5
36
4
3
35
2
1
34
08
09
10
Ivy House Farm
Harden Hall
The Malt Shovel (PH)
Ruin Bank Wood
Black Hills
Shipley Golf Course
HAZEL BECK
Cottingley Wood Estate
Round Hill
LEECH LA
GOIT STOCK TERR
GOIT STOCK LA
WILSDEN RD
THE BULLFIELD
WILSDEN OLD RD
FIRBECK
HARBECK DR
MILL HILL TOP
SANDY BANKS
Harden Beck
Mill
Bank Top
BD16
Crag Wood
CHERRY TREE ROW
HARDEN LA
Wilsden Beck
Lee Farm
March Cote Farm
GLEN MOUNT
GLEN DALE
GLEN DENE
BECKFIELD RD
WOODSIDE AVE
WOODSIDE CRES
WOODSIDE DR
WOODSIDE VIEW 1
CROSSWAY 2
WOODWAY 3
MARCH COTE LA
Lower Bents Farm
CROSS LA
STONEYS FOLD
Coplowe Hill
LEE LA
Birket Hill
MOORVIEW DR
MOORVIEW CRES
Middle Bents
BENTS LA
BIRCHLANDS GR
BIRCHLANDS AVE
FLORENCE AVE
MAYFIELD GR
BUTTERFIELD HOMES
LEE CL
SMITHY LA
MOSS ROW
STAPPER GN
Mill
MANOR HOUSE RD
SPRING PARK RD
Coplowe Hall
COPLOWE LA
Nab La
TAN HOUSE LA
HALLAS LA
WILSDEN HILL RD
CHAPEL ROW
NORR GREEN TERR
DYE HOUSE LA
MAINSPRING RD
SPRING FARM MEWS
WELL ST
TWEEDY ST
Wilsden Fst Sch
Norr
VILLAGE MEWS
CRANFORD PL
SCHOOL ST
Wilsden Hill
HIGH MEADOWS
BRIGGLAND CT
FIRTH LA
PO
ALBION FOLD
LISTER VILLE
Nor Hill
CRACK LA
P
MAIN ST
Wilsden
Cemy
Bents Head Farm
TOWNFIELD
CLUB ROW
NORTH VIEW
LINGFIELD RD
BIRKSHEAD
Mill
Stocka House Farm
WEST
ROYD
ROYD ST
HORNS EA DR
LINGFIELD GR
1 KINGSTON CL
2 DEWHIRST ST
3 BURNISTON CL
4 MOORSIDE RD
5 WELLINGTON ST
Birkshead Farm
SHAY LA
PEEL ST
LAUREL PK
ALBERT ST
VICTORIA ST
QUEEN ST
PARK AVE
LING PARK AVE
Mill
LOW WOOD
GREEN MEADOW
BROWN LEE LA
High Cotes
ST MATTHEWS CL
WELLINGTON RD
ST MATTHEWS GR
GREENEY HILL
DERWENT AVE
FARNDALE RD
CROOKE LA
LING PARK APP
Mills
Harecroft
PH
Cemy
THORNFIELD TERR
LANE SIDE
HAWORTH RD
MOORLAND VIEW
GILLRENE AVE
WINDY GR
SHAY GATE
UPPER SWAIN ROYD MEWS
ASPEN RISE
ACACIA DR
HORNBEAM CL
MAGNOLIA
Upper Swain Royd Farm
STATION RD
Lingbob
BADGERGATE AVE
BD15
WILSDEN RD
Lower Swain Royd Farm
Pudding Hill
New Holland
Bob La
Gazeby Hall
B6144
WEST AVE
OLD ALLEN RD
HARROP LA
Harrop Lane
Bob Lane Farm
BACK LA
Prune Park Inn (PH)
STONY LA
GRASLEIGH WAY
PRUNE PARK LA
Old Allen Moor
Allen House Farm
STEPHENSON RD
Shay House Farm
Whinney Hill Farm
Harrop Edge
DALE CROFT RISE 1
CRESKELD WAY 2
TEWITT LA
Manor Farm
OLD ALLEN RD
Duke of York (PH)
MUTTON LA
CLIFFE VIEW
ROSEDALE AVE
ALLERTON RD
STREAM HEAD RD
HIGH ASH PK
BYLAND GR
BD13
Dean Lane Head
Dean Lane Head Farm
BLACK DYKE LA
Allen Park Farm
Upper Streamhead Farm
DEAN LA
Mustard Pot
LONG LA
Moorhouse Moor
Sandal Farm
TEN YARDS LA
Egypt
EGYPT RD

72
54

53
37

E8
1 HIRST WOOD CRES
2 WOODSIDE AVE
3 DALLAM GR
4 ALBERT WLK
5 PETERSGARTH

F8
1 AMELIA ST
2 WILLIAM HENRY ST
3 LOWER SCHOOL ST
4 HIGHER SCHOOL ST
5 LOCKWOOD ST
6 MAWSON ST
7 EXHIBITION RD
8 UPPER ADA ST
9 UPPER MARY ST
10 KATHERINE ST
11 MYRTLE PL
12 DAISY PL
13 HAROLD PL
14 ALEXANDRA SQ
15 FERNCLIFFE RD
16 RICHMOND PL
17 RICHMOND RD
18 VICTORIA CT

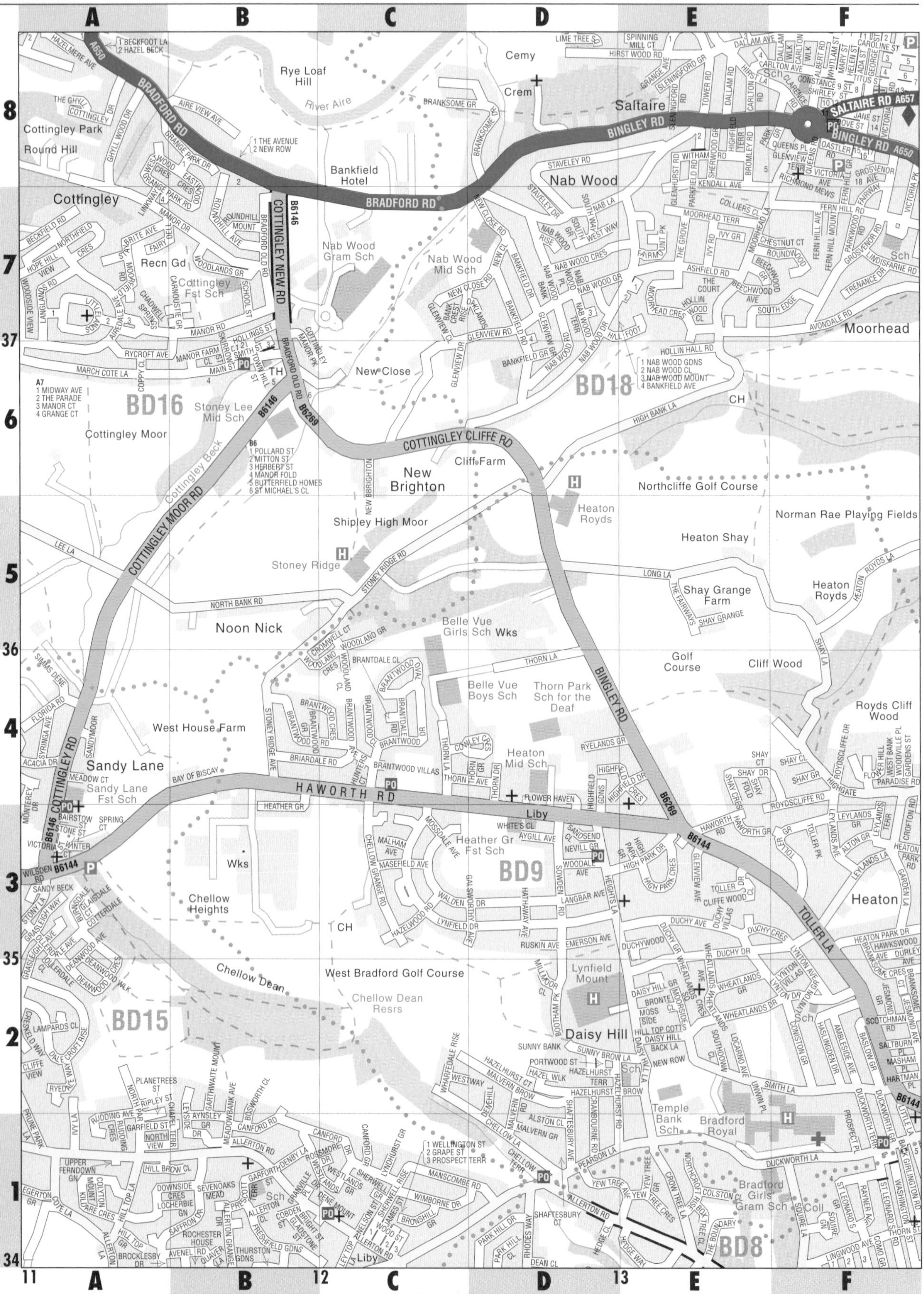

53
73

F1
1 COMO DR
2 COMO GDNS
3 COMO AVE
4 ST LEONARD'S CT
5 GIRLINGTON RD

38
56

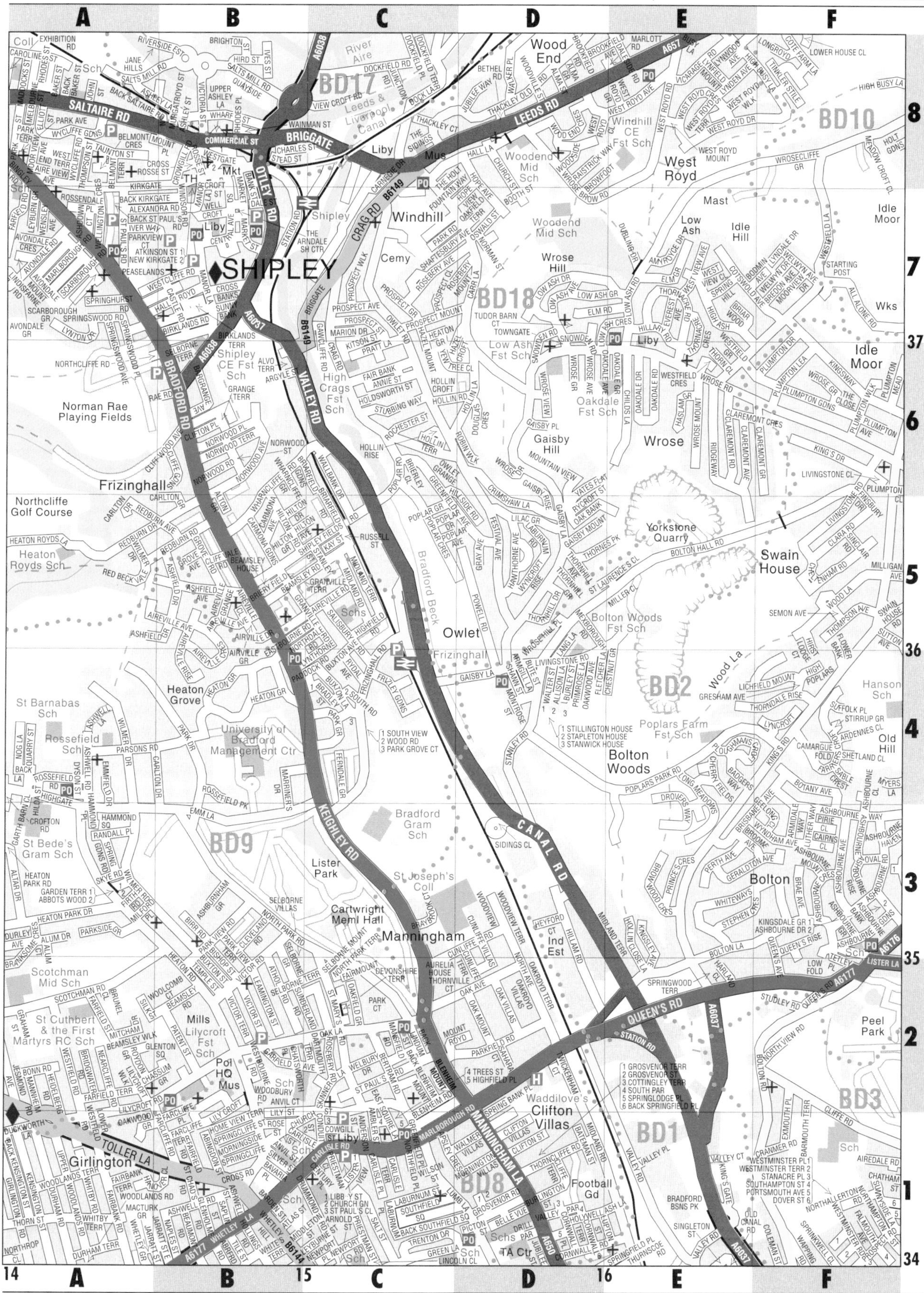
A
B
C
D
E
F
8
7
37
6
5
36
4
3
35
2
1
34
14
15
16
SHIPLEY
BD17
BD10
BD18
BD2
BD9
BD8
BD1
BD3
Wood End
Windhill
West Royd
Idle Moor
Idle Hill
Low Ash
Wrose Hill
Wrose
Gaisby Hill
Frizinghall
Northcliffe Golf Course
Heaton Royds Sch
Norman Rae Playing Fields
Yorkstone Quarry
Swain House
Owlet
Bradford Beck
Bolton Woods
Heaton Grove
University of Bradford Management Ctr
Rossefield Sch
St Barnabas Sch
Bradford Gram Sch
Lister Park
St Joseph's Coll
Cartwright Meml Hall
Manningham
Bolton
Old Hill
Peel Park
Scotchman Mid Sch
Mills
Lilycroft Fst Sch
Pol HQ Mus
Girlington
Clifton Villas
Football Gd
Bradford Bsns Pk
River Aire
Leeds & Liverpool Canal
SALTAIRE RD
LEEDS RD
BRIGGATE
OTLEY RD
BRADFORD RD
VALLEY RD
KEIGHLEY RD
CANAL RD
QUEEN'S RD
MANNINGHAM LA
TOLLER LA
WHETLEY LA
A6038
A657
A6037
B6149
A650
A6177
A6176
B6144

74
56

55
39

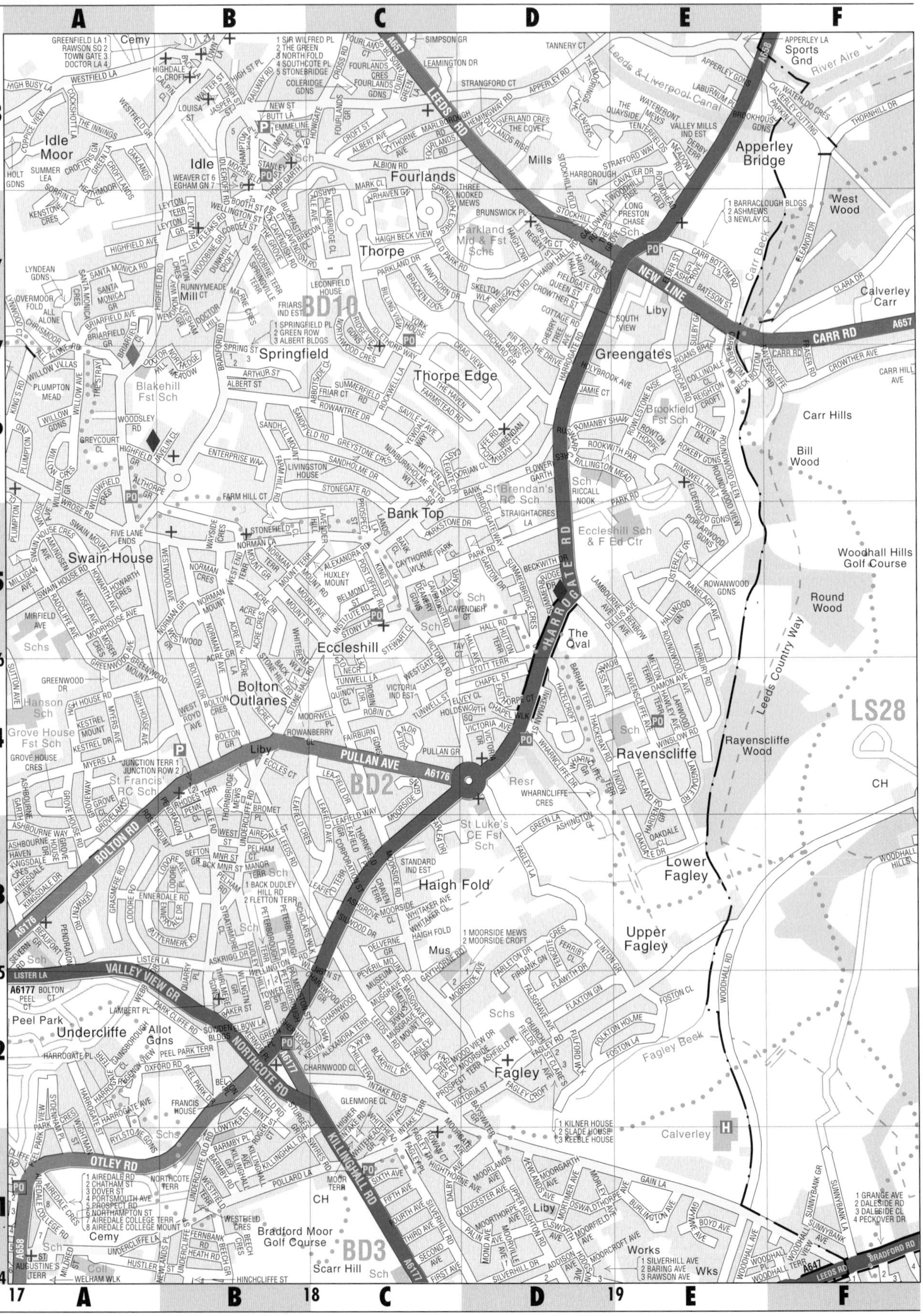
A
B
C
D
E
F
8
7
37
6
5
36
4
3
35
2
1
34
17
18
19
Idle Moor
Idle
Fourlands
Thorpe
Mills
Apperley Bridge
Sports Gnd
River Aire
Leeds & Liverpool Canal
West Wood
Calverley Carr
BD10
Springfield
Thorpe Edge
Greengates
Blakehill Fst Sch
Parkland Mid & Fst Schs
Carr Hills
Bill Wood
Brookfield Fst Sch
Bank Top
St Brendan's RC Sch
Eccleshill Sch & F Ed Ctr
Woodhall Hills Golf Course
Round Wood
Swain House
Eccleshill
The Oval
Leeds Country Way
LS28
Bolton Outlanes
Hanson Sch
Grove House Fst Sch
Ravenscliffe
Ravenscliffe Wood
St Francis' RC Sch
BD2
St Luke's CE Fst Sch
Haigh Fold
Lower Fagley
Upper Fagley
Peel Park
Undercliffe
Allot Gdns
Fagley
Fagley Beck
Calverley
Bradford Moor Golf Course
Scarr Hill
BD3
LEEDS RD
A657
A658
NEW LINE
CARR RD
HARROGATE RD
PULLAN AVE
A6176
BOLTON RD
VALLEY VIEW GR
NORTHCOTE RD
A6177
KILLINGHALL RD
OTLEY RD
LISTER LA
BRADFORD RD
A647

55
75

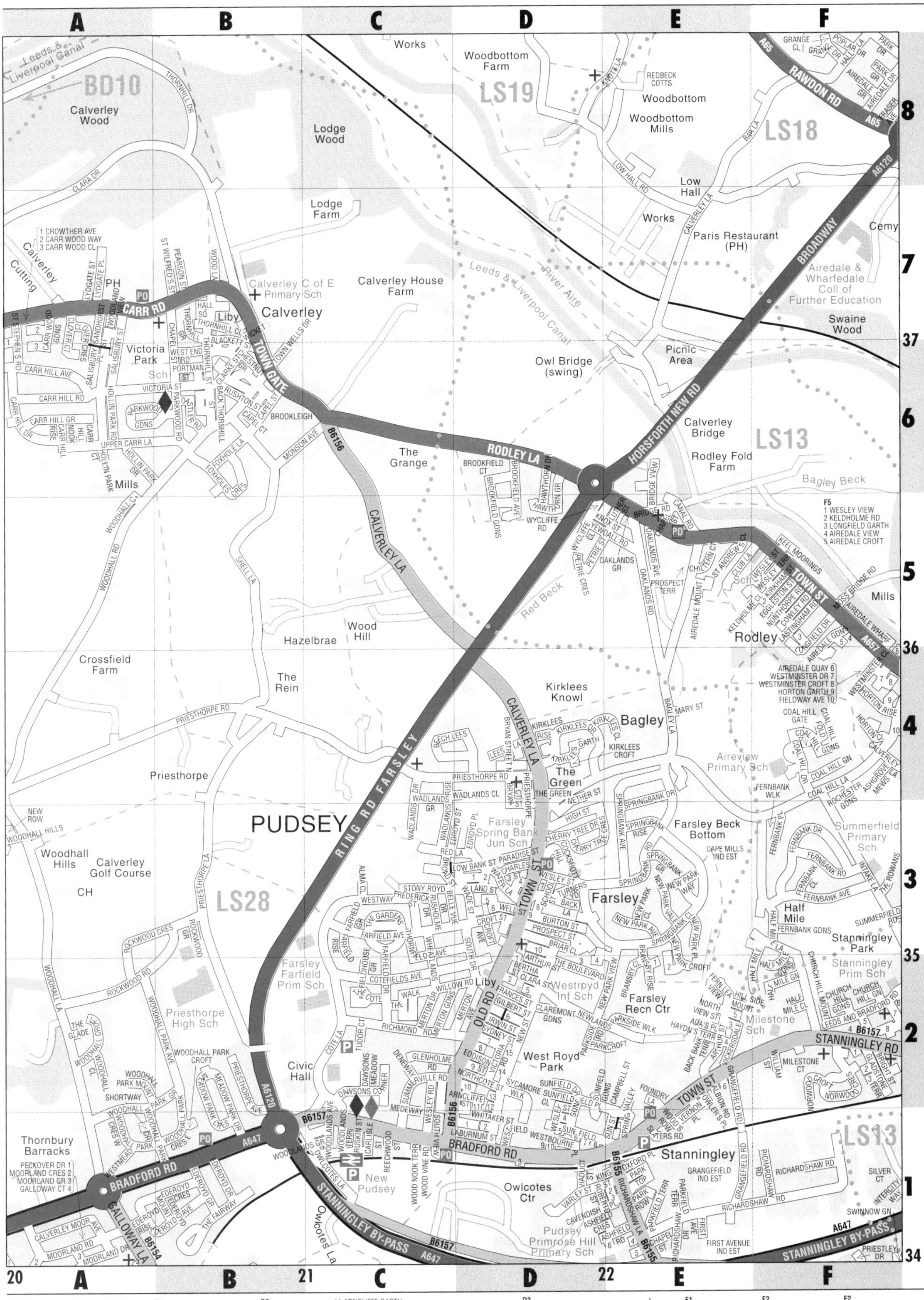

D1
1 HARKER TERR
2 HUDSON ST
3 STANHALL AVE
4 SPRINGFIELD TERR
5 CONWAY ST
6 WILSONS YD
7 DAWSON ST
8 WILLIAM ST
9 WEST TERRACE ST
10 WEST GROVE ST

D2
1 BECKBURY CL
2 BECKBURY ST
3 PROSPECT TERR
4 NEW PARK WLK
5 DONALD ST
6 PROVIDENCE ST
7 MELBOURNE ST
8 TENNYSON ST
9 ARMSTRONG ST
10 ANDREW ST
11 ARNCLIFFE GARTH
12 PROSPECT SQ
13 POPLAR SQ
14 ASHVILLE TERR
15 WEST VIEW

D3
1 GLADSTONE ST
2 OAKWELL TERR
3 MARSDEN CT
4 ANDREW ST
5 TURNER ST
6 EBENEZER ST
7 HAINSWORTH SQ
8 GAMBLES HILL
9 OLD FOLD
10 ST JOHN'S AVE

E1
1 TEMPERANCE ST
2 BOOCOCK ST
3 CAVENDISH SQ
4 PROVIDENCE PL
5 PRIMROSE HILL
6 ASHFIELD GR

E2
1 BRANSBY CT
2 TURBARY AVE
3 FERN TERR
4 GROVE ST
5 NORTH VIEW TERR
6 KEIGHLEY PL

F2
1 VICTORIA TERR
2 GRANVILLE ST
3 ROSEBERY TERR
4 STANNINGLEY CT
5 HARRISONS AVE
6 BROAD LA
7 BRITANNIA ST
8 BRITANNIA CL

B7
1 FEATHERBANK WLK
2 BACK FEATHERBANK TERR
3 FEATHERBANK TERR
4 SUNNYBANK AVE
5 BACK SUNNYBANK AVE
6 SUNNYBANK RD
7 BACK CLARENCE RD
8 WATERHOUSE CT
9 NEWLAY WOOD FOLD

57

B8
1 FEAST FIELD
2 STONEYTHORPE
3 STONEYCROFT
4 BROADWAY DR
5 FEATHERBANK GR
6 FEATHERBANK MOUNT

41

C7
1 WARWICK CT
2 NEWLAY BRIDLE PATH
3 NEWLAY WOOD GDNS
4 THROSTLE NEST VIEW
5 BACK OUTWOOD LA
6 BACK CRAGGWOOD RD
7 CRAGGWELL TERR
8 CRAGGWOOD TERR
9 WOODBINE TERR
10 REGENT CT

F8
1 RING RD WEST PK
2 CLAYTON GRANGE
3 LATCHMERE CROSS
4 LATCHMERE CREST
5 LATCHMERE GN
6 OLD FARM WLK
7 LINTON CROFT
8 MOOR GRANGE CT

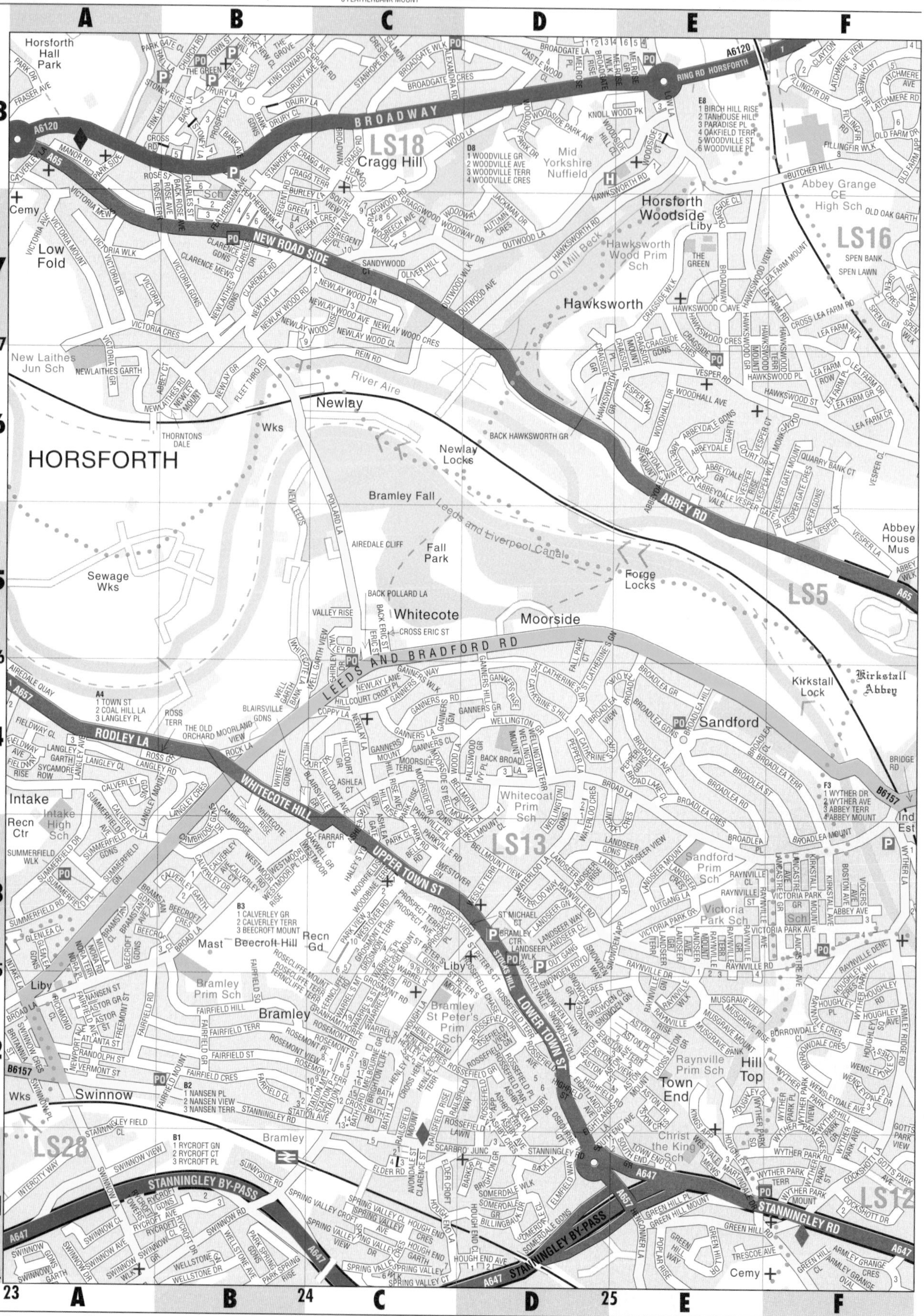

C1
1 ELDER MOUNT
2 ELDER PL
3 ELDER ST
4 CLEOPATRA PL
5 BRAMLEY ST
6 WEST CT
7 BRAMLEY GRANGE

C2
1 HENLEY AVE
2 HENLEY GR
3 HENLEY ST
4 WARREL'S ROW
5 BK ROSEMONT WLK
6 ROSEMONT WLK
7 ROSEMONT AVE
8 ROSEMONT GR
9 NANSEN AVE
10 NANSEN GR
11 NANSEN MOUNT
12 STATION GR
13 ASHDOWN ST
14 BATH GR
15 BACK BATH RD
16 HOUGH GR
17 HOUGH TERR
18 BACK MELBOURNE GR
19 WARREL'S TERR

57

C3
1 WESTOVER TERR
2 WESTOVER ST
3 WESTOVER GR
4 WARREL'S AVE
5 WESTOVER VIEW
6 WESTOVER AVE
7 HAYLEIGH TERR
8 HAYLEIGH ST
9 HAYLEIGH AVE
10 WESTOVER MOUNT

77

D1
1 HOUGH END CT
2 HOUGH END GDNS
3 DAISY ROW

D2
1 NEW SCARBRO' RD
2 DAISYFIELD RD
3 ROSSEFIELD CL
4 ASHBY MOUNT
5 ROSSEFIELD WLK
6 McLAREN FIELDS

D4
1 WESTMORELAND MOUNT
2 BACK WESTMORELAND MT
3 WELLINGTON GARTH
4 BELLMOUNT GN

E1
1 SOUTH END TERR
2 SOUTH END MOUNT
3 EASTLAND WLK

E2
1 BACK ASTON PL
2 BACK ASTON TERR
3 BACK ASTON VIEW
4 BACK HIGHFIELD RD

E3
1 RAYNVILLE APP
2 RAYNVILLE CT
3 RAYNVILLE GRANGE
4 RAYNVILLE PL

F1
1 WYTHER PARK CL
2 COCKSHOTT CL
3 ARMLEY GRANGE DR

F2
1 WENSLEYDALE MEWS
2 WENSLEYDALE CL
3 WENSLEYDALE RISE

A5
1 KEPSTORN RISE
2 WOODBRIDGE FOLD
3 LINTON CROFT
4 LATCHMERE WLK

A8
1 LATCHMERE AVE
2 OLD FARM GARTH

C5
1 BACK ROKEBY GDNS
2 WINSTON GDNS
3 BACK WINSTON GDNS
4 GRIMTHORPE AVE

D5
1 CHAPEL SQ
2 ASH TERR
3 ASH VIEW
4 CROSS CHAPEL ST
5 ARNDALE CTR
6 GRUNBERG ST
7 GRANBY MOUNT
8 CROSS GRANBY TERR
9 CHAPEL TERR
10 CHAPEL PL
11 TRELAWN CRES
12 ALMA COTTS

42

D6
1 HEATHFIELD SQ
2 BACK BURTON CRES
3 SOWDEN'S YD
4 ODDY PL
5 BACK HEATHFIELD TERR

60

E5
1 ASHFIELD PK
2 CONISTON AVE
3 BACK WOODLAND PARK RD

E6
1 MONK BRIDGE PL
2 MONK BRIDGE GR
3 BACK WILTON GR
4 HEDDON ST

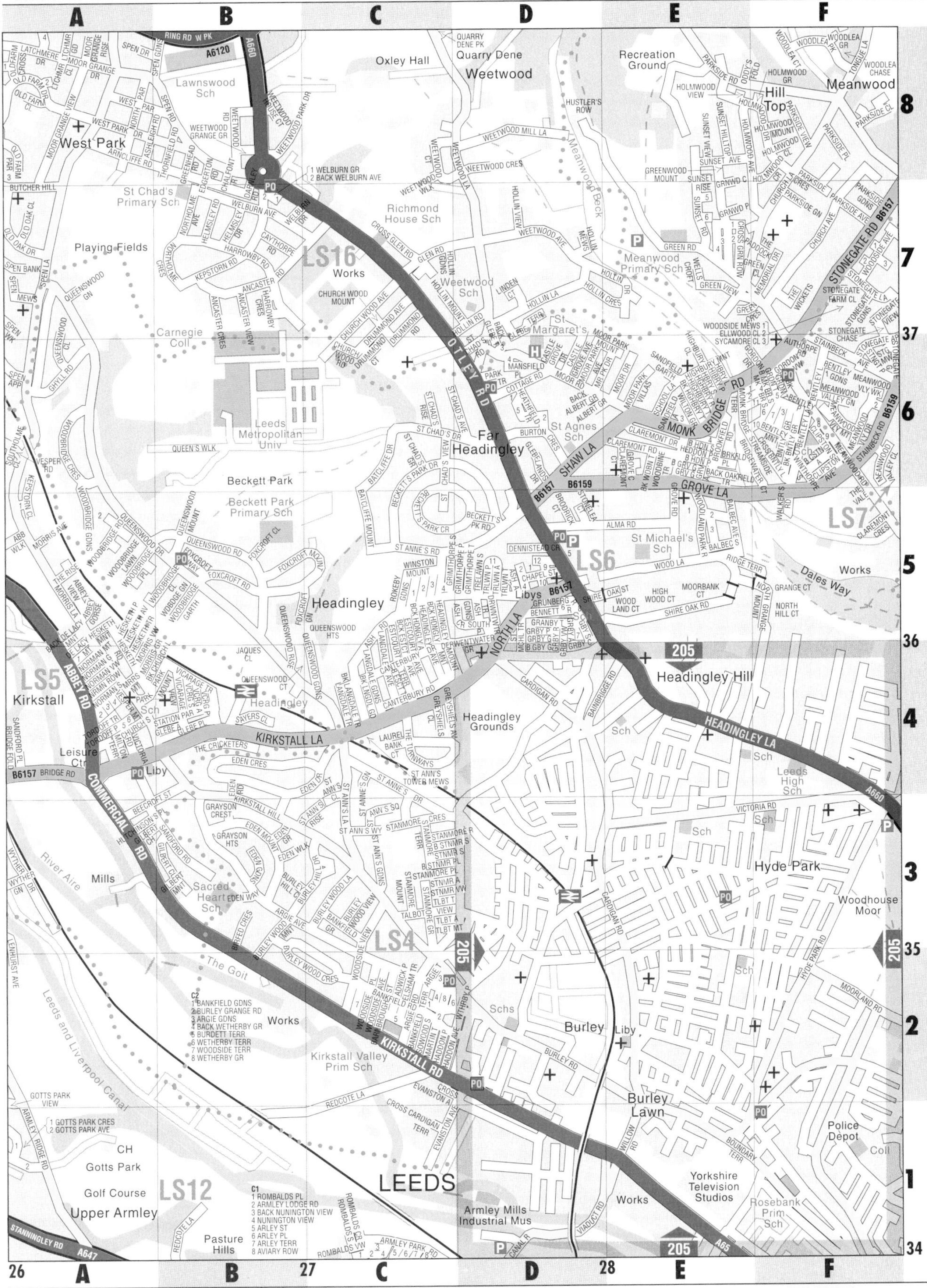

For full street detail of the highlighted area see page 205.

78

60

E7
1 CROSS GREENWOOD MOUNT
2 GREEN CHASE
3 GREEN ROW
4 BACK GREENWOOD MOUNT
5 SUNSET MOUNT
6 SUNSET DR

F6
1 BENTLEY CT
2 MEANWOOD VALLEY GR
3 BACK BENTLEY AVE
4 KING'S SQ
5 GORDON PL
6 MONK BRIDGE DR
7 BK MONK BRIDGE DR
8 CLIPSTON MOUNT
9 CLIPSTON TERR
10 MONK BRIDGE MOUNT
11 MONK BRIDGE AVE

59
43

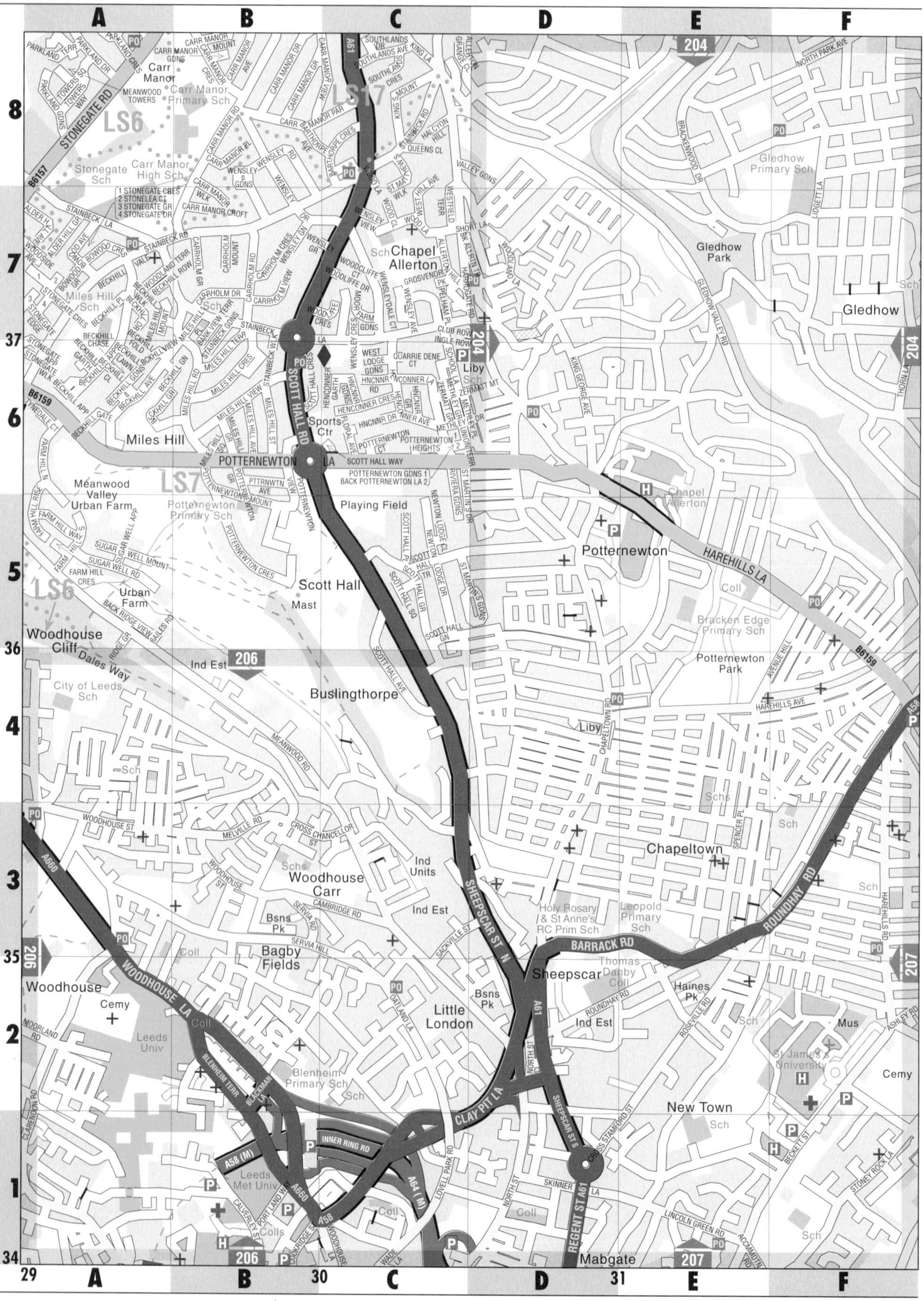

59
79

For full street detail of the highlighted area see pages 204, 206 and 207.

44
62

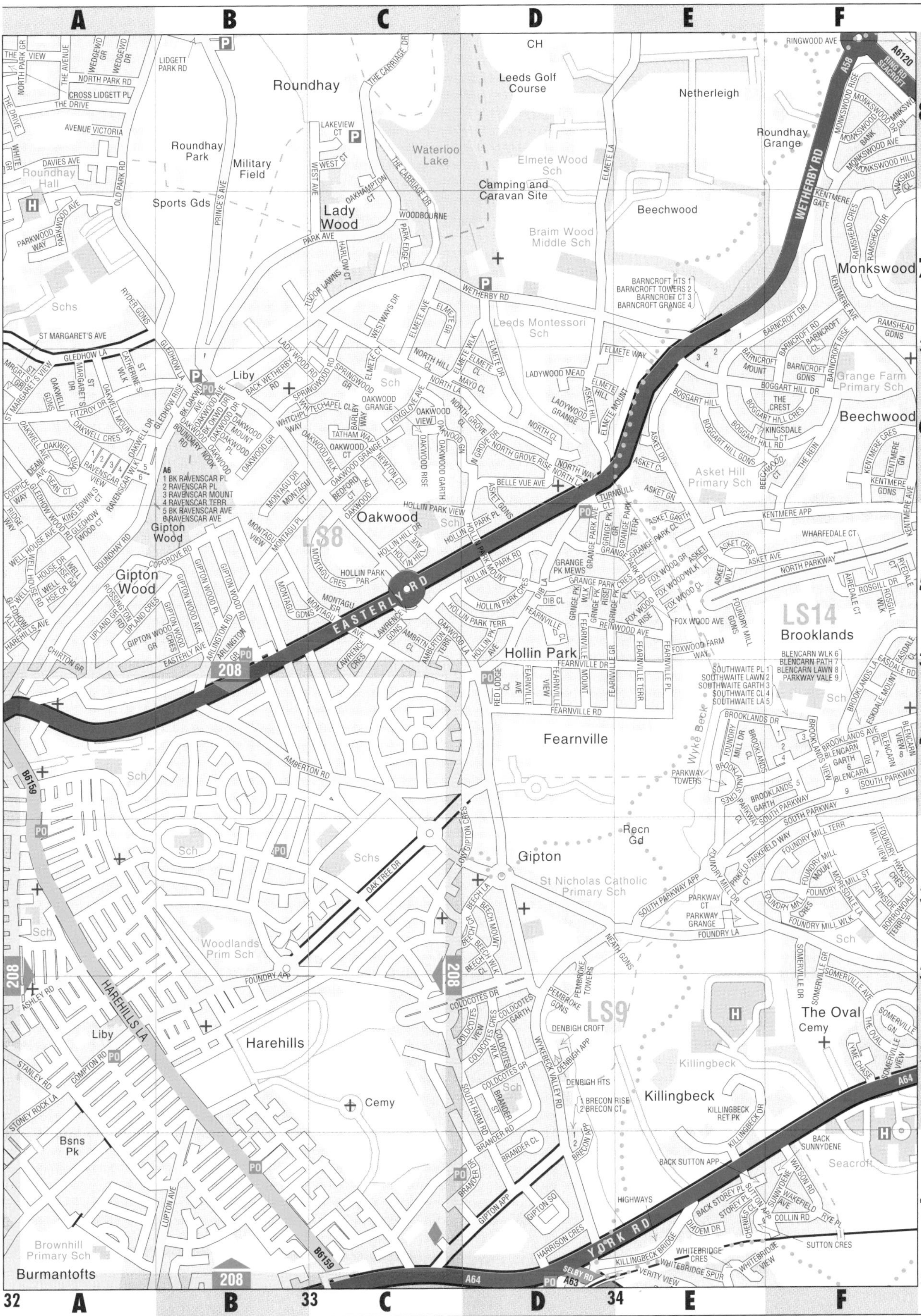

For full street detail of the highlighted area see page 208.

80
62

A5
1 RAMSHEAD HEIGHTS
2 BAILEY TOWERS
3 BROOKLAND TOWERS

B5
1 FOUNTAIN WLK
2 QUEENS PAR
3 MARKET SQ
4 QUEENS CT
5 SEACROFT ARC

61

B5
6 SEACROFT CHASE
7 EASTDEAN GATE
8 EASTDEAN GRANGE
9 SEACROFT GATE
10 HANSBY GRANGE

45

C5
1 BRAYTON TERR
2 BRAYTON WLK
3 FARNDALE CT
4 FARNDALE TERR
5 FARNDALE SQ
6 MILL GREEN GARTH

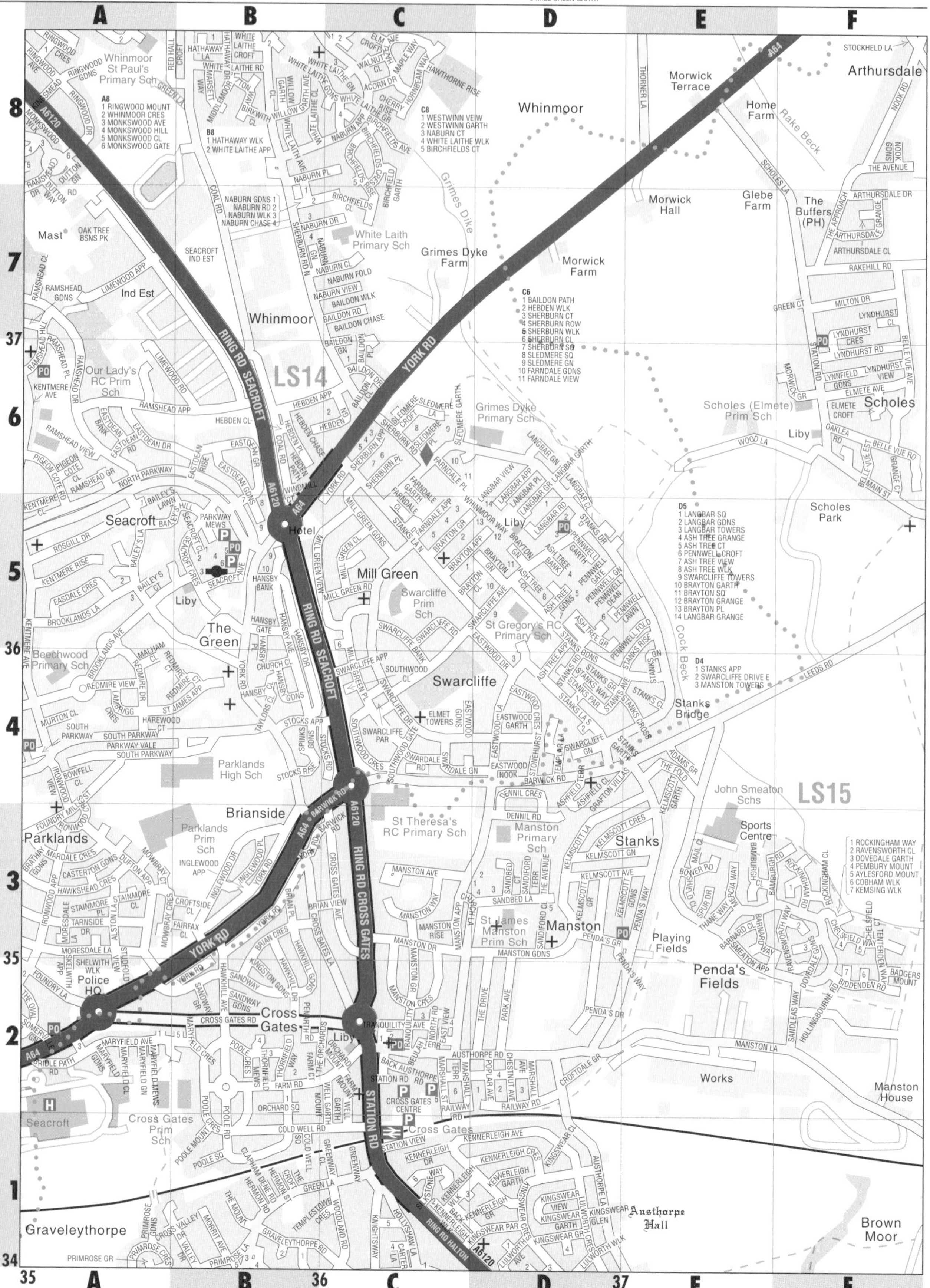

A2
1 MARYFIELD VALE
2 SOMERVILLE MOUNT
3 BRIDLE PATH WLK

B1
1 TEMPLESTOWE HILL
2 GRAVELEYTHORPE RISE
3 CROSS GREEN LA
4 WOODLAND HILL
5 GREEN LA

B2
1 ORCHARD RD
2 ORCHARD CROFT
3 THORNFIELD DR
4 THORNFIELD CT
5 MARYFIELD CT

61

C1
1 HOLLYSHAW CRES
2 KENNERLEIGH GLEN
3 KENNERLEIGH RISE
4 CARTER TERR
5 HOLLYSHAW WLK
6 SILKSTONE CT

81

C2
1 TRANQUILITY WLK
2 TRANQUILITY CT
3 NORTH TERR
4 SOUTH VIEW
5 BACK MARSHALL ST
6 BACK MARSHALL TERR

D1
1 LULWORTH CL
2 LULWORTH VIEW
3 LULWORTH DR
4 KINGSWEAR RISE

D2
1 BACK POPLAR AVE
2 BACK CHESTNUT AVE
3 BACK MARSHALL AVE
4 BACK AUSTHORPE RD

D3
1 OAK TERR
2 THE BUNGALOWS
3 SANDBED LAWNS
4 ROSEVILLE TERR
5 MANSTON TERR

46
64

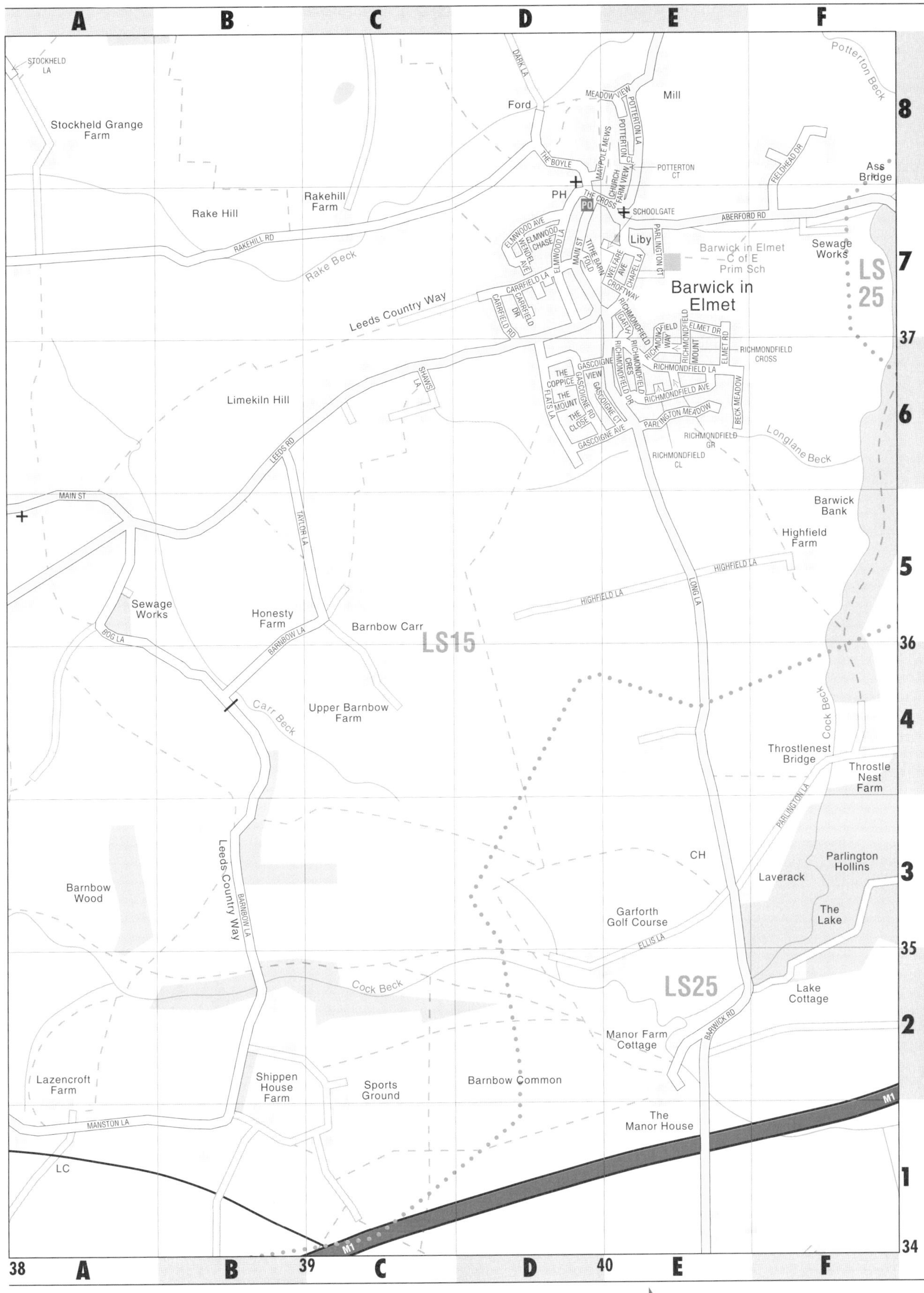
A
B
C
D
E
F
STOCKHELD LA
Stockheld Grange Farm
DARK LA
Ford
MEADOW VIEW
POTTERTON LA
Mill
Potterton Beck
MAYPOLE MEWS
POTTERTON CL
POTTERTON CT
CHURCH FARM VIEW
THE BOYLE
FIELDHEAD DR
Ass Bridge
PH
THE CROSS
PO
SCHOOLGATE
ABERFORD RD
Rake Hill
Rakehill Farm
RAKEHILL RD
Rake Beck
ELMWOOD AVE
ELMWOOD CHASE
WENDEL AVE
ELMWOOD LA
MAIN ST
TITHE BARN FOLD
WELFARE AVE
CHAPEL LA
CROFTWAY
PARLINGTON CT
Liby
Barwick in Elmet C of E Prim Sch
Sewage Works
LS 25
Barwick in Elmet
Leeds Country Way
CARRFIELD LA
CARRFIELD DR
CARRFIELD RD
RICHMONDFIELD GARTH
RICHMONDFIELD WAY
RICHMONDFIELD MOUNT
ELMET DR
ELMET RD
RICHMONDFIELD CROSS
THE COPPICE
GASCOIGNE VIEW
THE MOUNT
THE CLOSE
FLATS LA
GASCOIGNE RD
GASCOIGNE CT
GASCOIGNE AVE
RICHMONDFIELD CRES
RICHMONDFIELD DR
RICHMONDFIELD LA
RICHMONDFIELD AVE
BECK MEADOW
PARLINGTON MEADOW
RICHMONDFIELD GR
RICHMONDFIELD CL
Longlane Beck
SHAWS LA
Limekiln Hill
LEEDS RD
MAIN ST
Barwick Bank
TAYLOR LA
Highfield Farm
HIGHFIELD LA
LONG LA
Sewage Works
Honesty Farm
Barnbow Carr
LS15
BOG LA
BARNBOW LA
Carr Beck
Upper Barnbow Farm
Cock Beck
Throstlenest Bridge
Throstle Nest Farm
PARLINGTON LA
CH
Parlington Hollins
Laverack
Barnbow Wood
Leeds Country Way
BARNBOW LA
Garforth Golf Course
The Lake
ELLIS LA
LS25
Cock Beck
Lake Cottage
Manor Farm Cottage
BARWICK RD
Lazencroft Farm
Shippen House Farm
Sports Ground
Barnbow Common
MANSTON LA
The Manor House
M1
LC
M1
8
7
37
6
5
36
4
3
35
2
1
34
38
39
40

82
64

63
47

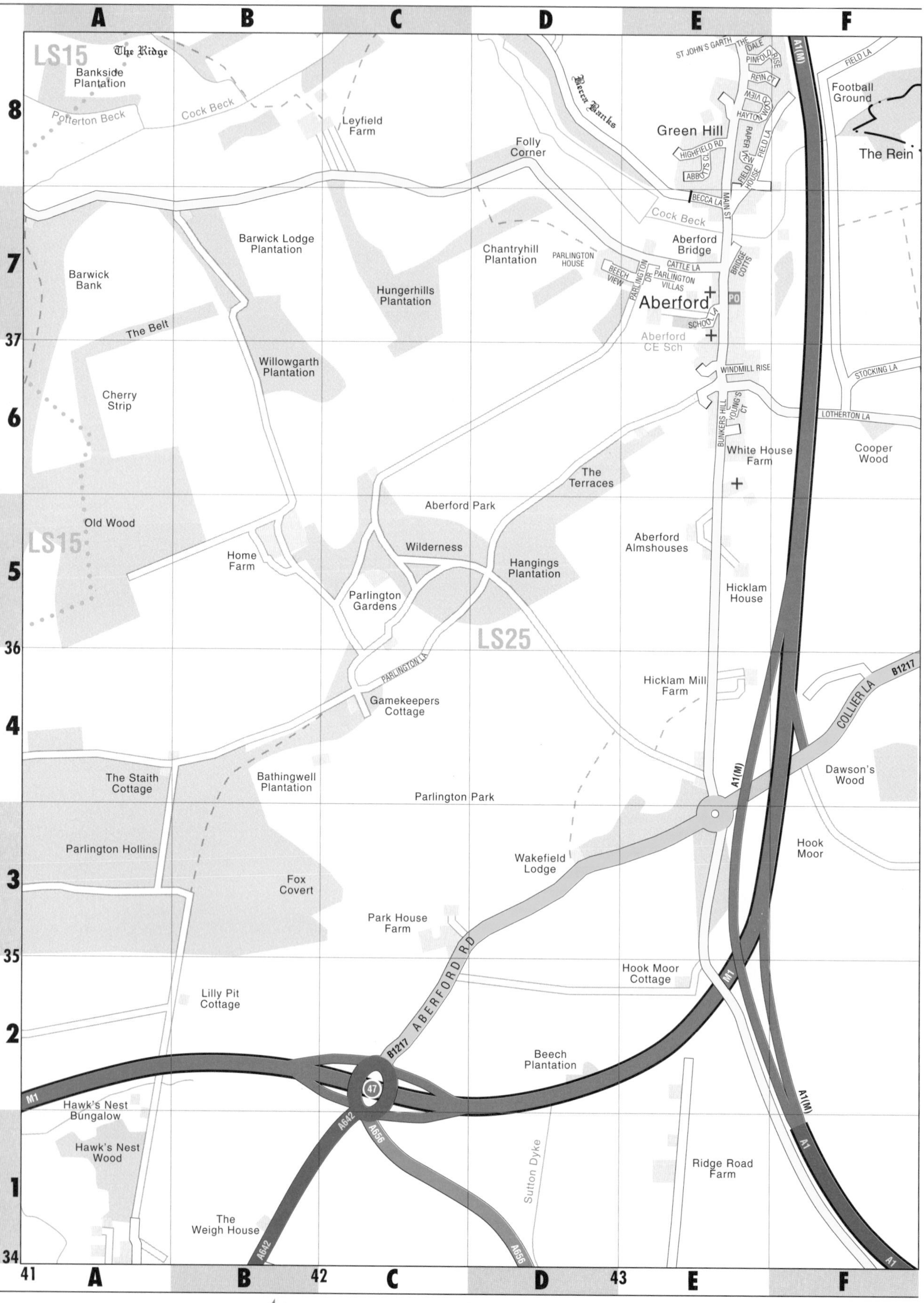
A
B
C
D
E
F
8
7
37
6
5
36
4
3
35
2
1
34
41
42
43
LS15
The Ridge
Bankside Plantation
Potterton Beck
Cock Beck
Leyfield Farm
Folly Corner
Hetcr Banks
ST JOHN'S GARTH
THE DALE
PINFOLD RISE
REIN CT
VIEW
HAYTON WOOD
Green Hill
HIGHFIELD RD
ABBOTTS CL
RAPER VIEW
FIELD LA
FIELD HOUSE
BECCA LA
MAIN ST
A1(M)
FIELD LA
Football Ground
The Rein
Cock Beck
Aberford Bridge
Barwick Lodge Plantation
Chantryhill Plantation
PARLINGTON HOUSE
BEECH VIEW
PARLINGTON DR
CATTLE LA
PARLINGTON VILLAS
BRIDGE COTTS
PO
Aberford
SCHOOL LA
Aberford CE Sch
Barwick Bank
Hungerhills Plantation
The Belt
Willowgarth Plantation
WINDMILL RISE
STOCKING LA
Cherry Strip
BUNKERS HILL
YOUNG'S CT
LOTHERTON LA
White House Farm
Cooper Wood
The Terraces
Aberford Park
Old Wood
LS15
Aberford Almshouses
Wilderness
Home Farm
Hangings Plantation
Parlington Gardens
Hicklam House
LS25
PARLINGTON LA
Hicklam Mill Farm
B1217
COLLIER LA
Gamekeepers Cottage
A1(M)
Dawson's Wood
The Staith Cottage
Bathingwell Plantation
Parlington Park
Parlington Hollins
Hook Moor
Wakefield Lodge
Fox Covert
Park House Farm
ABERFORD RD
Hook Moor Cottage
M1
Lilly Pit Cottage
B1217
Beech Plantation
M1
47
Hawk's Nest Bungalow
A642
A656
A1(M)
A1
Hawk's Nest Wood
Sutton Dyke
Ridge Road Farm
The Weigh House
A642
A656
A1

63
83

48

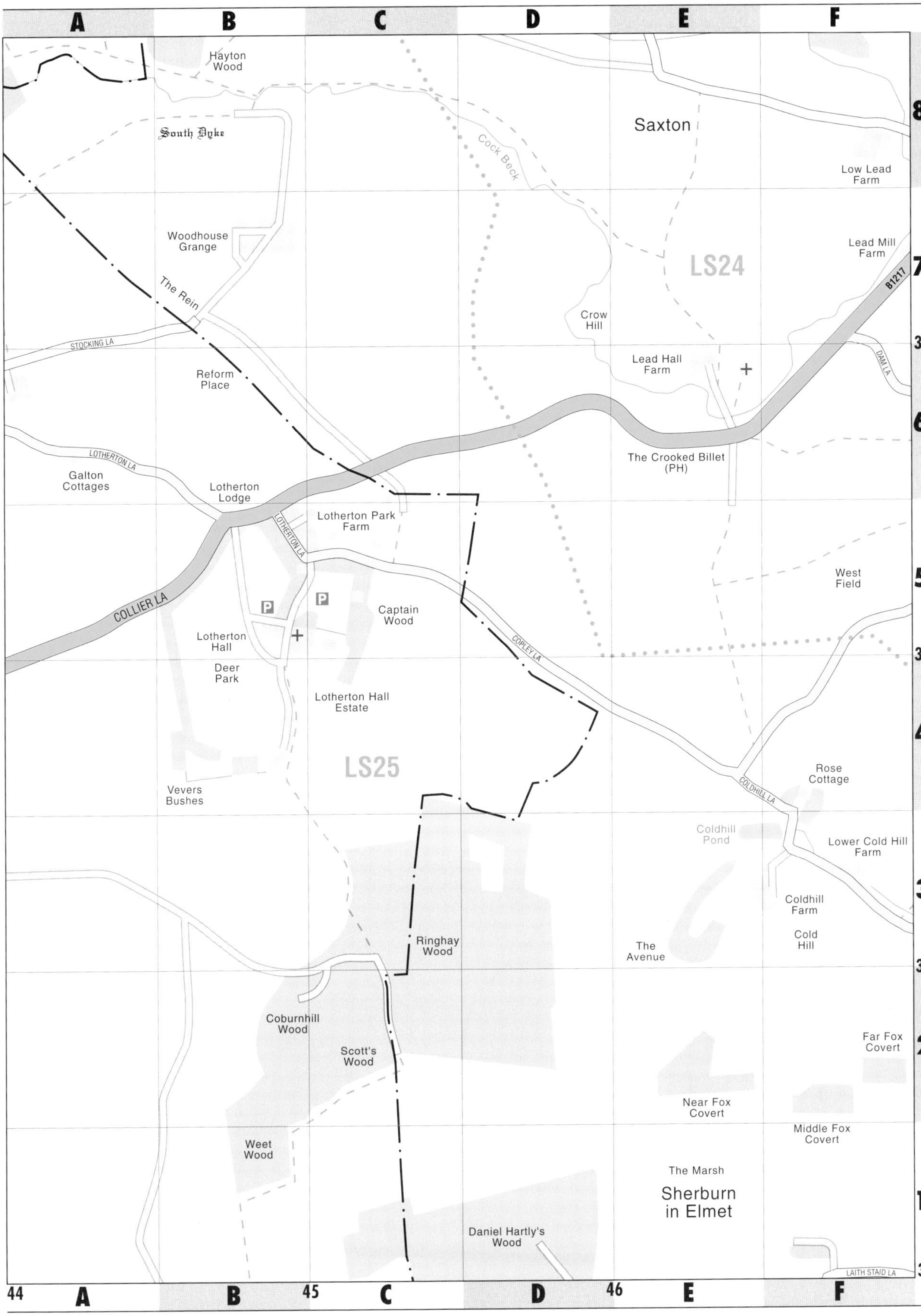

A
B
C
D
E
F
Hayton Wood
South Dyke
Saxton
Cock Beck
Low Lead Farm
Woodhouse Grange
The Rein
LS24
Lead Mill Farm
B1217
Crow Hill
STOCKING LA
Lead Hall Farm
DAM LA
Reform Place
LOTHERTON LA
The Crooked Billet (PH)
Galton Cottages
Lotherton Lodge
Lotherton Park Farm
LOTHERTON LA
West Field
COLLIER LA
P
P
Captain Wood
Lotherton Hall
COPLEY LA
Deer Park
Lotherton Hall Estate
LS25
Rose Cottage
COLDHILL LA
Vevers Bushes
Coldhill Pond
Lower Cold Hill Farm
Coldhill Farm
Ringhay Wood
Cold Hill
The Avenue
Coburnhill Wood
Scott's Wood
Far Fox Covert
Near Fox Covert
Middle Fox Covert
Weet Wood
The Marsh
Sherburn in Elmet
Daniel Hartly's Wood
LAITH STAID LA
8
7
37
6
5
36
4
3
35
2
1
34
44
45
46

84

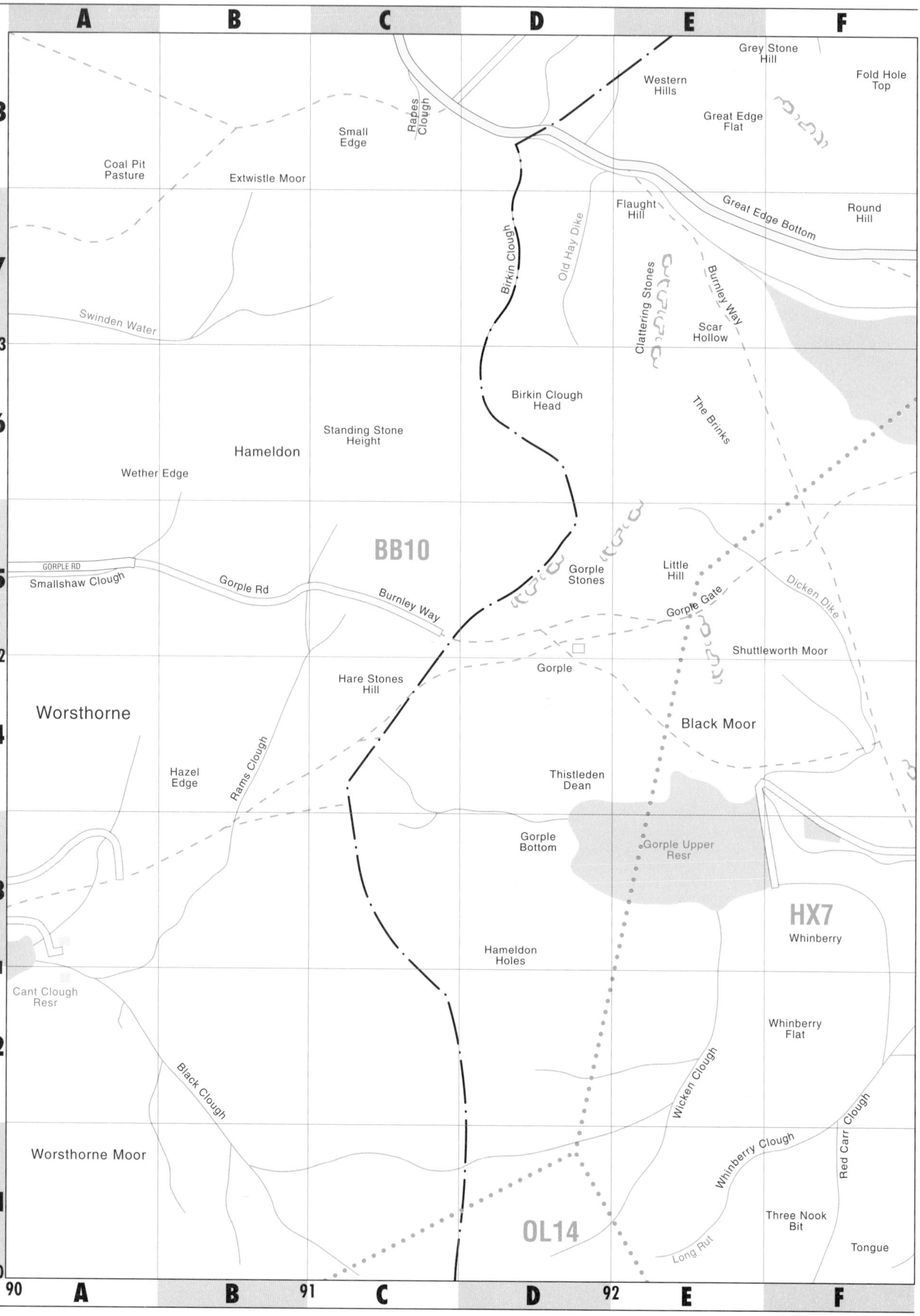
A
B
C
D
E
F
8
7
33
6
5
32
4
3
31
2
1
30
90
91
92
Grey Stone Hill
Fold Hole Top
Western Hills
Great Edge Flat
Rapes Clough
Small Edge
Coal Pit Pasture
Extwistle Moor
Flaught Hill
Great Edge Bottom
Round Hill
Old Hay Dike
Birkin Clough
Clattering Stones
Burnley Way
Scar Hollow
Swinden Water
Birkin Clough Head
The Brinks
Standing Stone Height
Hameldon
Wether Edge
BB10
GORPLE RD
Smallshaw Clough
Gorple Rd
Burnley Way
Gorple Stones
Little Hill
Dicken Dike
Gorple Gate
Shuttleworth Moor
Gorple
Hare Stones Hill
Worsthorne
Black Moor
Hazel Edge
Rams Clough
Thistleden Dean
Gorple Bottom
Gorple Upper Resr
HX7
Whinberry
Hameldon Holes
Cant Clough Resr
Whinberry Flat
Black Clough
Wicken Clough
Red Carr Clough
Worsthorne Moor
Whinberry Clough
Three Nook Bit
OL14
Long Rut
Tongue

86

68

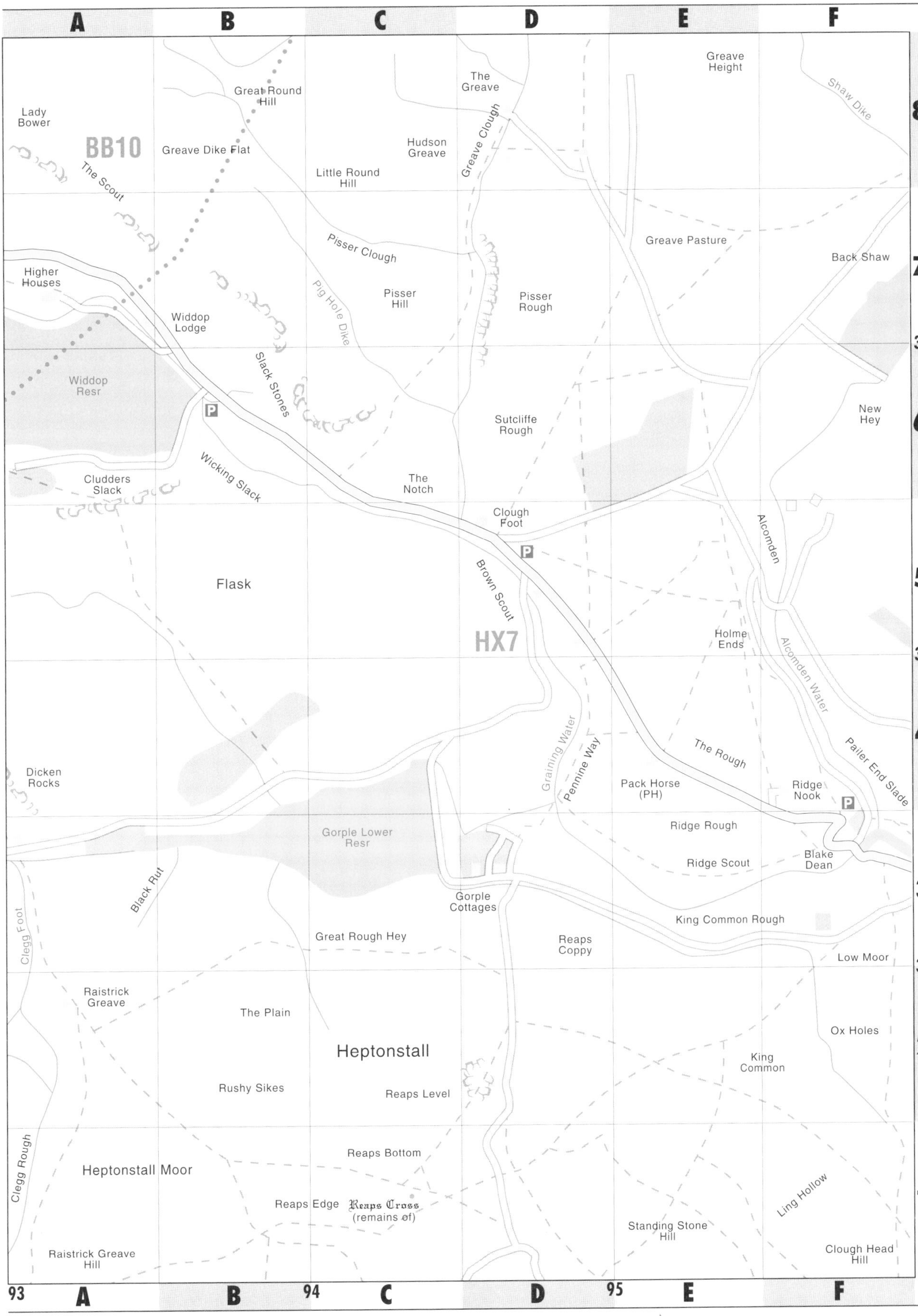
A
B
C
D
E
F
8
7
33
6
5
32
4
3
31
2
1
30
93
94
95
Lady Bower
BB10
The Scout
Great Round Hill
Greave Dike Flat
Little Round Hill
Hudson Greave
The Greave
Greave Clough
Greave Height
Shaw Dike
Greave Pasture
Back Shaw
Higher Houses
Widdop Lodge
Pisser Clough
Pig Hole Dike
Pisser Hill
Pisser Rough
Widdop Resr
Slack Stones
Sutcliffe Rough
New Hey
Cludders Slack
Wicking Slack
The Notch
Clough Foot
Alcomden
Flask
Brown Scout
HX7
Holme Ends
Alcomden Water
The Rough
Pailer End Slade
Dicken Rocks
Graining Water
Pennine Way
Pack Horse (PH)
Ridge Nook
Ridge Rough
Gorple Lower Resr
Ridge Scout
Blake Dean
Black Rut
Gorple Cottages
King Common Rough
Clegg Foot
Great Rough Hey
Reaps Coppy
Low Moor
Raistrick Greave
The Plain
Ox Holes
Heptonstall
King Common
Rushy Sikes
Reaps Level
Clegg Rough
Reaps Bottom
Heptonstall Moor
Ling Hollow
Reaps Edge
Reaps Cross (remains of)
Standing Stone Hill
Raistrick Greave Hill
Clough Head Hill

87

68

67
49

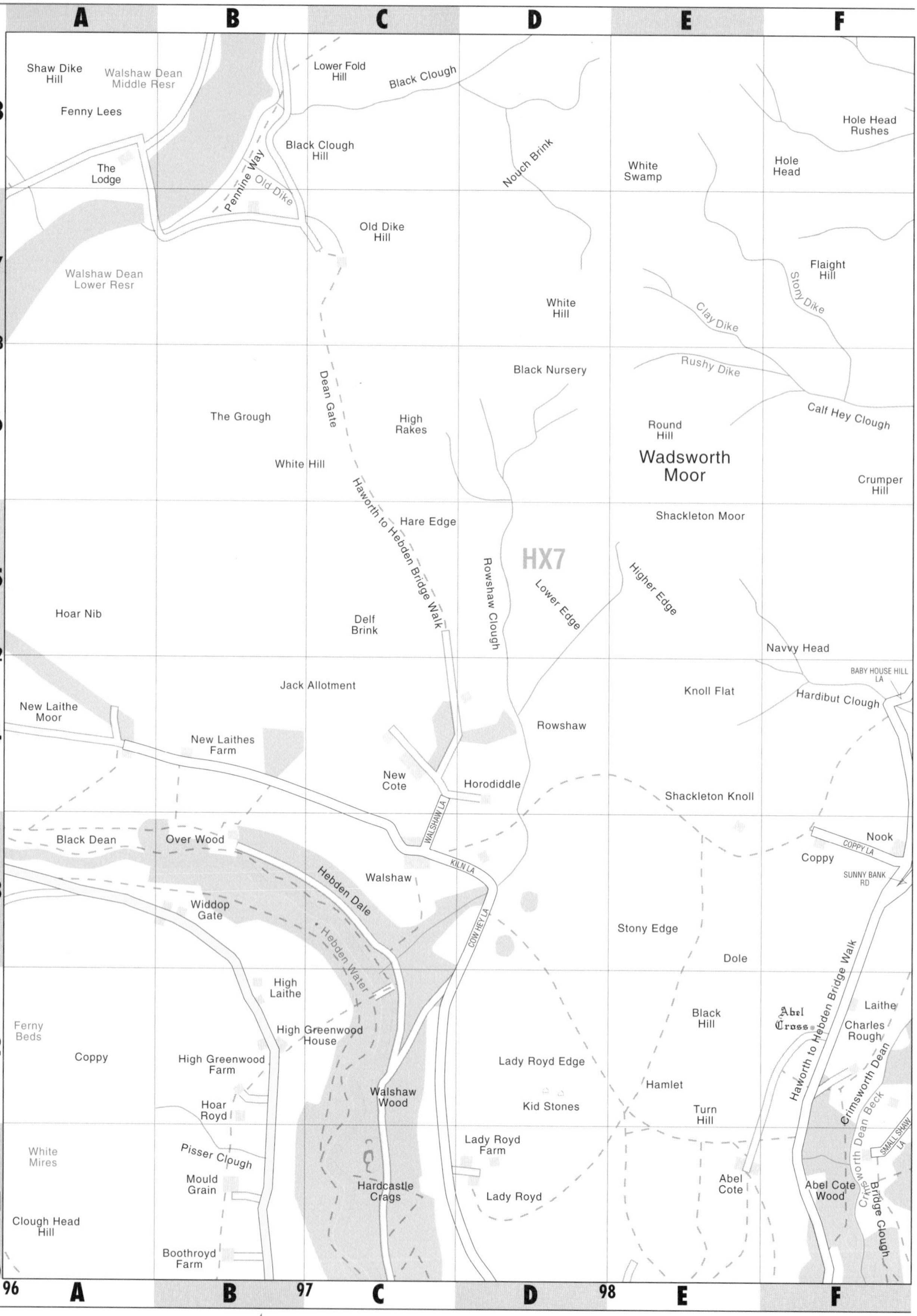
A
B
C
D
E
F
8
7
33
6
5
32
4
3
31
2
1
30
96
97
98
Shaw Dike Hill
Walshaw Dean Middle Resr
Lower Fold Hill
Black Clough
Fenny Lees
Black Clough Hill
Hole Head Rushes
Hole Head
The Lodge
Pennine Way
Old Dike
Nouch Brink
White Swamp
Old Dike Hill
Flaight Hill
Walshaw Dean Lower Resr
Stony Dike
White Hill
Clay Dike
Rushy Dike
Black Nursery
Dean Gate
Calf Hey Clough
The Grough
High Rakes
Round Hill
Wadsworth Moor
White Hill
Crumper Hill
Haworth to Hebden Bridge Walk
Hare Edge
Shackleton Moor
HX7
Rowshaw Clough
Lower Edge
Higher Edge
Hoar Nib
Delf Brink
Navvy Head
BABY HOUSE HILL LA
Jack Allotment
Knoll Flat
Hardibut Clough
New Laithe Moor
Rowshaw
New Laithes Farm
New Cote
Horodiddle
Shackleton Knoll
WALSHAW LA
Black Dean
Over Wood
Nook
COPPY LA
Coppy
Walshaw
KILN LA
SUNNY BANK RD
Hebden Dale
Widdop Gate
Hebden Water
COW HEY LA
Stony Edge
Dole
High Laithe
Black Hill
Abel Cross
Laithe
Ferny Beds
High Greenwood House
Charles Rough
Coppy
High Greenwood Farm
Lady Royd Edge
Crimsworth Dean
Hamlet
Walshaw Wood
Hoar Royd
Kid Stones
Turn Hill
Crimsworth Dean Beck
SMALL SHAW LA
White Mires
Pisser Clough
Lady Royd Farm
Mould Grain
Hardcastle Crags
Lady Royd
Abel Cote
Abel Cote Wood
Bridge Clough
Clough Head Hill
Boothroyd Farm

67
88

50
70

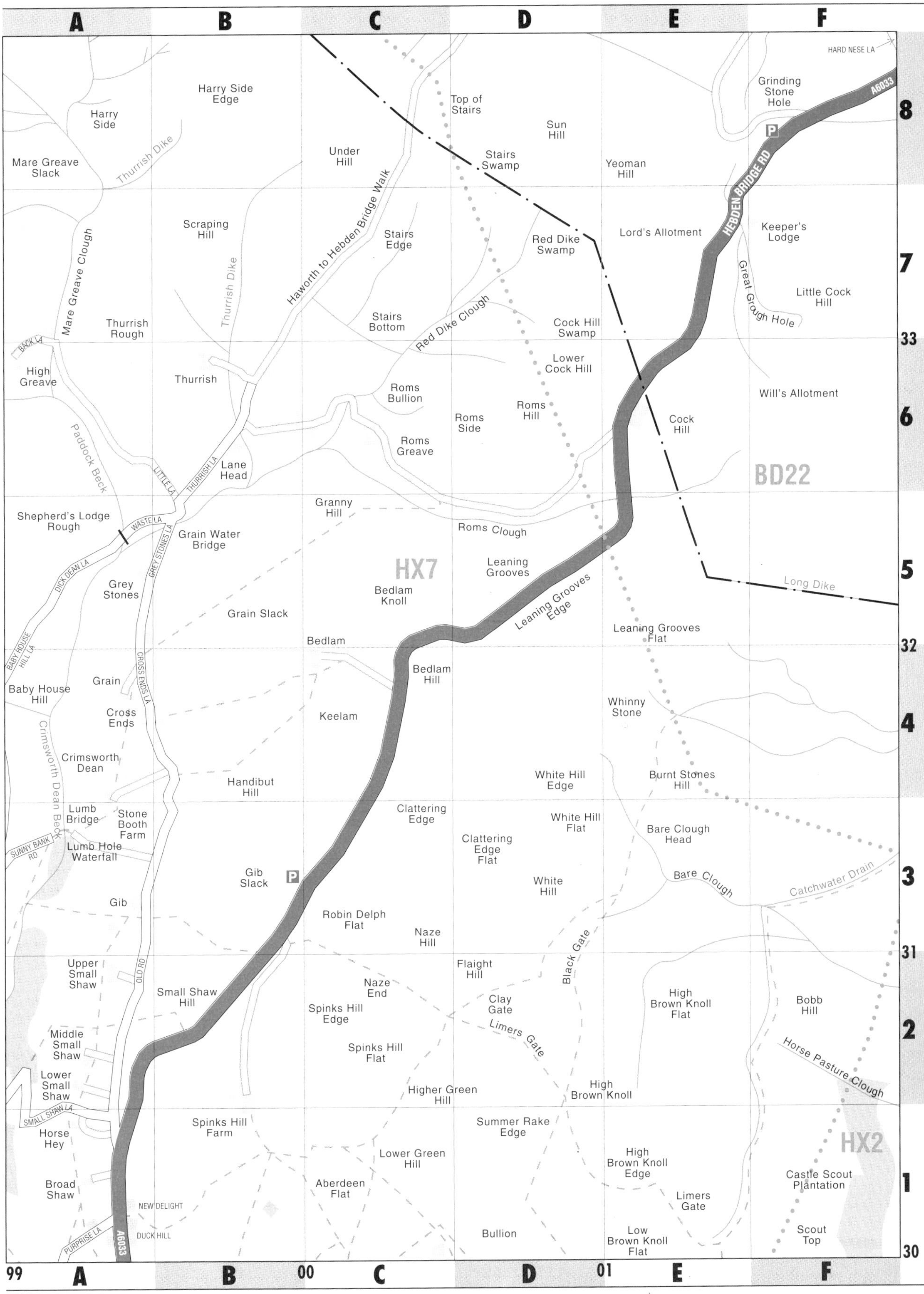
A
B
C
D
E
F
HARD NESE LA
Grinding Stone Hole
A6033
Harry Side Edge
Top of Stairs
Harry Side
8
Sun Hill
Mare Greave Slack
Thurrish Dike
Under Hill
Stairs Swamp
Yeoman Hill
HEBDEN BRIDGE RD
Scraping Hill
Haworth to Hebden Bridge Walk
Stairs Edge
Red Dike Swamp
Lord's Allotment
Keeper's Lodge
Mare Greave Clough
Thurrish Dike
7
Great Grough Hole
Little Cock Hill
Thurrish Rough
Stairs Bottom
Red Dike Clough
Cock Hill Swamp
BACK LA
33
High Greave
Thurrish
Lower Cock Hill
Roms Bullion
Will's Allotment
Roms Hill
Roms Side
Cock Hill
6
Paddock Beck
Roms Greave
LITTLE LA
THURRISH LA
Lane Head
BD22
Shepherd's Lodge Rough
Granny Hill
WASTE LA
Roms Clough
Grain Water Bridge
GREY STONES LA
DICK DEAN LA
Leaning Grooves
HX7
5
Long Dike
Grey Stones
Bedlam Knoll
Leaning Grooves Edge
Grain Slack
Leaning Grooves Flat
BABY HOUSE HILL LA
Bedlam
32
Bedlam Hill
Baby House Hill
Grain
CROSS ENDS LA
Whinny Stone
Cross Ends
Keelam
4
Crimsworth Dean Beck
Crimsworth Dean
Handibut Hill
White Hill Edge
Burnt Stones Hill
Lumb Bridge
Stone Booth Farm
Clattering Edge
White Hill Flat
Bare Clough Head
SUNNY BANK RD
Lumb Hole Waterfall
Clattering Edge Flat
Gib Slack
Bare Clough
Catchwater Drain
3
White Hill
Gib
Robin Delph Flat
Naze Hill
Black Gate
31
Upper Small Shaw
OLD RD
Flaight Hill
Naze End
Small Shaw Hill
Clay Gate
High Brown Knoll Flat
Bobb Hill
Spinks Hill Edge
2
Middle Small Shaw
Limers Gate
Spinks Hill Flat
Horse Pasture Clough
Lower Small Shaw
Higher Green Hill
High Brown Knoll
SMALL SHAW LA
Spinks Hill Farm
Summer Rake Edge
Horse Hey
HX2
Lower Green Hill
High Brown Knoll Edge
Castle Scout Plantation
Broad Shaw
1
Aberdeen Flat
Limers Gate
NEW DELIGHT
Scout Top
PURPRISE LA
DUCK HILL
A6033
Bullion
Low Brown Knoll Flat
30
99
A
B
00
C
D
01
E
F

89
70

69
51

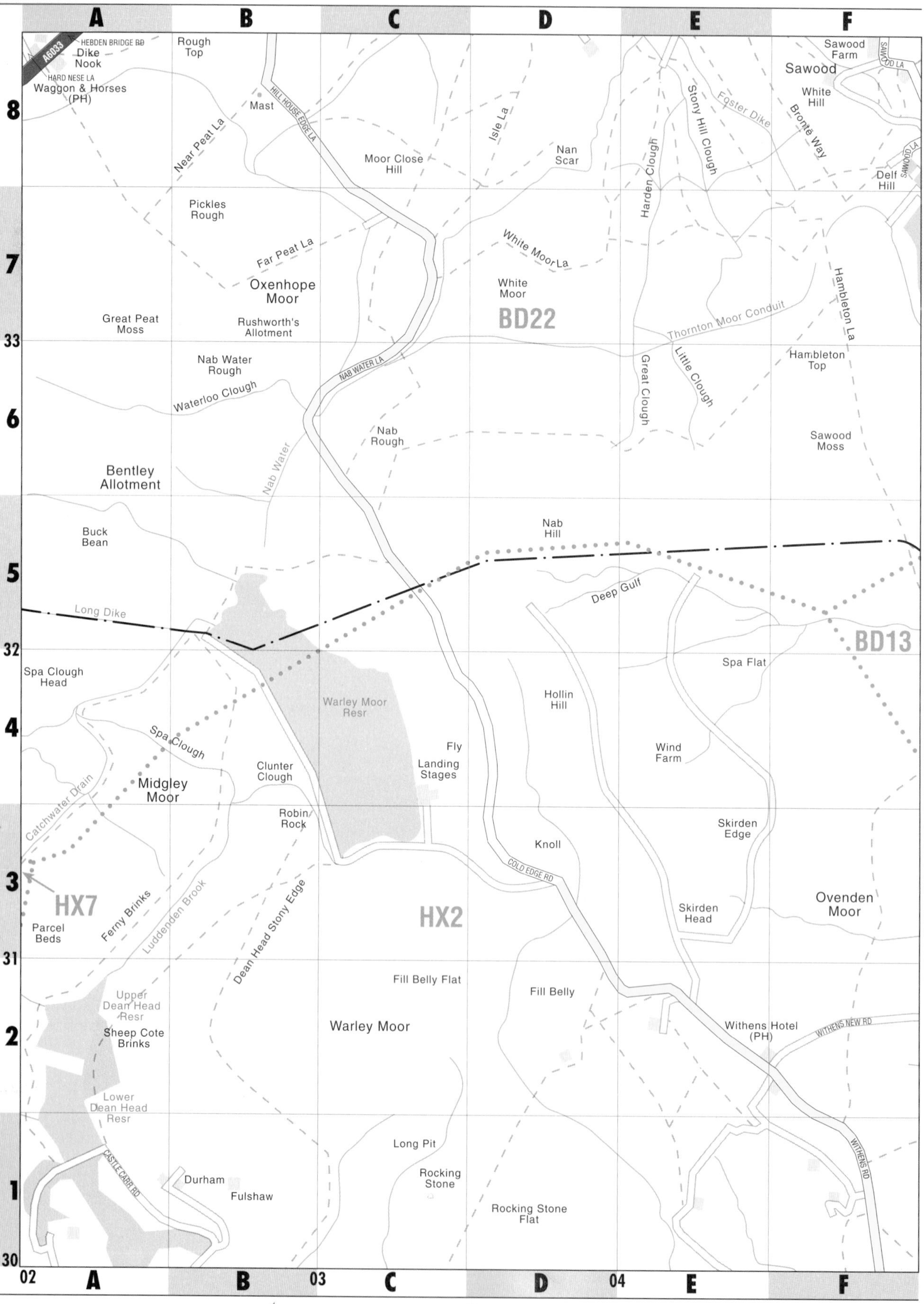
A
B
C
D
E
F
A6033
HEBDEN BRIDGE RD
Dike Nook
HARD NESE LA
Waggon & Horses (PH)
Rough Top
Mast
HILL HOUSE EDGE LA
Near Peat La
Moor Close Hill
Isle La
Nan Scar
Harden Clough
Stony Hill Clough
Foster Dike
Sawood Farm
Sawood
SAWOOD LA
White Hill
Brontë Way
Delf Hill
Pickles Rough
Far Peat La
White Moor La
White Moor
Oxenhope Moor
Great Peat Moss
Rushworth's Allotment
BD22
Thornton Moor Conduit
Hambleton La
Hambleton Top
Nab Water Rough
NAB WATER LA
Waterloo Clough
Great Clough
Little Clough
Nab Rough
Sawood Moss
Nab Water
Bentley Allotment
Buck Bean
Nab Hill
Long Dike
Deep Gulf
BD13
Spa Clough Head
Spa Flat
Warley Moor Resr
Hollin Hill
Spa Clough
Fly
Landing Stages
Wind Farm
Clunter Clough
Midgley Moor
Catchwater Drain
Robin Rock
Skirden Edge
Knoll
COLD EDGE RD
HX7
Ferny Brinks
Luddenden Brook
Dean Head Stony Edge
HX2
Skirden Head
Ovenden Moor
Parcel Beds
Fill Belly Flat
Fill Belly
Upper Dean Head Resr
Sheep Cote Brinks
Warley Moor
Withens Hotel (PH)
WITHENS NEW RD
Lower Dean Head Resr
Long Pit
CASTLE CARR RD
WITHENS RD
Durham
Fulshaw
Rocking Stone
Rocking Stone Flat
8
7
33
6
5
32
4
3
31
2
1
30
02
03
04

69
90

52
72

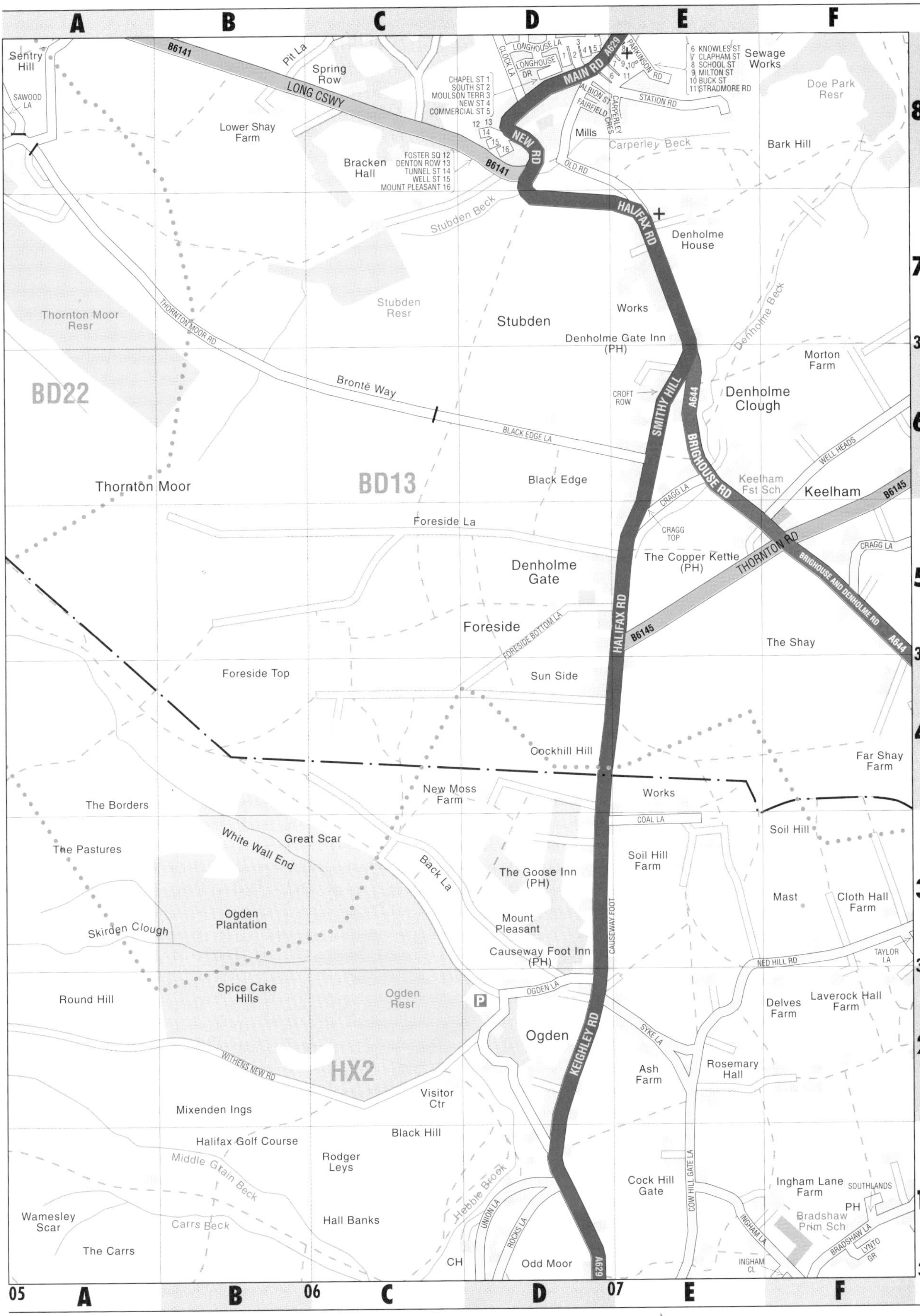
A
B
C
D
E
F
Sentry Hill
SAWOOD LA
B6141
LONG CSWY
Pit La
Spring Row
Lower Shay Farm
Bracken Hall
CHAPEL ST 1
SOUTH ST 2
MOULSON TERR 3
NEW ST 4
COMMERCIAL ST 5
FOSTER SQ 12
DENTON ROW 13
TUNNEL ST 14
WELL ST 15
MOUNT PLEASANT 16
CLOCK LA
LONGHOUSE LA
LONGHOUSE DR
MAIN RD
A629
NEW RD
PARKINSON RD
6 KNOWLES ST
7 CLAPHAM ST
8 SCHOOL ST
9 MILTON ST
10 BUCK ST
11 STRADMORE RD
Sewage Works
Doe Park Resr
STATION RD
ALBION ST
FAIRFIELD
CARPERLEY CRES
Mills
Carperley Beck
Bark Hill
OLD RD
HALIFAX RD
Denholme House
Stubden Beck
Thornton Moor Resr
THORNTON MOOR RD
Stubden Resr
Stubden
Works
Denholme Gate Inn (PH)
Denholme Beck
Morton Farm
BD22
Brontë Way
CROFT ROW
SMITHY HILL
A644
Denholme Clough
BLACK EDGE LA
BRIGHOUSE RD
WELL HEADS
Thornton Moor
BD13
Black Edge
Keelham Fst Sch
Keelham
B6145
CRAGG LA
CRAGG TOP
Foreside La
Denholme Gate
The Copper Kettle (PH)
THORNTON RD
BRIGHOUSE AND DENHOLME RD
Foreside
FORESIDE BOTTOM LA
HALIFAX RD
The Shay
Foreside Top
Sun Side
Cockhill Hill
Far Shay Farm
New Moss Farm
Works
The Borders
COAL LA
Soil Hill
White Wall End
Great Scar
The Pastures
Back La
Soil Hill Farm
The Goose Inn (PH)
Mast
Cloth Hall Farm
Ogden Plantation
Skirden Clough
Mount Pleasant
CAUSEWAY FOOT
Causeway Foot Inn (PH)
NED HILL RD
TAYLOR LA
Round Hill
Spice Cake Hills
Ogden Resr
P
OGDEN LA
Delves Farm
Laverock Hall Farm
Ogden
SYKE LA
KEIGHLEY RD
WITHENS NEW RD
HX2
Ash Farm
Rosemary Hall
Visitor Ctr
Mixenden Ings
Black Hill
Halifax Golf Course
Rodger Leys
Middle Grain Beck
Hebble Brook
Cock Hill Gate
COW HILL GATE LA
Ingham Lane Farm
SOUTHLANDS
PH
Bradshaw Prim Sch
Wamesley Scar
Carrs Beck
Hall Banks
UNION LA
ROCKS LA
INGHAM LA
BRADSHAW LA
LYNTON GR
The Carrs
CH
Odd Moor
INGHAM CL
8
7
33
6
5
32
4
3
31
2
1
30
05
06
07

91
72

71
53

D6
1 KING EDWARD TERR
2 KING EDWARD RD
3 VINE TERR
4 FIRTH ST
5 MARY ST
6 KIPPING PL
7 FOUNTAIN ST
8 ENDERLEY RD
9 ALDERSCHOLES CL
10 LOWER KIPPING LA
11 HIGH CLIFFE CL
12 BACK HIGH ST
13 ACKROYD CT
14 CHAPEL TERR
15 SOWDEN GRANGE

E6
1 BRIDGE ST
2 HAVELOCK SQ
3 INDUSTRY ST
4 THORNFIELD HALL
5 MARKET CT
6 SANDMOOR CL
7 NORTH CLIFFE CL
8 NORTH CLIFFE GR

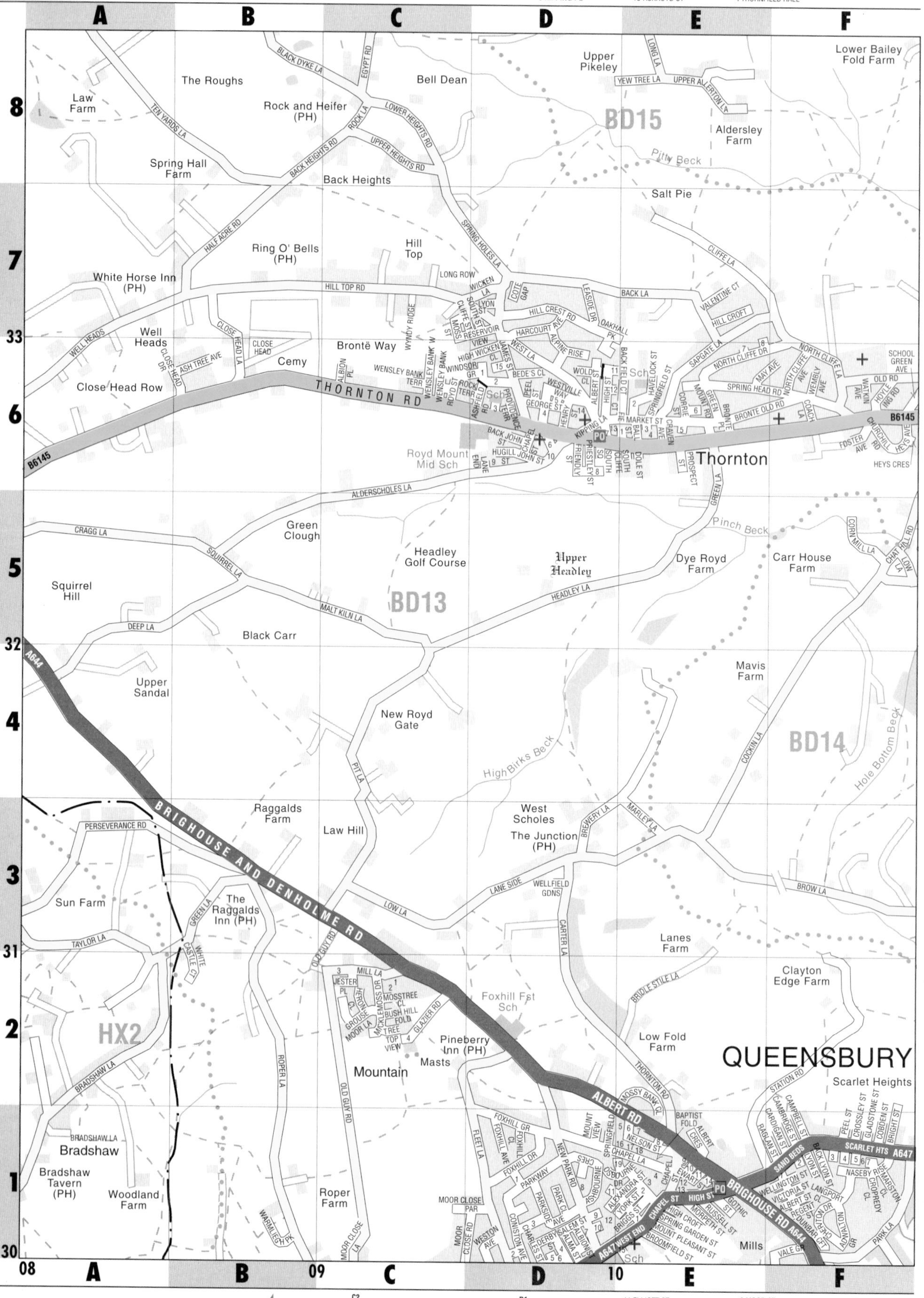
A
B
C
D
E
F
Law Farm
The Roughs
Rock and Heifer (PH)
Bell Dean
Upper Pikeley
Lower Bailey Fold Farm
BD15
Aldersley Farm
Spring Hall Farm
Back Heights
Pitty Beck
Salt Pie
Ring O' Bells (PH)
Hill Top
White Horse Inn (PH)
HILL TOP RD
Well Heads
Cemy
Brontë Way
Close Head Row
THORNTON RD
B6145
Royd Mount Mid Sch
Thornton
ALDERSCHOLES LA
CRAGG LA
Green Clough
Headley Golf Course
Upper Headley
Dye Royd Farm
Carr House Farm
Pinch Beck
Squirrel Hill
BD13
HEADLEY LA
Black Carr
Mavis Farm
Upper Sandal
A644
New Royd Gate
BD14
High Birks Beck
Hole Bottom Beck
Raggalds Farm
Law Hill
West Scholes
The Junction (PH)
BRIGHOUSE AND DENHOLME RD
Sun Farm
The Raggalds Inn (PH)
BROW LA
Lanes Farm
Clayton Edge Farm
Foxhill Fst Sch
HX2
Pineberry Inn (PH)
Masts
Mountain
Low Fold Farm
QUEENSBURY
Scarlet Heights
ALBERT RD
Bradshaw
Bradshaw Tavern (PH)
Woodland Farm
Roper Farm
Mills
SCARLET HTS A647
08
09
10
8
7
33
6
5
32
4
3
31
2
1
30

71
92

C2
1 FASCINATION PL
2 MONTROSE PL
3 LUDDENDON PL
4 RESERVOIR PL

D1
1 CONISTON AVE
2 LANGDALE DR
3 PARKFIELD DR
4 COMMERCIAL ST
5 BOOTH ST
6 LEE ST
7 THE GROVE
8 ADA ST
9 PARK GR
10 HENAGE ST
11 ELLIOTT CT
12 HIGH PEAL CT

E1
1 FOSTER ST
2 GRANBY ST
3 NORTH JOHN ST
4 ALBERT EDWARD ST
5 GOODWIN HOUSE
6 QUEENSBURY SQ
7 SMALL PAGE FOLD
8 NELSON PL
9 MOOR ST
10 CLIFTON ST
11 UNION ST
12 CROYDON ST
13 CAMBRIDGE PL
14 FOUNTAIN ST
15 RUSSELL HALL LA
16 WESTWARD HO
17 SPRING ROW
18 PROSPECT PL
19 LEWIS CL

F1
1 BRUNSWICK ST
2 NAPIER ST
3 SOUTH BANK
4 STONELEIGH
5 ROCK LEA
6 FERN LEA
7 EDGEHILL CL

A7
1 BEECROFT WLK
2 BARKSTON WLK
3 COXWOLD WLK
B7
1 BENTCLIFF WLK
2 MILNER HOUSE
3 GOLDCREST AVE
4 BLACKBIRD GDNS
B8
1 TOLWORTH FOLD
2 THURSTON GDNS
3 UPPER GRANGE AVE
4 UPTON WLK
5 KENILWORTH HOUSE
6 BLUEBELL CL
7 WHITBURN WAY
8 SNOWDROP MEWS
9 DAFFODIL CT
10 LINDHOLM GDNS
11 BOWMERE DR
12 CREDITON CT
C7
1 MALLARD CT
2 THE SQUARE
3 DUNLIN WAY
4 WHIMBREL CL
5 SANDPIPER MEWS
6 CHAFFINCH RD
7 SANDERLING CT
8 FULMAR MEWS

54

74

F8
1 LINGWOOD TERR
2 COMO GDNS
3 BUCKLAND RD
4 WASHINGTON ST
5 AGAR ST
6 AGAR TERR
7 WILLOW ST
8 WEST PARK TERR
9 CLEMENT ST
10 CRAVEN CT
11 THORNTON CT
12 COTTAGE GN

A B C D E F

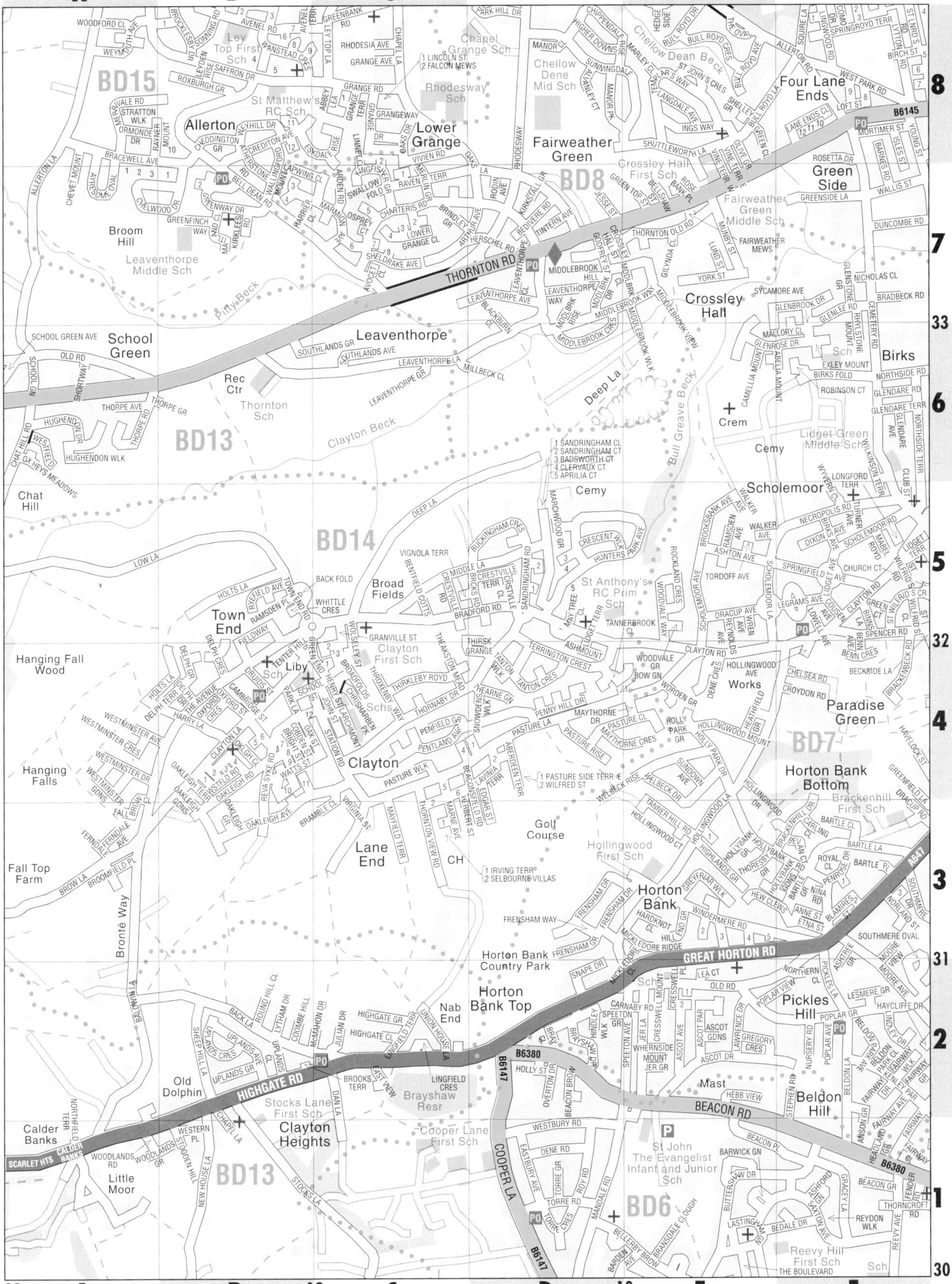

11 A B 12 C D 13 E F

B4
1 WOBURN TERR
2 WESTFIELD TERR
3 DERBY ST
4 CRANBROOK ST
5 ENDSLEIGH PL
6 GREENWELL ROW
7 GORDON ST
8 ARKWRIGHT ST
9 VICTORIA ST
10 ALEXANDER SQ
11 BROOMCROFT
12 NURSERY RD
C4
1 GREGORY CT
2 BEECH GR
3 BEECH SQ
4 PASTURE SIDE TERR W
5 CROSS ST
6 GAYTHORNE TERR

93

74

E2
1 BEACON ST
2 CRESSWELL TERR
E3
1 HIGHLANDS CL
2 YARWOOD GR
3 WINDERMERE TERR
4 CONISTON RD
5 ARKENDALE MEWS

F3
1 LYNCH AVE
2 BLAMIRES PL
3 ESMOND ST

C8
1 WHETLEY TERR
2 PRIMROSE ST
3 BACK WOOD ST
4 STALLABRASS ST
5 HIND ST
6 MENSTONE ST

73

55

For full street detail of the highlighted area see page 201.

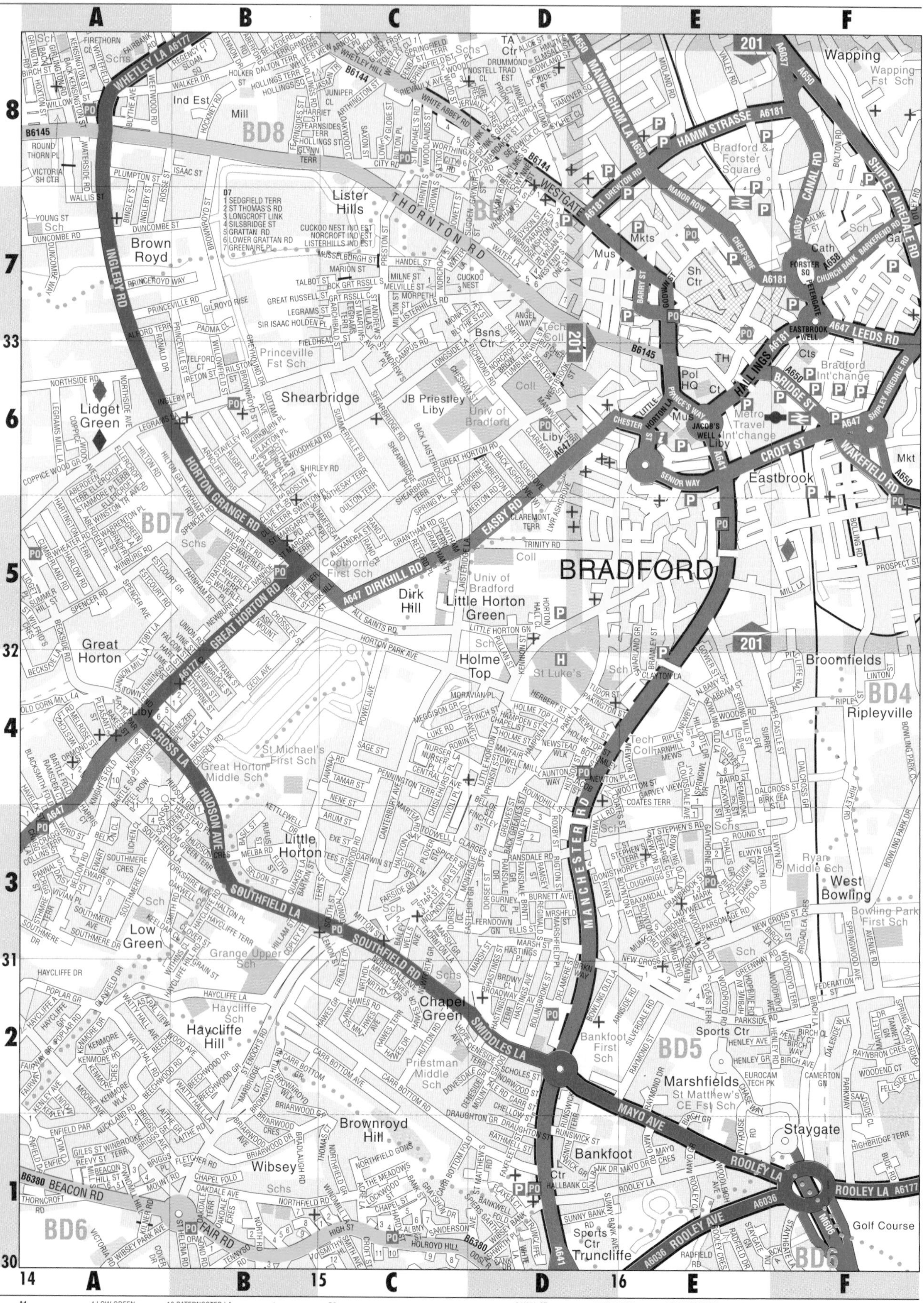

A1
1 KENLEY PAR
2 TANGLEWOOD CT
3 NEW LAITHE RD
4 ELLTON GR
5 LEVER ST
6 OVEREND ST
A3
1 UPPER GREEN
2 WATMOUGH ST
3 SOUTHMERE GR
4 LOW GREEN
A4
1 SAINT ST
2 WALSHAW ST
3 HUNT YD
4 SELLARS FOLD
5 CRABTREE PL
6 CRABTREE ST
7 JENNINGS ST
8 KINGSWOOD PL
9 KINGSWOOD TERR
10 PATERNOSTER LA
11 RUDD ST
12 PERSEVERANCE LA
B1
1 HOLDEN RD
2 BAGNALL TERR
3 WILMAN HILL
4 UPPER GEORGE ST
5 LOWER GEORGE ST
6 ODDY PL
7 ADAM ST
8 SCHOOL LA
9 ASHDOWN CL
10 OAKROYD RD

73

B3
1 HUDSON CL
2 STEPHENSON ST
B4
1 SHEPHERD ST
2 TODD TERR
3 FRANK PL
4 BEMPTON PL
5 BEMPTON CT
C1
1 PRIESTLEY TERR
2 BRADLAUGH TERR
3 BACK MARKET ST
4 MARKET ST
5 HORSLEY ST

94

6 HALL ST
7 HECTOR CL
8 HENDERSON PL
9 WARBURTON PL
10 LIGHTOWLER ST
11 SHARP ST
12 OAKROYD AVE
C3
1 CHRISTOPHER ST
2 CHRISTOPHER TERR
3 MURRAY ST
4 CENTRE ST
5 FOX ST
6 BACK SMITH ROW
7 BRUNEL GDNS
D3
1 MONT GR
2 CARLTON GR
3 STIRTON ST
4 LOW WELL RD
E2
1 LITTLE CROSS ST
2 CLIPSTONE ST
3 STONE ACRE CT
4 MOUNTBATTEN CT
E3
1 MOULSON CT
2 LONG ROW CT
3 CRANBROOK PL
4 TICHBORNE RD
5 MURDSTONE CL
E4
1 JACKIE SMART RD
2 CAULDWELL GDNS
3 MEGNAWAY
4 THIRKHILL CT
5 TILEY SQ
6 MERTON FOLD
7 VERE SQ
8 MITCHELL SQ
9 BOWBRIDGE RD

For full street detail of the highlighted area see page 201.

56

76

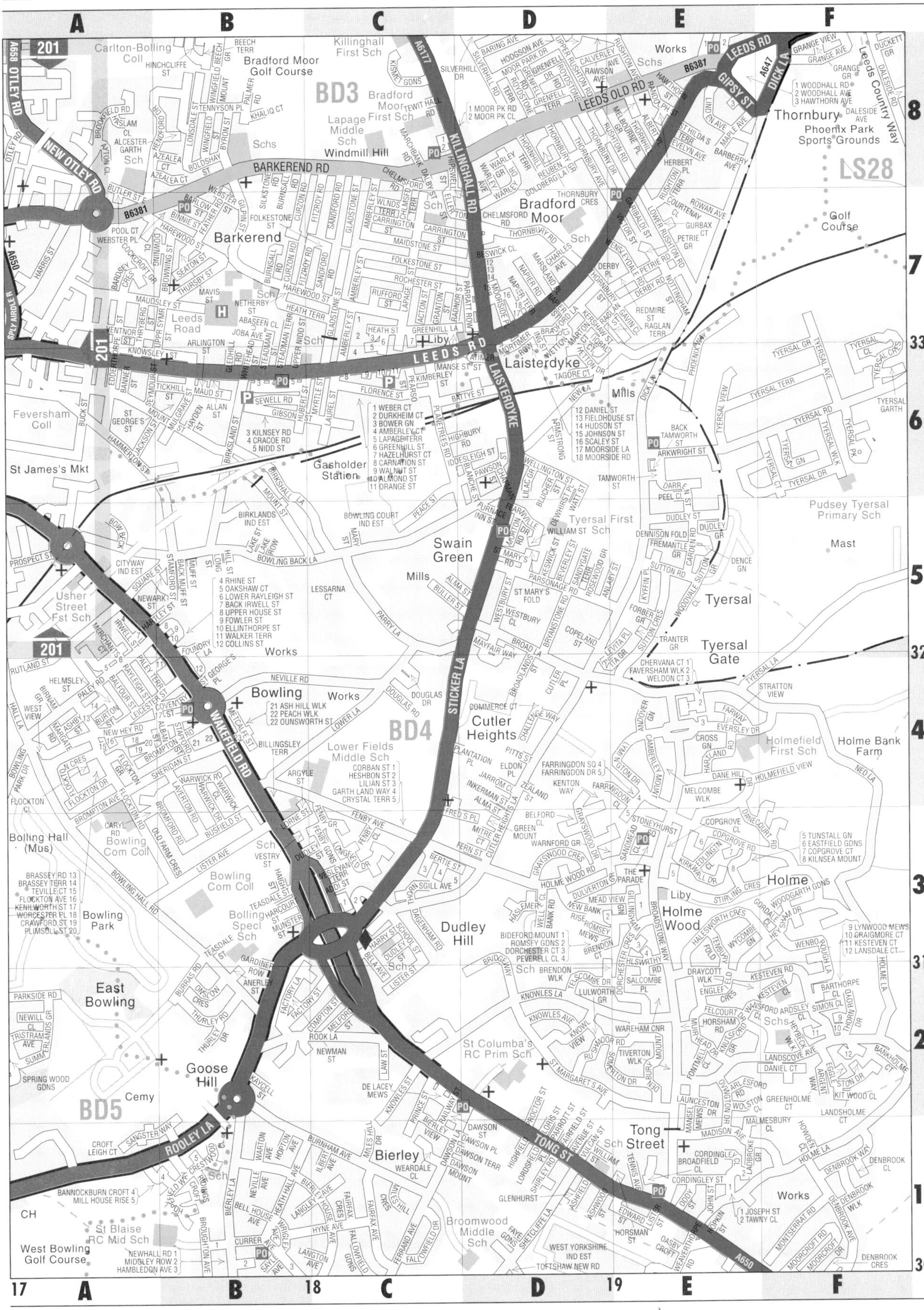

95

76

A8
1 CHATSWORTH AVE
2 CHATSWORTH DR
3 GALLOWAY CT
4 MOORLAND CRES
E5
1 HILLTHORPE SQ
2 HILLTHORPE ST
3 HILLTHORPE TERR
4 REGENCY PARK GR
E6
1 RADCLIFFE TERR
2 RADCLIFFE GR
3 CHAPEL FOLD

75

E6
4 SANDRINGHAM AVE
E7
1 CRAWSHAW CL
2 CRAWSHAW HILL
3 PARKFIELD TR
4 PARK AVE

57

E7
5 MANOR HOUSE ST
6 WESLEY SQ
E8
1 CLARENCE TR
2 CARLTON TR
3 RUTLAND CT
4 SURREY RD
5 PEMBROKE DR
6 CROFT HOUSE CT
7 BROUGHTON TR
8 OAKROYD TR
9 NORTH ST
10 WESLEY ROW
11 CLIFTON CT
F5
1 WEAVERS CT
2 LEAFIELD DR
3 MARLOWE CL
F7
1 LONGFIELD MNT
2 LONGFIELD GR
3 LONGFIELD AVE
4 HAMMERTON GR
5 HUGGAN ROW
6 ALBION ST
7 HILLSIDE GR
F8
1 WHITELANDS
2 MNT PLEASANT ST
3 ROSEMONT AVE
4 ROSEMONT ST
5 EAST VIEW CTS
6 MUSGRAVE BG
7 FAIRFIELD AVE
8 TOWNEND PL

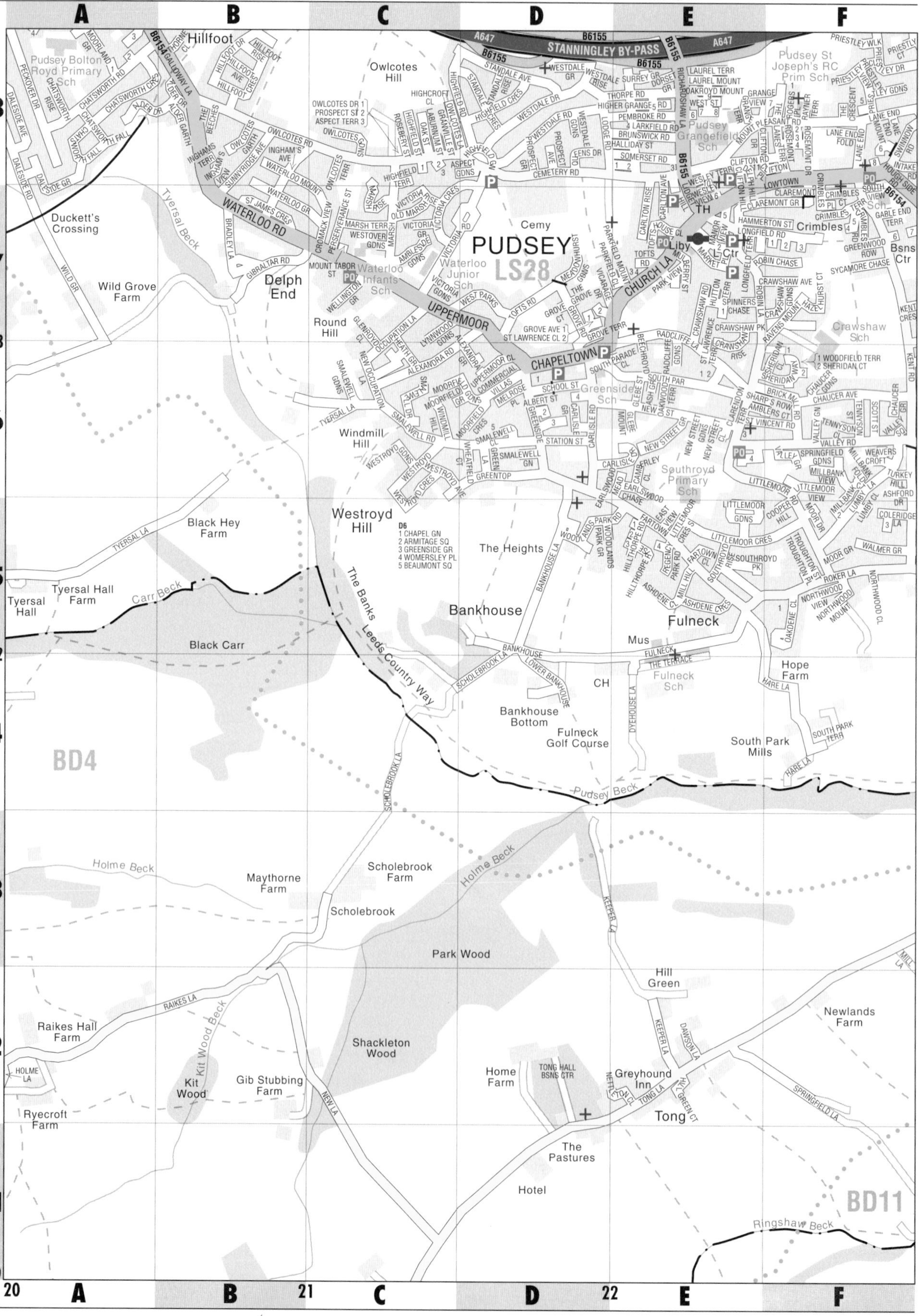

75
96

A
B
C
D
E
F
8
7
6
5
4
3
2
1
33
32
31
30
23
24
25
Swinnow Moor
Liby
Hough End
LS13
Park Spring Primary Sch
Gamble Hill
Hough Side
PUDSEY RD
HOUGH SIDE RD
STANNINGLEY BY-PASS
A647
A6110 RING ROAD BRAMLEY
REGINA HOUSE
Cemy
St Mary's
Hill End
Upper Wortley Recn Ctr
Farnley Beck
Park Spring
Post Hill
Beulah Farm
Mount Pleasant
RING ROAD FARNLEY
TONG RD
B6154
Swallow Hill
LAKESIDE IND EST
Acres Hall
Troy Dale
LS28
Pudsey Beck
Ryecroft Prim Sch
Silver Royd Hill
RING ROAD LOW WORTLEY
Wortley Beck
The Beulah (PH)
VALLEY RD
ACRES HALL DR
Littlemoor Bottom
Troydale
HALL LA
Farnley Hall
Farnley
Farnley Cemy
Farnley Park
Lawns Park Prim Sch
A6110
Low Farm
East House
LS12
Farnley Park High Sch
Cobden Primary Sch
Roker Lane Bottom
Park Side Farm
Barker's Well Farm
WHITEHALL TRAD EST
A58
New Farnley
Resr
Cockers Dale
Upland Farm
Nan Whins Wood
Leeds Country Way
TONG LA
BD4
BACK LA
Harper Farm
Castle Hill
Church Farm
Farnley Wood
Low Moor Side
WHITEHALL RD
MILL LA
Tong Beck
Corn Mill Farm
Mast
WALSH LA
Wentworth Farm
WOOD LA
Cemy
Farnley Wood Side
Upper Moor Side
Cud Hill Farm
B6126 GILDERSOME LA
SPRINGFIELD LA
BD11
DALE RD
Farnley Wood Beck
LS27
GAMBLE HILL WALK 1
GAMBLE HILL CROSS 2
GAMBLE HILL CHASE 3
GAMBLE HILL CROFT 4
GAMBLE HILL GRANGE 5
GAMBLE HILL FOLD 6
1 PRIESTLEY DR
2 SWINNOW GN
3 LANE END
4 BRITANNIA CT
5 PORTLAND ST
6 RICHMOND GDNS
7 HILLSIDE GR
8 CAVENDISH RISE
STONECLIFFE VIEW 1
STONECLIFFE WLK 2
STONECLIFFE PL 3
STONECLIFFE MOUNT 4
STONECLIFFE LAWN 5
STONECLIFFE GARTH 6
STONECLIFFE CL 7
STONECLIFFE BANK 8
9 BAWN WLK
10 BAWN PATH
WHINCOVER CROSS 11
WHINCOVER VIEW 12
WHINCOVER GRANGE 13
PINDER VIEW 14
PINDER GR 15
PINDER AVE 16
COBDEN PL 17
COBDEN ST 18
STEPHENSON WAY 1
NEWTON SQ 2
WEST END 3
SCHOOL CL 4
CASTLE INGS CL 5
ENNERDALE WAY 6
LOW MOORSIDE CL 7
LOW MOORSIDE CT 8

77
59

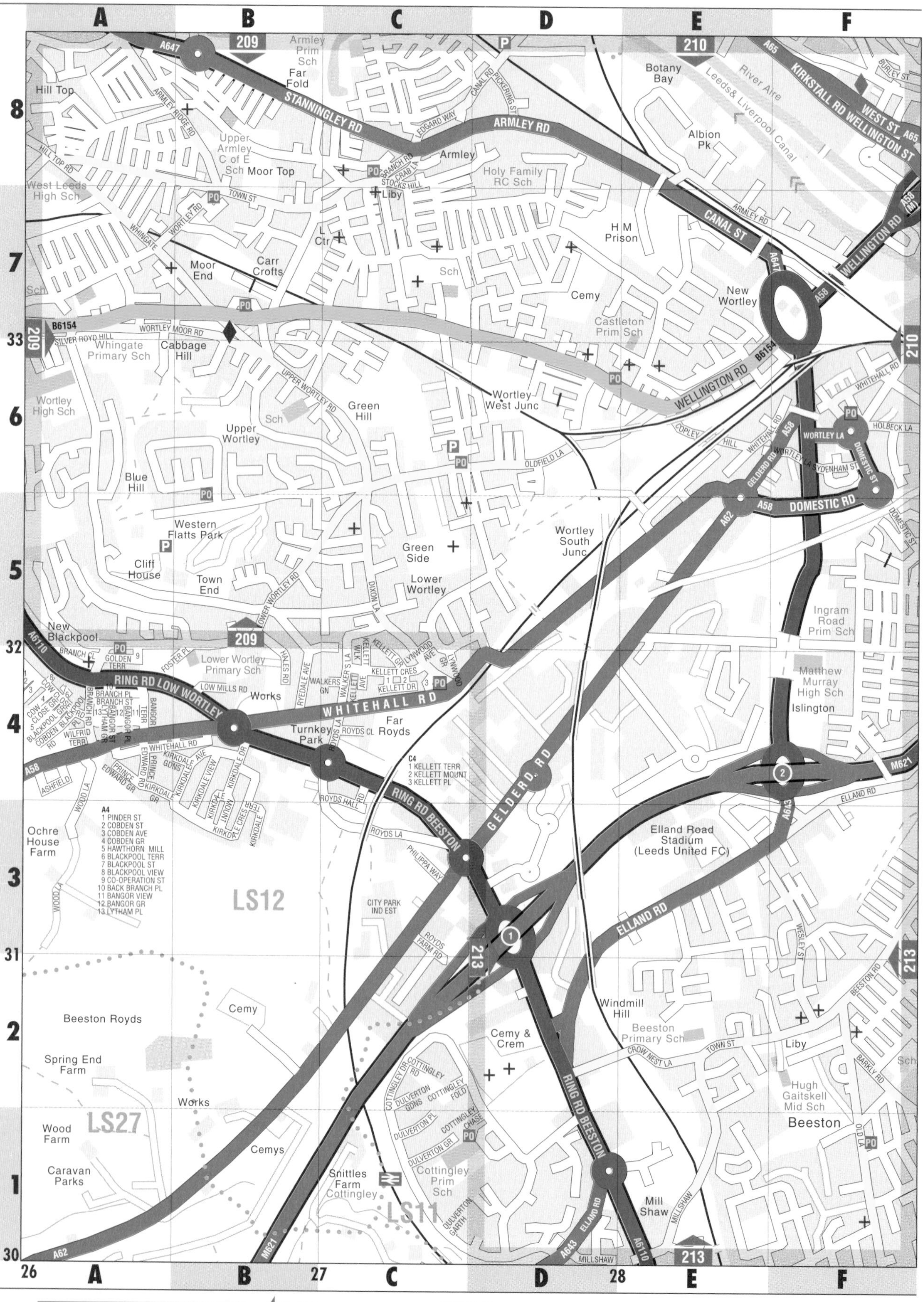

For full street detail of the highlighted area see pages 209, 210 and 213.

77
98

60
80

99

For full street detail of the highlighted area see pages 211, 212, 214 and 215.

A7
1 TEMPLE VIEW RD
2 GLENSDALE MOUNT
3 GLENSDALE ST
4 CHARLTON MOUNT
5 CHARLTON GR
6 CHARLTON ST
7 EAST PARK MOUNT
8 EAST PARK TERR
9 GARTON VIEW
10 BACK EAST PARK RD
11 RAINCLIFFE MOUNT
12 RAINCLIFFE TERR
13 ECCLESBURN TERR

79

A8
1 APPLETON WAY
2 BACK GLENTHORPE TERR
3 VINERY GR
4 VINERY ST
5 BACK ST ELMO GR
6 ST ELMO GR

61

7 CROSS IVY MOUNT
8 IVY VIEW
9 BACK IVY MOUNT
10 IVY CRES
11 BACK IVY AVE
12 BACK IVY ST
13 RAINCLIFFE ST

B8
1 DAWLISH PL
2 BACK DAWLISH MOUNT
3 BACK DAWLISH AVE
4 BACK DAWLISH RD
5 BACK VICTORIA GR
6 BACK VICTORIA AVE
7 CROSS DAWLISH GR
8 HEPTON CT

E8
1 BACK WILLIAM AVE
2 WILLIAM AVE
3 VERITY VIEW

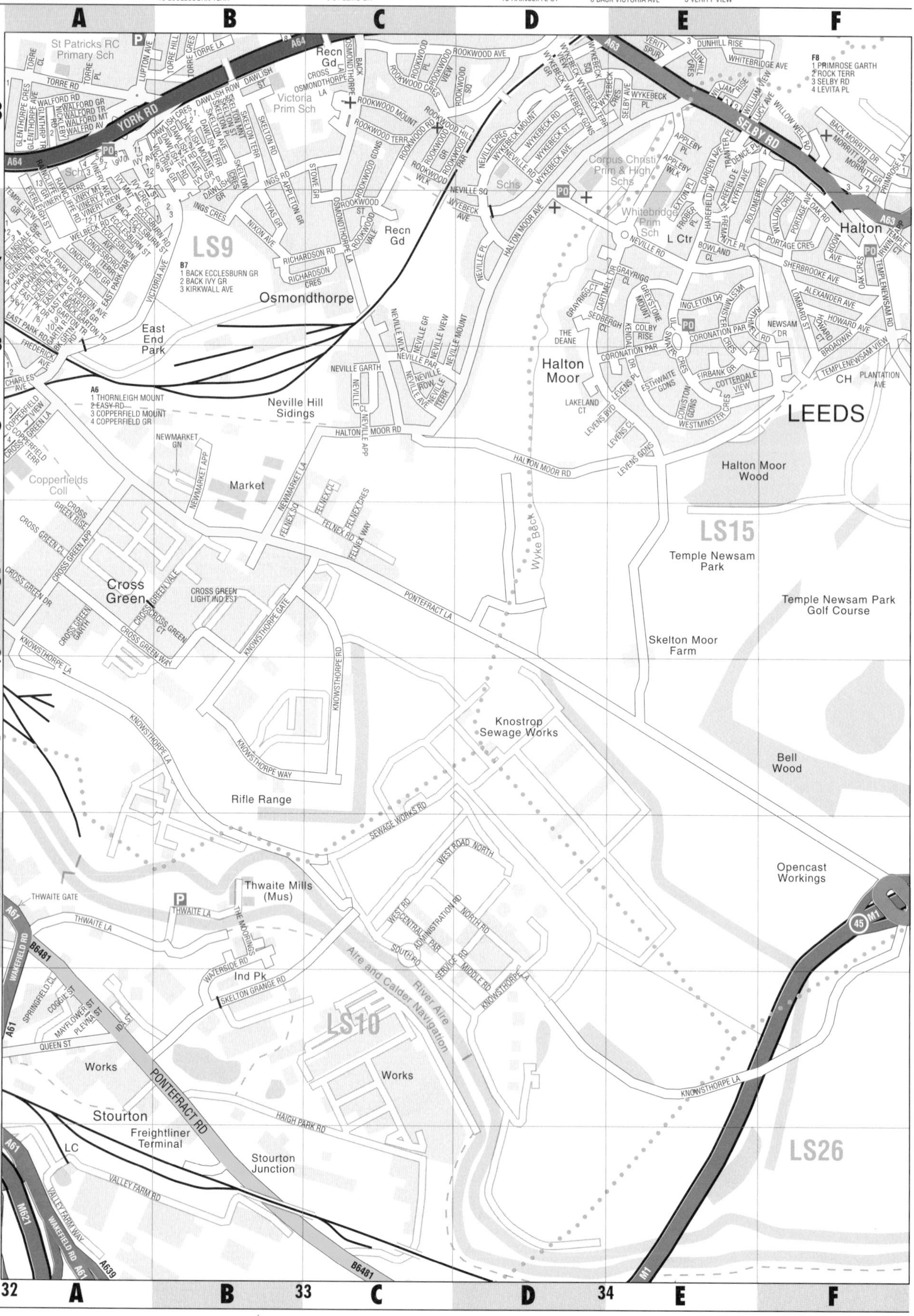

79
100

A8
1 PRIMROSE CRES
2 PRIMROSE AVE
3 BARLEY FIELD CT
4 OVERDALE TERR
5 BACK OVERDALE TERR
6 BACK GRAVELEY ST
7 CROSS PARK ST
8 PARK VIEW TERR
9 WHEATON CT

B8
1 GREEN LA
2 WILFRED ST
3 CHARLOTTE GR
4 PROSPECT GDNS
5 TEMPLESTOWE GDNS
6 TEMPLESTOWE HILL

C8
1 GRAVELEYTHORPE RD
2 CARTER AVE
3 TEMPLESTOWE DR
4 HOLLYSHAW TERR
5 BACK HOLLYSHAW TERR
6 CARTER LA

62
82

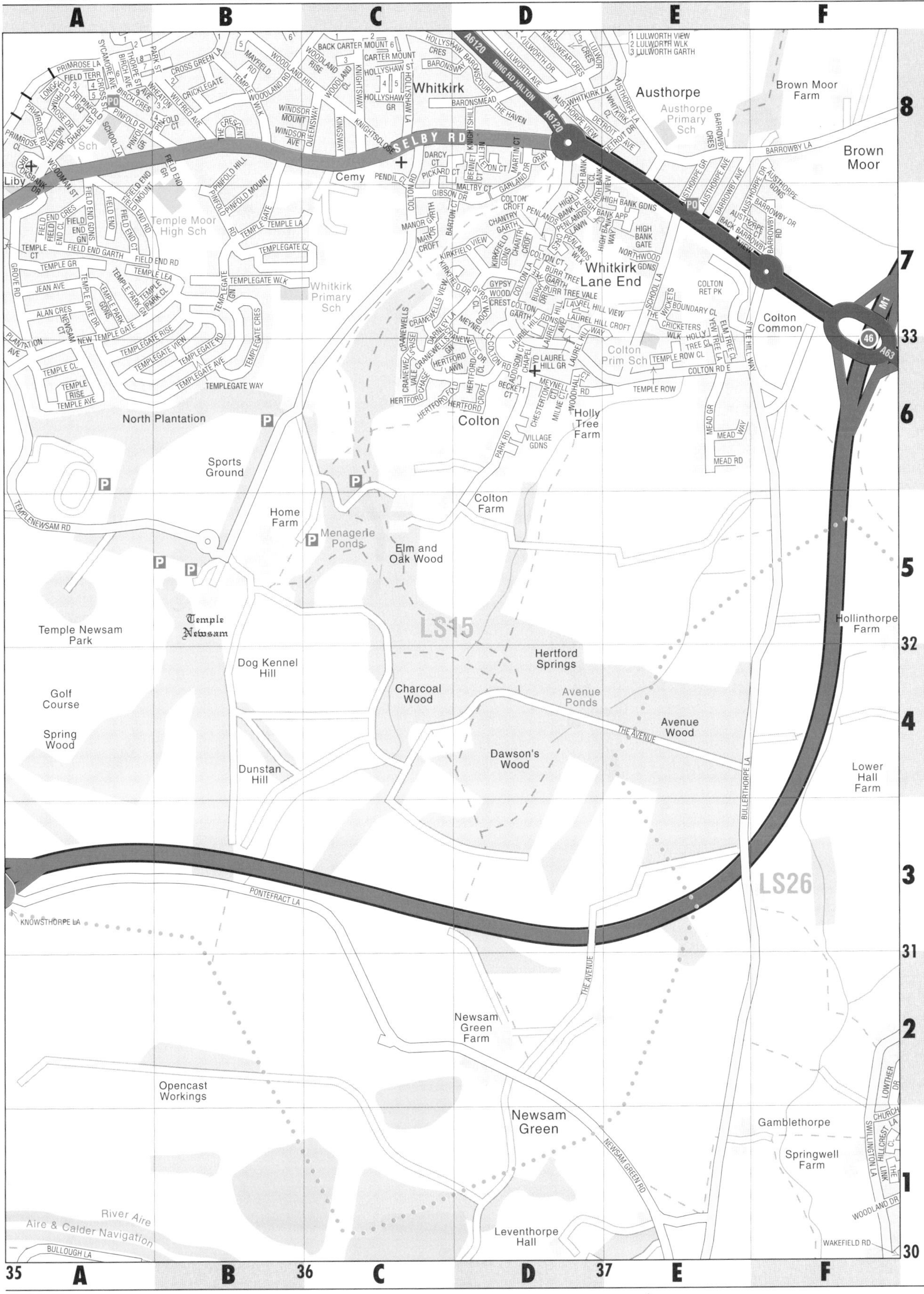

101
82

81
63

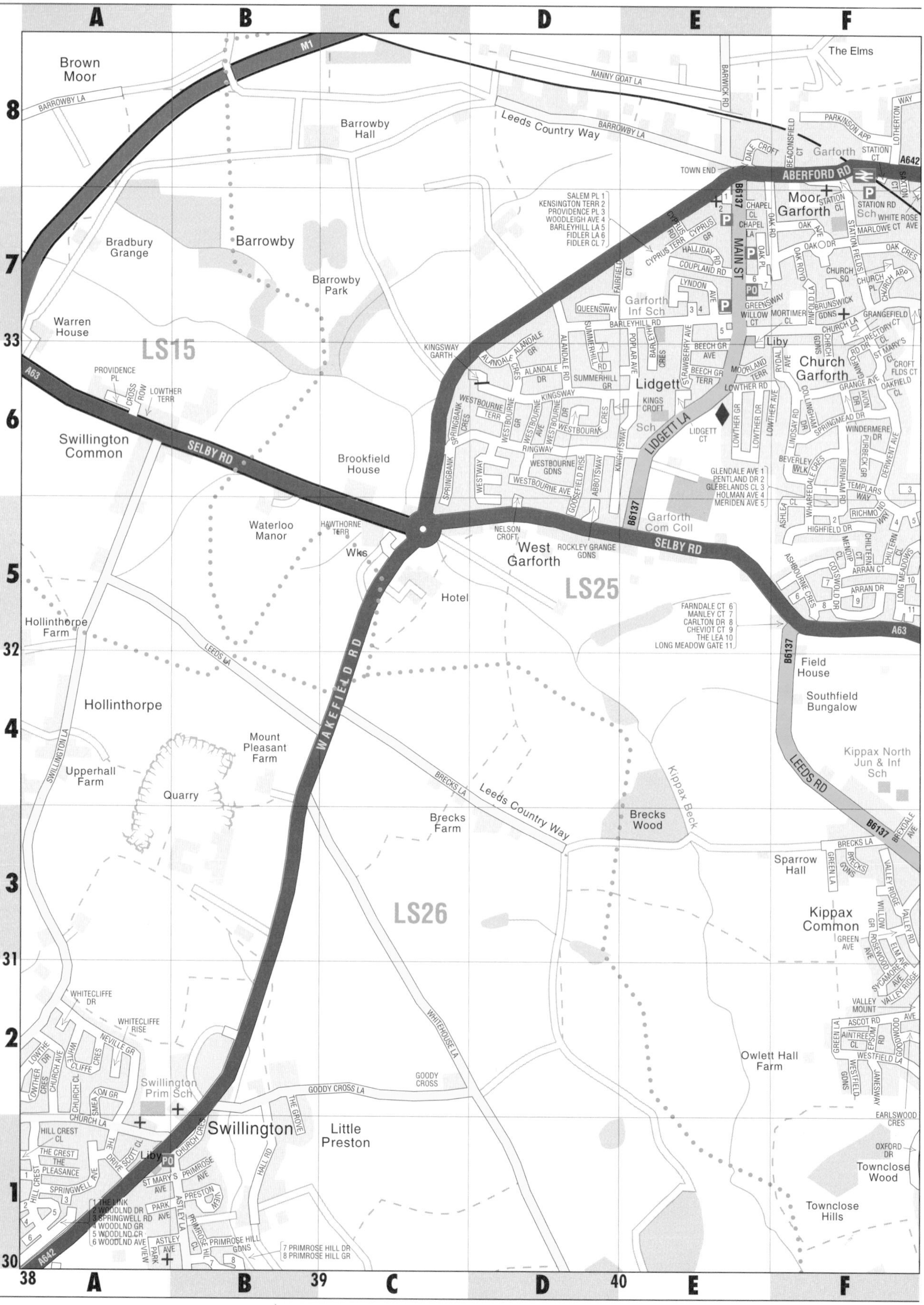
A
B
C
D
E
F
8
7
33
6
5
32
4
3
31
2
1
30
38
39
40
Brown Moor
BARROWBY LA
M1
NANNY GOAT LA
BARWICK RD
The Elms
Barrowby Hall
Leeds Country Way
BARROWBY LA
PARKINSON APP
LOTHERTON WAY
Garforth
STATION CT
A642
TOWN END
ABERFORD RD
Moor Garforth
STATION RD
WHITE ROSE AVE
MARLOWE CT
Bradbury Grange
Barrowby
Barrowby Park
SALEM PL 1
KENSINGTON TERR 2
PROVIDENCE PL 3
WOODLEIGH AVE 4
BARLEYHILL LA 5
FIDLER LA 6
FIDLER CL 7
CYPRUS TERR
CHAPEL CL
MAIN ST
B6137
Garforth Inf Sch
QUEENSWAY
BARLEYHILL RD
Warren House
LS15
KINGSWAY GARTH
ALANDALE DR
SUMMERHILL GR
Lidgett
Church Garforth
Liby
GRANGEFIELD CT
A63
PROVIDENCE PL
CROSS ROW
LOWTHER TERR
WESTBOURNE TERR
KINGSWAY
KINGS CROFT
Sch
LIDGETT LA
LIDGETT CT
LOWTHER RD
Swillington Common
SELBY RD
RINGWAY
WESTBOURNE GDNS
WESTBOURNE AVE
Brookfield House
GLENDALE AVE 1
PENTLAND DR 2
GLEBELANDS CL 3
HOLMAN AVE 4
MERIDEN AVE 5
WINDERMERE DR
TEMPLARS WAY
RICHMOND WAY
HIGHFIELD DR
Waterloo Manor
HAWTHORNE TERR
Wks
NELSON CROFT
West Garforth
ROCKLEY GRANGE GDNS
Garforth Com Coll
SELBY RD
Hotel
LS25
ARRAN CT
ARRAN DR
FARNDALE CT 6
MANLEY CT 7
CARLTON DR 8
CHEVIOT CT 9
THE LEA 10
LONG MEADOW GATE 11
Hollinthorpe Farm
LEEDS LA
WAKEFIELD RD
Field House
Southfield Bungalow
Hollinthorpe
Mount Pleasant Farm
SWILLINGTON LA
Upperhall Farm
Quarry
Kippax Beck
Kippax North Jun & Inf Sch
LEEDS RD
BRECKS LA
Leeds Country Way
Brecks Farm
Brecks Wood
BREXDALE AVE
BRECKS LA
Sparrow Hall
LS26
Kippax Common
VALLEY RIDGE
VALLEY MOUNT
ASCOT RD
AINTREE CL
WESTFIELD LA
WHITECLIFFE DR
WHITECLIFFE RISE
WHITEHOUSE LA
Owlett Hall Farm
Swillington Prim Sch
GOODY CROSS
GOODY CROSS LA
CHURCH LA
HILL CREST CL
THE CREST
Swillington
Little Preston
HALL RD
EARLSWOOD CRES
OXFORD DR
Townclose Wood
1 THE LINK
2 WOODLND DR
3 SPRINGWELL RD
4 WOODLND GR
5 WOODLND CR
6 WOODLND AVE
ST MARY'S AVE
PRIMROSE AVE
PRESTON VIEW
ASTLEY AVE
PRIMROSE HILL GDNS
7 PRIMROSE HILL DR
8 PRIMROSE HILL GR
Townclose Hills
A642

81
102

64
84

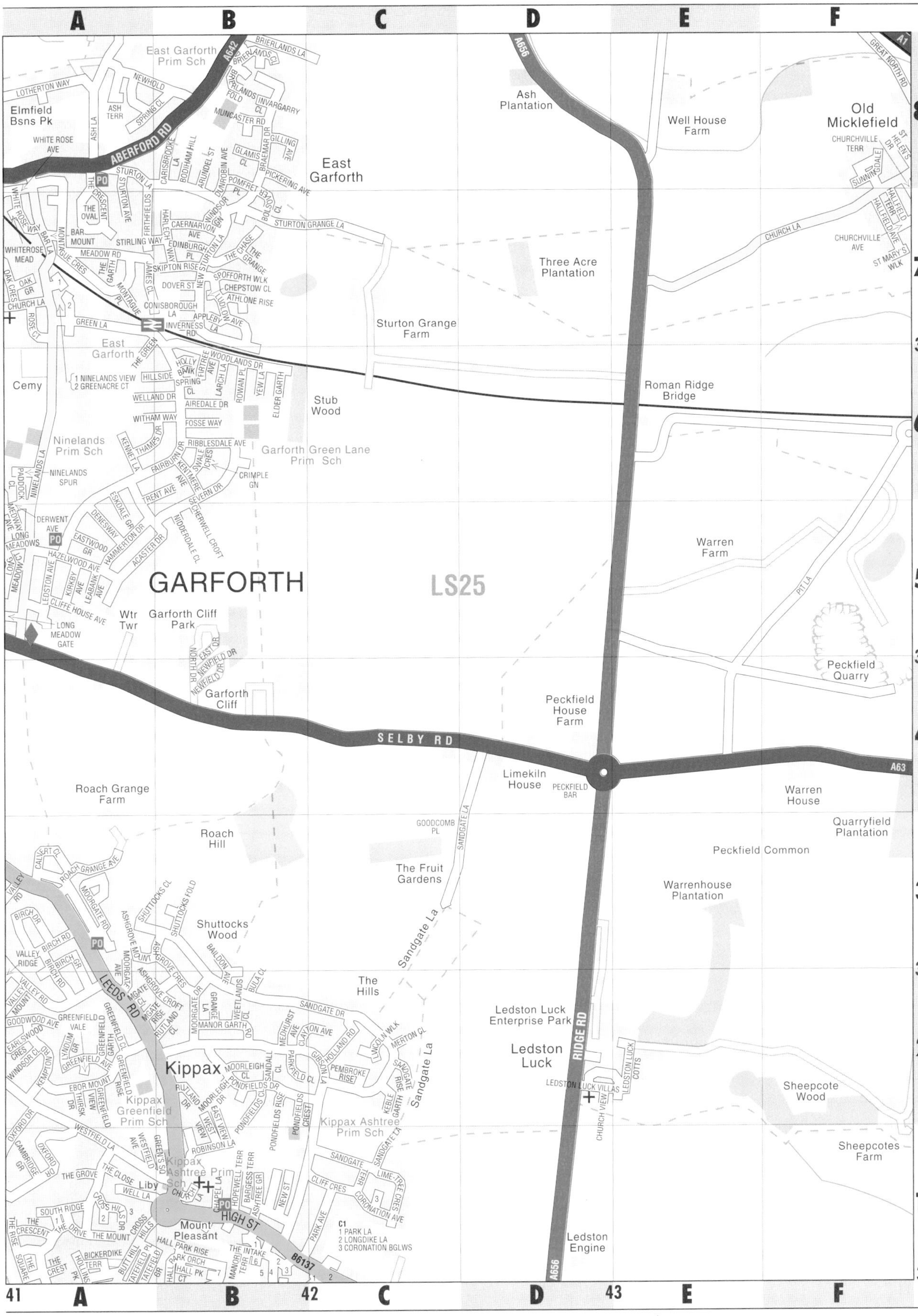

A1
1 THE GREEN
2 CROSS HILLS GDNS
3 CROSS HILLS CT

B1
1 ROGER FOLD
2 MALT KILN LA
3 LONGDIKE CT
4 MOUNT PLEASANT
5 MOUNT PLEASANT GDNS
6 PARK VIEW
7 HALL PARK CROFT

103
84

83
65

A
B
C
D
E
F
A1
LAITH STAID LA
Huddleston Hall
Old Micklefield
CHURCH CL
CHURCH LA
ST HELEN'S DR
Grange Farm
CHURCHVILLE
CHURCHVILLE DR
PO
Hartly Wood Cottages
Hartly Wood
Huddleston Old Wood
Manor House Farm
1 CHURCHVILLE AVE
2 CHURCHVILLE TERR
3 ST MARY'S WLK
Micklefield CE Prim Sch
Sheep Dike
Sewage Works
Micklefield
PIT LA
P
GREAT NORTH RD
GARDEN VILLAGE
Newthorpe Farm
RAILWAY COTTS
Micklefield
PIT LA
PROSPECT TERR 1
CLIFF TERR 2
WEST VIEW 3
SUNNYBANK
THE CRESCENT
EAST VIEW
Brookfield House
Newthorpe Barrack
Highroyds Wood
New Micklefield
Newton Farm
Newthorpe Beck
Newthorpe Grange
Woodlands
Newthorpe Quarry
HALL LA
Peckfield Quarry
Castle Hills
Highfield
LC
The New Inn (PH)
LS25
HIGHFIELD LA
B1222
Micklefield Plantation
Peckfield Plantation
WHITECOTE LA
A63
SELBY RD
A63
Quarryfield Plantation
The Boot and Shoe (PH)
Beacon Plantation
Whitecote Plantation
Pointer Farm
South Milford
B1222
Wellington Plantation
Ledston Lodge
Peckfield Lodge
WESTFIELD LA
Ledston Park
NEW RD
Hundred Acre Plantation
Scat House Farm
Long Plantation
Sheepcote Farm
Old Vicarage
Selby Fork Hotel
Dale Plantation
PARK LA
WF10
A1
8
7
33
6
5
32
4
3
31
2
1
30
44
45
46

83
104

86

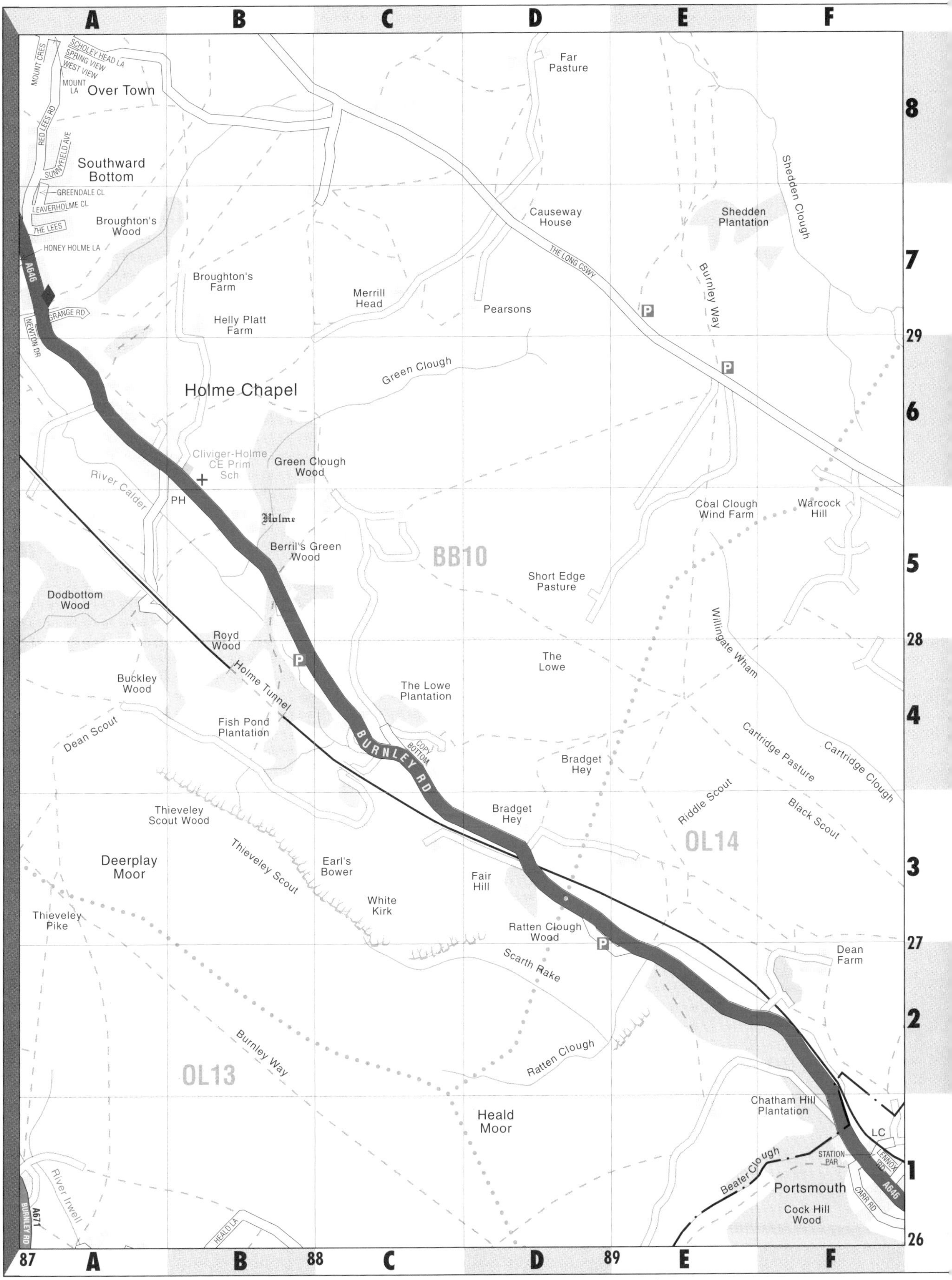
A
B
C
D
E
F
8
7
29
6
5
28
4
3
27
2
1
26
87
88
89
SCHOLEY HEAD LA
SPRING VIEW
WEST VIEW
MOUNT CRES
MOUNT LA
Over Town
RED LEES RD
SUNNYFIELD AVE
Southward Bottom
GREENDALE CL
LEAVERHOLME CL
THE LEES
Broughton's Wood
HONEY HOLME LA
A646
GRANGE RD
NEWTON DR
Broughton's Farm
Helly Platt Farm
Far Pasture
Causeway House
THE LONG CSWY
Shedden Plantation
Shedden Clough
Burnley Way
Merrill Head
Pearsons
Green Clough
Holme Chapel
Cliviger-Holme CE Prim Sch
Green Clough Wood
River Calder
PH
Holme
Berril's Green Wood
BB10
Coal Clough Wind Farm
Warcock Hill
Short Edge Pasture
Dodbottom Wood
Royd Wood
Holme Tunnel
Buckley Wood
The Lowe
The Lowe Plantation
Willingate Wham
Fish Pond Plantation
Dean Scout
BURNLEY RD
COPY BOTTOM
Bradget Hey
Cartridge Pasture
Cartridge Clough
Riddle Scout
Black Scout
Thieveley Scout Wood
Deerplay Moor
Thieveley Scout
Earl's Bower
OL14
Fair Hill
White Kirk
Thieveley Pike
Ratten Clough Wood
Scarth Rake
Dean Farm
Burnley Way
OL13
Ratten Clough
Heald Moor
Chatham Hill Plantation
LC
STATION PAR
LENNOX RD
Beater Clough
Portsmouth
CARR RD
Cock Hill Wood
River Irwell
A671
BURNLEY RD
HEALD LA

106

86

85
66

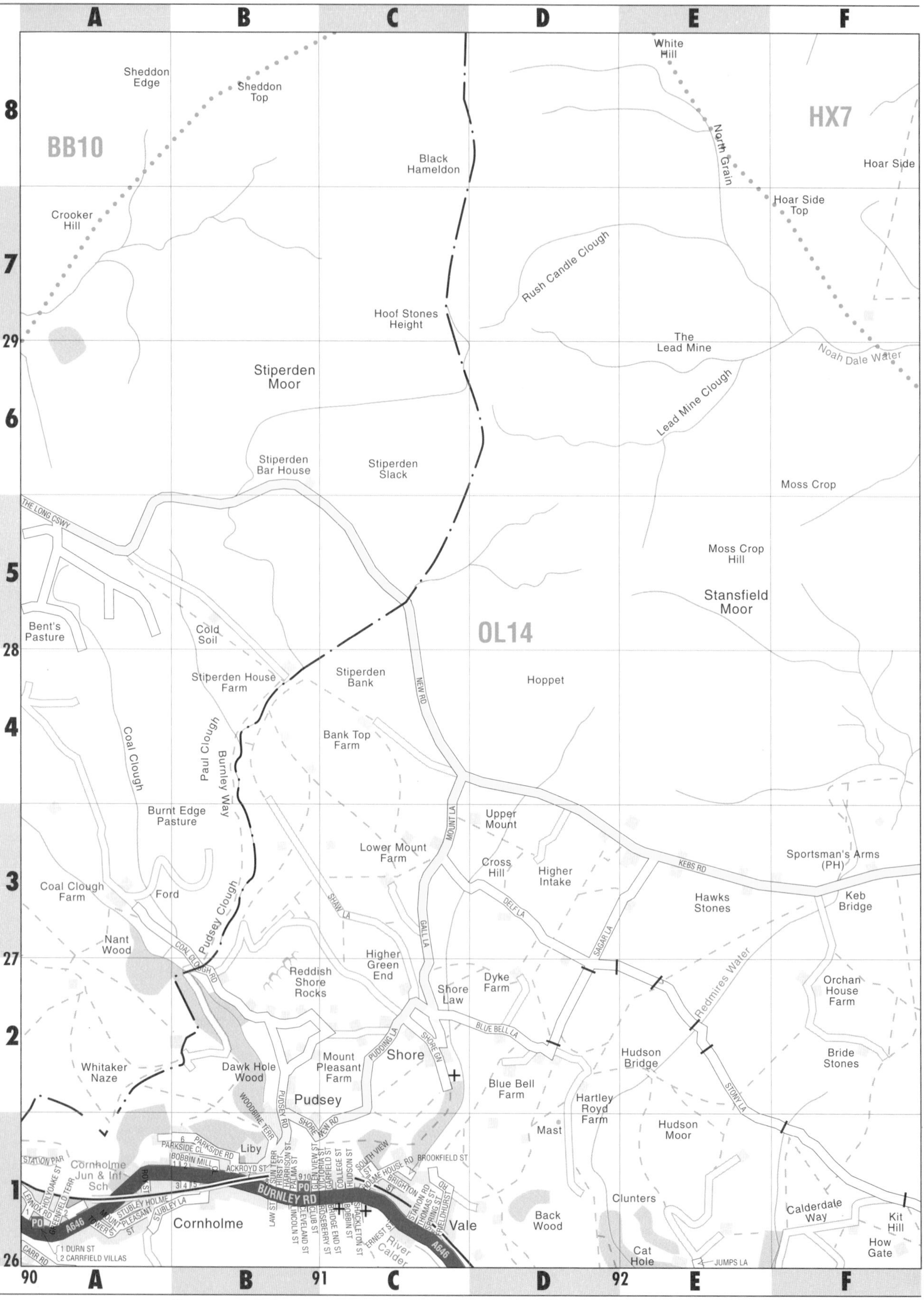
A
B
C
D
E
F
8
7
29
6
5
28
4
3
27
2
1
26
90
91
92
BB10
HX7
OL14
Sheddon Edge
Sheddon Top
Crooker Hill
Black Hameldon
White Hill
North Grain
Hoar Side
Hoar Side Top
Rush Candle Clough
Hoof Stones Height
The Lead Mine
Noah Dale Water
Stiperden Moor
Lead Mine Clough
Stiperden Bar House
Stiperden Slack
Moss Crop
THE LONG CSWY
Moss Crop Hill
Stansfield Moor
Bent's Pasture
Cold Soil
Stiperden House Farm
Stiperden Bank
NEW RD
Hoppet
Coal Clough
Paul Clough
Burnley Way
Bank Top Farm
Burnt Edge Pasture
Upper Mount
MOUNT LA
Lower Mount Farm
Cross Hill
Higher Intake
KEBS RD
Sportsman's Arms (PH)
Coal Clough Farm
Ford
Pudsey Clough
SHAW LA
DELF LA
Hawks Stones
Keb Bridge
GALL LA
SAGAR LA
Nant Wood
COAL CLOUGH RD
Higher Green End
Reddish Shore Rocks
Shore Law
Dyke Farm
Redmires Water
Orchan House Farm
BLUE BELL LA
PUDDING LA
SHORE GN
Whitaker Naze
Dawk Hole Wood
Mount Pleasant Farm
Shore
Hudson Bridge
Bride Stones
Blue Bell Farm
Pudsey
Hartley Royd Farm
WOODBINE TERR
PUDSEY RD
SHORE NEW RD
STONY LA
Mast
Hudson Moor
Liby
PARKSIDE CL
PARKSIDE RD
BOBBIN MILL CL
ACKROYD ST
STATION PAR
Cornholme Jun & Inf Sch
BROOKFIELD ST
BURNLEY RD
PO
A646
Clunters
Calderdale Way
Kit Hill
Cornholme
Vale
Back Wood
River Calder
Cat Hole
JUMPS LA
How Gate
1 DURN ST
2 CARRFIELD VILLAS
CARR RD

B1
1 BROWN BIRKS ST
2 DAISY BANK ST
3 PEAR PL
4 PEAR ST
5 SPRING VILLAS
6 STANSFIELD TERR
7 CORNHOLME TERR
8 OAKLEIGH TERR
9 SUNNY BANK TERR
10 GLADSTONE ST

85
107

67
88

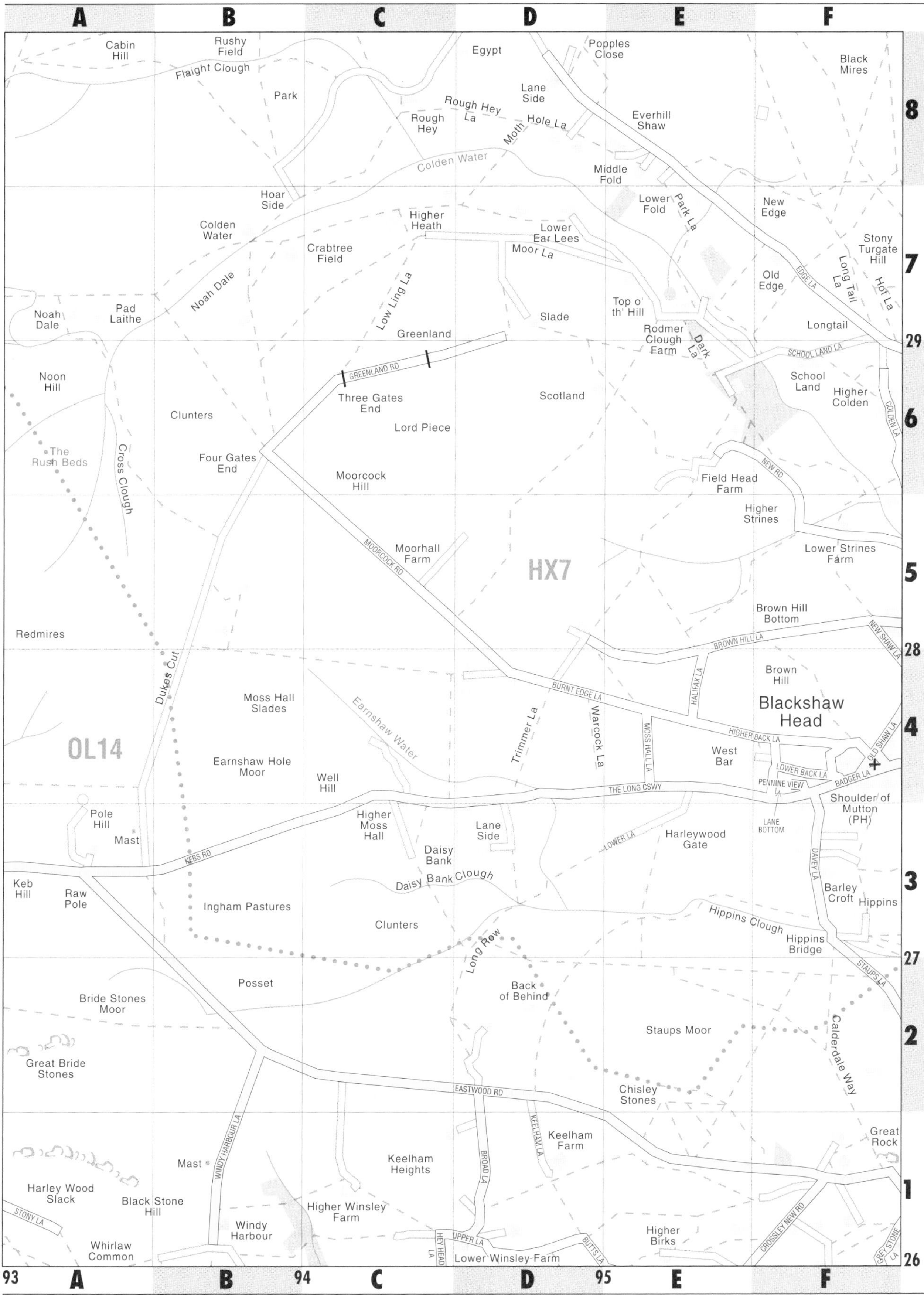
A
B
C
D
E
F
Cabin Hill
Rushy Field
Flaight Clough
Park
Egypt
Popples Close
Black Mires
Lane Side
Rough Hey La
Rough Hey
Moth Hole La
Everhill Shaw
Colden Water
Middle Fold
Hoar Side
Lower Fold
Park La
New Edge
Colden Water
Higher Heath
Lower Ear Lees
Crabtree Field
Moor La
Stony Turgate Hill
Noah Dale
Long Tail La
Hof La
Old Edge
Edge La
Noah Dale
Pad Laithe
Low Ling La
Slade
Top o' th' Hill
Longtail
Greenland
Rodmer Clough Farm
Dark La
School Land La
Noon Hill
Greenland Rd
School Land
Higher Colden
Three Gates End
Scotland
Colden La
Clunters
Lord Piece
The Rush Beds
Cross Clough
Four Gates End
Moorcock Hill
New Rd
Field Head Farm
Higher Strines
Moorcock Rd
Moorhall Farm
HX7
Lower Strines Farm
Brown Hill Bottom
Redmires
New Shaw La
Brown Hill La
Dukes Cut
Brown Hill
Burnt Edge La
Halifax La
Moss Hall Slades
Earnshaw Water
Trimmer La
Warcock La
Blackshaw Head
OL14
Moss Hall La
Higher Back La
Old Shaw La
Earnshaw Hole Moor
West Bar
Well Hill
Lower Back La
Pennine View
Badger La
The Long Cswy
Pole Hill
Higher Moss Hall
Shoulder of Mutton (PH)
Lane Side
Lane Bottom
Mast
Harleywood Gate
Lower La
Kebs Rd
Daisy Bank
Davey La
Keb Hill
Raw Pole
Daisy Bank Clough
Barley Croft
Hippins
Ingham Pastures
Hippins Clough
Clunters
Hippins Bridge
Long Row
Posset
Staups La
Back of Behind
Bride Stones Moor
Calderdale Way
Staups Moor
Great Bride Stones
Chisley Stones
Eastwood Rd
Great Rock
Keelham La
Keelham Farm
Windy Harbour La
Broad La
Mast
Keelham Heights
Harley Wood Slack
Black Stone Hill
Higher Winsley Farm
Stony La
Windy Harbour
Higher Birks
Crossley New Rd
Whirlaw Common
Hey Head La
Upper La
Butts La
Lower Winsley Farm
Grey Stone La
8
7
29
6
5
28
4
3
27
2
1
26
93
94
95

108
88

87
68

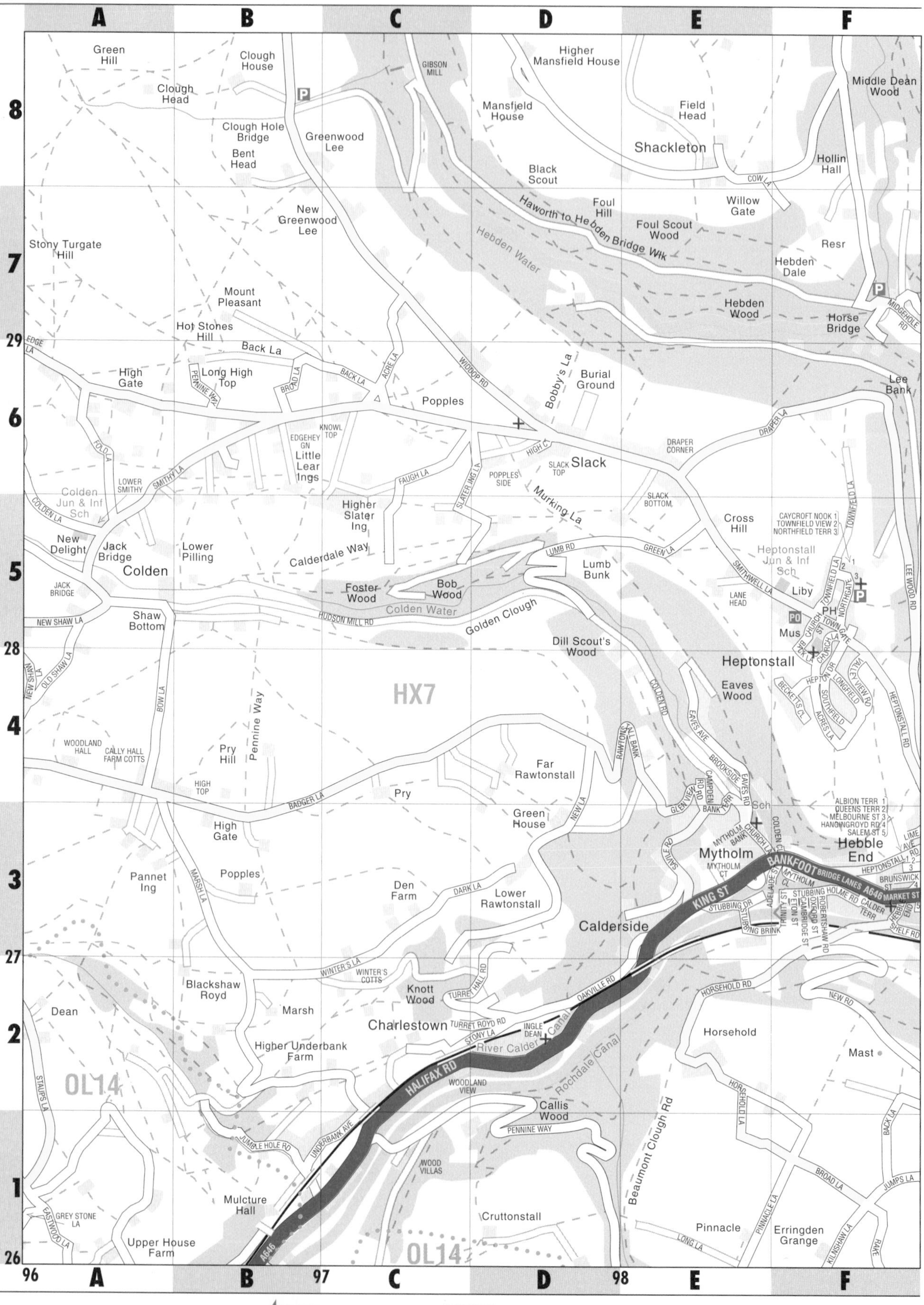
A
B
C
D
E
F
8
7
29
6
5
28
4
3
27
2
1
26
96
97
98
Green Hill
Clough House
Clough Head
Gibson Mill
Higher Mansfield House
Middle Dean Wood
Mansfield House
Field Head
Clough Hole Bridge
Greenwood Lee
Shackleton
Bent Head
Black Scout
Hollin Hall
Cow La
Foul Hill
Willow Gate
Haworth to Hebden Bridge Wlk
Foul Scout Wood
New Greenwood Lee
Hebden Water
Stony Turgate Hill
Resr
Hebden Dale
Mount Pleasant
Hebden Wood
Midgehole Rd
Horse Bridge
Hot Stones Hill
Edge La
Back La
High Gate
Long High Top
Pennine Way
Broad La
Acre La
Widdop Rd
Bobby's La
Burial Ground
Lee Bank
Popples
Knowl Top
Edgehey Gn
Little Lear Ings
Fold La
Smithy La
High Cl
Slack Top
Slack
Draper Corner
Draper La
Lower Smithy
Faugh La
Slater Ing La
Popples Side
Colden Jun & Inf Sch
Colden La
Higher Slater Ing
Murking La
Slack Bottom
Cross Hill
Caycroft Nook 1
Townfield View 2
Northfield Terr 3
Townfield La
New Delight
Jack Bridge
Lower Pilling
Lumb Rd
Green La
Heptonstall Jun & Inf Sch
Calderdale Way
Lumb Bunk
Colden
Jack Bridge
Foster Wood
Bob Wood
Smithwell La
Liby
Lane Head
Northgate
Lee Wood Rd
Colden Water
PH
New Shaw La
Shaw Bottom
Hudson Mill Rd
Golden Clough
Mus
Town Gate
Church La
Dill Scout's Wood
Old Shaw La
New Shaw
Heptonstall
Eaves Wood
HX7
Hepton Dr
Longfield
Valley View Rd
Becketts Cl
Southfield
Acres La
Colden Rd
Eaves Ave
Bow La
Heptonstall Rd
Rawtonstall Bank
Woodland Hall
Cally Hall Farm Cotts
Pry Hill
Far Rawtonstall
Brookside
Eaves Rd
High Top
Badger La
Pry
Glen View Rd
Camden Bank Terr
Sch
Green House
New La
Albion Terr 1
Queens Terr 2
Melbourne St 3
Hangingroyd Rd 4
Salem St 5
High Gate
Mytholm Bank
Mytholm
Saville Rd
Hebble End
Bankfoot
Bridge Lanes
A646
Market St
Heptonstall Rd
Pannet Ing
Marsh La
Popples
Mytholm Ct
Mytholm Cl
Brunswick St
Den Farm
Dark La
Lower Rawtonstall
King St
Stubbing Dr
Adelaide St
Trinity St
Stubbing Holme Rd
Oxford St
Robertshaw Rd
Eton St
Cambridge St
Calder Terr
Shelf Rd
Calderside
Stubbing Brink
Winter's La
Winter's Cotts
Turret Hall Rd
Blackshaw Royd
Knott Wood
Turret Royd Rd
Horsehold Rd
New Rd
Oakville Rd
Dean
Marsh
Charlestown
Ingle Dean
Canal
Stony La
River Calder
Horsehold
Mast
Higher Underbank Farm
Rochdale Canal
Halifax Rd
OL14
Staups La
Woodland View
Callis Wood
Horsehold La
Pennine Way
Back La
Beaumont Clough Rd
Jumble Hole Rd
Underbank Ave
Wood Villas
Broad La
Jumps La
Mulcture Hall
Grey Stone La
Eastwood La
Cruttonstall
Pinnacle La
Pinnacle
Erringden Grange
Long La
Kilnshaw La
Rake
Upper House Farm
OL14

87
109

69
90

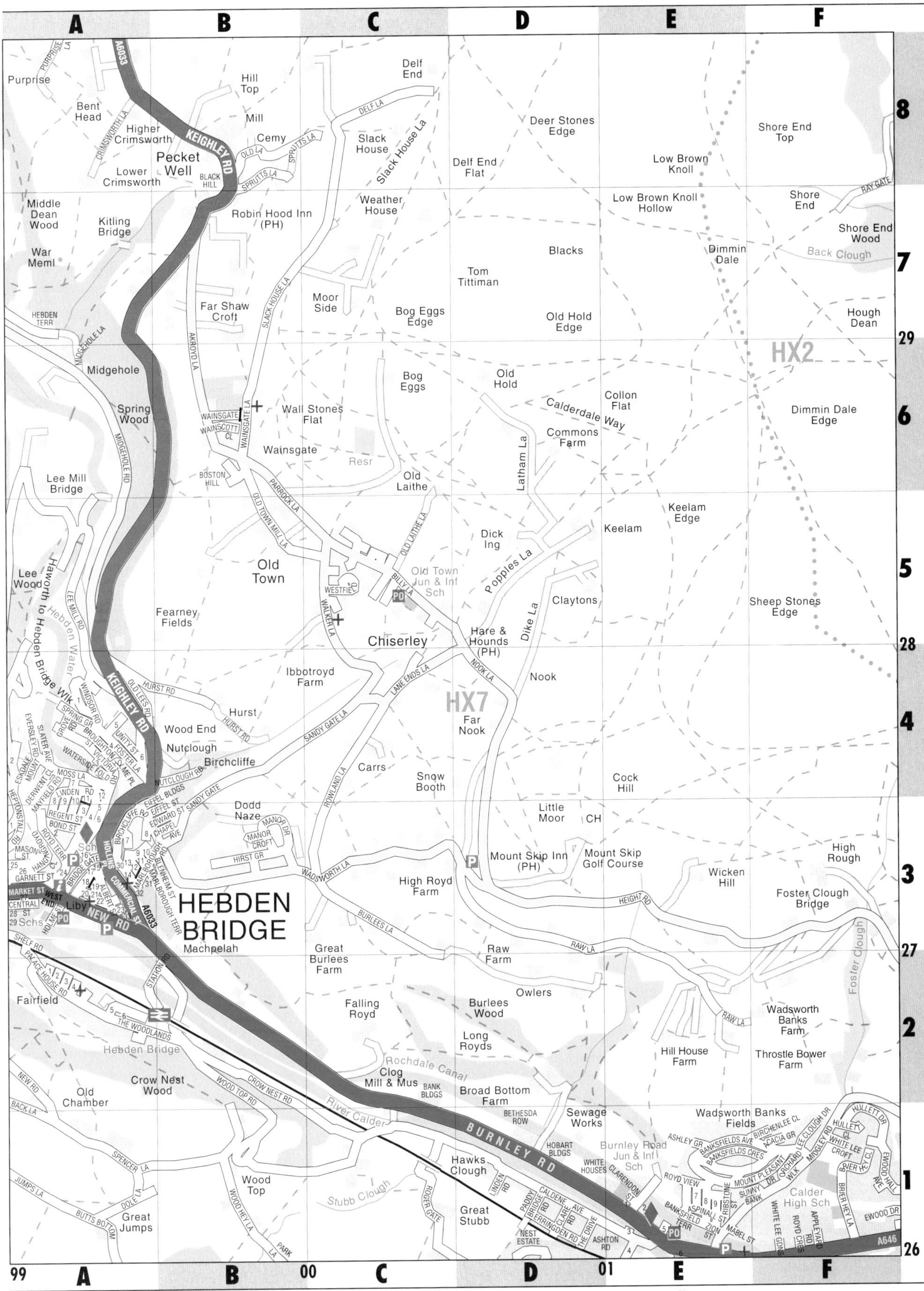

A2
1 ESSEX ST
2 YORK ST
3 NORFOLK ST
4 GUILDFORD ST
5 NEALE ST
6 MITCHELL ST

A3
1 LIME AVE
2 ROYD SQ
3 CLEVELAND PL
4 HANGINGROYD LA
5 GREENWOOD ST
6 VALLEY RD
7 ST JOHN'S CL
8 ALEXANDRA RD
9 CLIFFE ST
10 STEPHEN ST
11 GARDEN TERR
12 BALMORAL ST
13 SCHOOL ST
14 OSBORNE ST
15 LEES YD
16 ST GEORGE'S ST
17 ST GEORGE'S SQ
18 CROWN ST
19 CARLTON ST
20 CHEETHAM ST
21 HOPE ST
22 CROFT ST
23 TANPITS
24 OLD GATE
25 MELBOURNE ST
26 HANGINGROYD RD
27 HILTON ST
28 FIELDING ST
29 FOUNTAIN ST
30 HOLLINS CRES
31 MARLBOROUGH GR
32 OSBORNE PL
33 CROSSLEY TERR

A4
1 WINDSOR VIEW
2 LEE WOOD RD
3 BROOK ST
4 PALESTINE RD
5 HIGHFIELD CRES
6 LEES RD
7 ROSE GR
8 REGENT PL

A4
9 OAK ST
10 SACKVILLE ST
11 LINDEN PL
12 BAKER'S ST

E1
1 ACRE VILLAS
2 WESTFIELD TERR
3 CALDER GR
4 THRUSH HILL RD
5 WEST END TERR
6 NEW RD
7 ALBERT ST
8 BANKSFIELD RD
9 JUBILEE ST

89
70

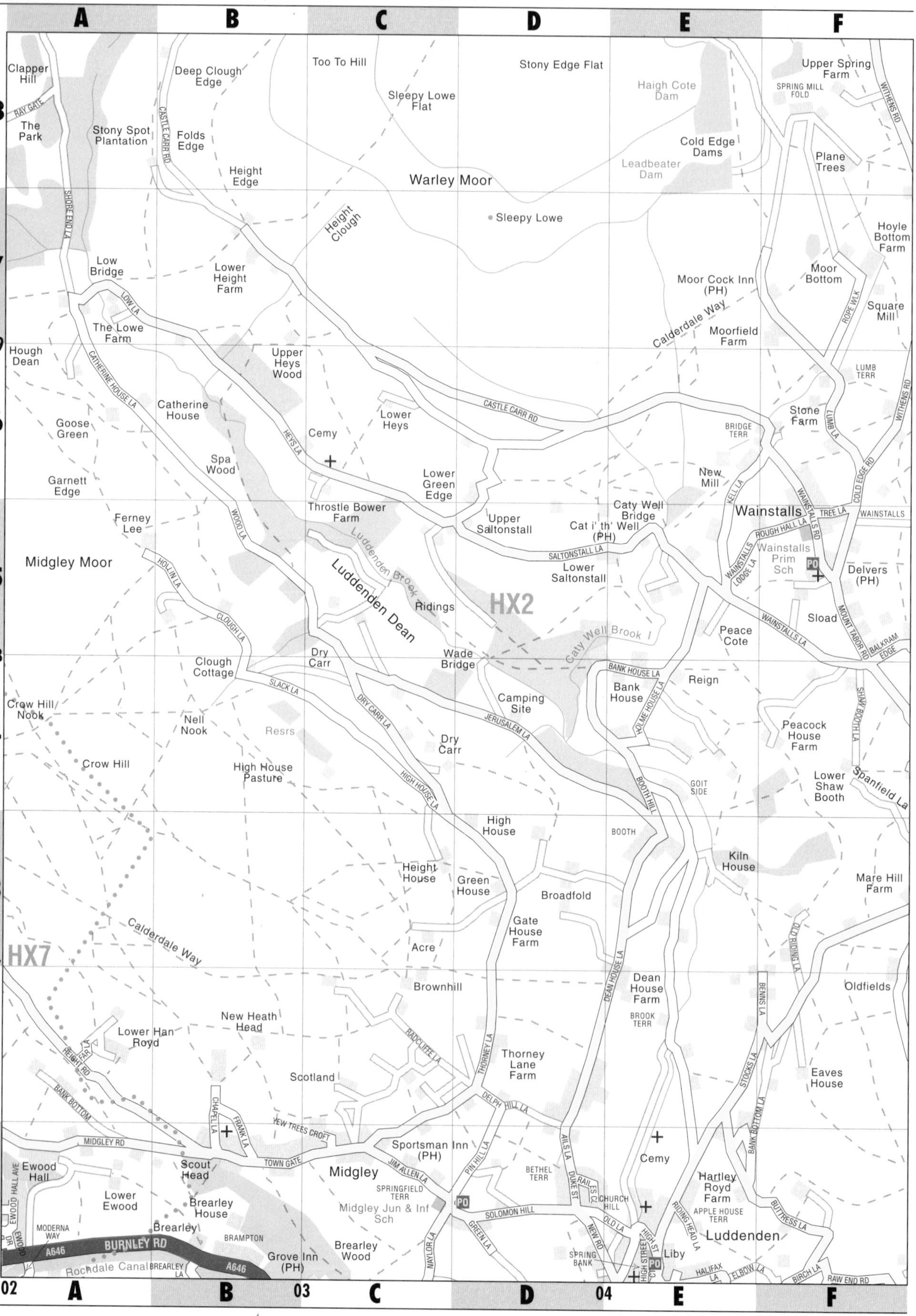
A
B
C
D
E
F
Clapper Hill
Deep Clough Edge
Too To Hill
Sleepy Lowe Flat
Stony Edge Flat
Haigh Cote Dam
Upper Spring Farm
SPRING MILL FOLD
WITHENS RD
RAY GATE
The Park
Stony Spot Plantation
CASTLE CARR RD
Folds Edge
Height Edge
Cold Edge Dams
Leadbeater Dam
Plane Trees
Warley Moor
SHORE END LA
Sleepy Lowe
Height Clough
Hoyle Bottom Farm
Low Bridge
Lower Height Farm
Moor Cock Inn (PH)
Moor Bottom
Calderdale Way
Square Mill
ROPE WLK
LOW LA
The Lowe Farm
Moorfield Farm
Hough Dean
Upper Heys Wood
LUMB TERR
CATHERINE HOUSE LA
Catherine House
Goose Green
Lower Heys
CASTLE CARR RD
Stone Farm
WITHENS RD
BRIDGE TERR
HEYS LA
Cemy
LUMB LA
Garnett Edge
Spa Wood
Lower Green Edge
New Mill
COLD EDGE RD
Throstle Bower Farm
Caty Well Bridge
KELL LA
Wainstalls
WAINSTALLS RD
TREE LA
WAINSTALLS
Ferney Lee
WOOD LA
Upper Saltonstall
Cat i' th' Well (PH)
ROUGH HALL LA
Luddenden Brook
SALTONSTALL LA
Wainstalls Prim Sch
Midgley Moor
HOLLIN LA
Luddenden Dean
Lower Saltonstall
WAINSTALLS LA
LODGE LA
PO
Delvers (PH)
HX2
Ridings
Sload
CLOUGH LA
Caty Well Brook
Peace Cote
MOUNT TABOR RD
BALKRAM EDGE
Dry Carr
Wade Bridge
Clough Cottage
BANK HOUSE LA
Reign
SLACK LA
Bank House
Crow Hill Nook
Camping Site
HOLME HOUSE LA
DRY CARR LA
SHAW BOOTH LA
Nell Nook
JERUSALEM LA
Peacock House Farm
Resrs
Dry Carr
Crow Hill
High House Pasture
Lower Shaw Booth
GOIT SIDE
Spanfield La
HIGH HOUSE LA
BOOTH HILL
High House
BOOTH
Kiln House
Height House
Green House
Broadfold
Mare Hill Farm
Gate House Farm
Calderdale Way
OLD RIDING LA
Acre
HX7
DEAN HOUSE LA
Dean House Farm
Oldfields
Brownhill
BENNS LA
New Heath Head
BROOK TERR
Lower Han Royd
RADCLIFFE LA
HEIGHT RD
THORNEY LA
Thorney Lane Farm
Scotland
STOCKS LA
Eaves House
BANK BOTTOM
DELPH HILL LA
CHAPEL LA
FRANK LA
YEW TREES CROFT
BANK BOTTOM LA
MIDGLEY RD
Cemy
Sportsman Inn (PH)
Ewood Hall
TOWN GATE
Scout Head
Midgley
JIM ALLEN LA
PIN HILL LA
BETHEL TERR
AILS LA
DUKE ST
Hartley Royd Farm
EWOOD HALL AVE
Lower Ewood
SPRINGFIELD TERR
RAIL ES
CHURCH HILL
BUTTRESS LA
Brearley House
Midgley Jun & Inf Sch
PO
SOLOMON HILL
OLD LA
APPLE HOUSE TERR
MODERNA WAY
Brearley
GREEN LA
NEW RD
RIDING HEAD LA
Luddenden
EWOOD DR
BRAMPTON
NAYLOR LA
HIGH ST
A646
BURNLEY RD
Brearley Wood
SPRING BANK
HIGH STREET CT
Liby
Grove Inn (PH)
HALIFAX LA
ELBOW LA
BIRCH LA
Rochdale Canal
BREARLEY LA
A646
RAW END RD
8
7
29
6
5
28
4
3
27
2
1
26
02
03
04

89
111

71
92

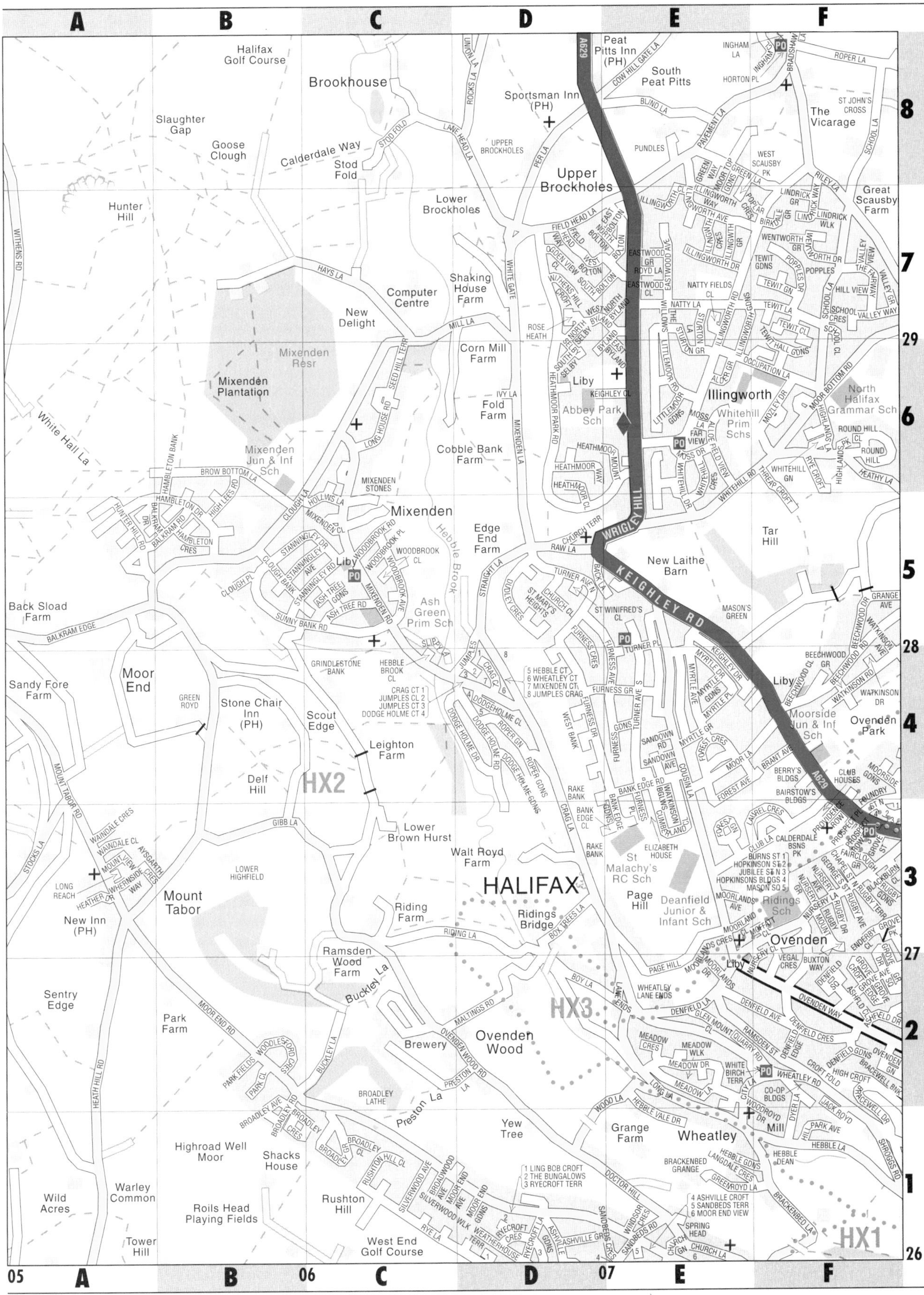
A
B
C
D
E
F
Halifax Golf Course
Brookhouse
Peat Pitts Inn (PH)
South Peat Pitts
Sportsman Inn (PH)
The Vicarage
Slaughter Gap
Goose Clough
Calderdale Way
Stod Fold
Upper Brockholes
Lower Brockholes
Hunter Hill
Great Scausby Farm
Computer Centre
New Delight
Shaking House Farm
Mixenden Resr
Mixenden Plantation
Corn Mill Farm
Liby
Illingworth
North Halifax Grammar Sch
Abbey Park Sch
Whitehill Prim Schs
Fold Farm
White Hall La
Mixenden Jun & Inf Sch
Cobble Bank Farm
Mixenden
Edge End Farm
Hebble Brook
Tar Hill
New Laithe Barn
WRIGLEY HILL
KEIGHLEY RD
Back Sload Farm
Ash Green Prim Sch
Moor End
Sandy Fore Farm
Stone Chair Inn (PH)
Scout Edge
Leighton Farm
Moorside Jun & Inf Sch
Ovenden Park
HX2
Delf Hill
Lower Brown Hurst
Walt Royd Farm
St Malachy's RC Sch
HALIFAX
Mount Tabor
New Inn (PH)
Page Hill
Deanfield Junior & Infant Sch
Ridings Sch
Ridings Bridge
Riding Farm
Ovenden
Ramsden Wood Farm
Sentry Edge
Park Farm
HX3
Ovenden Wood
Brewery
Yew Tree
Grange Farm
Wheatley
Mill
Highroad Well Moor
Shacks House
Warley Common
Wild Acres
Roils Head Playing Fields
Rushton Hill
Tower Hill
West End Golf Course
HX1
A629
8
7
29
6
5
28
4
3
27
2
1
26
05
06
07

112
92

91

C8
1 MOOR CLOSE FARM MEWS
2 CLARENDON PL
3 SUNNY VIEW TERR
4 MYRTLE GR
5 OXFORD RD

72

D8
1 CONISTON AVE
2 CONISTON CL
3 LEE ST
4 HAINSWORTH MOOR GARTH
5 HAINSWORTH MOOR CRES
6 HAINSWORTH MOOR DR

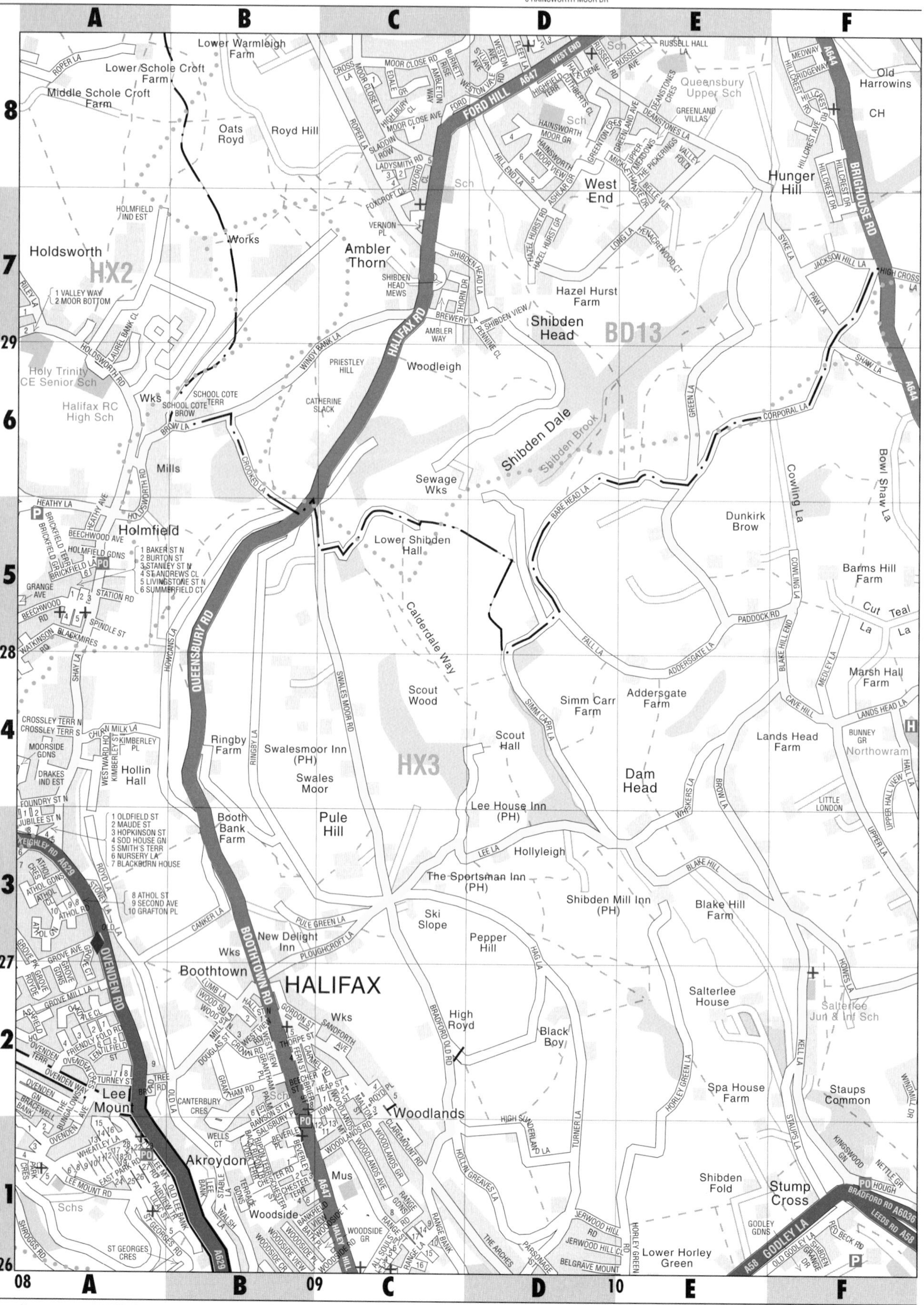

A1
1 BRACEWELL DR
2 BRACEWELL GR
3 WHEATLEY CL
4 WHEATLEY RD
5 LEE MOUNT GDNS
6 PEABODY ST
7 ELLISON ST
8 BUXTON ST
9 MATLOCK ST
10 GRANGE ST
11 LIVINGSTONE ST
12 TENNYSON ST
13 CLIFTON ST
14 LAWRENCE ST
15 OVENDEN CL
16 RUSHWORTH ST
17 GARFIELD ST
18 COLUMBUS ST
19 ASHVILLE ST
20 WASHINGTON ST
21 BRIGHTON ST
22 MELBOURNE ST
23 INGHAMS CT
24 RUSKIN TERR
25 WOODVILLE ST
26 MELROSE ST
27 CONCRETE ST
28 BATLEY ST
A2
1 FRIENDLY ST
2 BETHEL ST
3 AMY ST

91

A2
4 CLEVEDON PL
5 EARL TERR
6 LENTILFIELD TERR
7 EASTWOOD ST
8 ROBERT ST
9 OVENDEN ROAD TERR
B1
1 CHESTER CT
2 CHESTER GR
3 CHESTER CL

113

B1
4 CHESTER PL
5 GILMOUR ST
6 LINCOLN WAY
B2
1 TURNER'S CT
2 McBURNEY CL
3 BRUNEL CT
4 UTTLEY ST
5 SIMPSON ST
6 CATHCART ST
7 FERNFIELD TERR
8 IONA PL
C1
1 SUNNY SIDE ST
2 ALL SOULS' TERR
3 ALL SOULS' ST
4 SUNNY BANK TERR
5 LAURA ST
6 ADA ST
7 BACK LYTTON ST
8 WOODLANDS VIEW
9 LOWER RANGE
10 AMBLERS TERR
11 BROUGHAM RD
12 BROUGHAM ST
13 BROUGHAM TERR
14 OLD SCHOOLS GDNS
15 CHURCH SIDE CL
16 CHURCH SIDE DR
17 SCHOOL YARD VIEW
C2
1 BREWERY ST
2 ROBERT ST N
3 CLAREMOUNT TERR
4 ROYD MOUNT
5 THORN VIEW

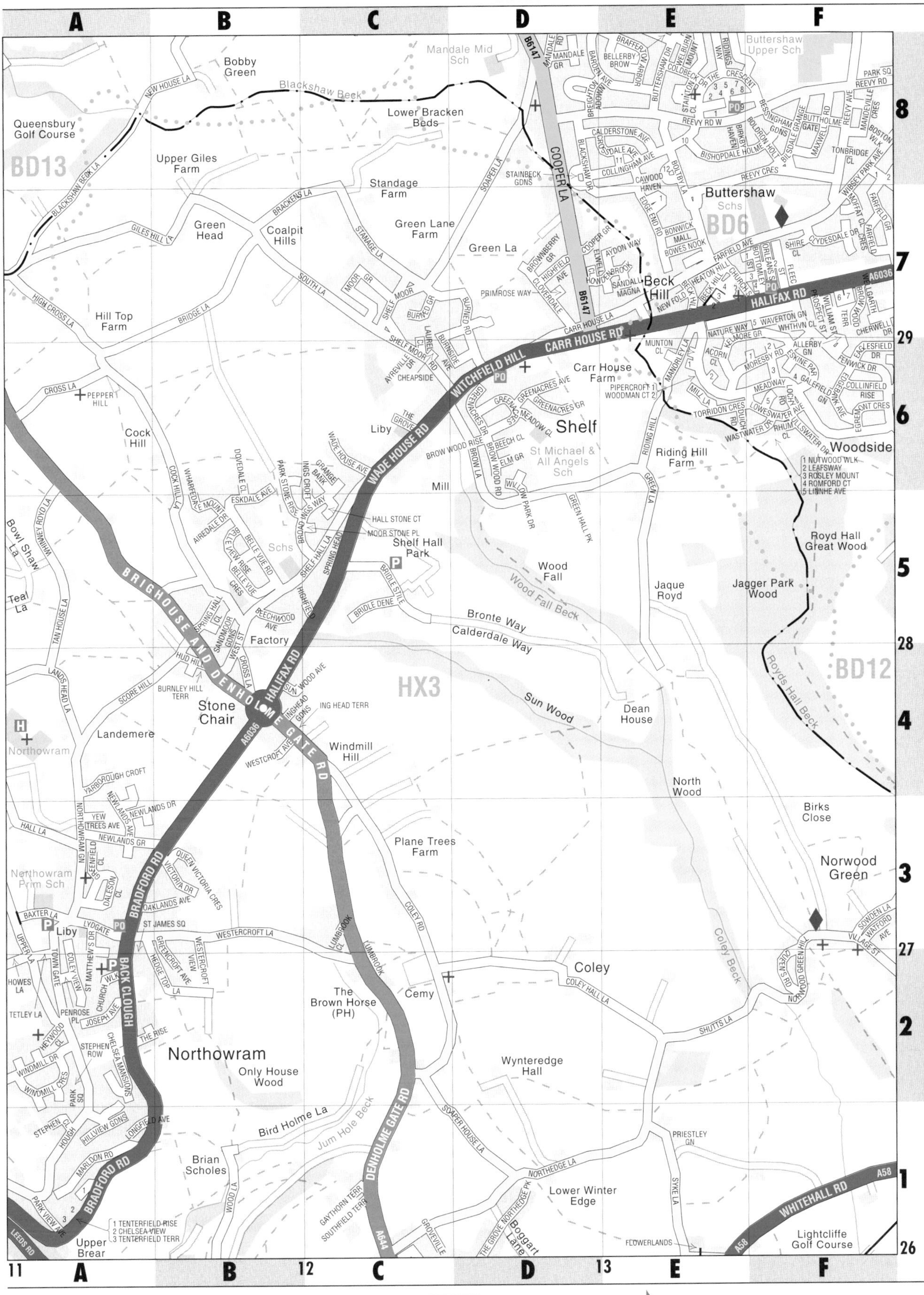
A
B
C
D
E
F
8
7
29
6
5
28
4
3
27
2
1
26
11
12
13
Mandale Mid Sch
Bobby Green
Blackshaw Beck
Queensbury Golf Course
BD13
Lower Bracken Beds
Upper Giles Farm
Standage Farm
Green Head
Coalpit Hills
Green Lane Farm
Green La
Buttershaw
Buttershaw Upper Sch
Schs
BD6
Beck Hill
HALIFAX RD
A6036
COOPER LA
B6147
Hill Top Farm
CARR HOUSE RD
WITCHFIELD HILL
Carr House Farm
Shelf
St Michael & All Angels Sch
Woodside
1 NUTWOOD WLK
2 LEAFSWAY
3 ROSLEY MOUNT
4 ROMFORD CT
5 LINNHE AVE
Cock Hill
Liby
Mill
Riding Hill Farm
WADE HOUSE RD
Bowl Shaw La
Teal La
Schs
Shelf Hall Park
Wood Fall
Wood Fall Beck
Jaque Royd
Jagger Park Wood
Royd Hall Great Wood
Bronte Way
Calderdale Way
Factory
BRIGHOUSE AND DENHOLME GATE RD
HX3
Sun Wood
Dean House
BD12
Royds Hall Beck
Stone Chair
Landemere
Northowram
Windmill Hill
North Wood
Birks Close
Plane Trees Farm
Northowram Prim Sch
Norwood Green
BRADFORD RD
BACK CLOUGH
Liby
Coley
Cemy
The Brown Horse (PH)
Coley Beck
Northowram
Only House Wood
Wynteredge Hall
Bird Holme La
Jum Hole Beck
DENHOLME GATE RD
A644
Brian Scholes
Lower Winter Edge
Boggart Lane
WHITEHALL RD
A58
Lightcliffe Golf Course
Upper Brear
LEEDS RD
1 TENTERFIELD RISE
2 CHELSEA VIEW
3 TENTERFIELD TERR
FLOWERLANDS
PRIESTLEY GN
SYKE LA
SOAPER HOUSE LA
NORTHEDGE LA
SHUTTS LA
COLEY HALL LA
COLEY RD
WESTERCROFT LA
ST JAMES SQ
YEW TREES AVE
NEWLANDS GR
HALL LA
BAXTER LA
TOWN GATE
WINDMILL DR
STEPHEN ROW
PARK SQ
HILLVIEW GDNS
LONGFIELD AVE
MARLDON RD
PARK VIEW AVE
GAYTHORN TERR
SOUTHFIELD TERR
GROVEVILLE
WOOD LA
SCORE HILL
BURNLEY HILL TERR
ING HEAD TERR
WESTCROFT AVE
YARBOROUGH CROFT
NEWLANDS DR
TAN HOUSE LA
LANDS HEAD LA
CROSS LA
PEPPER HILL
HIGH CROSS LA
BLACKSHAW BECK LA
GILES HILL LA
NEW HOUSE LA
BRACKENS LA
STANAGE LA
SOUTH LA
BRIDGE LA
SHELF MOOR
CHEAPSIDE
HALL STONE CT
MOOR STONE PL
BRIDLE STILE
BRIDLE DENE
RIDING HILL
GREEN LA
PRIMROSE WAY
STAINBECK GDNS
REEVY RD W
REEVY CRES
PIPERCROFT
WOODMAN CT
TORRIDON CRES
WASTWATER DR
NATURE WAY
MUNTON CL

A8
1 PARK SQ
2 COVER DR
3 BREARCLIFFE CL
B6
1 GREENTREES
2 WINTON GN

93

B6
3 ALFRED E BRIGGS ALMSHOUSES
4 SHAW ST
5 BARRACLOUGH ST
B8
1 WILMAN HILL
2 FOLLY HALL CL

74

B8
3 FOLLY HALL WLK
4 TORDOFF GN
5 ALEXANDER ST
6 ORMOND RD
7 NORTH RD

C6
1 EDWARD TURNER CL
2 AVERY TULIP CT
3 SALISBURY RD
D8
1 WHITE LANE TOP
2 WHITE LA

3 SCOTT ST
4 PEARSON RD W
5 MANCHESTER RD
6 SUTCLIFFE PL
7 COLL PL
8 GLENFIELD MNT
9 ODSAL PL

10 TAYLOR RD
11 PEARSON RD
12 WOODHOUSE TR
E5
1 RAILWAY TERR
2 TERRY RD
3 BOLLAND ST

4 MOORLAND PL
5 STATION RD
6 OLYMPIC CT
E6
1 FOURTH ST
2 THIRD ST
3 WESLEY AVE S

4 BREAKS RD
5 TORDOFF RD

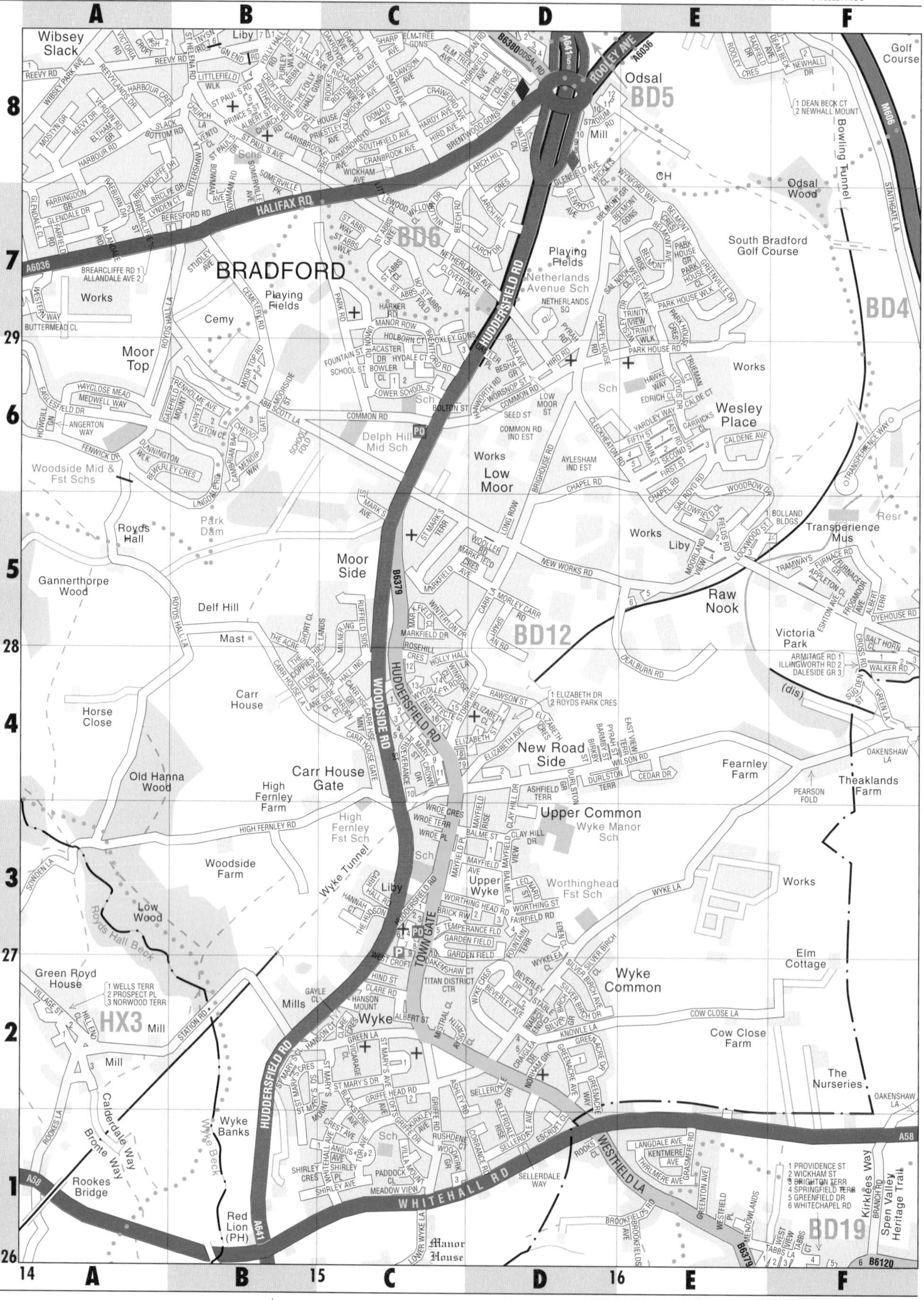

93

115

C1
1 CAMERON AVE
2 METHUEN OVAL
3 GREENGATES AVE
C2
1 ST MARY'S GDNS
2 GRIFFE HEAD CRES
C3
1 WAINMAN ST
2 WAINMAN SQ
3 CARR RD

4 GANNERTHOPRE CL
5 DAISY HILL
6 LAVERACK FIELD
7 HANSON PL
8 HANSON FOLD
9 WILKINSON FOLD
10 CLEGG ST
C4
1 COURTS LEET
2 MAIN ST
3 ROYD ST

4 ABEL ST
5 PROVIDENCE PL
6 PYRAH FOLD
7 SADDLER ST
8 CROWTHER ST
9 CROWN ST
10 HIGH FERNLEY CT
11 FERNLEY GDNS
12 WAVERTREE PK GDNS
13 WESTCOMBE CT
14 WEDGEMOOR CL

15 WORSNOP BLDGS
16 SCHOOL PL
17 BELL ST
18 BARRACLOUGH SQ
19 BACK RD
D2
1 GREENACRE CL
2 WATERLOO FOLD
3 BINKS FOLD
4 HOBSON FOLD
5 ALBERT TERR

D3
1 MAYFIELD TERR
2 WORTHING HEAD CL
3 PEARSON ROW
4 BENTLEY ST

75
96

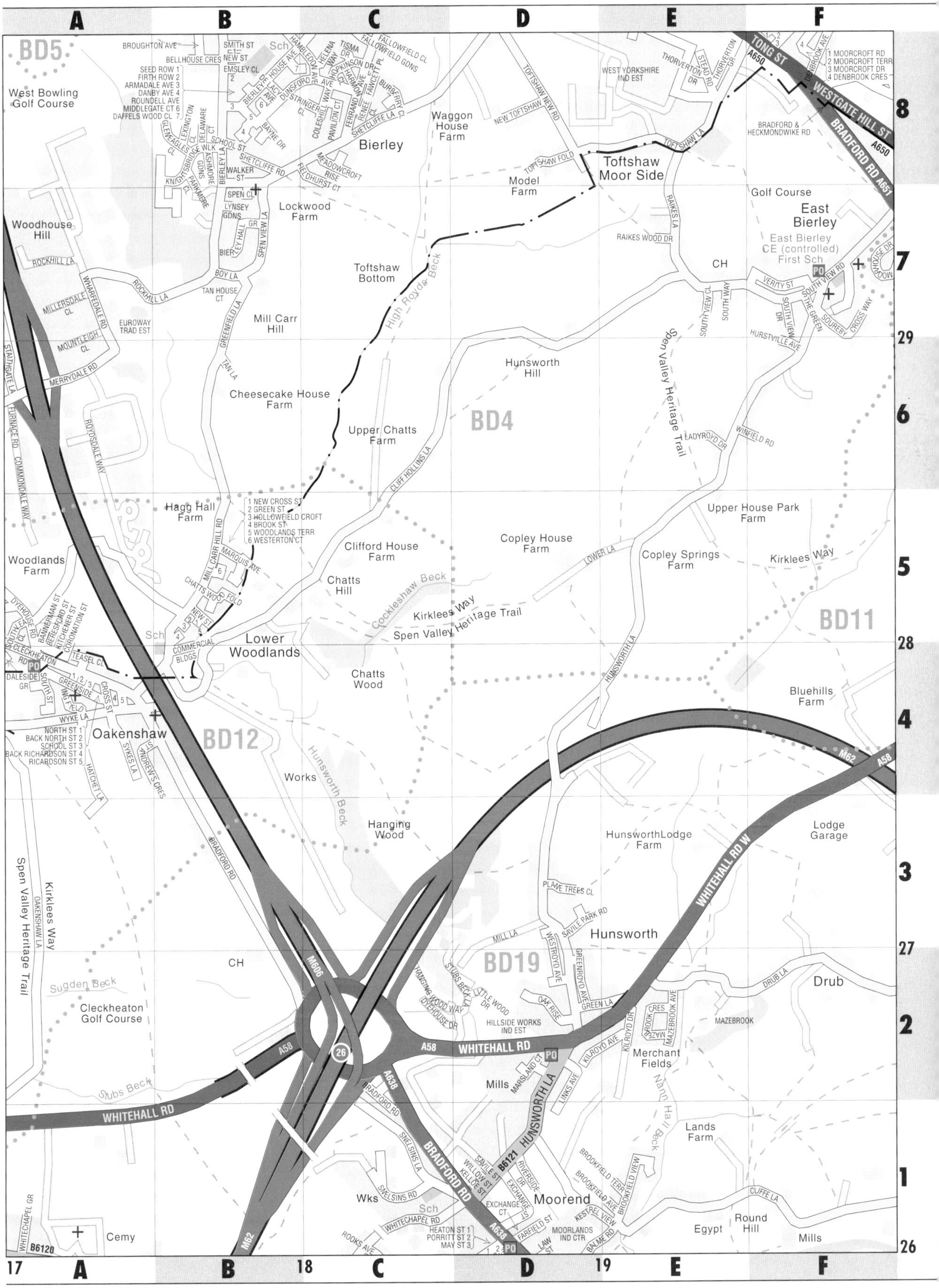
A
B
C
D
E
F
BD5
West Bowling Golf Course
BROUGHTON AVE
SMITH ST
BELLHOUSE CRES
NEW ST
EMSLEY CL
SEED ROW 1
FIRTH ROW 2
ARMADALE AVE 3
DANBY AVE 4
ROUNDELL AVE
MIDDLEGATE CT 6
DAFFELS WOOD CL 7
Sch
HAMBLEDON AVE
HELENA WAY
TISMA DR
FALLOWFIELD CL
FALLOWFIELD GDNS
BIERLEY HOUSE AVE
DE LACY AVE
DUNSFORD AVE
HOPKINSON DR
HARMON CL
STRINGER CL
COLESHILL WAY
PAVILION CT
FERRAND AVE
RENEE CL
FAWCETT PL
BURBERRY CL
SHETCLIFFE LA
BAYNE DR
GLENEAGLES CL
LEXINGTON CL
DELAWARE CT
KNIGHTSBRIDGE WLK
ASHMORE GDNS
PARKMERE CL
BIERLEY LA
SCHOOL ST
WALKER ST
SHETCLIFFE RD
MEADOWCROFT RISE
FIELDHURST CT
SPEN CL
LYNSEY GDNS
LEY HALL
SPEN VIEW LA
GR
BIER
Bierley
Waggon House Farm
NEW TOFTSHAW
TOFTSHAW NEW RD
WEST YORKSHIRE IND EST
THORVERTON DR
STEAD RD
THORVERTON GR
TONG ST
A650
WESTGATE HILL ST
BRADFORD RD A651
DENBROOK AVE
1 MOORCROFT RD
2 MOORCROFT TERR
3 MOORCROFT DR
4 DENBROOK CRES
BRADFORD & HECKMONDWIKE RD
TOFTSHAW LA
TOFTSHAW FOLD
Toftshaw Moor Side
Model Farm
Golf Course
East Bierley
East Bierley CE (controlled) First Sch
RAIKES LA
RAIKES WOOD DR
CH
PO
VERITY ST
SOUTH VIEW RD
SOUTH VIEW CL
SOUTH WAY
SOUTH VIEW DR
THE GREEN
SOUREBY CROSS WAY
HURSTVILLE AVE
Woodhouse Hill
ROCKHILL LA
Lockwood Farm
BOY LA
TAN HOUSE CT
ROCKHILL LA
MILLERSDALE CL
WHARFEDALE RD
MOUNTLEIGH CL
EUROWAY TRAD EST
GREENFIELD LA
Mill Carr Hill
Toftshaw Bottom
High Royds Beck
STAITHGATE LA
MERRYDALE RD
FURNACE RD
COMMONDALE WAY
ROYDSDALE WAY
TAN LA
Cheesecake House Farm
Upper Chatts Farm
Hunsworth Hill
BD4
Spen Valley Heritage Trail
LADYROYD DR
WINFIELD RD
CLIFF HOLLINS LA
Hagg Hall Farm
1 NEW CROSS ST
2 GREEN ST
3 HOLLOWFIELD CROFT
4 BROOK ST
5 WOODLANDS TERR
6 WESTERTON CT
MILL CARR HILL RD
MARQUIS AVE
Clifford House Farm
Copley House Farm
Upper House Park Farm
LOWER LA
Copley Springs Farm
Kirklees Way
Woodlands Farm
CHATTS WOOD FOLD
Chatts Hill
Cockleshaw Beck
Kirklees Way
Spen Valley Heritage Trail
BD11
DYEHOUSE RD
BANNERMAN ST
BERESFORD ST
KITCHENER ST
CORONATION ST
SOUTHLEASE RD
CLECKHEATON RD
NEW ST
Sch
COMMERCIAL BLDGS
Lower Woodlands
TEASEL CL
DALESIDE GR
GREENSIDE
SOUTH ST
CROSS ST
ING FIELD
WYKE LA
Chatts Wood
HUNSWORTH LA
Bluehills Farm
NORTH ST 1
BACK NORTH ST 2
SCHOOL ST 3
BACK RICHARDSON ST 4
RICARDSON ST 5
Oakenshaw
SYKES LA
ST ANDREW'S CRES
HATCHET LA
BD12
Hunsworth Beck
Works
M62
A58
Hanging Wood
BRADFORD RD
HunsworthLodge Farm
Lodge Garage
WHITEHALL RD W
Spen Valley Heritage Trail
Kirklees Way
OAKENSHAW LA
PLANE TREES CL
SAVILE PARK RD
Hunsworth
MILL LA
WESTROYD AVE
GREENROYD AVE
BD19
CH
M606
HANGING WOOD WAY
STUBS BECK LA
LITTLE WOOD DR
DYEHOUSE DR
OAK RISE
GREEN LA
HILLSIDE WORKS IND EST
KILROYD DR
BROOK CRES
MAZEBROOK AVE
MAZEBROOK
DRUB LA
Drub
Sugden Beck
Cleckheaton Golf Course
A58
26
A58 WHITEHALL RD
PO
KILROYD AVE
Merchant Fields
A638
Mills
MARSLAND CT
LINKS AVE
Nann Hall Beck
Stubs Beck
WHITEHALL RD
BRADFORD RD
SNELSINS LA
BRADFORD RD
B6121 HUNSWORTH LA
Lands Farm
MAZE
SAVILE ST
WILLOW ST
KELLOE ST
RIVERSIDE DR
EXCHANGE ST
BROOKFIELD TERR
BROOKFIELD VIEW
BROOKFIELD AVE
CLIFFE LA
SNELSINS RD
Wks
Sch
Moorend
EXCHANGE CT
KESTREL VIEW
Round Hill
Egypt
Mills
WHITECHAPEL GR
Cemy
WHITECHAPEL RD
HEATON ST 1
PORRITT ST 2
MAY ST 3
FARFIELD ST
MOORLANDS IND CTR
BALME RD
ROOKS AVE
LAW ST
A638
B6120
M62
8
7
29
6
5
28
4
3
27
2
1
26
17
18
19

116
96

95
76

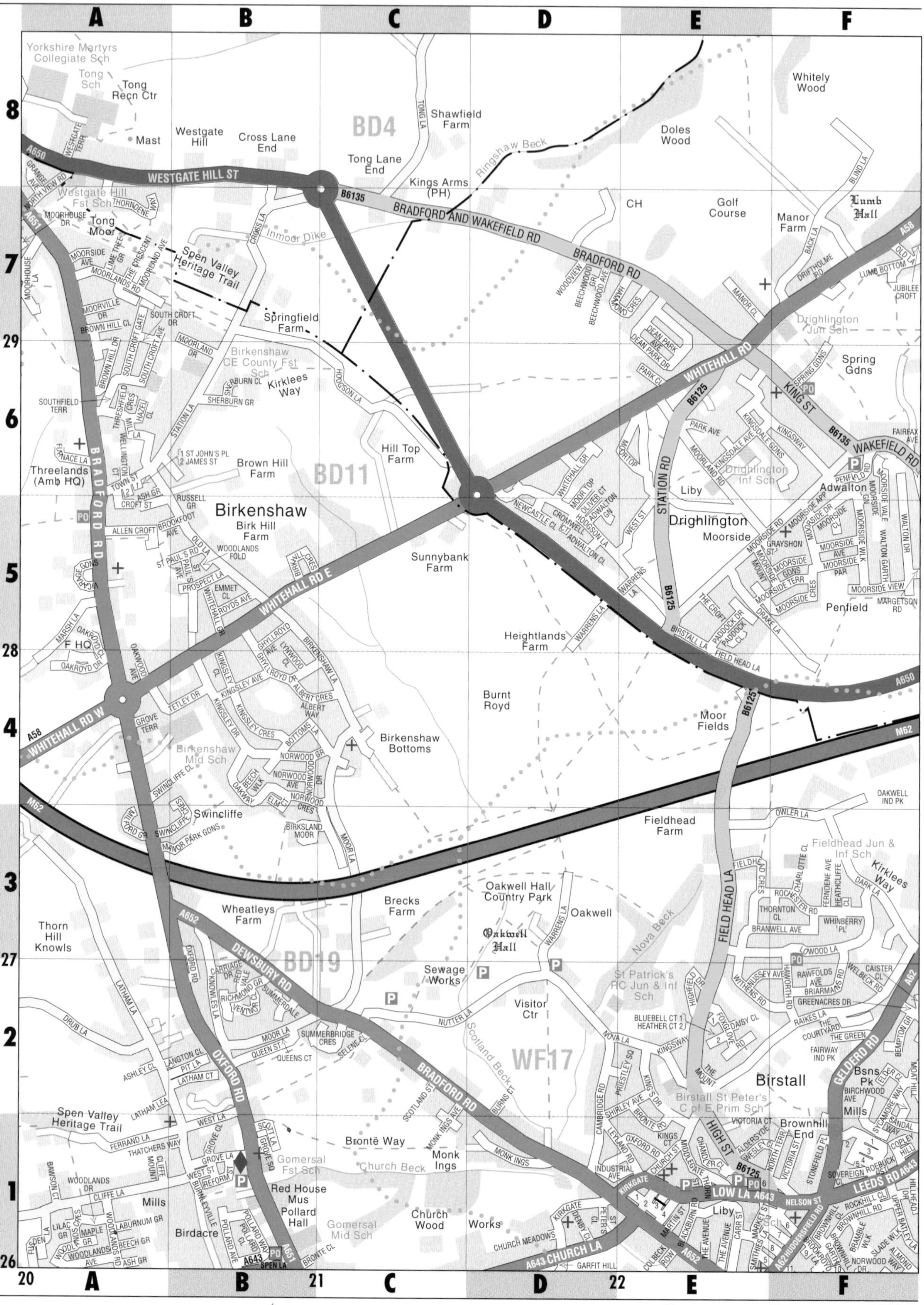

95
117

E1
1 COLLEGE ST
2 MUSGRAVE ST
3 SEDGEWICK ST
4 WHEWELL ST
5 JOHN ST
6 BOND ST

F1
1 SOUTH VIEW
2 CORONATION TERR
3 ALEXANDRA AVE
4 SPRINGWELL VIEW
5 SUNNYMOUNT TERR
6 CHAPEL LA
7 SCHOOL ST
8 UNION ST
9 JOHN NELSON CL
10 QUARRY LA
11 CHURCH RD

77
98

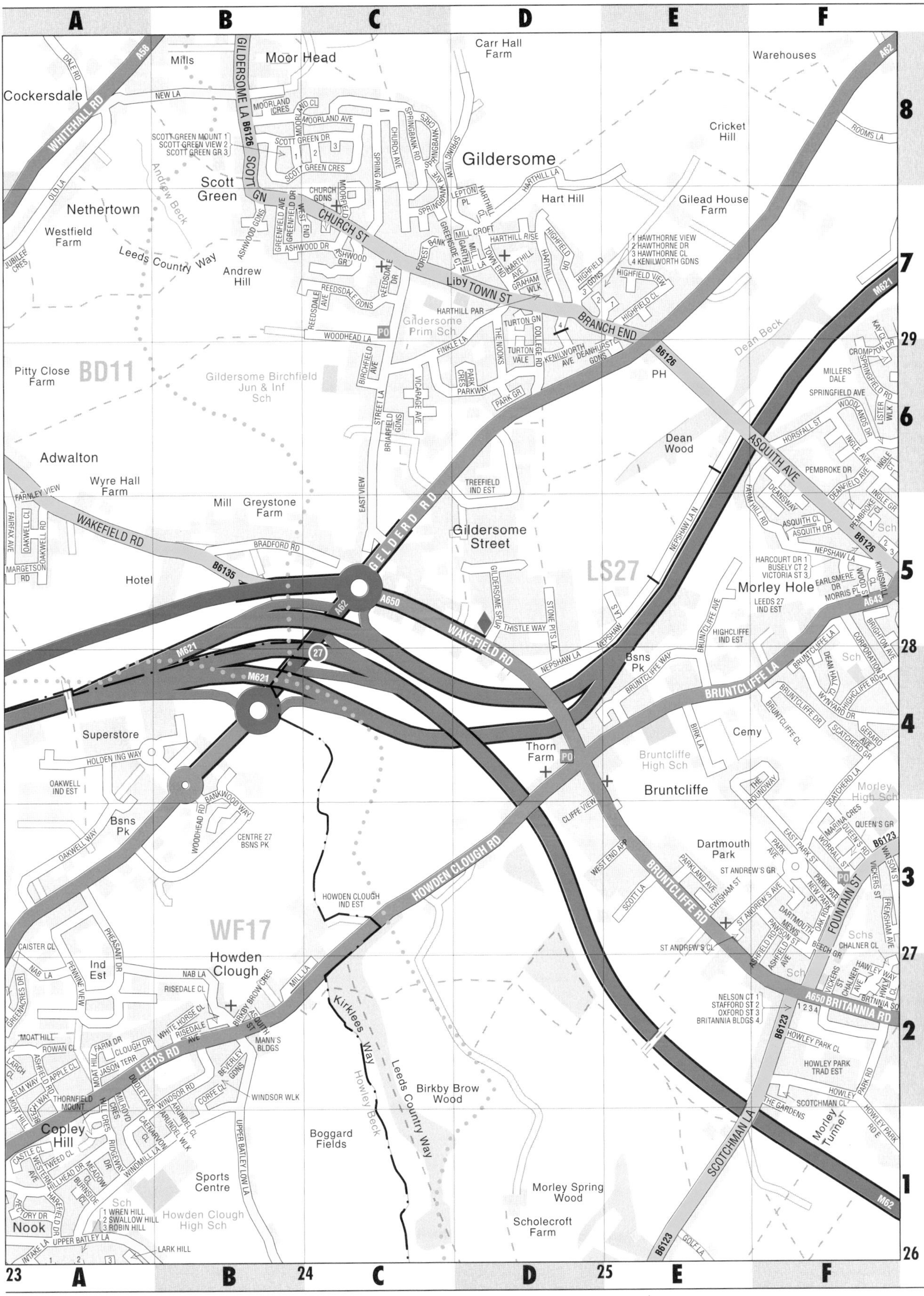
A
B
C
D
E
F
8
7
29
6
5
28
4
3
27
2
1
26
23
24
25
Cockersdale
Mills
Moor Head
Carr Hall Farm
Warehouses
A58
A62
WHITEHALL RD
NEW LA
DALE RD
GILDERSOME LA
B6126
SCOTT GN
MOORLAND CRES
MOORLAND CL
MOORLAND AVE
SCOTT GREEN MOUNT 1
SCOTT GREEN VIEW 2
SCOTT GREEN GR 3
SCOTT GREEN DR
SCOTT GREEN CRES
CHURCH AVE
SPRING AVE
SPRINGBANK RD
SPRINGBANK CRES
SPRING VIEW
Gildersome
Cricket Hill
ROOMS LA
HARTHILL LA
Hart Hill
Gilead House Farm
Scott Green
Nethertown
Westfield Farm
Andrew Beck
OLD LA
Leeds Country Way
Andrew Hill
JUBILEE CRES
ASHWOOD GDNS
GREENFIELD AVE
GREENFIELD DR
WEST END
CHURCH GDNS
MOORFIELD
CHURCH ST
ASHWOOD DR
ASHWOOD GR
REEDSDALE DR
REEDSDALE AVE
REEDSDALE GDNS
FOREST BANK
SPRINGBANK AVE
LEPTON PL
HARTHILL CL
MILL CROFT
MILL GARTH
MILL LA
GREENSIDE CL
TOWN END
HARTHILL RISE
HARTHILL AVE
HARTHILL
HIGHFIELD DR
HIGHFIELD GDNS
GRAHAM WLK
1 HAWTHORNE VIEW
2 HAWTHORNE DR
3 HAWTHORNE CL
4 KENILWORTH GDNS
HIGHFIELD VIEW
HIGHFIELD CL
Liby
TOWN ST
BRANCH END
HARTHILL PAR
Gildersome Prim Sch
WOODHEAD LA
PO
TURTON GN
TURTON VALE
THE NOOKS
COLLEGE RD
KENILWORTH AVE
DEANHURST GDNS
FINKLE LA
Dean Beck
KAY CL
CROMPTON DR
SPRINGFIELD RD
MILLERS DALE
SPRINGFIELD AVE
Pitty Close Farm
BD11
Gildersome Birchfield Jun & Inf Sch
BIRCHFIELD AVE
STREET LA
VICARAGE AVE
PARK CRES
PARKWAY
PARK GR
B6126
PH
BRIARFIELD GDNS
WOODLANDS DR
LISTER WLK
HORSFALL ST
Dean Wood
ASQUITH AVE
INGLE AVE
INGLE CL
Adwalton
Wyre Hall Farm
PEMBROKE DR
DEANFIELD AVE
EAST VIEW
TREEFIELD IND EST
DEANSWAY
FARM HILL RD
INGLE GR
PEMBROKE GR
FARNLEY VIEW
FAIRFAX AVE
OAKWELL CL
OAKWELL RD
Mill
Greystone Farm
GELDERD RD
Gildersome Street
NEPSHAW LA N
ASQUITH CL
ASQUITH DR
Sch
WAKEFIELD RD
BRADFORD RD
NEPSHAW LA
HARCOURT DR 1
BUSELY CT 2
VICTORIA ST 3
MARGETSON RD
Hotel
B6135
A62
A650
GILDERSOME SPUR
LS27
Morley Hole
EARLSMERE DR
WOOD ST
MORRIS PL
KINGSMILL CL
LEEDS 27 IND EST
A643
THISTLE WAY
STONE PITS LA
NEPSHAW
HIGHCLIFFE IND EST
BRUNTCLIFFE AVE
M621
27
NEPSHAW LA
Bsns Pk
BRUNTCLIFFE WAY
BRUNTCLIFFE LA
DEAN HALL CL
CORPORATION ST
BRIGHTON AVE
WYNYARD DR
HIGHCLIFFE RD
Superstore
HOLDEN ING WAY
BIRK LA
Cemy
BRUNTCLIFFE DR
BRUNTCLIFFE CL
SCATCHERD GR
GERARD AVE
Thorn Farm
PO
Bruntcliffe High Sch
OAKWELL IND EST
THE ROUNDWAY
Bruntcliffe
SCATCHERD LA
Morley High Sch
MARINA CRES
QUEEN'S RD
QUEEN'S GR
BANKWOOD WAY
WOODHEAD RD
Bsns Pk
OAKWELL WAY
CENTRE 27 BSNS PK
CLIFFE VIEW
EAST PARK ST
PARK AVE
Dartmouth Park
WORRALL ST
B6123
WATSON ST
HOWDEN CLOUGH RD
WEST END APP
PARKLAND AVE
ST ANDREW'S GR
LEWISHAM ST
SCOTT LA
BRUNTCLIFFE RD
ST ANDREW'S AVE
PARK PAR
NEW PARK ST
FOUNTAIN ST
VICKERS ST
FRENSHAM AVE
HOWDEN CLOUGH IND EST
DARTMOUTH MEWS
PAWSON ST
OAK RD
Schs
CHALNER CL
WF17
CAISTER CL
PHEASANT DR
ST ANDREW'S CL
ASHFIELD RD
ASHFIELD AVE
BEECH GR
Sch
HAWLEY WAY
Ind Est
NAB LA
Howden Clough
PENNINE VIEW
RISEDALE CL
BIRKBY BROW CRES
MILL LA
GREENACRES DR
VICKERS ST
CHALNER AVE
BRITANNIA SQ
NELSON CT 1
STAFFORD ST 2
OXFORD ST 3
BRITANNIA BLDGS 4
A650
BRITANNIA RD
MOAT HILL
ROWAN CL
FARM DR
WHITE HORSE CL
RISEDALE AVE
ASQUITH ST
MANN'S BLDGS
Kirklees Way
Leeds Country Way
B6123
HOWLEY PARK CL
HOWLEY PARK TRAD EST
ASHFIELD CL
LARCH CL
APPLE CL
JASON TERR
CLOUGH DR
LEEDS RD
BEVERLEY GDNS
MOAT HILL
ELM WAY
BEECH WAY
THORNFIELD MOUNT
DUDLEY AVE
MILGROVE GDNS
WINDSOR RD
CORFE CL
WINDSOR WLK
Howley Beck
Birkby Brow Wood
HOWLEY PARK RD
THE GARDENS
SCOTCHMAN CL
HOWLEY PARK RD E
Copley Hill
HILL CRES
ARUNDEL CL
ARUNDEL WLK
Boggard Fields
Morley Tunnel
CASTLE CL
WESTERN AVE
TWEED CL
HILLHEAD DR
MEADOW CL
BURNSIDE CL
HAREFIELD DR
CAERNARVON CL
RIDGEWAY
WINDMILL LA
UPPER BATLEY LOW LA
Sports Centre
SCOTCHMAN LA
Morley Spring Wood
M62
RECTORY DR
Nook
Sch
1 WREN HILL
2 SWALLOW HILL
3 ROBIN HILL
Howden Clough High Sch
Scholecroft Farm
INTAKE LA
UPPER BATLEY LA
LARK HILL
B6123
GOLF LA

118
98

A5
1 NELSON PL
2 BANK SQ
3 CHURCH WAY
4 VICTORIA GRANGE WAY
5 PROVIDENCE CT
6 VICTORIA MEWS
7 FOSTER CRES
8 FOSTER CL
9 COBDEN ST
10 COBDEN MEWS
11 FOSTER ST
12 CO-OPERATIVE ST

97

A6
1 ARKWRIGHT WLK
2 WINDERS DALE
3 SANDMEAD WAY
B7
1 DAFFIL GRANGE MEWS
2 HINDLE PL

78

B7
3 CLIFFORD PL
4 MOSS LEA
5 THORNVILLE
6 HODGSON PL
7 WALKER PL
8 GRANGE TERR
9 GRANGE PARK CL
10 GRANGE PARK MEWS
11 LANESIDE FOLD
C8
1 UNION ST
2 CO-OPERATIVE ST
3 FOUNTAIN ST
4 OLD SCHOOL MEWS
5 SUNNY GR
6 ALFRED ST
7 LITTLE LA
8 LITTLE LANE CT

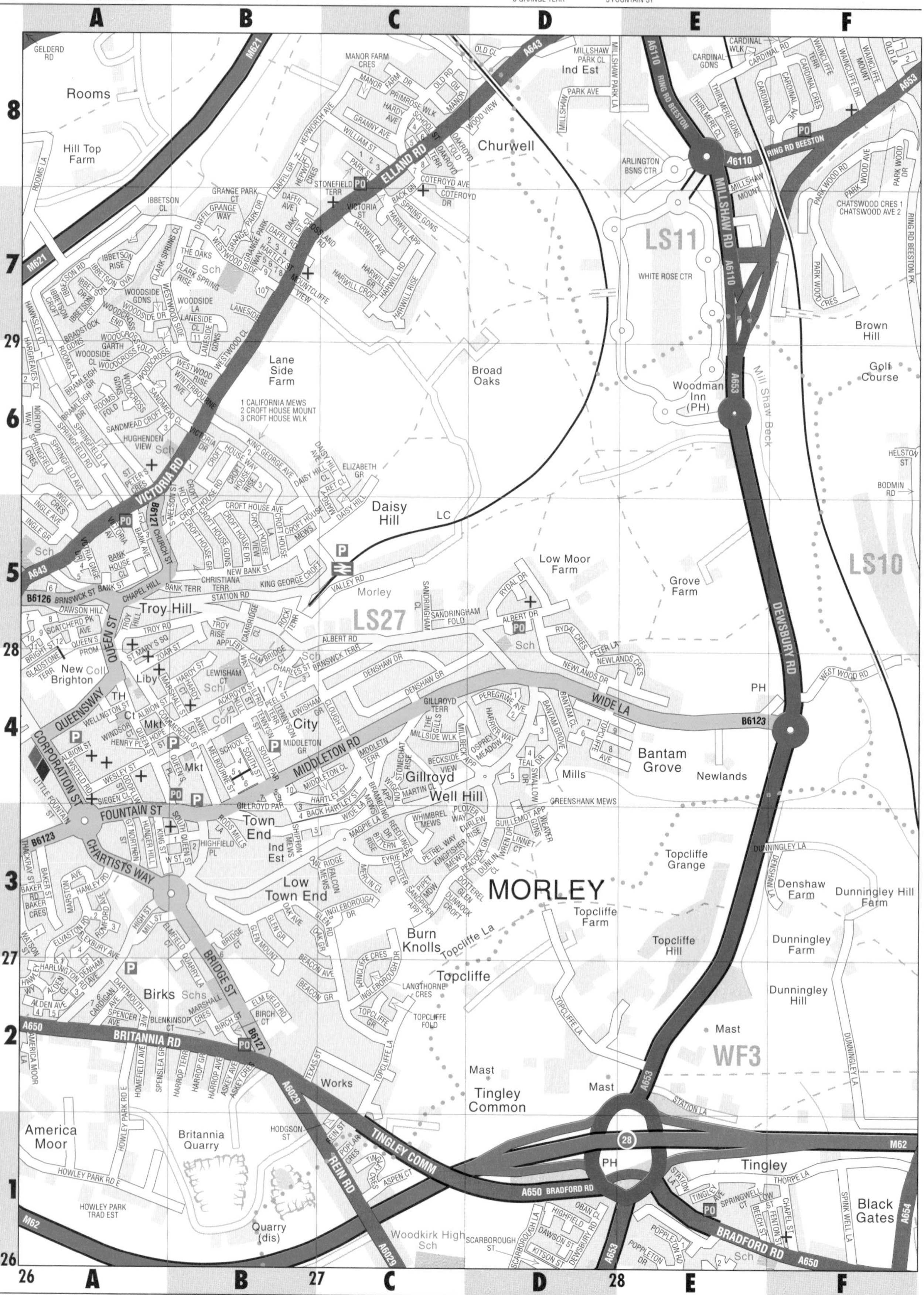

26 A B 27 C D 28 E F

A2
1 LENHAM CL
2 BARNET GR
3 HARLINGTON CT
4 ALDEN FOLD
5 ALDEN CT
6 LORD'S BLDGS
7 JOWETT TERR
A3
1 PENTLAND WAY
2 SUTTON GR
3 RICHMOND CL
4 FINCHLEY WAY
B3
1 ST PAUL'S ST
2 AUTY SQ
3 HARTLEY PL
4 RODS VIEW
5 CHATSWORTH MEWS
6 HARTLEY'S BLDGS
B4
1 JOHNSON TERR
2 CROSS PEEL ST
3 BRUNSWICK PL
4 JUBILEE TERR
5 JUBILEE PL
6 JUBILEE ST
7 GILLROYD PL
8 AIREDALE TERR
9 FLORENCE TERR
10 CALIFORNIA ST

97

119

D4
1 TAWNY CL
2 KESTREL GARTH
3 MALLARD WAY
4 HERON CT
5 PARTRIDGE CL
6 TOPCLIFFE MEAD
7 TOPCLIFFE GN
8 TOPCLIFFE CT
9 TOPCLIFFE MEWS

E1
1 POPPLETON CT
2 POPPLETON RISE

A8
1 GROVEHALL DR
2 OAKHURST ST
3 OAKHURST AVE
D5
1 CHAPEL HILL
2 STAITHE GDNS
3 TURNSTONE CT
4 AVOCET GARTH
5 SANDERLING GARTH
6 DUNLIN CT
7 DUNLIN FOLD
8 DUNLIN CROFT
D8
1 WINROSE HILL
2 CORNUS GDNS
3 THE SPINDLES
4 BLACKTHORNE CT
5 GORSE LEA
6 WHITEBEAM LA
F7
1 LEA PARK GDNS
2 LEA PARK GARTH
3 HOPES FARM MOUNT
4 HOPES FARM RD
5 HOPES FARM VIEW
6 GRANGE FIELDS MOUNT

79 100

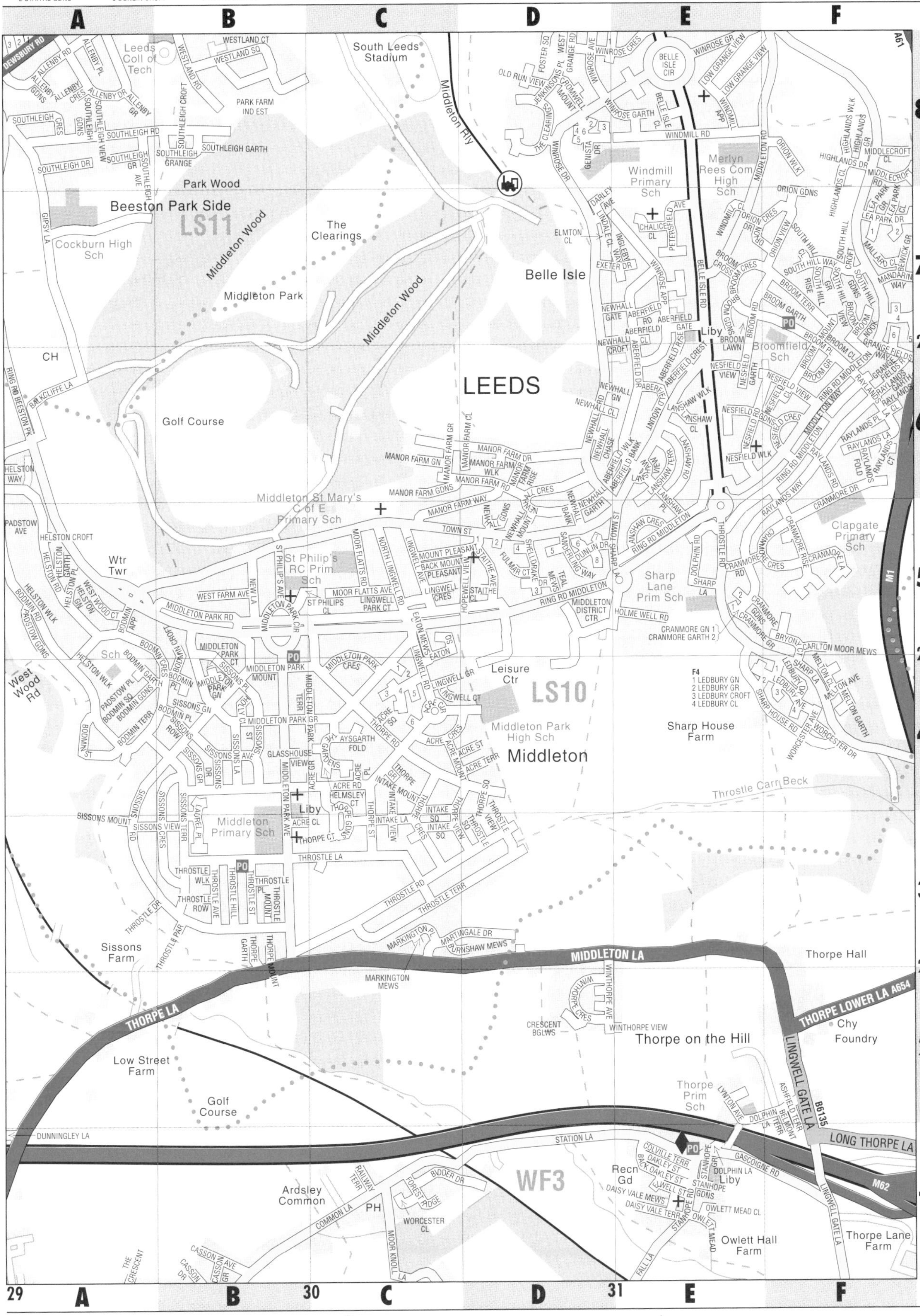

C4
1 LINGWELL MEWS
2 LINGWELL VIEW
3 LINGWELL GDNS
4 LINGWELL APP
5 LINGWELL WLK
6 LINGWELL GN

120 100

99
80

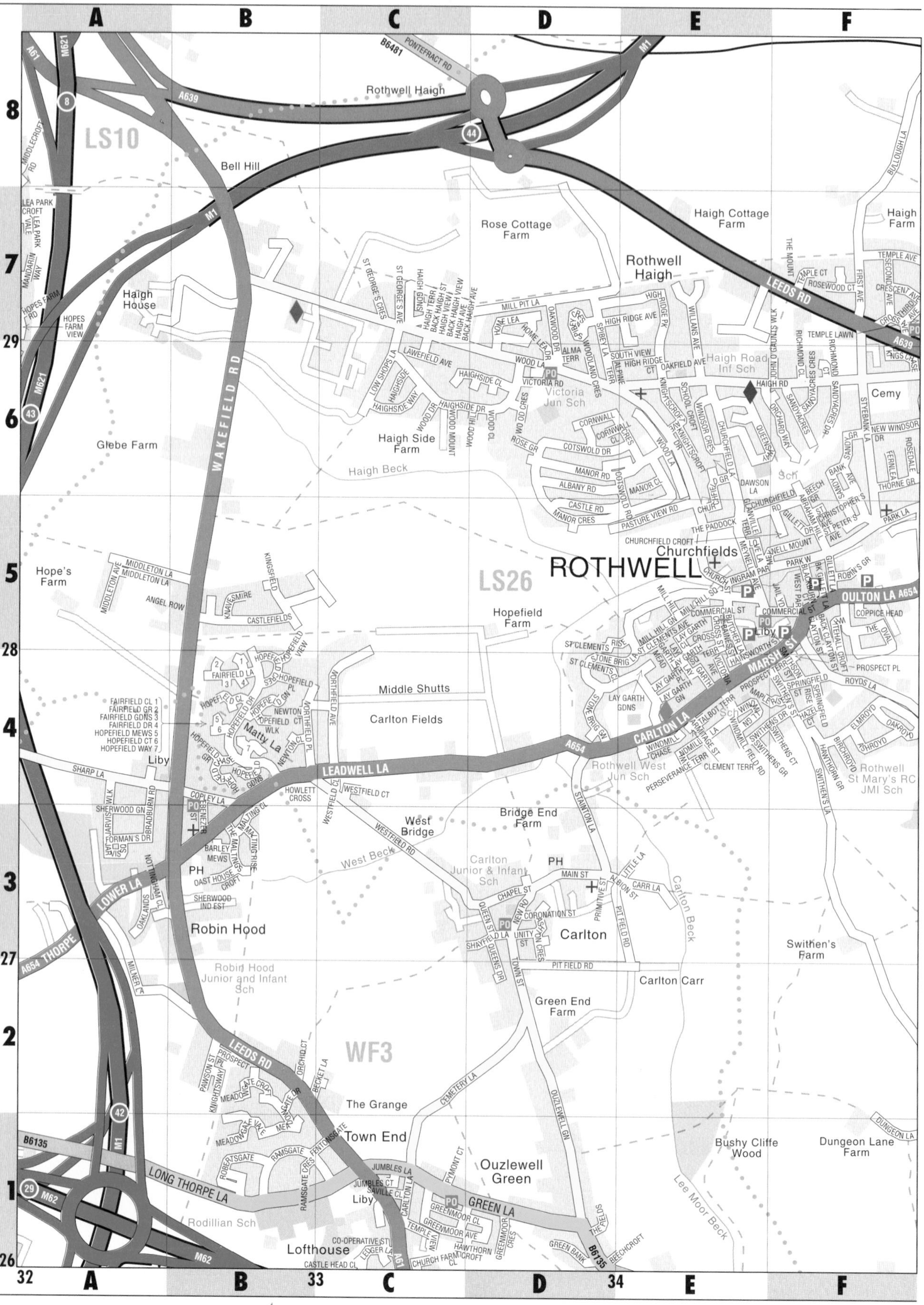
A
B
C
D
E
F
8
7
29
6
5
28
4
3
27
2
1
26
32
33
34
LS10
LS26
WF3
ROTHWELL
Rothwell Haigh
Bell Hill
Haigh House
Glebe Farm
Rose Cottage Farm
Haigh Cottage Farm
Haigh Farm
Haigh Side Farm
Haigh Beck
Hope's Farm
Hopefield Farm
Churchfields
Middle Shutts
Carlton Fields
Matty La
West Bridge
Bridge End Farm
West Beck
Carlton Junior & Infant Sch
Carlton
Robin Hood
Robin Hood Junior and Infant Sch
Carlton Carr
Green End Farm
Swithen's Farm
Rothwell St Mary's RC JMI Sch
Rothwell West Jun Sch
Victoria Jun Sch
Haigh Road Inf Sch
Cemy
The Grange
Town End
Ouzlewell Green
Bushy Cliffe Wood
Dungeon Lane Farm
Lee Moor Beck
Carlton Beck
Rodillian Sch
Lofthouse
Liby
PH
WAKEFIELD RD
LEEDS RD
LEADWELL LA
CARLTON LA
MARSH ST
OULTON LA A654
LOWER LA
A654 THORPE
LONG THORPE LA
GREEN LA
B6135
B6481
PONTEFRACT RD
A639
A61
M621
M1
M62
SHARP LA
COPLEY LA
MIDDLETON LA
CASTLEFIELDS
NORTHFIELD AVE
WESTFIELD RD
STAINTON LA
PIT FIELD RD
CEMETERY LA
OUZLEWELL GN
TOWN ST
BECKET LA
DUNGEON LA
COMMERCIAL ST
HAIGH RD
LAWEFIELD AVE
MILL PIT LA
CHURCHFIELD LA
BUTCHER LA
PARK LA
BULLOUGH LA

99
121

C5
1 LEVENTHORPE CT
2 BENTLEY SQ
3 WILLOW SQ
C6
1 NORTHGATE
2 MARGATE
3 BACK ROBERTS ST
4 ROBERTS ST
5 KITCHENER ST
6 BULLER ST
7 WHITE ST
8 CLAREMONT VIEW
9 BACK CLAREMONT ST

D6
1 AIREDALE VIEW
2 AIREDALE TERR
3 AIREDALE GR
4 ESHALD MANSIONS
5 RUTLAND CL

81
102

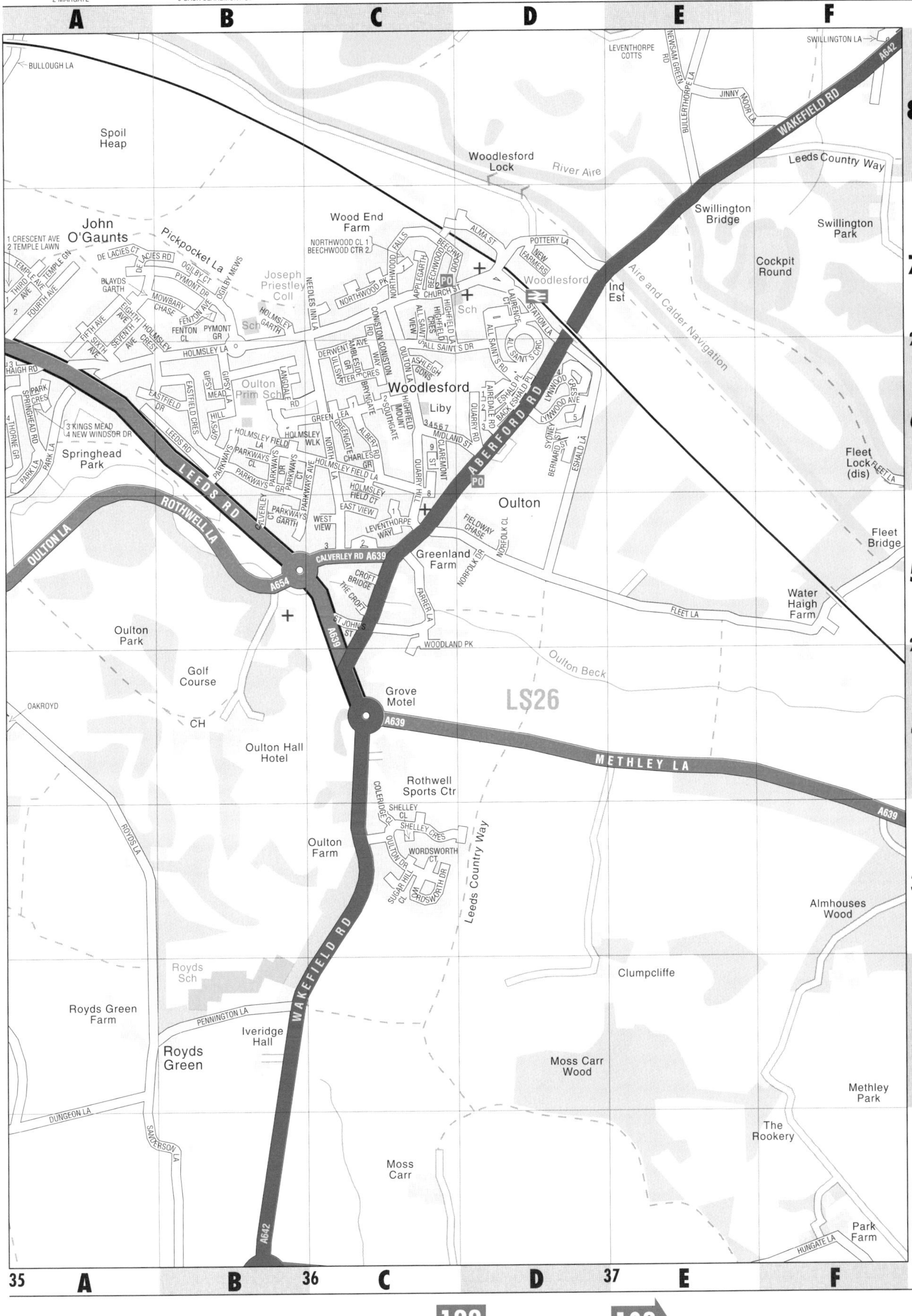

122
102

101
82

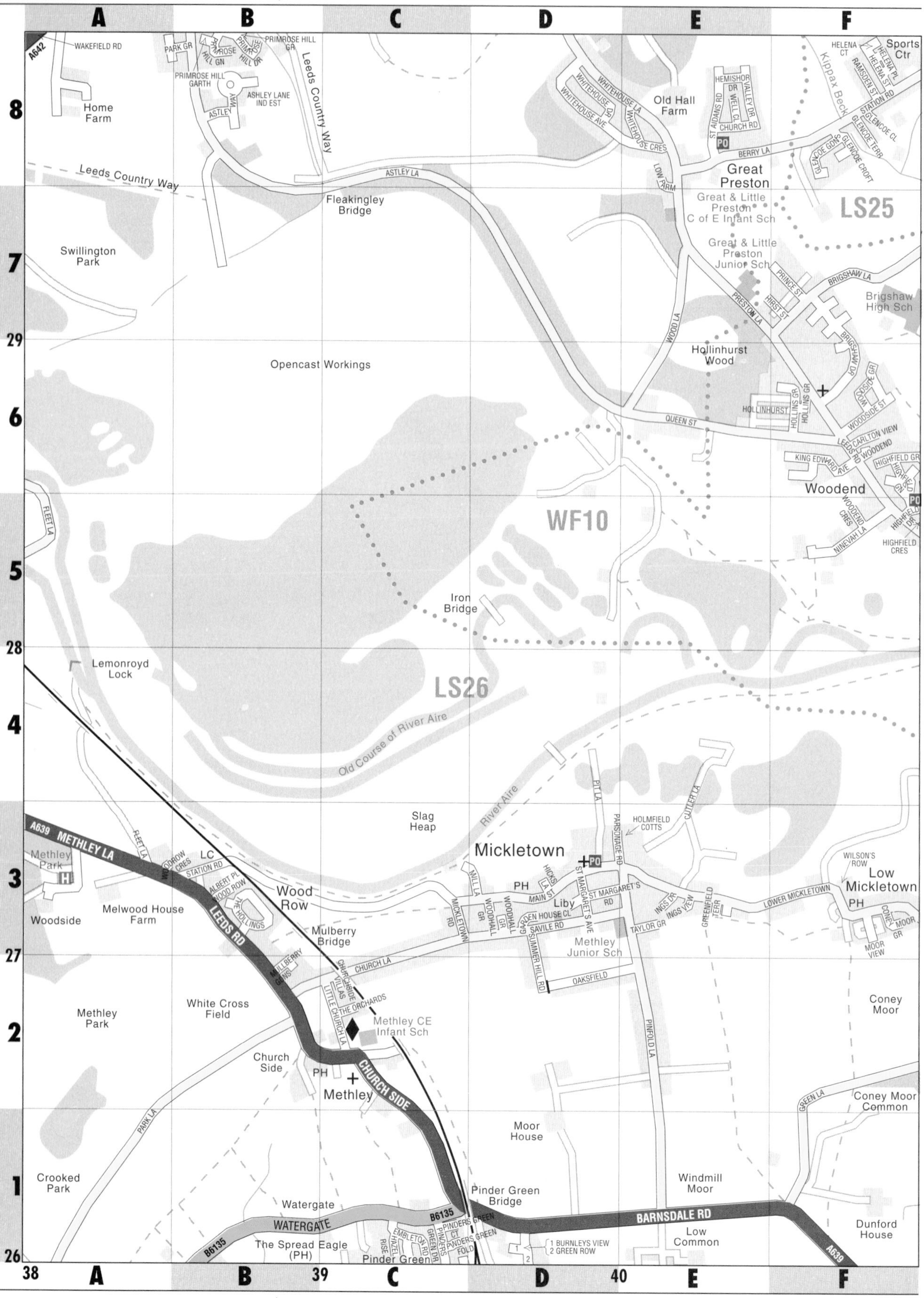

101
123

83
104

124
104

103
84

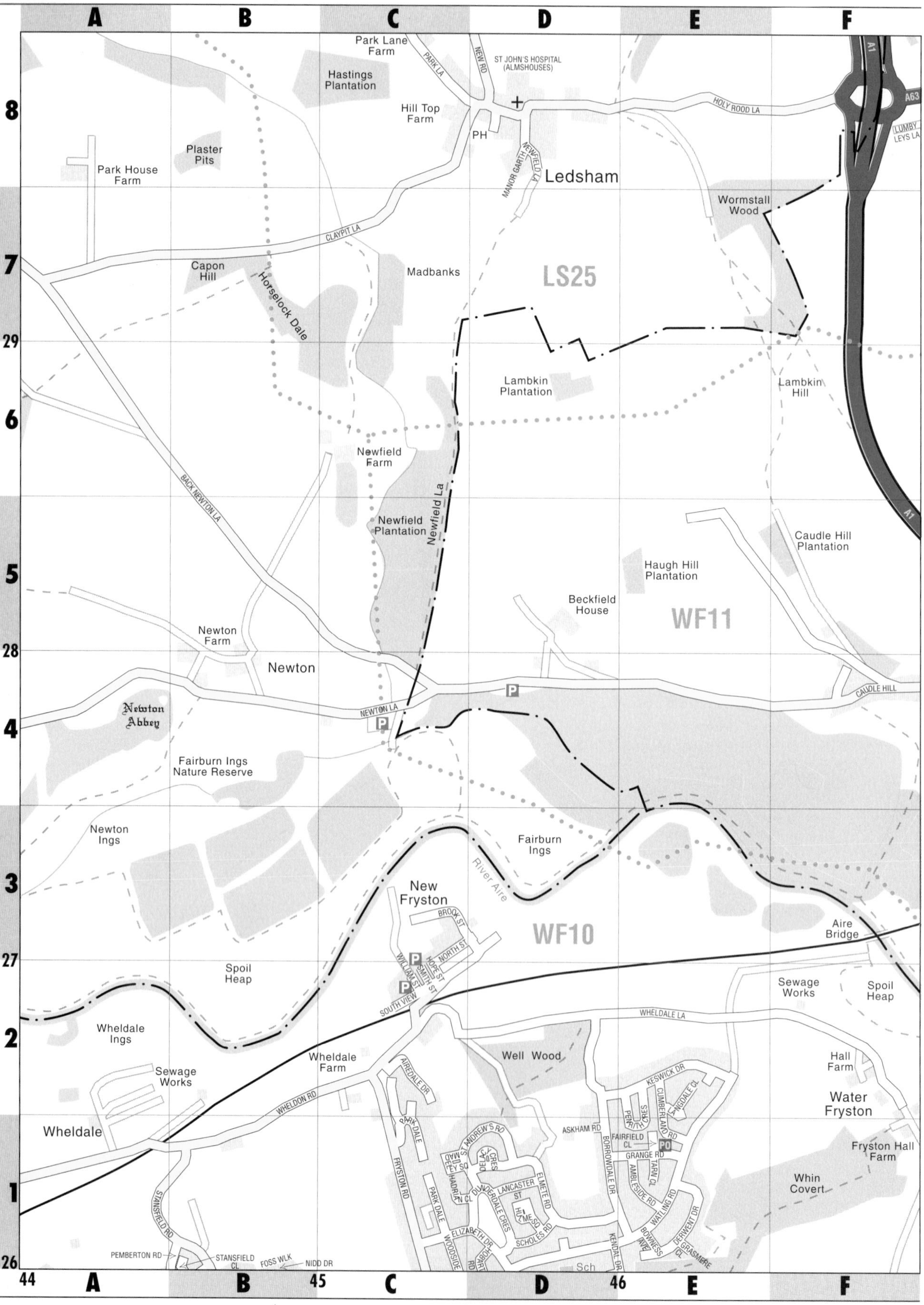

103
125

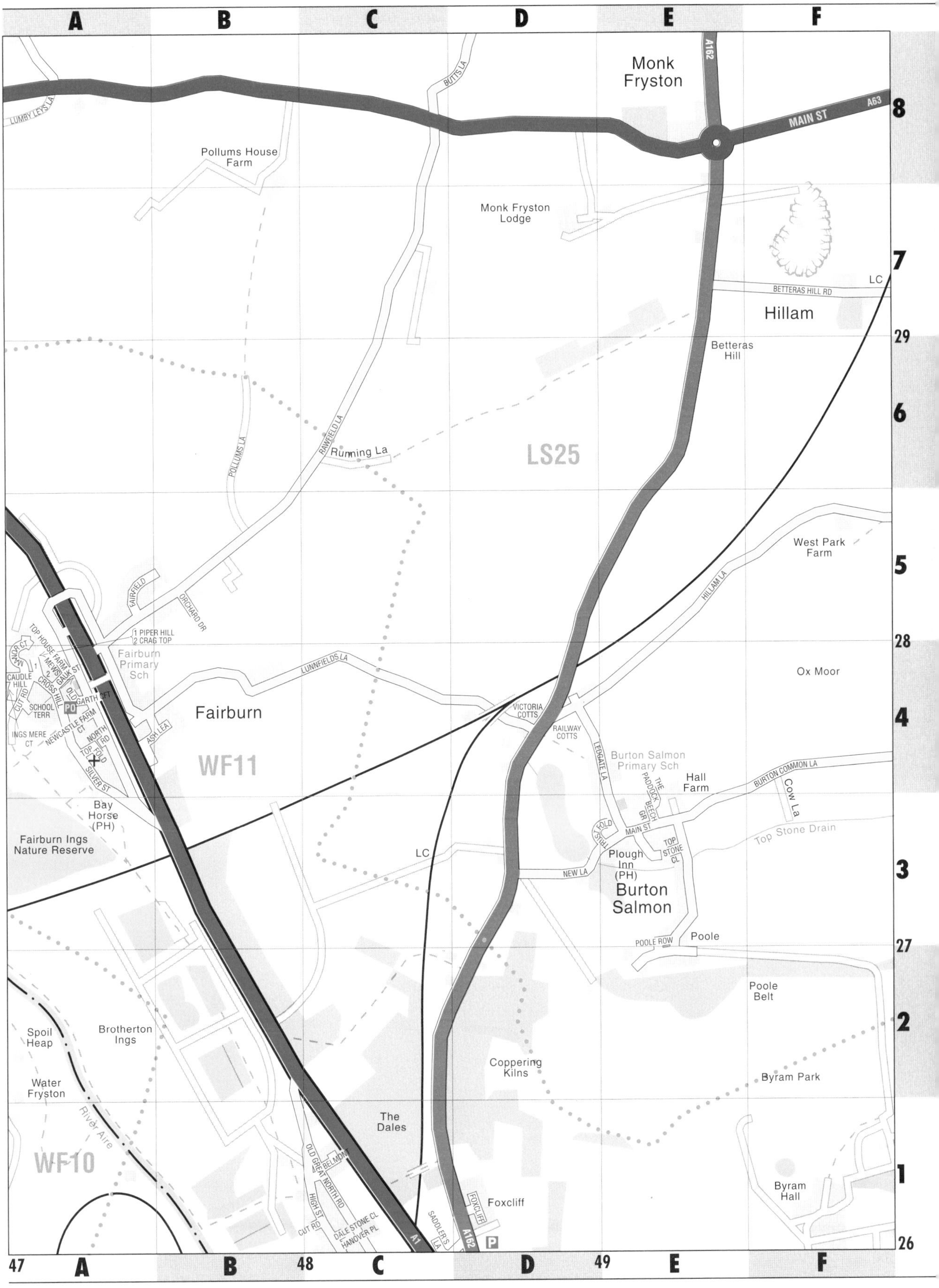
A
B
C
D
E
F
Monk
Fryston
A162
A63
MAIN ST
LUMBY LEYS LA
BUTTS LA
Pollums House
Farm
Monk Fryston
Lodge
BETTERAS HILL RD
LC
Hillam
Betteras
Hill
RAWFIELD LA
Running La
POLLUMS LA
LS25
West Park
Farm
HILLAM LA
FAIRFIELD
ORCHARD DR
1 PIPER HILL
2 CRAG TOP
Fairburn
Primary
Sch
LUNNFIELDS LA
Ox Moor
Fairburn
VICTORIA
COTTS
RAILWAY
COTTS
WF11
ASH LEA
Burton Salmon
Primary Sch
LEDGATE LA
THE
PADDOCK
BEECH
GR
Hall
Farm
BURTON COMMON LA
Cow La
TRUS FOLD
MAIN ST
TOP
STONE
CL
Top Stone Drain
Plough
Inn
(PH)
Burton
Salmon
NEW LA
LC
MANOR CT
TOP HOUSE FARM MEWS
GAUK ST
CAUDLE HILL
CROSS HILL
CUT RD
SCHOOL TERR
OLD GARTH CFT
PO
NEWCASTLE FARM CT
INGS MERE CT
NORTH RD
TOP FOLD
SILVER ST
Bay
Horse
(PH)
Fairburn Ings
Nature Reserve
POOLE ROW
Poole
Poole
Belt
Spoil
Heap
Brotherton
Ings
Coppering
Kilns
Byram Park
Water
Fryston
River Aire
The
Dales
WF10
OLD GREAT NORTH RD
BELMONT
HIGH ST
CUT RD
DALE STONE CL
HANOVER PL
A1
SADDLERS LA
FOXCLIFF
A162
Foxcliff
P
Byram
Hall
8
7
29
6
5
28
4
3
27
2
1
26
47
48
49

126

85

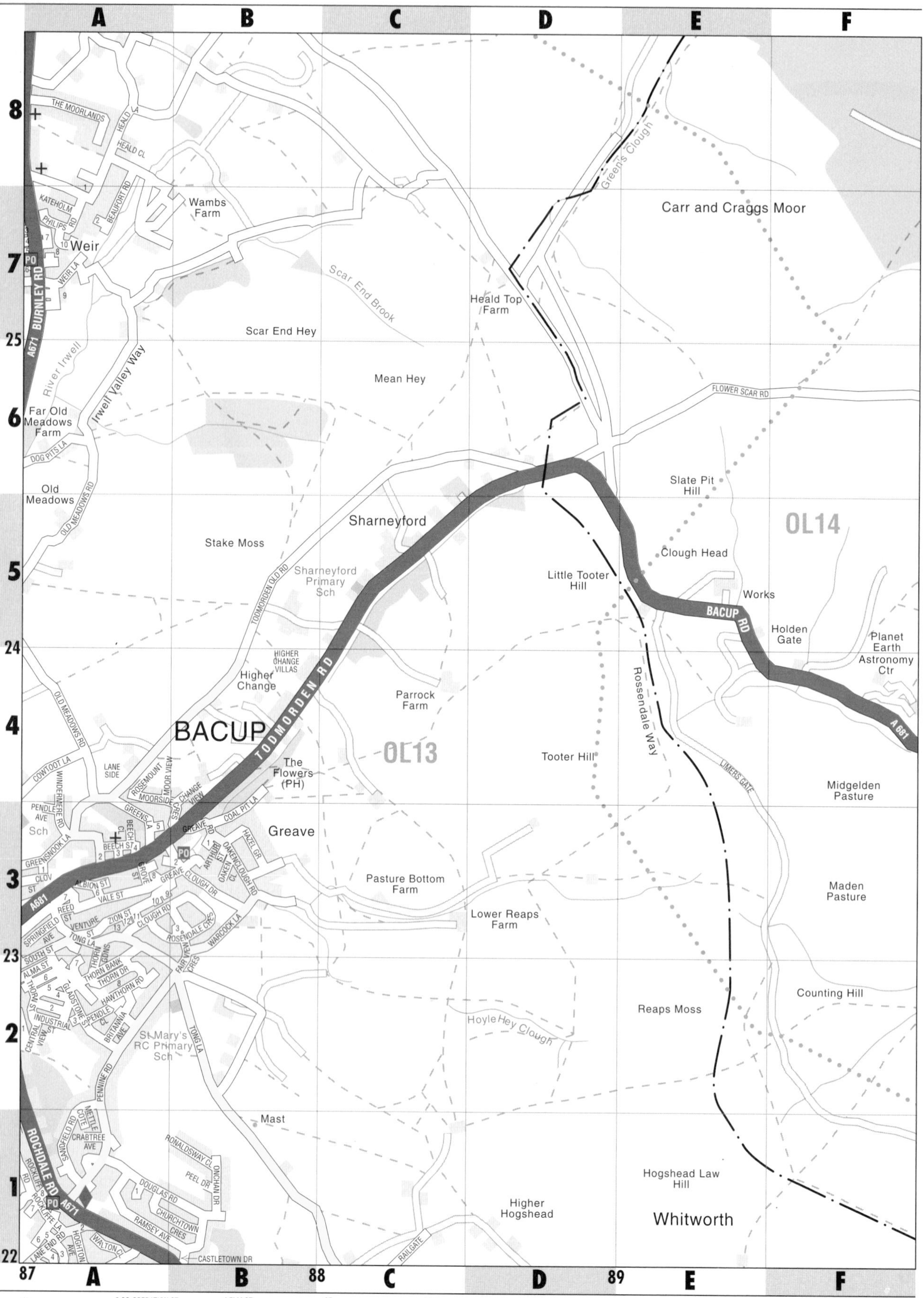

A1
1 FOXDALE CL
2 LANE END LA
3 THE FERNS
4 MERSEY ST
5 BRIAR ST
6 MOORLANDS TERR
7 PINE ST
8 GREEN HILL RD

A2
2 CO-OPERATION ST
3 GLADSTONE CRES
4 REGENT ST
5 CRIMEA ST
6 INKERMAN ST
7 THORN CRES
8 THORN CL

A3
1 GREENSNOOK TERR
2 CARLTON ST
3 CHRIST CHURCH ST
4 ELM ST
5 THE COURTYARD
6 CROSS ST
7 SPRING GDNS
8 GREEN END CL
9 EDWARD ST
10 BEAVER TERR
11 HANNAH ST
12 ASHWORTH ST
13 COWGILL ST

A7
1 WESLEY TERR
2 ROCHESTER CL
3 RICHARD ST
4 COMET ST
5 WRIGHT ST
6 HILLSIDE CRES
7 CAPTAIN ST
8 HALLEY ST
9 MELROSE TERR
10 NICOLA CL

B3
1 NUTTALL ST
2 GREAVE CLOUGH CL
3 ROSENDALE CL

86
108

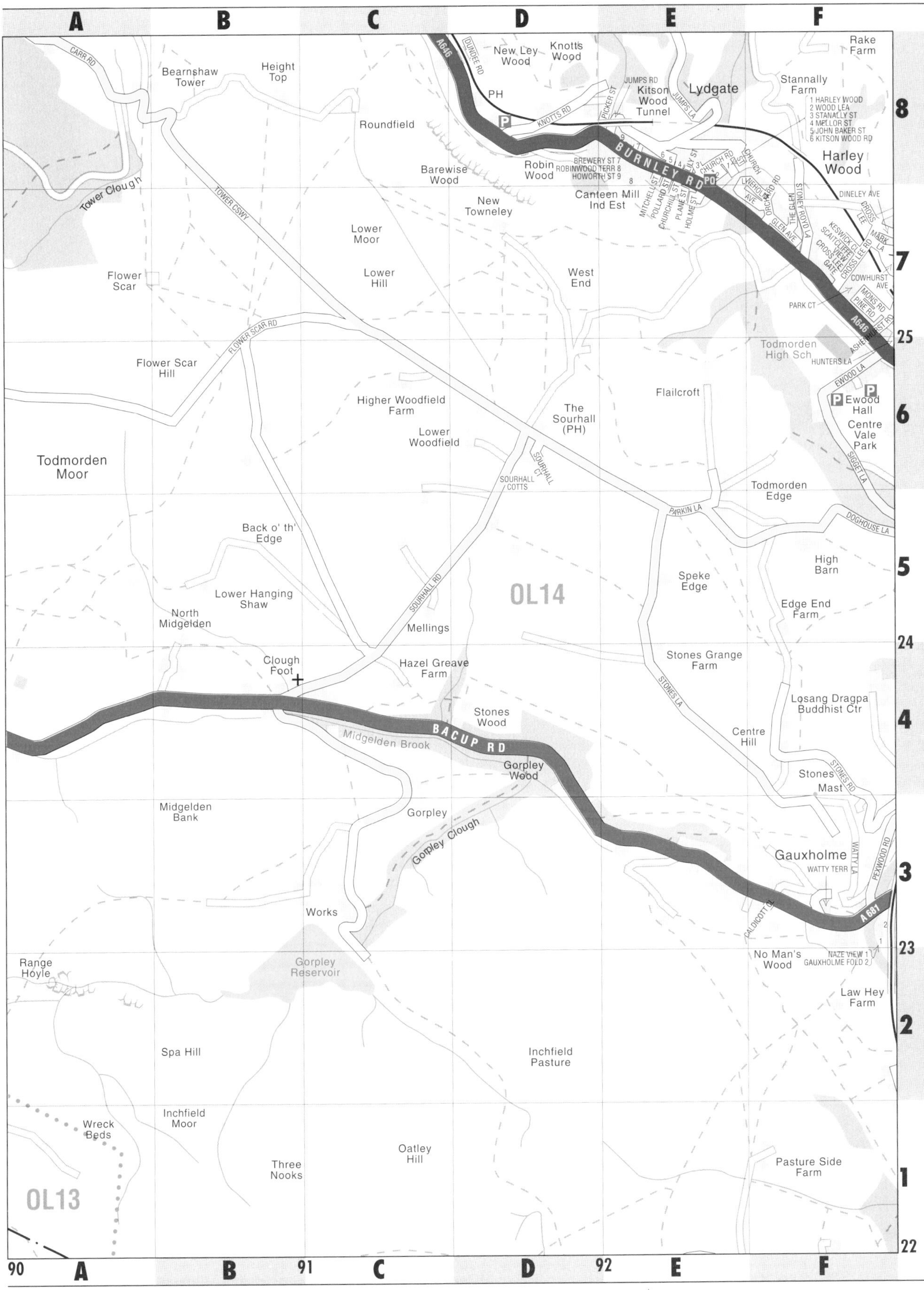

128
108

B5
1 CRESCENT ST
2 RAGLAN ST
3 BATH ST
4 JOHN ST
5 SHORT ST
6 COUPLAND ST
7 MOUNT PLEASANT VIEW
8 WHITE HART FOLD
9 SCHOOL LA
10 BROOK ST
11 ROOMFIELD CT
12 CAMBRIDGE PL
13 GEORGE ST
14 YORK PL
15 CROSSLEY ST
16 BUCKLEY WOOD BOTTOM
B6
1 COWFOLD ST
2 GLEDHILL ST
3 ADELAIDE ST

107

87

B6
4 BACK BYROM ST
5 HAMMERTON TERR
6 NUTFIELD ST
7 JOSHUA ST
8 STANSFIELD ST
9 HAWTHORN PL
10 UPPER RAGLAN ST
11 SCHOLFIELD ST
12 WHITEPLATTS ST
13 PICKLES CT
C5
1 HEY ST
2 SANWORTH ST
3 OSBORNE PL
4 ANCHOR ST
5 LOWER GEORGE ST
6 GIBSON ST
7 BACK DER ST
8 RICHMOND ST
9 EVERY ST
10 GORDON ST
11 HOPE BLDGS
12 ERRINGDEN ST
13 KILNHURST AVE
14 HOLDERNESS ST
15 HAVEN ST
16 BACK COMMERICAL ST
17 OLD CROSS STONE RD
D6
1 CARR HOUSE FOLD
2 WALTON FOLD
3 CORNFIELD ST
4 CHAPEL ST

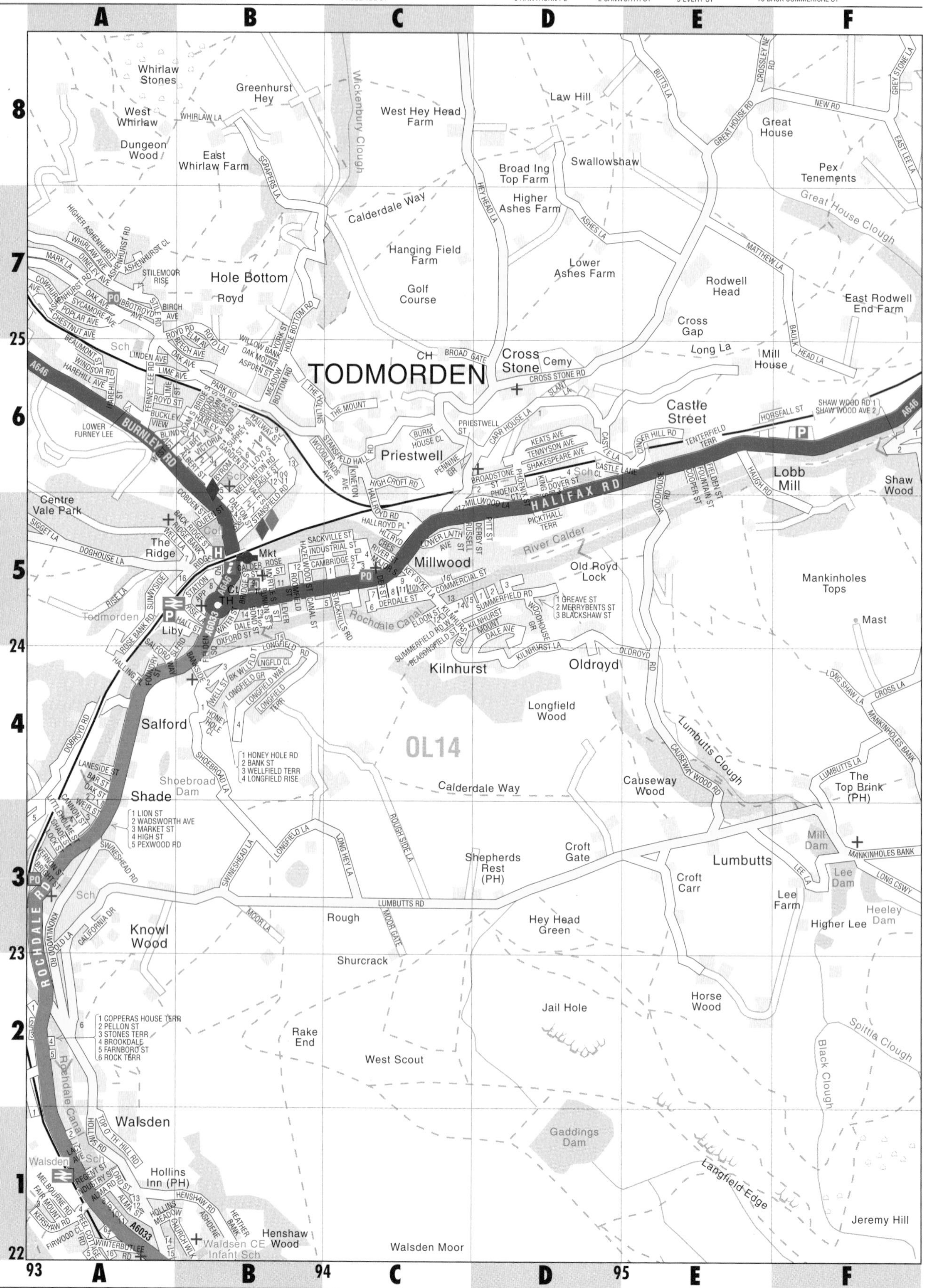

107

129

A1
1 MONA'S TERR
2 GRANVILLE ST
3 CALF HEY TERR
4 CLOUGH RD
5 PEEL COTT ST
6 BARNES ST
7 CHAPEL ST S
8 QUEBEC ST
9 MONTREAL ST
10 SAXON ST
11 VULCAN ST
12 WHARF ST
13 HOLLINS PL
14 KNOWSLEY AVE
15 DAMPIER ST
16 WINTERBUTLEE GR

88 110

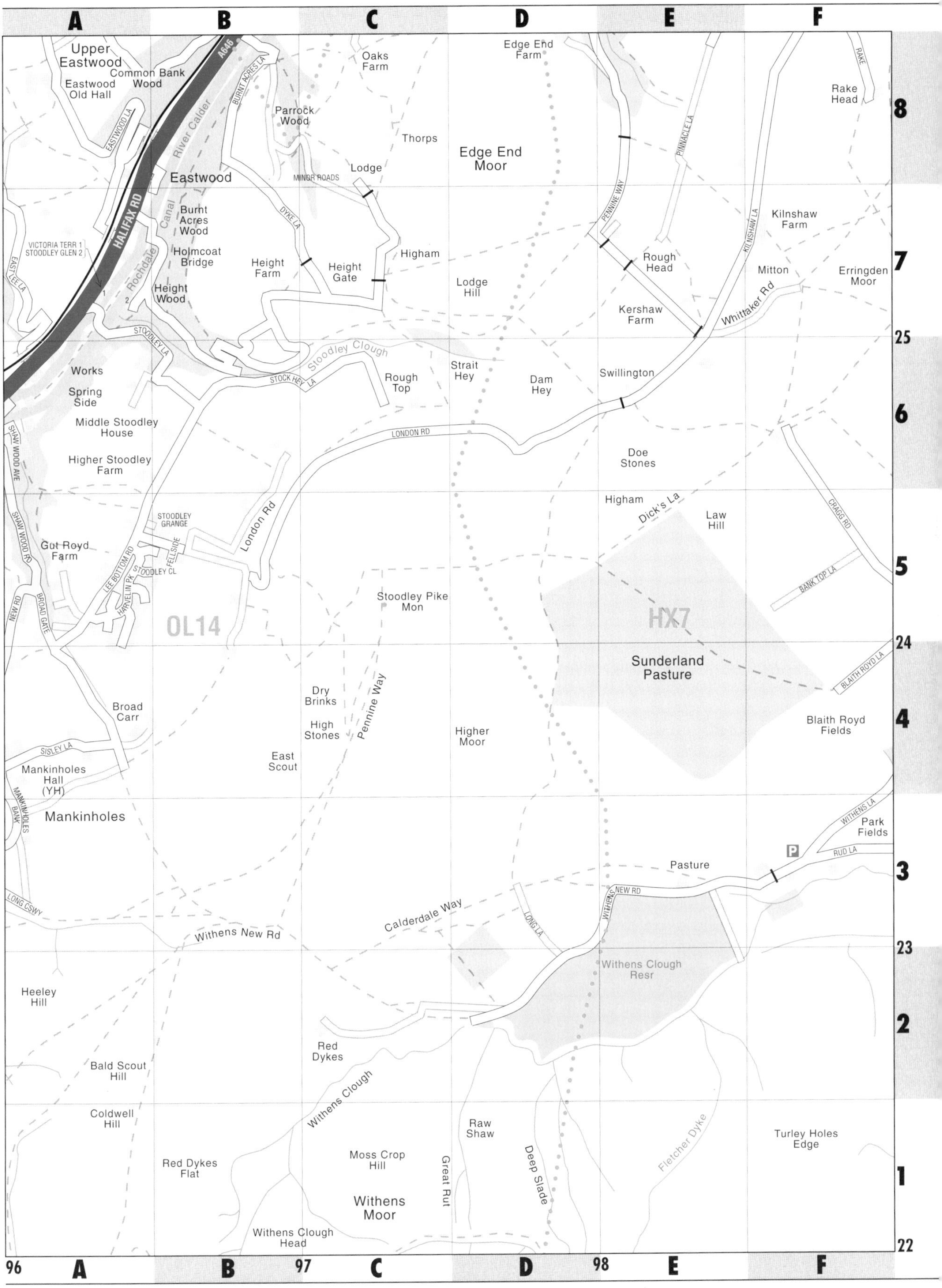

130 110

109
89

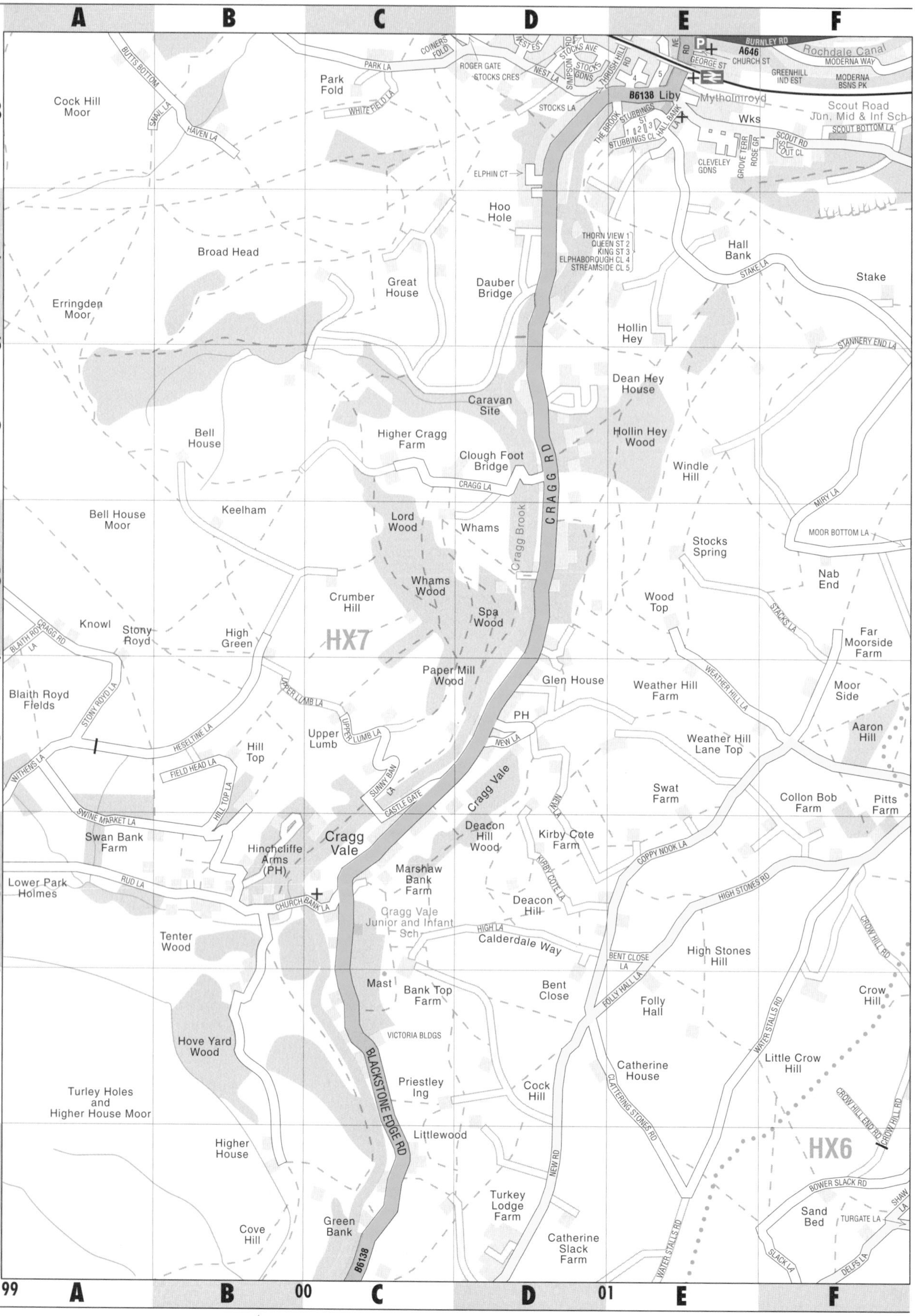

109
131

90
112

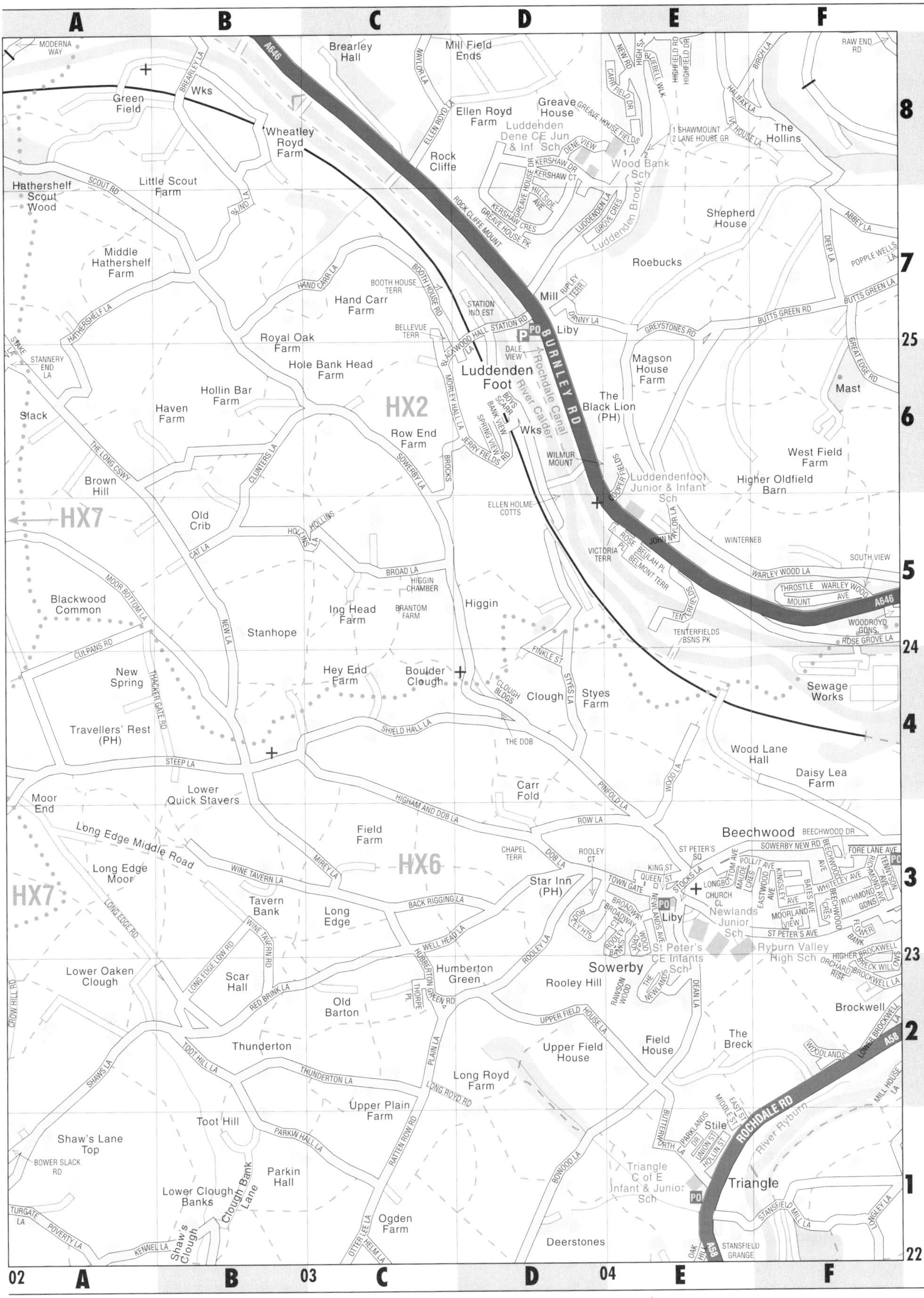
A
B
C
D
E
F
MODERNA WAY
A646
Brearley Hall
Mill Field Ends
NAYLOR LA
NEW RD
HIGH ST
HIGHFIELD RD
HIGHFIELD DR
RAW END RD
BIRCH LA
Green Field
BREARLEY LA
Wks
Wheatley Royd Farm
ELLEN ROYD LA
Ellen Royd Farm
Greave House
GREAVE HOUSE FIELDS
CARR FIELD DR
Luddenden Dene CE Jun & Inf Sch
1 SHAWMOUNT
2 LANE HOUSE GR
HALIFAX LA
IVE HOUSE LA
The Hollins
8
Hathershelf Scout Wood
SCOUT RD
Little Scout Farm
BLIND LA
Rock Cliffe
DENE VIEW
KERSHAW DR
KERSHAW CT
Wood Bank Sch
Luddenden Brook
LUDDENDEN LA
GROVE CRES
GREAVE HOUSE DR
HILLSIDE AVE
KERSHAW CRES
GREAVE HOUSE PK
ROCK CLIFFE MOUNT
Shepherd House
ABBEY LA
Middle Hathershelf Farm
HAND CARR LA
BOOTH HOUSE TERR
BOOTH HOUSE RD
Hand Carr Farm
STATION IND EST
Mill
RIPLEY TERR
Roebucks
DEEP LA
POPPLE WELLS LA
7
BUTTS GREEN LA
BUTTS GREEN RD
DANNY LA
HATHERSHELF LA
STAKE LA
STANNERY END LA
Royal Oak Farm
BELLEVUE TERR
BLACKWOOD HALL LA
STATION RD
P
PO
Liby
BURNLEY RD
GREYSTONES RD
25
Hole Bank Head Farm
DALE VIEW
Luddenden Foot
Rochdale Canal
River Calder
Magson House Farm
GREAT EDGE RD
Hollin Bar Farm
Haven Farm
HX2
MORLEY HALL LA
BOYS SCARR
BANK VIEW
The Black Lion (PH)
Mast
Slack
Row End Farm
SPRING VIEW
Wks
6
THE LONG CSWY
JERRY FIELDS RD
SOWERBY LA
BROCKS
WILMUR MOUNT
West Field Farm
Brown Hill
CLUNTERS LA
COOPER FIELDS
Luddendenfoot Junior & Infant Sch
Higher Oldfield Barn
HX7
Old Crib
ELLEN HOLME COTTS
HOLLINS
HOLLINS LA
ROSE PL
BEULAH PL
JOHN NAYLOR LA
WINTERNEB
CAT LA
VICTORIA TERR
BELMONT TERR
SOUTH VIEW
MOOR BOTTOM LA
BROAD LA
HIGGIN CHAMBER
WARLEY WOOD LA
THROSTLE MOUNT
WARLEY WOOD AVE
5
Blackwood Common
Ing Head Farm
BRANTOM FARM
Higgin
TENTERFIELDS
A646
NEW LA
Stanhope
TENTERFIELDS BSNS PK
WOODROYD GDNS
ROSE GROVE LA
CULPANS RD
FINKLE ST
24
New Spring
THACKER GATE RD
Hey End Farm
Boulder Clough
CLOUGH BLDGS
Clough
STYES LA
Styes Farm
Sewage Works
Travellers' Rest (PH)
SHIELD HALL LA
THE DOB
4
STEEP LA
Wood Lane Hall
WOOD LA
Daisy Lea Farm
PINFOLD LA
Moor End
Lower Quick Stavers
Carr Fold
HIGHAM AND DOB LA
ROW LA
Long Edge Middle Road
Field Farm
Beechwood
BEECHWOOD DR
CHAPEL TERR
DOB LA
ST PETER'S SQ
SOWERBY NEW RD
FORE LANE AVE
Long Edge Moor
WINE TAVERN LA
MIREY LA
HX6
ROOLEY CT
KING ST
QUEEN ST
STOCKS LA
LONGBOTTOM AVE
POLLIT AVE
TENNYSON AVE
RICHMOND AVE
PO
HX7
Star Inn (PH)
TOWN GATE
CHURCH CL
MAUDE CRES
EASTWOOD AVE
KINGSLEY AVE
WHITELEY AVE
BATES AVE
3
Tavern Bank
Long Edge
BACK RIGGING LA
BROADWAY
ROOLEY HTS
NEWLANDS AVE
Liby
Newlands Junior Sch
MOORLAND VIEW
RICHMOND GDNS
LONG EDGE RD
WINE TAVERN RD
WELL HEAD LA
FLOWER BANK
ST PETER'S AVE
LONG EDGE LOW RD
Scar Hall
HUMBERTON GREEN RD
Humberton Green
ROOLEY LA
St Peter's CE Infants Sch
Ryburn Valley High Sch
HIGHER BROCKWELL
BRECK WILLOWS
23
Lower Oaken Clough
RED BRINK LA
THORPE PL
Sowerby
Rooley Hill
RAWSON WOOD
THE NEWLANDS
DEAN LA
ORCHARD RISE
BROCKWELL LA
CROW HILL RD
Old Barton
UPPER FIELD HOUSE LA
Brockwell
LOWER BROCKWELL LA
2
TOOT HILL LA
Thunderton
PLAIN LA
Field House
The Breck
WOODLANDS
A58
SHAWS LA
THUNDERTON LA
Upper Field House
Long Royd Farm
LONG ROYD RD
MILL HOUSE LA
Upper Plain Farm
ROCHDALE RD
River Ryburn
Toot Hill
RATTEN ROW RD
BUTTERWORTH LA
PARKLANDS DR
MIDDLE ST
EAST ST
Stile
UNION ST
HOLLIN ST
Shaw's Lane Top
PARKIN HALL LA
BOWER SLACK RD
Parkin Hall
BOWOOD LA
Triangle C of E Infant & Junior Sch
Triangle
1
Lower Clough Banks
Clough Bank Lane
PO
STANSFIELD MILL LA
LONGLEY LA
TURGATE LA
POVERTY LA
Shaw's Clough
KENWELL LA
OTTER LEE LA
Ogden Farm
HELM LA
Deerstones
OAK HILL
A58
STANSFIELD GRANGE
22
02
03
04

132
112

111
91
For full street detail of the highlighted area see page 202.

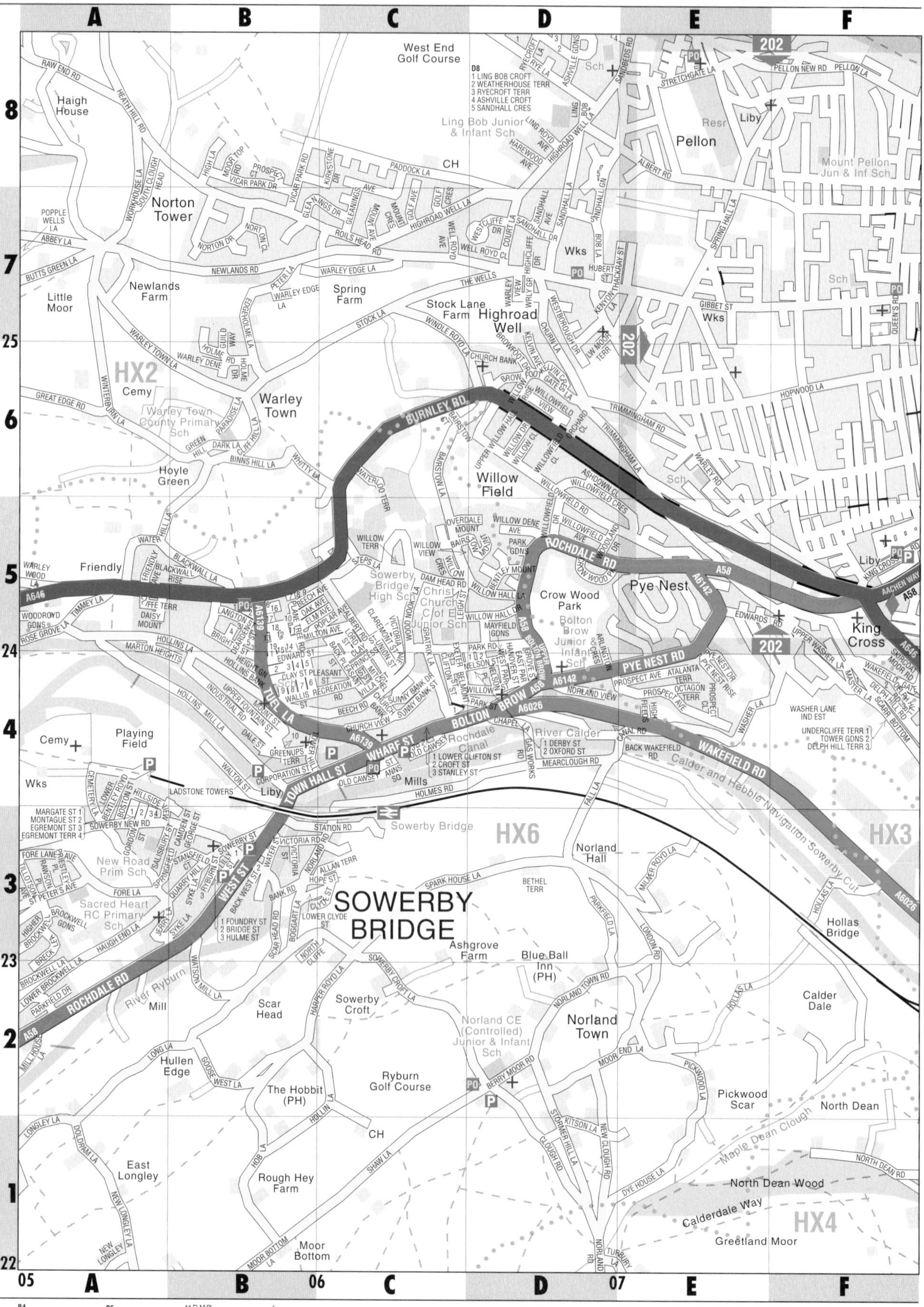

B4
1 ANNIE ST
2 JOHN ST W
3 CHESTER ST
4 ARNOLD ST
5 CLEMENT ST
6 BELGRAVE ST
7 EGERTON ST
8 PEEL ST
9 NEWTON ST
10 HOUGHTON TWRS

B5
1 HILL CREST
2 DALTON ST
3 HILL CREST AVE
4 FERN LEA ST
5 DENBY PL
6 BYRON AVE
7 MALTON ST
8 CHATHAM ST
9 BEECH VIEW
10 OAK PL
11 ELM PL
12 CLEVELEYS GDNS
13 PERSEVERANCE ST
14 CLEVELEYS AVE
15 CHARLES ST
16 BYRON ST
17 REGENT PL
18 OAK ST
19 MILTON ST

111
133

For full street detail of the highlighted area see pages 202 and 203.

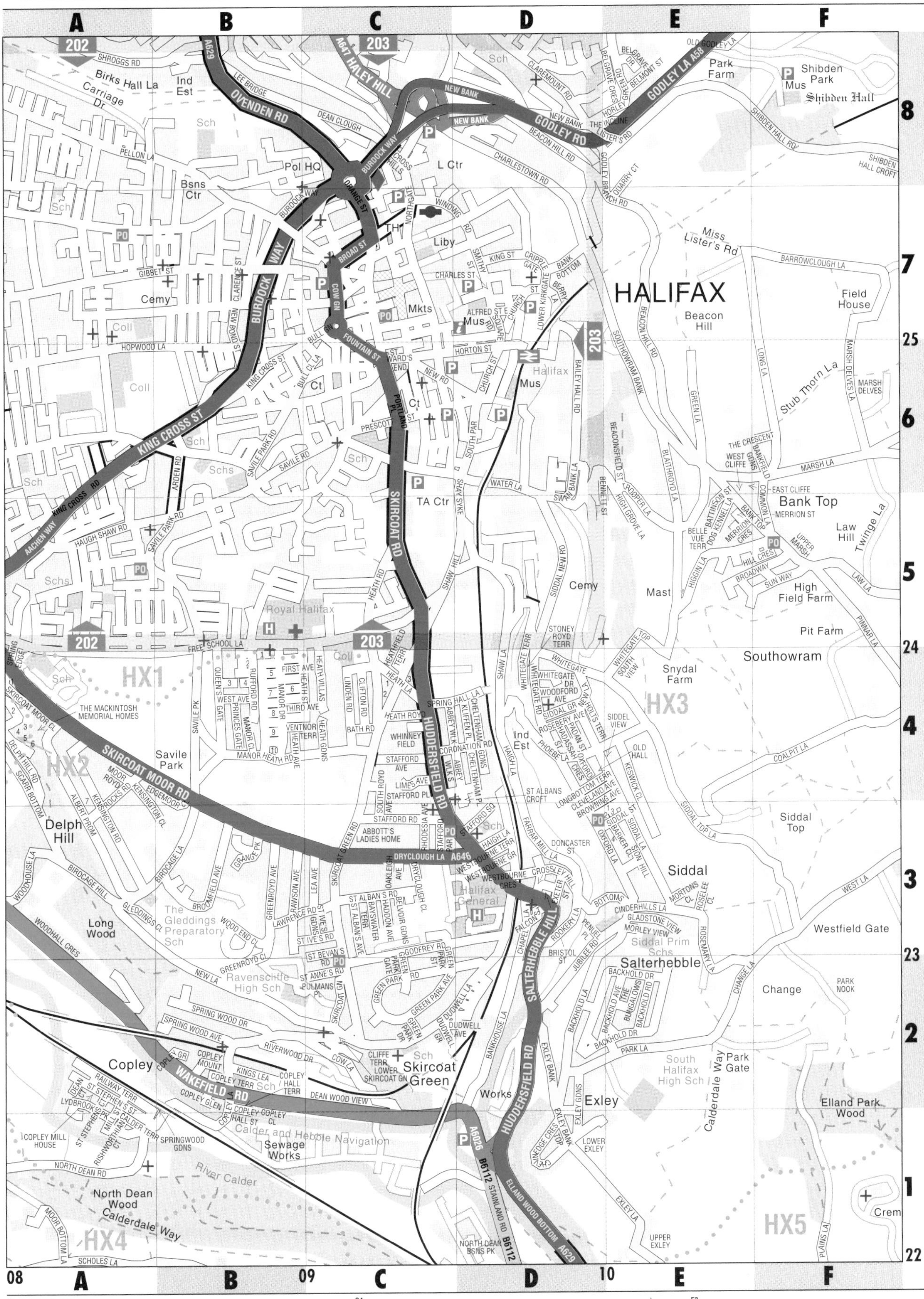

A4
1 STONE CLIFFE
2 ROSE TERR
3 ROCKS VIEW
4 VICTORIA TERR
5 DELPH HILL
6 NORLAND VIEW
7 EASTWOOD CT

B4
1 WARWICK CL
2 RUFFORD PL
3 HEATHERSTONES
4 RUFFORD VILLAS
5 GRANDSMERE PL
6 SECOND AVE
7 MARLBOROUGH AVE
8 AVONDALE PL
9 LEICESTER TERR
10 PARKSIDE

C4
1 HEATHFIELD GR
2 HEATHFIELD PL
3 ELM VIEW

E3
1 ASHGROVE AVE
2 DYSON PL
3 ASHGROVE PL
4 BARKER HOUSE

113
93

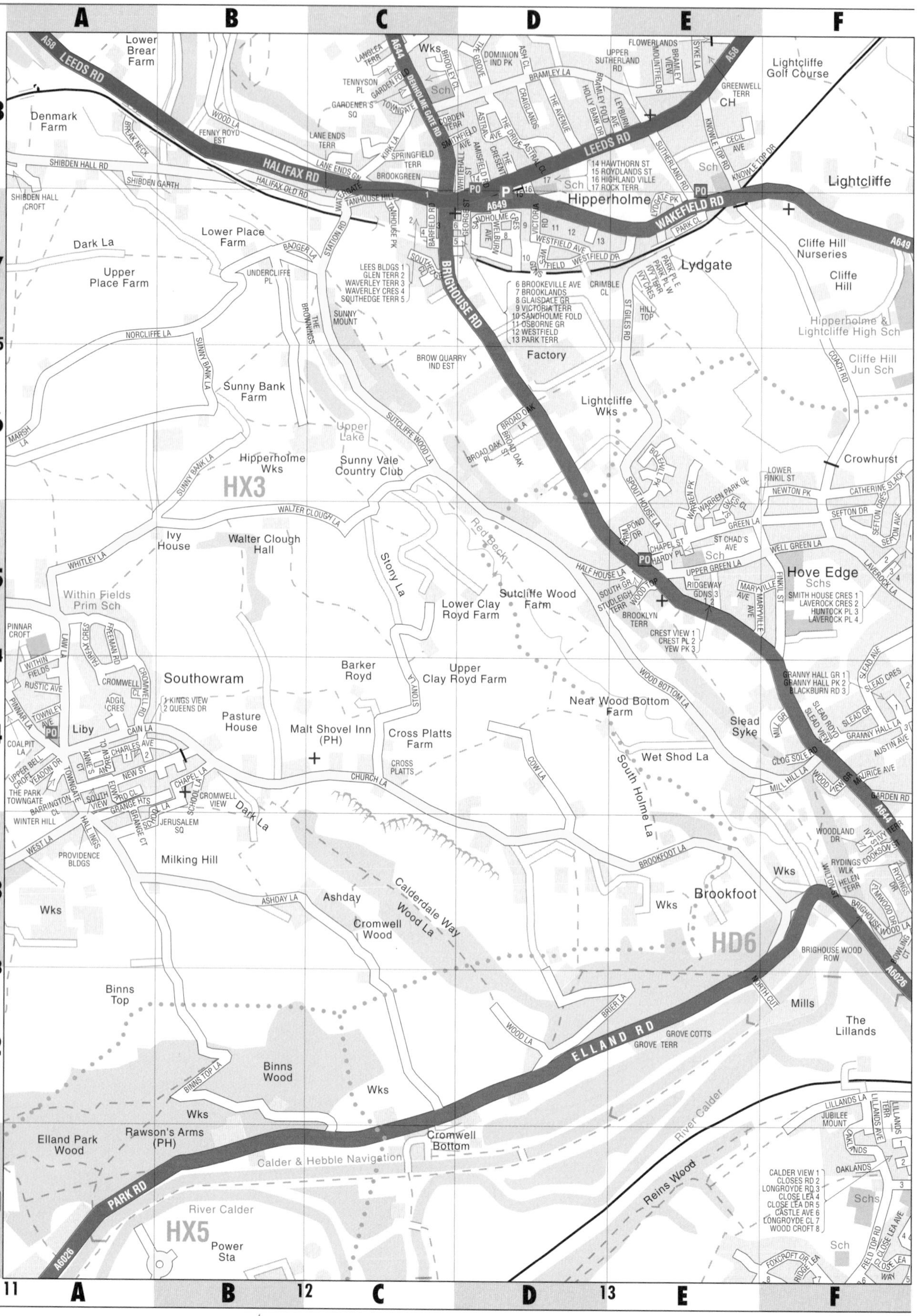

113
135

94

116

F8
1 WICKHAM ST
2 BRIGHTON TERR
3 WALKER ST
4 TABBS LA
5 NAYLOR'S BLDGS
6 GREENFIELD DR
7 WHITECHAPEL RD
8 ACER WAY
9 COWDRAY DR
10 UPPER GREEN AVE
11 LOWER GREEN AVE
12 THE PADDOCK
13 INDUSTRIAL ST

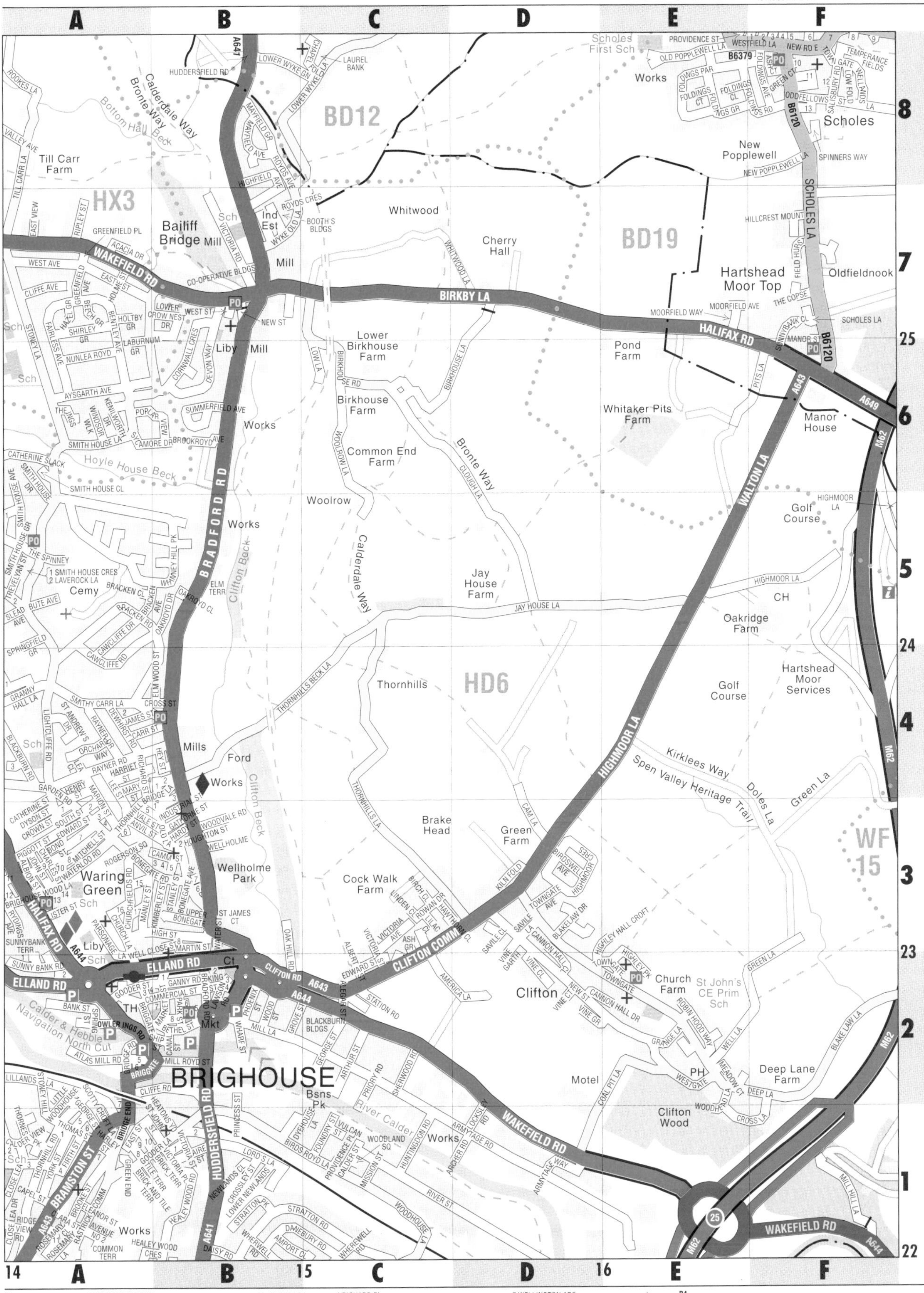

14 A B 15 C D 16 E F

A1
1 THORNHILL PL
2 CLOSES RD
3 LONGROYDE RD
4 DENHAM ST
5 BRYAN ST
6 ASH GROVE TERR
7 HARLEY PL
8 LAURA ST
9 BACK WILLIAM ST
10 WILLIAM ST
11 BRAMSTON GDNS

A2
1 SUNNYBANK GRANGE
2 PROSPECT PL
3 CHURCH LA
4 HEATON ST
5 DAISY ST
6 CROFT ST
7 SCOTTY BANK

A3
1 WILLIAM HENRY ST
2 WEST ST
3 EAST MOUNT
4 EAST MOUNT PL
5 FIRTH AVE
6 SUNDERLAND CT
7 ST MARTIN'S VIEW
8 BACK NEW ST
9 FRANCES ST
10 BACK CHARLES ST
11 RYDINGS CL
12 RYDINGS DR
13 ALBION PL
14 SCULPTOR PL
15 ROCK ST
16 HAIGH ST
17 BARTON ST

A4
1 GRANNY HALL PK
2 TRINITY GR
3 YE FARRE CL
4 RICHARD PL

B1
1 BACK GOODER LA
2 RAILWAY ST

B2
1 HUTCHINSON LA
2 HANGRAM ST
3 CLIFTON RD
4 WAKEFIELD RD
5 HALL ST
6 PARK ROW
7 WELLINGTON ARC
8 WEST PARK ST

B3
1 BARBER ST
2 OLD LANE CT
3 THE CRESCENT
4 EMPSALL ROW
5 ALFRED ST
6 LANE COURT NO 1
7 LANE COURT NO 2
8 EASTWOOD ST

B4
1 CROFT PL
2 BOTTOMLEY ST
3 ODDFELLOWS ST

136

116

115
95

D7
1 CARLTON CL
2 CARLTON WAY
3 GLADSTONE ST
4 BADEN TERR
5 CROSS CROWN ST
6 HOLDSWORTH CT
7 PLATT SQ
8 BUTTS YD
9 OLD ROBIN
D8
1 BEATRICE ST
2 ALICE ST
3 JOHN WILLIAM ST
4 TENNYSON PL
5 LYNTON TERR
6 CROWTHER ST
7 CLAREMONT ST
8 YORK PL
9 WHITFIELD ST
10 CAROLINE ST
11 PROSPECT ST
E7
1 MARKET PL
2 HORNCASTLE ST
3 SPRINGFIELD HOUSE
4 CHURCH GRANGE
5 CENTRAL ARC
6 CENTRAL PAR
7 ST JOHN'S PL
8 CROSS CHURCH ST
9 FAIRFIELD TERR
10 ASHFIELD TERR
11 SUNFIELD TERR
12 MAYFIELD TERR
13 BEECHFIELD TERR
14 WOODHEAD ST
15 PAVEMENT ST
E8
1 COACH LA
2 PROVIDENCE ST

115
137

A5
1 GARDEN PAR
2 GARDEN WLK
3 SPRING VALLEY SQ
4 SPRING VALLEY ST
5 SPRING VALLEY CL
6 YEW TREE CT

A5
7 CARTWRIGHT HOUSE
8 LUDDITE HOUSE
9 ARKWRIGHT HOUSE
10 LEE CT
11 VICAR ST

96

D5
1 MILTON ST
2 GROSVENOR ST

118

F7
1 THE BOWER
2 EALAND CRES
3 LONSDALE AVE
4 EALAND AVE

F8
1 YARD NO 4
2 WENSLEYDALE PAR
3 BROOKROYD GDNS
4 OAK VIEW TERR
5 ROMAN RD

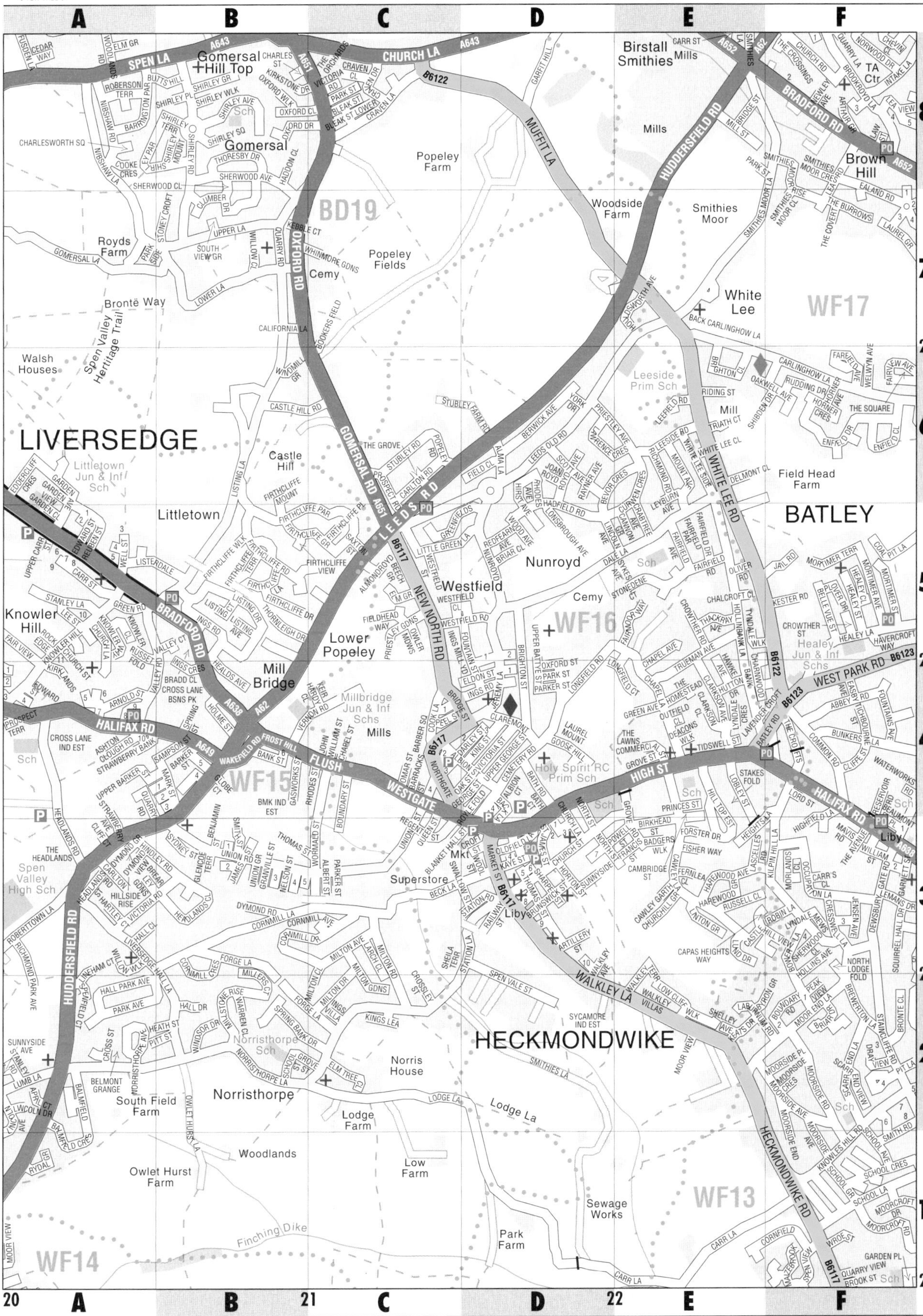

A4
1 RIPLEY RD
2 BURNSALL RD
3 THE HUSTINGS
4 ALEXANDRA ST
5 CHURCHFIELD CL
6 CHURCHFIELD TERR
7 ROUSE ST
8 JAMES ST
9 THOMAS ST
10 GEORGE ST

B3
1 JOHN WILLIAM ST
2 BIRCHWOOD CT
3 WELLINGTON ST
4 MELBOURNE ST
5 FREDERICK ST

B4
1 ALBION ST
2 WILLIAM ST
3 ALFRED ST
4 WHARTON ST
5 BENNETT ST
6 SOUTH ST

C4
1 CENTRE ST
2 WEST ST
3 CARR ST
4 GREENSIDE

D3
1 TOWER BLDGS
2 STRAWBERRY SQ
3 WHARTON TERR
4 ALFRED ST
5 BREWERY ST
6 GARDEN ST
7 STANNINGLEY GR
8 BROOKE ST
9 JOHN ST
10 WALKLEY GR

138

D4
1 GROSVENOR TERR
2 CLARYDON PL
3 PARK RD
4 FRANK PEEL CL

118

F2
1 LOWER BOWER LA
2 HOLLINS RD
3 PROSPECT TERR
4 STAINCLIFFE CRES
5 HEALDS RD
6 KNOWLES HILL
7 NORTH VIEW TERR
8 KNOWLES CROFT

F3
1 STAINCLIFFE HALL RD
2 HILLARY ST
3 CHURWELL AVE
4 WETHERILL TERR
5 SQUIRREL WLK

117
97

C5
1 CHURCHFIELD ST
2 HENRIETTA ST
3 BK HENRIETTA ST
4 BK PROVIDENCE ST
5 MARKET SQ
6 BRUNSWICK ST
7 HUME CREST
8 COBDEN CL
9 BAYLDONS PL
10 WARDS HILL CT

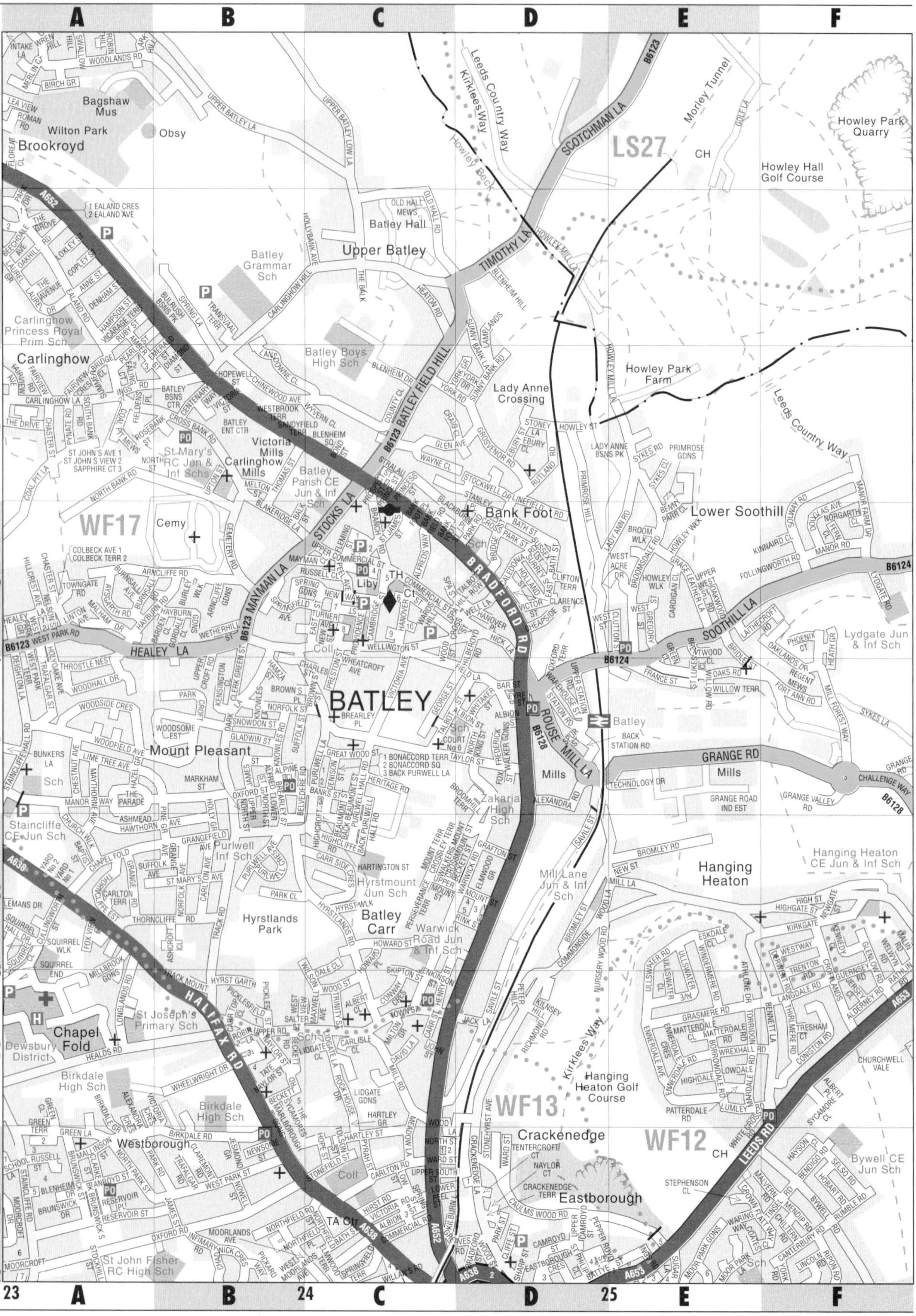

A1
1 SCHOOL CRES
2 BACK LEATHAM ST
3 GLADSTONE CT
4 HANOVER CT
5 FAIRFIELD CRES
6 FIR BANK
7 STAINCLIFFE CL

B2
1 TOP OF CARR
2 NORTH VIEW TERR
3 MITCHELL AVE
4 SOUTH VIEW TERR
5 MARLBRO' TERR

C1
1 LOWER CROSS ST
2 UPPER CROSS ST
3 BRIGHT ST
4 SPINKWELL RD

D1
1 UPPER PEEL ST
2 DEWSBURY RING RD
3 ERNEST ST
4 BACK MARRIOT ST

D3
1 MOUNT AVE
2 BACK MOUNT AVE
3 CROSS RINK ST
4 RINK TERR
5 RINK PAR

E1
1 ALFRED ST
2 JOHN ST
3 WELL ST
4 HOLLINROYD RD
5 VICTORIA BLDGS
6 MOOR PARK CT

117
139

98
120

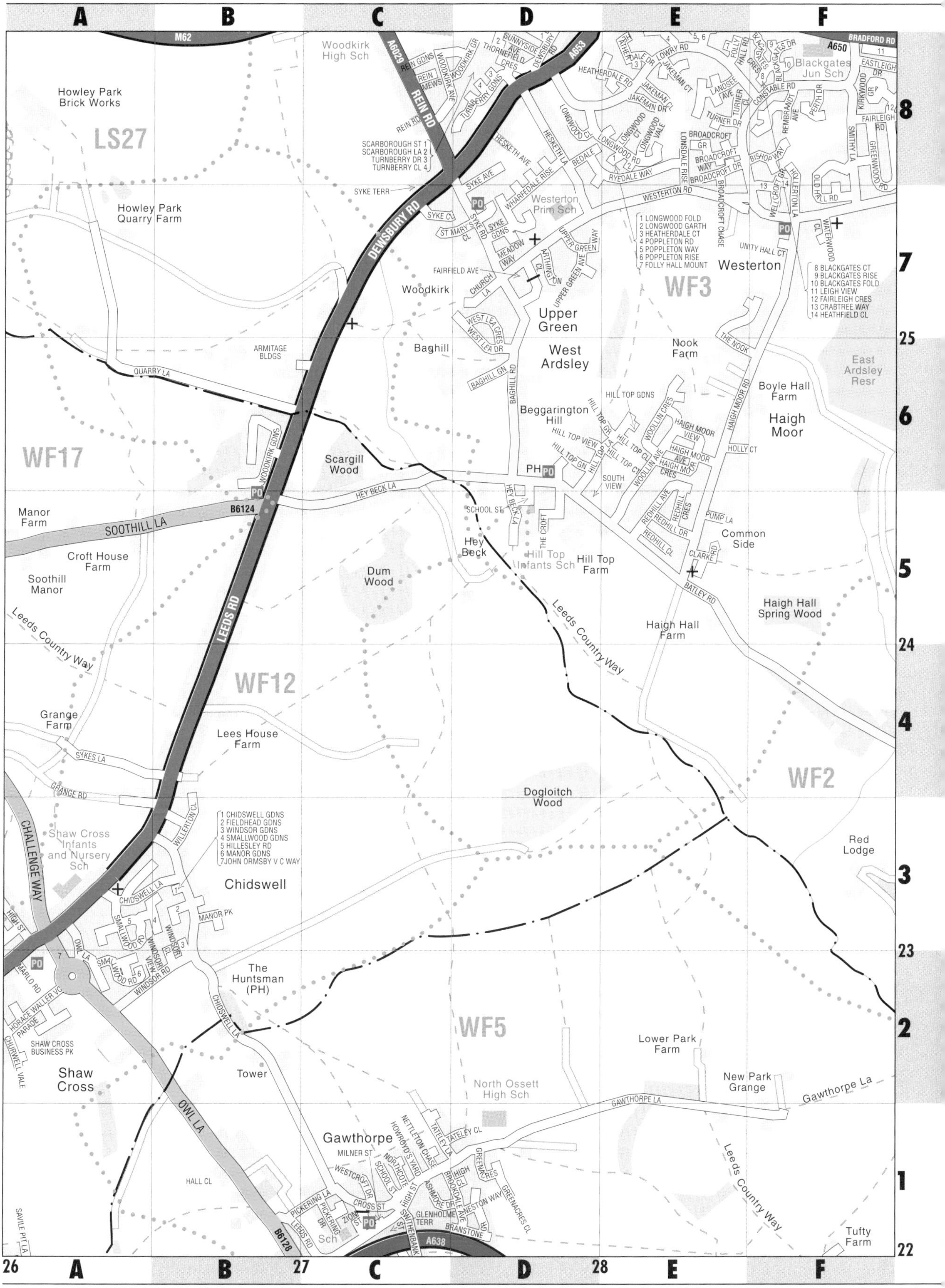

140
120

119
99

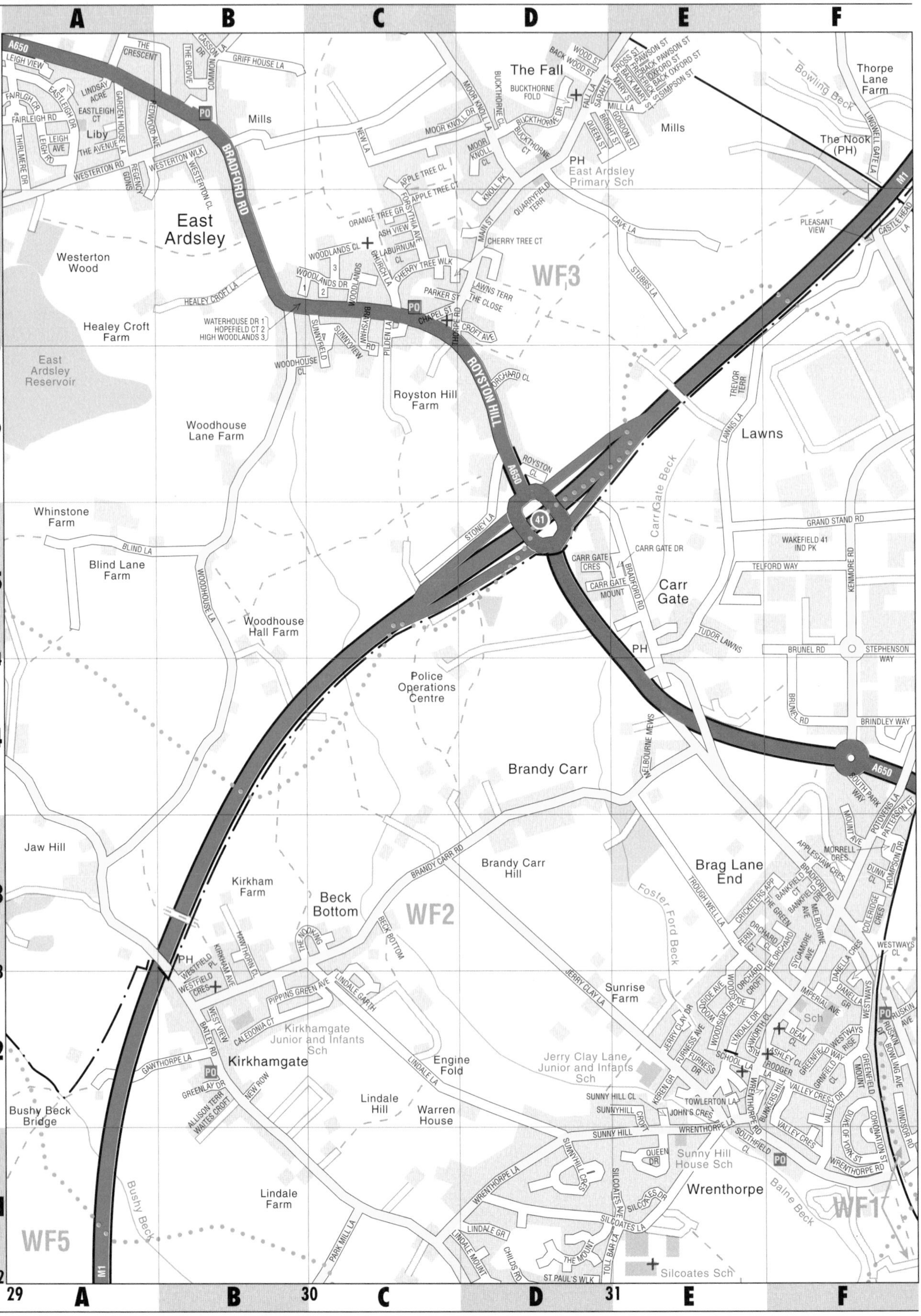
A
B
C
D
E
F
8
7
25
6
5
24
4
3
23
2
1
22
29
30
31
A650
M1
East Ardsley
Westerton Wood
Healey Croft Farm
East Ardsley Reservoir
Woodhouse Lane Farm
Whinstone Farm
Blind Lane Farm
Woodhouse Hall Farm
Jaw Hill
Kirkham Farm
Beck Bottom
Kirkhamgate
Kirkhamgate Junior and Infants Sch
Bushy Beck Bridge
Lindale Farm
Lindale Hill
Warren House
Engine Fold
Police Operations Centre
Brandy Carr
Brandy Carr Hill
Royston Hill Farm
The Fall
Mills
Liby
East Ardsley Primary Sch
Thorpe Lane Farm
The Nook (PH)
Lawns
Carr Gate
Brag Lane End
Sunrise Farm
Jerry Clay Lane Junior and Infants Sch
Sunny Hill House Sch
Wrenthorpe
Silcoates Sch
WF1
WF2
WF3
WF5
BRADFORD RD
ROYSTON HILL
GRAND STAND RD
WAKEFIELD 41 IND PK
TELFORD WAY
BRUNEL RD
STEPHENSON WAY
BRINDLEY WAY
BRANDY CARR RD
JERRY CLAY LA
TROUGH WELL LA
SUNNY HILL
WRENTHORPE LA
LINDALE LA
WOODHOUSE LA
BLIND LA
WATERHOUSE DR 1
HOPEFIELD CT 2
HIGH WOODLANDS 3
Foster Ford Beck
Carr Gate Beck
Bowling Beck
Balne Beck
Bushy Beck

100
122

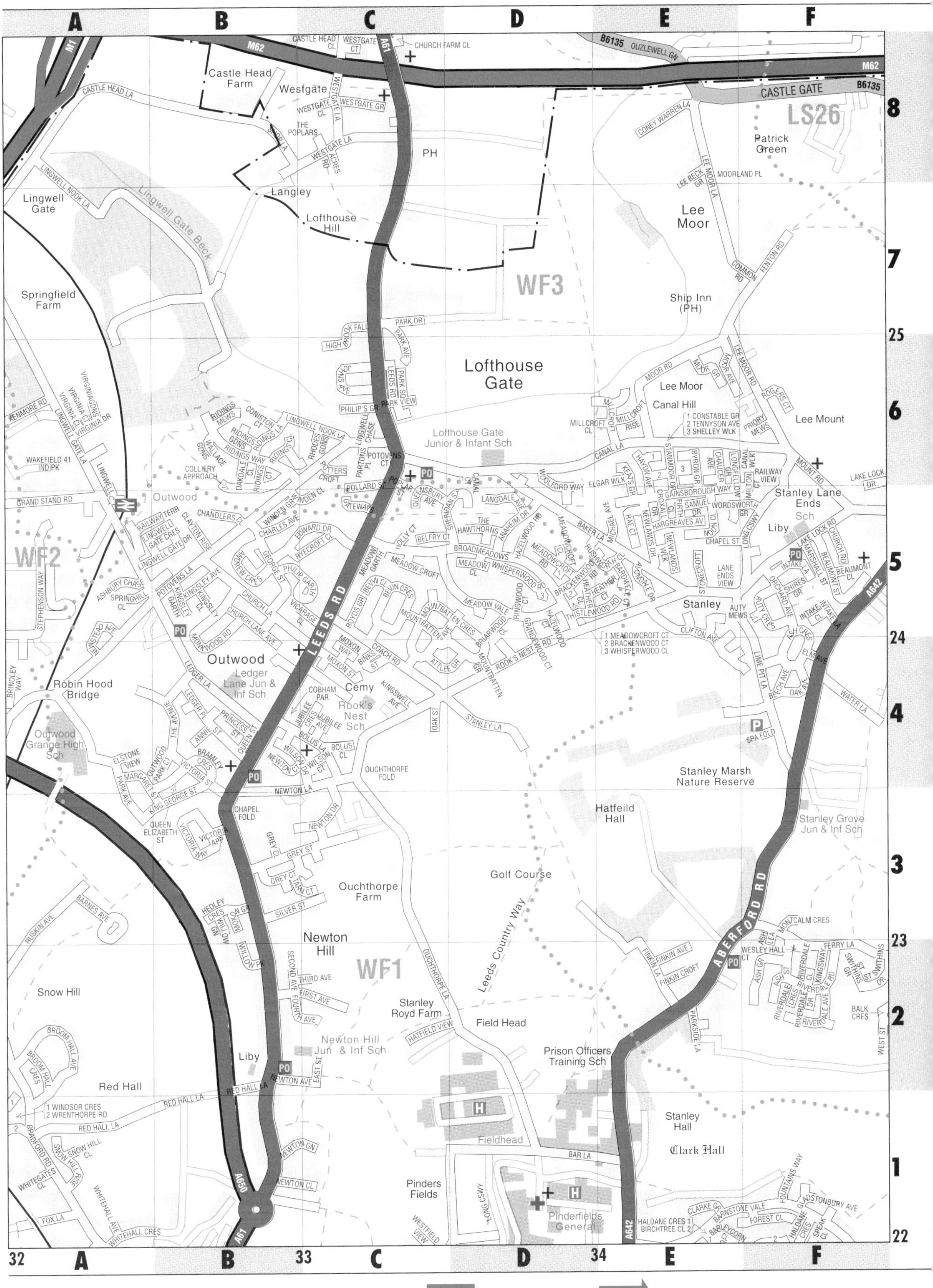

142
122

121
101

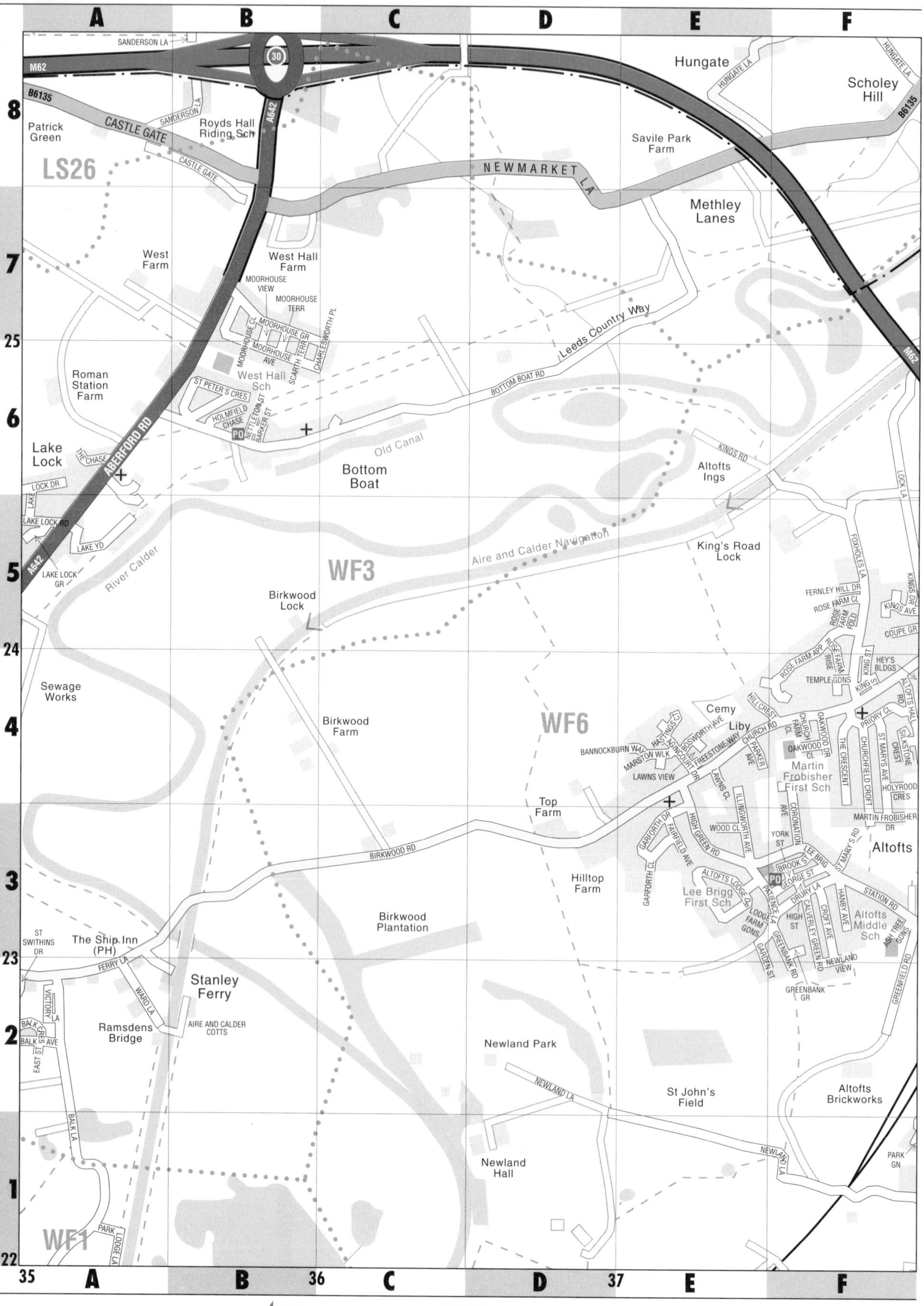

121
143

102
124

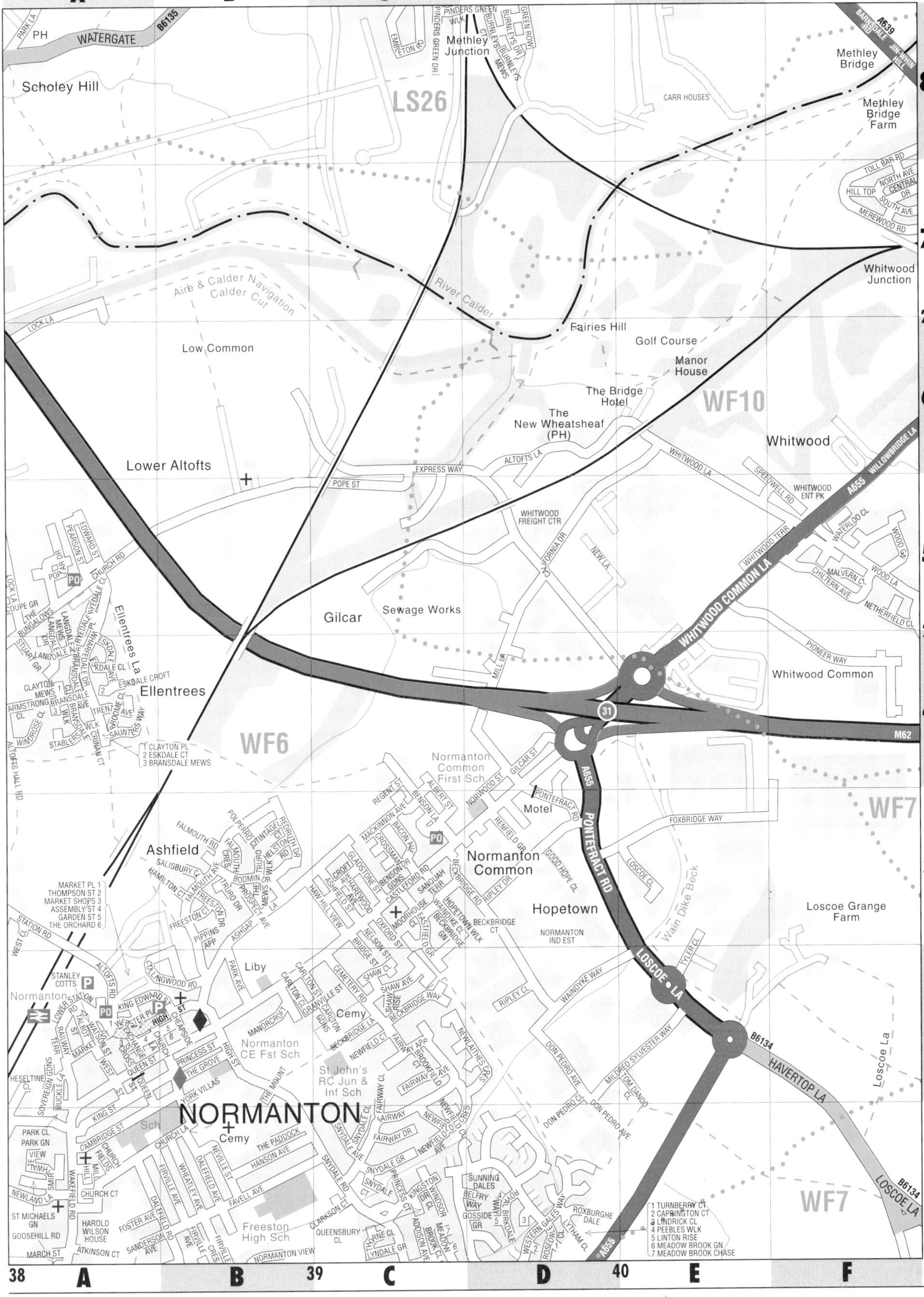

144
124

123
103

D8
1 ST MARY'S PL
2 RECTORY AVE
3 RECTORY ST
4 PERSEVERANCE ST
5 AIRE TERR
6 ST OSWALD ST
7 WESLEY ST
8 COMMERCIAL ST
9 SYKES ST
10 HOPE ST E

E7
1 ROBIN HOOD ST
2 ST HELENS PL
3 POPLAR HO
4 LAUREL HO
5 SYCAMORE HO
6 HOLLY HO
7 BIRCH HO
8 ACACIA HO
9 OAK HO
10 CYPRESS HO
11 MAGNOLIA HO
12 MULBERRY HO

123
145

104
126

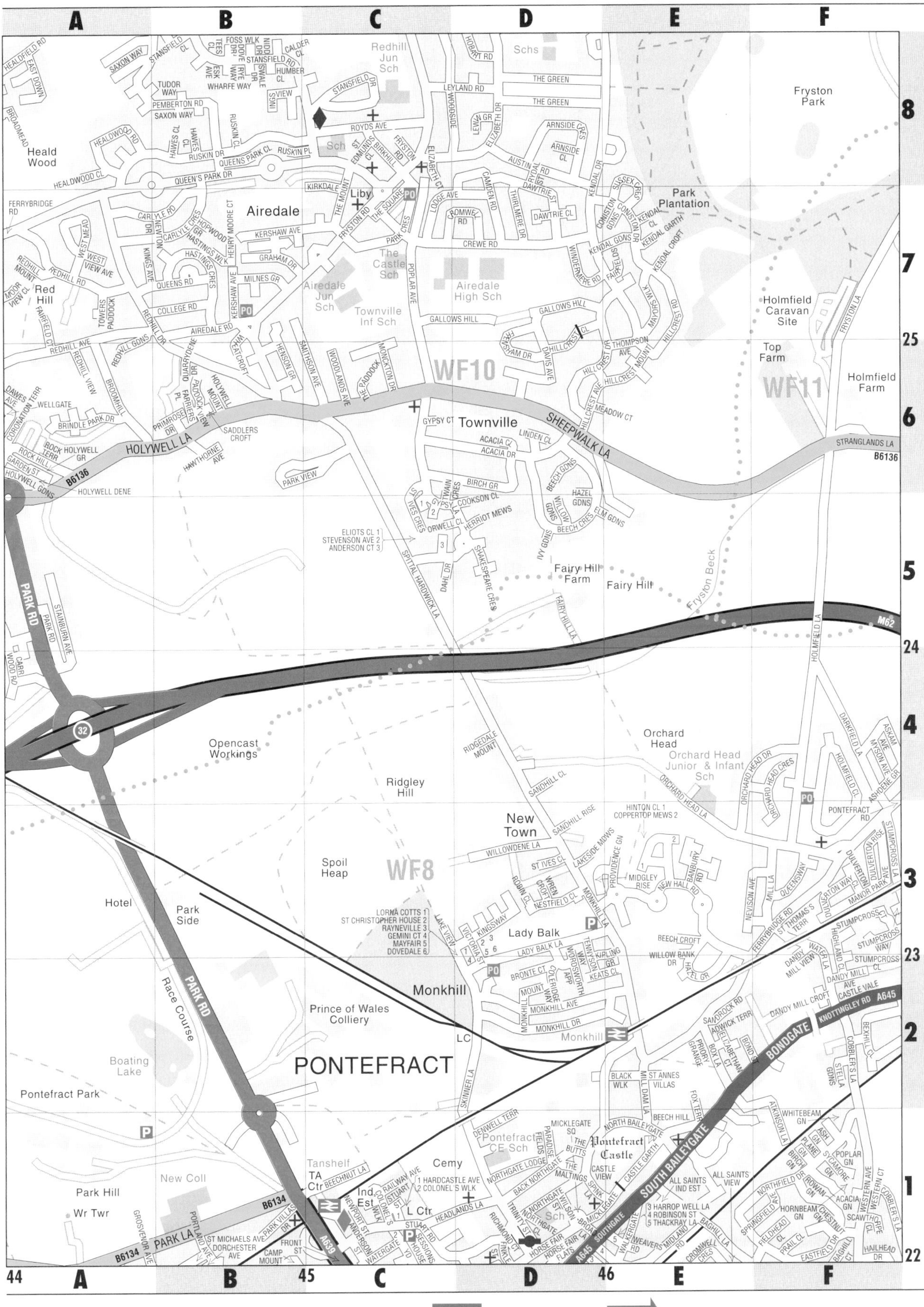

146
126

125
105

125
147

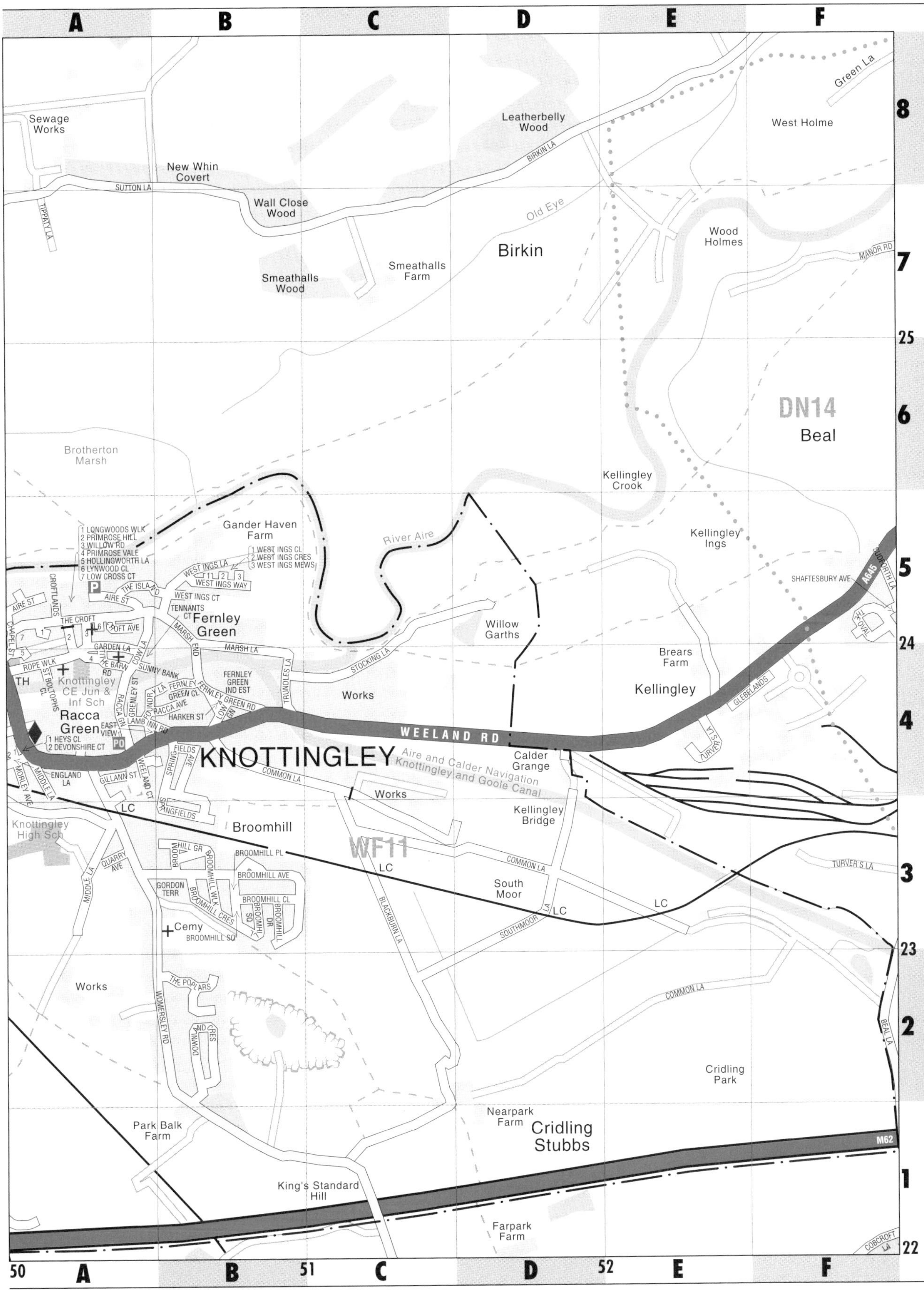
A
B
C
D
E
F
8
7
25
6
5
24
4
3
23
2
1
22
50
51
52
Sewage Works
New Whin Covert
SUTTON LA
TIPPATY LA
Wall Close Wood
Leatherbelly Wood
BIRKIN LA
Green La
West Holme
Old Eye
Birkin
Wood Holmes
MANOR RD
Smeathalls Farm
Smeathalls Wood
DN14
Beal
Brotherton Marsh
Kellingley Crook
Gander Haven Farm
River Aire
Kellingley Ings
1 LONGWOODS WLK
2 PRIMROSE HILL
3 WILLOW RD
4 PRIMROSE VALE
5 HOLLINGWORTH LA
6 LYNWOOD CL
7 LOW CROSS CT
1 WEST INGS CL
2 WEST INGS CRES
3 WEST INGS MEWS
WEST INGS LA
WEST INGS WAY
WEST INGS CT
SHAFTESBURY AVE
A645
SUDFORTH LA
CROFTLANDS
AIRE ST
THE ISLAND
TENNANTS CT
Fernley Green
THE CROFT
CROFT AVE
CHAPEL ST
MARSH END
MARSH LA
Willow Garths
Brears Farm
GARDEN LA
ROPE WLK
STOCKING LA
TRUNDLES LA
FERNLEY GREEN IND EST
SUNNY BANK
TH
Knottingley CE Jun & Inf Sch
ST BOTOLPHS CL
RACCA GN
FERNLEY GREEN CL
FERNLEY GREEN RD
RACCA AVE
HARKER ST
Works
Kellingley
GLEBELANDS
Racca Green
EAST VIEW
1 HEYS CL
2 DEVONSHIRE CT
LAMB INN RD
WEELAND RD
TURVER'S LA
KNOTTINGLEY
Calder Grange
Aire and Calder Navigation
Knottingley and Goole Canal
ENGLAND LA
GILLANN ST
WEELAND CT
COMMON LA
SPRINGFIELDS AVE
MIDDLE LA
MORLEY AVE
LC
Works
Kellingley Bridge
Knottingley High Sch
SPRINGFIELDS
Broomhill
WF11
BROOMHILL GR
BROOMHILL PL
BROOMHILL AVE
QUARRY AVE
COMMON LA
TURVER'S LA
South Moor
GORDON TERR
BROOMHILL WLK
BROOMHILL CL
BROOMHILL CRES
BROOMHILL SQ
BROOMHILL DR
BLACKBURN LA
SOUTHMOOR LA
Cemy
BROOMHILL SQ
Works
THE POPLARS
COMMON LA
WOMERSLEY RD
DOWNLAND CRES
BEAL LA
Cridling Park
Nearpark Farm
Cridling Stubbs
Park Balk Farm
M62
King's Standard Hill
Farpark Farm
COBCROFT LA

107

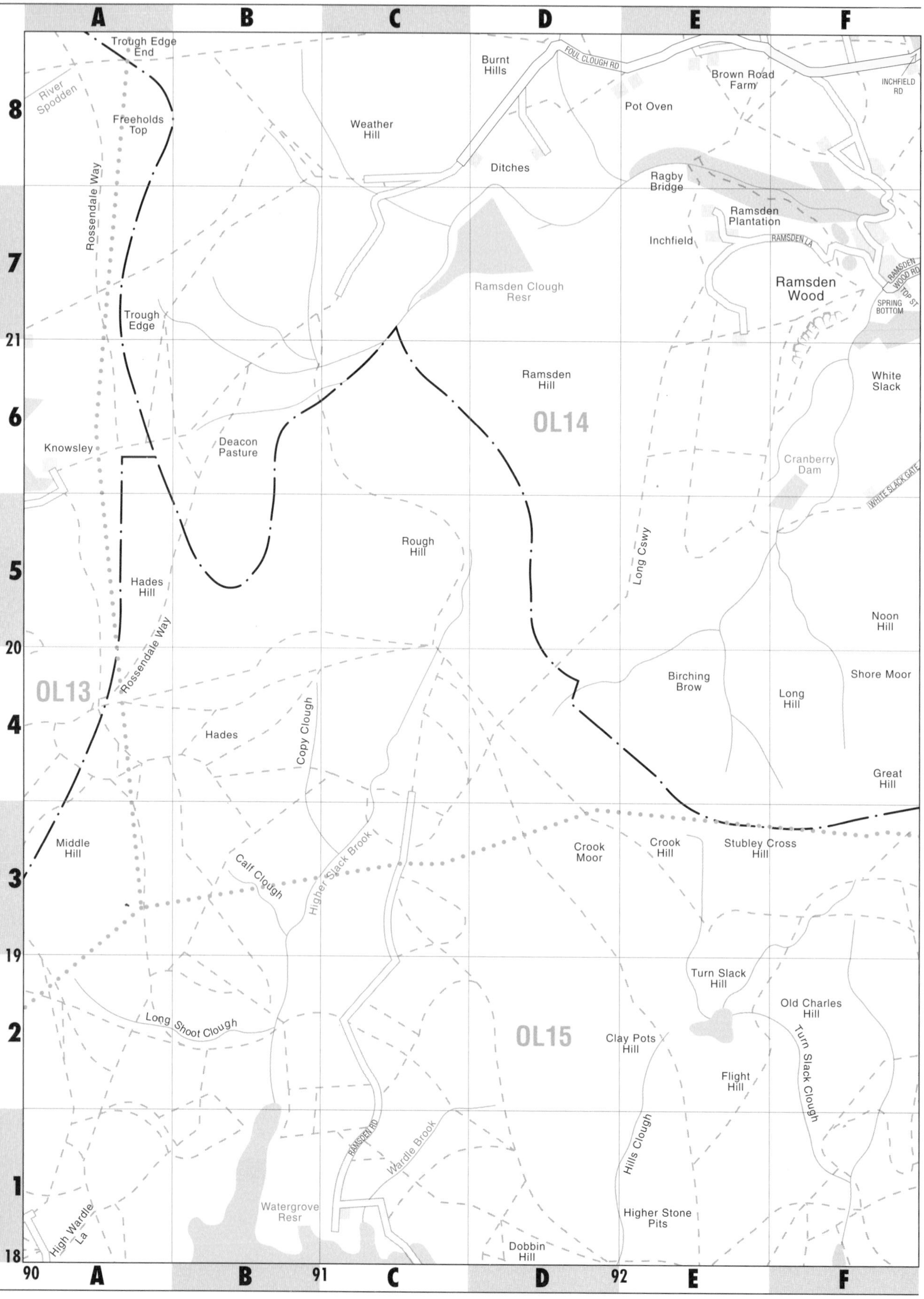

A
B
C
D
E
F
8
7
21
6
5
20
4
3
19
2
1
18
90
91
92
Trough Edge End
River Spodden
Freeholds Top
Rossendale Way
Weather Hill
Burnt Hills
FOUL CLOUGH RD
Brown Road Farm
INCHFIELD RD
Pot Oven
Ditches
Ragby Bridge
Ramsden Plantation
Inchfield
RAMSDEN LA
Ramsden Wood
RAMSDEN WOOD RD
TOP ST
SPRING BOTTOM
Ramsden Clough Resr
Trough Edge
Ramsden Hill
White Slack
OL14
Knowsley
Deacon Pasture
Cranberry Dam
WHITE SLACK GATE
Rough Hill
Long Cswy
Hades Hill
Rossendale Way
Noon Hill
OL13
Birching Brow
Shore Moor
Long Hill
Hades
Copy Clough
Great Hill
Middle Hill
Calf Clough
Higher Slack Brook
Crook Moor
Crook Hill
Stubley Cross Hill
Turn Slack Hill
Old Charles Hill
Long Shoot Clough
OL15
Clay Pots Hill
Turn Slack Clough
Flight Hill
RAMSDEN RD
Wardle Brook
Hills Clough
High Wardle La
Watergrove Resr
Higher Stone Pits
Dobbin Hill

108
130

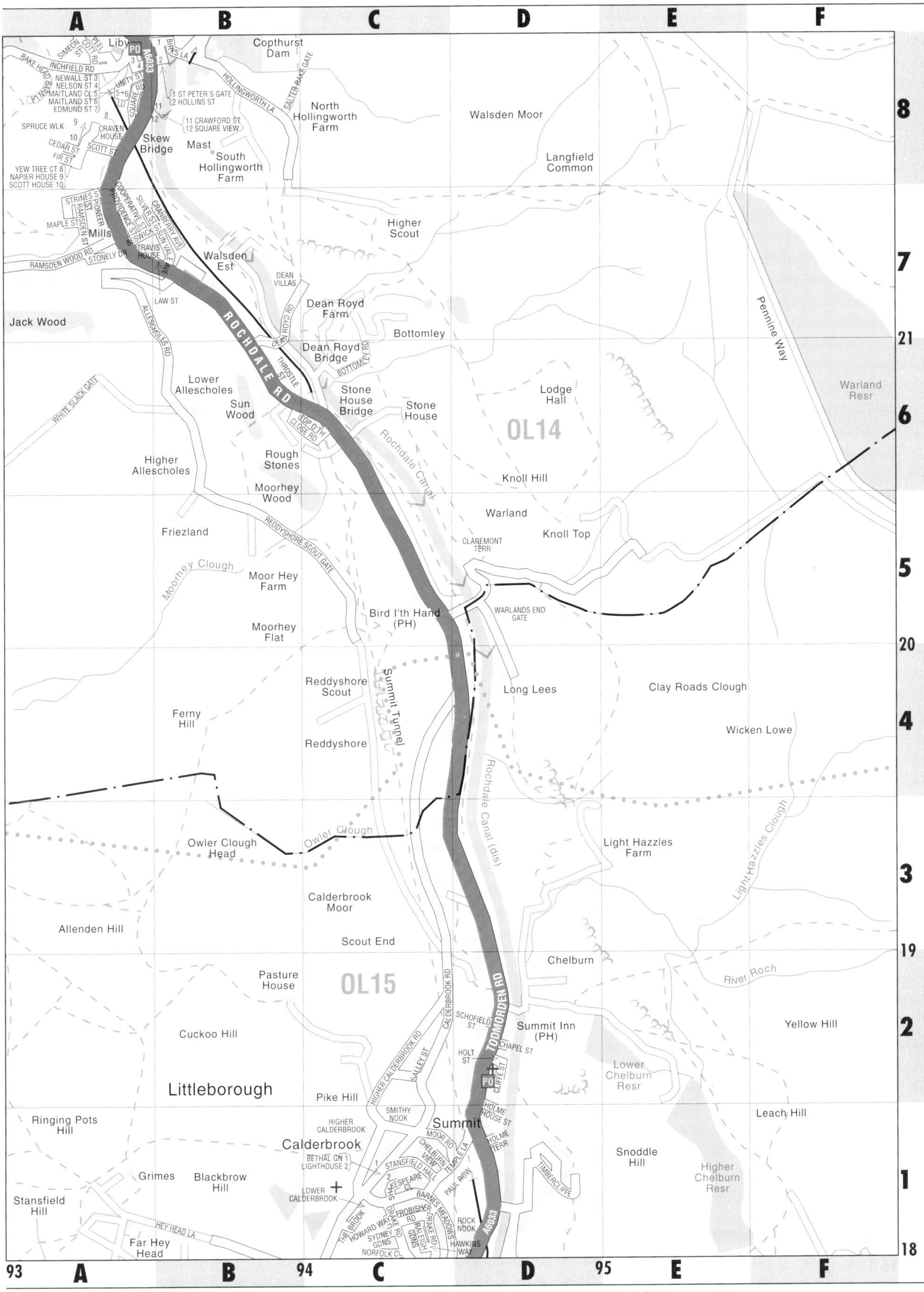
A
B
C
D
E
F
8
7
21
6
5
20
4
3
19
2
1
18
93
94
95
Liby
PO
A6033
SIMEON ST
COTT RD
PEEL ST
BAKE HEAD BARN LA
INCHFIELD RD
NEWALL ST 3
NELSON ST 4
MAITLAND CL 5
MAITLAND ST 6
EDMUND ST 7
UNITY ST
SQUARE RD
BIRKS LA
1 ST PETER'S GATE
2 HOLLINS ST
11 CRAWFORD ST
12 SQUARE VIEW
HOLLINGWORTH LA
SALTER RAKE GATE
Copthurst Dam
North Hollingworth Farm
Walsden Moor
Langfield Common
SPRUCE WLK
CRAVEN HOUSE
CEDAR ST
SCOTT ST
FIR ST
YEW TREE CT 8
NAPIER HOUSE 9
SCOTT HOUSE 10
Skew Bridge
Mast
South Hollingworth Farm
STRINES ST
MAPLE ST
RAMSDEN ST
PIONEER ST
COOPERATIVE ST
PROVIDENCE ST
SILVER ST
CRANBERRY AVE
Mills
TRAVIS HOUSE
STONELY DR
RAMSDEN WOOD RD
Walsden Est
Higher Scout
DEAN VILLAS
LAW ST
ALLESCHOLES RD
Jack Wood
ROCHDALE RD
DEAN ROYD RD
Dean Royd Farm
Bottomley
Dean Royd Bridge
BOTTOMLEY RD
THROSTLE ST
Pennine Way
Lower Allescholes
WHITE SLACK GATE
Sun Wood
TOP O'TH CLOSE RD
Stone House Bridge
Stone House
Lodge Hall
OL14
Warland Resr
Rochdale Canal
Higher Allescholes
Rough Stones
Knoll Hill
Moorhey Wood
Warland
Friezland
REDDYSHORE SCOUT GATE
CLAREMONT TERR
Knoll Top
Moorhey Clough
Moor Hey Farm
WARLANDS END GATE
Bird I'th Hand (PH)
Moorhey Flat
Reddyshore Scout
Summit Tunnel
Long Lees
Clay Roads Clough
Ferny Hill
Wicken Lowe
Reddyshore
Rochdale Canal (dis)
Owler Clough
Owler Clough Head
Light Hazzles Farm
Light Hazzles Clough
Calderbrook Moor
Allenden Hill
Scout End
Chelburn
River Roch
Pasture House
OL15
CALDERBROOK RD
TODMORDEN RD
SCHOFIELD ST
Summit Inn (PH)
Yellow Hill
Cuckoo Hill
HIGHER CALDERBROOK RD
SALLEY ST
HOLT ST
CHAPEL ST
CLIFFE ST
Lower Chelburn Resr
Littleborough
Pike Hill
HOLME HOUSE ST
Ringing Pots Hill
SMITHY NOOK
Summit
Leach Hill
HIGHER CALDERBROOK
Calderbrook
MOOR RD
CHELBURN VIEW
TEMPLE LA
HOLME TERR
Snoddle Hill
BETHAL GN 1
LIGHTHOUSE 2
STANSFIELD HALL
SHAKESPEARE CL
TIMBERCLIFFE
Higher Chelburn Resr
Grimes
Blackbrow Hill
LOWER CALDERBROOK
PAUL ROW
Stansfield Hill
BARNES MEADOWS
THE BROOK
HOWARD WAY
FROBISHER
DRAKE RD
RALEIGH GDNS
SYDNEY GDNS
NORFOLK CL
ROCK NOOK
HAWKINS WAY
HEY HEAD LA
Far Hey Head

130

129
109

129
148

A B C D E F
8
7
21
6
5
20
4
3
19
2
1
18
99 00 01
MOORLAND COTTS
B6138
Shooting Box
Turley Holes & Higher House Moor
Trimming Dale
Lark Hall
NEW RD
Round Hill
WATER STALLS RD
SLACK LA
DELFS LA
Delfs
NOOK LA
Rake Head
Noah Dale Clough
WICKING LA
Warcock Hill
Slate Delfs Hill
Sykes Farm
SYKES GATE
WASHFORD RD
BLACKSTONE EDGE RD
Washford Bridge
Calderdale Way
Flints Hall
Flints
HX7
Little Manshead Hill
Trap Bridge Hill
ASH HALL LA
Plain
Cabin Holes
Wicken Hill
GREAVE RD
Greave Head
Great Greave
Blackshaw Clough
Great Manshead Hill
Liberty Rush Bed
Far Slack
SLACK LA
COAL GATE RD
Green Holes
FLIGHT HOUSE RD
HX6
Manshead End
Colin Hill
Soyland Moor
RIPPONDEN OLD LA
Baitings Pasture
Clay Clough
Maiden Stones
Blue Ball Inn (PH)
Resr
Lower Shaw
BLUE BALL RD
BLUE BALL LA
BEESTONHIRST
New Inn
HOLLIN LA
A58
Greenwood Clough
Manshead End
Horse Hey Clough
Baitings
ROCHDALE RD
Baitings Gate Moor
Baitings Gate Pasture
Baitings Reservoir
River Ryburn
Ryburn Reservoir
Hanson Wood
Many Gates
BAITINGS GATE RD
Baitings Viaduct
Upper Schole Carr
Higher Wormald
BACK O' TH' HEIGHT
Schole Carr Moor
Height
LOWER WORMALD
Parrock Nook
Black Hill
Hutch Royd
Hutch Brook
Grey Stone Height
Mires
LONG CSWY
Hutch Bridge
New Gate
Warm Withens

131
111

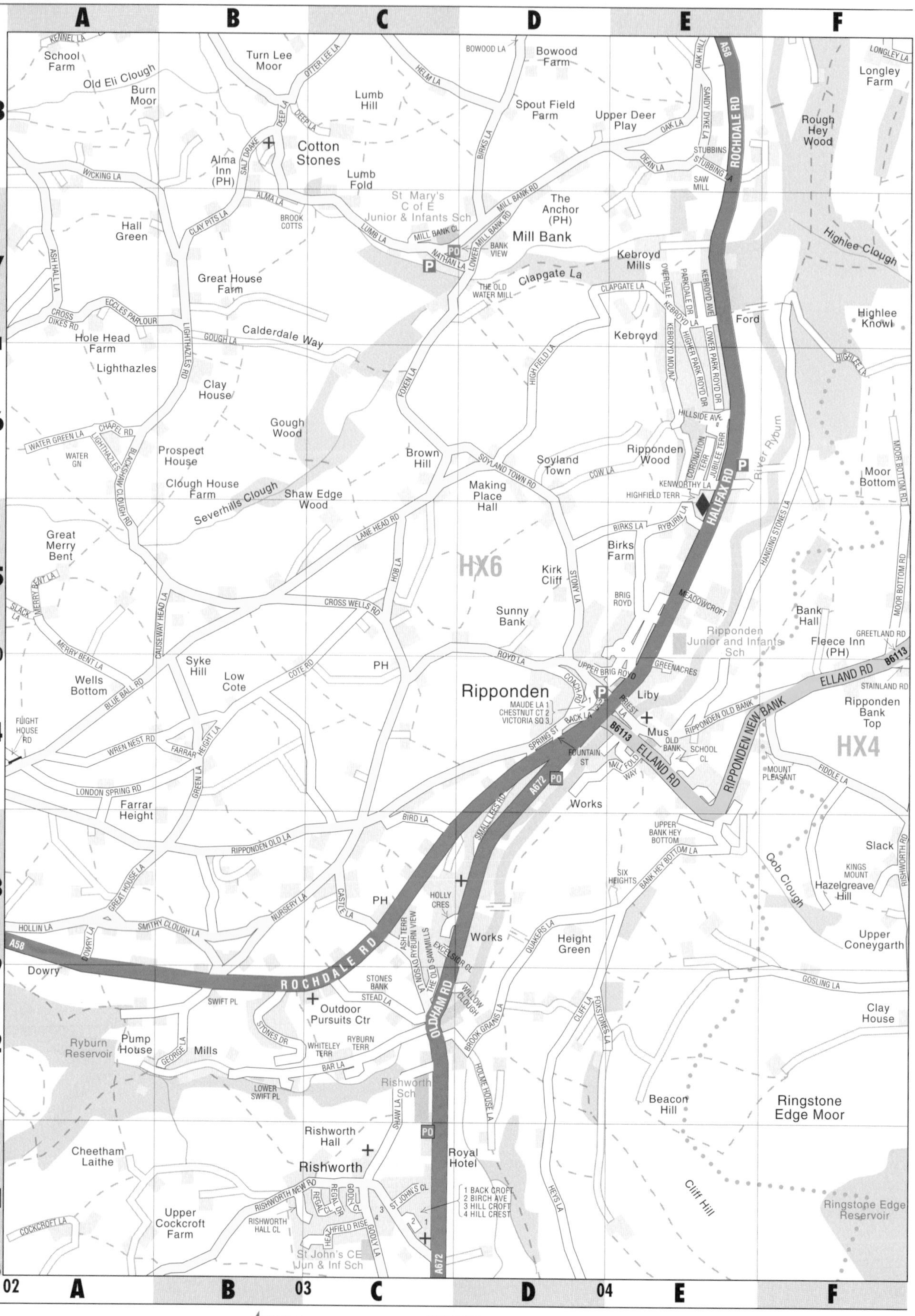

131
150

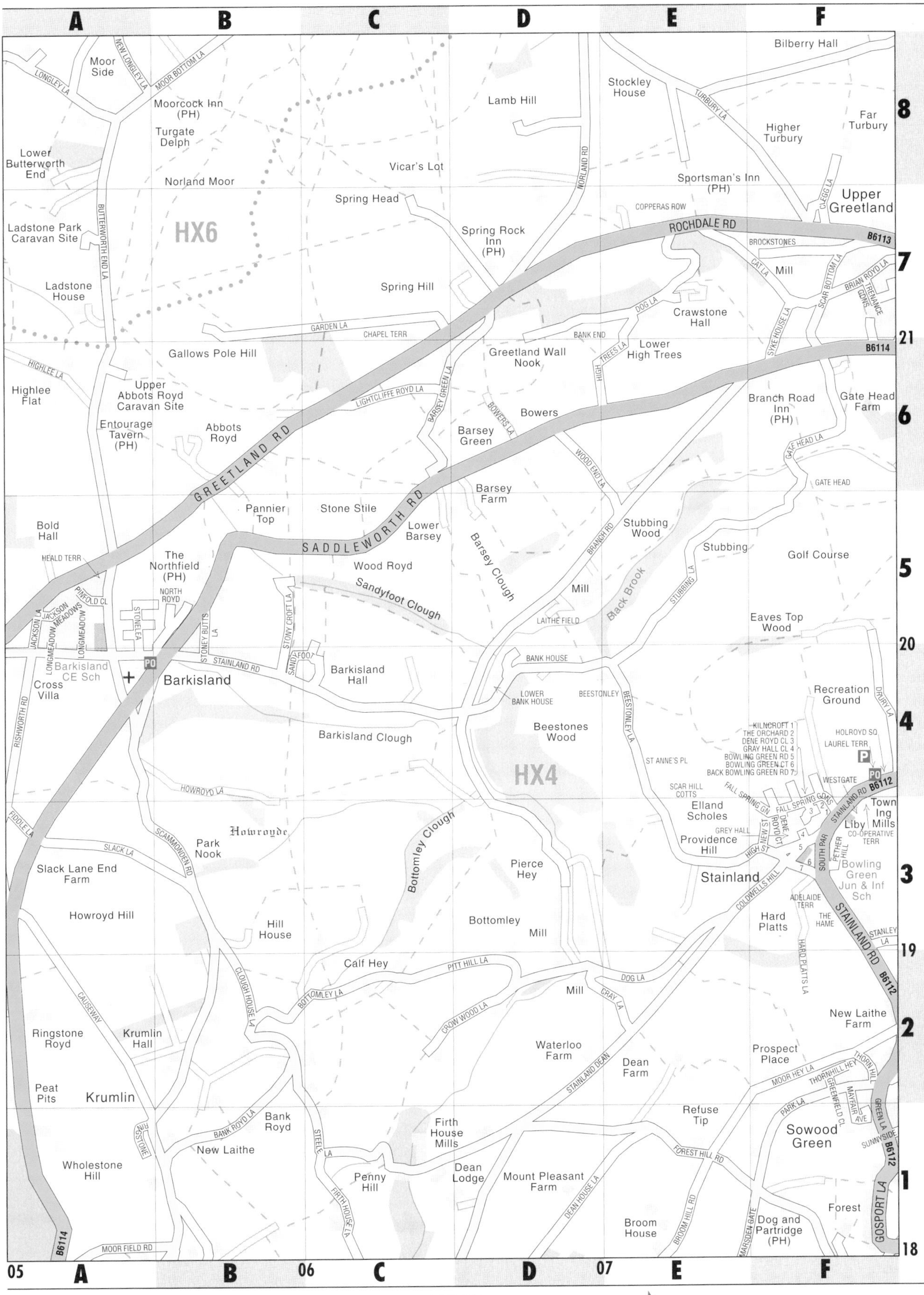
A
B
C
D
E
F
8
7
21
6
5
20
4
3
19
2
1
18
05
06
07
Moor Side
NEW LONGLEY LA
MOOR BOTTOM LA
LONGLEY LA
Moorcock Inn (PH)
Turgate Delph
Lower Butterworth End
Norland Moor
BUTTERWORTH END LA
HX6
Ladstone Park Caravan Site
Ladstone House
Lamb Hill
Vicar's Lot
Spring Head
Spring Rock Inn (PH)
Spring Hill
NORLAND RD
Stockley House
TURBURY LA
Bilberry Hall
Higher Turbury
Far Turbury
Sportsman's Inn (PH)
COPPERAS ROW
CLEGG LA
Upper Greetland
ROCHDALE RD
B6113
BROCKSTONES
CAT LA
Mill
SCAR BOTTOM LA
BRIAN ROYD LA
TRENANCE GDNS
Crawstone Hall
DOG LA
BANK END
Lower High Trees
HIGH TREES LA
SYKE HOUSE LA
B6114
GARDEN LA
CHAPEL TERR
Gallows Pole Hill
Greetland Wall Nook
HIGHLEE LA
Highlee Flat
Upper Abbots Royd Caravan Site
Entourage Tavern (PH)
Abbots Royd
LIGHTCLIFFE ROYD LA
BARSEY GREEN LA
BOWERS LA
Bowers
Barsey Green
Branch Road Inn (PH)
Gate Head Farm
GATE HEAD LA
GATE HEAD
WOOD END LA
GREETLAND RD
Pannier Top
Stone Stile
SADDLEWORTH RD
Barsey Farm
Lower Barsey
Stubbing Wood
BRANCH RD
Stubbing
Golf Course
Bold Hall
HEALD TERR
The Northfield (PH)
Wood Royd
Barsey Clough
Sandyfoot Clough
Mill
Black Brook
STUBBING LA
NORTH ROYD
PINFOLD CL
JACKSON LA
JACKSON MEADOWS
LONGMEADOW
STONELEA
STONEY BUTTS LA
STONY CROFT LA
LAITHE FIELD
Eaves Top Wood
Barkisland CE Sch
PO
STAINLAND RD
SANDYFOOT
Barkisland Hall
BANK HOUSE
Cross Villa
Barkisland
LOWER BANK HOUSE
BEESTONLEY
BEESTONLEY LA
Recreation Ground
DRURY LA
RISHWORTH RD
Barkisland Clough
Beestones Wood
KILNCROFT 1
THE ORCHARD 2
DENE ROYD CL 3
GRAY HALL CL 4
BOWLING GREEN RD 5
BOWLING GREEN CT 6
BACK BOWLING GREEN RD 7
HOLROYD SQ
LAUREL TERR
P
PO
ST ANNE'S PL
HX4
HOWROYD LA
SCAR HILL COTTS
FALL SPRING GDNS
WESTGATE
B6112
FIDDLE LA
Elland Scholes
FALL SPRING GN
Town Ing Mills
Liby
CO-OPERATIVE TERR
Howroyde
SCAMMONDEN RD
Park Nook
SLACK LA
GREY HALL
NEW ST
DENE ROYD CT
Providence Hill
HIGH ST
PETHER HILL
SOUTH PAR
Bowling Green Jun & Inf Sch
Slack Lane End Farm
Bottomley Clough
Pierce Hey
Stainland
COLDWELLS HILL
ADELAIDE TERR
Howroyd Hill
Hill House
Bottomley
Mill
Hard Platts
THE HAME
STANLEY LA
HARD PLATTS LA
Calf Hey
PITT HILL LA
CLOUGH HOUSE LA
DOG LA
BOTTOMLEY LA
CAUSEWAY
Mill
CRAY LA
CROW WOOD LA
New Laithe Farm
Ringstone Royd
Krumlin Hall
Waterloo Farm
Prospect Place
Dean Farm
THORN HILL
MOOR HEY LA
THORNHILL HEY
Peat Pits
Krumlin
STAINLAND DEAN
Bank Royd
BANK ROYD LA
Refuse Tip
GREENFIELD CL
MAYFAIR AVE
PARK LA
GREEN LA
Sowood Green
RINGSTONE
New Laithe
Firth House Mills
STEEL LA
FOREST HILL RD
SUNNYSIDE
Wholestone Hill
Penny Hill
Dean Lodge
Mount Pleasant Farm
DEAN HOUSE LA
Forest
FIRTH HOUSE LA
BROOM HILL RD
Broom House
MARSDEN GATE
Dog and Partridge (PH)
GOSPORT LA
B6114
MOOR FIELD RD

C7
1 LINDWELL PL
2 LINDWELL GR
3 LOWER WELLGATE
4 ROAD END
5 LINDWELL AVE
6 HOLLYNS TERR

D6
1 MIDDLE DEAN ST
2 BACK QUEEN ST
3 EXCHANGE ST
4 FEATHERBED CL
5 FEATHER BED LA
6 WOODSIDE TERR

133

D7
1 ELIZABETH ST
2 LAMBERT ST
3 PRINCESS ST
4 NORTH ST
5 GEORGE ST
6 UNION ST
7 CROSS ST
8 HIGH ST
9 GARWICK TERR

113

F6
1 NORTHFIELD CL
2 TALBOT HOUSE
3 TIMBER ST
4 TOWN HALL ST
5 ROCHESTER PL
6 GRANVILLE ST
7 BEDFORD ST
8 DEAN ST
9 AINLEY ST
10 BURLEY ST
11 FRANCES ST
12 ALBION ST
13 JOHN WILLIAM ST
14 PARKFIELD AVE
15 CATHERINE CRES

F7
1 TOWNGATE HOUSE
2 WEST HOUSE
3 MEXBOROUGH HOUSE
4 YORK HOUSE
5 RIPON HOUSE
6 REGENT HOUSE
7 SAVILE HOUSE
8 ELAND HOUSE
9 MARLBOROUGH HOUSE
10 CALDER HOUSE
11 CROFT HOUSE
12 ST MARYS GATE
13 CHURCH HOUSE
14 PORTLAND HOUSE
15 CONISTON HOUSE
16 CORNWALL HOUSE
17 CASTLEGATE HOUSE
18 PROVIDENCE ST

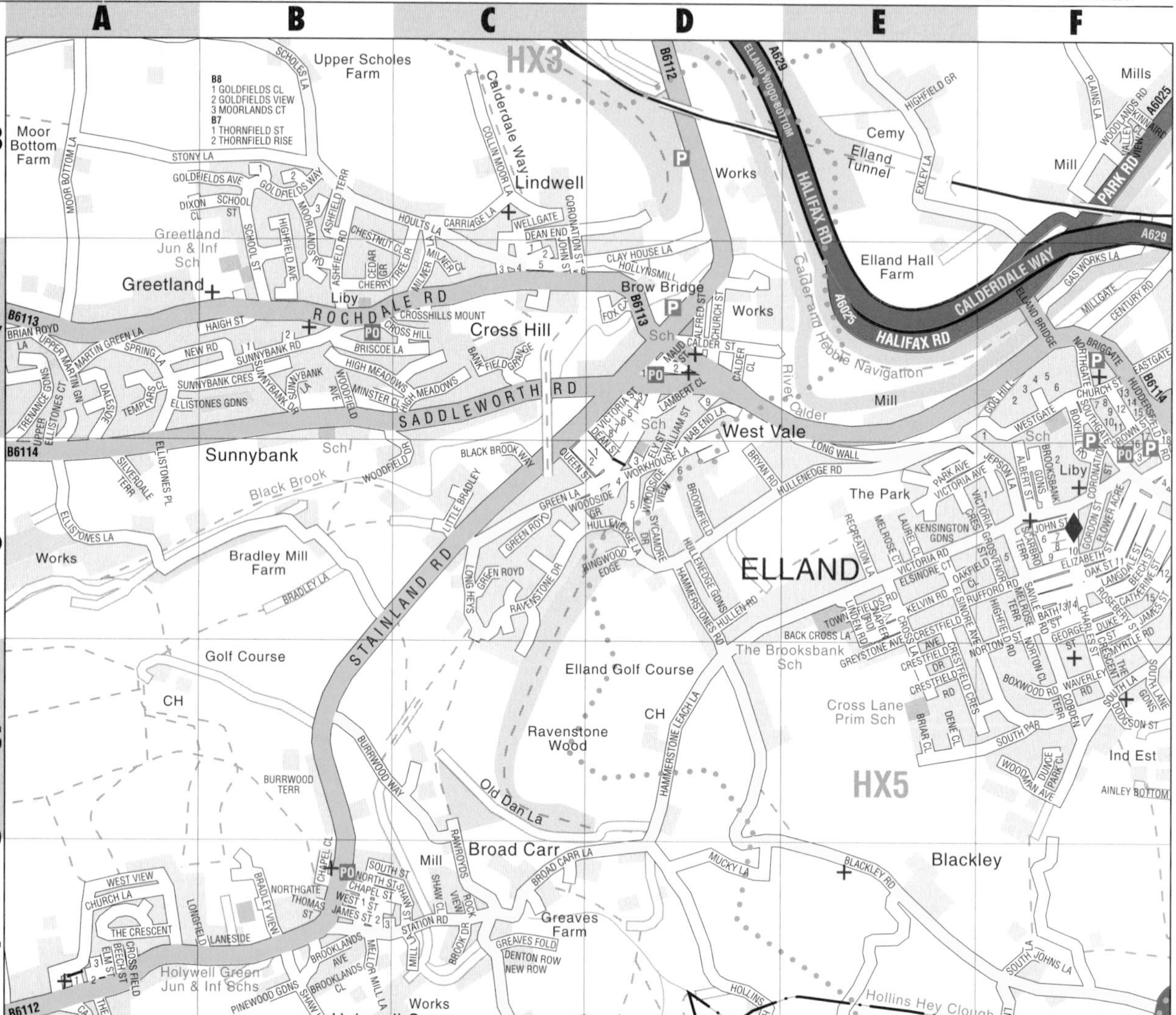

A4
1 THORNE ST
2 OAK TERR
3 GLADSTONE ST

B4
1 CROSS ST
2 WELL ST
3 GREEN ST

133

152

F1
1 MAPLIN DR
2 DEER CROFT RD
3 DEER CROFT CRES
4 RYNDLESIDE
5 LOW HILLS LA

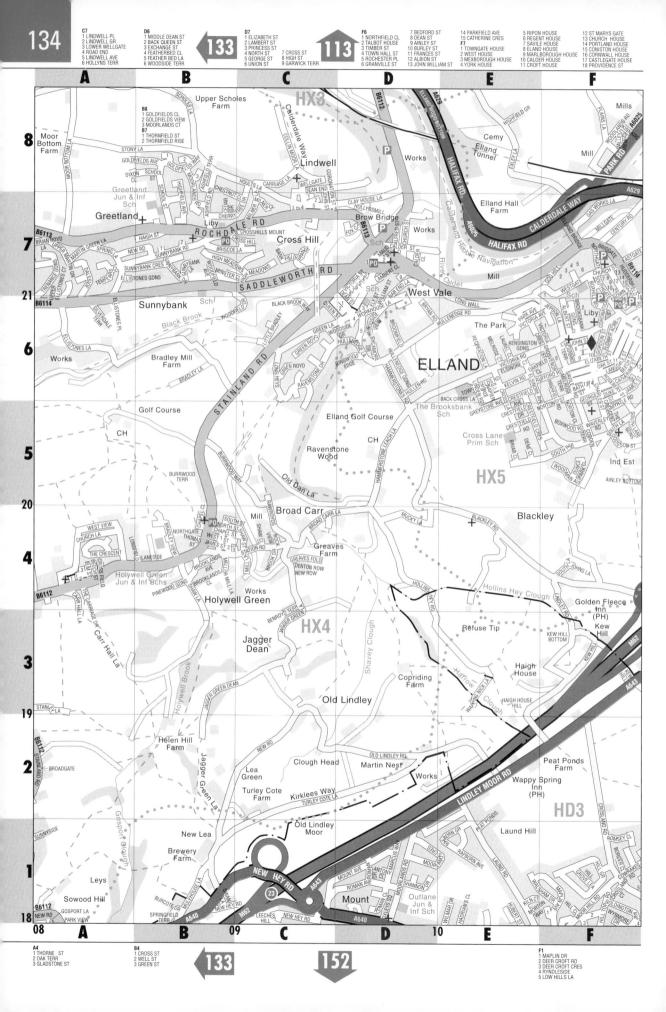

114
136

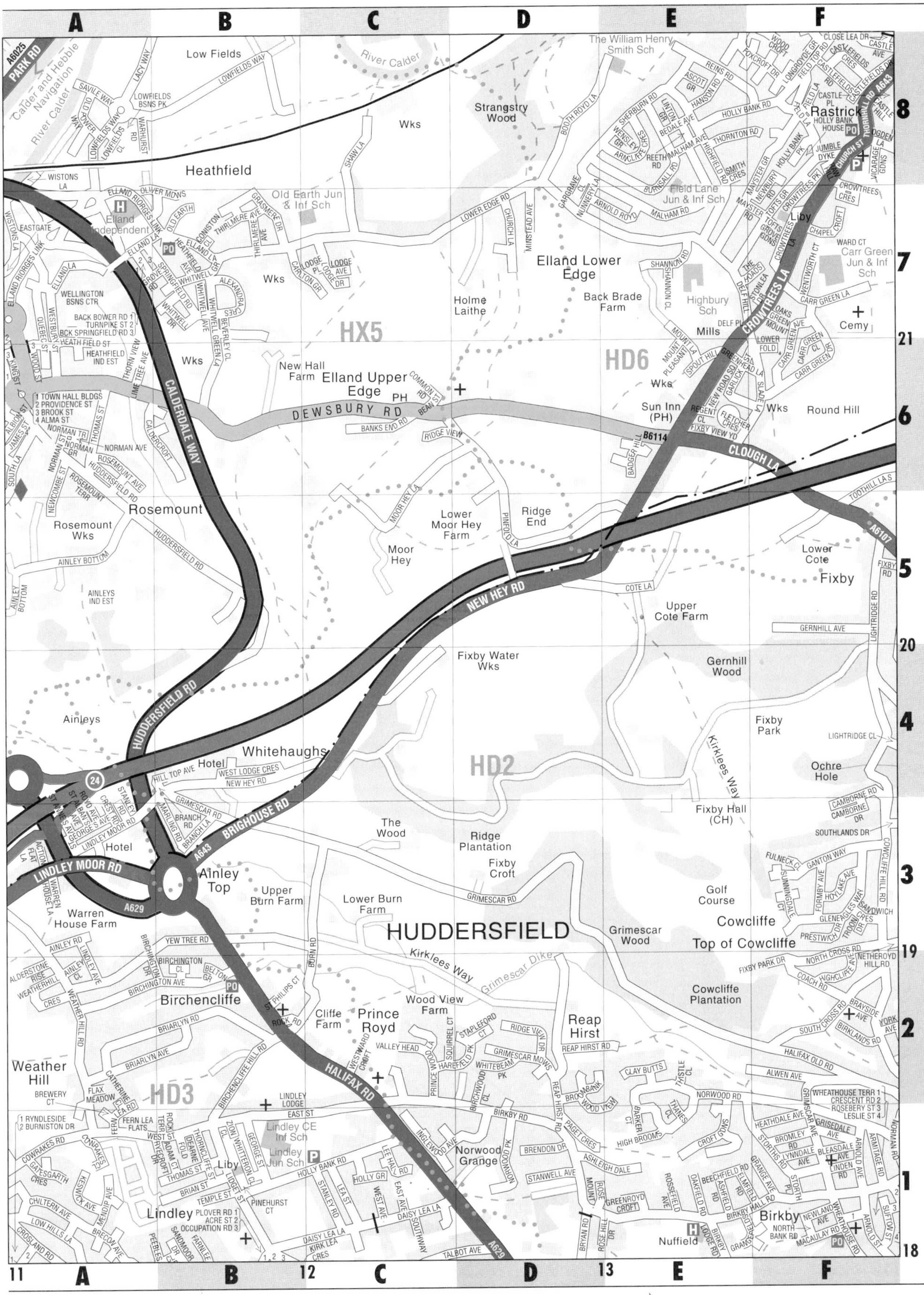

153
136

135
115

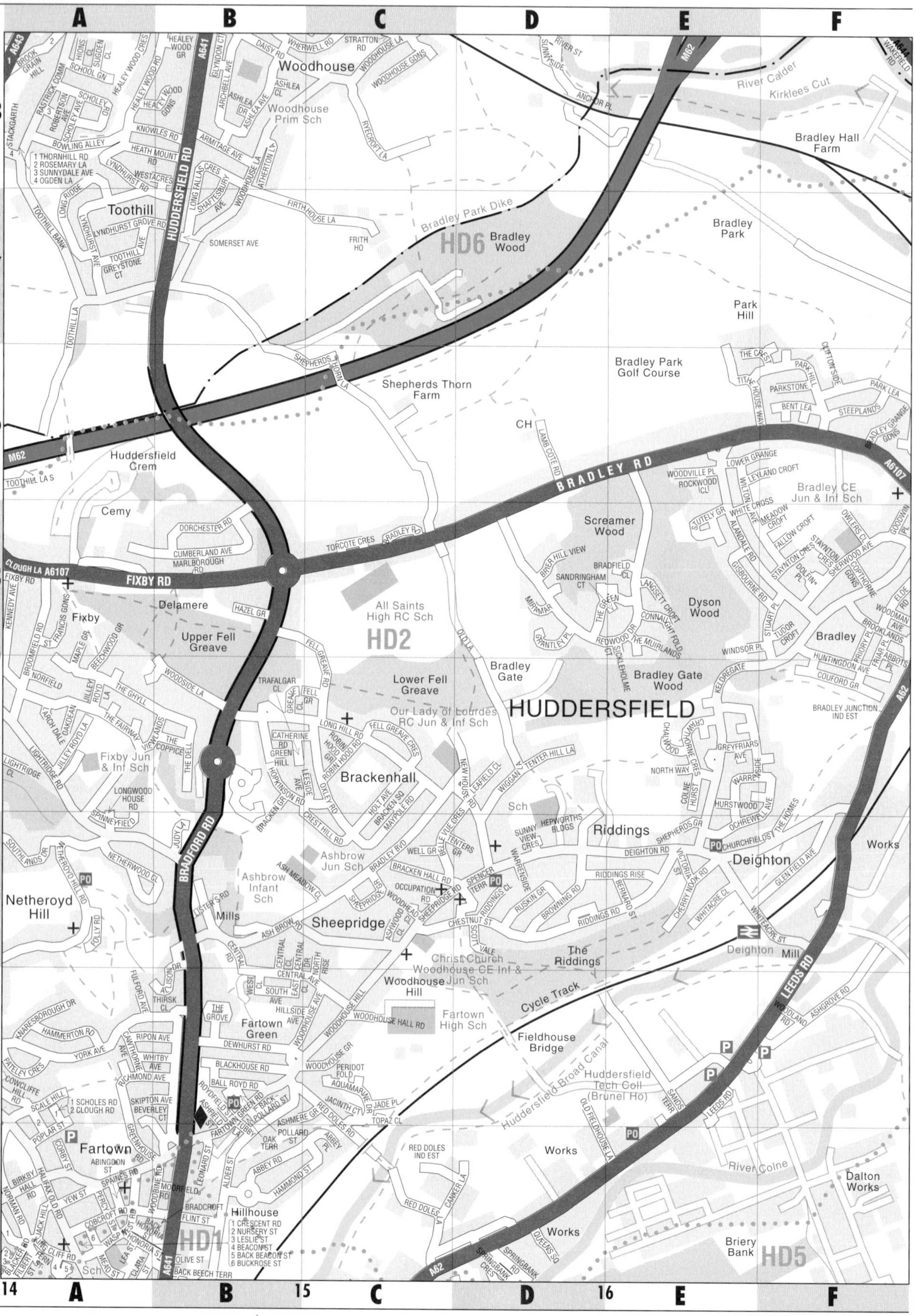

135
154

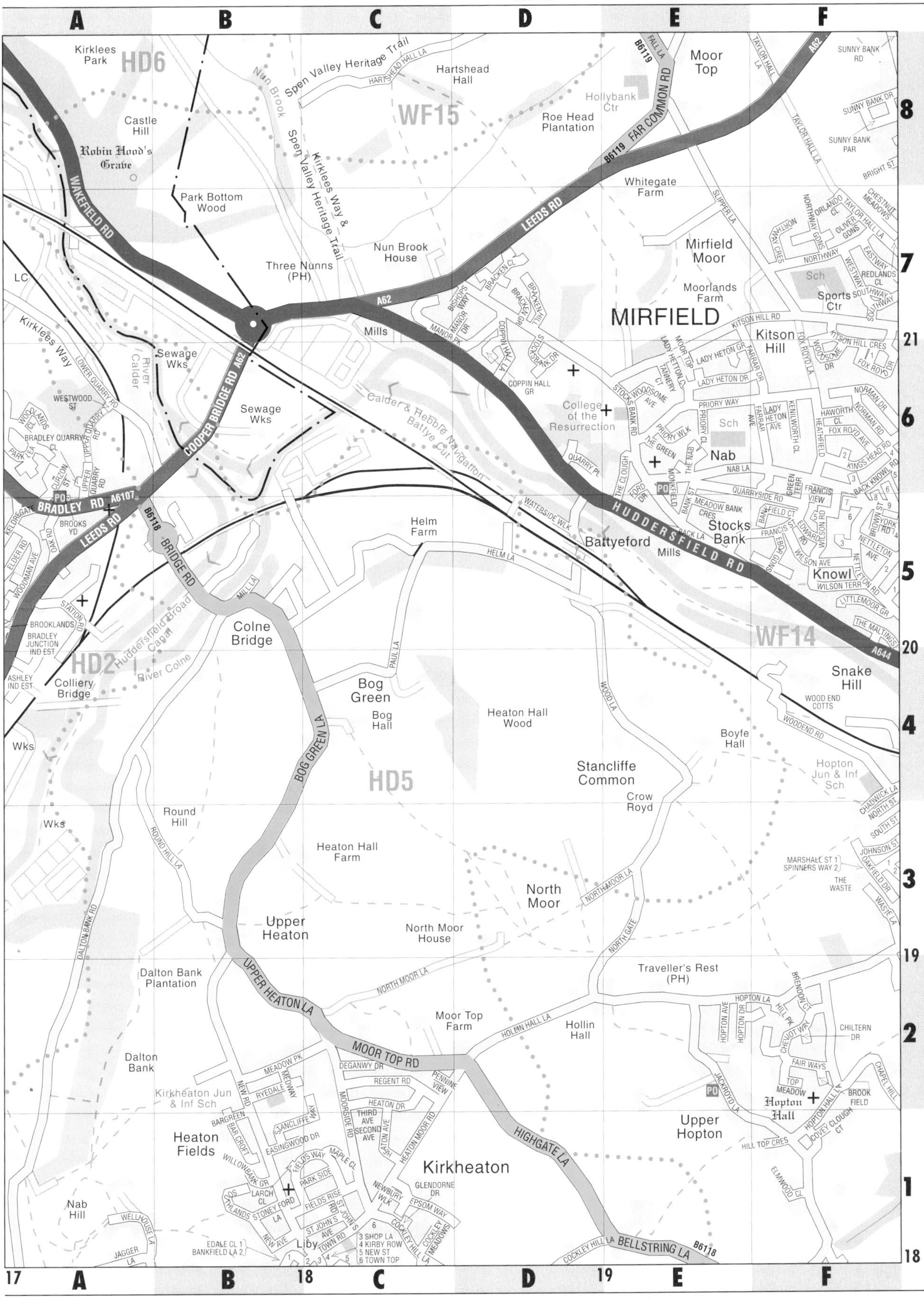
A
B
C
D
E
F
Kirklees Park
HD6
Castle Hill
Robin Hood's Grave
WAKEFIELD RD
Park Bottom Wood
Spen Valley Heritage Trail
HARTSHEAD HALL LA
Nun Brook
Kirklees Way & Spen Valley Heritage Trail
Hartshead Hall
WF15
Roe Head Plantation
Hollybank Ctr
FAR COMMON RD
B6119
FALL LA
Moor Top
TAYLOR HALL LA
A62
SUNNY BANK RD
SUNNY BANK DR
SUNNY BANK PAR
BRIGHT ST
LEEDS RD
Whitegate Farm
SLIPPER LA
Mirfield Moor
Nun Brook House
Three Nunns (PH)
Moorlands Farm
MIRFIELD
Sch
Sports Ctr
NORTHWAY
KITSON HILL RD
Kitson Hill
KITSON HILL CRES
LC
Kirklees Way
Mills
MANOR PK
BRACKEN CL
BRACKEN GR
COPPIN HALL LA
COPPIN HALL GR
STOCKSBANK DR
LADY HETON GR
LADY HETON DR
MOOR TOP
FARRAR DR
FOX ROYD LA
FOX ROYD DR
Sewage Wks
River Calder
COOPER BRIDGE RD
LOWER QUARRY RD
WESTWOOD ST
BRADLEY QUARRY CL
College of the Resurrection
STOCKS BANK RD
PRIORY WAY
PRIORY CL
PRIORY WLK
THE GREEN
THE NAB
Nab
NAB LA
KENILWORTH CL
HAWORTH CL
NORMAN RD
FOX ROYD AVE
HEATHFIELD
KINGS HEAD RD
Calder & Hebble Navigation
Battye Cut
QUARRY PL
THE CLOUGH
FORD DR
MONKFIELD
QUARRYSIDE RD
BANK ST
MEADOW BANK CRES
GREEN TERR
FRANCIS VIEW
BACK KNOWL RD
BRADLEY RD
A6107
PO
CURZON ST
UPPER QUARRY RD
HUDDERSFIELD RD
WATERSIDE WLK
BACK LA
Battyeford
Mills
Stocks Bank
FRANCIS ST
EDWARD ST
WILSON RD
Helm Farm
HELM LA
B6118
BRIDGE RD
LEEDS RD
BROOKS YD
ELDER RD
WOODMAN AVE
OAK RD
KELDREGATE
WILSON AVE
Knowl
WILSON TERR
NETTLETON AVE
LITTLEMOOR GR
THE MALTINGS
STATION RD
BROOKLANDS
BRADLEY JUNCTION IND EST
MILL LA
Colne Bridge
Huddersfield Broad Canal
River Colne
HD2
ASHLEY IND EST
Colliery Bridge
Bog Green
Bog Hall
PAUL LA
WF14
A644
Snake Hill
WOOD END COTTS
WOODEND RD
Boyfe Hall
Heaton Hall Wood
WOOD LA
Wks
BOG GREEN LA
HD5
Stancliffe Common
Crow Royd
Hopton Jun & Inf Sch
CHADWICK LA
NORTH ST
SOUTH ST
JOHNSON ST
Round Hill
ROUND HILL LA
Heaton Hall Farm
MARSHALL ST
SPINNERS WAY
THE WASTE
OAKFIELD DR
WASTE LA
North Moor
NORTH MOOR LA
Upper Heaton
North Moor House
NORTH GATE
DALTON BANK RD
Dalton Bank Plantation
UPPER HEATON LA
NORTH MOOR LA
Traveller's Rest (PH)
HOPTON LA
HOPTON AVE
HOPTON DR
BRENDON CT
HILL PK
CHEVIOT WAY
CHILTERN DR
Moor Top Farm
HOLLIN HALL LA
Hollin Hall
Dalton Bank
MOOR TOP RD
MEADOW PK
MEDWAY
DEGANWY DR
REGENT RD
PENNINE VIEW
FAIR WAYS
TOP MEADOW
Hopton Hall
BROOK FIELD
CHAPEL HILL
HOPTON HALL LA
COVEY CLOUGH CT
Kirkheaton Jun & Inf Sch
NEW RD
RYEDALE
HEATON DR
THIRD AVE
SECOND AVE
JACKROYD LA
Upper Hopton
HILL TOP CRES
BARGREEN
BAR CROFT
SANCLIFFE WAY
EASINGWOOD DR
MOORSIDE RD
LATON AVE
HEATON MOOR RD
HIGHGATE LA
Heaton Fields
WILLOWBANK GR
FIELDS WAY
MAPLE CL
Kirkheaton
GLENDORNE DR
ELMWOOD CL
PARK SIDE
LARCH CL
STONEY FORD LA
FIELDS RISE
ST JOHN'S AVE
NEWBURY WLK
EPSOM WAY
Nab Hill
WELLHOUSE LA
JAGGER LA
EDALE CL 1
BANKFIELD LA 2
NEW AVE
Liby
TOWN RD
3 SHOP LA
4 KIRBY ROW
5 NEW ST
6 TOWN TOP
COCKLEY HILL LA
COCKLEY MEADOWS
BELLSTRING LA
B6118
17
18
19
20
21
1
2
3
4
5
6
7
8

137
117

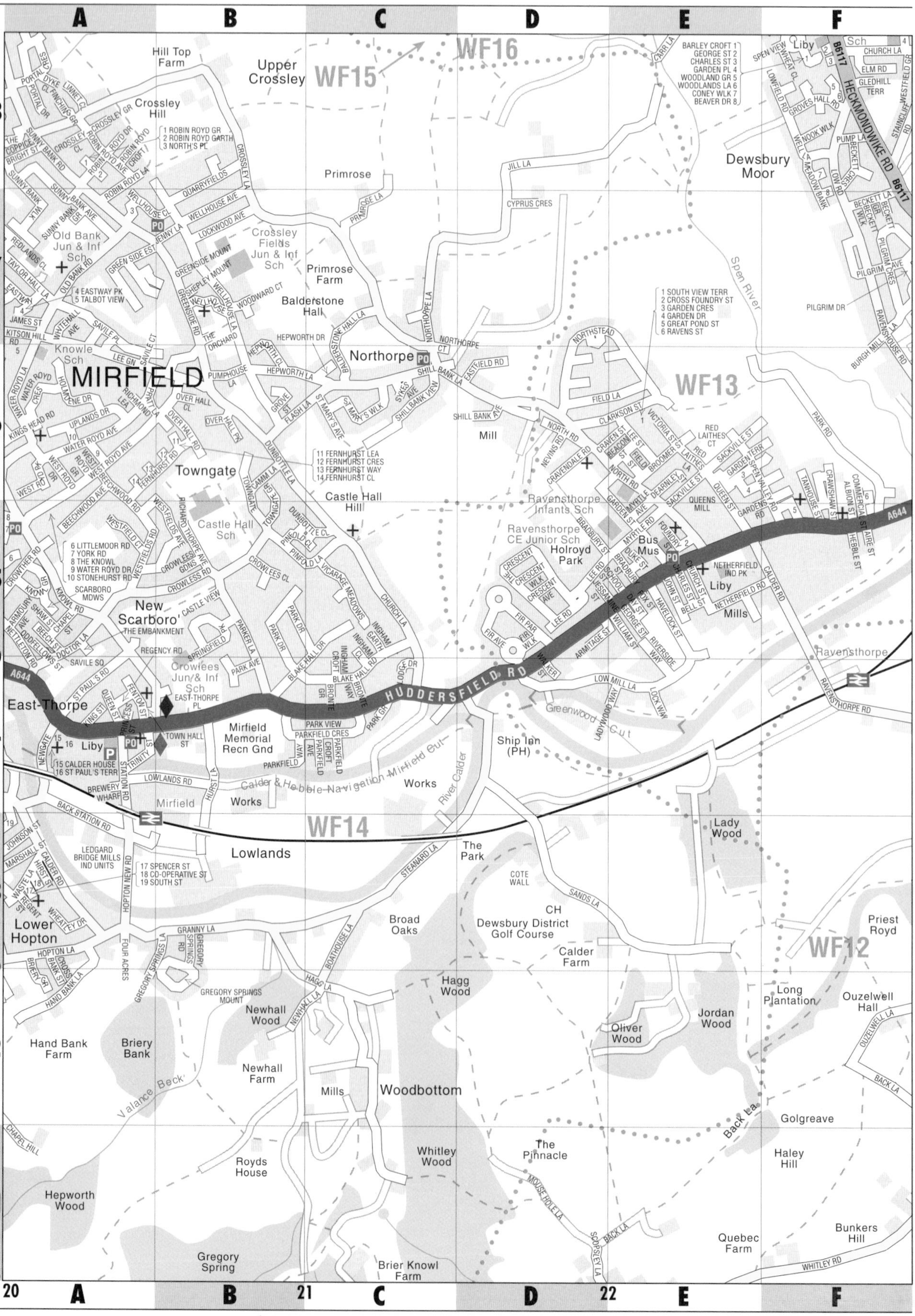

137
156

A8
1 STAINCLIFFE CL
2 CHURCH LA
A6
1 SCOUT HILL VIEW
2 SCOUT HILL TERR
3 THORNVILLE MOUNT
B7
1 WHITWORTH RD
2 CROW NEST TERR
3 JUNCTION RD
4 BROOK RD
B8
1 TWEEDALE ST
2 SUSSEX WLK
3 KENT WLK
4 DEVON WLK
5 NORFOLK WLK
6 DORSET WLK
7 RUTLAND WLK
8 TRAVIS LACEY TERR
9 PRINCESS GDNS
10 BROOK GDNS
11 DICKINSON GDNS
C8
1 DAWSON GDNS
2 HALLILEY GDNS
3 BK WEBSTER ST
4 ELIM WLK
5 BEECH WLK
6 SAVILE WLK
7 BARBER WLK
8 WELLINGTON WK
9 MILTON WLK
10 WELLINGTON RD E
11 WELLINGTON ST
C8
12 WHEELWRIGHT ST
13 WESTGATE TERR
14 BACK NELSON ST
15 SOUTHGATE
D8
1 KINGSWAY
2 PRINCE ST
3 MARKET ST
4 THE PRINCESS OF WALES PREC
5 THE ARCADE
6 WAKEFIELD OLD RD
7 CAMROYD ST
8 ERNEST ST
9 HIGHBURY TERR
10 HIGHGATE TERR

118
140

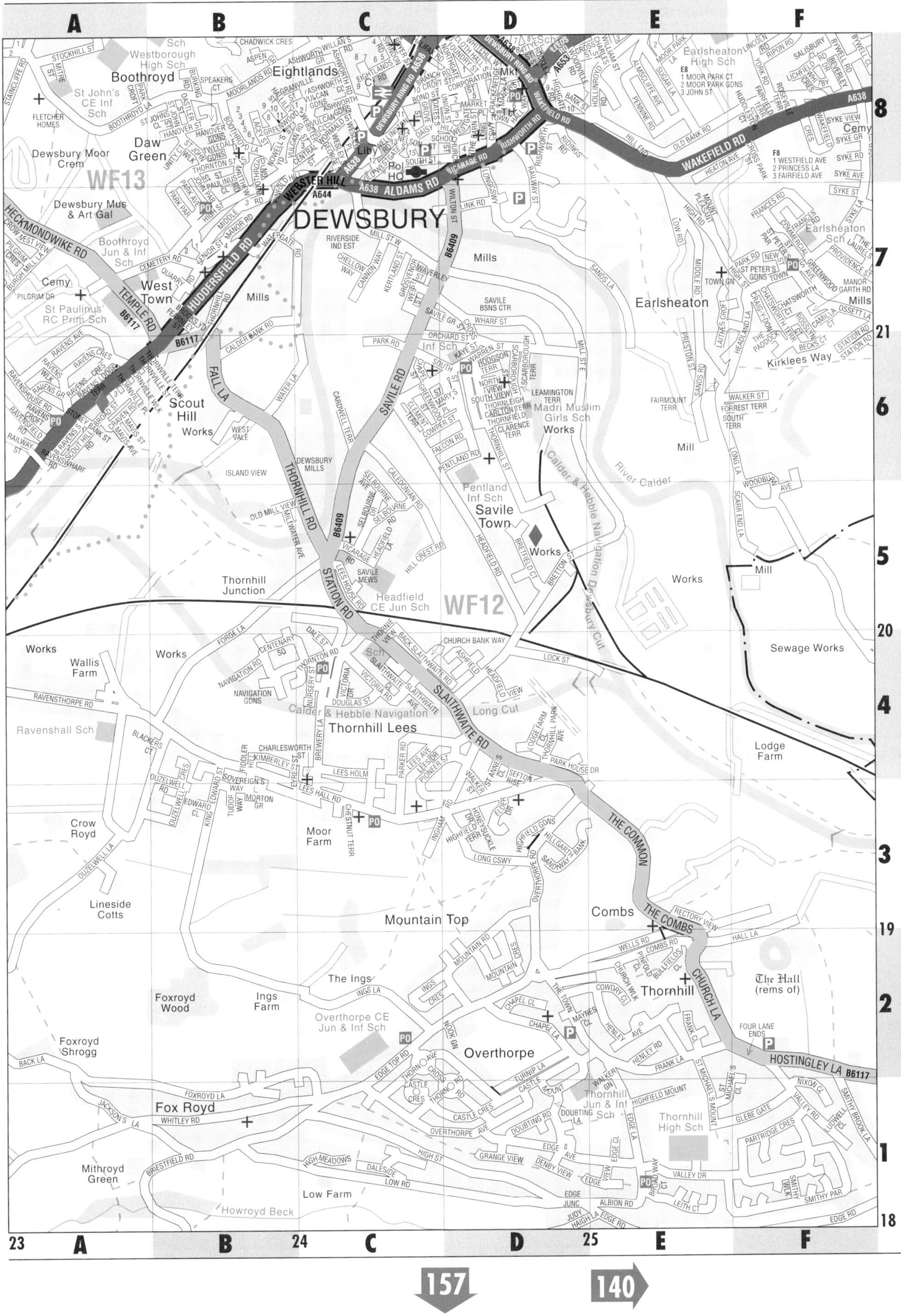

157
140

139
119

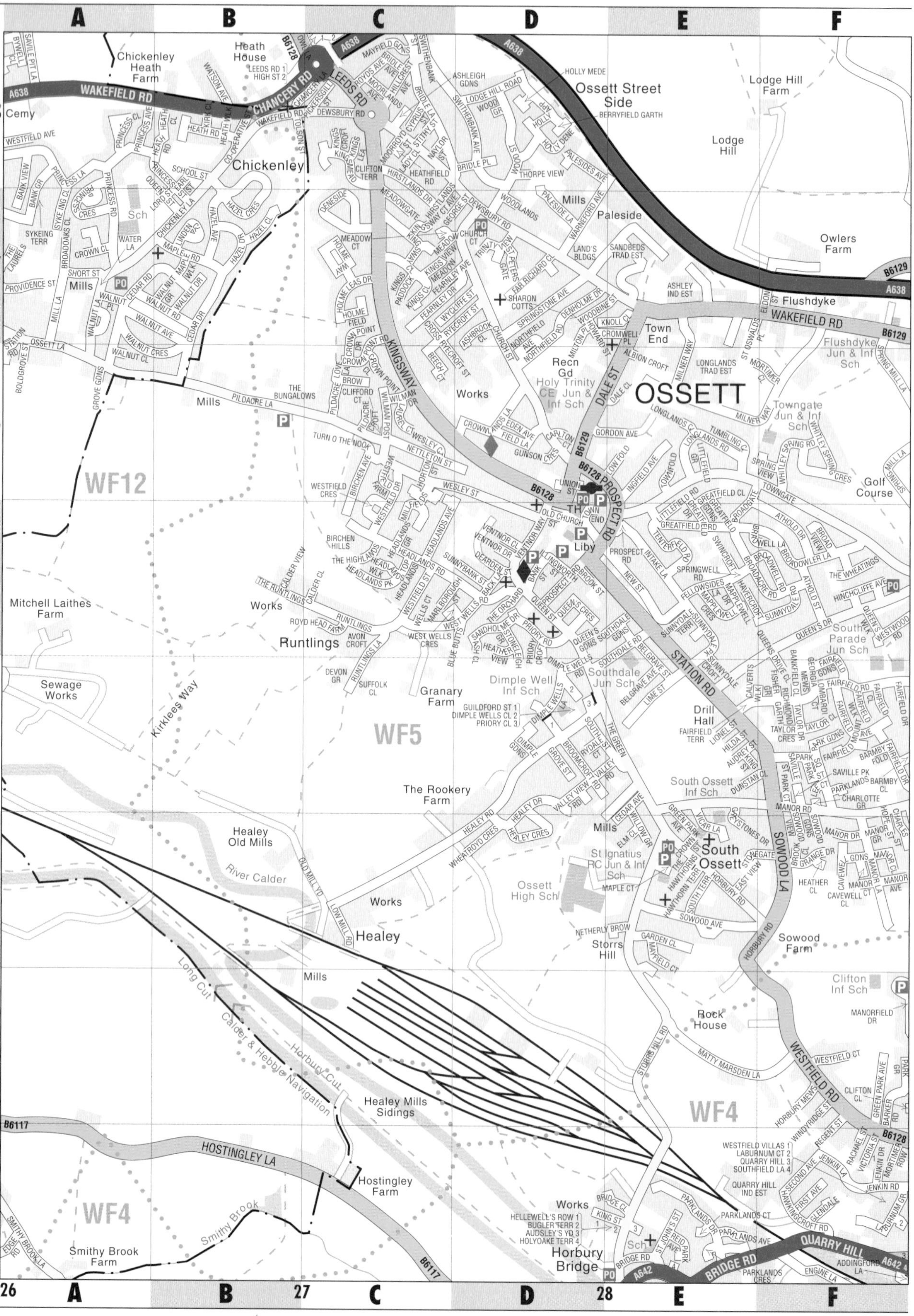

139
158

120
142

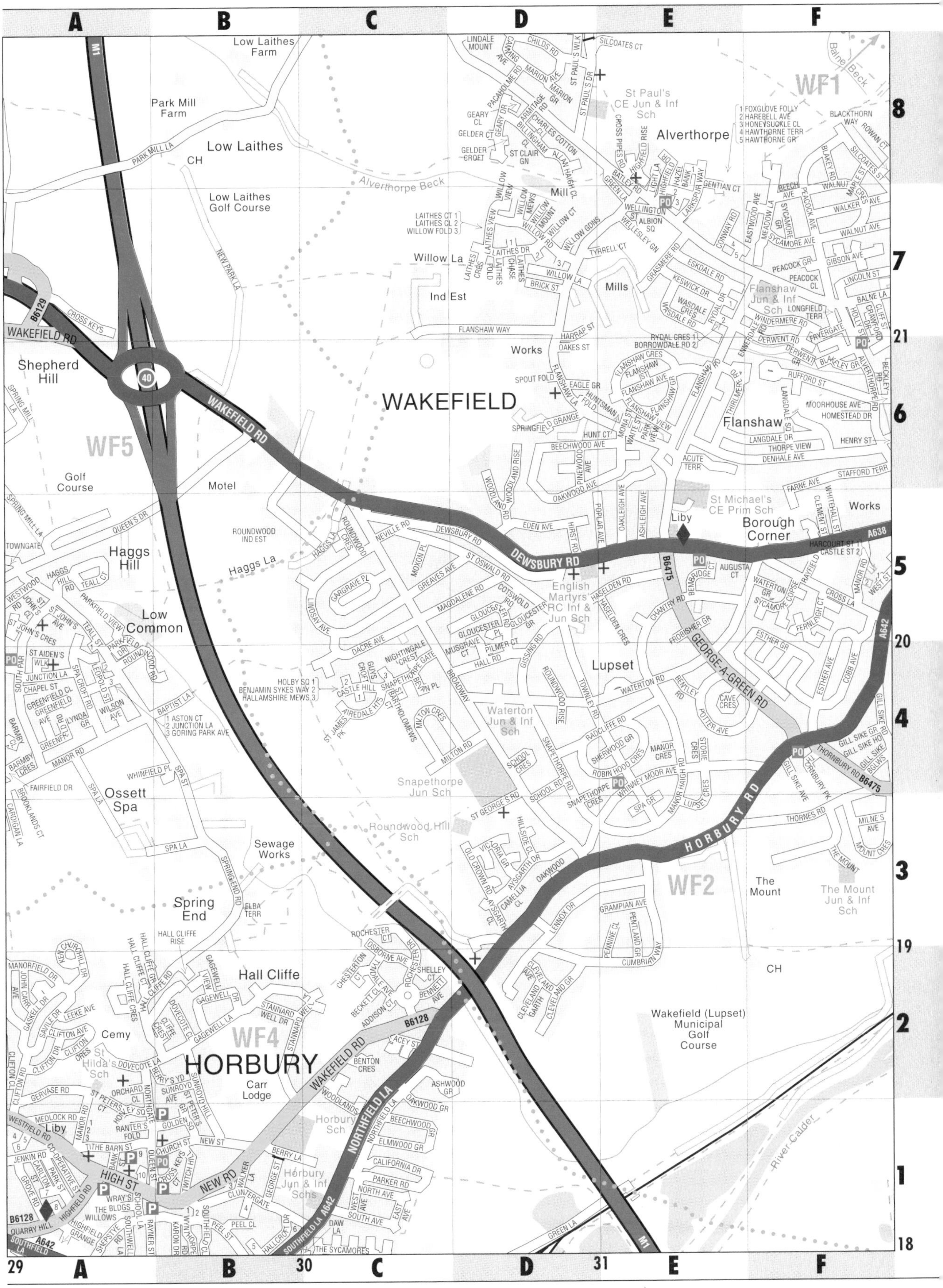

A1
1 MANOR PL
2 CLAYTON COTTS
3 CHARLESWORTH'S BLDGS
4 WESTFIELD TERR
5 WENSLEY ST
6 WENSLEY ST E
7 CROSS PARK ST
8 CLUBHOUSES CROFT
9 RING O'BELLS YD
10 FEARNSIDE'S CL

B1
1 WHITEHALL CT
2 CROSS ST
3 DAWSON HILL YD
4 STRINGER LA
5 HALLCROFT CL
6 NORMAN PL

159
142

141

121

For full street detail of the highlighted area see page 216.

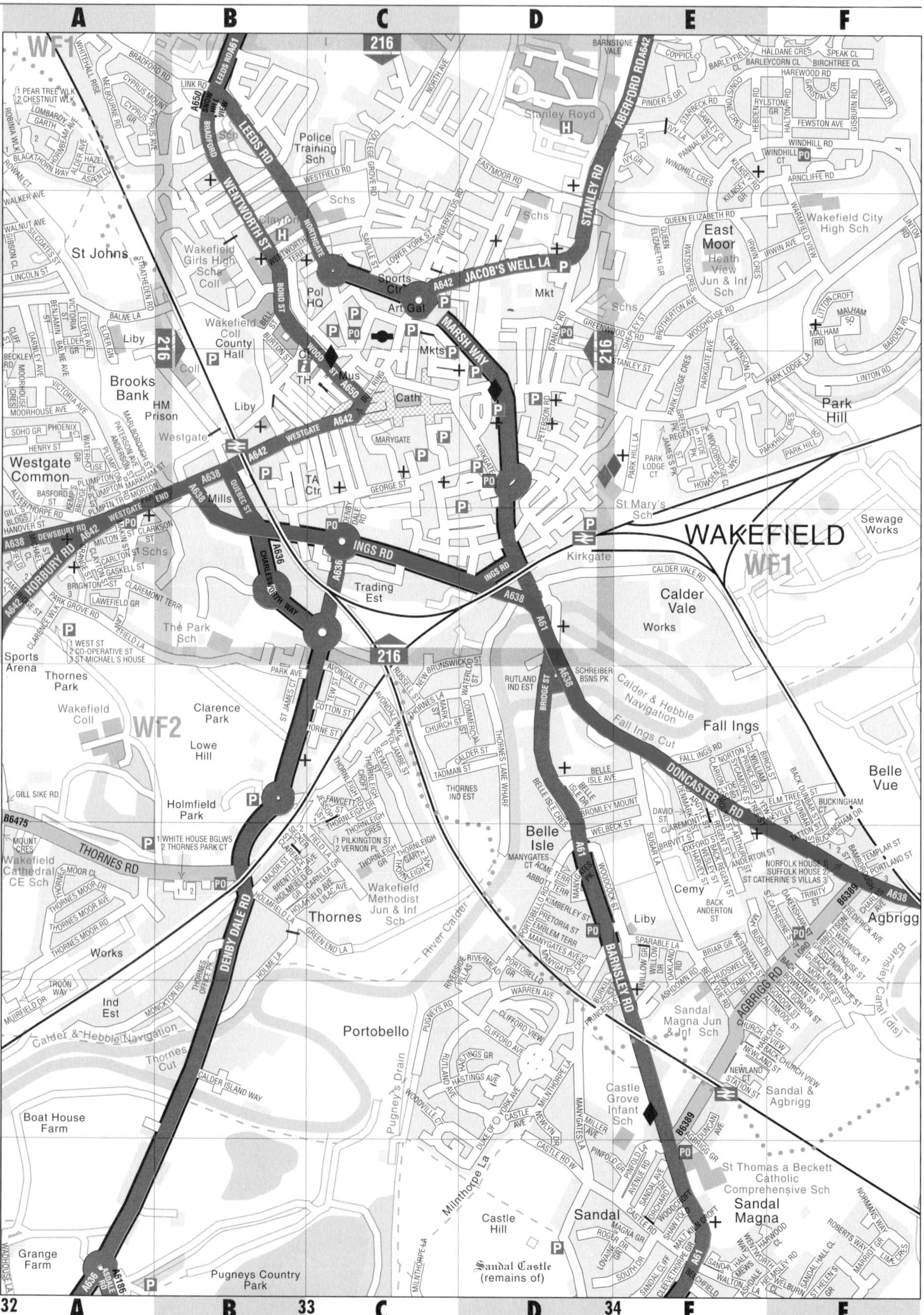
WAKEFIELD
WF1
WF2
St Johns
Brooks Bank
Westgate Common
HM Prison
Wakefield Girls High Schs
Wakefield Coll
County Hall
Police Training Sch
Clayton
Stanley Royd
East Moor
Heath View Jun & Inf Sch
Wakefield City High Sch
Park Hill
Sewage Works
Calder Vale
Works
Trading Est
Kirkgate
Westgate
St Mary's Sch
Cath
Mkts
Art Gal
Sports Ctr
Pol HQ
Mus
TA Ctr
Mills
The Park Sch
Sports Arena
Thornes Park
Clarence Park
Lowe Hill
Holmfield Park
Wakefield Cathedral CE Sch
Thornes
Wakefield Methodist Jun & Inf Sch
Fall Ings
Belle Vue
Belle Isle
Cemy
Agbrigg
Sandal Magna Jun & Inf Sch
Sandal & Agbrigg
Portobello
Castle Grove Infant Sch
St Thomas a Beckett Catholic Comprehensive Sch
Sandal Magna
Sandal
Castle Hill
Sandal Castle (remains of)
Pugneys Country Park
Boat House Farm
Grange Farm
Ind Est
Thornes Cut
Calder & Hebble Navigation
River Calder
Barnsley Canal (dis)
Pugney's Drain
LEEDS RD
WENTWORTH ST
NORTHGATE
JACOB'S WELL LA
MARSH WAY
STANLEY RD
ABERFORD RD A642
INGS RD
WESTGATE
DEWSBURY RD
HORBURY RD
DENBY DALE RD
THORNES RD
DONCASTER RD
BARNSLEY RD
AGBRIGG RD
CALDER VALE RD
CHARLESWORTH WAY
216
A B C D E F
8 7 21 6 5 20 4 3 19 2 1 18
32 33 34

122
144

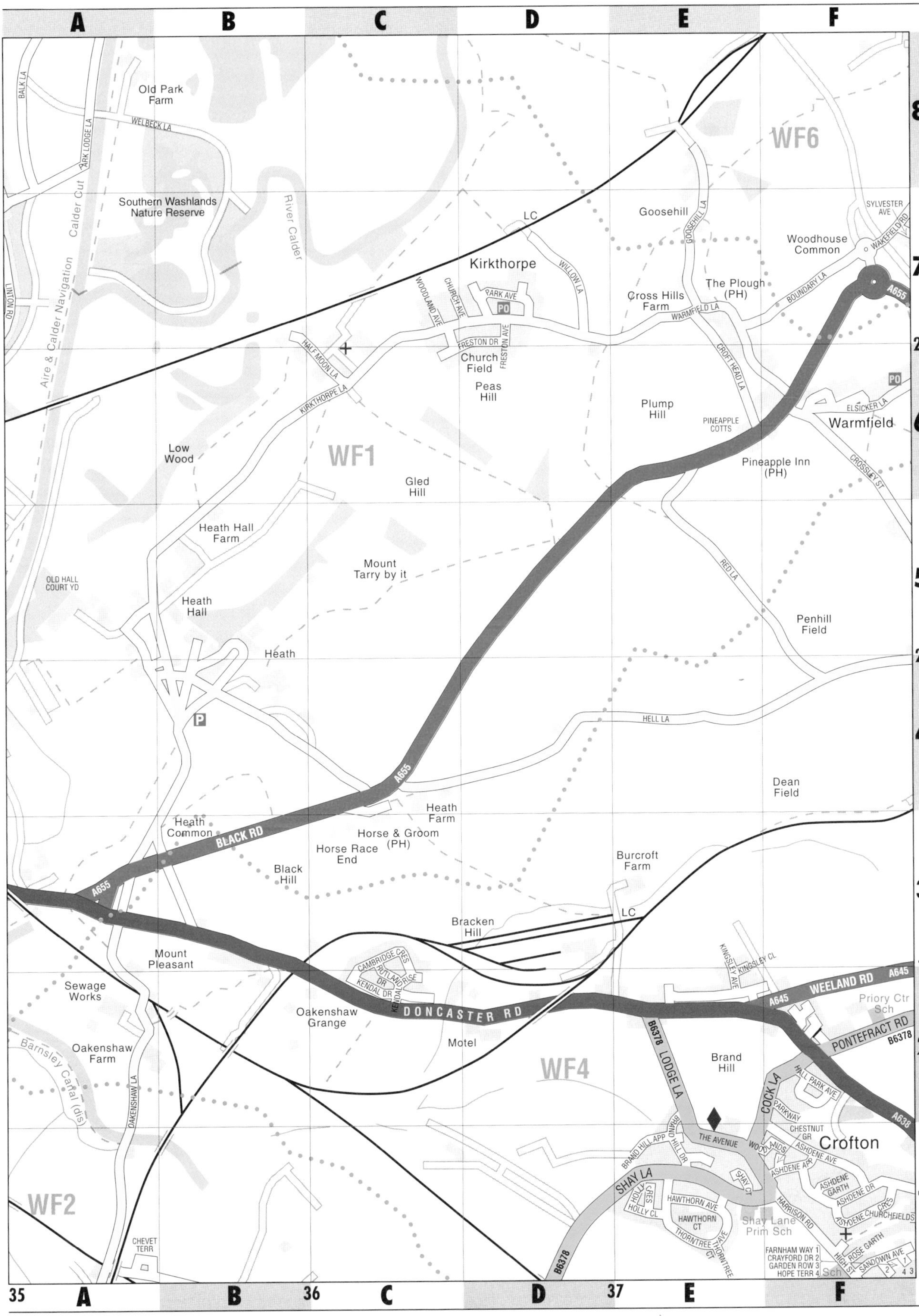

161
144

143
123

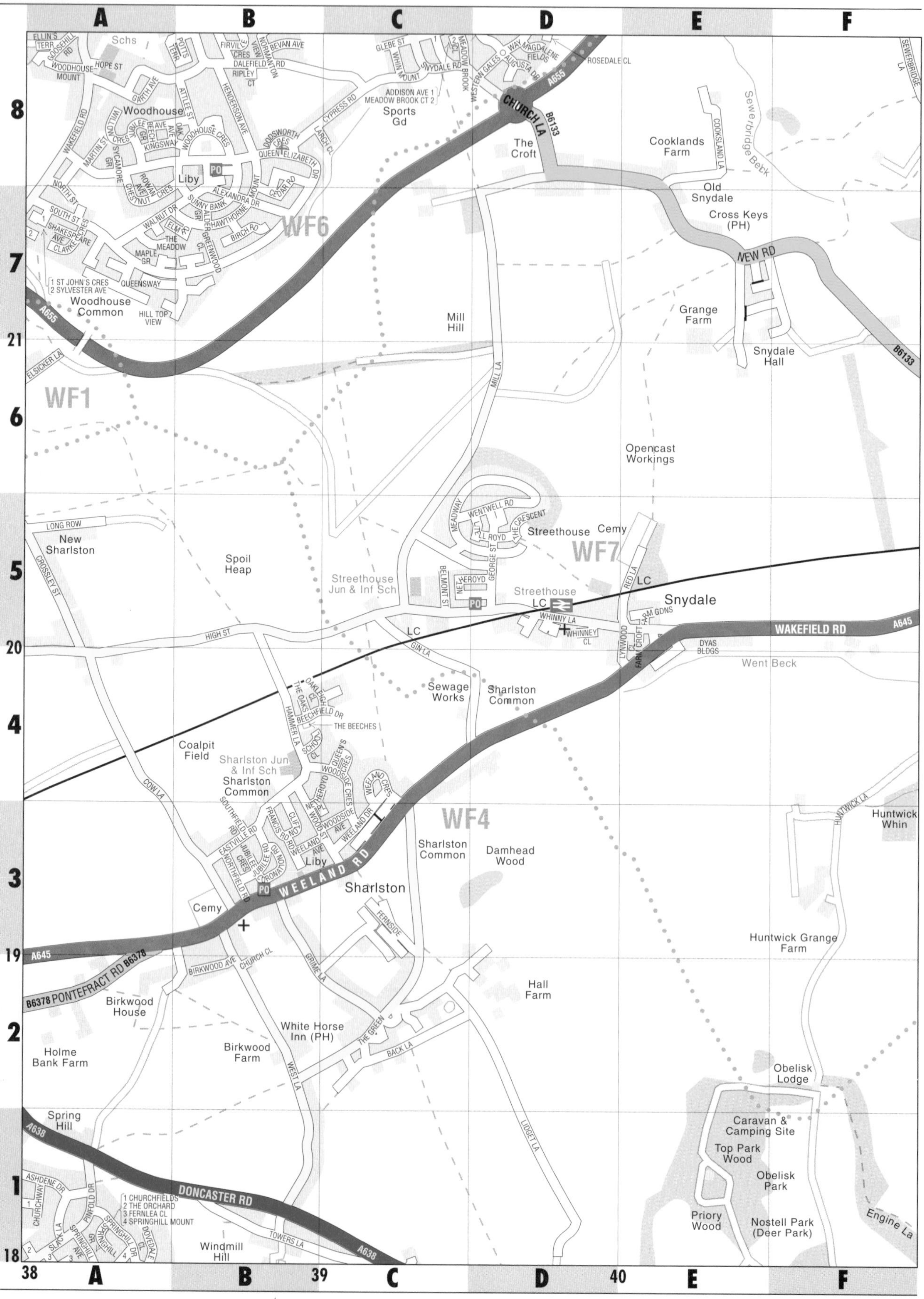

143
162

124
146

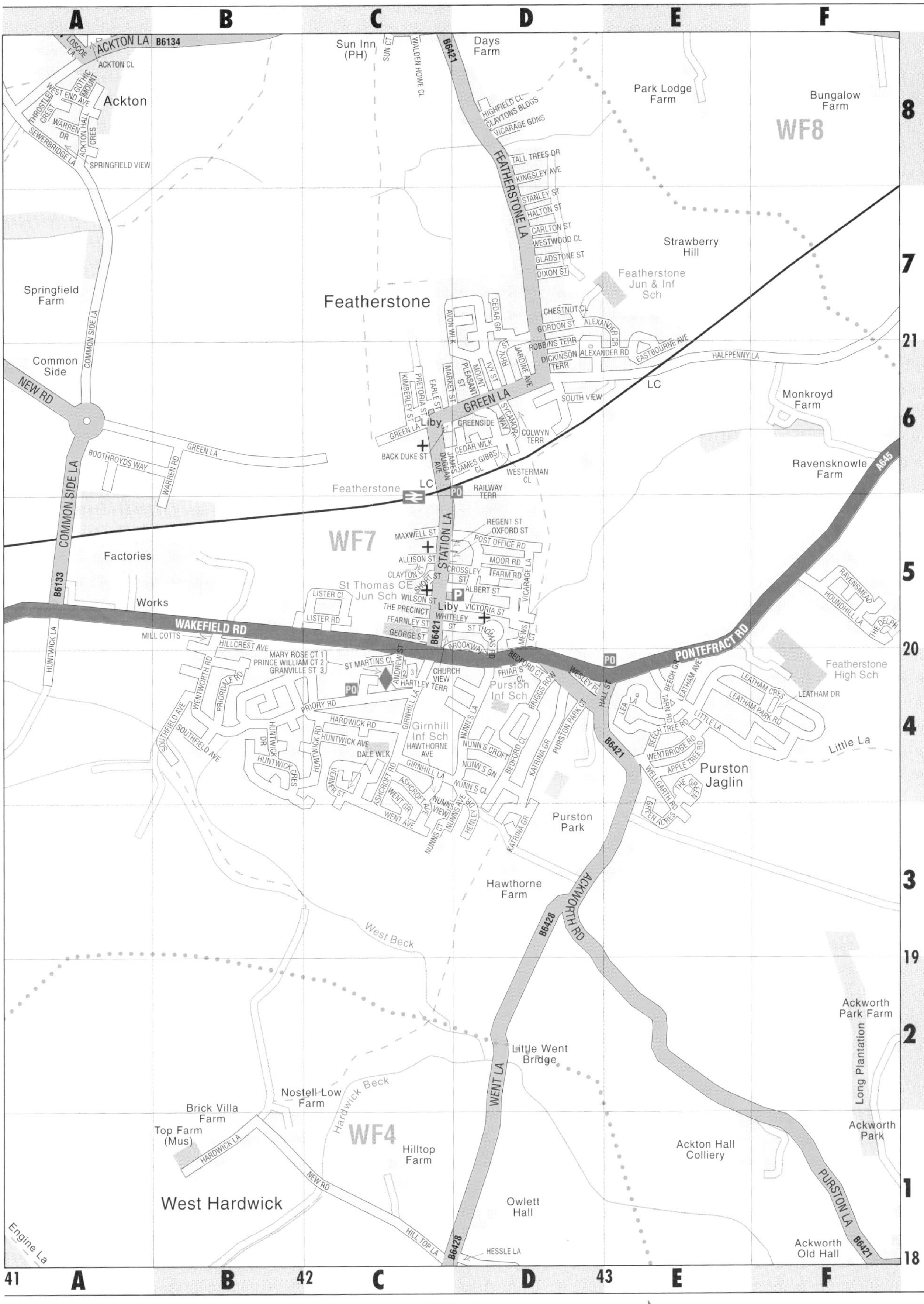

163
146

B7
1 BEECHWOOD
2 ARMSTRONG TERR
C7
1 WESTBOURNE AVE
2 WESTBOURNE MOUNT

B8
1 ST MICHAELS AVE
2 WOLSEY AVE
3 ARGYLL AVE
4 QUEENS TERR
5 CLIFTON VIEW
6 CLIFTON AVE

145

C8
1 ELM TERR
2 SWALES' YD
3 CROWN & ANCHOR YD
4 ROPERGATE END
5 WOODBINE AVE
6 GRANVILLE AVE

125

C8
7 CLIFF VILLAS
8 CLIFF ST
9 BLACKBURN CT
10 BANKS MOUNT
11 WEST MOUNT ST
12 CRAG MOUNT

D8
1 SALTER ROW
2 CHURCH LA
3 CROSS ST
4 SHOE MARKET
5 VALLEY RD
6 WOOLMARKET
7 BRIDGE ST
8 FINKLE ST
9 HORSE FAIR
10 BAXTERGATE
11 HORSE FAIR FLATS
12 HARROP WELL LA

E8
1 MIDLAND RD
2 ALL SAINTS' VIEW

F8
1 HAILHEAD DR
2 HAREFIELD RD
3 SCHOOLBOARDS LA
4 SOUTH VIEW GDNS
5 EASTBOURNE VIEW

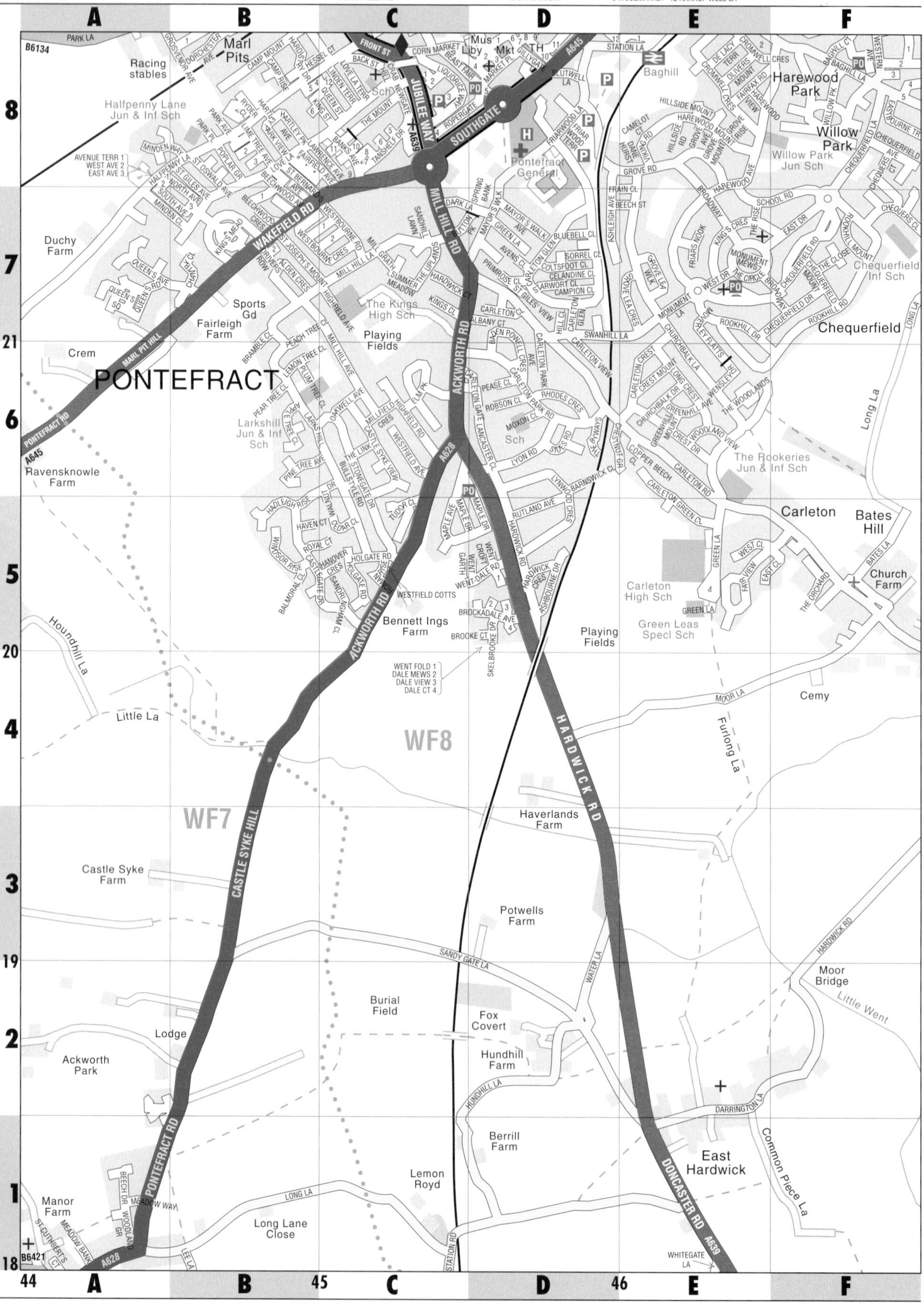

145
164

126

A
B
C
D
E
F
Cobbler's Lane Junior & Infant Sch
Greavefield Closes
GROVEHALL LA
GREAVEFIELD LA
GROVE HALL PARK HOMES
Grove Hall Farm
Grove Hall
LEYS LA
Trinity Farm
1 SHARNALEY CT
2 POMFRET CT
3 LAYTHORPE CT
EASTBOURNE VIEW
EASTBOURNE TERR
CHEQUERS CL
HAREFIELD RD
COBBLER'S LA
SOUTH VIEW GDNS
WF11
A1
Spital Gap
Hodgewood Farm
Hodge Wood
LONG LA
STREET FURLONG LA
SPITALGAP LA
HODGEWOOD LA
Golf Course
Hunters Wood
Bickering Wood
Millhill Fields
Darrington
Church Farm
Darrington CE Junior & Infant Sch
Bates Hill
MARLPIT LA
LEYS RD
HAVERCROFT LA
CH
Valley Plantation
ASH GR
ELM CL
SOTHERON CROFT
PARK CL
DENBY RD
PARK AVE
BEECH CRES
PHILIP'S LA
DENBY CREST
MILL HILL CL
NORTH PARK RISE
HILL CROFT CL
PO
NORWOOD
TUMBLING HILL
CARLETON RD
West End Farm
ESTCOURT RD
CHURCH LA
WENTWORTH DR
MANOR PK
MANOR PARK RISE
ORCHARD LA
NEW ROW COTTS
ORCHARD VIEW
GREENROYD CT
THORNTREE CL
MILNER'S LA
ESTCOURT DR
FAIRWAYS CT
VALLEY RD
BANK WOOD RD
NORTH LODGE LA
Manasseh
Machir
Darrington Windmill (disused)
WF8
Darrington Hall
West Valley
Chestnut House Hotel
HARDWICK RD
West Field
Long Plantation
Stapleton Park
WESTFIELD LA
Womersley
Fletcher's Spring
WEST PARK TERR
PH
WEST PARK DR
MOOR LA
Thorntree Closes
Round Ash Closes
Went Hill
Kirkdike Plantation
B6474
Dale Field
Long Plantation
Horse Race Closes
Wenthill Plantation
8
7
21
6
5
20
4
3
19
2
1
18
47
48
49

165

130

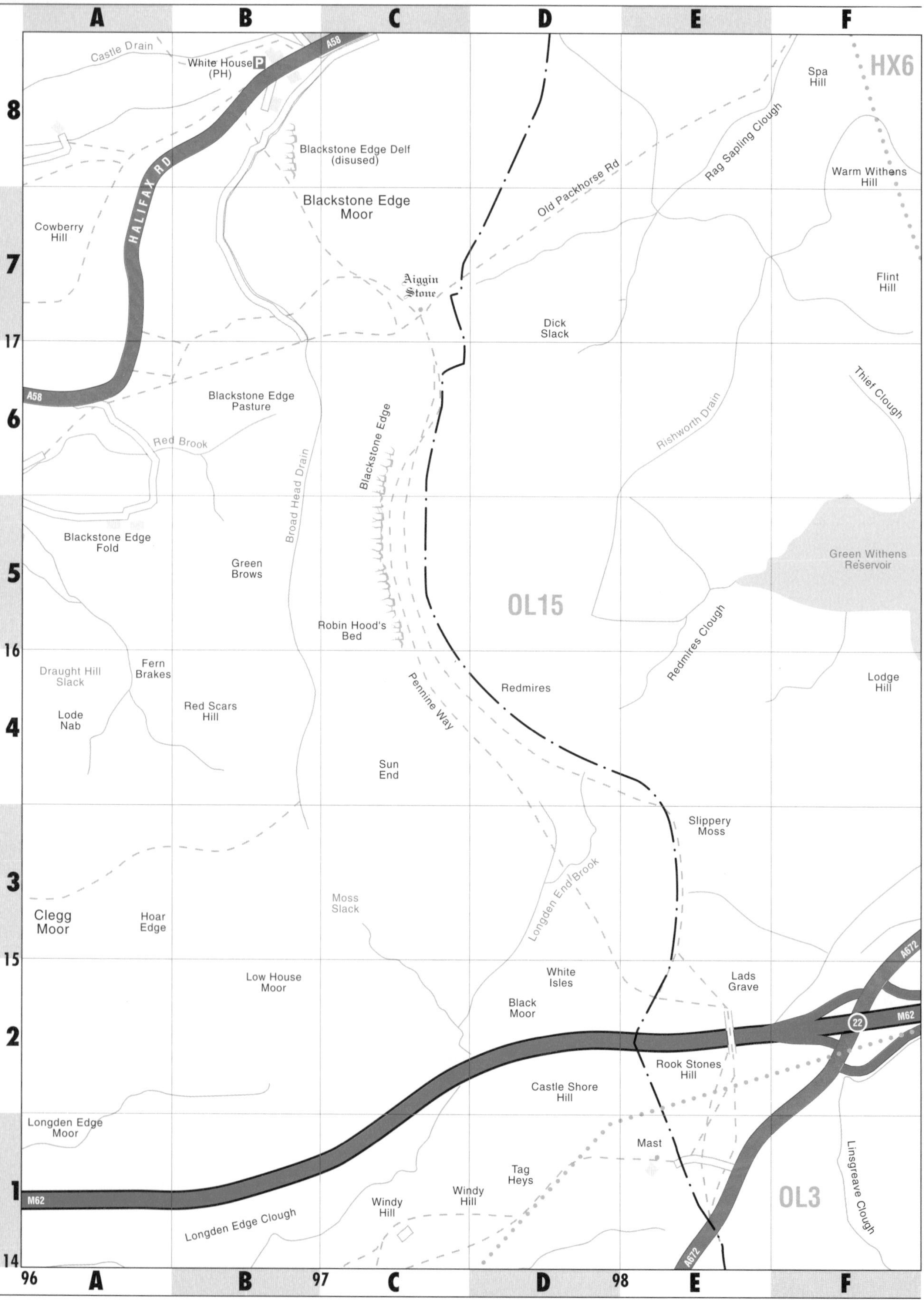
A
B
C
D
E
F
8
7
17
6
5
16
4
3
15
2
1
14
96
97
98
Castle Drain
White House
(PH)
A58
HALIFAX RD
Blackstone Edge Delf
(disused)
Blackstone Edge
Moor
Cowberry
Hill
Aiggin
Stone
Old Packhorse Rd
Rag Sapling Clough
Spa
Hill
HX6
Warm Withens
Hill
Flint
Hill
Dick
Slack
Thief Clough
Blackstone Edge
Pasture
Red Brook
Broad Head Drain
Blackstone Edge
Rishworth Drain
Blackstone Edge
Fold
Green
Brows
OL15
Green Withens
Reservoir
Robin Hood's
Bed
Redmires Clough
Draught Hill
Slack
Fern
Brakes
Lode
Nab
Red Scars
Hill
Pennine Way
Redmires
Lodge
Hill
Sun
End
Slippery
Moss
Clegg
Moor
Hoar
Edge
Moss
Slack
Longden End Brook
Low House
Moor
White
Isles
Lads
Grave
Black
Moor
A672
M62
22
Rook Stones
Hill
Castle Shore
Hill
Longden Edge
Moor
Mast
Tag
Heys
Windy
Hill
Windy
Hill
OL3
Linsgreave Clough
Longden Edge Clough

131
150

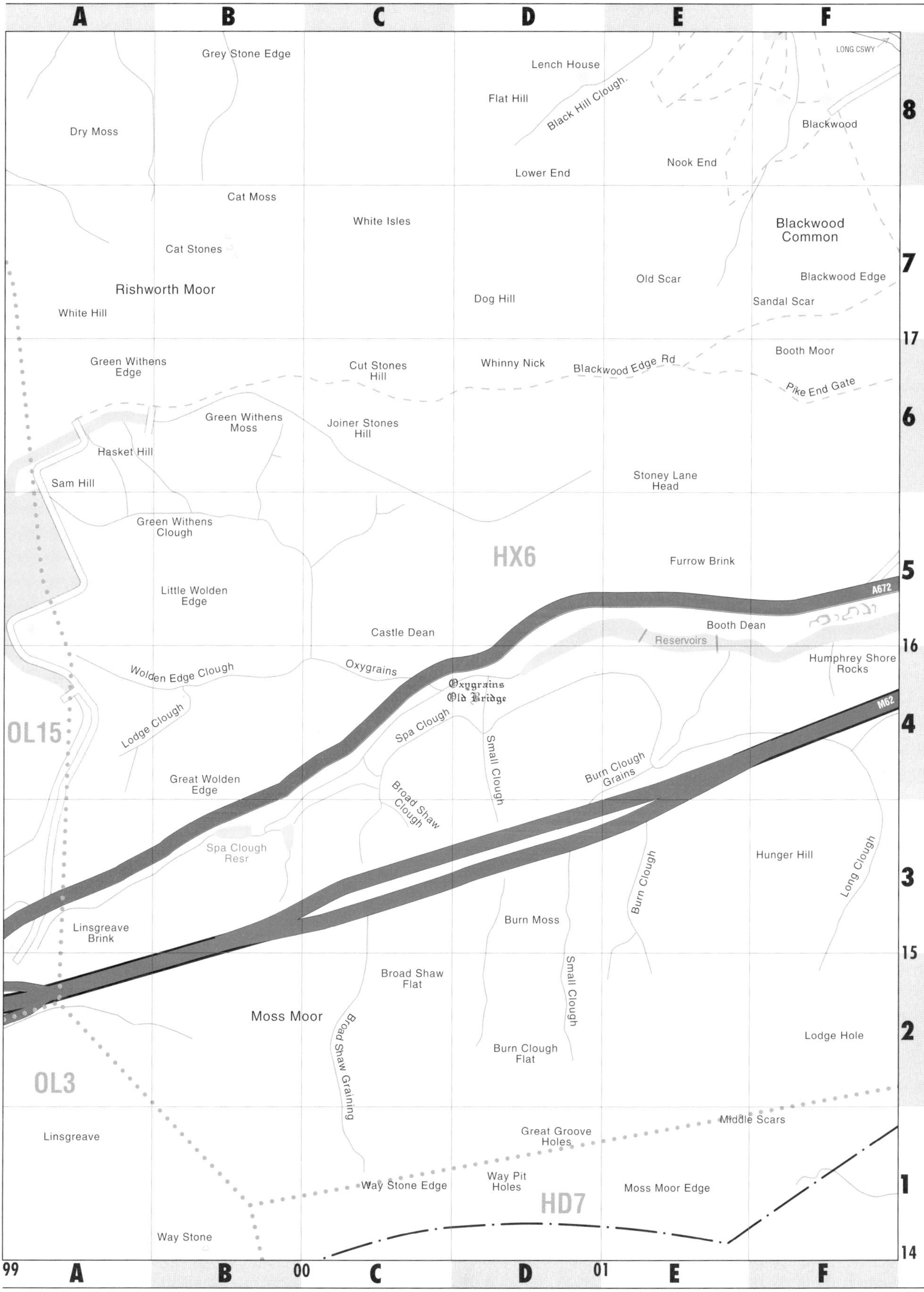

167
150

149
132

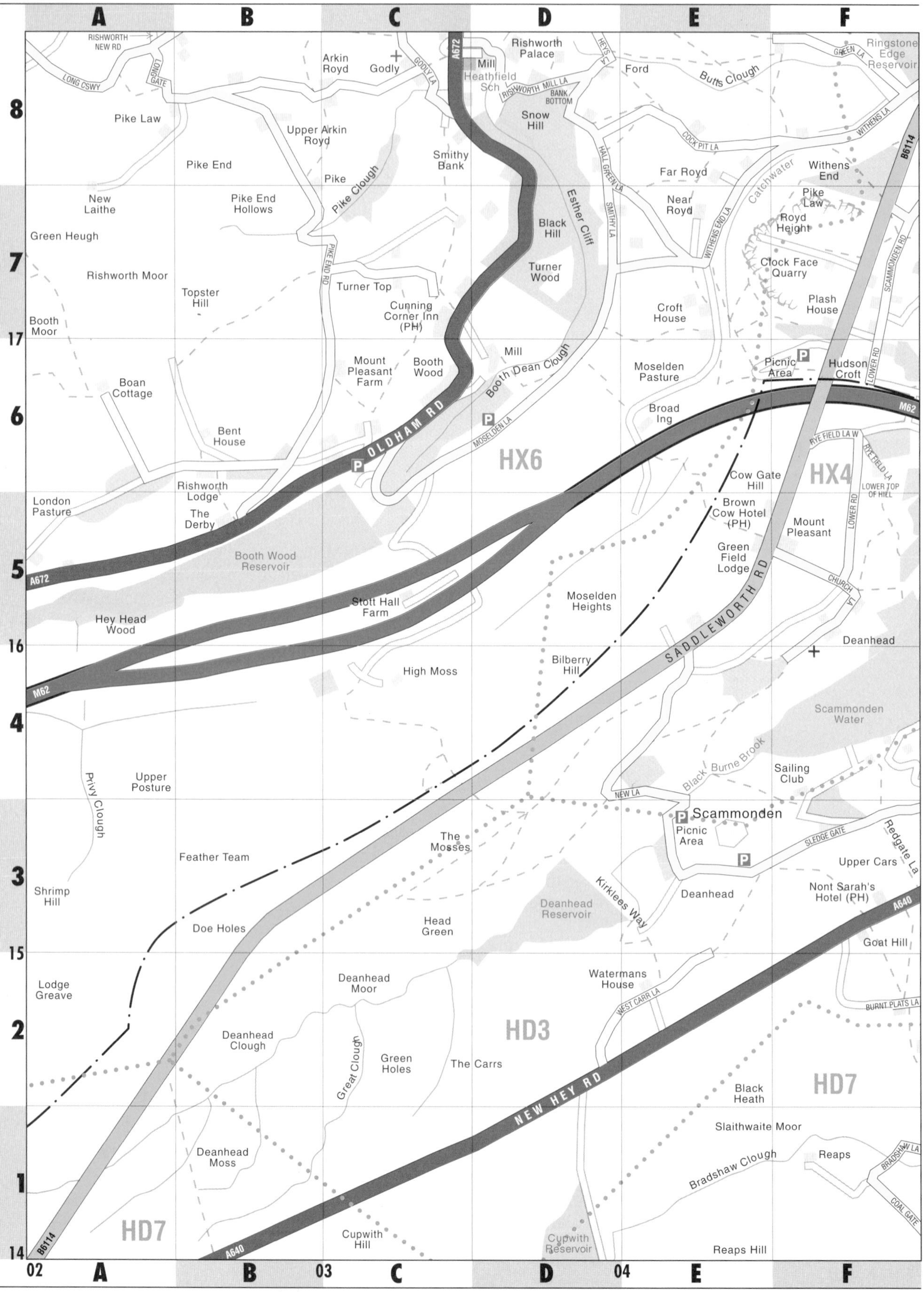

149
168

133
152

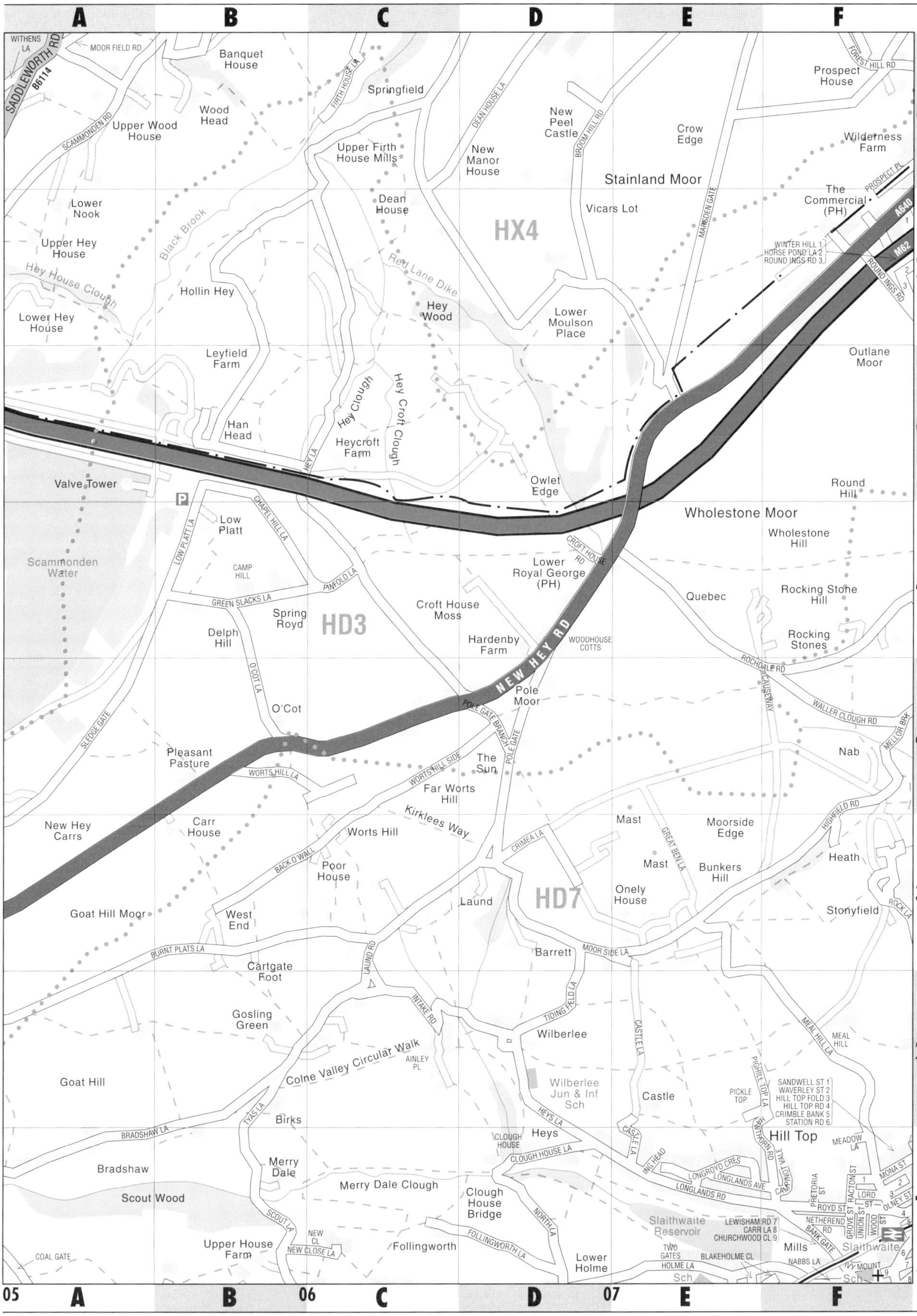

169
152

151
134

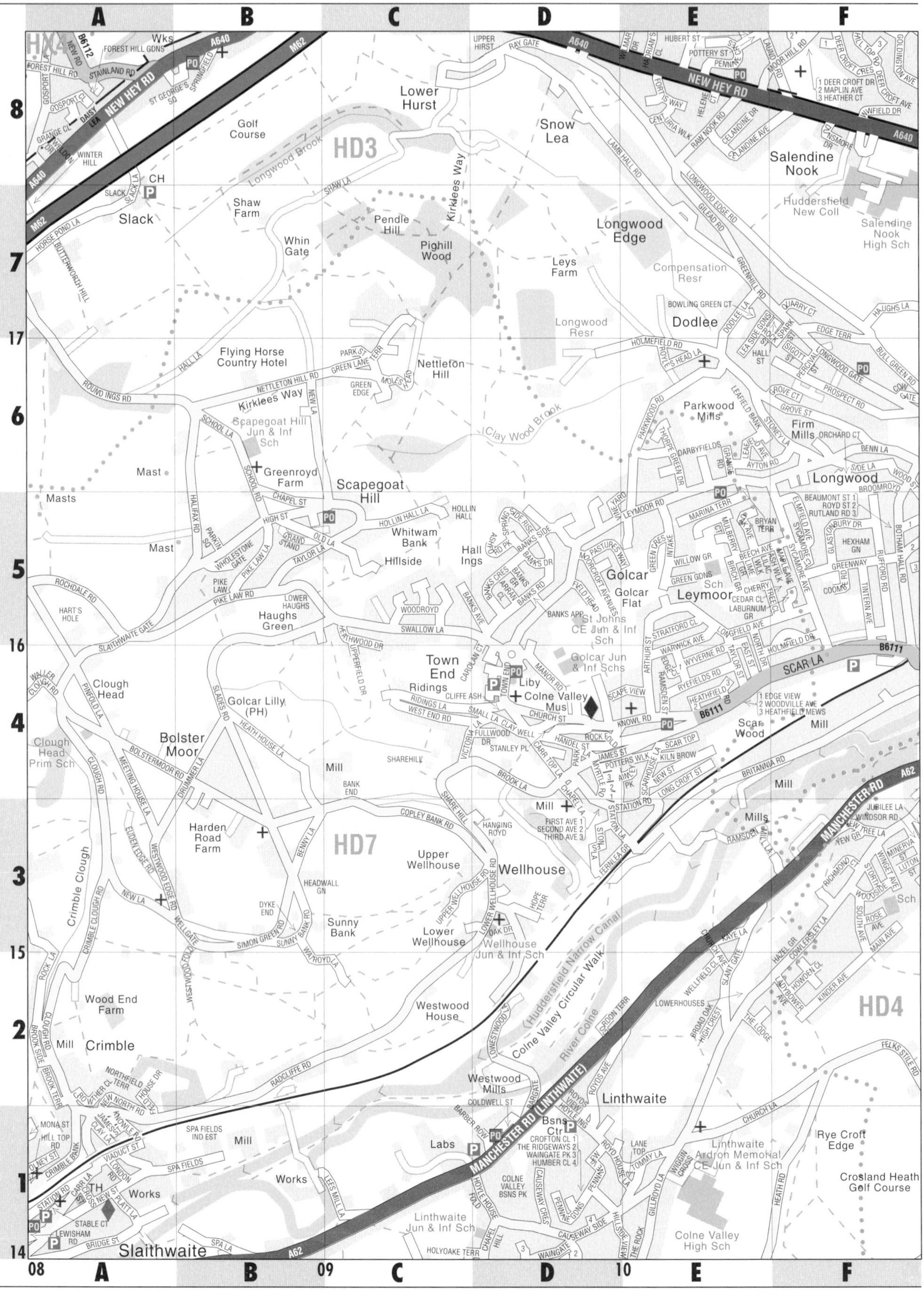

151
170

135
154

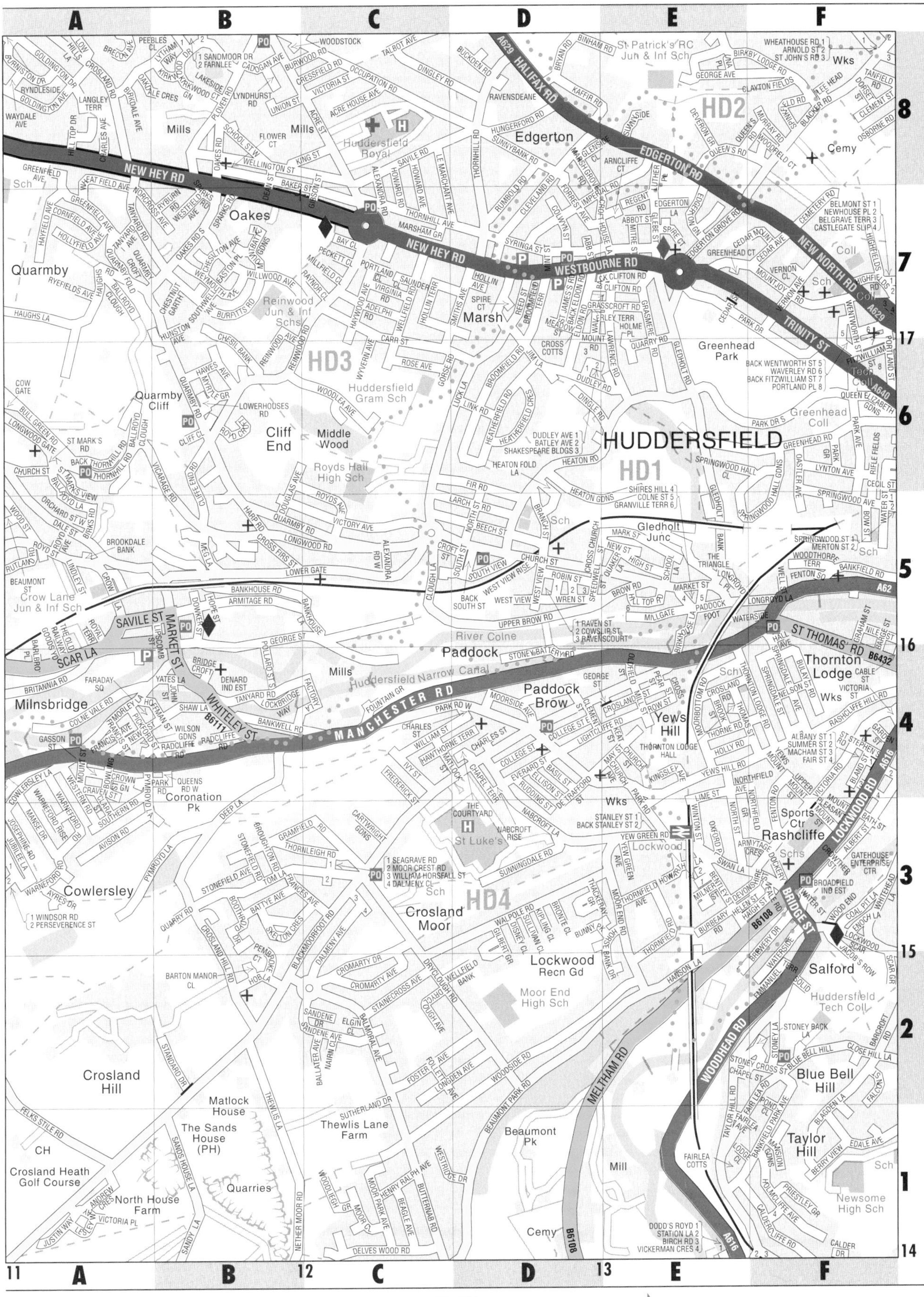

171
154

A5
1 SWALLOW ST
2 CORPORATION ST
3 PRINCESS ST
4 ALFRED ST
5 PEEL ST
6 CROSS GROVE ST

A6
1 GREENHEAD RD
2 BACK GREENHEAD RD
3 UPPER GEORGE ST
4 BACK SPRING ST
5 RICHARDSON SQ
6 SPRINGWOOD SQ

153

A6
7 SPRING ST
8 BACK CECIL ST
9 CECIL ST
10 SPRINGWOOD ST
11 UPPERHEAD ROW
12 GEORGE ST

136

A6
13 HALF MOON ST
14 SERGEANTSON ST
15 CHERRY TREE CTR
16 TEMPLE CL
17 BROOK'S YD
18 ST GEORGE'S SQ
19 CHANCERY LA
20 CHANCERY CL
21 LOCKWOOD'S YD
22 BYRAM ARC
23 IMPERIAL ARC
24 QUEEN TAP YD
25 DUNDAS ST
26 WARD SQ

A7
1 BELMONT CL
2 NEWHOUSE PL
3 HIGHFIELDS RD
4 ELMWOOD AVE
5 ELMWOOD CL
6 LITTLE BRUNSWICK ST

A8
1 THREE SISTERS SQ
2 ELEANOR ST
3 KING CLIFFE FLATS
4 COMMON RD

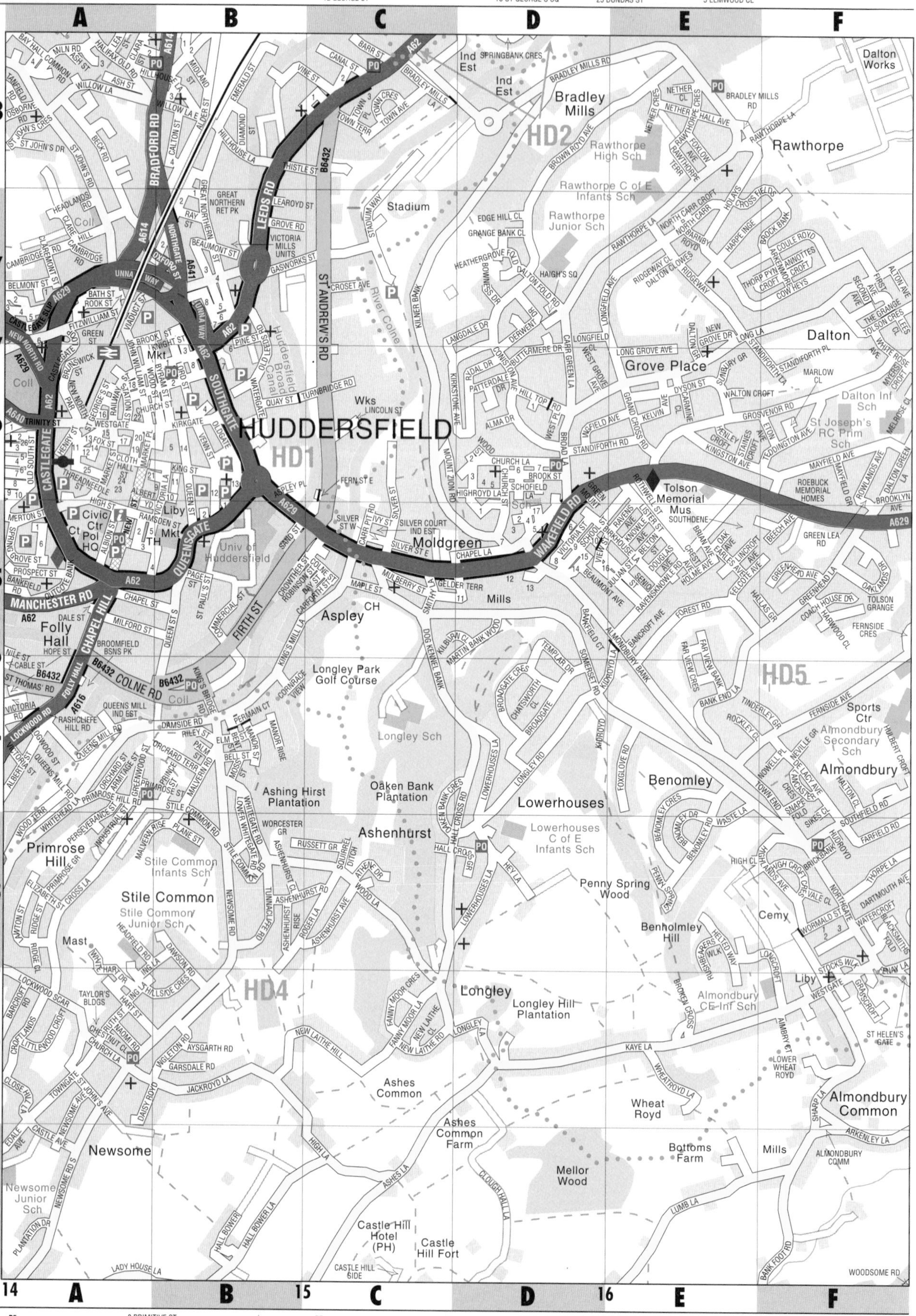

B5
1 RICE ST
2 BACK QUEEN ST

B6
1 NORTHUMBERLAND ST
2 ST PETER'S ST
3 FRIENDLY ST
4 BEAST MARKET
5 PACK HORSE CTR
6 IBBOTSON FLATS
7 LONSBROUGH FLATS
8 PRIMITIVE ST
9 MARKET AVE
10 PRINCESS ALEXANDRA WLK
11 THE SHAMBLES
12 ZETLAND ST
13 BRADLEY ST
14 CROSS CHURCH ST

B7
1 MYRTLE ST
2 LOWER VIADUCT ST
3 WILLIAM ST

153

B7
4 LOWER FITZWILLIAM ST
5 BACK UNION ST
6 UNION ST
7 RICHMOND FLATS
8 BROADWAY

B8
1 SHEARING CROSS GDNS
2 WHITESTONE LA
3 CROFT COTTAGE LA
4 HEBBLE ST

172

C8
1 GALLOWAY ST
2 FIELDHOUSE RD
3 MINI MARKET

D5
1 HIGHROYD CRES
2 HANDEL TERR
3 ELMFIELD TERR
4 THE AVENUE
5 OLD WAKEFIELD RD
6 VICTORIA PL
7 CHAPEL ST
8 EASTWOOD ST
9 TREVELYAN ST
10 DIAMOND ST
11 POPLAR ST
12 TOLSON'S YD
13 OLD BANK FOLD
14 BEAUMONT ST
15 OSBORNE ST
16 ROSEDALE AVE
17 POPLAR TERR

D6
1 MOUNT PLEASANT ST
2 BRIGGS TERR
3 HAMPSHIRE ST
4 PORCHESTER HOUSE
5 REDWOOD GR
6 LEEF ST
7 BATLEY ST

F3
1 HOUGHTON'S ALMSHOUSES
2 PARKIN'S ALMSHOUSES
3 NETTLETON'S ALMSHOUSES

137
156

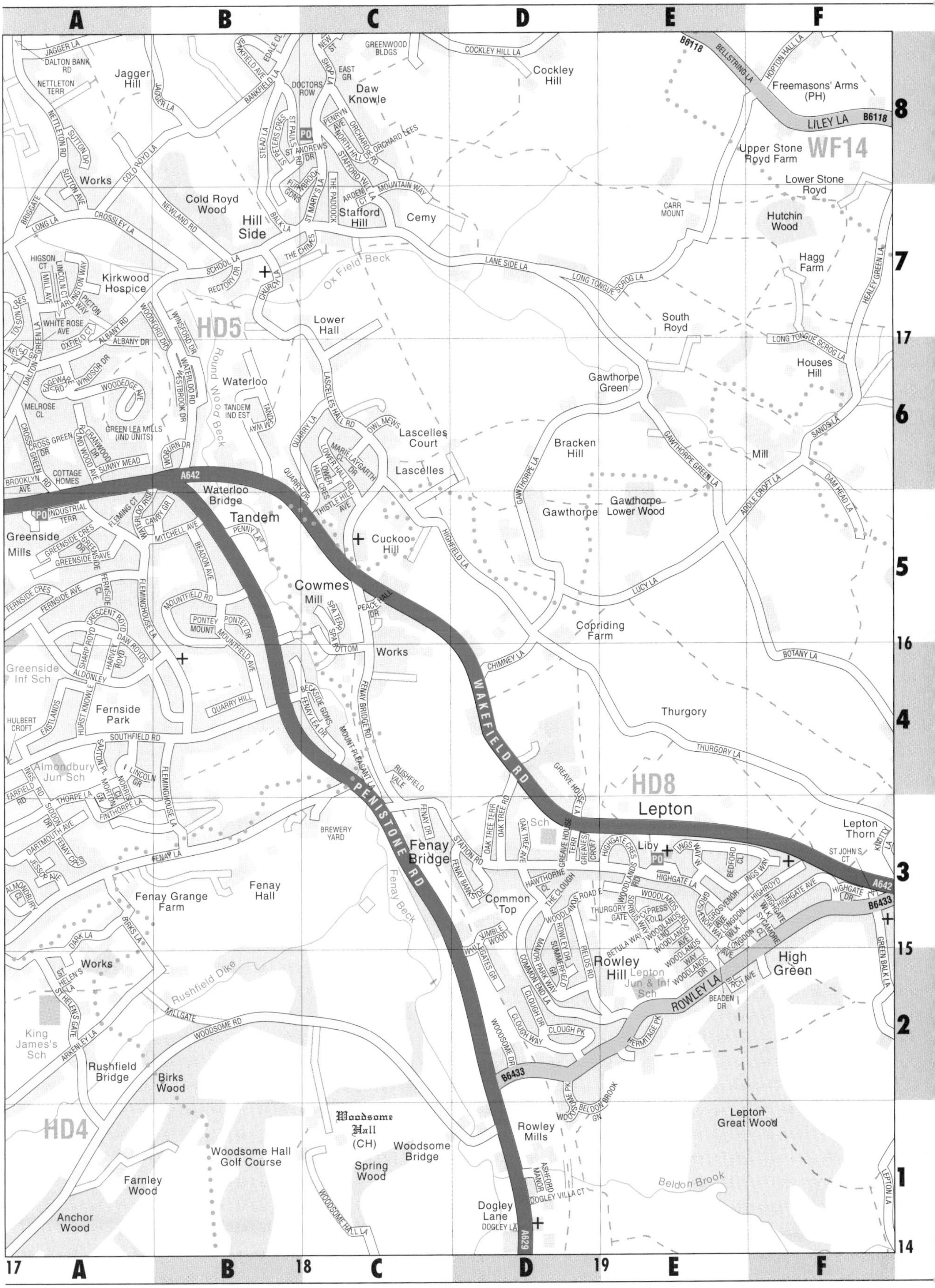

173
156

155
138

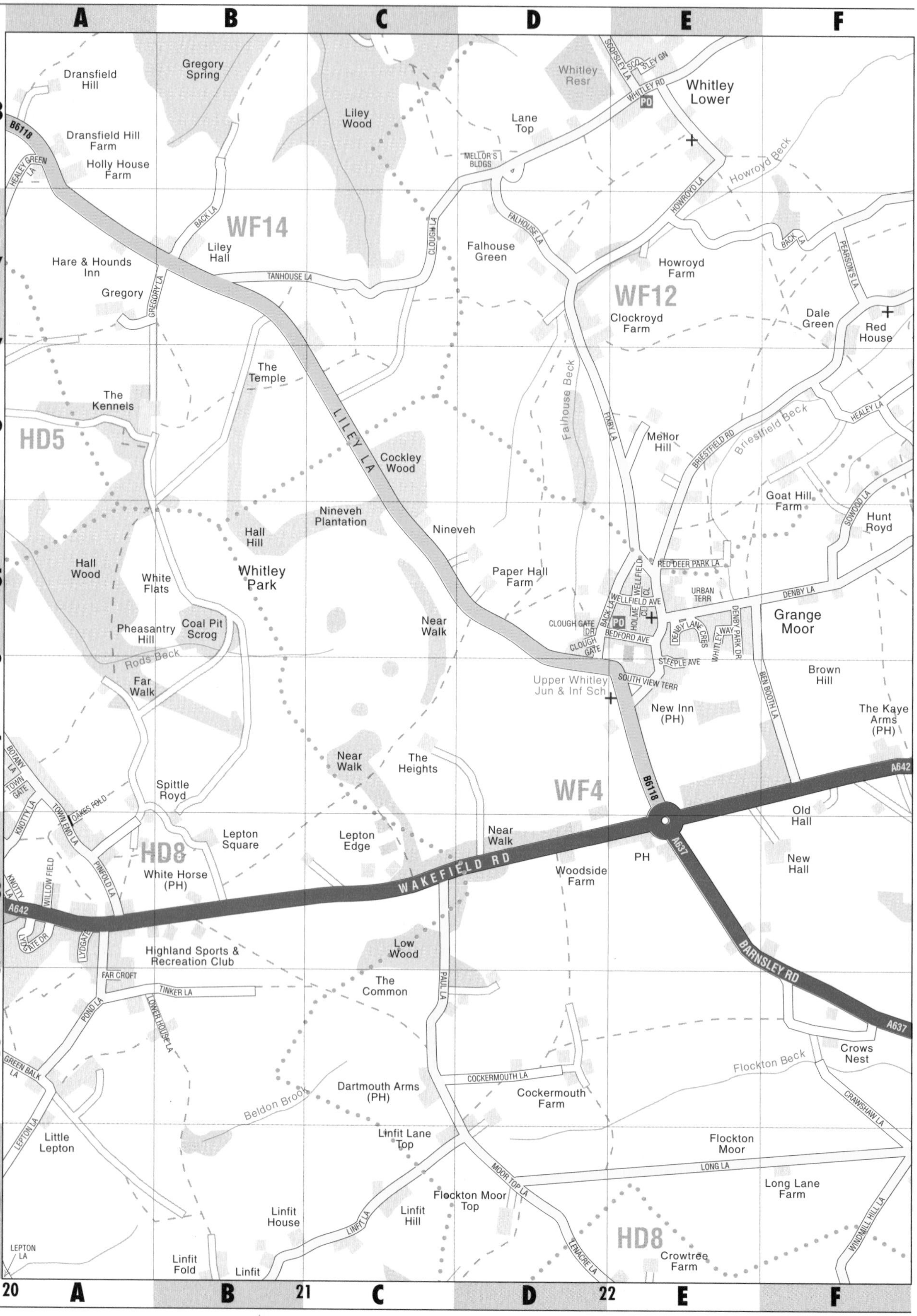

155
174

139
158

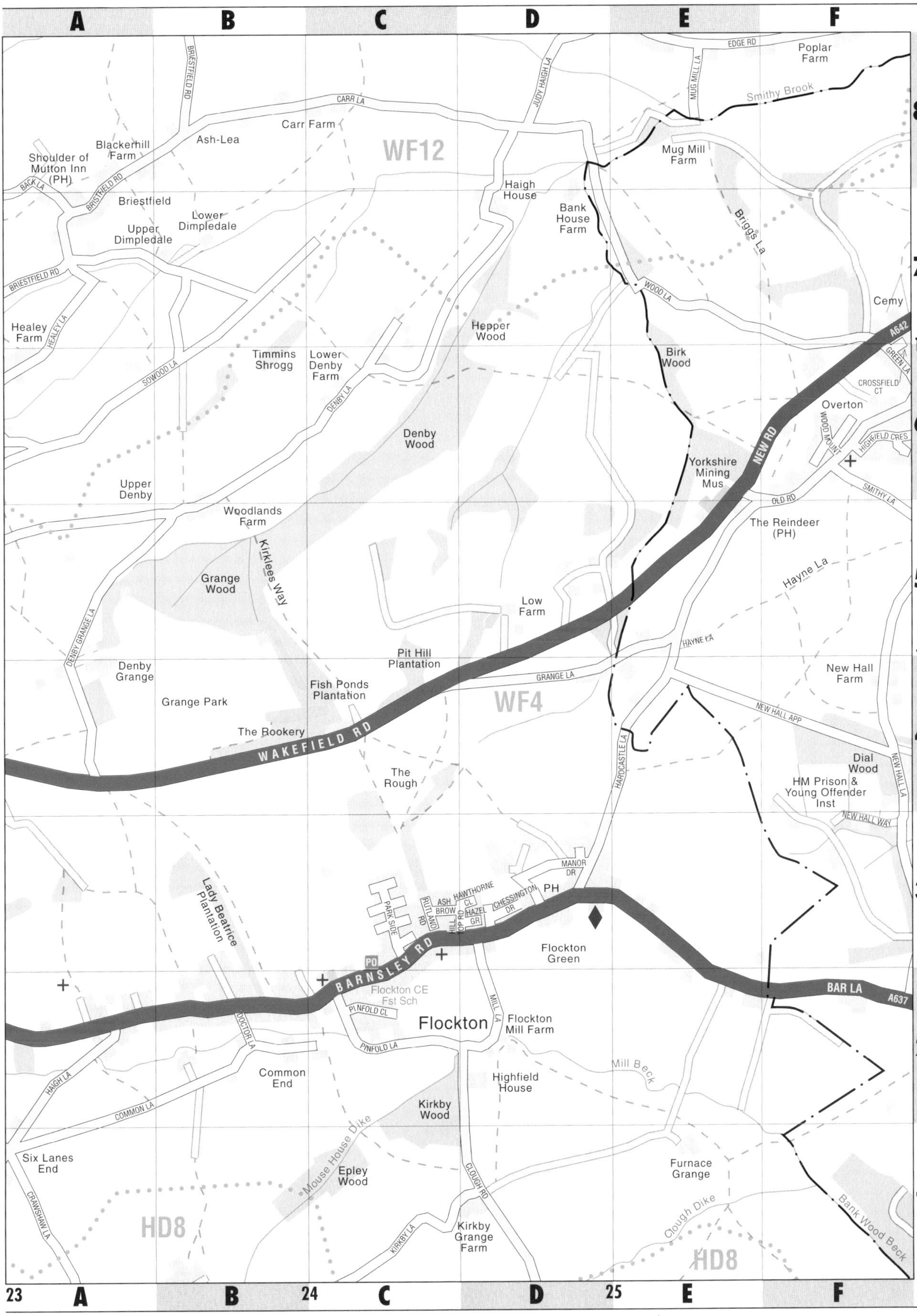

175
158

157
140

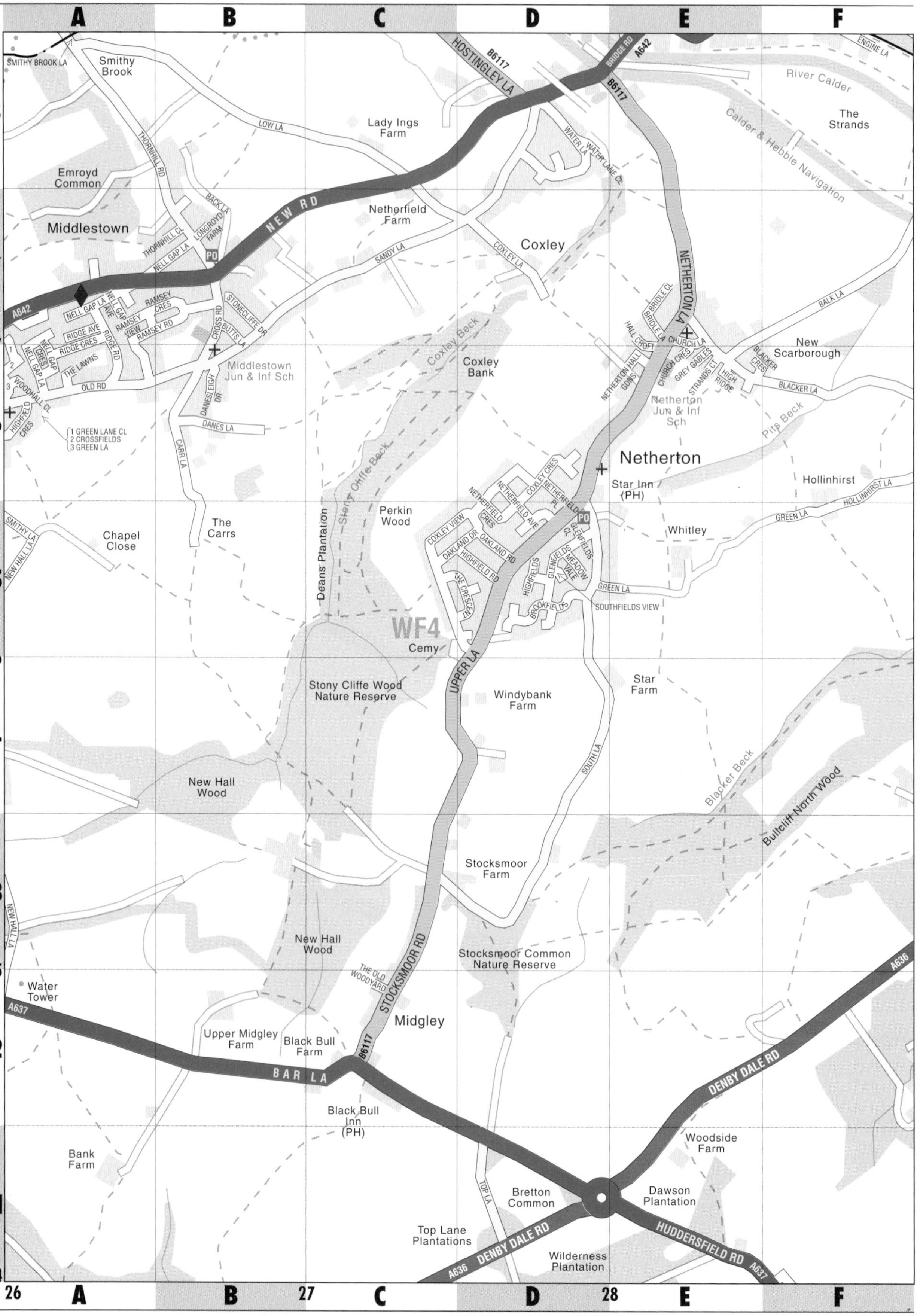
A
B
C
D
E
F
8
7
17
6
5
16
4
3
15
2
1
14
26
27
28
SMITHY BROOK LA
Smithy Brook
HOSTINGLEY LA
B6117
BRIDGE RD
A642
ENGINE LA
River Calder
The Strands
Calder & Hebble Navigation
LOW LA
Lady Ings Farm
THORNHILL RD
Emroyd Common
WATER LA
WATER LANE CL
BACK LA
NEW RD
Netherfield Farm
Middlestown
THORNHILL CL
LONGROYD FARM
PO
NELL GAP LA
SANDY LA
Coxley
COXLEY LA
NETHERTON LA
BALK LA
A642
NELL GAP LA
NELL GAP AVE
RAMSEY CRES
RAMSEY VIEW
RAMSEY RD
CROSS RD
STONECLIFFE DR
BUTTS LA
RIDGE AVE
RIDGE CRES
RIDGE RD
THE LAWNS
NELL GAP CRES
NELL GAP LA
OLD RD
WOODHALL CL
HIGHFIELD CRES
Middlestown Jun & Inf Sch
Coxley Beck
Coxley Bank
BRIDLE CL
BRIDLE LA
HALL CROFT
CHURCH LA
CHURCH CRES
GREY GABLES
STRANDS CT
HIGH RIDGE
BLACKER CRES
New Scarborough
BLACKER LA
NETHERTON HALL GDNS
Netherton Jun & Inf Sch
Pits Beck
DANESLEIGH DR
DANES LA
1 GREEN LANE CL
2 CROSSFIELDS
3 GREEN LA
CARR LA
Stony Cliffe Beck
Netherton
COXLEY CRES
NETHERFIELD PL
NETHERFIELD AVE
NETHERFIELD CRES
COXLEY VIEW
OAKLAND DR
OAKLAND RD
HIGHFIELD RD
Star Inn (PH)
Hollinhirst
HOLLINHIRST LA
GREEN LA
Whitley
SMITHY LA
NEW HALL LA
Chapel Close
The Carrs
Deans Plantation
Perkin Wood
GLENFIELDS
GLENFIELDS CL
MEADOW VALE
HIGHFIELDS
THE CRESCENT
BROOKFIELDS
GREEN LA
SOUTHFIELDS VIEW
WF4
Cemy
UPPER LA
Stony Cliffe Wood Nature Reserve
Windybank Farm
Star Farm
SOUTH LA
New Hall Wood
Blacker Beck
Bullcliff North Wood
Stocksmoor Farm
NEW HALL LA
New Hall Wood
Stocksmoor Common Nature Reserve
THE OLD WOODYARD
STOCKSMOOR RD
A636
Water Tower
A637
Midgley
Upper Midgley Farm
Black Bull Farm
B6117
BAR LA
DENBY DALE RD
Black Bull Inn (PH)
Woodside Farm
Bank Farm
TOP LA
Bretton Common
Dawson Plantation
Top Lane Plantations
A636
DENBY DALE RD
HUDDERSFIELD RD
A637
Wilderness Plantation

157
176

141
160

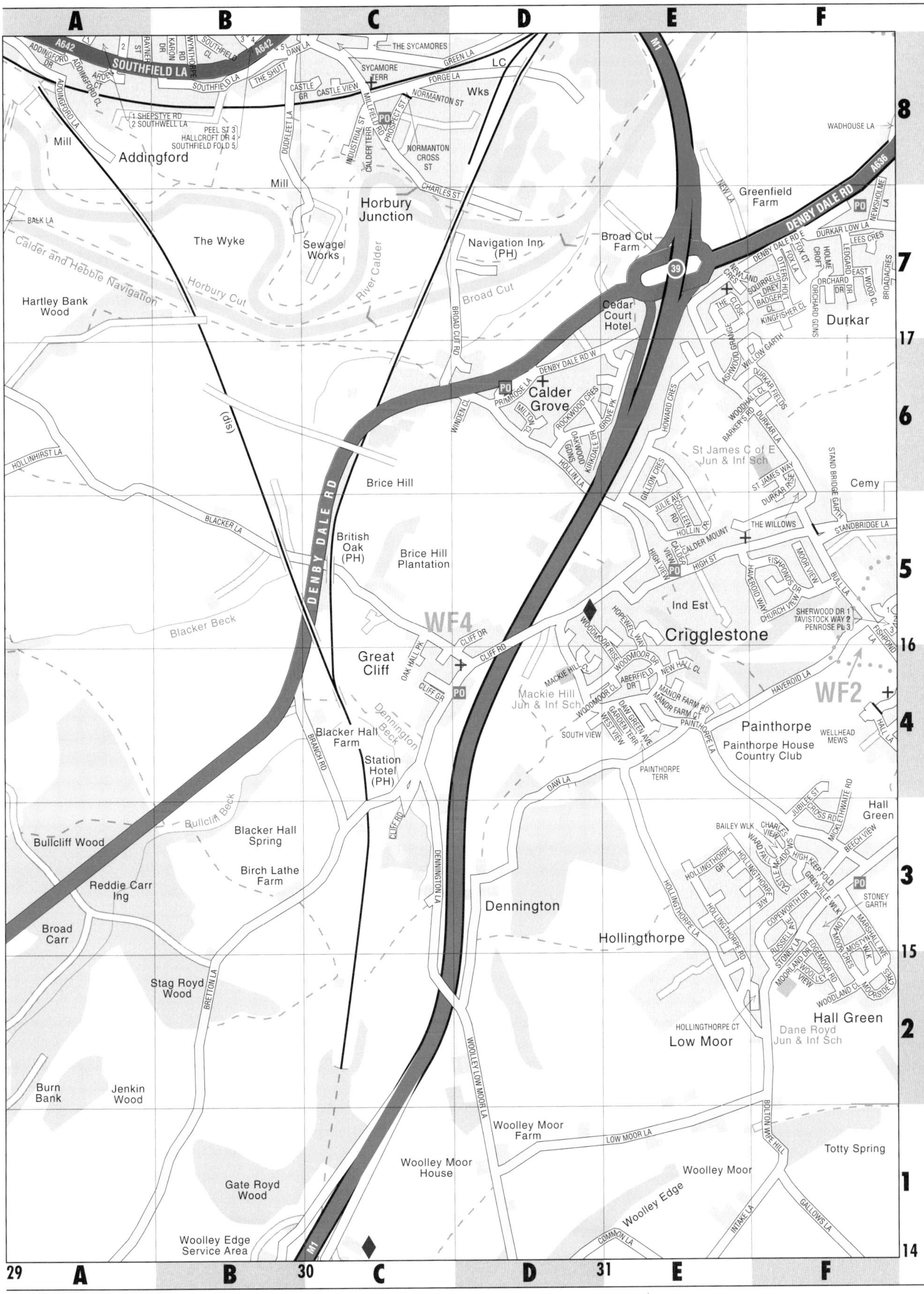
A
B
C
D
E
F
8
7
17
6
5
16
4
3
15
2
1
14
29
30
31
A642
SOUTHFIELD LA
ADDINGFORD DR
ADDINGFORD CL
ADDINGFORD LA
ARDEN CT
RAYNER ST
KARON DR
WYNTHORPE RD
SOUTHFIELD CL
SOUTHFIELD LA
THE SHUTT
DAW LA
CASTLE GR
CASTLE VIEW
THE SYCAMORES
SYCAMORE TERR
GREEN LA
FORGE LA
LC
Wks
NORMANTON ST
1 SHEPSTYE RD
2 SOUTHWELL LA
PEEL ST 3
HALLCROFT DR 4
SOUTHFIELD FOLD 5
Mill
Addingford
DUDFLEET LA
INDUSTRIAL ST
CALDER TERR
MILLFIELD RD
PROSPECT ST
NORMANTON CROSS ST
CHARLES ST
Mill
Horbury Junction
BALK LA
The Wyke
Sewage Works
Calder and Hebble Navigation
Horbury Cut
River Calder
Hartley Bank Wood
Navigation Inn (PH)
Broad Cut
BROAD CUT RD
Broad Cut Farm
M1
39
Greenfield Farm
NEW LA
WADHOUSE LA
A636
DENBY DALE RD
NEWSHOLME LA
DURKAR LOW LA
LEES CRES
DENBY DALE RD E
NEWLAND CRES
SQUIRRELS DREY
OTTERS HOLT
FOX CT
BADGER CL
KINGFISHER CL
HOLME CROFT
LEDGARD DR
EAST DR
ORCHARD DR
ORCHARD GDNS
WOOD CL
BROADACRES
THE CLOSE
Cedar Court Hotel
Durkar
DENBY DALE RD W
PRIMROSE LA
MILTON CT
WINDEN CL
Calder Grove
ROCKWOOD CRES
OAKWOOD GDNS
KIRKDALE DR
GROVE PK
HOLLIN LA
HOWARD CRES
ASHWOOD GRANGE
WILLOW GARTH
DURKAR FIELDS
DURKAR CL
WOODHALL CL
BARKER'S RD
DURKAR LA
St James C of E Jun & Inf Sch
ST JAMES WAY
DURKAR RISE
STANDBRIDGE GARTH
Cemy
HOLLINHIRST LA
(dis)
Brice Hill
GILLION CRES
JULIE AVE
COLLEEN RD
HOLLIN DR
BLACKER LA
DENBY DALE RD
British Oak (PH)
Brice Hill Plantation
THE WILLOWS
STANDBRIDGE LA
CALDER MOUNT
CALDER VIEW
HIGH VIEW
HIGH ST
HAVEROID WAY
FISHPONDS DR
MOOR VIEW
BULL LA
Ind Est
CHURCH VIEW
SHERWOOD DR 1
TAVISTOCK WAY 2
PENROSE PL 3
FISHPOND LA
Blacker Beck
WF4
CLIFF DR
CLIFF RD
HOPEWELL WAY
WOODMOOR RISE
Crigglestone
WOODMOOR DR
Great Cliff
OAK HALL PK
MACKIE HILL CL
ABERFIELD DR
NEW HALL CL
HAVEROID LA
WF2
CLIFF GR
Mackie Hill Jun & Inf Sch
WOODMOOR CL
MANOR FARM RD
MANOR FARM CT
GARDEN TERR
DAW GREEN AVE
WEST VIEW
SOUTH VIEW
PAINTHORPE LA
Painthorpe
Painthorpe House Country Club
WELLHEAD MEWS
HALL LA
BRANCH RD
Blacker Hall Farm
Dennington Beck
Station Hotel (PH)
PAINTHORPE TERR
DAW LA
JUBILEE ST
CROSS RD
MICKLETHWAITE RD
Hall Green
Bullcliff Beck
Blacker Hall Spring
CLIFF RD
BAILEY WLK
CHARLES VIEW
WARD FALL
HOLLINGTHORPE GR
HOLLINGTHORPE AVE
CASTLE MEADOWS
HIGH KEEP FOLD
GRENVILLE WLK
BEECH VIEW
Bullcliff Wood
Birch Lathe Farm
Reddie Carr Ing
DENNINGTON LA
STONEY GARTH
COPEWORTH DR
Dennington
HOLLINGTHORPE LA
HOLLINGTHORPE RD
RUSSELL AVE
STONEY LA
MARSHALL AVE
MOORLAND DR
EDGEMOOR RD
WOOLLEY VIEW
MOSTYN WLK
MOOR CRES
MOORSIDE CRES
WOODLAND CL
Broad Carr
Hollingthorpe
Stag Royd Wood
BRETTON LA
Hall Green
HOLLINGTHORPE CT
Low Moor
Dane Royd Jun & Inf Sch
WOOLLEY LOW MOOR LA
Burn Bank
Jenkin Wood
BOLTON WIFE HILL
Woolley Moor Farm
LOW MOOR LA
Totty Spring
Woolley Moor House
Woolley Moor
Gate Royd Wood
Woolley Edge
INTAKE LA
GALLOWS LA
COMMON LA
Woolley Edge Service Area
M1

177
160

159
142
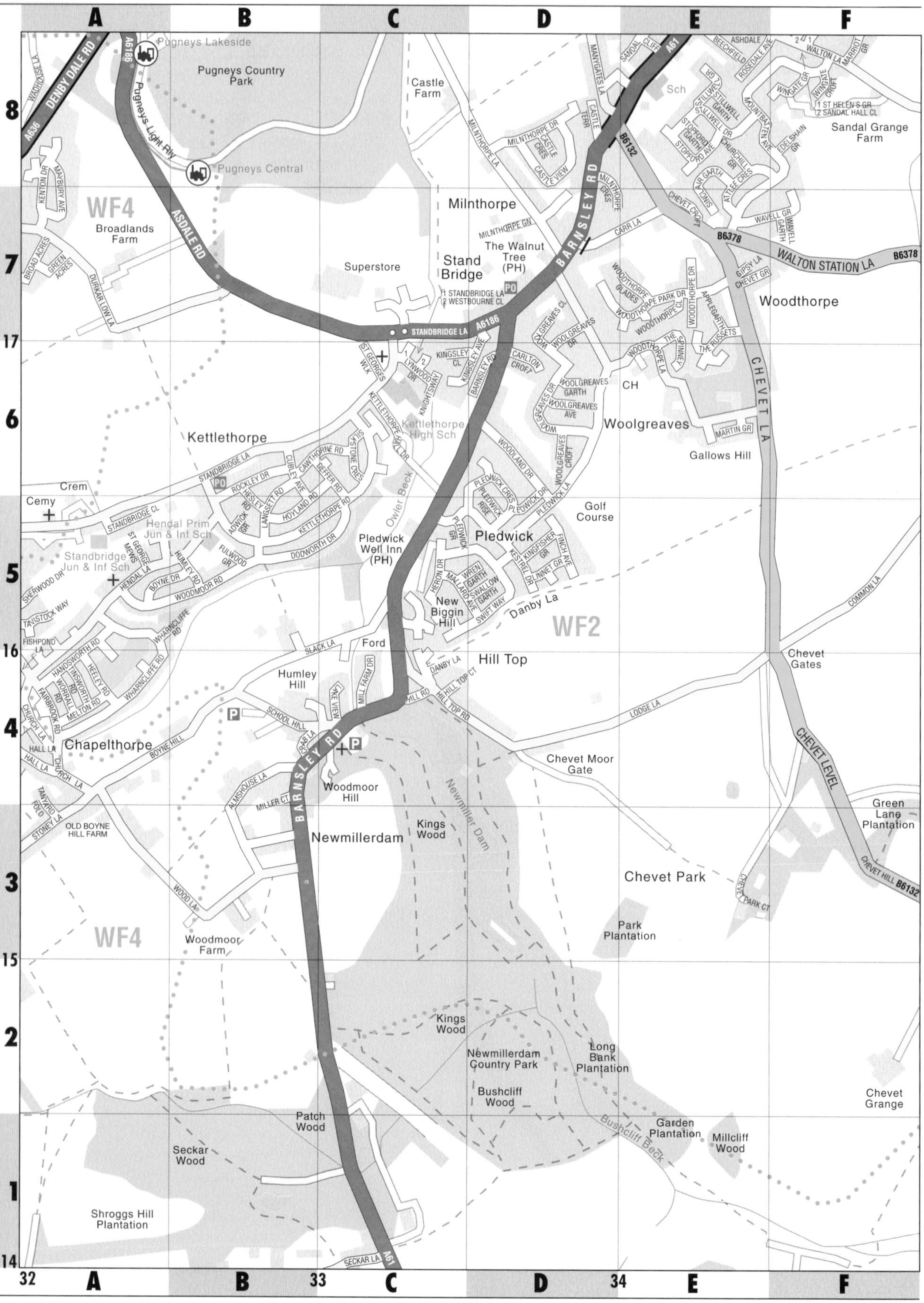

159
178

143
162

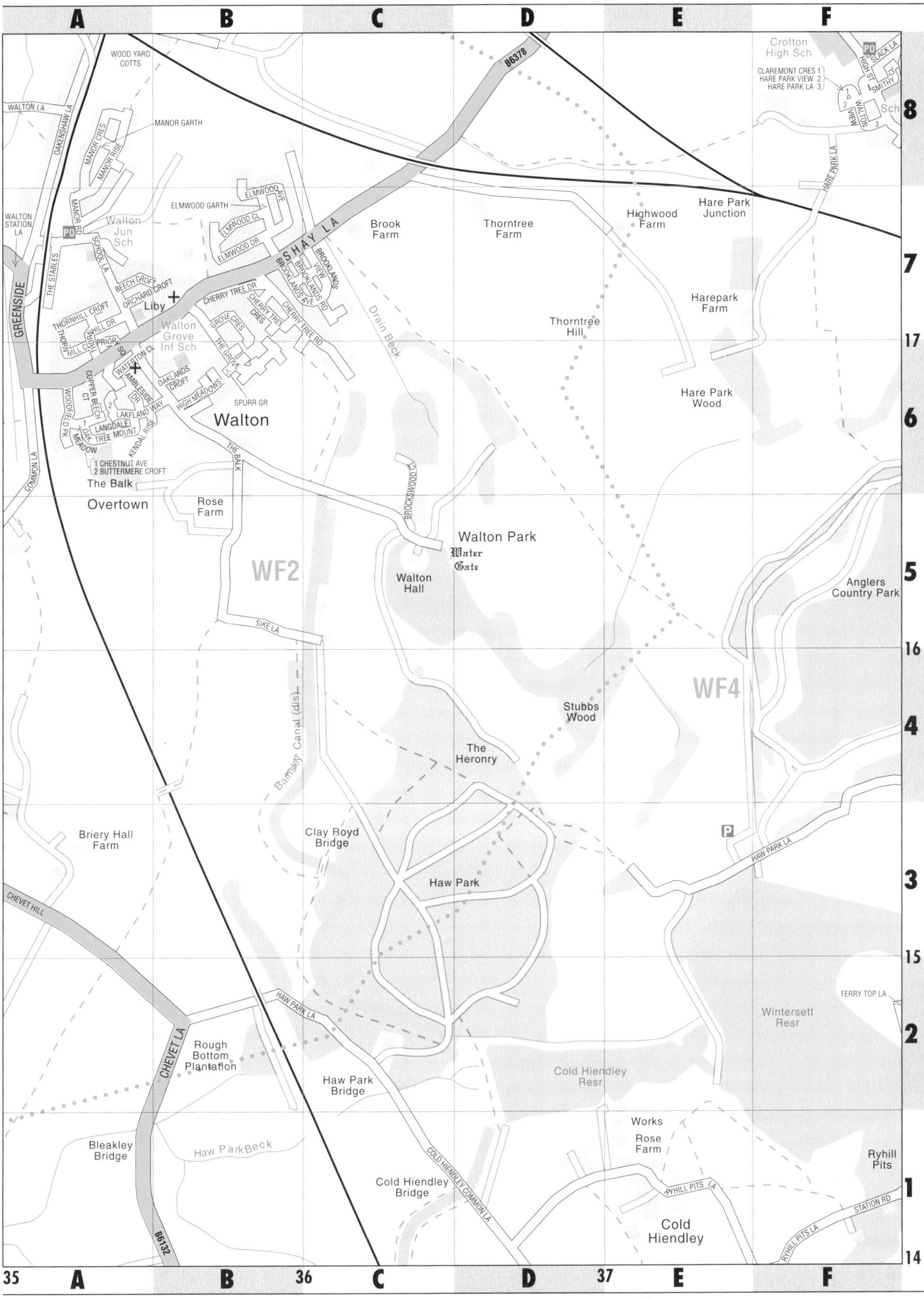
A
B
C
D
E
F
WOOD YARD COTTS
WALTON LA
OAKENSHAW LA
MANOR GARTH
MANOR CRES
MANOR RISE
MANOR RD
WALTON STATION LA
Walton Jun Sch
SCHOOL LA
THE STABLES
GREENSIDE
ELMWOOD GARTH
ELMWOOD AVE
ELMWOOD CL
ELMWOOD DR
SHAY LA
B6378
BROOKLANDS VIEW
BROOKLANDS RD
BROOKLANDS AVE
BEECH CROFT
ORCHARD CROFT
Liby
CHERRY TREE DR
CHERRY TREE CRES
CHERRY TREE RD
THORNHILL CROFT
THORNHILL DR
THORNHILL CL
PRIORY SQ
Walton Grove Inf Sch
GROVE CRES
THE GROVE
WATERTON CL
AMBLESIDE DR
OAKLANDS CROFT
HIGH MEADOWS
COPPER BEECH CT
WOODFIELD PK
LAKELAND WAY
LANGDALE MOUNT
KENDAL RISE
OAK TREE MEADOW
SPURR GR
Walton
1 CHESTNUT AVE
2 BUTTERMERE CROFT
The Balk
THE BALK
Overtown
Rose Farm
COMMON LA
Brook Farm
Thorntree Farm
Highwood Farm
Hare Park Junction
Drain Beck
Harepark Farm
Thorntree Hill
Hare Park Wood
BROCKSWOOD LA
Walton Park
Water Gate
Walton Hall
WF2
SIKE LA
WF4
Anglers Country Park
Stubbs Wood
The Heronry
Barnsley Canal (dis)
Clay Royd Bridge
Briery Hall Farm
Haw Park
HAW PARK LA
CHEVET HILL
CHEVET LA
Rough Bottom Plantation
Haw Park Bridge
Cold Hiendley Resr
Wintersett Resr
FERRY TOP LA
Works
Rose Farm
Ryhill Pits
Bleakley Bridge
Haw Park Beck
Cold Hiendley Bridge
COLD HIENDLEY COMMON LA
RYHILL PITS LA
STATION RD
Cold Hiendley
B6132
Crofton High Sch
CLAREMONT CRES 1
HARE PARK VIEW 2
HARE PARK LA 3
HIGH ST
SLACK LA
SMITHY
WALTON VIEW
Sch
HARE PARK LA
8
7
17
6
5
16
4
3
15
2
1
14
35
36
37

179
162

161
144

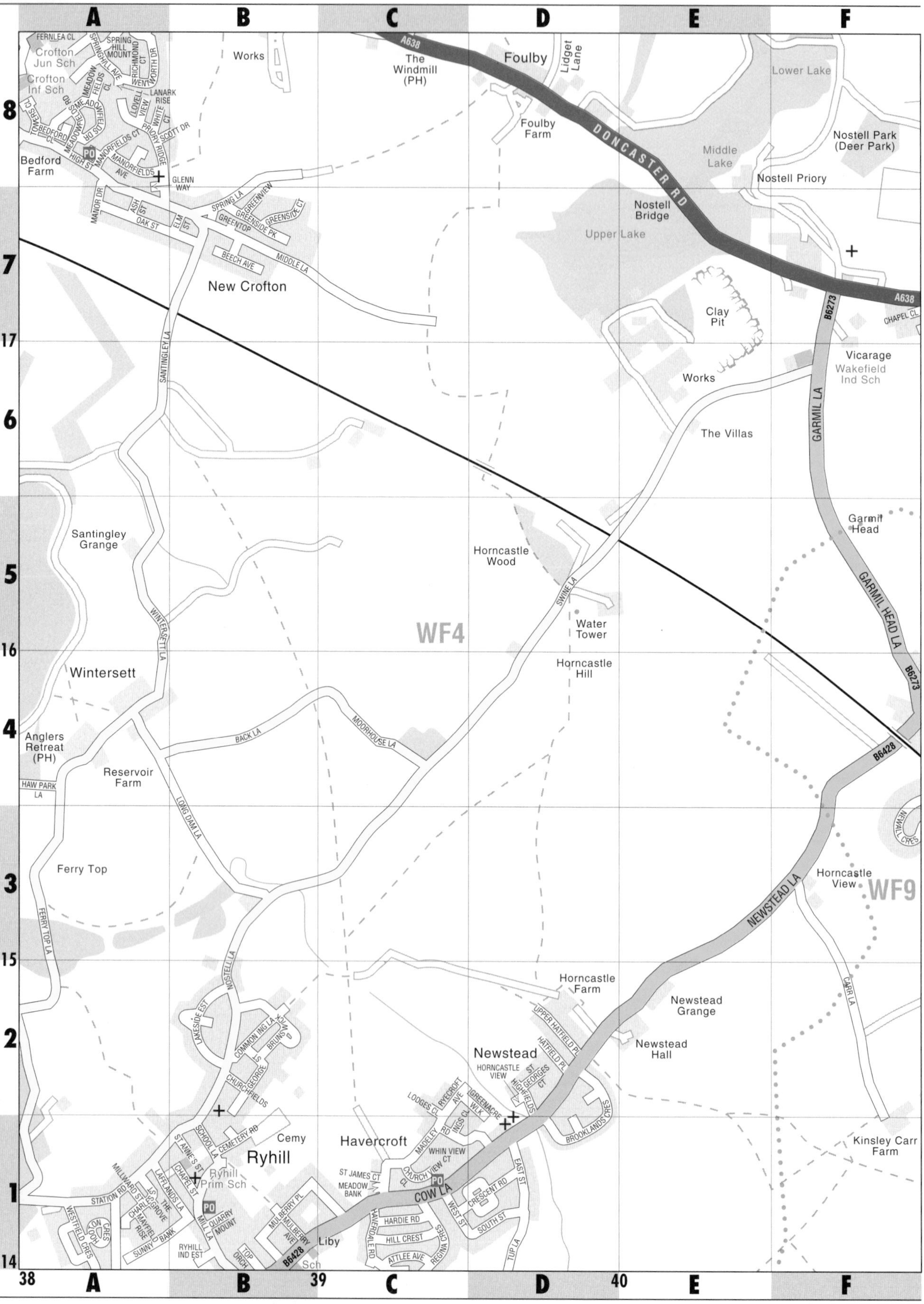
A
B
C
D
E
F
8
7
17
6
5
16
4
3
15
2
1
14
38
39
40
Crofton Jun Sch
Crofton Inf Sch
FERNLEA CL
SPRING HILL MOUNT
Works
The Windmill (PH)
A638
Foulby
Lidget Lane
Lower Lake
Foulby Farm
DONCASTER RD
Nostell Park (Deer Park)
Middle Lake
Nostell Priory
Bedford Farm
HIGH ST
MANORFIELDS AVE
PRIORY RIDGE
SCOTT DR
GLENN WAY
SPRING LA
GREENVIEW
GREENSIDE PK
GREENSIDE CT
GREENTOP
MANOR DR
ASH ST
OAK ST
ELM ST
BEECH AVE
MIDDLE LA
Nostell Bridge
Upper Lake
New Crofton
Clay Pit
B6273
CHAPEL CL
Vicarage
Wakefield Ind Sch
Works
SANTINGLEY LA
The Villas
GARMIL LA
Santingley Grange
Garmil Head
Horncastle Wood
GARMIL HEAD LA
SWINE LA
Water Tower
WF4
WINTERSETT LA
Wintersett
Horncastle Hill
Anglers Retreat (PH)
BACK LA
MOORHOUSE LA
B6428
Reservoir Farm
HAW PARK LA
LONG DAM LA
NEWALL CRES
Ferry Top
Horncastle View
WF9
NEWSTEAD LA
FERRY TOP LA
NOSTELL LA
CARR LA
Horncastle Farm
LAKESIDE EST
COMMON ING LA
UPPER HATFIELD PL
HATFIELD PL
Newstead Grange
Newstead Hall
Newstead
HORNCASTLE VIEW
ST GEORGES CT
HIGHFIELDS
CHURCHFIELDS
LODGES CL
RYECROFT AVE
GREENACRE WLK
INGS CL
MADELEY RD
SCHOOL LA
CEMETERY RD
Cemy
Havercroft
WHIN VIEW CT
BROOKLANDS CRES
Kinsley Carr Farm
Ryhill
ST ANNE'S ST
CHAPEL ST
MILLWARD ST
Ryhill Prim Sch
ST JAMES CT
MEADOW BANK
CHURCH VIEW CL
PO
COW LA
CRESCENT RD
EAST ST
WEST ST
STATION RD
WESTFIELD CRES
QUARRY MOUNT
MILL LA
SUNNY BANK
RYHILL IND EST
MULBERRY PL
MULBERRY AVE
Liby
HAVERDALE RD
HARDIE RD
HILL CREST
ATTLEE AVE
REGINA CRES
SOUTH ST
TUP LA
TOP ORCH
Sch

145
164

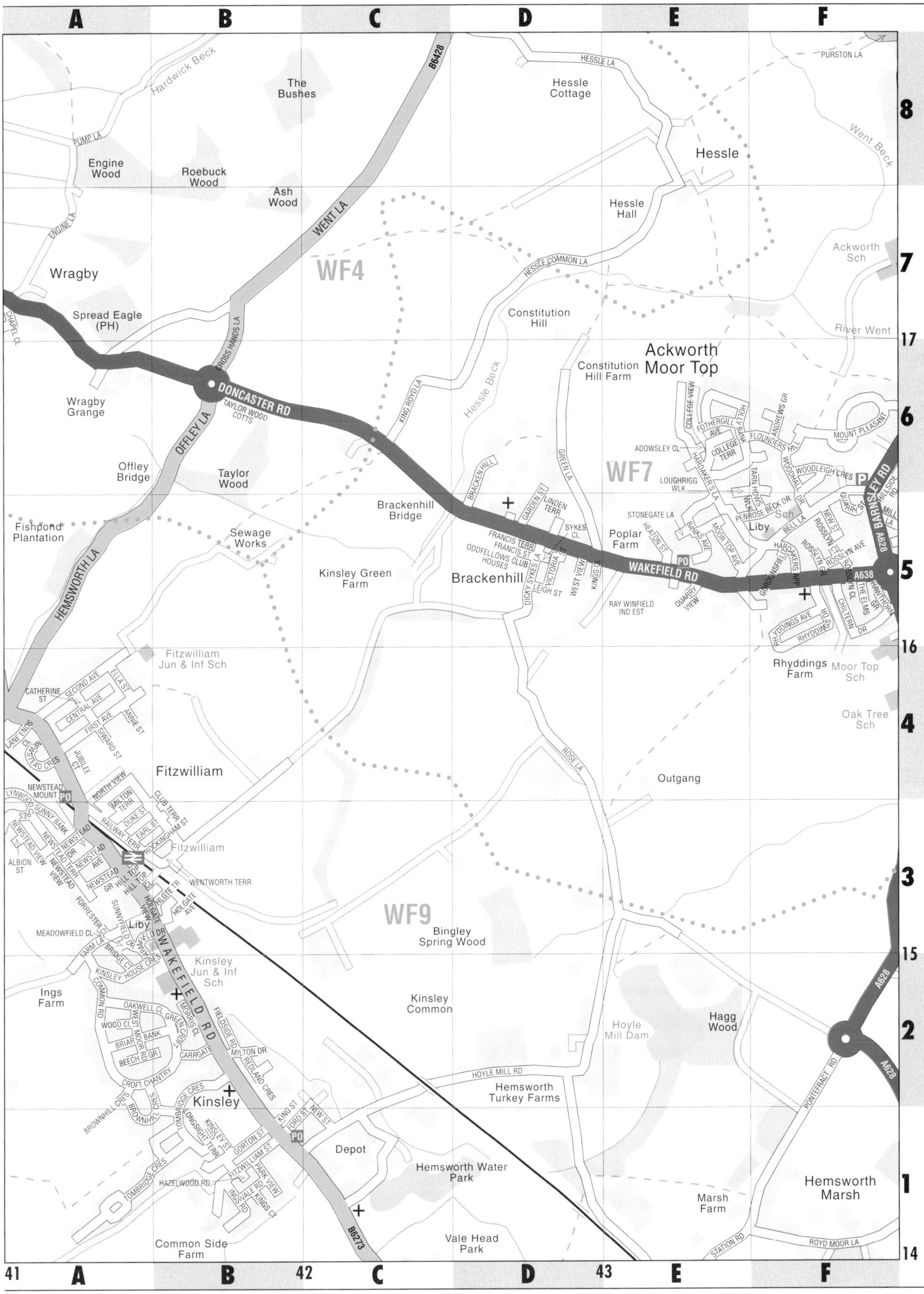

181
164

163
146

163
182

A B C D E F

8

Wenthill Plantation

Wentbridge Ings

Jackson's Hill Plantation

Jackson's Hill

B6474

A1

MOOR LA

Wentbridge

Castle Hill

7

PO

River Went

B6474

Thorpe Marsh

Blue Bell Inn (PH)

Wentbridge Viaduct

Sayle's Plantation

SMEATON IND PK

JACKSON'S LA

17

WENT EDGE RD

Went Edge Road Bridge

WENT EDGE RD

Summersfield Nurseries

WENTBRIDGE LA

WF8

6

Wentdale

Standing Flat Bridge

Broom Hill

Thorp Plantation

Peartree Field

B6474

Sunnydale Bungalow

Pear Tree Farm

5

BRENTWOOD CL

WENT VIEW

KINBERRY CL

Fox and Hounds (PH)

Kennels Hillthorpe

PEARTREE FIELD LA

Gingerbread Plantation

HADRIAN CL

SANDAL RISE

HILLTHORPE DR

PO

Hillthorpe Farm

Hillthorpe House

DONCASTER RD

FORUM VIEW

PALL GARTH RD

CHARIOT WAY

OAKFIELD PK

DARNING LA

16

THORPE LA

Went Farm

CAUSEWAY GARTH LA

WATCHIT HOLE LA

Thorpe Manor

Shooters Hill Farm

A1

4

THORPE GATE EST

BRIDGE LA

Thorpe Audlin

Hepworth Farm

Barr's Drain

COMMON LA

Thorpe Grange Farm

COAL PIT LA

Poultry Farm

3

A639

15

Walton Wood House

2

WF9

Walton Wood

Walton Wood LA

Harewood LA

Beacon Covert

GREEN LA

Tower

Sheepwalk LA

1

BEACONFIELD RD

B6474

Coal Pit Plantation

SHINWELL DR

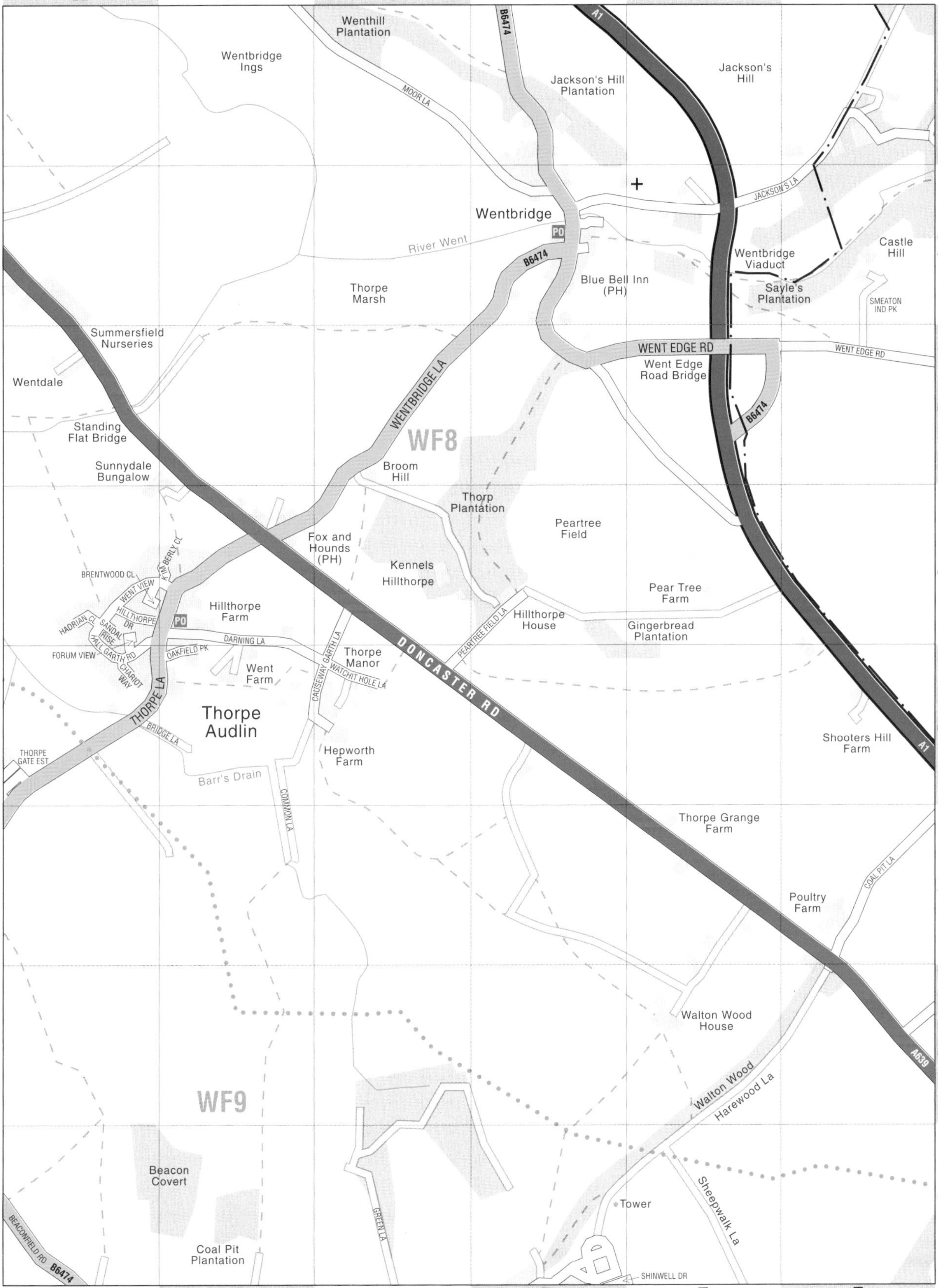

165

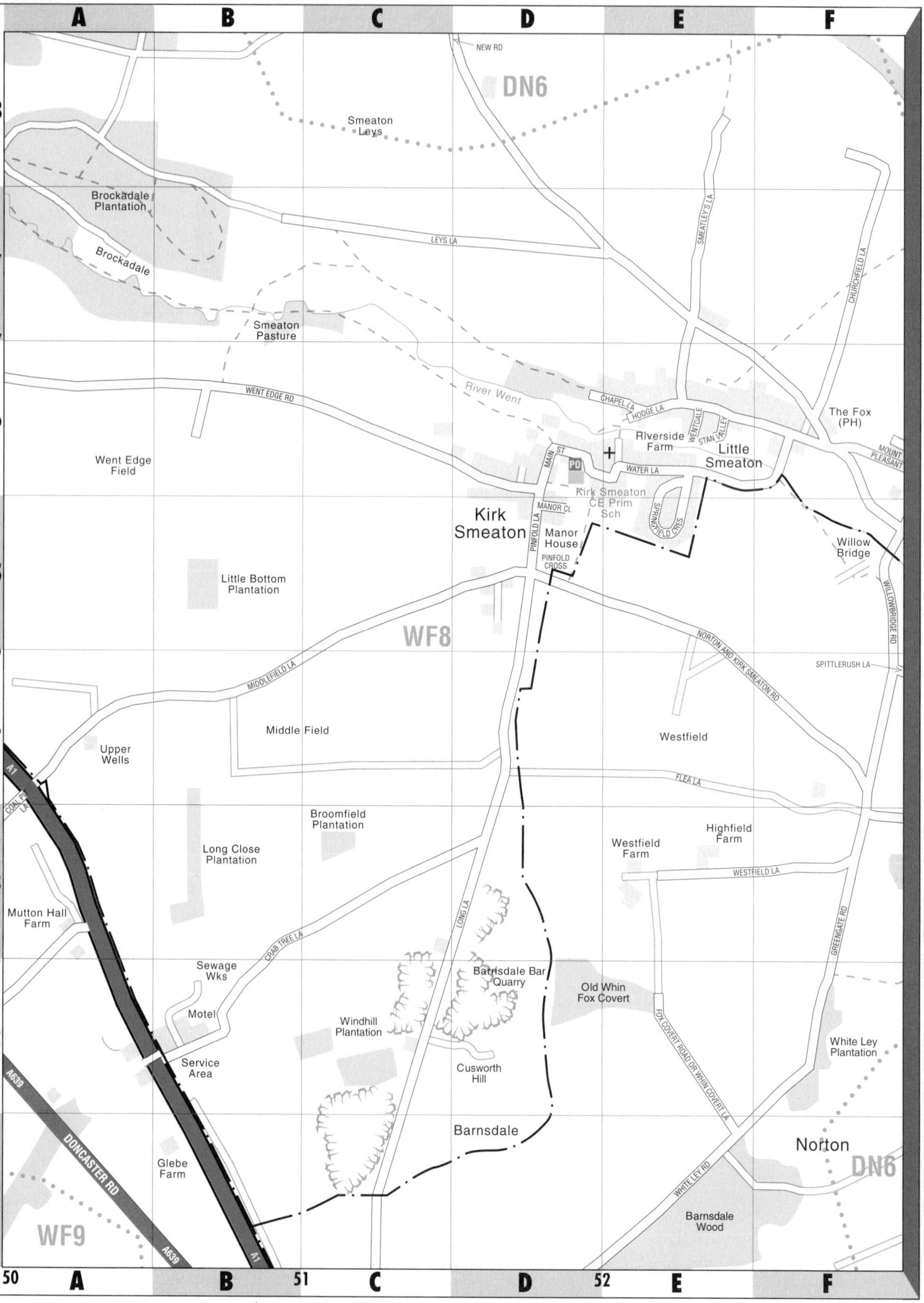

A
B
C
D
E
F
8
7
17
6
5
16
4
3
15
2
1
14
50
51
52
NEW RD
DN6
Smeaton Leys
Brockadale Plantation
Brockadale
LEYS LA
SMEATLEY'S LA
CHURCHFIELD LA
Smeaton Pasture
River Went
WENT EDGE RD
CHAPEL LA
HODGE LA
WENTDALE
STAN VALLEY
The Fox (PH)
MOUNT PLEASANT
Riverside Farm
Little Smeaton
MAIN ST
PO
WATER LA
Went Edge Field
Kirk Smeaton CE Prim Sch
MANOR CL
SPRINGFIELD CRES
Kirk Smeaton
PINFOLD LA
Manor House
PINFOLD CROSS
Willow Bridge
Little Bottom Plantation
WILLOWBRIDGE RD
WF8
NORTON AND KIRK SMEATON RD
SPITTLERUSH LA
MIDDLEFIELD LA
Middle Field
Westfield
Upper Wells
A1
COAL PIT LA
FLEA LA
Broomfield Plantation
Highfield Farm
Long Close Plantation
Westfield Farm
WESTFIELD LA
Mutton Hall Farm
LONG LA
GREENGATE RD
CRAB TREE LA
Sewage Wks
Barnsdale Bar Quarry
Old Whin Fox Covert
Motel
Windhill Plantation
FOX COVERT ROAD OR WHIN COVERT LA
White Ley Plantation
Service Area
Cusworth Hill
A639
DONCASTER RD
Barnsdale
Norton
DN6
Glebe Farm
WHITE LEY RD
Barnsdale Wood
WF9
A639
A1

165

184

149
168

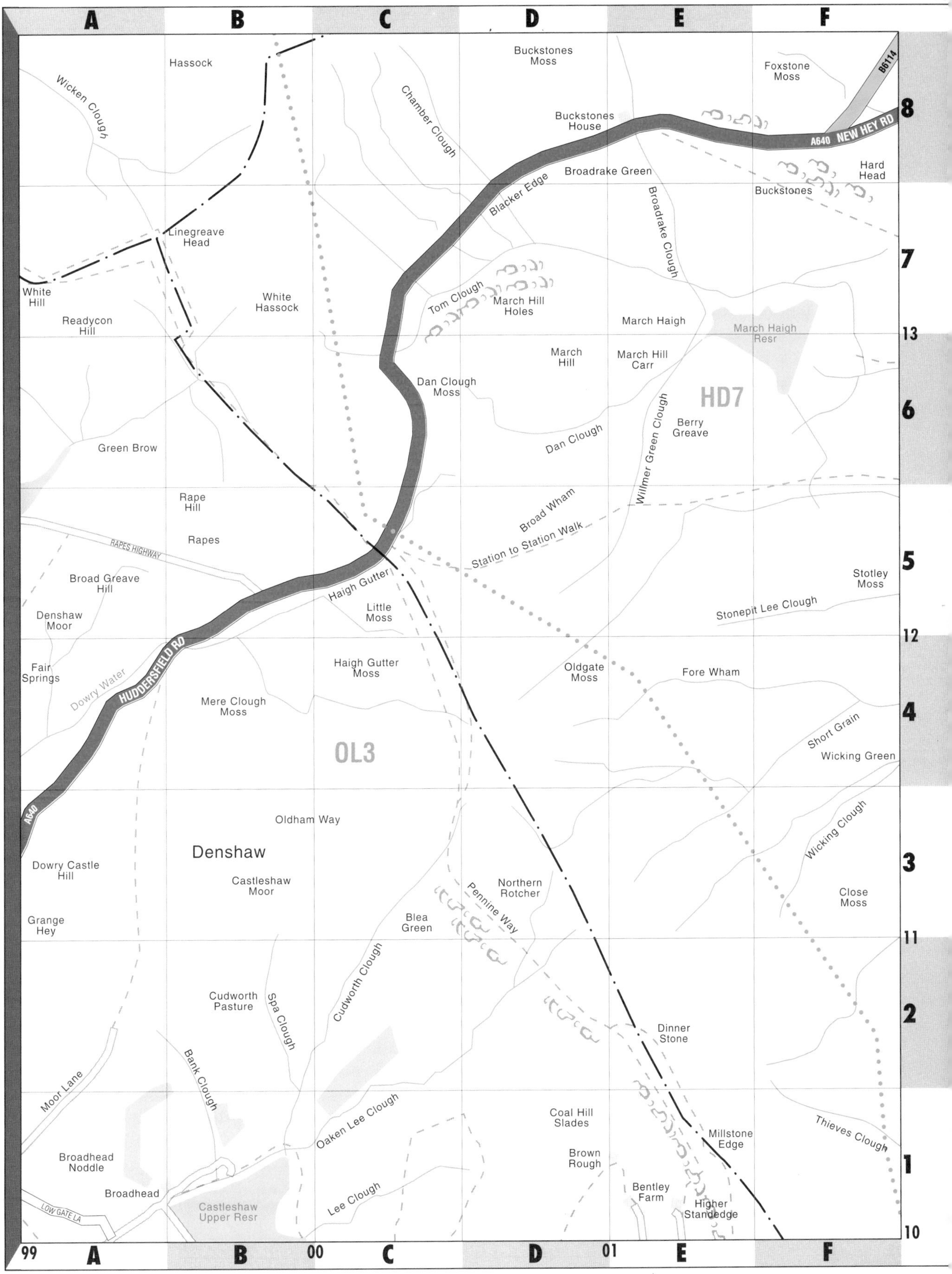
A
B
C
D
E
F
Hassock
Wicken Clough
Buckstones Moss
Chamber Clough
Foxstone Moss
B6114
8
Buckstones House
A640 NEW HEY RD
Hard Head
Broadrake Green
Buckstones
Blacker Edge
Broadrake Clough
Linegreave Head
7
White Hill
Tom Clough
March Hill Holes
White Hassock
Readycon Hill
March Haigh
March Haigh Resr
13
March Hill
March Hill Carr
Dan Clough Moss
HD7
Willmer Green Clough
Berry Greave
6
Dan Clough
Green Brow
Rape Hill
Broad Wham
Rapes
Station to Station Walk
RAPES HIGHWAY
5
Haigh Gutter
Broad Greave Hill
Stotley Moss
Little Moss
Stonepit Lee Clough
Denshaw Moor
12
Fair Springs
Haigh Gutter Moss
Oldgate Moss
Fore Wham
Dowry Water
HUDDERSFIELD RD
Mere Clough Moss
4
Short Grain
OL3
Wicking Green
A640
Oldham Way
Wicking Clough
Denshaw
Dowry Castle Hill
3
Castleshaw Moor
Northern Rotcher
Pennine Way
Close Moss
Grange Hey
Blea Green
11
Cudworth Clough
Cudworth Pasture
Spa Clough
2
Dinner Stone
Bank Clough
Moor Lane
Coal Hill Slades
Oaken Lee Clough
Millstone Edge
Thieves Clough
Broadhead Noddle
Brown Rough
1
Broadhead
Bentley Farm
Lee Clough
Castleshaw Upper Resr
Higher Standedge
LOW GATE LA
10
99
00
01

168

167
150

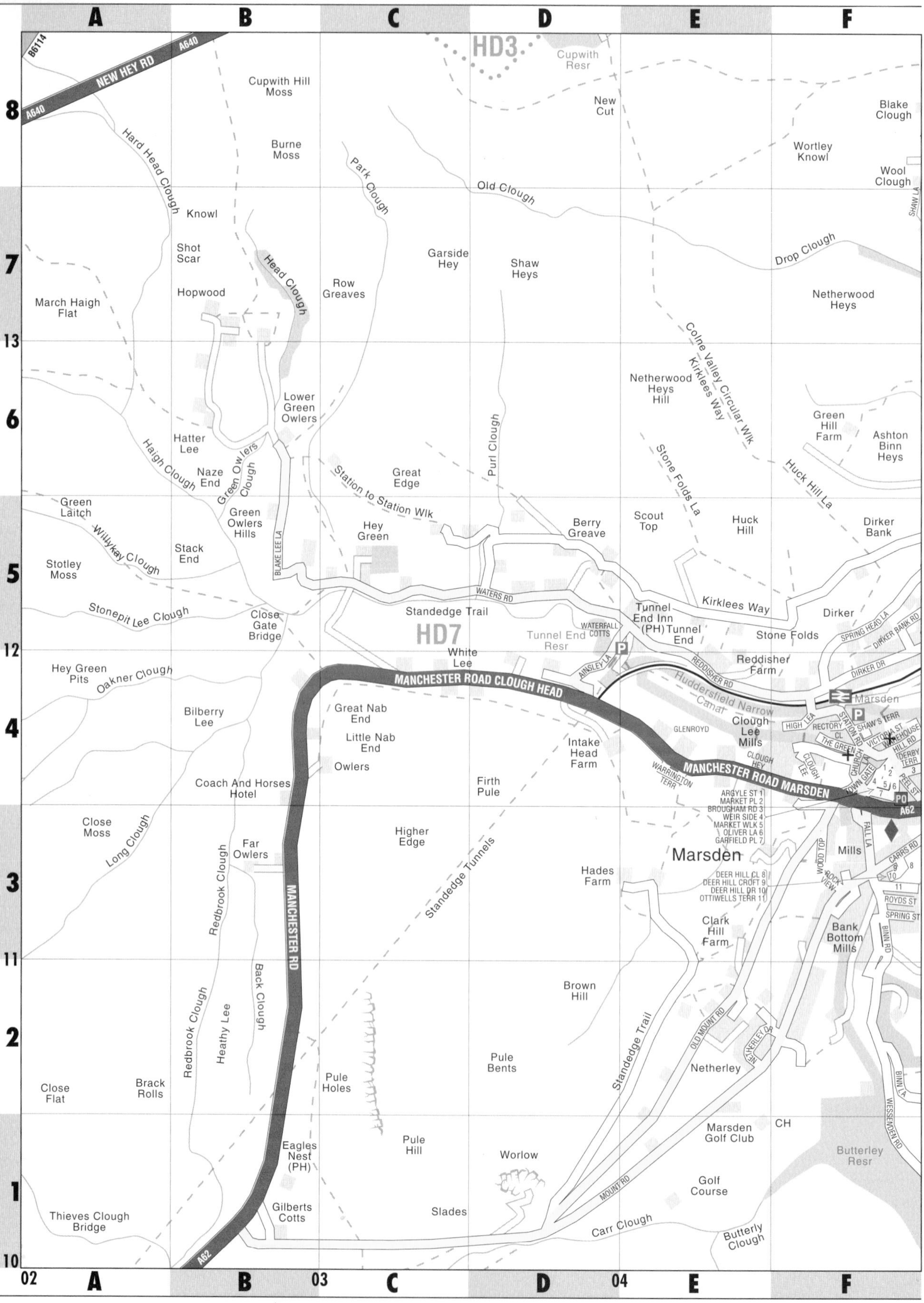

167
185

151
170

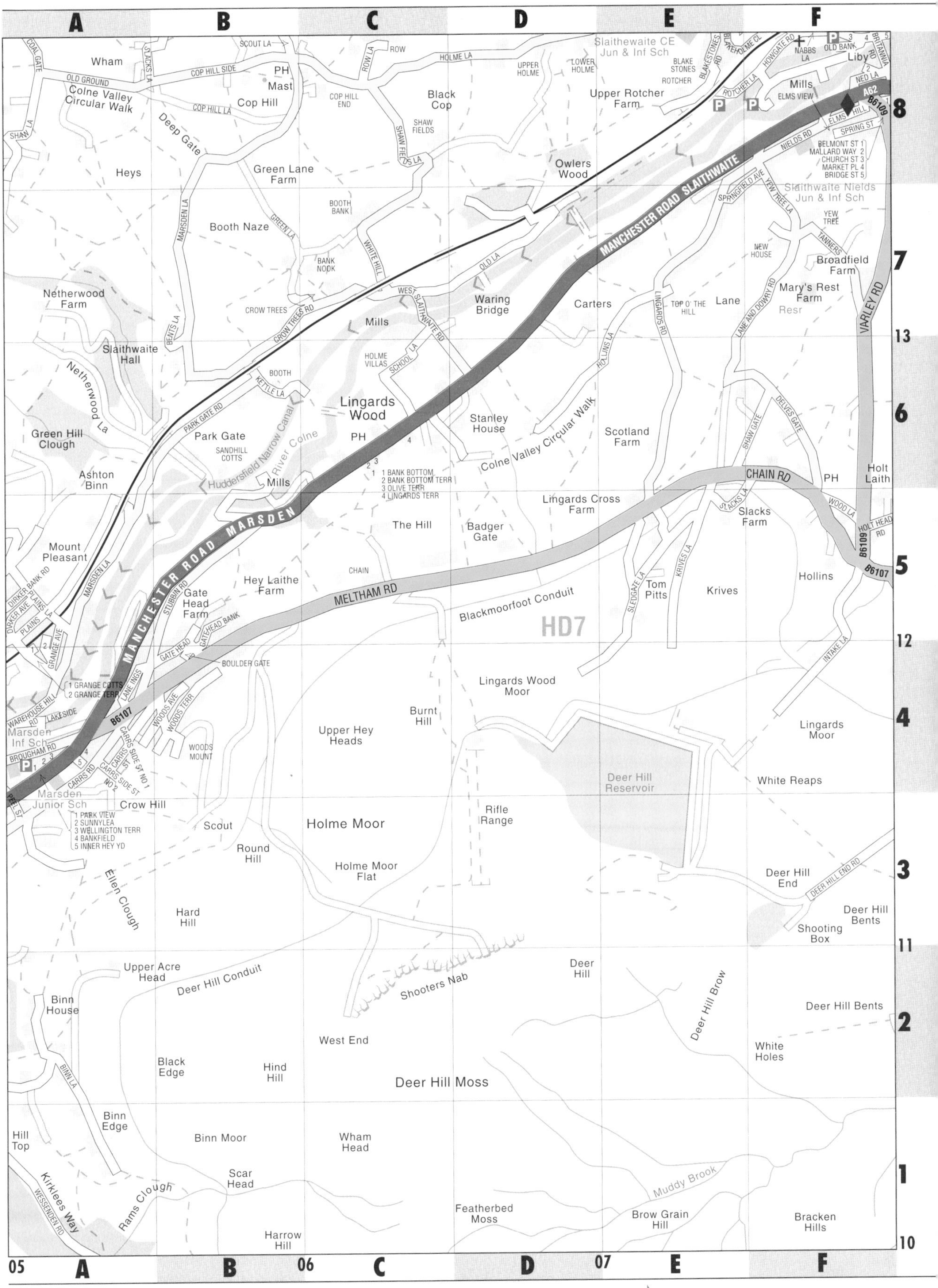

186
170

169
152

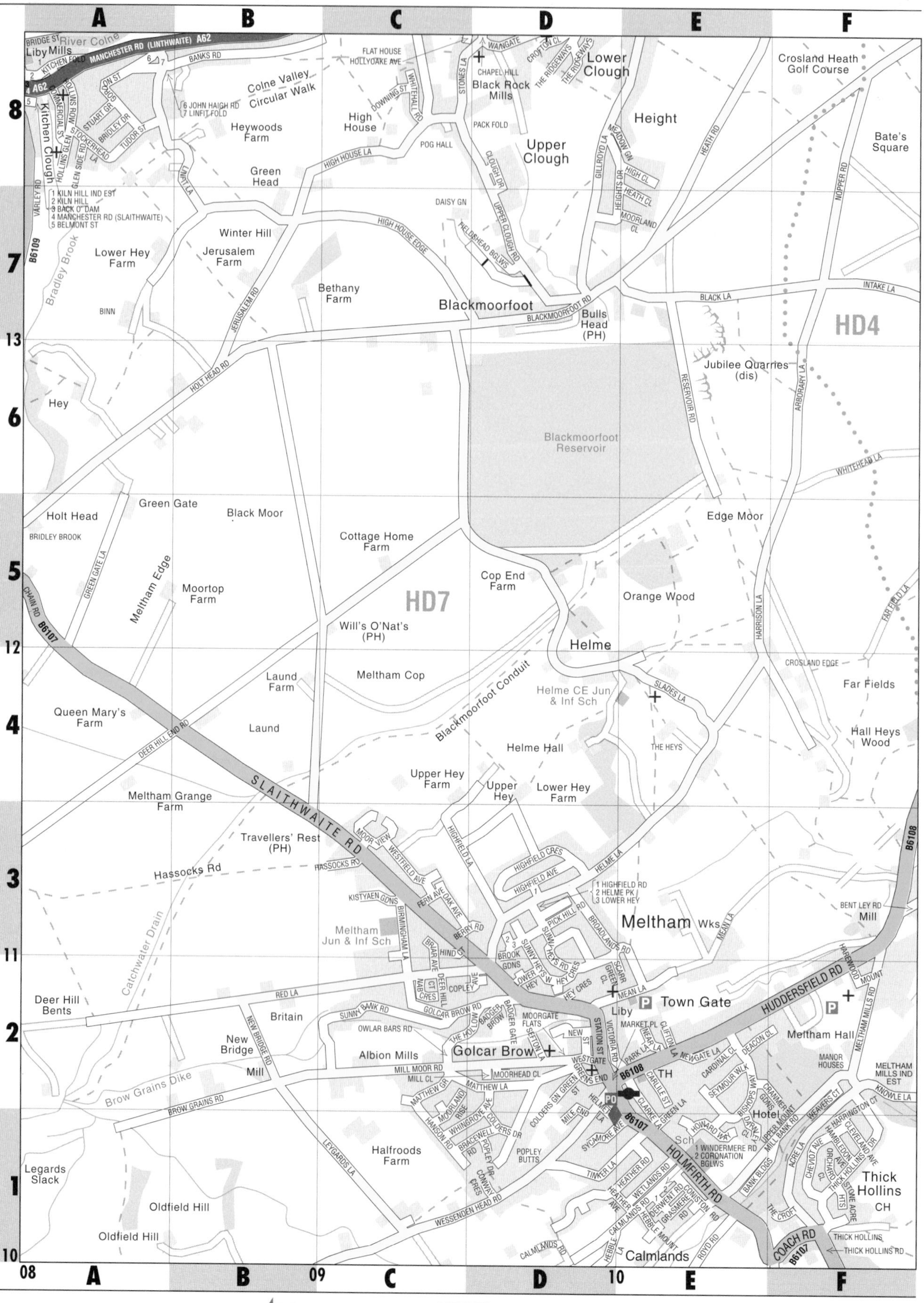

169
187

153
172

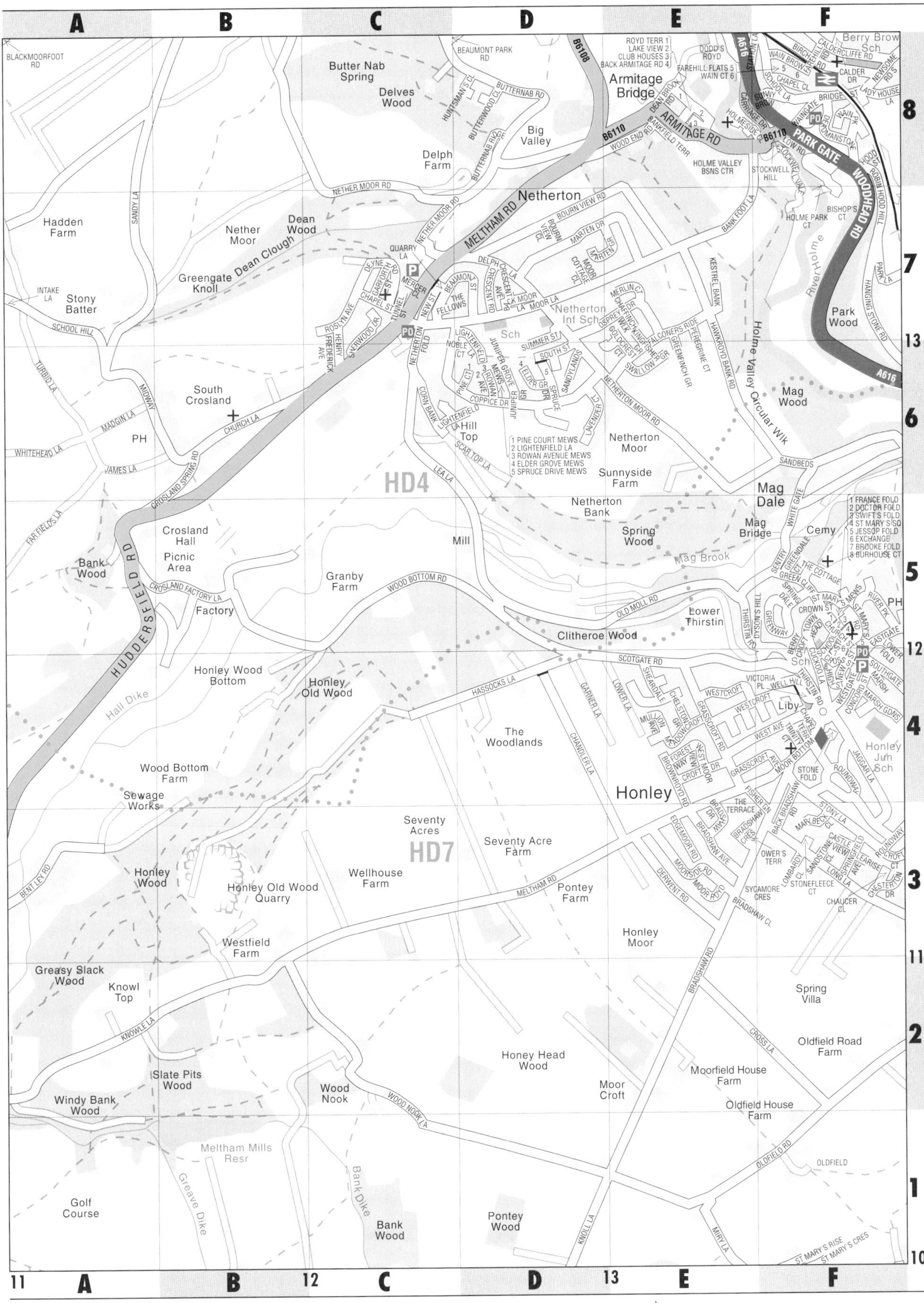

188
172

171
154

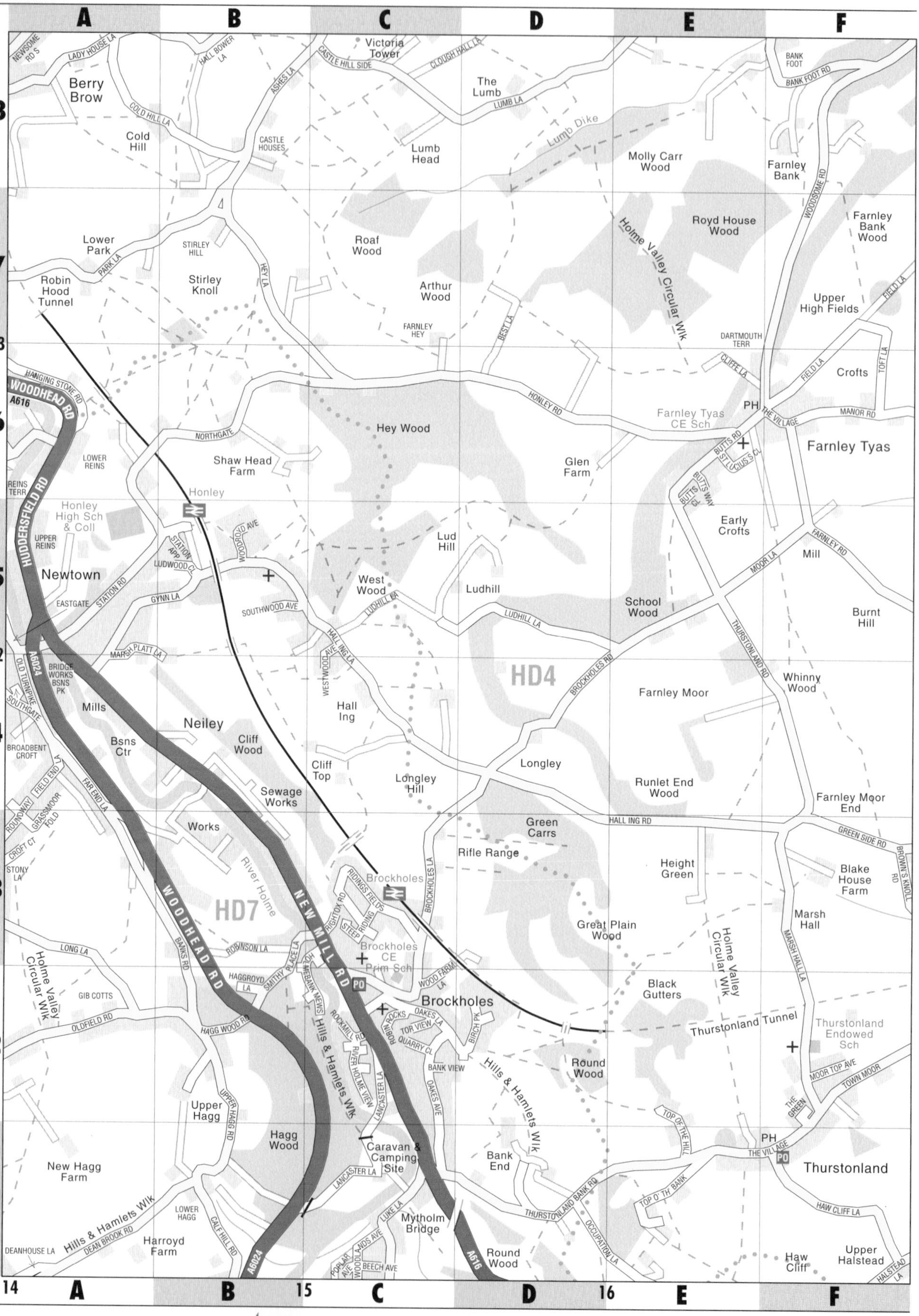

171
189

155
174

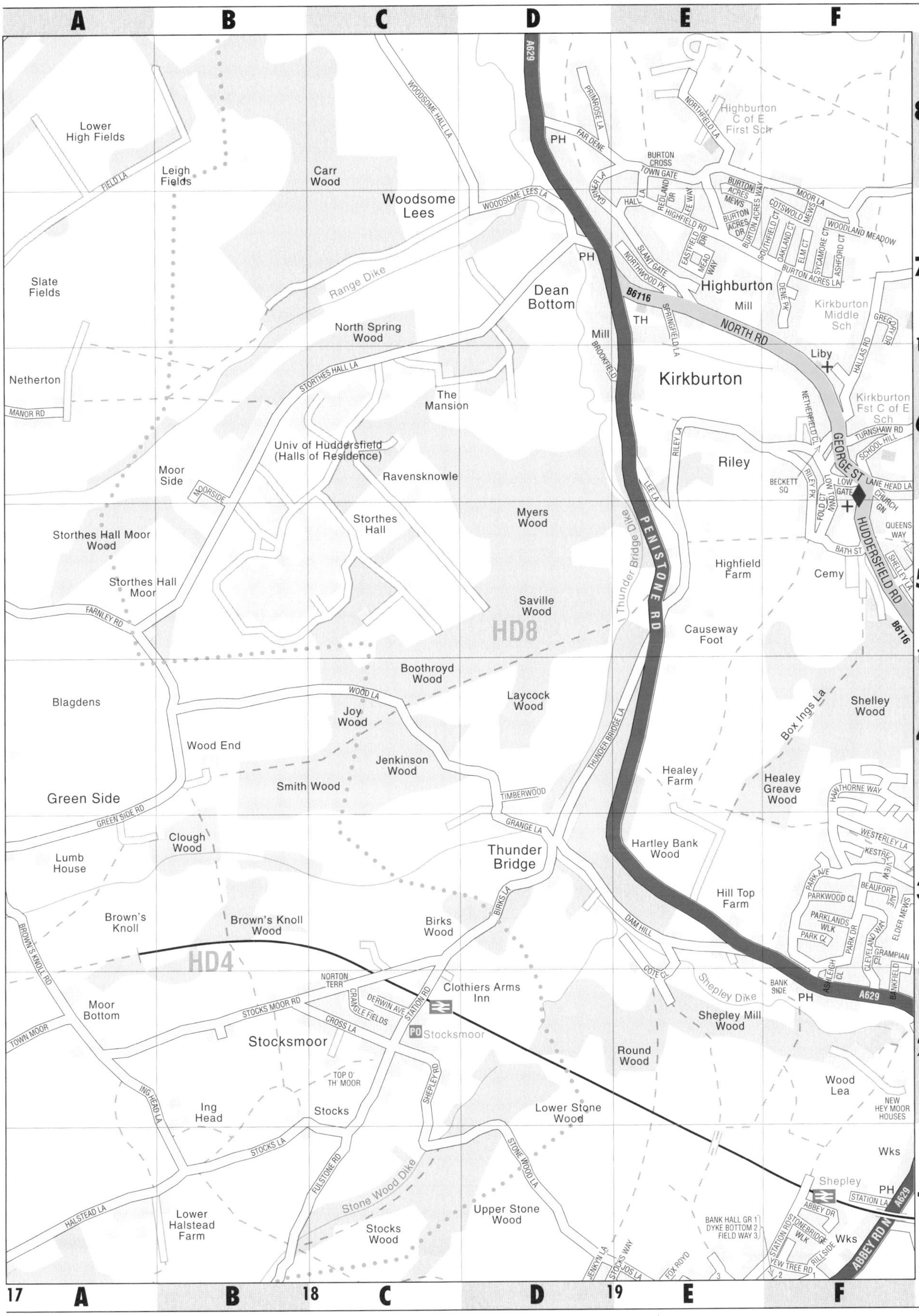

190
174

173
156

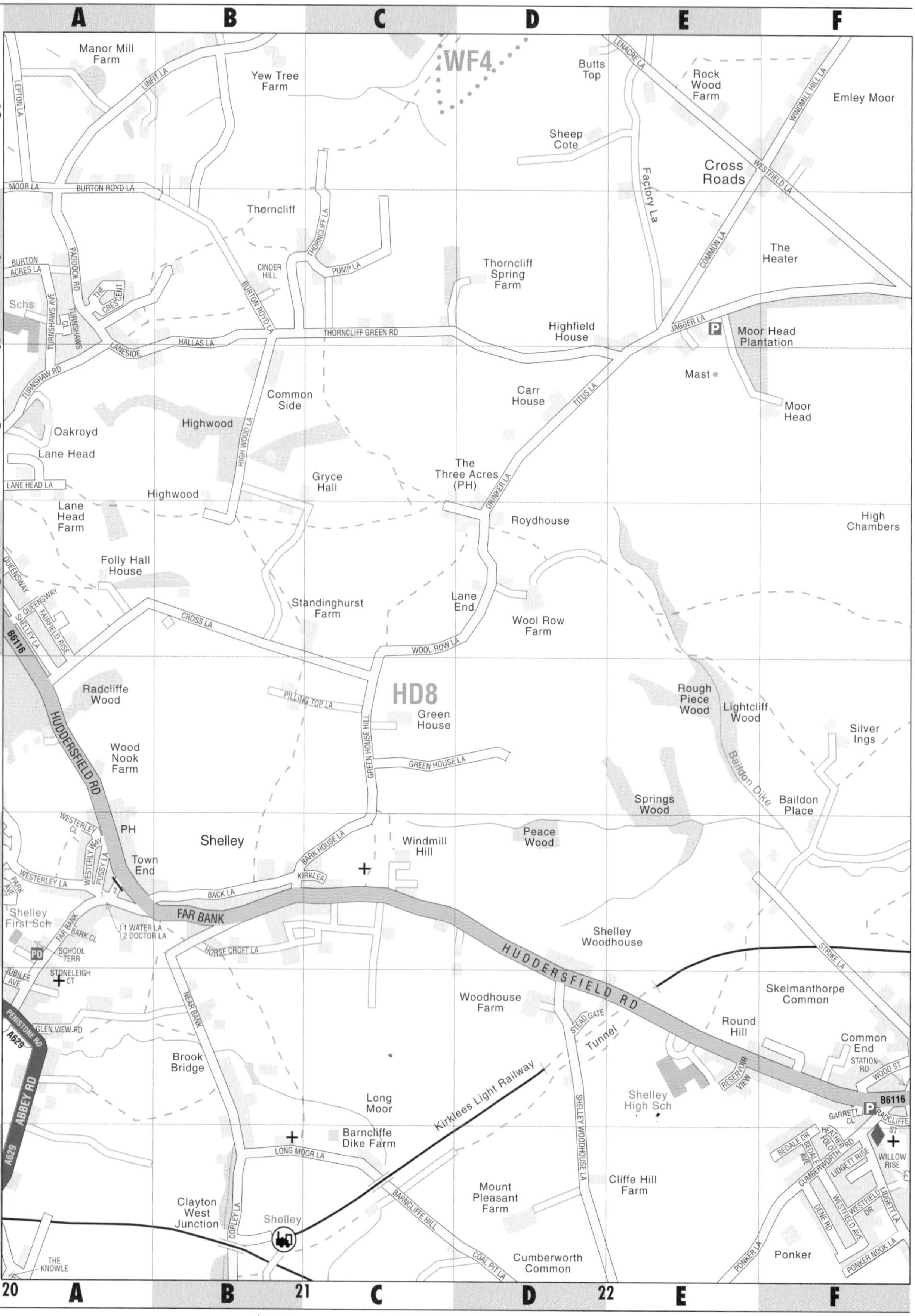
A
B
C
D
E
F
8
7
13
6
5
12
4
3
11
2
1
10
20
21
22
Manor Mill Farm
Yew Tree Farm
WF4
Butts Top
Rock Wood Farm
Emley Moor
LEPTON LA
LINFIT LA
Sheep Cote
LENACRE LA
WINDMILL HILL LA
Cross Roads
Factory La
WESTFIELD LA
MOOR LA
BURTON ROYD LA
Thorncliff
THORNCLIFF LA
CINDER HILL
PUMP LA
BURTON ROYD LA
PADDOCK RD
BURTON ACRES LA
THE CRESCENT
TURNSHAWS AVE
TURNSHAWS CL
Schs
Thorncliff Spring Farm
COMMON LA
The Heater
Highfield House
JAGGER LA
Moor Head Plantation
THORNCLIFF GREEN RD
HALLAS LA
LANESIDE
TURNSHAW RD
Mast
Carr House
TITUS LA
Common Side
Moor Head
Highwood
HIGH WOOD LA
Oakroyd
Lane Head
LANE HEAD LA
Gryce Hall
The Three Acres (PH)
DRINKER LA
Highwood
Lane Head Farm
Roydhouse
High Chambers
Folly Hall House
QUEENSWAY
SHELLEY LA
FAIRFIELD RISE
B6116
Standinghurst Farm
CROSS LA
Lane End
Wool Row Farm
WOOL ROW LA
Radcliffe Wood
HD8
PILLING TOP LA
Green House
GREEN HOUSE HILL
GREEN HOUSE LA
Rough Piece Wood
Lightcliff Wood
Silver Ings
HUDDERSFIELD RD
Wood Nook Farm
Baildon Dike
Springs Wood
Baildon Place
WESTERLEY CL
WESTERLEY WAY
PUSSY LA
PH
Shelley
BARK HOUSE LA
Windmill Hill
Peace Wood
Town End
KIRKLEA
WESTERLEY LA
PARK AVE
BACK LA
FAR BANK
Shelley First Sch
FAR BANK CL
1 WATER LA
2 DOCTOR LA
PO
SCHOOL TERR
HORSE CROFT LA
Shelley Woodhouse
STRIKE LA
HUDDERSFIELD RD
JUBILEE AVE
STONELEIGH CT
Woodhouse Farm
Skelmanthorpe Common
NEAR BANK
STEAD GATE
Tunnel
Round Hill
PENISTONE RD
A629
GLEN VIEW RD
Common End
STATION RD
WOOD ST
Brook Bridge
RESERVOIR VIEW
ABBEY RD
Kirklees Light Railway
Shelley High Sch
B6116
Long Moor
GARRETT CL
RADCLIFFE ST
Barncliffe Dike Farm
LONG MOOR LA
SHELLEY WOODHOUSE LA
HEATHER FOLD
BEDALE DR
BEDALE AVE
CUMBERWORTH RD
LIDGETT RISE
WILLOW RISE
Mount Pleasant Farm
Cliffe Hill Farm
Clayton West Junction
COPLEY LA
Shelley
BARNCLIFFE HILL
DENE RD
WESTFIELD AVE
WESTFIELD DR
LIDGETT LA
COAL PIT LA
Cumberworth Common
PONKER LA
Ponker
PONKER NOOK LA
THE KNOWLE

157
176

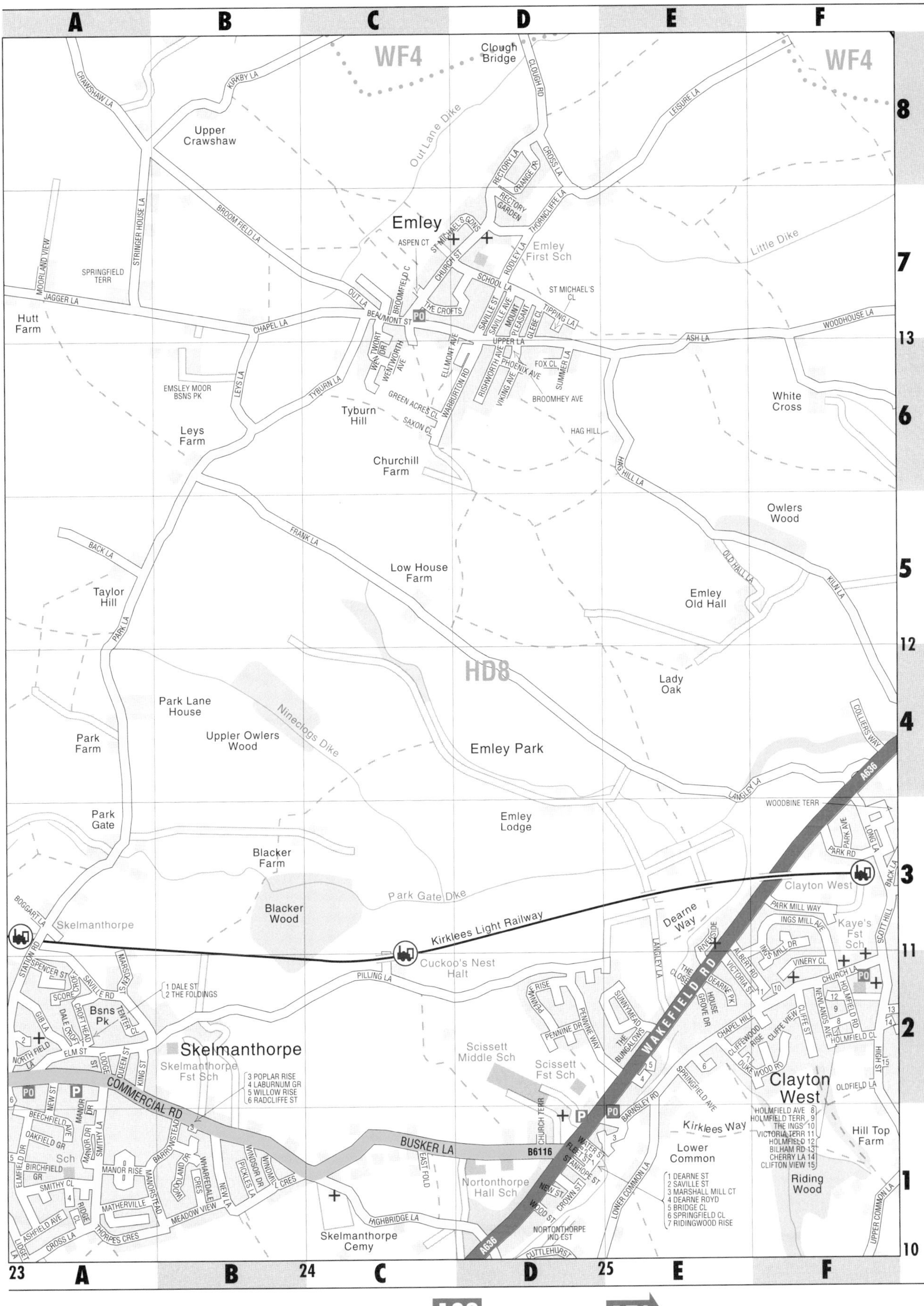
A
B
C
D
E
F
8
7
13
6
5
12
4
3
11
2
1
10
23
24
25
WF4
Clough Bridge
CLOUGH RD
CRAWSHAW LA
KIRKBY LA
Upper Crawshaw
Out Lane Dike
LEISURE LA
CROSS LA
RECTORY LA
GRANGE DR
RECTORY GARDEN
THORNCLIFFE LA
BROOM FIELD LA
STRINGER HOUSE LA
MOORLAND VIEW
SPRINGFIELD TERR
Emley
ASPEN CT
ST MICHAEL'S GDNS
CHURCH ST
RODLEY LA
Emley First Sch
Little Dike
JAGGER LA
OUT LA
BROOMFIELD C
SCHOOL LA
ST MICHAEL'S CL
THE CROFTS
SAVILLE ST
SAVILLE AVE
MOUNT PLEASANT
GLEBE CL
TIPPING LA
WOODHOUSE LA
Hutt Farm
CHAPEL LA
BEAUMONT ST
PO
UPPER LA
ASH LA
WENTWORTH DR
WENTWORTH AVE
ELLMONT AVE
FOX CL
PHOENIX AVE
SUMMER LA
EMSLEY MOOR BSNS PK
LEYS LA
TYBURN LA
WARBURTON RD
RISHWORTH AVE
VIKING AVE
BROOMHEY AVE
White Cross
Tyburn Hill
GREEN ACRES CL
SAXON CL
Leys Farm
HAG HILL
Churchill Farm
HAG HILL LA
Owlers Wood
FRANK LA
BACK LA
OLD HALL LA
Low House Farm
KILN LA
Taylor Hill
Emley Old Hall
PARK LA
HD8
Lady Oak
Park Lane House
Ninecloqs Dike
Uppler Owlers Wood
COLLIERS WAY
Park Farm
Emley Park
A636
LANGLEY LA
WOODBINE TERR
Park Gate
Emley Lodge
PARK AVE
LONG LA
PARK RD
Blacker Farm
BACK LA
Clayton West
Park Gate Dike
PARK MILL WAY
BOGGART LA
Blacker Wood
Dearne Way
INGS MILL AVE
Kaye's Fst Sch
SCOTT HILL
Skelmanthorpe
Kirklees Light Railway
STATION RD
RIVERSIDE
INGS MILL DR
MARSDEN ST
SPENCER ST
Cuckoo's Nest Halt
LANGLEY LA
THE CLOSE
ALBERT RD
VINERY CL
CHURCH LA
PILLING LA
VICTORIA ST
SAVILLE RD
1 DALE ST
2 THE FOLDINGS
PENNINE RISE
DEARNE PK
SCORE
CROFT HEAD
TENTER CL
HOUSE GROVE DR
HOLMFIELD RD
Bsns Pk
DALE CROFT
SUNNYMEAD
WAKEFIELD RD
NEWLANDS AVE
GIB LA
PENNINE DR
PENNINE WAY
CHAPEL HILL
CLIFFE ST
HOLMFIELD CL
NORTH FIELD LA
ELM ST
Skelmanthorpe
THE BUNGALOWS
CLIFFEWOOD RISE
CLIFFE VIEW
Scissett Middle Sch
Scissett Fst Sch
DUKE WOOD RD
HIGH ST
LODGE ST
QUEEN ST
KING ST
Skelmanthorpe Fst Sch
3 POPLAR RISE
4 LABURNUM GR
5 WILLOW RISE
6 RADCLIFFE ST
SPRINGFIELD AVE
Clayton West
OLDFIELD LA
COMMERCIAL RD
NEW ST
MANOR DR
BEECHFIELD AVE
BARNSLEY RD
HOLMFIELD AVE 8
HOLMFIELD TERR 9
THE INGS 10
VICTORIA TERR 11
HOLMFIELD 12
BILHAM RD 13
CHERRY LA 14
CLIFTON VIEW 15
Hill Top Farm
OAKFIELD GR
SMITHY LA
BARROWSTEAD
CHURCH TERR
Kirklees Way
BUSKER LA
B6116
WATER ST
Sch
WOODLAND DR
WHARFEDALE CRES
WINDSOR DR
WINDMILL CRES
Lower Common
ELMFIELD DR
BIRCHFIELD GR
MANOR RISE
MANORSTEAD
PICKLES LA
EAST FOLD
STANHOPE ST
SMITHY CL
NEW LA
Nortonthorpe Hall Sch
NEW ST
CROWN ST
LOWER COMMON LA
1 DEARNE ST
2 SAVILLE ST
3 MARSHALL MILL CT
4 DEARNE ROYD
5 BRIDGE CL
6 SPRINGFIELD CL
7 RIDINGWOOD RISE
Riding Wood
UPPER COMMON LA
MATHERVILLE
MEADOW VIEW
RIDGE CL
ASHFIELD AVE
CROSS LA
THORPES CRES
HIGHBRIDGE LA
Skelmanthorpe Cemy
WOOD ST
NORTONTHORPE IND EST
CUTTLEHURST
LIDGET
P

192
176

175
158

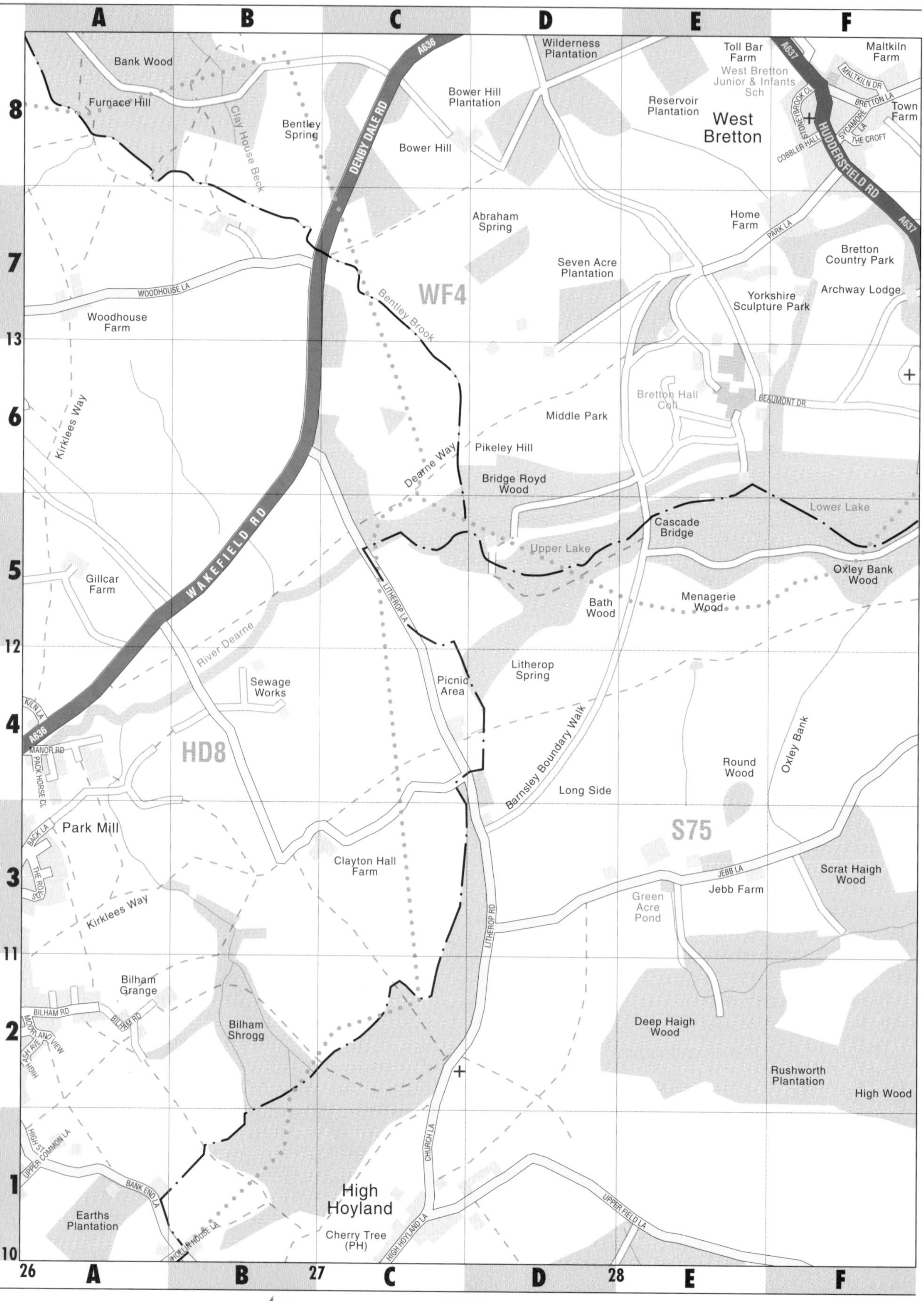

175
193

159
178

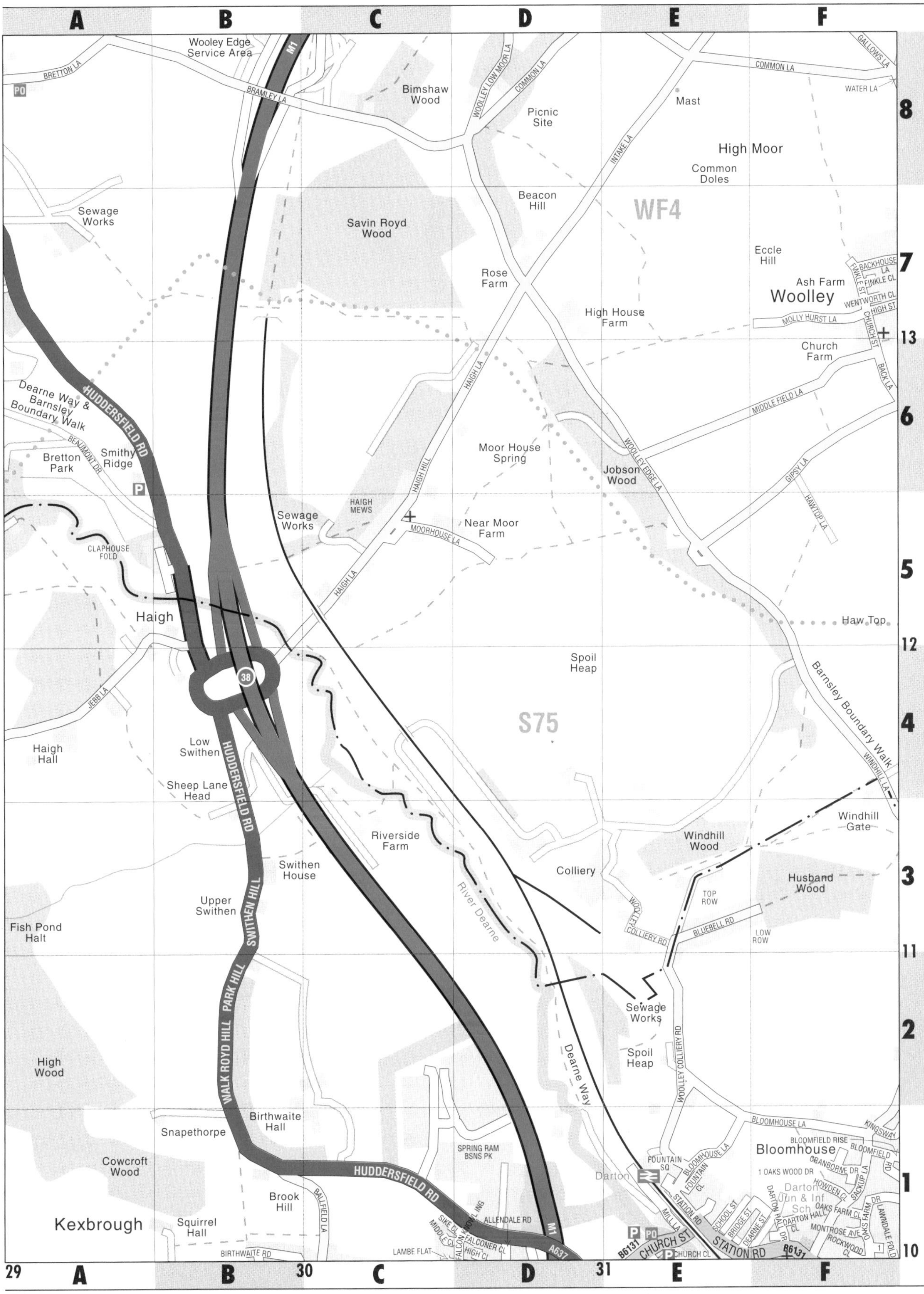
A
B
C
D
E
F
Wooley Edge
Service Area
BRETTON LA
PO
BRAMLEY LA
M1
Bimshaw
Wood
WOOLLEY LOW MOOR LA
COMMON LA
Picnic
Site
Mast
COMMON LA
GALLOWS LA
WATER LA
High Moor
Common
Doles
INTAKE LA
Beacon
Hill
WF4
Sewage
Works
Savin Royd
Wood
Rose
Farm
Eccle
Hill
Ash Farm
Woolley
BACKHOUSE LA
FINKLE CL
FINKLE ST
WENTWORTH CL
HIGH ST
MOLLY HURST LA
CHURCH ST
High House
Farm
Church
Farm
BACK LA
HAIGH LA
MIDDLE FIELD LA
HUDDERSFIELD RD
Dearne Way &
Barnsley
Boundary Walk
BEAUMONT DR
Bretton
Park
Smithy
Ridge
P
Moor House
Spring
WOOLLEY EDGE LA
Jobson
Wood
HAIGH HILL
GIPSY LA
HAWTOP LA
HAIGH
MEWS
Sewage
Works
Near Moor
Farm
MOORHOUSE LA
CLAPHOUSE
FOLD
HAIGH LA
Haigh
Haw Top
38
Spoil
Heap
Barnsley Boundary Walk
JEBB LA
S75
WINDHILL LA
Haigh
Hall
Low
Swithen
Sheep Lane
Head
HUDDERSFIELD RD
Windhill
Gate
Riverside
Farm
Windhill
Wood
Swithen
House
Colliery
Husband
Wood
Upper
Swithen
SWITHEN HILL
River Dearne
TOP
ROW
Fish Pond
Halt
WOOLLEY COLLIERY RD
BLUEBELL RD
LOW
ROW
Sewage
Works
PARK HILL
WALK ROYD HILL
Spoil
Heap
High
Wood
Dearne Way
WOOLLEY COLLIERY RD
Birthwaite
Hall
Snapethorpe
BLOOMHOUSE LA
KINGSWAY
BLOOMFIELD RISE
Bloomhouse
BLOOMFIELD RD
SPRING RAM
BSNS PK
Cowcroft
Wood
FOUNTAIN
SQ
BLOOMHOUSE LA
1 OAKS WOOD DR
CRANBORNE DR
SACKUP LA
HUDDERSFIELD RD
Darton
FOUNTAIN CL
Darton
Jun & Inf
Sch
HOWDEN CL
Brook
Hill
BALLFIELD LA
KNOLL ING
STATION RD
SCHOOL ST
BRIDGE ST
DEARNE ST
DARTON HALL DR
DARTON HALL CL
OAKS FARM CL
OAKS FARM DR
LAWNDALE FOLD
Kexbrough
Squirrel
Hall
SIKE CL
MIDDLE CL
FALCON KNOLL ING
ALLENDALE RD
M1
MILL LA
P
PO
MONTROSE AVE
ROCKWOOD CL
BIRTHWAITE RD
LAMBE FLAT
FALCONER CL
HIGH CL
A637
B6131
CHURCH ST
P
CHURCH CL
STATION RD
B6131
8
7
13
6
5
12
4
3
11
2
1
10
29
30
31

178

177
160

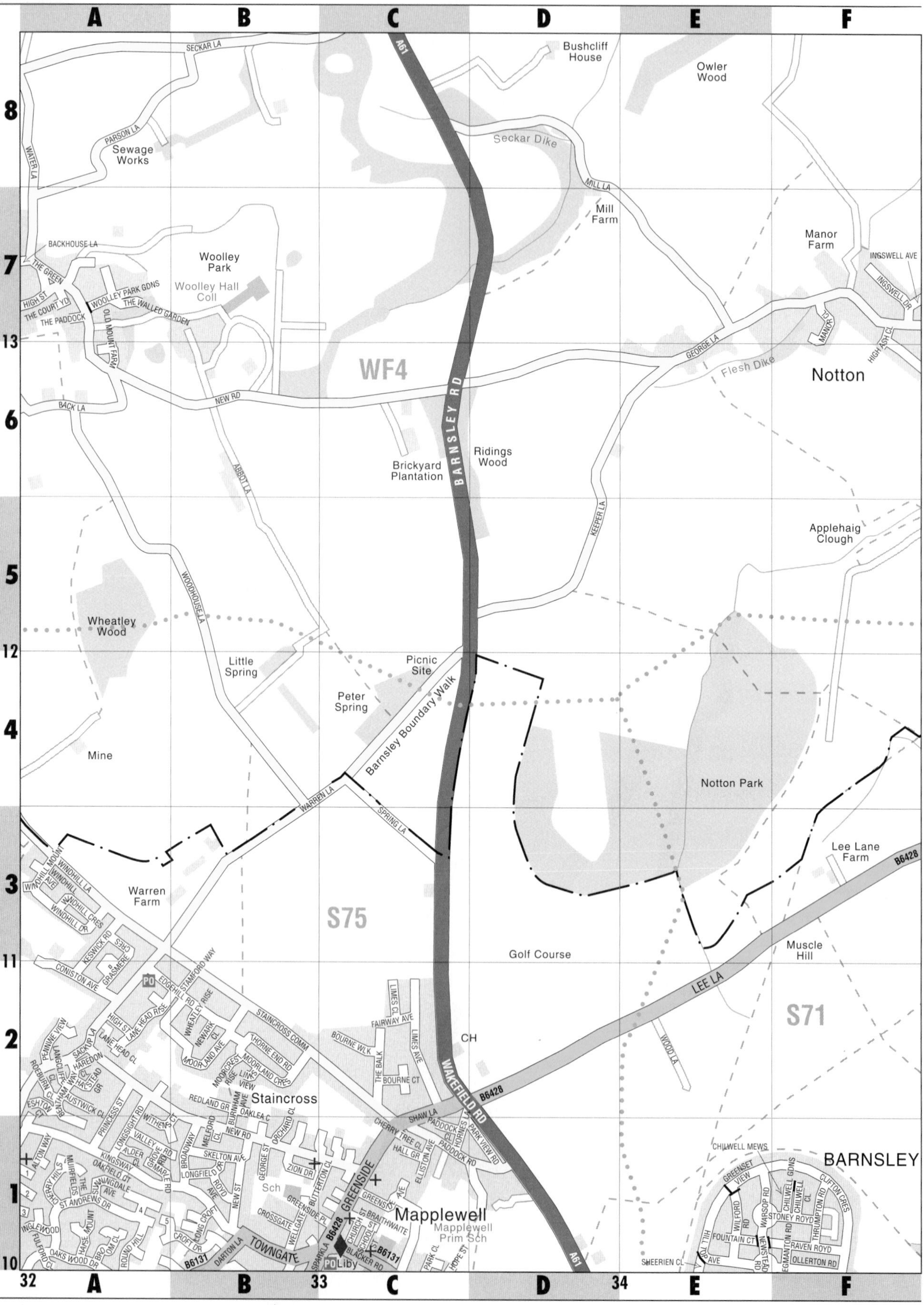

A1
1 BLOOMFIELD RISE
2 BLOOMFIELD RD
3 OAKS FARM DR
4 PRIEST ROYD
5 CROFT CL

177

161
180

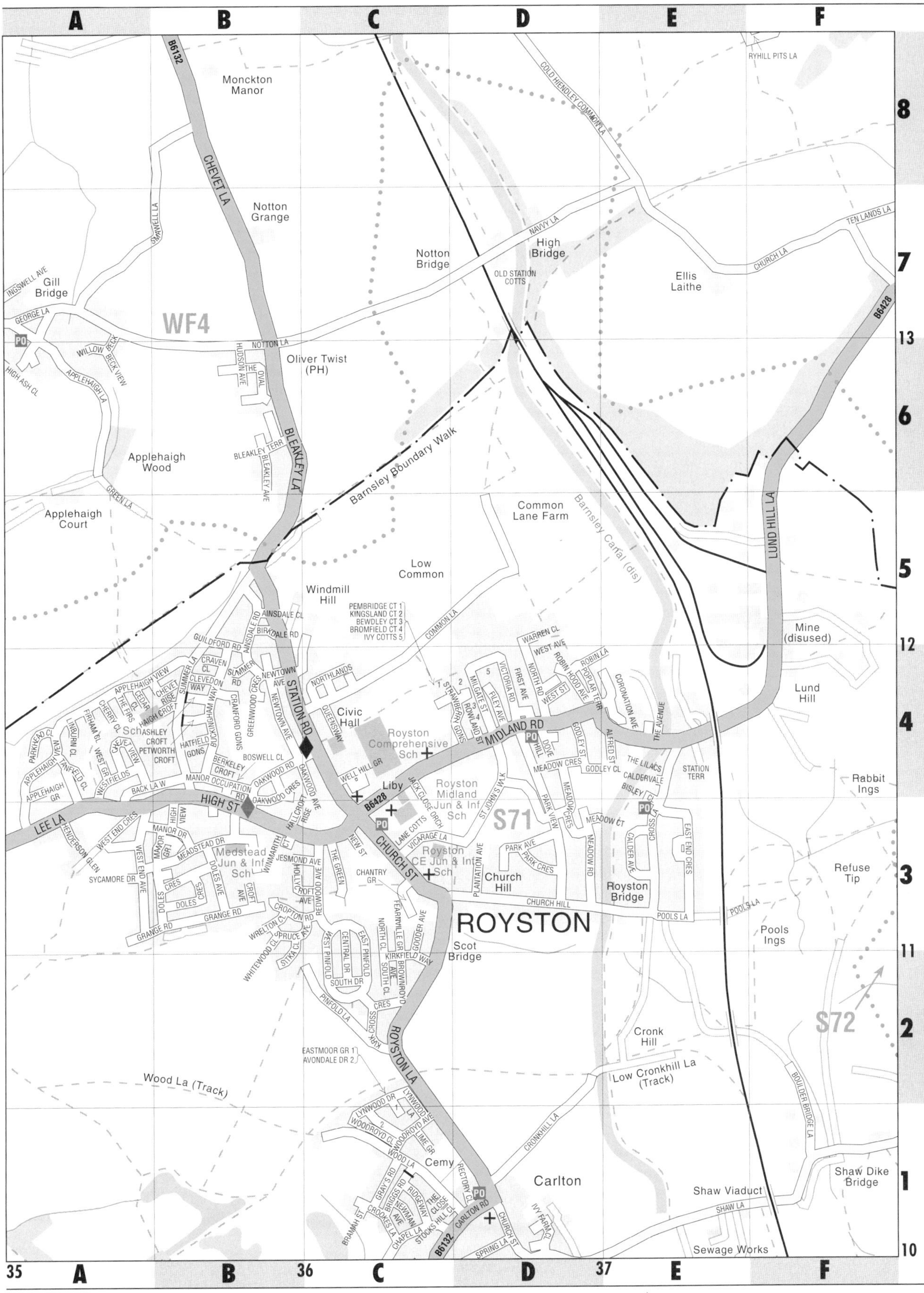
A
B
C
D
E
F
8
7
13
6
5
12
4
3
11
2
1
10
35
36
37
B6132
Monckton Manor
RYHILL PITS LA
COLD HIENDLEY COMMON LA
CHEVET LA
Notton Grange
SMAWELL LA
NAVVY LA
High Bridge
TEN LANDS LA
CHURCH LA
Notton Bridge
OLD STATION COTTS
Ellis Laithe
INGSWELL AVE
Gill Bridge
GEORGE LA
WF4
B6428
PO
NOTTON LA
HUDSON AVE
THE OVAL
Oliver Twist (PH)
WILLOW BECK
BECK VIEW
HIGH ASH CL
APPLEHAIGH LA
BLEAKLEY LA
Applehaigh Wood
BLEAKLEY TERR
BLEAKLEY AVE
Barnsley Boundary Walk
GREEN LA
Common Lane Farm
Barnsley Canal (dis)
Applehaigh Court
LUND HILL LA
Low Common
Windmill Hill
AINSDALE CL
PEMBRIDGE CT 1
KINGSLAND CT 2
BEWDLEY CT 3
BROMFIELD CT 4
IVY COTTS 5
COMMON LA
Mine (disused)
GUILDFORD RD
AINSDALE RD
BIRKDALE RD
WARREN CL
WEST AVE
ROBIN HOOD AVE
ROBIN LA
POPLAR TERR
CORONATION AVE
Lund Hill
NORTHLANDS
NEWTOWN AVE
STATION RD
CRAVEN CL
SUMMER RD
SUMMER LA
CLEVEDON WAY
APPLEHAIGH VIEW
CHEVET RISE
HAIGH CROFT
CEDAR CL
THE FIRS
CHERRY CL
FIRHAM CL
LINBURN CL
PARKHEAD CL
Sch
ASHLEY CROFT
PETWORTH CROFT
HATFIELD GDNS
BUCKINGHAM WAY
CRANFORD GDNS
GREENWOOD CRES
NEWTOWN AVE
QUEENSWAY
Civic Hall
Royston Comprehensive Sch
STRAWBERRY GDNS
ROWLAND ST
MILGATE ST
FILEY AVE
VICTORIA RD
FIRST AVE
NORTH RD
WEST ST
MIDLAND RD
HILL
DOVE
GODLEY ST
ALFRED ST
THE AVENUE
THE LILACS
STATION TERR
CALDERVALE
BISLEY CL
Rabbit Ings
GODLEY CL
MEADOW CRES
APPLEHAIGH CL
TANFIELD CL
WEST GR
WESTFIELDS
CHEVET VIEW
BERKELEY CROFT
BOSWELL CL
WELL HILL GR
Liby
JACK CLOSE ORCH
Royston Midland Jun & Inf Sch
ST JOHN'S WALK
PARK VIEW
MEADOW CT
APPLEHAIGH GR
BACK LA W
MANOR OCCUPATION RD
OAKWOOD RD
OAKWOOD AVE
OAKWOOD CRES
HALLCROFT RISE
HIGH ST
LANE COTTS
VICARAGE LA
S71
CROSS LA
EAST END CRES
CALDER AVE
LEE LA
HENDERSON GLEN
WEST END CRES
HIGH VIEW
MANOR DR
MANOR GR
MEADSTEAD DR
Medstead Jun & Inf Sch
WINMARITH CT
JESMOND AVE
THE GREEN
NEW ST
CHURCH ST
Royston CE Jun & Inf Sch
PLANTATION AVE
PARK AVE
PARK CRES
MEADOW RD
Refuse Tip
SYCAMORE DR
WEST END AVE
DOLES CRES
DOLES AVE
DOLES
CROFT AVE
HOLLYCROFT AVE
REDWOOD AVE
CHANTRY GR
Church Hill
Royston Bridge
CHURCH HILL
POOLS LA
GRANGE RD
CROPTON RD
WRELTON CL
SPRUCE AVE
FEARNVILLE GR
GODDER AVE
ROYSTON
Pools Ings
WHITEWOOD CL
STIKA CL
WEST PINFOLD
CENTRAL DR
EAST PINFOLD
NORTH CL
KIRKFIELD WAY
SOUTH CL
BROWNROYD AVE
Scot Bridge
SOUTH DR
CRES
PINFOLD LA
KIRK CROSS
ROYSTON LA
S72
Cronk Hill
EASTMOOR GR 1
AVONDALE DR 2
Wood La (Track)
Low Cronkhill La (Track)
BOULDER BRIDGE LA
LYNWOOD DR
LYNWOOD CL
WOODROYD CL
WOODROYD AVE
LIME GR
WOOD LA
Cemy
CRONKHILL LA
Carlton
Shaw Dike Bridge
GRAY'S RD
BRIGGS RD
NEWMAN AVE
RIDGEWAY
THE CLOSE
RECTORY CL
Shaw Viaduct
SHAW LA
BRAMAH ST
CROOKES LA
CHAPEL LA
STOCKS HILL CL
CARLTON RD
IVY FARM CL
SPRING LA
Sewage Works

180

179
162

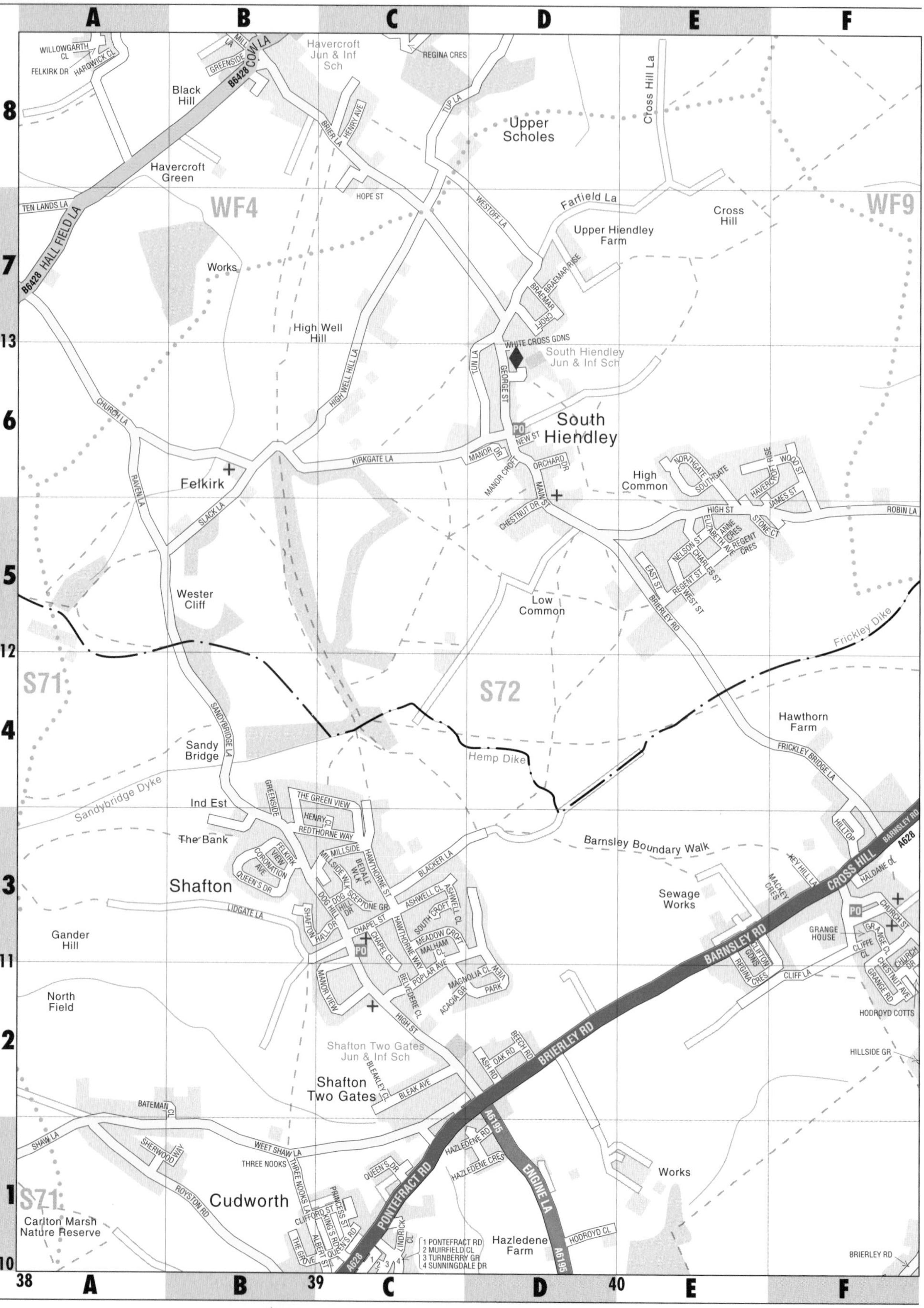
A
B
C
D
E
F
8
7
13
6
5
12
4
3
11
2
1
10
38
39
40
WILLOWGARTH CL
HARDWICK CL
FELKIRK DR
MILL LA
GREENSIDE
B6428 COW LA
Havercroft Jun & Inf Sch
REGINA CRES
Black Hill
HENRY AVE
BRIER LA
TUP LA
Upper Scholes
Cross Hill La
Havercroft Green
TEN LANDS LA
B6428 HALL FIELD LA
WF4
HOPE ST
WESTOFF LA
Farfield La
Cross Hill
WF9
Upper Hiendley Farm
BRAEMAR RISE
BRAEMAR CROFT
Works
High Well Hill
WHITE CROSS GDNS
South Hiendley Jun & Inf Sch
TUN LA
GEORGE ST
HIGH WELL HILL LA
CHURCH LA
PO
NEW ST
South Hiendley
KIRKGATE LA
MANOR DR
MANOR CROFT
ORCHARD DR
NORTHGATE
SOUTHGATE
HAVERCROFT RISE
WOOD ST
JAMES ST
High Common
Felkirk
RAVEN LA
SLACK LA
MAIN ST
CHESTNUT DR
HIGH ST
ANNE CRES
ELIZABETH AVE
STONE CT
ROBIN LA
REGENT CRES
NELSON ST
CHARLES ST
EAST ST
REGENT ST
WEST ST
BRIERLEY RD
Wester Cliff
Low Common
Frickley Dike
S71
S72
SANDYBRIDGE LA
Hawthorn Farm
Sandy Bridge
Hemp Dike
FRICKLEY BRIDGE LA
Sandybridge Dyke
Ind Est
GREENSIDE
THE GREEN VIEW
HENRY CL
REDTHORNE WAY
The Bank
Barnsley Boundary Walk
HILLTOP
BARNSLEY RD
A628
FELKIRK VIEW
CORONATION AVE
QUEEN'S DR
MILLSIDE
MILLSIDE WALK
BEDALE WALK
HAWTHORNE ST
BLACKER LA
KEY HILL LA
MACKEY CRES
CROSS HILL
HALDANE CL
Shafton
DOG HILL DR
SCEPTONE GR
ASHWELL CL
ASHWELL CROFT
Sewage Works
LIDGATE LA
SHAFTON HALL DR
CHAPEL ST
CHAPEL CL
HAWTHORNE WAY
SOUTH CROFT
MEADOW CROFT
MALHAM CL
CHURCH ST
GRANGE HOUSE
GRANGE CL
CLIFFE CL
CHURCH DR
CHESTNUT AVE
Gander Hill
POPLAR AVE
MAGNOLIA CL
PARK VIEW
ACACIA GR
BARNSLEY RD
CLIFTON GDNS
REGINA CRES
CLIFF LA
GRANGE RD
North Field
MANOR VIEW
BELVEDERE CL
HODROYD COTTS
HIGH ST
BRIERLEY RD
BEECH RD
OAK RD
ASH RD
Shafton Two Gates Jun & Inf Sch
BLEAKLEY CL
HILLSIDE GR
Shafton Two Gates
BLEAK AVE
BATEMAN CL
A6195
SHAW LA
SHERWOOD WAY
WEET SHAW LA
HAZLEDENE RD
HAZLEDENE CRES
ENGINE LA
THREE NOOKS
THREE NOOKS LA
QUEEN'S DR
Works
ROYSTON RD
Cudworth
PRINCESS ST
PONTEFRACT RD
CLIFFORD ST
KING'S RD
QUEEN'S RD
LINDRICK CL
Carlton Marsh Nature Reserve
ALBERT ST
THE GROVE
1 PONTEFRACT RD
2 MUIRFIELD CL
3 TURNBERRY GR
4 SUNNINGDALE DR
Hazledene Farm
HODROYD CL
BRIERLEY RD

179

163
182

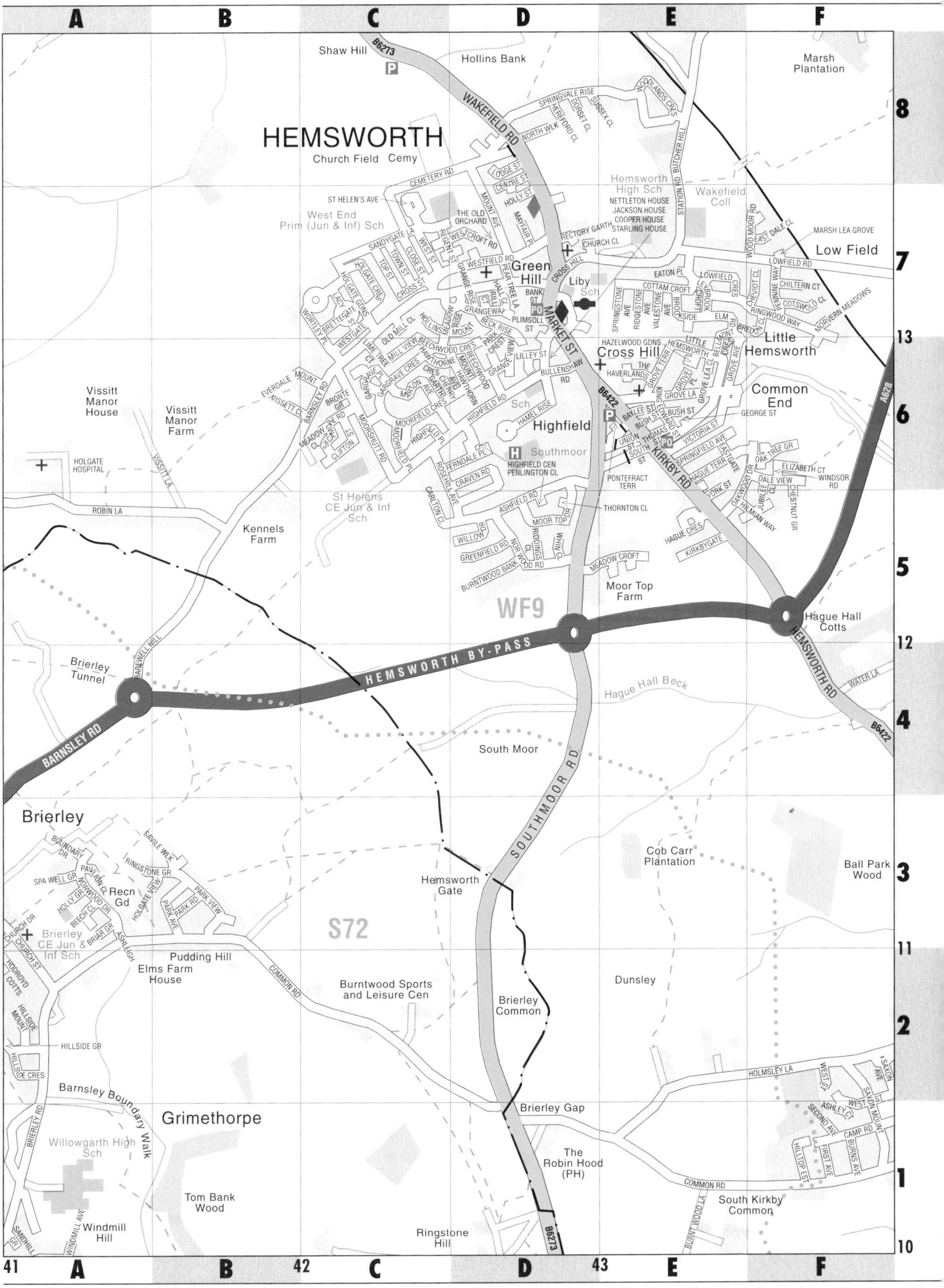
A
B
C
D
E
F
8
7
13
6
5
12
4
3
11
2
1
10
41
42
43
HEMSWORTH
Shaw Hill
Hollins Bank
Marsh Plantation
Church Field
Cemy
WAKEFIELD RD
B6273
SPRINGVALE RISE
SUSSEX CL
DORSET CL
HEREFORD CL
WOODLANDS CRES
NORTH WLK
STATION RD
BUTCHER HILL
Hemsworth High Sch
NETTLETON HOUSE
JACKSON HOUSE
COOPER HOUSE
STARLING HOUSE
Wakefield Coll
WOOD MOOR RD
EAST DALE CL
MARSH LEA GROVE
Low Field
LOWFIELD RD
CHILTERN CT
COTSWOLD CL
FENNINE WAY
MORVERN MEADOWS
RINGWOOD WAY
CEMETERY RD
LODGE ST
CENTRE ST
HOLLY ST
ST HELEN'S AVE
West End Prim (Jun & Inf) Sch
THE OLD ORCHARD
MOUNT AVE
MAYFAIR PL
RECTORY GARTH
CHURCH CL
WESTCROFT RD
SANDYGATE LA
WEST ST
REGENT ST
TOWN ST
CLOSE ST
TOP ST
CROSS ST
WESTFIELD RD
Green Hill
CROSS HILL
Liby
Sch
EATON PL
LOWFIELD CRES
COTTAM CROFT
HOLGATE CRES
HOLGATE GDNS
LACY ST
BRETTEGATE
WORTLEY PL
WESTGATE
GRANGE RISE
GRANGEWAY
HALL CL
PEAR TREE LA
BANK ST
PO
MARKET ST
PLIMSOLL ST
SPRINGSTONE AVE
RIDGESTONE AVE
VALESTONE AVE
BROOKSIDE
ELM RD
BREDON CL
CHEVIOT CL
OLD MILL CL
HOLLINS MEADOW
BECK RISE
PARK CREST
MILL VIEW
BEECHWOOD CRES
LIME TREE CT
GARGRAVE CRES
HAWTHORNE CRES
CHERRY TREE AVE
BEECHWOOD MOUNT
HAWTHORN MOUNT
GRANGE VIEW
LILLEY ST
BULLENSHAW RD
HAZELWOOD GDNS
Cross Hill
HEMSWORTH
HAVERLANDS
THE GROVE
GROVE TERR
GROVE LEA CL
BELLMONT CRES
GROVE AVE
Little Hemsworth
Common End
EVERDALE MOUNT
BARNSLEY RD
VISSITT CL
BRONTE GR
MOORFIELD CRES
HIGHFIELD RD
Sch
HAMEL RISE
Highfield
B6422
BAYLEE ST
BUSH ST
KING EDWARD ST
GROVE LA
GEORGE ST
Vissitt Manor House
Vissitt Manor Farm
MEADOW CL
SACKVILLE RD
CLIFTON RD
MOORSHUTT RD
MOORFIELD PL
HIGHFIELD PL
UNION ST
SOUTH ST
THOMAS ST
VICTORIA ST
SPRINGFIELD AVE
OAK TREE GR
ELIZABETH CT
WINDSOR RD
H
Southmoor
HIGHFIELD CEN
PENLINGTON CL
FERNDALE PL
CRAVEN RD
ROSEHILL AVE
PONTEFRACT TERR
KIRKBY RD
HAGUE TERR
EASTGATE
YORK ST
DALE VIEW
JUBILEE CL
CHESTNUT GR
HILMIAN WAY
OAKWOOD DR
HOLGATE HOSPITAL
VISSITT LA
ROBIN LA
St Helens CE Jun & Inf Sch
CARLTON CL
ASHFIELD RD
MOOR TOP
THORNTON CL
Kennels Farm
WILLOW RD
GREENFIELD RD
RIDDINGS CL
NIWIH CL
HAGUE CRES
KIRKBYGATE
BURNTWOOD BANK
NORWOOD RD
MEADOW CROFT
Moor Top Farm
WF9
A628
Hague Hall Cotts
HEMSWORTH BY-PASS
HEMSWORTH RD
BAREWELL HILL
Brierley Tunnel
Hague Hall Beck
WATER LA
B6422
BARNSLEY RD
South Moor
SOUTHMOOR RD
Brierley
BOUNDARY DR
SAVILE WLK
RINGSTONE GR
SPA WELL GR
PAVILION CL
NORWOOD DR
HOLLY GR
BEECH CL
Recn Gd
HOLGATE VIEW
PARK AVE
PARK RD
PARK VIEW
Cob Carr Plantation
Hemsworth Gate
Ball Park Wood
CHURCH DR
CHURCH ST
Brierley CE Jun & Inf Sch
BRIAR GR
ASHLEIGH
S72
Pudding Hill
Elms Farm House
COMMON RD
HOOROYD COTTS
HILLSIDE MOUNT
Burntwood Sports and Leisure Cen
Brierley Common
Dunsley
HILLSIDE GR
HILLSIDE CRES
HOLMSLEY LA
WEST ST
SAXON AVE
ASHLEY CT
SECOND AVE
WEST ST
SAXON MOUNT
Barnsley Boundary Walk
Brierley Gap
CAMP RD
BURNS AVE
FIRST AVE
HILLTOP EST
Grimethorpe
BRIERLEY RD
Willowgarth High Sch
The Robin Hood (PH)
COMMON RD
Tom Bank Wood
South Kirkby Common
BURNT WOOD LA
SANDHILL GR
WINDMILL AVE
Windmill Hill
Ringstone Hill
B6273

182

181
164

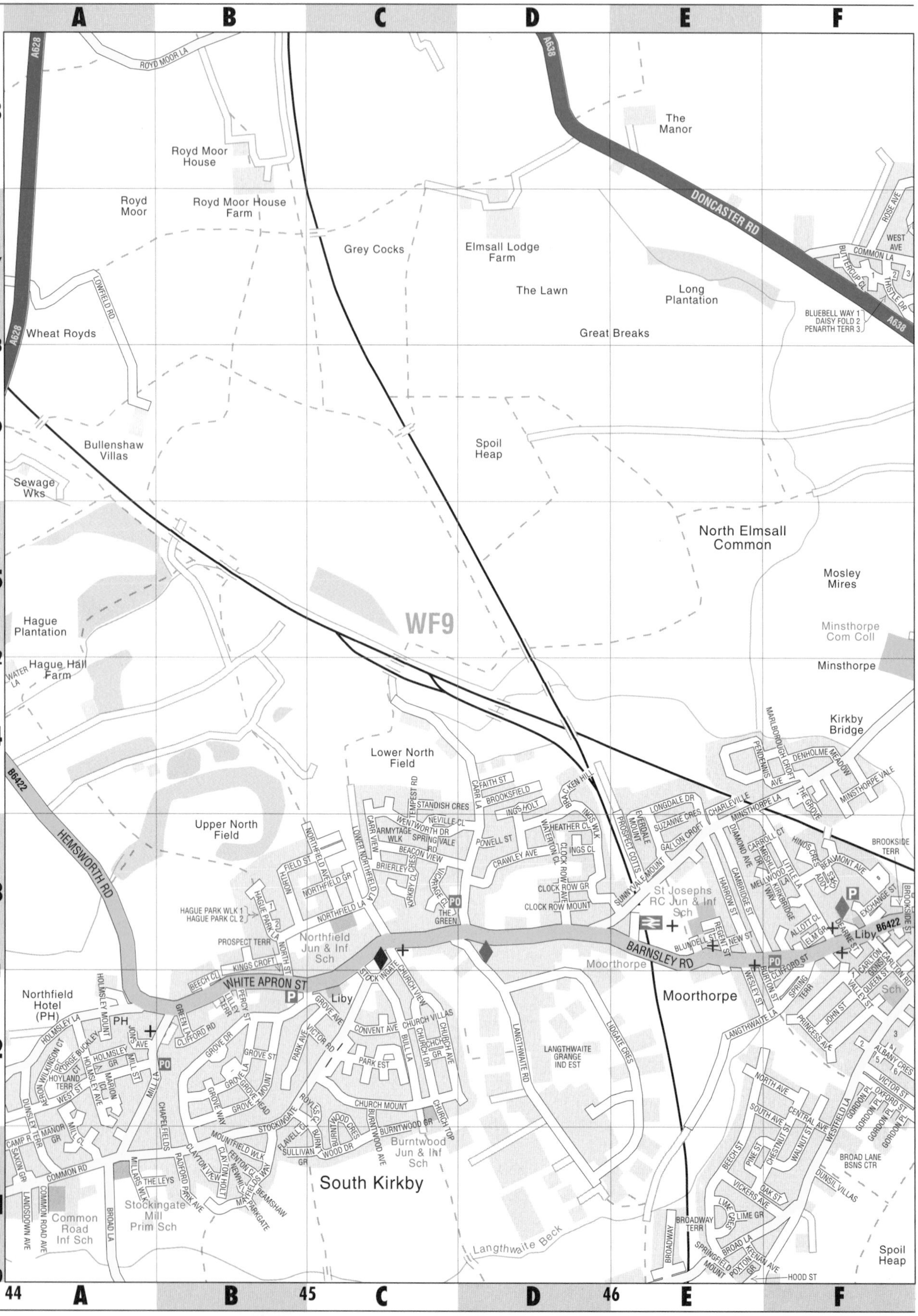
A
B
C
D
E
F
8
7
13
6
5
12
4
3
11
2
1
10
44
45
46
A628
ROYD MOOR LA
A638
The Manor
Royd Moor House
Royd Moor
Royd Moor House Farm
DONCASTER RD
Grey Cocks
Elmsall Lodge Farm
The Lawn
Long Plantation
Great Breaks
LOWFIELD RD
Wheat Royds
ROSE AVE
WEST AVE
COMMON LA
BUTTERCUP CL
THISTLE DR
BLUEBELL WAY 1
DAISY FOLD 2
PENARTH TERR 3
Bullenshaw Villas
Spoil Heap
Sewage Wks
North Elmsall Common
Mosley Mires
Hague Plantation
WF9
Minsthorpe Com Coll
WATER LA
Hague Hall Farm
Minsthorpe
Kirkby Bridge
Lower North Field
B6422
HEMSWORTH RD
Upper North Field
FAITH ST
BROOKSFIELD
STANDISH CRES
NEVILLE CL
ARMYTAGE WLK
WENTWORTH DR
SPRING VALE RD
BEACON VIEW
BRIERLEY CRES
KIRKBY CL
VICARAGE CL
INGS HOLT
POWELL ST
CRAWLEY AVE
HEATHER CL
WATERTON CL
CLOCK ROW AVE
INGS CL
INGS WLK
BRACKEN HILL
CLOCK ROW GR
CLOCK ROW MOUNT
PROSPECT COTTS
EVERDALE MOUNT
LONGDALE DR
SUZANNE CRES
GALLON CROFT
CHARLEVILLE
MINSTHORPE LA
MINSTHORPE VALE
PENDENNIS AVE
MARLBOROUGH CROFT
DENHOLME MEADOW
THE GROVE
BROOKSIDE TERR
DIAMOND AVE
CARROLL CT
MELLWOOD LA
HINDS CRES
BEAUMONT AVE
HARROW ST
CAMBRIDGE ST
SUNNYVALE MOUNT
St Josephs RC Jun & Inf Sch
EXCHANGE ST
NORTHFIELD AVE
NORTH ST
FIELD ST
NORTHFIELD GR
NORTHFIELD LA
LOWER NORTHFIELD LA
CARR VIEW
TEMPEST RD
CARR LA
HAGUE PARK WLK 1
HAGUE PARK CL 2
HAGUE PARK LA
PROSPECT TERR
Northfield Jun & Inf Sch
THE GREEN
BARNSLEY RD
BLUNDELL ST
REGENT ST
NEW ST
ALLOTT CL
ELM GR
DEARNE ST
Liby
BROOKSIDE ST
Moorthorpe
KINGS CROFT
BEECH CL
WHITE APRON ST
STOCKINGATE
CHURCH VIEW
WESLEY ST
BURTON ST
CLIFFORD ST
CARLTON ST
SPRING TERR
VALLEY ST
QUEEN ST
Sch
Northfield Hotel (PH)
PH
HOLMSLEY MOUNT
JONS AVE
GREEN LA
TILLER TERR
PERCY ST
CLIFFORD RD
GROVE AVE
VICTOR RD
CONVENT AVE
CHURCH VILLAS
CHURCH AVE
CHURCH DR
BULL LA
LANGTHWAITE RD
LIDGATE CRES
LANGTHWAITE LA
JOHN ST
PRINCESS AVE
HOLMSLEY LA
AARON WILKINSON CT
GEORGE BUCKLEY CT
HOLMSLEY GR
HOYLAND TERR
HOLMSLEY AVE
MARION ST
MILL ST
WEST ST
MILL LA
GROVE DR
GROVE ST
PARK AVE
PARK EST
LANGTHWAITE GRANGE IND EST
GROVE WAY
GROVE LA
GROVE MOUNT
GROVE HEAD
NORTH AVE
CENTRAL AVE
SOUTH AVE
ALBANY CRES
VICTOR ST
OXFORD ST
GORDON PL
GORDON ST
DUNSLEY TERR
MANOR GR
CAMP RD
SAXON GR
COMMON RD
CHAPELFIELDS
CLAYTON VIEW
CLAYTON HOLT
MOUNTFIELD WLK
FENTON CL
NEWHILL
FIELDS WAY
CHURCH MOUNT
ROYLE CL
HOOD CRES
BURNTWOOD GR
BURNTWOOD AVE
CHURCH TOP
FLAVELL CL
BURN WLK
SULLIVAN GR
WOOD DR
Burntwood Jun & Inf Sch
WESTFIELD LA
CHESTNUT ST
WALNUT ST
BEECH ST
PINE ST
OAK ST
VICKERS AVE
BROAD LANE BSNS CTR
DUNSIL VILLAS
LANDSDOWN AVE
COMMON ROAD AVE
Common Road Inf Sch
BROAD LA
MILLARDS WLK
THE LEYS
RADFORD PARK AVE
Stockingate Mill Prim Sch
BEAMSHAW
PARKGATE
South Kirkby
Langthwaite Beck
BROADWAY TERR
BROADWAY
SPRINGFIELD MOUNT
LIME CRES
LIME GR
BROAD LA
POXTON GR
KEENAN AVE
HOOD ST
Spoil Heap

181
194

F2
1 GRIMETHORPE ST
2 FIELD CRES
3 WESTFIELD BGLWS
4 ALBANY ST
5 ALBANY PL
6 WOODLEA

165
184

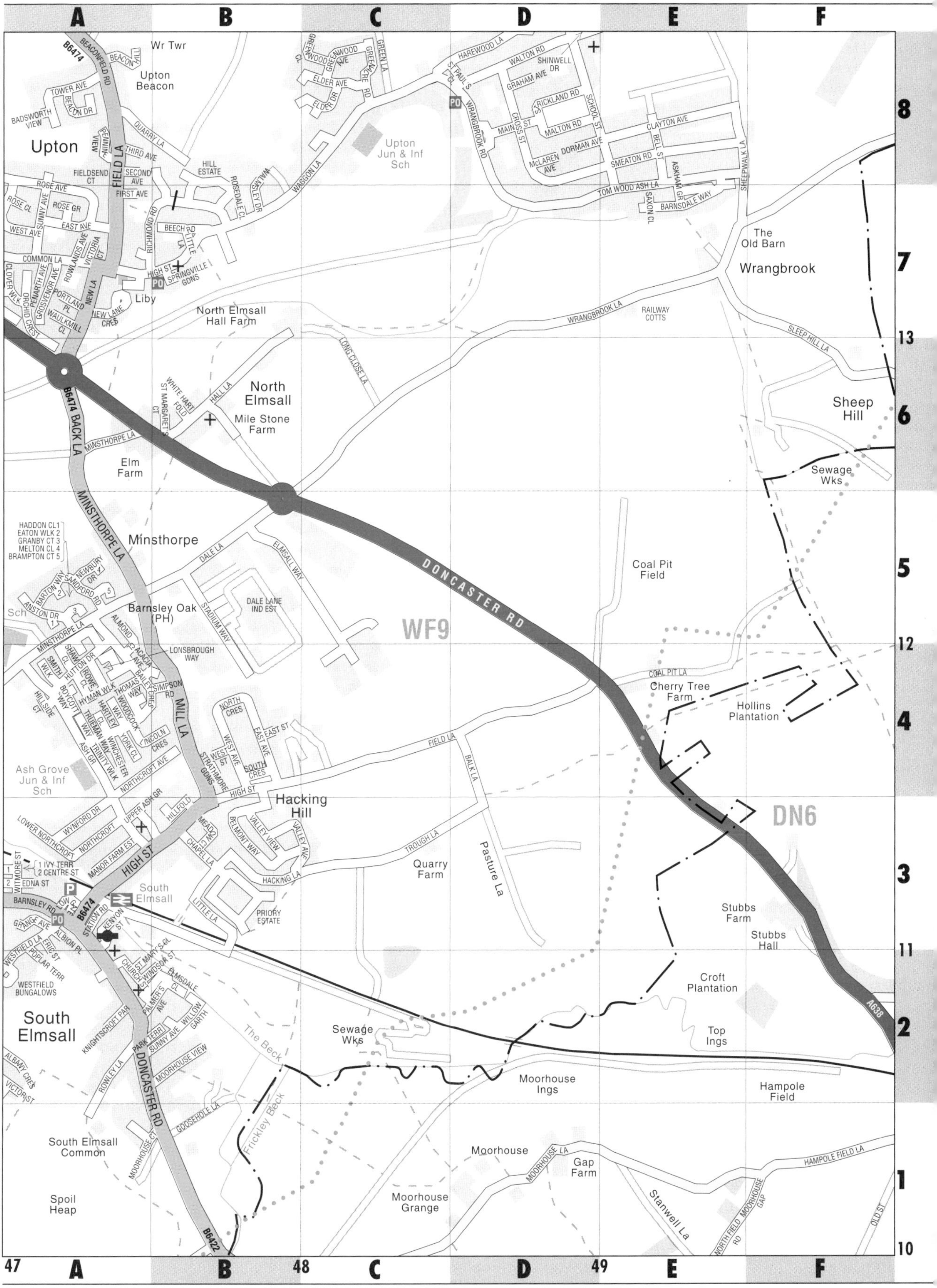

195
184

183
166

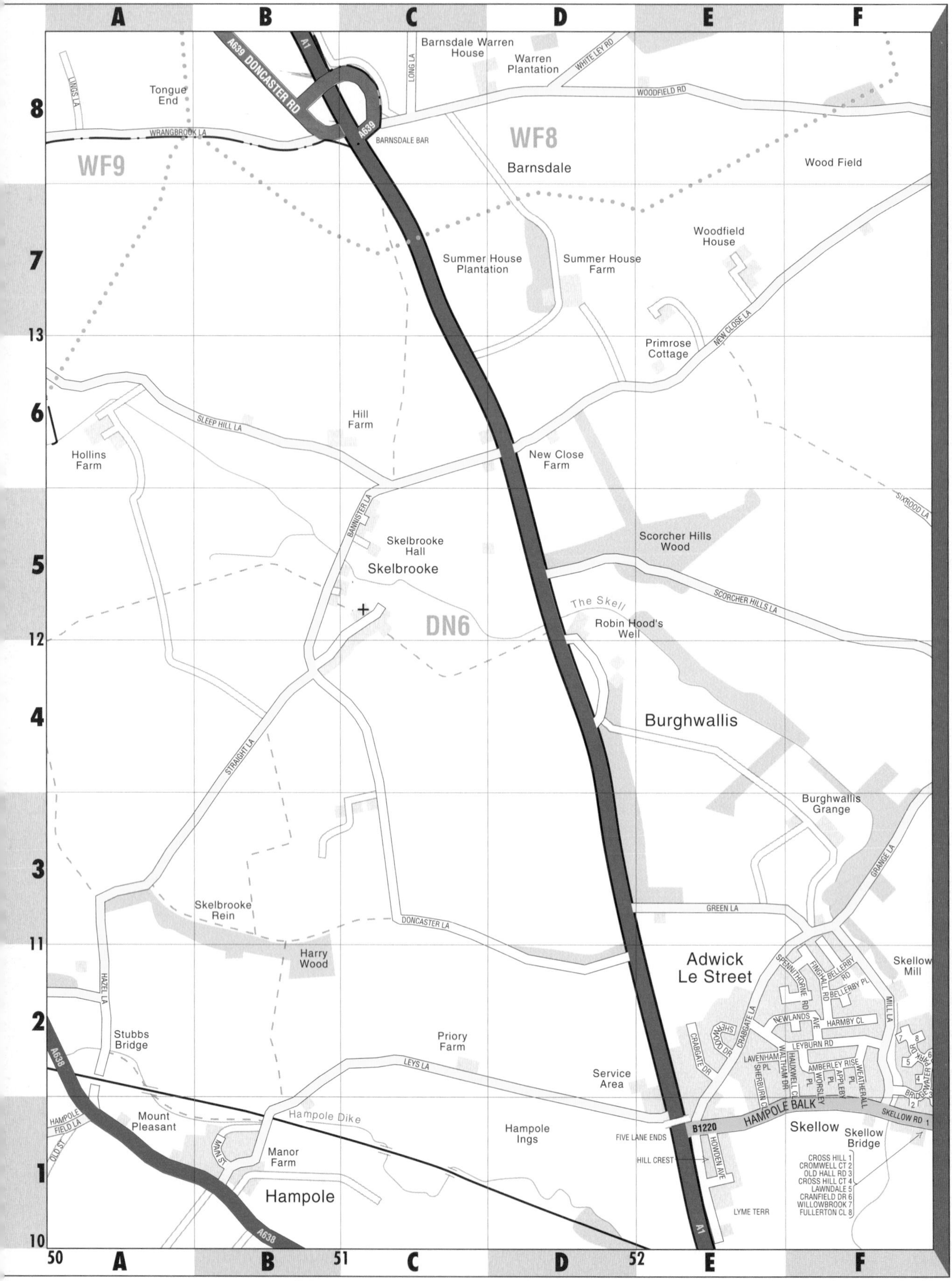
A
B
C
D
E
F
8
7
13
6
5
12
4
3
11
2
1
10
50
51
52
Tongue End
LINGS LA
WRANGBROOK LA
WF9
A639 DONCASTER RD
A1
A639
BARNSDALE BAR
Barnsdale Warren House
Warren Plantation
LONG LA
WHITE LEY RD
WOODFIELD RD
WF8
Barnsdale
Wood Field
Woodfield House
Summer House Plantation
Summer House Farm
Primrose Cottage
NEW CLOSE LA
SLEEP HILL LA
Hill Farm
Hollins Farm
New Close Farm
SIXROOD LA
BANNISTER LA
Skelbrooke Hall
Skelbrooke
Scorcher Hills Wood
SCORCHER HILLS LA
The Skell
DN6
Robin Hood's Well
Burghwallis
STRAIGHT LA
Burghwallis Grange
GRANGE LA
GREEN LA
Skelbrooke Rein
DONCASTER LA
Harry Wood
Adwick Le Street
Skellow Mill
HAZEL LA
SPENNITHORNE RD
FINGHALL RD
BELLERBY RD
BELLERBY PL
NEWLANDS AVE
HARMBY CL
MILL LA
Stubbs Bridge
Priory Farm
CRABGATE LA
CRABGATE DR
SHERWOOD DR
LEYBURN RD
LAVENHAM PL
WALTHAM DR
HAUXWELL CL
SHERBURN CL
AMBERLEY RISE
WORSLEY PL
APPLEBY PL
WEATHERALL
BRIDGEWATER PARK DR
LEYS LA
Service Area
A638
HAMPOLE FIELD LA
OLD ST
Mount Pleasant
Hampole Dike
Hampole Ings
FIVE LANE ENDS
B1220
HAMPOLE BALK
Skellow
SKELLOW RD
Skellow Bridge
MAIN ST
Manor Farm
HILL CREST
HOWDEN AVE
Hampole
LYME TERR
CROSS HILL 1
CROMWELL CT 2
OLD HALL RD 3
CROSS HILL CT 4
LAWNDALE 5
CRANFIELD DR 6
WILLOWBROOK 7
FULLERTON CL 8

183

168
186

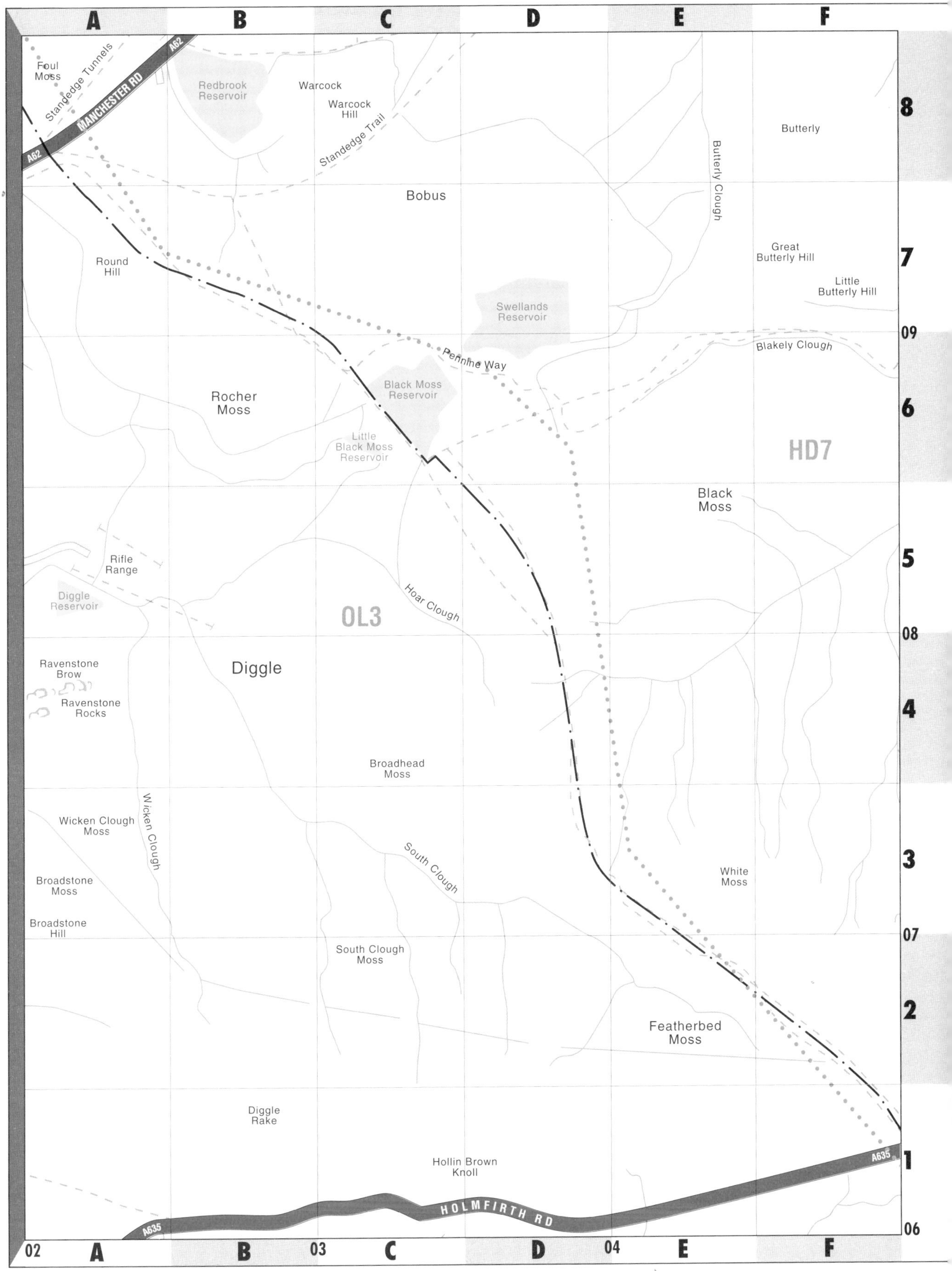
A
B
C
D
E
F
8
7
09
6
5
08
4
3
07
2
1
06
02
03
04
Foul Moss
Standedge Tunnels
A62
MANCHESTER RD
Redbrook Reservoir
Warcock
Warcock Hill
Standedge Trail
Butterly
Butterly Clough
Bobus
Round Hill
Great Butterly Hill
Little Butterly Hill
Swellands Reservoir
Blakely Clough
Pennine Way
Black Moss Reservoir
Rocher Moss
Little Black Moss Reservoir
HD7
Black Moss
Rifle Range
Diggle Reservoir
Hoar Clough
OL3
Ravenstone Brow
Ravenstone Rocks
Diggle
Broadhead Moss
Wicken Clough Moss
Wicken Clough
South Clough
White Moss
Broadstone Moss
Broadstone Hill
South Clough Moss
Featherbed Moss
Diggle Rake
Hollin Brown Knoll
A635
HOLMFIRTH RD

186

185
169

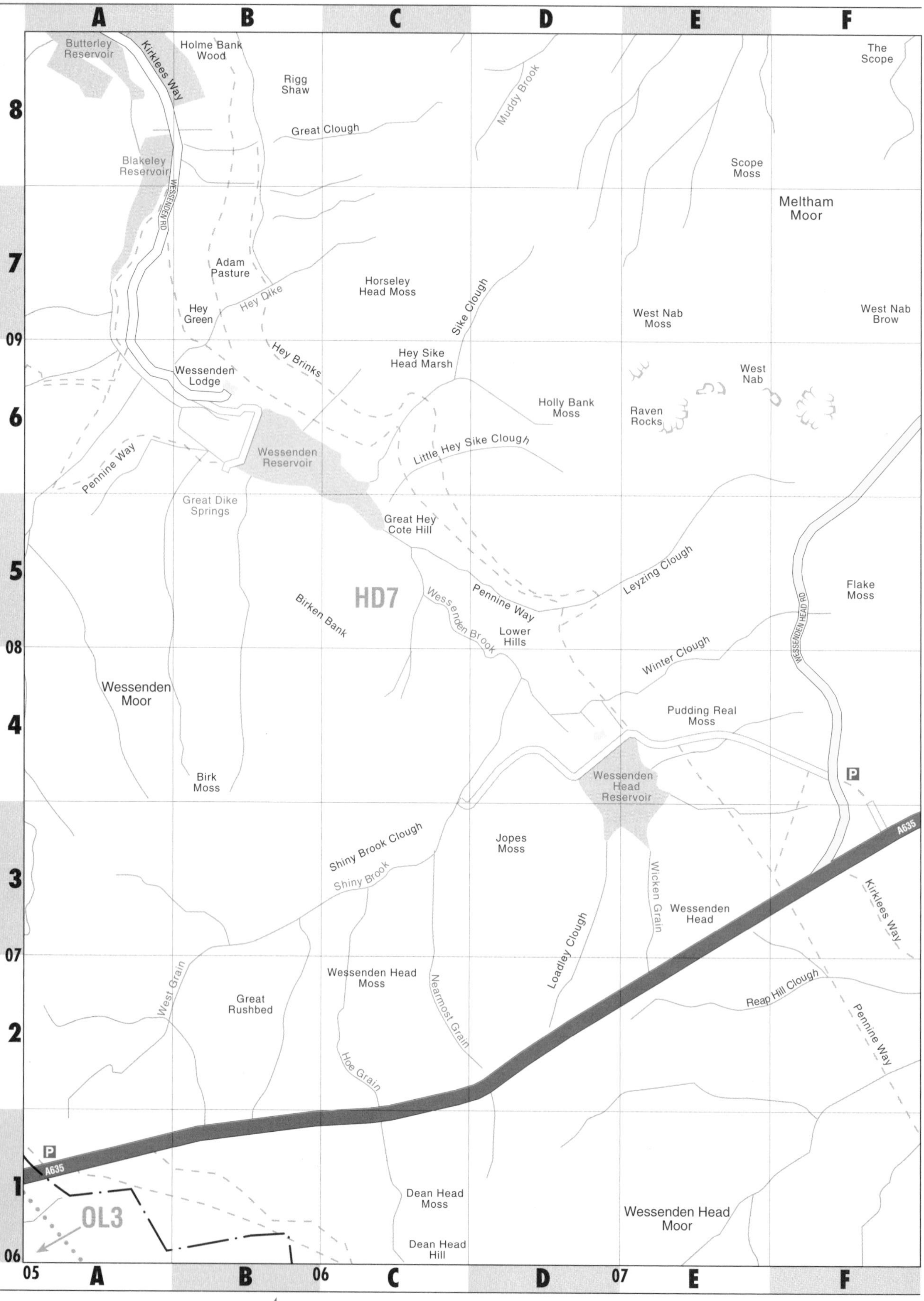
A
B
C
D
E
F
8
7
09
6
5
08
4
3
07
2
1
06
05
06
07
Butterley Reservoir
Kirklees Way
Holme Bank Wood
Rigg Shaw
Great Clough
Muddy Brook
The Scope
Blakeley Reservoir
WESSENDEN RD
Scope Moss
Meltham Moor
Adam Pasture
Horseley Head Moss
Sike Clough
Hey Dike
Hey Green
West Nab Moss
West Nab Brow
Hey Brinks
Hey Sike Head Marsh
Wessenden Lodge
West Nab
Holly Bank Moss
Raven Rocks
Little Hey Sike Clough
Pennine Way
Wessenden Reservoir
Great Dike Springs
Great Hey Cote Hill
Leyzing Clough
Flake Moss
HD7
Birken Bank
Wessenden Brook
Pennine Way
Lower Hills
WESSENDEN HEAD RD
Winter Clough
Wessenden Moor
Pudding Real Moss
Birk Moss
Wessenden Head Reservoir
P
Jopes Moss
A635
Shiny Brook Clough
Shiny Brook
Wicken Grain
Kirklees Way
Wessenden Head
Loadley Clough
Wessenden Head Moss
Nearmost Grain
West Grain
Great Rushbed
Reap Hill Clough
Pennine Way
Hoe Grain
P
A635
OL3
Dean Head Moss
Wessenden Head Moor
Dean Head Hill

185
196

170
188

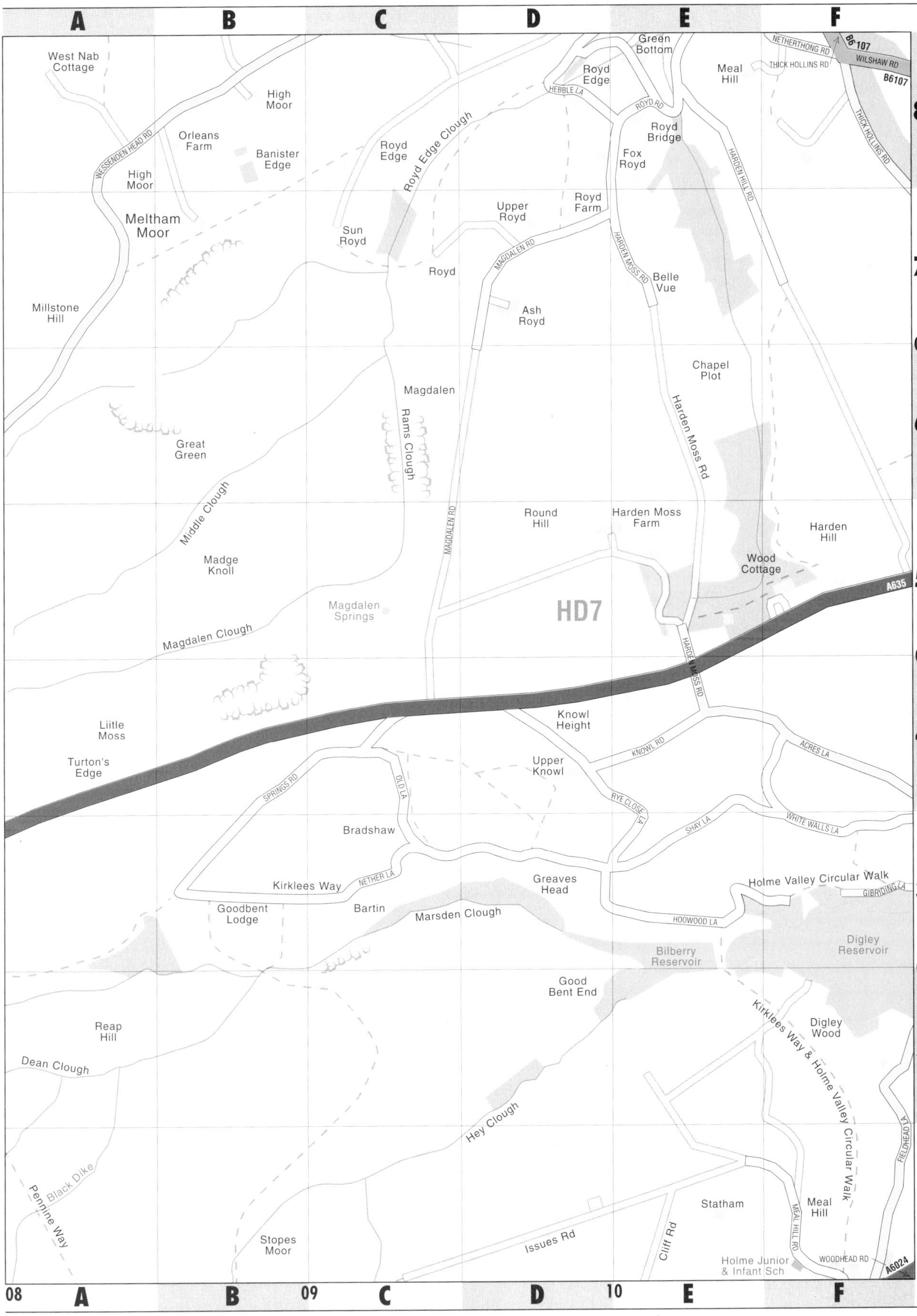
A
B
C
D
E
F
West Nab Cottage
Green Bottom
Royd Edge
Meal Hill
NETHERTHONG RD
B6107
WILSHAW RD
THICK HOLLINS RD
B6107
High Moor
HEBBLE LA
ROYD RD
8
Orleans Farm
Banister Edge
Royd Edge
Royd Edge Clough
Royd Bridge
Fox Royd
HARDEN HILL RD
THICK HOLLINS RD
WESSENDEN HEAD RD
High Moor
Meltham Moor
Upper Royd
Royd Farm
Sun Royd
MAGDALEN RD
HARDEN MOSS RD
Belle Vue
Royd
7
Millstone Hill
Ash Royd
09
Chapel Plot
Magdalen
Harden Moss Rd
Rams Clough
6
Great Green
Middle Clough
Round Hill
Harden Moss Farm
Harden Hill
MAGDALEN RD
Madge Knoll
Wood Cottage
5
A635
Magdalen Springs
HD7
Magdalen Clough
HARDEN MOSS RD
08
Knowl Height
Liitle Moss
4
Turton's Edge
KNOWL RD
ACRES LA
Upper Knowl
SPRINGS RD
OLD LA
RYE CLOSE LA
SHAY LA
WHITE WALLS LA
Bradshaw
Greaves Head
Holme Valley Circular Walk
Kirklees Way
NETHER LA
3
GIBRIDING LA
Goodbent Lodge
Bartin
Marsden Clough
HOOWOOD LA
Digley Reservoir
Bilberry Reservoir
07
Good Bent End
Kirklees Way & Holme Valley Circular Walk
Digley Wood
Reap Hill
2
Dean Clough
Hey Clough
FIELDHEAD LA
Black Dike
Pennine Way
1
Statham
Meal Hill
MEAL HILL RD
Cliff Rd
Stopes Moor
Issues Rd
WOODHEAD RD
Holme Junior & Infant Sch
A6024
06
08
A
B
09
C
D
10
E
F

197
188

187
171

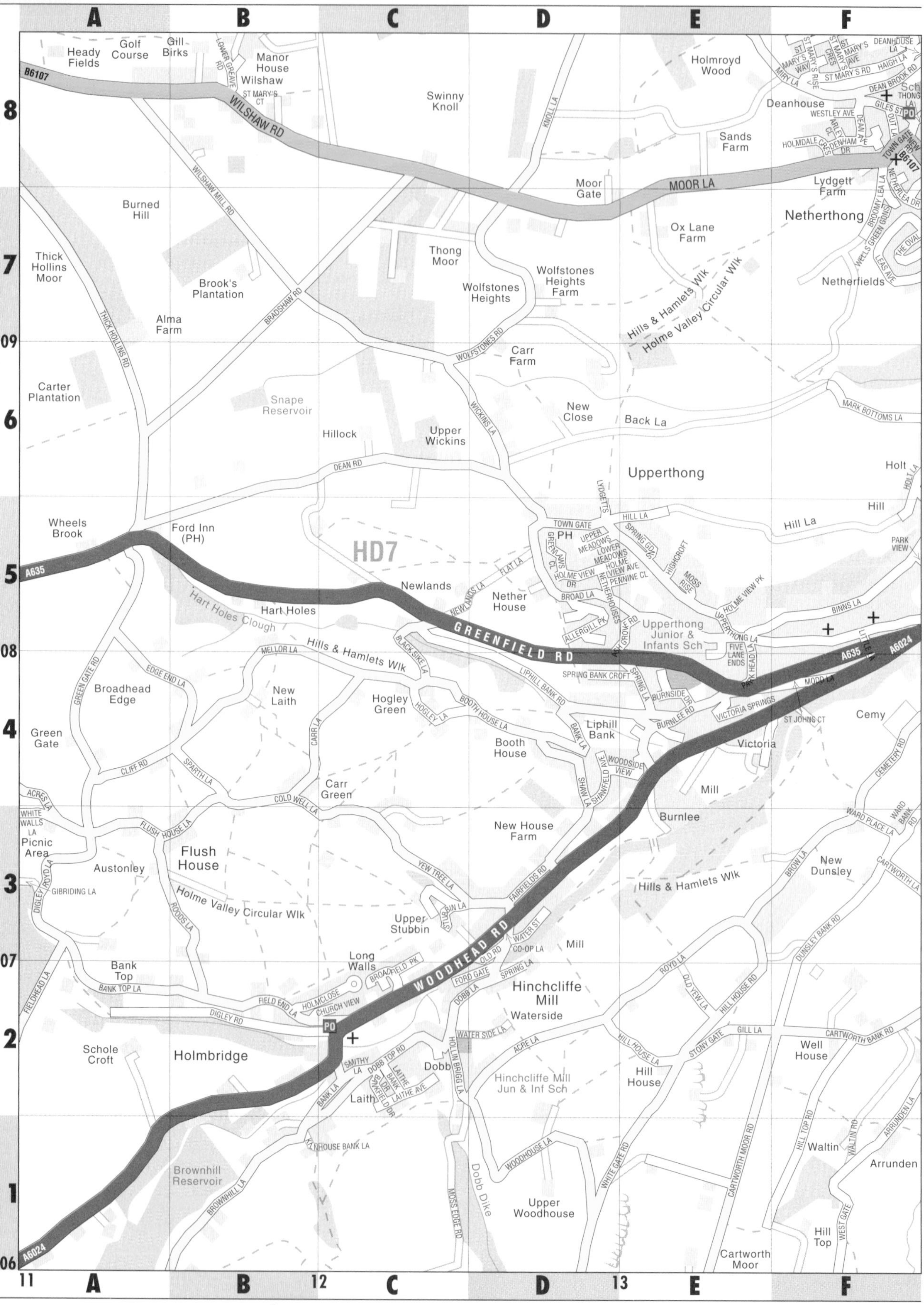
A
B
C
D
E
F
8
7
09
6
5
08
4
3
07
2
1
06
11
12
13
Heady Fields
Golf Course
Gill Birks
Manor House
Wilshaw
B6107
WILSHAW RD
Swinny Knoll
Holmroyd Wood
Deanhouse
Sands Farm
Moor Gate
MOOR LA
Lydgett Farm
Netherthong
Burned Hill
Thick Hollins Moor
Brook's Plantation
Alma Farm
Thong Moor
Wolfstones Heights
Wolfstones Heights Farm
Ox Lane Farm
Netherfields
Hills & Hamlets Wlk
Holme Valley Circular Wlk
Carr Farm
Carter Plantation
Snape Reservoir
New Close
Back La
Hillock
Upper Wickins
Upperthong
Holt
Hill
Hill La
Wheels Brook
Ford Inn (PH)
HD7
Newlands
Nether House
A635
Hart Holes
Hart Holes Clough
GREENFIELD RD
Upperthong Junior & Infants Sch
Broadhead Edge
New Laith
Hogley Green
Liphill Bank
Booth House
Victoria
Cemy
Green Gate
Carr Green
Mill
Burnlee
New House Farm
Picnic Area
Austonley
Flush House
Holme Valley Circular Wlk
Upper Stubbin
New Dunsley
Bank Top
Long Walls
WOODHEAD RD
Hinchcliffe Mill
Waterside
Well House
Schole Croft
Holmbridge
Dobb
Laith
Hinchcliffe Mill Jun & Inf Sch
Hill House
Brownhill Reservoir
Dobb Dike
Upper Woodhouse
Waltin
Arrunden
Hill Top
Cartworth Moor
A6024

172
190

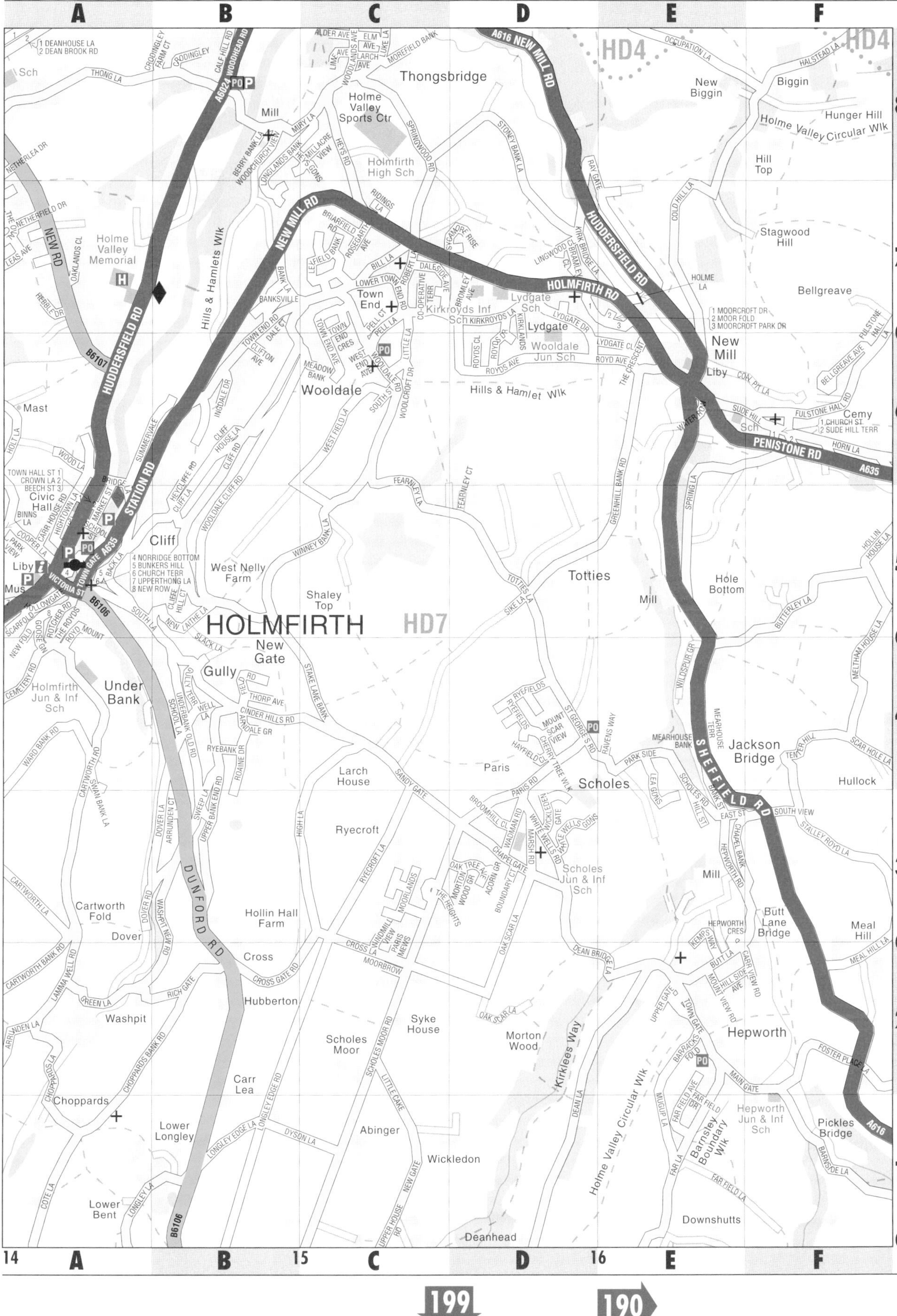

199
190

189
173

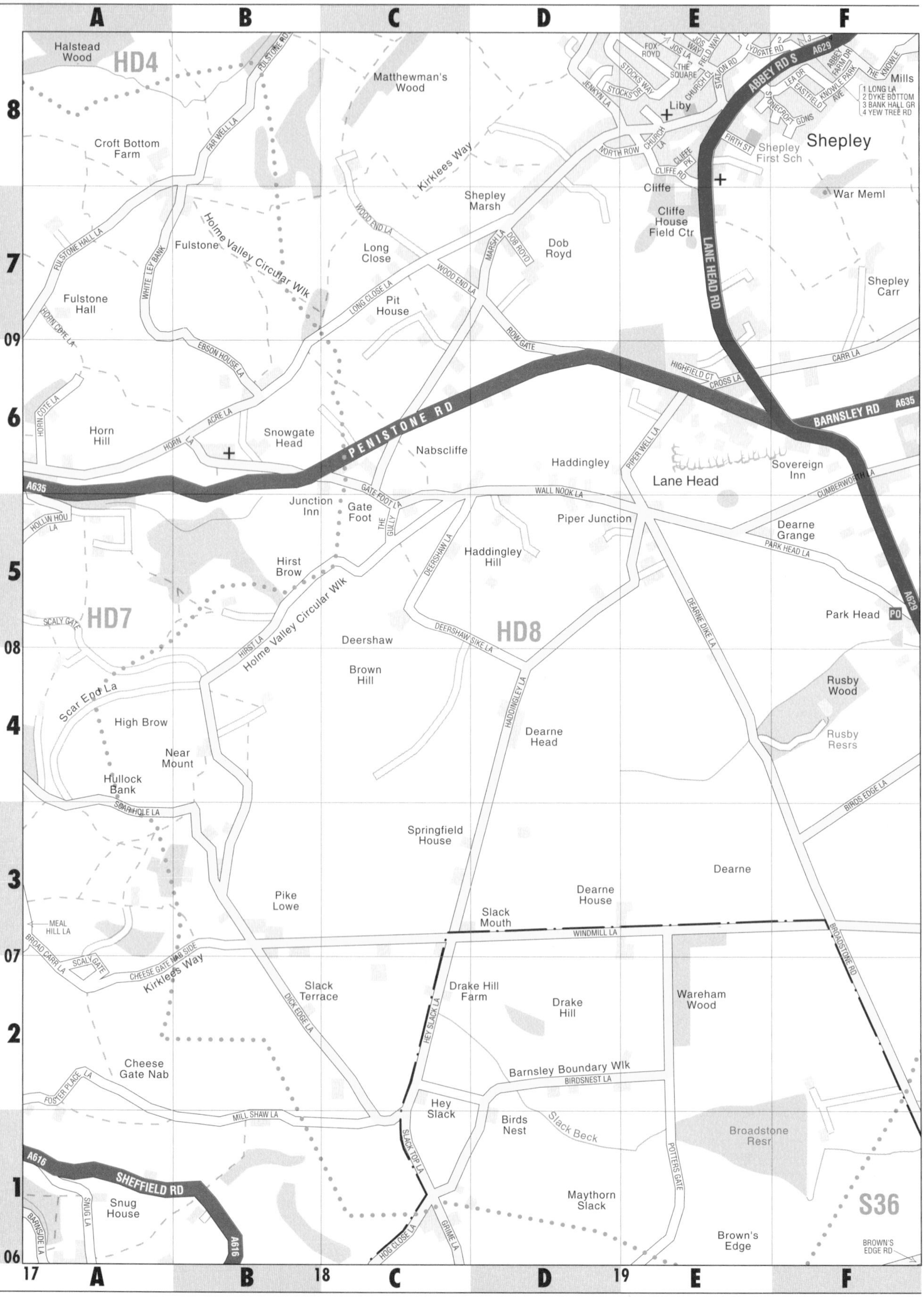
A
B
C
D
E
F
8
7
09
6
5
08
4
3
07
2
1
06
17
18
19
Halstead Wood
HD4
FULSTONE RD
Matthewman's Wood
FOX ROYD
JOS LA
JOS WAY
FIELD WAY
THE SQUARE
STOCKS WAY
STOCKS DR
JENKYN LA
CHURCH CL
STATION RD
LYDGATE RD
ABBEY RD S
A629
ABBEY FARM DR
THE KNOWLE
Mills
LEA DR
EASTFIELD
KNOWLE PARK AVE
STONECROFT GDNS
1 LONG LA
2 DYKE BOTTOM
3 BANK HALL GR
4 YEW TREE RD
Liby
Shepley
FIRTH ST
Shepley First Sch
NORTH ROW
CHURCH LA
CLIFFE PK
CLIFFE RD
Cliffe
War Meml
Croft Bottom Farm
FAR WELL LA
Kirklees Way
Shepley Marsh
Cliffe House Field Ctr
WOOD END LA
MARSH LA
DOB ROYD
Dob Royd
LANE HEAD RD
Fulstone
Holme Valley Circular Wlk
Long Close
FULSTONE HALL LA
WHITE LEY BANK
Fulstone Hall
Pit House
LONG CLOSE LA
Shepley Carr
HORN COTE LA
EBSON HOUSE LA
ROW GATE
CARR LA
HIGHFIELD CT
CROSS LA
HORN COTE LA
ACRE LA
PENISTONE RD
BARNSLEY RD
A635
Horn Hill
Snowgate Head
Nabscliffe
HORN LA
PIPER WELL LA
Haddingley
Sovereign Inn
Lane Head
A635
GATE FOOT LA
WALL NOOK LA
CUMBERWORTH LA
Junction Inn
Gate Foot
THE GULLY
Piper Junction
Dearne Grange
HOLLIN HOU LA
PARK HEAD LA
DEERSHAW LA
Haddingley Hill
Hirst Brow
SCALY GATE
HD7
DEARNE DIKE LA
Park Head
PO
A629
Holme Valley Circular Wlk
HD8
DEERSHAW SIKE LA
Deershaw
HIRST LA
Brown Hill
Rusby Wood
Scar End La
HADDINGLEY LA
High Brow
Dearne Head
Rusby Resrs
Near Mount
Hullock Bank
BIRDS EDGE LA
SCAR HOLE LA
Springfield House
Dearne
Pike Lowe
Dearne House
MEAL HILL LA
Slack Mouth
WINDMILL LA
BROADSTONE RD
BROAD CARR LA
SCALY GATE
CHEESE GATE NAB SIDE
Kirklees Way
Slack Terrace
Drake Hill Farm
Wareham Wood
DICK EDGE LA
HEY SLACK LA
Drake Hill
Cheese Gate Nab
Barnsley Boundary Wlk
BIRDSNEST LA
FOSTER PLACE LA
Hey Slack
MILL SHAW LA
Birds Nest
Slack Beck
Broadstone Resr
SLACK TOP LA
POTTERS GATE
A616
SHEFFIELD RD
Snug House
SNUG LA
Maythorn Slack
S36
BARNSIDE LA
A616
HOG CLOSE LA
GRIME LA
Brown's Edge
BROWN'S EDGE RD

189
200

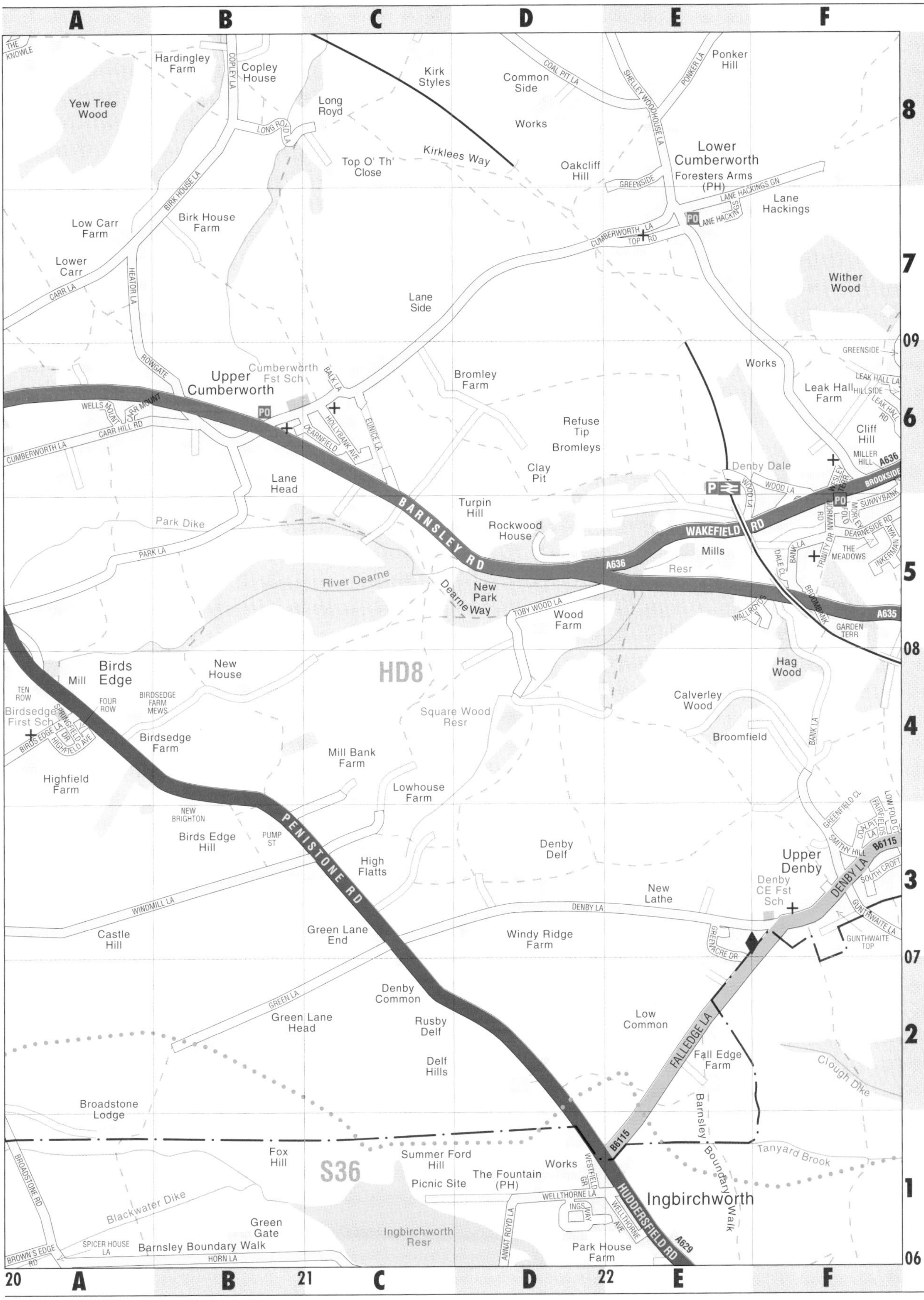
A
B
C
D
E
F
Hardingley Farm
Copley House
Yew Tree Wood
Long Royd
Kirk Styles
Common Side
Works
Ponker Hill
Top O' Th' Close
Kirklees Way
Oakcliff Hill
Lower Cumberworth
Foresters Arms (PH)
Lane Hackings
Low Carr Farm
Birk House Farm
Lower Carr
Lane Side
Wither Wood
Upper Cumberworth
Cumberworth Fst Sch
Bromley Farm
Works
Leak Hall Farm
Refuse Tip
Bromleys
Cliff Hill
Clay Pit
Denby Dale
Lane Head
Turpin Hill
Rockwood House
Park Dike
Mills
River Dearne
Resr
New Park
Dearne Way
Wood Farm
Birds Edge
Mill
New House
HD8
Hag Wood
Calverley Wood
Birdsedge First Sch
Square Wood Resr
Birdsedge Farm
Broomfield
Mill Bank Farm
Highfield Farm
Lowhouse Farm
Birds Edge Hill
Denby Delf
Upper Denby
High Flatts
Denby CE Fst Sch
New Lathe
Castle Hill
Green Lane End
Windy Ridge Farm
Denby Common
Low Common
Green Lane Head
Rusby Delf
Fall Edge Farm
Delf Hills
Clough Dike
Broadstone Lodge
Barnsley Boundary Walk
Tanyard Brook
Fox Hill
Summer Ford Hill
S36
Works
The Fountain (PH)
Picnic Site
Ingbirchworth
Blackwater Dike
Green Gate
Ingbirchworth Resr
Barnsley Boundary Walk
Park House Farm
BARNSLEY RD
WAKEFIELD RD
PENISTONE RD
HUDDERSFIELD RD
FALLEDGE LA
DENBY LA
WINDMILL LA
GREEN LA
CUMBERWORTH LA
CARR HILL RD
CARR LA
PARK LA
HEATOR LA
BIRK HOUSE LA
COPLEY LA
LONG ROYD LA
COAL PIT LA
SHELLEY WOODHOUSE LA
PONKER LA
TOBY WOOD LA
BANK LA
BROADSTONE RD
HORN LA
A636
A635
A629
B6115
8
7
6
5
4
3
2
1
09
08
07
06
20
21
22

191
175

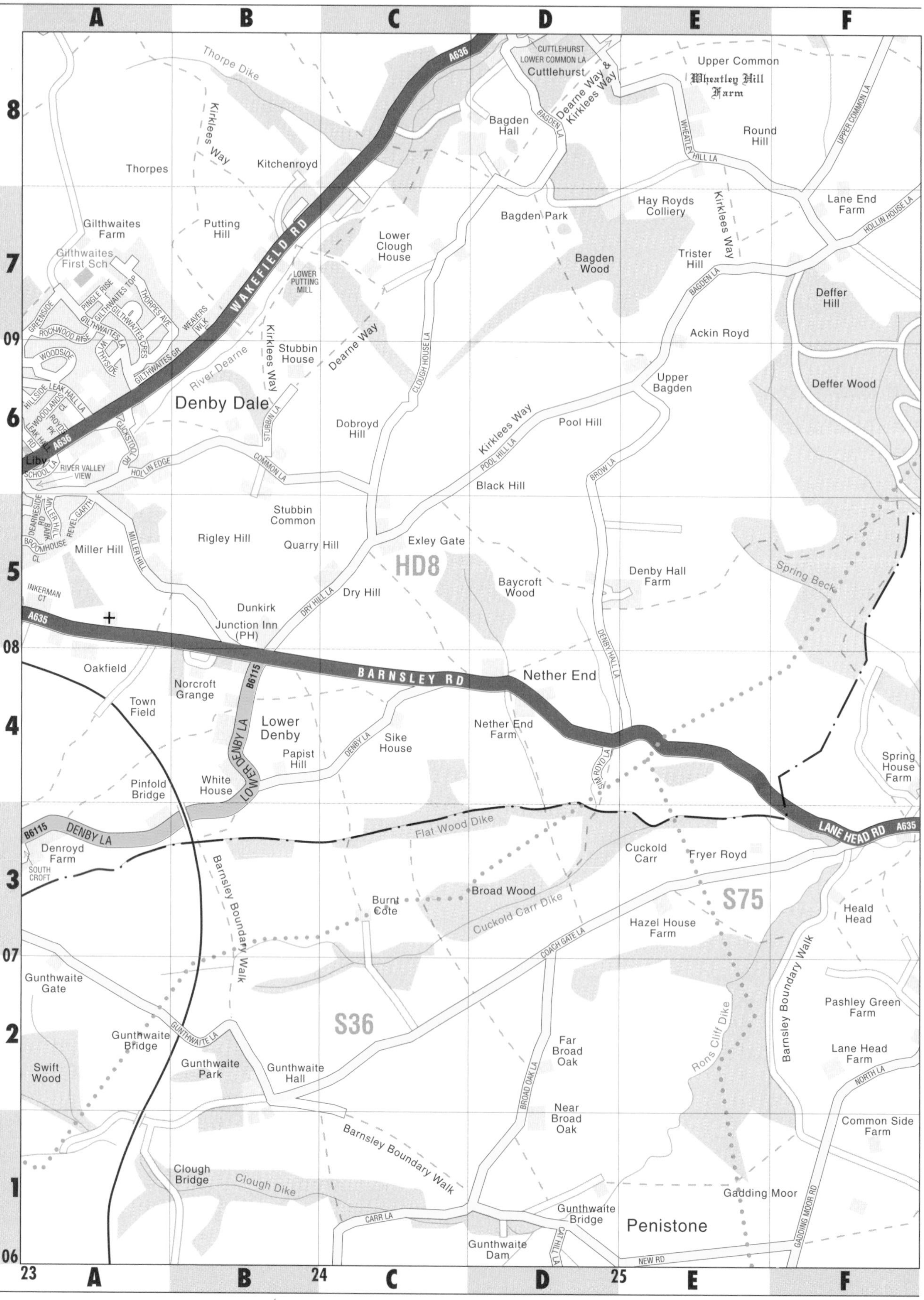
A
B
C
D
E
F
8
7
09
6
5
08
4
3
07
2
1
06
23
24
25
Thorpe Dike
Kirklees Way
Thorpes
Kitchenroyd
A636
WAKEFIELD RD
CUTTLEHURST
LOWER COMMON LA
Cuttlehurst
Dearne Way & Kirklees Way
BAGDEN LA
Bagden Hall
Upper Common
Wheatley Hill Farm
WHEATLEY HILL LA
Round Hill
UPPER COMMON LA
Giltwaites Farm
Putting Hill
Lower Clough House
Bagden Park
Hay Royds Colliery
Lane End Farm
HOLLIN HOUSE LA
Gilthwaites First Sch
LOWER PUTTING MILL
Bagden Wood
Trister Hill
Deffer Hill
GREENSIDE
PINGLE RISE
GILTHWAITES TOP
THORPES AVE
GILTHWAITES LA
GILTHWAITES CRES
ROCKWOOD RISE
WEAVERS WLK
Stubbin House
Dearne Way
Ackin Royd
WOODSIDE
WYTHSIDE
GILTHWAITES GR
River Dearne
CLOUGH HOUSE LA
Upper Bagden
Deffer Wood
HILLSIDE
LEAK HALL CL
WOODLANDS CL
ROYDS PK
LEAK HALL RD
Denby Dale
STUBBIN LA
Dobroyd Hill
Kirklees Way
Pool Hill
POOL HILL LA
CUCKSTOOL RD
Liby
SCHOOL LA
RIVER VALLEY VIEW
HOLLIN EDGE
COMMON LA
BROW LA
Black Hill
DEARNESIDE RD
MILLER HILL BANK
REVEL GARTH
Stubbin Common
Rigley Hill
Quarry Hill
Exley Gate
BROOMHOUSE CL
Miller Hill
MILLER HILL
HD8
Denby Hall Farm
Spring Beck
INKERMAN CT
Dry Hill
DRY HILL LA
Baycroft Wood
Dunkirk
A635
Junction Inn (PH)
DENBY HALL LA
Oakfield
B6115
BARNSLEY RD
Nether End
Norcroft Grange
Town Field
Lower Denby
Nether End Farm
LOWER DENBY LA
Sike House
DENBY LA
Papist Hill
SIM ROYD LA
Spring House Farm
Pinfold Bridge
White House
Flat Wood Dike
B6115
DENBY LA
LANE HEAD RD
A635
Denroyd Farm
SOUTH CROFT
Cuckold Carr
Fryer Royd
Barnsley Boundary Walk
Broad Wood
S75
Burnt Cote
Cuckold Carr Dike
Heald Head
Hazel House Farm
COACH GATE LA
Gunthwaite Gate
S36
Pashley Green Farm
Rons Cliff Dike
Barnsley Boundary Walk
Gunthwaite Bridge
GUNTHWAITE LA
Far Broad Oak
Lane Head Farm
Swift Wood
Gunthwaite Park
Gunthwaite Hall
BROAD OAK LA
NORTH LA
Near Broad Oak
Common Side Farm
Barnsley Boundary Walk
Clough Bridge
Clough Dike
Gadding Moor
GADDING MOOR RD
CARR LA
Gunthwaite Bridge
Penistone
Gunthwaite Dam
CAT HILL LA
NEW RD

191

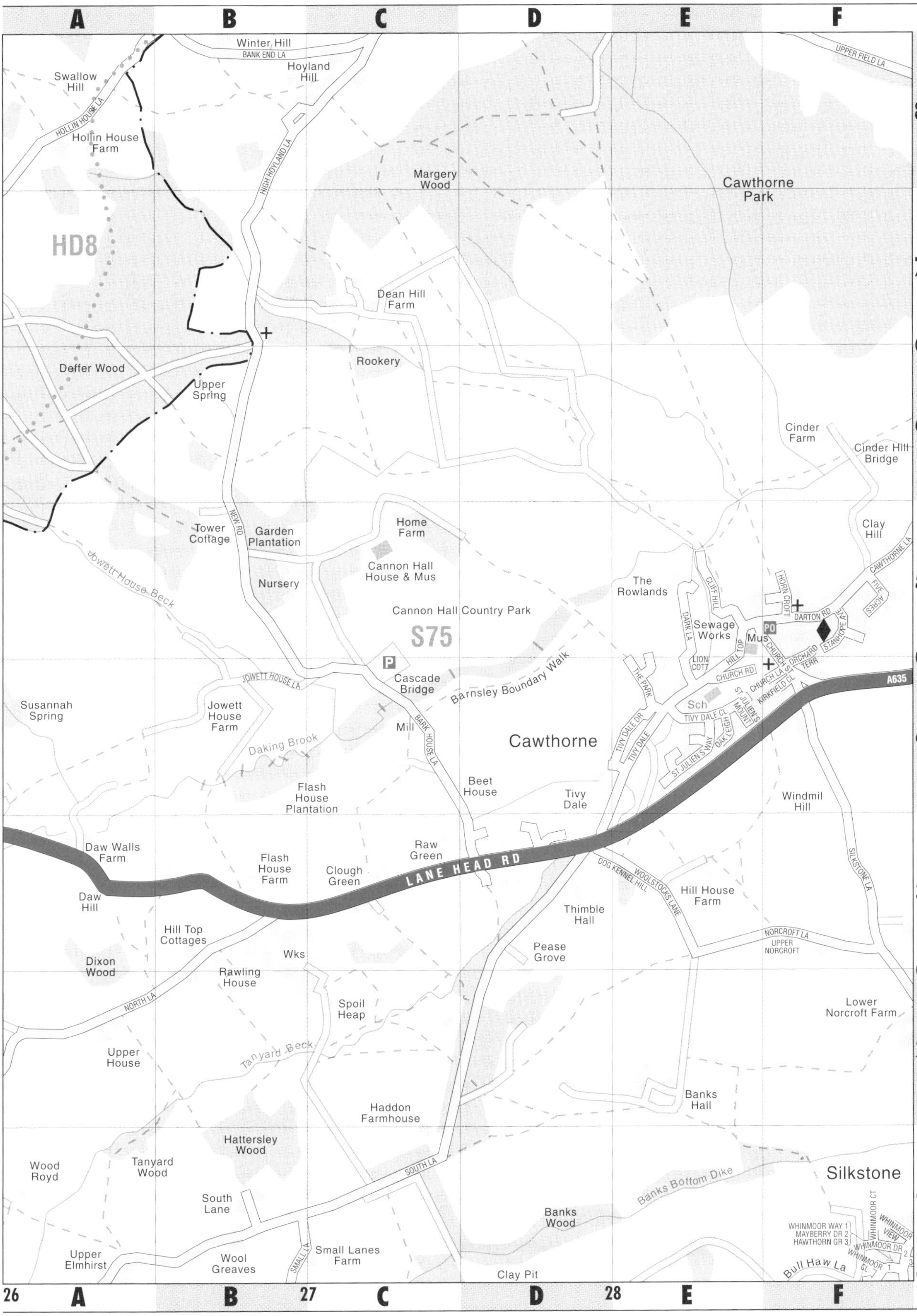
A
B
C
D
E
F
Winter Hill
BANK END LA
Hoyland Hill
Swallow Hill
HOLLIN HOUSE LA
Hollin House Farm
HIGH HOYLAND LA
UPPER FIELD LA
Margery Wood
Cawthorne Park
HD8
Dean Hill Farm
Deffer Wood
Upper Spring
Rookery
Cinder Farm
Cinder Hill Bridge
Tower Cottage
NEW RD
Garden Plantation
Home Farm
Clay Hill
Jowett House Beck
Nursery
Cannon Hall House & Mus
The Rowlands
CLIFF HILL
HORN CROFT
CAWTHORNE LA
FIVE ACRES
Cannon Hall Country Park
DARK LA
Sewage Works
DARTON RD
STANHOPE AVE
S75
PO
Mus
CHURCH ST
ORCHARD TERR
LION COTT
HILL TOP
CHURCH RD
CHURCH LA
KIRKFIELD CL
THE PARK
Cascade Bridge
JOWETT HOUSE LA
Barnsley Boundary Walk
A635
Susannah Spring
Jowett House Farm
Sch
TIVY DALE CL
ST JULIEN'S MOUNT
HIGH
OAK LEIGH
Daking Brook
Mill
BARK HOUSE LA
TIVY DALE DR
TIVY DALE
Cawthorne
ST JULIEN'S WAY
Flash House Plantation
Beet House
Tivy Dale
Windmil Hill
Daw Walls Farm
Raw Green
LANE HEAD RD
Flash House Farm
Clough Green
DOG KENNEL HILL
WOOLSTOCKS LANE
Hill House Farm
SILKSTONE LA
Daw Hill
Thimble Hall
Hill Top Cottages
Pease Grove
NORCROFT LA
UPPER NORCROFT
Dixon Wood
Wks
Rawling House
NORTH LA
Spoil Heap
Lower Norcroft Farm
Upper House
Tanyard Beck
Haddon Farmhouse
Banks Hall
Hattersley Wood
Wood Royd
Tanyard Wood
SOUTH LA
Silkstone
Banks Bottom Dike
South Lane
Banks Wood
WHINMOOR CT
WHINMOOR VIEW
WHINMOOR WAY 1
MAYBERRY DR 2
HAWTHORN GR 3
WHINMOOR DR
WHINMOOR CL
Upper Elmhirst
Wool Greaves
SMALL LA
Small Lanes Farm
Clay Pit
Bull Haw La
8
7
09
6
5
08
4
3
07
2
1
06
26
27
28

182

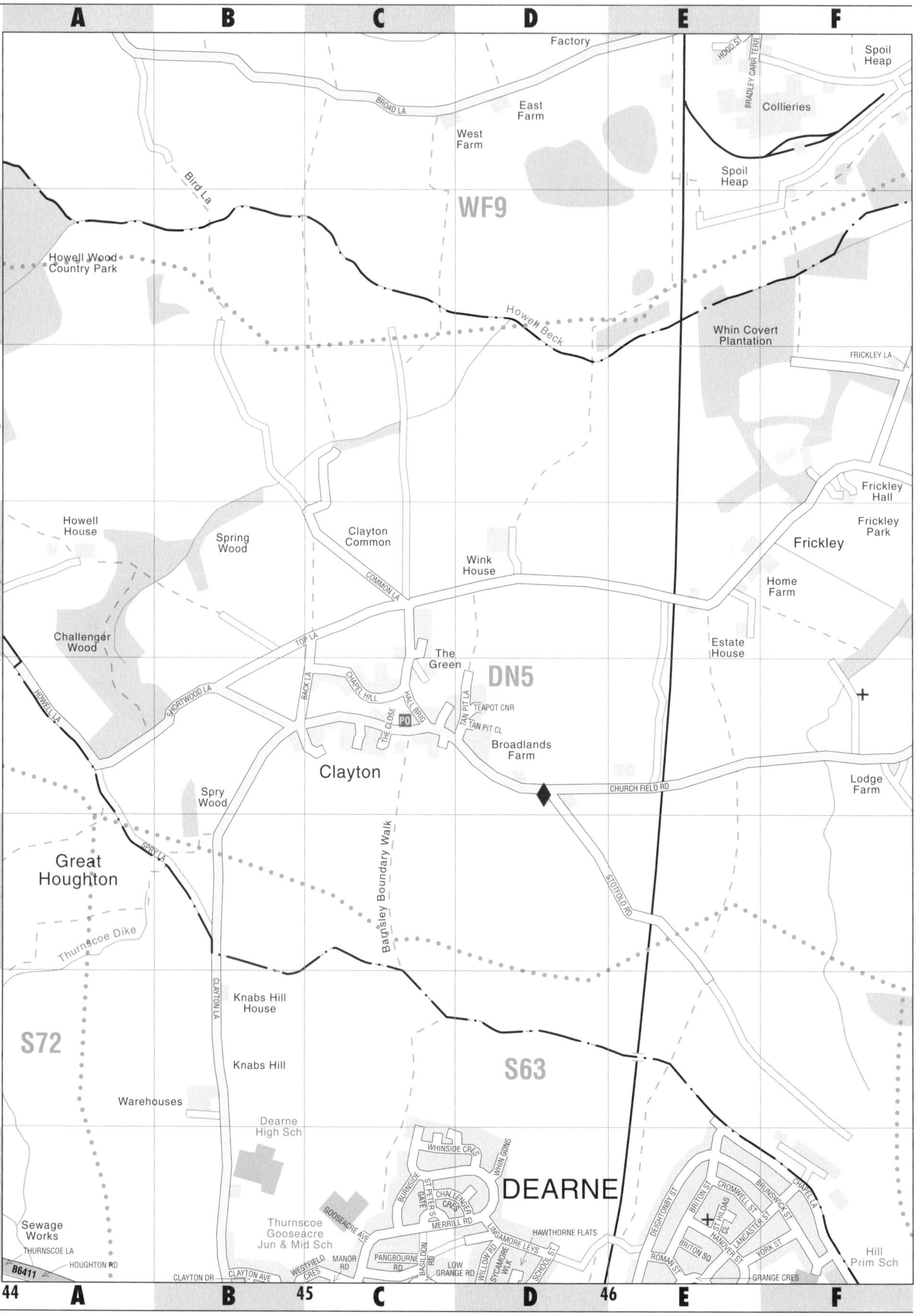
A
B
C
D
E
F
8
7
09
6
5
08
4
3
07
2
1
06
44
45
46
Factory
Spoil Heap
HOOD ST
BRADLEY CARR TERR
Collieries
BROAD LA
East Farm
West Farm
Spoil Heap
Bird La
WF9
Howell Wood Country Park
Howell Beck
Whin Covert Plantation
FRICKLEY LA
Frickley Hall
Howell House
Spring Wood
Clayton Common
Frickley Park
Frickley
Wink House
COMMON LA
Home Farm
Challenger Wood
TOP LA
Estate House
The Green
DN5
BACK LA
CHAPEL HILL
HALL BRIG
TAN PIT LA
TEAPOT CNR
TAN PIT CL
HOWELL LA
SHORTWOOD LA
THE CLOSE
PO
Broadlands Farm
Clayton
Spry Wood
CHURCH FIELD RD
Lodge Farm
Great Houghton
SPRY LA
Barnsley Boundary Walk
STOTFOLD RD
Thurnscoe Dike
CLAYTON LA
Knabs Hill House
S72
Knabs Hill
S63
Warehouses
Dearne High Sch
WHINSIDE CRES
WHIN GDNS
BURNSIDE
ST PETER S
GATE
CHALLENGER CRES
DEARNE
DEIGHTONBY ST
BRITON ST
CROMWELL ST
BRUNSWICK ST
CHAPEL LA
GOOSEACRE AVE
MERRILL RD
LINGAMORE LEYS
ST HILDAS CL
LANCASTER ST
Sewage Works
Thurnscoe Gooseacre Jun & Mid Sch
HAWTHORNE FLATS
HANOVER ST
BRITON SQ
THURNSCOE LA
B6411
HOUGHTON RD
WESTFIELD CRES
MANOR RD
PANGBOURNE RD
BASILDON RD
LOW GRANGE RD
WILLOW RD
SYCAMORE WLK
SCHOOL ST
ROMAN ST
YORK ST
Hill Prim Sch
CLAYTON DR
CLAYTON AVE
GRANGE CRES

183

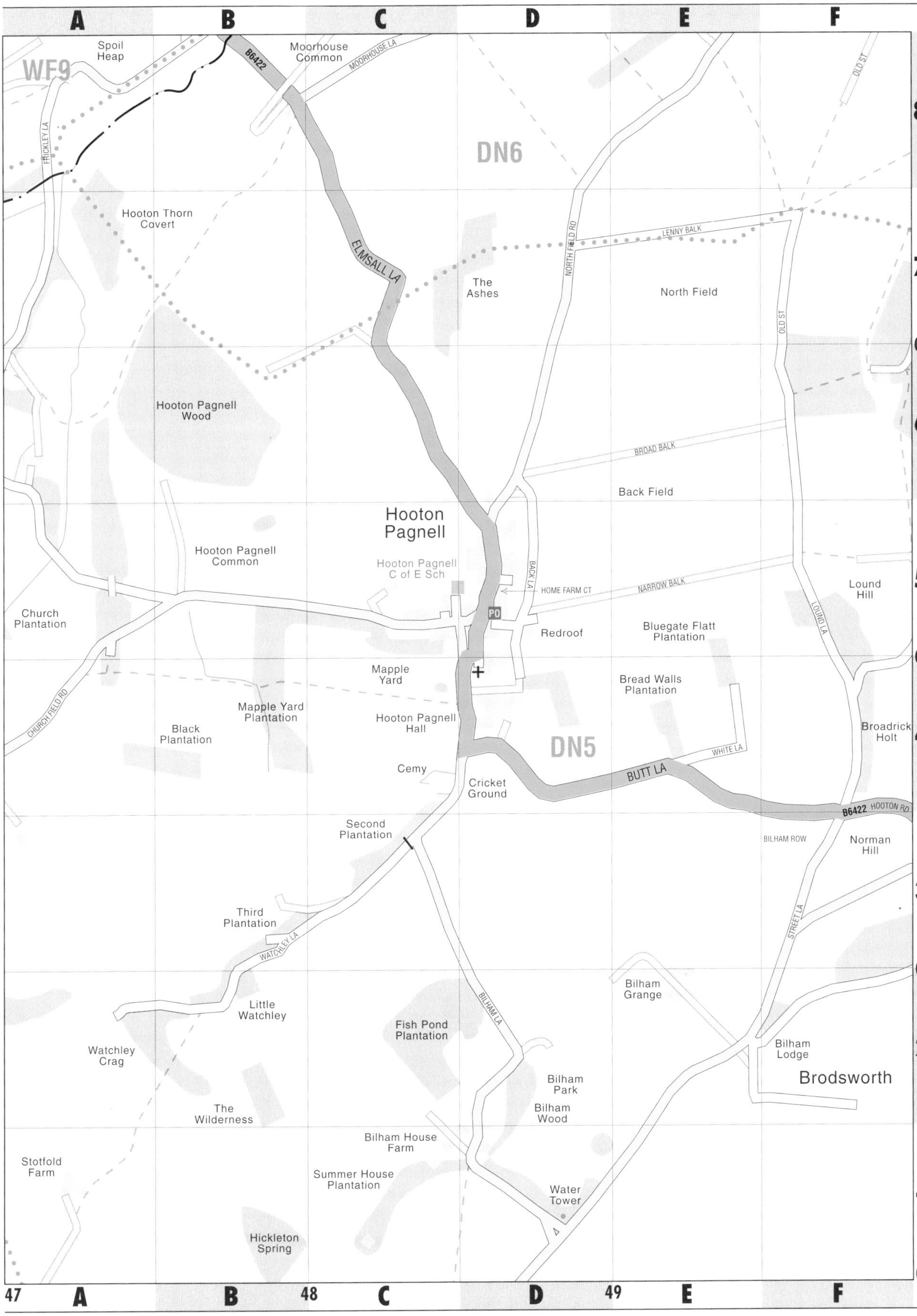
A
B
C
D
E
F
Spoil Heap
WF9
B6422
Moorhouse Common
MOORHOUSE LA
OLD ST
8
FRICKLEY LA
DN6
Hooton Thorn Covert
ELMSALL LA
NORTH FIELD RD
LENNY BALK
7
The Ashes
North Field
OLD ST
09
Hooton Pagnell Wood
6
BROAD BALK
Back Field
Hooton Pagnell
Hooton Pagnell Common
Hooton Pagnell C of E Sch
BACK LA
5
HOME FARM CT
NARROW BALK
Lound Hill
Church Plantation
PO
LOUND LA
Redroof
Bluegate Flatt Plantation
08
Mapple Yard
Bread Walls Plantation
Mapple Yard Plantation
Black Plantation
Hooton Pagnell Hall
DN5
Broadrick Holt
4
CHURCH FIELD RD
WHITE LA
Cemy
BUTT LA
Cricket Ground
B6422
HOOTON RD
Second Plantation
BILHAM ROW
Norman Hill
3
Third Plantation
STREET LA
WATCHLEY LA
07
Bilham Grange
Little Watchley
BILHAM LA
Fish Pond Plantation
Watchley Crag
Bilham Lodge
2
Brodsworth
Bilham Park
The Wilderness
Bilham Wood
Bilham House Farm
Stotfold Farm
Summer House Plantation
Water Tower
1
Hickleton Spring
06
47
A
B
48
C
D
49
E
F

186

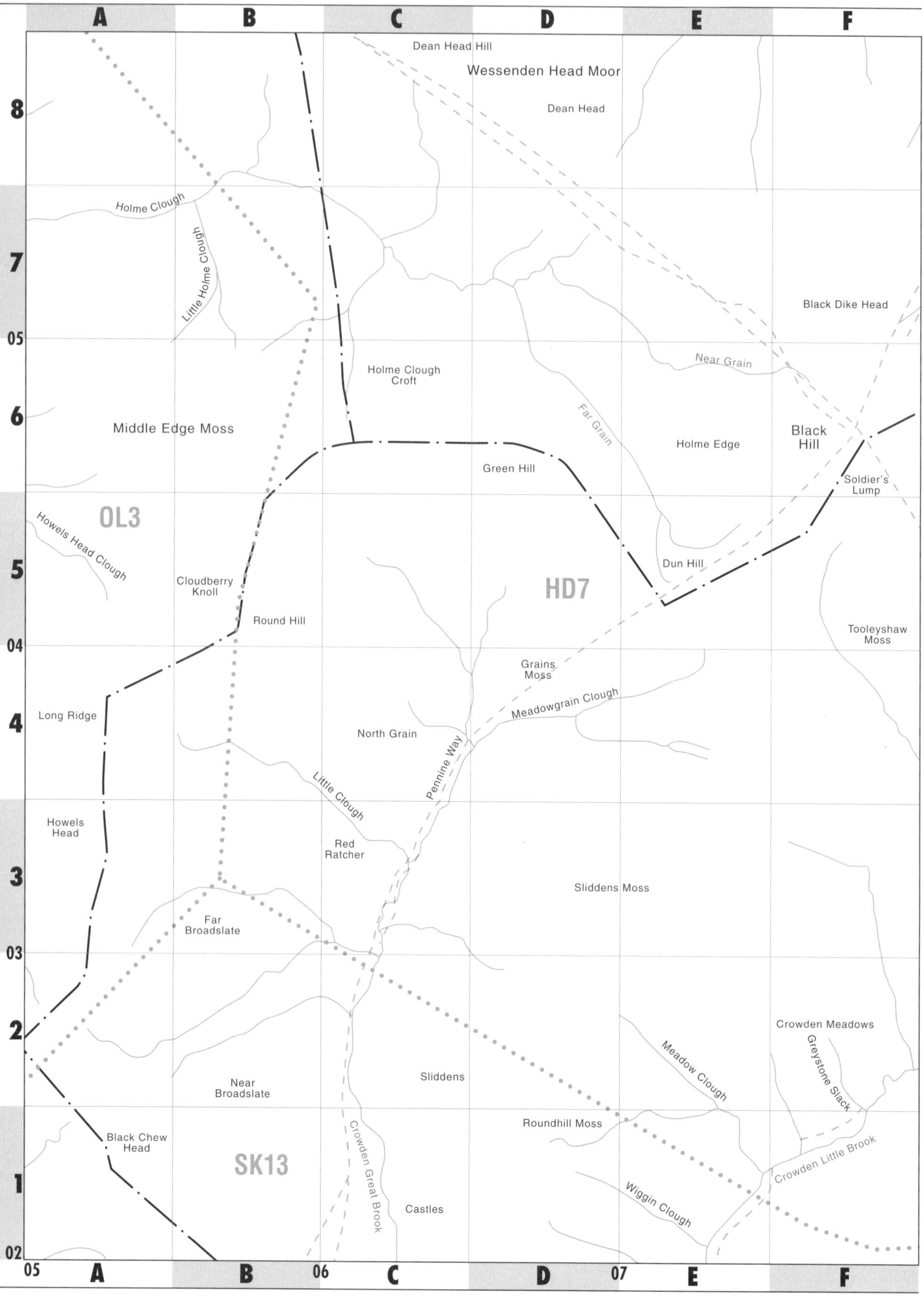
A
B
C
D
E
F
8
7
05
6
5
04
4
3
03
2
1
02
05
06
07
Dean Head Hill
Wessenden Head Moor
Dean Head
Holme Clough
Little Holme Clough
Black Dike Head
Near Grain
Holme Clough Croft
Far Grain
Middle Edge Moss
Holme Edge
Black Hill
Green Hill
Soldier's Lump
OL3
Howels Head Clough
Dun Hill
Cloudberry Knoll
HD7
Round Hill
Tooleyshaw Moss
Grains Moss
Meadowgrain Clough
Long Ridge
North Grain
Pennine Way
Little Clough
Howels Head
Red Ratcher
Sliddens Moss
Far Broadslate
Crowden Meadows
Meadow Clough
Greystone Slack
Near Broadslate
Sliddens
Roundhill Moss
Black Chew Head
Crowden Little Brook
SK13
Crowden Great Brook
Wiggin Clough
Castles

187
198

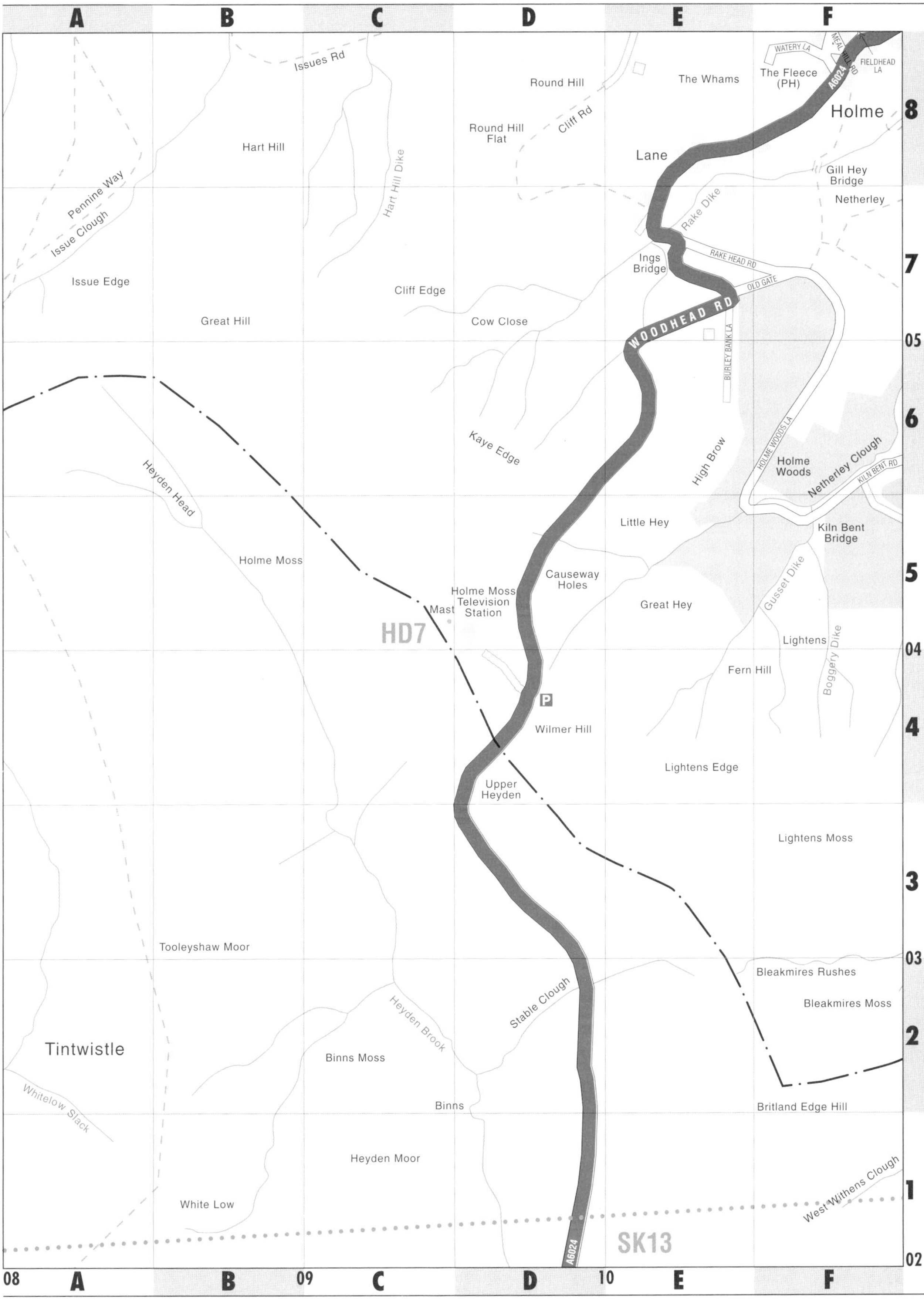
A
B
C
D
E
F
Issues Rd
Round Hill
The Whams
WATERY LA
MEAL HILL RD
FIELDHEAD LA
The Fleece (PH)
A6024
Holme
Cliff Rd
Round Hill Flat
Hart Hill
Hart Hill Dike
Lane
Gill Hey Bridge
Netherley
Pennine Way
Issue Clough
Rake Dike
RAKE HEAD RD
Ings Bridge
Issue Edge
Cliff Edge
OLD GATE
WOODHEAD RD
Great Hill
Cow Close
BURLEY BANK LA
Kaye Edge
HOLME WOODS LA
High Brow
Holme Woods
Netherley Clough
KILN BENT RD
Heyden Head
Little Hey
Kiln Bent Bridge
Holme Moss
Causeway Holes
Gusset Dike
Holme Moss Television Station
Mast
Great Hey
HD7
Lightens
Boggery Dike
Fern Hill
P
Wilmer Hill
Lightens Edge
Upper Heyden
Lightens Moss
Tooleyshaw Moor
Bleakmires Rushes
Bleakmires Moss
Stable Clough
Heyden Brook
Tintwistle
Binns Moss
Whitelow Slack
Binns
Britland Edge Hill
Heyden Moor
West Withens Clough
White Low
SK13
8
7
05
6
5
04
4
3
03
2
1
02
08
09
10

198

197
188

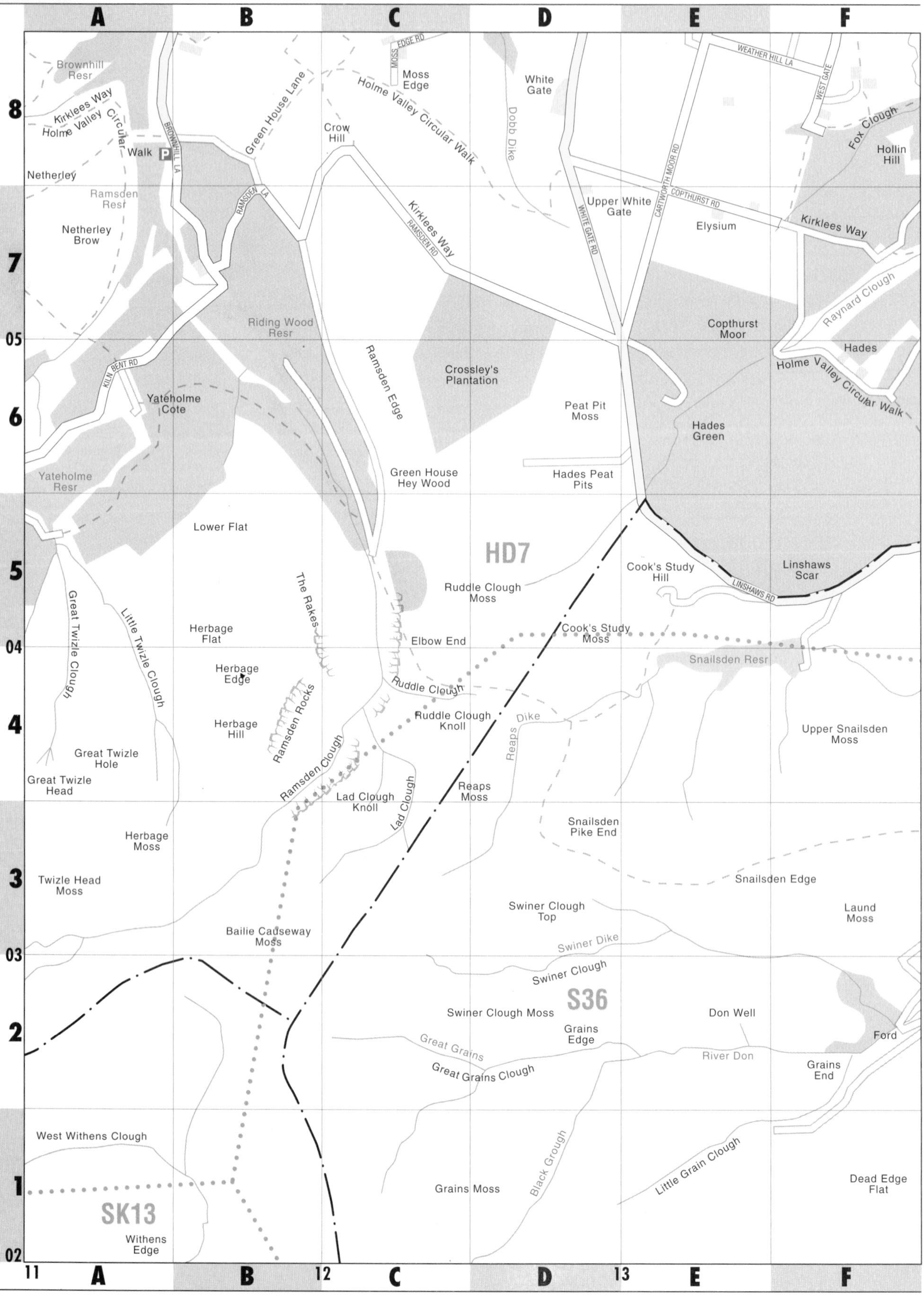
A
B
C
D
E
F
8
7
05
6
5
04
4
3
03
2
1
02
11
12
13
Brownhill Resr
Kirklees Way
Holme Valley Circular Walk
Netherley
Ramsden Resr
Netherley Brow
BROWNHILL LA
Green House Lane
RAMSDEN LA
MOSS EDGE RD
Moss Edge
Crow Hill
Holme Valley Circular Walk
Dobb Dike
White Gate
WEATHER HILL LA
WEST GATE
Fox Clough
Hollin Hill
Kirklees Way
RAMSDEN RD
WHITE GATE RD
Upper White Gate
CARTWORTH MOOR RD
COPTHURST RD
Elysium
Kirklees Way
Raynard Clough
Copthurst Moor
Hades
Holme Valley Circular Walk
Riding Wood Resr
KILN BENT RD
Yateholme Cote
Ramsden Edge
Crossley's Plantation
Peat Pit Moss
Hades Green
Yateholme Resr
Green House Hey Wood
Hades Peat Pits
Lower Flat
HD7
Cook's Study Hill
Linshaws Scar
LINSHAWS RD
Great Twizle Clough
Little Twizle Clough
The Rakes
Ruddle Clough Moss
Herbage Flat
Elbow End
Cook's Study Moss
Snailsden Resr
Herbage Edge
Ruddle Clough
Ramsden Rocks
Ruddle Clough Knoll
Reaps Dike
Herbage Hill
Upper Snailsden Moss
Great Twizle Hole
Great Twizle Head
Ramsden Clough
Lad Clough Knoll
Lad Clough
Reaps Moss
Snailsden Pike End
Herbage Moss
Twizle Head Moss
Snailsden Edge
Swiner Clough Top
Laund Moss
Bailie Causeway Moss
Swiner Dike
Swiner Clough
S36
Swiner Clough Moss
Grains Edge
Don Well
Ford
Great Grains
River Don
Great Grains Clough
Grains End
West Withens Clough
Black Grough
Little Grain Clough
Dead Edge Flat
Grains Moss
SK13
Withens Edge

197

189
200

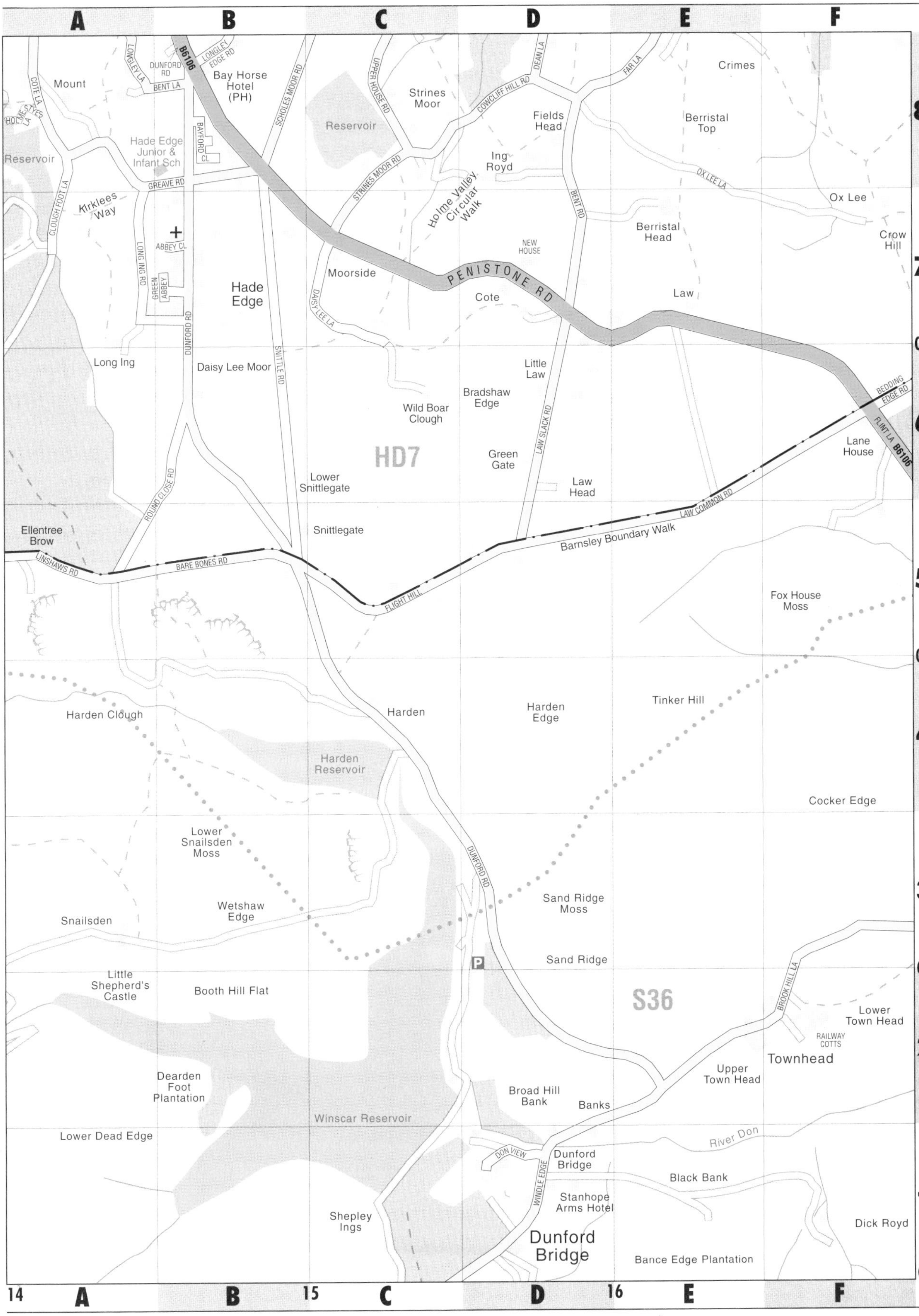
A
B
C
D
E
F
8
7
05
6
5
04
4
3
03
2
1
02
14
15
16
Mount
COTE LA
HOLMES LA
LONGLEY LA
DUNFORD RD
BENT LA
LONGLEY EDGE RD
B6106
Bay Horse Hotel (PH)
SCHOLES MOOR RD
UPPER HOUSE RD
Strines Moor
DEAN LA
COWCLIFF HILL RD
FAR LA
Crimes
Reservoir
Fields Head
Berristal Top
Hade Edge Junior & Infant Sch
BAYFORD CL
Reservoir
GREAVE RD
STRINES MOOR RD
Ing Royd
OX LEE LA
Ox Lee
CLOUGH FOOT LA
Kirklees Way
Holme Valley Circular Walk
BENT RD
Berristal Head
Crow Hill
ABBEY CL
LONG ING RD
GREEN ABBEY
NEW HOUSE
Moorside
PENISTONE RD
Hade Edge
DAISY LEE LA
Cote
Law
DUNFORD RD
Long Ing
Daisy Lee Moor
SNITTLE RD
Little Law
BEDDING EDGE RD
Bradshaw Edge
Wild Boar Clough
LAW SLACK RD
FLINT LA
Lane House
HD7
Green Gate
Lower Snittlegate
Law Head
ROUND CLOSE RD
LAW COMMON RD
Snittlegate
Ellentree Brow
Barnsley Boundary Walk
LINSHAWS RD
BARE BONES RD
FLIGHT HILL
Fox House Moss
Harden Clough
Harden
Harden Edge
Tinker Hill
Harden Reservoir
Cocker Edge
Lower Snailsden Moss
DUNFORD RD
Sand Ridge Moss
Wetshaw Edge
Snailsden
Sand Ridge
P
Little Shepherd's Castle
Booth Hill Flat
S36
BROOK HILL LA
Lower Town Head
RAILWAY COTTS
Townhead
Upper Town Head
Dearden Foot Plantation
Broad Hill Bank
Banks
Winscar Reservoir
Lower Dead Edge
River Don
DON VIEW
Dunford Bridge
WINDLE EDGE
Black Bank
Stanhope Arms Hotel
Shepley Ings
Dick Royd
Dunford Bridge
Bance Edge Plantation

200

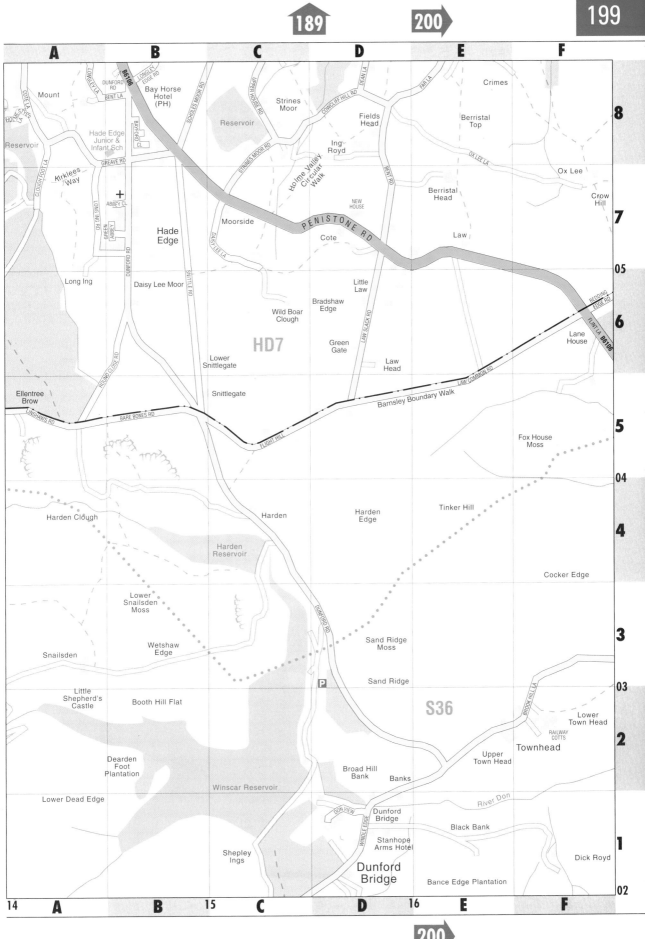

199 190
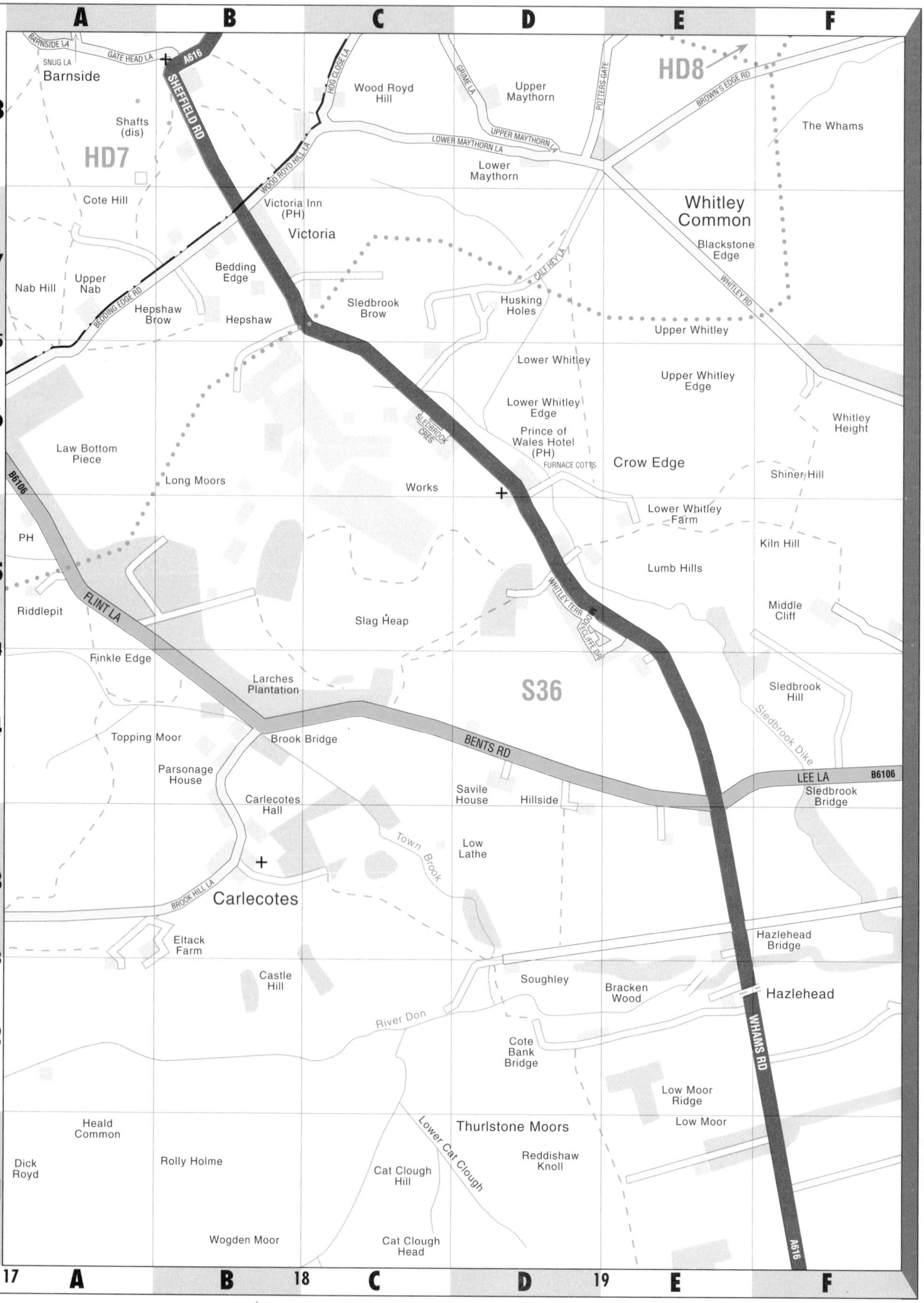
A B C D E F
8 7 05 6 5 04 4 3 03 2 1 02
17 18 19
BARNSIDE LA
SNUG LA
Barnside
GATE HEAD LA
A616
SHEFFIELD RD
HOG CLOSE LA
Wood Royd Hill
GRIME LA
Upper Maythorn
POTTERS GATE
HD8
BROWN'S EDGE RD
The Whams
Shafts (dis)
HD7
WOOD ROYD HILL LA
UPPER MAYTHORN LA
LOWER MAYTHORN LA
Lower Maythorn
Cote Hill
Victoria Inn (PH)
Victoria
Whitley Common
Blackstone Edge
Bedding Edge
CALF HEY LA
Nab Hill
Upper Nab
BEDDING EDGE RD
Hepshaw Brow
Hepshaw
Sledbrook Brow
Husking Holes
WHITLEY RD
Upper Whitley
Lower Whitley
Upper Whitley Edge
Lower Whitley Edge
SLEDBROOK CRES
Whitley Height
Law Bottom Piece
Prince of Wales Hotel (PH)
FURNACE COTTS
Crow Edge
Long Moors
Works
Shiner Hill
B6106
PH
Lower Whitley Farm
Kiln Hill
Lumb Hills
WHITLEY TERR
ECLIFFE DR
Riddlepit
FLINT LA
Slag Heap
Middle Cliff
Finkle Edge
Larches Plantation
S36
Sledbrook Hill
Topping Moor
Brook Bridge
BENTS RD
Sledbrook Dike
LEE LA
B6106
Parsonage House
Savile House
Hillside
Sledbrook Bridge
Carlecotes Hall
Town Brook
Low Lathe
BROOK HILL LA
Carlecotes
Eltack Farm
Hazlehead Bridge
Castle Hill
Soughley
Bracken Wood
Hazlehead
River Don
WHAMS RD
Cote Bank Bridge
Low Moor Ridge
Low Moor
Heald Common
Lower Cat Clough
Thurlstone Moors
Dick Royd
Rolly Holme
Cat Clough Hill
Reddishaw Knoll
Wogden Moor
Cat Clough Head
A616
199

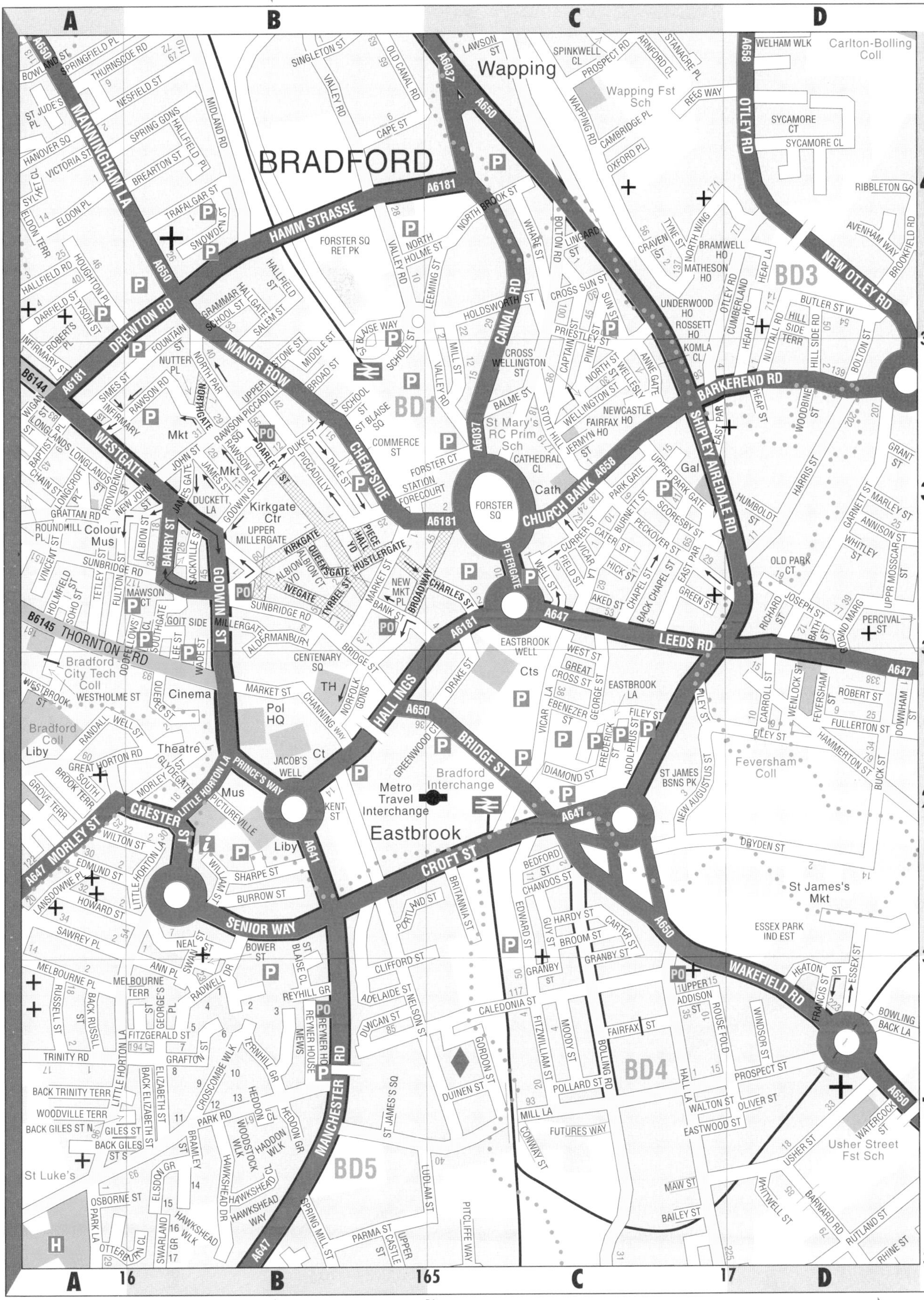

B1
1 DOUGLAS TOWERS
2 BUCHAN TOWERS
3 EVANS TOWERS
4 TIVERTON HO
5 CRITCHELL HO
6 ASHTON HO
7 LYDFORD HO
8 WALDRON HO
9 OSMOND HO
10 HASELBURY HO
11 TAUNTON HO
12 SHEPTON HO
13 BRIDGWATER HO
14 BOLINGBROKE CT
15 HAPSBURG CT

B1
16 WINDSOR CT
17 TUDOR CT

C3
1 WOLSLEY TERR
2 OAK TERR
3 ROSE TERR
4 OAK LA
5 BOWMAN PL
6 BOWMAN ST
7 BAKER FOLD
8 RAGLAN CT
9 CRYSTAL CT
10 LIGHTOWLER CL
11 GROSVENOR TERR
12 BACK CAVENDISH TERR
13 CAVENDISH TERR
14 CAVENDISH ST
15 GLADSTONE RD
16 HEYWOOD ST

Scale: 7 inches to 1 mile
0 110 yards 1/8 mile
0 125m 250m

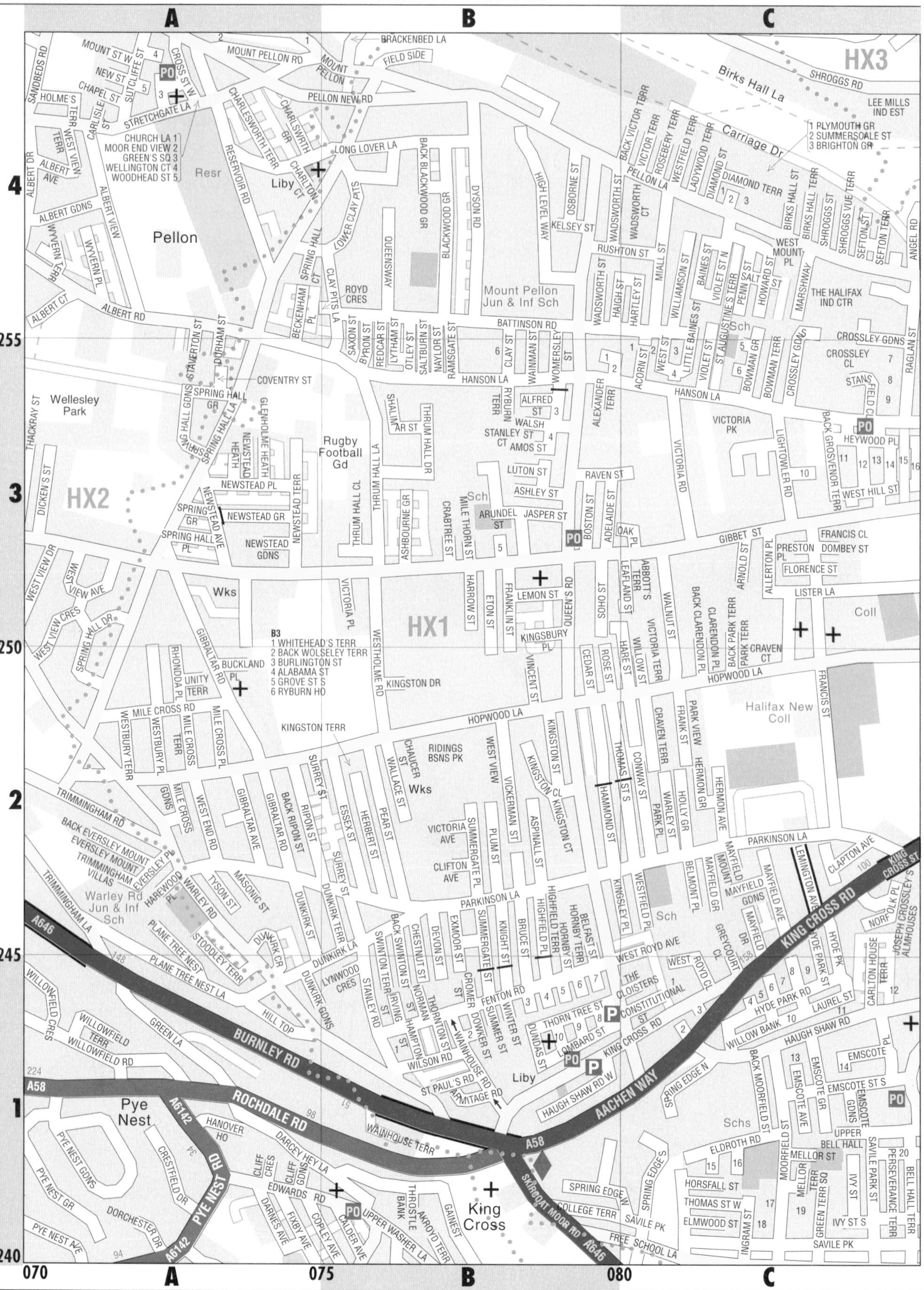

B1
1 VAUGHN ST
2 THORNTON TERR
3 AUTUMN ST
4 POHLMAN ST
5 RALEIGH ST
6 BURLEIGH ST
7 MAPLE ST

B1
8 CANNON ST
9 MOORGATE ST
10 LEADENHALL ST

C1
1 WEST ROYD VILLAS
2 TRAFALGAR SQ
3 TRAFALGAR ST
4 HAWTHORN ST
5 HAWTHORN TERR
6 WOODBINE ST
7 WOODBINE TERR
8 MAYFIELD ST
9 MAYFIELD TERR S
10 UPPER HAUGH SHAW
11 LAUREL BANK
12 FIELDHOUSE COTTS
13 HAUGH SHAW CROFT
14 LAUREL MOUNT
15 ROCKVILLE TERR
16 ELDROTH MOUNT
17 SAVILE PARK TERR
18 INGRAM SQ
19 WALSH'S SQ
20 BELL HALL MOUNT

One-way streets

House numbers

1 59 HIGH ST

D3
1 CROMWELL TERR
2 BACK CROMWELL TERR
3 MILTON TERR
4 BRUNSWICK GDNS
5 SUNDERLAND ST

92

E3
1 CULVER ST
2 TOWN HALL ST E
3 WESLEY CT
4 GILL'S CT
5 THE OLD ARCADE

113

E3
6 BLACK SWAN PAS
7 BLACK SWAN GINNELL
8 GEORGE SQ
9 BARUM TOP
10 POWELL ST
11 BACK COMMERCIAL ST
12 CARRIER ST

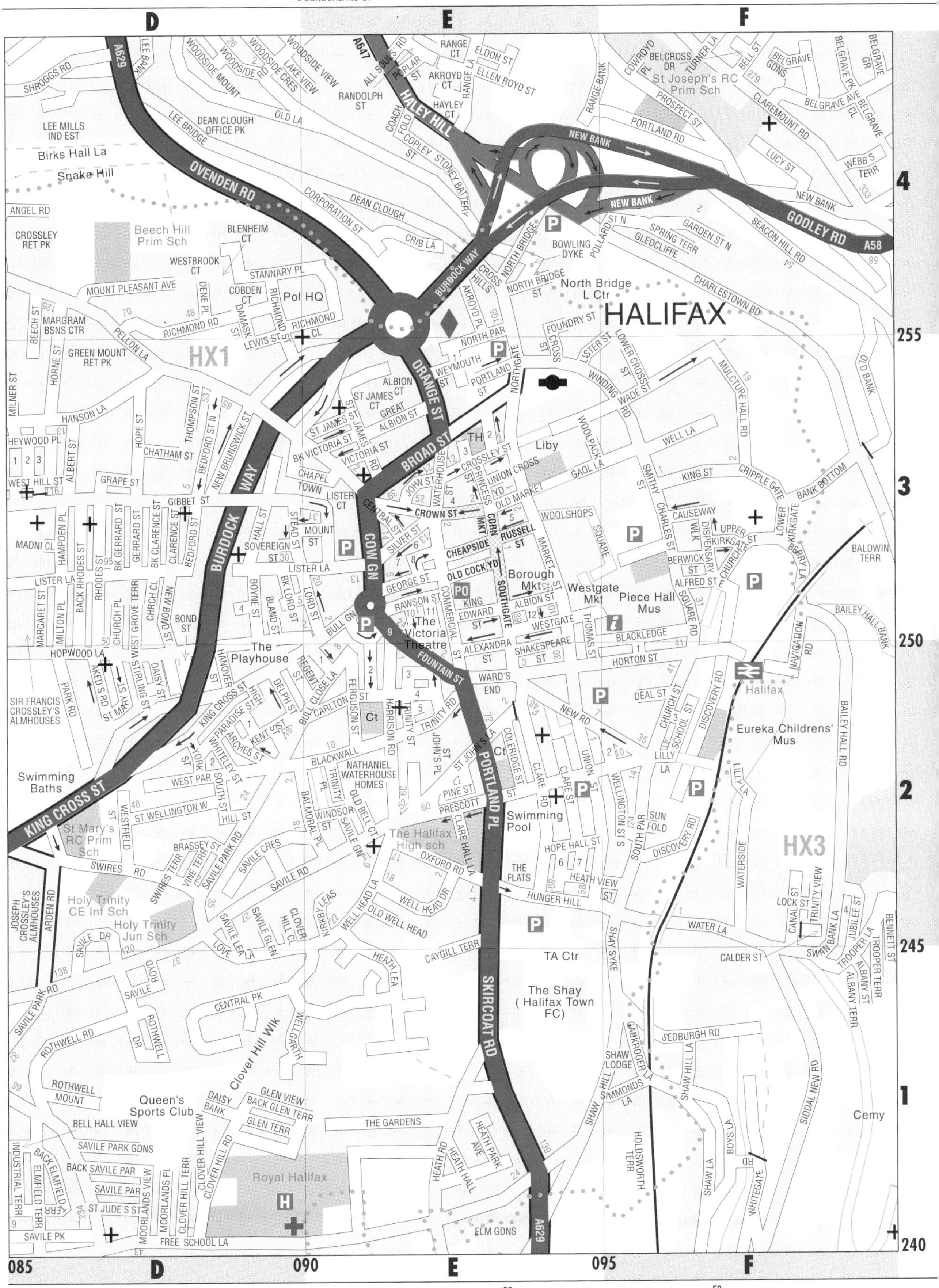

D2
1 HENRY ST
2 W PARADE FLATS

113

E2
1 CARLTON PL
2 BACK FERGUSON ST
3 CADNEY CROFT
4 CARLTON TERR
5 SEDAN ST
6 HOPE HALL TERR
7 BACK HOPE HALL TERR

113

F2
1 CROSS ST
2 WELLINGTON PL
3 BATH ST
4 JUBILEE TERR

60 43 61

A3
1 NORTHBROOK CROFT
2 HILL VIEW TERR
3 HAWTHORN MOUNT
4 HAWTHORN CRES
5 HAWTHORN VIEW
6 HAWTHORN LA
7 HAWTHORNE VALE
8 TOWN STREET WLK

Scale: 7 inches to 1 mile
0 110 yards 1/8 mile
0 125m 250m

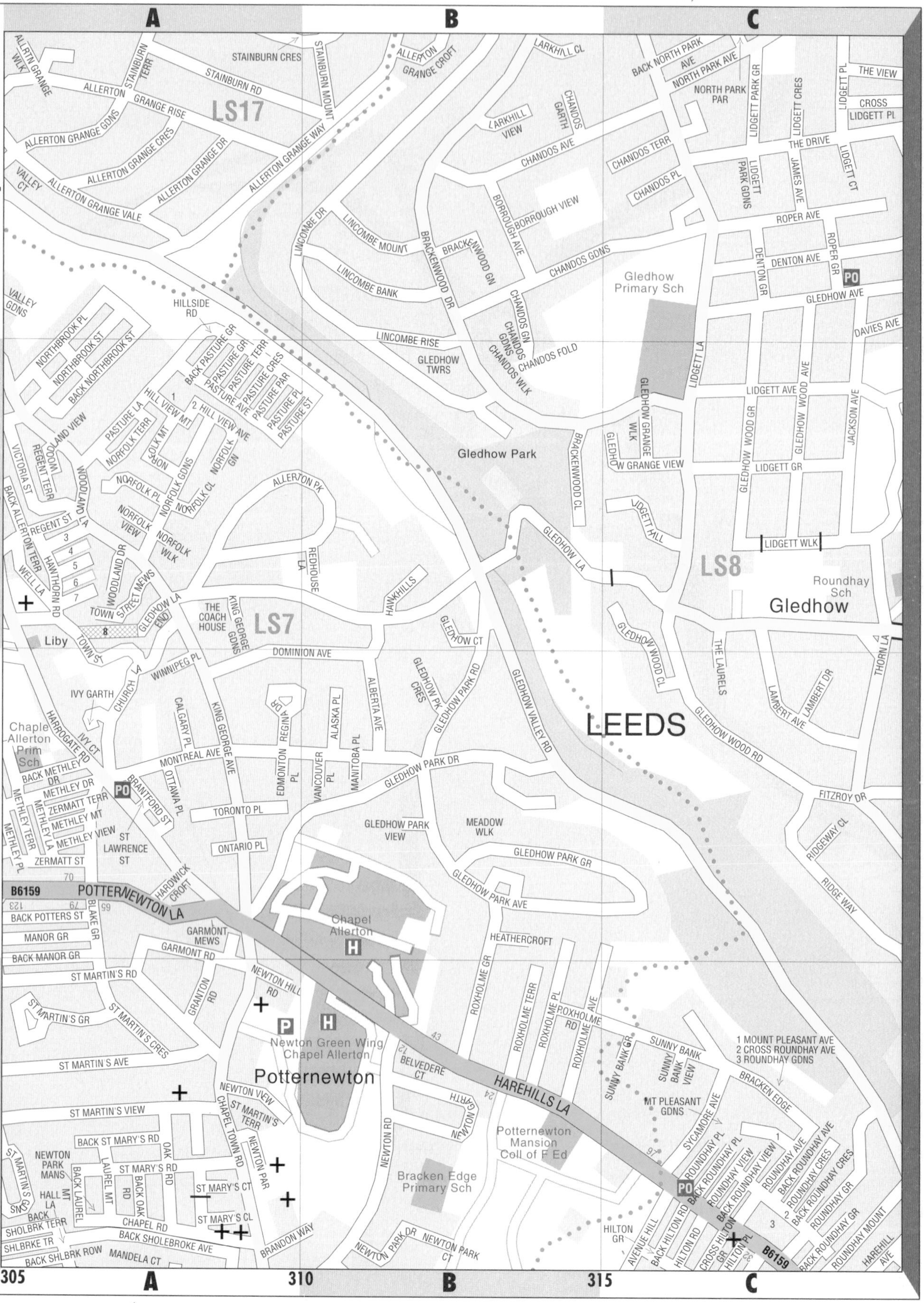

60 207 61

Scale: 7 inches to 1 mile
0 110yards 1/8mile
0 125m 250m

House numbers
1 59
HIGH ST

D3
1 BACK NEWPORT MT
2 BACK NEWPORT GDNS
3 BROOMFIELD ST
4 BACK BROOMFIELD PL
5 BACK NEWPORT PL

59

D3
6 BEECHWOOD ROW
7 BACK BEECHWOOD GR
8 BEECHWOOD RD
9 BACK BEECHWOOD RD
10 KNOWLE GR

206

D3
11 KNOWLE PL
12 BACK KNOWLE MOUNT

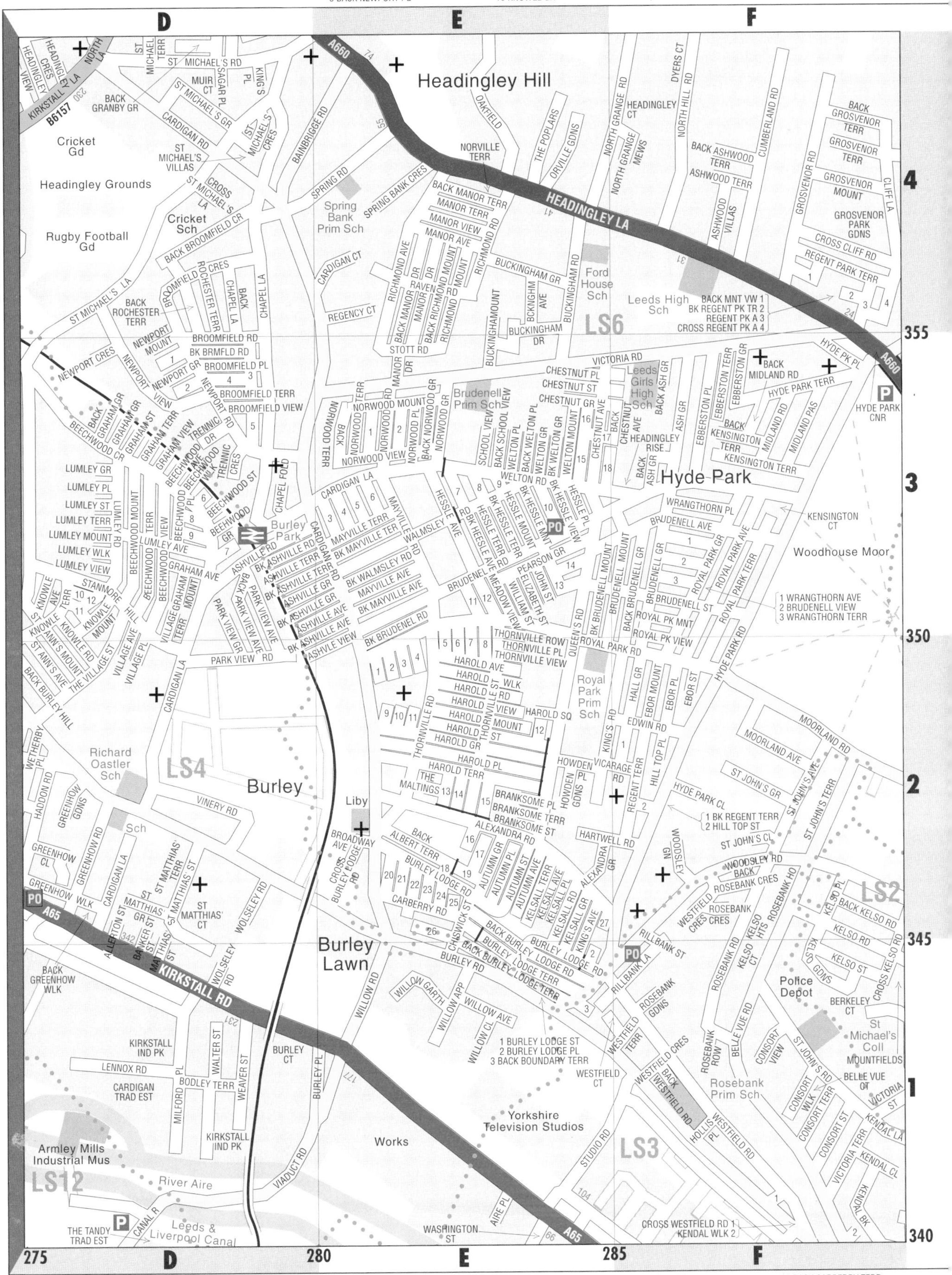

E3
1 BACK NORWOOD RD
2 BACK NORWOOD PL
3 BACK MAYVILLE ST
4 MAYVILLE ST
5 MAYVILLE PL
6 BACK MAYVILLE PL
7 HESSLE RD
8 HESSLE WLK
9 HESSLE ST
10 HESSLE VIEW
11 THORNVILLE CRES
12 BACK MEADOW VIEW
13 PEARSON AVE
14 PEARSON TERR
15 BACK WELTON MOUNT
16 CROSS CHESTNUT GR
17 CHESTNUT RD
18 BACK WELTON AVE

59

E2
1 BEAMSLEY TERR
2 BACK BEAMSLEY TERR
3 BEAMSLEY MOUNT
4 BACK BEAMSLEY MOUNT
5 THORNVILLE MOUNT
6 THORNVILLE GR
7 THORNVILLE TERR

210

E2
8 THORNVILLE AVE
9 BACK BEAMSLEY GR
10 BEAMSLEY GR
11 BEAMSLEY PL
12 HOPEWELL PL
13 SPRING GROVE WLK
14 BACK SPRING GROVE WLK

206

E2
15 SPRING GROVE VIEW
16 BACK AUTUMN TERR
17 AUTUMN TERR
18 SPRING GROVE TERR
19 BACK AUTUMN RD
20 BACK CARBERRY PL
21 CARBERRY PL
22 BACK CARBERRY TERR
23 CARBERRY TERR
24 BACK CHISWICK TERR
25 CHISWICK TERR
26 BACK CARBERRY RD
27 BACK KING'S AVE

205

60

A4
1 CLIFF CT
2 BACK MONTPELIER TR
3 MONTPELIER TERR
4 BACK LUCAS ST
5 BACK HARTLEY GR
6 QUARRY MOUNT ST
7 QUARRY MOUNT PL
8 QUARRY MOUNT TERR
9 BACK QUARRY MOUNT TERR
10 BACK CLARKSON VIEW
11 BACK PROVIDENCE AVE
12 PENNINGTON CT
13 PENNINGTON TERR
14 PENNINGTON GR
15 CROSS QUARRY ST

Scale: 7 inches to 1 mile
0 110 yards 1/8 mile
0 125m 250m

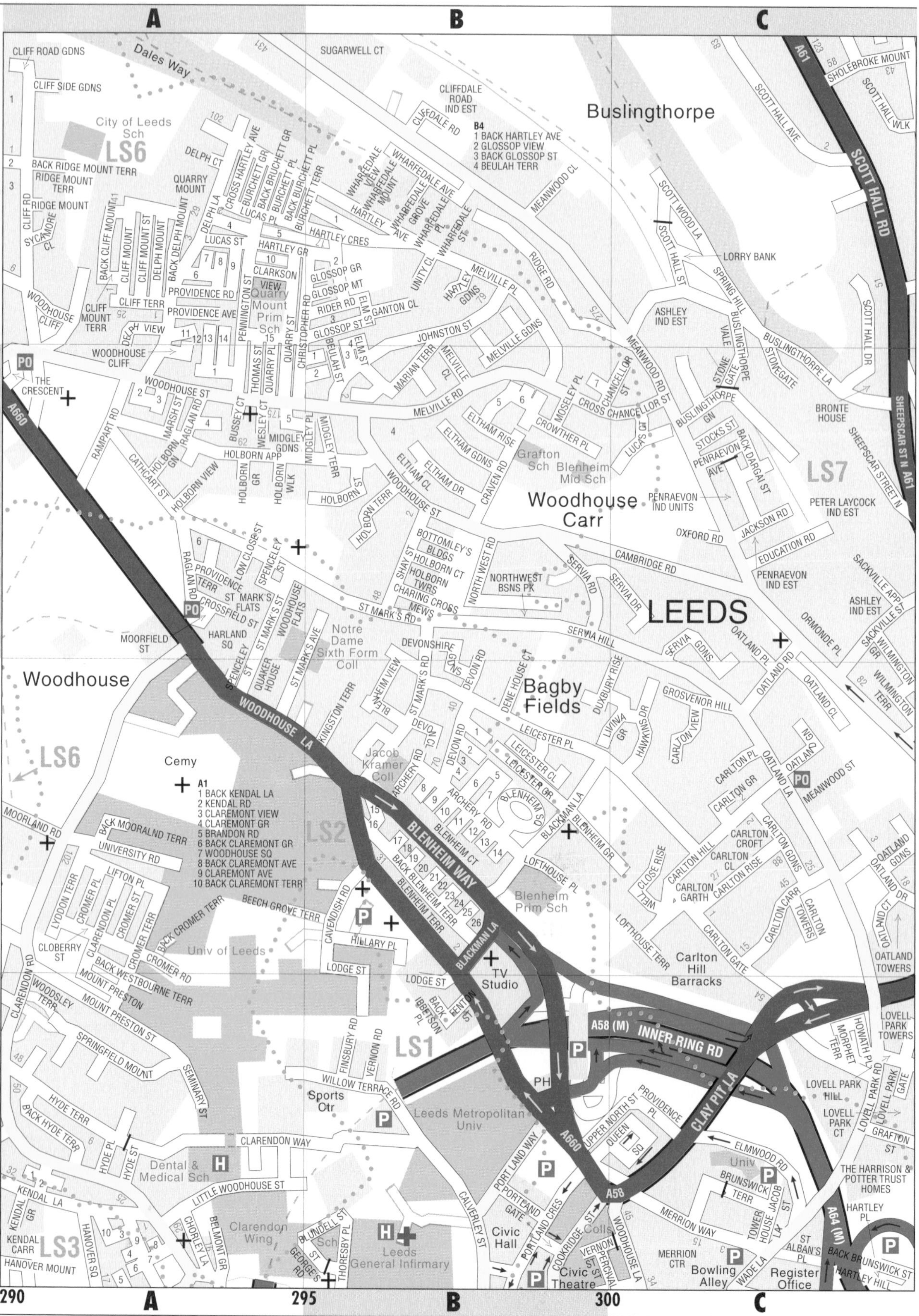

205

211

A3
1 PENNINGTON PL
2 PLEASANT CT
3 MARSH VALE
4 HOLBURN GDNS
5 LESLIE TERR
6 THE HARRISON & POTTER TRUST HOMES

A3
7 ST MARK'S FLATS
8 MOORFIELD ST
9 QUAKER HOUSE

B2
1 WINFIELD PL
2 WINFIELD TERR
3 BACK WINFIELD GR

B2
4 WINFIELD GR
5 BLENHEIM CRES
6 BLENHEIM AVE
7 BACK BLENHEIM AVE
8 BACK ARCHERY PL
9 ARCHERY PL
10 BACK ARCHERY TERR
11 ARCHERY TERR
12 BACK ARCHERY ST
13 ARCHERY ST
14 BACK ARCHERY RD
15 CROSS WOODSTOCK ST
16 BACK WOODSTOCK ST
17 MALBOROUGH GDNS
18 BACK MALBOROUGH GDNS
19 MALBOROUGH GR
20 BACK MALBOROUGH GR
21 BLANDFORD GDNS
22 BACK BLANDFORD GDNS
23 BLANDFORD GR
24 BACK BLANDFORD GR
25 CHURCHILL GDNS
26 BACK CHURCHILL GDNS

B3
1 BEULAH VIEW
2 BEULAH MOUNT
3 BEULAH GR
4 ELTHAM CT
5 CROSS SPEEDWELL ST
6 SPEEDWELL MOUNT
7 SPEEDWELL ST

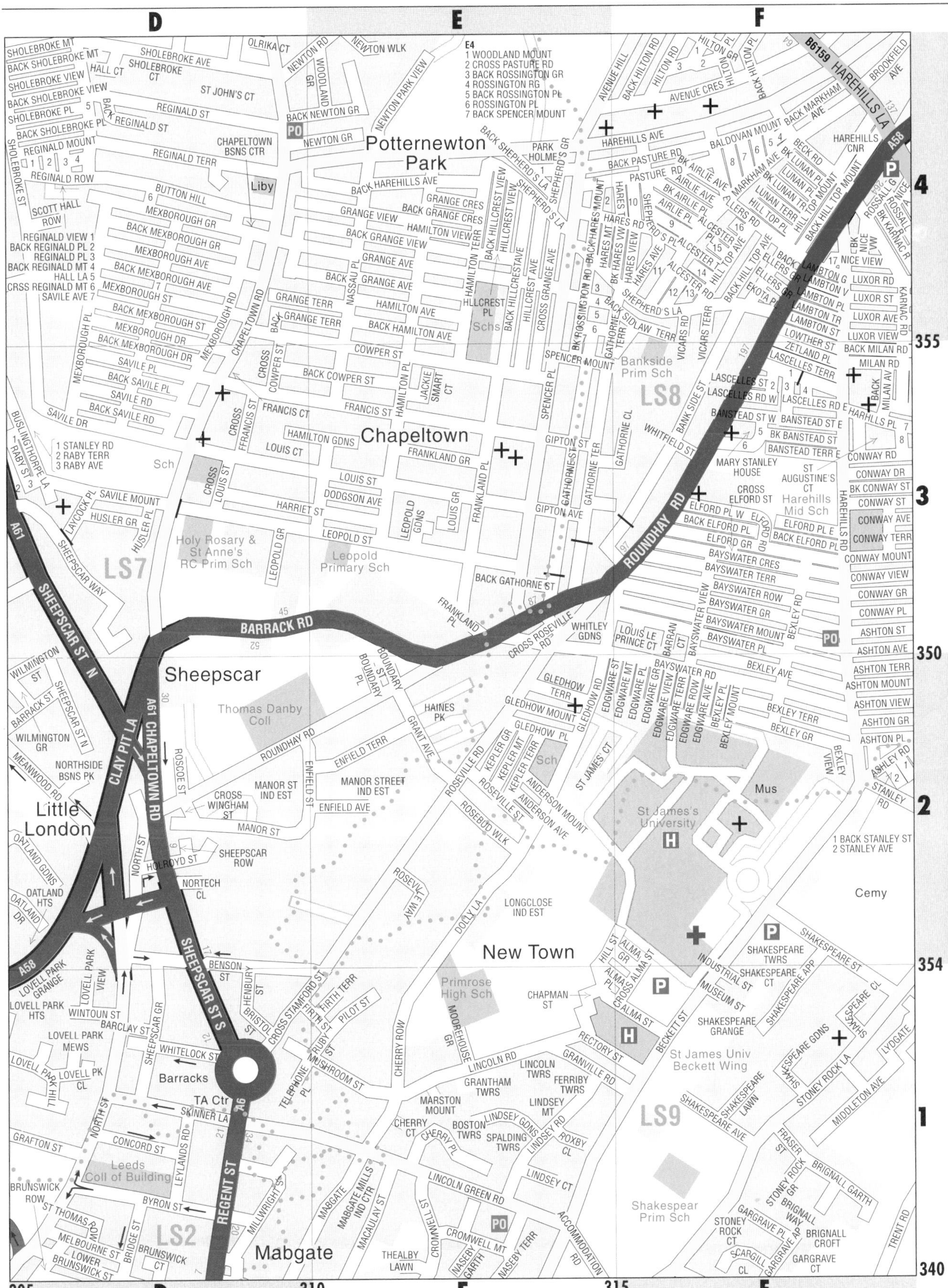

F3
1 BACK LASCELLES TERR
2 LASCELLES PL
3 LASCELLES VIEW
4 LASCELLES MOUNT
5 CROSS BANSTEAD ST
6 BANSTEAD TERR W
7 BACK HAREHILLS PL
8 DARFIELD GR

F4
1 BACK HILTON GR
2 HILTON ST
3 HILTON TERR
4 CROSS BECK RD
5 BALDOVAN PL
6 BACK BALBOVAN TERR
7 BALDOVAN TERR

F4
8 BACK ELLERS RD
9 BACK SHEPHERD'S PL
10 BACK HARES TERR
11 BACK HARES AVE
12 CROSS ALCESTER RD
13 ALCESTER ST
14 BACK ALCESTER RD

F4
15 BACK ALCESTER TERR
16 BK ALCESTER PL
17 BK LAMBTON GR

207

A3
1 BK STRATHMORE DR
2 BK SEAFORTH PL
3 BK SEAFORTH TERR

A4
1 BK HOVINGHAM TERR
2 BK HOVINGHAM MOUNT
3 BK DORSET RD
4 BK DORSET MOUNT

61

House numbers
1 59
HIGH ST

61

Scale: 7 inches to 1 mile
0 110 yards 1/8 mile
0 125 m 250 m

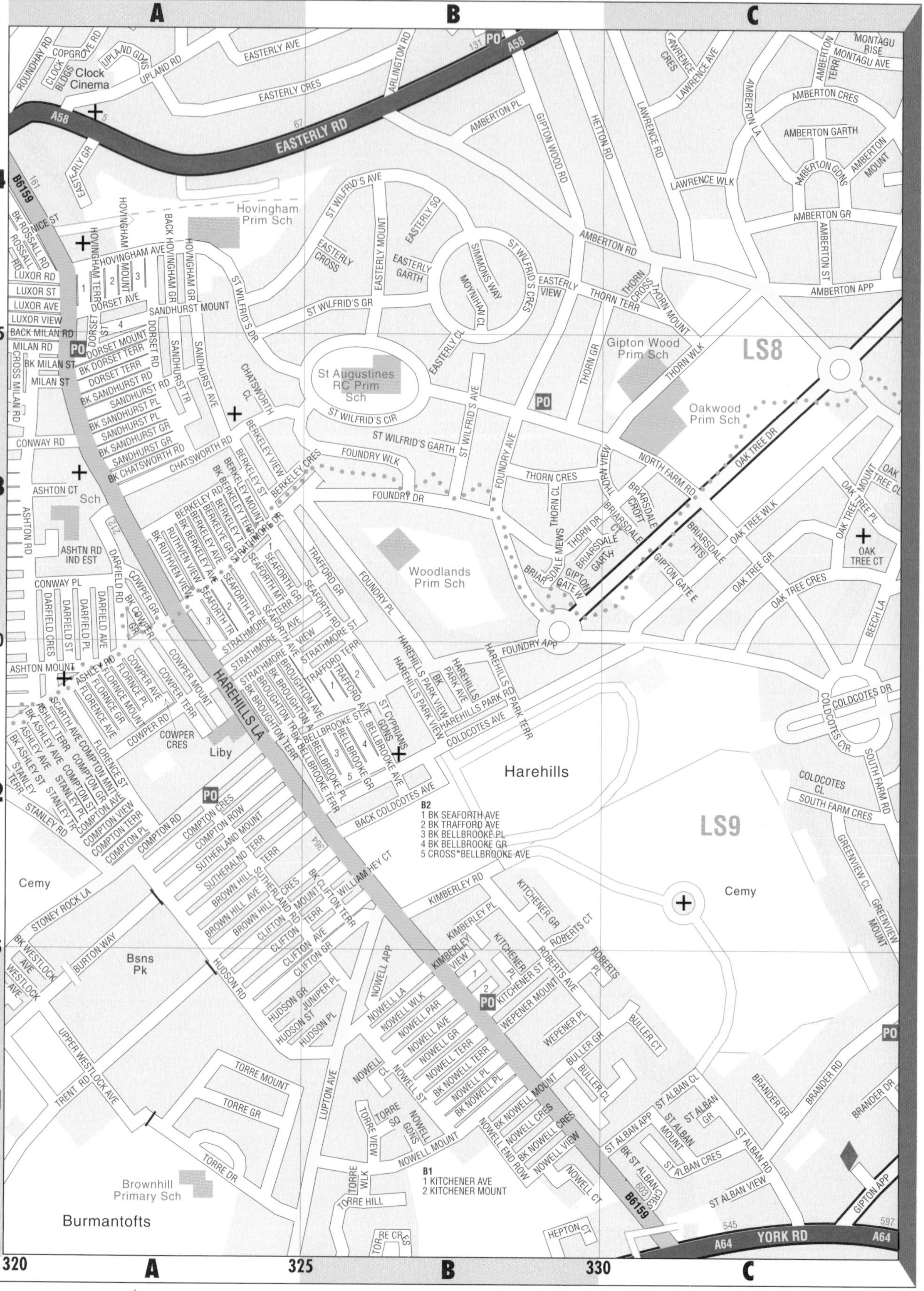

207

80

61

House numbers
1 59
HIGH ST

D4
1 GREENOCK TERR
2 GREENOCK PL
3 HIGHTHORNE GR
4 BACK HIGHTHORNE GR
5 PAISLEY VIEW
6 HIGHTHORNE VIEW

E4
1 BACK HIGHTHORNE VIEW
2 PAISLEY GR
3 PAISLEY PL
4 PAISLEY TERR
5 OBAN PL
6 OBAN TERR

59

F3
1 BACK ATHLONE AVE
2 BACK ATHLONE GR
3 BACK ATHLONE TERR
4 WESLEY AVE
5 WESLEY PL

210

F3
6 ORIENTAL ST
7 LAUREL GR
8 BRENTWOOD GR
9 LAUREL FOLD
10 LAUREL ST
11 BRENTWOOD ST
12 BRENTWOOD TERR

F4
1 BACK AVIARY RD
2 NUNINGTON AVE
3 NUNINGTON TERR

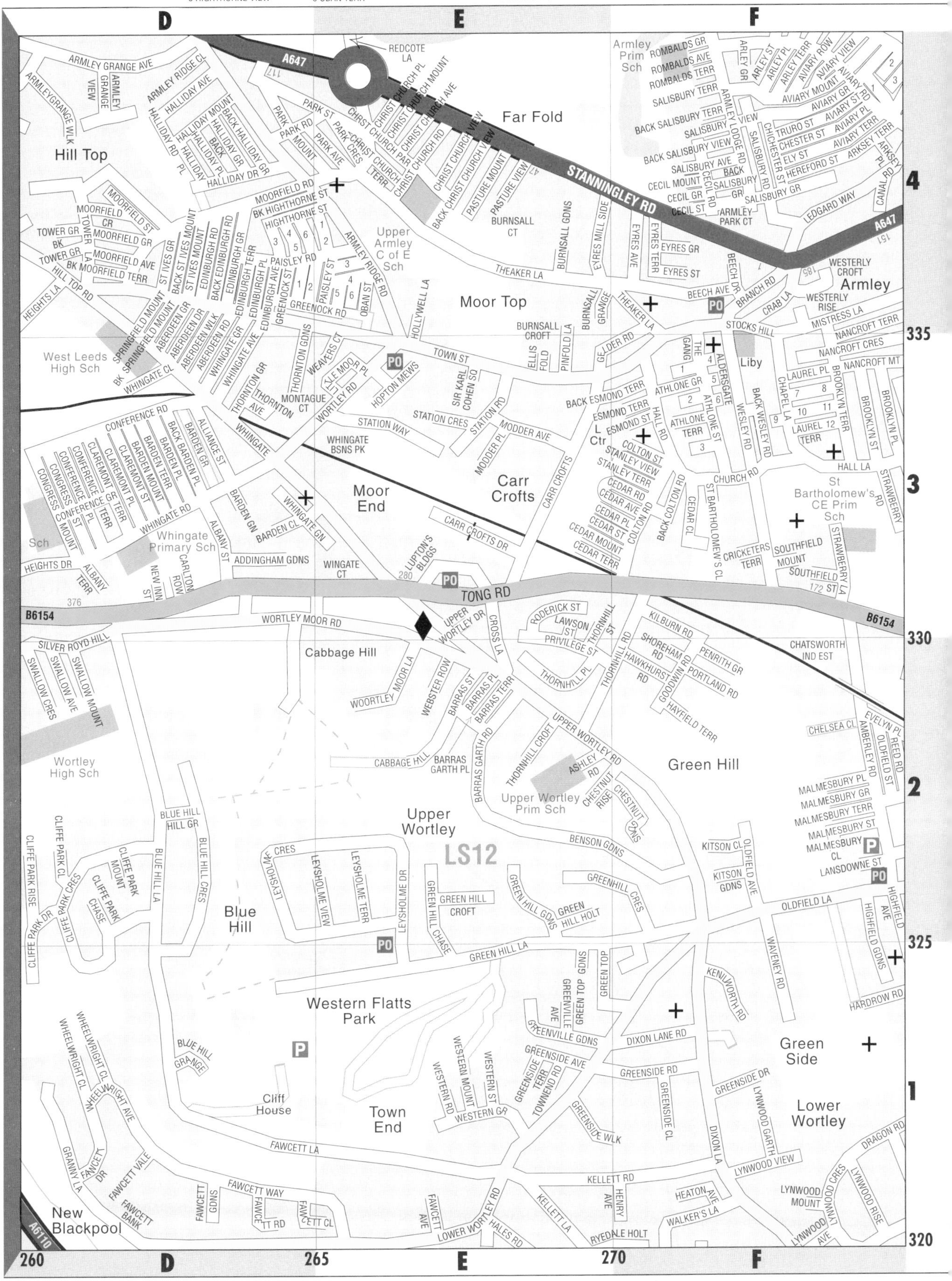

78
210

209
205

Scale: 7 inches to 1 mile
0 110 yards 1/8 mile
0 125m 250m

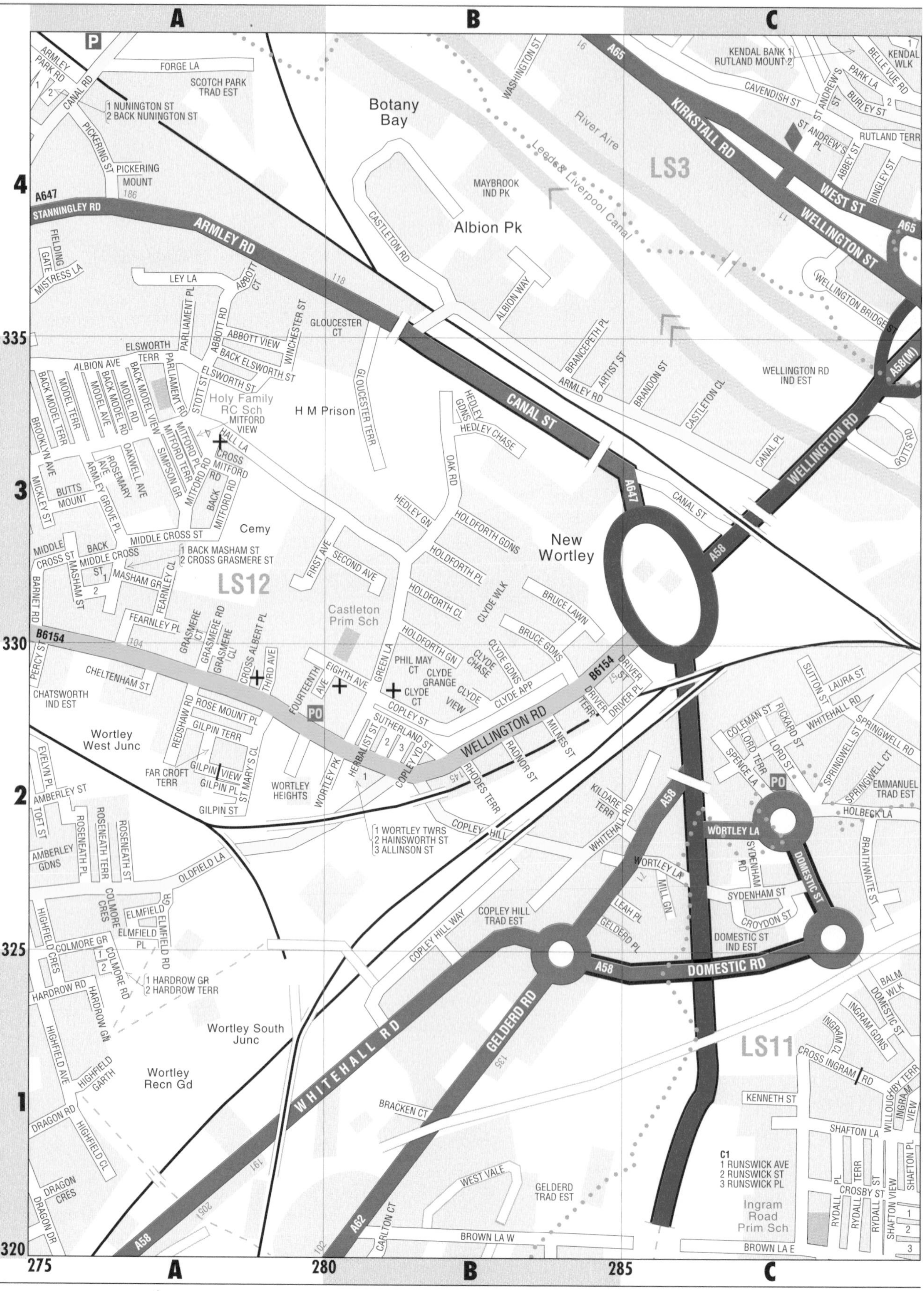

209
213

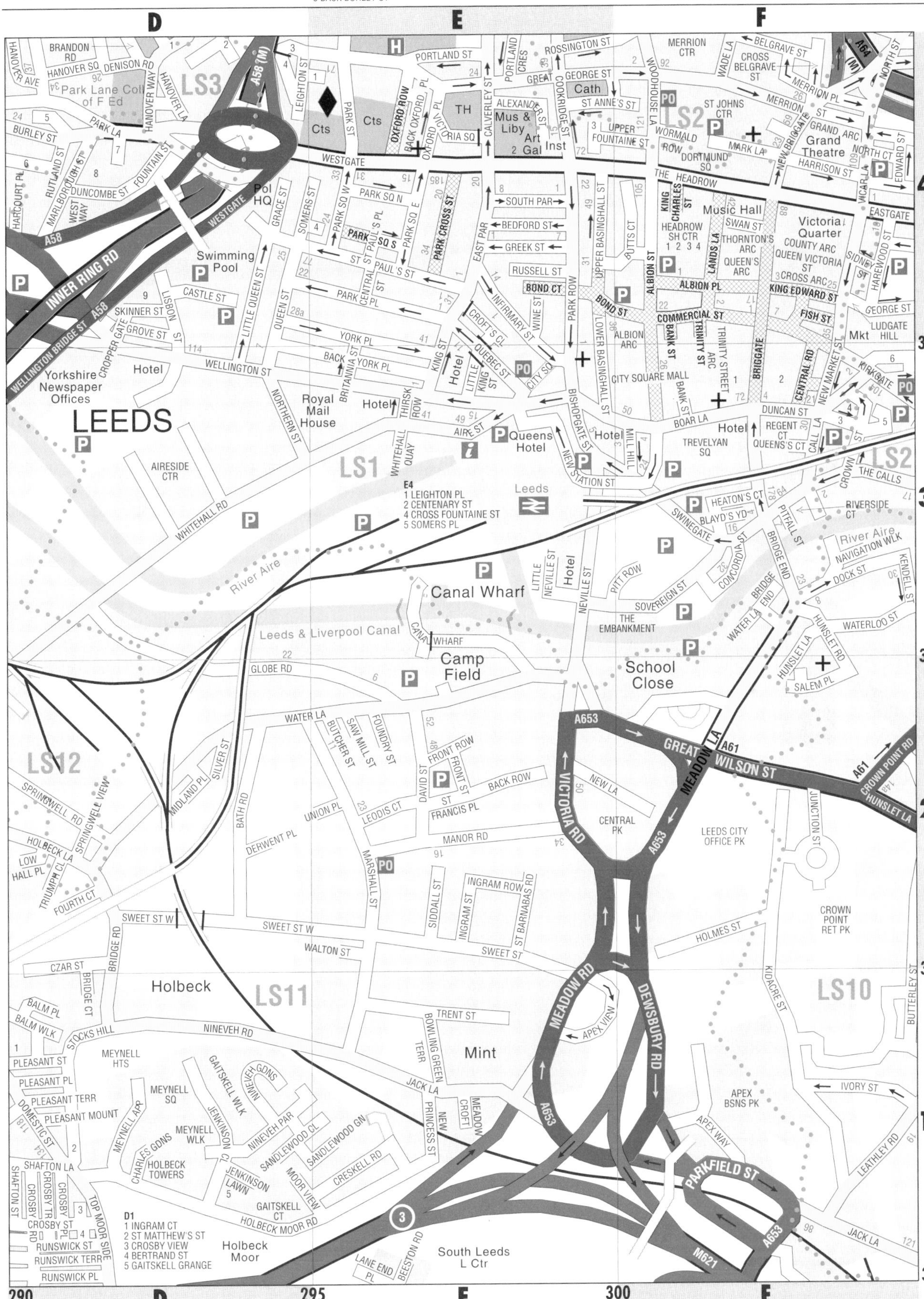
D
E
F
4
3
2
1
335
330
325
320
290
295
300
LEEDS
LS1
LS2
LS3
LS10
LS11
LS12
E4
1 LEIGHTON PL
2 CENTENARY ST
4 CROSS FOUNTAINE ST
5 SOMERS PL
D1
1 INGRAM CT
2 ST MATTHEW'S ST
3 CROSBY VIEW
4 BERTRAND ST
5 GAITSKELL GRANGE
BRANDON RD
HANOVER SQ
DENISON RD
HANOVER AVE
HANOVER WAY
HANOVER LA
Park Lane Coll of F Ed
A58 (M)
LEIGHTON ST
PORTLAND ST
PORTLAND CRES
ROSSINGTON ST
MERRION CTR
BELGRAVE ST
CROSS BELGRAVE ST
MERRION PL
MERRION ST
NORTH ST
A64 (M)
GREAT GEORGE ST
Cath
ST ANNE'S ST
ST JOHNS CTR
UPPER FOUNTAINE ST
WORMALD ROW
DORTMUND SQ
MARK LA
NEW BRIGGATE
GRAND ARC
Grand Theatre
NORTH CT
HARRISON ST
VICAR LA
EDWARD ST
Cts
TH
Mus & Liby
Art Gal
Inst
OXFORD ROW
BACK OXFORD PL
OXFORD PL
VICTORIA SQ
CALVERLEY ST
ALEXANDER ST
COOKRIDGE ST
WOODHOUSE LA
WADE LA
PARK LA
BURLEY ST
PARK ST
WESTGATE
THE HEADROW
EASTGATE
RUTLAND ST
MARLBOROUGH ST
HARCOURT PL
DUNCOMBE ST
FOUNTAIN ST
WEST WAY
Pol HQ
GRACE ST
SOMERS ST
PARK SQ W
PARK SQ N
PARK SQ E
PARK SQ S
PARK CROSS ST
SOUTH PAR
BEDFORD ST
GREEK ST
EAST PAR
UPPER BASINGHALL ST
BUTTS CT
KING CHARLES ST
Music Hall
HEADROW SH CTR
SWAN ST
THORNTON'S ARC
QUEEN'S ARC
LANDS LA
Victoria Quarter
COUNTY ARC
QUEEN VICTORIA ST
CROSS ARC
SIDNEY ST
HAREWOOD ST
A58
INNER RING RD
Swimming Pool
ST PAUL'S PL
ST PAUL'S ST
CENTRAL ST
PARK PL
RUSSELL ST
BOND CT
BOND ST
ALBION ST
ALBION PL
KING EDWARD ST
COMMERCIAL ST
FISH ST
GEORGE ST
LUDGATE HILL
Mkt
CASTLE ST
SKINNER ST
GROVE ST
LISBON ST
LITTLE QUEEN ST
QUEEN ST
INFIRMARY ST
CROFT'S CL
QUEBEC ST
WINE ST
PARK ROW
LOWER BASINGHALL ST
ALBION ARC
BANK ST
TRINITY ST
TRINITY STREET ARC
BRIGGATE
CENTRAL RD
NEW MARKET ST
KIRKGATE
WELLINGTON BRIDGE ST
CROPPER GATE
YORK PL
BACK YORK PL
BRITANNIA ST
KING ST
LITTLE KING ST
CITY SQ
Hotel
WELLINGTON ST
Yorkshire Newspaper Offices
NORTHERN ST
Royal Mail House
THIRSK ROW
BISHOPGATE ST
CITY SQUARE MALL
DUNCAN ST
BOAR LA
REGENT CT
QUEENS'S CT
CALL LA
AIRE ST
Queens Hotel
MILL HILL
TREVELYAN SQ
CROWN ST
THE CALLS
WHITEHALL QUAY
NEW STATION ST
AIRESIDE CTR
Leeds
HEATON'S CT
BLAYD'S YD
SWINEGATE
PITFALL ST
RIVERSIDE CT
WHITEHALL RD
River Aire
LITTLE NEVILLE ST
NEVILLE ST
PITT ROW
CONCORDIA ST
BRIDGE END
NAVIGATION WLK
DOCK ST
KENDELL ST
Canal Wharf
SOVEREIGN ST
THE EMBANKMENT
WATER LA
HUNSLET RD
WATERLOO ST
Leeds & Liverpool Canal
CANAL WHARF
Camp Field
GLOBE RD
School Close
HUNSLET LA
SALEM PL
A653
GREAT WILSON ST
A61
MEADOW LA
CROWN POINT RD
FOUNDRY ST
SAW MILL ST
BUTCHER ST
FRONT ROW
DAVID ST
FRONT ST
BACK ROW
ST FRANCIS PL
NEW LA
SILVER ST
MIDLAND PL
SPRINGWELL RD
SPRINGWELL VIEW
BATH RD
UNION PL
LEODIS CT
VICTORIA RD
CENTRAL PK
LEEDS CITY OFFICE PK
JUNCTION ST
HOLBECK LA
LOW HALL PL
TRIUMPH CL
FOURTH CT
DERWENT PL
MANOR RD
MARSHALL ST
PO
INGRAM ROW
ST BARNABAS RD
SIDDALL ST
INGRAM ST
CROWN POINT RET PK
SWEET ST W
SWEET ST
WALTON ST
HOLMES ST
BRIDGE RD
CZAR ST
BRIDGE CT
Holbeck
MEADOW RD
DEWSBURY RD
KIDACRE ST
BUTTERLEY ST
BALM PL
BALM WLK
STOCKS HILL
NINEVEH RD
TRENT ST
APEX VIEW
BOWLING GREEN TERR
PLEASANT ST
MEYNELL HTS
GAITSKELL WLK
NINEVEH GDNS
Mint
IVORY ST
PLEASANT PL
PLEASANT TERR
PLEASANT MOUNT
DOMESTIC ST
MEYNELL SQ
JACK LA
MEADOW CROFT
APEX BSNS PK
MEYNELL APP
MEYNELL WLK
JENKINSON CL
NINEVEH PAR
SANDLEWOOD CL
SANDLEWOOD GN
NEW PRINCESS ST
APEX WAY
LEATHLEY RD
CHARLES GDNS
HOLBECK TOWERS
SHAFTON LA
SHAFTON ST
CROSBY TERR
CROSBY ST
CROSBY PL
CROSBY RD
JENKINSON LAWN
MOOR VIEW
CRESKELL RD
GAITSKELL CT
PARKFIELD ST
TOP MOOR SIDE
RUNSWICK ST
RUNSWICK TERR
RUNSWICK PL
HOLBECK MOOR RD
Holbeck Moor
BEESTON RD
LANE END PL
South Leeds L Ctr
M621

211

A3
1 NEW YORK ST
2 PINE CT
3 BACK YORK ST

A4
1 BELL ST
2 CROSS BELL ST
3 BACK GEORGE ST

B4
1 THEALBY PL
2 CROMWELL HTS
3 NASEBY GRANGE
4 NASEBY GDNS

207

One-way Streets

80

Scale: 7 inches to 1 mile
0 110 yards 1/8 mile
0 125 m 250 m

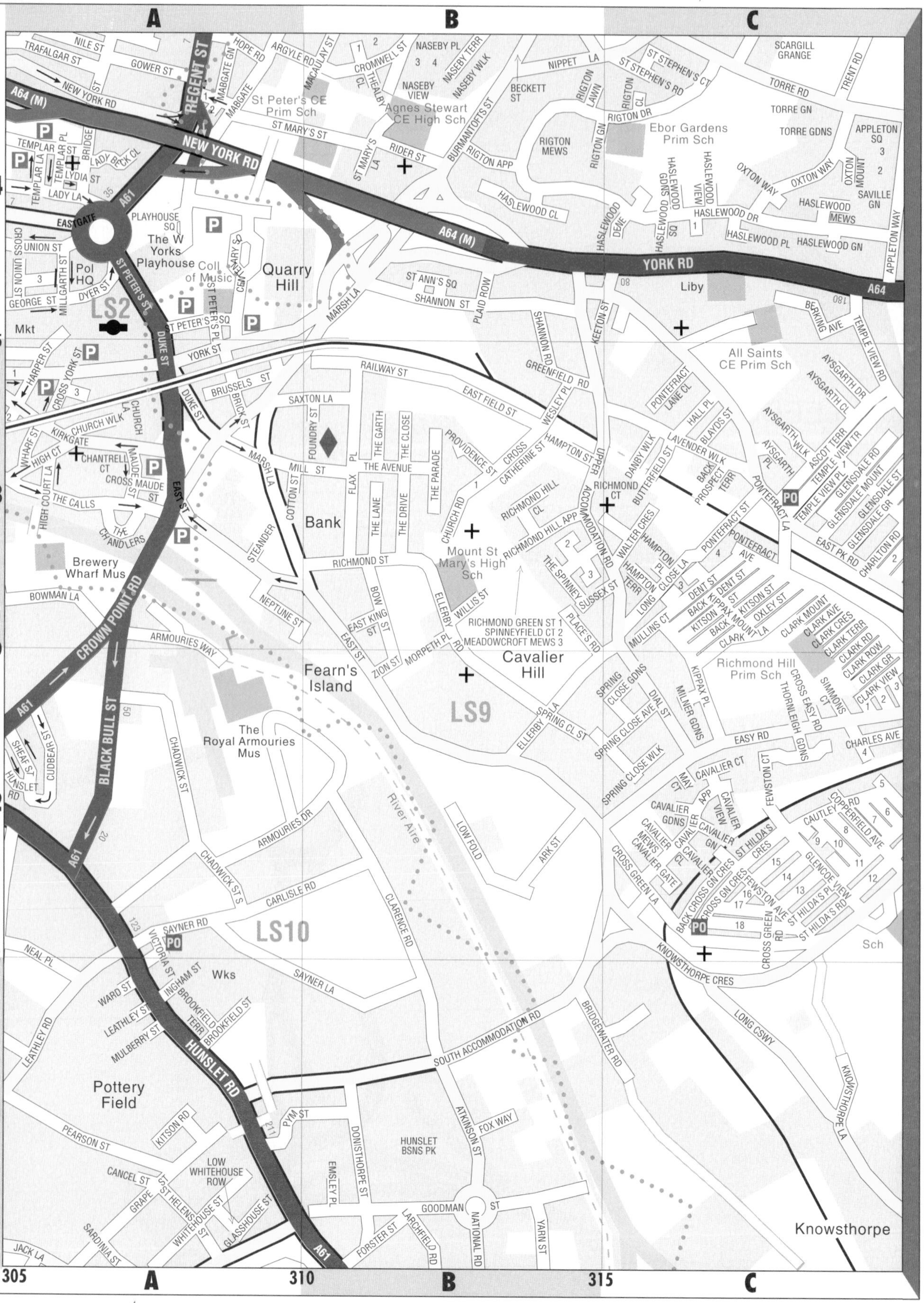

A
B
C
4
335
3
330
2
325
1
320
305
310
315
A64 (M)
NEW YORK RD
REGENT ST
YORK RD
A64
A61
EASTGATE
LS2
LS9
LS10
Quarry Hill
The W Yorks Playhouse
Coll of Music
Pol HQ
Mkt
St Peter's CE Prim Sch
Agnes Stewart CE High Sch
Ebor Gardens Prim Sch
Liby
All Saints CE Prim Sch
Bank
Mount St Mary's High Sch
Cavalier Hill
Fearn's Island
Richmond Hill Prim Sch
Brewery Wharf Mus
The Royal Armouries Mus
River Aire
Wks
Pottery Field
HUNSLET BSNS PK
LOW WHITEHOUSE ROW
Knowsthorpe
Sch
CROWN POINT RD
BLACK BULL ST
HUNSLET RD
DUKE ST
EAST ST
ST PETER'S ST
MARSH LA
SHANNON ST
PLAID ROW
RICHMOND ST
RAILWAY ST
EAST FIELD ST
PONTEFRACT LA
SOUTH ACCOMMODATION RD
ARMOURIES DR
ARMOURIES WAY
CHADWICK ST
CARLISLE RD
SAYNER RD
SAYNER LA
CLARENCE RD
BRIDGEWATER RD
KNOWSTHORPE CRES
KNOWSTHORPE LA
LONG CSWY
ATKINSON ST
GOODMAN ST
NATIONAL RD
YARN ST
LARCHFIELD RD
FORSTER ST
DONISTHORPE ST
EMSLEY PL
FOX WAY
PYM ST
KITSON RD
PEARSON ST
CANCEL ST
GRAPE ST
ST HELENS ST
WHITEHOUSE ST
GLASSHOUSE ST
SARDINIA ST
JACK LA
LEATHLEY RD
NEAL PL
WARD ST
MULBERRY ST
INGHAM ST
BROOKFIELD ST
VICTORIA ST
BOWMAN LA
THE CALLS
HIGH COURT LA
KIRKGATE
CHURCH WALK
YORK ST
GEORGE ST
MILLGARTH ST
DYER ST
UNION ST
CROSS UNION ST
TEMPLAR ST
LADY LA
NILE ST
TRAFALGAR ST
GOWER ST
HOPE RD
ARGYLE RD
MACAULAY ST
CROMWELL ST
NASEBY PL
NASEBY TERR
NASEBY WLK
NASEBY VIEW
BURMANTOFTS ST
BECKETT ST
NIPPET LA
ST STEPHEN'S RD
RIGTON DR
RIGTON APP
RIGTON MEWS
HASLEWOOD CL
HASLEWOOD DR
HASLEWOOD PL
HASLEWOOD GN
OXTON WAY
TORRE RD
TORRE GN
TORRE GDNS
TRENT RD
SCARGILL GRANGE
APPLETON SQ
APPLETON WAY
SAVILLE GN
TEMPLE VIEW RD
AYSGARTH DR
EAST PK RD
CHARLTON RD
CLARK AVE
CLARK CRES
CLARK TERR
CLARK ROW
CLARK GR
CLARK VIEW
EASY RD
CHARLES AVE
CAVALIER CT
CAVALIER GDNS
CROSS GREEN LA
ST HILDA'S CRES
COPPERFIELD RD
CAUTLEY RD
GLENCOE VIEW
FEWSTON AVE
FEWSTON CT
SPRING CLOSE WLK
SPRING CLOSE AVE
ELLERBY LA
ELLERBY RD
LOW FOLD
ARK ST
RICHMOND HILL APP
UPPER ACCOMMODATION RD
HAMPTON ST
CATHERINE ST
PROVIDENCE ST
CHURCH RD
WILLIS ST
MORPETH PL
ZION ST
EAST KING ST
BOW ST
NEPTUNE ST
STEANDER
COTTON ST
THE AVENUE
THE PARADE
THE LANE
THE DRIVE
THE CLOSE
THE GARTH
FOUNDRY ST
SAXTON LA
BRUSSELS ST
GREENFIELD RD
KEETON ST
WESLEY PL
RICHMOND GREEN ST 1
SPINNEYFIELD CT 2
MEADOWCROFT MEWS 3

211

C2
1 THORNLEIGH GR
2 THORNLEIGH VIEW
3 THORNLEIGH MOUNT
4 THORNLEIGH ST
5 COPPERFIELD TERR
6 COPPERFIELD WLK
7 COPPERFIELD ROW
8 COPPERFIELD DR
9 COPPERFIELD PL
10 COPPERFIELD CRES
11 COPPERFIELD VIEW
12 COPPERFIELD GR
13 ST HILDA'S MOUNT
14 ST HILDA'S AVE

215

C2
15 ST HILDA'S GR
16 CROSS GREEN GR
17 CROSS GREEN AVE
18 BACK CROSS GREEN LA

C3
1 EAST PARK DR
2 CHARLTON MOUNT
3 CAIN CL
4 O'GRADY SQ

80

C4
1 HASLEWOOD CT
2 APPLETON CT
3 APPLETON CL

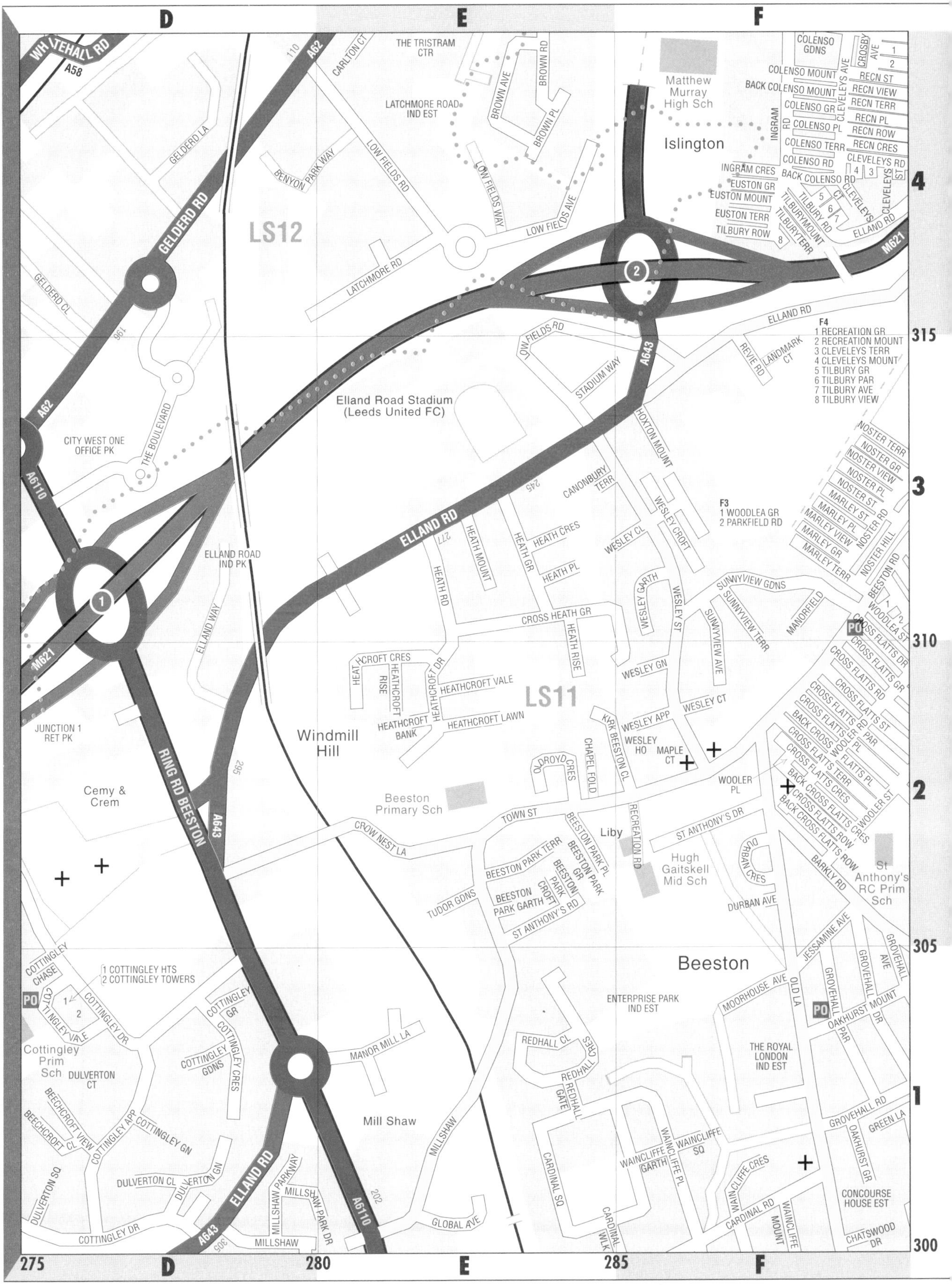
D
E
F
4
3
2
1
315
310
305
300
275
280
285
WHITEHALL RD
A58
A62
CARLTON CT
THE TRISTRAM CTR
BROWN AVE
BROWN RD
BROWN PL
Matthew Murray High Sch
COLENSO GDNS
CROSBY AVE
COLENSO MOUNT
BACK COLENSO MOUNT
COLENSO GR
COLENSO PL
COLENSO TERR
COLENSO RD
BACK COLENSO RD
CLEVELEYS AVE
CLEVELEYS RD
CLEVELEYS ST
CLEVELEYS
RECN ST
RECN VIEW
RECN TERR
RECN PL
RECN ROW
RECN CRES
INGRAM RD
INGRAM CRES
EUSTON GR
EUSTON MOUNT
EUSTON TERR
TILBURY ROW
TILBURY RD
TILBURYMOUNT
TILBURYTERR
ELLAND RD
Islington
LATCHMORE ROAD IND EST
GELDERD LA
BENYON PARK WAY
LOW FIELDS RD
LOW FIELDS WAY
LOW FIELDS AVE
LS12
GELDERD RD
LATCHMORE RD
GELDERD CL
M621
F4
1 RECREATION GR
2 RECREATION MOUNT
3 CLEVELEYS TERR
4 CLEVELEYS MOUNT
5 TILBURY GR
6 TILBURY PAR
7 TILBURY AVE
8 TILBURY VIEW
LOW FIELDS RD
STADIUM WAY
A643
REVIE RD
LANDMARK CT
Elland Road Stadium (Leeds United FC)
THE BOULEVARD
CITY WEST ONE OFFICE PK
A6110
HOXTON MOUNT
CANONBURY TERR
NOSTER TERR
NOSTER GR
NOSTER VIEW
NOSTER PL
NOSTER ST
NOSTER RD
NOSTER HILL
MARLEY ST
MARLEY PL
MARLEY VIEW
MARLEY GR
MARLEY TERR
F3
1 WOODLEA GR
2 PARKFIELD RD
WESLEY CROFT
WESLEY CL
WESLEY GARTH
WESLEY ST
WESLEY GN
WESLEY CT
WESLEY APP
WESLEY HO
ELLAND RD
HEATH MOUNT
HEATH GR
HEATH CRES
HEATH PL
HEATH RD
HEATH RISE
CROSS HEATH GR
ELLAND ROAD IND PK
ELLAND WAY
SUNNYVIEW GDNS
SUNNYVIEW TERR
SUNNYVIEW AVE
MANORFIELD
BEESTON RD
WOODLEA ST
CROSS FLATTS DR
CROSS FLATTS GR
CROSS FLATTS RD
CROSS FLATTS ST
CROSS FLATTS PAR
CROSS FLATTS PL
CROSS FLATTS TERR
CROSS FLATTS CRES
CROSS FLATTS ROW
BACK CROSS FLATTS CRES
BACK CROSS FLATTS ROW
BACK CROSS WOOLER PL
WOOLER ST
WOOLER PL
HEATHCROFT CRES
HEATHCROFT RISE
HEATHCROFT DR
HEATHCROFT VALE
HEATHCROFT BANK
HEATHCROFT LAWN
LS11
KIRK BEESTON CL
CHAPEL FOLD
OLDROYD CRES
MAPLE CT
Windmill Hill
JUNCTION 1 RET PK
RING RD BEESTON
Cemy & Crem
Beeston Primary Sch
TOWN ST
CROW NEST LA
Liby
RECREATION RD
ST ANTHONY'S DR
DURBAN CRES
DURBAN AVE
Hugh Gaitskell Mid Sch
BARKLY RD
St Anthony's RC Prim Sch
BEESTON PARK PL
BEESTON PARK TERR
BEESTON PARK GR
BEESTON PARK CROFT
BEESTON PARK GARTH
ST ANTHONY'S RD
TUDOR GDNS
JESSAMINE AVE
GROVEHALL AVE
GROVEHALL RD
GROVEHALL PAR
GROVEHALL DR
OAKHURST MOUNT
Beeston
MOORHOUSE AVE
OLD LA
ENTERPRISE PARK IND EST
THE ROYAL LONDON IND EST
COTTINGLEY CHASE
1 COTTINGLEY HTS
2 COTTINGLEY TOWERS
COTTINGLEY VALE
COTTINGLEY DR
COTTINGLEY GR
COTTINGLEY GDNS
COTTINGLEY CRES
Cottingley Prim Sch
DULVERTON CT
MANOR MILL LA
REDHALL CL
REDHALL CRES
REDHALL GATE
GROVEHALL RD
GREEN LA
OAKHURST GR
BEECHCROFT VIEW
BEECHCROFT CL
COTTINGLEY APP
COTTINGLEY GN
Mill Shaw
MILLSHAW
WAINCLIFFE GARTH
WAINCLIFFE PL
WAINCLIFFE SQ
WAINCLIFFE CRES
CARDINAL SQ
DULVERTON SQ
DULVERTON CL
DULVERTON GN
ELLAND RD
MILLSHAW PARKWAY
MILLSHAW PARK DR
GLOBAL AVE
CARDINAL WLK
CARDINAL RD
WAINCLIFFE MOUNT
CONCOURSE HOUSE EST
CHATSWOOD DR
COTTINGLEY DR
MILLSHAW
PO

◄ 213

A3
1 BACK MIDDLETON VIEW
2 BACK TEMPEST RD
3 WOOD PL
4 HARDY VIEW
5 HARDY GR

A4
1 RECREATION ROW
2 RECREATION CRES
3 RECREATION AVE
4 ST LUKE'S VIEW

211 ▲

C3
1 BK CROSSLAND TERR
2 BACK LINDEN GR
3 LINDEN PL
4 CROSS LINDEN TERR
5 LINDEN GDNS

6 ROWLAND TERR
7 BACK ROWLAND TERR
8 CAMBERLEY ST
9 BACK CAMBERLEY ST
10 BACK STRATFORD ST

Scale: 7 inches to 1 mile
0 110 yards 1/8 mile
0 125 m 250 m

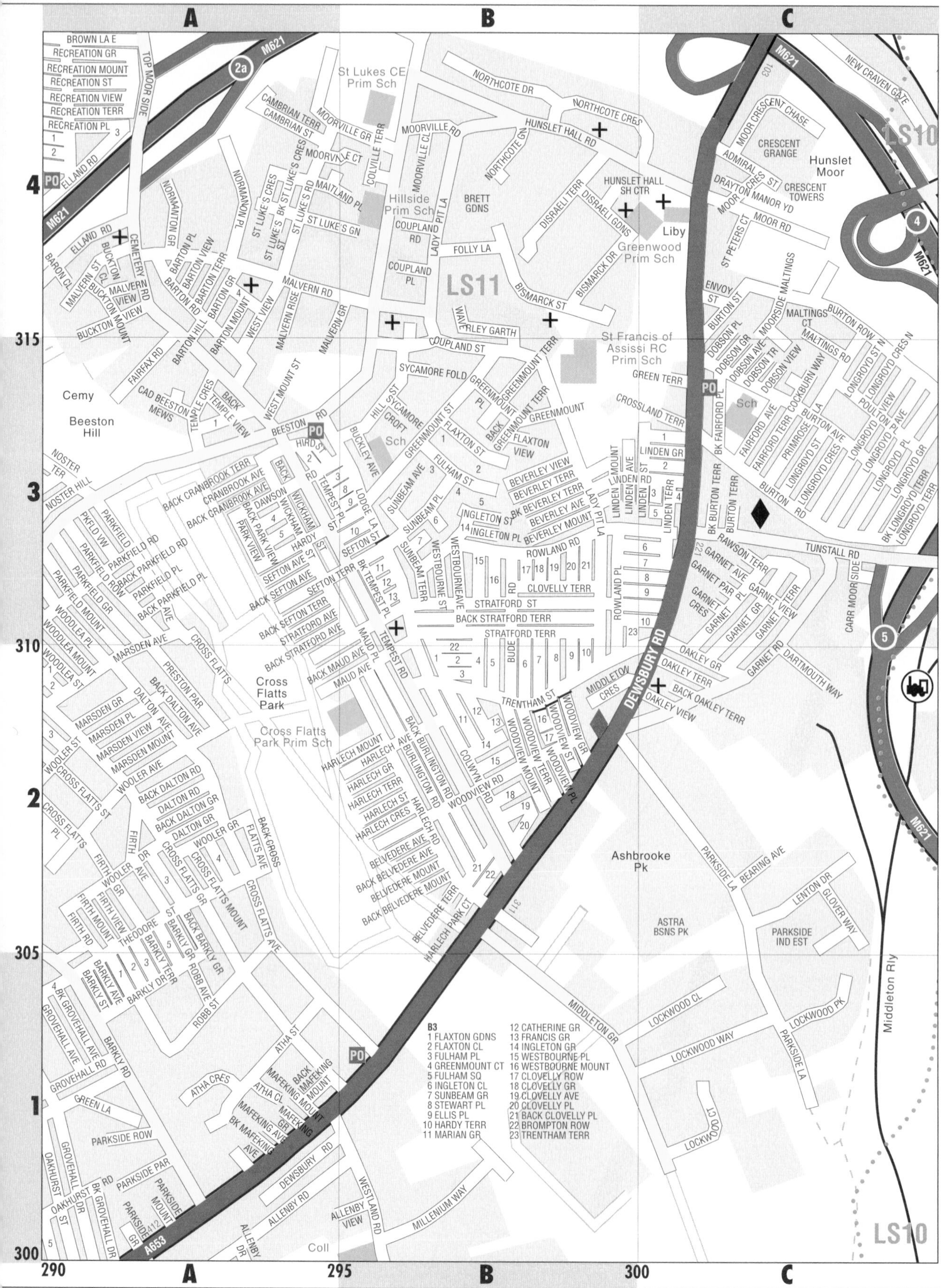

A1
1 BARKLY PL
2 BARKLY PAR
3 BACK BARKLY PAR
4 OAKHURST MOUNT
5 OAKHURST AVE

◄ 213

A2
1 WOOLER RD
2 CROSS FLATTS DR
3 BACK CROSS FLATTS GR
4 BACK CROSS FLATTS MOUNT
5 BACK BARKLY TERR

99

B2
1 BACK LODGE LA
2 BROMPTON GR
3 BROMPTON VIEW
4 BROMPTON TERR
5 BROMPTON MOUNT
6 TRENTHAM ROW
7 TRENTHAM GR

8 TRENTHAM AVE
9 TRENTHAM PL
10 BACK TRENTHAM PL
11 BACK COLWYN VIEW
12 COLWYN VIEW
13 LODGE TERR
14 COLWYN AVE
15 COLWYN MOUNT

16 UPPER WOODVIEW PL
17 CROSS WOODVIEW ST
18 COLWYN TERR
19 COLWYN PL
20 BACK COLWYN PL
21 BURLINGTON PL
22 BACK BURLINGTON PL

B3
1 FLAXTON GDNS
2 FLAXTON CL
3 FULHAM PL
4 GREENMOUNT CT
5 FULHAM SQ
6 INGLETON CL
7 SUNBEAM GR
8 STEWART PL
9 ELLIS PL
10 HARDY TERR
11 MARIAN GR

12 CATHERINE GR
13 FRANCIS GR
14 INGLETON GR
15 WESTBOURNE PL
16 WESTBOURNE MOUNT
17 CLOVELLY ROW
18 CLOVELLY GR
19 CLOVELLY AVE
20 CLOVELLY PL
21 BACK CLOVELLY PL
22 BROMPTON ROW
23 TRENTHAM TERR

D E F

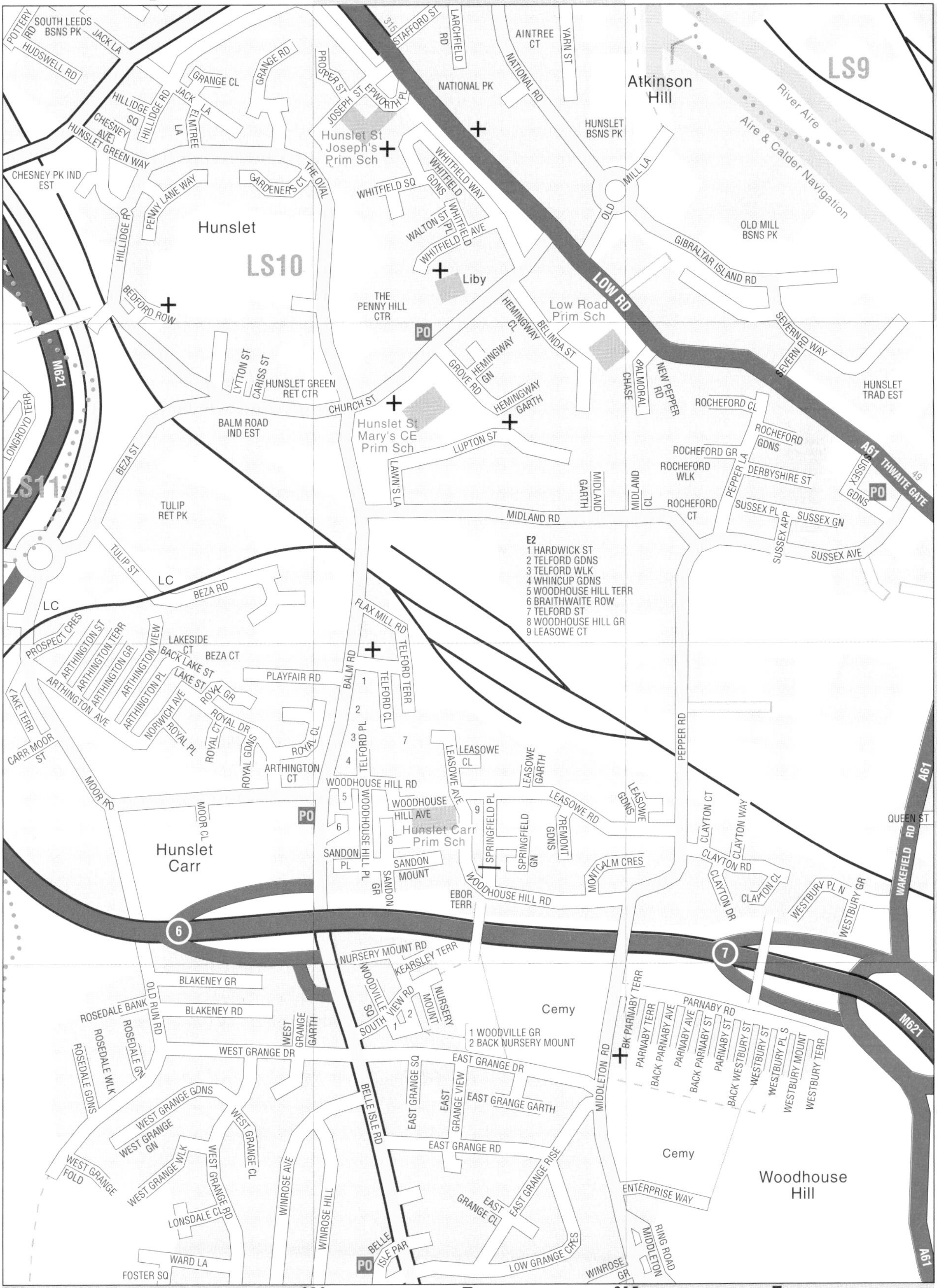

305 D 310 E 315 F

142
121

One-way streets

House numbers
1 59 HIGH ST

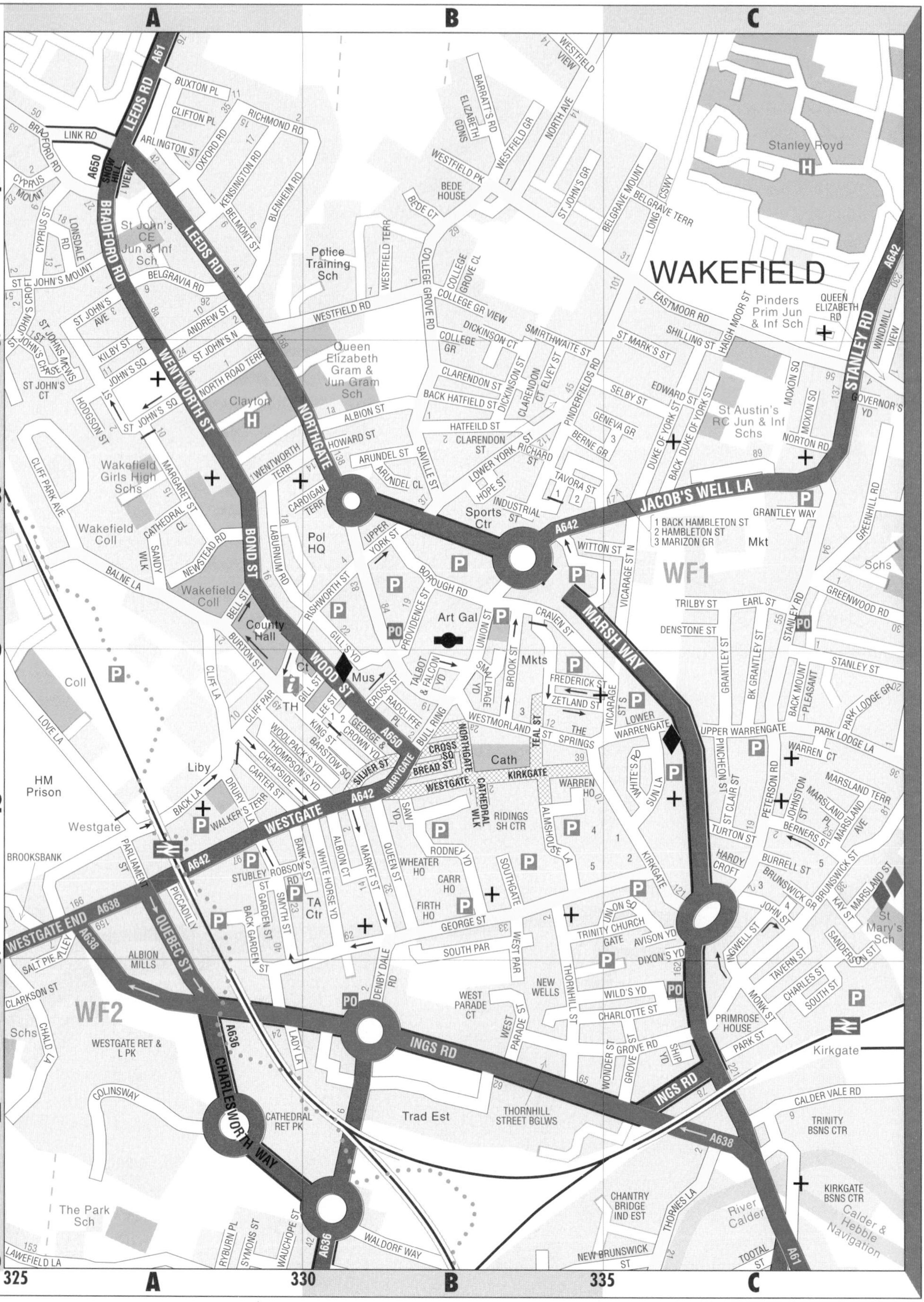

142
142
142

Scale: 7 inches to 1 mile
0 110 yards 1/8 mile
0 125 m 250 m

B2
1 TAMMY HALL ST
2 CHANCERY LA
3 WESTMORLAND HO
4 TUDOR HO
5 GREENWOOD HO

C2
1 TRINITY HO
2 MANOR HO
3 INGWELL CT
4 CRYSTAL PL
5 BRUNSWICK STREET BGLWS

Index

Street names are listed alphabetically and show the locality, the Postcode District, the page number and a reference to the square in which the name falls on the map page

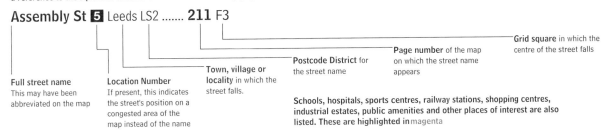

Assembly St **5** Leeds LS2 .... **211** F3

Full street name This may have been abbreviated on the map

Location Number If present, this indicates the street's position on a congested area of the map instead of the name

Town, village or locality in which the street falls.

Postcode District for the street name

Page number of the map on which the street name appears

Grid square in which the centre of the street falls

Schools, hospitals, sports centres, railway stations, shopping centres, industrial estates, public amenities and other places of interest are also listed. These are highlighted in magenta

Abbreviations used in the index

App	Approach	Cl	Close	Espl	Esplanade	Mdw	Meadows	S	South
Arc	Arcade	Comm	Common	Est	Estate	N	North	Sq	Square
Ave	Avenue	Cnr	Corner	Gdns	Gardens	Orch	Orchard	Strs	Stairs
Bvd	Boulevard	Cotts	Cottages	Gn	Green	Par	Parade	Stps	Steps
Bldgs	Buildings	Ct	Court	Gr	Grove	Pk	Park	St	Street, Saint
Bsns Pk	Business Park	Ctyd	Courtyard	Hts	Heights	Pas	Passage	Terr	Terrace
Bsns Ctr	Business Centre	Cres	Crescent	Ho	House	Pl	Place	Tk	Track
Bglws	Bungalows	Dr	Drive	Ind Est	Industrial Estate	Prec	Precinct	Trad Est	Trading Estate
Cswy	Causeway	Dro	Drove	Intc	Interchange	Prom	Promenade	Wlk	Walk
Ctr	Centre	E	East	Junc	Junction	Ret Pk	Retail Park	W	West
Circ	Circle	Emb	Embankment	La	Lane	Rd	Road	Yd	Yard
Cir	Circus	Ent	Enterprise	Mans	Mansions	Rdbt	Roundabout		

Town and village index

Aberford 64 E7
Ackworth Moor Top . 163 E6
Addingham 6 E8
Adwick Le Street 184 E2
Arthington 25 D6
Askwith 9 F5
Bacup 106 B4
Badsworth 164 E2
Baildon 38 C3
Bardsey 28 D4
Barnsley 178 F1
Barwick in Elmet 63 E7
Batley 118 C4
Beal 127 F6
Beamsley 2 F5
Bickerton 15 C7
Bingley 37 C4
Birkenshaw 96 B5
Birkin 127 D7
Blackshaw Head 87 F4
Bolton Abbey 2 E8
Boston Spa 30 D7
Bradford 74 E8
Bradford 201 B4
Bramham 30 E3
Bramhope 24 D3
Brierley 181 A3
Brighouse 115 B2
Brodsworth 195 F2
Brotherton 126 D8
Burghwallis 184 E4
Burley in Wharfdale 9 D1
Burton Salmon 105 E3
Byram 126 E7
Carlecotes 200 B3
Castleford 124 F8
Castley 25 B8
Cawthorne 193 D4
Clayton 194 C4
Clayton West 175 F2
Cleckheaton 116 C6
Clifton 10 E5
Collingham 29 B8
Cononley 4 A3
Cowling 32 C7
Cridling Stubbs 127 D1
Crigglestone 159 E5
Crofton 143 F1
Cudworth 180 B1
Cullingworth 52 C6
Darrington 147 C5
Dearne 194 D1
Denby Dale 192 B6
Denholme 52 D1
Denshaw 167 B3
Denton 9 A6
Dewsbury 139 C7
Diggle 185 B4
Draughton 1 D5
Dunford Bridge 199 D1
East Ardsley 120 B7
East Carlton 23 D3
East Keswick 28 C6
Elland 134 E6
Emley 175 C7
Fairburn 105 B4
Farnhill 4 D1
Farnley 11 D4
Featherstone 145 C7
Flockton 157 C2
Garforth 83 B5
Gildersome 97 D8
Glusburn 16 C6
Great Houghton 194 A3
Grimethorpe 181 B1
Guiseley 39 C8
Halifax 113 E7
Halifax 203 F4
Halton East 1 E8
Hampole 184 B1
Harden 36 B1
Harewood 27 A7
Haworth 51 B7
Hazlewood 3 B8
Hebden Bridge 89 B3
Hemsworth 181 C8
Heptonstall 67 C2
High Hoyland 176 C1
Hillam 105 F7
Holme 197 F8
Holme Chapel 85 B6
Holmfirth 189 B5
Honley 171 E4
Hooton Pagnell 195 C5
Horbury 141 B2
Horsforth 41 A2
Huddersfield 154 C6
Hunger Hill 8 B8
Ilkley 8 C4
Ingbirchworth 191 E1
Keighley 35 D6
Kexbrough 177 A1
Kippax 83 B2
Kirk Deighton 13 C8
Kirk Smeaton 166 D5
Kirkburton 173 E6
Kirkheaton 137 C1
Knottingley 127 B4
Leathley 24 C8
Ledsham 104 D8
Ledston 103 E6
Leeds 79 A7
Leeds 211 D3
Lepton 155 E3
Lindley 11 E7
Littleborough 129 B2
Liversedge 117 A6
Lofthouse Gate 121 D6
Low Bradley 4 D5
Mapplewell 178 C1
Marsden 168 E3
Meltham 170 E3
Menston 22 A4
Micklefield 84 A7
Mickletown 102 D3
Middleton 99 D4
Mirfield 138 A6
Monk Fryston 105 E8
Morley 98 D3
Nesfield 7 C8
Netherton 158 E6
Normanton 123 B1
Northowram 93 B2
Norton 166 F1
Notton 178 F6
Oakworth 34 D2
Ossett 140 E6
Otley 23 B8
Oxenhope 51 D2
Penistone 192 E1
Pontefract 146 B6
Pool 24 D7
Pudsey 76 D7
Queensbury 72 F2
Ripponden 132 D4
Rothwell 100 E5
Royston 179 D3
Ryhill 162 B1
Saxton 65 E8
Scarcroft 45 D8
Shafton 180 B3
Shelf 93 D6
Shepley 190 F8
Sherburn in Elmet 65 E1
Shipley 55 B7
Sicklinghall 12 C5
Silkstone 193 F1
Silsden 5 F1
Skelmanthorpe 175 B2
Skipton 4 B8
Slaithwaite 152 A1
South Elmsall 183 A2
South Hiendley 180 D6
South Kirkby 182 C1
South Milford 84 F3
Sowerby Bridge 112 C3
Spofforth 12 C8
Steeton 17 D5
Stutton 48 C5
Sutton-in-Craven 16 E5
Swillington 82 B1
Tadcaster 31 E3
Thorner 45 E5
Thornton 72 E6
Thorp Arch 14 F1
Thorpe Audlin 165 B4
Tintwistle 197 A2
Todmorden 108 C6
Trawden 32 A2
Upton 183 A8
Wadsworth Moor 68 E6
Wakefield 142 E5
Wakefield 216 C4
Walton 161 B6
West Bretton 176 E8
West Hardwick 145 B1
Wetherby 13 C6
Whitley Common 200 E7
Whitworth 106 E1
Wighill 15 F3
Wilsden 53 D5
Womersley 147 F3
Woolley 177 F7
Worsthorne 66 A4
Yeadon 40 D5

A1 Bsns Pk WF11 ... 126 C3
Aachen Way HX1 ... 202 C1
Abaseen Cl BD3 ... 75 B7
Abb Scott La BD12, BD6 ... 94 B6
Abb St HD1 ... 153 D7
Abbey Ave LS5 ... 58 F3
Abbey Cl Addingham LS29 ... 7 A8
Holmfirth HD7 ... 199 B7
Abbey Ct LS18 ... 58 B6
Abbey Dr HD8 ... 173 F1
Abbey Farm Dr HD8 ... 190 F8
Abbey Gorse LS5 ... 59 A5
Abbey Grange C of E High Sch LS16 ... 58 F8
Abbey House Mus LS5 ... 58 F5
Abbey La HX2 ... 111 F7
Abbey Lea BD15 ... 73 C8
Abbey Mount 4 LS5 ... 58 F3
Abbey Park Sch HX2 ... 91 D6
Abbey Pl HD2 ... 136 C1
Abbey Rd Batley WF17 ... 117 F4
Huddersfield HD2 ... 136 B1
Leeds LS5 ... 58 E6
Shepley HD8 ... 174 A2
Abbey Rd N HD8 ... 173 F1
Abbey Rd S HD8 ... 190 F8
Abbey St LS3 ... 210 C4
Abbey Terr 3 LS5 ... 58 F3
Abbey View LS5 ... 59 A5
Abbey Wlk Halifax HX3 ... 113 C4
Leeds LS5 ... 58 F5
Abbey Wlk S HX3 ... 113 D4
Abbeydale Garth LS5 ... 58 E6
Abbeydale Gdns LS5 ... 58 E6
Abbeydale Gr LS5 ... 58 E6
Abbeydale Mount LS5 ... 58 E6
Abbeydale Oval LS5 ... 58 E6
Abbeydale Vale LS5 ... 58 E6
Abbeydale Way LS5 ... 58 E6
Abbot La WF4 ... 178 B6
Abbot St HD1 ... 153 E7
Abbots Pl HD2 ... 136 F5
Abbots Wood BD9 ... 55 A3
Abbotside Cl BD10 ... 56 C6
Abbotsway LS25 ... 82 D6
Abbott Ct LS12 ... 210 A4
Abbott Rd LS12 ... 210 A4
Abbott Terr WF1 ... 142 D3
Abbott View LS12 ... 210 A4
Abbott's Ladies Home HX3 ... 113 C3
Abbotts Cl LS25 ... 64 E8
Abel St 4 BD12 ... 94 C4
Abelia Mount BD7 ... 73 F6
Aberdeen Dr LS12 ... 209 D4
Aberdeen Gr LS12 ... 209 D4
Aberdeen Pl BD7 ... 74 A5
Aberdeen Rd LS12 ... 209 D3
Aberdeen Terr
Bradford BD14 ... 73 D4
Bradford, Lidget Green BD7 ... 74 A6
Aberdeen Wlk LS12 ... 209 D3
Aberfield Bank LS10 ... 99 E6
Aberfield Cl LS10 ... 99 E7
Aberfield Crest LS10 ... 99 E6
Aberfield Dr
Crigglestone WF4 ... 159 E4
Middleton LS10 ... 99 E6
Aberfield Gate LS10 ... 99 E7
Aberfield Mount LS10 ... 99 E6
Aberfield Rd LS10 ... 99 E7
Aberfield Rise LS10 ... 99 E7
Aberfield Wlk LS10 ... 99 E6
Aberford C of E Sch LS25 ... 64 E7
Aberford Rd Aberford LS25 ... 64 C2
Barwick in E LS15 ... 63 E7
Bradford BD8 ... 74 B8
Bramham LS23 ... 30 D2
Garforth LS25 ... 83 A8
Lofthouse Gate WF3 ... 121 F3
Rothwell LS26 ... 101 D6
Wakefield WF1 ... 142 E8
Abingdon St Bradford BD8 ... 55 B1
Huddersfield HD2 ... 136 A1
Abraham Hill LS26 ... 100 F5
Abraham Ormerod Day Hospl OL14 ... 108 B5
Abram St BD5 ... 74 E4
Acacia Ave WF9 ... 183 A4
Acacia Cl WF10 ... 125 D6
Acacia Dr Bradford BD15 ... 54 A4
Brighouse HX3 ... 115 A7
Castleford WF10 ... 125 D6
Acacia Gn WF8 ... 125 F1
Acacia Gr Hebden Bridge HX7 ... 89 F1
Shafton S72 ... 180 C2
Acacia House 8 WF10 ... 124 E7
Acacia Park Cres BD10 ... 39 F2
Acacia Park Dr BD10 ... 39 F2
Acacia Park Terr LS19 ... 40 A2
Acacia Wlk WF11 ... 126 D3
Acaster Dr Bradford BD12 ... 94 C6
Garforth LS25 ... 83 B5
Accommodation Rd LS7 ... 60 A7
Acer Way 8 BD19 ... 115 F8
Ackroyd Ct 13 BD13 ... 72 D6
Ackroyd St Morley LS27 ... 98 B4
Todmorden OL14 ... 86 B1
Ackton Cl WF7 ... 145 A8
Ackton Hall Cres WF7 ... 145 A8
Ackton La WF7 ... 124 C1
Ackton Pasture La WF7 ... 124 B4
Ackton Pastures Junior & Infants Sch WF10 ... 124 A6
Ackworth Ave LS19 ... 40 C6
Ackworth Bridle Rd WF8 ... 164 E6
Ackworth Cres LS19 ... 40 C6
Ackworth Dr LS19 ... 40 D6
Ackworth House Cl WF7 ... 164 A8
Ackworth Rd
Featherstone WF7 ... 145 D3
Pontefract WF7, WF8 ... 146 C5
Ackworth Sch WF7 ... 164 A7
Ackworth St BD5 ... 74 E4
Acme Terr WF1 ... 142 D3
Acorn Bsns Pk BD23 ... 4 A7
Acorn Cl BD6 ... 93 E6
Acorn Dr LS14 ... 62 C8
Acorn Gr HD7 ... 189 D3
Acorn Pk BD17 ... 38 E2
Acorn St Halifax HX1 ... 202 C3
Keighley BD21 ... 35 B5
Acre Ave BD2 ... 56 B5
Acre Cir LS10 ... 99 C4
Acre Cl Bradford BD2 ... 56 B5
Middleton LS10 ... 99 C4
Acre Cres Bradford BD2 ... 56 B5
Middleton LS10 ... 99 C4
Acre Dr BD2 ... 56 B5
Acre Fold LS29 ... 6 E8
Acre Gr Bradford BD2 ... 56 B5
Middleton LS10 ... 99 C4
Acre House Ave HD3 ... 153 C8
Acre La
Bradford, Bolton Outlanes BD2 ... 56 B4
Bradford, Brownroyd Hill BD6 ... 74 C1
Haworth BD22 ... 51 C7
Heptonstall HX7 ... 88 C6
Holmfirth, Hinchcliffe Mill HD7 ... 188 D2
Holmfirth, Snowgate Head HD7 ... 190 B6
Meltham HD7 ... 170 F1
Acre Mount LS10 ... 99 C4
Acre Pl LS10 ... 99 C4
Acre Rd LS10 ... 99 C4
Acre Rise BD17 ... 38 C4
Acre Sq LS10 ... 99 C4
Acre St Huddersfield HD3 ... 153 C8
Middleton LS10 ... 99 D4
Acre Terr LS10 ... 99 D4
Acre The BD12 ... 94 B5
Acre Villas 1 HX7 ... 89 E1
Acrehowe Rise BD17 ... 38 E4
Acres Hall Ave LS28 ... 77 A6
Acres Hall Cres LS28 ... 77 A6
Acres Hall Dr LS28 ... 77 A6
Acres La Heptonstall HX7 ... 88 F4
Holmfirth HD7 ... 187 F4
Acres Rd WF3 ... 121 C8
Acres St BD21 ... 35 B6
Acres The Addingham LS29 ... 7 A8
Beamsley LS29 ... 3 A1
Sutton in C BD20 ... 16 C4
Acton Flat La HD3 ... 135 A3
Acton St BD3 ... 75 C7
Acute Terr WF2 ... 141 E6
Ada St Baildon BD17 ... 38 E2
6 Halifax HX3 ... 92 C1
11 Keighley BD21 ... 35 A7
8 Queensbury BD13 ... 72 D1
Shipley BD18 ... 54 F8
Ada's Pl LS28 ... 57 E2
Adam Croft BD13 ... 52 D6
Adam Ct HD3 ... 135 B1
Adam St 7 Bradford BD6 ... 74 B1
Todmorden OL14 ... 108 B6
Adams Gr LS15 ... 62 E4
Addersgate La HX13 ... 92 E4
Addi St BD4 ... 75 C3
Addingford Cl WF4 ... 159 A8
Addingford Dr WF4 ... 159 A8
Addingford La WF4 ... 159 A8
Addingham First Sch LS29 ... 2 E1
Addingham Gdns LS12 ... 209 D3
Addingham Middle Sch LS29 ... 2 F1
Addison Ave Bradford BD3 ... 56 D1
Normanton WF6 ... 123 C1
Addison Ct Horbury WF4 ... 141 C2
Leeds LS15 ... 81 D6
Addle Croft La HD8 ... 155 F5
Addlethorpe La LS22 ... 12 A5
Addy Cres WF9 ... 182 F3
Adel Garth LS16 ... 42 D5
Adel Gn LS16 ... 42 D4
Adel Grange Cl LS16 ... 42 C2
Adel Grange Croft LS16 ... 42 C2
Adel Grange Mews LS16 ... 42 C2
Adel La LS16 ... 42 C3
Adel Mead LS16 ... 42 D4
Adel Mill LS16 ... 42 D6
Adel Park Cl LS16 ... 42 C3
Adel Park Croft LS16 ... 42 C3
Adel Park Ct LS16 ... 42 C3
Adel Park Dr LS16 ... 42 C3
Adel Park Gdns LS16 ... 42 C3
Adel Pasture LS16 ... 42 C3
Adel Prim Sch LS16 ... 42 D3
Adel St John the Baptist CE Primary Sch LS16 ... 42 D4
Adel Towers Cl LS16 ... 42 D3
Adel Towers Ct LS16 ... 42 D3
Adel Vale LS16 ... 42 D4
Adel Wood Cl LS16 ... 42 D3
Adel Wood Dr LS16 ... 42 D3
Adel Wood Gdns LS16 ... 42 D3
Adel Wood Gr LS16 ... 42 D3
Adel Wood Pl LS16 ... 42 D3
Adel Wood Rd LS16 ... 42 D3
Adelaide House BD16 ... 37 B2
Adelaide Rise 1 BD17 ... 38 C1
Adelaide St Bradford BD5 ... 201 B1
Halifax HX1 ... 202 B3
Hebden Bridge HX7 ... 88 F3
3 Todmorden OL14 ... 108 B6
Adelaide Terr HX4 ... 133 F3
Adelphi Rd HD3 ... 153 C7
Adgil Cres HX3 ... 114 A4
Administration Rd LS9 ... 80 C3
Admiral St LS11 ... 214 C4
Adolphus St BD1 ... 201 C2
Adowsley Cl WF7 ... 163 E6
Adwalton Cl BD11 ... 96 D5
Adwalton Gn BD11 ... 96 D5
Adwalton Gr BD13 ... 72 F1
Adwick Gr WF2 ... 160 B5
Adwick Pl LS4 ... 59 C2
Adwick Terr WF8 ... 125 E2
Aeron Wilkinson Ct WF9 ... 182 A2
Agar St 5 BD8 ... 73 F8
Agar Terr 6 BD8 ... 73 F8
Agbrigg Gr WF2 ... 142 E2
Agbrigg Rd WF1, WF2 ... 142 E2
Agincourt Dr WF6 ... 122 E4
Agnes St BD20 ... 18 C1
Agnes Stewart CE High Sch LS9 ... 212 B4
Ails La HX2 ... 90 D1
Aimbry Ct HD5 ... 154 F2
Ainley Bottom HX5 ... 135 A5
Ainley Cl HD3 ... 135 A2
Ainley Pk HD7 ... 152 E4
Ainley Pl HD7 ... 151 C2
Ainley Rd HD3 ... 135 A3
Ainley St 9 HX5 ... 134 F6
Ainleys Ind Est HX5 ... 135 A5
Ainsbury Ave Baildon BD10 ... 39 B3
Bradford BD10 ... 39 C3
Ainsdale Cl S71 ... 179 B5
Ainsdale Gr BD13 ... 52 E6
Ainsdale Rd S71 ... 179 B5
Ainsley La HD7 ... 168 D4
Ainsty Cres LS22 ... 13 E7
Ainsty Dr LS22 ... 13 E7
Ainsty Garth LS22 ... 13 E7
Ainsty Rd LS22 ... 13 D7
Ainsty View LS22 ... 13 E7
Aintree Cl LS25 ... 82 F2
Aintree Ct LS10 ... 215 E4
Aire & Calder Cotts WF3 ... 122 B2
Aire Cl BD17 ... 38 B1
Aire Cres BD20 ... 16 E6
Aire Ct BD20 ... 17 E8
Aire Gr LS19 ... 40 C6
Aire Mount LS22 ... 13 D7
Aire Pl LS3 ... 205 E1
Aire Rd LS22 ... 13 D7
Aire St Bingley BD16 ... 36 E6
Bradford BD10 ... 39 A1
Brighouse HD6 ... 115 B1
Castleford WF10 ... 124 D8
Dewsbury WF13 ... 138 F5
Glusburn BD20 ... 16 E6
3 Haworth BD22 ... 51 D7
Keighley BD21 ... 35 D8
Knottingley WF11 ... 127 A5
Leeds LS1 ... 211 E3
Aire Terr WF10 ... 103 D1
Aire Valley Cl BD20 ... 4 B6
Aire Valley Dr BD20 ... 4 B6
Aire View Brotherton WF11 ... 126 C8
Cononley BD20 ... 4 A2
Keighley BD20 ... 18 F2
Knottingley WF11 ... 126 D5
Silsden BD20 ... 5 E1
Yeadon LS19 ... 40 C6
Aire View Ave Shipley BD16 ... 54 B8
Shipley BD18 ... 55 A8
Aire View Dr BD20 ... 36 C7
Aire View Infants Sch BD20 ... 5 E1
Aire Way BD17 ... 38 A1
Airebank BD16 ... 36 F3
Aireborough L Ctr LS20 ... 39 E8
Aireburn Ave BD20 ... 17 D5
Airedale Ave BD16 ... 54 A7
Airedale Bsns Ctr BD23 ... 4 A8
Airedale Cliff LS13 ... 58 C5
Airedale College Mount BD3 ... 56 A1
Airedale College Rd BD3 ... 56 A1
Airedale College Terr BD3 ... 56 A1
Airedale Cres BD3 ... 56 A1
Airedale Croft 5 LS13 ... 57 F5
Airedale Ct LS14 ... 61 F5
Airedale Dr
Castleford WF10 ... 104 C2
Garforth LS25 ... 83 B6
Horsforth LS18 ... 57 F8
Shelf HX3 ... 93 B5
Airedale Gdns LS13 ... 57 F5
Airedale General Hospl BD20 ... 17 B6
Airedale Gr Horsforth LS18 ... 57 F8
3 Rothwell LS26 ... 101 D6
Airedale High Sch WF10 ... 125 D7
Airedale Hts WF2 ... 141 C4
Airedale Mews BD20 ... 5 E1
Airedale Mount
Keighley BD20 ... 36 C8
Pudsey LS13 ... 57 E5
Airedale Pl 4 BD17 ... 38 E2
Airedale Quay LS13 ... 58 A4
Airedale Rd Bradford BD3 ... 55 F1
Castleford WF10 ... 125 B7
Keighley BD21 ... 35 F8
Rothwell LS26 ... 101 D6
Airedale St Bingley BD16 ... 36 F3
Bradford BD2 ... 56 B3
4 Keighley BD21 ... 35 E8
Airedale Terr Baildon BD17 ... 38 D2
8 Morley LS27 ... 98 B4
2 Rothwell LS26 ... 101 D6
Airedale Trad Pk BD20 ... 16 E7
Airedale View
Glusburn BD20 ... 16 D7
4 Pudsey LS13 ... 57 F5
1 Rothwell LS26 ... 101 D6
Airedale Wharf LS13 ... 57 F4
Airedale & Wharfdale Coll of Further Education LS18 ... 57 F7
Aireside BD20 ... 4 B2
Aireside Ave BD20 ... 4 B2
Aireside Ctr LS1 ... 211 D3
Aireside Terr BD20 ... 4 A3
Airevalley Rd BD21 ... 36 B7
Aireview Cres BD17 ... 38 A1
Aireview Primary Sch LS13 ... 57 F4
Aireview Terr Keighley BD20 ... 36 B8
Keighley, Long Lea BD21 ... 35 E6
Aireville Ave BD9 ... 55 B5
Aireville Cl Keighley BD20 ... 18 A2
Shipley BD18 ... 55 B5
Aireville Cres Shipley BD9 ... 55 B4
Silsden BD20 ... 5 F1
Aireville Dr BD20 ... 5 F1
Aireville Grange BD18 ... 55 B5
Aireville Mount BD20 ... 36 C8
Aireville Rise BD20 ... 5 F1
Aireville Rd BD9 ... 55 C5
Aireville Rise BD9 ... 55 B4
Aireville St BD20 ... 18 A2
Aireville Terr LS29 ... 9 E1
Aireworth Cl BD21 ... 18 E1
Aireworth Gr BD21 ... 35 E8
Aireworth Rd BD21 ... 35 E8
Aireworth St BD21 ... 35 B6
Airey St BD21 ... 35 A7
Airlie Ave LS8 ... 207 F4
Airlie Pl LS8 ... 207 F4
Airville Dr BD18 ... 55 B5
Airville Gr BD18 ... 55 B5
Akam Rd BD1 ... 74 D7
Aked St BD1 ... 201 C3
Aked's Rd HX1 ... 203 D2
Aketon Dr WF10 ... 124 C6
Aketon Rd WF10 ... 124 C6
Akroyd Ct HX3 ... 203 E4
Akroyd La HX7 ... 89 B6
Akroyd Pl HX1 ... 203 E4
Akroyd Terr HX2 ... 202 B1
Alabama St 4 HX1 ... 202 B3
Alan Cres LS15 ... 81 A7
Alandale Cres LS25 ... 82 D6
Alandale Dr LS25 ... 82 D6
Alandale Gr LS25 ... 82 D6
Alandale Rd Garforth LS25 ... 82 D6
Huddersfield HD2 ... 136 E5
Alaska Pl LS7 ... 204 B2
Alban St BD4 ... 75 B4
Albans Cl LS17 ... 28 E5
Albany Cres WF9 ... 182 F2
Albany Ct Keighley BD20 ... 35 A8
Pontefract WF8 ... 146 D7
Albany Dr HD5 ... 155 A6
Albany Pl 5 WF9 ... 182 F2
Albany Rd Huddersfield HD5 ... 155 A7
Rothwell LS26 ... 100 D6
Albany St Bradford BD5 ... 74 E4
Bradford, Brownroyd Hill BD6 ... 74 C1
Halifax HX3 ... 203 F1
Huddersfield HD1 ... 153 F4
Leeds LS12 ... 209 D3
South Elmsall WF9 ... 182 F2
Albany Terr Halifax HX3 ... 203 F1
Leeds LS12 ... 209 D3
Albany Wlk LS29 ... 8 B3
Albert Ave Bradford BD10 ... 56 C8
Halifax HX2 ... 202 A4
Shipley BD18 ... 37 F1
Albert Bldgs BD10 ... 56 B6
Albert Cl WF17 ... 118 C2
Albert Cres Birkenshaw BD11 ... 96 B4
Queensbury BD13 ... 72 E1
Albert Ct HX2 ... 202 A4
Albert Dr Halifax HX2 ... 202 A4
Morley LS27 ... 98 D5
Albert Edward St 4 BD13 ... 72 E1
Albert Gdns HX2 ... 202 A4
Albert Gr LS6 ... 59 D6
Albert La OL14 ... 108 B6
Albert Pl Batley WF12 ... 118 F2
Bradford BD3 ... 75 E8
Horsforth LS18 ... 41 C1
Mickletown LS26 ... 102 B3
Albert Prom HX3 ... 113 A3
Albert Rd Clayton West HD8 ... 175 E2
Glusburn BD20 ... 16 D6
Halifax, Pellon HX2 ... 202 A4
Morley LS27 ... 98 C5
Queensbury BD13 ... 72 E2
Rothwell LS26 ... 101 C6
Shipley BD18 ... 54 F8
Sowerby Bridge HX6 ... 112 C5
Albert Sq Silsden BD20 ... 5 E1
Yeadon LS19 ... 40 C7
Albert St 2 Baildon BD17 ... 38 C1
Bradford BD6 ... 94 B8
Bradford, Springfield BD10 ... 56 B6
Bradford, Wyke BD12 ... 94 C2
Brighouse HD6 ... 115 C2
Castleford WF10 ... 124 D8
Cleckheaton BD19 ... 116 D8
Cudworth S72 ... 180 C1
Elland HX5 ... 134 F6
Featherstone WF7 ... 145 D5
Halifax HX1 ... 203 D3
Albert St continued
1 Haworth BD22 ... 51 F8
Hebden Bridge HX7 ... 89 A3
7 Hebden Bridge, Wadsworth Banks Fields HX7 ... 89 E1
Huddersfield HD1 ... 153 F3
Keighley BD21 ... 35 B7
Liversedge WF15 ... 117 C3
Normanton WF6 ... 123 C3
Pudsey LS28 ... 76 D6
Queensbury BD13 ... 72 F1
Sutton in C BD20 ... 16 E5
Thornton BD13 ... 72 D6
Todmorden OL14 ... 108 B6
Wilsden BD15 ... 53 C4
Albert Terr
Bradford, Raw Nook BD12 ... 94 F5
5 Bradford, Wyke Common BD12 ... 94 D2
Shipley BD18 ... 37 F1
Yeadon LS19 ... 40 C7
Albert View HX2 ... 202 A4
Albert Way BD11 ... 96 B4
Albert Wlk 4 BD18 ... 54 E8
Albert Yd HD1 ... 154 A5
Alberta Ave LS7 ... 204 B2
Albion Arc LS1 ... 211 F4
Albion Ave LS12 ... 210 A3
Albion Cl LS23 ... 30 D5
Albion Croft WF5 ... 140 E6
Albion Ct Batley WF16 ... 117 D4
Bradford BD1 ... 201 B3
Halifax HX1 ... 203 E3
Wakefield WF1 ... 216 B2
Albion Fold BD15 ... 53 C5
Albion Mills WF2 ... 216 A1
Albion Pk LS12 ... 210 B4
Albion Pl
13 Brighouse HD6 ... 115 A3
Guiseley LS20 ... 22 E1
Leeds LS1 ... 211 F4
South Elmsall WF9 ... 183 A3
Thornton BD13 ... 72 C6
Albion Rd Bradford BD10 ... 56 C8
Dewsbury WF12 ... 139 E1
Pudsey LS28 ... 57 E2
Albion Sq WF2 ... 141 E7
Albion St Bacup OL13 ... 106 A3
Batley WF17 ... 118 D4
Batley, Heckmondwike WF16 ... 117 D4
Boston Spa LS23 ... 30 D5
Bradford BD1 ... 201 B3
3 Bradford, Buttershaw BD6 ... 93 F7
Brighouse HD6 ... 115 A3
Castleford WF10 ... 124 C8
Cleckheaton BD19 ... 116 E7
Denholme BD13 ... 71 D8
Dewsbury WF13 ... 118 C1
Dewsbury, Ravensthorpe WF13 ... 138 F5
Elland HX5 ... 135 A6
Halifax HX1 ... 203 E3
Haworth BD22 ... 51 E8
Hemsworth WF9 ... 163 A3
Huddersfield HD1 ... 154 A5
Leeds LS1, LS2 ... 211 F4
1 Liversedge WF15 ... 117 B4
Morley LS27 ... 98 A4
Otley LS21 ... 23 B7
6 Pudsey LS28 ... 76 F7
Queensbury BD13 ... 72 D1
Rothwell WF3 ... 100 D3
Wakefield WF1 ... 216 B3
Albion Terr Boston Spa LS23 ... 30 D5
Hebden Bridge HX7 ... 88 F3
Albion Way LS12 ... 210 B4
Albion Yd BD1 ... 201 B3
Alcester Garth BD3 ... 75 B8
Alcester Pl LS8 ... 207 F4
Alcester Rd LS8 ... 207 F4
Alcester St 13 LS8 ... 207 F4
Alcester Terr LS8 ... 207 F4
Aldams Rd WF12 ... 139 C7
Alden Ave LS27 ... 98 A2
Alden Cl LS27 ... 98 A2
Alden Cres WF8 ... 146 B7
Alden Ct 5 LS27 ... 98 A2
Alden Fold 4 LS27 ... 98 A2
Alder Ave Holmfirth HD7 ... 189 C8
Keighley BD21 ... 35 E5
Wakefield WF2 ... 142 A8
Alder Carr BD17 ... 38 B3
Alder Cl S75 ... 178 A1
Alder Dr LS28 ... 76 A8
Alder Garth LS28 ... 76 B8
Alder Gr Halifax HX2 ... 91 E6
Normanton WF6 ... 144 B7
Alder Hill Ave LS7 ... 60 A7
Alder Hill Gr LS7 ... 60 A7
Alder St HD1, HD2 ... 136 B1
Aldermanbury BD1 ... 201 B3
Alderney Rd WF12 ... 118 F2
Alderscholes Cl 9 BD13 ... 72 D6
Alderscholes La BD13 ... 72 C5
Aldersgate LS12 ... 209 F3
Alderson St 2 BD6 ... 93 E7
Alderstone Rise HD3 ... 135 A2
Aldersyde WF17 ... 96 E1
Alderton Bank LS17 ... 42 F2
Alderton Cres LS17 ... 43 A2
Alderton Hts LS17 ... 42 F2
Alderton Mount LS17 ... 42 F2
Alderton Pl LS17 ... 42 F2
Alderton Rise LS17 ... 43 A2
Aldonley HD5 ... 155 A4
Alegar St HD6 ... 115 C2
Alexander Ave LS15 ... 80 F7

Alexander Cres WF7 .... 145 E7
Alexander Ct BD20 .... 36 D7
Alexander Rd WF7 .... 145 D6
Alexander Sq 10 BD14 .... 73 B4
Alexander St
5 Bradford BD6 .... 94 B8
Leeds LS1 .... 211 E4
Alexander Terr HX1 .... 202 B3
Alexandra Ave 3 WF17 .... 96 F1
Alexandra Cres
Dewsbury WF13 .... 118 A2
Elland HX5 .... 135 B7
Ilkley LS29 .... 8 A4
Alexandra Dr WF6 .... 144 B7
Alexandra Gr Leeds LS6 .... 205 E2
Pudsey LS28 .... 76 D6
Alexandra Rd Batley WF17 . 118 D4
Bradford BD2 .... 56 C5
8 Hebden Bridge HX7 .... 89 A3
Horsforth LS18 .... 58 C8
Huddersfield HD3 .... 153 C7
Leeds LS6 .... 205 E2
Pudsey LS28 .... 76 C6
Shipley BD18 .... 55 A7
Alexandra Rd W HD3 .... 153 C5
Alexandra Sq 14 BD18 .... 54 F8
Alexandra St Bradford BD7 ... 74 C5
Halifax HX1 .... 203 E3
4 Liversedge WF15 .... 117 A4
Queensbury BD13 .... 72 E1
Alexandra Terr
Bradford BD2 .... 56 C2
6 Yeadon LS19 .... 40 C7
Alford Terr BD7 .... 74 A7
Alfred E Briggs Almshouses
3 BD12 .... 94 B6
Alfred St
4 Batley, Heckmondwike WF16 .... 117 D3
Batley, Mount Pleasant WF17 .... 118 B4
5 Brighouse HD6 .... 115 B3
1 Dewsbury WF13 .... 118 E1
Elland HX4 .... 134 D7
Halifax HX1 .... 202 B3
4 Huddersfield HD1 .... 154 A5
3 Liversedge WF15 .... 117 B4
6 Morley LS27 .... 98 C8
Royston S71 .... 179 E4
Alfred St E HX1 .... 203 F3
Alfreds Way WF17 .... 118 C5
Alice St Bradford BD8 .... 74 D8
2 Cleckheaton BD19 .... 116 D8
5 Haworth BD22 .... 51 C6
Keighley BD21 .... 35 C7
Alkincote St BD21 .... 35 C6
All Alone BD10 .... 56 A7
All Alone Rd BD10 .... 56 A6
All Saint's Circ LS26 .... 101 D6
All Saint's Dr LS26 .... 101 C6
All Saint's Rd LS26 .... 101 D6
All Saint's View LS26 .... 101 C7
All Saints C of E Jun & Inf Sch WF7 .... 124 D1
All Saints C of E Junior Sch LS21 .... 23 A8
All Saints' CE Fst Sch BD5 .. 74 D5
All Saints' CE Junior & Infant Sch HX3 113 C2
All Saints CE Primary Sch LS9 .... 212 C4
All Saints' First Sch LS29 .... 8 B5
All Saints High RC Sch HD2 .... 136 C5
All Saints Ind Est WF8 .... 125 E1
All Saints Rd BD7 .... 74 C5
All Saints' View 2 WF8 .... 146 E8
All Souls' Rd HX3 .... 92 C1
All Souls' St 3 HX3 .... 92 C1
All Souls' Terr 2 HX3 .... 92 C1
Allan Haigh Cl WF2 .... 141 D8
Allan St BD3 .... 75 B6
Allan Terr HX6 .... 112 C3
Allanbridge Cl BD10 .... 56 C7
Allandale Ave BD6 .... 94 A7
Allandale Rd BD6 .... 94 A7
Allanfield Terr LS22 .... 13 E8
Allen Croft BD11 .... 96 A5
Allenby Cres LS11 .... 99 A8
Allenby Dr LS11 .... 99 A8
Allenby Gdns LS11 .... 99 A8
Allenby Gr LS11 .... 99 A8
Allenby Pl LS11 .... 99 A8
Allenby Rd LS11 .... 99 A8
Allenby View LS11 .... 214 B1
Allendale Rd S75 .... 177 D1
Allerby Gn BD6 .... 93 F6
Allergill Pk HD7 .... 188 D5
Allerton Ave LS17 .... 43 D2
Allerton Bywater Prim Sch WF10 .... 103 B5
Allerton Cl BD15 .... 54 B1
Allerton Dr LS17 .... 28 C6
Allerton First & Middle Sch BD15 .... 54 B1
Allerton Gr LS17 .... 43 D2
Allerton Grange Ave LS17 .. 43 E1
Allerton Grange Cl LS17 .. 60 C8
Allerton Grange Cres LS17 204 A4
Allerton Grange Croft LS8 204 B4
Allerton Grange Dr
Bradford BD15 .... 54 B1
Leeds LS17 .... 204 A4
Allerton Grange Gdns LS17 .... 204 A4
Allerton Grange High Sch LS17 .... 43 E1
Allerton Grange Rise LS17 204 A4
Allerton Grange Vale LS17 204 A4
Allerton Grange Way LS17, LS8 .... 204 A4
Allerton Grange Wlk LS17 204 A4
Allerton High Sch LS17 .... 43 B3
Allerton Hill LS7 .... 60 C7
Allerton La
Bradford BD13, BD15 .... 73 A7
Thornton BD13, BD15 .... 73 A7
Allerton Pk LS7 .... 204 B3
Allerton Pl Halifax HX1 .... 202 C3
Leeds LS17 .... 43 D2
Allerton Rd BD15 .... 54 B1
Allerton St LS4 .... 205 D2
Allescholes Rd OL14 .... 129 B7
Alliance St LS12 .... 209 D3
Allinson St LS12 .... 210 B2
Allison Dr HD2 .... 136 B2
Allison La BD2 .... 55 D4
Allison St WF7 .... 145 C5
Allison Terr WF2 .... 120 B2
Alloe Field View HX2 .... 91 E6
Allott Cl WF9 .... 182 F3
Allums La LS21 .... 25 F5
Alma Cl LS28 .... 57 C3
Alma Cotts 12 LS6 .... 59 D5
Alma Dr HD5 .... 154 D6
Alma Gr Leeds LS9 .... 207 F2
Shipley BD18 .... 55 D8
Alma La Batley WF16 .... 117 D6
Ripponden HX6 .... 132 B7
Alma Pl Keighley BD21 .... 35 C5
Leeds BD3 .... 207 E2
Alma Rd Leeds LS6 .... 59 E5
Todmorden OL14 .... 108 A1
Alma St Bacup OL13 .... 106 A2
Bradford, Cutler Heights BD4 . 75 D3
Bradford, Swain Green BD4 ... 75 D5
Elland HX5 .... 135 A6
Haworth BD22 .... 51 C8
Keighley BD21 .... 35 C5
Leeds LS9 .... 207 F1
Queensbury BD13 .... 72 D1
Rothwell LS26 .... 101 D7
Shipley BD18 .... 55 D8
Todmorden OL14 .... 108 A1
Yeadon LS19 .... 40 C7
Alma Terr Keighley BD21 .... 35 C5
Keighley, Green End BD20 .... 19 E1
Rothwell LS26 .... 100 D6
Almhouses BD21 .... 35 A3
Almond Cl WF9 .... 183 A5
Almond St BD3 .... 75 C6
Almond Way WF17 .... 96 F1
Almondbury Bank HD5 .... 154 E5
Almondbury CE Inf Sch HD5 .... 154 F2
Almondbury Cl HD5 .... 155 A3
Almondbury Comm HD4 .... 154 F1
Almondbury County Junior Sch HD5 . 155 A4
Almondbury Secondary Sch HD5 .... 154 F4
Almondroyd WF16 .... 117 C5
Almscliffe Ave WF12 .... 139 E8
Almshouse Hill LS23 .... 30 D2
Almshouse La
Crigglestone WF2 .... 160 B4
Wakefield WF1 .... 216 B2
Alpha St BD21 .... 35 D6
Alpine Cl WF17 .... 118 B4
Alpine Rise BD13 .... 72 D6
Alpine Terr LS26 .... 100 D6
Alston Cl BD9 .... 54 D1
Alston La LS14 .... 62 A3
Alston Rd BD21 .... 18 D1
Altar Dr Bradford BD9 .... 55 A3
Keighley BD20 .... 19 A1
Altar La BD16 .... 36 C4
Altar View BD16 .... 36 E5
Althorpe Gr BD10 .... 56 A6
Altinkool St WF1 .... 142 F2
Altofts Hall Rd WF6 .... 122 F4
Altofts La WF10 .... 123 D6
Altofts Lodge Dr WF6 .... 122 E3
Altofts Middle Sch WF6 .... 122 F3
Altofts Rd WF6 .... 123 A2
Alton Ave HD5 .... 154 F7
Alton Gr Bradford BD9 .... 54 F3
Shipley BD18 .... 55 B5
Alton Way S75 .... 178 A1
Alum Ct BD9 .... 55 A3
Alum Dr BD9 .... 55 A3
Alvanley Ct BD8 .... 73 D8
Alverthorpe Rd WF2 .... 141 F6
Alvo Terr BD18 .... 55 B6
Alwen Ave HD2 .... 135 F2
Alwoodley Chase LS17 .... 43 E5
Alwoodley Court Gdns LS17 .... 43 A6
Alwoodley Ct LS17 .... 42 F5
Alwoodley Gdns LS17 .... 43 A5
Alwoodley Golf Course LS17 .... 43 F6
Alwoodley La LS17 .... 43 C6
Alwoodley Primary Sch LS17 .... 43 A3
Amber St WF17 .... 118 A6
Amberley Ct BD3 .... 75 C6
Amberley Gdns LS12 .... 209 F2
Amberley Rd LS12 .... 209 F2
Amberley Rise DN6 .... 184 F2
Amberley St Bradford BD3 ... 75 C7
Leeds LS12 .... 210 A2
Amberton App LS8 .... 208 C4
Amberton Cl LS8 .... 61 C5
Amberton Cres LS8 .... 208 C4
Amberton Garth LS8 .... 208 C4
Amberton Gdns LS8 .... 208 C4
Amberton Gr LS8 .... 208 C4
Amberton La LS8 .... 208 C4
Amberton Mount LS8 .... 208 C4
Amberton Pl LS8 .... 208 B4
Amberton Rd LS8, LS9 .... 208 C4
Amberton St LS8 .... 208 C4
Amberton Terr LS8 .... 61 C5
Amble Tonia BD13 .... 52 E1
Ambler St Bradford BD8 .... 55 C1
Castleford WF10 .... 124 E7
Keighley BD21 .... 35 D7
Ambler Way BD13 .... 92 C7
Amblers Croft BD10 .... 39 B2
Amblers Ct LS28 .... 76 E6
Amblers Mews
4 Baildon BD17 .... 38 C4
Keighley BD20 .... 36 D8
Amblers Terr 10 HX3 .... 92 C1
Ambleside Ave BD9 .... 54 F2
Ambleside Dr WF2 .... 161 A6
Ambleside Gdns LS28 .... 76 C7
Ambleside Gr LS26 .... 101 C6
Ambleside Rd WF10 .... 104 E1
Ambleside Wlk LS22 .... 13 B6
Ambleton Way BD13 .... 92 C8
Amelia St 1 BD18 .... 54 F8
America La Brighouse HD6 . 115 C2
Sutton in C BD20 .... 16 E1
America Moor La LS27 .... 98 A2
Amisfield Rd HX3 .... 114 D8
Amos St HX1 .... 202 B3
Amport Cl HD6 .... 115 B1
Amundsen Ave BD2 .... 56 A5
Amy St 9 Bingley BD16 .... 37 A3
3 Halifax HX3 .... 92 A2
Amyroyce Dr BD18 .... 55 E7
Anaheim Dr WF1 .... 121 D5
Ancaster Cres LS16 .... 59 B7
Ancaster Rd LS16 .... 59 B7
Ancaster View LS16 .... 59 B7
Anchor Pl HD6 .... 136 D8
Anchor St Huddersfield HD1 154 B7
4 Todmorden OL14 .... 108 C5
Anchorage The BD16 .... 36 F4
Anderson Ave LS8 .... 207 E2
Anderson Ct WF10 .... 125 C5
Anderson House BD17 .... 38 B1
Anderson Mount LS8 .... 207 E2
Anderson St Bradford BD8 .... 55 C1
Pontefract WF8 .... 125 C1
Wakefield WF2 .... 142 A6
Anderton St Glusburn BD20 ... 16 D7
Wakefield WF1 .... 142 E3
Andover Gn BD4 .... 75 E4
Andrew Cl HX3 .... 114 A4
Andrew Cres
Huddersfield HD4 .... 153 A1
Lofthouse Gate WF1 .... 121 B5
Andrew St
Featherstone WF7 .... 145 C4
10 Pudsey LS28 .... 57 D2
4 Pudsey, Farsley LS28 .... 57 D3
Wakefield WF1 .... 216 A4
Andrews Gr WF7 .... 163 F6
Anerley St BD4 .... 75 B2
Angel Rd HX1 .... 202 C4
Angel Row LS26 .... 100 B5
Angel St BD17 .... 38 D4
Angel Way BD7 .... 74 D6
Angerton Way BD6 .... 94 A6
Anglers Country Pk WF4 .... 161 F5
Angus Ave BD12 .... 94 C1
Anlaby St BD4 .... 75 D5
Ann Pl BD5 .... 201 B1
Ann St Denholme BD13 .... 52 D1
Haworth BD22 .... 51 D7
Keighley BD21 .... 35 B6
Annat Royd La S36 .... 191 D1
Anne Cres S72 .... 180 E5
Anne Gate BD1 .... 201 C3
Anne St Batley WF17 .... 118 A7
Bradford BD7 .... 73 F3
Anne's Ct HX3 .... 114 A4
Annie St Haworth BD22 .... 51 F8
Hemsworth WF9 .... 163 A4
Keighley BD21 .... 18 C1
Lofthouse Gate WF1 .... 121 B4
Morley LS27 .... 98 B4
Shipley BD18 .... 55 C6
1 Sowerby Bridge HX6 .... 112 B4
Annison St BD3 .... 201 D3
Annotes Croft HD5 .... 154 F7
Anroyd St WF13 .... 118 A1
Anson Gr BD7 .... 73 F2
Anston Dr WF9 .... 183 A5
Anthony La BD16 .... 36 B2
Antony Cl HD3 .... 134 D1
Anvil Ct BD8 .... 55 B1
Anvil St Bradford BD8 .... 55 B1
Brighouse HD6 .... 115 A3
Apex Bsns Ctr LS11 .... 211 F1
Apex View LS11 .... 211 E1
Apex Way LS11 .... 211 F1
Apperley Gdns BD10 .... 56 E8
Apperley La BD10, LS19 .... 39 F2
Apperley Rd BD10 .... 56 D8
Apple Cl WF17 .... 97 A2
Apple House Terr HX2 .... 90 E1
Apple St Keighley BD21 .... 35 A3
Oxenhope BD22 .... 51 C2
Apple Tree Cl
East Ardsley WF3 .... 120 C8
Pontefract WF8 .... 146 B6
Apple Tree Ct WF3 .... 120 C7
Apple Tree Gdns LS29 .... 7 F4
Apple Tree Rd WF7 .... 145 E4
Appleby La LS25 .... 83 B7
Appleby Pl Adwick Le S DN6 184 F2
Leeds LS15 .... 80 E8
Appleby Way Morley LS27 .... 98 B4
Wetherby LS22 .... 13 E7
Appleby Wlk LS15 .... 80 E8
Applegarth Rothwell LS26 ... 101 C7
Wakefield WF2 .... 160 E7
Applehaigh Gr S71 .... 179 A4
Applehaigh La WF4 .... 179 A6
Applehaigh View S71 .... 179 A4
Appleshaw Cres WF2 .... 120 F3
Appleton Cl Bingley BD16 .... 37 B5
Bradford BD12 .... 94 F5
3 Leeds LS9 .... 212 C4
Appleton Ct 2 LS9 .... 212 C4
Appleton Gr LS9 .... 80 B7
Appleton Sq LS9 .... 212 C4
Appleton Way LS9 .... 212 C4
Appletree Cl LS23 .... 30 D7
Appleyard Rd HX7 .... 89 F1
Approach The LS15 .... 62 F7
April Ct WF15 .... 117 A2
Aprilia Ct BD14 .... 73 D5
Apsley Cres BD8 .... 55 C1
Apsley St 7 Haworth BD22 ... 51 D7
8 Keighley BD21 .... 35 B5
Oakworth BD22 .... 34 D3
Apsley Terr BD22 .... 34 D3
Aquamarine Dr HD2 .... 136 C2
Aquila Way WF15 .... 116 D5
Arborary La HD4, HD7 .... 170 F6
Arbour The Farnhill BD20 .... 4 D1
Ilkley LS29 .... 8 A6
Arcade The 5
Dewsbury WF12 .... 139 D8
Knottingley WF11 .... 126 E4
Arcadia St 12 BD21 .... 35 B5
Archbell Ave HD6 .... 136 B8
Archbishop Cranmer CE Prim Sch LS17 .... 43 B3
Archer Rd HD6 .... 115 D1
Archer St WF10 .... 124 C6
Archery Pl 9 LS2 .... 206 B2
Archery Rd LS2 .... 206 B2
Archery St 13 LS2 .... 206 B2
Archery Terr 11 LS2 .... 206 B2
Arches St HX1 .... 203 D2
Arches The HX3 .... 92 D1
Archibald St BD7 .... 74 C7
Arctic Par BD7 .... 74 A4
Arctic St 6 Haworth BD22 .... 51 E8
Keighley BD20 .... 18 B1
Arden Ct Horbury WF4 .... 159 A8
Kirkheaton HD5 .... 155 C7
Arden Rd Bradford BD8 .... 73 C7
Halifax HX1 .... 203 D2
Ardennes Cl BD2 .... 55 F4
Ardsley Cl BD4 .... 75 F2
Argent Way BD4 .... 75 F2
Argie Ave LS4 .... 59 B3
Argie Gdns 3 LS4 .... 59 C2
Argie Rd LS4 .... 59 C2
Argie Terr LS4 .... 59 C2
Argyl Mews LS17 .... 28 C5
Argyle Rd Knottingley WF11 126 C5
Leeds LS9 .... 212 A4
Argyle St Bradford BD4 .... 75 B4
Keighley BD21 .... 35 B7
Marsden HD7 .... 168 F4
Shipley BD18 .... 55 B6
Wakefield WF1 .... 142 E4
Argyll Ave 1 WF8 .... 146 B8
Argyll Cl Baildon BD17 .... 38 E2
Horsforth LS18 .... 41 B4
Ark St LS9 .... 212 B2
Arkendale Mews 5 BD7 .... 73 E3
Arkenley La HD4 .... 155 A2
Arkenmore HD5 .... 154 F7
Arksey Pl LS12 .... 209 F4
Arksey Terr LS12 .... 209 F4
Arkwright House 9 WF15 117 A5
Arkwright St
Bradford, Clayton BD14 .... 73 B4
Bradford, Tyersal BD4 .... 75 E6
Arkwright Wlk 1 LS27 .... 98 A6
Arlesford Rd BD4 .... 75 E2
Arley Cl HD7 .... 188 F8
Arley Gr LS12 .... 209 F4
Arley Pl LS12 .... 209 F4
Arley St 5 LS12 .... 59 C1
Arley Terr LS12 .... 209 F4
Arlington Bsns Ctr LS11 .... 98 E8
Arlington Cres HX2 .... 112 D4
Arlington Gr
Castleford WF10 .... 124 F7
Leeds LS8 .... 61 B5
Arlington Rd LS8 .... 61 B5
Arlington St Bradford BD3 .... 75 B6
Wakefield WF1 .... 216 A4
Arlington Way HD5 .... 155 A7
Armadale Ave BD4 .... 95 B8
Armgill La BD2 .... 55 D4
Armidale Way BD2 .... 55 F3
Armitage Ave HD6 .... 136 B8
Armitage Bldgs WF12 .... 119 B6
Armitage Rd Bradford BD12 .. 94 F4
Halifax HX1 .... 202 B1
Huddersfield HD3 .... 153 B5
Huddersfield, Armitage Bridge HD4 .... 171 E8
Huddersfield, Birkby HD2 .... 135 F1
Wakefield WF2 .... 141 D8
Armitage Sq 2 LS28 .... 76 D6
Armitage St
Castleford WF10 .... 124 C8
Dewsbury WF13 .... 138 D5
Huddersfield HD4 .... 154 A4
Rothwell LS26 .... 100 E4
Armley Grange Ave LS12 .. 209 D4
Armley Grange Cres LS12 .... 58 F1
Armley Grange Dr LS12 .... 77 F8
Armley Grange Mount LS12 77 F8
Armley Grange Oval LS12 .... 58 F1
Armley Grange Rise 4 LS12 77 F8
Armley Grange View LS12 209 D4
Armley Grange Wlk LS12 . 209 D4
Armley Grove Pl LS12 .... 210 A3
Armley Lodge Rd LS12 .... 209 F4
Armley Mills Ind Mus LS12 .... 205 D1
Armley Park Ct LS12 .... 209 F4
Armley Park Rd LS12 .... 59 C1
Armley Prim Sch LS12 .... 209 F4
Armley Primary Sch LS12 . 209 F4
Armley Rd LS12 .... 210 B3
Armley Ridge Cl LS12 .... 209 D4
Armley Ridge Rd
Leeds, Moor Top LS12 .... 209 E4
Leeds, Upper Armley LS12 .... 59 A1
Armouries Dr LS10 .... 212 A2
Armouries Way LS10 .... 212 A3
Armoury Ave WF14 .... 138 A5
Armstrong Cl WF6 .... 123 A4
Armstrong St Bradford BD4 .. 75 D6
9 Pudsey LS28 .... 57 D2
Armstrong Terr 2 WF8 .... 146 B7
Armytage Cres HD1 .... 153 F3
Armytage Rd HD6 .... 115 D1
Armytage Way HD6 .... 115 D1
Armytage Wlk WF9 .... 182 C3
Arncliffe Ave 1 BD22 .... 35 A5
Arncliffe Cres
Brighouse HD6 .... 135 E8
Morley LS27 .... 98 C2
Arncliffe Ct HD1 .... 153 E7
Arncliffe Dr WF11 .... 126 C4
Arncliffe Garth 11 LS28 .... 57 D2
Arncliffe Gdns WF17 .... 118 B5
Arncliffe Gr 17 BD22 .... 35 A6
Arncliffe Grange LS17 .... 43 D2
Arncliffe Rd Batley WF17 .... 118 B5
Keighley BD22 .... 35 A6
Leeds LS16 .... 59 A8
Wakefield WF1 .... 142 F8
Arncliffe St LS28 .... 57 D2
Arncliffe Terr BD7 .... 74 B6
Arndale Ctr 5 LS6 .... 59 D5
Arndale Gr HD7 .... 189 B4
Arndale Sh Ctr The BD18 .... 55 B7
Arnford Cl BD3 .... 201 C4
Arnold Ave HD2 .... 135 F1
Arnold Pl BD8 .... 74 C8
Arnold Royd HD6 .... 135 E7
Arnold St Bradford BD8 .... 55 C1
Halifax HX1 .... 202 C3
Huddersfield HD2 .... 135 F1
Liversedge WF15 .... 117 A4
4 Sowerby Bridge HX6 .... 112 B4
Arnside Ave BD20 .... 18 E1
Arnside Cl WF10 .... 125 D8
Arnside Cres WF10 .... 125 D8
Arnside Rd BD5 .... 74 E2
Arran Cl HD7 .... 152 D5
Arran Ct LS25 .... 82 F5
Arran Dr Garforth LS25 .... 82 F5
Horsforth LS18 .... 41 B4
Arrunden Ct HD7 .... 189 B3
Arrunden La HD7 .... 188 F2
Arthington Ave LS10 .... 215 D2
Arthington Cl WF3 .... 119 D7
Arthington Ct LS10 .... 215 D2
Arthington Garth LS21 .... 24 F6
Arthington Gr LS10 .... 215 D2
Arthington La
Arthington LS21 .... 25 D6
Pool LS21 .... 24 E6
Arthington Lawns LS21 .... 24 E6
Arthington Pl LS10 .... 215 D2
Arthington Rd LS16 .... 25 C2
Arthington St Bradford BD8 .. 74 C8
Leeds LS10 .... 215 D2
Arthington Terr LS10 .... 215 D2
Arthington View LS10 .... 215 D2
Arthur Ave BD8 .... 73 D7
Arthur Gr WF17 .... 117 F8
Arthur St Bacup OL13 .... 106 B3
Bingley BD16 .... 36 F3
Bradford BD10 .... 56 B6
Brighouse HD6 .... 115 C2
Huddersfield HD7 .... 152 E4
Oakworth BD22 .... 34 C2
Pudsey LS28 .... 57 E2
Pudsey, Farsley LS28 .... 57 D2
Wakefield WF1 .... 142 E3
Arthursdale Cl LS15 .... 62 F7
Arthursdale Dr LS15 .... 62 F7
Arthursdale Grange LS15 .... 62 F7
Artillery St WF16 .... 117 D3
Artist St LS12 .... 210 B3
Arum St BD5 .... 74 C3
Arundel Cl Batley WF17 .... 97 B2
Wakefield WF1 .... 216 B3
Arundel St Garforth LS25 .... 83 B8
Halifax HX1 .... 202 B3
Wakefield WF1 .... 216 B3
Arundel Wlk WF17 .... 97 B1
Ascot Ave BD7 .... 73 E2
Ascot Dr BD7 .... 73 E2
Ascot Gdns BD7 .... 73 E2
Ascot Gr HD6 .... 135 E8
Ascot Par BD7 .... 73 E2
Ascot Rd LS25 .... 82 F2
Ascot Terr LS9 .... 212 C3

Asdale Rd Crigglestone WF2 160 B7
Wakefield WF2 160 B7
Ash Ave LS6 59 D5
Ash Brow WF4 157 C3
Ash Brow Rd HD2 136 B3
Ash Cl Brighouse HX3 114 D8
Ilkley LS29 7 E4
Ossett WF5 140 D5
Ash Cres Leeds LS6 59 D5
Lofthouse Gate WF3 121 F5
Ash Croft BD6 94 A8
Ash Ct BD19 115 F8
Ash Gdns LS6 59 D5
Ash Ghyll Gdns BD16 36 F4
Ash Gn WF8 125 F1
Ash Gr Bingley BD16 37 A1
Birkenshaw BD11 96 A6
Brighouse HD6 115 C2
Cleckheaton BD19 116 B6
Cleckheaton, Birdacre BD19 96 A1
Darrington WF8 147 C5
Horsforth LS18 41 C2
Ilkley LS29 8 C5
Keighley BD21 35 B4
Leeds LS6 205 F3
Lofthouse Gate WF3 121 F2
Otley LS21 22 F7
Pudsey LS28 76 E6
South Elmsall WF9 183 A4
Steeton BD20 17 D5
Sutton in C BD20 16 D5
Ash Green Prim Sch HX2 91 C5
Ash Grove Jun & Inf Sch WF9 183 A4
Ash Grove Rd HD7 188 E5
Ash Grove Terr 6 HD6 115 A1
Ash Hall La HX6 132 A7
Ash Hill Dr LS17 44 F4
Ash Hill Garth LS17 44 F4
Ash Hill Gdns LS17 44 F4
Ash Hill La LS17 44 F4
Ash Hill Wlk BD4 75 B4
Ash La Emley HD8 175 E7
Garforth LS25 83 A8
Ash Lea Fairburn WF11 105 B4
Lofthouse Gate WF3 121 F3
Ash Meadow Cl HD2 136 C3
Ash Mount Bradford BD7 74 B5
Keighley BD21 35 A5
Ash Rd Leeds LS6 59 C5
Shafton S72 180 D2
Ash St Cleckheaton BD19 116 C7
Crofton WF4 162 A7
Glusburn BD20 16 D6
Huddersfield HD1 154 A8
Ilkley LS29 8 C5
Lofthouse Gate WF3 121 F2
Oxenhope BD22 51 C3
Ash Terr Bingley BD16 36 F2
Garforth LS25 83 A8
2 Leeds LS6 59 D5
Ripponden HX6 132 C3
Ash Tree App LS14 62 D4
Ash Tree Ave BD13 72 B6
Ash Tree Bank LS14 62 D5
Ash Tree Cl LS14 62 D5
Ash Tree Ct 5 LS14 62 D5
Ash Tree Gdns Halifax HX2 91 C5
Leeds LS14 62 D5
Normanton WF6 122 F3
Ash Tree Gr LS14 62 D5
Ash Tree Grange 4 LS14 62 D5
Ash Tree Rd HX2 91 C5
Ash Tree View 7 LS14 62 D5
Ash Tree Wlk
Burley in W LS29 9 E1
8 Leeds LS14 62 D5
Ash View East Ardsley WF3 120 C7
3 Leeds LS6 59 D5
Ash Wlk HD7 152 E5
Ashbourne Ave
Bradford BD2 55 F3
Cleckheaton BD19 116 D6
Ashbourne Bank BD2 55 F3
Ashbourne Cl BD2 55 F4
Ashbourne Cres
Bradford BD2 55 F3
Garforth LS25 82 F5
Queensbury BD13 72 D1
Ashbourne Croft BD19 116 D6
Ashbourne Dr Bradford BD2 55 F3
Cleckheaton BD19 116 D6
Pontefract WF8 146 D5
Ashbourne Garth BD2 56 A4
Ashbourne Gdns
Bradford BD2 55 F3
Cleckheaton BD19 116 D6
Ashbourne Gr Bradford BD2 55 F3
Halifax HX1 202 B3
Ashbourne Haven BD2 55 F3
Ashbourne Mount BD2 55 F3
Ashbourne Oval BD2 55 F3
Ashbourne Rd Bradford BD2 55 F3
Keighley BD21 35 A5
Ashbourne Rise BD2 55 F3
Ashbourne View BD19 116 D6
Ashbourne Way
Bradford BD2 55 F3
Cleckheaton BD19 116 D6
Ashbrook Cl WF5 140 D7
Ashbrooke Pk LS11 214 C2
Ashbrow Infants Sch HD2 136 B3
Ashburn Cl LS22 13 D7
Ashburn Croft LS22 13 D7
Ashburn Dr LS22 13 D7
Ashburn Gr Baildon BD17 38 C4
Wetherby LS22 13 D7
Ashburn Pl LS29 8 A3
Ashburn Way LS22 13 D7
Ashburnham Gr BD9 55 B3
Ashbury Chase WF1 121 A5
Ashby Ave LS13 58 D1
Ashby Cl WF15 116 F1
Ashby Cres LS13 58 D1
Ashby Mount 4 LS13 58 D2
Ashby Sq LS13 58 D2
Ashby St BD4 75 A4
Ashby Terr LS13 58 D2
Ashby View LS13 58 D2
Ashcombe Dr WF11 126 F3
Ashcroft Ave WF7 145 C4
Ashcroft Cl WF17 118 B3
Ashcroft Rd WF7 145 C4
Ashdale WF2 142 E1
Ashdale La LS22 13 D8
Ashday La Brighouse HX3 114 B3
Halifax HX3 114 B3
Ashdene Gildersome LS12 77 D3
Todmorden OL14 108 B1
Ashdene App WF4 143 F1
Ashdene Ave WF4 143 F1
Ashdene Cl LS28 76 E5
Ashdene Cres Crofton WF4 143 F1
Pudsey LS28 76 E5
Ashdene Ct BD13 52 D6
Ashdene Dr WF4 143 F1
Ashdene Garth WF4 143 F1
Ashdene Gr WF8 125 F4
Ashdown Cl
9 Bradford BD6 74 B1
Halifax HX2 112 D6
Ashdown Ct BD18 55 A7
Ashdown Rd WF1 142 E3
Ashdown St 13 LS13 58 C2
Ashenhurst Ave HD4 154 C3
Ashenhurst Cl
Huddersfield HD4 154 B3
Todmorden OL14 108 A7
Ashenhurst Rd
Huddersfield HD4 154 B3
Todmorden OL14 108 A7
Ashenhurst Rise HD4 154 B3
Ashes La Huddersfield HD4 154 C1
Todmorden OL14 108 D7
Ashfield Bradford BD4 75 D1
Dewsbury WF12 139 D4
Leeds LS12 78 A4
Wetherby LS22 13 F6
Ashfield Ave Morley LS27 97 F3
Shipley BD18 55 B5
Skelmanthorpe HD8 175 A1
Ashfield Cl Halifax HX3 91 F2
Leeds, New Farnley LS12 77 F4
Leeds, Stanks LS15 62 D4
Ashfield Cres Bingley BD16 37 A2
Pudsey LS28 57 E1
Ashfield Ct 5 BD16 37 A2
Ashfield Dr Baildon BD17 38 D3
Halifax HX3 92 A2
Shipley BD9 55 B5
Ashfield Gr 6 Pudsey LS28 57 E1
Shipley BD9 55 B5
Ashfield Pk 1 LS6 59 E5
Ashfield Pl BD2 56 D2
Ashfield Rd Batley WF17 97 A2
Bradford BD10 39 C1
Elland HX4 134 B7
Hemsworth WF9 181 D5
Huddersfield HD2 135 E1
Morley LS27 97 F3
Pudsey LS28 57 E1
Shipley BD18 54 E7
Thornton BD13 72 D6
Ashfield Residential Sch BD10 39 C1
Ashfield St
Huddersfield HD2 136 B2
9 Keighley BD21 35 B6
Normanton WF6 123 C3
Ashfield Terr Bradford BD12 94 D4
10 Cleckheaton BD19 116 E7
Elland HX4 134 B8
11 Haworth BD22 51 C6
Leeds LS15 62 D4
Middleton WF3 99 F2
Ashfield Way LS12 77 F4
Ashford Ct HD8 173 F7
Ashford Dr LS28 76 F6
Ashford Gn BD6 73 F1
Ashford Manor HD8 155 D1
Ashford Pk HD7 152 D5
Ashgap La WF6 123 B3
Ashgrove Bradford BD7 74 D6
Bradford, Greengates BD10 56 E7
Bradford, Haigh Fold BD2 56 C3
Ashgrove Ave 1 HX3 113 E3
Ashgrove Cres LS25 83 B3
Ashgrove Croft LS25 83 B2
Ashgrove Mews LS13 57 F4
Ashgrove Mount LS25 83 A3
Ashgrove Pl 3 HX3 113 E3
Ashgrove Rd
Huddersfield HD2 136 F2
Keighley BD20 18 A2
Ashington Cl BD2 56 D3
Ashlands First Sch LS29 8 C5
Ashlands Rd LS29 8 C5
Ashlar Gr Castleford WF10 124 F6
Queensbury BD13 92 D8
Ashlea Ave HD6 136 B8
Ashlea Cl Brighouse HD6 136 B8
Garforth LS25 82 F5
Ashlea Ct LS13 58 C3
Ashlea Dr HD6 136 B8
Ashlea Gate LS13 58 C3
Ashlea Gn LS13 58 C3
Ashleigh S72 181 A3
Ashleigh Ave
Pontefract WF8 146 D7
Wakefield WF2 141 E5
Ashleigh Cl HD8 173 F2
Ashleigh Dale HD2 135 E1
Ashleigh Gdns Ossett WF5 140 C8
Rothwell LS26 101 C6
Ashleigh Rd LS16 59 A8
Ashleigh St BD21 35 C8
Ashley Ave LS9 208 A2
Ashley Cl Cleckheaton BD19 96 A2
Wakefield WF2 120 F2
Ashley Croft S71 179 B4
Ashley Ct WF9 181 F1
Ashley Gr HX7 89 E1
Ashley Ind Est
Huddersfield HD2 137 A4
Leeds LS7 206 C3
Leeds LS7 206 C4
Ossett WF5 140 E7
Ashley La BD17 55 B8
Ashley Rd Bingley BD16 37 A2
Bradford BD12 94 C2
Leeds LS9 208 A2
Leeds, Upper Wortley LS12 209 E2
Ashley St Halifax HX1 202 B3
Shipley BD17 55 B8
Ashley Terr LS9 208 A2
Ashmead Batley WF17 118 A3
Boston Spa LS23 30 D5
Ashmere Gr HD2 136 C2
Ashmews BD10 56 E7
Ashmore Dr WF5 119 C1
Ashmore Gdns BD4 95 B8
Ashmount BD14 73 D4
Ashroyd LS26 100 F4
Ashtofts Mount LS20 22 E1
Ashton Ave Bradford BD7 73 E5
Leeds LS8 207 F3
Ashton Clough Rd WF15 117 A4
Ashton Cres WF3 100 D3
Ashton Ct LS8 208 A3
Ashton Gr LS8 207 F2
Ashton Ho 6 BD5 201 B1
Ashton Mount LS8 208 A2
Ashton Pl LS8 207 F2
Ashton Rd Castleford WF10 124 D6
Hebden Bridge HX7 89 E1
Leeds LS8 208 A3
Ashton Road Ind Est LS8 208 A3
Ashton St Bradford BD1 74 D7
Castleford WF10 124 D7
Leeds LS8 207 F3
Ashton Terr LS8 207 F2
Ashton View LS8 207 F2
Ashtree Gr Bradford BD7 73 F3
Kippax LS25 83 B1
Ashville Ave LS6 205 E3
Ashville Croft 4 HX2 112 D8
Ashville Gdns HX2 112 D8
Ashville Gr Halifax HX2 91 D1
Leeds LS6 205 D3
Ashville Rd LS4, LS6 205 D3
Ashville St 19 HX3 92 A1
Ashville Terr Glusburn BD20 16 D6
Leeds LS6 205 D3
Oakworth BD22 34 D3
14 Pudsey LS28 57 D2
Ashville View LS6 205 E2
Ashwell Cl S72 180 C3
Ashwell La BD9 55 A4
Ashwell Rd Bradford BD8 55 B1
Shipley BD9 55 A4
Ashwell St BD8 55 B1
Ashwood LS14 45 B1
Ashwood Cl HD2 136 C3
Ashwood Dr
Gildersome LS27 97 C7
Keighley BD20 19 A1
Ashwood Gdns LS27 97 B7
Ashwood Gr
Gildersome LS27 97 C7
Horbury WF4 141 C2
Ashwood Grange WF4 159 E6
Ashwood St BD4 75 D1
Ashwood Terr LS6 205 F4
Ashwood Villas LS6 205 F4
Ashworth Cl WF13 139 C8
Ashworth Gdns WF13 139 C8
Ashworth Gr WF13 139 C8
Ashworth Pl BD6 74 D1
Ashworth Rd WF13 139 C8
Ashworth St 12 OL13 106 A3
Askam Ave WF8 125 F4
Asket Ave LS14 61 F5
Asket Cl LS14 61 E6
Asket Cres LS14 61 E5
Asket Dr LS14 61 E6
Asket Garth LS14 61 E5
Asket Gdns LS8 61 D6
Asket Gn LS14 61 E6
Asket Hill LS8 61 D6
Asket Pl LS14 61 E5
Asket Wlk LS14 61 E5
Askey Ave LS27 98 B2
Askey Cres LS27 98 B2
Askham Gr WF9 183 E7
Askham Rd WF10 104 D1
Askrigg Dr BD2 56 B3
Askwith County Primary Sch LS21 9 F5
Askwith La LS21 10 A6
Aspden St OL14 108 B6
Aspect Gdns LS28 76 D8
Aspect Terr LS28 76 C8
Aspen Cl Keighley BD21 35 E5
Wakefield WF2 142 A8
Aspen Ct Emley HD8 175 C7
Morley WF3 98 C1
Aspen Gr WF13 139 B8
Aspen Mount LS16 41 E2
Aspen Rise BD15 53 F4
Aspinall St Halifax HX1 202 B2
Hebden Bridge HX7 89 E1
Aspley Pl HD1 154 B6
Asquith Ave LS27 97 F6
Asquith Cl LS27 97 F5
Asquith Dr LS27 97 F5
Asquith St WF17 97 B2
Assembly St 5 Leeds LS2 211 F3
Normanton WF6 123 A2
Astley Ave LS26 82 A1
Astley La LS26 102 C8
Astley Lane Ind Est LS26 102 B8
Astley Way LS26 102 B8
Aston Ave LS13 58 E2
Aston Cl WF15 116 F2
Aston Cres LS13 58 E2
Aston Ct WF5 141 A4
Aston Dr LS13 58 E2
Aston Gr LS13 58 E2
Aston Mount LS13 58 E2
Aston Pl LS13 58 E2
Aston Rd Bradford BD5 74 E3
Leeds LS13 58 D2
Aston St LS13 58 D2
Aston Terr LS13 58 E2
Aston View LS13 58 E2
Astor Gr LS13 58 A2
Astor St LS13 58 A2
Astra Bsns Pk LS11 214 C2
Astral Ave HX3 114 D8
Astral Cl HX3 114 D8
Astral View BD6 74 A2
Atalanta Terr HX2 112 E4
Atha Cl LS11 214 A1
Atha Cres LS11 214 A1
Atha St LS11 214 A1
Athelstan La LS21 11 A1
Athene Dr HD4 154 C3
Atherstone Rd BD15 73 B7
Atherton La HD6 136 B8
Athlone Dr WF12 118 E2
Athlone Gr LS12 209 F3
Athlone Rise LS25 83 B7
Athlone St LS12 209 F3
Athlone Terr LS12 209 F3
Athol Cl HX3 92 A3
Athol Cres HX3 92 A3
Athol Gdns HX3 92 A3
Athol Gn HX3 92 A3
Athol Rd Bradford BD9 55 B2
Halifax HX3 92 A3
Athol St Halifax HX3 92 A3
Keighley BD21 18 E1
Athold Dr WF5 140 F5
Athold St WF5 140 F5
Atkinson Ct WF6 123 A1
Atkinson La WF8 125 F2
Atkinson St Leeds LS10 212 B1
Shipley BD18 55 B8
Atlanta St LS13 58 A2
Atlas First Sch BD8 74 C8
Atlas Mill Rd HD6 115 A2
Atlas St BD8 55 B1
Attlee Ave WF4 162 C1
Attlee Cres WF2 160 E8
Attlee Gr WF1 121 C4
Attlee St WF6 144 B8
Auckland Rd BD6 74 A1
Audby Cl LS22 13 F6
Audby La LS22 13 F6
Audrey St WF5 140 E4
Audsley's Yd WF4 140 E1
Augusta Ct WF2 141 F5
Augusta Dr WF6 144 D8
Aurelia House BD8 55 C2
Austhorpe Ave LS15 81 E7
Austhorpe Ct LS15 81 E7
Austhorpe Dr LS15 81 E7
Austhorpe Gdns LS15 81 F8
Austhorpe Gr LS15 81 E8
Austhorpe La LS15 62 D1
Austhorpe Primary Sch LS15 81 E8
Austhorpe Rd LS15 62 D2
Austhorpe View LS15 81 D8
Austin Ave HD6 114 F4
Austin Rd WF10 125 D8
Austin St 11 BD21 35 D8
Austwick Cl S75 178 A2
Authorpe Rd LS6 59 F6
Autumn Ave Leeds LS6 205 E2
Wetherby LS22 13 E8
Autumn Cres LS18 58 D7
Autumn Gr LS6 205 E2
Autumn Pl LS6 205 E2
Autumn St 3 Halifax HX1 202 B1
Leeds LS6 205 E2
Autumn Terr 17 LS6 205 E2
Auty Cres WF3 121 F5
Auty Mews WF3 121 F5
Auty Sq 2 LS27 98 B3
Avenel Rd BD15 73 B8
Avenel Terr BD15 73 B8
Avenham Way BD3 201 D4
Avens Cl WF8 146 D7
Avenue A LS23 15 B3
Avenue B LS23 15 B1
Avenue C E LS23 15 C2
Avenue C W LS23 15 C2
Avenue Cres LS8 207 F4
Avenue D LS23 15 B1
Avenue Des Hirondelles LS21 24 D6
Avenue E E LS23 15 C1
Avenue E W LS23 31 B8
Avenue F LS23 15 D1
Avenue G LS23 15 D2
Avenue Gdns LS17 43 A5
Avenue Hill LS8 207 F4
Avenue Lawns LS17 42 F5
Avenue No 2 HD6 115 A1
Avenue Rd Bradford BD5 74 F3
Wakefield WF2 142 E1
Avenue St BD4 75 D1
Avenue Terr Otley LS21 22 F7
Pontefract WF8 146 A8
Avenue The Barwick in E LS15 62 F8
Batley WF17 117 F3
Batley, Birstall WF17 96 E1
Batley, Carlinghow WF17 118 A7
Bradford BD14 73 B4
Brighouse HX3 114 D8
Collingham LS22 13 A1
Crofton WF4 143 E1
East Ardsley WF3 120 A8
Guiseley BD10 39 E2
Harewood LS17 27 A6
Horsforth LS18 40 F1
4 Huddersfield HD5 154 D5
Leeds LS15 81 E3
Leeds, Alwoodley LS17 43 A5
Leeds, Bank LS9 212 B3
Leeds, Park Villas LS8 44 A1
2 Leeds, Stanks LS15 62 D3
Lofthouse Gate WF1 121 B4
Royston S71 179 E4
Shipley BD16 54 B8
Avenue Victoria LS8 61 A8
Averingcliffe Rd BD10 56 D6
Avery Tulip Ct 2 BD12 94 C6
Aviary Gr LS12 209 F4
Aviary Mount LS12 209 F4
Aviary Pl LS12 209 F4
Aviary Rd LS12 209 F4
Aviary Row LS12 209 F4
Aviary St LS12 209 F4
Aviary Terr LS12 209 F4
Aviary View LS12 209 F4
Avison Rd HD4 153 A3
Avison Yd WF1 216 C2
Avocet Cl BD8 73 C7
Avocet Garth 4 LS10 99 D5
Avon Cl LS17 44 F4
Avon Croft WF5 140 C5
Avon Ct LS17 44 E5
Avon Dr LS25 82 F6
Avon Wlk WF7 145 C7
Avondale BD20 35 A8
Avondale Cres BD18 55 A7
Avondale Ct LS17 43 D3
Avondale Dr
Lofthouse Gate WF3 121 E5
Royston S71 179 C1
Avondale Gr BD18 55 A7
Avondale Mount BD18 55 A7
Avondale Pl 8 HX3 113 B4
Avondale Rd BD18 54 F7
Avondale St Leeds LS13 58 C1
Wakefield WF2 142 C4
Avondale Way WF2 142 C4
Aydon Way HX3 93 E7
Aygill Ave BD9 54 D3
Aylesbury St 3 BD21 35 A4
Aylesford Mount LS15 62 F3
Aylesham Ind Est BD12 94 D6
Aynholme Cl LS29 6 F8
Aynholme Dr LS29 6 F8
Aynsley Gr BD15 54 B1
Ayres Dr HD4 153 A3
Ayresome Ave LS8 44 A2
Ayresome Oval BD15 73 A7
Ayresome Terr LS8 43 F2
Ayreville Dr HX3 93 C6
Ayrton Cres 18 BD16 37 A3
Aysgarth Ave HX3 115 A6
Aysgarth Cl Bradford BD12 94 C2
Leeds LS9 212 C3
Wakefield WF2 141 D3
Aysgarth Cres HX2 91 A3
Aysgarth Dr Leeds LS9 212 C3
Wakefield WF2 141 D3
Aysgarth Fold LS10 99 C4
Aysgarth Pl LS9 212 C3
Aysgarth Rd Batley WF17 118 A5
Huddersfield HD4 154 B2
Aysgarth Wlk LS9 212 C3
Ayton Cl BD3 75 A8
Ayton Rd HD3 152 E6
Azealea Ct BD3 75 B8

Baby House Hill La HX7 69 A4
Bachelor La LS18 41 C2
Back Acres St 8 BD21 35 B6
Back Ada St 10 BD21 35 A7
Back Aireview Terr BD21 35 E6
Back Aireville St BD20 18 A2
Back Airlie Pl LS8 207 F4
Back Albert Gr LS6 59 D6
Back Albert Terr LS6 205 E2
Back Alcester Pl 16 LS8 207 F4
Back Alcester Rd 14 LS8 207 F4
Back Alcester Terr 15 LS8 207 F4
Back Allerton Terr LS7 204 A3
Back Alma St 5 LS19 40 C7
Back Anderton St WF1 142 E3
Back Ann St BD13 52 E1
Back Archery Pl 8 LS2 206 B2
Back Archery Rd 14 LS2 206 B2

Back Archery St 12 LS2 ... 206 B2
Back Archery Terr 10 LS2 ... 206 B2
Back Armitage Rd HD4 ... 171 E8
Back Ash Gr LS6 ... 205 F3
Back Ashgrove (W) BD7 ... 74 D6
Back Ashley Ave LS9 ... 208 A2
Back Ashley St LS9 ... 208 A2
Back Ashville Ave LS6 ... 205 E3
Back Ashville Gr LS6 ... 205 E3
Back Ashville Rd LS6 ... 205 D3
Back Ashville Terr LS6 ... 205 D3
Back Ashwood Terr LS6 ... 205 F4
Back Aston Pl 1 LS13 ... 58 E2
Back Aston Rd LS13 ... 58 D2
Back Aston St LS13 ... 58 D2
Back Aston Terr 2 LS13 ... 58 E2
Back Aston View 3 LS13 ... 58 E2
Back Athlone Ave 1 LS12 ... 209 F3
Back Athlone Gr 2 LS12 ... 209 F3
Back Athlone Terr 3 LS12 ... 209 F3
Back Atlanta St LS13 ... 58 A2
Back Austhorpe Rd 4 LS15 ... 62 D2
Back Autumn Rd 19 LS6 ... 205 E2
Back Autumn Terr 16 LS6 ... 205 E2
Back Aviary Rd 1 LS12 ... 209 F4
Back Aylesbury St 4 BD21 ... 35 A4
Back Baker St BD18 ... 55 A8
Back Balbovan Terr 6 LS8 ... 207 F4
Back Balfour St
Bingley BD16 ... 36 F2
5 Keighley BD21 ... 35 B6
Back Bank St WF10 ... 124 D8
Back Bank Terr LS28 ... 57 E2
Back Banstead St LS8 ... 207 F3
Back Barden Pl LS12 ... 209 D3
Back Barkly Gr LS11 ... 214 A2
Back Barkly Par 3 LS11 ... 214 A1
Back Barkly Terr 5 LS11 ... 214 A2
Back Barrowby View LS15 ... 81 F7
Back Bath Rd 15 LS13 ... 58 C2
Back Beacon St HD2 ... 136 A1
Back Beamsley Gr 9 LS6 ... 205 E2
Back Beamsley Mount 4 LS6 ... 205 E2
Back Beamsley Terr 2 LS6 ... 205 E2
Back Beaumont St WF17 ... 118 C3
Back Beck La LS29 ... 6 F8
Back Beech St BD16 ... 36 F2
Back Beech Terr HD1 ... 136 B1
Back Beechwood Gr 7 LS4 ... 205 D3
Back Beechwood Rd 9 LS4 ... 205 D3
Back Bellbrooke Gr LS9 ... 208 B2
Back Bellbrooke Pl LS9 ... 208 B2
Back Bellbrooke Terr LS9 ... 208 B2
Back Belvedere Ave LS11 ... 214 B2
Back Belvedere Mount LS11 ... 214 B2
Back Bentley Ave 3 LS6 ... 59 F6
Back Bentley Gr LS6 ... 59 F6
Back Berkeley Ave LS8 ... 208 A3
Back Berkeley Terr LS8 ... 208 A3
Back Beverley Terr LS11 ... 214 B3
Back Blackwood Gr HX1 ... 202 B4
Back Blandford Gdns 22 LS2 ... 206 B2
Back Blandford Gr 24 LS2 ... 206 B2
Back Blenheim Ave 7 LS2 ... 206 B2
Back Blenheim Mount BD8 ... 55 C2
Back Blenheim Terr LS2 ... 206 B2
Back Boundary Terr LS3 ... 205 E1
Back Bower Rd HX5 ... 135 A7
Back Bowling Green Rd HX4 ... 133 F3
Back Bowman St WF1 ... 142 F3
Back Bradshaw Rd HD7 ... 171 F3
Back Branch Pl 10 LS12 ... 78 A4
Back Breary Ave LS18 ... 41 D1
Back Breary Terr LS18 ... 41 D1
Back Briggate BD20 ... 5 E2
Back Broad La LS13 ... 58 D4
Back Broomfield Cres LS6 ... 205 D4
Back Broomfield Pl 4 LS6 ... 205 D3
Back Broomfield Rd
5 Keighley BD21 ... 35 B7
Leeds LS4 ... 205 D3
Back Broomfield St 6 BD21 ... 35 B7
Back Broughton Ave LS9 ... 208 A2
Back Broughton Terr LS9 ... 208 A2
Back Brudenell Gr LS6 ... 205 F3
Back Brudenell Mount LS6 ... 205 E3
Back Brudenell Rd LS6 ... 205 E3
Back Brunswick St
Dewsbury WF13 ... 118 A1
Leeds LS2 ... 206 C1
Back Burchett Gr LS6 ... 206 A4
Back Burchett Pl LS6 ... 206 A4
Back Burley Hill LS4 ... 205 D2
Back Burley Lodge Rd LS6 ... 205 E1
Back Burley Lodge Terr LS6 ... 205 E1
Back Burley St 5 LS3 ... 211 D4
Back Burlington Pl 22 LS11 ... 214 B2
Back Burlington Rd LS11 ... 214 B2
Back Burton Cres 2 LS6 ... 59 D6
Back Burton Terr LS11 ... 214 C3
Back Buxton St 4 BD21 ... 35 D7
Back Byrl St BD21 ... 18 C1
Back Byrom St 4 OL14 ... 108 B6
Back Caister St 4 BD21 ... 35 B4
Back Camberley St 9 LS11 ... 214 C3
Back Carberry Pl 20 LS6 ... 205 E2
Back Carberry Rd 26 LS6 ... 205 E2
Back Carberry Terr 22 LS6 ... 205 E2
Back Carlinghow La WF17 ... 117 E7
Back Carter Mount LS15 ... 81 C8
Back Cartmel Rd 12 BD21 ... 35 A7
Back Castle Rd BD21 ... 35 B8
Back Cavendish Rd BD10 ... 56 B7
Back Cavendish St BD21 ... 35 C7
Back Cavendish Terr 12 HX1 ... 202 C3
Back Cecil St 8 HD1 ... 154 A6
Back Chapel La LS6 ... 205 D4
Back Chapel St BD1 ... 201 C3
Back Charles St 10 HD6 ... 115 A3
Back Chatsworth Rd LS8 ... 208 A3
Back Chestnut Ave 2
Leeds, Cross Gates LS15 ... 62 D2
Leeds, Hyde Park LS6 ... 205 F3
Back Chiswick Terr 24 LS6 ... 205 E2
Back Christ Church View LS12 ... 209 E4
Back Church La
Leeds, Adel LS16 ... 42 D5
Leeds, Kirkstall LS5 ... 59 A4
Back Church View WF1 ... 142 F2
Back Churchill Gdns 26 LS2 ... 206 B2
Back Claremont Ave 8 LS3 ... 206 A1
Back Claremont Gr 6 LS3 ... 206 A1
Back Claremont St 9 LS26 ... 101 C6
Back Claremont Terr 10 LS3 ... 206 A1
Back Clarence Rd 7 LS18 ... 58 B7
Back Clarence St HX1 ... 203 D3
Back Clarendon Pl HX1 ... 202 C2
Back Clarkson View 10 LS6 ... 206 A4
Back Clayton St LS26 ... 100 F5
Back Cliff Mount LS6 ... 206 A4
Back Clifton Rd HD1 ... 153 E7
Back Clifton Terr LS9 ... 208 B2
Back Clipston Ave LS6 ... 59 F6
Back Clough HX3 ... 93 A2
Back Clovelly Pl 21 LS11 ... 214 B3
Back Coldcotes Ave LS9 ... 208 B2
Back Colenso Mount LS11 ... 213 F4
Back Colenso Rd
Keighley BD21 ... 18 E1
Leeds LS11 ... 213 F4
Back Colne Rd BD20 ... 16 D6
Back Colton Rd LS12 ... 209 F3
Back Colwyn Pl 20 LS11 ... 214 B2
Back Colwyn View 11 LS11 ... 214 B2
Back Commercial St 11 HX1 ... 203 E3
Back Commerical St 16 OL14 ... 108 C5
Back Compton St 9 BD21 ... 35 D8
Back Conway St LS8 ... 207 F3
Back Cowper Gr LS8 ... 208 A3
Back Cowper St LS7 ... 207 E3
Back Craggwood Rd 6 LS18 ... 58 C7
Back Cranbrook Ave LS11 ... 214 A3
Back Cranbrook Terr LS11 ... 214 A3
Back Croft HX6 ... 132 C1
Back Croft House La BD20 ... 18 A2
Back Cromer Ave 16 BD21 ... 35 B5
Back Cromer Gr 1 BD21 ... 35 B4
Back Cromer Terr LS2 ... 206 A2
Back Cromwell Terr 2 HX1 ... 203 D3
Back Cross Flatts Ave LS11 ... 214 A2
Back Cross Flatts Cres LS11 ... 213 F2
Back Cross Flatts Gr 3 LS11 ... 214 A2
Back Cross Flatts Mount 4 LS11 ... 214 A2
Back Cross Flatts Pl LS11 ... 213 F2
Back Cross Flatts Row LS11 ... 213 F2
Back Cross Green Cres LS9 ... 212 C2
Back Cross Green La 18 LS9 ... 212 C2
Back Cross La HX5 ... 134 E6
Back Crossland Terr 1 LS11 ... 214 C3
Back Cunliffe St LS29 ... 8 B4
Back Dalton Ave LS11 ... 214 A2
Back Dalton Gr LS11 ... 214 A2
Back Dalton Rd LS11 ... 214 A2
Back Dargai St LS7 ... 206 C3
Back Dawlish Ave 3 LS9 ... 80 B8
Back Dawlish Mount 2 LS9 ... 80 B8
Back Dawlish Rd 4 LS9 ... 80 B8
Back De Lacy Mount LS5 ... 59 A5
Back Delph Mount LS6 ... 206 A4
Back Dent St LS9 ... 212 C3
Back Der St 7 OL14 ... 108 C5
Back Devonshire La LS8 ... 44 A2
Back Dorset Mount 4 LS8 ... 208 A4
Back Dorset Rd 3 LS8 ... 208 A4
Back Dorset Terr LS8 ... 208 A3
Back Dudley Hill Rd BD2 ... 56 B2
Back Duke of York St WF1 ... 216 C3
Back Duke St WF7 ... 145 C6
Back Dunbar St WF1 ... 142 F4
Back East Park Rd 10 LS9 ... 80 A7
Back Eaton St 2 BD21 ... 35 A4
Back Ecclesburn Gr 1 LS9 ... 80 B7
Back Ecclesburn St LS9 ... 80 A7
Back Edensor Rd 9 BD21 ... 35 A7
Back Edinburgh Rd LS12 ... 209 D4
Back Eldon Rd HD1 ... 153 D7
Back Elford Pl LS8 ... 207 F3
Back Elizabeth St
Bradford BD5 ... 201 B1
Bradford BD5 ... 201 B1
Back Ellers Gr LS8 ... 207 F4
Back Ellers Rd 8 LS8 ... 207 F4
Back Elmfield Terr HX1 ... 203 D1
Back Elsworth St LS12 ... 210 A3
Back Emily St 16 BD21 ... 35 D8
Back Eric St Keighley BD21 ... 35 C8
Leeds LS13 ... 58 C5
Back Eshald Pl LS26 ... 101 D6
Back Esmond Terr LS12 ... 209 F3
Back Estcourt Ave LS6 ... 59 C4
Back Estcourt Terr LS6 ... 59 C4
Back Eversley Mount HX2 ... 202 A2
Back Fairford Pl LS11 ... 214 C3
Back Featherbank Terr 2 LS18 ... 58 B7
Back Ferguson St 2 HX1 ... 203 E2
Back Field Ct BD13 ... 72 D6
Back Fitzwilliam St HD1 ... 153 F6
Back Florist St BD21 ... 18 E1
Back Fold BD14 ... 73 B5
Back Foster Rd 2 BD21 ... 35 B4
Back Garden St
Castleford WF10 ... 124 D6
Wakefield WF1 ... 216 A2
Back Garton Rd LS9 ... 80 A7
Back Garton Terr LS9 ... 80 A7
Back Gathorne St LS8 ... 207 E3
Back George St 3 LS2 ... 212 A4
Back Gerrard St HX1 ... 203 D3
Back Giles St N
Bradford BD5 ... 74 D5
Bradford BD5 ... 201 B1
Back Giles St S
Bradford BD5 ... 74 D5
Bradford BD5 ... 201 B1
Back Gillett La LS26 ... 100 F5
Back Girlington Rd BD8 ... 54 F1
Back Gladstone St BD16 ... 36 F2
Back Glebe Terr LS16 ... 59 D7
Back Glen Terr HX1 ... 203 D1
Back Glenthorpe Terr 2 LS9 ... 80 A8
Back Glossop St LS6 ... 206 B4
Back Gn LS27 ... 98 C7
Back Gooder La 1 HD6 ... 115 B1
Back Gordon St WF1 ... 142 F2
Back Gordon Terr LS6 ... 59 F6
Back Graham Gr LS4 ... 205 D3
Back Granby Gr LS6 ... 205 D4
Back Grange Ave LS7 ... 207 E4
Back Grange Cres LS7 ... 207 E4
Back Grange Terr LS7 ... 207 D4
Back Grange View LS7 ... 207 E4
Back Grant St BD21 ... 35 A7
Back Grantley St WF1 ... 216 C2
Back Graveley St 6 LS15 ... 81 A8
Back Great Russell St BD7 ... 74 C7
Back Greaves St BD5 ... 74 D3
Back Greenhead Rd 2 HD1 ... 154 A6
Back Greenhow Wlk LS4 ... 205 D2
Back Greenmount Terr LS11 ... 214 B3
Back Greenwood Mount 4 LS6 ... 59 E7
Back Grosvenor Terr
Halifax HX1 ... 202 C3
Leeds LS6 ... 205 F4
Back Grouse St BD21 ... 35 D8
Back Grove Gdns LS6 ... 59 E6
Back Grove Rd LS29 ... 8 B4
Back Grovehall Ave LS11 ... 214 A1
Back Grovehall Dr LS11 ... 214 A1
Back Haigh Ave LS26 ... 100 C7
Back Haigh St LS26 ... 100 C7
Back Haigh View LS26 ... 100 C7
Back Halliday Gr LS12 ... 209 D4
Back Halliday Pl LS12 ... 209 D4
Back Hambleton St WF1 ... 216 B3
Back Hamilton Ave LS7 ... 207 E4
Back Hamilton View LS7 ... 207 E4
Back Harehills Ave LS7 ... 207 E4
Back Harehills Park View LS9 ... 208 B2
Back Harehills Pl 7 LS8 ... 207 F3
Back Hares Ave 11 LS8 ... 207 F4
Back Hares Mount LS8 ... 207 E4
Back Hares Terr 10 LS8 ... 207 F4
Back Hares View LS8 ... 207 F4
Back Harold Gr LS6 ... 205 E2
Back Hartley Ave LS6 ... 206 B4
Back Hartley Gr 5 LS6 ... 206 A4
Back Hartley St LS27 ... 98 C3
Back Hatfield St WF1 ... 216 B3
Back Hawksworth Gr LS5 ... 58 F6
Back Headingley Ave LS6 ... 59 C5
Back Headingley Mount LS6 ... 59 C5
Back Heathfield Terr 5 LS6 ... 59 D6
Back Heddon Pl LS6 ... 59 E6
Back Heddon St LS6 ... 59 E6
Back Heights Rd BD13 ... 72 B8
Back Henrietta St 3 WF17 ... 118 C5
Back Hessle Ave LS6 ... 205 E3
Back Hessle Mount LS6 ... 205 E3
Back Hessle Terr LS6 ... 205 E3
Back Hessle View LS6 ... 205 E3
Back High St 12 BD13 ... 72 D6
Back Highbury Terr LS6 ... 59 E6
Back Highfield Rd 4 LS13 ... 58 E2
Back Highthgorne View 1 LS12 ... 209 E4
Back Highthorne Gr 4 LS12 ... 209 D4
Back Highthorne St LS12 ... 209 D4
Back Hill Top Ave LS8 ... 207 F4
Back Hill Top Mount LS8 ... 207 F4
Back Hillcrest Ave LS7 ... 207 E4
Back Hillcrest View LS7 ... 207 E4
Back Hilton Gr 1 LS8 ... 207 F4
Back Hilton Pl LS8 ... 207 F4
Back Hilton Rd LS8 ... 207 F4
Back Hird St 7 BD22 ... 35 B6
Back Hollyshaw Terr 5 LS15 ... 81 C8
Back Honoria St HD1 ... 136 A1
Back Hope Hall Terr 7 HX1 ... 203 E2
Back Hovingham Gr LS8 ... 208 A4
Back Hovingham Mount 2 LS8 ... 208 A4
Back Hovingham Terr 1 LS8 ... 208 A4
Back Hyde Gr BD21 ... 35 D8
Back Hyde Terr LS2 ... 206 A1
Back Ibbetson Pl LS2 ... 206 B1
Back Ingledew Cres LS8 ... 44 B2
Back Irwell St BD4 ... 75 A5
Back Ivy Ave 11 LS9 ... 80 A8
Back Ivy Gr 2 LS9 ... 80 B7
Back Ivy Mount 9 LS9 ... 80 A8
Back Ivy St 12 LS9 ... 80 A8
Back John St BD13 ... 72 D6
Back Kelso Rd LS2 ... 205 F2
Back Kendal La 1 LS3 ... 206 A1
Back Kennerleigh Wlk LS15 ... 62 C1
Back Kensington St
Bradford, Brown Royd BD8 ... 74 A8
Bradford, Girlington BD8 ... 55 A1
Back Kensington Terr LS6 ... 205 F3
Back King's Ave 27 LS6 ... 205 E2
Back Kirby St BD21 ... 35 D8
Back Kirkgate BD18 ... 55 A7
Back Kitson St LS9 ... 212 C3
Back Knowl Rd WF14 ... 137 F6
Back Knowle Mount 12 LS4 ... 205 D3
Back La Badsworth WF9 ... 164 E2
Batley WF16 ... 117 D4
Birkenshaw BD11 ... 96 F7
Bradford, Clayton Heights BD13, BD14 ... 73 B2
Bradford, Idle BD10 ... 56 B8
Bramham LS23 ... 30 D3
Burley in W LS29 ... 9 F1
Clayton DN5 ... 194 C4
Clayton West HD8 ... 176 A3
Crofton WF4 ... 144 C2
Dewsbury WF12 ... 138 F2
Dewsbury, Whitley Lower WF12 ... 156 F7
Emley HD8 ... 175 A5
Flockton WF4 ... 156 E5
Gildersome LS12 ... 77 C3
Guiseley LS20 ... 39 D8
Halifax HX2 ... 91 D5
Haworth BD22 ... 50 C6
Hebden Bridge HX7 ... 88 F1
Heptonstall HX7 ... 88 F4
Holmfirth HD7 ... 189 A5
Hooton Pagnell DN5 ... 195 D5
Horsforth LS18 ... 58 B8
Keighley, East Morton BD20 ... 19 D1
Keighley, Laycock BD22 ... 34 B7
Kippax WF10 ... 103 B4
Leeds LS13 ... 58 D1
Lepton WF14 ... 156 B7
Mirfield WF14 ... 137 E5
Netherton WF4 ... 158 B7
Ossett WF5 ... 140 D5
Otley LS29 ... 10 A1
Pudsey LS28 ... 57 D3
Ripponden HX6 ... 132 D4
Ryhill WF4 ... 162 B4
Shepley HD8 ... 174 B3
Shipley BD9 ... 55 A4
Sicklinghall LS22 ... 12 C5
Silsden BD20 ... 5 E2
Skipton BD23 ... 4 C8
South Elmsall WF9 ... 183 A6
Thornton BD13 ... 72 E7
Wadsworth Moor HX7 ... 69 A6
Wakefield WF1 ... 216 A2
Wilsden BD15 ... 53 D3
Woolley WF4 ... 178 A6
Yeadon LS19 ... 40 A6
Back La W S71 ... 179 A4
Back Laisteridge La BD7 ... 74 C6
Back Lake St LS10 ... 215 D2
Back Lambton Gr 17 LS8 ... 207 F4
Back Landseer Ave LS13 ... 58 E3
Back Landseer Gr LS13 ... 58 E3
Back Landseer Terr LS13 ... 58 E3
Back Langdale Gdns LS6 ... 59 C4
Back Langdale Terr LS6 ... 59 C4
Back Lascelles Terr 1 LS8 ... 207 F3
Back Laurel Mount LS7 ... 204 A1
Back Leatham St 2 WF13 ... 118 A1
Back Leeming BD22 ... 51 D1
Back Lime St BD21 ... 35 B3
Back Linden Gr 2 LS11 ... 214 C3
Back Lindum St BD8 ... 55 C2
Back Lodge La 1 LS11 ... 214 B2
Back Lombard St LS19 ... 40 A4
Back Longroyd Terr LS11 ... 214 C3
Back Lord St HX1 ... 203 D3
Back Low La LS18 ... 41 D1
Back Lucas St 4 LS6 ... 206 A4
Back Lunan Pl LS8 ... 207 F4
Back Lunan Terrr LS8 ... 207 F4
Back Lyon St BD13 ... 72 F1
Back Lytton St 7 HX3 ... 92 C1
Back Mafeking Ave LS11 ... 214 A1
Back Mafeking Mount LS11 ... 214 A1
Back Malt St 9 BD22 ... 35 A4
Back Mannville Rd 10 BD21 ... 35 A6
Back Manor Dr LS6 ... 205 E4
Back Manor Gr LS7 ... 204 A2
Back Manor St BD2 ... 56 B3
Back Manor Terr LS6 ... 205 E4
Back Market St 3 BD6 ... 74 C1
Back Markham Ave LS8 ... 207 F4
Back Marlborough Gdns 18 LS2 ... 206 B2
Back Marlborough Gr 20 LS2 ... 206 B2
Back Marriot St 4 WF13 ... 118 D1
Back Marshall Ave 3 LS15 ... 62 D2
Back Marshall St 5 LS15 ... 62 C2
Back Marshall Terr 6 LS15 ... 62 C2
Back Mary St
East Ardsley WF3 ... 120 E8
Glusburn BD20 ... 16 D8
Back Masham St LS12 ... 210 A3
Back Maud Ave LS11 ... 214 B2
Back Mayville Ave LS6 ... 205 E3
Back Mayville Pl 6 LS6 ... 205 E3
Back Mayville St 3 LS6 ... 205 E3
Back Mayville Terr LS6 ... 205 E3
Back Meadow View 12 LS6 ... 205 E3
Back Melbourne Gr 18 LS13 ... 58 C2
Back Methley Dr LS7 ... 204 A2
Back Mexborough Ave LS7 ... 207 D4
Back Mexborough Dr LS7 ... 207 D4
Back Mexborough Gr LS7 ... 207 D4
Back Mexborough St LS7 ... 207 D4
Back Middle Cross St LS12 ... 210 A3
Back Middleton Rd LS29 ... 8 A4
Back Middleton View 1 LS11 ... 214 A3
Back Midland Rd LS6 ... 205 F3
Back Milan Ave LS8 ... 207 F3
Back Milan Rd LS8 ... 207 F3
Back Milan St LS8 ... 208 A3
Back Mitchell Terr BD16 ... 36 F2
Back Mitford Rd LS12 ... 210 A3
Back Model Rd LS12 ... 210 A3
Back Model Terr LS12 ... 210 A3
Back Model View LS12 ... 210 A3
Back Monk Bridge Dr 7 LS6 ... 59 F6
Back Monk Bridge St LS6 ... 59 F6
Back Montague St WF1 ... 142 F3
Back Montpelier Terr 2 LS6 ... 206 A4
Back Moor La HD4 ... 171 D7
Back Moorfield St HX1 ... 202 C1
Back Moorfield Terr LS12 ... 209 D4
Back Moorland Terr LS2 ... 206 A2
Back Morning St 14 BD21 ... 35 B4
Back Morritt Dr LS15 ... 80 F8
Back Mount Ave 2 WF17 ... 118 D3
Back Mount Pleasant
Middleton LS10 ... 99 C5
Wakefield WF1 ... 216 C2
Back Mount View LS6 ... 205 F4
Back Muff St BD4 ... 75 B5
Back Myrtle Ave BD16 ... 36 F2
Back Myrtle Terr BD22 ... 34 F1
Back Nansen St LS13 ... 58 A2
Back Nelson St 14 WF13 ... 139 C8
Back New St 8 HD6 ... 115 A3
Back New York St 6 LS2 ... 211 F3
Back Newport Gdns 2 LS6 ... 205 D3
Back Newport Mount 1 LS6 ... 205 D3
Back Newport Pl 5 LS6 ... 205 D3
Back Newton Gr LS7 ... 207 E4
Back Newton La
Ledsham WF10 ... 104 B5
Ledston WF10 ... 103 E7
Back Nice View LS8 ... 207 F4
Back Norman Mount 1 LS5 ... 59 A4
Back Norman Pl LS8 ... 44 A2
Back Norman Terr LS8 ... 44 A2
Back North Park Ave LS8 ... 204 C4
Back North St BD12 ... 95 A4
Back Northbrook St LS7 ... 204 A3
Back Northgate WF8 ... 125 D1
Back Norwood Gr LS6 ... 205 E3
Back Norwood Pl 2 LS6 ... 205 E3

Back Norwood Rd 1 LS6 205 E3
Back Norwood Terr LS6 205 E3
Back Nowell Cres LS9 208 B1
Back Nowell Mount LS9 208 B1
Back Nowell Pl LS9 208 B1
Back Nowell Terr LS9 208 B1
Back Nunington St LS12 210 A4
Back Nunington View 3 LS12 59 C1
Back Nunroyd Rd LS17 43 D1
Back Nursery Mount LS10 215 E1
Back O' Dam HD7 170 A8
Back o' Th' Height HX6 131 D1
Back O' the Mill BD16 36 A1
Back O'Wall HD7 151 B3
Back Oak Ave BD16 36 F2
Back Oak Rd LS7 204 A1
Back Oakfield Terr LS6 59 E6
Back Oakley St WF3 99 E1
Back Oakley Terr LS11 214 C2
Back Oakwood Ave LS8 61 B6
Back Oakwood Dr LS8 61 B6
Back Osmondthorpe La LS9 80 C8
Back Otterburn St 2 BD21 35 C8
Back Outwood La 5 LS18 58 C7
Back Overdale Terr 5 LS15 81 A8
Back Oxford Pl LS1 211 E4
Back Oxford St
East Ardsley WF3 120 E8
7 Keighley BD21 35 A6
Back Paget St 8 BD21 35 A7
Back Parish Ghyll Rd LS29 8 B4
Back Park Cres LS8 44 B2
Back Park Terr HX1 202 C2
Back Park View LS11 214 A3
Back Park View Ave LS4 205 D3
Back Parkfield Pl LS11 214 A3
Back Parkfield Rd LS11 214 A3
Back Parnaby Ave LS10 215 F1
Back Parnaby St LS10 215 F1
Back Parnaby Terr LS10 215 F1
Back Pasture Gr LS7 204 A3
Back Pasture Rd LS8 207 F4
Back Pawson St WF3 120 E8
Back Pleasant St HX6 112 C4
Back Pollard La LS13 58 C5
Back Pollard St HD2 136 B2
Back Poplar Ave 1 LS15 62 D2
Back Potternewton La LS7 60 C6
Back Potters St LS7 204 A2
Back Prospect Pl BD21 35 B6
Back Prospect Terr LS9 212 C3
Back Providence Ave 11 LS6 206 A4
Back Providence St 4 WF17 118 C5
Back Purlwell Hall Rd WF17 118 C3
Back Purwell La WF17 118 C4
Back Quarry Mount Terr 9 LS6 206 A4
Back Queen St
2 Elland HX4 134 D6
2 Huddersfield HD1 154 B5
Back Ravens St WF13 139 A6
Back Ravenscar Ave 5 LS8 61 A6
Back Ravenscar Pl 1 LS8 61 A6
Back Raynville Mount LS13 58 E3
Back Rd 19 BD12 94 C4
Back Regent Park Terr LS6 205 F4
Back Regent St WF1 142 E3
Back Regent Terr LS6 205 F2
Back Reginald Mount LS7 207 D4
Back Reginald Pl LS7 207 D4
Back Reginald St LS7 207 D4
Back Rhodes St HX1 203 D3
Back Ribble St BD21 35 F8
Back Richardson St BD12 95 A4
Back Richmond Mount LS6 205 E4
Back Ridge Mount Terr LS6 206 A4
Back Ridge St OL14 108 B5
Back Ridge View LS7 60 A5
Back Rigging La HX6 111 C3
Back Ripley St BD20 18 F1
Back Ripon St HX1 202 A2
Back Ripon Terr HX3 92 B1
Back River St 5 BD22 51 D7
Back Roberts St 3 LS26 101 C6
Back Rochester Terr LS6 205 D4
Back Rokeby Gdns 1 LS6 59 C5
Back Roman Gr LS8 44 A2
Back Roman Pl LS8 44 B2
Back Roman St LS8 44 B2
Back Rose Ave LS18 58 B7
Back Rosebank Cres LS3 205 F2
Back Rosemont Wlk 5 LS13 58 C2
Back Rossall Rd LS8 208 A4
Back Rossington Gr 3 LS8 207 E4
Back Rossington Pl 5 LS8 207 E4
Back Rossington Rd LS8 207 E4
Back Roundhay Ave LS8 204 C1
Back Roundhay Cres LS8 204 C1
Back Roundhay Gr LS8 204 C1
Back Roundhay Pl LS8 204 C1
Back Roundhay View LS8 204 C1
Back Row LS11 211 E2
Back Rowland Terr 7 LS11 214 C3
Back Rowsley St 2 BD21 35 D7
Back Rupert St BD21 35 C8
Back Russell St BD5 201 A1
Back Ruthven View LS8 208 A3
Back Rydal St 5 BD22 35 A6
Back Rylstone St 1 BD21 35 E8
Back Saint Ives Mount LS12 209 D4
Back Salisbury Gr LS12 209 F4
Back Salisbury Terr LS12 209 F4
Back Salisbury View LS12 209 F4
Back Saltaire Rd N BD17 55 B8
Back Sandhurst Gr LS8 208 A3
Back Sandhurst Pl LS8 208 A3
Back Sandhurst Rd LS8 208 A3
Back Savile Par HX1 203 D1
Back Savile Pl LS7 207 D3
Back Savile Rd LS7 207 D3
Back School View LS6 205 E3
Back Seaforth Ave LS9 208 B2
Back Seaforth Pl 2 LS9 208 A3
Back Seaforth Terr 3 LS9 208 A3
Back Sefton Ave LS11 214 A3
Back Sefton Terr LS11 214 A3
Back Shaftesbury Ave LS8 44 A2
Back Shaw La BD21 35 D3
Back Shepherd's La LS7 207 E4
Back Shepherd's Pl 9 LS8 207 F4
Back Sholebroke Ave LS7 204 A1
Back Sholebroke Mount LS7 207 D4
Back Sholebroke Pl LS7 207 D4
Back Sholebroke Row LS7 204 A1
Back Sholebroke Terr LS7 204 A1
Back Sholebroke View LS7 207 D4
Back Sidlaw Terr LS8 207 F4
Back Simpson St 1 BD21 35 A7
Back Sladen St 5 BD21 35 A7
Back Slaithwaite Rd WF12 139 C4
Back Smith Row 6 BD5 74 C3
Back South End Gr LS13 58 E1
Back South St HD1 153 D5
Back Southfield Sq BD8 55 C1
Back Spencer Mount 7 LS8 207 E4
Back Spring Grove Wlk 14 LS6 205 E2
Back Spring St 4 HD1 154 A6
Back Springfield Mount LS12 209 D4
Back Springfield Pl BD8 55 D1
Back Springfield Rd HX5 135 A7
Back St Bramham LS23 30 C2
Pontefract WF8 146 C8
Back St Alban Cres LS9 208 C1
Back St Elmo Gr 5 LS9 80 A8
Back St Luke's Cres LS11 214 A4
Back St Mary's Rd LS7 204 A1
Back St Paul's Rd BD18 55 A7
Back Stanley St
Huddersfield HD1 153 E3
Leeds LS9 207 F2
Back Stanmore Pl LS4 59 C3
Back Stanmore St LS4 59 C3
Back Station Rd
Batley WF17 118 D4
Glusburn BD20 16 D7
Mirfield WF14 138 A3
Back Stone Hill Rd BD2 56 B4
Back Storey Pl LS14 61 E1
Back Stratford Ave LS11 214 A3
Back Stratford St 10 LS11 214 C3
Back Stratford Terr LS11 214 B3
Back Strathmore Dr 1 LS9 208 A3
Back Sunnybank Ave 5 LS18 58 B7
Back Sunnydene LS14 61 F1
Back Sutton App LS14 61 E1
Back Swinton St HX1 202 B2
Back Sycamore Ave BD16 36 F2
Back Tamworth St BD4 75 E6
Back Tempest Rd 2 LS11 214 A3
Back Temple View LS11 214 A3
Back Thornhill Rd HD3 153 A6
Back Thornhill St LS28 57 B6
Back Tower Gr LS12 209 D4
Back Trafford Ave LS9 208 B2
Back Trentham Pl 10 LS11 214 B2
Back Trinity Terr BD5 201 A1
Back Union St 5 HD1 154 B7
Back Unity St N BD16 36 F2
Back Unity St S 6 BD16 37 A2
Back Victor Terr HX1 202 C4
Back Victoria Ave 6 LS9 80 B8
Back Victoria Gr 5 LS9 80 B8
Back Victoria St HX1 203 E3
Back Wakefield Rd HX6 112 E4
Back Walmsley Rd LS6 205 E3
Back Walnut St 16 BD21 35 B4
Back Webster St 3 WF13 139 C8
Back Welburn Ave LS16 59 B7
Back Wellfield Terr OL14 108 B4
Back Welton Ave 18 LS6 205 E3
Back Welton Gr LS6 205 E3
Back Welton Mount 15 LS6 205 E3
Back Welton Pl LS6 205 E3
Back Wentworth St HD1 153 F7
Back Wesley Rd LS12 209 F3
Back Wesley St WF10 124 D8
Back West St HX6 112 B3
Back Westbourne Terr LS2 206 A2
Back Westbury St LS10 215 F1
Back Westfield Rd LS3 205 F1
Back Westlock Ave LS9 208 A1
Back Westmoreland Mount 2 LS13 58 D4
Back Weston Rd LS29 8 B4
Back Westover Rd LS13 58 C3
Back Wetherby Gr 4 LS4 59 C2
Back Wetherby Rd LS8 61 B6
Back Wheat St 7 BD22 35 A4
Back Wickham St LS11 214 B3
Back William Ave 1 LS15 80 E8
Back William St 9 HD6 115 A1
Back Wilton Gr 3 LS6 59 E6
Back Winfield Gr 3 LS2 206 B2
Back Winston Gdns 3 LS6 59 C5
Back Winterburn St BD21 35 C8
Back Wolsley Terr 2 HX1 202 B3
Back Wood St 3
Bradford BD8 74 C8
East Ardsley WF3 120 D8
Back Woodbine Terr LS6 59 E6
Back Woodland Park Rd 3 LS6 59 E5
Back Woodstock St 16 LS2 206 B2
Back Wright Ave BD22 34 D3
Back York Pl LS1 211 E3
Back York St 3 LS2 212 A3
Backhold Ave HX3 113 E2
Backhold Dr HX3 113 E2
Backhold La HX3 113 D2
Backhold Rd HX3 113 E2
Backhouse La WF4 177 F7
Backstone Gill La LS17 27 E1
Backstone La LS29 8 C3
Backstone Way LS29 8 D4
Bacon Ave WF6 123 C3
Bacon St LS20 39 F8
Bacup Rd OL14 107 D4
Baddeley Gdns BD10 39 A1
Baden Powell Cres WF8 146 D7
Baden St BD22 51 C8
Baden Terr 4 BD19 116 D7
Badger Brow HD7 170 D2
Badger Cl WF4 159 F7
Badger Gate HD7 170 D2
Badger Hill HD6 135 E6
Badger La
Blackshaw Head HX7 88 B4
Brighouse HX3 114 B7
Badger Wood Glade LS22 13 E7
Badgergate Ave BD15 53 C4
Badgers Gate LS29 3 E4
Badgers Mount LS15 62 F2
Badgers Way BD2 55 E4
Badgers Wlk WF16 117 E3
Badsworth CE Jun & Inf Sch WF9 164 E2
Badsworth Ct
Badsworth WF9 164 E3
Bradford BD14 73 D5
Badsworth Mews WF9 164 E2
Badsworth View WF9 183 A8
Bagden La Denby Dale HD8 192 D8
Denby Dale, Trister Hill HD8 192 E7
Baghill Ct WF8 146 F8
Baghill Gn WF3 119 D6
Baghill La WF8 146 F8
Baghill Rd WF3 119 D6
Baghill Sta WF8 146 E8
Bagley La LS28 57 E4
Bagnall Terr 2 BD6 74 B1
Bagshaw Mus WF17 118 A8
Baildon Ave LS25 83 B3
Baildon CE First Sch BD17 38 D4
Baildon Chase LS14 62 C7
Baildon Cl LS14 62 C6
Baildon Dr LS14 62 C6
Baildon Gn LS14 62 C6
Baildon Golf Course BD17 38 A6
Baildon Holmes BD17 38 C1
Baildon Path 1 LS14 62 C6
Baildon Pl LS14 62 C6
Baildon Rd Baildon BD17 38 D2
Leeds LS14 62 C7
Baildon Sta BD17 38 E3
Baildon Wlk LS14 62 C7
Baildon Wood Ct BD17 38 C2
Bailes Rd LS7 60 A5
Bailey Cres WF9 183 A4
Bailey Hall Bank HX3 203 F3
Bailey Hall Rd HX3 203 F2
Bailey Hills Rd BD16 36 E4
Bailey St BD4 201 C1
Bailey Towers 2 LS14 62 A5
Bailey Walk WF4 159 F3
Bailey Wells Ave BD5 74 C3
Bailey's Ct LS14 62 A5
Bailey's Hill LS14 62 B5
Bailey's La LS14 62 A5
Bailey's Lawn LS14 62 A5
Bailiff Bridge Junior & Infants Sch HD6 115 B7
Bainbridge Wharf BD20 4 D1
Bainbrigge Rd LS6 205 D4
Baines St Halifax HX1 202 C4
Rothwell LS26 100 E5
Baird St BD5 74 E4
Bairstow Ct HX6 112 C6
Bairstow La HX6 112 C6
Bairstow Mount HX6 112 D5
Bairstow St BD15 54 A3
Bairstow's Bldgs HX2 91 F4
Baitings Gate Rd HX6 131 C2
Baker Cres LS27 98 A3
Baker Fold 7 HX1 202 C3
Baker La WF3 121 D5
Baker Rd LS27 98 A3
Baker St Bradford BD2 56 B2
Huddersfield HD3 153 B8
Morley LS27 98 A3
Shipley BD18 55 A8
Baker St N HX2 92 A5
Baker's St 12 HX7 89 A4
Bakes St BD7 74 A4
Balbec Ave LS6 59 E5
Balbec St LS6 59 E5
Balderstone Hall La WF14 138 C7
Baldovan Mount LS8 207 F4
Baldovan Pl 5 LS8 207 F4
Baldovan Terr 7 LS8 207 F4
Baldwin La
Bradford BD13, BD14 73 A2
Queensbury BD13, BD14 73 A2
Baldwin Terr HX3 203 F3
Balfour St Bingley BD16 36 F2
Bradford BD4 75 A4
6 Keighley BD21 35 B6
Balk Ave WF3 122 A2
Balk Cres WF3 122 A2
Balk La Bradford BD7 74 B4
Denby Dale HD8 191 C6
Kirkheaton HD5 155 B7
Lofthouse Gate WF3 122 A1
Netherton WF4 158 F7
South Elmsall WF9 183 D4
Wakefield WF3 122 A1
Balk St WF17 118 B5
Balk The Batley WF17 118 C7
Mapplewell S75 178 C2
Walton WF2 161 B6
Balkcliffe La LS10 99 A6
Balkram Dr HX2 91 A5
Balkram Edge HX2 91 A5
Balkram Rd HX2 91 B5
Balks WF15 116 F4
Ball Royd Rd HD2 136 B2
Ball St BD13 72 E6
Ballantyne Rd BD10 39 A2
Ballater Ave HD4 153 C2
Ballfield La S75 177 C1
Ballroyd Clough
Huddersfield HD3 153 A6
Huddersfield, Quarmby HD3 153 A7
Ballroyd La HD3 153 A5
Balm Pl LS11 211 D1
Balm Rd LS10 215 E2
Balm Road Ind Est LS10 215 D3
Balm Wlk LS11 211 D1
Balme La BD12 94 D3
Balme Rd BD19 116 D8
Balme St Bradford BD1 201 C3
Bradford, Upper Common BD12 94 D3
Balmfield WF15 117 A2
Balmfield Cres WF15 117 A1
Balmoral Ave HD4 153 C2
Balmoral Chase LS10 215 F3
Balmoral Cl WF8 146 B5
Balmoral Dr WF11 126 C4
Balmoral Pl HX1 203 E2
Balmoral St 12 HX7 89 A3
Balmoral Way LS19 40 D6
Balne Ave WF2 142 A7
Balne La WF2 142 A7
Bamborough St WF1 142 F3
Bamburgh Cl LS15 62 E3
Bamburgh Rd LS15 62 E3
Bamlett Brow BD22 51 D8
Banbury Rd WF8 125 E3
Bancroft Ave HD5 154 E5
Bancroft St BD22 51 F8
Bangor Gr 12 LS12 78 A4
Bangor Pl LS12 78 A4
Bangor St LS12 78 A4
Bangor Terr LS12 78 A4
Bangor View 11 LS12 78 A4
Bank Bradford BD10 56 D6
Oxenhope BD22 51 E1
Bank Ave Horsforth LS18 58 B8
Morley LS27 98 A5
Bank Bldgs
Hebden Bridge HX7 89 C2
Meltham HD7 170 E1
Bank Bottom Halifax HX3 203 F3
Hebden Bridge HX7 90 A2
Marsden HD7 169 C6
Ripponden HX6 150 D8
Bank Bottom La HX2 90 E1
Bank Bottom Terr HD7 169 C6
Bank Cl BD10 56 C5
Bank Crest BD17 38 C3
Bank Crest Rise BD18 54 C7
Bank Dr BD6 74 D1
Bank Edge Cl HX2 91 E3
Bank Edge Gdns HX2 91 E3
Bank Edge Rd HX2 91 E4
Bank End Elland HX4 133 D7
Slaithwaite HD7 152 C4
Bank End La
Clayton West HD8 176 A1
High Hoyland HD8 176 A1
Huddersfield HD5 154 E4
Bank End Rd HD7 152 C3
Bank Field Grange HX4 134 C7
Bank Field Rd WF17 118 C5
Bank Foot HD4 172 F8
Bank Foot La HD4 171 E7
Bank Foot Pl WF17 118 C5
Bank Foot Rd HD4 172 F8
Bank Foot St WF17 118 C5
Bank Gate HD7 151 F1
Bank Gdns LS18 58 B8
Bank Gr WF12 140 A7
Bank Hall Gr HD8 190 F8
Bank Hey Bottom La HX6 132 E3
Bank House HX4 133 D4
Bank House Cl LS27 98 A5
Bank House La HX2 90 E4
Bank La Denby Dale HD8 191 F4
Holmfirth HD7 188 C2
Holmfirth, Liphill Bank HD7 188 D4
Holmfirth, Town End HD7 189 B7
Silsden BD20 5 E8
Bank Nook HD7 169 C7
Bank Par LS21 22 F7
Bank Rd Glusburn BD20 16 D7
Sowerby Bridge HX6 112 B3
Bank Royd La HX4 133 B1
Bank Side HD8 173 F2
Bank Side St LS8 207 F3
Bank Sq 2 LS27 98 A5
Bank St Bradford BD1 201 B3
Bradford, Brownroyd Hill BD6 74 C1
Brighouse HD6 115 A2
Castleford WF10 124 D8
Cleckheaton BD19 116 C7
Dewsbury WF12 139 D8
Hemsworth WF9 181 D7
Holmfirth HD7 189 E4
Horbury WF4 141 A1
5 Keighley BD21 35 C7
Leeds LS27 211 F3
Liversedge WF15 117 B4
Mirfield WF14 137 E5
Morley LS27 98 A5
Ossett WF5 140 D5
Shipley BD18 55 B7
Todmorden OL14 108 B4
Wakefield WF1 216 B2
Wetherby LS22 13 E5
Bank Terr
Hebden Bridge HX7 88 E4
Morley LS27 98 B5
Bank Top HX3 113 F5
Bank Top Dr BD20 18 F2
Bank Top La
Hebden Bridge HX7 109 F5
Holmfirth HD7 188 A2
Bank Top Way BD21 35 F6
Bank View Baildon BD17 38 B2
Dewsbury WF12 140 A8
Honley HD7 172 C2
Sowerby Bridge, Luddenden Foot HX2 111 D6
Sowerby Bridge, Mill Bank HX6 132 D7
Bank View Terr LS7 60 B7
Bank Wlk BD17 38 C4
Bank Wood Rd WF8 147 F4
Banker St LS4 205 D2
Bankfield Bardsey LS17 28 D4
Marsden HD7 169 A4
Shepley HD8 173 F2
Bankfield Ave
Kirkheaton HD5 155 B8
Shipley BD18 54 D7
Bankfield Cl WF5 140 F4
Bankfield Ct
Huddersfield HD5 154 D5
Mirfield WF14 137 F5
Wakefield WF2 120 F3
Bankfield Dr Holmfirth HD7 188 C2
Keighley BD22 34 E7
Shipley BD18 54 D7
Wakefield WF2 120 F3
Bankfield Gdns Halifax HX3 113 F6
1 Leeds LS4 59 C2
Bankfield Gr Leeds LS4 59 C3
Shipley BD18 54 D6
Bankfield La HD5 155 B8
Bankfield Mount BD22 34 E7
Bankfield Park Ave HD4 153 F1
Bankfield Rd
Huddersfield HD1 153 F5
Keighley BD22 34 E8
Leeds LS4 59 C2
Shipley BD18 54 D7
Bankfield St BD22 34 E8
Bankfield Terr Baildon BD17 38 D2
Huddersfield HD4 171 E8
Leeds LS4 59 C2
Bankfield View HX3 92 B1
Bankfield Wlk BD22 34 E7
Bankfoot HX7 88 F3
Bankfoot First Sch BD5 74 D2
Bankholme Ct BD4 75 F2
Bankhouse LS28 76 D5
Bankhouse La Halifax HX3 113 D2
Huddersfield HX3 153 C5
Pudsey LS28 76 D5
Bankhouse Rd HD3 153 B5
Banklands BD20 5 E2
Banklands Ave BD20 5 F2
Banklands La BD20 5 F2
Banks App HD7 152 D5
Banks Ave
Ackworth M T WF7 163 E5
Huddersfield HD7 152 D5
Pontefract WF8 146 C8
Banks Cres HD7 152 D5
Banks Dr HD7 152 D5
Banks End Rd HX5 135 C6
Banks Garth WF11 126 F4
Banks Gr HD7 152 D5
Banks La Keighley BD20 18 E3
Knottingley WF11 126 F4
Banks Mount 10 WF8 146 C8
Banks Rd Honley HD7 172 B3
Huddersfield HD7 152 D5
Slaithwaite HD7 170 B8

Banks Side HD7 152 D5
Banks St WF17 118 C4
Banksfield Ave LS19 40 B8
Banksfield Cl LS19 40 B8
Banksfield Cres LS19 40 B8
Banksfield Gr LS19 40 B8
Banksfield Mount LS19 40 B8
Banksfield Rd 8 HX7 89 E1
Banksfield Rise LS19 40 B8
Banksfield Terr HX7 89 E1
Banksfields Ave HX7 89 E1
Banksfields Cres HX7 89 E1
Bankside OL14 108 B4
Bankside Primary Sch LS8 207 F3
Bankside Terr BD17 38 B2
Banksville HD7 189 B7
Bankwell Fold BD6 74 D1
Bankwell Rd HD3 153 B4
Bankwood WF17 97 B4
Bankwood Way WF17 97 B3
Banner St BD3 75 A6
Bannerman St BD12 95 A5
Bannister La DN6 184 C5
Bannockburn Croft BD5 75 B1
Bannockburn Way WF6 122 E4
Banstead St E LS8 207 F3
Banstead St W LS8 207 F3
Banstead Terr E LS8 207 F3
Banstead Terr W 6 LS8 207 F3
Bantam Cl LS27 98 D4
Bantam Grove La LS27 98 D4
Bantree Ct BD10 39 A2
Baptist Fold BD13 72 F1
Baptist La WF5 141 B4
Baptist Pl BD1 201 A3
Baptist St WF17 118 A3
Bar Croft HD5 137 B1
Bar House La BD20 17 F3
Bar La Bramham LS23 31 A6
Garforth LS25 83 A7
Horsforth LS18 57 F8
Keighley BD20 18 F1
Lofthouse Gate WF1 121 D1
Netherton WF4 158 B2
Ripponden HX6 132 C2
West Bretton WF4 158 B2
Bar Mount LS25 83 A7
Bar St Batley WF17 118 D4
Todmorden OL14 108 A4
Barber Row HD7 152 D1
Barber Sq WF16 117 C4
Barber St 1 HD6 115 B3
Barber Wlk 7 WF13 139 C8
Barberry Ave BD3 75 E8
Barclay Cl BD13 52 E6
Barclay St LS7 207 D1
Barcroft BD22 51 F8
Barcroft Gr LS19 40 A6
Barcroft Rd HD4 154 A2
Barden Ave BD6 93 D8
Barden Cl Batley WF17 118 B5
Leeds LS12 209 D3
Barden Dr BD16 37 C4
Barden Gn LS12 209 D3
Barden Gr LS12 209 D3
Barden Mount LS12 209 D3
Barden Pl LS12 209 D3
Barden Rd WF1 142 F7
Barden St BD8 55 B1
Barden Terr LS12 209 D3
Bardsey County Primary Sch LS17 28 C3
Bardsey Cres BD3 75 A7
Bardwell Ct WF3 121 E5
Bare Bones Rd HD7 199 B5
Bare Head La HX3 92 D5
Barewell Hill S72 181 A4
Barfield Ave LS19 40 A6
Barfield Cres LS17 43 F5
Barfield Dr LS19 40 A6
Barfield Gr LS17 44 A5
Barfield Mount LS17 44 A5
Barfield Rd HX3 114 C7
Bargate HD7 152 D1
Barge St HD1 153 F4
Bargess Terr LS25 83 B1
Bargrange Ave BD18 55 B6
Bargreen HD5 137 B1
Barham Terr BD10 56 D4
Baring Ave BD3 75 D8
Baring Sq BD20 16 D4
Bark Cl HD8 174 A3
Bark House La
Cawthorne S75 193 C4
Shepley HD8 174 C3
Bark La LS29 7 A8
Barker Cl HX3 113 E3
Barker Ct HD2 135 E1
Barker House 4 HX3 113 E3
Barker Pl LS13 58 D1
Barker Rd WF4 140 F2
Barker St Liversedge WF15 117 B4
Lofthouse Gate WF3 122 B6
Todmorden OL14 108 B6
Barker's Rd WF4 159 E6
Barkerend First Sch BD3 75 A8
Barkerend Rd BD1, BD3 75 B8
Barkers Well Fold LS12 77 D4
Barkers Well Garth LS12 77 E3
Barkers Well Gate LS12 77 E3
Barkers Well Lawn LS12 77 E3
Barkisland CE Sch HX4 133 A5
Barkly Ave LS11 214 A1
Barkly Dr LS11 214 A1
Barkly Gr LS11 214 A2
Barkly Par 2 LS11 214 A1
Barkly Pl 1 LS11 214 A1
Barkly Rd LS11 214 A1
Barkly St LS11 214 A1
Barkly Terr LS11 214 A2
Barkston Wlk 2 BD15 73 A7
Barlbro' Pl HD4 153 A4
Barlby Way LS8 61 C6
Barley Cote Ave BD20 19 A2
Barley Cote Gr BD20 19 A2
Barley Cote Rd BD20 19 A2
Barley Croft WF13 138 F8
Barley Field Ct 3 LS15 81 A8
Barley Mews WF3 100 B3
Barley St BD22 35 A4
Barleycorn Cl WF3 121 E1
Barleyfield Cl WF1 142 E8
Barleyfields Cl LS22 13 E7
Barleyfields Ct LS22 13 E6
Barleyfields La LS22 13 E6
Barleyfields Rd LS22 13 E7
Barleyfields Terr LS22 13 E6
Barleyfields Wlk LS22 13 E6
Barleyhill Cres LS25 82 E6
Barleyhill La LS25 82 E7
Barleyhill Rd LS25 82 E7
Barlow Rd BD21 35 B8
Barlow St BD3 75 B7
Barmby Cl WF5 140 F4
Barmby Cres WF5 141 A4
Barmby Fold WF5 140 F4
Barmby Pl BD2 56 B1
Barmby Rd BD2 56 B1
Barmby St BD12 94 D4
Barmouth Terr BD3 55 F2
Barn Cl LS29 21 F4
Barn St BD22 51 C2
Barnaby Rd BD16 37 C4
Barnard Cl LS15 62 E3
Barnard Rd BD4 201 D1
Barnard Way LS15 62 E3
Barnbow La
Barwick in E LS15 63 B5
Leeds LS15 63 B3
Barnbrough St LS4 59 C2
Barnby Royd HD5 154 F7
Barncliffe Hill HD8 174 C1
Barncroft Cl LS14 61 F7
Barncroft Ct LS14 61 E6
Barncroft Dr LS14 61 F7
Barncroft Gdns LS14 61 F6
Barncroft Grange LS14 61 E6
Barncroft Hts LS14 61 E7
Barncroft Mount LS14 61 E6
Barncroft Rd LS14 61 F7
Barncroft Rise LS14 61 F6
Barncroft Towers LS14 61 E6
Barnes Ave WF1 121 A3
Barnes Meadows OL15 129 C1
Barnes Rd Bradford BD8 73 F7
Castleford WF10 124 D6
Barnes St 6 OL14 108 A1
Barnet Gr 2 LS27 98 A2
Barnet Rd LS12 210 A3
Barnett House 5 BD6 93 E8
Barnsdale Bar DN6 184 C8
Barnsdale Est WF10 124 B6
Barnsdale Rd Kippax WF10 103 D4
Mickletown LS26 102 E1
Barnsdale Way WF9 183 E7
Barnside La HD7 189 F1
Barnsley Beck Gr BD17 38 D3
Barnsley Rd
Ackworth M T WF7 164 A6
Brierley S72 181 A4
Clayton West HD8 175 E1
Crigglestone WF2, WF4 160 B4
Denby Dale HD8 191 C5
Flockton WF4 157 C3
Hemsworth WF9 181 C6
Notton WF4 178 E5
South Elmsall WF9 182 E3
South Kirkby WF9 182 E3
Wakefield WF1, WF2 160 D7
Woolley WF4 178 C6
Barnstone Vale WF1 121 E1
Barnswick Cl WF8 146 D6
Barnswick View LS16 41 E4
Baron Cl LS11 214 A4
Baronscourt LS15 81 D8
Baronsmead LS15 81 D8
Baronsway LS15 81 C8
Barr St HD1 154 C8
Barrack Rd LS7 207 D3
Barrack St LS7 207 D2
Barracks Fold HD7 189 E2
Barracks St WF16 117 C4
Barraclough Bldgs BD10 56 E7
Barraclough Sq 18 BD12 94 C4
Barraclough St 5 BD12 94 B6
Barran Ct LS8 207 F3
Barran St 8 BD16 37 A3
Barras Garth Pl LS12 209 E2
Barras Garth Rd LS12 209 E2
Barras Pl LS12 209 E2
Barras St LS12 209 E2
Barras Terr LS12 209 E2
Barratt's Rd WF1 216 B4
Barrett St BD20 5 D1
Barrington Cl HX3 114 A4
Barrington Par BD19 117 A8
Barrowby Ave LS15 81 E7
Barrowby Cl LS29 22 B4
Barrowby Cres LS15 81 E8
Barrowby Dr LS15 81 F7
Barrowby La Garforth LS25 82 E8
Leeds LS15 81 F8
Barrowby Rd LS15 81 F7
Barrowclough La HX3 113 F7
Barrows La BD20 17 C4
Barrowstead HD8 175 B1
Barry St BD1 201 B3
Barsey Green La HX4 133 C6
Barstow Sq WF1 216 B2
Barthorpe Ave LS17 60 B8
Barthorpe Cl BD4 75 F2
Barthorpe Cres LS17 60 C8
Bartle Cl BD7 73 F3
Bartle Fold BD7 74 A4
Bartle Gill Dr BD17 38 E4
Bartle Gill Rise BD17 38 E4
Bartle Gill View BD17 38 E4
Bartle Gr BD7 73 F3
Bartle La BD7 73 F3
Bartle Pl BD7 73 F3
Bartle Sq BD7 74 A4
Barton Ct LS15 81 D7
Barton Gr LS11 214 A4
Barton Hill LS11 214 A4
Barton Manor Cl HD4 153 B2
Barton Mount LS11 214 A4
Barton Pl LS11 214 A4
Barton Rd LS11 214 A4
Barton St Bradford BD5 74 B3
17 Brighouse HD6 115 A3
Barton Terr LS11 214 A4
Barton View LS11 214 A4
Barton Way WF9 183 A5
Barum Top 9 HX1 203 E3
Barwick Gn BD6 73 E1
Barwick in Elmet C of E Primary Sch LS15 63 E7
Barwick Rd
Barwick in E LS15, LS25 63 E2
Leeds LS14, LS15 62 D4
Basford St WF2 142 A5
Basil St Bradford BD5 74 B3
Huddersfield HD4 153 D4
Basildon Rd S63 194 C1
Baslow Gr BD9 54 F2
Bassenthwaite Wlk WF11 126 E2
Batcliffe Dr LS6 59 C6
Batcliffe Mount LS6 59 C5
Bateman Cl S72 180 B2
Bateman St BD8 55 D1
Bates Ave HX6 111 F3
Bates La WF8 146 F5
Bateson St BD10 56 E7
Bath Cl LS13 58 C2
Bath Ct WF16 117 D4
Bath Gr 14 LS13 58 C2
Bath La LS13 58 C2
Bath Pl Cleckheaton BD19 116 D7
Halifax HX3 92 B1
Bath Rd Batley WF16 117 D4
Cleckheaton BD19 116 D7
Halifax HX3 113 C4
Leeds LS13 58 C2
Leeds, Holbeck LS11 211 D2
Bath St 1 Bacup OL13 106 A2
Batley WF17 118 D5
Bradford BD3 201 D3
Dewsbury WF13 118 C1
Elland HX5 134 F6
3 Halifax HX1 203 F2
Huddersfield HD1 154 A7
Huddersfield, Rashcliffe HD1 153 F3
Ilkley LS29 8 C5
Keighley BD21 35 B7
Kirkburton HD8 173 F5
3 Todmorden OL14 108 B5
Batley Ave HD1 153 D6
Batley Boys High Sch WF17 118 C6
Batley Bsns Ctr WF17 118 B6
Batley Ct BD17 38 D4
Batley Enterprise Ctr WF17 118 B6
Batley Field Hill WF17 118 C6
Batley Grammar Sch WF17 118 B7
Batley Parish CE Jun & Inf Sch WF17 118 C6
Batley Rd Batley WF16 117 F4
East Ardsley WF3 119 E5
Wakefield WF2 120 B2
Batley St 28 Halifax HX3 92 A1
7 Huddersfield HD5 154 D6
Batley Sta WF17 118 D4
Batter La LS19 40 C4
Battinson Rd HX1 202 B4
Battinson St HX3 113 E5
Battye Ave HD4 153 B3
Battye St BD4 75 D6
Battyeford CE (C) Junior & Infants Sch WF14 137 E6
Baulk Head La OL14 108 F6
Bavaria Pl BD8 55 B1
Bawn App LS12 77 F5
Bawn Ave LS12 77 F6
Bawn Dr LS12 77 E6
Bawn Gdns LS12 77 E6
Bawn La LS12 77 E6
Bawn Path LS12 77 F6
Bawn Vale LS12 77 E6
Bawn Wlk LS12 77 F6
Bawson Ct BD19 96 A1
Baxandall St BD5 74 E3
Baxter La HX3 93 A3
Baxter Wood BD20 16 C7
Baxtergate 10 WF8 146 D8
Bay Cl HD3 153 C7
Bay Hall Common Rd HD1 154 A8
Bay Horse La Scarcroft LS14 45 A6
Thorner LS17 45 A6
Bay of Biscay BD9 54 B4
Bayford Cl HD7 199 B8
Bayldons Pl 9 WF17 118 C5
Baylee St WF9 181 E6
Bayne Dr BD4 95 B8
Bayswater Cres LS8 207 F3
Bayswater Gr Bradford BD2 56 D2
Leeds LS8 207 F3
Bayswater Mount LS8 207 F3
Bayswater Pl LS8 207 F3
Bayswater Rd LS8 207 F2
Bayswater Row LS8 207 F3
Bayswater Terr Halifax HX3 113 C3
Leeds LS8 207 F3
Bayswater View LS8 207 F3
Bayton La LS19 40 E5
Beacon Ave LS27 98 C2
Beacon Brow BD6 73 D2
Beacon Cl BD16 37 B3
Beacon Dr WF9 183 A8
Beacon Gr Bradford BD6 73 F1
Morley LS27 98 C2
Beacon Hill WF9 183 A8
Beacon Hill Rd HX3 113 E7
Beacon Pl BD6 73 E1
Beacon Rd BD6 73 E2
Beacon Rise LS29 7 E4
Beacon St Addingham LS29 7 A8
Bradford BD6 74 A1
1 Bradford, Horton Bank BD7 73 E2
Dewsbury WF13 138 E6
Huddersfield HD2 136 A1
Beacon View WF9 182 C3
Beaconfield Rd WF9 164 F1
Beaconsfield Ct LS25 82 F8
Beaconsfield Rd BD14 73 D4
Beaconsfield St
Halifax HX3 113 E6
Todmorden OL14 108 C5
Beaden Dr HD8 155 E3
Beadon Ave HD5 155 B5
Beagle Ave HD4 153 C1
Beal La DN14 127 F2
Beamshaw WF9 182 B1
Beamsley Gr Bingley BD16 37 B3
10 Leeds LS6 205 E2
Beamsley House BD18 55 B5
Beamsley La BD23 2 F6
Beamsley Mount 3 LS6 205 E2
Beamsley Pl 11 LS6 205 E2
Beamsley Rd Bradford BD9 55 B2
Shipley BD18 55 B5
Beamsley Terr 1 LS6 205 E2
Beamsley View LS29 7 E4
Beamsley Wlk BD9 55 A2
Bean St HX5 135 C6
Beancroft Rd WF10 124 D7
Beancroft St WF10 124 C6
Beanlands Dr BD20 16 C6
Beanlands Par LS29 8 C5
Beanlands Pl BD20 16 C7
Bearing Ave LS11 214 C2
Beast Fair WF8 146 C8
Beast Market 4 HD1 154 B6
Beatrice St
1 Cleckheaton BD19 116 D8
Keighley BD20 18 C1
5 Oxenhope BD22 51 C2
Beaufort Ave HD8 173 F3
Beaufort Gr BD2 56 A3
Beaufort Rd OL13 106 A7
Beaumont Ave
Huddersfield HD5 154 D5
Leeds LS8 44 A2
South Elmsall WF9 182 F3
Beaumont Cl WF3 121 F5
Beaumont Dr WF4 176 F6
Beaumont Park Rd HD4 153 D2
Beaumont Pl WF17 117 F3
Beaumont Rd BD8 55 B1
Beaumont Sq 15 LS28 76 D6
Beaumont St Batley WF17 118 C3
Emley HD8 175 C7
Huddersfield HD1 154 B7
Huddersfield, Longwood HD3 152 F5
14 Huddersfield, Moldgreen HD5 154 D5
Huddersfield, Netherton HD4 171 D7
Lofthouse Gate WF3 121 F5
Todmorden OL14 108 A6
Beauvais Dr BD20 36 B8
Beaver Dr WF13 138 F7
Beaver Terr 10 OL13 106 A3
Becca La LS25 64 E7
Beck Bottom Pudsey LS28 56 E6
Wakefield WF2 120 C3
Beck Hill BD6 93 E7
Beck La Bingley BD16 37 A4
Collingham LS22 13 B1
Liversedge WF16 117 C3
Beck Meadow LS15 63 E6
Beck Rd Bingley BD16 36 E8
Huddersfield HD1 154 A8
Leeds LS8 207 F4
Beck Rise WF9 181 D7
Beck Side 3 BD21 35 C6
Beck St BD21 35 C6
Beck View WF4 179 A6
Beckbridge Ct WF6 123 C3
Beckbridge Gn WF6 123 C3
Beckbridge La WF6 123 C2
Beckbridge Rd WF6 123 C3
Beckbridge Way WF6 123 C2
Beckbury Cl 1 LS28 57 D2
Beckbury St 2 LS28 57 D2
Beckenham Pl HX1 202 A4
Becket La WF3 100 C2
Beckett Cl WF4 141 C2
Beckett Cres WF13 138 F8
Beckett Ct LS15 81 D6
Beckett Gr WF13 138 F7
Beckett La WF13 138 F7
Beckett Park Primary Sch LS6 59 B5
Beckett Rd WF13 118 B2
Beckett Sq HD8 173 F6
Beckett St Batley WF17 118 D3
Leeds LS9 207 F1
Beckett Terr LS9 207 F1
Beckett Wlk WF13 138 F7
Beckett's Park Cres LS6 59 C5
Beckett's Park Dr LS6 59 C6
Beckett's Park Rd LS6 59 D5
Becketts Cl HX7 88 F4
Beckfield Cl BD20 16 E6
Beckfield Rd BD16 54 A7
Beckfoot Grammar Sch BD16 37 A1
Beckfoot La BD16 36 F1
Beckfoot Mill BD16 36 E1
Beckhill App LS7 60 A6
Beckhill Ave LS7 60 A6
Beckhill Chase LS7 60 A6
Beckhill Cl LS7 60 A6
Beckhill Dr LS7 60 A7
Beckhill Fold LS7 60 A7
Beckhill Garth LS7 60 A6
Beckhill Gate LS7 60 A6
Beckhill Gdns LS7 60 A6
Beckhill Gn LS7 60 B6
Beckhill Gr LS7 60 A6
Beckhill Lawn LS7 60 A6
Beckhill Pl LS7 60 A7
Beckhill Row LS7 60 A7
Beckhill View LS7 60 A6
Beckhill Wlk LS7 60 A7
Beckley Rd WF2 142 A6
Becks Ct WF12 139 F6
Becks Rd BD21 35 A6
Beckside Cl Addingham LS29 6 F8
Burley in W LS29 9 E1
Beckside Gdns HD5 155 C4
Beckside La BD7 74 A4
Beckside Rd BD7 74 A5
Beckside View LS27 98 C4
Beckwith Dr BD10 56 D5
Bedale WF3 119 D8
Bedale Ave Brighouse HD6 135 E8
Skelmanthorpe HD8 174 F1
Bedale Dr Bradford BD6 73 F1
Skelmanthorpe HD8 174 F1
Bedale Wlk S72 180 C3
Bedding Edge Rd HD7 200 A7
Bede Ct WF1 216 B4
Bede House WF1 216 B4
Bede's Cl BD13 72 D6
Bedford Ave WF5 156 E5
Bedford Cl Crofton WF4 162 A8
Featherstone WF7 145 D4
Leeds LS16 41 E3
Lepton HD8 155 E3
Bedford Ct
Featherstone WF7 145 D4
Leeds LS8 61 C6
Bedford Dr LS16 41 E3
Bedford Garth LS16 41 E3
Bedford Gdns LS16 41 E3
Bedford Gn LS16 41 E3
Bedford Gr LS16 41 E2
Bedford Mount LS16 41 E2
Bedford Row LS10 215 D4
Bedford St Bradford BD4 201 C2
Cleckheaton BD19 116 C7
7 Elland HX5 134 F6
Halifax HX1 203 D3
Keighley BD21 35 B7
Leeds LS1 211 E4
Bedford St N HX1 203 D3
Bedford View LS16 41 E3
Bedivere Rd BD8 73 D7
Bedlam La LS21 25 F4
Beech Ave Crofton WF4 162 B7
Denholme BD13 52 C3
Holmfirth HD7 172 C1
Horsforth LS18 58 C7
Huddersfield HD5 154 F5
Huddersfield, Leymoor HD7 152 E5
Leeds LS12 209 F4
Lofthouse Gate WF3 121 F4
Sowerby Bridge HX6 112 B5
Todmorden OL14 108 B6
Wakefield WF2 141 F7
Beech Cl Bacup OL13 106 A3
Bradford BD10 39 B2
Brierley S72 181 A3
Leeds LS9 61 D3
Menston LS29 22 A6
Shelf HX3 93 D6
South Kirkby WF9 182 B2
Beech Cres Baildon BD17 37 F1
Bradford BD3 56 B1
Castleford WF10 125 D5
Darrington WF8 147 C5
Leeds LS9 61 D3
Beech Croft Pontefract WF8 125 E3
Walton WF2 161 A7
Beech Ct Baildon BD17 38 B1
Castleford WF10 124 E6
Ossett WF5 140 C6
Beech Dr
Ackworth M T WF7 146 A1
Denholme BD13 52 C3
Leeds LS12 209 F4
Beech Gdns WF10 125 D6

Beech Gr Bingley BD16 37 C5
Bradford BD3 56 B1
2 Bradford, Clayton BD14 73 C4
Brighouse HX3 115 A7
Burton Salmon LS25 105 E3
Cleckheaton BD19 96 A1
Featherstone WF7 145 E4
Hemsworth WF9 163 A2
Liversedge WF16 117 C5
Morley LS27 97 F3
Normanton WF6 144 A8
Rothwell LS26 100 F6
Silsden BD20 5 D1
Beech Grove Ave LS25 82 E6
Beech Grove Terr
Garforth LS25 82 E6
Leeds LS2 206 B2
Beech Hill Otley LS21 23 A8
Pontefract WF8 125 E1
Beech Hill Primary Sch
HX1 203 D4
Beech Junior & Infants
Sch HD7 152 E5
Beech La LS9 208 C3
Beech Lees LS28 57 C4
Beech Mount LS9 61 D3
Beech Rd Boston Spa LS23 30 C8
Bradford BD6 94 C7
Shafton S72 180 D2
Sowerby Bridge HX6 112 C4
Upton WF9 183 B7
Beech Spinney LS22 13 E8
Beech Sq 3 BD14 73 C4
Beech St Bacup OL13 106 A3
Bingley BD16 36 F2
East Ardsley WF3 98 E1
Elland HX5 134 F6
Elland, Holywell Green HX4 134 A4
Glusburn BD20 16 D6
Halifax HX1 203 D4
Holmfirth HD7 189 A5
Huddersfield HD1 153 D5
Keighley BD21 35 E8
Mirfield WF14 138 A5
Pontefract WF8 146 E7
South Elmsall WF9 182 E1
Steeton BD20 17 C5
Beech Terr BD3 75 B8
Beech Tree Rd WF7 145 E4
Beech View Aberford LS25 64 D7
Crigglestone WF4 159 F3
9 Sowerby Bridge HX6 112 B5
Beech Way WF17 97 A2
Beech Wlk Birkenshaw BD11 96 B4
5 Dewsbury WF13 139 C8
Leeds LS16 42 D2
Leeds, Gipton LS9 61 D3
Beechcroft WF3 100 D1
Beechcroft Cl LS11 213 D1
Beechcroft Mead LS17 44 A4
Beechcroft View LS11 213 D1
Beechdale Ave WF17 118 A7
Beecher St Halifax HX3 92 B2
Keighley BD21 18 E1
Beeches End LS23 30 E7
Beeches Rd BD21 35 E8
Beeches The Baildon BD17 38 D4
Guiseley LS20 22 E2
Pudsey LS28 76 B8
Beechfield Gildersome LS12 77 D3
Wakefield WF2 160 E8
Beechfield Ave HD8 175 A1
Beechfield Dr WF4 144 B4
Beechfield Rd HD2 135 E1
Beechfield Terr 13 BD19 116 E7
Beechmount Cl BD17 38 D4
Beechnut La WF8 125 C1
Beechroyd LS28 76 E6
Beechroyd Terr BD16 36 F2
Beechtree Ct BD17 38 A2
Beechwood 1
Pontefract WF8 146 B7
Rothwell LS26 101 D7
Beechwood Ave
Birkenshaw BD11 96 D7
Bradford BD6 74 B2
Halifax HX2, HX3 92 A5
Keighley BD20 18 F1
Leeds LS4 205 D3
Mirfield WF14 138 A5
Pontefract WF8 146 B7
Shelf HX3 93 B5
Shipley BD18 54 E7
Sowerby Bridge HX6 111 F3
Wakefield WF2 141 D6
Beechwood Cl Halifax HX2 91 F4
Horsforth LS18 41 A3
Beechwood Cres
Hemsworth WF9 181 C6
Leeds LS4 205 D3
Pontefract WF8 146 B7
Sowerby Bridge HX6 111 F3
Beechwood Ct Leeds LS16 42 B5
Leeds, Beechwood LS14 61 F6
Beechwood Ctr LS26 101 C7
Beechwood Dale WF7 164 B7
Beechwood Dr Bradford BD6 74 B2
Halifax HX2 91 F5
Sowerby Bridge HX6 111 F3
Beechwood Gr
Birkenshaw BD11 96 D7
Bradford BD6 74 B2
Halifax HX2 91 F4
Horbury WF4 141 C1
Huddersfield HD2 136 A4
Beechwood Gr continued
Ilkley LS29 7 F4
Leeds LS4 205 D3
Shipley BD18 54 E7
Beechwood Mount
Hemsworth WF9 181 D6
Leeds LS4 205 D3
Beechwood Pl LS4 205 D3
Beechwood Primary Sch
LS14 62 A4
Beechwood Rd
Bradford BD6 74 A2
Halifax HX2 91 F4
8 Leeds LS4 205 D3
Mirfield WF14 138 A6
Beechwood Rise LS22 13 E7
Beechwood Row 6 LS4 205 D3
Beechwood St Leeds LS4 205 D3
Pudsey LS28 57 C1
Beechwood Terr LS4 205 D3
Beechwood View LS4 205 D3
Beechwood Wlk LS4 205 D3
Beecroft Cl LS13 58 B3
Beecroft Cres LS13 58 B3
Beecroft Gdns LS13 58 A3
Beecroft Mount 3 LS13 58 B3
Beecroft St Keighley BD21 35 D7
Leeds LS5 59 A3
Beecroft Wlk 1 BD15 73 A7
Beehive St 6 BD6 93 F7
Beehive Yd 7 BD6 93 F7
Beeston Park Croft LS11 213 E2
Beeston Park Garth LS11 213 E2
Beeston Park Gr LS11 213 E2
Beeston Park Pl LS11 213 E2
Beeston Park Terr LS11 213 E2
Beeston Primary Sch
LS11 213 E2
Beeston Rd LS11 214 A3
Beestonley HX4 133 E4
Beestonley La HX4 133 E4
Bela Ave BD4 75 C3
Belcross Dr HX3 203 F4
Beldon Brook Gn HD8 155 D1
Beldon La BD7 73 F2
Beldon Park Ave BD7 73 F2
Beldon Park Cl BD7 73 F2
Beldon Pl BD2 56 B2
Beldon Rd BD7 74 A3
Belfast St HX1 202 B1
Belford Cl BD4 75 D3
Belfry Ct WF1 121 C5
Belfry The LS19 40 C6
Belfry Way WF6 123 D1
Belgrave Ave Halifax HX3 203 F4
Ossett WF5 140 E4
Belgrave Cl HX3 203 F4
Belgrave Cres HX3 113 E8
Belgrave Dr HX3 113 E8
Belgrave Gdns HX3 203 F4
Belgrave Gr HX3 203 F4
Belgrave Mews LS19 40 A4
Belgrave Mount
Halifax HX3 92 D1
Wakefield WF1 216 C4
Belgrave Pk HX3 203 F4
Belgrave Rd Bingley BD16 37 A3
Keighley BD21 35 B8
Belgrave St Leeds LS2 211 F4
Ossett WF5 140 E4
6 Sowerby Bridge HX6 112 B4
Belgrave Terr
Huddersfield HD1 153 F7
Wakefield WF1 216 C4
Belgravia Rd WF1 216 A4
Belinda St LS10 215 E3
Bell Bank View BD16 36 E4
Bell Dean Rd BD15, BD8 73 B7
Bell Hall Mount 20 HX1 202 C1
Bell Hall Terr HX1 202 C1
Bell Hall View HX1 203 D1
Bell House Ave BD4 75 B1
Bell La Ackworth M T WF7 163 F5
Leeds LS13 58 D3
Bell Lane Jun & Inf Sch
WF7 163 F5
Bell Rd LS13 58 C3
Bell Sq BD20 5 E2
Bell St 17 Bradford BD12 94 C4
Dewsbury WF13 138 E5
Halifax HX3 203 F4
Huddersfield HD4 154 B4
1 Leeds LS9 212 A4
Upton WF9 183 E8
Wakefield WF1 216 A3
Bellbrooke Ave LS9 208 B2
Bellbrooke Gr LS9 208 B2
Bellbrooke Pl LS9 208 B2
Bellbrooke St LS9 208 B2
Belle Isle Ave WF1 142 D4
Belle Isle Cir LS10 99 E8
Belle Isle Cl LS10 99 E8
Belle Isle Cres WF1 142 D4
Belle Isle Dr WF1 142 D4
Belle Isle Par LS10 215 E1
Belle Isle Rd Haworth BD22 51 C7
Middleton LS10 99 E7
Belle View Rise HX3 93 B5
Belle Vue Bradford BD8 55 D1
Ilkley LS29 8 C3
Queensbury BD13 92 E7
Belle Vue Ave
Barwick in E LS15 62 F6
Leeds LS8 61 D6
Belle Vue Boys Sch BD9 54 C4
Belle Vue Cres
Huddersfield HD2 136 C3
Shelf HX3 93 B5
Belle Vue Ct LS3 205 F1
Belle Vue Dr LS28 57 C3
Belle Vue Est LS15 62 F6
Belle Vue First Sch BD8 55 D1
Belle Vue Girls Sch BD9 54 C5
Belle Vue Rd
Barwick in E LS15 62 F6
Leeds LS3 205 F1
Shelf HX3 93 B5
Wakefield WF1 142 E2
Belle Vue St WF17 117 F5
Belle Vue Terr
Guiseley LS20 39 E8
Halifax HX3 113 E5
Bellerby Brow BD6 73 E1
Bellerby Pl DN6 184 F2
Bellerby Rd DN6 184 F2
Bellevue Terr HX2 111 C7
Bellgreave Ave HD7 189 F6
Bellhouse Cres BD4 95 B8
Bellmont Cres WF9 181 E6
Bellmount Cl LS13 58 D3
Bellmount Gdns LS13 58 C4
Bellmount Gn 4 LS13 58 D4
Bellmount Pl LS13 58 D4
Bellmount View LS13 58 D3
Belloe St BD5 74 D4
Bellshaw St BD8 73 E7
Bellstring La WF14 137 E1
Bellwood Ave LS23 30 D6
Belmont WF11 105 C1
Belmont Ave Baildon BD17 38 B3
Bradford BD12 94 E7
Otley LS21 10 F1
Belmont Cl Baildon BD17 38 B3
1 Huddersfield HD1 154 A7
Belmont Cres
Bradford BD12 94 E7
Shipley BD18 55 A8
Belmont Gdns BD12 94 D7
Belmont Gr Bradford BD6 94 D7
Leeds LS2 206 A1
Yeadon LS19 40 C5
Belmont Grange WF15 117 A2
Belmont Middle Sch BD17 38 B3
Belmont Pl HX1 202 C2
Belmont Rd LS29 8 E4
Belmont Rise Baildon BD17 38 B3
Bradford BD12 94 E7
Belmont St Bradford BD2 56 C5
Featherstone WF7 144 C5
Halifax HX3 113 E8
Huddersfield HD1 154 A7
Slaithwaite HD7 169 F8
Sowerby Bridge HX6 112 C4
Wakefield WF1 216 A4
Belmont Terr Halifax HX2 111 E5
Middleton WF3 99 F2
Shipley BD18 55 A8
Belmont Way WF9 183 B3
Belton Cl BD7 74 A3
Belton Gr HD3 135 B2
Belton Rd BD20 17 E8
Belton St HD5 154 E5
Belvedere Ave Leeds LS17 43 D4
Leeds LS11 214 B2
Belvedere Cl S72 180 C2
Belvedere Ct Leeds LS17 43 E4
Leeds, Potternewton LS7 204 B1
Belvedere Gr LS17 43 D4
Belvedere Mount LS11 214 B2
Belvedere Rd Batley WF17 118 B4
Leeds LS17 43 D4
Belvedere Terr
Bradford BD8 74 B8
Leeds LS11 214 B2
Belvedere View LS17 43 E4
Belvoir Dr WF11 126 E4
Belvoir Gdns HX3 113 C3
Bembridge Ct WF2 141 E5
Bempton Ct 5 BD7 74 B4
Bempton Gr WF17 96 F2
Bempton Pl 4 BD7 74 B4
Ben Booth La WF4 156 F4
Ben Rhydding Dr LS29 8 F3
Ben Rhydding Rd LS29 8 D3
Ben Rhydding Sta LS29 8 E4
Benbow Ave BD10 56 E5
Bendigo Rd WF12 118 F1
Benjamin St
Liversedge WF15 117 B3
Wakefield WF2 142 A7
Benjamin Sykes Way WF2 141 C4
Benn Ave BD7 73 F4
Benn Cres BD7 73 F4
Benn La HD3 152 F6
Bennet Ct LS15 81 D8
Bennett Ave WF4 141 C2
Bennett Ct LS21 10 F1
Bennett La WF12 118 F2
Bennett Rd LS6 59 D5
Bennett St Halifax HX3 203 F2
5 Liversedge WF15 117 B4
Benns La HX2 90 F2
Benny La HD7 152 B3
Benny Parr Cl WF17 118 E5
Benomley Cres HD5 154 E4
Benomley Dr HD5 154 E3
Benomley Rd HD5 154 E3
Benroyd Terr HX4 134 C4
Benson Gdns Leeds LS12 209 E2
Normanton WF6 123 C3
Benson La WF6 123 C3
Benson St LS7 207 D2
Bent Close La HX7 110 E3
Bent Cotts BD20 16 B5
Bent La Holmfirth HD7 199 B8
Sutton in C BD20 16 C5
Bent Lea HD2 136 F6
Bent Ley Rd HD7 171 A3
Bent Rd HD7 199 D7
Bent St HD4 154 B4
Bentcliff Wlk 1 BD15 73 B7
Bentcliffe Ave LS17 43 E2
Bentcliffe Cl LS17 43 E1
Bentcliffe Ct LS17 43 E1
Bentcliffe Dr LS17 43 E2
Bentcliffe Gdns LS17 43 E1
Bentcliffe Gr LS17 43 E1
Bentcliffe La LS17 43 D2
Bentcliffe Mount LS17 43 E1
Bentfield Cotts BD14 73 C5
Bentham Way S75 178 A2
Bentley Ave HX3 115 A7
Bentley Cl BD17 38 B4
Bentley Ct 1 LS6 59 F6
Bentley Gdns LS6 59 F6
Bentley Gr LS6 59 F6
Bentley La LS6, LS7 59 F6
Bentley Mount Leeds LS6 59 F6
Sowerby Bridge HX6 112 D5
Bentley Par LS6 59 F6
Bentley Primary Sch LS6 59 F6
Bentley Rd WF2 141 E4
Bentley Sq 2 LS26 101 C5
Bentley St 4 Bradford BD12 94 D3
Huddersfield HD1 153 E3
Benton Cres WF4 141 C2
Benton Park Ave 2 LS19 40 C5
Benton Park Cres LS19 40 C5
Benton Park Dr LS19 40 C5
Benton Park Rd LS19 40 C5
Benton Park Sch LS19 40 B5
Bents La Marsden HD7 169 B6
Wilsden BD15 53 A6
Bents Rd S36 200 D4
Benyon Park Way LS12 213 D4
Beresford Rd BD6 94 B7
Beresford St BD12 95 A5
Berkeley Ave LS8 208 A3
Berkeley Cres LS8 208 A3
Berkeley Croft S71 179 B4
Berkeley Ct LS3 205 F1
Berkeley Gr LS8 208 A3
Berkeley Mount LS8 208 A3
Berkeley Rd LS8 208 A3
Berkeley St LS8 208 A3
Berkeley Terr LS8 208 A3
Berkeley View LS8 208 A3
Berking Ave LS9 212 C4
Bermondsey St LS21 23 B8
Bernard St
Huddersfield HD2 136 E3
Rothwell LS26 101 D6
Berne Gr WF1 216 B3
Berners St WF1 216 C2
Berrington Way BD22 34 B3
Berry Bank La HD7 189 B8
Berry Brow Infant Sch
HD4 171 F8
Berry Croft HD7 171 F5
Berry La Halifax HX3 203 F3
Horbury WF4 141 B1
Keighley BD21 35 B6
Swillington LS26 102 E8
Berry Moor Rd HX6 112 D2
Berry Rd HD7 170 C3
Berry St 6 BD21 35 D7
Berry View HD4 153 F1
Berry's Bldgs HX2 91 F4
Berry's Yd WF4 141 B2
Berryfield Garth WF5 140 D8
Bertha St Keighley BD21 35 C7
Pudsey LS28 57 D2
Bertie St BD4 75 C3
Bertram Dr BD17 38 B2
Bertram Rd BD8 55 C2
Bertrand St 4 LS11 211 D1
Berwick Ave WF16 117 D6
Berwick St HX1 203 F3
Bescaby Gr BD17 38 E3
Besha Ave BD12 94 D6
Besha Gr BD12 94 D6
Bessingham Gdns BD6 93 F8
Best La Kirkburton HD4 172 D7
Oxenhope BD22 51 C2
Beswick Cl BD3 75 D7
Beswick St OL14 129 A7
Bethal Gn OL15 129 C1
Bethel Rd BD18 55 D8
Bethel St Brighouse HD6 115 B2
2 Halifax HX3 92 A2
Keighley BD20 36 D8
Bethel Terr Halifax HX2 90 D1
Sowerby Bridge HX6 112 D3
Bethesda Row HX7 89 D1
Betteras Hill Rd LS25 105 F7
Betula Way HD8 155 E3
Beulah Gr 3 LS6 206 B3
Beulah Mount 2 LS6 206 B3
Beulah Pl HX2 111 E5
Beulah St LS6 206 B3
Beulah Terr Leeds LS6 206 B4
Leeds, Cross Gates LS15 62 C2
Beulah View 1 LS6 206 B3
Bevan Ave WF6 144 B8
Bevan Ct BD7 73 F3
Bevan Pl WF2 141 C4
Bevedere Gdns LS17 43 E4
Beverley Ave Bradford BD12 94 D2
Leeds LS11 214 B3
Beverley Cl HX5 135 B7
Beverley Ct HD2 136 B2
Beverley Dr Bradford BD12 94 D2
Dewsbury WF12 139 F8
Beverley Garth WF7 164 A5
Beverley Gdns WF17 97 B2
Beverley Mount LS11 214 B3
Beverley Pl HX3 92 B1
Beverley Rise LS29 7 E4
Beverley St BD4 75 D5
Beverley Terr Halifax HX3 92 B1
Leeds LS11 214 B3
Beverley View LS11 214 B3
Beverley Wlk LS25 82 F6
Bevin Cl WF1 121 C5
Bevin Cres WF1 121 C5
Bevor Cres WF16 117 D6
Bewdley Ct S71 179 D4
Bewerley Cres BD6 94 A6
Bewick Gr LS10 99 F7
Bexhill Cl WF8 125 F2
Bexley Ave LS8 207 F2
Bexley Gr LS8 207 F2
Bexley Mount LS8 207 F2
Bexley Pl LS8 207 F2
Bexley Rd LS8 207 F3
Bexley Terr LS8 207 F2
Bexley View LS8 207 F2
Beza Ct LS10 215 D2
Beza Rd LS10 215 D3
Beza St LS10 215 D3
Bickerdike Pl WF10 103 B4
Bickerdike Terr LS25 83 A1
Bickerton Way LS21 10 E1
Biddenden Rd LS15 62 F2
Bidder Dr WF3 99 C1
Bideford Ave LS8 43 F2
Bideford Mount BD4 75 E3
Bierley C of E First Sch
BD4 75 B1
Bierley Hall Gr BD4 95 B7
Bierley House Ave BD4 75 C1
Bierley La BD4 95 B8
Bierley View BD4 75 C1
Big Meadow Dr LS29 6 D8
Bilham La DN5 195 D2
Bilham Rd HD8 176 A2
Bilham Row DN5 195 F3
Bill La HD7 189 C7
Billam's Hill LS21 10 F1
Billey La LS12 77 E4
Billing Ct LS19 40 D3
Billing Dr LS19 40 E3
Billing View Bradford BD10 56 C7
Yeadon LS19 40 D3
Billingbauk Dr LS13 58 D1
Billingham Cl WF2 141 D8
Billingsley Terr BD4 75 B4
Billingwood Dr LS19 40 D3
Billy La HX7 89 C5
Bilsdale Grange BD6 93 F8
Bilsdale Way BD17 38 A2
Bilton Pl BD8 74 C8
Bingley Bank LS17 28 C2
Bingley C of E First Sch
BD16 36 F3
Bingley Five Rise Locks
BD16 36 F4
Bingley Grammar Sch
BD16 36 E4
Bingley Hospl BD16 37 A3
Bingley Rd Baildon BD17 38 B6
Bradford BD9 54 D4
Cullingworth BD13 35 B1
Guiseley LS29 21 C2
Menston LS29 21 F3
Shipley BD18 54 E8
Bingley St Bradford BD8 74 A7
Leeds LS3 210 C4
Bingley (St Ives)
Municipal Golf Course
BD16 36 B4
Bingley Sta BD16 36 F3
Binham Rd HD2 153 D8
Binks Fold 3 BD12 94 D2
Binks St WF1 121 C4
Binn HD7 170 A7
Binn La HD7 169 A2
Binn Rd HD7 168 F3
Binnie St BD3 75 B7
Binns Hill La HX2 112 B6
Binns La Bradford BD7 73 F5
Glusburn BD20 16 A6
Holmfirth HD7 188 F5
Binns St BD16 37 A3
Binns Top La HX3 114 B2
Binswell Fold 9 BD17 38 C4
Birch Ave Bradford BD5 74 F2
Leeds LS15 81 A8
Lepton HD8 155 E2
Ripponden HX6 132 C1
Todmorden OL14 108 A7
Birch Cl Bradford BD5 74 F2
Brighouse HD6 115 C3
Birch Cliff BD17 38 B2
Birch Close La BD16 37 F8
Birch Cres LS15 81 A8
Birch Ct LS27 98 B2
Birch Dr LS25 83 A3
Birch Gn WF8 125 F1
Birch Gr Batley WF17 118 A8
Bradford BD5 74 E1
Castleford WF10 125 D6
Huddersfield HD7 152 E5
Keighley BD21 35 B4
Kippax LS25 83 A3
Birch Hill Rise 1 LS18 58 E8
Birch House 7 WF10 124 E7
Birch La Bradford BD5 74 E3
Bradford, Staygate BD5 74 F2
Halifax HX2 111 F8
Birch Mews LS16 42 D2
Birch Pk HD7 172 D2

Birch Rd Huddersfield HD4 171 F8
Kippax LS25 83 A3
Normanton WF6 144 B7
Birch St Bradford BD8 74 A8
Morley LS27 98 B2
Wakefield WF1 142 F4
Birch Tree Gdns BD21 35 E6
Birch Way BD5 74 F2
Bircham Cl BD16 37 C5
Birchcliffe Rd HX7 89 A3
Birchdale BD16 36 F5
Birchen Ave WF5 140 C6
Birchen Hills WF5 140 C5
Birchencliffe Hill Rd HD3 135 B2
Birchenlee Cl HX7 89 F1
Birches The Bramhope LS16 24 F2
Guiseley LS20 22 E2
Birchfield Ave LS27 97 C6
Birchfield Garth LS14 62 C8
Birchfield Gr HD8 175 A1
Birchfields Ave LS14 62 C8
Birchfields Cl LS14 62 C7
Birchfields Cres LS14 62 C8
Birchfields Ct 5 LS14 62 C8
Birchfields Rise LS14 62 C8
Birchington Ave HD3 135 B2
Birchington Cl HD3 135 B2
Birchington Dr HD3 135 A2
Birchlands Ave BD15 53 B6
Birchlands Gr BD15 53 B6
Birchroyd LS26 100 F4
Birchtree Cl WF1 142 F8
Birchtree Way LS16 41 E2
Birchtree Wlk WF11 126 D3
Birchwood Ave
Batley WF17 96 F2
Keighley BD20 18 B2
Leeds LS17 44 A3
Birchwood Cl HD2 135 D2
Birchwood Ct Ilkley LS29 8 A4
2 Liversedge WF15 117 B3
Birchwood Dr BD20 18 B2
Birchwood Hill LS17 44 A4
Birchwood Mount LS17 44 A4
Birchwood Rd BD20 18 A2
Bird La HX6 132 C3
Birdale Field La LS22 29 D8
Birdcage Hill HX3 113 A3
Birdcage La HX3 113 B3
Birdcage Wlk LS21 23 A6
Birds Edge La HD8 190 F4
Birds Royd La HD6 115 C1
Birdsedge Farm Mews
HD8 191 A4
Birdsedge First Sch HD8 191 A4
Birdsnest La HD7 190 D2
Birdswell Ave HD6 115 D3
Birfed Cres LS4 59 B3
Birk House La HD8 191 B8
Birk La LS27 97 E4
Birk Lea St BD5 74 F4
Birkby Brow Cres WF17 97 B2
Birkby Hall Rd HD2 135 E1
Birkby Haven BD6 93 E8
Birkby Junior Sch HD1 136 A1
Birkby La HD6 115 D7
Birkby Lodge Rd HD2 153 F8
Birkby Rd HD2 135 D1
Birkby St BD12 94 D4
Birkdale Ave HD3 153 A8
Birkdale Cl
Cullingworth BD13 52 E6
Leeds LS17 43 B4
Birkdale Ct BD20 18 A3
Birkdale Dr LS17 43 B4
Birkdale Gn LS17 43 B4
Birkdale Gr
Dewsbury WF13 118 A1
Halifax HX2 91 F7
Leeds LS17 43 A4
Birkdale High Sch
Dewsbury WF13 118 B2
Dewsbury, Chapel Fold
WF13 118 A2
Birkdale Mount LS17 43 B4
Birkdale Pl LS17 43 A4
Birkdale Rd
Dewsbury WF13 118 B1
Royston S71 179 B5
Birkdale Rise LS17 43 A4
Birkdale Way LS17 43 B4
Birkdale Wlk LS17 43 A4
Birkenshaw CE
County Fst Sch BD11 96 B6
Birkenshaw La BD11 96 C4
Birkenshaw Middle Sch
BD11 96 B4
Birkett St BD19 116 D8
Birkhead St WF16 117 E3
Birkhill WF10 125 C8
Birkhill Cres BD11 96 B5
Birkhouse La
Brighouse HD6 115 D6
Huddersfield HD5 154 E5
Huddersfield, Yews Hill
HD1, HD4 153 E5
Birkhouse Rd HD6 115 C6
Birkin La WF11 127 D8
Birklands Rd
Huddersfield HD2 135 F2
Shipley BD18 55 B7
Birklands Terr BD18 55 B7
Birks Ave BD7 73 F5
Birks Fold BD7 73 F6
Birks Hall St HX1 202 C4
Birks Hall Terr HX1 202 C4
Birks La Huddersfield HD4 155 A3
Kirkburton HD8 173 D3
Birks La continued
Ripponden HX6 132 E5
Sowerby Bridge HX6 132 D8
Todmorden OL14 129 B8
Birks Rd HD3 153 A5
Birkshall La BD4, BD3 75 B6
Birkshead BD15 53 D5
Birksland Ind Est BD4 75 B5
Birksland Moor BD11 96 B3
Birksland St BD3 75 B6
Birkwith Cl LS14 62 B8
Birkwood Ave WF4 144 B2
Birkwood Rd WF6 122 C3
Birmingham La HD7 170 C3
Birnam Gr BD4 75 A4
Birr Rd BD9 55 B3
Birstall County Junior
& Infants Sch WF17 96 F1
Birstall La BD11 96 E5
Birstall St Peter's C of E
Primary Sch WF17 96 E2
Birthwaite Rd S75 177 B1
Bishop St BD9 55 B2
Bishop Way WF3 119 F8
Bishop's Ct HD4 171 F7
Bishopdale Dr LS22 13 A1
Bishopdale Holme BD6 93 E8
Bishopgate St LS1 211 E3
Bishops Way Meltham HD7 170 E2
Mirfield WF14 137 D7
Bisley Cl S71 179 E4
Bismarck Dr LS11 214 B4
Bismarck St LS11 214 B4
Bittern Rise LS27 98 C3
Black Abbey La BD20 16 C6
Black Brook Way HX4 134 C6
Black Bull St LS10 212 A2
Black Dyke La BD13 53 B1
Black Edge La BD13 71 D6
Black Gates Ct WF3 119 F8
Black Gates Rise WF3 119 F8
Black Hill HX7 89 B8
Black Hill La Bramhope LS16 25 D1
Keighley BD20 17 E1
Black Hill Rd LS21 25 C5
Black La HD7 170 E7
Black Moor Rd Leeds LS17 43 A2
Oxenhope BD22 51 E4
Black Rd WF4 143 B3
Black Sike La HD7 188 C5
Black Swan Ginnell 7
HX1 203 E3
Black Swan Pas 6 HX1 203 E3
Black Wlk WF8 125 E2
Black Wood Gr LS16 41 D3
Black Wood Mount LS16 41 D3
Black Wood Rise LS16 41 D3
Blackbird Gdns 4 BD8 73 B7
Blackburn Bldgs HD6 115 C2
Blackburn Cl Bradford BD8 73 D7
Halifax HX3 91 F3
Blackburn Ct 9
Pontefract WF8 146 C8
Rothwell LS26 100 F5
Blackburn House HX3 92 A3
Blackburn La WF11 127 C3
Blackburn Pl WF17 118 D5
Blackburn Rd Batley WF17 96 E1
Brighouse HD6 115 A4
Blacker Cres WF4 158 E6
Blacker La Netherton WF4 159 B5
Shafton S72 180 C3
Blacker Rd
Huddersfield HD1, HD2 153 F8
Mapplewell S75 178 C1
Blackers Ct WF12 139 B4
Blackett St LS28 57 B7
Blackgates Cres WF3 119 F8
Blackgates Dr WF3 119 F8
Blackgates Fold WF3 119 F8
Blackgates Infant Sch
WF3 98 E1
Blackgates Junior Sch
WF3 119 F8
Blackhouse Rd HD2 136 B2
Blackledge HX1 203 F3
Blackley Rd HX5 134 E4
Blackman La LS2 206 B2
Blackmires HX2 92 A5
Blackmoor Ct LS17 42 F5
Blackmoor La LS17 28 A1
Blackmoorfoot Rd
Huddersfield HD4 153 E4
Slaithwaite HD7 170 D7
Blackpool Gr LS12 78 A4
Blackpool Pl LS12 78 A4
Blackpool St 7 LS12 78 A4
Blackpool Terr 6 LS12 78 A4
Blackpool View 8 LS12 78 A4
Blackshaw Beck La BD13 93 A8
Blackshaw Clough Rd HX6 132 A6
Blackshaw Dr BD6 93 D8
Blackshaw St OL14 108 D5
Blacksmith Fold BD7 74 A4
Blacksmith La LS16 25 F1
Blacksmiths Fold HD5 154 F3
Blackstone Ave BD12 94 C2
Blackstone Edge Rd
Hebden Bridge HX7 131 B7
Ripponden HX6 130 F5
Blackthorn Way WF2 142 A8
Blackthorne Ct 4 LS10 99 D8
Blackwall HX1 203 E2
Blackwall La HX6 112 B5
Blackwall Rise HX6 112 B5
Blackwood Ave LS16 41 D3
Blackwood Gdns LS16 41 D3
Blackwood Gr HX1 202 B4
Blackwood Hall La HX2 111 D7
Blacup Moor View BD19 116 D7
Blagden La HD4 153 F1
Blairsville Gdns LS13 58 B4
Blairsville Gr LS13 58 C4
Blaith Royd La HX7 109 F4
Blaithroyd La HX3 113 E6
Blake Cres LS20 39 F8
Blake Gr LS7 204 A2
Blake Hall Dr WF14 138 C4
Blake Hall Rd WF14 138 C4
Blake Hill HX3 92 E3
Blake Hill End HX3 92 F5
Blake Law La
Brighouse WF15 115 F2
Liversedge HD6 116 A2
Blake Lee La HD7 168 B5
Blake Stones HD7 169 E8
Blakehill Ave BD2 56 C2
Blakehill First Sch BD10 56 A6
Blakehill Terr BD2 56 C2
Blakeholme Cl HD7 169 E8
Blakelaw Dr HD6 115 D3
Blakeley Gr WF2 141 F6
Blakeney Gr LS10 215 D1
Blakeney Rd LS10 215 D1
Blakeridge La WF17 118 B5
Blakestones Rd HD7 169 E8
Blakey Rd WF2 141 F8
Blamires Pl 2 BD7 73 F3
Blamires St BD7 73 F3
Blanche St BD4 75 D6
Bland St Halifax HX1 203 D3
Huddersfield HD1 153 F4
Bland's Cl WF10 124 E7
Blandford Gdns 21 LS2 206 B2
Blandford Gr 23 LS2 206 B2
Blands Ave WF10 103 A5
Blands Cres WF10 103 A5
Blands Gr WF10 103 A5
Blands Terr WF10 103 A5
Blanket Hall St WF16 117 D3
Blantyre Ct BD13 52 D6
Blayd's Yd LS1 211 F3
Blayds Garth LS26 101 A7
Blayds St LS9 212 C3
Bleach Mill La LS29 21 E5
Bleak Ave S72 180 C2
Bleak St BD19 117 C8
Bleak St Lower BD19 117 C8
Bleakley Ave WF4 179 B6
Bleakley Cl S72 180 C2
Bleakley La WF4 179 B6
Bleakley Terr WF4 179 B6
Bleasdale Ave
Huddersfield HD2 135 F1
Knottingley WF11 126 F4
Blencarn Cl LS14 61 F4
Blencarn Garth LS14 61 F4
Blencarn Lawn LS14 61 F4
Blencarn Path LS14 61 F4
Blencarn Rd LS14 61 F4
Blencarn View LS14 61 F4
Blencarn Wlk LS14 61 F4
Blenheim Ave 6 LS2 206 B2
Blenheim Cl WF11 126 C4
Blenheim Cres 5 LS2 206 B2
Blenheim Ct Halifax HX1 203 D4
Leeds LS2 206 B2
Blenheim Dr Batley WF17 118 C6
Dewsbury WF13 118 A1
Blenheim Gr LS2 206 B2
Blenheim Hill WF17 118 D7
Blenheim Middle Sch
LS6 206 B3
Blenheim Mount BD8 55 C2
Blenheim Pl BD10 39 B1
Blenheim Primary Sch
LS2 206 B2
Blenheim Rd Bradford BD8 55 C2
Wakefield WF1 216 A4
Blenheim Sq Batley WF17 118 C6
Leeds LS2 206 B2
Blenheim St
Hebden Bridge HX7 89 B3
10 Keighley BD21 35 B5
Blenheim Terr LS2 206 B2
Blenheim View LS2 206 B2
Blenheim Wlk LS2 206 B2
Blenkinsop Ct LS27 98 B2
Blind La Bickerton LS24 15 F8
Birkenshaw BD11 96 F8
East Ardsley WF3 120 A5
Halifax HX2 91 E8
Harden BD16 36 D3
Hebden Bridge HX2 111 B7
Thorner LS17 44 E4
Todmorden OL14 108 B6
Bloomfield Rd S75 177 F1
Bloomfield Rise S75 177 F1
Bloomhouse La S75 177 F1
Blucher St BD4 75 D6
Blue Ball La HX6 131 E3
Blue Ball Rd HX6 131 D3
Blue Bell Hill HD4 153 F2
Blue Bell La OL14 86 D2
Blue Butts WF5 140 D5
Blue Hill BD13 52 D1
Blue Hill Cres LS12 209 D2
Blue Hill Gr LS12 209 D2
Blue Hill Grange LS12 209 D1
Blue Hill La LS12 209 D2
Bluebell Cl 6
Bradford BD15 73 B8
Pontefract WF8 146 D7
Bluebell Ct WF17 96 E2
Bluebell Rd S75 177 E3
Bluebell Way WF9 182 F7
Bluebell Wlk HX2 111 E8
Blundell St Leeds LS1 206 B1
South Elmsall WF9 182 E3
Blythe Ave BD8 74 A8
Blythe St BD7 74 D7
Bmk Ind Est WF15 117 B4
Boar La LS1 211 F3
Boardman St OL14 108 B6
Boat La Kippax WF10 103 B3
Mickletown WF10 103 A3
Boathouse La WF14 138 C3
Bob La HX2 112 D7
Bobbin Mill Cl
Steeton BD20 17 C5
Todmorden OL14 86 B1
Bobbin Mill Ct BD20 17 C5
Bobbin St OL14 86 C1
Bodiham Hill LS25 83 B8
Bodington Hall LS16 42 C2
Bodkin La BD22 50 E3
Bodley Terr LS4 205 D1
Bodmin App LS10 99 A5
Bodmin Ave BD18 55 F7
Bodmin Cres LS10 99 B5
Bodmin Croft LS10 99 B4
Bodmin Dr WF6 123 B3
Bodmin Garth LS10 99 A4
Bodmin Gdns LS10 99 A4
Bodmin Pl LS10 99 B4
Bodmin Rd LS10 99 A5
Bodmin Sq LS10 99 A4
Bodmin St LS10 99 A4
Bodmin Terr LS10 99 A4
Bog Green La HD5 137 C4
Bog La LS15 63 A5
Boggart Hill LS14 61 E6
Boggart Hill Cres LS14 61 F6
Boggart Hill Dr LS14 61 F6
Boggart Hill Gdns LS14 61 E6
Boggart Hill Rd LS14 61 E6
Boggart La
Skelmanthorpe HD8 175 A3
Sowerby Bridge HX6 112 B3
Boland Cres BD22 34 E3
Boldgrove St WF12 140 A6
Boldmere Rd LS15 80 E7
Boldron Holt BD6 93 F8
Boldshay St BD3 75 B8
Bolehill Pk HD6 114 E6
Bolingbroke Ct 14 BD5 201 B1
Bolingbroke St BD5 74 D2
Bolland Bldgs BD12 94 F5
Bolland St 3 BD12 94 E5
Bolling Hall (Mus) BD4 75 A3
Bolling Rd Bradford BD4 201 C1
Ilkley LS29 8 D4
Bolling Rd First Sch LS29 8 E4
Bolling Specl Sch BD4 75 B3
Bolsover Cl LS25 83 B7
Bolstermoor Rd HD7 152 A4
Boltby La BD6 93 E8
Bolton HX2 91 E7
Bolton Abbey Sta BD23 2 C7
Bolton Bridge Rd LS29 8 A4
Bolton Brow HX6 112 D4
Bolton Brow
Junior & Infants Sch
HX6 112 D4
Bolton Cres BD2 56 B4
Bolton Ct BD2 56 A2
Bolton Dr BD2 56 B4
Bolton Gdns LS19 40 C6
Bolton Gr BD2 56 B4
Bolton Hall Rd Bradford BD2 55 E5
Shipley BD2 55 E5
Bolton La BD2 55 E3
Bolton Lane First Sch BD2 55 F3
Bolton Rd Addingham LS29 2 F4
Bradford BD2, BD3 55 F2
Draughton LS29 2 F4
Silsden BD20, LS29 5 F4
Yeadon LS19 40 C6
Bolton Royd Primary Sch
LS28 76 A8
Bolton St Bradford BD3 201 D3
Bradford, Low Moor BD12 94 C6
Bolton Terr BD20 5 E2
Bolton Way LS23 30 C7
Bolton Wife Hill WF4 159 F1
Bolton Woods First Sch
BD2 55 D4
Bolus Cl WF1 121 C4
Bolus La WF1 121 C4
Bonaccord Sq WF17 118 C4
Bonaccord Terr WF17 118 C4
Bond Ct LS1 211 E4
Bond St Batley WF17 118 C6
6 Batley, Birstall WF17 96 E1
Brighouse HD6 115 A3
Dewsbury WF13 139 C8
Halifax HX1 203 D2
Hebden Bridge HX7 89 A3
Leeds LS1 211 E4
Pontefract WF8 125 E2
Todmorden OL14 108 B5
Wakefield WF1 216 A3
Bondgate Harewood LS17 27 A7
Otley LS21 23 A7
Pontefract WF8 125 F2
Bonegate Ave HD6 115 B3
Bonegate Rd HD6 115 B3
Bonn Rd BD9 55 A2
Bonwick Mall BD6 93 E7
Boocock St 2 LS28 57 E1
Bookers Cl DB19 117 C7
Bookers Field BD19 117 C7
Booth Halifax HX2 90 E3
Marsden HD7 169 B6
Booth Bank HD7 169 C7
Booth Hill HX2 90 E4
Booth House La HD7 188 D4
Booth House Rd HX2 111 C7
Booth House Terr HX2 111 C7
Booth Royd BD10 39 B1
Booth Royd Dr BD10 39 B1
Booth Royd La HD6 135 D8
Booth St Bradford BD10 56 B7
Burley in W LS29 9 E2
Castleford WF10 124 D8
Cleckheaton BD19 116 D8
5 Queensbury BD13 72 D1
Shipley BD18 55 D7
Booth's Bldgs HD6 115 B7
Bootham Pk BD9 54 D2
Boothman Wlk 4 BD21 35 A5
Boothroyd Dr HD4 153 B3
Boothroyd Gn WF13 139 B8
Boothroyd Jun & Inf Sch
WF13 139 A7
Boothroyd
Junior & Infants Sch
WF13 139 A7
Boothroyd La WF13 139 A8
Boothroyds Way WF7 145 A6
Boothtown Rd HX3 92 B2
Border Cl HD3 134 F1
Borough Ave LS8 204 B4
Borough Market HX1 203 E3
Borough Rd WF1 216 B3
Boroughgate LS21 23 A8
Borrins Way BD17 38 D3
Borrough View LS8 204 B4
Borrowdale Cres LS12 58 F2
Borrowdale Croft LS19 40 B7
Borrowdale Dr WF10 104 D1
Borrowdale Rd
Batley WF12 118 E2
Wakefield WF2 141 E7
Borrowdale Terr LS14 61 F3
Boston Ave LS5 58 F3
Boston Hill HX7 89 B6
Boston Mews LS23 30 E7
Boston Rd Boston Spa LS23 30 D6
Wetherby LS22 13 E3
Boston Spa C of E
Primary Sch LS23 30 E7
Boston Spa
Comprehensive Sch LS23 30 B7
Boston Spa Junior Sch
LS23 30 D7
Boston Spa Specl Sch
LS23 30 D7
Boston St Castleford WF10 124 E8
Halifax HX1 202 B3
Sowerby Bridge HX6 112 A3
Boston Towers LS9 207 E1
Boston Wlk BD6 93 F8
Boswell Cl S71 179 B4
Bosworth Ave WF6 122 E4
Bosworth Cl BD15 54 B1
Botany Ave BD2 55 F4
Botany Dr BD20 19 E2
Botany La HD8 155 F4
Botham Hall Rd HD3 152 F5
Bottom Boat Rd WF3 122 D6
Bottomley La HX4 133 C2
Bottomley Rd OL14 129 C6
Bottomley St Bradford BD5 74 D4
Bradford, Buttershaw BD6 93 F7
2 Brighouse HD6 115 B4
Bottomley's Bldgs LS6 206 B3
Bottoms HX3 113 D3
Bottoms La BD11 96 B4
Boulder Bridge La S71 179 F1
Boulder Gate HD7 169 B4
Boulevard The Leeds LS12 213 D3
Pudsey LS28 57 D2
Boundary Ave BD20 16 D6
Boundary Cl LS15 81 E7
Boundary Ct HD7 189 D3
Boundary Dr S72 181 A3
Boundary Farm Rd LS17 43 A3
Boundary La WF6 143 F7
Boundary Pl LS7 207 E2
Boundary Rd WF13 117 F2
Boundary St Leeds LS7 207 E2
Liversedge WF16 117 C4
Boundary The BD8 54 E1
Bourbon Cl BD6 94 B8
Bourn View Cl HD4 171 D7
Bourn View Rd HD4 171 D7
Bourne Ct S75 178 C2
Bourne St BD10 39 B2
Bourne Wlk S75 178 C2
Bow Beck BD4 75 A5
Bow Gn BD7 73 D4
Bow La HX7 88 A4
Bow St Huddersfield HD1 153 F5
Keighley BD21 35 C7
Leeds LS9 212 B3
Bowbridge Rd 9 BD5 74 E4
Bowcliffe Rd LS23 30 D2
Bower Gn BD3 75 C7
Bower La WF13 117 F3
Bower Rd LS15 62 E3
Bower Slack Rd HX6 110 F1
Bower St BD5 201 B2
Bower The 1 WF17 117 F7
Bowers La HX4 133 D6
Bowes Nook BD6 93 E7
Bowfell Cl LS14 62 A4
Bowland Ave BD17 37 E1
Bowland Cl LS15 80 E7

Bowland St BD1 74 D8
Bowler Cl BD12 94 C6
Bowling Alley HD6 136 A8
Bowling Ave WF2 120 F2
Bowling Back La BD4 75 B5
Bowling Com Coll
Bradford BD4 75 A3
Bradford BD4 75 B4
Bowling Court Ind Est BD4 75 C5
Bowling Ct HD6 114 F3
Bowling Dyke HX1 203 E4
Bowling Green Ct HD3 152 E7
Bowling Green Junior & Infants Sch HX4 133 F3
Bowling Green Rd HX4 133 F3
Bowling Green Terr LS11 211 E1
Bowling Hall Rd BD4 75 A3
Bowling Old La
Bradford BD5 74 E4
Bradford, Bankfoot BD5 74 D2
Bowling Park Cl BD4 74 F4
Bowling Park Dr BD4 74 F3
Bowling Park First Sch BD5 74 F3
Bowling St HD4 153 A4
Bowman Ave BD6 94 B7
Bowman Gr HX1 202 C3
Bowman La LS10 212 A3
Bowman Pl 5 HX1 202 C3
Bowman Rd BD6 94 B7
Bowman St 6 Halifax HX1 202 C3
Wakefield WF1 142 F3
Bowman Terr HX1 202 C3
Bowmere Dr 11 BD15 73 B8
Bownas Rd LS23 30 C8
Bowness Ave Bradford BD10 56 D4
Castleford WF10 104 E1
Bowness Dr HD5 154 D7
Bowood Ave LS7 60 A7
Bowood Cres LS7 60 A7
Bowood Gr LS7 60 A7
Bowood La HX6 111 D1
Bowwood Dr BD20 36 C8
Box La WF8 125 E2
Box Tree Cl BD8 54 E1
Box Trees La HX2 91 D3
Boxhill Rd HX5 134 F7
Boxwood Rd HX5 134 F5
Boy La Bradford BD4 95 B7
Halifax HX3 91 D2
Boycott Dr WF7 164 A5
Boycott Way WF9 183 A4
Boyd Ave BD3 56 E1
Boyle & Petyt Sch The BD23 2 F6
Boyle The LS15 63 D8
Boyne Dr WF2 160 A5
Boyne Hill WF4 160 A4
Boyne St HX1 203 D3
Boynton St BD5 74 E3
Boynton Terr BD5 74 E3
Boys La HX3 203 F1
Boys Scarr HX2 111 D6
Bracewell Ave BD15 73 A8
Bracewell Bank HX3 92 A2
Bracewell Dr HX3 91 F2
Bracewell Gr 2 HX3 92 A1
Bracewell Rd HD7 170 D1
Bracewell St BD21 35 F7
Bracken Ave HD6 115 A5
Bracken Bank Ave BD22 34 F3
Bracken Bank Cres BD22 35 A3
Bracken Bank Gr BD22 34 F3
Bracken Bank Way BD22 34 F3
Bracken Bank Wlk BD22 34 F2
Bracken Cl Brighouse HD6 115 A5
Mirfield WF14 137 D7
Bracken Ct Leeds LS17 43 C1
Leeds LS12 210 B1
Bracken Edge
Bradford BD10 56 C7
Leeds LS8 204 C1
Bracken Edge Primary Sch LS7 204 B1
Bracken Ghyll Dr BD20 5 D2
Bracken Ghyll Golf Course LS29 2 E1
Bracken Gr
Huddersfield HD2 136 B4
Mirfield WF14 137 D7
Bracken Hall Countryside Ctr BD17 37 E3
Bracken Hall Rd HD2 136 C3
Bracken Hill
Ackworth M T WF7 163 D6
Leeds LS17 43 C1
Mirfield WF14 137 D7
South Kirkby WF9 182 D4
Bracken Mount BD20 5 D2
Bracken Pk Bingley BD16 37 C3
Scarcroft LS14 45 A7
Bracken Rd Brighouse HD6 115 A5
Keighley BD22 35 A4
Steeton BD20 17 A5
Bracken Sq HD2 136 C4
Bracken St BD21 35 B4
Brackenbeck Rd BD7 73 F4
Brackenbed Grange HX2 91 E1
Brackenbed La HX2 91 F1
Brackendale BD10 39 A2
Brackendale Ave BD10 39 A2
Brackendale Dr BD10 38 F2
Brackendale Gr BD10 38 F2
Brackendale Par BD10 38 F2
Brackendale Pl BD10 39 A2
Brackenhill Dr BD7 73 F3
Brackenhill First Sch BD7 73 F3
Brackenholme Royd 10 BD6 93 E8
Brackens La HX3 93 B7
Brackenwood Cl Ilkley LS29 8 E4
Leeds LS8 204 B3
Brackenwood Ct WF1 121 D5
Brackenwood Dr LS8 204 B4
Brackenwood Gn LS8 204 B4
Brackenwood Rd WF1 121 D5
Bradbeck Rd BD7 73 F7
Bradburn Rd WF3 100 A3
Bradbury St WF13 138 E5
Bradcroft HD1 136 B1
Bradd Cl WF15 117 B5
Bradfield Cl HD2 136 E5
Bradford Bsns Pk BD1 55 E1
Bradford City Tech Coll
Bradford BD7 74 D7
Bradford BD5 74 E4
Bradford Forster Sq Sta BD1 201 B3
Bradford Girls' Grammar Sch BD9 54 E1
Bradford Golf Course LS20 39 A7
Bradford Grammar Sch BD9 55 C3
Bradford & Heckmondwike Rd BD4 95 F8
Bradford & Ilkley Com Coll
Bradford BD7 74 D6
Ilkley LS29 8 A3
Bradford & Ilkley Com Coll McMillan Bldg BD5 74 D5
Bradford Ind Mus BD2 56 C3
Bradford Interchange Sta BD1 201 C2
Bradford La BD3 75 D7
Bradford Moor First Sch BD3 75 C8
Bradford Moor Golf Course BD2 56 B1
Bradford Old Rd Halifax HX3 92 C2
Shipley BD16 54 B7
Bradford Rd Batley WF17 118 D5
Bingley BD16 37 A1
Birkenshaw BD11 96 A5
Birkenshaw, Drighlington BD11 96 D7
Bradford, Clayton BD14 73 D5
Bradford, Oakenshaw BD12, BD19 95 B3
Bradford, Springfield BD10 56 B6
Brighouse HD6 115 B2
Brighouse HD6 115 B5
Burley in W LS29 21 F8
Cleckheaton BD19 116 E8
Cleckheaton, Birstall BD19 96 C2
Dewsbury WF13 118 D1
East Ardsley WF3 120 B8
Gildersome LS27 97 B5
Guiseley LS29 22 B3
Huddersfield HD1, HD2 136 B3
Keighley BD20, BD21 18 E1
Liversedge WF15 117 B4
Lofthouse Gate WF2 120 E5
Menston LS29 22 B3
Northowram HX3 93 A1
Northowram HX3 93 A3
Otley LS21 22 D6
Pudsey LS28 57 C1
Shipley, Frizinghall BD18 55 B6
Shipley, Nab Wood BD18 54 C7
Wakefield WF2 120 F3
Bradford Royal Infmy BD9 54 F1
Bradford St
Dewsbury WF13 118 D1
Keighley BD21 35 D8
Bradford & Wakefield Rd BD4, BD11 96 C7
Bradfords Cl LS23 30 C3
Bradlaugh Rd BD6 74 B1
Bradlaugh Terr 2 BD6 74 C1
Bradley Ave
Castleford WF10 124 C8
Silsden BD20 5 D2
Bradley Bvd HD2 136 C3
Bradley Carr Terr WF9 194 E8
Bradley CE Jun & Inf Sch HD2 136 F5
Bradley Dr BD20 5 D2
Bradley Gr BD20 5 D2
Bradley Grange Gdns HD2 136 F6
Bradley Junction Ind Est HD2 136 F4
Bradley La Elland HX4 134 B6
Pudsey LS28 76 B7
Bradley Mills La HD1 154 C8
Bradley Mills Rd HD5 154 D8
Bradley Park Golf Course HD2 136 E6
Bradley Quarry Cl HD2 137 A6
Bradley Rd
Huddersfield HD2 136 D6
Silsden BD20 5 D2
Bradley Rise BD20 5 D2
Bradley St Bingley BD16 36 F3
Castleford WF10 124 D8
13 Huddersfield HD1 154 B6
Shipley BD9 55 C4
Bradley Terr LS17 44 A4
Bradley View HX4 134 B4
Bradleys Both County Primary Sch BD20 4 C6
Bradshaw Ave HD7 171 E3
Bradshaw Cl HD7 171 E3
Bradshaw Cres HD7 171 E3
Bradshaw Dr HD7 171 E3
Bradshaw La Halifax HX2 72 A2
Marsden HD7 151 A1
Bradshaw Primary Sch HX2 71 F1
Bradshaw Rd Honley HD7 171 E2
Meltham HD7 188 B7
Bradstock Gdns LS27 98 A6
Bradwell La WF5 140 E5
Brae Ave BD2 55 F3
Braemar Croft S72 180 D7
Braemar Dr LS25 83 B8
Braemar Rise S72 180 D7
Brafferton Arbor BD6 93 E8
Braim Wood Middle Sch LS8 61 D7
Braine Rd LS22 13 F6
Braithwaite Ave BD22 34 F7
Braithwaite Cres BD22 34 F7
Braithwaite Dr BD22 34 F7
Braithwaite Edge Rd BD22 34 D8
Braithwaite Gr BD22 34 F7
Braithwaite Rd BD22 34 E8
Braithwaite Row 6 LS10 215 E2
Braithwaite Sch BD22 34 E8
Braithwaite St Leeds LS11 210 C2
Mapplewell S75 178 C1
Braithwaite Way BD22 34 F7
Braithwaite Wlk BD22 34 F7
Bramah St S71 179 C1
Bramble Ave LS23 30 B7
Bramble Cl Bradford BD14 73 C3
Pontefract WF8 146 B7
Bramble Wlk WF17 96 F1
Brambles The LS29 7 F4
Brambling Mews LS27 98 C3
Bramham Dr BD17 38 D4
Bramham La LS23 29 B3
Bramham Park LS23 46 F8
Bramham Primary Sch LS23 30 D4
Bramham Rd Bingley BD16 37 A4
Boston Spa LS23 30 D4
Castleford WF10 124 A6
Thorner LS14 46 C7
Bramhope Old La LS21 23 E4
Bramhope Primary Sch LS16 24 E2
Bramhope Rd BD19 116 C8
Bramleigh Dr LS27 98 A6
Bramleigh Gr LS27 98 A6
Bramley Cl Holmfirth HD7 189 D7
Oakworth BD22 34 B3
Bramley Cres WF1 121 B4
Bramley Ctr LS13 58 D3
Bramley Fold HX3 114 D8
Bramley Gdns LS14 45 C1
Bramley Grange 7 LS13 58 C1
Bramley Grange Coll LS14 45 D1
Bramley Hill Primary Sch LS13 58 B2
Bramley La Brighouse HX3 114 D8
West Bretton WF4 177 B8
Bramley St Bradford BD5 74 E4
5 Leeds LS13 58 C1
Bramley Sta LS13 58 B1
Bramley View HX3 114 E8
Brampton HX2 90 B1
Brampton Ct WF9 183 A5
Bramstan Ave LS13 58 A3
Bramstan Cl LS13 58 A3
Bramstan Gdns LS13 58 A3
Bramstan Recn Ctr LS13 58 A4
Bramston Gdns 11 HD6 115 A1
Bramston St HD6 115 A1
Bramwell Ho BD3 201 C4
Bran St 8 BD21 35 B4
Brancepeth Pl LS12 210 B3
Branch Cl LS12 78 A4
Branch End LS27 97 E7
Branch La HD2 135 B3
Branch Pl LS12 78 A4
Branch Rd Batley WF17 118 C5
Brighouse BD19 94 F1
Crigglestone WF4 159 C4
Dewsbury WF13 139 C8
Elland HX4 133 D5
Huddersfield HD2 135 B4
Leeds LS12 78 A4
Leeds, Armley LS12 209 F4
Branch St
Huddersfield HD1 153 D5
Leeds LS12 78 A4
Brand Hill App WF4 143 E1
Brand Hill Dr WF4 143 E1
Brander App LS9 61 D1
Brander Cl LS9 61 D1
Brander Dr LS9 61 D1
Brander Gr LS9 208 C1
Brander Rd LS9 61 D1
Brander St LS9 61 D2
Brandfort St BD7 74 A5
Brandon Cres LS17 44 F6
Brandon Ct LS17 44 C5
Brandon La LS17 44 F6
Brandon Rd 5 LS3 206 A1
Brandon St LS12 210 C3
Brandon Terr LS17 44 C5
Brandon Way LS7 204 A1
Brandy Carr Rd WF2 120 C3
Branksome Cres BD9 54 F2
Branksome Ct BD9 54 F2
Branksome Dr BD18 54 D8
Branksome Gr BD18 54 C8
Branksome Pl LS6 205 E2
Branksome St LS6 205 E2
Branksome Terr LS6 205 E2
Bransby Cl LS28 57 E2
Bransby Ct 1 LS28 57 E2
Bransby Rise LS28 57 E2
Bransdale Ave Guiseley LS20 39 E8
Normanton WF6 123 A4
Bransdale Cl Baildon BD17 38 A2
Guiseley LS20 39 E8
Normanton WF6 123 A4
Bransdale Clough BD6 73 E1
Bransdale Garth LS20 39 E8
Bransdale Gdns LS20 39 E8
Bransdale Mews WF6 123 A4
Bransdale Wlk WF6 123 A4
Branshaw Dr BD22 34 E5
Branshaw Golf Course BD22 34 D4
Branshaw Gr BD22 34 E5
Branshaw Mount BD22 34 E5
Branshaw Sch BD22 35 A6
Branstone Gr WF5 119 D1
Brant Ave HX2 91 F4
Brant Bank La LS29 7 D6
Brantcliffe Dr BD17 38 C4
Brantcliffe Way BD17 38 C5
Brantdale Cl BD9 54 C4
Brantdale Rd BD9 54 C4
Brantford St LS7 204 A2
Brantom Farm HX2 111 C5
Brantwood Ave BD9 54 C4
Brantwood Cl BD9 54 C4
Brantwood Cres BD9 54 C4
Brantwood Dr BD9 54 C4
Brantwood Gr BD9 54 B4
Brantwood Oval BD9 54 C4
Brantwood Rd BD9 54 B4
Brantwood Villas BD9 54 C4
Branwell Ave WF17 96 F3
Branwell Dr BD22 51 C8
Branxholme Ind Est HD6 115 B7
Brassey Rd BD4 75 A4
Brassey St HX1 203 D2
Brassey Terr BD4 75 A4
Brathay Gdns LS14 62 A3
Bray Cl BD7 73 D2
Braybrook Ct BD8 55 C3
Brayshaw Dr BD7 73 D2
Brayshaw Rd WF3 120 C7
Brayside Ave HD2 135 F2
Brayton App LS14 62 C5
Brayton Cl LS14 62 C5
Brayton Garth 10 LS14 62 D5
Brayton Gn LS14 62 D5
Brayton Gr LS14 62 C5
Brayton Grange 12 LS14 62 D5
Brayton Pl 13 LS14 62 D5
Brayton Sq 11 LS14 62 D5
Brayton Terr 1 LS14 62 C5
Brayton Wlk 2 LS14 62 C5
Brazil St WF10 124 E8
Bread St WF1 216 B2
Break Neck HX3 114 A8
Breakmoor Ave BD20 5 E3
Breaks Rd 4 BD12 94 E6
Brear Ley Gdns WF15 117 A3
Brearcliffe Cl 3 BD6 94 A8
Brearcliffe Dr BD6 94 A8
Brearcliffe Gr BD6 94 A7
Brearcliffe Rd BD6 94 B7
Brearcliffe St BD6 94 A7
Brearley La HX2 111 B8
Brearley St WF17 118 B4
Brearton St BD1 201 B4
Breary Ave LS18 41 D1
Breary Ct LS16 24 E3
Breary La LS16 24 E3
Breary La E LS16 25 A3
Breary Rise LS16 24 E3
Breary Terr LS18 41 D1
Breary Wlk LS18 41 D1
Breck Lea HX6 112 A3
Breck Willows HX6 111 F2
Brecks Gdns LS25 82 F3
Brecks La Kippax LS25 82 F3
Swillington LS26 82 C4
Brecks Rd BD14 73 D5
Brecon App LS9 61 D1
Brecon Ave HD3 135 A1
Brecon Cl BD10 56 B7
Brecon Ct LS9 61 D1
Brecon Rise LS9 61 D1
Bredon Ave BD18 55 F7
Bredon Cl WF9 181 F7
Breighton Adown BD6 93 D8
Bremner St LS21 23 B8
Brendan Ct BD10 56 D6
Brendon Ct Bradford BD4 75 D3
Mirfield WF14 137 F2
Brendon Dr HD2 135 D1
Brendon Wlk BD4 75 D2
Brentford Rd BD12 94 C6
Brentlea Ave WF2 142 B3
Brentwood Cl Batley WF17 118 E5
Thorpe Audlin WF8 165 A5
Brentwood Gdns BD6 94 D8
Brentwood Gr 8 LS12 209 F3
Brentwood St 11 LS12 209 F3
Brentwood Terr 12 LS12 209 F3
Bretfield Ct WF12 139 D5
Brett Gdns LS11 214 B4
Brettegate WF9 181 C7
Bretton Country Pk WF4 176 F7
Bretton Hall Coll
Wakefield WF2 142 D2
West Bretton WF4 176 E6
Bretton Hall Coll (Annexe) WF10 124 C7
Bretton La Crigglestone WF4 159 C3
West Bretton WF4 159 B2
Bretton St WF12 139 D5
Brevitt St WF1 142 E3
Brewerton La WF13 117 F2
Brewery Ct HD3 135 A1
Brewery Dr HD4 153 F2
Brewery La
Dewsbury WF12 139 C4
Knottingley WF11 126 F4
Queensbury BD13 72 D3
Queensbury, Shibden Head BD13 92 C7
Brewery Rd Ilkley LS29 8 C4
Keighley BD21 35 A3
Brewery St 5 Batley WF16 117 D3
1 Halifax HX3 92 C2
Keighley BD21 35 D7
Todmorden OL14 107 E8
Brewery Wharf WF14 138 A4
Brewery Wharf Mus LS2 212 A3
Brewery Yard HD5 155 C3
Brexdale Ave LS25 82 F3
Brian Ave HD5 154 E5
Brian Cres LS15 62 B3
Brian Pl LS15 62 B3
Brian Royd La HX4 133 F7
Brian St HD3 135 B1
Brian View LS15 62 C3
Briar Ave HD7 170 C3
Briar Bank WF9 163 A2
Briar Cl Batley WF16 117 D5
Elland HX5 134 E5
Pudsey LS28 57 D3
Briar Dr WF13 117 F2
Briar Gate LS22 13 E7
Briar Gr Brierley S72 181 A3
Wakefield WF1 142 E3
Briar Rhydding BD17 38 E2
Briar St 5 OL13 106 A1
Briar Wood BD18 55 E7
Briardale Rd BD9 54 B4
Briarfield Ave BD10 56 A7
Briarfield Cl Bradford BD10 56 A7
Ilkley LS29 8 D3
Briarfield Gdns
Gildersome LS27 97 C6
Shipley BD18 55 C6
Briarfield Gr BD10 56 A7
Briarfield Rd Holmfirth HD7 189 C7
Shipley BD18 55 C5
Briarlea Cl LS19 39 F5
Briarlyn Ave HD3 135 A2
Briarlyn Rd HD3 135 B2
Briarmains Rd WF17 96 F2
Briarsdale Croft LS8 208 C3
Briarsdale Ct LS8 208 C3
Briarsdale Garth LS8 208 B3
Briarsdale Hts LS9 208 C3
Briarsdale Mews LS8 208 B3
Briarwood Ave
Bradford BD6 74 B1
Keighley BD20 18 F1
Briarwood Cl WF1 121 D5
Briarwood Cres BD6 74 B1
Briarwood Dr BD6 74 B1
Briarwood Gr BD6 74 B2
Brick Mill Rd LS28 76 F6
Brick Row BD12 94 C3
Brick St Cleckheaton BD19 116 C7
Leeds LS9 212 A3
Wakefield WF2 141 D7
Brick Terr HD6 115 B1
Brick & Tile Terr HD6 115 A1
Brickbank HD5 154 F3
Brickfield Gr HX2 92 A5
Brickfield La HX2 92 A5
Brickfield Terr HX2 92 A5
Brickyard 7 WF14 137 F5
Bride St OL14 108 B6
Bridge Ave LS21 23 A8
Bridge Cl Boston Spa LS23 30 E8
Clayton West HD8 175 E2
Horbury WF4 140 E1
Bridge Cotts LS25 64 E7
Bridge Croft HD3 153 B4
Bridge Ct Hemsworth WF9 163 A2
Leeds LS11 211 D1
Morley LS27 98 B3
Bridge End Brighouse HD6 115 A1
Glusburn BD20 16 B6
Leeds LS1 211 F3
Bridge End St OL14 86 C1
Bridge Fold LS5 59 A4
Bridge Foot LS23 30 E8
Bridge Garth LS23 30 D6
Bridge Gate HX7 89 A3
Bridge La Holmfirth HD7 189 A6
Ilkley LS29 8 A4
Knottingley WF11 126 F5
Shelf HX3 93 B7
Thorpe Audlin WF8 165 B4
Bridge Lanes HX7 88 F3
Bridge Paddock LS22 13 B1
Bridge Rd Boston Spa LS23 30 E8
Brighouse HD6 115 A2
Horbury WF4 140 E1
Huddersfield HD2 137 B5
Leeds, Holbeck LS11 211 D2
Leeds, Kirkstall LS5 59 A4
Pudsey LS13 57 E5
Silsden BD20 5 E2
Sutton in C BD20 16 D5
Bridge St
Batley, Bank Foot WF17 118 D5
Batley, Birstall Smithies WF17 117 E8
Bradford BD1 201 C2
Castleford WF10 124 E8
Huddersfield HD4 171 F8

Bridge St continued
Huddersfield, Rashcliffe HD4 153 F3
Keighley BD21 35 B6
Leeds LS2 212 A4
Liversedge WF16 117 C4
Mapplewell S75 177 E1
Morley LS27 98 B2
Normanton WF6 123 C3
Oakworth BD22 34 B2
Otley LS21 23 A8
[7] Pontefract WF8 146 D8
Silsden BD20 5 E2
Slaithwaite HD7 152 A1
Sowerby Bridge HX6 112 B3
[1] Thornton BD13 72 E6
Todmorden OL14 108 B5
Wakefield WF1 142 D4
Bridge Terr HX2 90 E6
Bridge View LS13 57 E6
Bridge Wood Cl LS18 41 D2
Bridge Wood View LS18 41 D2
Bridge Works Bsns Pk HD7 172 A4
Bridgegate Way BD10 56 D5
Bridgehouse La BD22 51 C6
Bridgewater Ct LS6 59 F6
Bridgewater Park Dr DN6 184 F2
Bridgewater Rd LS9 212 C1
Bridgeway BD4 75 D3
Bridgland Ave LS29 22 A5
Bridgwater Ho [13] BD5 201 B1
Bridgwater Rd BD9 55 A2
Bridle Ave WF5 140 C8
Bridle Cl WF4 158 E7
Bridle Dene HX3 93 C5
Bridle La Netherton WF4 158 E7
Ossett WF5 140 C8
Bridle Path Rd
Harewood LS17 44 E5
Leeds LS15 62 A2
Bridle Path Wlk [3] LS15 62 A2
Bridle Pl WF5 140 D8
Bridle St WF17 118 E5
Bridle Stile HX3 93 C5
Bridle Stile La BD13 72 E2
Bridley Brook HD7 170 A5
Bridley Dr HD7 170 A8
Brier Hey Cl HX7 89 F1
Brier Hey La HX7 89 F1
Brier Hill Cl BD19 116 A6
Brier Hill View HD2 136 D5
Brier La Brighouse HD6 114 E2
Ryhill WF4 180 C8
Brier St Halifax HX3 92 B2
Keighley BD21 35 B4
Brierdene BD20 5 E2
Brierlands Cl LS25 83 B8
Brierlands Fold LS25 83 B8
Brierlands La LS25 83 B8
Brierley C of E First Sch S72 181 A3
Brierley Cl BD18 55 C6
Brierley Cres WF9 182 C3
Brierley Rd
Grimethorpe S72 181 A1
Shafton S72 180 D2
South Hiendley S72 180 E5
Briery Cl LS29 7 E4
Briery Field BD18 55 B5
Briery Gr WF14 138 A2
Briestfield Rd WF12 156 E6
Brig Royd HX6 132 E5
Brigg Gdns BD22 34 F7
Brigg's Ave WF10 124 E6
Briggate Brighouse HD6 115 A2
Elland HX5 134 F7
Huddersfield HD5 155 A7
Leeds LS1 211 F3
Shipley BD17 55 B8
Shipley BD18 55 C7
Silsden BD20 5 E2
Briggland Ct BD15 53 C5
Briggs Ave BD6 74 A1
Briggs Gr BD6 74 A1
Briggs Pl BD6 74 A1
Briggs Rd S71 179 C1
Briggs Row WF7 145 D4
Briggs St BD13 72 E1
Briggs Terr [2] HD5 154 D6
Brighouse & Denholme Gate Rd
Northowram HX3 93 B4
Queensbury HX3 92 F6
Shelf HX3 93 B4
Brighouse & Denholme Rd BD13 72 B3
Brighouse High Sch
Brighouse HD6 115 A2
Brighouse, Hove Edge HD6 114 F5
Brighouse Liby & Smith Art Gal HD6 115 A3
Brighouse Rd Bradford BD12 94 D6
Brighouse HX3 114 D7
Denholme BD13 71 E6
Huddersfield HD3 135 B3
Queensbury BD13 92 F7
Shelf BD13, HX3 92 F7
Brighouse Wood La HD6 114 F3
Brighouse Wood Row HD6 114 F3
Bright St Bradford BD15 54 B1
Bradford, Clayton BD14 73 B4
[3] Dewsbury WF13 118 C1
East Ardsley WF3 120 E8
Farnhill BD20 4 D1
[8] Haworth BD22 51 D7
Mirfield WF14 138 A8
Morley LS27 98 A4
Pudsey LS28 57 F2
Bright St continued
Queensbury BD13 72 F1
Sowerby Bridge HX6 112 B5
Todmorden OL14 108 A3
Brighton Ave LS27 97 F5
Brighton Cl WF17 117 E6
Brighton Cliff LS13 58 C2
Brighton Gr Halifax HX1 202 C4
Leeds LS13 58 D1
Brighton Rd LS29 8 E3
Brighton St Batley WF16 117 D4
Bradford BD10 39 A1
[21] Halifax HX3 92 A1
Shipley BD17 55 B8
Todmorden OL14 86 C1
Wakefield WF2 142 A5
Brighton Terr BD19 94 F1
Brignall Croft LS9 207 F1
Brignall Garth LS9 207 F1
Brignall Way LS9 207 F1
Brigshaw Dr WF10 102 F6
Brigshaw High Sch WF10 102 F7
Brigshaw La LS25, WF10 103 A8
Brindle Park Dr WF10 125 A6
Brindley Gr BD8 73 C7
Brindley Rd BD20 17 F8
Brindley Way WF2 120 F4
Brisbane Ave BD2 55 E3
Briscoe La HX4 134 B7
Bristfield Rd WF12 157 A8
Bristol Ave BD20 36 B8
Bristol St Halifax HX3 113 D3
Leeds LS7 207 D1
Britannia Ave OL13 106 A2
Britannia Bldgs LS27 97 F2
Britannia Cl [8] LS28 57 F2
Britannia Ct LS13 77 A8
Britannia Rd
Huddersfield HD3, HD7 152 F4
Morley LS27 98 A2
Slaithwaite HD7 169 F8
Britannia Sq LS27 97 F2
Britannia St Bingley BD16 37 A3
Bradford BD5 201 C2
Leeds LS1 211 E3
Pudsey LS28 58 A2
Britannia Terr BD19 116 D8
British Liby Document Supply Ctr The LS23 15 B3
Briton Sq S63 194 E1
Briton St S63 194 E1
Britton St BD19 116 F6
Broad Acres WF4 160 A7
Broad Balk DN5 195 E6
Broad Carr La Elland HX4 134 C4
Holmfirth HD7 190 A2
Broad Cut Rd WF4 159 D7
Broad Gate
Todmorden OL14 109 A5
Todmorden, Cross Stone OL14 108 D6
Broad Head La BD20 33 D3
Broad Ings Way HX3 93 C5
Broad La Bradford BD4 75 D5
Hebden Bridge HX7 88 F1
Heptonstall HX7 88 B6
Holmfirth HD7 188 D5
Huddersfield HD5 154 D6
Leeds LS5, LS13, LS28 58 C3
Pontefract WF8 125 D1
South Elmsall WF9 182 E1
South Kirkby WF9 194 C8
Sowerby Bridge HX2 111 C5
Todmorden OL14 87 D1
Broad Lane Bsns Ctr WF9 182 F1
Broad Lane Cl LS13 58 E4
Broad Oak HD7 152 E2
Broad Oak La
Brighouse HX3 114 D6
Ingbirchworth S36 192 D2
Broad Oak Pl HX3 114 D6
Broad Oak St HX3 114 D6
Broad St Bradford BD1 201 B3
Dewsbury WF13 139 A6
Halifax HX1 203 E3
Pudsey LS28 57 C3
Todmorden OL14 108 B6
Broad Tree Rd HX3 92 A2
Broad View WF5 140 F5
Broad Way Ct WF12 139 E1
Broadacre Rd WF5 140 F5
Broadbent Croft HD7 172 A4
Broadcroft Chase WF3 119 E7
Broadcroft Dr WF3 119 E8
Broadcroft Gr WF3 119 E8
Broadcroft Way WF3 119 E8
Broadfield Cl BD4 75 E1
Broadfield Ind Est HD1 153 F3
Broadfield Pk HD7 188 C2
Broadfield Way LS29 6 D8
Broadfolds BD14 73 C4
Broadgate Elland HX4 134 A2
Huddersfield HD5 154 D4
Ossett WF5 140 E5
Broadgate Ave LS18 41 D1
Broadgate Cres
Horsforth LS18 58 C8
Huddersfield HD5 154 D4
Broadgate Dr LS18 41 D1
Broadgate La LS18 41 C1
Broadgate Primary Sch LS18 41 C1
Broadgate Rise LS18 58 D8
Broadgate Wlk LS18 58 C8
Broadlands BD20 35 A8
Broadlands Rd HD7 170 D3
Broadlands St BD4 75 D4
Broadlea Ave LS13 58 E4
Broadlea Cl LS13 58 E4
Broadlea Cres
Bradford BD5 74 F3
Leeds LS13 58 E4
Broadlea Gdns LS13 58 E4
Broadlea Gr LS13 58 E4
Broadlea Hill LS13 58 E4
Broadlea Mount LS13 58 F3
Broadlea Oval LS13 58 E4
Broadlea Pl LS13 58 E3
Broadlea Rd LS13 58 E4
Broadlea St LS13 58 E4
Broadlea Terr LS13 58 F4
Broadlea View LS13 58 D4
Broadley Ave HX2 91 B2
Broadley Cl HX2 91 C1
Broadley Cres HX2 91 C1
Broadley Gr HX2 91 C1
Broadley Lathe HX2 91 C2
Broadley Rd HX2 91 B1
Broadmead WF10 124 F8
Broadmeadows WF1 121 D5
Broadoaks Cl WF12 140 A7
Broadowler La WF5 140 F5
Broadstone Rd
Denby Dale HD8 190 F3
Ingbirchworth S36 191 A1
Broadstone St OL14 108 D6
Broadstone Way BD4 75 E3
Broadwalk LS21 10 E1
Broadway Bingley BD16 37 A2
Bradford BD1 201 C3
Guiseley LS20 39 C8
Halifax HX3 113 F5
Horsforth LS18 58 C8
[8] Huddersfield HD1 154 B7
Leeds, Halton LS15 80 F7
Leeds, Hawksworth LS5 58 E7
Mapplewell S75 178 B1
Pontefract WF8 146 E7
South Elmsall WF9 182 E1
Sowerby Bridge HX6 111 E3
Wakefield WF2 141 D4
Broadway Ave
Bradford BD5 74 D2
Leeds LS6 205 E2
Broadway Cl BD5 74 D2
Broadway Ct HX6 111 E3
Broadway Dr [4] LS18 58 B8
Broadway Terr WF9 182 E1
Broadwell Rd WF5 140 F5
Broadwood Ave HX2 91 C1
Brock Bank HD5 154 F7
Brockadale Ave WF8 146 D5
Brockholes C of E Primary Sch HD7 172 C2
Brockholes La HD7 172 C3
Brockholes Rd
Honley HD4 172 D4
Kirkburton HD4 172 D4
Brockholes Sta HD7 172 C3
Brocklesby Dr BD15 73 B8
Brocks HX2 111 C6
Brockstones HX4 133 F7
Brockswood Ct WF2 161 C5
Brockwell Gdns HX6 112 A3
Brockwell La HX6 112 A2
Brodetsky Primary Sch LS17 43 C4
Brodley Cl HX3 114 C8
Brodrick Ct LS6 59 D5
Broken Cross HD5 154 E2
Broken Way BD5 74 D2
Bromet Pl BD2 56 B4
Bromfield Ct S71 179 D4
Bromford Rd BD4 75 B3
Bromley Ave HD7 189 D7
Bromley Gr BD22 34 E5
Bromley Mount WF1 142 D4
Bromley Rd Batley WF17 118 E3
Bingley BD16 36 F4
Huddersfield HD2 135 F1
Shipley BD18 54 E8
Bromley St WF17 118 D3
Brompton Ave BD4 75 A4
Brompton Gr [2] LS11 214 B2
Brompton Mount [5] LS11 214 B2
Brompton Rd BD4 75 B4
Brompton Row [22] LS11 214 B3
Brompton Terr [4] LS11 214 B2
Brompton View [3] LS11 214 B2
Bronshill Gr BD15 54 C1
Bronte Ave WF11 126 B4
Bronte Bridge BD22 50 B4
Bronte Cl Batley WF13 117 F2
Bradford BD9 54 E2
Cleckheaton BD19 96 B1
Huddersfield HD4 153 D3
Bronte Ct WF8 125 D2
Bronte Dr BD22 34 F3
Bronte Gr Hemsworth WF9 181 C6
Mirfield WF14 138 C4
Bronte House LS7 206 C3
Bronte House Sch BD10 39 F2
Bronte Middle Sch BD22 34 E3
Bronte Old Rd BD13 72 E6
Bronte Parsonage Mus BD22 51 B7
Bronte Pl BD13 72 E6
Bronte Rd WF17 96 E1
Bronte St [1] Haworth BD22 51 B7
Keighley BD21 35 D8
Bronte Villas BD22 51 F8
Bronte Way WF14 138 C4
Brook Cl WF5 140 F3
Brook Cotts HX6 132 B7
Brook Dr HX4 134 C4
Brook Field WF14 137 F2
Brook Gdns
[10] Dewsbury WF13 139 B8
Meltham HD7 170 D3
Brook Grain Hill HD6 136 A8
Brook Grains La HX6 132 D2
Brook Hill BD17 38 D3
Brook Hill La
Carlecotes S36 200 B3
Dunford Bridge S36 199 F2
Brook La Cleckheaton WF15 116 C4
Huddersfield HD7 152 D4
Brook Rd [4] WF12 139 B7
Brook Side HD7 152 A2
Brook St Bradford BD12 95 B5
Castleford WF10 104 C3
Dewsbury WF13 117 F1
Elland HX5 135 A6
[3] Hebden Bridge HX7 89 A4
Huddersfield HD1 154 A7
Huddersfield, Moldgreen HD5 154 D6
Huddersfield, Yews Hill HD1 153 E4
Ilkley LS29 8 B4
[11] Keighley BD21 35 B5
Normanton WF6 122 F3
Ossett WF5 140 D5
[10] Todmorden OL14 108 B5
Wakefield WF1 216 B2
Brook Terr Halifax HX2 90 E2
Slaithwaite HD7 152 A2
Brook The
Hebden Bridge HX7 110 E8
Littleborough OL15 129 C1
Brook's Yd [17] HD1 154 A6
Brookdale OL14 108 A2
Brookdale Ave WF5 119 D1
Brookdale Bank HD3 153 A5
Brooke Ct WF8 146 D5
Brooke St [8] Batley WF16 117 D3
Brighouse HD6 115 A1
Cleckheaton BD19 116 E7
Brookeville Ave HX3 114 C7
Brookfield HD8 173 E6
Brookfield Ave
Castleford WF10 124 F7
Cleckheaton BD19 95 E1
Leeds LS8 207 F4
Pudsey LS13 57 D6
Shipley BD18 55 D8
Brookfield Ct
Normanton WF6 123 C2
Pudsey LS13 57 D6
Brookfield Dr WF7 164 C8
Brookfield First Sch BD10 56 E6
Brookfield Gdns LS13 57 D6
Brookfield Pl LS6 59 E6
Brookfield Rd Bradford BD3 75 A8
Leeds LS6 59 E6
Shipley BD18 55 D8
Brookfield St Leeds LS10 212 A1
Todmorden OL14 86 C1
Brookfield Terr
Cleckheaton BD19 95 E1
Leeds LS10 212 A1
Brookfield View BD19 95 E1
Brookfields WF4 158 D5
Brookfields Ave BD12 94 E1
Brookfields Rd BD12 94 E1
Brookfoot Ave BD11 96 A5
Brookfoot La HD6 114 E3
Brookgreen HX3 114 C8
Brookhill Ave LS17 43 E4
Brookhill Cl LS17 43 E4
Brookhill Cres LS17 43 E4
Brookhill Dr LS17 43 E4
Brookhill Gr LS17 43 E4
Brookhouse Gdns BD10 56 F8
Brookland Towers [3] LS14 62 A5
Brooklands Brighouse HX3 114 D7
East Keswick LS17 28 C5
Huddersfield HD2 136 F5
Brooklands Ave Elland HX4 134 B4
Leeds LS14 62 A4
Walton WF2 161 B7
Brooklands Cl Elland HX4 134 B4
Leeds LS14 61 E4
Menston LS29 22 B5
Brooklands Cres Leeds LS14 61 E4
Ryhill WF4 162 D1
Yeadon LS19 40 B6
Brooklands Ct WF5 141 A4
Brooklands Dr Leeds LS14 61 E4
Yeadon LS19 40 B6
Brooklands Garth LS14 61 F4
Brooklands Gr LS29 22 B5
Brooklands La Leeds LS14 61 F4
Menston LS29 22 B5
Brooklands Rd WF2 161 C7
Brooklands View
Leeds LS14 61 F4
Walton WF2 161 C7
Brooklands Way LS29 22 A5
Brooklands Wlk LS29 22 B5
Brookleigh LS28 57 B6
Brooklyn Ave
Huddersfield HD5 155 A6
Leeds LS12 210 A3
Brooklyn Ct BD19 116 D8
Brooklyn Dr BD19 116 D8
Brooklyn Pl LS12 209 F3
Brooklyn Rd BD19 116 D8
Brooklyn St Keighley BD20 18 A2
Leeds LS12 209 F3
Brooklyn Terr
Brighouse HD6 114 E5
Leeds LS12 209 F3
Brookroyd Ave HD6 115 B6
Brookroyd Gdns [3] WF17 117 F8
Brookroyd La WF17 117 F8
Brooks Terr BD13 73 B2
Brooks Yd Dewsbury WF13 139 B7
Huddersfield HD2 137 A5
Brooksbank WF2 216 A2
Brooksbank Ave BD7 73 E5
Brooksbank Dr LS15 81 A8
Brooksbank Gdns HX5 134 F6
Brooksbank Sch The HX5 134 E6
Brooksfield WF9 182 D4
Brookside Collingham LS22 29 B8
Denby Dale HD8 191 F6
Hebden Bridge HX7 88 E4
Hemsworth WF9 181 E7
Leeds LS17 43 E5
Brookside Fold [2] BD22 51 C2
Brookside St WF9 182 F3
Brookside Terr WF9 182 F3
Brookway WF7 145 D5
Broom Cl Mapplewell S75 178 A1
Middleton LS10 99 F7
Broom Cres LS10 99 E7
Broom Cross LS10 99 E7
Broom Field La HD8 175 B7
Broom Garth LS10 99 F7
Broom Gdns LS10 99 E7
Broom Gr LS10 99 F6
Broom Hall Ave WF1 121 A2
Broom Hall Cres WF1 121 A2
Broom Hill Rd HX4 151 D8
Broom Lawn LS10 99 E7
Broom Mount LS10 99 F6
Broom Nook LS10 99 F7
Broom Pl LS10 99 F6
Broom Rd LS10 99 E7
Broom St Bradford BD4 201 C2
Cleckheaton BD19 116 B6
[7] Keighley BD21 35 C6
Broom Terr LS10 99 F7
Broom View LS10 99 F7
Broom Wlk WF17 118 E5
Broombank Denby Dale HD8 191 F5
Huddersfield HD2 135 D2
Broomcroft [11] BD14 73 B4
Broomcroft Rd WF5 140 D4
Broome Ave BD2 55 E3
Broome Cl WF6 123 A4
Broomer St WF13 138 E6
Broomfield Elland HX5 134 D6
Leeds LS16 42 B4
Broomfield Ave HX3 113 B3
Broomfield Bsns Pk HD1 154 A4
Broomfield Cl HD8 175 C7
Broomfield Cres LS6 205 D4
Broomfield Pl
Bradford BD14 73 A3
[3] Keighley BD21 35 B7
Leeds LS6 205 D3
Broomfield Rd
Huddersfield HD2 136 A5
Huddersfield, Marsh HD1 153 D6
[4] Keighley BD21 35 B7
Leeds LS6 205 D4
Broomfield Sch LS10 99 F7
Broomfield St
Keighley BD21 35 B7
[3] Leeds LS6 205 D3
Queensbury BD13 72 E1
Broomfield Terr
Cleckheaton BD19 116 B7
Huddersfield HD1 153 D7
Leeds LS6 205 D3
Broomfield View LS6 205 D3
Broomhey Ave HD8 175 D6
Broomhill WF10 125 A6
Broomhill Ave Keighley BD21 35 A5
Knottingley WF11 127 B3
Leeds LS17 43 D1
Broomhill Cl Holmfirth HD7 189 D3
Knottingley WF11 127 B3
Broomhill Cres
Knottingley WF11 127 B3
Leeds LS17 43 D2
Broomhill Dr [2]
Keighley BD21 35 A5
Knottingley WF11 127 B3
Leeds LS17 43 C1
Broomhill Gr Keighley BD21 35 A5
Knottingley WF11 127 B3
Broomhill Mount BD21 35 A5
Broomhill Pl WF11 127 B3
Broomhill Sq WF11 127 B3
Broomhill St BD21 35 A4
Broomhill Terr WF17 118 D4
Broomhill Way BD21 35 B5
Broomhill Wlk
Keighley BD21 35 A5
Knottingley WF11 127 B3
Broomhouse Cl HD8 192 A5
Broomroyd HD3 152 F6
Broomsdale Rd WF17 118 E5
Broomwood Middle Sch BD4 75 D1
Broomy Lea La HD7 188 F7
Broster Ave BD22 34 F7
Brotherton Ave WF1 142 E7
Brotherton Primary Sch WF11 126 C8
Brougham Rd [11]
Halifax HX3 92 C1
Marsden HD7 169 A4
Brougham St [12] HX3 92 C1
Brougham Terr [13] HX3 92 C1
Broughton Ave Bradford BD4 75 B1
Leeds LS9 208 A2

Broughton Rd HD4 153 B3
Broughton St HX7 89 A4
Broughton Terr Leeds LS9 208 A2
7 Pudsey LS28 76 E8
Broughtons Yd WF11 126 C5
Brow Bottom La HX2 91 B6
Brow Foot Gate La HX2 112 D6
Brow Grains Rd HD7 170 B2
Brow La Denby Dale HD8 192 D6
Halifax HX3 92 B6
Holmfirth HD7 188 F3
Northowram HX3 92 E4
Shelf HX3 93 D6
Thornton BD14 72 F3
Brow Quarry Ind Est HX3 114 D6
Brow Rd Haworth BD22 51 D6
Huddersfield HD1 153 E5
Brow St BD21 35 D6
Brow Top Rd BD22 51 E7
Brow Wood Cres BD2 55 E3
Brow Wood Rd HX3 93 D6
Brow Wood Rise HX3 93 D6
Browcliff BD20 5 E2
Browfield Terr BD20 5 E2
Browfield View BD22 34 E5
Browfoot BD18 55 D8
Browfoot Dr HX2 112 D6
Browgate BD17 38 C4
Brown Ave LS11 213 E4
Brown Bank La BD20 6 B4
Brown Bank Terr BD20 16 E7
Brown Birks St 1 OL14 86 B1
Brown Hill Ave LS9 208 A2
Brown Hill Cl BD11 96 A7
Brown Hill Cres LS9 208 A2
Brown Hill Dr BD11 96 A6
Brown Hill La HX7 87 E5
Brown Hill Terr LS9 208 A2
Brown La E LS11 210 C1
Brown La W LS11, LS12 210 B1
Brown Lee La BD15 53 A4
Brown Pl LS11 213 E4
Brown Rd LS11 213 E4
Brown Royd Ave HD5 154 D8
Brown St 15 Keighley BD21 35 D8
Mirfield WF14 137 F5
Brown's Edge Rd S36 200 E8
Brown's Knoll Rd HD4 173 A3
Brown's Pl WF17 118 B4
Brown's St WF17 118 C4
Brownberrie Ave LS18 41 C3
Brownberrie Cres LS18 41 B3
Brownberrie Dr LS18 41 C3
Brownberrie Gdns LS18 41 B3
Brownberrie La LS18 41 B3
Brownberrie Wlk LS18 41 C3
Brownberry Gr HX3 93 D7
Brownhill Cl WF17 96 F1
Brownhill Cres WF9 163 A1
Brownhill Garth WF17 96 F1
Brownhill Inf Sch WF17 97 A1
Brownhill La HD7 198 B8
Brownhill Primary Sch LS9 208 A1
Brownhill Rd WF17 96 F1
Browning Ave HX3 113 D4
Browning Rd HD2 136 D3
Browning St BD3 75 B7
Brownings The HX3 114 C7
Brownlea Cl LS19 39 F5
Brownroyd Ave S71 179 C2
Brownroyd Hill Rd BD6 74 B2
Brownroyd Rd HD7 171 E4
Brownroyd St Bradford BD8 74 B7
Bradford, Shearbridge BD7 74 B6
Brownroyd Wlk BD6 74 B2
Browns Ct BD20 4 C6
Browsfield Rd LS29 6 D8
Browsholme St 2 BD21 35 C6
Browwood Terr BD6 93 F7
Bruce Gdns LS12 210 B3
Bruce Lawn LS12 210 B3
Bruce St HX1 202 B2
Brudenell Ave LS6 205 F3
Brudenell Gr LS6 205 F3
Brudenell Mount LS6 205 F3
Brudenell Primary Sch LS6 205 E3
Brudenell Rd LS6 205 E3
Brudenell St LS6 205 F3
Brudenell View LS6 205 F3
Brunel Cl BD9 55 A2
Brunel Ct 3 HX3 92 B2
Brunel Gdns 7 BD5 74 C3
Brunel Rd WF2 120 F4
Brunswick WF4 162 B2
Brunswick Arc 8 BD21 35 C7
Brunswick Ct LS2 207 D1
Brunswick Dr WF13 118 A1
Brunswick Gdns
Garforth LS25 82 F7
4 Halifax HX1 203 D3
Brunswick Gr WF1 216 C2
Brunswick House BD16 37 B2
Brunswick Pl
Bradford BD10 56 D7
3 Morley LS27 98 B4
Brunswick Rd
Bradford BD10 56 D7
Pudsey LS28 76 E8
Brunswick Row LS2 207 D1
Brunswick St
6 Batley WF17 118 C5
Batley, Heckmondwike WF16 117 D3
Brunswick St continued
Bingley BD16 37 B3
Cullingworth BD13 52 E6
Dearne S63 194 F1
Dewsbury WF13 118 A1
Hebden Bridge HX7 88 F3
Huddersfield HD1 154 A6
Morley LS27 98 A5
1 Queensbury BD13 72 F1
Wakefield WF1 216 C2
Brunswick Street Bglws 5 WF1 216 C2
Brunswick Terr
Leeds LS2 206 C1
Morley LS27 98 B4
Bruntcliffe Ave LS27 97 E5
Bruntcliffe Cl LS27 97 F4
Bruntcliffe Dr LS27 97 F4
Bruntcliffe High Sch LS27 97 E4
Bruntcliffe La LS27 97 E4
Bruntcliffe Rd LS27 97 E3
Bruntcliffe Way LS27 97 E4
Brunthwaite Bridge La BD20 18 A8
Brunthwaite La BD20 6 B1
Brussels St LS9 212 A3
Bryan Cl WF10 124 A8
Bryan Rd Elland HX5 134 D6
Huddersfield HD2 135 D1
Bryan St 5
Brighouse HD6 115 A1
Pudsey LS28 57 D3
Bryan St N LS28 57 D4
Bryan Terr HD3 152 E6
Bryanstone Rd BD4 75 D5
Bryer St WF13 139 C8
Bryngate LS26 101 C6
Bryony Ct LS10 99 F5
Buchan Towers 2 BD5 201 B1
Buck La BD17 38 F3
Buck Mill La BD10 39 A2
Buck St Bradford BD3 201 D2
Denholme BD13 71 E8
Buck Stone Ave LS17 42 F4
Buck Stone Cl LS17 43 A4
Buck Stone Cres LS17 43 A4
Buck Stone Dr LS17 42 F4
Buck Stone Gdns LS17 43 A4
Buck Stone Gn LS17 42 F4
Buck Stone Gr LS17 42 F4
Buck Stone La BD20 16 A1
Buck Stone Mount LS17 42 F4
Buck Stone Oval LS17 42 F4
Buck Stone Rd LS17 42 F5
Buck Stone Rise LS17 42 F4
Buck Stone View LS17 42 F4
Buck Stone Way LS17 42 F4
Buckden Ct BD20 5 E2
Buckden Rd HD3 153 D8
Buckfast Ct BD10 56 B7
Buckingham Ave LS6 205 E4
Buckingham Cres BD14 73 D5
Buckingham Ct WF1 142 F4
Buckingham Dr Leeds LS6 205 E4
Wakefield WF1 142 F3
Buckingham Gr LS6 205 E4
Buckingham Mount LS6 205 E3
Buckingham Rd LS6 205 E4
Buckingham Way
Byram WF11 126 E7
Royston S71 179 B4
Buckland Pl HX1 202 A2
Buckland Rd 3 BD8 73 F8
Buckle La Menston LS29 22 C4
Normanton WF6 123 A2
Buckley Ave LS11 214 B3
Buckley La HX2 91 C2
Buckley View OL14 108 A6
Buckley Wood Bottom 16 OL14 108 B5
Buckrose St HD1 136 A1
Buckstone Dr LS19 40 B3
Buckthorne Cl WF3 120 D8
Buckthorne Ct WF3 120 D8
Buckthorne Dr WF3 120 D8
Buckthorne Fold WF3 120 D8
Buckton Cl LS11 214 A4
Buckton Mount LS11 214 A4
Buckton View LS11 214 A4
Bude Rd Bradford BD5 74 F1
Leeds LS11 214 B3
Bugler Terr WF4 140 E1
Bula Cl LS25 83 B2
Bulay Rd HD1 153 F4
Bull Close La HX1 203 E2
Bull Gn HX1 203 E3
Bull Green Rd HD3 152 F6
Bull Hill BD22 51 C1
Bull La Crigglestone WF4 159 F5
South Kirkby WF9 182 C2
Bull Ring WF1 216 B2
Bull Royd Ave BD8 73 E8
Bull Royd Cres BD8 73 E8
Bull Royd Dr BD8 73 E8
Bull Royd La BD8 73 E8
Bullace Trees La WF15 116 E3
Bullenshaw Rd WF9 181 D6
Buller Cl LS9 208 B1
Buller Ct LS9 208 C1
Buller Gr LS9 208 B1
Buller St Bradford BD4 75 C5
6 Rothwell LS26 101 C6
Bullerthorpe La LS15, LS26 81 E4
Bullfield The BD16 53 B8
Bullfields Cl WF12 139 E2
Bullough La Leeds LS26 81 A1
Rothwell LS26 100 F8
Bullstyle Rd WF8 146 C6
Bulrush Bsns Pk WF17 118 B7
Bungalow Rd BD20 16 C6
Bungalows The
Clayton West HD8 175 E2
Halifax HX2 91 D1
Halifax, Lee Mount HX3 92 A2
Halifax, Salterhebble HX3 113 E2
Leeds LS15 62 D3
Normanton WF6 123 A5
Ossett WF5 140 C6
Bunker's Hill La BD22 34 D5
Bunkers Hill
Aberford LS25 64 E6
Guiseley BD17 39 B5
Holmfirth HD7 189 A5
Wakefield WF2 120 F2
Bunkers La WF17 117 F4
Bunney Gr HX3 92 F4
Bunny Pk HD4 153 D3
Burbeary Rd HD1 153 E3
Burberry Cl BD4 95 C8
Burchett Gr LS6 206 A4
Burchett Pl LS6 206 A4
Burchett Terr LS6 206 B4
Burcote Dr HD3 134 B1
Burdale Pl BD7 74 B6
Burdett Terr 5 LS4 59 C2
Burdock Way HX1 203 D3
Burfitts Rd HD3 153 B7
Burgh Mill La WF13 139 A7
Burhouse Ct HD7 171 F4
Burkill St WF1 142 D2
Burking Rd WF13 139 B8
Burlees La HX7 89 C3
Burleigh St 6 HX1 202 B1
Burley Bank La HD7 197 E6
Burley C E First Sch LS29 9 E1
Burley Ct Leeds LS4 205 D1
Steeton BD20 17 C5
Burley Grange Rd 2 LS4 59 C2
Burley Hill Cres LS4 59 B3
Burley Hill Dr LS4 59 C3
Burley in Wharfedale Sta LS29 21 E8
Burley La Horsforth LS18 58 B7
Menston LS29 21 F5
Burley Lodge Pl LS6 205 E1
Burley Lodge Rd LS6 205 E2
Burley Lodge St LS6 205 E1
Burley Lodge Terr LS6 205 E1
Burley Mews BD20 17 C5
Burley Middle Sch LS29 9 F1
Burley Park Sta LS4 205 D3
Burley Pl LS4 205 E1
Burley Rd Leeds LS3, LS4 205 D2
Menston LS29 22 A6
Burley St 10 Elland HX5 134 F6
Leeds LS3 210 C4
Shipley BD2 55 D4
Burley St Matthias' Sch LS4 205 D2
Burley Wlk WF17 118 B5
Burley Wood Cres LS4 59 C2
Burley Wood La LS4 59 C3
Burley Wood Mount LS4 59 B3
Burley Wood View LS4 59 C3
Burley & Woodhead C of E Sch LS29 21 F8
Burlington Ave BD3 56 E1
Burlington Pl 21 LS11 214 B2
Burlington Rd LS11 214 B2
Burlington St Bradford BD8 55 D1
3 Halifax HX1 202 B3
Burlington Works BD3 56 E1
Burmantofts St LS9 212 B4
Burn Rd HD2, HD3 135 C3
Burned Gr HX3 93 C7
Burned Rd HX3 93 D7
Burneston Gdns 12 BD6 93 E8
Burnett Ave BD5 74 D3
Burnett Pl BD5 74 D3
Burnett Rise BD13 92 C8
Burnett St BD1 201 C3
Burnham Ave Bradford BD4 75 C1
Mapplewell S75 178 B1
Burnham Ct LS22 13 C6
Burnham Rd LS25 82 F6
Burnhill La WF9 164 F5
Burniston Cl BD15 53 C4
Burniston Dr HD3 153 A8
Burnlee Rd HD7 188 E4
Burnley Hill Terr HX3 93 B4
Burnley Rd Bacup OL13 85 A1
Halifax, Luddenden Foot HX2 111 D6
Halifax, Willow Field HX2, HX6 112 C6
Holme Chapel BB10 85 C4
Todmorden OL14 85 C4
Burnley Road Jun & Inf Sch HX7 89 E1
Burnleys Ct LS26 123 D8
Burnleys Dr LS26 123 D8
Burnleys Mews LS26 123 D8
Burnleys View LS26 102 D1
Burnleyville BD19 96 B1
Burnroyd Ave BD20 16 D6
Burns Ave WF9 181 F1
Burns Ct WF17 96 D2
Burns Hill LS29 6 E8
Burns St HX3 91 F3
Burns Way LS23 30 D5
Burnsall Ave WF17 118 A5
Burnsall Croft LS12 209 E3
Burnsall Ct LS12 209 E4
Burnsall Gdns LS12 209 E4
Burnsall Grange LS12 209 E4
Burnsall Mews BD20 5 E2
Burnsall Rd Batley WF17 118 A5
Bradford BD3 75 B7
Brighouse HD6 135 E8
Liversedge WF15 116 F4
Burnsdale BD15 54 A3
Burnshaw Mews LS10 99 C3
Burnside S63 194 C1
Burnside Ave HX3 93 C6
Burnside Cl WF17 97 A1
Burnside Dr HD7 188 E4
Burnt Acres La OL14 109 B8
Burnt Edge La HX7 87 D4
Burnt House Cl OL14 108 C6
Burnt Plats La HD7 151 B3
Burnt Side Rd LS12 77 C2
Burnt Wood Cres WF9 182 C2
Burnt Wood La WF9 181 E1
Burntwood Ave WF9 182 C2
Burntwood Bank WF9 181 D5
Burntwood Dr WF9 182 C1
Burntwood Gr WF9 182 C1
Burntwood Jun & Inf Sch WF9 182 C2
Burntwood Sports & Leisure Ctr S72 181 C2
Burnup Gr BD19 116 C7
Burnwells BD10 39 A2
Burnwells Ave BD10 39 A2
Burr Tree Dr LS15 81 D7
Burr Tree Garth LS15 81 D7
Burr Tree Vale LS15 81 D7
Burrage St BD16 36 F3
Burras Ave LS21 22 F7
Burras Dr LS21 22 F7
Burras La LS21 22 F7
Burras Rd BD4 75 B2
Burrel Cl LS22 14 A5
Burrell St WF1 216 C2
Burrow St BD5 201 B2
Burrows The WF17 117 F7
Burrwood Terr HX4 134 B5
Burrwood Way HX4 134 B5
Burton Acres Dr HD8 173 E7
Burton Acres La HD8 173 F7
Burton Acres Mews HD8 173 E7
Burton Acres Way HD8 173 E7
Burton Arc 1 LS1 211 F3
Burton Ave LS11 214 C3
Burton Common La LS25 105 F4
Burton Cres LS6 59 D6
Burton Cross HD8 173 E8
Burton Mews LS17 43 D5
Burton Rd LS11 214 C3
Burton Row LS11 214 C4
Burton Royd La HD8 174 A7
Burton Salmon Primary Sch LS25 105 E3
Burton St Bradford BD4 75 A4
Halifax HX2 92 A5
Keighley BD20 18 B2
Leeds LS11 214 C4
Pudsey LS28 57 D3
South Elmsall WF9 182 F2
Wakefield WF1 216 A3
Burton Terr LS11 214 C3
Burton Way LS9 208 A1
Burwood Rd HD3 153 C8
Busely Ct LS27 97 F5
Busfield St Bingley BD16 36 F3
Bradford BD4 75 B3
Bush St WF9 181 E6
Bushill Fold BD13 72 C2
Busker La HD8 175 C1
Buslingthorpe Gn LS7 206 C3
Buslingthorpe La LS7 206 C4
Buslingthorpe Vale LS7 206 C4
Bussey Ct LS6 206 A3
Busy La BD18 38 E1
Butcher Hill
Hemsworth WF9 181 E8
Leeds LS16, LS18 58 F8
Butcher La LS26 100 E5
Butcher St Bradford BD7 74 D7
Leeds LS11 211 E2
Bute Ave HD6 115 A5
Bute St BD2 55 D4
Butler La BD17 38 D4
Butler St E BD3 75 A7
Butler St W BD3 201 D4
Butt Hill LS25 83 A1
Butt La Bradford BD10 56 B8
Haworth BD22 51 C7
Holmfirth HD7 189 E2
Hooton Pagnell DN5 195 E4
Leeds LS12, LS13 77 D6
Butterbowl Dr LS12 77 F5
Butterbowl Garth LS12 77 E5
Butterbowl Gdns LS12 77 F5
Butterbowl Gr LS12 77 E5
Butterbowl Lawn LS12 77 E5
Butterbowl Mount LS12 77 F5
Butterbowl Rd LS12 77 F5
Buttercup Cl WF9 182 F7
Butterfield Homes
Glusburn BD20 16 C6
5 Shipley BD16 54 B6
Wilsden BD15 53 B6
Butterfield St LS9 212 C3
Butterley La HD7 189 F5
Butterley St LS10 211 F2
Buttermead Cl BD6 94 A7
Buttermere Ave LS22 13 C6
Buttermere Croft WF2 161 A6
Buttermere Dr HD5 154 D6
Buttermere Rd BD2 56 B3
Buttermere Wlk WF11 126 E2
Butternab Rd HD4 171 D8
Butternab Ridge HD4 171 D8
Buttershaw Dr BD6 73 E1
Buttershaw First Sch BD6 93 F7
Buttershaw La Bradford BD6 94 B8
Cleckheaton WF15 116 B5
Buttershaw Middle Sch BD6 93 F7
Buttershaw Upper Sch BD6 93 F8
Butterton Cl S75 178 C1
Butterwick Gdns LS22 13 C5
Butterwood Cl HD4 171 D8
Butterworth End La HX6 133 A7
Butterworth Hill HD3 152 A7
Butterworth La HX6 111 E1
Buttholme Gate BD6 93 F8
Button Hill LS7 207 D4
Button Pk WF8 146 C7
Buttress La HX2 90 F1
Butts Cl HD4 172 E6
Butts Ct LS1 211 F4
Butts Garth LS14 45 F5
Butts Garth View LS14 45 F5
Butts Green La HX2 112 A7
Butts Green Rd HX2 111 F7
Butts Hill BD19 117 B8
Butts La Guiseley LS20 22 E1
Monk Fryston LS25 105 D8
Netherton WF4 158 B7
South Milford LS25 105 D8
Todmorden OL14 108 E8
Butts Mount LS12 210 A3
Butts Rd HD4 172 E6
Butts Terr LS20 22 E1
Butts The Keighley BD20 36 D8
Pontefract WF8 125 D1
Butts Way HD4 172 E6
Butts Yd 8 BD19 116 D7
Buxton Ave BD9 55 C4
Buxton La BD9 55 C4
Buxton Pl WF1 216 A4
Buxton St Bradford BD9 55 B2
8 Halifax HX3 92 A1
3 Keighley BD21 35 D7
Buxton Way HX3 91 F3
Byeway LS20 22 C1
Byland HX2 91 E7
Byland Cl LS23 30 C7
Byland Gr BD15 53 F1
Bylands Ave BD20 18 E2
Byram Arc 22 HD1 154 A6
Byram Park Ave WF11 126 E8
Byram Park Rd WF11 126 E8
Byram St HD1 154 B6
Byrom St OL14 108 B6
Byron Ave 6 HX6 112 B5
Byron Cl WF11 126 B4
Byron First Sch BD3 75 B8
Byron Gr Batley WF13 117 E2
Lofthouse Gate WF3 121 E6
Byron St Bradford BD3 75 B8
Halifax HX1 202 B3
Leeds LS2 207 D1
16 Sowerby Bridge HX6 112 B5
Byways The WF8 146 D6
Bywell CE Jun Sch WF12 118 F1
Bywell Cl WF12 140 A8
Bywell Rd WF12 118 F1

Cabbage Hill LS12 209 E2
Cabin Rd LS21 24 B5
Cable St HD1 154 A4
Cad Beeston Mews LS11 214 A3
Cadney Croft 3 HX1 203 E2
Cadogan Ave HD3 153 B8
Caenarvon Cl WF17 97 A1
Caernarvon Ave LS25 83 B7
Cain Cl 3 LS9 212 C3
Cain La HX3 114 A4
Cairns Cl BD2 55 F3
Caister Cl WF17 97 A2
Caister Gr 5 BD21 35 B4
Caister St 3 BD21 35 B4
Caister Way BD21 35 B4
Calde Ct BD12 94 E6
Caldene Ave Bradford BD12 94 E6
Hebden Bridge HX7 89 D1
Calder Ave Halifax HX2 202 B1
Royston S71 179 E3
Calder Bank Rd WF13 139 B7
Calder Banks BD13 73 A1
Calder Cl Castleford WF10 125 B8
Elland HX4 134 D7
Ossett WF5 140 C5
Wetherby LS22 13 D8
Calder Coll of F Ed OL14 108 B5
Calder Dr HD4 171 F8
Calder Gr 3 HX7 89 E1
Calder High Sch HX7 89 F1
Calder House
10 Elland HX5 134 F7
Mirfield WF14 138 A4
Calder Island Way WF2 142 B2
Calder Mount WF4 159 E5
Calder Rd Dewsbury WF13 138 F5
Mirfield WF14 138 A3
Calder St Brighouse HD6 115 C1
Castleford WF10 124 C8
Elland HX4 134 D7
Halifax HX4 203 F2
Todmorden OL14 108 B5
Wakefield WF1 142 D4
Calder Terr Elland HX3 113 A1
Hebden Bridge HX7 88 F3
Horbury WF4 159 C8
Calder Vale Rd WF1 142 E5
Calder View Brighouse HD6 115 A1
Crigglestone WF4 159 E5
Ossett WF5 140 B5
Calder Way BD20 17 E8
Calderbrook Rd OL15 129 C2

Caldercliffe Rd HD4 153 F1
Caldercroft HX5 135 B6
Calderdale Bsns Pk HX2 91 F3
Calderdale Way HX5 135 B6
Calderstone Ave BD6 93 E8
Caldervale S71 179 E4
Caldicott Cl OL14 107 F3
Caledonia Ct WF2 120 B2
Caledonia Rd Batley WF17 118 D5
Keighley BD21 35 D8
Caledonia St BD4, BD5 201 C1
Caledonian Rd WF12 139 C5
Calf Hey La S36 200 D7
Calf Hey Terr 3 OL14 108 A1
Calf Hill Rd HD7 172 B1
Calgary Pl LS7 204 A2
California Dr
Castleford WF10 123 D5
Horbury WF4 141 C1
Todmorden OL14 108 A3
California La DB19 117 B7
California Mews LS27 98 B6
California St 10 LS27 98 B4
Call La LS1 211 F3
Calls The LS2 212 A3
Cally Hall Farm Cotts HX7 88 A4
Calmlands Rd HD7 170 D1
Calpin Cl BD10 56 B8
Calton Gr BD21 35 F6
Calton Rd BD21 35 F6
Calton St Huddersfield HD1 154 B8
Keighley BD21 35 B6
Calver Ave BD21 35 A8
Calver Gr BD21 35 A7
Calver Rd BD21 35 A7
Calverley Ave Bradford BD3 75 D8
Leeds LS13 58 B3
Calverley C of E Primary Sch LS28 57 B7
Calverley Ct Leeds LS13 58 B3
Rothwell LS26 101 B5
Calverley Cutting BD10 56 F8
Calverley Dr LS13 58 B3
Calverley Garth LS13 58 B3
Calverley Gdns LS13 58 A4
Calverley Gr 1 LS13 58 B3
Calverley Green Rd WF6 122 F3
Calverley La Horsforth LS18 58 A8
Leeds LS13 58 A3
Pudsey LS28 57 C5
Yeadon LS18 57 E7
Calverley Moor Ave LS28 57 A1
Calverley Parkside Primary Sch LS28 57 B6
Calverley Rd LS26 101 C5
Calverley St LS1 206 B1
Calverley Terr 2 LS13 58 B3
Calversyke Middle Sch BD22 34 F7
Calversyke St BD21 35 A7
Calvert Cl LS25 83 A3
Calverts Wlk WF5 140 E4
Cam La HD6 115 D3
Camargue Fold BD2 55 F4
Cambell St BD21 35 C7
Camberley Cl LS28 76 E6
Camberley Mount BD4 75 E4
Camberley St 8 LS11 214 C3
Camborne Dr HD2 135 F3
Camborne Rd HD2 135 F4
Camborne Way BD22 34 E5
Cambrian Bar BD12 94 B6
Cambrian St LS11 214 A4
Cambrian Terr LS11 214 A4
Cambridge Cl LS27 98 B5
Cambridge Cres WF4 143 C3
Cambridge Ct LS27 98 B4
Cambridge Dr Leeds LS13 58 B3
Otley LS21 23 C7
Cambridge Gdns LS13 58 B3
Cambridge Gr Kippax LS25 83 A1
Otley LS21 23 B7
Cambridge Pl
Bradford BD3 201 C4
13 Queensbury BD13 72 E1
12 Todmorden OL14 108 B5
Cambridge Rd Batley WF17 96 D2
Huddersfield HD1 154 A7
Leeds LS7 206 C3
Cambridge St Batley WF16 117 E4
Batley WF17 118 C5
Bradford BD7 74 B4
Bradford, Town End BD14 73 B4
Castleford WF10 124 D7
Guiseley LS20 22 E1
Hebden Bridge HX7 88 F3
Normanton WF6 123 A1
Otley LS21 23 B7
13 Queensbury BD13 72 F1
South Elmsall WF9 182 E3
Todmorden OL14 108 C5
Wakefield WF2 142 A5
Cambridge Terr LS21 23 B7
Cambridge Way LS21 23 B7
Camden Rd WF10 125 D8
Camden St HX6 112 B3
Camellia Cl WF2 141 D3
Camellia Mount BD7 73 E6
Camelot Ct WF8 146 E8
Cameron Ave 1 BD12 94 C1
Camerton Gn BD5 74 F2
Camilla Ct WF12 139 F7
Camm La WF14 138 B6
Camm St HD6 115 B3
Camp Hill HD3 151 B5
Camp Mount WF8 146 B8
Camp Rd Bramhope LS16 24 E1
South Kirkby WF9 181 F1
Camp Rise WF8 146 B8
Camp Sq LS14 45 F5
Campbell St Glusburn BD20 16 D7
Pudsey LS28 57 E2
Queensbury BD13 72 F1
Campden Rd HX7 88 E4
Campinot Vale HD7 151 F1
Campion Cl WF8 146 D7
Campus Rd BD7 74 C6
Camroyd St WF13 118 D1
Canada Cres LS19 40 C4
Canada Dr LS19 40 C5
Canada Rd LS19 40 C5
Canada Terr LS19 40 C4
Canal Ct WF3 121 D6
Canal La
Lofthouse Gate WF3 121 E6
Silsden BD20 18 A7
Canal Pl LS12 210 C3
Canal Rd Bingley BD16 36 F5
Bradford BD1 201 C4
Halifax HX6 112 E4
Keighley BD20 18 E1
Leeds LS12 210 A4
Pudsey LS13 57 E5
Shipley BD1, BD2 55 D3
Canal St Brighouse HD6 115 B2
Halifax HX3 203 F2
Huddersfield HD1 154 C8
Leeds LS12 210 B3
Todmorden OL14 108 B5
Canal Wharf LS11 211 E3
Canal Wlk WF3 121 F6
Canary St BD19 116 D8
Canberra Cl 6 BD22 51 F8
Canberra Dr BD22 51 F8
Canby Gr HD5 155 B5
Cancel St LS10 212 A1
Canford Dr BD15 54 C1
Canford Gr BD15 54 C1
Canford Rd BD15 54 B1
Canker La Halifax HX3 92 B3
Huddersfield HD2 136 D1
Canning Ave WF2 141 D8
Cannon Gr WF16 117 E5
Cannon Hall Cl HD6 115 D2
Cannon Hall Country Pk S75 193 D5
Cannon Hall Dr HD6 115 D2
Cannon Hall House & Mus S75 193 C5
Cannon Mill La BD7 74 A4
Cannon St Bingley BD16 37 A2
Castleford WF10 124 E5
8 Halifax HX1 202 B1
Todmorden OL14 108 A3
Cannon Way WF13 139 C7
Canonbury Terr LS11 213 E3
Canteen Mill Ind Est OL14 107 E8
Canterbury Ave BD5 74 C4
Canterbury Cres HX3 92 B1
Canterbury Dr LS6 59 C4
Canterbury Rd
Dewsbury WF12 118 F1
Leeds LS6 59 C4
Capas Heights Way WF16 117 E3
Cape Mills Ind Est LS28 57 E3
Cape St BD1 201 B4
Capel Ct LS28 57 B6
Capel St Brighouse HD6 115 A1
Pudsey LS28 57 B6
Caprington Ct WF6 123 D1
Captain St 7 Bacup OL13 106 A7
Bradford BD1 201 C4
Carberry Pl 21 LS6 205 E2
Carberry Rd LS6 205 E2
Carberry Terr 23 LS6 205 E2
Cardan Dr LS29 8 E4
Carden Ave LS15 80 E8
Carden Rd BD4 75 E5
Cardigan Ave LS27 98 A2
Cardigan Cl WF17 118 E5
Cardigan Ct LS6 205 E4
Cardigan La Leeds LS4, LS6 205 E3
Leeds, Burley LS4, LS6 205 D2
Ossett WF5 141 A3
Cardigan St BD13 72 F1
Cardigan Terr WF1 216 B3
Cardigan Trad Est LS4 205 D1
Cardinal Ave LS11 98 F8
Cardinal Cl HD7 170 E2
Cardinal Cres LS11 98 F8
Cardinal Gdns LS11 98 E8
Cardinal Gr LS11 98 E8
Cardinal Heenan High Sch LS6 43 A1
Cardinal Rd LS11 213 F1
Cardinal Sq LS11 213 E1
Cardinal Wlk LS11 98 F8
Cardwell Terr WF12 139 C6
Carforth St HD1 154 C5
Carisbrooke Cres BD6 94 C8
Carisbrooke La LS25 83 B8
Cariss St LS10 215 D3
Cark Rd BD21 35 C8
Carlby Gr 3 BD22 35 A6
Carlby St BD22 35 A6
Carleton Cl Boston Spa LS23 30 B8
Pontefract WF8 146 D7
Carleton Crest WF8 146 E6
Carleton Dr LS23 30 B7
Carleton Gate WF8 146 D6
Carleton Glen WF8 146 D7
Carleton Green Cl WF8 146 E5
Carleton High Sch WF8 146 E5
Carleton House 1 BD6 93 E8
Carleton Park Ave WF8 146 D6
Carleton Park Jun & Inf Sch WF8 146 D6
Carleton Park Rd WF8 146 D6
Carleton Rd WF8 146 E6
Carleton St BD20 18 C1
Carleton View WF8 146 D6
Carlile St HD7 170 E2
Carling Cl BD7 73 F3
Carlinghow Hill WF17 118 B7
Carlinghow La WF17 117 F6
Carlinghow Mills WF17 118 B6
Carlinghow Princess Royal Prim Sch WF17 118 A7
Carlisle Ave LS19 40 C6
Carlisle Cl WF13 118 C2
Carlisle Dr LS28 76 E6
Carlisle Gr LS28 76 D6
Carlisle Pl BD8 55 C1
Carlisle Rd Bradford BD8 55 C1
Leeds LS10 212 A2
Pudsey LS28 76 D6
Carlisle St Bradford BD8 55 C1
Halifax HX2 202 A4
Keighley BD21 35 D7
Pudsey LS28 57 C1
Carlisle Terr BD8 55 C1
Carlrayne La LS29 22 A5
Carlton App LS22 13 C6
Carlton Ave Batley WF17 118 B3
Castleford WF10 124 F7
Pudsey LS28 76 E7
Shipley BD18 54 F8
Carlton Carr LS7 206 C2
Carlton Cl
1 Cleckheaton BD19 116 D7
Hemsworth WF9 181 C5
Leeds LS7 206 C2
Normanton WF6 123 B2
Carlton Croft Leeds LS7 206 C2
Wakefield WF2 160 D6
Carlton Ct
Cleckheaton BD19 116 D8
Leeds LS12 213 E4
Ossett WF5 140 D6
Carlton Dr Baildon BD17 38 C4
Garforth LS25 82 F5
Guiseley LS20 22 F2
Shipley BD9 55 B4
Shipley, Frizinghall BD18 55 A5
Carlton Garth Leeds LS7 206 C2
Leeds, Blackwood LS17 44 A5
Carlton Gate LS7 206 C2
Carlton Gdns Leeds LS7 206 C2
Normanton WF6 123 C2
South Elmsall WF9 182 F3
Carlton Gr 2 Bradford BD5 74 D3
Elland HX5 135 C7
Leeds LS7 206 C2
Shipley BD18 55 B5
Carlton Hill LS2, LS7 206 C2
Carlton House Terr HX1 202 C1
Carlton Junior & Infant Sch WF13 118 B2
Carlton Junior & Infant Sch WF3 100 D3
Carlton La East Carlton LS19 23 C3
Guiseley LS20 23 C3
Rothwell LS26 100 E4
Rothwell, Lofthouse WF3 100 C1
Carlton Marsh Nature Reserve S71, S72 180 A1
Carlton Moor Mews LS10 99 F5
Carlton Mount LS19 40 C8
Carlton Pl 1 Halifax HX1 203 E2
Leeds LS7 206 C2
Carlton Rd Batley WF16 117 C6
Dewsbury WF13 118 C1
Liversedge WF15 117 A3
Royston S71 179 D1
Shipley BD18 54 E8
South Elmsall WF9 182 F3
Carlton Rise Leeds LS7 206 C2
Pudsey LS28 76 E7
Carlton Row LS12 209 D3
Carlton St 2 Bacup OL13 106 A3
Bradford BD7 74 D6
Castleford WF10 124 D8
Featherstone WF7 145 D7
Halifax HX1 203 E2
10 Haworth BD22 51 D7
19 Hebden Bridge HX7 89 A3
Horbury WF4 141 A1
Normanton WF6 123 C2
Otley LS21 23 B7
Wakefield WF2 142 A5
Carlton Terr Batley WF17 118 A3
Dewsbury WF12 139 D6
4 Halifax HX1 203 E2
2 Pudsey LS28 76 E8
Yeadon LS19 40 C7
Carlton Towers LS7 206 C2
Carlton View Kippax WF10 102 F6
Leeds LS7 206 C2
Carlton Way 2 BD19, OL2 116 D7
Carlton Wlk BD18 54 F8
Carlton-Bolling Coll BD3 56 A1
Carlyle Cres WF10 125 B7
Carlyle Rd WF10 125 B7
Carmel Rd HX3 92 C2
Carmine Cl HD5 154 E6
Carmona Ave BD18 55 B5
Carmona Gdns BD18 55 B5
Carnaby Rd BD7 73 E2
Carnegie Coll LS6 59 B6
Carnegie Dr BD18 55 C7
Carnlea Gr WF2 142 C3
Carnoustie Gr BD16 54 B7
Carolan Ct HD7 152 D5
Caroline St
10 Cleckheaton BD19 116 D8
Shipley BD18 54 F8
Carperley Cres BD13 71 E8
Carr Bank Keighley BD20 19 C1
Otley LS21 11 A2
Carr Bank Bottom LS21 10 F2
Carr Bottom Ave BD5 74 C2
Carr Bottom Fold BD5 74 C1
Carr Bottom Gr BD5 74 B2
Carr Bottom Rd
Bradford, Brownroyd Hill BD5 74 C2
Bradford, Greengates BD10 56 E7
Carr Bridge Ave LS16 41 D3
Carr Bridge Cl LS16 41 D3
Carr Bridge Dr LS16 41 D3
Carr Bridge View LS16 41 D3
Carr Cl LS19 40 D3
Carr Crofts LS12 209 E3
Carr Crofts Dr LS12 209 E3
Carr Field Dr HX2 111 E8
Carr Gate Cres WF2 120 D5
Carr Gate Dr WF2 120 E5
Carr Gate Mount WF2 120 D5
Carr Gr BD20 19 A1
Carr Green Ave HD6 135 F6
Carr Green Cl HD6 135 F6
Carr Green Dr HD6 135 F6
Carr Green Junior & Infants Sch HD6 135 F7
Carr Green La
Brighouse HD6 135 F7
Huddersfield HD5 154 D6
Carr Hall La HX4 134 A4
Carr Hall Rd BD12 94 C3
Carr Head La BD20 16 A5
Carr Hill Ave LS28 57 A6
Carr Hill Dr LS28 57 A6
Carr Hill Gr LS28 57 A6
Carr Hill Nook LS28 57 A6
Carr Hill Rd
Denby Dale HD8 191 A6
Pudsey LS28 57 A6
Carr Hill Rise LS28 57 A6
Carr House WF1 216 B2
Carr House Fold 1 OL14 108 D6
Carr House Gate BD12 94 C4
Carr House Gr BD12 94 C4
Carr House La
Bradford BD12 94 B4
Shelf HX3 93 D7
Todmorden OL14 108 D6
Carr House Mount BD12 94 C4
Carr House Rd
Holmfirth HD7 189 A5
Shelf HX3 93 D7
Carr Houses LS26 123 E8
Carr La Bingley BD16 36 E8
Bradford BD12 94 D5
Castleford WF10 124 F5
Denholme BD13 52 E2
Dewsbury WF12 157 C8
Dewsbury, Heckmondwike WF16 117 E1
Hemsworth WF4, WF9 162 F2
Holmfirth HD7 188 B4
Ingbirchworth S36 192 C1
Keighley, East Morton BD20 36 C8
Keighley, Riddlesden BD20 19 A1
Netherton WF4 158 B6
Rothwell WF3 100 E3
Shepley HD8 190 F6
Shipley BD18 55 D7
Slaithwaite HD7 152 A1
South Kirkby WF9 182 D4
Thorner LS14 45 D5
Wakefield WF2 160 E7
Wetherby LS22 14 A7
Yeadon LS19 40 D3
Carr Lane Ave WF10 124 E5
Carr Manor Ave LS17 43 B1
Carr Manor Cres LS17 60 B8
Carr Manor Croft LS17 60 B7
Carr Manor Dr LS17 60 B8
Carr Manor Garth LS17 43 B1
Carr Manor Gdns LS17 60 B8
Carr Manor Gr LS17 60 B8
Carr Manor High Sch LS7 60 A7
Carr Manor Mount LS17 60 B8
Carr Manor Par LS17 60 B8
Carr Manor Pl LS17 60 B8
Carr Manor Primary Sch LS17 60 B8
Carr Manor Rd LS17 60 B8
Carr Manor View LS17 60 C8
Carr Manor Wlk LS17 60 B7
Carr Moor Side LS11 214 C3
Carr Moor St LS10 215 D2
Carr Mount Denby Dale HD8 191 A6
Kirkheaton HD5 155 E7
Carr Pit Rd HD5 154 C5
Carr Rd 3 Bradford BD12 94 C3
Pudsey LS28 57 A7
Todmorden OL14 107 A8
Carr Side Cres WF17 118 C3
Carr St 3 Batley WF16 117 C4
Batley, Batley Carr WF17 118 C2
Batley, Birstall WF17 96 E1
Bradford BD5 74 D2
Brighouse HD6 115 A4
Cleckheaton BD19 116 D7
Huddersfield HD3 153 C7
Keighley BD21 35 C7
Liversedge WF15 117 A5
Carr Top Cl WF17 118 B2
Carr Top La HD7 152 D4
Carr View WF9 182 C3
Carr View Rd HD7 189 F2
Carr Wood Cl LS28 57 A6
Carr Wood Gdns LS28 57 A7
Carr Wood Ind Est WF10 124 F5
Carr Wood Rd WF10 124 F5
Carr Wood Way LS28 57 A7
Carr's Cl WF13 117 F3
Carrfield Dr LS15 63 D7
Carrfield La LS15 63 D7
Carrfield Rd LS15 63 D7
Carrfield Villas OL14 86 A1
Carrgate WF9 163 B2
Carrholm Cres LS7 60 B7
Carrholm Dr LS7 60 B7
Carrholm Gr LS7 60 B7
Carrholm Mount LS7 60 B7
Carrholm Rd LS7 60 B7
Carrholm View LS7 60 B7
Carriage Dr
Cleckheaton BD19 96 B2
Huddersfield HD4 171 F8
Carriage Dr The
Elland HX4 134 A4
Leeds LS8 61 C8
Carriage La HX4 134 C8
Carricks Cl BD12 94 E6
Carrier St 12 HX1 203 E3
Carrington St BD3 75 C7
Carrington Terr LS20 39 D8
Carroll Ct WF9 182 E3
Carroll St BD3 201 D2
Carrs Rd HD7 169 A4
Carrs Side St No 1 HD7 169 A4
Carrs Side St No 2 HD7 169 A4
Carrs St HD7 169 A4
Carter Ave 2 LS15 81 C8
Carter La 6 Leeds LS15 81 C8
Queensbury BD13 72 D3
Carter Mount LS15 81 C8
Carter St Bradford BD4 201 C2
Wakefield WF1 216 A2
Carter Terr 4 LS15 62 C1
Carter's La LS29 8 E7
Cartmel Rd BD21 35 A7
Cartmell Dr LS15 80 D7
Cartworth Bank Rd HD7 188 F2
Cartworth La HD7 189 A3
Cartworth Moor Rd
Holme HD7 198 E8
Holmfirth HD7 188 E1
Cartworth Rd HD7 189 A4
Cartwright Gdns HD4 153 C3
Cartwright Hall Art Gall BD9 55 C3
Cartwright House 7 WF15 117 A5
Cartwright St BD19 116 F6
Carver St BD19 116 D8
Caryl Rd BD4 75 A3
Cashmere St BD21 35 A7
Casson Ave WF3 99 B1
Casson Dr WF3 120 B8
Casson Gr WF3 99 B1
Casterton Gdns LS14 62 A3
Castle Ave Brighouse HD6 135 F8
Huddersfield HD4 154 A1
Wakefield WF2 142 D2
Castle Carr Rd Halifax HX2 90 D6
Wadsworth Moor HX2 70 A1
Castle Cl Bardsey LS17 28 D3
Batley WF17 97 A1
Castle Cres Dewsbury WF12 139 D1
Wakefield WF2 160 D8
Castle Croft BD16 36 A1
Castle Ct 1 BD21 35 C8
Castle Garth WF8 125 E1
Castle Gate
Hebden Bridge HX7 110 C4
Ilkley LS29 8 B4
Lofthouse Gate LS26 122 A8
Wetherby LS22 13 E5
Castle Gr Bardsey LS17 28 D3
Harden BD16 36 A1
Horbury WF4 159 C8
Castle Grove Ave LS6 59 D6
Castle Grove Dr LS6 59 D6
Castle Grove Inf Sch WF2 142 E2
Castle Hall Sch WF14 138 B5
Castle Head Cl WF3 100 C1
Castle Head La WF3 121 A8
Castle Hill Brighouse HD6 135 F8
Ilkley LS29 8 B4
Wakefield WF2 141 C4
Castle Hill Fort HD4 154 C1
Castle Hill Junior & Infants Sch OL14 108 D6
Castle Hill Rd BD19 117 B6
Castle Hill Side HD4 172 C8
Castle Hill View WF16 117 F3
Castle Houses HD4 172 B8
Castle Ings Cl LS12 77 D3
Castle Ings Dr LS12 77 D3
Castle Ings Gdns LS12 77 D2
Castle La Ripponden HX6 132 C3
Slaithwaite HD7 151 E2
Todmorden OL14 108 D6
Castle Lane Cl OL14 108 D6
Castle Meadows WF4 159 F3
Castle Mount WF12 139 D1
Castle Par WF10 124 F6
Castle Pl HD6 135 F8
Castle Rd Ilkley LS29 8 B4
Keighley BD21 35 B8
Rothwell LS26 100 D5
Shipley BD18 55 B7
Wakefield WF2 142 E1

Castle Rd W WF2 142 D1
Castle Sch The WF10 125 C7
Castle St Leeds LS1 211 D4
Wakefield WF2 141 F5
Castle Syke Hill WF8 146 B3
Castle Syke View WF8 146 C6
Castle Terr WF2 160 D8
Castle Vale WF8 125 F2
Castle View Honley HD7 171 F3
Horbury WF4 159 C8
Leeds LS17 43 B1
Mirfield WF14 138 B5
Pontefract WF8 125 D1
Wakefield WF2 160 D8
Castle Wood Cl
Harewood LS17 27 A7
Horsforth LS18 58 D8
Castle Yd LS29 8 B4
Castlefield Ct WF10 124 D8
Castlefields LS26 100 B5
Castlefields Cres HD6 135 F8
Castlefields Dr HD6 135 F8
Castlefields Ind Est BD16 36 D5
Castlefields Infants Sch HD6 114 F1
Castlefields La BD16 36 E5
Castlefields Rd
Bingley BD16 36 D6
Brighouse HD6 135 F8
Castleford Airedale Jun & Inf Sch WF10 125 C7
Castleford High Sch WF10 124 F8
Castleford La
Featherstone WF7 124 B2
Knottingley WF11 126 B5
Castleford Normanton & District Hospl (General) WF10 124 B6
Castleford Rd WF6 123 C3
Castleford Sta WF10 124 D7
Castleford Three Lane Ends Jun & Inf Schs WF10 124 A8
Castleford Townville Inf Sch WF10 125 C7
Castleford Wheldon Inf Sch WF10 124 D8
Castlegate HD1 154 A6
Castlegate Dr
Bradford BD10 56 C6
Pontefract WF8 146 C5
Castlegate House 17 HX5 134 F7
Castlegate Loop HD1 154 A6
Castlegate Slip HD1 154 A7
Castlemore Rd BD17 38 D2
Castleton Cl LS12 210 C3
Castleton Primary Sch LS12 210 B3
Castleton Rd LS12 210 B4
Castletown Dr OL13 106 B1
Castley La Castley LS21 25 B8
Leathley LS21 24 E8
Cat Hill La S36 192 D1
Cat La Elland HX4 133 F7
Sowerby Bridge HX2 111 B5
Cater St BD1 201 C3
Cath Ch of St Peter The BD1 201 C3
Cathcart St 6 Halifax HX3 92 B2
Leeds LS6 206 A3
Cathedral Church of All Saints The WF1 216 B2
Cathedral Cl Bradford BD1 201 C3
Wakefield WF1 216 A3
Cathedral Ret Pk WF2 216 A1
Cathedral Wlk WF1 216 B2
Catherine Cl HD3 135 A2
Catherine Cres 15 HX5 134 F6
Catherine Gr 12 LS11 214 B3
Catherine House La HX2 90 A6
Catherine Rd HD2 136 B4
Catherine Slack
Brighouse HD6 114 F6
Queensbury BD13 92 C6
Catherine St
Brighouse HD6 115 A3
Elland HX5 134 F6
Hemsworth WF9 163 A4
5 Keighley BD21 35 B5
Catlow St WF10 124 C7
Cattle La LS25 64 E7
Cattle Market St LS21 23 A8
Cattlelaith La WF11 126 D2
Caudle Hill WF11 104 F4
Cauldwell Gdns 2 BD5 74 E4
Caulms Wood Rd WF13 118 D1
Causeway Halifax HX1 203 F3
Ripponden HX4 133 A2
Causeway Cres HD7 152 D1
Causeway Foot HX2 71 D3
Causeway Garth La WF8 165 C4
Causeway Head La HX6 132 B5
Causeway Side HD7 152 D1
Causeway Wood Rd OL14 108 E4
Cautley Rd LS9 212 C2
Cavalier App LS9 212 C2
Cavalier Cl LS9 212 C2
Cavalier Ct LS9 212 C2
Cavalier Dr BD10 56 E8
Cavalier Gate LS9 212 C2
Cavalier Gdns LS9 212 C2
Cavalier Gn LS9 212 C2
Cavalier Mews LS9 212 C2
Cavalier View LS9 212 C2
Cave Cres WF2 141 E4
Cave Hill HX3 92 F4
Cave La WF3 120 E7
Cavendish Ct
Bradford BD10 56 C5
2 Keighley BD21 35 C7
Cavendish Dr Bingley BD16 37 B4
Guiseley LS20 39 D8
Cavendish First Sch BD10 56 D5
Cavendish Gr LS20 39 D8
Cavendish Mews LS17 43 D4
Cavendish Pl LS28 57 E1
Cavendish Rd
Bradford, Eccleshill BD2 56 C5
Bradford, Thorpe BD10 56 B7
Guiseley LS20 39 D8
Leeds LS2 206 B2
Cavendish Rise LS28 77 A7
Cavendish Sq 3 LS28 57 E1
Cavendish St
14 Halifax HX1 202 C3
Keighley BD21 35 C7
Leeds LS3 210 C4
Pudsey LS28 77 A7
3 Yeadon LS19 40 C7
Cavendish Terr 13 HX1 202 C3
Cavewell Cl WF5 140 F3
Cavewell Gdns WF5 140 F3
Cawcliffe Dr HD6 115 A5
Cawcliffe Rd HD6 115 A4
Cawley Garth WF16 117 E3
Cawley La WF16 117 E3
Cawley Lane Jun & Inf Sch WF16 117 E4
Cawood Haven BD6 93 E8
Cawthorne Ave HD2 136 A2
Cawthorne C of E Jun & Inf Sch S75 193 E4
Cawthorne La S75 193 F5
Cawthorne Rd WF2 160 B6
Caxton Rd LS21 22 E7
Caxton St LS22 13 E5
Caycroft Nook HX7 88 F5
Caygill Terr HX1 203 E2
Caythorne Wlk BD10 56 C5
Caythorpe Rd LS16 59 B7
Cecil Ave Baildon BD17 38 C4
Bradford BD7 74 B4
Brighouse HX3 114 E8
Cecil Gr LS12 209 F4
Cecil Mount LS12 209 F4
Cecil Rd LS12 209 F4
Cecil St 11 Haworth BD22 51 E8
9 Huddersfield HD1 154 A6
Leeds LS12 209 F4
Cedar Ave
Huddersfield HD1 153 F7
Leeds LS12 209 F3
Ossett WF5 140 E4
Cedar Cl Huddersfield HD7 152 F5
Leeds LS12 209 F3
Pontefract WF8 146 C5
Royston S71 179 A4
Cedar Covert LS22 13 E8
Cedar Ct WF10 124 E7
Cedar Dr Bradford BD12 94 E4
Dewsbury WF12 140 B7
Cedar Gr Elland HX4 134 B7
Featherstone WF7 145 D7
Sutton in C BD20 16 C5
Cedar Mount
Huddersfield HD1 153 F7
Leeds LS12 209 F3
Cedar Pl LS12 209 F3
Cedar Rd Dewsbury WF12 140 A7
Leeds LS12 209 F3
Normanton WF6 144 B7
Cedar St Bingley BD16 36 E5
Halifax HX1 202 B2
Huddersfield HD1 153 E7
Keighley BD21 35 B4
Leeds LS12 209 F3
Todmorden OL14 129 A8
Cedar Terr LS12 209 F3
Cedar Way BD19 117 A8
Cedar Wlk
Featherstone WF7 145 D6
Knottingley WF11 126 E2
Cedars The LS16 24 F2
Celandine Ave HD3 152 E8
Celandine Cl WF8 146 D7
Celandine Dr HD3 152 E8
Cemetery La Halifax HX6 112 A4
Keighley BD20 18 B2
Rothwell WF3 100 C2
Cemetery Rd Batley WF17 118 B5
Batley, Heckmondwike WF16 117 D4
Bingley BD16 36 E4
Bradford, Birks BD7, BD8 73 F6
Bradford, Moor Top BD12, BD6 94 B7
Dewsbury WF13 139 B7
Haworth BD22 50 F6
Hemsworth WF9 181 C8
Holmfirth HD7 188 F4
Huddersfield HD1 153 F7
Leeds LS11 214 A4
Normanton WF6 123 C2
Pudsey LS28 76 D8
Ryhill WF4 162 B1
Yeadon LS19 40 C8
Centenary Rd BD17 38 F4
Centenary Sq
Bradford BD1 201 B2
Dewsbury WF12 139 B4
Leeds LS2, LS9 212 A4
Centenary St 2 LS1 211 E4
Centenary Way WF17 118 B6
Central Arc BD19 116 E7
Central Ave Baildon BD17 38 B2
Bradford BD5 74 C4
Cleckheaton WF15 116 B5
Hemsworth WF9 163 A4
Huddersfield HD2 136 B2
Keighley BD22 34 F3
Shipley BD18 55 B7
South Elmsall WF9 182 F2
Central Ave E WF15 116 B5
Central Cl HD2 136 B3
Central Dr
Castleford WF10 124 A7
Huddersfield HD2 136 B3
Keighley BD22 34 F3
Royston S71 179 C3
Central Par
6 Cleckheaton BD19 116 E7
Leeds LS9 80 C3
Central Pk Halifax HX1 203 D1
Leeds LS11 211 E2
Central Rd
Huddersfield HD2 136 B3
Leeds LS1 211 F3
Central St
Dewsbury WF13 139 C8
Halifax HX1 203 E3
Hebden Bridge HX7 89 A3
Leeds LS1 211 E4
Central Street Infant Sch HX7 89 A3
Central View OL13 106 A2
Centre 27 Bsns Pk WF17 97 B3
Centre St 4 Bradford BD5 74 C3
Hemsworth WF9 181 D8
1 Liversedge WF16 117 C4
South Elmsall WF9 183 A3
Centuria Wlk HD3 152 E8
Century Pl BD8 55 C1
Century Rd HX5 134 F7
Ceres Rd LS22 14 A5
Chaddlewood Cl LS18 41 C1
Chadwell Springs BD16 54 A7
Chadwick Cres WF13 118 B1
Chadwick La WF14 137 F4
Chadwick St LS10 212 A2
Chadwick St S LS10 212 A2
Chaffinch Rd 6 BD8 73 C7
Chaffinch Wlk HD4 171 E7
Chain HD7 169 C5
Chain Rd Meltham HD7 170 A5
Slaithwaite HD7 169 F6
Chain St Bradford BD1 201 A3
Castleford WF10 124 C8
Chalcroft Cl WF16 117 E5
Chald La WF2 216 A1
Chalfont Rd LS16 59 B8
Chalice Cl LS10 99 E7
Challenge Way
Batley WF12 119 A3
Bradford BD4 75 D4
Challenger Cres S63 194 D1
Challis Gr BD5 74 E3
Chalner Ave LS27 97 F2
Chalner Cl LS27 97 F2
Chalwood HD2 136 E4
Chancellor St LS6 206 C3
Chancery Cl 20 HD1 154 A6
Chancery La 19
Huddersfield HD1 154 A6
Ossett WF5 140 C8
2 Wakefield WF1 216 B2
Chancery Rd WF5 140 B8
Chandler Cl WF17 96 E1
Chandler La HD7 171 D4
Chandlers Cl WF1 121 B5
Chandlers The LS2 212 A3
Chandos Ave LS8 204 B4
Chandos Fold LS8 204 B3
Chandos Garth LS8 204 B4
Chandos Gdns LS8 204 B4
Chandos Gn LS8 204 B4
Chandos Pl LS8 204 C4
Chandos St Bradford BD4 201 C2
4 Keighley BD21 35 B5
Chandos Terr LS8 204 C4
Chandos Wlk LS8 204 B3
Change La HX3 113 E2
Change View OL13 106 B4
Changegate BD22 51 B7
Changegate Ct 2 BD22 51 B7
Channing Way BD1 201 B2
Chantrell Ct LS2 212 A3
Chantry Bridge Ind Est WF1 216 C1
Chantry Cl Ilkley LS29 8 B3
Pontefract WF8 146 B7
Chantry Croft LS15 81 D7
Chantry Dr LS29 8 B4
Chantry Garth LS15 81 D7
Chantry Gr S71 179 C3
Chantry La LS24 48 E5
Chantry Rd WF2 141 E5
Chapel Allerton Hospl LS7 204 B2
Chapel Allerton Primary Sch LS7 204 A2
Chapel Ave Batley WF16 117 E5
Hebden Bridge HX7 89 B3
Chapel Bank HD7 189 E3
Chapel Cl Dewsbury WF12 139 D2
Elland HX4 134 B4
Garforth LS25 82 E7
Huddersfield HD4 171 F8
Shafton S72 180 C3
West Hardwick WF4 163 A7
Chapel Croft HD6 135 F7
Chapel Fold Batley WF17 118 A3
Bradford BD6 74 B1
Brighouse BD12 115 C8
Leeds, Beeston LS11 213 E2
Leeds, Burley LS6 205 D3
Lofthouse Gate WF1 121 B3
8 Pudsey LS28 76 E6
Chapel Garth WF7 164 A6
Chapel Gn 1 LS28 76 D6
Chapel Gr BD16 36 E5
Chapel Grange Sch BD15 73 D8
Chapel Hill Clayton DN5 194 C4
Clayton West HD8 175 E2
Huddersfield HD1 154 A5
1 Middleton LS10 99 D5
Mirfield WF14 137 F2
Morley LS27 98 A5
Slaithwaite HD7 152 D1
2 Yeadon LS19 40 B7
Chapel Hill La HD3 151 B5
Chapel House Rd BD12 94 D7
Chapel La Badsworth WF9 164 E2
Barwick in E LS15 63 E7
Batley WF16 117 E4
6 Batley, Birstall WF17 96 F1
Boston Spa LS23 30 D5
Bradford, Clayton Heights BD13 73 B2
Bradford, Lower Grange BD15 73 C8
Dearne S63 194 F1
Dewsbury WF12 139 D2
Emley HD8 175 B7
Garforth LS25 82 E7
Guiseley BD17 39 C5
Halifax HX3 113 D3
Halifax, Midgley HX2 90 B2
Halifax, Southowram HX3 114 B4
Halton East BD23 1 E8
Huddersfield, Moldgreen HD5 154 D5
Huddersfield, Wellhouse HD7 152 D4
Ilkley LS29 8 A4
Keighley BD21 35 B7
Keighley, Laycock BD22 34 C7
Kippax LS25 83 B1
Kirk Smeaton WF8 166 E6
Leeds, Armley LS12 209 F3
Leeds, Farnley LS12 77 E5
Leeds, Headingley Hill LS6 205 D4
Queensbury BD13 72 E1
Royston S71 179 C1
South Elmsall WF9 183 B3
Sowerby Bridge HX6 112 D4
Yeadon LS19 40 B7
Chapel Pl 10 LS6 59 D5
Chapel Rd Bingley BD16 36 E5
Bradford BD12 94 E6
Bradford, Low Moor BD12 94 D6
Leeds LS7 204 A1
Steeton BD20 17 C5
Chapel Row BD15 53 C6
Chapel Sq 1 LS6 59 D5
Chapel St Addingham LS29 6 F8
Bingley BD16 36 E5
Bradford BD1 201 C3
Bradford, Brownroyd Hill BD6 74 C1
Bradford, Eccleshill BD2 56 D4
Bradford, Holme Top BD5 74 D4
Brighouse HD6 114 E5
Cleckheaton BD19 116 E8
Cleckheaton, Hightown WF15 116 C5
Denholme BD13 71 D8
Dewsbury WF12 139 C6
East Ardsley WF3 120 C7
East Ardsley, Black Gates WF3 98 F1
Elland HX4 134 B4
Halifax HX2 202 A4
Huddersfield HD1 154 A5
Huddersfield, Blue Bell Hill HD4 153 E2
7 Huddersfield, Moldgreen HD5 154 D5
Huddersfield, Netherton HD4 171 C7
Knottingley WF11 127 A5
Leeds, Halton LS15 81 A8
Leeds, Headingley LS6 59 D5
Littleborough OL15 129 D2
Liversedge WF15 117 C4
Lofthouse Gate WF3 121 E5
Mirfield WF14 138 A5
Ossett WF5 141 A4
Pudsey, Calverley LS28 57 B6
Pudsey, Rodley LS13 57 E5
Pudsey, Stanningley LS28 57 E1
Queensbury BD13 72 E1
Rothwell WF3 100 D3
Ryhill WF4 162 B1
Shafton S72 180 C3
Silsden BD20 5 E2
Slaithwaite HD7 152 B5
Thornton BD13 72 D6
4 Todmorden OL14 108 D6
Yeadon LS19 40 B4
Chapel St N HX3 91 F3
Chapel St S 7 OL14 108 A1
Chapel Terr Bradford BD15 54 B1
Honley HD7 171 F4
Huddersfield HD4 153 D4
9 Leeds LS6 59 D5
Ripponden HX6 133 C7
Sowerby Bridge HX6 111 D3
14 Thornton BD13 72 D6
Chapel Wlk Bingley BD16 36 F3
Bradford BD2 56 D4
Chapel Yd LS15 81 D6
Chapelfields WF9 182 B1
Chapelgate HD7 189 D3
Chapeltown Halifax HX1 203 D3
Pudsey LS28 76 D6
Chapeltown Bsns Ctr LS7 207 D4
Chapeltown Rd LS7 207 D4
Chapman St Bradford BD4 75 D6
Leeds LS9 207 E1
Charing Cross Mews LS6 206 B3
Chariot Way WF8 165 A4
Charles Ave Bradford BD3 75 D7
Halifax HX3 114 A4
Huddersfield HD3 153 A8
Leeds LS9 212 C2
Lofthouse Gate WF1 121 B5
Wakefield WF1 142 F3
Charles Cotton Cl WF2 141 D8
Charles Ct 7 BD22 51 C2
Charles Gdns LS11 211 D1
Charles Gr LS26 101 C6
Charles St Batley WF17 118 C4
Bingley BD16 36 F3
Bradford BD1 201 C3
Brighouse HD6 115 A3
Castleford WF10 124 E7
Cleckheaton BD19 117 B8
Dewsbury WF12 139 E8
Dewsbury, Dewsbury Moor WF13 138 F8
Dewsbury, Ravensthorpe WF13 138 E5
Elland HX5 134 F6
Halifax HX1 203 F3
Horbury WF4 159 D7
Horsforth LS18 58 B7
Huddersfield HD4 153 D4
Morley LS27 98 B4
Ossett WF5 140 F3
Otley LS21 23 A7
Pudsey LS28 57 D3
Queensbury BD13 72 D1
Ryhill WF4 162 A1
Shipley BD17 55 B8
South Hiendley S72 180 E5
15 Sowerby Bridge HX6 112 B5
Wakefield WF1 216 C1
Charles View WF4 159 F3
Charlestown Est WF7 164 A4
Charlestown Rd HX3 203 F4
Charlesworth Gr HX2 202 A4
Charlesworth Pl WF3 122 C6
Charlesworth Sq BD19 117 A8
Charlesworth St WF12 139 C4
Charlesworth Terr HX2 202 A4
Charlesworth Way WF2 216 A1
Charlesworth's Bldgs 3 WF4 141 A1
Charleville WF9 182 E4
Charlotte Cl WF17 96 F3
Charlotte Ct BD22 51 E8
Charlotte Gr 3 Leeds LS15 81 B8
Ossett WF5 140 F4
Charlotte St WF1 216 C1
Charlton Ct HX2 202 A4
Charlton Gr 6 Leeds LS9 80 A7
Silsden BD20 17 F8
Charlton Mount 2 LS9 212 C3
Charlton Pl LS9 80 A7
Charlton Rd LS9 80 A7
Charlton St LS9 80 A7
Charnwood Bank WF16 117 E4
Charnwood Cl BD2 56 C2
Charnwood Gr BD2 56 C2
Charnwood Rd BD2 56 C2
Charterhouse Rd BD10 39 B1
Charteris Rd BD8 73 C7
Chartists Way LS27 98 A3
Chartwell Ct LS17 44 B5
Charville Gdns LS17 44 F3
Chase The Burley in W LS29 22 A7
Garforth LS25 83 B7
Keighley BD21 34 F8
Lofthouse Gate WF3 122 A6
Wetherby LS22 13 F6
Yeadon LS19 40 A4
Chase Way BD5 74 E2
Chassum Gr BD9 55 B2
Chaster St WF17 118 A6
Chat Hill Rd BD13 72 F5
Chatham St Bradford BD3 56 A1
Halifax HX1 203 D3
8 Sowerby Bridge HX6 112 B5
Chatswood Ave LS11 98 F8
Chatswood Cres LS11 98 F8
Chatswood Dr LS11 213 F1
Chatsworth Ave 1 LS28 76 A8
Chatsworth Cl
Huddersfield HD5 154 D4
Leeds LS8 208 A3
Chatsworth Cres LS28 76 A8
Chatsworth Ct WF12 139 F7
Chatsworth Dr
2 Pudsey LS28 76 A8
Wetherby LS22 13 C6
Chatsworth Fall LS28 76 A8
Chatsworth Ind Est LS12 210 A2
Chatsworth Mews 5 LS27 98 B3
Chatsworth Pl BD8 55 B2
Chatsworth Rd Leeds LS8 208 A3
Pudsey LS28 76 A8
Chatsworth Rise LS28 76 A8
Chatsworth St BD21 35 D7
Chatsworth Terr WF12 139 F7
Chatts Wood Fold BD12 95 B5
Chaucer Ave
Lofthouse Gate WF3 121 E6
Pudsey LS28 76 F6
Chaucer Cl HD7 171 F3

Chaucer Gdns LS28 76 F6
Chaucer Gr LS28 76 F6
Chaucer St HX1 202 B2
Cheapside Batley WF17 118 D5
Bradford BD1 201 B3
Cleckheaton BD19 116 E7
Halifax HX1 203 E3
Normanton WF6 123 B2
Shelf HX3 93 C6
Wakefield WF1 216 A2
Cheddington Gr BD15 73 B8
Cheese Gate Nab Side HD7 190 A2
Cheetham St 20 HX7 89 A3
Chelburn View OL15 129 C1
Chellow Dene Mid Sch BD8 73 D8
Chellow Grange Rd BD9 54 C3
Chellow La BD9 54 D1
Chellow St BD5 74 D2
Chellow Terr BD9 54 D1
Chellow Way WF12 139 C7
Chelmsford Rd BD3 75 C8
Chelmsford Terr BD3 75 C7
Chelsea Cl LS12 209 F2
Chelsea Mansions HX3 93 A2
Chelsea Rd BD7 73 F4
Chelsea St BD21 35 B6
Chelsfield Ct LS15 62 F3
Chelsfield Way LS15 62 F3
Chelston Gr HD7 171 E4
Cheltenham Ave LS29 8 F4
Cheltenham Gdns HX3 113 D4
Cheltenham Pl HX3 113 D4
Cheltenham Rd BD2 55 F5
Cheltenham St LS12 210 A2
Chelwood Ave LS8 43 E3
Chelwood Cres LS8 43 F2
Chelwood Dr
Bradford BD15 73 A7
Leeds LS8 43 F2
Chelwood Gr LS8 43 F3
Chelwood Mount LS8 43 F3
Chelwood Pl LS8 43 E3
Chenies Cl LS14 61 E1
Chepstow Cl LS25 83 B7
Chequerfield Ave WF8 146 F8
Chequerfield Cl WF10 124 A6
Chequerfield Dr WF8 146 F7
Chequerfield Infant Sch WF8 146 F7
Chequerfield La WF8 146 F8
Chequerfield Mount WF8 146 F7
Chequerfield Rd WF8 146 F7
Chequers Cl WF8 146 F7
Chequers Ct WF8 146 F8
Cheriton Dr BD13 72 F1
Cherry Cl S71 179 A4
Cherry Ct LS9 207 E1
Cherry Fields BD2 55 E4
Cherry Garth WF9 181 C6
Cherry Gr LS29 7 F4
Cherry Hills S75 178 A1
Cherry La HD8 175 F2
Cherry Lea Ct LS19 40 B5
Cherry Nook Rd HD2 136 E3
Cherry Pl LS9 207 E1
Cherry Rise LS14 62 C8
Cherry Row LS9 207 E1
Cherry St 2 Haworth BD22 51 E8
Keighley BD21 35 E8
Cherry Tree Ave
Bradford BD10 56 D7
Knottingley WF11 126 E3
Cherry Tree Cl
Huddersfield HD7 152 F5
Mapplewell S75 178 C1
Cherry Tree Cres
Pudsey LS28 57 D3
Walton WF2 161 B7
Cherry Tree Ct WF3 120 C7
Cherry Tree Ctr 15 HD1 154 A6
Cherry Tree Dr Elland HX4 134 C7
Pudsey LS28 57 D3
Walton WF2 161 B7
Cherry Tree Gdns BD10 38 F1
Cherry Tree Rd WF2 161 B7
Cherry Tree Rise BD21 35 E6
Cherry Tree Row BD16 53 B7
Cherry Tree Wlk
East Ardsley WF3 120 C7
Holmfirth HD7 189 D4
Cherrywood Cl LS14 45 B1
Cherrywood Gdns LS14 45 B1
Chervana Ct BD4 75 E4
Cherwell Croft LS25 83 B5
Cherwell Dr BD6 93 F7
Chesham St Bradford BD7 74 C6
Keighley BD21 35 D8
Chesil Bank HD3 153 B6
Chesilton Ave HD3 153 B7
Chesney Ave LS10 215 D4
Chesney Pk Ind Est LS10 215 D4
Chesnut End LS23 30 E7
Chessington Dr WF4 157 D3
Chester Cl 3 HX3 92 B1
Chester Ct 1 HX3 92 B1
Chester Gr 2 HX3 92 B1
Chester Pl 4 HX3 92 B1
Chester Rd HX3 92 B1
Chester St Bradford BD5 201 B2
Halifax, Woodside HX3 92 B1
Leeds LS12 209 F4
3 Sowerby Bridge HX6 112 B4
Chester Terr HX3 92 B1
Chesterton Ct
Horbury WF4 141 C2
Leeds LS15 81 D6
Chesterton Dr HD7 171 F3
Chestnut Ave Batley WF17 118 A4
Boston Spa LS23 30 C8
Brierley S72 180 F2
Leeds, Cross Gates LS15 62 D2
Leeds, Hyde Park LS6 205 E3
Todmorden OL14 108 A7
Walton WF2 161 A6
Wetherby LS22 13 D6
Chestnut Cl Elland HX4 134 B7
Featherstone WF7 145 D7
Huddersfield HD4 154 A2
Ilkley LS29 8 E3
Keighley BD22 34 F6
Chestnut Cres WF6 144 A7
Chestnut Ct
Ripponden HX6 132 D4
Shipley BD18 54 F7
Chestnut Dr Leeds LS16 42 B5
South Hiendley S72 180 D5
Chestnut Garth HD3 153 B7
Chestnut Gdns LS12 209 E2
Chestnut Gn WF8 125 F1
Chestnut Gr
Boston Spa LS23 30 C8
Crofton WF4 143 F1
Hemsworth WF9 181 F6
Leeds LS6 205 E3
Pontefract WF8 146 D6
Pudsey LS28 57 B6
Shipley BD2 55 E4
Chestnut Meadows WF14 137 F8
Chestnut Pl LS6 205 E3
Chestnut Rd 17 LS6 205 E3
Chestnut Rise LS12 209 E2
Chestnut St Glusburn BD20 16 D6
Halifax HX1 202 B2
Huddersfield HD2 136 D3
Leeds LS6 205 E3
South Elmsall WF9 182 F1
Chestnut Terr WF12 139 C3
Chestnut Way LS16 42 B5
Chestnut Wlk
Knottingley WF11 126 D3
Wakefield WF2 142 A8
Chestnuts The WF8 126 A4
Chevet Croft WF2 160 E7
Chevet Gr WF2 160 E7
Chevet Hill WF2 160 F3
Chevet La Notton WF4 179 B8
Wakefield WF2, WF4 160 F6
Walton WF2 161 B2
Walton, Woolgreaves WF2, WF4 160 F6
Chevet Level WF2 160 F4
Chevet Mount BD15 73 A8
Chevet Park Ct WF2 160 E3
Chevet Rise S71 179 B4
Chevet Terr WF1 143 A1
Chevet View S71 179 A4
Chevin Ave Menston LS29 22 A5
Otley LS21 23 B6
Chevin End Rd LS20 22 D3
Chevin Forest Park LS21 23 D5
Chevin Side LS21 23 A6
Chevinedge Cres HX3 113 D1
Chevington Ct LS19 40 A3
Chevins Cl WF17 117 F8
Cheviot Ave HD7 170 F1
Cheviot Cl WF9 181 F7
Cheviot Ct LS25 82 F5
Cheviot Gate BD12 94 B6
Cheviot Pl WF11 126 F4
Cheviot Way WF14 137 F2
Cheyne Wlk 12 BD22 35 A6
Chichester St LS12 209 F4
Chickenley La WF12 140 B7
Chickenly Com Jun & Inf Sch WF12 140 A7
Chidswell Gdns WF12 119 B3
Chidswell La Batley WF12 119 A3
Ossett WF5 119 B2
Child La WF15 116 F1
Childs La BD18 55 E6
Childs Rd WF2 141 D8
Chiltern Ave
Castleford WF10 123 F5
Huddersfield HD3 135 A1
Knottingley WF11 126 E4
Chiltern Cl LS25 82 F5
Chiltern Ct Garforth LS25 82 F5
Hemsworth WF9 181 F7
Pudsey LS13 57 E5
Chiltern Dr
Ackworth M T WF7 163 F5
Mirfield WF14 137 F2
Chiltern Rd WF12 118 F1
Chiltern Way WF15 116 D5
Chilwell Cl S71 178 F1
Chilwell Gdns S71 178 F1
Chilwell Mews S71 178 F1
Chimes The HD5 155 C7
Chimney La HD8 155 D4
Chinewood Ave WF17 118 B6
Chippendale Ct LS29 22 B4
Chippendale Rise
Bradford BD8 73 D8
Otley LS21 11 A1
Chirton Gr LS8 61 A5
Chislehurst Pl BD5 74 C4
Chiswick St LS6 205 E2
Chiswick Terr 25 LS6 205 E2
Choppards Bank Rd HD7 189 A2
Choppards La HD7 189 A2
Chorley La 2 LS2 211 D4
Chrisharben Pk BD14 73 C4
Chrismoor BD10 56 A7
Christ Church Ave LS12 209 E4
Christ Church C of E Jun & Inf Sch HX2 112 D8
Christ Church C of E Junior Sch HX6 112 C5
Christ Church Mount LS12 209 E4
Christ Church Par LS12 209 E4
Christ Church Pl LS12 209 E4
Christ Church Rd LS12 209 E4
Christ Church St 3 OL13 106 A3
Christ Church Terr LS12 209 E4
Christ Church View LS12 209 E4
Christ Church Woodhouse CE Inf & Jun Sch
Huddersfield, Riddings HD2 136 D4
Huddersfield, Sheepridge HD2 136 C3
Christ the King RC Primary Sch LS13 58 E1
Christiana Terr LS27 98 B5
Christopher Rd LS6 206 A4
Christopher St 1 BD5 74 C3
Christopher Terr 2 BD5 74 C3
Church App LS25 82 F7
Church Ave Crofton WF1 143 D7
Gildersome LS27 97 C8
Horsforth LS18 41 B1
Huddersfield, Linthwaite HD7 152 E2
Huddersfield, Yews Hill HD4 153 E4
Leeds LS6 59 F7
South Kirkby WF9 182 C2
Swillington LS26 82 A2
Church Bank
Bradford BD1 201 C3
Halifax, Highroad Well HX2 112 D6
Sowerby Bridge HX6 112 C4
Church Bank La HX7 110 C3
Church Bank Way WF12 139 C4
Church Cl Crofton WF4 144 B2
Halifax HX1 203 D3
Halifax, Ovenden HX2 91 D5
Hemsworth WF9 181 D7
Leeds LS14 62 B4
Mapplewell S75 177 E1
Micklefield LS25 84 A8
Pool LS21 24 C7
Shepley HD8 190 E8
Sowerby Bridge HX6 111 E3
Swillington LS26 82 A2
Church Cres
Horsforth LS18 41 B1
Leeds LS17 43 C3
Netherton WF4 158 E6
Swillington LS26 82 B1
Yeadon LS19 40 A6
Church Cswy LS23 14 F1
Church Ct Bradford BD7 73 F5
Keighley BD20 18 F2
Normanton WF6 123 A1
Ossett WF5 140 D7
Yeadon LS19 40 B6
Church Dr Brierley S72 180 F3
East Keswick LS17 28 B5
South Kirkby WF9 182 C2
Church Farm LS14 45 F6
Church Farm Cl
Normanton WF6 122 F4
Rothwell WF3 100 C1
Church Farm View LS15 63 E7
Church Field Rd DN5 194 E4
Church Fields BD2 56 D2
Church Fields Mews WF10 124 F6
Church Garth
Castleford WF10 124 F6
Pool LS21 24 C7
Church Gate LS18 41 B1
Church Gdns
Garforth LS25 82 F6
Gildersome LS27 97 C7
Leeds LS17 43 D3
Church Gn Halifax HX2 91 E1
Kirkburton HD8 173 F6
Church Gr Horsforth LS18 41 B1
South Kirkby WF9 182 C2
Church Grange 4 BD19 116 E7
Church Hill Baildon BD17 38 D4
Bramham LS23 30 D2
Bramhope LS16 24 D3
Halifax HX2 90 D1
Royston S71 179 D3
Thorner LS14 46 A6
Church Hill Gdns LS28 57 F2
Church Hill Gn LS28 57 F2
Church Hill Mount LS28 57 F2
Church House 13 HX5 134 F7
Church La Bardsey LS17 28 C2
Batley WF16 117 D3
Bradford BD6 94 B8
3 Brighouse HD6 115 A2
Brighouse, Elland Lower Edge HD6 135 D7
Brighouse, Southowram. HX3 114 C4
Brighouse, Waring Green HD6 115 A3
Cawthorne S75 193 F4
Clayton West HD8 175 F2
Cleckheaton BD19 117 C8
Clifton LS21 10 B2
Collingham LS22 13 B1
Crigglestone WF4 160 A4
Darrington WF8 147 D5
Dewsbury, Dewsbury Moor WF13 138 F8
Dewsbury, Thornhill WF12 139 E2
East Ardsley WF3 120 C7
Church La continued
East Ardsley, Upper Green WF3 119 D7
Elland HX4 134 A4
Featherstone WF7 124 C1
Garforth LS25 82 F7
Guiseley BD17 39 C5
Halifax HX2 91 E1
Harewood LS17 26 F7
Hebden Bridge HX7 88 E3
Heptonstall HX7 88 F5
High Hoyland S75 176 C1
Horsforth LS18 41 B1
Huddersfield HD4 171 B6
Huddersfield, Linthwaite HD7 152 E1
Huddersfield, Moldgreen HD5 154 D6
Huddersfield, Newsome HD4 154 A2
Kippax LS25 83 B1
Kirkheaton HD5 155 B7
Leeds LS6 59 F7
Leeds LS2 212 A3
Leeds, Adel LS16 42 C5
Leeds, Chapel Allerton LS7 204 A2
Leeds, Manston LS15 62 D3
Liversedge WF15 116 B3
Liversedge, Knowler Hill WF15 117 A5
Lofthouse Gate WF1 121 B5
Marsden HD7 168 F4
Marsden, Scammonden HX4 150 F5
Micklefield LS25 83 F7
Mickletown LS26 102 C2
Mirfield WF14 138 C5
Netherton WF4 158 E7
Normanton WF6 123 A1
Normanton WF7 144 D8
2 Pontefract WF8 146 D8
Pool LS21 24 C7
Pudsey LS28 76 E7
Ryhill S71 179 F7
Shepley HD8 190 E8
Swillington LS26 82 A1
Church Lane Ave WF1 121 B5
Church Meadows
Batley WF17 96 D1
Bramham LS23 30 D3
Church Mews
Boston Spa LS23 30 D8
5 Bradford BD6 93 E7
Church Mount
Horsforth LS18 41 B1
South Kirkby WF9 182 C2
Church Pk WF15 116 E2
Church Pl Garforth LS25 82 F7
Halifax HX1 203 D3
Church Rd Batley WF17 117 F8
Bradford BD6 94 B8
Cawthorne S75 193 E4
Horsforth LS18 41 B1
Leeds LS12 209 F3
Leeds, Bank LS9 212 B3
Liversedge FW15 116 E2
Lofthouse Gate WF3 121 F5
Normanton WF6 122 E4
Sutton in C BD20 16 D5
Swillington LS26 102 E8
Todmorden OL14 107 E8
Church Row LS29 9 A6
Church Sch The BD13 72 E6
Church Side LS26 102 C2
Church Side Cl 15 HX3 92 C1
Church Side Dr 16 HX3 92 C1
Church Sq LS25 82 F7
Church St Addingham LS29 7 A8
Batley, Birstall WF17 96 E1
Batley, Heckmondwike WF16 117 D3
Bingley BD16 37 A2
Boston Spa LS23 30 D8
Bradford BD8 55 C1
Bradford, Beck Hill BD6 93 E7
Brighouse HD6 135 F8
Brotherton WF11 126 C8
Castleford WF10 124 D8
Cawthorne S75 193 F4
Cleckheaton BD19 116 E7
Cleckheaton, Hightown WF15 116 C5
Cullingworth BD13 52 D6
Dewsbury WF13 139 D8
Dewsbury, Ravensthorpe WF13 138 E5
Elland HX5 134 F7
Elland, West Vale HX4 134 D7
Emley HD8 175 C7
Gildersome LS27 97 C7
Glusburn BD20 16 D7
Guiseley LS20 22 F1
Halifax HX1 203 F2
Haworth BD22 51 B7
Hebden Bridge HX7 110 E8
Heptonstall HX7 88 F5
Holmfirth HD7 189 F6
Honley HD7 171 F5
Horbury WF4 141 B1
Huddersfield HD1 154 B6
Huddersfield, Longwood HD3 153 A6
Huddersfield, Moldgreen HD5 154 D6
Huddersfield, Paddock HD1 153 D5
Huddersfield, Town End HD7 152 D4
Huddersfield, Yews Hill HD4 153 E4
Ilkley LS29 8 B4
Keighley BD21 35 C6
Keighley, Eastwood BD21 35 D7
Church St continued
Leeds LS10 215 E3
Leeds, Kirkstall LS5 59 A4
Liversedge WF15 117 A5
Mapplewell S75 178 C1
Mapplewell, Bloomhouse S75 177 E1
Morley LS27 98 A5
Ossett WF5 140 D7
8 Oxenhope BD22 51 C2
Rothwell, Churchfields LS26 100 E5
Rothwell, Woodlesford LS26 101 C7
Royston S71 179 C3
Royston, Carlton S71 179 D1
Shipley BD18 55 D8
Slaithwaite HD7 169 F8
South Elmsall WF9 183 A2
Todmorden OL14 107 E8
Wakefield WF1 142 C4
Wetherby LS22 13 E5
Woolley WF4 177 F7
Yeadon LS19 40 A6
Church Terr
Clayton West HD8 175 D1
Halifax HX4 91 D5
Holmfirth HD7 189 A5
Church Top WF9 182 C2
Church View
Cleckheaton BD19 116 B8
Crigglestone WF4 159 F5
Featherstone WF7 145 C5
Holmfirth HD7 188 C2
Kippax LS25 83 D2
South Kirkby WF9 182 C2
Sowerby Bridge HX6 112 C4
Thorner LS14 45 F6
Wakefield WF1 142 E2
Church View Cl WF4 162 C1
Church View Mews LS23 30 D5
Church Villas WF9 182 C2
Church Way Keighley BD21 35 C6
3 Morley LS27 98 A5
Church Wlk Batley WF17 118 A3
Dewsbury WF12 139 E2
Leeds LS2 212 A3
Northowram HX3 93 A2
Todmorden OL14 108 B1
Church Wood Ave LS16 59 C7
Church Wood Mount LS16 59 C7
Church Wood Rd LS16 59 C6
Churchbalk Dr WF8 146 E6
Churchbalk La WF8 146 E6
Churchfarm Garth LS17 44 F4
Churchfield Cl 5 WF15 117 A4
Churchfield Croft
Normanton WF6 122 F4
Rothwell LS26 100 F5
Churchfield Gr LS26 100 E6
Churchfield La
Castleford WF10 124 F7
Kirk Smeaton WF8 166 F7
Rothwell LS26 100 E6
Churchfield Rd LS26 100 F5
Churchfield St 1 WF17 118 C5
Churchfield Terr 6 WF15 117 A4
Churchfields Crofton WF4 144 A1
Huddersfield HD2 136 F3
Ryhill WF4 162 B2
Churchfields Rd HD6 115 A3
Churchgate LS16 24 D3
Churchill Flats LS21 24 C7
Churchill Gdns 25 LS2 206 B2
Churchill Gr Batley WF16 117 E3
Wakefield WF2 160 E8
Churchill Rd BD13 72 F6
Churchill St OL14 107 E8
Churchill Way BD20 16 E7
Churchside Villas LS26 102 C2
Churchtown Cres OL13 106 B1
Churchville LS25 84 A8
Churchville Ave LS25 83 F7
Churchville Dr LS25 84 A7
Churchville Terr LS25 84 A7
Churchway WF4 144 A1
Churchwood Cl HD7 151 F1
Churn La HX2 112 D7
Churn Milk La HX3 92 A4
Churwell Ave 3 WF13 117 F3
Churwell Cl WF10 124 D6
Churwell Primary Sch LS27 98 B7
Churwell Vale WF12 119 A2
Cinder Hill HD8 174 B7
Cinder Hill Rd OL14 108 E6
Cinder Hills Rd HD7 189 B4
Cinder La Boston Spa LS23 30 E6
Castleford WF10 124 C8
Lindley LS21 11 F5
Cinderhills La HX3 113 E3
Circle The S66 146 E7
City La HX3 91 E2
City of Leeds Coll of Music LS2 206 B1
City of Leeds Sch LS6 206 A4
City Park Ind Est LS12 78 C3
City Rd BD8 74 C8
City Sq LS1 211 E3
City Square Mall LS1 211 F3
City Varieties Music Hall LS1 211 F4
City West One Office Pk LS12 213 D3
Cityway Ind Est BD4 75 A5
Clapgate LS21 23 A8
Clapgate La HX6 132 E7

Clapgate Primary Sch
LS10 99 F5
Clapham Dene Rd LS15 62 B1
Clapham St BD13 71 E8
Claphouse Fold S75 177 A5
Clapton Ave HX1 202 C2
Clara Dr LS28 57 A8
Clara Rd BD2 55 F5
Clara St Brighouse HD6 115 A1
Huddersfield HD1 154 A8
Huddersfield, Cowlersley HD4 153 A3
Huddersfield, Fartown HD1 136 A1
Pudsey LS28 57 D2
Clare Cres BD12 94 C2
Clare Hall La HX1 203 E2
Clare Hill HD1 154 A7
Clare Rd Bradford BD12 94 C2
Cleckheaton BD19 116 D7
Halifax HX1 203 E2
Hebden Bridge HX7 89 D1
Clare St HX1 203 E2
Claremont Batley WF16 117 D4
Bradford BD7 74 D6
Pudsey LS28 76 F8
Claremont Ave
9 Leeds LS3 206 A1
Shipley BD18 55 E6
Claremont Cres
Crofton WF4 161 F8
Leeds LS6 59 F5
Shipley BD18 55 E6
Claremont Ct LS6 59 E6
Claremont Dr LS6 59 E6
Claremont Gdns
Bingley BD16 37 A4
Pudsey LS28 57 D2
Claremont Gr
4 Leeds LS3 206 A1
Pudsey LS28 76 E7
Shipley BD18 55 F6
Claremont Pl LS12 209 D3
Claremont Rd
Dewsbury WF13 118 B1
Leeds LS6 59 E6
Shipley BD18 55 E6
Claremont St
7 Cleckheaton BD19 116 D8
Huddersfield HD1 154 A7
Leeds LS12 209 D3
Rothwell LS26 101 C6
Sowerby Bridge HX6 112 C5
Wakefield WF1 142 E4
Claremont Terr
Bradford BD5 74 D6
Leeds LS12 209 D3
Todmorden OL14 129 D5
Wakefield WF2 142 A5
Claremont View 3
Leeds LS3 206 A1
8 Rothwell LS26 101 C6
Claremount Rd HX3 92 C1
Claremount Terr 3 HX3 92 C2
Clarence Dr Horsforth LS18 58 B7
Menston LS29 21 F6
Clarence Gdns LS18 58 B7
Clarence Mews LS18 58 B7
Clarence Rd Horsforth LS18 58 B7
Leeds LS10 212 B2
Shipley BD18 54 F8
Wakefield WF2 142 B3
Clarence St Batley WF17 118 D5
Cleckheaton BD19 116 D7
Halifax HX1 203 D3
Leeds LS13 58 C1
Clarence Terr
Dewsbury WF12 139 D6
1 Pudsey LS28 76 E8
Clarence Wlk WF2 142 A5
Clarendon Ct WF1 216 B3
Clarendon Pl Halifax HX1 202 C2
Leeds LS2 206 A2
2 Queensbury BD13 92 C8
Clarendon Rd Bingley BD16 37 B4
Boston Spa LS23 30 C8
Leeds LS2 206 A1
Clarendon St
9 Haworth BD22 51 C6
Hebden Bridge HX7 89 E1
Keighley BD21 35 B5
Wakefield WF1 216 B3
Clarendon Terr LS28 76 E6
Clarendon Way LS2 206 A1
Clarges St BD5 74 D3
Clarion Field LS29 22 D5
Clarion St WF1 142 E4
Clark Ave LS9 212 C3
Clark Cres LS9 212 C3
Clark Gr LS9 212 C2
Clark La LS9 212 C3
Clark Mount LS9 212 C3
Clark Rd LS9 212 C3
Clark Row LS9 212 C2
Clark Spring Cl LS27 98 A7
Clark Spring Rise LS27 98 B7
Clark Terr LS9 212 C3
Clark View LS9 212 C2
Clarke Cres WF6 144 A7
Clarke Gr WF1 121 E1
Clarke La HD7 170 E2
Clarke Rd WF3 119 E5
Clarke St Dewsbury WF13 118 A1
Pudsey LS28 57 B6
Clarkson Ave WF16 117 E4
Clarkson Cl WF16 117 E4
Clarkson Ct WF6 123 C1
Clarkson St Dewsbury WF13 138 E6
Wakefield WF2 142 A5
Clarkson View LS6 206 A4
Clarydon Pl 2 WF16 117 D4
Clattering Stones Rd HX7 110 E2
Clay Butts HD2 135 E2
Clay Hill Dr BD12 94 D4
Clay House La HX4 134 D7
Clay La HD7 152 A1
Clay Pit La LS2, LS7 206 C1
Clay Pits La Halifax HX1 202 B4
Ripponden HX6 132 B7
Clay St Halifax HX1 202 B3
Sowerby Bridge HX6 112 B4
Sowerby Bridge HX6 112 C5
Clay Well HD7 152 D4
Clayborn View BD19 116 E6
Clayfield Bglws WF11 126 C4
Clayfield Dr BD7 74 A2
Claypit La Ledsham LS25 104 C7
Thorner LS14 45 F5
Clayton Ave Dearne S63 194 B1
Kippax LS25 83 C2
Upton WF9 183 E8
Clayton C of E First Sch
BD14 73 C4
Clayton (CE) First Sch
BD14 73 B4
Clayton Cl LS10 215 F2
Clayton Cotts 2 WF4 141 A1
Clayton Ct
Featherstone WF7 145 C5
Leeds LS16 58 F8
Leeds LS10 215 F2
Clayton Dr LS10 215 F2
Clayton Fields HD2 153 F8
Clayton Gr LS19 40 B7
Clayton Grange 2 LS16 58 F8
Clayton Hall Rd BD20 16 E6
Clayton Holt WF9 182 B1
Clayton Hospl WF1 216 A3
Clayton La Bradford BD5 74 E4
Bradford, Clayton BD14 73 B4
Dearne S63 194 B2
Clayton Mews WF6 123 A4
Clayton Middle Sch BD14 73 C4
Clayton Pl WF6 123 A4
Clayton Rd Bradford BD7 73 F5
Leeds LS10 215 F2
Clayton Rise Keighley BD20 35 A8
Lofthouse Gate WF1 121 B5
Clayton St Rothwell LS26 100 F5
Wakefield WF2 142 A5
Clayton Terr BD13 52 D5
Clayton View WF9 182 B1
Clayton Way LS10 215 F2
Clayton West Sta HD8 175 F3
Clayton Wood Bank LS16 41 F1
Clayton Wood Cl LS16 41 F1
Clayton Wood Ct LS16 41 F1
Clayton Wood Rd LS16 41 F1
Clayton Wood Rise LS16 41 F1
Claytons Bldgs WF7 145 D8
Clearings The LS10 99 D8
Cleasby Rd LS29 22 A4
Cleavesty La LS17 28 B6
Cleckheaton Golf Course
BD19 95 A2
Cleckheaton Rd BD12 94 D6
Cleeve Hill LS19 40 B4
Cleevethorpe Gr WF2 142 E1
Clegg La HX4 133 F7
Clegg St 10 BD12 94 C3
Clement St 9 Bradford BD8 73 F8
Huddersfield HD1 153 F8
Huddersfield, Paddock Brow HD4 153 D4
5 Sowerby Bridge HX6 112 B4
Wakefield WF2 141 F5
Clement Terr
Dewsbury WF12 139 C6
Rothwell LS26 100 E4
Cleopatra Pl 4 LS13 58 C1
Clerk Green St WF17 118 B4
Clervaux Ct BD14 73 D5
Clevedon Pl 4 HX3 92 A2
Clevedon Way S71 179 B4
Cleveland Ave Halifax HX3 113 D4
Horbury WF2 141 D2
Knottingley WF11 126 E4
Meltham HD7 170 F1
Cleveland Garth WF2 141 D2
Cleveland Gr WF2 141 D2
Cleveland Pl 3 HX7 89 A3
Cleveland Rd Bradford BD9 55 B3
Huddersfield HD1 153 D7
Cleveland St OL14 86 B1
Cleveland Way HD8 173 F3
Cleveley Gdns HX7 110 E8
Cleveleys Ave Leeds LS11 213 F4
14 Sowerby Bridge HX6 112 B5
Cleveleys Ct LS11 213 F4
Cleveleys Gdns 12 HX6 112 B5
Cleveleys Mount 4 LS11 213 F4
Cleveleys Rd LS11 213 F4
Cleveleys St LS11 213 F4
Cleveleys Terr 3 LS11 213 F4
Cliff Cl HD3 153 B6
Cliff Cres Halifax HX2 202 A1
Kippax LS25 83 C1
Cliff Ct 1 Leeds LS6 206 A4
Liversedge WF15 117 A3
Cliff Dr WF4 159 D5
Cliff Gdns HX2 202 A1
Cliff Gr WF4 159 C4
Cliff Hill S75 193 E5
Cliff Hill La HX2 112 B6
Cliff Hollins La BD12, BD4 95 C6
Cliff House La HD7 189 B6
Cliff La Brierley S72 180 F2
Holmfirth HD7 189 B5
Leeds LS6 205 F4
Ripponden HX6 132 D2
Wakefield WF1 216 A2
Cliff Mount LS6 206 A4
Cliff Mount St LS6 206 A4
Cliff Mount Terr LS6 206 A4
Cliff Par WF1 216 A2
Cliff Park Ave WF1 216 A3
Cliff Rd Crigglestone WF4 159 D4
Holmfirth, Cliff HD7 189 B6
Holmfirth, Flush House HD7 188 A4
Leeds LS6 206 A4
Cliff Road Gdns LS6 206 A4
Cliff Side Gdns LS6 206 A4
Cliff St Haworth BD22 51 D7
8 Pontefract WF8 146 C8
Wakefield WF2 141 F7
Cliff Terr Leeds LS6 206 A4
Micklefield LS25 84 B6
Cliff Vale Rd BD18 55 B5
Cliff Villas 7 WF8 146 C8
Cliff Wood Ave BD18 55 B6
Cliffdale Rd LS7 206 B4
Cliffdale Road Ind Est
LS7 206 B4
Cliffdale Road
Light Ind Est LS7 206 B4
Cliffe Ash HD7 152 D4
Cliffe Ave Baildon BD17 38 C3
Brighouse HX3 115 A7
Harden BD16 36 A1
Cliffe Castle Mus BD20 18 B1
Cliffe Cl S72 180 F3
Cliffe Cres BD20 36 B8
Cliffe Crest WF4 141 B2
Cliffe Ct BD21 35 B8
Cliffe Dr LS19 40 B3
Cliffe End Rd HD3 153 B6
Cliffe Gdns BD18 55 B6
Cliffe Hill Ct HD7 189 B5
Cliffe Hill Junior School
HX3 115 A6
Cliffe House Ave LS25 83 A5
Cliffe La Baildon BD17 38 C1
Cleckheaton BD19 95 F1
Kirkburton HD4 172 E6
Thornton BD13 72 E7
Yeadon LS19 40 C3
Cliffe La S BD17 38 C1
Cliffe La W BD17 38 C2
Cliffe Mill Fold BD20 36 E8
Cliffe Mount BD19 96 A1
Cliffe Park Chase LS12 209 D2
Cliffe Park Cl LS12 209 D2
Cliffe Park Cres LS12 209 D2
Cliffe Park Dr LS12 209 D2
Cliffe Park Mount LS12 209 D2
Cliffe Park Rise LS12 209 D2
Cliffe Pk HD8 190 E8
Cliffe Rd Bradford BD3 55 F1
Brighouse HD6 115 B2
Keighley BD21 35 B4
Shepley HD8 190 E8
Cliffe St Batley WF17 117 F4
Clayton West HD8 175 F2
Dewsbury WF13 118 D1
9 Hebden Bridge HX7 89 A3
Keighley BD21 35 B8
Littleborough OL15 129 D2
Thornton BD13 72 D7
Cliffe Terr Baildon BD17 38 C1
Bradford BD8 55 D1
Halifax, Skircoat Green HX3 113 C2
Keighley BD21 35 C4
Sowerby Bridge HX6 112 A5
Wetherby LS22 13 E5
Cliffe View Bradford BD15 53 F2
Clayton West HD8 175 F2
Morley LS27 97 D3
Cliffe Wood Cl BD9 54 E3
Cliffestone Dr BD20 36 D8
Cliffewood Rise HD8 175 E2
Clifford Ave Ilkley LS29 8 A5
Wakefield WF2 142 D2
Clifford Ct WF5 140 C6
Clifford Jun & Inf Sch
LS23 30 E5
Clifford Moor Rd LS23 30 C7
Clifford Pl 3 LS27 98 B7
Clifford Rd Baildon BD17 38 C2
Boston Spa LS23 30 E7
Bramham LS23 30 D3
Ilkley LS29 8 A5
South Kirkby WF9 182 B2
Clifford St Bradford BD5 201 B1
Cudworth S72 180 C1
Silsden BD20 5 D2
South Elmsall WF9 182 F2
Clifford View WF2 142 D2
Clifton Ave Halifax HX1 202 B2
Holmfirth HD7 189 B6
Horbury WF4 141 A2
Leeds LS9 208 B2
Lofthouse Gate WF1 121 E5
6 Pontefract WF8 146 B8
Clifton Cl WF4 141 A2
Clifton Comm HD6 115 C3
Clifton Cres Barnsley S71 178 F1
Horbury WF4 141 A2
Clifton Ct 11 LS28 76 E8
Clifton Dr Horbury WF4 141 A2
Pudsey LS28 76 E8
Clifton Forge Bsns Pk
WF11 126 E4
Clifton Gdns S72 180 E3
Clifton Gr LS9 208 B1
Clifton Hill LS28 76 E8
Clifton Infant Sch WF4 140 F2
Clifton La Clifton LS21 10 E5
Meltham HD7 170 E2
Clifton Mount LS9 208 A2
Clifton Pl Pudsey LS28 76 F8
Shipley BD18 55 B6
Wakefield WF1 216 A4
Clifton Rd
3 Brighouse HD6 115 B2
Crofton WF4 144 B3
Halifax HX3 113 C4
Horbury WF4 141 A2
Huddersfield HD1 153 E7
Ilkley LS29 8 D3
Pudsey LS28 76 E8
Clifton Side HD2 136 F6
Clifton St Bradford BD8 55 D1
13 Halifax HX3 92 A1
Hemsworth WF9 181 C6
Keighley BD22 35 A6
10 Queensbury BD13 72 E1
Sowerby Bridge HX6 112 C4
Clifton Terr Batley WF17 118 D5
Leeds LS9 208 A2
Ossett WF5 140 C8
Clifton View
Clayton West HD8 175 F2
5 Pontefract WF8 146 B8
Clifton Villas BD8 55 D1
Clipston Ave LS6 59 F6
Clipston Mount 8 LS6 59 F6
Clipston St LS6 59 F6
Clipston Terr 9 LS6 59 F6
Clipstone St 2 BD5 74 E2
Clive Pl BD7 74 B5
Clive Terr BD7 74 B5
Cliviger-Holme CE
Primary Sch BB10 85 B6
Cloberry St LS2 206 A2
Clock Bldgs LS8 208 A4
Clock La BD13 71 D8
Clock Row Ave WF9 182 D3
Clock Row Gr WF9 182 D3
Clock Row Mount WF9 182 D3
Clock View St BD20 18 B2
Clog Bridge BD20 5 E1
Clog Mill & Mus HX7 89 C2
Clog Sole Rd HD6 114 F4
Cloisters The HX1 202 C1
Close Head BD13 72 B6
Close Head Dr BD13 72 B6
Close Head La BD13 72 B6
Close Hill La HD4 153 F2
Close Lea HD6 115 A1
Close Lea Ave HD6 114 F1
Close Lea Dr HD6 114 F1
Close Lea Way HD6 114 F1
Close Rd WF10 124 F7
Close St WF9 181 C7
Close The Barwick in E LS15 63 D6
Boston Spa LS23 30 E8
Bradford BD2 55 F6
Clayton DN5 194 C4
Clayton West HD8 175 E2
Collingham LS22 29 B8
Crigglestone WF4 159 E7
East Ardsley WF3 120 D7
East Keswick LS17 28 C5
Guiseley LS20 39 C8
Kippax LS25 83 A1
Leeds, Alwoodley LS17 43 A5
Leeds, Bank LS9 212 B3
Pontefract WF8 146 F7
Royston S71 179 C1
Thorner LS14 46 A6
Closes Rd 2 HD6 115 A1
Cloth Hall St
Dewsbury WF13 139 D8
Huddersfield HD1 154 A6
3 Leeds LS2 211 F3
Cloudsdale Ave BD5 74 E4
Clough Ave BD20 17 C6
Clough Bank HX2 91 B5
Clough Bank La BD22 34 B6
Clough Bldgs HX6 111 D4
Clough Dr Batley WF17 97 A2
Lepton HD8 155 D2
Slaithwaite HD7 170 D8
Clough Foot La HD7 199 A7
Clough Gate Flockton WF4 156 D5
Oakworth BD22 34 D2
Clough Gate Dr WF4 156 D5
Clough Hall La HD4 154 D1
Clough Head Primary Sch
HD7 152 A4
Clough Hey HD7 168 E4
Clough House HD7 151 D1
Clough House La
Denby Dale HD8 192 C6
Ripponden HX4 133 B2
Slaithwaite HD7 151 D1
Clough Houses BD22 34 C2
Clough La Brighouse HD6 115 D6
Brighouse, Fixby HD6 135 F6
Halifax HX2 91 B5
Huddersfield, Fixby HD6 135 F6
Huddersfield, Paddock
HD1, HD2 153 C5
Lepton WF14 156 C7
Liversedge WF15 116 D3
Oakworth BD22 34 D3
Wadsworth Moor HX2 90 B5
Clough Lee HD7 168 F4
Clough Pk HD8 155 D2
Clough Pl HX2 91 B5
Clough Rd Bacup OL13 106 A3
Emley WF4 157 D1
Huddersfield HD2 136 A2
Slaithwaite HD7 152 A4
Slaithwaite, Crimble HD7 152 A2
Sowerby Bridge HX6 112 D1
4 Todmorden OL14 108 A1
Clough St Bradford BD5 74 E3
Morley LS27 98 C4
Clough The Lepton HD8 155 D3
Mirfield WF14 137 E6
Clough Way HD8 155 D2
Clovelly Ave 19 LS11 214 B3
Clovelly Gr 18 LS11 214 B3
Clovelly Pl 20 LS11 214 B3
Clovelly Row 17 LS11 214 B3
Clovelly Terr LS11 214 B3
Clover Cres LS28 57 A7
Clover Ct LS28 57 A7
Clover Hill WF15 116 D5
Clover Hill Cl HX1 203 D2
Clover Hill Rd HX1 203 D1
Clover Hill Terr HX1 203 D1
Clover Hill View HX1 203 D1
Clover St Bacup OL13 106 A3
Bradford BD5 74 B3
Clover Wlk WF9 183 A7
Cloverdale HX3 93 D7
Cloverville App BD6 94 C7
Club Houses Halifax HX2 91 F3
Huddersfield HD4 171 E8
Club La Halifax HX2 91 F3
Pudsey LS13 57 E5
Club Row Leeds LS7 204 A3
Wilsden BD15 53 C5
Yeadon LS19 40 C7
Club St Bradford BD7 73 F5
Todmorden OL14 86 B1
Club Terr WF9 163 B3
Clubhouses Croft 8 WF4 141 A1
Clumber Dr BD19 117 B7
Cluntergate WF4 141 B1
Clunters La HX2 111 B6
Clutton St WF17 118 E5
Clyde App LS12 210 B2
Clyde Chase LS12 210 B2
Clyde Ct LS12 210 B2
Clyde Gdns LS12 210 B2
Clyde Grange LS12 210 B2
Clyde St Bingley BD16 36 F3
Sowerby Bridge HX6 112 C3
Wakefield WF1 142 E4
Clyde View LS12 210 B2
Clyde Wlk LS12 210 B3
Clydesdale Dr BD6 93 F7
Co-op Bldgs HX3 91 F2
Co-op La HD7 188 D3
Co-operation St
2 Bacup OL13 106 A2
9 Leeds LS12 78 A4
Co-operative Bldgs HD6 115 B7
Co-operative St
Dewsbury WF12 140 B8
Horbury WF4 141 A1
Keighley BD21 35 A3
Mirfield WF14 138 A3
2 Morley LS27 98 C8
12 Morley, Churwell LS27 98 A5
Rothwell WF3 100 C1
Todmorden OL14 129 A7
Wakefield WF2 142 A5
Co-operative Terr
Elland HX4 133 F4
Holmfirth HD7 189 C7
Coach Fold HX3 203 E4
Coach Gate La S36 192 D3
Coach House The LS7 204 A3
Coach La
1 Cleckheaton BD19 116 E8
Lindley LS21 11 F6
Thornton BD13 72 F6
Coach Rd Baildon BD17 38 A1
Brighouse HD6 114 F6
Gildersome LS12 77 E3
Guiseley LS20 39 D7
Huddersfield HD2 135 F2
Lofthouse Gate WF1 121 C4
Meltham HD7 170 F1
Ripponden HX6 132 D4
Coal Clough Rd OL14 86 B2
Coal Gate HD7 151 A1
Coal Gate Rd HX6 131 F5
Coal Hill Dr LS13 57 F4
Coal Hill Fold LS13 57 F4
Coal Hill Gate LS13 57 F4
Coal Hill Gdns LS13 57 F4
Coal Hill Gn LS13 57 F4
Coal Hill La LS28, LS13 57 F4
Coal La HX2 71 E3
Coal Pit La Bacup OL13 106 B3
Batley WF17 118 A6
Brighouse HD6 115 E2
Denby Dale HD8 191 D8
Holmfirth HD7 189 F6
Huddersfield HD4 153 F3
South Elmsall WF9 183 E4
Upton WF8 165 F3
Coal Pit Mews WF17 118 A6
Coal Rd Bardsey LS17 44 E8
Harewood LS17 44 E8
Leeds LS14 45 A2
Leeds, Whinmoor LS14 62 B6
Coalpit La Denby Dale HD8 191 F3
Halifax HX3 113 F4
Coate's La BD20 4 F4
Coates Cl WF12 118 F1
Coates St BD5 74 D4
Coates Terr BD5 74 D4

Cobb Ave WF2 ... 141 F4
Cobble Hall Golf Course LS8 ... 44 D1
Cobbler Hall WF4 ... 176 F8
Cobbler's La WF8 ... 147 A8
Cobbler's Lane Infants Sch WF8 ... 126 A1
Cobbler's Lane Junior Sch WF8 ... 147 A8
Cobbydale Ct BD20 ... 5 D1
Cobcroft La WF11 ... 127 F1
Cobcroft Rd HD1, HD2 ... 136 A1
Cobden Ave 3 LS12 ... 78 A4
Cobden Cl 8 WF17 ... 118 C5
Cobden Ct HX1 ... 203 D4
Cobden Gr 4 LS12 ... 78 A4
Cobden Mews 10 LS27 ... 98 A5
Cobden Pl LS12 ... 77 F4
Cobden Primary Sch LS12 ... 77 F4
Cobden Rd Leeds LS12 ... 77 F4
Leeds, New Blackpool LS12 ... 78 A4
Cobden St Bradford BD15 ... 54 B1
Bradford, Clayton BD14 ... 73 B4
Bradford, Idle BD10 ... 56 B7
Leeds LS12 ... 77 F4
9 Morley LS27 ... 98 A5
Queensbury BD13 ... 72 F1
Todmorden OL14 ... 108 B5
Cobden Terr
Brighouse HX3 ... 114 C8
Elland HX5 ... 134 F5
Leeds LS12 ... 77 F4
Cobham Par WF1 ... 121 B4
Cobham Wlk LS15 ... 62 F2
Cock Hill La HX3 ... 93 B6
Cock La WF4 ... 143 F2
Cock Pit La HX4 ... 150 E8
Cockburn High Sch LS11 ... 99 A7
Cockburn Way LS11 ... 214 C3
Cockcroft Gr BD3 ... 75 A7
Cockcroft La HX6 ... 132 A1
Cockermouth La WF4 ... 156 D2
Cockin La BD14 ... 72 E4
Cocking End LS29 ... 7 C5
Cocking La LS29 ... 6 E6
Cockley Hill La HD5 ... 155 D8
Cockley Meadows HD5 ... 137 C1
Cockshott Cl 2 LS12 ... 58 F1
Cockshott Dr LS12 ... 58 F1
Cockshott Hill LS28 ... 57 D3
Cockshott La
Bradford BD10 ... 56 A8
Leeds LS12 ... 58 F1
Cockshott Pl LS29 ... 6 E8
Coggil St LS10 ... 80 A2
Coiners Fold HX7 ... 110 C8
Colbeck Row WF17 ... 96 E1
Colbert Ave LS29 ... 8 E5
Colby Rise LS15 ... 80 E7
Cold Edge Rd Halifax HX2 ... 70 D3
Halifax, Wainstalls HX2 ... 90 F6
Cold Hiendley Common La WF2 ... 161 D1
Cold Hill La Holmfirth HD7 ... 189 E7
Huddersfield HD4 ... 172 A8
Cold Royd La HD5 ... 155 A8
Cold St BD22 ... 51 C6
Cold Well La HD7 ... 188 B4
Cold Well Rd LS15 ... 62 B1
Cold Well Sq LS15 ... 62 B1
Coldbeck Dr BD6 ... 93 E8
Coldcotes Ave LS9 ... 208 B2
Coldcotes Cir LS9 ... 208 C2
Coldcotes Cl LS9 ... 208 C2
Coldcotes Cres LS9 ... 61 D2
Coldcotes Dr LS9 ... 208 C2
Coldcotes Garth LS9 ... 61 D2
Coldcotes Gr LS9 ... 61 D2
Coldcotes View LS9 ... 61 D2
Coldcotes Wlk LS9 ... 61 D2
Colden Cl HX7 ... 88 F3
Colden Junior & Infants Sch HX7 ... 88 B6
Colden La HX7 ... 88 A6
Colden Rd HX7 ... 88 E4
Colders Dr HD7 ... 170 D1
Colders Gn HD7 ... 170 D2
Coldhill La Saxton LS24 ... 65 E4
Sherburn in E LS25 ... 65 E4
Coldshaw Top BD22 ... 51 C6
Coldwell St HD7 ... 152 D1
Coldwells Hill HX4 ... 133 F3
Coleman St Bradford BD1 ... 55 F1
Leeds LS12 ... 210 C2
Colenso Gdns LS11 ... 213 F4
Colenso Gr Keighley BD21 ... 18 E1
Leeds LS11 ... 213 F4
Colenso Mount LS11 ... 213 F4
Colenso Pl LS11 ... 213 F4
Colenso Rd LS11 ... 213 F4
Colenso Terr LS11 ... 213 F4
Colenso Way BD21 ... 18 E1
Colenso Wlk BD21 ... 18 E1
Coleridge Cl LS26 ... 101 C3
Coleridge Cres WF2 ... 120 F3
Coleridge Gdns BD10 ... 56 C8
Coleridge La LS28 ... 76 F5
Coleridge St HX1 ... 203 E2
Coleridge Way WF8 ... 125 D2
Coles Way BD20 ... 18 D2
Coleshill Way BD4 ... 95 C8
Coley Hall La HX3 ... 93 D2
Coley Rd Northowram HX3 ... 93 C3
Shelf HX3 ... 93 C3
Coley View HX3 ... 93 A2
Colinsway WF2 ... 216 A1
Coll of Music LS9 ... 212 A4
Coll of the Resurrection WF14 ... 137 E6
Coll Pl 7 BD6 ... 94 D8
Collbrook Ave BD6 ... 94 C8
Colleen Rd WF4 ... 159 E5
College Ct BD20 ... 4 C5
College Farm La LS22 ... 13 B3
College Gr Castleford WF10 ... 124 A6
Wakefield WF1 ... 216 B4
College Grove Cl WF1 ... 216 B4
College Grove Rd WF1 ... 216 B4
College Grove View WF1 ... 216 B4
College La BD20 ... 4 D6
College Rd Bingley BD16 ... 37 A6
Castleford WF10 ... 125 B7
Gildersome LS27 ... 97 D6
Low Bradley BD20 ... 4 D5
College St 1 Batley WF17 ... 96 E1
Huddersfield HD4 ... 153 D4
Todmorden OL14 ... 86 C1
College St E HD4 ... 153 D4
College Terr
Ackworth M T WF7 ... 163 E6
Halifax HX1 ... 202 B1
College View WF7 ... 163 E6
College Wlk 6 BD21 ... 35 C7
Collier La Aberford LS25 ... 65 A5
Baildon BD17 ... 38 C4
Colliers Cl BD18 ... 54 E7
Colliers La LS17 ... 44 E4
Colliers Way HD8 ... 175 F4
Colliery App WF3 ... 121 B6
Collin Moor La HX4 ... 134 C8
Collin Rd LS14 ... 61 F1
Collindale Cl BD10 ... 56 E6
Collinfield Rise BD6 ... 93 F6
Collingham Ave BD6 ... 93 E8
Collingham Dr LS25 ... 82 F6
Collingwood Rd WF6 ... 123 B2
Collins Cl 18 BD22 ... 51 E8
Collins St
Bradford, Bowling BD4 ... 75 B4
Bradford, Low Green BD7 ... 74 A3
Collinson St BD19 ... 116 D8
Collyer View LS29 ... 8 E5
Colmore Gr LS12 ... 210 A2
Colmore Rd LS12 ... 210 A1
Colmore St LS12 ... 210 A2
Colne Hurst HD2 ... 136 E4
Colne Rd Glusburn BD20 ... 16 B6
Huddersfield HD1 ... 154 A4
Colne Rd (Chapel La) BD22 ... 34 C2
Colne Rd (Church St) BD22 ... 34 B2
Colne Rd (Goodley) BD22 ... 34 C2
Colne St Huddersfield HD1 ... 153 E5
Huddersfield, Aspley HD1 ... 154 C5
Colne Vale Rd HD3 ... 153 A4
Colne Valley Bsns Pk HD7 ... 152 D1
Colne Valley High Sch HD7 ... 152 E1
Colne Valley Mus HD7 ... 152 D4
Colonel's Wlk WF8 ... 125 C1
Colour Mus BD1 ... 74 D7
Colston Cl BD8 ... 54 E1
Colton Croft LS15 ... 81 D7
Colton Ct LS15 ... 81 D7
Colton Garth LS15 ... 81 D7
Colton La LS15 ... 81 D7
Colton Primary Sch LS15 ... 81 E6
Colton Rd Leeds LS15 ... 81 C7
Leeds, Armley LS12 ... 209 F3
Leeds, Colton LS15 ... 81 D6
Colton Rd E LS15 ... 81 E6
Colton Ret Pk LS15 ... 81 E7
Colton St LS12 ... 209 F3
Coltsfoot Cl WF8 ... 146 D7
Columbus St 13 HX3 ... 92 A1
Colville Terr
East Ardsley WF3 ... 99 E1
Leeds LS11 ... 214 B4
Colwyn Ave 14 LS11 ... 214 B2
Colwyn Mount 15 LS11 ... 214 B2
Colwyn Pl 19 LS11 ... 214 B2
Colwyn Rd LS11 ... 214 B2
Colwyn St HD1 ... 153 D7
Colwyn Terr
Featherstone WF7 ... 145 D6
18 Leeds LS11 ... 214 B2
Colwyn View 12 LS11 ... 214 B2
Colyton Mount BD15 ... 54 A1
Combs Rd WF12 ... 139 E2
Combs The WF12 ... 139 E3
Comet St 4 OL13 ... 106 A7
Commerce Ct BD4 ... 75 D4
Commerce St BD1 ... 201 B3
Commercial Bldgs BD12 ... 95 B4
Commercial Rd
Dewsbury WF13 ... 118 C1
Leeds LS5 ... 59 A3
Skelmanthorpe HD8 ... 175 B2
Commercial St
Batley WF17 ... 118 C5
Batley, Heckmondwike WF16 ... 117 E4
Brighouse HD6 ... 115 B2
8 Castleford WF10 ... 124 D8
Cleckheaton BD19 ... 116 E7
Denholme BD13 ... 71 D8
Dewsbury, Earlsheaton WF12 ... 139 F7
Dewsbury, Ravensthorpe WF13 ... 138 F5
Halifax HX1 ... 203 E3
Hebden Bridge HX7 ... 89 A3
Huddersfield HD1 ... 154 B5
Commercial St continued
Leeds LS1 ... 211 F4
Morley LS27 ... 98 B4
Oakworth BD22 ... 34 B2
4 Queensbury BD13 ... 72 D1
Rothwell LS26 ... 100 F5
Shipley BD18 ... 55 B8
Slaithwaite HD7 ... 170 A8
Todmorden OL14 ... 108 C5
Wakefield WF1 ... 142 D4
Commercial Villas LS28 ... 76 D6
Common End La HD8 ... 155 D2
Common Holme La LS29 ... 7 E6
Common Ing La WF4 ... 162 B2
Common La Clayton DN5 ... 194 C5
Denby Dale HD8 ... 192 B6
East Ardsley WF3 ... 99 C1
Emley HD8 ... 174 E7
Flockton WF4 ... 157 A2
Halifax HX3 ... 113 F5
Knottingley, Broomhill WF11 ... 127 B4
Knottingley, South Moor WF11 ... 127 D3
Royston S71 ... 179 C5
Thorpe Audlin WF8 ... 165 B3
Wakefield WF2 ... 160 F5
Woolley WF4 ... 177 D8
Common Rd Batley WF17 ... 117 F4
Bradford BD12 ... 94 C6
Brierley S72 ... 181 B2
Elland HX5 ... 135 C6
Hemsworth WF9 ... 163 A2
4 Huddersfield HD1 ... 154 A8
Lofthouse Gate WF3 ... 121 F7
South Kirkby WF9 ... 181 E1
Common Road Ave WF9 ... 182 A1
Common Road Ind Est BD12 ... 94 D6
Common Road Infant Schs WF9 ... 182 A1
Common Side La WF7 ... 145 A6
Common Terr HD6 ... 115 A1
Common The WF12 ... 139 E3
Commondale Way BD4 ... 95 A6
Commonside Batley WF17 ... 118 D3
Liversedge FW15 ... 116 E2
Como Ave 3 BD8 ... 54 F1
Como Dr BD8 ... 73 F8
Como Gdns 2 BD8 ... 54 F1
Como Gr BD8 ... 54 F1
Compeigne Ave BD21 ... 18 F1
Compton Ave LS9 ... 208 A2
Compton Cres LS9 ... 208 A2
Compton Gr LS9 ... 208 A2
Compton La LS22 ... 29 B6
Compton Mount LS9 ... 208 A2
Compton Pl LS9 ... 208 A2
Compton Rd LS9 ... 208 A2
Compton Row LS9 ... 208 A2
Compton St Bradford BD4 ... 75 C2
10 Keighley BD21 ... 35 D8
Leeds LS9 ... 208 A2
Compton Terr LS9 ... 208 A2
Compton View LS9 ... 208 A2
Concord St Honley HD7 ... 171 F4
Leeds LS2 ... 207 D1
Concordia St LS1 ... 211 F3
Concourse House Est LS11 ... 213 F1
Concrete St 27 HX3 ... 92 A1
Conduit St BD8 ... 55 C1
Coney La BD21 ... 35 C7
Coney Moor Gr LS26 ... 102 F3
Coney Warren La WF3 ... 121 E8
Coney Wlk WF13 ... 138 F8
Conference Gr LS12 ... 209 D3
Conference Pl LS12 ... 209 D3
Conference Rd LS12 ... 209 D3
Conference Terr LS12 ... 209 D3
Congress Mount LS12 ... 209 D3
Congress St LS12 ... 209 D3
Congreve App LS17 ... 28 E6
Congreve Way LS17 ... 28 E6
Conisborough La LS25 ... 83 B7
Coniston Ave
Huddersfield HD5 ... 154 D6
2 Leeds LS6 ... 59 E5
Mapplewell S75 ... 178 A2
1 Queensbury BD13 ... 72 D1
Coniston Cl Elland HX5 ... 135 B7
2 Queensbury BD13 ... 92 D8
Coniston Ct WF3 ... 121 B6
Coniston Dr WF10 ... 125 E7
Coniston Gdns
Castleford WF10 ... 125 E7
Leeds LS15 ... 80 E6
Coniston Gr Baildon BD17 ... 37 F1
Bradford BD9 ... 54 F2
Coniston House 15 HX5 ... 134 F7
Coniston Pl WF11 ... 126 E1
Coniston Rd Batley WF12 ... 118 F2
4 Bradford BD7 ... 73 E3
Meltham HD7 ... 170 E1
Rothwell LS26 ... 101 C7
Coniston Way
Rothwell LS26 ... 101 C6
Wetherby LS22 ... 13 B5
Conistone Cres WF1 ... 142 E8
Connaught Fold HD2 ... 136 E5
Connaught Rd LS29 ... 8 D3
Cononley County Primary Sch BD20 ... 4 A3
Cononley La BD20 ... 4 B2
Cononley Rd BD20 ... 16 B8
Cononley Sta BD20 ... 4 A2
Consort St LS3 ... 205 F1
Consort Terr LS3 ... 205 F1
Consort View LS3 ... 205 F1
Consort Wlk LS3 ... 205 F1
Constable Gr WF3 ... 121 E6
Constable Rd
East Ardsley WF3 ... 119 F8
Ilkley LS29 ... 8 E3
Constance St BD18 ... 54 F8
Constitutional St HX1 ... 202 C1
Convent Ave WF9 ... 182 C2
Conway Ave LS8 ... 207 F3
Conway Cres Batley WF17 ... 118 C2
Meltham HD7 ... 170 D1
Conway Dr LS8 ... 207 F3
Conway Gr LS8 ... 207 F3
Conway Mount LS8 ... 207 F3
Conway Pl LS8 ... 208 A3
Conway Rd Leeds LS8 ... 208 A3
Wakefield WF2 ... 141 E7
Conway St Bradford BD4 ... 201 C1
Halifax HX1 ... 202 C2
Leeds LS8 ... 207 F3
5 Pudsey LS28 ... 57 D1
Conway Terr LS8 ... 207 F3
Conway View LS8 ... 207 F3
Cook La WF16 ... 117 C4
Cooke Cres BD19 ... 117 A8
Cooke La BD21 ... 35 C7
Cooke St 3 BD21 ... 35 C7
Cookridge Ave LS16 ... 41 E6
Cookridge Dr LS16 ... 41 E6
Cookridge Gr LS16 ... 41 E6
Cookridge Hall Golf Course LS16 ... 41 F6
Cookridge Hospl LS16 ... 41 E2
Cookridge La LS16 ... 41 E7
Cookridge Primary Sch LS16 ... 41 E4
Cookridge St LS1, LS2 ... 211 E4
Cooksland La WF7 ... 144 E8
Cookson Cl WF10 ... 125 D5
Cookson St HD6 ... 114 F3
Coombe Hill BD13 ... 73 B2
Coombe Rd HD3 ... 152 F5
Cooper Bridge Rd HD5, WF14 ... 137 B6
Cooper Cl BD16 ... 37 A5
Cooper Fields HX2 ... 111 E6
Cooper Gr HX3 ... 93 D7
Cooper Hill LS28 ... 76 F5
Cooper House WF9 ... 181 D6
Cooper La Bradford BD6 ... 93 D8
Holmfirth HD7 ... 189 A5
Shelf BD6, HX3 ... 93 D8
Cooper Lane First Sch BD6 ... 73 D1
Cooper Rd LS22 ... 13 E5
Cooper St OL14 ... 108 E6
Cop Hill End HD7 ... 169 C8
Cop Hill La HD7 ... 169 B8
Cop Hill Side HD7 ... 169 B8
Copeland St BD4 ... 75 D5
Copeworth Dr WF4 ... 159 F3
Copgrove Cl BD4 ... 75 E3
Copgrove Ct BD4 ... 75 E3
Copgrove Rd
Bradford BD4 ... 75 E3
Leeds LS8 ... 61 B5
Copley Ave Halifax HX2 ... 202 B1
Meltham HD7 ... 170 D2
Copley Bank Rd HD7 ... 152 C3
Copley Cl HX3 ... 113 B1
Copley Glen HX3 ... 113 B2
Copley Gr HX3 ... 113 B2
Copley Hall St HX3 ... 113 B2
Copley Hall Terr HX3 ... 113 B2
Copley Hill Batley WF17 ... 96 F1
Leeds LS12 ... 210 B2
Copley Hill Trad Est LS12 ... 210 B2
Copley Hill Way LS12 ... 210 B2
Copley Junior & Infant Sch HX3 ... 113 B2
Copley La Aberford LS25 ... 65 D5
Halifax HX3 ... 113 B2
Rothwell WF3 ... 100 B4
Saxton LS25 ... 65 D5
Shepley HD8 ... 174 B1
Copley Mill House HX3 ... 113 A2
Copley Mount HX3 ... 113 B2
Copley St Batley WF17 ... 118 A7
Bradford BD5 ... 74 B3
Halifax HX3 ... 203 E4
Leeds LS12 ... 210 B2
Copley Terr HX3 ... 113 B2
Copley Yd LS12 ... 210 B2
Coplowe La BD15 ... 53 D6
Copmanroyd LS21 ... 11 A3
Copper Beech Cl WF8 ... 146 E6
Copper Beech Ct WF2 ... 161 A6
Copperas House Terr OL14 ... 108 A2
Copperas Row HX4 ... 133 E7
Copperfield Ave LS9 ... 212 C2
Copperfield Cres 10 LS9 ... 212 C2
Copperfield Dr 8 LS9 ... 212 C2
Copperfield Gr 4 LS9 ... 80 A6
Copperfield Mount 3 LS9 ... 80 A6
Copperfield Pl 9 LS9 ... 212 C2
Copperfield Row 7 LS9 ... 212 C2
Copperfield Terr LS9 ... 80 A6
Copperfield View 11 LS9 ... 212 C2
Copperfield Wlk 6 LS9 ... 212 C2
Copperfields Coll LS9 ... 80 A6
Coppertop Mews WF8 ... 125 E3
Coppice Cl WF1 ... 142 E8
Coppice Dr HD4 ... 171 D6
Coppice Head LS26 ... 100 F5
Coppice The
Barwick in E LS15 ... 63 D6
Glusburn BD20 ... 16 C6
Huddersfield HD2 ... 136 B4
Ilkley LS29 ... 8 A6
Mirfield WF14 ... 138 A8
Yeadon LS19 ... 40 B8
Yeadon, Westfield LS19 ... 39 F5
Coppice View BD10 ... 56 A8
Coppice Way LS8 ... 61 A6
Coppice Wood Ave BD7 ... 74 A6
Coppice Wood Cl LS20 ... 23 A1
Coppice Wood Cres LS19 ... 23 B1
Coppice Wood Gr
Bradford BD7 ... 74 A6
Yeadon LS20 ... 40 A8
Coppice Wood Rise LS19 ... 40 B8
Coppies The BD12 ... 94 B4
Coppin Hall Gr WF14 ... 137 D6
Coppin Hall La WF14 ... 137 D6
Coppy Cl BD16 ... 54 A6
Coppy La Haworth BD22 ... 33 C7
Leeds LS13 ... 58 C4
Wadsworth Moor HX7 ... 68 F3
Coppy Nook La HX7 ... 110 E3
Coppy Rd Addingham LS29 ... 6 E8
Steeton BD20 ... 17 B5
Coppy Row BD22 ... 34 B2
Coppy Wood Dr LS29 ... 8 B7
Copse The Bingley BD16 ... 37 D3
Brighouse BD19 ... 115 F7
Burley in W LS29 ... 21 E8
Featherstone WF7 ... 124 C1
Copt Royd Gr LS19 ... 40 A7
Copthorne First Sch BD7 ... 74 C5
Copthorne Gdns HD2 ... 136 F5
Copthurst Rd HD7 ... 198 E7
Copy Bottom BB10 ... 85 C4
Corban St BD4 ... 75 C3
Corby St HD2 ... 136 A1
Cordingley Cl BD4 ... 75 E1
Cordingley St BD4 ... 75 E1
Corfe Cl WF17 ... 97 B2
Corn Bank HD4 ... 171 C6
Corn Exchange 4 LS1 ... 211 F3
Corn Market Halifax HX1 ... 203 E3
Pontefract WF8 ... 146 C8
Corn Mill LS29 ... 22 B4
Corn Mill Ct LS13 ... 77 D7
Corn Mill La Otley LS29 ... 10 A1
Thornton BD13 ... 72 F5
Corn St 6 BD21 ... 35 A4
Cornerstones Cl LS29 ... 7 A8
Cornfield WF13 ... 117 F1
Cornfield Ave HD3 ... 153 A7
Cornfield St 3 OL14 ... 108 D6
Cornholme Junior & Infants Sch OL14 ... 86 A1
Cornholme Terr 7 OL14 ... 86 B1
Cornmill Ave WF15 ... 117 C3
Cornmill Cl LS17 ... 28 D3
Cornmill Cres WF15 ... 117 B2
Cornmill Dr WF15 ... 117 B3
Cornmill La Bardsey LS17 ... 28 D3
Liversedge WF15 ... 117 B3
Cornrace View HD4 ... 154 B4
Cornus Gdns 2 LS10 ... 99 D8
Cornwall Ave BD20 ... 5 C1
Cornwall Cl LS26 ... 100 D6
Cornwall Cres
Baildon BD17 ... 38 B4
Brighouse HD6 ... 115 B6
Rothwell LS26 ... 100 D6
Cornwall House 16 HX5 ... 134 F7
Cornwall Pl BD8 ... 55 D1
Cornwall Rd Bingley BD16 ... 37 B2
Bradford BD8 ... 55 D1
Keighley BD21 ... 18 E1
Cornwall Terr BD8 ... 55 D1
Coronation Ave
Guiseley BD10 ... 39 D4
Kippax LS25 ... 83 C1
Normanton WF6 ... 122 F3
Royston S71 ... 179 E4
Shafton S72 ... 180 B3
Coronation Bglws
3 Kippax LS25 ... 83 C1
Knottingley WF11 ... 126 D4
Meltham HD7 ... 170 E1
Coronation Bsns Ctr BD21 ... 18 D1
Coronation Hospl LS29 ... 8 C3
Coronation Mount BD22 ... 34 F7
Coronation Par LS15 ... 80 E7
Coronation Rd Crofton WF4 ... 144 B3
Halifax HX3 ... 113 D4
Coronation St Bradford BD12 ... 95 A4
Castleford WF10 ... 103 F1
Elland HX5 ... 134 F6
Elland, Lindwell HX4 ... 134 C7
Rothwell WF3 ... 100 D3
Wakefield WF2 ... 120 F1
Coronation Terr
2 Batley WF17 ... 96 F1
Castleford WF10 ... 125 A6
Ripponden HX6 ... 132 E6
Coronation Way BD22 ... 34 F8
Coronation Wlk BD22 ... 34 F8
Corporal La HX3 ... 92 F6
Corporation St
Bradford BD2 ... 56 C3
Dewsbury WF13 ... 139 D8
Halifax HX1 ... 203 E4
2 Huddersfield HD1 ... 154 A5
Morley LS27 ... 98 A4
Sowerby Bridge HX6 ... 112 B4

Corpus Christi High Sch LS9 80 E8
Corpus Christi Primary Sch LS9 80 D8
Corrance Rd BD12 94 D1
Corrie St BD13 72 E6
Cote Cl HD8 173 E2
Cote Farm Cotts BD10 38 F1
Cote Farm La Bradford BD17 38 F1
Shipley BD10 55 F8
Cote Gap BD13 72 D7
Cote La Bradford BD15 54 A1
Brighouse HD2 135 E5
Holmfirth HD7 199 A8
Pudsey LS28 57 C2
Cote Rd HX6 132 B4
Cote The LS28 57 C2
Cote Wall WF14 138 D3
Cotefields Ave LS28 57 C2
Coteroyd Ave LS27 98 C8
Coteroyd Dr LS27 98 C7
Cotewall Rd BD5 74 D3
Cotswold Ave BD18 55 E7
Cotswold Cl WF9 181 F7
Cotswold Dr
Cleckheaton WF15 116 D5
Garforth LS25 82 F5
Knottingley WF11 126 E4
Rothwell LS26 100 D6
Cotswold Mews HD8 173 F7
Cotswold Rd Rothwell LS26 100 E6
Wakefield WF2 141 D5
Cottage Gn 12 BD8 73 F8
Cottage Homes HD5 155 A6
Cottage Rd Bradford BD10 56 D7
Leeds LS6 59 D6
Cottage The HD7 171 F5
Cottam Ave BD7 74 B6
Cottam Croft WF9 181 E7
Cottam Terr BD7 74 B6
Cotterdale BD15 54 A3
Cotterdale Holt LS22 13 A1
Cotterdale View LS15 80 E6
Cotterill Rd WF11 126 D3
Cottingley App LS11 213 D1
Cottingley Chase LS11 213 D1
Cottingley Cliffe Rd BD16 54 C6
Cottingley County Primary Sch LS11 78 C1
Cottingley Cres LS11 213 D1
Cottingley Dr Morley LS11 78 C2
Shipley BD16 54 A8
Cottingley First Sch BD16 54 B7
Cottingley Fold LS11 78 C2
Cottingley Gdns LS11 213 D1
Cottingley Gn LS11 213 D1
Cottingley Gr LS11 213 D1
Cottingley Heights LS11 213 D1
Cottingley Manor Pk BD16 54 B7
Cottingley Moor Rd BD16 54 A5
Cottingley New Rd BD16 54 B7
Cottingley Prim Sch LS11 78 C1
Cottingley Rd
Bradford BD15 54 A4
Morley LS11 78 C2
Cottingley Sta LS11 78 C1
Cottingley Terr BD8 55 D1
Cottingley Towers LS11 213 D1
Cottingley Vale LS11 213 D1
Cotton St Leeds LS9 212 A3
Wakefield WF2 142 C4
Couford Gr HD2 136 F4
Coule Royd HD5 154 F7
Coultas Cl LS29 22 B4
County Arc LS1 211 F4
County Cl WF17 118 C6
Coupe Gr WF6 122 F5
Coupland Pl LS11 214 B4
Coupland Rd Garforth LS25 82 E7
Leeds LS11 214 B4
Coupland St Leeds LS11 214 B3
6 Todmorden OL14 108 B5
Court Dr LS5 58 E6
Court La HX2 112 D7
Court No 6 WF17 118 C4
Court The Leeds LS17 42 F5
Liversedge WF15 116 E4
Shipley BD18 54 E7
Court Way The WF7 164 B8
Court Yard Mews BD20 17 F6
Court Yd The WF4 178 A7
Courtenay Cl BD3 75 E7
Courthouse St LS21 23 A8
Courts Leet 1 BD12 94 C4
Courtyard The
5 Bacup OL13 106 A3
Batley WF17 96 F2
Huddersfield HD4 153 D4
Cousen Ave BD7 73 F5
Cousen Rd BD7 74 B4
Cousin La HX2 91 E4
Coutances Way LS29 9 B3
Coventry St Bradford BD4 75 B4
Halifax HX2 202 A3
Cover Dr 2 BD6 94 A8
Coverdale Garth LS22 29 A8
Coverdale Way BD17 38 E4
Coverley Garth LS19 39 F7
Coverley Rise LS19 39 F7
Covert The WF17 117 F7
Covet The BD10 56 D8
Covey Clough Ct WF14 137 F1
Cow & Calf LS29 8 E2
Cow Close Gr LS12 78 A4
Cow Close La BD12 94 E2
Cow Close Rd LS12 78 A4
Cow Gate HD3 152 F6
Cow Gn HX1 203 E3
Cow Hey La HX7 68 D3
Cow Heys HD5 154 F7
Cow Hill Gate La HX2 71 E1
Cow La Brighouse HX3 114 D4
Crofton WF4 144 A4
Halifax HX3 113 C2
Knottingley WF11 127 A4
Ripponden HX6 132 D6
Ryhill WF4 162 C1
Wadsworth Moor HX7 88 E8
Cowcliff Hill Rd HD7 199 D8
Cowcliffe Hill Rd HD2 135 F3
Cowdray Dr 9 BD19 115 F8
Cowdry Cl WF12 139 E2
Cowfold St 1 OL14 108 B6
Cowgill St 13 Bacup OL13 106 A3
Bradford BD8 55 C1
Cowhurst Ave OL14 108 A7
Cowlersley Junior & Infants Sch HD4 152 F3
Cowlersley La HD4 152 F3
Cowley Cres BD9 54 D4
Cowley Rd LS13 57 F5
Cowpasture Rd LS29 8 C3
Cowper Ave LS9 208 A2
Cowper Cres LS9 208 A2
Cowper Gr LS8 208 A3
Cowper Mount LS9 208 A2
Cowper Rd LS9 208 A2
Cowper St
Dewsbury WF12 139 C6
Leeds LS7 207 E3
Cowper Terr LS9 208 A2
Cowrakes Cl HD3 135 A1
Cowrakes Rd HD3 135 A1
Cowroyd Pl HX3 203 F4
Cowslip St HD1 153 D5
Cowtoot La OL13 106 A4
Coxley Cres WF4 158 D6
Coxley La WF4 158 D7
Coxley View WF4 158 C5
Coxwold Hill LS22 13 E7
Coxwold View LS22 13 E6
Coxwold Wlk 3 BD15 73 A7
Crab Hill WF8 146 C8
Crab La Crigglestone WF2 160 B4
Leeds LS12 209 F4
Crab Tree La WF8 166 B3
Crabgate Dr DN6 184 E2
Crabgate La DN6 184 E2
Crabtree Ave Bacup OL13 106 A1
Batley WF16 117 E5
Crabtree Gn LS22 29 B7
Crabtree Hill LS22 29 B8
Crabtree La LS17 28 C7
Crabtree Pl 5 BD7 74 A4
Crabtree St
6 Bradford BD7 74 A4
Halifax HX1 202 B3
Crabtree Way WF3 119 F7
Crack La BD15 53 D5
Crackenedge La WF13 118 D1
Crackenedge Terr WF13 118 D1
Cracoe Rd BD3 75 B6
Crag Cl Halifax HX2 91 D4
Sutton in C BD20 16 C5
Crag Ct HX2 91 D4
Crag Gdns LS23 30 D2
Crag Hill Ave LS16 41 E6
Crag Hill Rd BD10 39 A2
Crag Hill View LS16 41 E6
Crag La Halifax HX2 91 D3
Leeds LS17 42 F5
Low Bradley BD20 4 C4
Sutton in C BD20 16 C4
Crag Mount 12 WF8 146 C8
Crag Pl BD21 35 C4
Crag Rd BD18 55 C7
Crag The LS23 30 D2
Crag Top WF11 105 A4
Crag Vale Terr BD20 16 B6
Crag View Bradford BD10 56 D6
Cononley BD20 4 A1
Sutton in C BD20 16 C5
Cragg Ave LS18 58 C8
Cragg Bottom Rd BD22 49 E8
Cragg Dr LS29 8 F3
Cragg Hill LS18 58 C8
Cragg La Bradford BD7 74 A3
Denholme BD13 71 E6
Hebden Bridge HX7 110 D6
Thornton BD13 72 A5
Cragg Rd
Hebden Bridge HX7 109 F5
Hebden Bridge HX7 110 D6
Horsforth LS18 58 C8
Cragg St BD7 74 A3
Cragg Terr Bradford BD7 74 A3
Horsforth LS18 58 B8
Yeadon LS19 40 B2
Cragg Top BD13 71 E5
Cragg Vale Junior & InfantSch HX7 110 C3
Cragg View BD20 5 E2
Cragg Wood Dr LS19 40 A2
Craggwell Terr 7 LS18 58 C7
Craggwood Cl LS18 58 C7
Craggwood Rd LS18 58 C7
Craggwood Terr 8 LS18 58 C7
Cragside BD10 38 F1
Cragside Cl LS5 58 E7
Cragside Cres LS5 58 E7
Cragside Gdns LS5 58 E7
Cragside Gr LS5 58 D6
Cragside Mount LS5 58 E7
Cragside Pl LS5 58 E6
Cragside Wlk LS5 58 E7
Craig Cl WF17 118 C6
Craig-y-don WF12 139 F7
Craiglands HX3 114 D8
Craiglands Pk LS29 8 C3
Craiglands Rd LS29 8 C3
Craiglea Dr BD12 94 D2
Craigmore Ct BD4 75 F2
Craigmore Dr LS29 8 E4
Cranberry Ave OL14 129 B7
Cranborne Dr S75 177 F1
Cranbourne Rd BD9 54 D1
Cranbrook Ave
Bradford BD6 94 C8
Leeds LS11 214 A3
Cranbrook Pl 3 BD5 74 E3
Cranbrook St Bradford BD5 74 E3
4 Bradford,Clayton BD14 73 B4
Cranbrook View LS28 77 A5
Cranewells Dr LS15 81 D6
Cranewells Gn LS15 81 C6
Cranewells Rise LS15 81 C6
Cranewells Vale LS15 81 C6
Cranewells View LS15 81 C7
Cranfield Dr DN6 184 F2
Cranford Gdns S71 179 B4
Cranford Pl BD15 53 C5
Crangle Fields HD4 173 C2
Cranleigh Mount BD21 35 A5
Cranmer Bank LS17 43 A3
Cranmer Cl LS17 43 A3
Cranmer Gdns Leeds LS17 43 A3
Meltham HD7 170 F2
Cranmer Rd Bradford BD3 55 F1
Leeds LS17 43 A3
Cranmer Rise LS17 43 A3
Cranmore Cres LS10 99 E5
Cranmore Dr LS10 99 F6
Cranmore Garth LS10 99 E5
Cranmore Gdns LS10 99 E5
Cranmore Gn LS10 99 E5
Cranmore Gr LS10 99 E5
Cranmore La LS10 99 F5
Cranmore Rd LS10 99 E5
Cranmore Rise LS10 99 F5
Cranwood Dr HD5 155 A6
Craven Ave Silsden BD20 5 E1
Thornton BD13 72 E6
Craven Cl
Cleckheaton BD19 117 C8
Royston S71 179 B4
Craven Cres LS29 6 E8
Craven Ct 10 Bradford BD8 73 F8
Halifax HX1 202 C2
Silsden BD20 5 F1
Craven Dr
Cleckheaton BD19 117 C8
Silsden BD20 5 E1
Craven Gr BD20 5 F1
Craven House OL14 129 A8
Craven La BD19 117 C8
Craven Pk LS29 21 F5
Craven Rd Dewsbury WF13 139 A6
Hemsworth WF9 181 D6
Keighley BD21 35 E8
Leeds LS6 206 B3
Craven St Bradford BD3 201 C4
Dewsbury WF13 138 E6
Huddersfield HD4 153 A4
Otley LS21 23 B7
Wakefield WF1 216 B3
Craven Terr Bradford BD2 56 C3
Halifax HX1 202 C2
Otley LS21 23 B7
Cravendale Rd WF13 138 D6
Crawford Ave BD6 94 C8
Crawford Dr WF2 141 F7
Crawford St Bradford BD4 75 A4
Todmorden OL14 129 B8
Crawley Ave WF9 182 D3
Crawshaw Ave LS28 76 F7
Crawshaw Cl 1 LS28 76 E7
Crawshaw Gdns LS28 76 F7
Crawshaw Hill 2 LS28 76 E7
Crawshaw La Emley HD8 175 A8
Flockton WF4 156 F2
Flockton, Six Lanes End WF4 157 A1
Crawshaw Pk LS28 76 E7
Crawshaw Rd LS28 76 E7
Crawshaw Rise LS28 76 E6
Crawshaw St WF13 138 F6
Crawthorne Cres HD2 136 E4
Cray La HX4 133 E2
Crayford Dr WF4 143 F1
Crediton Ave BD15 73 B8
Crediton Ct 12 BD15 73 B8
Crescent Ave
Dewsbury WF13 138 D5
Huddersfield HD4 171 D7
Rothwell LS26 100 F7
Crescent Bglws WF3 99 D2
Crescent Grange LS11 214 C4
Crescent Rd
Huddersfield, Fartown HD2 136 A1
Huddersfield, Netherton HD4 171 D7
Ryhill WF4 162 D1
Crescent Royd HD5 155 A5
Crescent St 1 OL14 108 B5
Crescent Terr LS29 8 B4
Crescent The Baildon BD17 38 C2
Bingley BD16 36 E6
Birkenshaw BD11 96 A7
Bradford BD6 93 E8
3 Brighouse HD6 115 B3
Burley in W LS29 21 E8
Castleford WF10 124 F6
Crescent The continued
Cleckheaton WF15 116 D5
Dewsbury WF13 138 D5
East Ardsley WF3 120 A8
Elland HX5 134 F5
Elland, Holywell Green HX4 134 A4
Featherstone WF7 144 D5
Garforth LS25 83 A7
Guiseley LS20 39 C8
Halifax HX3 113 F6
Holmfirth HD7 189 E6
Ilkley LS29 8 E5
Kippax LS25 83 A1
Kirkburton HD8 174 A7
Leeds LS16 42 B4
Leeds, Alwoodley LS17 42 F6
Leeds, Whitkirk LS15 81 B8
Leeds, Woodhouse LS6 206 A3
Menston LS29 22 B4
Micklefield LS25 84 A6
Netherton WF4 158 D5
Normanton WF6 122 F4
Otley LS21 11 A2
Pudsey LS28 76 F8
Sicklinghall LS22 12 C5
Crescent Towers LS11 214 C4
Crescent View
Keighley BD22 35 A3
Leeds LS17 42 F6
Crescent Wlk
Bradford BD14 73 D5
Dewsbury WF13 138 D5
Cresent The HX3 114 D8
Creskeld Cres LS16 24 F3
Creskeld Dr LS16 24 F3
Creskeld Garth LS16 24 F3
Creskeld Gdns LS16 24 F3
Creskeld La
Arthington LS21 25 A5
Bramhope LS16 24 F3
Creskeld Pk LS16 24 F3
Creskeld Way BD15 53 F2
Creskell Rd LS11 211 E1
Cressfield Rd HD3 153 C8
Cresswell La WF13 117 F3
Cresswell Mount BD7 73 E2
Cresswell Pl BD7 73 E2
Cresswell Terr 2 BD7 73 E2
Crest Ave Bradford BD12 94 C1
Huddersfield HD5 154 E5
Crest Dr WF8 146 E6
Crest Hill Rd HD2 136 C3
Crest Mount WF8 146 E6
Crest Pl HD6 114 E5
Crest Rd HD3 135 A3
Crest The
Huddersfield HD2 136 E6
Kippax LS25 83 A1
Leeds LS14 61 E6
Swillington LS26 82 A1
Crest View HD6 114 E5
Crestfield Ave HX5 134 E6
Crestfield Cres HX5 134 E5
Crestfield Dr Elland HX5 134 E5
Halifax HX2 202 A1
Crestfield Rd HX5 134 E5
Crestville Cl BD14 73 D5
Crestville Rd BD14 73 C5
Crestville Terr BD14 73 D5
Crestwood Cl BD5 75 B1
Crewe Ave WF11 126 B4
Crewe Rd WF10 125 D7
Crib La HX1 203 E4
Cricketers App WF2 120 E3
Cricketers Cl WF7 164 A5
Cricketers Gn LS19 40 C5
Cricketers Terr LS12 209 F3
Cricketers The LS5 59 B4
Cricketers Wlk
Leeds LS15 81 E7
Steeton BD20 17 D5
Cricklegate LS15 81 B8
Crimble Bank HD7 152 A1
Crimble Cl HX3 114 E7
Crimble Clough Rd HD7 152 A3
Crimbles Ct LS28 76 F7
Crimbles Pl LS28 76 F7
Crimbles Rd LS28 76 F7
Crimbles Terr LS28 76 F7
Crimea La HD7 151 E4
Crimea St 5 OL13 106 A2
Crimple Gn LS25 83 B6
Crimshaw La BD18 55 D5
Crimsworth Dean HX7 68 F2
Crimsworth La HX7 89 A8
Crinan Ct WF6 123 A4
Cringles La BD20 5 F7
Cripplegate HX1 203 F3
Critchell Ho 5 BD5 201 B1
Crodingley HD7 189 B8
Crodingley Farm Ct HD7 189 B8
Croft Ave Bingley BD16 36 D6
East Ardsley WF3 120 D7
Knottingley WF11 127 A5
Normanton, Altofts WF6 122 F3
Normanton, Normanton Common WF6 123 C3
Otley LS21 10 F1
Pudsey LS28 57 D3
Royston S71 179 B3
Croft Bridge LS26 101 C5
Croft Chantry WF9 163 A2
Croft Cl Mapplewell S75 178 A1
Menston LS29 21 F4
Croft Cottage La 3 HD1 154 B8
Croft Ct Honley HD7 171 F3
Horsforth LS18 41 C1
Menston LS29 21 F4
Croft Dr Bramham LS23 30 D3
Honley HD7 171 E4
Mapplewell S75 178 B1
Menston LS29 22 A4
Croft End LS22 13 C5
Croft Field BD20 17 E8
Croft Fold HX3 91 F3
Croft Foulds Ct LS25 82 F7
Croft Gdns HD2 135 E1
Croft Head Guiseley LS20 22 E1
Skelmanthorpe HD8 175 A2
Croft Head La WF1 143 E6
Croft Head Terr BD20 16 C6
Croft Hill BD20 16 C5
Croft House 11 HX2 134 F7
Croft House Ave LS27 98 B5
Croft House Cl
Bradford BD6 94 B8
Morley LS27 98 B5
Croft House Ct 6 LS28 76 E8
Croft House Dr Morley LS27 98 B5
Otley LS21 10 F1
Croft House Fold LS29 7 A8
Croft House Gdns LS27 98 B5
Croft House Gr LS27 98 B5
Croft House La
Huddersfield HD1 153 E7
Keighley BD20 18 A2
Morley LS27 98 B5
Croft House Mews LS27 98 B5
Croft House Mount LS27 98 B6
Croft House Rd
Bradford BD6 94 B8
Morley LS27 98 B5
Slaithwaite HD3 151 D5
Croft House Rise LS27 98 B6
Croft House View LS27 98 B5
Croft House Way LS27 98 B6
Croft House Wlk LS27 98 B6
Croft La Tadcaster LS24 31 E6
Thorp Arch LS23 15 A4
Croft Leigh Ct BD5 75 A1
Croft Pk LS29 21 F4
Croft Pl 1 HD6 115 B4
Croft Rd Bingley BD16 36 D6
Bramham LS23 30 D3
Keighley BD20 19 D1
Croft Rise LS29 22 A4
Croft Row BD13 71 E6
Croft St Birkenshaw BD11 96 A5
Bradford, Brownroyd Hill BD6 74 C1
Bradford, Eastbrook BD5 201 C2
Bradford, Fourlands BD10 56 C8
6 Brighouse HD6 115 A2
Dewsbury WF13 139 C8
Glusburn BD20 16 C6
Haworth BD22 51 C7
22 Hebden Bridge HX7 89 A3
Huddersfield HD1 153 C5
Keighley BD21 35 B6
Liversedge WF16 117 D3
Otley LS21 23 B7
Pudsey LS28 57 D3
Shipley BD18 55 B8
Sowerby Bridge HX6 112 C4
Steeton BD20 17 C5
Croft Terr LS12 77 E3
Croft The Badsworth WF9 164 D3
Birkenshaw BD11 96 E5
Castleford WF10 124 F6
Collingham LS22 29 A8
Draughton BD23 1 D5
East Ardsley WF12 119 D5
Knottingley WF11 127 A5
Leeds LS15 62 B1
Meltham HD7 170 F1
Rothwell LS26 101 C5
Scarcroft LS14 45 D8
West Bretton WF4 176 F8
Croft Way LS29 22 A4
Croft's Ct LS1 211 E4
Croftdale Gr LS15 62 D2
Crofters Gn BD10 56 A8
Crofters Lea LS19 39 F7
Croftlands Batley WF12 118 F2
Bradford BD10 56 A8
Huddersfield HD4 154 A2
Knottingley WF11 127 A5
Crofton Cl HD7 170 D8
Crofton High Sch WF4 161 F8
Crofton Infant Sch WF4 162 A8
Crofton Junior Sch WF4 162 A8
Crofton Rd Bradford BD9 54 F3
Shipley BD9 55 A4
Crofton Rise LS17 45 A4
Crofton Terr LS17 45 A4
Crofts The Batley WF17 117 F4
Emley HD8 175 D7
Farnhill BD20 4 E1
Sutton in C BD20 16 C4
Croftside Cl LS14 62 B3
Croftway LS15 63 E7
Croisdale Cl WF15 116 E4
Cromack View LS28 76 C7
Cromarty Ave HD4 153 C2
Cromarty Dr HD4 153 C2
Cromer Ave 15 15 BD21 35 B5
Cromer Gr 17 BD21 35 B5
Cromer Pl LS2 206 A2
Cromer Rd Keighley BD21 35 B5
Leeds LS2 206 A2
Cromer St Halifax HX1 202 B1
14 Keighley BD21 35 B5
Leeds LS2 206 A2
Cromer Terr LS2 206 A2
Crompton Dr LS27 97 F6
Cromwell Cl Byram WF11 126 D8
Halifax HX3 114 A4

Cromwell Cres WF8 146 E8
Cromwell Ct
Adwick Le S DN6 184 F1
Birkenshaw BD11 96 D5
Shipley BD9 54 C5
Cromwell Hts 2 LS9 212 B4
Cromwell Mount Leeds LS9 207 E1
Middleton LS10 99 D8
Cromwell Pl WF5 140 E7
Cromwell Rd
Castleford WF10 125 D7
Halifax HX3 114 A4
Cromwell Rise LS25 103 B8
Cromwell St Dearne S63 194 E1
Leeds LS9 207 E1
Cromwell Terr 1 HX1 203 D3
Cromwell View HX3 114 B4
Cronkhill La S71 179 D1
Crooke La BD15 53 C4
Crooked La Bradford BD10 39 A1
Halifax HX3 92 B6
Crookes La S71 179 C1
Cropper Gate LS1 211 D4
Cropredy Cl BD13 72 F1
Cropstones LS23 30 D2
Cropton Rd S71 179 B3
Crosby Ave LS11 213 F4
Crosby Pl LS11 211 D1
Crosby Rd LS11 211 D1
Crosby St Keighley BD21 35 B8
Leeds LS11 210 C1
Crosby Terr LS11 211 D1
Crosby View 3 LS11 211 D1
Croscombe Wlk BD5 201 B1
Croset Ave HD1 154 C7
Crosland Ct HD3 134 F1
Crosland Edge HD7 170 F4
Crosland Factory La HD4 171 B5
Crosland Heath Golf Course HD4 152 F1
Crosland Hill Rd HD4 153 B3
Crosland Moor Infants Sch HD4 153 C3
Crosland Rd
Huddersfield, Lidley HD3 135 A1
Huddersfield, Yews Hill HD1 153 E4
Crosland Spring Rd HD4 171 B6
Crosland St HD4 153 E4
Crosley View BD16 37 C2
Crosley Wood Rd BD16 37 B2
Cross Albert Pl LS12 210 A2
Cross Alcester Rd 12 LS8 207 F4
Cross Alma St LS9 207 F1
Cross Arc LS1 211 F4
Cross Aston Gr LS13 58 E2
Cross Ave LS26 100 F7
Cross Bank Rd WF17 118 B6
Cross Bank St WF14 138 A2
Cross Banks BD18 55 B7
Cross Banstead St 5 LS8 207 F3
Cross Bath Rd LS13 58 C2
Cross Beck Rd 4 LS8 207 F4
Cross Belgrave St LS2 211 F4
Cross Bell St 2 LS9 212 A4
Cross Bellbrooke Ave LS9 208 B2
Cross Bentley La LS6 59 F6
Cross Burley Lodge Rd LS6 205 E2
Cross Cardigan Terr LS4 59 C1
Cross Catherine St LS9 212 B3
Cross Chancellor St LS6 206 B3
Cross Chapel St 4 LS6 59 D5
Cross Chestnut Gr 16 LS6 205 E3
Cross Church St
8 Cleckheaton BD19 116 E7
14 Huddersfield HD1 154 B6
Huddersfield, Paddock HD1 153 D5
Cross Cliff Rd LS6 205 F4
Cross Cotts HD1 153 D7
Cross Cowper St LS7 207 D3
Cross Crown St 5 BD19 116 D7
Cross Dawlish Gr 7 LS9 80 B8
Cross Dikes Rd HX6 132 A7
Cross Easy Rd LS9 212 C2
Cross Elford St LS8 207 F3
Cross Emily St 11 BD21 35 C8
Cross End Fold LS29 7 A8
Cross Ends La HX7 69 A4
Cross Eric St LS13 58 C5
Cross Evanston Ave LS4 59 C2
Cross Farm Ct BD22 51 C3
Cross Field HX4 134 A4
Cross Fields HD5 154 E7
Cross Firs St HD3 153 B5
Cross Flatts LS11 214 A2
Cross Flatts Ave LS11 214 A2
Cross Flatts Cres LS11 213 F2
Cross Flatts Dr LS11 213 F2
Cross Flatts Gr LS11 214 A2
Cross Flatts Mount LS11 214 A2
Cross Flatts Par LS11 213 F2
Cross Flatts Park Primary Sch LS11 214 B2
Cross Flatts Pl LS11 213 F2
Cross Flatts Rd LS11 213 F2
Cross Flatts Row LS11 213 F2
Cross Flatts St LS11 213 F2
Cross Flatts Terr LS11 213 F2
Cross Foundry St WF13 138 E5
Cross Fountaine St 3 LS2 211 E4
Cross Francis St LS7 207 D3
Cross Gate Rd HD7 189 B2
Cross Gates Ave LS15 62 C3
Cross Gates Ctr LS15 62 C2
Cross Gates La
Harden BD16 36 C3
Leeds LS15 62 B3
Cross Gates Prim Sch LS15 62 A2
Cross Gates Rd LS15 62 B2
Cross Gates Sta LS15 62 C1
Cross Glen Rd LS16 59 C7
Cross Gn Bradford BD4 75 E4
Otley LS21 23 B8
Cross Granby Terr 8 LS6 59 D5
Cross Grange Ave LS7 207 E4
Cross Grasmere St LS12 210 A3
Cross Green App LS9 80 A5
Cross Green Ave 17 LS9 212 C2
Cross Green Cl LS9 80 A5
Cross Green Cres LS9 212 C2
Cross Green Ct LS9 80 B5
Cross Green Dr
Huddersfield HD5 155 A6
Leeds LS9 80 A5
Cross Green Garth LS9 80 A5
Cross Green Gr 16 LS9 212 C2
Cross Green La Leeds LS15 81 B8
Leeds, Knowsthorpe LS9 212 C2
Cross Green Light Ind Est LS9 80 B5
Cross Green Rd
Huddersfield HD5 155 A6
Leeds LS9 212 C2
Cross Green Rise LS9 80 A5
Cross Green Row LS6 59 E7
Cross Green Vale LS9 80 B5
Cross Green Way LS9 80 A5
Cross Greenwood Mount 1 LS6 59 E7
Cross Grove St 6 HD1 154 A5
Cross Hands La WF4 163 B6
Cross Hartley Ave LS6 206 A4
Cross Heath Gr LS11 213 E3
Cross Henley Rd LS13 58 C2
Cross Hill Adwick Le S DN6 184 F1
Brierley S72 180 F3
Elland HX4 134 C7
Fairburn WF11 105 A4
Hemsworth WF9 181 D7
Cross Hill Ct DN6 184 F2
Cross Hill La WF15 116 C1
Cross Hills Halifax HX1 203 E4
Kippax LS25 83 B1
Cross Hills Ct 3 LS25 83 A1
Cross Hills Dr LS25 83 A1
Cross Hills Ent Ctr BD20 16 E7
Cross Hills Gdns 2 LS25 83 A1
Cross Hilton Gr LS8 204 C1
Cross Ingledew Cres LS8 44 B2
Cross Ingram Rd LS11 210 C1
Cross Ivy Mount 7 LS9 80 A8
Cross Kelso Rd LS2 205 F1
Cross Keys WF5 141 A7
Cross Keys Ct WF4 141 B1
Cross La Bingley BD16 36 F3
Birkenshaw BD11 96 B7
Bradford BD7 74 A4
Brighouse HD6 115 F1
Elland HX5 134 E6
Emley HD8 175 D8
Guiseley LS20 23 A4
Holmfirth HD7 189 C2
Honley HD7 171 F2
Huddersfield HD4 154 A3
Kirkburton HD8 174 B5
Kirkburton, Stocksmoor HD4 173 C2
Leeds LS12 209 E3
Leeds, Farnley LS12 77 E5
Oxenhope BD22 51 C3
Queensbury BD13 92 C8
Royston S71 179 E3
Shelf HX3 93 A6
Shelf, Stone Chair HX3 93 B4
Shepley HD8 190 E6
Skelmanthorpe HD8 175 A1
Todmorden OL14 108 F4
Wakefield WF2 141 F5
Wilsden BD16 53 D7
Cross Lane Bsns Pk WF15 117 B4
Cross Lane Prim Sch HX5 134 E5
Cross Lea Farm Rd LS5 58 F7
Cross Lee OL14 107 F7
Cross Lee Gate OL14 107 F7
Cross Lee Rd OL14 107 F7
Cross Leeds St 13 BD21 35 B7
Cross Lidgett Pl LS8 204 C4
Cross Linden Terr 4 LS11 214 C3
Cross Louis St LS7 207 D3
Cross Maude St LS2 212 A3
Cross Milan Rd LS8 208 A3
Cross Mitford Rd LS12 210 A3
Cross Osmondthorpe La LS9 80 C8
Cross Park Ave WF10 124 F7
Cross Park St Batley WF17 118 D5
Dewsbury WF12 139 F8
7 Horbury WF4 141 A1
7 Leeds LS15 81 A8
Cross Pasture Rd 2 LS7 207 E4
Cross Peel St 2 LS27 98 B4
Cross Pipes Rd WF2 141 E8
Cross Platts HX3 114 C4
Cross Quarry St 15 LS6 206 A4
Cross Queen St WF6 123 A2
Cross Rd
Bradford, Fourlands BD10 56 C8
Bradford, Girlington BD8 55 B1
Bradford, Oakenshaw BD12 94 F4
Crigglestone WF4 159 F3
Dewsbury WF12 139 D1
Horsforth LS18 58 A8
Netherton WF4 158 B7
Cross Reginald Mount LS7 207 D4
Cross Rink St 3 WF17 118 D3
Cross River St BD21 18 E1
Cross Roseville Rd LS8 207 E3
Cross Rosse St BD18 55 B8
Cross Roundhay Ave LS8 204 C1
Cross Row LS15 82 A6
Cross Rydal St 6 BD22 35 A6
Cross Ryecroft St WF5 140 C7
Cross Speedwell St 5 LS6 206 B3
Cross Sq WF1 216 B2
Cross St 6 Bacup OL13 106 A3
Batley WF17 118 C5
2 Bradford, Buttershaw BD6 93 F7
5 Bradford, Clayton BD14 73 C4
Bradford, Oakenshaw BD12 95 A4
Brighouse HD6 115 B4
Castleford WF10 124 B8
Castleford WF10 124 C8
Dewsbury WF12 139 E8
Dewsbury, Savile Town WF12 139 D7
East Ardsley WF3 120 E8
1 Elland, Holywell Green HX4 134 B4
7 Elland, West Vale HX4 134 D7
Halifax HX1 203 E3
1 Halifax HX1 203 F2
Hemsworth WF9 181 C7
Honley HD7 171 F4
2 Horbury WF4 141 B1
Huddersfield HD4 153 E4
Leeds LS15 81 A8
Liversedge WF15 117 A2
Ossett WF5 119 C1
3 Pontefract WF8 146 D8
Rothwell LS26 100 E5
Slaithwaite HD7 152 A1
Upton WF9 183 D8
Wakefield WF1 216 B2
Wetherby LS22 13 E5
Cross St Michael's La LS6 205 D4
Cross St W HX2 202 A4
Cross Stamford St LS7 207 D1
Cross Stone Rd OL14 108 D6
Cross Sun St BD1 201 C4
Cross Terr LS26 100 E5
Cross The Barwick in E LS15 63 E7
Bramhope LS16 24 D3
Cross Union St LS2 212 A4
Cross Valley Dr LS15 62 B1
Cross Wellington St BD1 201 C3
Cross Wells Rd HX6 132 C5
Cross Westfield Rd LS3 205 F1
Cross Wingham St LS7 207 D2
Cross Woodstock St 15 LS2 206 B2
Cross Woodview St 17 LS11 214 B2
Cross York St LS2 212 A3
Crossbeck Cl LS29 8 B3
Crossbeck Rd LS29 8 C3
Crossdale Ave BD6 93 E8
Crossfield Cl BD22 51 B3
Crossfield Ct WF4 157 F6
Crossfield Rd BD22 51 C3
Crossfield St LS2 206 A3
Crossfields WF4 158 A6
Crossflatts First Sch BD16 36 E6
Crossflatts Sta BD16 36 E5
Crossgate Mapplewell S75 178 B1
Otley LS21 23 A7
Crosshills Mount HX4 134 C7
Crosshills Rd BD20 4 A2
Crossings The WF17 117 F8
Crossland Rd LS27 98 B7
Crossland Terr LS11 214 C3
Crosslane Ind Est WF15 117 A4
Crossley Cl Halifax HX1 202 C3
Mirfield WF14 138 A8
Crossley Fields Jun & Inf Sch WF14 138 B7
Crossley Gdns HX1 202 C4
Crossley Gr WF14 138 A8
Crossley Hall First Sch BD8 73 E8
Crossley Hall St BD8 73 D7
Crossley Heath Sch HX4 113 A4
Crossley Hill HX3 113 D3
Crossley La
Huddersfield HD5 155 A7
Mirfield WF14 138 B8
Crossley New Rd OL14 87 F1
Crossley Ret Pk HX1 203 D4
Crossley St Batley WF15 117 C2
Bradford BD7 74 B5
Brighouse HD6 115 B1
Crofton WF4 143 F6
Featherstone WF7 145 D5
Halifax HX1 203 E3
Queensbury BD13 72 F1
15 Todmorden OL14 108 B5
Wetherby LS22 13 E5
Crossley Terr Batley WF17 118 C3
33 Hebden Bridge HX7 89 A3
Crossley Terr N HX3 92 A4
Crossley Terr S HX3 92 A4
Crossman Dr WF6 123 C3
Crossmoor Cl BD20 5 C1
Crossmount St WF17 118 C3
Crossroads Cotts LS24 47 E5
Crossway BD16 53 F7
Crossways The LS21 11 A2
Crow Hill End Rd HX6 110 F2
Crow Hill Rd HX6, HX7 110 F2
Crow La Huddersfield HD3 153 A5
Otley LS21 23 A7
Crow Lane Jun & Inf Sch HD3 153 A5
Crow Nest La LS11 213 E2
Crow Nest Rd HX7 89 B2
Crow Nest Terr 2 WF13 139 B7
Crow Nest View WF13 139 A7
Crow Tree Cl BD17 38 D3
Crow Tree La BD8 54 E1
Crow Trees HD7 169 C7
Crow Trees Pk LS19 40 B4
Crow Trees Rd HD7 169 B7
Crow Wood La HX4 133 D2
Crow Wood Pk HX2 112 D5
Crowgill Rd BD18 55 B8
Crowlees C of E Sch WF14 138 B4
Crowlees Cl WF14 138 B5
Crowlees Gdns WF14 138 B5
Crowless Rd WF14 138 B5
Crown & Anchor Yd 3 WF8 146 C8
Crown Cl WF12 140 A7
Crown Dr BD12 94 C4
Crown Flatt Way WF12 118 E1
Crown Gn HD4 153 A4
Crown La HD7 189 A5
Crown Point Cl WF5 140 C6
Crown Point Dr WF5 140 C7
Crown Point Rd
Leeds LS10 212 A2
Ossett WF5 140 C6
Crown Point Ret Pk LS10 211 F2
Crown Rd HX3 92 B2
Crown St
9 Bradford, Carr House Gate BD12 94 C4
Bradford, Lister Hills BD1 74 C7
Brighouse HD6 115 A3
Burley in W LS29 9 F1
Clayton West HD8 175 D1
Cleckheaton BD19 116 D7
Elland HX5 134 F7
Halifax HX1 203 E3
18 Hebden Bridge HX7 89 A3
Honley HD7 171 F5
Leeds LS2 211 F3
Ossett WF5 140 E3
Crownest La BD16 37 A3
Crownest Rd BD16 37 A3
Crownlands La WF5 140 D6
Crowther Ave LS28 56 F6
Crowther Cl HD7 152 A2
Crowther Fold BD16 36 B1
Crowther Pl
Castleford WF10 124 D7
Leeds LS6 206 B3
Crowther Rd Batley WF16 117 E5
Mirfield WF14 138 A5
Crowther St Batley WF17 117 F5
8 Bradford, Carr House Gate BD12 94 C4
Bradford, Greengates BD10 56 D7
Castleford WF10 124 D7
6 Cleckheaton BD19 116 D8
Huddersfield, Aspley HD1 154 B5
Huddersfield, Rashcliffe HD1 153 F3
Crowtrees Cres HD6 135 F7
Crowtrees Ct LS19 40 B3
Crowtrees La HD6 135 F7
Crowtrees Pk HD6 135 F8
Croxall Dr WF3 121 E5
Croydon Rd BD7 73 F4
Croydon St Leeds LS11 210 C2
12 Queensbury BD13 72 E1
Crumack La BD22 51 F3
Crummock Pl WF11 126 E2
Cryer Row BD20 16 D4
Crystal Ct 9 HX1 202 C3
Crystal Pl 4 WF1 216 C2
Crystal Terr BD4 75 C3
Cubley Ave WF2 160 B6
Cuckoo La HD7 171 F4
Cuckoo Nest BD7 74 C7
Cuckoo Nest Ind Est BD7 74 C7
Cuckoo's Nest Halt HD8 175 C2
Cuckstool Rd HD8 192 A6
Cudbear St LS10 212 A2
Cullingworth First Sch BD13 52 D6
Cullingworth Rd BD13 52 E5
Cullingworth St WF13 118 A3
Culpans Rd HX6 111 A5
Culver St 1 HX1 203 E3
Cumberland Ave HD2 136 B5
Cumberland Cl HX2 91 E3
Cumberland Ho BD3 201 D4
Cumberland Rd
Bradford BD7 74 A5
Castleford WF10 104 E2
Leeds LS6 205 F4
Cumberworth C of E First Sch HD8 191 B6
Cumberworth La
Denby Dale HD8 190 F6
Denby Dale, Lower Cumberworth HD8 191 E7
Cumberworth Rd HD8 174 F1
Cumbrian Way WF2 141 E2
Cunliffe La BD17 39 B5
Cunliffe Rd Bradford BD8 55 D3
Ilkley LS29 8 B4
Cunliffe Terr BD8 55 D2
Cunliffe Villas BD8 55 D3
Cure Hill BD22 34 B3
Curlew Cl Castleford WF10 124 D6
Ilkley LS29 7 E4
Curlew Ct BD20 17 B6
Curlew Rise LS27 98 D3
Curlew St BD5 74 C3
Curly Hill LS29 8 B6
Currer Ave BD4 75 B1
Currer La LS29 3 C4
Currer St BD1 201 C3
Currer Wlk BD20 17 B6
Curwen Cres WF16 117 E6
Curzon Rd BD3 75 B7
Curzon St HD2 137 A6
Cut Rd Brotherton WF11 105 C1
Fairburn WF11 105 A4
Cuthberts Cl BD13 92 D8
Cutler Heights La BD4 75 D3
Cutler La LS26 102 E4
Cutler Pl BD4 75 D4
Cutsyke Ave WF10 124 B5
Cutsyke Crest WF10 124 B5
Cutsyke Hill WF10 124 B6
Cutsyke Rd Castleford WF7 124 B3
Featherstone WF7 124 B3
Cypress Fold HD8 155 E3
Cypress House 10 WF10 124 E7
Cypress Rd WF6 144 C8
Cyprus Ave Bradford BD10 38 F1
Wakefield WF1 142 A8
Cyprus Cres WF14 138 D7
Cyprus Dr BD10 39 A1
Cyprus Gr Garforth LS25 82 E7
Wakefield WF1 142 A8
Cyprus Mount WF1 142 A8
Cyprus Rd LS25 82 E7
Cyprus St WF1 216 A4
Cyprus Terr LS25 82 E7
Czar St LS11 211 D2

Dacre Ave WF2 141 C4
Dacre Cl WF15 116 F5
Daffels Wood Cl BD4 95 B8
Daffil Ave LS27 98 B7
Daffil Gr LS27 98 B8
Daffil Grange Mews 1 LS27 98 B7
Daffil Grange Way LS27 98 B7
Daffil Rd LS27 98 B7
Daffodil Ct 9 BD15 73 B8
Dagenham Rd BD4 75 C3
Dahl Dr WF10 125 C5
Daisy Bank HX1 203 D1
Daisy Bank St 2 OL14 86 B1
Daisy Cl WF17 96 E2
Daisy Croft BD20 5 F1
Daisy Fold WF9 182 F7
Daisy Gn HD7 170 C7
Daisy Hill
5 Bradford BD12 94 C3
Dewsbury WF13 139 C8
Morley LS27 98 C5
Silsden BD20 5 F1
Daisy Hill Ave LS27 98 C6
Daisy Hill Back La BD9 54 E2
Daisy Hill Cl LS27 98 C6
Daisy Hill Gr BD9 54 E2
Daisy Hill La BD9 54 E2
Daisy Hill Middle Sch BD9 54 E2
Daisy Lea HD3 152 A8
Daisy Lea La HD3 135 C1
Daisy Lee La HD7 199 C7
Daisy Mount HX6 112 A5
Daisy Pl 12 BD18 54 F8
Daisy Rd HD6 136 B8
Daisy Row 3 LS13 58 D1
Daisy Royd HD4 154 A2
Daisy St Bradford BD7 74 A3
5 Brighouse HD6 115 A2
Halifax HX1 203 D2
1 Haworth BD22 51 E8
Daisy Vale Mews WF3 99 E1
Daisy Vale Terr WF3 99 E1
Daisyfield Rd 2 LS13 58 D2
Dalby Ave BD3 56 C1
Dalby St BD3 75 C8
Dalcross Gr BD5 74 F4
Dalcross St BD5 74 F4
Dale Ave OL14 108 D5
Dale Cl Batley WF17 118 C3
Denby Dale HD8 191 F5
Guiseley LS20 39 B8
Ossett WF5 140 E6
Dale Cres BD20 17 C5
Dale Croft Garforth LS25 82 E8
Ilkley LS29 7 E4
Skelmanthorpe HD8 175 A2
Dale Croft Rise BD15 54 A2
Dale Ct Holmfirth HD7 189 B7
Pontefract WF8 146 D5
Dale Garth BD17 38 B3
Dale Gr BD10 38 E1
Dale La Batley WF16 117 E5
South Elmsall WF9 183 B5
Dale Lane Ind Est WF9 183 B5
Dale Mews WF8 146 D5
Dale Park Ave LS16 41 D4
Dale Park Cl LS16 41 D4
Dale Park Gdns LS16 41 D4
Dale Park Rise LS16 41 D4
Dale Park View LS16 41 D4
Dale Park Wlk LS16 41 D4
Dale Rd BD11 97 A8
Dale St Bradford BD1 201 B3
Dewsbury WF12 139 C4
Huddersfield HD3 153 A5
Huddersfield, Folly Hall HD1 154 A5
Keighley BD21 18 E1

Dale St continued
Ossett WF5 140 D6
Shipley BD18 55 B7
Skelmanthorpe HD8 175 A2
Sowerby Bridge HX6 112 B4
Todmorden OL14 108 B5
Dale Stone Cl WF11 105 C1
Dale The LS25 47 E1
Dale View Halifax HX2 111 D6
Hemsworth WF9 181 F6
Ilkley LS29 7 E4
Pontefract WF8 146 D5
Silsden BD20 5 E2
Steeton BD20 17 C5
Dale View Cl BD21 35 E6
Dale View Gr BD21 35 E6
Dale View Rd BD21 35 E6
Dale Wlk WF7 145 C4
Dalefield Ave WF6 123 B1
Dalefield Rd WF6 144 B8
Dales Dr LS20 39 B8
Dales Way LS20 39 B8
Daleside Dewsbury WF12 139 C1
Elland HX4 134 A7
Daleside Ave
Holmfirth HD7 189 C7
Pudsey LS28 76 A8
Daleside Cl LS28 56 F1
Daleside Gr Bradford BD12 94 F4
Pudsey LS28 76 A7
Daleside Rd Keighley BD20 19 A1
Pudsey LS28 75 F8
Shipley BD18 55 E8
Daleside Wlk BD5 74 F2
Daleson Cl HX3 93 A3
Dalesway BD16 37 B5
Daleview Ct BD17 38 A2
Dallam Ave BD18 54 E8
Dallam Gr 3 BD18 54 E8
Dallam Rd BD18 54 E8
Dallam Wlk BD18 54 F8
Dalmeny Ave HD4 153 C3
Dalmeny Cl HD4 153 C3
Dalton Ave LS11 214 A2
Dalton Bank Rd HD5 137 A3
Dalton Clowes HD5 154 E7
Dalton Fold Rd HD5 154 D7
Dalton Gr Huddersfield HD5 154 E7
Leeds LS11 214 A2
Dalton Green La HD5 155 A6
Dalton Infants Sch HD5 154 F6
Dalton La Collingham LS23 29 E3
Keighley BD21 35 E7
Dalton Rd Keighley BD21 35 E7
Leeds LS11 214 A2
Dalton St
2 Sowerby Bridge HX6 112 B5
Todmorden OL14 108 B5
Dalton Terr Bradford BD8 74 B8
Castleford WF10 124 D7
Keighley BD21 35 E8
Dalton Works HD5 136 F1
Dam Head La HD8 155 F5
Dam Head Rd HX6 112 C5
Dam Hill HD8 173 E3
Dam La Saxton LS24 65 F6
Yeadon LS19 40 C7
Damask St HX1 203 D4
Damems La BD22 35 A2
Damems Rd BD21 35 A3
Damems Sta BD22 35 A2
Damon Ave BD10 56 E4
Dampier St 15 OL14 108 A1
Damside BD21 35 B6
Damside Rd HD4 154 B4
Dan La BD13 73 C2
Danby Ave BD4 95 B8
Danby La WF2 160 C4
Danby Wlk LS9 212 C3
Dandy Mill Ave WF8 125 F2
Dandy Mill Croft WF8 125 F2
Dandy Mill View WF8 125 F3
Dane Hill Dr BD4 75 E3
Dane Royd Jun & Inf Sch WF4 159 F2
Danebury Rd HD6 115 B1
Danecourt Rd BD4 75 F3
Danefield Terr LS21 23 B8
Danehurst WF8 146 E8
Danella Cres WF2 120 F3
Danella Gr WF2 120 F2
Danes La WF4 158 D6
Danesleigh Dr WF4 158 B6
Daniel Ct BD4 75 F2
Daniel St BD3 75 D7
Danny La HX2 111 D7
Dansk Way LS29 8 D5
Danum Dr BD17 38 C2
Darbyfields HD7 152 E6
Darcey Hey La HX2 202 A1
Darcy Ct LS15 81 C8
Darfield Ave LS8 208 A3
Darfield Cres LS8 208 A2
Darfield Gr 6 LS8 207 F3
Darfield Pl LS8 208 A3
Darfield Rd LS8 208 A3
Darfield St Bradford BD1 201 A4
Leeds LS8 208 A3
Dark La Barwick in E LS15 63 D8
Batley, Birstall WF17 96 F3
Batley, Mount Pleasant WF17 118 B4
Blackshaw Head HX7 88 C3
Cawthorne S75 193 E5
Halifax HX2 112 B6
Dark La continued
Haworth BD22 33 F1
Huddersfield HD4 155 A3
Oxenhope BD22 51 D3
Pontefract WF8 146 C7
Darkfield La WF8 125 F4
Darkwood Cl LS17 44 A4
Darkwood Way LS17 44 A4
Darley Ave LS10 99 D7
Darley Rd WF15 116 F5
Darley St Batley WF16 117 D4
Bradford BD1 201 B3
Keighley BD20 18 B1
Darnes Ave HX2 202 A1
Darning La WF8 165 B5
Darnley Ave WF2 142 A6
Darnley Cl HD7 170 E1
Darnley La LS15 81 C7
Darnley Rd LS16 59 B7
Darren St BD4 75 E6
Darrington C of E Junior & Infants Sch WF8 147 D5
Darrington La WF8 146 E2
Dartmouth Ave
Huddersfield HD5 155 A3
Morley LS27 98 A2
Dartmouth Mews LS27 97 F3
Dartmouth Terr
Bradford BD8 55 C2
Kirkburton HD4 172 E6
Dartmouth Way LS11 214 C2
Darton Hall Cl S75 177 F1
Darton Hall Dr S75 177 F1
Darton Jun & Inf Sch S75 177 F1
Darton La S75 178 B1
Darton Rd S75 193 F5
Darton Sta S75 177 E1
Darwin St BD5 74 C3
Davey La HX7 87 F3
David La WF13 118 C2
David St Castleford WF10 124 B7
Leeds LS11 211 E2
Wakefield WF1 142 E4
Davies Ave LS8 61 A8
Davis Ave WF10 125 D6
Daw Green Ave WF4 159 E4
Daw La Crigglestone WF4 159 D4
Horbury WF4 159 C8
Daw Royds HD5 155 A4
Dawes Ave WF10 124 F6
Dawlish Ave LS9 80 B8
Dawlish Cres LS9 80 B8
Dawlish Gr LS9 80 B7
Dawlish Mount LS9 80 B8
Dawlish Pl 1 LS9 80 B8
Dawlish Rd LS9 80 B8
Dawlish Row LS9 80 B8
Dawlish St LS9 80 B8
Dawlish Terr LS9 80 B8
Dawnay Rd BD5 74 C4
Dawson Ave BD6 94 C8
Dawson Gdns 1 WF13 139 C8
Dawson Hill LS27 98 A5
Dawson Hill Yd 3 WF4 141 B1
Dawson La Birkenshaw BD4 76 E2
Bradford BD4 75 C1
Rothwell LS26 100 E6
Dawson Mount BD4 75 C1
Dawson Pl Bradford BD4 75 D1
Keighley BD21 35 C5
Dawson Rd
Huddersfield HD4 154 B3
Keighley BD21 35 C5
Leeds LS11 214 A3
Dawson St
Bradford, Bierley BD4 75 C2
Bradford, Thackley BD10 39 B2
East Ardsley WF3 98 D1
7 Pudsey LS28 57 D1
Dawson Terr BD4 75 C1
Dawson Way BD21 35 C5
Dawson's Corner LS28 57 C2
Dawsons Meadow LS28 57 C2
Dawtrie Cl WF10 125 D7
Dawtrie St WF10 125 D7
Day St Dewsbury WF13 138 E5
Huddersfield HD1 154 C5
De Lacey Mews BD4 75 C2
De Lacies Ct LS26 101 A7
De Lacies Rd LS26 101 B8
De Lacy Ave Bradford BD4 95 B8
Featherstone WF7 124 C1
Huddersfield HD5 154 F4
De Lacy Mount LS5 59 A4
De Lacy Terr WF8 146 E8
De Trafford St HD4 153 D4
Deacon Cl HD7 170 E2
Deaconess Ct LS29 8 B3
Deacons Wlk WF16 117 E4
Deadmanstone HD4 171 F8
Deal St Halifax HX1 203 F2
Keighley BD21 35 E8
Dealburn Rd BD12 94 E4
Dean Ave Holmfirth HD7 188 F8
Leeds LS8 61 A6
Dean Beck Ave BD6 74 E1
Dean Beck Ct BD6 94 F8
Dean Bridge La HD7 189 E2
Dean Brook Rd
Holmfirth HD7 172 A1
Huddersfield HD4 171 E8
Dean Cl Bradford BD8 54 D1
Wakefield WF2 120 F2
Dean Clough HX1 203 E4
Dean Clough Office Pk HX3 203 D4
Dean Ct Elland HX3 113 A2
Leeds LS8 61 A6
Dean Edge Rd BD22 50 A8
Dean End HX4 134 C8
Dean Hall Cl LS27 97 F4
Dean Head LS18 41 A8
Dean House La HX2 90 E2
Dean La East Carlton LS16 24 A1
Guiseley LS20 38 F8
Holmfirth HD7 189 D1
Horsforth LS18 41 A8
Keighley BD22 33 F6
Sowerby Bridge HX6 132 E8
Sowerby Bridge, Sowerby HX6 111 E2
Wilsden BD13 53 C1
Dean Park Ave BD11 96 E7
Dean Park Dr BD11 96 E6
Dean Rd Bradford BD6 94 D8
Holmfirth HD7 188 C6
Dean St 8 Elland HX5 134 F6
Elland, West Vale HX4 134 D7
Haworth BD22 51 D7
Huddersfield HD3 153 B8
Ilkley LS29 8 C5
Dean Villas OL14 129 B7
Dean Wood View HX3 113 C2
Deane The LS15 80 D7
Deanery Gdns BD10 56 C5
Deanfield Ave LS27 97 F6
Deanfield Junior & Infants Sch HX2 91 E3
Deanhouse La HD7 189 A8
Deanhurst Gdns LS27 97 E6
Deanhurst Ind Ctr LS27 97 D6
Deanroyd Rd OL14 129 B7
Deanstones Cres BD13 92 E8
Deanstones La BD13 92 E8
Deansway LS27 97 F6
Deanswood Cl LS17 43 A3
Deanswood Dr LS17 42 F3
Deanswood Garth LS17 43 A3
Deanswood Gdns LS17 42 F3
Deanswood Gn LS17 42 F3
Deanswood Hill LS17 43 A3
Deanswood Pl LS17 43 A3
Deanswood Rise LS17 43 A3
Deanswood View LS17 43 A3
Deanwood Ave BD15 54 A3
Deanwood Cres BD15 54 A2
Deanwood Wlk BD15 54 A2
Dearden St Ossett WF5 140 D5
Sowerby Bridge HX6 112 B5
Dearne Croft LS22 13 E8
Dearne Dike La HD8 190 E5
Dearne Fold HD3 135 B1
Dearne High Sch S63 194 B1
Dearne Pk HD8 175 E2
Dearne Royd HD8 175 E2
Dearne St
Clayton West HD8 175 D1
Mapplewell S75 177 F1
South Elmsall WF9 182 F3
Dearneside Rd HD8 191 F5
Dearnfield HD8 191 C6
Dearnley St WF13 138 E6
Dee Ct BD22 34 C2
Deep Dale LS23 14 C1
Deep La Bradford BD13 73 C5
Brighouse HD6 115 F2
Halifax HX2 111 F7
Huddersfield HD4 153 B3
Sowerby Bridge HX6 132 B8
Thornton BD13 72 A5
Deepdale Cl BD17 38 A2
Deepdale La LS23 14 C1
Deer Croft Ave HD3 152 F8
Deer Croft Cres HD3 152 F8
Deer Croft Dr HD3 152 F8
Deer Croft Rd 2 HD3 134 F1
Deer Hill Cl HD7 168 F3
Deer Hill Croft HD7 168 F3
Deer Hill Ct HD7 170 C2
Deer Hill Dr HD7 168 F3
Deer Hill End Rd HD7 170 A4
Deershaw La HD7 190 C5
Deershaw Sike La HD7 190 C5
Deerstone Ridge LS22 13 E8
Defarge Ct BD5 74 E3
Deffer Rd WF2 160 C6
Deganwy Dr HD5 137 C2
Deighton Cl LS22 13 F6
Deighton Gates Junior & Infants Sch LS22 13 E8
Deighton La WF17 118 A4
Deighton Rd
Huddersfield HD2 136 E3
Wetherby LS22 13 E7
Deighton Sta HD2 136 E3
Deightonby St S63 194 E1
Delacy Cres WF10 104 D1
Delamere St BD5 74 D2
Delaware Ct BD4 95 B8
Delf Hill HD6 135 E7
Delf La Todmorden OL14 86 D3
Wadsworth Moor HX7 89 C8
Delf Pl HD6 135 E7
Delfs La HX6 110 F1
Delius Ave BD10 56 E5
Dell Croft BD20 5 C2
Dell The Bardsey LS17 28 D3
Castleford WF10 124 A6
Cullingworth BD13 52 E6
Huddersfield HD2 136 B4
Dellside Fold BD13 52 D6
Delmont Cl WF17 117 E6
Delph Cres BD14 73 B4
Delph Croft View BD21 35 D6
Delph Ct LS6 206 A4
Delph Dr BD14 73 B4
Delph Gr BD14 73 B4
Delph Hill 10 Baildon BD17 38 C4
5 Halifax HX2 113 A4
Pudsey LS28 76 E8
Delph Hill La HX2 90 D2
Delph Hill Middle Sch BD12 94 C6
Delph Hill Rd HX2 112 F4
Delph Hill Terr 3 HX2 112 F4
Delph La Huddersfield HD4 171 D7
Leeds LS6 206 A4
Delph Mount LS6 206 A4
Delph St HX1 203 D2
Delph Terr BD14 73 B4
Delph The WF7 145 F5
Delph View LS6 206 A4
Delph Wood Cl BD16 37 C3
Delverne Gr BD2 56 C3
Delves Gate HD7 169 F6
Delves Wood Rd HD4 153 C1
Denard Ind Est HD4 153 B4
Denbigh App LS9 61 D2
Denbigh Croft LS9 61 D2
Denbigh Hts LS9 61 D2
Denbrook Ave BD4 75 F1
Denbrook Cl BD4 75 F1
Denbrook Cres BD4 95 F8
Denbrook Way BD4 75 F1
Denbrook Wlk BD4 75 F1
Denbury Mount BD4 75 E2
Denby C of E Fst Sch HD8 191 F3
Denby Cl Batley WF17 96 D1
Liversedge WF15 116 F5
Denby Crest WF8 147 D5
Denby Ct BD22 34 B2
Denby Dale Rd
Crigglestone WF4 159 C5
Wakefield WF2 142 B3
West Bretton WF4 158 E2
Denby Dale Rd E WF4 159 F7
Denby Dale Rd W WF4 159 D6
Denby Dale Sta HD8 191 E6
Denby Dr BD17 38 B1
Denby Grange La WF4 157 A5
Denby Hall La HD8 192 D4
Denby Hill Rd BD22 34 B2
Denby La Bradford BD15 54 B1
Denby Dale, Lower Denby HD8 192 C4
Denby Dale, Upper Denby HD8 191 F3
Denby Lane Cres WF4 156 E5
Denby Mount BD22 51 C2
Denby Park Dr WF4 156 E5
Denby Pl 5 HX6 112 B5
Denby Rd Darrington WF8 147 C5
Keighley BD21 35 C5
Denby St BD8 74 C8
Denby View WF12 139 D1
Dence Gn BD4 75 E5
Dence Pl LS15 80 E8
Dene Cl HX5 134 E5
Dene Cres BD7 73 E4
Dene Gr BD20 5 E2
Dene Hill BD17 37 F3
Dene Mount BD15 54 C1
Dene Pk HD8 173 F7
Dene Pl HX1 203 D4
Dene Rd Bradford BD6 73 D1
Skelmanthorpe HD8 174 F1
Dene Royd Cl HX4 133 F3
Dene Royd Ct HX4 133 F3
Dene View HX2 111 D8
Denehill BD9 54 D2
Deneside WF5 140 C7
Deneside Mount BD5 74 D2
Deneside Terr BD5 74 D2
Denesway LS25 83 A5
Deneway LS28 57 C2
Denfield Ave HX3 91 F2
Denfield Cres HX3 91 F2
Denfield Edge HX3 91 F2
Denfield Gdns HX3 91 F2
Denfield La HX3 91 E2
Denfield Sq HX3 91 F2
Denhale Ave WF2 141 F6
Denham Ave LS27 98 A2
Denham Dr HD7 188 F8
Denham St Batley WF17 118 A7
4 Brighouse HD6 115 A1
Denholme Dr WF5 140 D7
Denholme First Sch BD13 52 D1
Denholme Gate Rd
Brighouse HX3 93 C1
Northowram HX3 93 C1
Denholme Meadow WF9 182 F4
Denholme Rd BD22 51 D1
Denison Rd LS3 211 D4
Denison St Batley WF17 118 C4
Yeadon LS19 40 B7
Denmark St WF1 142 E4
Dennil Cres LS15 62 D4
Dennil Rd LS15 62 D3
Dennington La WF4 159 C3
Dennis La BD20 5 A4
Dennison Fold BD4 75 E5
Dennison Hill LS21 23 B8
Dennistead Cres LS6 59 D5
Denshaw Dr LS27 98 C4
Denshaw Gr LS27 98 C4
Denshaw La WF3 98 F3
Denstone St WF1 216 C3
Dent Dr WF1 142 F8
Dent St LS9 212 C3
Denton Ave LS8 204 C4
Denton Dr BD16 37 C4
Denton Gdns WF7 164 A5
Denton Gr LS8 204 C4
Denton House 9 BD6 93 E8
Denton Rd Denton LS29 9 A6
Ilkley LS29 8 D5
Denton Row Denholme BD13 71 D8
Elland HX4 134 C4
Denton Terr WF10 124 E8
Denwell Terr WF8 125 D1
Der St OL14 108 C5
Derby Pl BD3 75 D7
Derby Rd Bradford BD3 75 E7
Yeadon LS19 40 B4
Derby St Bingley BD16 36 F3
3 Bradford, Clayton BD14 73 B4
Bradford, Great Horton BD7 74 B4
Queensbury BD13 72 D1
Sowerby Bridge HX6 112 D4
Todmorden OL14 108 D5
Derby Terr Bradford BD10 56 E8
Marsden HD7 168 F4
Derbyshire St LS10 215 F3
Derdale St OL14 108 C5
Derry Hill LS29 21 F4
Derry Hill Gdns LS29 21 F4
Derry La LS29 21 F4
Derwent Ave Baildon BD17 37 E1
Garforth LS25 82 F6
Rothwell LS26 101 C6
Wilsden BD15 53 C4
Derwent Cl HX7 89 A4
Derwent Ct BD20 17 E8
Derwent Dr
Castleford WF10 104 E1
Huddersfield HD5 154 D7
Leeds LS16 42 D4
Derwent Gr WF2 141 F6
Derwent Pl
Knottingley WF11 126 E1
Leeds LS11 211 D2
Derwent Rd Batley WF12 118 F2
Bradford BD2 56 A3
Honley HD7 171 E3
Meltham HD7 170 E1
Wakefield WF2 141 F6
Derwent Rise LS22 13 D8
Derwent St BD21 35 F8
Derwentwater Gr LS6 59 D5
Derwentwater Terr LS6 59 D5
Derwin Ave HD4 173 C2
Detroit Ave LS15 81 E8
Detroit Dr LS15 81 E8
Deveron Gr HD2 153 E8
Devon Cl LS2 206 B2
Devon Gr WF5 140 C4
Devon Rd LS2 206 B2
Devon St HX1 202 B2
Devon Way HD6 115 B6
Devon Wlk 4 WF13 139 B8
Devonshire Ave LS8 44 A2
Devonshire Cl LS8 44 A2
Devonshire Cres LS8 44 A1
Devonshire Ct WF11 127 A4
Devonshire Gdns LS2 206 B3
Devonshire La LS8 44 A2
Devonshire Pl 3 LS19 40 B7
Devonshire St
Huddersfield HD1 153 E3
Keighley BD21 35 B7
Devonshire St W BD21 35 A7
Devonshire Terr BD9 55 C2
Dewar Cl LS22 13 B1
Dewhirst Cl BD17 38 D2
Dewhirst Pl BD4 75 D6
Dewhirst Rd Baildon BD17 38 D2
Brighouse HD6 115 A4
Dewhirst St BD15 53 C5
Dewhurst Rd HD2 136 B2
Dewsbury Bus Mus WF13 138 E5
Dewsbury Coll
Batley WF17 118 C5
Dewsbury WF13 118 C1
Dewsbury District Golf Course WF14 138 D3
Dewsbury District Hospl WF13 118 A2
Dewsbury Gate Rd WF13 117 F3
Dewsbury Mills WF12 139 C6
Dewsbury Moor Infant Sch WF13 117 F2
Dewsbury Mus & Art Gal WF13 139 A7
Dewsbury Rd
Brighouse HD6 135 C6
Cleckheaton BD19 96 B2
Cleckheaton, Marsh BD19 116 E7
East Ardsley WF12 119 C7
Elland HX5 135 C6
Leeds LS11 214 C2
Middleton LS27 98 F5
Ossett WF5 140 D7
Wakefield WF2 141 D5
Dewsbury Sta WF13 139 C8
Deyne Rd HD4 171 C7
Diadem Dr LS14 61 E1
Dial St LS9 212 C2
Diamond Ave WF9 182 E3
Diamond St Batley WF17 118 B6
Bradford BD1 201 C2
Halifax HX1 202 C4
Huddersfield HD1 154 B8
10 Huddersfield, Moldgreen HD5 154 D5
Keighley BD22 35 A4
Diamond Terr HX1 202 C4
Dib Cl LS8 61 D5
Dib La LS8 61 D5
Dibb La LS19 39 F7
Dick Dean La HX7 69 A5

Dick Edge La HD7 ... 190 B2
Dick La BD3, BD4 ... 75 E6
Dick's Garth Rd LS29 ... 21 F4
Dicken's St HX2 ... 202 A3
Dickens St BD5 ... 74 E3
Dickinson Ct WF1 ... 216 B4
Dickinson Gdns 11 WF13 ... 139 B8
Dickinson St
Horsforth LS18 ... 41 C2
Wakefield WF1 ... 216 B3
Dickinson Terr WF7 ... 145 D6
Dickson Fold WF15 ... 116 F4
Dicky Sykes La WF7 ... 163 D5
Digby Rd LS29 ... 22 A4
Digley Rd HD7 ... 188 B2
Digley Royd La HD7 ... 188 A3
Dimple Gdns WF5 ... 140 D4
Dimple Well Infant Sch
WF5 ... 140 D4
Dimple Wells Cl WF5 ... 140 D4
Dimple Wells La WF5 ... 140 D4
Dimple Wells Rd WF5 ... 140 D4
Dimples La Haworth BD22 ... 51 B6
Keighley BD20 ... 36 D8
Dineley Ave OL14 ... 108 A7
Dingle Rd HD1 ... 153 D6
Dingley Rd HD3 ... 153 C8
Dinsdale's Bldgs LS19 ... 40 A6
Dirker Ave HD7 ... 169 A5
Dirker Bank Rd HD7 ... 168 F5
Dirker Dr HD7 ... 168 F4
Dirkhill Rd BD7 ... 74 C5
Dirkhill St BD7 ... 74 B5
Discovery Rd HX1 ... 203 F2
Dish Hill Fly-over WF11 ... 126 D8
Disney Cl HD4 ... 153 D3
Dispensary Wlk HX1 ... 203 F3
Disraeli Gdns LS11 ... 214 B4
Disraeli Terr LS11 ... 214 B4
Dixon Ave BD7 ... 73 F5
Dixon Cl Elland HX4 ... 134 B8
Steeton BD20 ... 17 C5
Dixon La LS12 ... 209 F1
Dixon Lane Rd LS12 ... 209 F1
Dixon St
Featherstone WF7 ... 145 D7
Sutton in C BD20 ... 16 E5
Dixon's Yd WF1 ... 216 C2
Dob La HX6 ... 111 D3
Dob Park Rd LS21 ... 10 E8
Dob Royd HD8 ... 190 D7
Dob The HX6 ... 111 D3
Dobb Kiln La BD16 ... 37 B1
Dobb La HD7 ... 188 C2
Dobb Top Rd HD7 ... 188 C2
Dobroyd Rd OL14 ... 108 A4
Dobson Ave LS11 ... 214 C3
Dobson Gr LS11 ... 214 C3
Dobson Pl LS11 ... 214 C3
Dobson Terr LS11 ... 214 C3
Dobson View LS11 ... 214 C3
Dobsons Wharf BD20 ... 17 E8
Dock La BD17, BD18 ... 55 C8
Dock St LS10 ... 211 F3
Dockery HD1 ... 153 F3
Dockfield Pl BD17 ... 55 C8
Dockfield Rd BD17 ... 55 C8
Dockfield Terr BD17 ... 55 C8
Dockroyd La BD22 ... 34 D2
Doctor Fold HD7 ... 171 F5
Doctor Hill Bradford BD10 ... 56 A6
Bradford, Springfield BD10 ... 56 B7
Halifax HX2 ... 91 E1
Doctor La Bradford BD10 ... 39 B1
Flockton WF4 ... 157 B2
Mirfield WF14 ... 138 A5
Shepley HD8 ... 174 A3
Dodd's Royd HD4 ... 171 E8
Dodge Holme Ct HX2 ... 91 D4
Dodge Holme Dr HX2 ... 91 D4
Dodge Holme Gdns HX2 ... 91 D4
Dodge Holme Rd HX2 ... 91 D4
Dodgeholme Cl HX2 ... 91 D4
Dodgson Ave LS7 ... 207 E3
Dodgson St HX5 ... 134 F5
Dodlee La HD3 ... 152 E7
Dodsworth Cres WF6 ... 144 B8
Dodworth Dr WF2 ... 160 B5
Dog Hill S72 ... 180 C3
Dog Hill Dr S72 ... 180 C3
Dog Kennel Bank HD5 ... 154 C4
Dog Kennel Hill S75 ... 193 E3
Dog Kennel La HX3 ... 113 E5
Dog La
Elland, Stainland HX4 ... 133 E2
Elland, Upper Greetland HX4 ... 133 E7
Dog Pits La OL13 ... 106 A6
Doghouse La OL14 ... 108 A5
Dogley La HD4 ... 155 D1
Dogley Villa Ct HD8 ... 155 D1
Doldram La HX6 ... 112 A1
Dole La HX7 ... 89 A1
Dole St BD13 ... 72 E6
Doles Ave S71 ... 179 B3
Doles Cres S71 ... 179 B3
Dolfin Pl HD2 ... 136 F5
Doll La BD13 ... 52 E4
Dolly La LS9 ... 207 E2
Dolphin La WF3 ... 99 F2
Dolphin Rd LS10 ... 99 E5
Dombey St HX1 ... 202 C3
Domestic Rd LS12 ... 210 C1
Domestic St LS11 ... 210 C1
Domestic St Ind Est LS11 ... 210 C2
Dominion Ave LS7 ... 204 B3
Dominion Ind Pk HX3 ... 114 C8
Don Ave LS22 ... 13 D8
Don Ct BD20 ... 5 E1
Don Pedro Ave WF6 ... 123 D2
Don Pedro Cl WF6 ... 123 D2
Don St BD21 ... 35 B8
Don View S36 ... 199 D1
Donald Ave BD6 ... 94 C8
Donald St 5 LS28 ... 57 D2
Doncaster La DN6 ... 184 C3
Doncaster Rd
Ackworth M T WF4 ... 163 B6
Crofton WF4 ... 143 D2
Darrington WF7 ... 164 B3
Hampole WF9 ... 183 D5
Knottingley WF11 ... 126 C4
South Elmsall WF9 ... 183 D5
Thorpe Audlin WF8 ... 165 C4
Upton WF9 ... 182 E7
Upton, Barnsdale WF8 ... 166 A1
Wakefield WF1 ... 142 E4
West Hardwick WF4 ... 163 B6
Doncaster Road Est WF7 ... 164 A5
Doncaster Sq WF11 ... 126 D5
Doncaster St HX3 ... 113 D3
Donisthorpe St
Bradford BD5 ... 74 E3
Leeds LS10 ... 212 B1
Dorchester Ave WF8 ... 146 B8
Dorchester Cres
Baildon BD17 ... 38 F4
Bradford BD4 ... 75 E2
Dorchester Ct BD4 ... 75 E3
Dorchester Dr Halifax HX2 ... 202 A1
Yeadon LS19 ... 40 D6
Dorchester Rd HD2 ... 136 B5
Dorian Cl BD10 ... 56 C6
Dorman Ave WF9 ... 183 D8
Dorothy St BD21 ... 35 A3
Dorset Ave LS8 ... 208 A4
Dorset Cl Bradford BD5 ... 74 C3
Hemsworth WF9 ... 181 D8
Dorset Gr LS28 ... 76 E8
Dorset Mount LS8 ... 208 A3
Dorset Rd LS8 ... 208 A3
Dorset St Bradford BD5 ... 74 D3
Huddersfield HD1 ... 153 F8
Leeds LS8 ... 208 A4
Dorset Terr LS8 ... 208 A3
Dorset Wlk 6 WF13 ... 139 B8
Dortmund Sq LS2 ... 211 F4
Dotterel Glen LS27 ... 98 C3
Doubting La WF12 ... 139 D1
Doubting Rd WF12 ... 139 D1
Douglas Ave Batley WF17 ... 118 F5
Huddersfield HD5 ... 154 E5
Huddersfield, Cliff End HD3 ... 153 B6
Douglas Cres BD18 ... 55 D6
Douglas Dr BD4 ... 75 C4
Douglas Rd Bacup OL13 ... 106 A1
Bradford BD4 ... 75 C4
Douglas St Dewsbury WF12 ... 139 C4
Halifax HX3 ... 92 B2
8 Haworth BD22 ... 51 E8
Douglas Towers 1 BD5 ... 201 B1
Dove Cl LS22 ... 13 E8
Dove Dr WF10 ... 125 B8
Dove St 16 Haworth BD22 ... 51 D7
Shipley BD18 ... 54 F8
Dovecote Cl WF4 ... 141 B2
Dovecote Dr WF10 ... 103 E6
Dovecote La WF4 ... 141 A2
Dovedale Cl Crofton WF4 ... 144 A1
Shelf HX3 ... 93 B6
Dovedale Garth LS15 ... 62 F3
Dovedale Gdns LS15 ... 62 F3
Dovelands BD20 ... 16 D4
Dover La HD7 ... 189 B3
Dover Rd HD7 ... 189 A3
Dover St Bradford BD3 ... 56 A1
Garforth LS25 ... 83 B7
Todmorden OL14 ... 108 D5
Dovesdale Gr BD5 ... 74 D2
Dovesdale Rd BD5 ... 74 D2
Dowkell La LS23 ... 14 F1
Dowker St Halifax HX1 ... 202 B1
Huddersfield HD3 ... 153 B5
Dowley Gap La BD16 ... 37 B1
Downham St BD3 ... 201 D2
Downing Cl BD3 ... 75 B7
Downing St HD7 ... 170 C8
Downland Cres WF11 ... 127 B2
Downside Cres BD15 ... 54 A1
Dowry La HX6 ... 132 A3
Dracup Ave BD7 ... 73 E5
Dracup Rd BD7 ... 73 F3
Dradishaw Rd BD20 ... 5 D1
Dragon Cres LS12 ... 210 A1
Dragon Dr LS12 ... 210 A1
Dragon Rd LS12 ... 210 A1
Drake La BD11 ... 96 E5
Drake Rd OL15 ... 129 C1
Drake St Bradford BD1 ... 201 C2
Keighley BD21 ... 35 C8
Drakes Ind Est HX3 ... 92 A4
Draper Corner HX7 ... 88 E6
Draper La HX7 ... 88 F6
Draughton Gr BD5 ... 74 D1
Draughton St BD5 ... 74 D1
Dray View WF13 ... 117 F2
Draycott Wlk BD4 ... 75 E2
Drayton Manor Yd LS11 ... 214 C4
Drewry Rd BD21 ... 35 B7
Drewton Rd BD1 ... 201 B4
Driftholme Rd BD11 ... 96 F7
Drighlington Inf Sch
BD11 ... 96 E6
Drighlington Junior Sch
BD11 ... 96 F7
Drill Par BD8 ... 55 D1
Drill St 10 Haworth BD22 ... 51 C6
Keighley BD21 ... 35 C7
Drinker La HD8 ... 174 D6
Drive The Bardsey LS17 ... 28 D5
Batley WF17 ... 118 A6
Bingley BD16 ... 36 E6
Bradford BD10 ... 56 D6
Brighouse HX3 ... 114 D8
Burley in W LS29 ... 21 E8
Hebden Bridge HX7 ... 89 D1
Kippax LS25 ... 83 A1
Leeds LS8 ... 204 C4
Leeds, Alwoodley LS17 ... 43 A6
Leeds, Bank LS9 ... 212 B3
Leeds, Manston LS15 ... 62 D2
Swillington LS26 ... 82 A1
Driver Pl LS12 ... 210 B2
Driver St LS12 ... 210 B2
Driver Terr Leeds LS12 ... 210 B2
Silsden BD20 ... 5 E2
Drivers Row WF8 ... 146 B7
Drovers Way BD2 ... 55 E4
Drub La BD19 ... 95 F2
Druggist La LS29 ... 6 F8
Druids St BD14 ... 73 B4
Druids View BD16 ... 36 D6
Drummer La HD7 ... 152 B4
Drummond Ave LS16 ... 59 C7
Drummond Ct LS16 ... 59 C6
Drummond Middle Sch
BD8 ... 55 C1
Drummond Rd
Bradford BD8 ... 55 C1
Leeds LS16 ... 59 C7
Drummond Trad Est BD8 ... 74 D8
Drury Ave LS18 ... 58 B8
Drury Cl LS18 ... 58 B8
Drury La Elland HX4 ... 133 F4
Horsforth LS18 ... 58 B8
Normanton WF6 ... 122 F3
Wakefield WF1 ... 216 A2
Dry Carr La HX2 ... 90 C4
Dry Hill La HD8 ... 192 B5
Dryclough Ave HD4 ... 153 C2
Dryclough CE Inf Sch
HD4 ... 153 C3
Dryclough Cl HX3 ... 113 C3
Dryclough La HX3 ... 113 C3
Dryclough Rd HD4 ... 153 C2
Dryden St Bingley BD16 ... 36 F3
Bradford BD1 ... 201 D2
Dubb La BD16 ... 37 A3
Duchy Ave BD9 ... 54 E3
Duchy Cres BD9 ... 54 E3
Duchy Dr BD9 ... 54 E3
Duchy Gr BD9 ... 54 E3
Duchy Villas BD9 ... 54 E3
Duchywood BD9 ... 54 E3
Ducie St BD10 ... 39 B1
Duck Hill HX7 ... 69 A1
Duckett Gr LS28 ... 75 F8
Duckett La BD1 ... 201 B3
Duckworth Gr BD9 ... 54 F1
Duckworth La BD9 ... 54 F1
Duckworth Terr BD9 ... 54 F1
Dudfleet La WF4 ... 159 B8
Dudley Ave Batley WF17 ... 97 A2
Huddersfield HD1 ... 153 D6
Dudley Cres HX2 ... 91 D5
Dudley Gr BD4 ... 75 E5
Dudley Hill First Sch BD4 ... 75 C3
Dudley Hill Rd BD2 ... 56 B3
Dudley Rd HD1 ... 153 D6
Dudley St Bradford BD4 ... 75 B3
Bradford, Dudley Hill BD4 ... 75 C3
Bradford, Tyersal BD4 ... 75 E5
Dudwell Ave HX3 ... 113 C2
Dudwell Gr HX3 ... 113 C2
Dudwell La HX3 ... 113 C2
Dufton App LS14 ... 62 A3
Duich Rd BD6 ... 93 E6
Duinen St BD5 ... 201 C1
Duke of York Ave WF2 ... 142 D1
Duke of York St
Wakefield WF1 ... 216 C3
Wakefield, Wrenthorpe WF2 ... 120 F1
Duke St Bradford BD1 ... 201 B3
Castleford WF10 ... 124 B8
Dewsbury WF13 ... 138 E5
Elland HX5 ... 134 F6
Halifax HX2 ... 90 D1
11 Haworth BD22 ... 51 D7
Hemsworth WF9 ... 163 A3
Keighley BD20 ... 18 C1
Leeds LS9 ... 212 A3
Duke Wood Rd HD8 ... 175 F2
Dulverton Cl Morley LS11 ... 213 D1
Pontefract WF8 ... 125 F3
Dulverton Ct LS11 ... 213 D1
Dulverton Garth LS11 ... 78 C1
Dulverton Gdns LS11 ... 78 C2
Dulverton Gn LS11 ... 213 D1
Dulverton Gr Bradford BD4 ... 75 D3
Morley LS11 ... 78 C1
Dulverton Pl LS11 ... 78 C1
Dulverton Rise WF8 ... 125 F3
Dulverton Sq LS11 ... 213 D1
Dulverton Way WF8 ... 125 F3
Dunbar Cft BD13 ... 72 F1
Dunbar St WF1 ... 142 F4
Dunbottle Cl WF14 ... 138 C5
Dunbottle La WF14 ... 138 B6
Duncan Ave Otley LS21 ... 22 D6
Wakefield WF2 ... 142 E2
Duncan St Bradford BD5 ... 201 B1
Leeds LS1 ... 211 F3
Dunce Park Cl HX5 ... 134 F5
Duncombe Rd BD8 ... 74 A7
Duncombe St
Bradford BD8 ... 74 A7
Leeds LS1 ... 211 D4
Duncombe Way BD8 ... 74 A7
Dundas St Halifax HX1 ... 202 B1
25 Huddersfield HD1 ... 154 A6
Keighley BD21 ... 35 D6
Dundee Rd OL14 ... 107 D8
Dunderdale Cres WF10 ... 104 D1
Dunford Rd
Dunford Bridge HD7 ... 199 D3
Holmfirth HD7 ... 189 B3
Holmfirth, Hade Edge HD7 ... 199 B7
Dungeon La LS26 ... 101 A1
Dunhill Cres LS9 ... 80 E8
Dunhill Rise LS9 ... 80 E8
Dunkhill Croft BD10 ... 56 B7
Dunkirk Cres HX1 ... 202 A2
Dunkirk Gdns HX1 ... 202 A1
Dunkirk La HX1 ... 202 B2
Dunkirk Rise BD20 ... 18 E2
Dunkirk St HX1 ... 202 A2
Dunkirk Terr HX1 ... 202 B2
Dunlin Cl LS27 ... 98 C3
Dunlin Croft 8 LS10 ... 99 D5
Dunlin Ct 6 LS10 ... 99 D5
Dunlin Dr LS10 ... 99 D5
Dunlin Fold 7 LS10 ... 99 D5
Dunlin Way 3 BD8 ... 73 C7
Dunn Cl WF2 ... 120 F3
Dunningley La
Middleton WF3 ... 98 F3
Middleton, Black Gates WF3 ... 98 F2
Dunnington Wlk BD6 ... 94 A6
Dunnock Croft LS27 ... 98 C3
Dunrobin Ave LS25 ... 83 B8
Dunsford Ave BD4 ... 95 B8
Dunsil Villas WF9 ... 182 F1
Dunsley Bank Rd HD7 ... 188 F3
Dunsley Terr WF9 ... 182 A2
Dunsmore Dr HD3 ... 152 F8
Dunstan Cl WF5 ... 140 E4
Dunstarn Dr LS16 ... 42 D3
Dunstarn Gdns LS16 ... 42 E3
Dunstarn La LS16 ... 42 D2
Durban Ave LS11 ... 213 F2
Durban Cres LS11 ... 213 F2
Durham Rd BD8 ... 55 A1
Durham St Castleford WF10 ... 124 E6
Halifax HX2 ... 202 A3
Durham Terr BD8 ... 55 A1
Durkar Fields WF4 ... 159 F6
Durkar La WF4 ... 159 F6
Durkar Low La WF4 ... 160 A7
Durkar Rise WF4 ... 159 F6
Durkheim Ct BD3 ... 75 C7
Durley Ave BD9 ... 55 A3
Durling Dr BD18 ... 55 E7
Durlston Gr BD12 ... 94 D4
Durlston Terr BD12 ... 94 D4
Durn St OL14 ... 86 A1
Durrance St BD22 ... 34 F6
Durrant Cl LS22 ... 13 F4
Dutton Gn LS14 ... 62 A8
Dutton Way LS14 ... 62 A7
Duxbury Rise LS7 ... 206 B2
Dyas Bldgs WF7 ... 144 E5
Dye House La
Sowerby Bridge HX6 ... 112 E1
Wilsden BD15 ... 53 B5
Dyehouse Dr BD19 ... 95 C2
Dyehouse La Brighouse HD6 ... 115 B1
Pudsey LS28 ... 76 E4
Dyehouse Rd BD12 ... 95 A5
Dyer La HX3 ... 91 F2
Dyer St LS2 ... 212 A4
Dyers Ct LS6 ... 205 F4
Dyke Bottom HD8 ... 190 F8
Dyke Cl WF14 ... 138 A8
Dyke End HD7 ... 152 B3
Dyke La OL14 ... 109 B7
Dymond Gr WF15 ... 117 A3
Dymond Rd WF15 ... 117 B3
Dymond View WF15 ... 117 A3
Dyson La Holmfirth HD7 ... 189 C1
Ripponden HX6 ... 132 C2
Dyson Pl 2 HX3 ... 113 E3
Dyson Rd HX1 ... 202 B4
Dyson St Bradford BD1 ... 74 D7
Brighouse HD6 ... 115 A3
Huddersfield HD5 ... 154 E6
Shipley BD9 ... 55 A4
Dyson's Hill HD7 ... 171 E5
Eagle Gr WF2 ... 141 D6
Eagle St Haworth BD22 ... 51 E8
Keighley BD21 ... 35 B7
Todmorden OL14 ... 108 B6
Eaglesfield Dr BD6 ... 94 A6
Ealand Ave WF17 ... 118 A7
Ealand Cres WF17 ... 118 A7
Ealand Rd
Batley, Brown Hill WF17 ... 117 F7
Batley, Carlinghow WF17 ... 118 A7
Ealing Ct WF17 ... 118 A6
Earl Cowper Middle Sch
LS7 ... 207 E4
Earl St Dewsbury WF12 ... 140 B8
Haworth BD22 ... 51 C6
Hemsworth WF9 ... 163 A3
Keighley BD21 ... 35 B8
Wakefield WF1 ... 216 C3
Earl Terr 5 HX3 ... 92 A2
Earle St WF7 ... 145 C6
Earles Ave HD5 ... 154 E5
Earls View BD20 ... 16 C4
Earlsheaton High Sch
WF12 ... 139 E8
Earlsheaton Infants Sch
WF12 ... 139 F7
Earlsmere Dr LS27 ... 97 F5
Earlswood Ave LS8 ... 43 F2
Earlswood Chase LS28 ... 76 E6
Earlswood Cres LS25 ... 83 A2
Earlswood Mead LS28 ... 76 E6
Easby Ave WF17 ... 117 F4
Easby Cl LS29 ... 7 F4
Easby Dr LS29 ... 7 F4
Easby Rd BD7 ... 74 D5
Easdale Cl LS14 ... 61 F5
Easdale Cres LS14 ... 62 A5
Easdale Rd LS14 ... 61 F4
Easingwood Dr HD5 ... 137 B1
East Acres WF11 ... 126 E7
East Ardsley Primary Sch
WF3 ... 120 D8
East Ave Glusburn BD20 ... 16 D6
Horbury WF4 ... 141 C1
Huddersfield HD3 ... 135 C1
Keighley BD21 ... 35 C8
Pontefract WF8 ... 146 B7
South Elmsall WF9 ... 183 B4
Upton WF9 ... 183 A7
East Bath St WF17 ... 118 D5
East Beck Ct LS21 ... 9 F5
East Bierley CE (controlled)
First Sch BD4 ... 95 F7
East Bolton HX2 ... 91 E7
East Busk La LS21 ... 23 C8
East Byland HX2 ... 91 E6
East Causeway Cl LS16 ... 42 D5
East Causeway Cres LS16 ... 42 D4
East Causeway Vale LS16 ... 42 E4
East Chevin Rd LS21 ... 23 C5
East Cl Huddersfield HD2 ... 136 B2
Pontefract WF8 ... 146 F5
East Cliffe HX3 ... 113 E6
East Cswy LS16 ... 42 D5
East Dale Cl WF9 ... 181 F7
East Dene BD20 ... 5 E2
East Down WF10 ... 125 A8
East Dr Garforth LS25 ... 83 B5
Pontefract WF8 ... 146 F7
East End Cres S71 ... 179 E3
East Field St LS9 ... 212 B3
East Fold HD8 ... 175 C1
East Garforth Primary Sch
LS25 ... 83 B8
East Garforth Sta LS25 ... 83 A7
East Gr HD5 ... 155 C8
East Grange Cl LS10 ... 215 E1
East Grange Dr LS10 ... 215 E1
East Grange Garth LS10 ... 215 E1
East Grange Rd LS10 ... 215 E1
East Grange Rise LS10 ... 215 E1
East Grange Sq LS10 ... 215 E1
East Grange View LS10 ... 215 E1
East King St LS9 ... 212 B3
East Lee La OL14 ... 109 A7
East Leeds High Sch LS14 ... 61 F4
East Moor Ave LS8 ... 43 F1
East Moor Cres LS8 ... 43 F2
East Moor Dr LS8 ... 44 A1
East Moor La LS16 ... 42 D4
East Moor Rd LS8 ... 43 F2
East Morton First Sch
BD20 ... 36 D8
East Mount 3 HD6 ... 115 A3
East Mount Pl 4 HD6 ... 115 A3
East Par
Baildon BD17 ... 38 D4
Bradford BD1 ... 201 C3
Ilkley LS29 ... 8 C4
Keighley BD21 ... 35 C7
Leeds LS1 ... 211 E4
Menston LS29 ... 22 A4
Sowerby Bridge HX6 ... 112 D4
Steeton BD20 ... 17 D5
East Park Dr LS9 ... 80 A7
East Park Gr LS9 ... 80 A7
East Park Mount 7 LS9 ... 80 A7
East Park Par LS9 ... 80 A7
East Park Pl LS9 ... 80 A7
East Park Rd Halifax HX3 ... 92 A1
1 Leeds LS9 ... 212 C3
East Park St Leeds LS9 ... 80 A7
Morley LS27 ... 97 F3
East Park Terr 8 LS9 ... 80 A7
East Park View LS9 ... 80 A7
East Pinfold S71 ... 179 C2
East Rd BD12 ... 94 E6
East Riddlesden Hall
BD20 ... 18 F1
East Royd BD22 ... 34 D2
East Side Ct LS28 ... 77 A5
East Squire La BD8 ... 55 C1
East St Batley WF17 ... 118 C5
Brighouse HD6 ... 115 A1
Brighouse, Bailiff Bridge HX3 ... 115 A7
Holmfirth HD7 ... 189 E3
Huddersfield, Leymoor HD7 ... 152 E4
Huddersfield, Lindley HD3 ... 135 B1
Leeds LS2, LS9 ... 212 B3
Lofthouse Gate, Newton Hill WF1 ... 121 C2
Lofthouse Gate, Stanley Ferry WF3 ... 122 A2
Ryhill WF4 ... 162 D1
South Elmsall WF9 ... 183 B4
South Hiendley S72 ... 180 E5
Sowerby Bridge HX6 ... 111 E1
East Terr BD22 ... 51 E8

East View Bradford BD13 73 C2
Brighouse HX3 115 A7
Castleford WF10 124 A7
Cleckheaton BD19 116 A6
Gildersome LS27 97 C5
Glusburn BD20 16 D7
Kippax LS25 83 B2
Knottingley WF11 127 A4
Leeds LS15 62 C2
Micklefield LS25 84 B6
6 Mirfield WF14 137 F6
Ossett WF5 140 E3
Pudsey LS28 76 E5
Rothwell LS26 101 C5
Silsden BD20 5 E2
Yeadon LS19 40 C6
East View Cotts 5 LS28 76 F8
East View Rd LS19 40 C6
East View Terr
Bradford BD12 94 E4
Otley LS21 23 B7
East-Thorpe Pl WF14 138 B4
Eastborough Cres WF13 118 D1
Eastborough Junior & Infants Sch WF13 139 D8
Eastbourne Ave WF7 145 E6
Eastbourne Cl WF8 147 A7
Eastbourne Cres WF8 147 A8
Eastbourne Dr WF8 147 A8
Eastbourne Rd BD9 55 B5
Eastbourne Terr WF8 147 A8
Eastbourne View WF8 147 A8
Eastbrook La BD1 201 C2
Eastbrook Well BD1 201 C3
Eastburn Junior & Infant Sch BD20 16 F6
Eastbury Ave BD6 73 D1
Eastdean Bank LS14 62 A6
Eastdean Dr LS14 62 A6
Eastdean Gate 7 LS14 62 B5
Eastdean Gdns LS14 62 B6
Eastdean Gr LS14 62 B6
Eastdean Grange 8 LS14 62 B5
Eastdean Rd LS14 62 A6
Eastdean Rise LS14 62 B6
Easterly Ave LS8 208 B4
Easterly Cl LS8 208 B3
Easterly Cres LS8 208 A4
Easterly Cross LS8 208 B4
Easterly Garth LS8 208 B4
Easterly Gr LS8 208 A4
Easterly Mount LS8 208 B4
Easterly Rd LS8 61 C5
Easterly Sq LS8 208 B4
Easterly View LS8 208 B4
Eastfield HD8 190 F8
Eastfield Ave WF11 126 F3
Eastfield Cres LS26 101 B6
Eastfield Dr Kirkburton HD8 173 E7
Pontefract WF8 125 F1
Rothwell LS26 101 B6
Eastfield Gdns BD4 75 E3
Eastfield Gr WF6 123 C3
Eastfield La WF10 124 E8
Eastfield Pl BD20 16 D5
Eastfield Rd
Knottingley WF11 126 F3
Mirfield WF14 138 D6
Eastgate Bramhope LS16 24 D3
Elland HX5 134 F7
Hemsworth WF9 181 E6
Honley HD7 171 F5
Leeds LS2 212 A4
Easthorpe Ct BD2 56 D4
Eastland Wlk 3 LS13 58 E1
Eastlands HD5 155 A4
Eastleigh Ct WF3 120 A8
Eastleigh Dr WF3 120 A8
Eastleigh Gr BD5 74 C3
Eastmoor Gr S71 179 C2
Eastmoor Rd WF1 216 C4
Easton Pl HD3 153 B7
Eastville Rd WF4 144 B3
Eastway WF14 137 F7
Eastway Pk WF14 138 A7
Eastwood Ave Halifax HX2 91 E7
Sowerby Bridge HX6 111 F3
Wakefield WF2 141 E7
Eastwood Cl
Crigglestone WF4 159 F7
Halifax HX2 91 E7
Eastwood Cres Leeds LS14 62 D4
Shipley BD16 54 B8
Eastwood Ct 7 HX3 113 A4
Eastwood Dr LS14 62 D5
Eastwood First Sch BD21 35 D8
Eastwood Garth LS14 62 D4
Eastwood Gdns LS14 62 C4
Eastwood Gr Garforth LS25 83 A5
Halifax HX2 91 E7
Eastwood La LS14 62 D4
Eastwood Nook LS14 62 D4
Eastwood Rd OL14 87 D2
Eastwood St Bradford BD4 201 C1
8 Brighouse HD6 115 B3
7 Halifax HX3 92 A2
8 Huddersfield HD5 154 D5
Easy Rd LS9 212 C2
Eaton Hill LS16 41 F3
Eaton Mews LS10 99 C5
Eaton Pl WF9 181 E7
Eaton Rd LS29 8 A3
Eaton Sq LS10 99 C5
Eaton St 1 BD21 35 A4
Eaton Wlk WF9 183 A5
Eaves Ave HX7 88 E4
Eaves Rd HX7 88 E4
Ebberston Gr LS6 205 F3
Ebberston Pl LS6 205 F3
Ebberston Terr LS6 205 F3
Ebenezer Pl BD7 74 A4
Ebenezer St Bradford BD1 201 C2
6 Pudsey LS28 57 D3
Rothwell WF3 100 B3
Ebor Gardens Primary Sch LS9 212 C4
Ebor Gdns WF14 137 F5
Ebor La BD22 51 D8
Ebor Mount Kippax LS25 83 A2
Leeds LS6 205 F2
Ebor Pl LS6 205 F2
Ebor St LS6 205 F2
Ebor Terr LS10 215 E2
Ebridge Ct 17 BD16 37 A3
Ebson House La HD7 190 B6
Ebury Cl WF17 118 D6
Ebury St WF17 118 D6
Eccles Ct BD2 56 B4
Eccles Parlour HX6 132 A7
Ecclesburn Ave LS9 80 A7
Ecclesburn Rd LS9 80 A7
Ecclesburn St LS9 80 A7
Ecclesburn Terr 13 LS9 80 A7
Eccleshill North Middle Sch BD10 56 D6
Eccleshill Sch & Further Education Ctr BD10 56 E5
Eccup La Bramhope LS16 25 F2
Harewood LS16 26 A5
Eccup Moor Rd LS16 42 E8
Echo St WF15 116 F2
Edale Ave HD4 153 F1
Edale Cl HD5 137 B1
Edale Gr BD13 92 C8
Edale Way LS16 41 F3
Eddercliff Cres WF15 117 A6
Edderthorpe St BD3 75 A6
Eddison Cl LS16 42 D5
Eddison St LS28 57 D2
Eddison Wlk LS16 42 D5
Eddystone Rise WF11 126 D3
Edelshain Gr WF2 160 F8
Eden Ave Ossett WF5 140 D6
Wakefield WF2 141 D5
Eden Cl BD12 94 D3
Eden Cres LS4 59 B4
Eden Dr LS4 59 C4
Eden Gdns LS4 59 B3
Eden Gr LS4 59 B3
Eden Mount LS4 59 B3
Eden Rd LS4 59 B4
Eden Way LS4 59 B3
Eden Wlk LS4 59 B3
Edendale WF10 124 F8
Edensor Rd BD21 35 A7
Ederoyd Ave LS28 57 B1
Ederoyd Cres LS28 57 B1
Ederoyd Dr LS28 57 B1
Ederoyd Gr LS28 57 B1
Ederoyd Mount LS28 57 B1
Ederoyd Rise LS28 57 A1
Edgar St BD14 73 D3
Edgbaston Cl LS17 43 A6
Edgbaston Wlk LS17 43 A6
Edge Ave WF12 139 D1
Edge Cl Dewsbury WF12 139 E1
Huddersfield HD7 152 E4
Edge End BD13 52 E1
Edge End Gdns 1 BD6 93 E7
Edge End La HD7 188 A4
Edge End Rd BD6 93 E7
Edge Hill Cl HD5 154 D7
Edge Junc WF12 139 D1
Edge La Dewsbury WF12 139 E1
Heptonstall HX7 87 F7
Edge Rd WF12 139 F1
Edge Terr HD3 152 F7
Edge Top Rd WF12 139 C2
Edge View Dewsbury WF12 139 E1
Huddersfield HD7 152 E4
Edgebank Ave BD6 93 F6
Edgehey Gn HX7 88 B6
Edgehill Cl 6 BD13 72 F1
Edgehill Rd S75 178 B2
Edgeholme La HX2 112 B7
Edgemoor Cl HX3 113 B4
Edgemoor Rd
Crigglestone WF4 159 F2
Honley HD7 171 E3
Edgerton Gn HD1 153 E7
Edgerton Grove Rd HD1 153 E7
Edgerton La HD1 153 E7
Edgerton Rd
Huddersfield HD1 153 E8
Leeds LS16 59 B8
Edgeware Rd HD5 155 A6
Edgware Ave LS8 207 F2
Edgware Gr LS8 207 F2
Edgware Mount LS8 207 F2
Edgware Pl LS8 207 F2
Edgware Row LS8 207 F2
Edgware St LS8 207 E2
Edgware Terr LS8 207 F2
Edgware View LS8 207 F2
Edinburgh Ave LS12 209 D4
Edinburgh Gr LS12 209 D4
Edinburgh Pl
Garforth LS25 83 B7
Leeds LS12 209 D4
Edinburgh Rd LS12 209 D4
Edinburgh Terr LS12 209 D4
Edlington Cl BD4 75 E3
Edmonton Pl LS7 204 A2
Edmund St Bradford BD5 201 A2
Todmorden OL14 129 A8
Edna St WF9 183 A3
Edrich Cl BD12 94 E6
Edroyd Pl LS28 57 D3
Edroyd St LS28 57 D3
Education Rd LS7 206 C3
Edward Cl Dewsbury WF12 139 B3
Halifax HX3 114 A4
Edward Dr WF1 121 C5
Edward Rd WF14 137 F5
Edward St 9 Bacup OL13 106 A3
Bradford BD4 201 C2
Bradford, Tong Street BD4 75 E1
Brighouse HD6 115 C2
Brighouse, Waring Green HD6 115 A3
Hebden Bridge HX7 89 A3
Leeds LS2 211 F4
Liversedge, Knowler Hill WF15 117 A4
Liversedge, Littletown WF15 117 A5
Normanton WF6 123 A5
Shipley BD18 37 F1
Sowerby Bridge HX6 112 B4
Wakefield WF1 216 C3
Edward Turner Cl 1 BD12 94 C6
Edwards Rd HX2 202 A1
Edwin Rd LS6 205 F2
Eel Holme View St BD20 18 B2
Eel Mires Garth LS22 13 F6
Effingham Rd BD16 36 A1
Egerton Gr BD15 54 A1
Egerton St 7 HX6 112 B4
Egerton Terr LS19 40 D3
Eggleston Dr BD4 75 F2
Eggleston St LS13 57 F5
Egglestone Sq LS23 30 C7
Egham Gn BD10 56 B7
Egmanton Rd S71 178 F1
Egremont Cres BD6 93 F6
Egremont St HX6 112 A3
Egremont Terr HX6 112 A3
Egypt Rd BD13 72 C8
Eiffel Bldgs HX7 89 A3
Eiffel St HX7 89 A3
Eighth Ave
Cleckheaton WF15 116 B5
Leeds LS12 210 B2
Rothwell LS26 101 A7
Eightlands Ave LS13 58 D2
Eightlands La LS13 58 D2
Eightlands Rd WF13 139 C8
Ekota Pl LS8 207 F4
Elam Wood Rd BD20 18 C3
Eland House 8 HX5 134 F7
Elba Terr WF4 141 B3
Elbow La Bradford BD2 56 B2
Halifax HX2 90 E1
Elder Ave Upton WF9 183 C8
Wakefield WF2 142 A7
Elder Bank BD13 52 D6
Elder Cl WF17 96 F2
Elder Croft LS13 58 C1
Elder Dr Dewsbury WF12 139 D3
Upton WF9 183 C8
Elder Garth LS25 83 B6
Elder Gn WF2 142 A7
Elder Gr Huddersfield HD4 171 D6
Wakefield WF2 142 A7
Elder Grove Mews HD4 171 D6
Elder La HD2 137 A5
Elder Mount 1 LS13 58 C1
Elder Pl 2 LS13 58 C1
Elder Rd LS13 58 C1
Elder St Bradford BD10 56 E7
Keighley BD20 18 A2
3 Leeds LS13 58 C1
Elderwood Gdns BD10 56 E5
Eldon Pl Bradford BD1 201 A4
Bradford, Cutler Heights BD4 75 D4
Cleckheaton BD19 116 E7
Eldon Rd HD1 153 D7
Eldon St Batley WF16 117 D4
Halifax HX3 203 E4
Ossett WF5 140 F7
Todmorden OL14 108 C5
Eldon Terr BD1 201 A4
Eldroth Mount 16 HX1 202 C1
Eldroth Rd HX1 202 C1
Eldwick First Sch BD16 37 C5
Eleanor Dr LS28 56 F7
Eleanor St Brighouse HD6 115 A1
2 Huddersfield HD1 154 A8
Eleventh Ave WF15 116 C5
Elford Gr LS8 207 F3
Elford Pl E LS8 207 F3
Elford Pl W LS8 207 F3
Elford Rd LS8 207 F3
Elgar Wlk WF3 121 E6
Elgin Cl HD4 153 C2
Eli St BD5 74 F3
Elia St BD21 35 D8
Elim Wlk 4 WF13 139 C8
Eliot Gr LS20 39 F8
Eliots Cl WF10 125 C5
Elizabeth Ave Bradford BD12 94 D4
South Hiendley S72 180 E5
Elizabeth Cl BD12 94 D4
Elizabeth Cres BD12 94 D4
Elizabeth Ct
Castleford WF10 125 C8
Collingham LS22 29 A8
Hemsworth WF9 181 F6
Elizabeth Dr Bradford BD12 94 D4
Castleford WF10 125 D8
Knottingley WF11 126 C4
Elizabeth Gdns WF1 216 B4
Elizabeth Gr LS27 98 C5
Elizabeth House HX2 91 E3
Elizabeth St
15 Bingley BD16 37 A3
Bradford BD5 201 B1
Bradford, New Road Side BD12 94 D4
Elland HX5 134 F6
1 Elland, West Vale HX4 134 D7
Huddersfield HD4 154 A3
Leeds LS6 205 E3
Liversedge FW15 116 E4
Oakworth BD22 34 D3
Wakefield WF1 142 E2
Elizabethan Ct WF8 125 E2
Ella St WF9 163 A4
Elland Bridge HX5 134 F7
Elland C of E Sch HX5 134 F7
Elland Golf Course HX5 134 D5
Elland Independent Hospl HX5 135 A7
Elland La HX5 135 A7
Elland Rd
Brighouse HD6, HX5 114 E2
Halifax HD6, HX5 114 E2
Leeds LS11 213 E3
Leeds LS11 213 E3
Morley LS27 98 C8
Ripponden HX6 132 E4
Elland Road Ind Pk LS11 213 D3
Elland Road Stadium (Leeds Utd FC) LS11 213 E3
Elland St WF10 103 E1
Elland Way LS11 213 D3
Elland Wood Bottom HX3, HX5 113 D1
Elland-Riorges' Link HX5 135 A7
Ellar Carr Rd
Bradford BD10 39 C1
Cullingworth BD13 52 C7
Ellar Gdns LS29 22 B6
Ellen Holme Cotts HX2 111 D5
Ellen Royd La HX2 111 C8
Ellen Royd St HX3 203 E4
Ellen St 13 BD16 37 A3
Ellenthorpe Rd BD17 37 E2
Ellerby La LS9 212 B2
Ellerby Rd LS9 212 B3
Ellercroft Ave BD7 74 A6
Ellercroft Rd BD7 74 A6
Ellercroft Terr BD7 74 A6
Ellerker La LS14 46 B5
Ellerker Rd LS14 46 A6
Ellers Gr LS8 207 F4
Ellers Rd Leeds LS8 207 F4
Sutton in C BD20 16 D4
Ellerton St BD3 75 C7
Ellicott Ct LS29 22 A4
Ellin's Terr WF6 144 A8
Ellinthorpe St BD4 75 B5
Elliott Ct 11 BD13 72 D1
Elliott St Shipley BD18 55 A8
Silsden BD20 5 D1
Ellis Fold LS12 209 E3
Ellis La LS25 63 E3
~~Ellis Pl 9 LS11~~ 214 B3
Ellis St BD5 74 D3
Ellison St 7 Halifax HX3 92 A1
Huddersfield HD4 153 D4
Elliston Ave S75 178 C1
Ellistones Gdns HX4 134 A7
Ellistones La HX4 134 A6
Ellistones Pl HX4 134 A6
Ellmont Ave HD8 175 D7
Ellton Gr 4 BD6 74 A1
Ellwood Cl LS6 59 F7
Elm Ave Holmfirth HD7 189 C8
Kippax LS25 82 F3
Lofthouse Gate WF3 121 F4
Sowerby Bridge HX6 112 B5
Todmorden OL14 108 B6
Elm Cl Darrington WF8 147 C5
Ossett WF5 140 E3
Elm Cres BD20 36 D8
Elm Croft LS14 62 C8
Elm Ct Birkenshaw BD11 96 B4
Kirkburton HD8 173 F7
Elm Gdns WF10 125 D5
Elm Gr Burley in W LS29 21 F8
Cleckheaton BD19 117 A8
Keighley, East Morton BD20 36 D8
Keighley, Ingrow BD21 35 B4
Liversedge WF16 117 C5
Shelf HX3 93 D6
Shipley BD18 55 E7
Silsden BD20 5 D1
South Elmsall WF9 182 F3
Elm Pk WF8 146 C6
Elm Pl Knottingley WF11 126 E3
11 Sowerby Bridge HX6 112 B5
Elm Rd Dewsbury WF13 138 F8
Hemsworth WF9 181 E7
Normanton WF6 144 B7
Shipley BD18 55 D7
Sutton in C BD20 16 C5
Elm St 4 Bacup OL13 106 A3
Crofton WF4 162 B7
Elland HX4 134 A4
Huddersfield HD4 154 B4
Leeds LS6 206 B4
Oxenhope BD22 51 C3
Skelmanthorpe HD8 175 A2
Elm Terr Brighouse HD6 115 B5
Otley LS21 23 C8
1 Pontefract WF8 146 C8
Elm Tree Ave BD6 94 C8
Elm Tree Cl Batley WF15 117 C2
Bradford BD6 94 D8
Keighley BD21 35 D6
Leeds LS15 81 E6
Elm Tree Gdns BD6 94 C8
Elm Tree St WF1 142 F4
Elm View 3 Halifax HX3 113 C4
Steeton BD20 17 B6
Elm Way WF17 97 A2
Elm Wood St HD6 115 B4
Elmet Dr LS15 63 E7
Elmet Rd LS15 63 E6
Elmet Towers LS14 62 C4
Elmete Ave Barwick in E LS15 62 F6
Leeds LS8 61 C7
Elmete Cl LS8 61 D6
Elmete Croft LS15 62 F6
Elmete Ct LS8 61 C6
Elmete Dr LS8 61 D6
Elmete Gr LS8 61 C7
Elmete Grange LS29 22 A4
Elmete Hill LS8 61 D6
Elmete La LS8 44 E2
Elmete Mount LS8 61 D6
Elmete Rd WF10 104 D1
Elmete Way LS8 61 D6
Elmete Wlk LS8 61 D6
Elmete Wood Sch LS8 61 D8
Elmfield BD17 38 D3
Elmfield Ave HD3 152 F5
Elmfield Bsns Pk LS25 83 A8
Elmfield Ct LS27 98 B3
Elmfield Dr Bradford BD6 94 D8
Skelmanthorpe HD8 175 A1
Elmfield Gr LS12 210 A2
Elmfield Pl LS12 210 A2
Elmfield Rd Glusburn BD20 16 E7
Huddersfield HD2 135 E1
Leeds LS12 210 A2
Morley LS27 98 B2
Elmfield Terr Halifax HX1 203 D1
3 Huddersfield HD5 154 D5
Elmfield Way LS13 58 D1
Elmhurst Cl LS17 44 B4
Elmhurst Gdns LS17 44 A4
Elmhurst Gr WF11 126 F3
Elmore Terr BD20 16 E7
Elmroyd LS26 100 F4
Elms Hill HD7 169 F8
Elms The Ackworth M T WF7 163 F5
Guiseley LS20 22 E1
Elms View HD7 169 F8
Elmsall La DN6 195 C7
Elmsall St BD1 74 D8
Elmsall Way WF9 183 B5
Elmsdale Cl WF9 183 B2
Elmsley St BD20 17 C5
Elmton Cl LS10 99 D7
Elmtree La LS10 215 D4
Elmwood Ave
Barwick in E LS15 63 D7
4 Huddersfield HD1 154 A7
Walton WF2 161 B7
Elmwood Chase LS15 63 D7
Elmwood Cl
5 Huddersfield HD1 154 A7
Mirfield WF14 137 F1
Walton WF2 161 B7
Elmwood Dr Brighouse HD6 114 F3
Keighley BD22 35 A4
Walton WF2 161 B7
Elmwood Garth WF2 161 B7
Elmwood Gr Batley WF17 118 D3
Horbury WF4 141 C1
Elmwood La
Barwick in E LS15 63 D7
Leeds LS7 206 C1
Elmwood Rd Keighley BD22 34 F4
Leeds LS2 206 C1
Elmwood St HX1 202 C1
Elmwood Terr
Dewsbury WF13 118 C1
Keighley BD22 34 F4
Elphaborough Cl HX7 110 E8
Elphin Ct HX7 110 D8
Elsdon Gr BD5 201 B1
Elsham Terr LS4 59 C2
Elsicker La WF1 143 F6
Elsie St BD20 18 B2
Elsinore Ave HX5 134 F5
Elsinore Ct HX5 134 E6
Elstone View WF1 121 A4
Elsworth Ave BD3 56 D1
Elsworth St LS12 210 A3
Elsworth Terr LS12 210 A3
Eltham Cl LS6 206 B3
Eltham Ct 4 LS6 206 B3
Eltham Dr LS6 206 B3
Eltham Gdns LS6 206 B3
Eltham Gr BD6 94 A8
Eltham Rise LS6 206 B3
Eltofts Pk LS14 45 C5
Elvaston Rd LS27 98 A3
Elvey Cl BD2 56 D4
Elvey St WF1 216 B3
Elwell Cl HX3 93 D7
Elwell St WF3 99 E1
Elwyn Gr BD5 74 E3
Elwyn Rd BD5 74 F3
Ely St Elland HX4 134 D6
Leeds LS12 209 F4
Embankment The
Leeds LS1 211 F3
Mirfield WF14 138 A5
Emblem Terr WF1 142 D3
Embleton Rd LS26 123 C8
Embsay & Bolton Abbey Steam Railway BD23 1 C7

Emerald St Batley WF17 118 B6
Huddersfield HD1 154 B8
11 Keighley BD22 35 A4
Emerson Ave BD9 54 D3
Emily St BD21 35 D8
Emley First Sch HD8 175 D7
Emley Moor Bsns Pk HD8 175 B6
Emm La BD9 55 B3
Emmanuel Terr HD4 153 F2
Emmanuel Trad Est LS12 210 C2
Emmeline Cl BD10 56 B8
Emmet Cl BD11 96 B5
Emmfield Dr BD9 55 A4
Emmott Dr LS19 40 E3
Emmott Farm Fold 2 BD22 51 C6
Empsall Row 4 HD6 115 B3
Emscote Ave HX1 202 C1
Emscote Gdns HX1 202 C1
Emscote Gr HX1 202 C1
Emscote Pl HX1 202 C1
Emscote St S HX1 202 C1
Emsley Cl BD4 95 B8
Emsley Pl LS10 212 B1
Emville Ave LS17 44 C5
Enderby Wlk HX3 91 F3
Enderley Rd 8 BD13 72 D6
Endor Cres LS29 21 F7
Endor Gr LS29 21 F7
Endsleigh Pl 5 BD14 73 B4
Enfield LS19 40 B6
Enfield Ave LS7 207 E2
Enfield Cl WF17 117 F6
Enfield Dr Batley WF17 117 F6
Bradford BD6 74 A1
Enfield Par BD6 74 A1
Enfield Rd BD17 38 C2
Enfield Side Rd BD22 50 E5
Enfield St Keighley BD21 35 B7
Leeds LS7 207 D2
Enfield Terr LS7 207 E2
Enfield Wlk BD6 74 A1
Engine La Horbury WF4 140 F1
Shafton S72 180 D1
West Hardwick WF4 163 A7
England Lane Jun & Inf Sch WF11 126 F3
Englefield Cres BD4 75 E2
English Martyrs' RC Infant & Junior Sch WF2 141 D5
Ennerdale Ave WF12 118 E2
Ennerdale Cl LS22 13 C6
Ennerdale Cres WF12 118 E2
Ennerdale Dr Bradford BD2 56 B3
Knottingley WF11 126 E2
Ennerdale Rd Batley WF12 118 E2
Bradford BD2 56 B3
Gildersome LS12 77 D2
Wakefield WF2 141 F7
Ennerdale Way LS12 77 D3
Enoch La HD4 153 F3
Enterprise Park Ind Est LS11 213 F1
Enterprise Way
Bradford BD10 56 B6
Castleford WF10 124 C8
Middleton LS10 215 F1
Skipton BD23 4 A7
Envoy St LS11 214 C4
Epsom Rd LS25 82 F2
Epsom Way HD5 137 C1
Epworth Pl Leeds LS10 215 E4
Oakworth BD22 34 B3
Eric St Keighley BD21 35 C8
Leeds LS13 58 C5
South Elmsall WF9 183 A3
Ernest St 8
Dewsbury WF13 139 D8
Todmorden OL14 86 C1
Erringden Rd HX7 89 A4
Erringden St 12 OL14 108 C5
Escroft Cl BD12 94 D1
Eshald La LS26 101 D6
Eshald Mansions 4 LS26 101 D6
Eshald Pl LS26 101 D6
Esholt Ave LS20 39 D7
Esholt La Baildon BD17 38 F4
Guiseley BD17 39 A4
Eshton Ave BD12 94 F5
Eshton Ct S75 178 A2
Esk Ave WF10 125 B8
Esk Gdns LS22 13 E8
Eskdale Ave
Normanton WF6 123 A4
Shelf HX3 93 B5
Eskdale Cl Batley WF12 118 E3
Guiseley LS20 39 E8
Normanton WF6 123 A4
Eskdale Croft Guiseley LS20 39 E8
Normanton WF6 123 A4
Eskdale Ct WF6 123 A4
Eskdale Gr LS25 83 A5
Eskdale Mount
Hebden Bridge HX7 89 A4
Leeds LS14 61 F4
Eskdale Rd WF2 141 E7
Eskdale Rise BD15 73 C8
Eskine Par BD6 93 F6
Esmond St 3 Bradford BD7 73 F3
Leeds LS12 209 F3
Esmond Terr LS12 209 F3
Essex Park Ind Est BD4 201 D2
Essex St Bradford BD4 201 D1
Halifax HX1 202 B2
1 Hebden Bridge HX7 89 A2
Estcourt Ave LS6 59 C4
Estcourt Dr WF8 147 D4
Estcourt Gr BD7 74 A5
Estcourt Rd Bradford BD7 74 A5
Darrington WF8 147 C5
Estcourt Terr LS6 59 C4
Esther Ave WF2 141 F4
Esther Gr WF2 141 F5
Esthwaite Gdns LS15 80 E6
Ethel St Keighley BD20 18 B1
Sutton in C BD20 16 D4
Etna St BD7 73 F3
Eton Ave HD5 154 F6
Eton St Halifax HX1 202 B3
Hebden Bridge HX7 88 F3
Euden Edge Rd HD7 152 A3
Eunice La HD8 191 C6
Eureka Childrens' Mus HX1 203 F2
Eurocam Tech Pk BD5 74 E2
Euroway Trad Est BD4 95 A7
Euston Gr LS11 213 F4
Euston Mount LS11 213 F4
Euston Terr LS11 213 F4
Evans Towers 3 BD5 201 B1
Evanston Ave LS4 59 C1
Evelyn Ave BD3 75 E8
Evelyn Pl LS12 209 F2
Evens Terr BD5 74 E2
Everard St HD4 153 D4
Everdale Mount
Hemsworth WF9 181 C6
South Elmsall WF9 182 E3
Everest Ave BD18 55 E7
Everleigh St LS9 80 A7
Eversley Dr BD4 75 E4
Eversley Mount HX2 202 A2
Eversley Pl HX2 202 A2
Eversley Rd HX7 89 A4
Eversley View LS14 45 C7
Every St 9 OL14 108 C5
Evesham Gr BD10 56 B7
Ewart Pl BD7 74 A3
Ewart St Bradford BD7 74 A3
Queensbury BD13 72 E1
Ewood Dr HX7 90 A1
Ewood Hall Ave HX7 89 F1
Ewood La OL14 107 F6
Excelsior Cl HX6 132 C3
Exchange HD7 171 F5
Exchange Bldgs BD20 16 D7
Exchange Ct BD19 95 D1
Exchange St
Cleckheaton BD19 95 D1
3 Elland HX4 134 D6
Normanton WF6 123 A2
South Elmsall WF9 182 F3
Exe St BD5 74 C3
Exeter Dr LS10 99 E7
Exeter St Halifax HX3 113 D3
Sowerby Bridge HX6 112 C4
Exhibition Rd 7 BD18 54 F8
Exley Ave BD21 35 A4
Exley Bank HX3 113 D2
Exley Bank Top HX3 113 D1
Exley Cres BD21 35 A5
Exley Dr BD21 35 A5
Exley Gdns HX3 113 D2
Exley Gr BD21 35 A5
Exley Head View BD22 34 E8
Exley La Elland HX5 134 E8
Halifax HX5 113 E1
Exley Mount Bradford BD7 73 F6
Keighley BD21 35 A5
Exley Rd BD21 35 A5
Exley St 11 BD22 35 A6
Exley Way BD21 35 A4
Exmoor St HX1 202 B2
Exmouth Pl BD3 55 F1
Express Way WF10 123 D6
Exton Pl LS15 80 E7
Eyre St Batley WF17 118 D4
Dewsbury WF12 139 B4
Eyres Ave LS12 209 F4
Eyres Gr LS12 209 F4
Eyres Mill Side LS12 209 E4
Eyres St LS12 209 F4
Eyres Terr LS12 209 F4
Eyrie App LS27 98 C3

Factory La Bradford BD4 75 B2
Huddersfield HD3 153 B4
Factory St BD4 75 C2
Fagley Cres BD2 56 C2
Fagley Croft BD2 56 D2
Fagley Dr BD2 56 C2
Fagley First Sch BD2 56 D2
Fagley La BD2 56 D3
Fagley Pl BD2 56 C1
Fagley Rd BD2 56 D2
Fagley Terr BD2 56 C1
Fair Bank BD18 55 C6
Fair Lea Rd HD4 153 E1
Fair Mount OL14 108 A1
Fair Rd BD6 74 B1
Fair St HD1 153 F4
Fair View Liversedge WF15 116 F5
Pontefract WF8 146 E5
Fair View Cres OL13 106 B3
Fair Ways WF14 137 F2
Fairbank Rd BD8 55 A1
Fairbank Terr BD8 55 A1
Fairbourne House 8 BD6 93 E8
Fairbrook Rd WF2 160 A4
Fairburn Dr LS25 83 B6
Fairburn Gdns BD2 56 C4
Fairburn Ings Nature Reserve WF10 104 B4
Fairburn Primary Sch WF11 105 A4
Fairclough Gr HX3 91 F3
Fairfax Ave Birkenshaw BD11 97 A5
Bradford BD4 75 C1
Featherstone WF7 124 C1
Knottingley WF11 126 D3
Menston LS29 22 A5
Fairfax Cl LS14 62 B3
Fairfax Cres Bradford BD4 75 C1
Halifax HX3 114 A5
Fairfax Gdns LS29 22 A5
Fairfax Gr LS19 39 F7
Fairfax Ho BD1 201 C3
Fairfax Rd Bingley BD16 36 F5
Cullingworth BD13 52 E7
Leeds LS11 214 A3
Menston LS29 22 A5
Pontefract WF8 146 E8
Fairfax St Bradford BD4 201 C1
Haworth BD22 51 D7
Otley LS21 23 B7
Silsden BD20 5 D1
Fairfax View LS18 41 B4
Fairfield Denholme BD13 71 D8
Fairburn WF11 105 A5
Fairfield Ave Batley WF16 117 E5
3 Dewsbury WF12 139 F8
East Ardsley WF3 119 D7
Leeds LS13 58 A2
Normanton WF6 122 E3
Ossett WF5 140 F4
Pontefract WF8 146 B8
7 Pudsey LS28 76 F8
Fairfield Cl Castleford WF10 104 E1
Leeds LS13 58 B2
Ossett WF5 140 F4
Rothwell LS26 100 B4
Fairfield Cres
5 Dewsbury WF13 118 A1
Leeds LS13 58 B2
Fairfield Ct Baildon BD17 38 E4
Castleford WF10 125 A7
Garforth LS25 82 D7
Liversedge WF15 116 F4
Fairfield Dr Baildon BD17 38 E4
Batley WF16 117 E5
Ossett WF5 140 F4
Rothwell LS26 100 B4
Fairfield Gdns Ossett WF5 140 F5
Rothwell LS26 100 B4
Fairfield Gr Leeds LS13 58 B2
Rothwell LS26 100 B4
Fairfield Hill LS13 58 B2
Fairfield La LS26 100 B4
Fairfield Mount Leeds LS13 58 B2
Ossett WF5 140 F4
Fairfield Par WF16 117 E5
Fairfield Rd Batley WF16 117 E5
Bradford, Girlington BD8 55 B1
Bradford, Upper Wyke BD12 94 D3
Leeds LS13 58 A2
Ossett WF5 140 F4
Fairfield Rise HD8 174 A5
Fairfield Specl Sch WF16 117 E5
Fairfield Sq LS13 58 B2
Fairfield St Bradford BD4 75 D1
Leeds LS13 58 B2
Fairfield Terr
9 Cleckheaton BD19 116 E7
Dewsbury WF12 139 F8
Leeds LS13 58 B2
Ossett WF5 140 E4
Fairfield Wlk WF5 140 F4
Fairfields Castleford WF10 125 E7
Denby Dale HD8 191 F3
Fairfields Rd HD7 188 D3
Fairford Ave LS11 214 C3
Fairford Terr LS11 214 C3
Fairhaven Gn BD10 56 C7
Fairlea Ave HD4 153 E1
Fairlea Cotts HD4 153 E1
Fairleigh Cres WF3 120 A8
Fairleigh Rd WF3 120 A8
Fairless Ave HX3 115 A7
Fairmoor Way WF16 117 E5
Fairmount BD9 55 C2
Fairmount Pk BD18 54 E7
Fairmount Terr
Dewsbury WF12 139 E6
Keighley BD21 35 F6
Fairview Ave WF17 117 F6
Fairview Cres WF17 118 A6
Fairview Ct BD17 38 B1
Fairview Rd WF17 118 A6
Fairview Terr HX3 92 B1
Fairway Bradford BD7 73 F1
Guiseley LS20 22 C1
Normanton WF6 123 C1
Shipley BD18 54 F7
Yeadon LS19 40 A2
Fairway App WF6 123 C2
Fairway Ave Bradford BD7 73 F2
Mapplewell S75 178 C2
Normanton WF6 123 C2
Fairway Cl Bradford BD7 73 F1
Guiseley LS20 39 C8
Normanton WF6 123 C1
Fairway Cres BD22 51 D6
Fairway Dr Bradford BD7 73 F2
Normanton WF6 123 C1
Fairway Gr BD7 74 A2
Fairway Ind Pk WF17 96 F2
Fairway The
Featherstone WF7 124 D1
Halifax HX2 91 F7
Huddersfield HD2 136 A4
Leeds LS17 43 B6
Pudsey LS28 57 B1
Fairway Wlk BD7 73 F2
Fairways Ct WF8 147 E4
Fairways The Keighley BD20 18 A3
Shipley BD9 54 E5
Fairweather Green Middle Sch BD8 73 E7
Fairweather Mews BD8 73 E7
Fairy Dell BD16 54 B7
Fairy Hill La WF8 125 D5
Faith St WF9 182 D4
Falcon Cl LS21 23 A7
Falcon Cliffe BD20 17 D5
Falcon Dr WF10 124 C6
Falcon Knowl Ing S75 177 D1
Falcon Mews Bradford BD8 73 C8
Morley LS27 98 C3
Falcon Rd Bingley BD16 36 F5
Dewsbury WF12 139 D6
Falcon St Bradford BD7 74 B4
Halifax HX3 113 D3
Huddersfield HD4 153 F2
Falconer Cl S75 177 D1
Falconers Ride HD4 171 E7
Falhouse La WF4 156 D7
Falkland Cres LS17 43 C1
Falkland Gdns LS17 43 D1
Falkland Gr LS17 43 C1
Falkland Mount LS17 43 C1
Falkland Rd Bradford BD10 56 E4
Leeds LS17 43 C1
Falkland Rise LS17 43 C1
Falklands Ct LS17 43 C1
Fall Brow Cl BD14 73 A3
Fall Ings Rd WF1 142 E4
Fall La Dewsbury WF13 139 B6
East Ardsley WF3 120 D8
Liversedge WF15 116 D1
Marsden HD7 168 F3
Northowram HX3 92 D5
Sowerby Bridge HX6 112 D4
Fall Park Ct LS13 58 D5
Fall Rd WF14 137 E8
Fall Spring Gdns HX4 133 F3
Fall Spring Gn HX4 133 F3
Fall Wood St BD22 51 D6
Falledge La HD8 191 E2
Fallow Croft HD2 136 F5
Fallow La BD22 34 A6
Fallowfield Cl BD4 95 C8
Fallowfield Dr BD4 75 C1
Fallowfield Gdns BD4 75 C1
Fallswood Gr LS13 58 D4
Falmouth Ave Bradford BD3 55 F1
Normanton WF6 123 B3
Falmouth Cres WF6 123 B3
Falmouth Rd WF6 123 B3
Falsgrave Ave BD2 56 D2
Faltis Sq BD10 56 C6
Fanny Moor Cres HD4 154 C2
Fanny Moor La HD4 154 C2
Fanny St Keighley BD21 35 B6
Shipley BD18 37 F1
Far Bank HD8 174 B3
Far Common Rd WF14 137 E8
Far Croft HD8 156 A2
Far Croft Terr LS12 210 A2
Far Dene HD8 173 D8
Far End La HD7 172 A4
Far Field Ave HD7 189 E1
Far Field Dr HD7 189 E1
Far Field La Holmfirth HD7 189 E1
Meltham HD7, HD4 170 F5
Far Fields La HD7 171 A5
Far La Hebden Bridge HX2 90 A2
Holmfirth HD7 189 E1
Far Low Bank BD22 34 B3
Far Mead Croft LS29 9 E2
Far Moss LS17 43 A5
Far Reef Cl LS18 41 C2
Far Richard Cl WF5 140 D7
Far View HX2 91 E6
Far View Bank HD5 154 E4
Far View Cres HD5 154 E4
Far Well Fold LS19 40 D3
Far Well La HD4 190 B8
Far Well Rd LS19 40 D3
Faraday Sq HD3 153 A4
Farcliffe Pl BD8 55 B1
Farcliffe Rd BD8 55 B1
Farcliffe Terr BD8 55 B1
Fardene St BD20 5 D2
Fardew Ct BD16 36 F4
Fardew Golf Course BD20 36 C8
Farehill Flats HD4 171 F8
Farehill Rd HD4 171 F8
Farfield Ave Batley WF17 117 F6
Bradford BD6 93 E7
Pudsey LS28 57 C3
Farfield Cres BD6 93 F7
Farfield Ct LS17 43 E5
Farfield Dr LS28 57 C2
Farfield Gr Bradford BD6 93 F7
Pudsey LS28 57 C3
Farfield Rd Baildon BD17 38 D2
Bradford BD6 94 A7
Huddersfield HD5 154 F3
Shipley BD18 55 A7
Farfield Rise LS28 57 C3
Farfield St Bradford BD9 55 A2
Cleckheaton BD19 95 D1
Farfield Terr BD9 55 A2
Farlea Dr BD2 56 C3
Farleton Dr BD2 56 D3
Farley Cres BD22 34 B3
Farm Croft WF7 144 E5
Farm Ct LS15 62 B2
Farm Gdns WF7 144 E5
Farm Hill Cres LS7 60 A5
Farm Hill Ct BD10 56 B5
Farm Hill N LS7 60 A6
Farm Hill Rd Bradford BD10 56 B6
Morley LS27 97 F5
Farm Hill Rise LS7 60 A5
Farm Hill S LS7 60 A5
Farm Hill Way LS7 60 A5
Farm La WF9 163 A3
Farm Mount LS15 62 C2
Farm Pond Dr HD6 114 E5
Farm Rd Featherstone WF7 145 D5
Leeds LS15 62 B2
Farmfield Dr WF9 163 A3
Farmstead Rd BD10 56 C6
Farnboro St OL14 108 A2
Farndale App LS14 62 C5
Farndale Cl Leeds LS14 62 C5
Wetherby LS22 13 B6
Farndale Ct Garforth LS25 82 F5
3 Leeds LS14 62 C5
Farndale Garth LS14 62 C6
Farndale Gdns 10 LS14 62 C6
Farndale Pl LS14 62 C6
Farndale Rd Baildon BD17 38 A2
Wilsden BD15 53 C4
Farndale Sq 5 LS14 62 C5
Farndale Terr 4 LS14 62 C5
Farndale View 11 LS14 62 C6
Farne Ave WF2 141 F6
Farnham Cl Baildon BD17 38 D4
Leeds LS14 45 B1
Farnham Croft LS14 45 B1
Farnham First Sch BD7 74 B5
Farnham Rd BD7 74 B5
Farnham Way WF4 143 F1
Farnlee HD3 135 B1
Farnley C of E Primary Sch LS21 11 D5
Farnley Cl LS29 22 B4
Farnley Cres LS12 77 E6
Farnley Hey HD4 172 C7
Farnley La Farnley LS21 11 B3
Otley LS21 11 B3
Farnley Park High Sch LS12 77 E4
Farnley Pk LS21 11 E2
Farnley Rd Kirkburton HD4 172 F5
Menston LS29 22 B4
Farnley Tyas C of E Sch HD4 172 E6
Farnley View BD11 97 A6
Farr Royd LS29 9 E2
Farr Royd Terr LS29 9 E2
Farra St BD22 51 C2
Farrar Ave WF14 137 F6
Farrar Croft LS16 42 A4
Farrar Ct LS13 58 C3
Farrar Dr WF14 137 F6
Farrar Gr LS16 42 A4
Farrar Height La HX6 132 B4
Farrar La LS16 42 A4
Farrar Mill La HX3 113 D3
Farrer La LS26 101 C5
Farriers Croft BD2 55 F4
Farriers Pl WF10 125 B6
Farringdon Cl BD4 75 E4
Farringdon Dr BD4 75 E4
Farringdon Gr BD6 94 A7
Farringdon Sq BD4 75 E4
Farrow Bank LS12 77 E7
Farrow Gn LS12 77 F7
Farrow Hill LS12 77 F7
Farrow Rd LS12 77 F7
Farrow Vale LS12 77 E7
Farside Gn BD5 74 C3
Farsley Farfield Primary Sch LS28 57 C2
Farsley Springbank Junior Sch LS28 57 D3
Fartown LS28 76 E5
Fartown Cl LS28 76 E5
Fartown Green Rd HD2 136 B2
Fartown High Sch HD2 136 C2
Farway BD4 75 E4
Fascination Pl 1 BD13 72 C2
Faugh La HX7 88 C6
Favell Ave WF6 123 B1
Faversham Wlk BD4 75 E4
Fawcett Ave LS12 209 E1
Fawcett Bank LS12 209 D1
Fawcett Cl LS12 209 D1
Fawcett Dr LS12 209 D1
Fawcett Gdns LS12 209 D1
Fawcett La LS12 209 E1
Fawcett Pl BD4 95 C8
Fawcett Rd LS12 209 D1
Fawcett St WF2 142 C4
Fawcett Vale LS12 209 D1
Fawcett Way LS12 209 D1
Fawkes Dr LS21 22 D6
Faxfleet St BD5 74 D2
Faye Gdns BD4 75 D1
Fearnley Ave WF5 140 D7
Fearnley Cl LS12 210 A3
Fearnley Ct HD7 189 D5
Fearnley Dr WF5 140 C7
Fearnley La HD7 189 C6
Fearnley Pl LS12 210 A3
Fearnley St Dewsbury WF13 139 B7
Featherstone WF7 145 C5
Fearnside's Cl 10 WF4 141 A1
Fearnsides St BD8 74 B8
Fearnsides Terr BD8 74 B8
Fearnville Ave LS8 61 D4
Fearnville Cl LS8 61 D5
Fearnville Dr Bradford BD4 75 D5
Leeds LS8 61 D4

Fearnville Gr Leeds LS8 61 D4
Royston S71 179 C3
Fearnville Mount LS8 61 D4
Fearnville Pl LS8 61 E4
Fearnville Rd LS8 61 D4
Fearnville Terr LS8 61 E4
Fearnville View LS8 61 D4
Feast Field LS18 41 B1
Feather Bed La 5 HX4 134 D6
Feather Rd BD3 75 B7
Feather St BD21 35 D6
Featherbank Ave LS18 58 B7
Featherbank Gr 5 LS18 58 B8
Featherbank La LS18 58 B7
Featherbank Mount 6 LS18 58 B8
Featherbank Terr 3 LS18 58 B7
Featherbank Wlk 1 LS18 58 B7
Featherbed Cl 4 HX4 134 D6
Featherbed La
Bickerton LS24 15 E6
Wighill LS24 15 E6
Featherstone High Sch WF7 145 F4
Featherstone Junior & Infants Sch WF7 145 E7
Featherstone La WF7 145 D7
Featherstone Sta WF7 145 C6
Federation St BD5 74 F2
Feetham's Fold LS9 212 B3
Felbrigg Ave BD22 35 A6
Felcote Ave HD5 154 E5
Felcourt Dr BD4 75 E2
Felkirk Dr WF4 180 A8
Felkirk View S72 180 B3
Felks Stile Rd HD4 153 A1
Fell Cres BD22 34 F6
Fell Gr Huddersfield HD2 136 C4
Keighley BD22 34 F6
Fell Greave Cres HD2 136 C4
Fell Greave Rd HD2 136 C4
Fell La BD22 34 F6
Fellows The HD4 171 C7
Fellowsides La WF5 140 E5
Fellside OL14 109 B5
Fellside Cl BD5 74 F2
Fellwood Ave BD22 51 E8
Fellwood Cl BD22 51 E8
Felnex Cl LS9 80 C6
Felnex Cres LS9 80 C5
Felnex Rd LS9 80 C5
Felnex Sq LS9 80 B5
Felnex Way LS9 80 C5
Fenay Bankside HD8 155 D3
Fenay Bridge Rd HD8 155 C4
Fenay Cres HD5 155 A3
Fenay Dr HD8 155 C3
Fenay La HD5 155 B3
Fenay Lea Dr HD5 155 C4
Fenby Ave BD4 75 C3
Fenby Cl BD4 75 C3
Fenby Gdns BD4 75 C3
Fenby Gr BD4 75 C3
Fencote Cres BD2 56 D3
Fender Rd BD6 73 F1
Fennec Rd BD17 38 E4
Fenny Royd Est HX3 114 B8
Fenton Ave LS26 101 B7
Fenton Cl Rothwell LS26 101 B7
South Kirkby WF9 182 B1
Fenton Rd Halifax HX1 202 B1
Huddersfield HD1 153 F3
Lofthouse Gate WF3 121 F7
Fenton Sq HD1 153 F5
Fenton St Burley in W LS29 9 F1
East Ardsley WF3 98 F1
Leeds LS2 206 B1
Mirfield WF14 138 A4
Fentonsgate WF3 100 C1
Fenwick Dr BD6 94 A6
Ferguson St HX1 203 E2
Fern Ave HD7 170 C3
Fern Bank LS21 23 B8
Fern Chase LS14 45 A7
Fern Cl WF17 118 F5
Fern Croft
Cleckheaton WF15 116 C4
Scarcroft LS14 45 A7
Fern Ct Keighley BD20 18 A2
Wakefield WF2 120 E3
Fern Gdns LS29 8 A3
Fern Hill Ave BD18 54 F7
Fern Hill Gr BD18 54 F7
Fern Hill Mount BD18 54 F7
Fern Hill Rd BD18 54 F7
Fern Lea BD13 72 F1
Fern Lea Flats HD3 135 A1
Fern Lea Rd HD3 135 A1
Fern Lea St 4 HX6 112 B5
Fern Lea View LS28 57 E2
Fern St Bradford BD4 75 D3
Halifax HX3 92 B2
8 Haworth BD22 51 C6
Huddersfield HD1 136 A1
Keighley BD21 35 C8
Fern St E HD1 154 C6
Fern Terr 3 LS28 57 E2
Fern Way LS14 45 A7
Fernbank Ave 14
Bingley BD16 37 A3
Keighley BD22 34 F4
Pudsey LS13 57 F3
Fernbank Cl LS13 57 F3
Fernbank Dr Baildon BD17 38 A1
Bingley BD16 37 B3
Pudsey LS13 57 F3
Fernbank Gdns LS13 57 F3
Fernbank Pl LS13 57 F3
Fernbank Rd Bradford BD3 56 B1
Pudsey LS13 57 F3
Fernbank St BD16 37 A3
Fernbank Terr BD16 37 A3
Fernbank Wlk LS13 57 F3
Ferncliffe Dr Baildon BD17 38 B3
Keighley BD20 18 A2
Ferncliffe Rd Bingley BD16 37 A3
Leeds LS13 58 C2
15 Shipley BD18 54 F8
Ferncliffe Terr LS13 58 C2
Ferndale Ave BD14 73 A3
Ferndale Gr BD9 55 C4
Ferndale Pl WF9 181 D6
Ferndene BD16 37 B2
Ferndene Ave WF17 96 F3
Ferndown Gn BD5 74 D3
Ferney Lee Junior & Infants Sch OL14 108 A6
Ferney Lee Rd OL14 108 A6
Fernfield Terr 7 HX3 92 B2
Fernhill BD16 37 A5
Fernhurst Cl WF14 138 A6
Fernhurst Cres WF14 138 B6
Fernhurst Lea WF14 138 B6
Fernhurst Rd WF14 138 B6
Fernhurst Way WF14 138 A6
Ferniehurst First Sch BD17 38 C2
Fernlea LS26 100 F6
Fernlea Cl Batley WF16 117 E3
Crofton WF4 162 A8
Fernlea Gr HD7 152 E3
Fernleigh Ct WF2 141 F5
Fernley Gdns 11 BD12 94 C4
Ferney Green Cl WF11 127 B4
Fernley Green Ind Est WF11 127 B4
Fernley Green Rd WF11 127 B4
Fernley Hill Dr WF6 122 F5
Ferns The 3 OL13 106 A1
Fernside WF4 144 C3
Fernside Ave HD5 154 F4
Fernside Cl HD5 155 A5
Fernside Cres HD5 155 A5
Fernwood LS8 44 A1
Fernwood Ct LS8 44 A1
Ferrand Ave BD4 95 C8
Ferrand La Bingley BD16 36 F3
Cleckheaton BD19 96 A1
Ferrand St BD16 37 A3
Ferrands Cl BD16 36 B1
Ferrands Park Way BD16 36 B1
Ferriby Cl BD2 56 D3
Ferriby Towers LS9 207 E1
Ferry La WF3 121 F2
Ferry Top La WF4 162 A3
Ferrybridge By-Pass WF11 126 C5
Ferrybridge Infant Sch WF11 126 B5
Ferrybridge Power Sta WF11 126 B7
Ferrybridge Rd
Castleford WF10 124 F7
Knottingley WF11 126 D4
Pontefract WF8 125 F3
Festival Ave BD18 55 D5
Feversham Coll BD3 201 D2
Feversham Fst Sch BD3 75 B7
Feversham St BD3 201 D2
Fewston Ave Leeds LS9 212 C2
Wakefield WF1 142 F8
Fewston Ct LS9 212 C2
Fiddle La HX4 132 F4
Fiddler Hill WF12 139 B4
Fidler Cl LS25 82 E7
Fidler La LS25 82 E7
Field Cl WF16 117 D6
Field Cres 2 WF9 182 F2
Field Ct BD13 72 E6
Field End LS15 81 A7
Field End Cl LS15 81 A7
Field End Cres LS15 81 A7
Field End Ct LS15 81 A7
Field End Garth LS15 81 A7
Field End Gdns LS15 81 A7
Field End Gn LS15 81 A7
Field End Gr LS15 81 B8
Field End La Holmfirth HD7 188 B2
Honley HD7 172 A4
Field End Mount LS15 81 A7
Field End Rd LS15 81 A7
Field Head HD7 152 D5
Field Head La Batley WF17 96 E3
Halifax HX2 91 D7
Hebden Bridge HX7 110 B4
Oxenhope BD22 51 A5
Field Head Way HX2 91 D7
Field House LS25 64 E8
Field House Cl LS22 13 C5
Field Hurst BD19 115 F7
Field La Aberford LS25 64 E8
Batley WF17 118 D4
Brighouse HD6 135 F8
Dewsbury WF13 138 D6
Kirkburton HD4 173 A8
Ossett WF5 140 D6
South Elmsall WF9 183 C4
Upton WF9 183 A8
Wakefield WF2 142 C3
Field Lane County Junior & Infants Sch WF17 118 D4
Field Lane Jun & Inf Sch HD6 135 E7
Field Pl WF2 142 A5
Field Rd HD7 189 B4
Field Side HX1 202 B4
Field St Bradford BD1 201 C3
Dewsbury WF13 138 E6
Field Terr LS15 81 A8
Field Top Rd HD6 114 F1
Field View WF10 124 A6
Field Way HD8 190 E8
Fieldcroft Ct 3 WF14 137 F5
Fieldedge La BD20 19 A2
Fielden Sq OL14 108 B4
Fielden St OL14 108 E6
Fieldens Pl WF17 118 A6
Fieldfares The BD20 5 E1
Fieldgate Rd BD10 56 D7
Fieldhead Cl WF8 125 F1
Fieldhead Cres WF17 96 E3
Fieldhead Ct LS23 30 C7
Fieldhead Dr
Barwick in E LS15 63 F8
Glusburn BD20 16 D7
Guiseley LS20 39 C8
Fieldhead Gdns WF12 119 B3
Fieldhead Gr LS20 39 C8
Fieldhead Hospl WF1 121 D1
Fieldhead Junior & Infants Sch WF17 96 F3
Fieldhead La HD7 187 F1
Fieldhead Paddock LS23 30 C8
Fieldhead Rd LS20 39 D8
Fieldhead St BD7 74 C7
Fieldhead Way WF16 117 C5
Fieldhouse Cl LS17 43 C2
Fieldhouse Cotts 12 HX1 202 C1
Fieldhouse Dr Leeds LS17 43 C2
Slaithwaite HD7 152 A1
Fieldhouse Gr LS28 57 C2
Fieldhouse Lawn LS17 43 C2
Fieldhouse Rd 2 HD1 154 C8
Fieldhouse St Bradford BD3 75 D7
Wakefield WF1 142 F3
Fieldhouse Wlk LS17 43 C2
Fieldhurst Ct BD4 95 C8
Fielding Gate LS12 210 A4
Fielding St 28 HX7 89 A3
Fields Rd Bradford BD12 94 E5
Lepton HD8 155 D2
Fields Rise HD5 137 C1
Fields The WF3 100 D1
Fields Way HD5 137 C1
Fieldsend Ct WF9 183 A7
Fieldshead Bglws HD7 170 D7
Fieldside BD13 52 D6
Fieldside Rd WF9 163 B2
Fieldway Bradford BD14 73 B5
Ilkley LS29 8 E4
Fieldway Ave LS13 58 A4
Fieldway Chase LS26 101 D5
Fieldway Cl LS13 58 A4
Fieldway Rise LS13 58 A4
Fife St 15 BD22 51 D7
Fifth Ave Bradford BD3 56 C1
Rothwell LS26 101 A7
Fifth Ave E WF15 116 B5
Fifth Ave W WF15 116 B5
Fifth St BD12 94 E6
Filbert St HD1 136 A1
Filey Ave S71 179 D4
Filey St BD1 201 C2
Filley Royd BD19 116 E6
Fillingfir Dr LS16 58 F8
Fillingfir Rd LS16 58 F8
Fillingfir Wlk LS16 58 F8
Finch Ave WF2 160 D5
Finch St BD5 74 D4
Finching Gr WF14 138 A8
Finchley St BD5 74 D3
Finchley Way 4 LS27 98 A3
Findon Terr BD10 56 E4
Fine Garth Cl LS23 30 D3
Finghall Rd DN6 184 F2
Fink Hill LS18 58 A8
Finkil St HD6 114 F5
Finkin Ave WF3 121 E2
Finkin Croft WF3 121 E2
Finkin La WF3 121 E2
Finkle Cl WF4 177 F7
Finkle La LS27 97 D6
Finkle St Pontefract WF8 125 D1
Sowerby Bridge HX6 111 D4
Woolley WF4 177 F7
Finsbury Dr BD2 55 F5
Finsbury Rd LS1 206 B1
Finthorpe La HD5 155 A3
Fir Ave WF13 138 D5
Fir Bank 6 WF13 118 A1
Fir Par WF13 138 D5
Fir Rd HD1 153 D6
Fir St Haworth BD22 51 C6
12 Keighley BD21 35 B4
Todmorden OL14 129 A8
Fir Tree App LS17 43 C3
Fir Tree Cl LS17 43 C4
Fir Tree Gdns
Bradford BD10 56 D7
Leeds LS17 43 B4
Fir Tree Gn LS17 43 C4
Fir Tree Gr LS17 43 C4
Fir Tree La LS17 43 D3
Fir Tree Primary Sch LS17 43 C3
Fir Tree Rise LS17 43 C3
Fir Tree Vale LS17 43 C3
Fir Wlk WF13 138 D5
Firbank Gn BD2 56 D3
Firbank Gr LS15 80 E6
Firbeck BD16 53 B8
Firbeck Rd LS23 30 D3
Firethorn Cl BD8 74 A8
Firham Cl S71 179 A4
Firs The Royston S71 179 A4
Scarcroft LS14 45 C7
First Ave Bardsey LS17 28 E5
Bradford BD3 56 C1
Cleckheaton WF15 116 C5
Halifax HX3 113 B4
Hemsworth WF9 163 A4
Horbury WF4 140 F1
Huddersfield, Dalton HD5 154 F7
Huddersfield, Town End HD7 152 D4
3 Keighley BD21 35 B6
Leeds LS12 210 A3
Lofthouse Gate WF1 121 C2
Pudsey LS28 57 E1
Rothwell LS26 100 F7
Royston S71 179 D4
South Kirkby WF9 181 F1
Upton WF9 183 A7
Wetherby LS22 13 F5
Yeadon LS19 40 C5
First Avenue Ind Est LS28 57 E1
First St BD12 94 E6
Firth Ave
5 Brighouse HD6 115 A3
Leeds LS11 214 A2
Firth Cl WF3 121 E5
Firth Gr LS11 214 A2
Firth House WF1 216 B2
Firth House La
Brighouse HD6 136 C7
Ripponden HX4 133 C1
Firth La BD15 53 C5
Firth Mount LS11 214 A2
Firth Rd Bradford BD9 55 A3
Leeds LS11 214 A2
Firth Row BD4 95 B8
Firth St Brighouse HD6 115 A1
Huddersfield HD1 154 B5
Leeds LS9 207 E1
Shepley HD8 190 E8
Firth St 4 BD13 72 D6
Firth Terr LS9 207 E1
Firth View LS11 214 A2
Firthcliffe Dr WF15 117 B5
Firthcliffe Gr WF15 117 C5
Firthcliffe La WF15 117 B5
Firthcliffe Mount WF15 117 B5
Firthcliffe Par WF15 117 B5
Firthcliffe Pl WF15 117 C5
Firthcliffe Rd WF15 117 B5
Firthcliffe Terr WF15 117 B5
Firthcliffe View WF15 117 B5
Firthcliffe Wlk WF15 117 B5
Firthfield La WF9 164 F4
Firthfields LS25 83 A7
Firtree Ave LS25 83 B6
Firville Ave WF6 123 B1
Firville Cres WF6 144 B8
Firwood Cl OL14 108 A1
Fish St LS1 211 F4
Fishbeck La BD20 6 A4
Fisher Gn HD7 171 F4
Fisher Gr WF5 140 F4
Fisher St WF11 126 E4
Fisher Way WF15 117 E3
Fishergate WF11 126 D5
Fishpond La WF2 159 F5
Fishponds Dr WF4 159 F5
Fitts La LS17 27 A8
Fitzgerald St BD5 201 B1
Fitzroy Dr LS8 61 A6
Fitzroy Rd BD3 75 C7
Fitzwilliam Jun & Inf Sch WF9 163 B4
Fitzwilliam St
Bradford BD4 201 C1
Hemsworth WF9 163 B1
Fitzwilliam Sta WF9 163 A3
Five Acres S75 193 F5
Five Lane Ends
Adwick Le S DN6 184 E1
Bradford BD2 56 A5
Holmfirth HD7 188 E5
Leeds LS16 42 D8
Five Oaks BD17 38 A2
Fixby Ave HX2 202 A1
Fixby Jun & Inf Sch HD2 136 A4
Fixby La WF4 156 E6
Fixby Park Dr HD2 135 F2
Fixby Rd HD2 136 A5
Fixby View Yd HD6 135 E6
Flanshaw Ave WF2 141 E6
Flanshaw Cres WF2 141 E6
Flanshaw Gr WF2 141 E6
Flanshaw Jun & Inf Sch WF2 141 F7
Flanshaw La WF2 141 D6
Flanshaw Rd WF2 141 E6
Flanshaw St WF2 141 E6
Flanshaw View WF2 141 E6
Flanshaw Way WF2 141 D7
Flappit Spring BD13 52 A6
Flasby St BD21 35 C8
Flash La WF14 138 B6
Flass La WF10 124 C5
Flat House HD7 170 C8
Flat La HD7 188 D5
Flat Nook BD16 37 B3
Flats La LS15 63 D6
Flats The HX1 203 E2
Flavell Cl WF9 182 B1
Flawith Dr BD2 56 D2
Flax Meadow HD3 135 A2
Flax Mill Rd LS10 215 E3
Flax Pl LS9 212 B3
Flaxen Ct BD6 74 D1
Flaxton Cl 2 LS11 214 B3
Flaxton Gdns 1 LS11 214 B3
Flaxton Gn BD2 56 D2
Flaxton Pl BD7 74 B6
Flaxton St LS11 214 B3
Flaxton View LS11 214 B3
Flea La WF8 166 E4
Fledborough Rd LS22 13 C5
Fleece St Bradford BD6 93 F7
Keighley BD21 35 C7
Fleet La Mickletown LS26 102 A3
Queensbury BD13 72 D1
Rothwell LS26 101 E5
Fleet St HD8 175 D1
Fleet Thro Rd LS18 58 B6
Fleming Ct HD5 155 A5
Fleming St WF17 118 C5
Fleminghouse La HD5 155 A5
Fletcher Ave BD20 5 E2
Fletcher Cres HD6 135 E6
Fletcher Homes WF13 139 A8
Fletcher La BD2 55 D4
Fletcher Rd BD6 74 B1
Fletton Terr BD2 56 B2
Flexbury Ave LS27 98 A3
Flight Hill HD7 199 C5
Flight House Rd HX6 131 F4
Flint La HD7, S36 200 A5
Flint St HD1 136 B1
Flintmill La LS23 14 D3
Flinton Gr BD2 56 D3
Flockton Ave BD4 75 A4
Flockton (C of E) First Sch WF4 157 C2
Flockton Cl BD4 75 A4
Flockton Cres BD4 75 A4
Flockton Dr BD4 75 A4
Flockton Gr BD4 75 A4
Flockton Rd BD4 75 A4
Floral Ave LS7 60 C6
Floreat Cl WF17 118 A8
Florence Ave Leeds LS9 208 A2
Wilsden BD15 53 B6
Florence Gr LS9 208 A2
Florence Mount LS9 208 A2
Florence Pl LS9 208 A2
Florence St Bradford BD3 75 C6
Castleford WF10 124 D8
Halifax HX1 202 C3
Leeds LS9 208 A2
Florence Terr 9 LS27 98 B4
Florida Rd BD15 54 A4
Florist St BD21 18 E1
Flounders Hill WF7 163 F6
Flower Acre HX5 134 F6
Flower Bank Bradford BD2 55 F4
Sowerby Bridge HX6 111 F3
Flower Cl LS19 40 A7
Flower Croft BD21 34 F5
Flower Garth BD10 56 D6
Flower Haven BD9 54 D4
Flower Hill BD9 54 F4
Flower Mount Baildon BD17 38 D4
8 Yeadon LS19 40 C7
Flower Scar Rd OL14 107 B7
Flowerlands HX3 114 E8
Floyd St BD5 74 B3
Flush WF15 117 C4
Flush House La HD7 188 A3
Flushdyke Junior & Infants Sch WF5 140 F7
Fold Ct HD8 173 F5
Fold La HX7 88 A6
Fold The 4 Haworth BD22 51 B7
Leeds LS15 62 E4
Foldings Ave BD19 115 F8
Foldings Cl BD19 115 E8
Foldings Ct BD19 115 E8
Foldings Gr BD19 115 E8
Foldings Par BD19 115 E8
Foldings Rd BD19 115 F8
Foldings The HD8 175 A2
Foljambe St WF2 142 C4
Folkestone St BD3 75 C7
Folkton Holme BD2 56 E2
Follett Ave HD4 153 C2
Follingworth La HD7 151 D1
Follingworth Rd WF17 118 F5
Folly Hall HD1 154 A4
Folly Hall Ave BD6 94 B8
Folly Hall Cl 2 BD6 94 B8
Folly Hall Gdns The BD6 94 B8
Folly Hall La HX7 110 E2
Folly Hall Mount WF3 119 E8
Folly Hall Rd Bradford BD6 94 B8
East Ardsley WF3 119 E8
Folly Hall Wlk 3 BD6 94 B8
Folly La Bramham LS23 30 D2
Leeds LS11 214 B4
Folly Rd HD2 136 A3
Folly View LS23 30 D2
Folly View Rd BD22 51 D6
Fontmell Cl BD4 75 E2
Football LS19 40 C6
Forber Gr BD4 75 E5
Ford BD13 92 C8
Ford Dr WF14 137 E6
Ford Gate HD7 188 D3
Ford Hill BD13 92 D8
Ford House Sch LS6 205 E4
Ford St Hemsworth WF9 163 B1
Keighley BD21 18 E1
Fore La HX6 112 A3
Fore Lane Ave HX6 112 A3
Foreside Bottom La BD13 71 D5
Forest Ave HX2 91 E4
Forest Bank LS27 97 C7
Forest Cl WF1 121 F1
Forest Cres HX2 91 E4
Forest Gate LS21 23 A7

Forest Gn HX2 91 E3
Forest Hill Gdns HD3 152 A8
Forest Hill Rd HX4 133 E1
Forest Rd HD5 154 E5
Forest Ridge WF3 99 C1
Forest Way HD7 171 E4
Forge Hill La WF11 126 E4
Forge La Batley WF15 117 C2
Dewsbury WF12 139 B4
Harewood LS17 27 D1
Horbury WF4 159 C8
Leeds LS12 210 A4
Liversedge WF15 117 B3
Forge Row LS12 77 D3
Forge View BD20 17 C5
Forman's Dr WF3 100 A3
Formby Ave HD2 135 F3
Forrest Ave HD1 153 D7
Forrest Terr WF12 139 E6
Forrester Cl WF9 163 A3
Forster Ct BD1 201 C3
Forster Dr WF16 117 E3
Forster Pl LS12 78 B4
Forster Sq BD1 201 C3
Forster Square Ret Pk BD1 201 B4
Forster St LS10 212 B1
Forsythia Ave WF3 120 C7
Fort Ann Rd WF17 118 F4
Fortis Way HD3 152 E8
Fortshot La LS17 27 B1
Forum View WF8 165 A5
Foss Ave LS22 13 D7
Foss Wlk WF10 104 B1
Fosse Way LS25 83 B6
Foster Ave
Huddersfield HD4 153 C2
Normanton WF6 123 A1
Silsden BD20 5 D2
Thornton BD13 72 F6
Foster Beaver Coll The BD9 54 F1
Foster Cl Burley in W LS29 9 F1
8 Morley LS27 98 A5
Foster Cres 7 LS27 98 A5
Foster Gdns BD22 34 F7
Foster La HX7 89 A4
Foster Park Gr BD13 52 E1
Foster Park Rd BD13 52 E1
Foster Park View BD13 52 E1
Foster Pk BD13 52 E1
Foster Place La HD7 189 F2
Foster Rd BD21 35 B4
Foster Sq Denholme BD13 71 D8
Middleton LS10 99 D8
Foster St 11 Morley LS27 98 A5
1 Queensbury BD13 72 E1
Foston Cl BD2 56 E2
Foston La BD2 56 E2
Fothergill Ave WF7 163 E6
Foul Clough Rd OL14 128 D8
Foulcauseway La LS21 23 D7
Foulds' Terr 6 BD16 37 A4
Foundry App LS9 208 B3
Foundry Ave LS8, LS9 208 B3
Foundry Dr LS9 208 B3
Foundry Hill BD16 36 F3
Foundry La Bradford BD4 75 B5
Knottingley WF11 127 A4
Leeds LS14, LS9 61 E3
Pudsey LS28 57 E2
Foundry Mill Cres LS14 61 F3
Foundry Mill Dr LS14 61 E3
Foundry Mill Gdns LS14 61 E5
Foundry Mill Mount LS14 61 F3
Foundry Mill St LS14 61 F3
Foundry Mill Terr LS14 61 F3
Foundry Mill View LS14 61 F3
Foundry Mill Wlk LS14 61 F3
Foundry Pl LS9 208 B3
Foundry St
Brighouse HD6 115 C1
Dewsbury WF13 139 D8
Dewsbury, Ravensthorpe WF13 138 E5
Halifax HX1 203 E4
Leeds, Bank LS9 212 B3
Leeds, Camp Field LS11 211 E2
Sowerby Bridge HX6 112 B3
Todmorden OL14 108 A4
Foundry St N HX3 91 F3
Foundry Terr BD19 116 E7
Foundry Wlk LS8 208 B3
Fountain Cl
Liversedge WF15 116 F1
Mapplewell S75 177 E1
Fountain Ct S71 178 E1
Fountain Dr WF15 116 F1
Fountain Gr HD4 153 C4
Fountain Sq S75 177 E1
Fountain St Batley WF16 117 D5
Bradford BD1 201 B4
Bradford, Low Moor BD12 94 C6
Halifax HX1 203 E2
29 Hebden Bridge HX7 89 A3
Leeds LS1 211 D4
Liversedge WF15 116 F1
3 Morley LS27 98 C8
14 Queensbury BD13 72 E1
Ripponden HX6 132 D4
7 Thornton BD13 72 D6
Todmorden OL14 108 E6
Fountain Terr BD12 94 D3
Fountain Way BD18 55 C7
Fountain Wlk 1 LS14 62 B5
Fountains Ave
Batley WF17 117 F4
Boston Spa LS23 30 C7
Fountains Way WF1 121 F1
Four Acres WF14 138 A3
Four Lane Ends
Castleford WF10 124 A6
Dewsbury WF12 139 F2
Guiseley LS20 39 C7
Four Row HD8 191 A4
Fourlands Cres BD10 56 C8
Fourlands Ct BD10 56 C8
Fourlands Dr BD10 56 C8
Fourlands Gdns BD10 56 C8
Fourlands Gr BD10 56 C8
Fourlands Rd BD10 56 C8
Fourteenth Ave LS12 210 A2
Fourth Ave Bradford BD3 56 C1
Cleckheaton WF15 116 B5
9 Keighley BD21 35 A6
Lofthouse Gate WF1 121 B2
Rothwell LS26 101 A7
Wetherby LS22 13 F5
Fourth Ct LS11 211 D2
Fourth St 1 BD12 94 E6
Fowler St BD4 75 B5
Fowler's Pl LS28 57 E2
Fowlers Garth BD22 34 D1
Fox Cl HD8 175 D6
Fox Covert Rd or Whin Covert La WF8 166 E2
Fox Ct Crigglestone WF4 159 F7
Elland HX4 134 D7
Fox Heads La LS22 12 A8
Fox La Crigglestone WF4 159 F7
Wakefield WF1 121 A1
Fox Royd HD8 173 E1
Fox Royd Ave WF14 137 F6
Fox Royd Dr WF14 137 F6
Fox Royd La 3 WF14 137 F6
Fox Royd View 4 WF14 137 F6
Fox St Batley WF17 118 D4
Bingley BD16 36 F3
5 Bradford BD5 74 C3
Cleckheaton BD19 116 B7
Dewsbury WF13 138 E5
Huddersfield HD1 154 A6
Fox Terr WF8 125 E1
Fox View WF13 118 A3
Fox Way LS10 212 B1
Fox Wood Ave LS8 61 E5
Fox Wood Cl LS8 61 E5
Fox Wood Gr LS8 61 E5
Fox Wood Rise LS8 61 E5
Fox Wood Wlk LS8 61 E5
Foxbridge Way WF6 123 E3
Foxcliff WF11 105 D1
Foxcroft Cl Leeds LS6 59 B5
Queensbury BD13 92 C7
Foxcroft Dr HD6 114 F1
Foxcroft Gn LS6 59 B5
Foxcroft Mount LS6 59 C5
Foxcroft Rd LS6 59 B5
Foxcroft Way LS6 59 B5
Foxdale Cl 1 OL13 106 A1
Foxen La HX6 132 C6
Foxglove Ave LS8 61 C6
Foxglove Folly WF2 141 E8
Foxglove Rd Batley WF17 96 E2
Huddersfield HD5 154 E4
Foxhill Baildon BD17 38 B3
Wetherby LS22 13 E6
Foxhill Ave Leeds LS16 42 C1
Queensbury BD13 72 D1
Foxhill Cl BD13 72 D1
Foxhill Cres LS16 42 D1
Foxhill Ct LS16 42 C1
Foxhill Dr Leeds LS16 42 D1
Queensbury BD13 72 D1
Foxhill First Sch BD13 72 D2
Foxhill Gn LS16 42 D1
Foxhill Gr Leeds LS16 42 D1
Queensbury BD13 72 D1
Foxhills The LS16 41 D4
Foxhole La LS28 57 B6
Foxholes Cres LS28 57 B6
Foxholes La WF6 122 F5
Foxlow Ave HD5 154 E8
Foxroyd La WF12 139 B1
Foxstone Rise BD17 38 E3
Foxstones La HX6 132 D2
Foxwood Farm Way LS8 61 E5
Foxwood Wlk LS22 13 F7
Frain Cl WF8 146 E7
France Fold HD7 171 F5
France St WF17 118 E4
Frances Ave HD4 153 C3
Frances Rd WF12 139 F7
Frances St
9 Brighouse HD6 115 A3
11 Elland HX5 134 F6
Keighley BD21 35 A8
Pudsey LS28 57 D2
Francis Ave HD3 153 A4
Francis Cl HX1 202 C3
Francis Ct LS7 207 D3
Francis Gr 13 LS11 214 B3
Francis House BD2 56 B2
Francis Rd WF4 144 B3
Francis St
Ackworth M T WF7 163 D5
Batley WF16 117 E3
Bradford BD4 201 D1
Castleford WF10 124 E8
Halifax HX1 202 C2
Huddersfield HD3 153 A4
Leeds LS7 207 E3
Mirfield WF14 137 F5
Francis Terr WF7 163 D5
Francis View WF14 137 F5
Frank Cl WF12 139 E2
Frank La Dewsbury WF12 139 E2
Emley HD8 175 C5
Hebden Bridge HX2 90 B1
Frank Parkinson Ct LS20 22 E1
Frank Parkinson Homes LS20 22 E1
Frank Peel Cl 4 WF16 117 D4
Frank Pl 3 BD7 74 B4
Frank St Bradford BD7 74 B4
Halifax HX1 202 C2
Frankland Gr LS7 207 E3
Frankland Pl LS7 207 E3
Franklin St HX1 202 B3
Fraser Ave LS18 58 A8
Fraser House 2 BD6 93 E8
Fraser Rd LS28 56 F6
Fraser St Bradford BD8 74 C8
Leeds LS9 207 F1
Freakfield La WF15 116 B2
Fred St BD21 35 B6
Fred's Pl BD4 75 C3
Frederick Ave Leeds LS9 80 A6
Wakefield WF1 142 F3
Frederick Cl BD10 38 F1
Frederick St Bradford BD1 201 C2
East Ardsley WF3 120 E8
Huddersfield HD4 153 C4
Keighley BD21 35 D7
5 Liversedge WF15 117 B3
Pudsey LS28 57 C3
Wakefield WF1 216 B2
Frederick Walker Gdns WF17 118 D4
Free School La HX1, HX3 203 D1
Freely La LS23 30 D2
Freeman Rd HX3 114 A5
Freemans Way LS22 14 A6
Freemont St LS13 58 A2
Freeston Ct WF6 123 B3
Freeston Dr WF6 123 B3
Freeston High Sch WF6 123 B1
Freestone Way WF6 122 E4
Fremantle Gr BD4 75 E5
Fremantle Pl LS15 80 E7
Frensham Ave LS27 97 F3
Frensham Dr Bradford BD7 73 D3
Castleford WF10 125 D6
Frensham Gr BD7 73 D3
Frensham Way BD7 73 D3
Freshfield Gdns BD15 54 B1
Freston Ave WF1 143 D7
Freston Dr WF1 143 D7
Friar Ct BD10 56 C6
Friar Pl HD2 136 F5
Friar's Cl WF7 145 D4
Friars Ind Est BD10 56 B7
Friars Nook WF8 146 E7
Friarwood La WF8 146 D8
Frickley Bridge La S72 180 F4
Frickley La Clayton WF9 195 A8
South Elmsall WF9 195 A8
Frieldhurst Rd OL14 86 C1
Friendly Ave HX6 112 A5
Friendly Fold Rd HX3 92 A2
Friendly St 1 Halifax HX3 92 A2
3 Huddersfield HD1 154 B6
Thornton BD13 72 D6
Friends Adult Sch LS27 98 B4
Frimley Dr BD5 74 C2
Frith House HD6 136 C7
Frith St 14 BD22 51 E8
Frizinghall First Sch BD9 55 C5
Frizinghall Mid Sch BD9 55 C5
Frizinghall Rd BD9 55 C4
Frizinghall Sta BD9 55 C4
Frizley Gdns BD9 55 C4
Frober Pl LS15 80 E7
Frobisher Gr WF2 141 E5
Frobisher Rd OL15 129 C1
Frogmoor Ave BD12 94 F5
Front Row LS11 211 E2
Front St Bramham LS23 30 C2
Castleford WF10 124 F6
Leeds LS11 211 E2
Pontefract WF8 146 C8
Frost Hill WF15 117 B4
Fruit St BD21 35 E8
Fryergate WF2 141 F7
Fryston La WF11 125 F7
Fryston Rd WF10 125 C7
Fulford Ave HD2 136 A2
Fulford Cl S75 178 A1
Fulford St WF10 124 C7
Fulford Wlk BD2 56 D2
Fulham Pl 3 LS11 214 B3
Fulham Sq 5 LS11 214 B3
Fulham St LS11 214 B3
Fullerton Cl DN6 184 F2
Fullerton St BD3 201 D2
Fullwood Dr HD7 152 D4
Fulmar Ct LS10 99 D5
Fulmar Mews 8 BD8 73 C7
Fulmar Rd WF10 124 C6
Fulneck LS28 76 E5
Fulneck Boys' Sch LS28 76 E4
Fulneck Cl HD2 135 F3
Fulneck Girls' Sch LS28 76 E5
Fulneck Golf Course LS28 76 D4
Fulstone Hall La HD7 190 A7
Fulstone Rd HD4 173 C1
Fulton St BD1 201 A3
Fulwood Gr WF2 160 B5
Furnace Cotts S36 200 D6
Furnace Gr BD12 94 F5
Furnace Inn St BD4 75 D5
Furnace La BD11 96 A6
Furnace Rd Bradford BD4 95 A6
Bradford, Raw Nook BD12 94 F5
Furnbrook Gdns HD5 155 C8
Furness Ave Halifax HX2 91 E4
Wakefield WF2 120 E2
Furness Cres HX2 91 D5
Furness Dr Halifax HX2 91 D4
Wakefield WF2 120 E2
Furness Gdns HX2 91 E4
Furness Gr HX2 91 E4
Furness Pl HX2 91 E3
Fusden La BD19 96 A1
Futures Way BD4 201 C1
Fyfe Cres BD17 38 D2
Fyfe Gr BD17 38 E2
Fyfe La BD17 38 E2
Gable End Terr LS28 76 F7
Gables The Baildon BD17 38 E3
13 Keighley BD21 35 A7
Gadding Moor Rd S75 192 F1
Gagewell Dr WF4 141 B2
Gagewell La WF4 141 B2
Gagewell View WF4 141 B2
Gain La BD2, BD3 56 E1
Gainest HX2 202 B1
Gainford Dr LS25 82 F6
Gainsborough Cl BD3 56 A2
Gainsborough Pl LS12 77 E3
Gainsborough Way WF3 121 E5
Gainsbro Ave LS16 42 B5
Gainsbro Dr LS16 42 B5
Gaisby La BD18 55 D5
Gaisby Mount BD18 55 D5
Gaisby Pl BD18 55 D6
Gaisby Rise BD18 55 D5
Gaitskell Ct LS11 211 D1
Gaitskell Grange 5 LS11 211 D1
Gaitskell Wlk LS11 211 D1
Gale St 5 Haworth BD22 51 F8
Keighley BD21 35 C8
Galefield Gn BD6 93 F6
Gall La OL14 86 C3
Gallon Croft WF9 182 E3
Galloway Ct 3 LS28 76 A8
Galloway La LS28 57 A1
Galloway Rd BD10 56 D7
Galloway St 1 HD1 154 C8
Gallows Hill WF10 125 D7
Gallows La WF4 159 F1
Galsworthy Ave BD9 54 D3
Gamble Hill LS13 77 D8
Gamble Hill Chase LS13 77 D8
Gamble Hill Cl LS13 77 D8
Gamble Hill Croft LS13 77 D8
Gamble Hill Cross LS13 77 D8
Gamble Hill Dr LS13 77 D8
Gamble Hill Fold LS13 77 D8
Gamble Hill Gn LS13 77 D8
Gamble Hill Grange LS13 77 D8
Gamble Hill Lawn LS13 77 D8
Gamble Hill Path LS13 77 D8
Gamble Hill Pl LS13 77 D8
Gamble Hill Rise LS13 77 D8
Gamble Hill Vale LS13 77 D8
Gamble Hill View LS13 77 D8
Gamble Hill Wlk LS13 77 D8
Gamble La LS12 77 C6
Gambles Hill 8 LS28 57 D3
Game Scar La or Goose Eye Brow BD22 34 B6
Gamel View BD20 17 B6
Gang The LS12 209 F3
Ganners Cl LS13 58 C4
Ganners Gn LS13 58 C4
Ganners Gr LS13 58 D4
Ganners Hill LS13 58 D4
Ganners La LS13 58 C4
Ganners Mount LS13 58 C4
Ganners Rd LS13 58 C4
Ganners Rise LS13 58 D4
Ganners Way LS13 58 C4
Ganners Wlk LS13 58 C4
Gannerthorpe Cl 4 BD12 94 C3
Gannet Cl WF10 124 C6
Ganny Rd HD6 115 B2
Ganton Cl LS6 206 B4
Ganton Way HD2 135 F3
Gaol La HX1 203 F3
Garden Ave WF15 117 A6
Garden Cl Bradford BD12 94 C4
Glusburn BD20 16 B6
Liversedge WF15 117 A5
Ossett WF5 140 E3
Garden Cres WF13 138 E6
Garden Dr WF13 138 E6
Garden Field BD12 94 D3
Garden Fold HX3 114 C8
Garden House Cl LS26 102 D3
Garden House La WF3 120 A8
Garden La Bradford BD9 54 F3
Knottingley WF11 127 A5
Ripponden HX6 133 C7
Garden Par 1 WF15 117 A5
Garden Pl Dewsbury WF13 117 F1
Sutton in C BD20 16 E5
Garden Rd HD6 115 A4
Garden St
Ackworth M T WF7 163 D5
6 Batley WF16 117 D3
Castleford WF10 124 D6
Castleford WF10 125 A6
Dewsbury WF13 138 E5
11 Haworth BD22 51 F8
Huddersfield HD1 153 F4
Normanton WF6 123 B2
Normanton, Altofts WF6 122 E3
Todmorden OL14 108 B6
Wakefield WF1 216 A2
Garden St N HX3 203 F4
Garden Terr Bradford BD9 55 A3
Crigglestone WF4 159 E4
Denby Dale HD8 191 F5
Dewsbury WF13 138 E6
11 Hebden Bridge HX7 89 A3
Garden View Bingley BD16 37 C3
Liversedge WF15 117 A6
Garden View Ct LS8 44 B1
Garden Village LS25 84 A6
Garden Wlk 2 WF15 117 A5
Gardener's Sq HX3 114 C8
Gardeners Ct LS10 215 D4
Gardens Rd WF13 138 F5
Gardens St BD9 54 F4
Gardens The Bingley BD16 37 D3
Halifax HX1 203 E1
Middleton LS10 99 C4
Morley LS27 97 F2
Pudsey LS28 57 C3
Gardiner Row BD4 75 B3
Garfield Ave BD8 55 B2
Garfield Pl HD7 168 F4
Garfield St Bradford BD15 54 A1
17 Halifax HX3 92 A1
Todmorden OL14 86 C1
Garforth Ave BD20 17 C6
Garforth Barleyhill Infants Sch LS25 82 E7
Garforth Cl WF6 122 E3
Garforth Com Coll LS25 82 E5
Garforth Dr WF6 122 E3
Garforth Golf Course LS15 63 E3
Garforth Green Lane Primary Sch LS25 83 B6
Garforth Infants Sch LS25 82 E7
Garforth Rd BD21 35 E8
Garforth St Bradford BD15 54 B1
Huddersfield HD4 171 C7
Garforth Sta LS25 82 F8
Gargrave App LS9 207 F1
Gargrave Cl HD6 135 D7
Gargrave Cres WF9 181 C6
Gargrave Ct LS9 207 F1
Gargrave Pl
Hemsworth WF9 181 C6
Leeds LS9 207 F1
Wakefield WF2 141 C5
Garibaldi St BD3 75 E7
Garland Dr LS15 81 D8
Garlick St HD6 135 E6
Garmil Head La WF9 162 F5
Garmil La WF4 162 F6
Garmont Mews LS7 204 A2
Garmont Rd LS7 204 A2
Garner La Honley HD7 171 D4
Kirkburton HD8 173 D8
Garnet Ave LS11 214 C3
Garnet Cres LS11 214 C3
Garnet Gr LS11 214 C3
Garnet La LS24 48 F8
Garnet Par LS11 214 C3
Garnet Pl LS11 214 C3
Garnet Rd LS11 214 C2
Garnet Terr LS11 214 C3
Garnet View LS11 214 C3
Garnett St Batley WF13 117 F3
Bradford BD3 201 D3
Hebden Bridge HX7 89 A3
Otley LS21 23 B8
Garrett Cl HD8 174 F2
Garsdale Ave BD10 56 C7
Garsdale Cres BD17 38 E4
Garsdale Fold LS22 13 A1
Garsdale Gr WF1 142 F8
Garsdale Rd HD4 154 B2
Garsdale Wlk WF11 126 E2
Garth Ave Collingham LS22 29 B8
Leeds LS17 43 B1
Normanton WF6 144 A8
Garth Barn Cl BD9 55 A4
Garth Dr LS17 43 B1
Garth End LS22 29 B8
Garth Gr LS29 22 A4
Garth Land Way BD4 75 C3
Garth Rd LS17 43 B1
Garth St Castleford WF10 124 C6
Keighley BD21 35 A7
Garth The Collingham LS22 29 B8
Garforth LS25 83 A7
Leeds LS9 212 B3
Garth Wlk LS17 43 C1
Garthwaite Mount BD15 54 B2
Garton Ave LS9 80 A7
Garton Dr DN5 56 D5
Garton Gr LS9 80 A7
Garton Rd LS9 80 A7
Garton Terr LS9 80 A7
Garton View 9 LS9 80 A7
Garvey View BD5 74 E4
Garwick Terr 9 HX4 134 D7
Gas St 4 BD22 51 D7
Gas Works La
Boston Spa LS23 30 F7
Elland HX5 134 F7
Gas Works Rd
Keighley BD21 35 F7
Sowerby Bridge HX6 112 D4
Gascoigne Ave LS15 63 D6
Gascoigne Ct LS15 63 E6
Gascoigne Rd
Barwick in E LS15 63 D6
East Ardsley WF3 99 E1
Gascoigne View LS15 63 D6
Gaskell Dr WF4 141 A2
Gaskell St WF2 142 A5

Gasson St HD3 153 A4
Gasworks St
Huddersfield HD1 154 B7
Liversedge WF15 117 B4
Gate Foot La HD8 190 C5
Gate Head Elland HX4 133 F6
Marsden HD7 169 B4
Gate Head La Elland HX4 133 F6
Holmfirth HD7 200 A8
Gate Way Dr LS19 40 A6
Gatefield Mount BD6 94 B6
Gatehead Bank HD7 169 B5
Gatehouse Enterprise Ctr HD1 153 F3
Gateland Dr LS17 44 E4
Gateland La LS17 44 E4
Gateon House La LS17 28 B4
Gatesgarth Cres HD3 135 A1
Gatesway BD16 36 B1
Gateways WF1 121 C5
Gateways Girls' Prep & High Sch LS17 27 A6
Gathorne Cl LS8 207 F3
Gathorne St Bradford BD7 74 B4
Brighouse HD6 115 B3
Leeds LS8 207 E3
Gathorne Terr LS8 207 E3
Gauk St Brotherton WF11 126 C8
Fairburn WF11 105 A4
Gaukroger La HX3 203 F1
Gauxholme Fold OL14 107 F3
Gavin Cl BD3 75 E7
Gaw La BD23 1 F8
Gawcliffe Rd BD18 55 C7
Gawthorpe Ave BD16 37 A5
Gawthorpe Dr BD16 37 A5
Gawthorpe Green La HD8 155 E6
Gawthorpe Jun & Inf Sch WF5 119 C1
Gawthorpe La Bingley BD16 37 A4
Kirkheaton HD8 155 D6
Ossett WF5 119 E2
Wakefield WF2 120 A2
Gay La LS21 23 A7
Gayle Cl BD12 94 C2
Gaynor St BD8 74 D8
Gaythorn Terr HX3 93 C1
Gaythorne Rd Bradford BD5 74 E3
Bradford, Haigh Fold BD2 56 C2
Gaythorne Terr 6 BD14 73 C4
Geary Cl WF2 141 D8
Geary Dr WF2 141 D8
Geecroft La LS22 12 B4
Geelong Cl BD2 55 F3
Gelder Croft WF2 141 D8
Gelder Ct WF2 141 D8
Gelder Rd LS12 209 F3
Gelder Terr HD5 154 C5
Gelderd Cl LS12 213 D4
Gelderd La LS12 213 D4
Gelderd Pl LS12 210 B2
Gelderd Rd Batley WF17 97 C5
Gildersome LS27 97 C5
Leeds LS12 213 D3
Gelderd Trad Est LS12 210 B1
General Infmy at Leeds The LS1 206 B1
Geneva Gr WF1 216 C3
Genista Dr LS10 99 D8
Gentian Ct WF2 141 E8
George Ave HD2 153 E8
George Buckley Ct WF9 182 A2
George & Crown Yd WF1 216 B2
George La Notton WF4 178 E6
Ripponden HX6 132 B2
George Sq 8 HX1 203 E3
George St Addingham LS29 6 F8
6 Baildon BD17 38 C1
Batley WF17 118 C4
Batley, Heckmondwike WF16 117 D4
Bradford BD1 201 C2
Brighouse HD6 115 A1
Brighouse HD6 115 C2
Brighouse, Hipperholme HX3 114 D7
Cleckheaton BD19 116 D8
Denholme BD13 52 E1
Dewsbury WF13 139 C8
Dewsbury, Dewsbury Moor WF13 138 F8
Dewsbury, Ravensthorpe WF13 138 E5
Elland HX5 134 F6
5 Elland, West Vale HX4 134 D7
Featherstone WF7 145 C5
Featherstone, Streethouse WF7 144 D5
Halifax HX1 203 E3
Hebden Bridge HX7 110 E8
Hemsworth WF9 181 E6
Horbury WF4 141 B1
12 Huddersfield HD1 154 A6
Huddersfield, Lindley HD3 135 B1
Huddersfield, Milnsbridge HD3 153 B5
Huddersfield, Paddock Brow HD1 153 E4
Kirkburton HD8 173 F6
10 Liversedge WF15 117 A4
Lofthouse Gate WF1 121 B5
Mapplewell S75 178 B1
Normanton WF6 122 F3
Ossett WF5 140 D7
Ryhill WF4 162 B2
George St continued
Shipley BD18 54 F8
South Hiendley S72 180 D6
Sowerby Bridge HX6 112 B3
Thornton BD13 72 D6
13 Todmorden OL14 108 B5
Wakefield WF1 216 B2
Yeadon LS19 40 B4
George's Sq
Cullingworth BD13 52 D6
Keighley BD21 35 B6
George's St HX3 91 F3
George-a-Green Rd WF2 141 E4
Georgia Mews WF5 140 F4
Geraldton Ave BD2 55 E3
Gerard Ave LS27 97 F4
Gernhill Ave HD2 135 F5
Gerrard St HX1 203 D3
Gervase Rd WF4 141 A2
Ghyll Beck Dr Otley LS21 22 D6
Yeadon LS19 40 E3
Ghyll Cl BD20 17 C5
Ghyll Mews LS29 8 A3
Ghyll Mount LS19 39 F6
Ghyll Rd LS6 59 A6
Ghyll Royd LS20 39 E7
Ghyll Royd Sch LS29 7 F3
Ghyll The Huddersfield HD2 136 A4
Shipley BD16 54 A8
Ghyll Way BD23 4 A8
Ghyll Wood LS29 7 E3
Ghyll Wood Dr BD16 54 A8
Ghyllbank BD20 5 E2
Ghyllroyd Ave BD11 96 B5
Ghyllroyd Dr BD11 96 B4
Gib Cotts HD7 172 A2
Gib La HD8 175 A2
Gibb La HX2 91 B3
Gibbet St HX1, HX2 202 A3
Gibraltar Ave HX1 202 A2
Gibraltar Island Rd LS10 215 F4
Gibraltar Rd Halifax HX1 202 A2
Pudsey LS28 76 B7
Gibraltar Terr BD20 16 C5
Gibriding La HD7 187 F3
Gibson Ave WF2 141 F7
Gibson Cl WF2 142 A7
Gibson Dr LS15 81 C7
Gibson La LS25 83 C2
Gibson Mill HX7 88 C8
Gibson St Bradford BD3 75 B6
Huddersfield HD3 153 C7
6 Todmorden OL14 108 C5
Gilbert Chase LS5 59 A3
Gilbert Cl LS5 59 B3
Gilbert Gr HD4 153 D3
Gilbert Mount LS5 59 B3
Gilbert St LS28 57 D2
Gilcar St WF6 123 D4
Gildersome Birchfield Jun & Inf Sch LS27 97 C6
Gildersome La LS27 77 B1
Gildersome Primary Sch LS27 97 C7
Gildersome Spur LS27 97 D5
Gilead Rd HD3 152 E7
Giles Hill La HX3 93 A7
Giles St Bradford BD6 74 A1
Bradford BD5 201 A1
Holmfirth HD7 188 F8
Gill Bank Rd LS29 8 A6
Gill Beck Cl BD17 38 E4
Gill Cl LS29 6 D8
Gill La Guiseley LS19 39 F4
Holmfirth HD7 188 E2
Keighley BD22 34 A4
Nesfield LS29 7 C7
Yeadon, Henshaw LS19 40 A5
Yeadon, Westfield LS19 39 F4
Gill Sike Ave WF2 141 F4
Gill Sike Bglws WF2 141 F4
Gill Sike Gr WF2 141 F4
Gill Sike House WF2 141 F4
Gill Sike Rd WF2 141 F4
Gill St WF1 216 B2
Gill's Bldgs WF2 142 A5
Gill's Ct 4 HX1 203 E3
Gill's Yd WF1 216 B3
Gillann St WF11 127 A4
Gillett Dr LS26 100 F5
Gillett La LS26 100 F5
Gilling Ave LS25 83 B8
Gillingham Gn BD4 75 E3
Gillion Cres WF4 159 E6
Gillrene Ave BD15 53 D4
Gillroyd La HD7 170 D8
Gillroyd Par LS27 98 B3
Gillroyd Pl 7 LS27 98 B4
Gillroyd Terr LS27 98 C4
Gills The Morley LS27 98 C4
Otley LS21 11 A2
Gillstone Dr BD22 51 D6
Gillygate WF8 146 D8
Gilmour St 5 HX3 92 B1
Gilpin Pl LS12 210 A2
Gilpin St Bradford BD3 75 B7
Leeds LS12 210 A2
Gilpin Terr LS12 210 A2
Gilpin View LS12 210 A2
Gilpin Rise BD7 74 B7
Gilstead Ct BD16 37 C3
Gilstead Dr BD16 37 C3
Gilstead La BD16 37 C3
Gilstead Middle Sch BD16 37 C4
Gilstead Way LS29 8 B5
Gilthwaites Cres HD8 192 A7
Gilthwaites First Sch HD8 192 A7
Gilthwaites Gr HD8 192 A6
Gilthwaites La HD8 192 A7
Gilthwaites Top HD8 192 A7
Gilynda Cl BD8 73 E7
Gin La WF7 144 C4
Ginnel The LS17 28 C2
Gipsy Hill LS26 101 B6
Gipsy La Leeds LS11 99 A7
Middleton LS11 99 A7
Rothwell LS26 101 B6
Wakefield WF2 160 E7
Woolley WF4 177 F6
Gipsy Mead LS26 101 B6
Gipsy St BD3 75 E8
Gipton App LS9 61 D1
Gipton Ave LS8 207 E3
Gipton Gate E LS9 208 C3
Gipton Gate W LS9 208 B3
Gipton Sq LS9 61 D1
Gipton St LS8 207 E3
Gipton Wood Ave LS8 61 B5
Gipton Wood Cres LS8 61 B5
Gipton Wood Gr LS8 61 B5
Gipton Wood Pl LS8 61 B5
Gipton Wood Primary Sch LS8 208 C3
Gipton Wood Rd LS8 61 B5
Girlington First Sch BD8 74 A8
Girlington Rd BD8 55 A1
Girnhill Infants Sch WF7 145 C4
Girnhill La WF7 145 C4
Gisbourne Rd HD2 136 E5
Gisburn Rd WF1 142 F8
Gisburn St BD21 35 B8
Gissing Rd WF2 141 D4
Glade The Pudsey LS28 57 A2
Scarcroft LS14 45 B7
Gladstonbury Ave WF1 121 F1
Gladstone Cres
3 Bacup OL13 106 A2
Yeadon LS19 40 B5
Gladstone Ct 3 WF13 118 A1
Gladstone Rd
15 Halifax HX1 202 C3
Yeadon LS19 40 B4
Gladstone St Bacup OL13 106 A2
Bingley BD16 36 F2
Bradford BD15 54 B1
Bradford, Barkerend BD3 75 C7
3 Cleckheaton BD19 116 D7
3 Elland HX4 134 A4
Featherstone WF7 145 D7
Keighley BD21 35 B6
Normanton WF6 123 C3
1 Pudsey LS28 57 D3
Queensbury BD13 72 F1
10 Todmorden OL14 86 B1
Gladstone Terr
Castleford WF10 124 E8
Morley LS27 98 A4
Pudsey LS28 57 F2
Gladstone View HX3 113 E3
Gladwin St WF17 118 B4
Glaisdale Cl BD20 17 E8
Glaisdale Ct BD15 54 A3
Glaisdale Gr HX3 114 D7
Glamis Cl LS25 83 B8
Glanville Terr LS26 100 E5
Glasshoughton Infant Sch WF10 124 F7
Glasshouse St LS10 212 A1
Glasshouse View LS10 99 B4
Glastonbury Dr HD3 152 F5
Glazier Rd BD13 72 C2
Gleanings Ave HX2 112 C7
Gleanings Dr HX2 112 C7
Glebe Ave LS5 59 B4
Glebe Cl HD8 175 D7
Glebe Field Chase LS22 13 D6
Glebe Field Cl LS22 13 D6
Glebe Field Croft LS22 13 D6
Glebe Field Dr LS22 13 D6
Glebe Field Garth LS22 13 D6
Glebe Field Holt LS22 13 D6
Glebe Gate WF12 139 F1
Glebe La WF11 126 F4
Glebe Mount LS28 76 E6
Glebe Pl LS5 59 B4
Glebe St Castleford WF10 124 D7
Huddersfield HD1 153 E7
Normanton WF6 144 C8
Pudsey LS28 76 E6
Glebe Terr LS16 59 D7
Glebelands WF11 127 E4
Glebelands Cl LS25 82 F6
Glebelands Dr LS6 59 D6
Gledcliffe HX3 203 F4
Gleddings Cl HX3 113 A3
Gleddings Preparatory Sch The HX3 113 A3
Gledhill Rd BD3 75 B6
Gledhill St 2 OL14 108 B6
Gledhill Terr WF13 138 F8
Gledholt Bank HD1 153 E5
Gledholt Rd HD1 153 E6
Gledhow Ave LS8 204 C4
Gledhow Ct LS7 204 B3
Gledhow Dr BD22 51 C4
Gledhow Grange View LS8 204 C3
Gledhow Grange Wlk LS8 204 C3
Gledhow La LS7, LS8 204 B3
Gledhow Mount LS8 207 E2
Gledhow Park Ave LS7 204 B2
Gledhow Park Cres LS7 204 B2
Gledhow Park Dr LS7 204 B2
Gledhow Park Gr LS7 204 B2
Gledhow Park Rd LS7 204 B2
Gledhow Park View LS7 204 B2
Gledhow Pl LS8 207 E2
Gledhow Primary Sch LS8 204 C4
Gledhow Rd LS8 207 E2
Gledhow Rise LS8 61 B6
Gledhow Terr LS8 207 E2
Gledhow Towers LS8 204 B3
Gledhow Valley Rd LS17, LS7, LS8 204 B2
Gledhow Wood Ave LS8 204 C3
Gledhow Wood Cl LS8 204 C3
Gledhow Wood Ct LS8 61 A5
Gledhow Wood Gr LS8 204 C3
Gledhow Wood Rd LS8 204 C2
Gledmow Lane End LS7 204 A3
Glen Ave Batley WF17 118 C6
Todmorden OL14 107 F7
Glen Ct WF10 124 A6
Glen Dale BD16 53 F7
Glen Dene Menston LS29 22 B4
Shipley BD16 53 F7
Glen Field Ave HD2 136 F3
Glen Garth BD21 35 D5
Glen Gr LS27 98 B3
Glen Lee La BD21 35 D5
Glen Mount Menston LS29 22 B3
Morley LS27 98 B3
Shipley BD16 53 F7
Glen Mount Cl HX3 91 E2
Glen Rd Baildon BD17 37 D4
Leeds LS16 59 C7
Morley LS27 98 C3
Glen Rise BD17 38 A2
Glen Side Rd HD7 170 A8
Glen Terr Brighouse HX3 114 C7
Halifax HX1 203 D1
Glen The OL14 107 F7
Glen View Halifax HX1 203 D1
Harden BD16 36 B1
Glen View Rd Bingley BD16 37 C5
Hebden Bridge HX7 88 E4
Shepley HD8 174 A2
Glen View St OL14 86 B1
Glen Way BD16 37 C6
Glenaire BD18 38 E1
Glenaire Dr BD17 38 A1
Glenaire First Sch BD17 38 A2
Glenbrook Dr BD7 73 F7
Glencoe Cl LS25 102 F8
Glencoe Croft LS25 102 F8
Glencoe Gdns LS25 102 F8
Glencoe Terr Kippax LS25 102 F8
Liversedge WF15 117 B3
Glencoe View LS9 212 C2
Glendale WF4 140 F1
Glendale Ave LS25 82 F6
Glendale Cl BD6 94 A7
Glendale Dr BD6 94 A7
Glendare Ave BD7 73 F6
Glendare Rd BD7 73 F6
Glendare Terr BD7 73 F6
Glendorne Dr HD5 137 C1
Glendower Pk LS16 42 D2
Gleneagles Cl BD4 95 B8
Gleneagles Rd
Featherstone WF7 124 D1
Leeds LS17 43 B4
Gleneagles Way HD2 135 F3
Glenfield BD18 38 E1
Glenfield Ave Bradford BD6 94 D8
Wetherby LS22 13 F4
Glenfield Mount 8 BD6 94 D8
Glenfields WF4 158 D5
Glenfields Cl WF4 158 D5
Glenholm Rd BD17 38 C3
Glenholm Rd W BD17 38 C2
Glenholme BD18 38 E1
Glenholme Heath HX1 202 A3
Glenholme Rd
Bradford BD8 55 B1
Pudsey LS28 57 C2
Glenholme Terr WF5 119 C1
Glenhurst BD4 75 D1
Glenhurst Ave BD21 35 C5
Glenhurst Dr BD21 35 D5
Glenhurst Gr BD21 35 D5
Glenhurst Rd BD18 54 E8
Glenlea Cl LS28 58 A3
Glenlea Gdns LS28 58 A3
Glenlee Rd BD7 73 F7
Glenlow Rd WF12 118 F3
Glenlyon Ave BD20 18 A1
Glenlyon Dr BD20 18 A1
Glenmere Mount LS19 40 D7
Glenmore Cl BD2 56 C1
Glenmore Ct LS16 24 E3
Glenn Way WF4 162 A8
Glenrose Dr BD7 73 E6
Glenroyd Marsden HD7 168 E4
Shipley BD18 38 E1
Glenroyd Ave BD6 94 D7
Glenroyd Cl LS28 76 C7
Glensdale Gr LS9 212 C3
Glensdale Mount LS9 212 C3
Glensdale Rd LS9 212 C3
Glensdale St LS9 212 C3
Glensdale Terr LS9 80 A7
Glenside Ave BD18 38 E1
Glenside Cl HD3 153 D8
Glenside Rd BD18 38 E1
Glenstone Gr BD7 73 F7
Glenthorpe Ave LS9 80 A8
Glenthorpe Cres LS9 80 A8
Glenthorpe Terr LS9 80 A8
Glenton Sq BD9 55 A2
Glenview Ave BD9 54 E3
Glenview Cl BD18 54 C7
Glenview Dr BD18 54 C6
Glenview Gr BD18 54 D7
Glenview Rd BD18 54 D7
Glenview Terr BD18 54 F8
Glenwood Ave BD17 37 E1
Global Ave LS11 213 E1
Globe Ct WF15 117 B4
Globe Fold BD8 74 C8
Globe Rd LS11 211 D2
Glossop Gr LS6 206 B4
Glossop Mount LS6 206 B4
Glossop St LS6 206 B4
Glossop View LS6 206 B4
Gloucester Ave
Bradford BD3 56 D1
Silsden BD20 5 C1
Gloucester Ct LS12 210 B4
Gloucester Gr WF2 141 D5
Gloucester Pl WF2 141 D5
Gloucester Rd
Bingley BD16 37 B2
Wakefield WF2 141 D5
Gloucester Terr LS12 210 B3
Glover Ct BD5 74 E4
Glover Way LS11 214 C2
Glovershaw La BD16 37 E6
Glusburn County Primary Sch BD20 16 C6
Glydegate BD5 201 B2
Glyndon Ct HD6 136 B8
Glynn Terr BD8 74 B8
Gobind Marg BD3 201 D3
Godfrey Rd HX3 113 C3
Godfrey St BD8 73 D7
Godley Branch Rd HX3 113 E8
Godley Cl S71 179 D4
Godley Gdns HX3 92 F1
Godley La Halifax HX3 113 E8
Northowram HX3 92 F1
Godley Rd HX3 203 F4
Godley St S71 179 D4
Godly Cl HX6 132 C1
Godwin St BD1 201 B3
Goff Well La BD21 35 C2
Gog Hill HX5 134 F7
Goit Side Bradford BD1 201 B3
Halifax HX2 90 E4
Goit Stock La BD16 53 B8
Goit Stock Terr BD16 53 B8
Golcar Brow Rd HD7 170 C2
Golcar Jun & Inf Sch HD7 152 D4
Goldcrest Ave 3 BD8 73 B7
Goldcrest Ct HD4 171 E6
Golden Acre Cnr LS16 25 A1
Golden Acre Pk & Gdns LS16 42 C8
Golden Bank LS18 41 C1
Golden Butts Rd LS29 8 C4
Golden Sq WF4 141 B1
Golden Terr LS12 78 A4
Golden View Dr BD21 35 F6
Goldfields Ave HX4 134 B8
Goldfields Cl 1 HX4 134 B8
Goldfields View 2 HX4 134 B8
Goldfields Way HX4 134 B8
Goldington Ave HD3 153 A8
Goldington Dr HD3 153 A8
Golf Ave HX2 112 C7
Golf Cres HX2 112 C7
Golf La LS27 118 E8
Gomersal First Sch BD19 96 B1
Gomersal La BD19 117 A7
Gomersal Middle Sch BD19 96 B1
Gomersal Rd WF16 117 C6
Gondal Ct BD5 74 C3
Good Hope Cl WF6 123 D3
Goodcomb Pl LS25 83 C3
Gooder Ave S71 179 C3
Gooder La HD6 115 B1
Gooder St HD6 115 A2
Goodman St LS10 212 B1
Goodrick La LS17 43 B7
Goodwin House 5 BD13 72 E1
Goodwin Pl HD2 136 F5
Goodwin Rd LS12 209 F2
Goodwood LS29 7 F6
Goodwood Ave LS25 83 A2
Goody Cross LS26 82 C2
Goody Cross La LS26 82 C2
Goose Cote La
Haworth BD22 34 E2
Keighley BD22 34 E2
Goose Cote Way BD22 34 E3
Goose Eye BD22 34 B6
Goose Gn HD7 189 A5
Goose Hill WF16 117 D4
Goose La LS20 21 C1
Goose West La HX6 112 B2
Gooseacre Ave S63 194 C1
Goosefield Rise LS25 82 D6
Goosehill La WF1 143 E7
Goosehill Rd WF6 144 A8
Goosehole La WF9 183 B1
Gordale Cl Batley WF17 118 B5
Bradford BD4 75 F3
Gordon Ave WF5 140 D6
Gordon Dr LS6 59 F6
Gordon Pl 5 Leeds LS6 59 F6
South Elmsall WF9 182 F2
Gordon St Bradford BD5 201 C1
7 Bradford, Clayton BD14 73 B4
East Ardsley WF3 120 E8
Elland HX5 134 F6
Featherstone WF7 145 D7
Halifax HX3 92 B2
10 Haworth BD22 51 E8
Ilkley LS29 8 C4
Keighley BD21 35 B7

Gordon St continued
Slaithwaite HD7 ... 170 A8
Sowerby Bridge HX6 ... 112 A3
Sutton in C BD20 ... 16 D5
10 Todmorden OL14 ... 108 C5
Wakefield WF1 ... 142 F2
Gordon Terr Bradford BD10 .. 39 B1
Knottingley WF11 ... 127 B3
Leeds LS6 ... 59 F6
Slaithwaite HD7 ... 152 D2
Gordon View LS6 ... 59 F6
Gordonsfield WF7 ... 163 F5
Goring Park Ave WF5 ... 141 A4
Gorple Rd BB10 ... 66 A5
Gorse Ave BD17 ... 37 E1
Gorse Lea 5 LS10 ... 99 D8
Gorse Rd HD3 ... 153 C6
Gorton St WF9 ... 163 B1
Gosling La HX4 ... 132 F2
Gosport Cl HD3 ... 152 A8
Gosport La Elland HD3 ... 152 A8
Elland, Sowood Green HX4 ... 133 F1
Gosside Gr WF6 ... 123 D1
Gothic Mount WF7 ... 145 A8
Gothic St BD13 ... 72 E1
Gott St BD22 ... 51 F8
Gott's Terr BD20 ... 18 A2
Gotts Park Ave LS12 ... 58 F1
Gotts Park View LS12 ... 59 A2
Gotts Rd LS12 ... 210 C3
Gough La HX6 ... 132 B7
Goulbourne St BD21 ... 35 B6
Governor's Yd WF1 ... 216 C3
Gower St Bradford BD5 ... 74 E4
Leeds LS2 ... 212 A4
Grace Leather La WF17 ... 118 E5
Grace St Keighley BD21 ... 35 D7
Leeds LS1 ... 211 D4
Gracechurch St BD8 ... 74 D8
Gracey La BD6 ... 73 F1
Grafton Cl Baildon BD17 ... 38 D4
Knottingley WF11 ... 126 F5
Grafton Pl HX3 ... 92 A3
Grafton Rd BD21 ... 35 A5
Grafton Sch LS6 ... 206 B3
Grafton St Batley WF17 ... 118 D3
Bradford BD5 ... 201 B1
Castleford WF10 ... 124 E5
Keighley BD21 ... 35 B5
Leeds LS7 ... 207 D1
Grafton Villas LS15 ... 62 D4
Graham Ave Leeds LS4 ... 205 D3
Upton WF9 ... 183 D8
Graham Dr WF10 ... 125 B7
Graham Gr LS4 ... 205 D3
Graham Mount LS4 ... 205 D3
Graham St Bradford BD9 ... 55 A2
Huddersfield HD1 ... 153 F5
Leeds LS4 ... 205 D3
Graham Terr LS4 ... 205 D3
Graham View LS4 ... 205 D3
Graham Wlk LS27 ... 97 D7
Grain St BD5 ... 74 B2
Gramfield Rd HD4 ... 153 C3
Grammar School St BD1 ... 201 B4
Grampian Ave WF2 ... 141 E3
Grampian Cl HD8 ... 173 F3
Granby Ave LS6 ... 59 D5
Granby Cl LS6 ... 59 D5
Granby Ct WF9 ... 183 A5
Granby Dr BD20 ... 18 F1
Granby Gr LS6 ... 59 D5
Granby La BD20 ... 18 F1
Granby Mount 7 LS6 ... 59 D5
Granby Pl LS6 ... 59 D5
Granby Rd LS6 ... 59 D5
Granby St Bradford BD4 ... 201 C2
Leeds LS6 ... 59 D5
2 Queensbury BD13 ... 72 E1
Granby Terr LS6 ... 59 D5
Granby View LS6 ... 59 D5
Grand Arc LS1 ... 211 F4
Grand Cross Rd HD5 ... 154 E6
Grand Stand HD7 ... 152 B5
Grand Stand Rd WF2 ... 120 F5
Grand Theatre LS1 ... 211 F4
Grandage Terr BD8 ... 74 B8
Grandsmere Pl 5 HX3 ... 113 B4
Grange Ave Batley WF17 ... 118 B3
Birkenshaw BD4 ... 96 A8
Bradford, Lower Grange BD15 ... 73 C8
Bradford, Thornbury BD3 ... 75 F8
Garforth LS25 ... 82 F6
Halifax HX2 ... 91 F5
Huddersfield HD2 ... 135 F1
Ilkley LS29 ... 8 D4
Leeds LS7 ... 207 E4
Marsden HD7 ... 169 A4
Menston LS29 ... 21 F5
Shipley BD18 ... 54 E8
South Elmsall WF9 ... 183 A3
Thorp Arch LS23 ... 15 A3
Yeadon LS19 ... 40 C6
Grange Bank HX3 ... 93 C6
Grange Bank Cl HD5 ... 154 D7
Grange Castle LS19 ... 40 D6
Grange Cl Badsworth WF9 ... 164 E2
Bardsey LS17 ... 28 D4
Brierley S72 ... 180 F3
Elland HD3 ... 152 A8
Horsforth LS18 ... 57 F8
Ilkley LS29 ... 8 D4
Knottingley WF11 ... 126 D4
Leeds LS10 ... 215 D4
Grange Cotts
Cleckheaton BD19 ... 116 C8
Marsden HD7 ... 169 A4
Grange Cres Dearne S63 ... 194 E1
Keighley BD20 ... 18 E2
Leeds LS7 ... 207 E4
Yeadon LS19 ... 40 C6
Grange Croft LS17 ... 43 C5
Grange Ct Badsworth WF9 ... 164 E2
Barwick in E LS15 ... 62 F6
Halifax HX3 ... 114 A4
Leeds, Alwoodley LS17 ... 43 C5
Leeds, Headingley Hill LS6 ... 59 F5
4 Shipley BD16 ... 54 A7
Grange Dr Bradford BD15 ... 73 C8
Emley HD8 ... 175 D8
Horsforth LS18 ... 57 F8
Ossett WF5 ... 140 F3
Grange Est LS29 ... 8 D4
Grange Farm Primary Sch LS14 ... 61 F6
Grange Fields Mount 6 LS10 ... 99 F7
Grange Fields Rd LS10 ... 99 F6
Grange Fields Way LS10 ... 99 F6
Grange Gr Bradford BD3 ... 75 F8
Keighley BD20 ... 18 E1
Grange Holt LS17 ... 43 C5
Grange House S72 ... 180 F3
Grange Hts HX3 ... 114 A4
Grange La Brighouse HD6 ... 115 E2
Burghwallis DN6 ... 184 F3
Flockton WF4 ... 157 D4
Haworth BD22 ... 33 F3
Kippax LS25 ... 83 B2
Kirkburton HD8 ... 173 D3
Grange Middle Sch BD20 ... 18 E2
Grange Mount LS19 ... 40 C6
Grange Park Ave LS8 ... 61 D5
Grange Park Cl
Kippax WF10 ... 103 A5
Leeds LS8 ... 61 E5
9 Morley LS27 ... 98 B7
Grange Park Cres LS8 ... 61 D5
Grange Park Ct LS27 ... 98 B7
Grange Park Dr Morley LS27 98 B7
Shipley BD16 ... 54 B8
Grange Park Gr LS8 ... 61 D5
Grange Park Mews
Leeds LS8 ... 61 D5
10 Morley LS27 ... 98 B7
Grange Park Pl LS8 ... 61 E5
Grange Park Rd Leeds LS8 ... 61 E5
Shipley BD16 ... 54 A7
Grange Park Rise LS8 ... 61 D5
Grange Park Terr LS8 ... 61 E5
Grange Park Way LS27 ... 98 B7
Grange Park Wlk LS8 ... 61 D5
Grange Pk Baildon BD17 ... 38 E3
Halifax HX3 ... 113 B3
Grange Rd Batley WF17 ... 118 A3
Batley, Chidswell WF17 ... 119 A4
Bingley BD16 ... 37 B4
Bradford BD15 ... 73 C8
Brierley S72 ... 180 F2
Burley in W LS29 ... 9 F1
Castleford WF10 ... 104 E1
Cleckheaton BD19 ... 116 C8
Farnhill BD20 ... 4 D1
Holme Chapel BB10 ... 85 A7
Huddersfield HD7 ... 152 E6
Keighley BD20 ... 18 E1
Leeds LS10 ... 215 D4
Royston S71 ... 179 B3
Steeton BD20 ... 17 A5
Yeadon LS19 ... 40 C6
Grange Rd First Sch BD7 ... 74 B5
Grange Rd The LS16 ... 42 B1
Grange Rise WF9 ... 181 D7
Grange Road Ind Est WF17 ... 118 E4
Grange St 10 Halifax HX3 ... 92 A1
Keighley BD21 ... 35 C8
Wakefield WF2 ... 142 A5
Grange Terr Bradford BD15 ... 73 C8
Leeds LS7 ... 207 D4
Marsden HD7 ... 169 A4
8 Morley LS27 ... 98 B7
Pudsey LS28 ... 76 E8
Shipley BD18 ... 55 B6
Steeton BD20 ... 17 A5
Grange The Garforth LS25 ... 83 B7
Huddersfield HD5 ... 154 F7
Grange Upper Sch BD5 ... 74 B2
Grange Valley Rd WF17 ... 118 F4
Grange View Bradford BD3 ... 75 F8
Dewsbury WF12 ... 139 D1
Hemsworth WF9 ... 181 D6
Leeds LS7 ... 207 E4
Otley LS21 ... 10 F1
Pudsey LS28 ... 76 E8
Steeton BD20 ... 17 A5
Wetherby LS22 ... 13 E4
Grange View Gdns LS17 ... 44 F1
Grangefield Ave
Batley WF17 ... 118 B3
Burley in W LS29 ... 9 F1
Grangefield Ct LS25 ... 82 F7
Grangefield Ind Est LS28 ... 57 E1
Grangefield Rd LS28 ... 57 E1
Grangefields HD2 ... 135 E1
Grangeway Bradford BD15 ... 73 C8
Hemsworth WF9 ... 181 D7
Grangewood Ct Leeds LS16 .. 42 B1
Lofthouse Gate WF1 ... 121 D5
Grangewood Gdns LS16 ... 42 B1
Granhamthorpe LS13 ... 58 C2
Granny Ave LS27 ... 98 C8
Granny Hall Gr HD6 ... 114 F4
Granny Hall La HD6 ... 114 F4
Granny Hall Pk HD6 ... 114 F4
Granny La Leeds LS12 ... 209 D1
Mirfield WF14 ... 138 B3
Grant Ave LS7 ... 207 E2
Grant St Bradford BD3 ... 201 D3
Keighley BD21 ... 35 A7
Oxenhope BD22 ... 51 C2
Grantham Pl Bradford BD7 ... 74 C5
Halifax HX3 ... 92 B2
Grantham Rd Bradford BD7 .. 74 C5
Halifax HX3 ... 92 B2
Grantham Terr BD7 ... 74 C5
Grantham Towers LS9 ... 207 E1
Grantley Pl HD2 ... 136 D5
Grantley St WF1 ... 216 C2
Grantley Way WF1 ... 216 C3
Granton Rd LS7 ... 204 A1
Granton St BD3 ... 75 C7
Granville Ave 6 WF8 ... 146 C8
Granville Mount LS21 ... 22 F7
Granville Pl Bradford BD15 ... 54 B1
Otley LS21 ... 22 F7
Granville Rd Leeds LS9 ... 207 E1
Shipley BD18 ... 55 C5
Granville St Bradford BD14 ... 73 C5
Castleford WF10 ... 124 C5
Dewsbury WF13 ... 139 B8
6 Elland HX5 ... 134 F6
Featherstone WF7 ... 145 C4
Keighley BD21 ... 35 B7
Liversedge WF15 ... 117 B3
Normanton WF6 ... 123 B2
Pudsey LS28 ... 76 C8
2 Pudsey, Stanningley LS28 . 57 F2
2 Todmorden OL14 ... 108 A1
Granville Terr Bingley BD16 ... 37 A3
Guiseley LS20 ... 22 F2
Huddersfield HD1 ... 153 E5
Otley LS21 ... 22 F7
Shipley BD18 ... 55 B5
2 Yeadon LS19 ... 40 C7
Grape St Bradford BD15 ... 54 C1
Halifax HX1 ... 203 D3
2 Keighley BD21 ... 35 E8
Leeds LS10 ... 212 A1
Grasleigh Ave BD15 ... 54 A3
Grasleigh Way BD15 ... 53 F2
Grasmere Ave LS22 ... 13 C5
Grasmere Cl
Castleford WF10 ... 104 E1
Leeds LS12 ... 210 A2
Grasmere Cres S75 ... 178 A3
Grasmere Ct LS12 ... 210 A3
Grasmere Dr Elland HX5 ... 135 B7
Wetherby LS22 ... 13 C5
Grasmere Rd Batley WF12 .. 118 E2
Bradford BD2 ... 56 A3
Brighouse BD12 ... 94 E1
Knottingley WF11 ... 126 E2
Leeds LS12 ... 210 A2
Meltham HD7 ... 170 E1
Wakefield WF2 ... 141 E7
Grasscroft HD5 ... 154 F2
Grasscroft Ave HD7 ... 171 F4
Grasscroft Rd Honley HD7 ... 171 E4
Huddersfield HD1 ... 153 E7
Grassmere Rd HD1 ... 153 E7
Grassmoor Fold HD7 ... 172 A3
Gratrix La HX6 ... 112 C5
Grattan Rd 5 BD1 ... 74 D7
Graveleythorpe Rd LS15 ... 62 B1
Graveleythorpe Rise 2 LS15 ... 62 B1
Gray Ave BD18 ... 55 D5
Gray Ct LS15 ... 81 D8
Gray Hall Cl HX4 ... 133 F3
Gray St FW15 ... 116 E4
Gray's Rd S71 ... 179 C1
Grayrigg Cl LS15 ... 80 E7
Grayrigg Ct LS15 ... 80 D7
Grayshon Dr BD6 ... 74 C1
Grayshon St BD11 ... 96 E5
Grayson Crest LS4 ... 59 B3
Grayson Hts LS4 ... 59 B3
Grayswood Cres BD4 ... 75 D3
Grayswood Dr BD4 ... 75 D3
Great Albion St HX1 ... 203 E3
Great Cross St BD1 ... 201 C2
Great Edge Rd HX2 ... 111 F6
Great George St
3 Leeds LS1 ... 211 D4
Leeds LS1, LS2 ... 211 E4
Great Horton Middle Sch BD7 ... 74 A4
Great Horton Rd
Bradford, Great Horton BD7 ... 74 B5
Bradford, Horton Bank BD7 ... 73 E3
Great House La HX6 ... 132 A3
Great House Rd OL14 ... 108 E8
Great & Little Preston C of E Infant Sch LS26 ... 102 E7
Great & Little Preston Junior Sch LS26 ... 102 E7
Great North Rd LS25 ... 84 A6
Great Northern Rd BD21 ... 35 C6
Great Northern Ret Pk HD1 ... 154 B7
Great Northern St
Huddersfield HD1 ... 154 B7
Morley LS27 ... 98 A3
Great Pasture LS29 ... 9 F2
Great Pond St WF13 ... 138 F5
Great Russell Ct BD7 ... 74 C7
Great Russell St BD7 ... 74 C7
Great Wilson St LS11 ... 211 F2
Great Wood St WF17 ... 118 C4
Greatfield Cl WF5 ... 140 E6
Greatfield Dr WF5 ... 140 E5
Greatfield Gdns WF5 ... 140 E6
Greatfield Rd WF5 ... 140 E5
Greave Cl HD2 ... 136 B4
Greave Clough Cl 2 OL13 ... 106 B3
Greave Clough Dr OL13 ... 106 B3
Greave House Dr HX2 ... 111 D7
Greave House Fields HX2 ... 111 E8
Greave House La HD8 ... 155 D3
Greave House Pk HX2 ... 111 D7
Greave House Terr HD8 ... 155 D3
Greave Rd Bacup OL13 ... 106 B3
Holmfirth HD7 ... 199 A8
Ripponden HX6 ... 131 E6
Greave St OL14 ... 108 D5
Greavefield La WF8 ... 126 B1
Greaves Ave WF2 ... 141 C5
Greaves Croft HD8 ... 155 D3
Greaves Fold HX4 ... 134 C4
Greaves Rd WF13 ... 118 D1
Greaves St Bradford BD5 ... 74 D3
Castleford WF10 ... 124 D8
Greek St Castleford WF10 ... 124 E8
Leeds LS1 ... 211 E4
Green Abbey HD7 ... 199 B7
Green Acre Cl BD17 ... 38 D3
Green Acres
Crigglestone WF4 ... 160 A7
Featherstone WF7 ... 145 E3
Green Acres Cl HD8 ... 175 C6
Green Ave Batley WF16 ... 117 E4
Kippax LS25 ... 82 F3
Silsden BD20 ... 5 D2
Green Balk La HD8 ... 155 F2
Green Bank WF3 ... 100 D1
Green Bank Ct BD17 ... 38 B1
Green Chase 2 LS6 ... 59 E7
Green Cl Batley WF17 ... 118 E5
Bradford BD8 ... 73 E8
Dewsbury WF13 ... 118 A2
Leeds LS6 ... 59 F7
Low Bradley BD20 ... 4 C6
Steeton BD20 ... 16 F6
Green Cliff HD7 ... 171 F5
Green Cres
Huddersfield HD7 ... 152 E5
Leeds LS6 ... 59 E7
Green Croft WF9 ... 163 B2
Green Ct Barwick in E LS15 ... 62 F7
Bradford BD7 ... 73 F5
Brighouse BD19 ... 115 F8
Green Edge HD7 ... 152 C6
Green End Bradford BD14 ... 73 B4
Brighouse HD6 ... 115 A1
Green End Cl 8 OL13 ... 106 A3
Green End La WF2 ... 142 C3
Green End Rd Bradford BD6 . 94 B8
Keighley BD20 ... 19 E2
Green Gate La HD7 ... 170 A5
Green Gate Rd HD7 ... 188 A4
Green Gdns HD7 ... 152 E5
Green Hall Pk HX3 ... 93 D5
Green Head Ave BD20 ... 18 A2
Green Head Dr BD20 ... 18 A2
Green Head La BD20 ... 18 A2
Green Head Rd BD20 ... 18 B2
Green Hill Halifax HX2 ... 112 B6
Huddersfield HD2 ... 136 B4
Green Hill Chase LS12 ... 209 E2
Green Hill Cl LS12 ... 58 F1
Green Hill Croft LS12 ... 209 E2
Green Hill Dr LS13 ... 58 E1
Green Hill Gdns LS12 ... 209 E2
Green Hill Holt LS12 ... 209 E2
Green Hill La LS12 ... 209 E1
Green Hill Mount LS13 ... 58 E1
Green Hill Pl LS13 ... 58 E1
Green Hill Rd
8 Bacup OL13 ... 106 A1
Leeds LS12, LS13 ... 58 E1
Green Hill Way LS13 ... 58 E1
Green House Hill HD8 ... 174 C4
Green House La HD8 ... 174 C4
Green La
Ackworth M T WF7 ... 163 D6
Addingham LS29 ... 2 E1
Adwick Le S DN6 ... 184 E3
Baildon BD17 ... 38 A4
Baildon, Baildon Wood Bottom BD17 ... 38 B1
Boston Spa LS23 ... 30 F6
Bradford BD8 ... 55 C1
Bradford, Fourlands BD10 ... 56 C8
Bradford, Idle Moor BD10 ... 56 A8
Bradford, Lidget Green BD7 ... 74 A5
Bradford, Oakenshaw BD12 ... 94 F4
Bradford, Ravenscliffe BD2 ... 56 D3
Bradford, Wyke BD12 ... 94 C2
Brighouse, Clifton HD6 ... 115 F2
Brighouse, Hove Edge HD6 ... 114 E5
Burley in W LS29 ... 9 E3
Castleford, Castleford Ings WF10 ... 103 F1
Castleford, Cutsyke WF10 ... 124 C5
Cleckheaton BD19 ... 95 E2
Collingham LS22 ... 29 A8
Denby Dale HD8 ... 191 B2
Dewsbury WF13 ... 118 A1
Elland, Sowood Green HX4 ... 133 F1
Elland, West Vale HX4 ... 134 C6
Featherstone WF7 ... 145 B6
Featherstone WF7 ... 145 D6
Garforth LS25 ... 83 A7
Glusburn BD20 ... 16 B7
Halifax, Bank Top HX3 ... 113 E6
Halifax, Illingworth HX2 ... 91 E8
Halifax, Midgley HX2 ... 90 D1
Halifax, Pye Nest HX2 ... 202 A1
Green La continued
Halifax, Shibden Dale HX2, HX3, HX4 ... 92 E6
Halton East BD23 ... 1 E8
Haworth BD22 ... 33 F4
Heptonstall HX7 ... 88 E5
Holmfirth HD7 ... 189 A2
Horbury WF4 ... 159 C8
Horsforth LS18 ... 58 B7
Kippax LS25 ... 82 F2
Kippax, Kippax Common LS25 ... 82 F3
Ledston WF10 ... 103 E6
Leeds LS11 ... 214 A1
Leeds, Cookridge LS16 ... 41 D5
5 Leeds, Cross Gates LS15 ... 62 B1
Leeds, Farnley LS12 ... 77 C5
Leeds, New Wortley LS12 ... 210 B2
Leeds, Whinmoor LS14 ... 62 A8
Liversedge WF15 ... 116 D3
Low Bradley BD20 ... 5 A6
Marsden HD7 ... 169 B7
Meltham HD7 ... 170 E1
Menston LS29 ... 21 C5
Mickletown LS26 ... 102 F2
Netherton WF4 ... 158 E5
Netherton WF4 ... 158 F5
Netherton, Overton WF4 ... 157 F6
Notton WF4 ... 179 A5
Oakworth BD22 ... 34 D2
Otley LS21 ... 10 F1
Pontefract WF8 ... 146 D7
Pontefract, Carleton WF8 ... 146 E5
Pudsey LS28 ... 76 D6
Queensbury BD13 ... 72 B3
Ripponden HX4 , HX6 ... 150 F8
Ripponden, Soyle Hill HX6 ... 132 B4
Rothwell WF3 ... 100 D1
Shelf HX3 ... 93 E6
South Kirkby WF9 ... 182 B2
Steeton BD20 ... 17 A6
Thornton BD13 ... 72 E6
Upton WF9 ... 165 C1
Wakefield WF2 ... 141 E7
Yeadon LS19 ... 40 B5
Green Lane Cl WF4 ... 158 A6
Green Lane First Sch BD8 ... 55 C1
Green Lane Terr HD7 ... 152 C6
Green Lea LS26 ... 101 C6
Green Lea Cl LS23 ... 30 E7
Green Lea Mills (Ind Units) HD5 ... 155 A6
Green Lea Rd HD5 ... 154 F6
Green Leas Special Sch WF8 ... 146 E5
Green Meadow BD15 ... 53 D4
Green Meadows Sch LS20 .. 22 C1
Green Mount Baildon BD17 ... 38 B2
Bradford BD4 ... 75 D3
Huddersfield HD5 ... 154 D6
Green Mount Rd BD13 ... 72 E6
Green Mount Ret Pk HX1 ... 203 D3
Green Park Ave
Halifax HX3 ... 113 C2
Horbury WF4 ... 140 F2
Ossett WF5 ... 140 E3
Green Park Dr HX3 ... 113 C2
Green Park Gate HX3 ... 113 C2
Green Park Rd HX3 ... 113 C2
Green Park St HX3 ... 113 C3
Green Pk Leeds LS17 ... 43 E2
Wakefield WF1 ... 142 E6
Green Pl BD2 ... 56 B2
Green Rd Baildon BD17 ... 38 C2
Leeds LS6 ... 59 E7
Liversedge WF15 ... 117 A5
Green Row Bradford BD10 ... 56 B6
3 Leeds LS6 ... 59 E7
Mickletown LS26 ... 102 D1
Green Royd Elland HX4 ... 134 C6
Halifax HX2 ... 91 B4
Green Side Rd HD4 ... 173 A3
Green Slacks La HD3 ... 151 B5
Green St Bradford BD1 ... 201 C3
Bradford, Lower Woodlands BD12 ... 95 B5
Castleford WF10 ... 103 D1
3 Elland HX4 ... 134 B4
Haworth BD22 ... 51 C6
Huddersfield HD1 ... 154 A7
Meltham HD7 ... 170 D2
4 Oxenhope BD22 ... 51 C2
Green Sykes Rd BD22 ... 34 A7
Green Terr
Dewsbury WF13 ... 118 A2
Guiseley LS20 ... 39 E8
Leeds LS11 ... 214 C3
Mirfield WF14 ... 137 F6
Green Terrace Sq HX1 ... 202 C1
Green The Batley WF17 ... 96 F2
Bingley BD16 ... 37 A6
Bingley BD16 ... 37 D3
Bingley, Eldwick Beck BD16 ... 37 D6
Bingley, Micklethwaite BD16 .. 36 E7
Birkenshaw BD4 ... 95 F7
Bradford BD10 ... 56 B8
Castleford WF10 ... 125 D8
Crofton WF4 ... 144 C2
Featherstone WF7 ... 145 E4
Garforth LS25 ... 83 A7
Guiseley LS20 ... 39 E8
Horsforth LS18 ... 58 B8
Huddersfield HD2 ... 136 D5
1 Kippax LS25 ... 83 A1

Green The continued
Kirkburton HD4 172 F2
Leeds, Hawksworth LS5 58 E7
Leeds, Moortown LS17 43 E2
Marsden HD7 168 F4
Mirfield WF14 137 E6
Ossett WF5 140 E4
Otley LS21 10 F1
Pudsey LS28 57 D4
Royston S71 179 C3
South Kirkby WF9 182 C3
Wakefield WF2 120 E3
Woolley WF4 178 A7
Green Top LS12 209 E1
Green Top Gdns LS12 209 E1
Green Top St BD8 73 E7
Green View Leeds LS6 59 E7
Scarcroft LS14 45 C8
Green View The S72 180 C4
Green Way Glusburn BD20 16 C7
Halifax HX2 91 E8
Scarcroft LS14 45 C8
Green Wood Pk LS6 59 E7
Green's Sq HX2 202 A4
Green's Sq LS25 83 B1
Greenacre Ave BD12 94 D2
Greenacre Cl 1 BD12 94 D2
Greenacre Ct LS25 83 A7
Greenacre Dr
Bradford BD12 94 D2
Denby Dale HD8 191 E3
Greenacre Park Ave LS19 40 B5
Greenacre Park Mews 1 LS19 40 C5
Greenacre Park Rise LS19 40 C5
Greenacre Pk LS19 40 B5
Greenacre Rd WF9 183 C8
Greenacre Way BD12 94 D2
Greenacre Wlk WF4 162 D2
Greenacres Ossett WF5 119 D1
Ripponden HX6 132 E4
Shelf HX3 93 D6
Greenacres Ave HX3 93 D6
Greenacres Cl WF5 119 D1
Greenacres Dr Batley WF17 97 A2
Keighley BD20 18 A1
Shelf HX3 93 D6
Greenacres Gr HX3 93 D6
Greenaire Pl 7 BD1 74 D7
Greenbank BD19 116 F6
Greenbank Cl WF10 124 A5
Greenbank Gr WF6 122 F3
Greenbank Rd
Bradford BD15 73 C8
Normanton WF6 122 F3
Greenbanks Ave LS18 41 C2
Greenbanks Cl LS18 41 C2
Greenbanks Dr LS18 41 B2
Greencliffe Ave BD17 38 C3
Greencroft Ave HX3 93 B3
Greendale Cl BB10 85 A7
Greendale Ct HD7 171 F5
Greendown Cl LS29 8 D4
Greeney Hill BD15 53 B4
Greenfell Cl BD22 34 F6
Greenfield BD22 51 C8
Greenfield Ave
Brighouse HX3 115 A7
Gildersome LS27 97 B7
Guiseley LS20 39 B7
Huddersfield HD3 153 A7
Kippax LS25 83 A2
Ossett WF5 141 A4
Shipley BD18 55 C5
Greenfield Cl
Denby Dale HD8 191 F3
Elland HX4 133 F2
Kippax LS25 83 A2
Northowram HX3 93 A3
Ossett WF5 141 A4
Wakefield WF2 120 F2
Greenfield Cres BD13 52 E6
Greenfield Ct Keighley BD21 35 A7
Leeds LS16 42 B4
Greenfield Dr
6 Brighouse BD19 115 F8
Gildersome LS27 97 B7
Greenfield Garth LS25 83 A2
Greenfield Gdns BD20 16 F6
Greenfield La
Bradford, Bierley BD4 95 B7
Bradford, Horton Bank Bottom BD7 73 F3
Bradford, Thackley BD10 39 B1
Guiseley LS20 39 B7
Greenfield Mount WF2 120 F2
Greenfield Pl Bradford BD8 55 C1
Brighouse HX3 115 A7
Greenfield Rd
Hemsworth WF9 181 D5
Holmfirth HD7 188 D5
Leeds LS9 212 B3
Normanton WF6 122 F2
Ossett WF5 141 A4
Greenfield Rise LS25 83 A2
Greenfield Sch BD10 39 B1
Greenfield Terr
Haworth BD22 51 C8
Mickletown LS26 102 E3
Todmorden OL14 86 A1
Greenfield Vale LS25 83 A2
Greenfield View LS25 83 A2
Greenfield Way WF2 120 F2
Greenfields WF16 117 C5
Greenfields Way LS29 21 F7
Greenfinch Gr HD4 171 E7
Greenfold La LS22 13 F5
Greengate Rothwell LS26 101 C6
Silsden BD20 5 D2
Greengate Rd
Keighley BD21 35 C6
Norton WF8 166 F3
Greengates Ave 3 BD12 94 C1
Greengates First Sch BD10 56 E7
Greenhead Ave HD5 154 F5
Greenhead Ct HD1 153 E7
Greenhead Grammar Sch BD20 18 B2
Greenhead La
Brighouse HD6 135 E6
Huddersfield HD5 154 F5
Greenhead Rd
Huddersfield HD1 153 F6
Leeds LS16 59 B8
Greenhill Ave WF8 146 E6
Greenhill Bank Rd HD7 189 E5
Greenhill Cres LS12 209 F2
Greenhill Dr BD16 36 E7
Greenhill Ind Est HX7 110 F8
Greenhill La Bingley BD16 36 F6
Bradford BD3 75 C7
Greenhill Middle Sch LS13 77 D8
Greenhill Mount WF8 146 E6
Greenhill Prim Sch
Leeds LS13 77 D8
Wakefield WF1 216 C3
Greenhill Rd
Huddersfield HD3 152 E7
Wakefield WF1 216 C3
Greenhill St BD3 75 C7
Greenhills LS19 40 C3
Greenholme Cl LS29 9 F2
Greenholme Ct BD4 75 F2
Greenholme Trad Est LS29 9 F2
Greenhouse Rd HD2 136 A1
Greenhow Cl LS4 205 D2
Greenhow Gdns LS4 205 D2
Greenhow Pk LS29 9 D1
Greenhow Rd LS4 205 D2
Greenhow Wlk LS4 205 D2
Greenland Ave BD13 92 E8
Greenland Rd HX7 87 C6
Greenland Villas BD13 92 E8
Greenlaws Cl HD7 188 D5
Greenlay Dr WF2 120 B2
Greenlea Ave LS19 39 F6
Greenlea Cl LS19 39 F5
Greenlea Fold LS19 39 F5
Greenlea Mount LS19 39 F6
Greenlea Rd LS19 39 F5
Greenmoor Ave WF3 100 C1
Greenmoor Cl WF3 100 C1
Greenmoor Cres WF3 100 D1
Greenmount Ct 4 LS11 214 B3
Greenmount La LS11 214 B3
Greenmount Pl LS11 214 B3
Greenmount Sch LS11 214 B3
Greenmount St LS11 214 B3
Greenmount Terr LS11 214 B3
Greenock Pl 2 LS12 209 D4
Greenock Rd LS12 209 D4
Greenock St LS12 209 D4
Greenock Terr 1 LS12 209 D4
Greenroyd Ave
Cleckheaton BD19 95 D2
Halifax HX3 113 B3
Greenroyd Cl HX3 113 B3
Greenroyd Croft HD2 135 E1
Greenroyd Ct WF8 147 C5
Greenroyd Dr BD20 16 D4
Greenroyd Gr BD20 16 D4
Greenroyd La HX2 91 E1
Greens End Rd HD7 170 D2
Greens La OL13 106 A3
Greenset View S71 178 E1
Greenshank Mews LS27 98 D3
Greenshaw Terr LS20 22 D1
Greenside Bradford BD12 95 A4
Cleckheaton BD19 116 E7
Denby Dale HD8 192 A7
Featherstone WF7 145 D6
4 Liversedge WF16 117 C4
Mapplewell S75 178 C1
Ryhill WF4 180 B8
Shafton S72 180 B4
Walton WF2 161 A7
Greenside Ave
Huddersfield HD5 155 A5
Leeds LS12 209 E1
Mapplewell S75 178 C1
Greenside Cl LS12 209 F1
Greenside County Infant Sch HD5 155 A4
Greenside Cres HD5 155 A5
Greenside Ct Crofton WF4 162 B7
Gildersome LS27 97 D7
Greenside Dr
Huddersfield HD5 155 A5
Leeds LS12 209 F1
Greenside Est WF14 138 A7
Greenside Gr 3 LS28 76 D6
Greenside La Bradford BD8 73 F7
Cullingworth BD13 52 E6
Greenside Mount WF14 138 B7
Greenside Pk WF4 162 B7
Greenside Pl S75 178 C1
Greenside Rd Leeds LS12 209 F1
Mirfield WF14 138 B7
Greenside Terr LS12 209 E1
Greenside Wlk LS12 209 E1
Greensnook La OL13 106 A3
Greensnook Terr 1 OL13 106 A3
Greensway LS25 82 E7
Greenthorpe Hill LS13 77 E8
Greenthorpe Mount LS13 77 E8
Greenthorpe Rd LS13 77 E8
Greenthorpe St LS13 77 E7
Greenthorpe Wlk LS13 77 E8
Greenthwaite Cl BD20 18 A1
Greenton Ave BD19 94 E1
Greenton Cres BD13 92 D8
Greentop Crofton WF4 162 B7
Pudsey LS28 76 D6
Greentrees 1 BD6 94 B6
Greenups Terr HX6 112 B4
Greenview WF4 162 B7
Greenview Cl LS9 208 C2
Greenview Mount LS9 61 D2
Greenville Ave LS12 209 E1
Greenville Dr BD12 94 E7
Greenville Gdns LS12 209 E1
Greenway Guiseley LS20 39 C7
Honley HD7 171 F5
Huddersfield HD3 152 F5
Leeds LS15 62 C1
Greenway Cl LS15 62 C1
Greenway Dr BD15 73 B7
Greenway Rd BD5 74 E2
Greenwell Row 6 BD14 73 B4
Greenwell Terr HX3 114 E8
Greenwood Ave
Bradford BD2 56 A4
Dewsbury WF12 139 F7
Upton WF9 183 C8
Greenwood Bldgs HD5 155 C8
Greenwood Cl
Normanton WF6 144 B7
Upton WF9 183 C8
Greenwood Cres S71 179 B4
Greenwood Ct
Bradford BD1 201 C2
Leeds LS6 59 E7
Greenwood Dr BD2 56 A4
Greenwood House 5 WF1 216 B2
Greenwood Mount
Bradford BD2 56 A4
Leeds LS6 59 E7
Greenwood Primary Sch LS11 214 C4
Greenwood Rd
Baildon BD17 38 B1
East Ardsley WF3 119 F7
Wakefield WF1 142 E7
Greenwood Row LS28 76 F7
Greenwood St
Dewsbury WF12, WF13 139 B8
Dewsbury, Savile Town WF12 139 C6
5 Hebden Bridge HX7 89 A3
Huddersfield HD4 154 A4
Greetland Junior & Infants Sch HX4 134 B7
Greetland Rd HX4 133 B6
Gregory Cres BD7 73 E2
Gregory Ct 1 BD14 73 C4
Gregory Dr HD8 173 F7
Gregory La WF14 156 A7
Gregory Rd WF10 124 E5
Gregory Springs La WF14 138 B3
Gregory Springs Mount WF14 138 B2
Gregory Springs Rd WF14 138 B3
Gregory St WF17 118 E5
Grenfell Dr BD3 75 D8
Grenfell Rd BD3 75 D8
Grenfell Terr BD3 75 D8
Grenley St WF11 127 A4
Grenville Wlk WF4 159 F3
Gresham Ave BD2 55 F4
Gresley Rd BD21 35 C7
Gresley Road Ind Est BD21 35 C7
Grey Cl WF1 121 B3
Grey Ct WF1 121 B3
Grey Gables WF4 158 E6
Grey Hall HX4 133 F3
Grey Scar Ct BD22 34 B2
Grey Scar Rd BD22 34 A2
Grey St WF1 121 B3
Grey Stone La OL14 108 F8
Grey Stones La HX7 69 B5
Greycourt Cl
Bradford BD10 56 A6
Halifax HX1 202 C1
Greyfriar Wlk BD7 73 E3
Greyfriars Ave HD2 136 E4
Greyhound Dr BD7 74 B6
Greyshiels Ave LS6 59 C4
Greyshiels Cl LS6 59 C4
Greystone Ave HX5 134 E5
Greystone Cl
Boston Spa LS23 30 E7
Burley in W LS29 9 E2
Greystone Cres BD10 56 C6
Greystone Ct HD6 136 A7
Greystone Mount LS15 80 E7
Greystone Pk LS25 47 E1
Greystones Cl LS25 47 E1
Greystones Dr
Keighley BD22 34 F3
Ossett WF5 140 E3
Greystones La BD22 33 D7
Greystones Mount BD22 34 F2
Greystones Rd HX2 111 E7
Greystones Rise BD22 34 F3
Griff House La WF3 120 B8
Griffe Dr BD12 94 C1
Griffe Gdns BD22 34 B2
Griffe Head Cres 2 BD12 94 C2
Griffe Head Rd BD12 94 C2
Griffe Rd Bradford BD12 94 C1
Haworth BD22 50 D8
Griffe View BD22 34 B2
Grime La Crofton WF4 144 B2
Whitley Common HD7 200 D8
Grimes Dyke Primary Sch LS14 62 D6
Grimescar Meadows HD2 135 D2
Grimescar Rd HD2 135 D3
Grimethorpe St 1 WF9 182 F2
Grimscar Ave HD2 135 F1
Grimthorpe Ave 4 LS6 59 C5
Grimthorpe Pl LS6 59 D5
Grimthorpe St LS6 59 C5
Grimthorpe Terr LS6 59 D5
Grindlestone Bank HX2 91 C4
Grisedale Ave HD2 135 F1
Grizedale Cl LS22 13 B6
Grosmont Pl LS13 58 C3
Grosmont Rd LS13 58 C2
Grosmont Terr LS13 58 C3
Grosvenor Ave
Lepton HD8 155 E3
Pontefract WF8 146 B8
Shipley BD18 54 F8
Upton WF9 183 A7
Grosvenor Ct LS16 41 D4
Grosvenor Hill LS7 206 C2
Grosvenor Mews LS19 40 A4
Grosvenor Mount LS6 205 F4
Grosvenor Park Gdns LS6 205 F4
Grosvenor Pk LS7 60 C7
Grosvenor Rd
Batley WF17 118 D6
Bradford BD8 55 D1
Huddersfield HD5 154 F6
Leeds LS6 205 F4
Shipley BD18 54 F7
Grosvenor St
2 Batley WF16 117 D5
Bradford BD8 55 D1
Dewsbury WF12 139 C7
Elland HX5 134 F6
Wakefield WF1 142 F3
Grosvenor Terr
1 Batley WF16 117 D4
Bradford BD8 55 D1
11 Halifax HX1 202 C3
Leeds LS6 205 F4
Otley LS21 23 B8
Wetherby LS22 13 E6
Grosvenor Way HD8 155 E3
Grouse Moor La BD13 72 C2
Grouse St 8 BD21 35 D8
Grove Ave Halifax HX3 92 A3
Hemsworth WF9 181 E6
Ilkley LS29 7 F3
Leeds LS6 59 E6
Pontefract WF8 146 E8
Pudsey LS28 76 D7
Shipley BD18 55 B5
South Kirkby WF9 182 C2
Grove Cl Bradford BD2 56 A4
Cleckheaton BD19 96 B1
Grove Convalescent Hospl The LS29 8 B3
Grove Cotts HD6 114 E2
Grove Cres
Boston Spa LS23 30 F7
Halifax HX2 111 E7
Walton WF2 161 B7
Grove Cres S LS23 30 F7
Grove Croft HX3 91 F2
Grove Ct Halifax HX3 92 A2
Huddersfield HD3 152 F6
Leeds LS6 59 E6
Pudsey LS28 76 D7
Grove Dr Halifax HX3 91 F3
South Kirkby WF9 182 B2
Grove Edge HX3 91 F2
Grove Farm Cl LS16 41 F4
Grove Farm Cres LS16 41 E4
Grove Farm Croft LS16 41 E4
Grove Farm Dr LS16 41 E4
Grove Gdns
Boston Spa LS23 30 F7
Dewsbury WF12 140 A6
Halifax HX3 92 A3
Leeds LS6 59 E6
Grove Hall Park Homes WF11 147 D8
Grove Head WF9 182 B2
Grove House Cres BD2 56 A4
Grove House Dr BD2 56 A3
Grove House First Sch BD2 56 A4
Grove House Rd BD2 56 A3
Grove La Badsworth WF9 164 E3
Cleckheaton BD19 96 B1
Hemsworth WF9 181 E6
Knottingley WF11 126 E4
Leeds LS6 59 E6
South Kirkby WF9 182 B2
Grove Lea Cl WF9 181 E6
Grove Lea Cres WF8 146 E7
Grove Lea Jun & Inf Sch WF9 181 E7
Grove Lea Wlk WF8 146 E7
Grove Mill La HX3 92 A2
Grove Mount
Pontefract WF8 146 E8
South Kirkby WF9 182 B2
Grove Pk Criggleston WF4 159 E6
Halifax HX3 92 A3
Grove Pl Boston Spa LS23 30 E7
Hemsworth WF9 181 E6
Grove Rd Batley WF16 117 E3
Boston Spa LS23 30 E7
Elland HX5 135 B7
Hebden Bridge HX7 89 A4
Horbury WF4 141 A1
Horsforth LS18 58 C8
Huddersfield HD1 154 B7
Ilkley LS29 7 F4
Leeds LS15 81 A7
Leeds, Headingley Hill LS6 59 E5
Leeds, Hunslet LS10 215 E3
Mapplewell S75 178 A1
Menston LS29 22 A4
Pontefract WF8 146 E8
Pudsey LS28 76 D7
Shipley BD18 55 B5
Wakefield WF1 216 C1
Grove Rise Leeds LS17 42 F5
Pontefract WF8 146 E8
Grove Royd HX3 92 A2
Grove Sq Cleckheaton BD19 96 B1
Halifax HX3 91 F2
Grove St Bacup OL13 106 A3
Batley, Heckmondwike WF16 117 E4
Batley, Norristhorpe WF15 117 C2
Brighouse HD6 115 B2
Dewsbury WF13 139 C8
Halifax, Ovenden HX2 91 F3
Huddersfield HD3 152 F6
Leeds LS1 211 D4
Mirfield WF14 138 B6
Ossett WF5 140 D4
4 Pudsey LS28 57 E2
Slaithwaite HD7 151 F1
South Kirkby WF9 182 B2
Sowerby Bridge HX6 112 D4
Wakefield WF1 216 C1
Grove St S 5 HX1 202 B3
Grove Terr
Birkenshaw BD11 96 A4
Boston Spa LS23 30 E7
Bradford BD7 201 A2
Brighouse HD6 114 E2
Hebden Bridge HX7 110 E8
Hemsworth WF9 181 E6
Pudsey LS28 76 D7
Grove The Baildon BD17 38 C4
Batley, Brookroyd WF17 118 A7
Batley, Nunroyd WF16 117 C6
Bingley BD16 36 E6
Bradford BD10 56 D7
Bradford, Idle BD10 56 B7
Brighouse HX3 114 D8
Cudworth S72 180 B1
East Ardsley WF3 120 B8
East Keswick LS17 28 B6
Horsforth LS18 41 B1
Huddersfield HD2 136 B2
Ilkley LS29 8 B4
Kippax LS25 83 A1
Leeds LS17 42 F5
Normanton WF6 123 B2
Pudsey LS28 76 D7
7 Queensbury BD13 72 D1
Ryhill WF4 162 A1
Shelf HX3 93 C6
Shipley BD18 54 E7
South Elmsall WF9 182 F4
Swillington LS26 82 B2
Walton WF2 161 B6
Yeadon LS19 40 B6
Grove Way WF9 182 B2
Grove Wilmington LS7 207 D2
Grovehall Ave LS11 214 A1
Grovehall La WF8, WF11 147 B8
Grovehall Par LS11 213 F1
Grovehall Rd LS11 213 F1
Grovelands BD2 56 A4
Groves Hall Rd WF13 138 F8
Groveville HX3 93 C1
Groveway BD2 56 A4
Grunberg Rd LS6 59 D5
Grunberg St 6 LS6 59 D5
Guard House Ave BD22 35 A7
Guard House Dr BD22 35 A7
Guard House First Sch BD22 34 F7
Guard House Gr BD22 34 F7
Guard House Rd BD22 35 A7
Guernsey Rd WF12 118 F2
Guild Way HX2 112 B7
Guildford Rd S71 179 B5
Guildford St
4 Hebden Bridge HX7 89 A2
Ossett WF5 140 D4
Guillemot App LS27 98 D3
Guiseley Dr LS29 22 B2
Guiseley Infant Sch LS20 22 E1
Guiseley Sch LS20 39 D8
Guiseley Sta LS20 22 D1
Guiseley Queensway Primary Sch LS19 40 A8
Gully Terr HD7 189 B4
Gully The HD7 190 C5
Gunson Cres WF5 140 D6
Gunter Rd LS22 14 A5
Gunthwaite La S36 192 B2
Gunthwaite Top HD8 191 F3
Gurbax Ct BD3 75 E7
Gurney Cl BD5 74 D3
Guy St BD4 201 C2
Guycroft LS21 22 F7
Guys Croft WF2 141 C4
Gwynne Ave BD3 56 E1
Gynn La HD7 172 B5

Gypsy Ct WF10 125 C6
Gypsy La WF10 125 C5
Gypsy Wood Cl LS15 81 D7
Gypsy Wood Crest LS15 81 D7

Hacking La WF9 183 B3
Hadassah St HX3 113 D4
Haddingley La HD7 190 D4
Haddon Ave Halifax HX3 113 C3
Leeds LS4 59 C2
Haddon Cl
Cleckheaton BD19 117 B8
South Elmsall WF9 183 A5
Haddon Pl LS4 59 C2
Haddon Rd LS4 205 D2
Hade Edge Jun & Inf Sch HD7 199 B8
Hadfield House 3 BD6 93 E8
Hadfield Rd WF16 117 D5
Hadleigh Ct LS17 43 D2
Hadleigh Rise WF8 146 B5
Hadrian Cl
Castleford WF10 104 C1
Thorpe Audlin WF8 165 A5
Hag Farm Rd
Burley in W LS29 21 E7
Menston LS29 21 E7
Hag Hill HD8 175 E6
Hag Hill La HD8 175 E6
Hag La HX3 92 D3
Hagg La WF14 138 C2
Hagg Wood Rd HD7 172 B2
Haggroyd La HD7 172 B2
Haggs Hill Rd WF5 141 A5
Haggs La WF2 141 C5
Hague Cres WF9 181 E5
Hague Park Cl WF9 182 B3
Hague Park La WF9 182 B3
Hague Park Wlk WF9 182 B3
Hague Terr WF9 181 E6
Haigh Ave LS26 100 C7
Haigh Beck View BD10 56 C7
Haigh Cnr BD10 56 D7
Haigh Croft S71 179 B4
Haigh Fold BD2 56 C3
Haigh Gdns LS26 100 C7
Haigh Hall BD10 56 D7
Haigh Hall Rd BD10 56 D7
Haigh Hill S75 177 C6
Haigh House Hill HD3 134 E3
Haigh La Flockton WF4 157 A2
Halifax HX3 113 D4
Holmfirth HD7 188 F8
Woolley S75, WF4 177 C5
Haigh Mews S75 177 C5
Haigh Moor Ave WF3 119 E6
Haigh Moor Cres WF3 119 E6
Haigh Moor Rd WF3 119 E6
Haigh Moor St WF1 216 C4
Haigh Moor View WF3 119 E6
Haigh Park Rd LS10 80 B2
Haigh Rd LS26 100 F6
Haigh Road Inf Sch LS26 100 E6
Haigh St Bradford BD4 75 B3
16 Brighouse HD6 115 A3
Elland HX4 134 B7
Halifax HX1 202 B4
Huddersfield HD1 153 F3
Haigh Terr LS26 100 C7
Haigh View LS26 100 C7
Haigh Wood Cres LS16 41 D3
Haigh Wood Gn LS16 41 D2
Haigh Wood Rd LS16 41 D2
Haigh's Sq HD5 154 D7
Haighside LS26 100 C6
Haighside Cl LS26 100 D6
Haighside Dr LS26 100 C6
Haighside Way LS26 100 C6
Hailhead Dr WF8 125 F1
Haincliffe Pl 11 BD21 35 B4
Haincliffe Rd BD21 35 B4
Haines Pk LS7 207 E2
Hainsworth Moor Cres 5 BD13 92 D8
Hainsworth Moor Dr 6 BD13 92 D8
Hainsworth Moor Garth 4 BD13 92 D8
Hainsworth Moor Gr BD13 92 D8
Hainsworth Moor Middle Sch BD13 92 D8
Hainsworth Moor View BD13 92 D8
Hainsworth Rd BD20 17 F8
Hainsworth Sq 7 LS28 57 D3
Hainsworth St Leeds LS12 210 B2
Rothwell BD20 100 E4
Hainworth Crag Rd BD21 35 A2
Hainworth La BD21 35 B3
Hainworth Rd
Keighley, Hainworth BD21 35 B3
Keighley, The Pitts BD21 35 C4
Hainworth Wood Rd BD21 35 B4
Hainworth Wood Rd N BD21 35 C5
Haise Mount S75 178 A1
Halcyon Hill LS7 60 C8
Halcyon Way BD5 74 C3
Haldane Cl S72 180 F3
Haldane Cres WF1 142 F8
Hales Rd LS12 78 B4
Halesworth Cres BD4 75 E3
Haley Hill HX3 203 E4
Haley's Yd LS13 58 C3
Half Acre Rd BD13 72 B7
Half Acres Jun & Inf Schs WF10 124 C7
Half House La HD6 114 D5
Half Mile LS13 57 F2
Half Mile Cl LS28 57 F2
Half Mile Gdns LS13 57 F2
Half Mile Gn LS28 57 F2
Half Mile La LS13 57 F3
Half Moon La WF1 143 C6
Half Moon St 13 HD1 154 A6
Half St BD21 35 B8
Halfpenny La WF8 146 A8
Halfpenny Lane Junior & Infants Sch WF8 146 B8
Halifax General Hospl HX3 113 D3
Halifax Golf Course HX2 71 B1
Halifax High Sch The
Halifax HX1 202 C1
Halifax HX1 203 E2
Halifax Ind Ctr The HX1 202 C4
Halifax La
Blackshaw Head HX7 87 E4
Halifax HX2 111 E8
Halifax New Coll HX1 202 C2
Halifax RC High Sch HX2 92 A6
Halifax Rd Batley WF17 118 B2
Bradford BD6 94 B7
Brighouse HD6 115 A3
Brighouse, Hartshead Moor Top HD6 115 E7
Brighouse, Hipperholme HX3 114 B8
Cleckheaton WF15 116 C5
Cullingworth BD13 52 D6
Cullingworth, Cullingworth Moor BD13 52 A5
Denholme, Denholme Gate BD13 71 E5
Denholme, Stubden BD13 71 E7
Dewsbury WF13 118 B2
Elland HX5 134 E7
Halifax HX3, HX5 134 E8
Hebden Bridge HX7 88 C2
Keighley BD21, BD22 35 A3
Littleborough OL15 148 A7
Northowram HX3 93 B4
Queensbury BD13 92 C7
Ripponden HX6 132 E6
Shelf HX3 93 B4
Slaithwaite HD7 152 B5
Todmorden OL14 108 D6
Halifax Sta HX1 203 F2
Hall Ave Bradford BD2 56 D5
Huddersfield HD1 153 F5
Sutton in C BD20 16 D4
Hall Bank Dr BD16 36 F4
Hall Bank La HX7 110 E8
Hall Bower HD4 154 B1
Hall Bower La HD4 154 B1
Hall Brig DN5 194 C4
Hall Cl Boston Spa LS23 30 E7
Bramhope LS16 24 E4
Burley in W LS29 9 D1
Hemsworth WF9 181 D7
Liversedge WF15 117 A3
Ossett WF5 119 B1
Sutton in C BD20 16 D4
Hall Cliffe Cres WF4 141 A2
Hall Cliffe Ct WF4 141 A2
Hall Cliffe Gr WF4 141 A2
Hall Cliffe Rd WF4 141 A2
Hall Cliffe Rise WF4 141 B2
Hall Croft WF4 158 E6
Hall Cross Gr HD5 154 D3
Hall Cross Rd HD5 154 D3
Hall Ct Brotherton WF11 126 C8
Leeds LS7 207 D4
Sutton in C BD20 16 D4
Hall Dr Bramhope LS16 24 E4
Burley in W LS29 9 D1
Liversedge WF15 117 B2
Sutton in C BD20 16 D4
Hall Field La WF4 180 A7
Hall Garth Rd WF8 165 A4
Hall Gdns BD20 4 E1
Hall Gr Leeds LS6 205 F2
Mapplewell S75 178 C1
Hall Green La HX6 150 D8
Hall Ing La HD7 172 C5
Hall Ing Rd Honley HD4 172 E3
Kirkburton HD4 172 E3
Hall Ings Bradford BD1 201 B2
Halifax HX3 114 A3
Hall La Askwith LS21 9 E6
Bradford BD4 201 C1
Dewsbury WF12 139 F2
Horsforth LS18 41 A1
Kirkburton HD8 173 E7
Ledston WF10 103 F6
Leeds LS12 210 A3
Leeds, Cookridge LS16 41 F6
Leeds, Farnley LS12 77 D5
Leeds, Potternewton LS7 207 D4
Northowram HX3 92 F4
Sherburn in E LS25 84 F5
Shipley BD18 55 D8
Slaithwaite HD3 152 B6
South Elmsall WF9 183 B6
Hall Mews LS23 30 E7
Hall Orchards Ave LS22 14 A6
Hall Park Ave Crofton WF4 143 F2
Horsforth LS18 41 A1
Liversedge WF15 117 A2
Hall Park Cl LS18 41 A1
Hall Park Croft LS25 103 B8
Hall Park Ct LS25 83 B1
Hall Park Garth LS18 41 A1
Hall Park Meadows LS25 103 B8
Hall Park Mount LS18 41 A1
Hall Park Orch LS25 83 B1
Hall Park Rd LS23 15 B5
Hall Park Rise
Horsforth LS18 41 B1
Kippax LS25 83 B1
Hall Pl LS9 212 C3
Hall Rd Bradford BD2 56 D5
Leeds LS12 209 F3
Swillington LS26 82 B1
Wakefield WF2 141 D4
Hall Rise Bramhope LS16 24 E3
Burley in W LS29 9 D1
Hall Rise Cl LS16 24 E3
Hall Rise Croft LS16 24 E3
Hall Royd BD18 55 B7
Hall Sq LS28 57 B7
Hall St 6 Bradford BD6 74 C1
5 Brighouse HD6 115 B2
Featherstone WF7 145 E4
Glusburn BD20 16 D7
Halifax HX1 203 D3
Haworth BD22 51 C6
Huddersfield HD3 152 F7
Oakworth BD22 34 D2
Todmorden OL14 108 B5
Hall St N HX3 92 B2
Hall Stone Ct HX3 93 C5
Hall Way BD20 16 D4
Hallam Field Houses LS20 39 E8
Hallam La LS21 10 B5
Hallam St LS20 39 D8
Hallamshire Mews WF2 141 C4
Hallas Bridge BD13 52 F6
Hallas Gr HD5 154 F5
Hallas Hall Farm Cotts BD13 52 E6
Hallas La Cullingworth BD13 52 E5
Kirkburton HD8 174 B6
Wilsden BD13 52 F5
Hallas Rd HD8 173 F6
Hallbank Cl BD5 74 D1
Hallbank Dr BD5 74 D1
Hallcliffe BD17 38 D4
Hallcroft 5 WF4 141 B1
Hallcroft Dr Addingham LS29 7 B7
Horbury WF4 141 B1
Hallcroft Rise S71 179 B3
Halley St 8 OL13 106 A7
Hallfield Ave LS25 83 F7
Hallfield Cres LS22 13 F5
Hallfield Dr BD17 38 C3
Hallfield La LS22 13 F5
Hallfield Pl BD1 201 B4
Hallfield Rd BD1 201 A4
Hallfield St BD1 201 B4
Hallfield Terr LS25 83 F7
Hallgate BD1 201 B4
Halliday Ave LS12 209 D4
Halliday Dr LS12 209 D4
Halliday Gr LS12 209 D4
Halliday Mount LS12 209 D4
Halliday Pl LS12 209 D4
Halliday Rd Garforth LS25 82 E7
Leeds LS12 209 D4
Halliday St LS28 76 E8
Halliley Gdns 2 WF13 139 C8
Halliley St WF13 139 B8
Halling Pl OL14 108 A4
Hallowes Gr BD13 52 D5
Hallowes Park Rd BD13 52 D6
Hallows Rd BD21 18 E1
Hallows The BD20 35 A8
Hallroyd Cres OL14 108 C5
Hallroyd Pl OL14 108 C5
Hallroyd Rd OL14 108 C5
Hallwood Gn BD10 56 E5
Halstead Dr LS29 22 A5
Halstead Gr S75 178 A2
Halstead La HD4 173 A1
Halstead Pl BD7 74 B3
Halsteads Way BD20 17 C6
Halton Cl HD5 154 F4
Halton Dr LS15 81 A8
Halton Moor Ave LS9 80 D7
Halton Moor Rd LS15, LS9 80 D6
Halton Pl BD5 74 B3
Halton Rd WF1 142 F8
Halton St WF7 145 D7
Hambledon Ave
Bradford BD4 95 B8
Meltham HD7 170 F1
Hambledon First Sch BD4 95 B8
Hambleton Bank HX2 91 B6
Hambleton Cotts BD23 2 B8
Hambleton Cres HX2 91 B5
Hambleton Dr HX2 91 B5
Hambleton St WF1 216 B3
Hame The HX4 133 F3
Hamel Rise WF9 181 D6
Hamilton Ave LS7 207 E4
Hamilton Ct WF6 123 B3
Hamilton Gdns LS7 207 E3
Hamilton Pl LS7 207 E3
Hamilton Primary Sch LS7 207 E4
Hamilton St BD1 74 D8
Hamilton Terr Leeds LS7 207 E4
Otley LS21 23 B8
Hamilton View LS7 207 E4
Hamm Strasse BD1 201 B4
Hammer La WF4 144 B4
Hammerstone Leach La HX5 134 D5
Hammerstones Rd HX5 134 D6
Hammerton Dr LS25 83 A5
Hammerton Gr 4 LS28 76 F7
Hammerton Rd HD2 136 A2
Hammerton St Bradford BD3 75 A6
Pudsey LS28 76 E7
Hammerton Terr 5 OL14 108 B6
Hammond Cres BD11 96 E7
Hammond Pl BD9 55 A3
Hammond Rd WF11 126 D3
Hammond Sq BD9 55 A3
Hammond St Halifax HX1 202 B2
Huddersfield HD2 136 B1
Hampden Cl WF11 126 B5
Hampden Pl Bradford BD5 74 D4
Halifax HX1 203 D3
Hampden St BD5 74 D4
Hampole Balk DN6 184 E1
Hampole Field La DN6 183 F1
Hampshire Cl LS29 8 D4
Hampshire St 3 HD5 154 D6
Hampson St WF17 118 A7
Hampton Pl Bradford BD10 56 B8
Leeds LS9 212 C3
Hampton St Halifax HX1 202 B1
Leeds LS9 212 B3
Hampton Terr LS9 212 C3
Hamworth Dr BD22 34 D2
Hamza St WF17 118 B4
Hanby Ave WF6 122 F3
Hand Bank La WF14 138 A2
Hand Carr La HX2 111 C7
Handel St Bradford BD7 74 C7
Huddersfield HD7 152 D4
Handel Terr 2 HD5 154 D5
Handsworth Rd WF2 160 A4
Hanging Gate La BD22 51 B5
Hanging Heaton CE Jun & Inf Sch WF17 118 F3
Hanging Royd HD7 152 D3
Hanging Stone Rd HD4 171 F7
Hanging Stones La HX6 132 F5
Hanging Wood Way BD19 95 C2
Hangingroyd Cl HX7 89 A3
Hangingroyd La 4 HX7 89 A3
Hangingroyd Rd 26 HX7 89 A3
Hangingstone Rd LS29 8 E2
Hangram St 2 HD6 115 B2
Hanley Rd LS27 98 A3
Hannah Ct BD12 94 C3
Hannah St 11 OL13 106 A3
Hanover Ave LS3 211 D4
Hanover Cl BD8 55 B1
Hanover Cres WF8 146 C5
Hanover Ct 4
Dewsbury WF13 118 A1
Keighley BD20 18 A2
Hanover Gdns
Burley in W LS29 21 E8
Dewsbury WF13 139 B8
Hanover House HX2 202 A1
Hanover La LS3 211 D4
Hanover Mount LS3 206 A1
Hanover Pl Batley WF17 118 D5
Brotherton WF11 105 C1
Hanover Sq Bradford BD1 74 D8
Leeds LS3 211 D4
Hanover St Batley WF17 118 C5
Dearne S63 194 E1
Dewsbury WF13 139 B8
Farnhill BD20 4 D1
Halifax HX1 203 D2
Keighley BD21 35 C7
Sowerby Bridge HX6 112 D4
Wakefield WF2 142 A5
Hanover Way
Burley in W LS29 21 E8
Leeds LS3 211 D4
Hansby Ave LS14 62 B5
Hansby Bank LS14 62 B5
Hansby Cl LS14 62 B4
Hansby Dr LS14 62 B4
Hansby Gate LS14 62 B5
Hansby Gdns LS14 62 B4
Hansby Grange 10 LS14 62 B5
Hansby Pl LS14 62 B5
Hanson Ave WF6 123 B1
Hanson Ct BD12 94 B2
Hanson Fold 8 BD12 94 C3
Hanson La Halifax HX1 202 C3
Huddersfield HD4 153 E2
Hanson Mount BD12 94 C2
Hanson Pl 7 BD12 94 C3
Hanson Rd Brighouse HD6 135 E8
Meltham HD7 170 C1
Hanson Sch BD2 56 A4
Hanworth Rd BD12 94 D6
Hapsburg Ct 15 BD5 201 B1
Harbeck Dr BD16 36 B1
Harborough Gn BD10 56 D8
Harbour Cres BD6 94 A8
Harbour Pk 2 BD6 93 F8
Harbour Rd BD6 94 A8
Harclo Rd BD21 35 E8
Harcourt Ave BD13 72 D7
Harcourt Dr Addingham LS29 2 F1
Morley LS27 97 F5
Harcourt Pl LS1 211 D4
Harcourt St Bradford BD4 75 B3
Wakefield WF2 141 F5
Hard Ings Rd BD21 18 C1
Hard Nese La
Oxenhope BD22 50 F1
Oxenhope, Upper Town BD22 51 B2
Hard Platts La HX4 133 F2
Hardaker La BD17 38 A2
Hardaker St BD8 74 D8
Hardaker's La WF7 163 E6
Hardakers App WF7 163 F5
Hardcastle Ave WF8 125 C1
Hardcastle Crags HX7 68 C1
Hardcastle La
Flockton WF4 157 E4
Netherton WF4 157 E4
Harden Brow La BD16 36 A1
Harden First Sch BD16 36 B1
Harden Gr Bradford BD10 56 E3
Keighley BD21 35 E5
Harden Hill Rd HD7 187 E8
Harden La Harden BD15 53 B7
Wilsden BD15 53 B7
Harden Moss Rd
Holmfirth HD7 187 E4
Meltham HD7 187 E7
Harden Rd Harden BD16 36 D2
Keighley BD21 35 F5
Hardgate La BD22 51 F7
Hardie Rd WF4 162 C1
Harding Houses BD20 16 E7
Hardings La Glusburn BD20 16 F7
Hunger Hill LS29 8 A8
Ilkley LS29 8 A7
Hardistry Dr WF8 146 B8
Hardknot Cl BD7 73 E3
Hardrow Gn LS12 210 A1
Hardrow Gr LS12 210 A1
Hardrow Rd LS12 210 A1
Hardrow Terr LS12 210 A1
Hardwick Cl WF4 180 A8
Hardwick Cres WF8 146 D5
Hardwick Croft LS7 204 A2
Hardwick Ct WF8 146 C7
Hardwick La WF4 145 B1
Hardwick Rd
Darrington WF7, WF8 146 F3
Featherstone WF7 145 C4
Pontefract WF7, WF8 146 D5
Hardwick St
8 Keighley BD21 35 A6
1 Leeds LS10 215 E2
Hardy Ave Bradford BD6 94 C8
Morley LS27 98 C8
Hardy Croft WF1 216 C2
Hardy Ct LS27 98 B4
Hardy Gr 5 LS11 214 A3
Hardy Pl HD6 114 E5
Hardy St Bradford BD4 201 C2
Bradford, Brownroyd Hill BD6 74 C1
Brighouse HD6 115 B3
Leeds LS11 214 A3
Morley LS27 98 B4
Hardy Terr 10 LS11 214 B3
Hardy View 4 LS11 214 A3
Hare Farm Ave LS12 77 D7
Hare Farm Cl LS12 77 D7
Hare La LS28 76 F4
Hare Park Ave WF15 116 C4
Hare Park Cl WF15 116 C4
Hare Park La
Cleckheaton WF15 116 C4
Crofton WF4 161 F8
Hare Park Mount LS12 77 D7
Hare Park View WF4 161 F8
Hare St HX1 202 C2
Harebell Ave WF2 141 E7
Harecroft Rd LS21 11 A1
Haredon Cl S75 178 A2
Harefield Cl BD20 17 A5
Harefield Dr WF17 97 A1
Harefield E LS15 80 E7
Harefield Pk HD2 135 D2
Harefield Rd 2 WF8 146 F8
Harefield W LS15 80 E8
Harehill Ave OL14 108 A6
Harehill Cl BD10 39 B1
Harehill Rd BD10 39 B1
Harehill St OL14 108 A6
Harehills Ave LS7, LS8 207 F4
Harehills Cnr LS8 207 F4
Harehills La
Haworth BD22 33 D1
Leeds LS7, LS8, LS9 208 B1
Harehills Park Ave LS9 208 B2
Harehills Park Rd LS9 208 B2
Harehills Park Terr LS9 208 B2
Harehills Park View LS9 208 B2
Harehills Pl LS8 207 F3
Harehills Primary Sch LS8 208 A3
Harehills Rd LS8 207 F3
Harepark Dr WF15 116 C4
Hares Ave LS8 207 F4
Hares Mount LS8 207 E4
Hares Rd LS8 207 F4
Hares Terr LS8 207 F4
Hares View LS8 207 F4
Harewood Ave
Batley WF16 117 E3
Halifax HX2 112 D8
Harewood LS17 27 D7
Normanton WF6 123 C3
Pontefract WF8 146 E8
Steeton BD20 17 A5
Harewood C of E Primary Sch LS17 27 A7
Harewood Cl WF11 126 C4
Harewood Cres BD22 34 E2
Harewood Ct Leeds LS17 43 D1
Leeds, The Green LS14 62 A4
Harewood Gate LS17 27 A7
Harewood Gr WF16 117 E3
Harewood House LS17 26 E6
Harewood La WF9 183 D8
Harewood Mews LS17 27 A7
Harewood Mount
Meltham HD7 170 F2
Pontefract WF8 146 E8
Harewood Pl HX2 202 A2

Harewood Rd
Collingham LS17 28 C7
East Keswick LS17 28 C7
Keighley BD22 34 F3
Wakefield WF1 142 F8
Harewood Rise BD22 34 F3
Harewood St Bradford BD3 75 B7
Leeds LS2 211 F4
Harewood View WF8 146 E8
Harewood Way LS13 77 B8
Hargrave Cres LS29 21 F4
Hargreaves Ave WF3 121 E5
Hargreaves Cl LS27 98 A6
Hargreaves St BD20 16 E6
Harker Rd BD12 94 C7
Harker St Knottingley WF11 127 B4
Sutton in C BD20 16 E5
Harker Terr 1 LS28 57 D1
Harland Cl BD2 55 E2
Harland Sq LS2 206 A3
Harlech Ave LS11 214 B2
Harlech Cres LS11 214 B2
Harlech Gr LS11 214 B2
Harlech Mount LS11 214 B2
Harlech Park Ct LS11 214 B2
Harlech Rd LS11 214 B2
Harlech St LS11 214 B2
Harlech Terr LS11 214 B2
Harlech Way LS25 83 B7
Harley Cl LS13 77 A8
Harley Ct LS13 77 A8
Harley Dr LS13 77 A8
Harley Gdns LS13 77 A8
Harley Gn LS13 77 A8
Harley Pl HD6 115 A1
Harley Rd LS13 77 A8
Harley Rise LS13 77 A8
Harley St
7 Brighouse HD6 115 A1
Todmorden OL14 108 B6
Harley Terr LS13 77 B8
Harley View LS13 77 A8
Harley Wlk LS13 77 A8
Harley Wood OL14 107 E8
Harlington Ct 3 LS27 98 A2
Harlington Rd LS27 98 A2
Harlock St WF1 142 E2
Harlow Ct LS8 61 C7
Harlow Rd BD7 74 A5
Harmby Cl DN6 184 F2
Harmon Cl BD4 95 C8
Harold Ave LS6 205 E2
Harold Gr LS6 205 E2
Harold Mount LS6 205 E2
Harold Pl Leeds LS6 205 E2
13 Shipley BD18 54 F8
Harold Rd LS6 205 E2
Harold Sq LS6 205 E2
Harold St Bingley BD16 36 E4
Leeds LS6 205 E2
Harold Terr LS6 205 E2
Harold View LS6 205 E2
Harold Wilson House
WF6 123 A1
Harold Wlk LS6 205 E2
Harp Rd HD3 153 B5
Harpe Inge HD5 154 E7
Harper Ave BD10 39 B1
Harper Cres BD10 39 C1
Harper Gr Bradford BD10 39 B1
Sutton in C BD20 16 D4
Harper La LS19 40 B6
Harper Rock LS19 40 B6
Harper Royd La HX6 112 C2
Harper St LS2 212 A3
Harper Terr 8 LS19 40 B6
Harpers Sq BD20 16 D4
Harrap St WF2 141 D7
Harrier Cl BD8 73 B7
Harrier Way LS27 98 D4
Harriet St Bradford BD8 74 B8
Brighouse HD6 115 A4
Leeds LS7 207 D3
Harrington Ct HD7 170 F1
Harris Ct BD7 74 A4
Harris St 3 Bingley BD16 37 A2
Bradford BD1 201 D3
Harrison Cres LS9 61 D1
Harrison La HD7 170 E5
Harrison Pl BD20 16 B6
Harrison & Potter
Trust Homes The
Leeds LS7 206 C1
6 Leeds, Woodhouse LS2 206 A3
Harrison Rd Crofton WF4 143 F1
Halifax HX1 203 E2
Harrison St Bingley BD16 37 A2
Leeds LS1 211 F4
Todmorden OL14 86 B1
Harrisons Ave 5 LS28 57 F2
Harrogate Ave BD3 56 A2
Harrogate Pl BD3 56 A2
Harrogate Rd
Bradford BD10, BD2 56 D5
East Carlton LS16 23 F2
Harewood LS17 27 A4
Leeds LS17 43 E5
Spofforth LS22 13 B7
Yeadon LS19 40 C5
Harrogate St BD3 56 A2
Harrogate Terr BD3 56 A2
Harrogate View LS17 44 C5
Harrop Ave LS27 98 B2
Harrop Gr LS27 98 B2
Harrop La BD15 53 B3
Harrop Terr LS27 98 B2
Harrop Well La 12 WF8 146 D8
Harrow St Halifax HX1 202 B3
South Elmsall WF9 182 E3
Harrowby Cres LS16 59 B7
Harrowby Rd LS16 59 B7
Harry La Bradford BD14 73 B4
Oxenhope BD22 51 C3
Harry St BD4 75 C3
Hart St Bradford BD7 74 B4
Huddersfield HD4 154 A2
Hart's Hole HD7 152 A5
Harthill LS27 97 D7
Harthill Ave LS27 97 D7
Harthill Cl LS27 97 D7
Harthill La LS27 97 D8
Harthill Par LS27 97 D7
Harthill Rise LS27 97 D7
Hartington Middle Sch
BD22 51 C7
Hartington St
Batley WF17 118 C3
9 Keighley BD21 35 C8
Hartington Terr BD7 74 A5
Hartland Rd BD4 75 E4
Hartley Ave LS6 206 B4
Hartley Cl WF9 183 A4
Hartley Cres LS6 206 B4
Hartley Ct WF15 117 A3
Hartley Gdns LS6 206 B4
Hartley Gr Dewsbury WF13 118 C1
Leeds LS6 206 A4
Hartley Hill LS2 206 C1
Hartley Park Ave WF8 146 B8
Hartley Park View WF8 146 B8
Hartley Pl Leeds LS2 206 C1
3 Morley LS27 98 B3
Hartley St Bradford BD4 75 B5
Castleford WF10 124 C7
Dewsbury WF13 118 C1
Glusburn BD20 16 A6
Halifax HX1 202 C4
Morley, Churwell LS27 98 B7
Morley, Town End LS27 98 C4
Hartley Terr WF7 145 C4
Hartley's Bldgs 6 LS27 98 B3
Hartley's Sq BD20 19 D1
Hartlington Ct BD17 38 E3
Hartman Pl BD9 54 F3
Hartshead Hall La WF15 116 D1
Hartshead Junior Mixed
& Infant Sch WF15 116 C2
Hartshead La WF15 116 C2
Hartshead Moor Sch
BD19 116 A6
Hartwell Rd LS6 205 E2
Harvelin Pk OL14 109 A5
Harvest Croft LS29 9 D1
Harvey Royd HD5 155 A4
Harvey St WF1 142 E3
Harwill App LS27 98 C7
Harwill Ave LS27 98 C7
Harwill Croft LS27 98 C7
Harwill Gr LS27 98 C7
Harwill Rd LS27 98 C7
Harwill Rise LS27 98 C7
Harwood Cl
Huddersfield HD5 154 F5
Wakefield WF2 142 E1
Haselbury Ho 10 BD5 201 B1
Haselden Cres WF2 141 E5
Haselden Rd WF2 141 E5
Haslam Cl BD3 75 A8
Haslam Gr BD18 55 E6
Haslemere Cl BD4 75 D3
Haslewood Cl LS9 212 B4
Haslewood Ct 1 LS9 212 C4
Haslewood Dene LS9 212 C4
Haslewood Dr LS9 212 C4
Haslewood Gdns LS9 212 C4
Haslewood Gn LS9 212 C4
Haslewood Mews LS9 212 C4
Haslewood Pl LS9 212 C4
Haslewood Sq LS9 212 C4
Haslewood View LS9 212 C4
Hasley Rd LS29 21 F8
Haslingden Dr BD9 54 F2
Hassocks La HD7 171 D4
Hassocks Rd HD7 170 C3
Haste St WF10 124 B8
Hastings Ave Bradford BD5 74 D2
Wakefield WF2 142 D2
Hastings Cres WF10 125 B7
Hastings Ct
Collingham LS22 29 B8
Normanton WF6 122 E4
Thorner LS17 44 E4
Hastings Gr WF2 142 D2
Hastings Pl BD5 74 D3
Hastings St BD5 74 D2
Hastings Terr BD5 74 D2
Hastings Way LS22 28 F8
Hastings Wlk WF10 125 B7
Hatchet La BD12 95 A4
Hatfield Gdns S71 179 B4
Hatfield Pl WF4 162 D2
Hatfield Rd BD2 56 B2
Hatfield St WF1 216 B3
Hatfield View WF1 121 C3
Hathaway Ave BD9 54 D3
Hathaway Dr LS14 45 B1
Hathaway La LS14 62 B8
Hathaway Mews LS14 45 B1
Hathaway Wlk 1 LS14 62 B8
Hathershelf La HX2 111 A7
Hatton Cl BD6 94 D8
Haugh End La HX6 112 A3
Haugh Rd OL14 108 E6
Haugh Shaw Croft 13
HX1 202 C1
Haugh Shaw Rd HX1 202 C1
Haugh Shaw Rd W HX1 202 B1
Haughs La HD3 153 A7
Haughs Rd HD3 153 A7
Hauxley Ct LS29 8 D5
Hauxwell Cl DN6 184 F2
Hauxwell Dr LS19 40 B6
Havelock Sq 2 BD13 72 E6
Havelock St Bradford BD7 74 A4
Dewsbury WF13 138 E5
Thornton BD13 72 E6
Haven Chase LS16 41 E3
Haven Croft LS16 41 F3
Haven Ct Leeds LS16 41 F3
Pontefract WF8 146 B5
Haven Garth LS16 41 E3
Haven Gdns LS16 41 E3
Haven Gn LS16 41 E3
Haven La HX7 110 B8
Haven Mount LS16 41 E3
Haven Rise LS16 41 E3
Haven St 15 OL14 108 C5
Haven The Bradford BD10 56 C6
Leeds LS15 81 D8
Haven View LS16 41 E3
Havercroft WF5 140 E5
Havercroft Jun & Inf Sch
WF4 180 B8
Havercroft La WF8 147 E5
Havercroft Rise S72 180 E6
Havercroft Way WF17 117 F5
Haverdale Rd WF4 162 C1
Haverlands The WF9 181 E6
Haveroid La WF4 159 F4
Haveroid Way WF4 159 F5
Haverthwaites Dr LS25 47 E1
Havertop La WF6 123 F2
Haw Ave LS19 40 C8
Haw Cliff La HD4 172 F1
Haw Hill View WF6 123 C3
Haw La LS19 40 B8
Haw Park La Ryhill WF4 161 F3
Walton WF2 161 B2
Haw View LS19 40 C8
Hawber Cote Dr BD20 5 F2
Hawber Cote La BD20 5 F2
Hawber La BD20 5 F1
Hawes Ave Bradford BD5 74 C2
Huddersfield HD3 153 B6
Hawes Cl WF10 125 B8
Hawes Cres BD5 74 C2
Hawes Dr BD5 74 C2
Hawes Gr BD5 74 C2
Hawes Mount BD5 74 C2
Hawes Rd BD5 74 C2
Hawes Terr BD5 74 C2
Haweswater Cl LS22 13 B5
Haweswater Pl WF11 126 E1
Hawk St 4 BD21 35 D8
Hawk's Nest Gdns E LS17 43 D4
Hawk's Nest Gdns S LS17 43 D4
Hawk's Nest Gdns W LS17 43 D4
Hawk's Nest Rise LS17 43 D4
Hawkcliffe View BD20 5 C1
Hawke Ave WF16 117 E4
Hawke Way BD12 94 E6
Hawkhill Ave Guiseley LS20 39 D8
Leeds LS15 62 B2
Hawkhill Dr LS15 62 B2
Hawkhill Gdns LS15 62 B2
Hawkhills LS7 204 B3
Hawkhurst Rd LS12 209 F2
Hawkingcroft Rd WF4 140 F1
Hawkins Dr LS7 206 C2
Hawkins Way OL15 129 C1
Hawkroyd Bank Rd HD4 171 E6
Hawksbridge La BD22 51 A3
Hawkshead Cl BD5 201 B1
Hawkshead Cres LS14 62 A3
Hawkshead Dr BD5 201 B1
Hawkshead Way BD5 201 B1
Hawkshead Wlk BD5 201 B1
Hawksley Ct LS27 98 A6
Hawkstone Ave LS20 39 C7
Hawkstone Dr BD20 18 A1
Hawkstone View LS20 39 D7
Hawkswood Ave
Bradford BD9 54 F3
Leeds LS5 58 E7
Hawkswood Cres LS5 58 E7
Hawkswood Gr LS5 58 E7
Hawkswood Mount LS5 58 E7
Hawkswood Pl LS5 58 F6
Hawkswood St LS5 58 F6
Hawkswood Terr LS5 58 F6
Hawkswood View LS5 58 E7
Hawksworth Ave LS20 39 D8
Hawksworth C of E
Primary Sch LS20 38 F8
Hawksworth Cl LS29 22 A3
Hawksworth Dr
Guiseley LS20 39 D7
Menston LS29 22 A4
Hawksworth Gr LS5 58 D6
Hawksworth Hall Sch
LS20 38 F8
Hawksworth La LS20 39 B7
Hawksworth Rd
Baildon BD17 38 C6
Horsforth LS18 58 D7
Hawksworth St LS29 8 B4
Hawksworth Wood
Primary Sch LS16 58 E7
Hawley Cl LS27 97 F2
Hawley Terr BD10 56 E4
Hawley Way LS27 97 F2
Haworth Cl WF14 137 F6
Haworth First Sch BD22 51 C7
Haworth Gr BD9 54 E3
Haworth La LS19 40 B7
Haworth Rd Batley WF17 96 F2
Bradford BD9 54 C4
Haworth BD22 51 E8
Wilsden BD15 53 C4
Haworth Sta BD22 51 C7
Hawthorn Ave
Batley WF17 118 A3
Bradford BD3 75 E8
Crofton WF4 143 E1
Knottingley WF11 126 E3
Yeadon LS19 40 C7
Hawthorn Cl
Brighouse HD6 115 C3
Wakefield WF2 120 B3
Hawthorn Cres
Baildon BD17 38 D3
4 Leeds LS7 204 A3
Yeadon LS19 40 B7
Hawthorn Croft WF3 100 C1
Hawthorn Ct S65 143 E1
Hawthorn Dr
Bradford BD10 56 C7
Pudsey LS13 57 D6
Yeadon LS19 40 C8
Hawthorn Gr
Ackworth M T WF7 163 F5
Burley in W LS29 21 F8
Pudsey LS13 57 D5
Rothwell LS26 100 F4
Silkstone S75 193 F1
Hawthorn La 6 LS7 204 A3
Hawthorn Mill 5 LS12 78 A4
Hawthorn Mount 3 LS7 204 A3
Hawthorn Pl 9 OL14 108 B6
Hawthorn Rd Bacup OL13 106 A2
Leeds LS7 204 A3
Slaithwaite HD7 151 F1
Yeadon LS19 40 C7
Hawthorn St Bradford BD3 75 E8
Brighouse HX3 114 D8
4 Halifax HX1 202 C1
Hawthorn Terr
5 Halifax HX1 202 C1
Huddersfield HX1 154 B8
Ossett WF5 140 E3
Hawthorn Vale 7 LS7 204 A3
Hawthorn View
Baildon BD17 38 E3
5 Leeds LS7 204 A3
Hawthorne Ave
Castleford WF10 125 B6
Featherstone WF7 145 C4
Hemsworth WF9 181 D6
Shipley BD18 55 D5
Wetherby LS22 13 D7
Hawthorne Cl
Flockton WF4 157 D3
Gildersome LS27 97 D7
Lepton HD8 155 D3
Hawthorne Cres WF9 181 C6
Hawthorne Dr LS27 97 D7
Hawthorne Flats S63 194 D1
Hawthorne Gdns LS16 42 B5
Hawthorne Gr WF2 141 E7
Hawthorne Mount WF6 144 B7
Hawthorne Rise LS14 62 C8
Hawthorne St Shafton S72 180 C3
Silsden BD20 5 D1
Hawthorne Terr
Huddersfield HD4 153 C4
Swillington LS25 82 C5
Wakefield WF2 141 E7
Hawthorne View LS27 97 E7
Hawthorne Way
Keighley BD20 36 E8
Shafton S72 180 C3
Shepley HD8 173 F3
Hawthorns The
Glusburn BD20 16 C6
Lofthouse Gate WF1 121 D5
Ossett WF5 140 E3
Hawtop La WF4 177 F5
Hayburn Gdns WF17 118 B5
Hayburn Rd WF17 118 A5
Haycliffe Ave BD7 74 A2
Haycliffe Dr BD7 73 F2
Haycliffe Gr BD7 74 A2
Haycliffe Hill Rd BD5 74 B3
Haycliffe La BD5, BD6 74 B2
Haycliffe Rd BD5 74 B3
Haycliffe Terr BD5 74 B3
Hayclose Mead BD6 94 A6
Hayden St BD3 75 B6
Haydn Ave WF3 121 E6
Haydn's Terr LS28 57 E2
Hayfield Ave
Boston Spa LS23 30 C8
Huddersfield HD3 153 A7
Hayfield Cl Baildon BD17 38 E4
Holmfirth HD7 189 D4
Hayfield Terr LS12 209 F2
Hayfields The BD22 51 C8
Haygill Nook BD23 1 E1
Hayhills La BD20 5 D4
Hayhills Rd BD20 5 E2
Hayleigh Ave 9 LS13 58 C3
Hayleigh Mount LS13 58 C3
Hayleigh St 8 LS13 58 C3
Hayleigh Terr 7 LS13 58 C3
Hayley Ct HX3 203 E4
Hayne La WF4 157 E5
Haynes St BD21 35 D6
Hays La HX2 91 C7
Hayson Cl WF12 118 F1
Haythorns Ave BD20 5 D1
Haythorns Mount BD20 5 D1
Hayton Dr LS22 13 F4
Hayton Wood View LS25 64 E8
Haywain The LS29 8 D3
Haywood Ave HD3 153 C7
Hazebrouck Dr BD17 38 B4
Hazel Ave Dewsbury WF12 140 B7
Leeds LS14 62 C8
Hazel Beck BD16 54 A8
Hazel Cl Birkenshaw BD11 96 A6
Dewsbury WF12 140 B7
Hazel Cres WF12 140 B7
Hazel Croft BD18 55 D7
Hazel Ct Rothwell LS26 100 F4
Wakefield WF2 142 A8
Hazel Dr WF12 140 B7
Hazel Gdns WF10 125 D6
Hazel Gr Bacup OL13 106 B3
Batley WF17 118 A4
Brighouse HX3 115 A7
Flockton WF4 157 D3
Huddersfield, Brackenhall
HD2 136 B5
Huddersfield, Cowlersley
HD7 152 F2
Pontefract WF8 125 E2
Sutton in C BD20 16 C5
Hazel Grove Rd BD20 16 C5
Hazel Hurst Gr BD13 92 D7
Hazel Hurst Rd BD13 92 D7
Hazel La DN6 184 A2
Hazel Mount BD18 55 C7
Hazel Rd WF11 126 E2
Hazel Rise LS26 102 C1
Hazel Wlk BD9 54 D2
Hazelcroft BD2 56 D4
Hazeldene BD13 92 D8
Hazeldene Cotts LS22 12 C5
Hazelheads BD17 38 C5
Hazelhurst Ave 1 BD16 37 A1
Hazelhurst Brow BD9 54 D2
Hazelhurst Ct Bradford BD9 75 C7
Bradford, Daisy Hill BD9 54 D2
Pudsey LS28 76 F7
Hazelhurst Rd BD9 54 D2
Hazelhurst Terr BD9 54 D2
Hazelmere Ave BD16 54 A8
Hazelwood Ave
Garforth LS25 83 A5
Keighley BD20 18 F1
Hazelwood Ct WF1 121 D5
Hazelwood Gdns WF9 181 E6
Hazelwood Rd
Bradford BD9 54 C3
Hemsworth WF9 163 B1
Lofthouse Gate WF1 121 D5
Hazelwood St OL14 108 B5
Hazill Bank WF2 141 E8
Hazledene Cres S72 180 D1
Hazledene Rd S72 180 D1
Headfield C of E Jun Sch
WF12 139 C5
Headfield La WF12 139 C5
Headfield Rd
Dewsbury WF12 139 D5
Huddersfield HD4 154 A3
Headfield View WF12 139 D4
Headingley Ave LS6 59 C5
Headingley Cres LS6 205 D4
Headingley Ct LS6 205 F4
Headingley Golf Course
LS16 42 D6
Headingley Grounds
(Cricket & Rugby League)
LS6 205 D4
Headingley La LS6 205 E4
Headingley Mount LS6 59 C5
Headingley Primary Sch
LS6 59 D5
Headingley Rise LS6 205 F3
Headingley Sta LS5 59 B4
Headingley View LS6 205 D4
Headland Gr BD6 73 F1
Headland La WF12 139 F6
Headlands Ave WF5 140 C5
Headlands CE Prim Sch
WF15 117 A4
Headlands Cl WF15 117 B3
Headlands Gr WF5 140 C5
Headlands La
Knottingley WF11 126 E4
Pontefract WF8 125 D1
Headlands Pk WF5 140 C5
Headlands Rd
Huddersfield HD1 154 A7
Liversedge WF15 117 A4
Ossett WF5 140 C5
Headlands St WF15 117 A3
Headlands The WF15 117 A3
Headlands Wlk WF5 140 C5
Headley Cotts LS24 48 A8
Headley Golf Course
BD13 72 C5
Headley La Bramham LS23 30 E1
Thornton BD13 72 D5
Headrow Sh Ctr LS1 211 F4
Headrow The LS1 211 F4
Headwall Gn HD7 152 B3
Heald Cl OL13 106 A8
Heald La OL13 106 A8
Heald St WF10 124 F8
Heald Terr HX4 133 A5
Healdfield Rd WF10 124 F8
Healds Ave WF15 117 B4
Healds Rd WF13 118 A2
Healdwood Cl WF10 125 A8
Healdwood Rd WF10 125 A8

Healey Ave BD16 37 A2
Healey Cl WF17 117 F5
Healey Cres WF5 140 D3
Healey Croft La WF3 120 B7
Healey Dr WF5 140 D4
Healey Green La
WF14, HD5 155 F7
Healey Junior Infants Sch
WF17 117 F5
Healey La Batley WF17 117 F5
Batley, WF17 118 B5
2 Bingley BD16 37 A2
Dewsbury WF12 157 A7
Healey Rd WF5 140 D3
Healey St WF17 117 F5
Healey Wood Cres HD6 115 A1
Healey Wood Gdns HD6 136 B8
Healey Wood Gr HD6 136 B8
Healey Wood Rd HD6 115 B1
Heap La BD3 201 D4
Heap St Bradford BD1 201 D3
Halifax HX3 92 C2
Heath Ave HX3 113 B4
Heath Cl Dewsbury WF12 140 B8
Slaithwaite HD7 170 E7
Heath Cres Leeds LS11 213 E3
Low Bradley BD20 4 C6
Heath Dr Boston Spa LS23 30 B7
Low Bradley BD20 4 C6
Heath Gdns HX3 113 C4
Heath Gr Batley WF17 118 F5
Keighley BD20 36 D8
Leeds LS11 213 E3
Pudsey LS28 76 C6
Heath Hall HX1 203 E1
Heath Hall Ave BD4 75 B1
Heath Hill Rd HX2 91 A2
Heath House La HD7 152 B4
Heath La HX3 113 C4
Heath Lea HX1 203 E2
Heath Mount LS11 213 E3
Heath Mount Rd HD6 136 A8
Heath Park Ave HX1 203 E1
Heath Pk LS29 7 F3
Heath Pl LS11 213 E3
Heath Rd Bradford BD3 56 B1
Dewsbury WF12 140 B8
Halifax HX1, HX3 203 E1
Huddersfield HD7 152 F1
Leeds LS11 213 E3
Slaithwaite HD7 170 E8
Heath Rise LS11 213 E2
Heath Royd HX3 113 C4
Heath St Bingley BD16 37 A3
Bradford BD3 75 C7
Halifax HX3 113 C4
Liversedge WF15 117 B2
Heath Terr BD3 75 C7
Heath View Jun & Inf Sch
WF1 142 E7
Heath View St HX1 203 F2
Heath Villas HX3 113 C4
Heath Wlk WF12 140 B8
Heathcliff BD22 51 B7
Heathcliffe Cl WF17 96 F3
Heathcote Ave LS14 45 F5
Heathcote Rise BD22 51 E8
Heathcroft Bank LS11 213 E2
Heathcroft Cres LS11 213 E2
Heathcroft Dr LS11 213 E2
Heathcroft Lawn LS11 213 E2
Heathcroft Rise LS11 213 E2
Heathcroft Vale LS11 213 E2
Heathdale Ave HD2 135 F1
Heather Ave HD7 170 E1
Heather Bank OL14 108 B1
Heather Bank Cl BD13 52 D5
Heather Cl
Lofthouse Gate WF1 121 D5
Ossett WF5 140 F3
South Kirkby WF9 182 D3
Heather Ct Batley WF17 96 E2
Bingley BD16 37 A5
Huddersfield HD3 152 F8
Lofthouse Gate WF3 121 E5
Heather Dr HX2 91 A3
Heather Fold HD8 174 F1
Heather Gdns Leeds LS13 77 E8
Scarcroft LS14 45 C7
Heather Gr Bradford BD9 54 B3
Keighley BD21 35 A8
Leeds LS13 77 E8
Heather Grove First Sch
BD9 54 D3
Heather Rd Baildon BD17 38 D4
Meltham HD7 170 E1
Heather Rise LS29 21 F8
Heather Side BD17 38 B4
Heather Vale LS14 45 B7
Heather View Bingley BD16 37 D5
Ossett WF5 140 D5
Heatherbank Ave BD22 34 F4
Heathercroft LS7 204 B2
Heatherdale Ct WF3 119 E8
Heatherdale Dr WF3 119 E8
Heatherdale Rd WF3 119 E8
Heatherfield Cres HD1 153 D6
Heatherfield Rd HD1 153 D6
Heathergrove Fold HD5 154 D7
Heatherlands Ave BD13 52 D2
Heatherstones 3 HX3 113 B4
Heathfield Leeds LS16 42 B4
Mirfield WF14 137 F6
Heathfield Ave HX5 135 B7
Heathfield Cl Bingley BD16 37 A4
East Ardsley WF3 119 F8
Heathfield Gr Bradford BD7 73 E4
1 Halifax HX3 113 C4
Heathfield Ind Est HX5 135 A6
Heathfield La LS23 30 B8
Heathfield Mews HD7 152 E4
Heathfield Pl 2 HX3 113 C4
Heathfield Rd
Huddersfield HD7 152 E4
Ossett WF5 140 C8
Heathfield Rise HX6 132 C1
Heathfield Sch HX6 150 C8
Heathfield Sq 1 LS6 59 D6
Heathfield St HX5 135 A6
Heathfield Terr
Halifax HX3 113 C4
Leeds LS6 59 D6
Heathfield Wlk LS16 42 A5
Heathmoor Cl
Bradford BD10 56 A7
Halifax HX2 91 D6
Heathmoor Mount HX2 91 E6
Heathmoor Park Rd HX2 91 D6
Heathmoor Way HX2 91 D6
Heathness Rd LS29 2 D1
Heathview Infants Sch
WF1 216 C3
Heathwood Dr HD7 152 C5
Heathy Ave HX2 92 A5
Heathy La HX2 92 A5
Heaton Ave
Cleckheaton BD19 116 C7
Dewsbury WF12 139 E8
Keighley BD20 36 C7
Kirkheaton HD5 137 C1
Leeds LS12 209 F1
Heaton Avenue First Sch
BD19 116 C7
Heaton Cl Baildon BD17 38 B4
Bingley BD16 37 B4
Heaton Cres Baildon BD17 38 B5
Bingley BD16 37 B4
Heaton Dr Baildon BD17 38 B4
Bingley BD16 37 B4
Kirkheaton HD5 137 C2
Heaton Fold La HD1 153 D6
Heaton Gdns HD1 153 D6
Heaton Gr
Cleckheaton BD19 116 C7
Shipley, Heaton Grove BD9 55 B4
Shipley, Windhill BD18 55 C7
Heaton Hill BD6 93 E7
Heaton Middle Sch BD9 54 D4
Heaton Moor Rd HD5 137 C1
Heaton Park Dr BD9 55 A3
Heaton Park Rd BD9 54 F3
Heaton Rd Batley WF17 118 C7
Bradford BD8, BD9 55 B2
Huddersfield HD1 153 D6
Heaton Royds Hospl BD9 54 D5
Heaton Royds La BD9 54 F5
Heaton Royds Sch BD18 55 A5
Heaton St
Ackworth M T WF7 163 E5
Bradford BD4 201 D1
4 Brighouse HD6 115 A2
Cleckheaton BD19 116 D8
Heaton's Ct LS1 211 F3
Heatons Yd HD6 115 B1
Heator La HD8 191 A7
Hebb View BD6 73 E2
Hebble Brook Cl HX2 91 C4
Hebble Ct HX2 91 D4
Hebble Dean HX2 91 F1
Hebble Dr HD7 189 A7
Hebble End HX7 88 F3
Hebble Gdns HX2 91 E1
Hebble La Halifax HX3 91 F1
Meltham HD7 187 D8
Hebble Mount HD7 170 E1
Hebble Row BD22 34 C1
Hebble St Dewsbury WF13 138 F5
4 Huddersfield HD1 154 B8
Hebble Vale Dr HX2 91 E1
Hebden App LS14 62 B6
Hebden Bridge Rd BD22 51 B1
Hebden Bridge Sta HX7 89 B2
Hebden Chase LS14 62 B6
Hebden Cl LS14 62 B6
Hebden Gn LS14 62 C6
Hebden Path LS14 62 B6
Hebden Pl LS14 62 B6
Hebden Rd Haworth BD22 51 D6
Wakefield WF1 142 E8
Hebden Royd C of E Junior
& Infant Sch HX7 88 E3
Hebden Terr HX7 89 B8
Hebden Wlk 2 LS14 62 C6
Heber Cl BD20 17 F8
Heber St BD21 35 B6
Heber's Ghyll Dr LS29 7 E3
Heber's Gr LS29 7 E4
Heckmondwike
Grammar Sch WF16 117 D4
Heckmondwike Rd
Batley WF13 117 F1
Dewsbury WF13 138 F8
Hector Cl 7 BD6 74 C1
Heddon Cl BD5 201 B1
Heddon Gr BD5 201 B1
Heddon Pl LS6 59 E6
Heddon St 4 LS6 59 E6
Heddon Wlk BD5 201 B1
Hedge Cl BD8 54 D1
Hedge Side BD8 73 E8
Hedge Top La HX3 93 B2
Hedge Way BD8 54 E1
Hedley Chase LS12 210 B3
Hedley Cres WF1 121 B3
Hedley Gdns LS12 210 B3
Hedley Gn LS12 210 B3
Heeley Rd WF2 160 A4
Heidelberg Rd BD9 55 A2
Height Gn HX6 112 B4
Height La Draughton BD23 1 D3
Oxenhope BD22 51 D2
Height Rd HX7 89 E3
Heights Bank LS12 77 F7
Heights Cl LS12 77 E7
Heights Dr Leeds LS12 77 F7
Slaithwaite HD7 170 D8
Heights E The LS12 77 F7
Heights Garth LS12 77 E7
Heights La Batley WF16 117 E3
Bingley BD16 37 B6
Bradford BD9 54 D3
Leeds LS12 77 F7
Silsden BD20 5 B4
Heights Par LS12 77 E7
Heights The HD7 189 C3
Heights W The LS12 77 E7
Heights Way LS12 77 F7
Heights Wlk LS12 77 F7
Helen Rose Ct BD18 38 E1
Helen St Huddersfield HD1 153 E3
Shipley BD18 54 F8
Helen Terr HD6 114 F3
Helena Ct LS25 102 F8
Helena Pl LS25 102 F8
Helena St LS25 102 F8
Helena Way BD4 95 C8
Helene Ct HD3 152 E8
Hell La WF4 143 E4
Hellewell St 4 BD6 93 F7
Hellewell's Rd WF5 140 D1
Hellwood La LS14 45 D7
Helm La Mirfield WF14 137 D5
Sowerby Bridge HX6 132 C8
Helme CE Junior
& Infants Sch HD7 170 E4
Helme La HD7 170 D3
Helme Pk HD7 170 D3
Helmet La HD7 170 D2
Helmsley Ct LS10 99 C4
Helmsley Dr LS16 59 B7
Helmsley Rd
Boston Spa LS23 30 C7
Leeds LS16 59 B7
Wakefield WF2 142 F1
Helmsley St BD4 75 A4
Helston Croft LS10 99 A5
Helston Garth LS10 99 A5
Helston Gn LS10 99 A5
Helston Pl LS10 99 A5
Helston Rd Middleton LS10 99 A5
Normanton WF6 123 B3
Helston St LS10 98 F6
Helston Way LS10 99 A6
Helston Wlk LS10 99 A5
Helted Way HD5 154 E3
Hemingway Cl LS10 215 E3
Hemingway Garth LS10 215 E3
Hemingway Gn LS10 215 E3
Hemingway Rd BD10 56 D8
Hemishor Dr LS26 102 E8
Hemsby Gr 7 BD21 35 B4
Hemsby Rd WF10 124 C6
Hemsby St 6 BD21 35 B4
Hemsworth By-Pass
WF9 181 D4
Hemsworth High Sch
WF9 181 E7
Hemsworth La WF9 163 A5
Hemsworth Rd WF9 181 F4
Hemsworth Water Pk
WF9 163 D1
Hen Holme La BD20 17 E7
Henacrewood Ct BD13 92 E7
Henage St 10 BD13 72 D1
Henbury St LS7 207 D1
Henconner Ave LS7 60 C6
Henconner Cres LS7 60 C6
Henconner Dr LS7 60 C6
Henconner Garth LS7 60 C6
Henconner Gdns LS7 60 C6
Henconner Gr LS7 60 C6
Henconner La
Leeds, Chapel Allerton LS7 60 C6
Leeds, Gamble Hill LS13 77 E8
Henconner Rd LS7 60 C6
Hendal La WF2 160 A5
Hendal Prim Jun & Inf Sch
WF2 160 B5
Henderson Ave WF6 144 B8
Henderson Glen S71 179 A3
Henderson Pl 8 BD6 74 C1
Hendford Dr BD3 75 B8
Henley Ave Bradford BD5 74 E2
Dewsbury WF12 139 E2
1 Leeds LS13 58 C2
Yeadon LS19 40 D3
Henley Cl LS19 40 D3
Henley Cres Leeds LS13 58 C2
Yeadon LS19 40 D3
Henley Croft HD5 154 E6
Henley Ct BD5 74 F2
Henley Dr
Featherstone WF7 145 D3
Yeadon LS19 40 C3
Henley Gr Bradford BD5 74 E2
2 Leeds LS13 58 C2
Henley Hill LS19 40 C3
Henley Mount LS19 40 D3
Henley Pl LS13 58 C2
Henley Rd Bradford BD5 74 F2
Dewsbury WF12 139 E2
Leeds LS13 58 C2
Henley St 3 LS13 58 C2
Henley Terr LS13 58 C2
Henley View LS13 58 C2
Henrietta St 2 WF17 118 C5
Henry Ave Leeds LS12 209 F1
Ryhill WF4 180 C8
Henry Cl S72 180 C3
Henry Frederick Ave HD4 171 C6
Henry Moore Ct WF10 125 B7
Henry Moore Inst LS1 211 E4
Henry Pl S64 98 A4
Henry Ralph Ave HD4 153 C1
Henry St Batley WF17 118 C2
Bradford BD14 73 C4
Brighouse HD6 115 A4
1 Halifax HX1 203 D2
Huddersfield HD1 154 A6
Keighley BD21 35 C7
Thornton BD13 72 D6
Wakefield WF2 142 A6
Henry Terr LS19 39 F7
Henshaw Ave LS19 40 B6
Henshaw Cres LS19 40 B6
Henshaw La LS19 40 B6
Henshaw Oval LS19 40 B6
Henshaw Rd OL14 108 B1
Henson Gr WF10 125 B6
Hepton Ct LS9 208 B1
Hepton Dr HX7 88 F4
Heptonstall Junior
& Infants Sch HX7 88 F5
Hepworth Ave LS27 98 B8
Hepworth Cl WF14 138 B6
Hepworth Cres
Holmfirth HD7 189 E3
Morley LS27 98 B8
Hepworth Dr WF14 138 C6
Hepworth Junior
& Infants Sch HD7 189 F1
Hepworth La WF14 138 B6
Hepworth Rd HD7 189 E3
Hepworth St WF10 103 F1
Hepworths Bldgs HD2 136 D3
Herbalist St LS12 210 B2
Herbert Pl BD3 75 E8
Herbert St Bingley BD16 37 A3
Bradford, Clayton BD14 73 C3
Bradford, Holme Top BD5 74 D4
Castleford WF10 124 D7
Halifax HX1 202 B2
Shipley, Cottingley BD16 54 B6
Shipley, Saltaire BD18 37 F1
Hereford Cl WF9 181 D8
Hereford St LS12 209 F4
Heritage Rd WF17 118 C4
Heritage Way BD22 34 C2
Hermit St BD21 35 A2
Hermitage Pk HD8 155 E2
Hermon Ave HX1 202 C2
Hermon Gr HX1 202 C2
Hermon Rd LS15 62 B1
Hermon St LS15 62 B1
Heron Cl Leeds LS17 43 F4
Queensbury BD13 72 C2
Steeton BD20 17 B6
Heron Ct 4 LS27 98 D4
Heron Dr WF2 160 C5
Heron Gr LS17 43 F4
Herries Ct LS29 22 B4
Herriot Mews WF10 125 D5
Herschel Rd BD8 73 D7
Hertford Chase LS15 81 C6
Hertford Cl LS15 81 D6
Hertford Croft LS15 81 D6
Hertford Fold LS15 81 C6
Hertford Lawn LS15 81 C6
Heseltine Cl WF6 123 A2
Heseltine La HX7 110 B4
Heshbon St BD4 75 C3
Hesketh Ave
East Ardsley WF3 119 D8
Leeds LS5 59 A5
Hesketh La WF3 119 D8
Hesketh Mount LS5 59 A5
Hesketh Pl LS5 59 A5
Hesketh Rd LS5 59 A4
Hesketh Terr LS5 59 A4
Hesley Rd WF2 160 B5
Hessel Ct WF8 146 B8
Hessle Ave LS6 205 E3
Hessle Common La WF7 163 D7
Hessle La WF7 163 D8
Hessle Mount LS6 205 E3
Hessle Pl LS6 205 E3
Hessle Rd 7 LS6 205 E3
Hessle St 9 LS6 205 E3
Hessle Terr LS6 205 E3
Hessle View 10 LS6 205 E3
Hessle Wlk 8 LS6 205 E3
Hetchell View LS17 28 D2
Hetton Dr BD3 75 D6
Hetton Rd LS8 208 B4
Heuthwaite Ave LS22 13 F4
Hew Clews BD7 73 E3
Hexham Gn HD3 152 F5
Hey Beck La WF12 119 C5
Hey Cres HD7 170 D2
Hey Head La
Littleborough OL15 129 A1
Todmorden OL14 108 D7
Hey La Huddersfield HD7 172 B7
Huddersfield, Lowerhouses
HD5 154 D3
Kirkburton HD7 172 B7
Ripponden HD3 151 B6
Hey Slack La HD7 190 C2
Hey St Bradford BD7 74 D7
Brighouse HD6 115 B4
1 Todmorden OL14 108 C5
Hey's Bldgs WF6 122 F4
Heybeck Wlk BD4 75 F2
Heycliffe Rd HD7 189 B5
Heyford Ct BD2 55 D3
Heygate Cl BD17 38 D4
Heygate La Baildon BD17 38 D4
Bramham LS23 30 F3
Heys Ave BD13 72 F6
Heys Cl WF11 127 A4
Heys Cres BD13 72 F6
Heys Gdns HD7 189 C8
Heys La Halifax HX2 90 B6
Ripponden HX6 132 D1
Slaithwaite HD7 151 D2
Heys Rd HD7 189 C8
Heys The HD7 170 E4
Heysham Dr BD4 75 F3
Heywood Cl HX3 93 A2
Heywood Pl HX1 203 D3
Heywood St 16 HX1 202 C3
Hick La WF17 118 D5
Hick St BD1 201 C3
Hicks La LS26 102 D3
Hicks Memorial Sch LS25 84 A7
Higgin Chamber HX2 111 C5
Higgin La HX3 113 E5
High Ash Leeds LS17 43 E5
Shipley BD18 55 E7
High Ash Ave
Clayton West HD8 176 A2
Leeds LS17 43 F5
High Ash Cl WF4 178 F7
High Ash Dr LS17 43 E5
High Ash Mount LS17 43 F5
High Ash Pk BD15 53 F1
High Bank BD20 4 C6
High Bank App LS15 81 D7
High Bank Cl
Addingham LS29 6 E8
Leeds LS15 81 D8
High Bank Gate LS15 81 D7
High Bank Gdns LS15 81 E7
High Bank La BD18 54 E6
High Bank Pl LS15 81 D7
High Bank View LS15 81 D7
High Bank Way LS15 81 E7
High Banks Cl BD20 18 F2
High Binns La BD22 51 D3
High Bradley La BD20 4 C7
High Brook Fall WF3 121 C7
High Brooms HD2 135 E1
High Bury Cl BD13 92 C8
High Busy La
Bradford BD10 56 A8
Shipley BD18 55 F8
High Cl Guiseley LS20 39 B8
Huddersfield HD5 154 E3
Kexbrough S75 177 D1
Ossett WF5 119 D1
Slaithwaite HD7 170 E8
Yeadon LS19 40 B3
High Cliffe Cl 11 BD13 72 D6
High Cliffe Terr LS22 13 E5
High Cote BD20 18 D2
High Court La LS2 212 A3
High Crags First Sch
BD18 55 C6
High Crest HD7 152 E2
High Croft Addingham LS29 6 F8
Halifax HX3 91 F3
Queensbury BD13 72 E1
High Croft Cres HD5 154 F3
High Croft Rd OL14 108 C6
High Croft Way BD20 4 D1
High Cross La HX3 93 A7
High Ct Heptonstall HX7 88 D6
Leeds LS2 212 A3
High End BD17 39 C5
High Farm Fold WF9 164 E2
High Farm Mdw WF9 164 E2
High Fernley Ct 10 BD12 94 C4
High Fernley First Sch
BD12 94 C3
High Fernley Rd BD12 94 B3
High Field La
Oakworth BD22 34 C3
Ripponden HX6 132 D6
High Fields HX6 112 E4
High Fold Baildon BD17 38 C4
Bingley BD16 36 E8
Keighley BD22 34 F5
High Fold La BD20 18 A2
High Green Dr BD20 5 D2
High Green Rd WF6 122 E3
High Grove La HX3 113 E5
High Holly Garth BD21 35 D6
High House Ave BD2 56 A4
High House Edge HD7 170 C7
High House La
Halifax HX2 90 C4
Slaithwaite HD7 170 C8
High House Mews LS29 6 F8
High House Rd BD2 56 A4
High Hoyland La S75 193 B8
High Keep Fold WF4 159 F3
High La Cowling BD22 32 A8
Halifax HX2 112 B8
Hebden Bridge HX7 110 D3
Holmfirth HD7 189 B3
Huddersfield HD4 154 C1
Spofforth HG3 12 A8
High Lea HD7 168 F4
High Lees Rd HX2 91 B5
High Level Way HX1 202 B4
High Malsis BD20 16 A5
High Meadow BD20 18 A1

High Meadows
Dewsbury WF12 139 C1
Elland HX4 134 C7
Walton WF2 161 B6
Wilsden BD15 53 C5
High Mill LS29 3 A1
High Mill La LS29 3 A1
High Moor Ave LS17 43 E2
High Moor Cl LS17 43 E3
High Moor Cres LS17 43 E3
High Moor Ct LS17 43 E2
High Moor Dr LS17 43 E3
High Moor Gr LS17 43 E3
High Oxford St WF10 124 C7
High Park Cres BD9 54 E3
High Park Dr BD9 54 E3
High Park Gr BD9 54 E3
High Peal Ct 12 BD13 72 D1
High Poplars BD2 55 F4
High Rd WF12 139 E7
High Ridge WF4 158 E6
High Ridge Ave LS26 100 E7
High Ridge Ct LS26 100 E6
High Ridge Pk LS26 100 E7
High Ridge Way LS16 24 F2
High Royds Dr LS29 22 B3
High Royds Hospl LS29 22 B2
High Spring Gardens La
BD20 35 A8
High Spring Rd BD21 35 F6
High St Batley WF16 117 E4
Batley, Birstall WF17 96 E1
Batley, Hanging Heaton
WF17 118 F3
Boston Spa LS23 30 D8
Boston Spa, Clifford LS23 30 E5
Bradford, Idle BD10 56 B8
Bradford, Wibsey BD6 74 C1
Bramham LS23 30 D2
Brighouse HD6 115 B3
Brotherton WF11 105 C1
Castleford WF10 124 C7
Clayton West HD8 175 F2
Cleckheaton BD19 116 D8
Crigglestone WF4 159 E5
Crofton WF4 161 F8
Crofton, Sharlston WF4 144 B5
Dewsbury, Daw Green
WF12, WF13 139 B7
Dewsbury, Earlsheaton
WF12 139 F7
Dewsbury, Overthorpe
WF12 139 C1
Elland, Stainland HX4 133 F3
8 Elland, West Vale HX4 134 D7
Halifax HX2 90 E1
Honley HD7 171 F4
Horbury WF4 141 A1
Huddersfield HD1 153 E5
Huddersfield HD1 154 A5
Keighley BD21 35 B7
Kippax LS25 83 B1
Knottingley WF11 126 C5
Mapplewell S75 178 A2
Morley LS27 98 A3
Normanton WF6 123 B2
Normanton, Altofts WF6 122 F3
Ossett WF5 119 C1
Pudsey LS28 57 D3
Queensbury BD13 72 E1
Royston S71 179 B3
Shafton S72 180 C2
Slaithwaite HD7 152 B5
South Elmsall WF9 183 A3
South Hiendley S72 180 E5
Steeton BD20 17 C5
Sutton in C BD20 16 D4
Thornton BD13 72 D6
Todmorden OL14 108 A3
Upton WF9 183 B7
Woolley WF4 178 A7
Yeadon LS19 40 C7
High Stones Rd HX7 110 E3
High Street Pl BD10 56 B8
High Sunderland La HX3 92 D1
High Top HX7 88 B4
High Trees La HX4 133 E6
High Trees Sch LS23 30 E6
High View
Crigglestone WF4 159 E5
Royston S71 179 B3
High Weardley La LS17 26 A6
High Well Hill La S72 180 C7
High Wheatley LS29 8 E3
High Wicken Cl BD13 72 D6
High Wood LS29 8 F3
High Wood Ct LS6 59 E5
High Wood La HD8 174 B6
High Woodlands WF3 120 C7
Higham & Dob La HX6 111 C3
Highbank First Sch WF15 116 B5
Highbridge La HD8 175 C1
Highbridge Terr BD5 74 F1
Highburton C of E
(Controlled) First Sch
HD8 173 E8
Highbury Cl LS6 59 E6
Highbury La LS6 59 E6
Highbury Mount LS6 59 E6
Highbury Pl Leeds LS6 59 E6
Pudsey LS13 77 A8
Highbury Rd Bradford BD4 75 C6
Leeds LS6 59 E6
Highbury Sch HD6 135 E7
Highbury St LS6 59 E6
Highbury Terr
9 Dewsbury WF12 139 D8
Leeds LS6 59 E6
Highcliffe Ave HD2 135 F2
Highcliffe Ct LS22 13 F5
Highcliffe Dr HX2 112 D7
Highcliffe Ind Est LS27 97 E5
Highcliffe Rd Batley WF17 118 C3
Morley LS27 97 F4
Highcroft Batley WF17 118 C3
Collingham LS22 29 A8
Holmfirth HD7 188 E5
Highcroft Cl LS28 76 C8
Highcroft Gdns BD21 35 F6
Highdale WF12 118 E2
Highdale Croft BD10 56 B8
Higher Ashenhurst OL14 108 A7
Higher Back La HX7 87 F4
Higher Brockwell HX6 112 A3
Higher Calderbrook
OL15 129 C1
Higher Calderbrook Rd
OL15 129 C2
Higher Change Villas
OL13 106 B4
Higher Coach Rd BD17 37 F2
Higher Downs BD8 73 D8
Higher Grange Rd LS28 76 E8
Higher Hartley St BD20 16 B6
Higher Intake Rd BD2 56 C1
Higher Lodge St BD20 16 B6
Higher Park Royd Dr HX6 132 E6
Higher Scholes BD22 33 F1
Higher School St 4 BD18 54 F8
Higherwood Cl BD21 35 E6
Highfell Rise BD22 34 E5
Highfield Bradford BD4 75 D1
East Ardsley WF3 98 D1
Shelf HX3 93 C5
Highfield Ave
Bradford BD10 56 A7
Brighouse HD6 115 B8
Denby Dale HD8 191 A4
Elland HX4 134 B7
Leeds LS12 210 A1
Meltham HD7 170 D3
Pontefract WF8 126 A4
Pontefract WF8 146 C7
Shelf HX3 93 D7
Highfield Cl
Featherstone WF7 145 D8
Gildersome LS27 97 E7
Keighley BD20 19 D1
Leeds LS12 210 A1
Highfield Cres Baildon BD17 38 C4
Bradford BD9 54 E4
5 Hebden Bridge HX7 89 A4
Kippax LS26 102 F5
Leeds LS12 210 A2
Meltham HD7 170 D3
Netherton WF4 157 F6
Pudsey LS28 76 D8
Rothwell LS26 101 C7
Highfield Ct
Castleford WF10 124 D6
Liversedge WF15 116 F2
Oakworth BD22 34 C2
Shepley HD8 190 E6
Highfield Ctr WF9 181 D6
Highfield Dr Batley WF17 96 E2
Bradford BD9 54 E4
Garforth LS25 82 F5
Gildersome LS27 97 D7
Halifax HX2 111 E8
Kippax LS26 102 F5
Liversedge FW15 116 E4
Wakefield WF2 141 E8
Yeadon LS19 40 C3
Highfield Garth LS12 210 A1
Highfield Gdns
Bradford BD9 54 D4
Dewsbury WF12 139 D3
Gildersome LS27 97 D7
Leeds LS12 209 F1
Highfield Gn Kippax WF10 102 F6
Pudsey LS28 76 D8
Highfield Gr Bradford BD10 56 A6
Halifax HX5 134 E8
Kippax WF10 102 F6
Highfield Grange WF4 141 A1
Highfield La
Barwick in E LS15 63 E5
Batley WF13 117 F4
Keighley BD21 35 B8
Lepton HD8 155 D5
Meltham HD7 170 C3
Rothwell LS26 101 C7
Sherburn in E LS25 84 D5
Silsden BD20 5 E2
Highfield Mews 1
Baildon BD17 38 C4
Keighley BD20 19 D1
Highfield Middle Sch BD21 35 B7
Highfield Mount
Dewsbury WF12 139 E1
Rothwell LS26 101 C6
Highfield Pl Bradford BD8 55 C1
Halifax HX1 202 B2
Hemsworth WF9 181 C6
Kippax WF10 103 A6
Morley LS27 98 B3
Highfield Primary Sch
LS17 43 E4
Highfield Rd Aberford LS25 64 E8
Bradford BD2, BD10 56 B7
Brighouse HD6 135 E8
Cleckheaton BD19 116 C7
Elland HX5 134 F6
Highfield Rd continued
Halifax HX2 111 E8
Hemsworth WF9 181 D6
Horbury WF4 141 A1
Keighley BD21 35 A8
Kirkburton HD8 173 E7
Leeds LS13 58 D2
Meltham HD7 170 D3
Netherton WF4 158 D5
Pontefract WF8 146 C6
Pudsey LS28 76 C8
Shipley BD9 55 C5
Slaithwaite HD7 151 F4
Highfield Rise WF2 141 E8
Highfield St Keighley BD21 35 B7
Leeds LS13 58 D2
Pudsey LS28 76 C8
Highfield Terr
Dewsbury WF12 139 D3
Halifax HX1 202 B2
Pudsey LS28 76 C8
Queensbury BD13 92 D8
Ripponden HX6 132 E6
Shipley BD18 54 E8
Yeadon LS19 40 C3
Highfield View LS27 97 E7
Highfields
Huddersfield HD1 153 F7
Netherton WF4 158 D5
Ryhill WF4 162 D2
Highfields Rd HD1 153 F7
Highfold LS19 40 A5
Highgate Bradford BD9 54 F4
Glusburn BD20 16 C7
Highgate Ave HD8 155 F3
Highgate Cl BD13 73 C2
Highgate Cres HD8 155 E3
Highgate Dr HD8 155 F3
Highgate Gr BD13 73 C2
Highgate La
Kirkheaton HD5 137 D1
Lepton HD8 155 E3
Highgate Rd
Bradford BD13 73 B2
Dewsbury WF12 139 D8
Highgate St WF17 118 F3
Highgate Terr 10 WF12 139 D8
Highgate Wlk HD8 155 F3
Highland Cl WF8 125 F3
Highland Ville HX3 114 D8
Highlands Ave HD5 154 F3
Highlands Cl
1 Bradford BD7 73 E3
Middleton LS10 99 F8
Highlands Dr LS10 99 F8
Highlands Gr Bradford BD7 73 E3
Middleton LS10 99 F8
Highlands La HX2 91 F6
Highlands Pk HX2 91 F6
Highlands The
Cleckheaton WF15 116 D5
Ossett WF5 140 C5
Highlands Wlk LS10 99 F8
Highlea Cl LS19 39 F5
Highlee La HX6, HX4 132 F6
Highley Hall Croft HD6 115 D3
Highley Pk HD6 115 E2
Highmoor BD17 38 A3
Highmoor Cres HD6 115 D3
Highmoor La
Brighouse HD6 115 F5
Brighouse, Clifton HD6 115 E4
Cleckheaton HD6 116 A6
Highmoor Wlk BD17 38 A2
Highroad Well La HX2 112 C7
Highroyd HD8 155 F3
Highroyd Cres 1 HD5 154 D5
Highroyd La HD5 154 D6
Highthorne Ave BD3 56 C1
Highthorne Dr LS17 43 F4
Highthorne Gr
3 Leeds LS12 209 D4
Leeds, Blackwood LS17 44 A4
Highthorne Mount LS17 43 F4
Highthorne St LS12 209 D4
Highthorne View 6 LS12 209 D4
Hightown La HD7 189 A5
Hightown Rd WF15 116 D6
Hightown Sch WF15 116 C5
Hightown View WF15 116 D5
Highway LS20 22 B1
Highways LS14 61 E1
Highwood Ave LS17 43 C3
Highwood Cres LS17 43 C3
Highwood Gr LS17 43 C2
Higson Ct HD5 155 A7
Hilberoyd Rd WF17 118 D5
Hilda St Ossett WF5 140 E4
Shipley BD9 55 A4
Hill Brow Cl BD15 54 A1
Hill Cl Baildon BD17 38 B2
Huddersfield HD3 134 F1
Pontefract WF8 146 D7
Hill Clough Gr BD22 34 D7
Hill Cres Batley WF17 97 A1
Burley in W LS29 21 F7
Halifax HX3 113 F5
Yeadon LS19 40 C5
Hill Crest Adwick Le S DN6 184 E1
Collingham LS22 28 E8
Ripponden HX6 132 C1
Ryhill WF4 162 C1
1 Sowerby Bridge HX6 112 B5
Swillington LS26 82 A1
Hill Crest Ave
Denholme BD13 52 E1
3 Sowerby Bridge HX6 112 B5
Hill Crest Dr BD13 52 D1
Hill Crest Mount BD13 52 D1
Hill Crest Rd
Denholme BD13 52 D1
Dewsbury WF12 139 C5
Thornton BD13 72 D7
Hill Crest View BD13 52 D1
Hill Croft Ripponden HX6 132 C1
Thornton BD13 72 E7
Hill Croft Cl WF8 147 D5
Hill Dr WF7 164 A8
Hill End WF12 139 E8
Hill End Cl Brighouse HX3 94 A2
Leeds LS12 77 F8
Hill End Cres LS12 77 F8
Hill End Gr BD7 73 E3
Hill End La
Cullingworth BD13 52 F8
Harden BD16 36 A1
Queensbury BD13 92 D8
Hill End Rd LS12 77 F8
Hill Estate WF9 183 B7
Hill Foot BD18 54 E7
Hill Gr HD3 134 F1
Hill Gr S LS10 99 F7
Hill Green Ct BD4 76 E2
Hill Grove Lea HD3 134 F1
Hill House Edge La BD22 70 B8
Hill House La
Holmfirth HD7 188 E2
Oxenhope BD22 51 C1
Hill House Rd HD7 188 E2
Hill La HD7 188 E5
Hill Lands BD12 94 C5
Hill Park Ave HX3 91 F1
Hill Pk WF14 137 F2
Hill Primary Sch S63 194 F1
Hill Rd Castleford WF10 124 F6
Wakefield WF2 160 C4
Hill Rise Ave LS13 58 C4
Hill Rise Gr LS13 58 C4
Hill Side Ave HD7 189 E2
Hill Side Mount LS28 57 E2
Hill Side Rd Bingley BD16 36 F3
Bradford BD3 201 D3
Hill Side Terr BD3 201 D4
Hill St Bradford, Bowling BD4 75 B5
Bradford, Wibsey BD6 74 A1
Cleckheaton BD19 116 C7
Halifax HX1 203 D2
Haworth BD22 51 C6
Holmfirth HD7 189 E3
Leeds LS11 214 B3
Leeds, New Town LS9 207 E2
Hill Top Brighouse HX3 114 E7
Burley in W LS29 9 E1
Castleford WF10 123 F7
Cawthorne S75 193 E5
Halifax HX2 202 A1
Hemsworth WF9 163 A3
Ilkley LS29 8 A2
Knottingley WF11 126 F4
Steeton BD20 17 C5
Hill Top Ave Barnsley S71 178 E1
Huddersfield HD2 135 B4
Leeds LS8 207 F4
Hill Top C of E First Sch
BD12 94 C6
Hill Top Cl
East Ardsley WF3 119 E6
Hemsworth WF9 163 A3
7 Leeds LS12 77 F8
Hill Top Cotts BD9 54 E2
Hill Top Cres WF14 137 F1
Hill Top Ct East Ardsley WF3 119 E6
Wakefield WF2 160 C4
Hill Top Dr HD3 153 A8
Hill Top Est WF16 117 E4
Hill Top Fold HD7 151 F1
Hill Top Gdns WF3 119 E6
Hill Top Gn WF3 119 D6
Hill Top Gr Bradford BD15 54 A1
East Ardsley WF3 119 E6
Hill Top Infants Sch WF2 119 D5
Hill Top La Bingley BD16 36 F8
Bradford BD15 54 A1
East Ardsley WF3 119 E6
Hebden Bridge HX7 110 B4
West Hardwick WF4 145 C1
Hill Top Mews WF11 126 F4
Hill Top Mount LS8 207 F4
Hill Top Pl Leeds LS8 207 F4
Leeds, Hyde Park LS6 205 F2
Hill Top Rd Flockton WF4 157 D3
Holmfirth HD7 188 F1
Huddersfield HD3 134 F1
Huddersfield, Grove Place
HD5 154 D6
Huddersfield, Paddock HD1 153 E5
Keighley BD21 35 A2
Leeds LS12 77 F8
Oakworth BD22 34 B2
Slaithwaite HD7 152 A1
Thornton BD13 72 C7
Wakefield WF2 160 C4
Hill Top Sch WF10 125 C7
Hill Top St LS6 205 F2
Hill Top View
East Ardsley WF3 119 D6
Normanton WF6 144 A7
Hill Top Way BD22 34 F7
Hill Top Wlk BD22 34 F7
Hill View HX2 91 F7
Hill View Ave LS7 204 A3
Hill View Mount LS7 204 A3
Hill View Terr 2 LS7 204 A3
Hillam La
Burton Salmon LS25 105 E5
Hillam LS25 105 E5
Hillam Rd BD2 55 D3
Hillam St BD5 74 B3
Hillary Pl LS2 206 B2
Hillary Rd BD18 55 E7
Hillary St 2 WF13 117 F3
Hillbrook Rise LS29 7 F3
Hillcote Dr BD5 74 E4
Hillcourt Ave LS13 58 C4
Hillcourt Croft LS13 58 C4
Hillcourt Dr LS13 58 C4
Hillcourt Gr LS13 58 C4
Hillcrest WF6 122 E4
Hillcrest Ave
Batley WF17 118 A5
Castleford WF10 125 D6
Featherstone WF7 145 B5
Leeds LS7 207 E4
Ossett WF5 140 C8
Queensbury BD13 92 F8
Silsden BD20 5 E2
Hillcrest Cl
Castleford WF10 125 D7
Swillington LS26 81 F1
Hillcrest Dr
Castleford WF10 125 E6
Queensbury BD13 92 F8
Hillcrest Mount
Brighouse BD19 115 F7
Castleford WF10 125 E6
Leeds LS16 41 E4
Hillcrest Pl LS7 207 F4
Hillcrest Rd
Castleford WF10 125 E7
Queensbury BD13 92 F8
Hillcrest Rise LS16 41 E4
Hillcrest View LS7 207 E4
Hillesley Rd WF12 119 A3
Hillfold WF9 183 B3
Hillfoot Ave LS28 76 B8
Hillfoot Cres LS28 76 B8
Hillfoot Dr LS28 76 B8
Hillfoot Rise LS28 76 B8
Hillgarth Dewsbury WF12 139 D3
Knottingley WF11 126 E3
Hillhead Dr WF17 97 A1
Hillhouse La HD1 154 B8
Hillidge Rd LS10 215 D4
Hillidge Sq LS10 215 D4
Hillingdon Way LS17 43 B6
Hillings La
Guiseley LS20, LS29 21 E3
Menston LS29 21 E3
Hillside Byram WF11 126 D7
Denby Dale HD8 192 A6
Garforth LS25 83 B6
Hillside Ave Guiseley LS20 22 D3
Halifax HX2 111 D7
Huddersfield HD2 136 B2
Oakworth BD22 34 B2
Ripponden HX6 132 E6
Hillside Cl Addingham LS29 6 E8
Wakefield WF2 141 D3
Hillside Cres
6 Bacup OL13 106 A7
Brierley S72 181 A2
Huddersfield HD4 154 B2
Hillside Ct Menston LS29 21 F4
South Elmsall WF9 183 A4
Hillside Gr Brierley S72 181 A2
Oakworth BD22 34 B2
7 Pudsey LS28 76 F7
Hillside Mount
Brierley S72 181 A2
Pontefract WF8 146 E8
Pudsey LS28 77 A7
Hillside Prim Sch LS11 214 B4
Hillside Rd
Ackworth M T WF7 164 A6
Leeds LS7 204 A3
Pontefract WF8 146 E8
Shipley BD18 55 D5
Hillside Rise Guiseley LS20 22 D3
Liversedge WF15 117 A3
Hillside Terr BD17 38 C3
Hillside View Halifax HX6 112 A4
Pudsey LS28 77 A7
Slaithwaite HD7 152 E1
Hillside Works Ind Est
BD19 95 D2
Hillthorpe Dr WF8 165 A5
Hillthorpe Rd LS28 76 E5
Hillthorpe Rise LS28 76 E5
Hillthorpe Sq 1 LS28 76 E5
Hillthorpe St 2 LS28 76 E5
Hillthorpe Terr 3 LS28 76 E5
Hilltop S72 180 F3
Hilltop Est WF9 181 F1
Hillview Gdns HX3 93 A1
Hillway LS20 39 C8
Hilmian Way WF9 181 F5
Hilton Ave BD18 55 B5
Hilton Cres BD17 38 C2
Hilton Ct LS16 24 A4
Hilton Dr BD18 55 B5
Hilton Gr Bradford BD7 74 B6
Leeds LS8 204 C1
Shipley BD18 55 B5
Hilton Grange LS16 24 B4
Hilton Mews LS16 24 A3
Hilton Pl LS8 207 F4
Hilton Rd Bradford BD7 74 A6
Leeds LS8 207 F4
Shipley BD18 55 B5
Hilton St
27 Hebden Bridge HX7 89 A3
2 Leeds LS8 207 F4
Hilton Terr 3 LS8 207 F4
Hinchcliffe Ave WF5 140 F5

Hinchcliffe Mill Junior & Infants Sch HD7 .... 188 C2
Hinchcliffe St BD3 .... 75 B8
Hinchliffe Ave BD17 .... 38 D2
Hind Ct HD7 .... 170 C3
Hind St 5 Bradford BD8 .... 74 C8
Bradford, Wyke BD12 .... 94 C2
Hindle Pl 2 LS27 .... 98 B7
Hindley Rd WF15 .... 117 A3
Hindley Wlk BD7 .... 73 D2
Hinds Cres WF9 .... 182 F3
Hinton Cl WF8 .... 125 E3
Hinton La WF11 .... 126 A6
Hions Cl HD6 .... 136 A8
Hipperholme Grammar Sch HX3 .... 114 C8
Hipperholme & Lightcliffe High Sch HX3 .... 114 F7
Hipswell St BD3 .... 75 C8
Hird Ave BD6 .... 94 C8
Hird Rd BD12 .... 94 D6
Hird St Keighley BD21 .... 35 B5
Leeds LS11 .... 214 A3
Shipley BD17 .... 55 B8
Hirst Ave WF16 .... 117 D6
Hirst Gr HX7 .... 89 B3
Hirst La Holmfirth HD7 .... 190 B5
Shipley BD18 .... 54 E8
Hirst Lodge Ct BD2 .... 55 F5
Hirst Mill Cres BD18 .... 37 E1
Hirst Rd Dewsbury WF13 .... 118 C1
Wakefield WF2 .... 141 D5
Hirst St Kippax WF10 .... 102 F7
Mirfield WF14 .... 138 A3
Todmorden OL14 .... 86 B1
Hirst Wood Cres 1 BD18 .... 54 E8
Hirst Wood Rd BD18 .... 54 E8
Hirstlands Ave WF5 .... 140 C7
Hirstlands Dr WF5 .... 140 C8
Hive St BD22 .... 35 A6
Hoads The HD6 .... 135 F7
Hob La Haworth BD22 .... 50 C7
Huddersfield HD4 .... 153 B2
Ripponden HX6 .... 132 C5
Sowerby Bridge HX6 .... 112 B1
Hobart Bldgs HX7 .... 89 D1
Hobart Rd Castleford WF10 .... 125 D8
Dewsbury WF12 .... 118 F1
Hobb Nook La LS21 .... 10 A7
Hobberley La LS17 .... 44 F3
Hobson Fold 4 BD12 .... 94 D2
Hockney Rd BD8 .... 74 B8
Hodge La WF8 .... 166 E6
Hodgewood La WF8 .... 147 D6
Hodgson Ave Bradford BD3 .... 56 E8
Leeds LS17 .... 44 A3
Hodgson Cres LS17 .... 44 A3
Hodgson La BD11 .... 96 C6
Hodgson Pl 6 LS27 .... 98 B7
Hodgson St Morley LS27 .... 98 C1
Wakefield WF1 .... 216 A3
Hodgson Terr WF12 .... 139 D6
Hodroyd Cl S72 .... 180 D1
Hodroyd Cotts S72 .... 180 F2
Hoffman St HD3 .... 153 A4
Hog Close La HD7 .... 200 C8
Hogley La HD7 .... 188 C4
Holays HD5 .... 154 E7
Holbeck La LS11 .... 210 C2
Holbeck Moor Rd LS11 .... 211 D1
Holbeck Towers LS11 .... 211 D1
Holborn App LS6 .... 206 A3
Holborn Ct Bradford BD12 .... 94 C6
Leeds LS6 .... 206 B3
Holborn Gdns 4 LS6 .... 206 A3
Holborn Gn LS6 .... 206 A3
Holborn Gr LS6 .... 206 A3
Holborn St LS6 .... 206 B3
Holborn Terr LS6 .... 206 B3
Holborn Towers LS6 .... 206 B3
Holborn View LS6 .... 206 A3
Holborn Wlk LS6 .... 206 A3
Holby Sq WF2 .... 141 C4
Holden Ing Way WF17 .... 97 A4
Holden La Baildon BD17 .... 38 D4
Silsden BD20 .... 18 C6
Holden Rd 1 BD6 .... 74 B1
Holden St BD22 .... 34 F5
Holderness Rd WF11 .... 126 E4
Holderness St 14 OL14 .... 108 C5
Holdforth Cl LS12 .... 210 B3
Holdforth Gdns LS12 .... 210 B3
Holdforth Gn LS12 .... 210 B3
Holdforth Pl LS12 .... 210 B3
Holdsworth Ct 6 BD19 .... 116 D7
Holdsworth Rd HX2, HX3 .... 92 A6
Holdsworth Sq BD2 .... 56 D4
Holdsworth St
Bradford BD1 .... 201 C4
Cleckheaton BD19 .... 116 D8
Shipley BD18 .... 55 C6
Holdsworth Terr HX1 .... 203 F1
Hole Bottom Rd OL14 .... 108 B7
Hole La BD20 .... 5 B3
Holes La WF11 .... 126 E4
Holgate Ave WF9 .... 163 B3
Holgate Cres WF9 .... 181 C7
Holgate Gdns WF9 .... 181 C7
Holgate Hospital WF9 .... 181 A6
Holgate Rd WF8 .... 146 C5
Holgate Terr WF9 .... 163 B3
Holgate View
Brierley S72 .... 181 B3
Hemsworth WF9 .... 163 B3
Holker St Bradford BD8 .... 74 B8
Keighley BD21 .... 35 C8
Holland Rd LS25 .... 83 C2
Holland St WF17 .... 118 D5
Hollas La Halifax HX3, HX6 .... 112 F3
Sowerby Bridge HX6 .... 112 E2
Hollerton La WF3 .... 119 F7
Hollin Ave HD3 .... 153 D7
Hollin Brigg La HD7 .... 188 C2
Hollin Close La BD2 .... 55 E3
Hollin Cres LS16 .... 59 E7
Hollin Dr
Crigglestone WF4 .... 159 E5
Leeds LS16 .... 59 E7
Hollin Edge HD8 .... 192 A6
Hollin Gate LS21 .... 10 D2
Hollin Gdns LS16 .... 59 C7
Hollin Greaves La HX3 .... 92 D1
Hollin Hall HD7 .... 152 C5
Hollin Hall Dr LS29 .... 7 E3
Hollin Hall La
Huddersfield HD7 .... 152 C5
Kirkheaton WF14 .... 137 D2
Hollin Hall Rd BD18 .... 54 E6
Hollin Head BD17 .... 38 F4
Hollin Hill Ave LS8 .... 61 C5
Hollin Hill Dr LS8 .... 61 C5
Hollin House La
Clayton West HD8 .... 193 A8
Holmfirth HD7 .... 189 F5
Hollin La
Crigglestone WF4 .... 159 D6
Leeds LS16 .... 59 D7
Ripponden HX6 .... 132 A3
Shipley BD18 .... 55 D6
Sowerby Bridge HX6 .... 112 C2
Wadsworth Moor HX2 .... 90 B5
Hollin Mews LS16 .... 59 D7
Hollin Mount LS16 .... 59 D7
Hollin Park Ave LS8 .... 61 D5
Hollin Park Cres LS8 .... 61 D5
Hollin Park Ct LS28 .... 57 A6
Hollin Park Dr LS28 .... 57 A6
Hollin Park Mount LS8 .... 61 D5
Hollin Park Par LS8 .... 61 C5
Hollin Park Pl LS8 .... 61 D5
Hollin Park Rd Leeds LS8 .... 61 D5
Pudsey LS28 .... 57 A6
Hollin Park Terr LS8 .... 61 D5
Hollin Park View LS8 .... 61 C5
Hollin Rd Leeds LS16 .... 59 D7
Shipley BD18 .... 55 C6
Hollin Rise BD18 .... 55 C6
Hollin St HX6 .... 111 E1
Hollin Terr
Huddersfield HD3 .... 153 C7
Shipley BD18 .... 55 C6
Hollin View LS16 .... 59 D7
Hollin Wood Cl BD18 .... 54 E7
Hollinbank La WF16 .... 117 E5
Hollingbourne Rd LS15 .... 62 F2
Hollings Rd BD8 .... 74 B8
Hollings Sq BD8 .... 74 B8
Hollings St Bradford BD8 .... 74 B8
Shipley BD16 .... 54 B7
Hollings Terr BD8 .... 74 B8
Hollings The LS26 .... 102 B3
Hollingthorpe Ave WF4 .... 159 F3
Hollingthorpe Ct WF4 .... 159 F2
Hollingthorpe Gr WF4 .... 159 E3
Hollingthorpe La WF4 .... 159 E3
Hollingthorpe Rd WF4 .... 159 E2
Hollingwood Ave BD7 .... 73 F4
Hollingwood Ct BD7 .... 73 E3
Hollingwood Dr BD7 .... 73 E4
Hollingwood First Sch BD7 .... 73 E3
Hollingwood Gate LS29 .... 7 F3
Hollingwood La BD7 .... 73 E3
Hollingwood Mount BD7 .... 73 E4
Hollingwood Rise LS29 .... 7 F3
Hollingworth La
Knottingley WF11 .... 127 A4
Todmorden OL14 .... 129 B8
Hollinhirst La WF4 .... 158 F6
Hollinhurst WF10 .... 102 F6
Hollinroyd Rd WF12 .... 139 E8
Hollins HX6 .... 111 C5
Hollins Ave WF13 .... 117 F3
Hollins Bank HX6 .... 112 B4
Hollins Bank La BD20 .... 17 E4
Hollins Cl BD20 .... 17 F2
Hollins Cres 30 HX7 .... 89 A3
Hollins Glen HD7 .... 170 A8
Hollins Gr WF10 .... 102 F6
Hollins Hey Rd HX4 .... 134 D4
Hollins Hill BD17, LS20 .... 39 B6
Hollins La
Halifax, Mixenden HX2 .... 91 C5
Keighley BD20 .... 17 F2
Slaithwaite HD7 .... 169 E6
Sowerby Bridge HX6 .... 111 C5
Sowerby Bridge HX6 .... 112 B5
Hollins Meadow OL14 .... 108 A1
Hollins Mill La HX6 .... 112 B4
Hollins Mount WF9 .... 181 C7
Hollins Pk LS25 .... 83 A1
Hollins Pl
Hebden Bridge HX7 .... 89 A3
13 Todmorden OL14 .... 108 A1
Hollins Rd 2 Batley WF13 .... 117 F2
Todmorden OL14 .... 108 A1
Hollins Row HD7 .... 170 A8
Hollins St OL14 .... 129 B8
Hollins The OL14 .... 108 B6
Hollinwood View BD16 .... 36 D7
Hollis Pl LS3 .... 205 F1
Hollow The HD7 .... 170 D2
Hollowfield Croft BD12 .... 95 B5
Hollowgate HD7 .... 189 A5
Holly App WF5 .... 140 D8
Holly Ave LS16 .... 41 D3
Holly Bank
Ackworth M T WF7 .... 163 E6
Garforth LS25 .... 83 B6
Guiseley LS20 .... 39 D8
Sutton in C BD20 .... 16 C5
Holly Bank Dr HX3 .... 114 D8
Holly Bank Pk HD6 .... 135 F8
Holly Bank Rd
Brighouse HD6 .... 135 F8
Huddersfield HD3 .... 135 C1
Holly Bush Ct LS23 .... 30 E7
Holly Cl Crofton WF4 .... 143 E1
Middleton LS10 .... 99 B4
Holly Cres Crofton WF4 .... 143 E1
Ripponden HX6 .... 132 C3
Holly Ct East Ardsley WF3 .... 119 E6
Guiseley LS20 .... 39 E8
Lofthouse Gate WF1 .... 121 C5
Holly Dene WF5 .... 140 D8
Holly Dr LS16 .... 41 D3
Holly Gr Batley WF17 .... 118 B3
Brierley S72 .... 181 A3
Halifax HX1 .... 202 C2
Huddersfield HD3 .... 135 C1
Holly Hall La BD12 .... 94 C4
Holly House 6 WF10 .... 124 E7
Holly Mede WF5 .... 140 D8
Holly Park Dr BD7 .... 73 E4
Holly Park Gr BD7 .... 73 E4
Holly Rd Boston Spa LS23 .... 30 B8
Huddersfield HD1 .... 153 E4
Holly St Bradford BD6 .... 73 D2
Hemsworth WF9 .... 181 D7
Wakefield WF2 .... 141 F7
Holly Terr HD1 .... 154 B8
Holly Tree Cl LS15 .... 81 E6
Hollybank Ave
Batley WF17 .... 118 C7
Denby Dale HD8 .... 191 C6
Hollybank Ctr WF14 .... 137 E8
Hollybank Gdns BD7 .... 73 F3
Hollybank Gr BD7 .... 73 E3
Hollybank House HD6 .... 135 F8
Hollybank Rd BD7 .... 73 F3
Hollybush Gn LS22 .... 29 C8
Hollycroft Ave S71 .... 179 B3
Hollycroft Ct LS16 .... 42 A3
Hollyfield Ave HD3 .... 153 A7
Hollyns Terr 6 HX4 .... 134 C7
Hollynsmill HX4 .... 134 D7
Hollyoake Ave HD7 .... 170 C8
Hollyshaw Cres LS15 .... 81 C8
Hollyshaw Gr LS15 .... 81 C8
Hollyshaw La LS15 .... 81 C8
Hollyshaw St LS15 .... 81 C8
Hollyshaw Terr 4 LS15 .... 81 C8
Hollyshaw Wlk 5 LS15 .... 62 C1
Hollywell La LS12 .... 209 E4
Holman Ave LS25 .... 82 F5
Holmcliffe Ave HD4 .... 153 F1
Holmclose HD7 .... 188 C2
Holmdale Cres HD7 .... 188 F8
Holmdene Dr WF14 .... 138 A6
Holme Ave HD5 .... 154 E5
Holme Cl Flockton WF4 .... 156 E5
Glusburn BD20 .... 16 D6
Holme Croft WF4 .... 159 F7
Holme Dr HX2 .... 112 B6
Holme Farm La LS23 .... 28 F3
Holme Field WF5 .... 140 C7
Holme Ghyll BD20 .... 16 B6
Holme Gr LS29 .... 21 F7
Holme House La
Halifax HX2 .... 90 E4
Keighley BD22 .... 34 C5
Holme House Rd OL14 .... 86 C1
Holme House St OL15 .... 129 D1
Holme House View HX6 .... 132 D2
Holme Ings LS29 .... 7 C7
Holme Jun & Inf Sch HD7 .... 187 F1
Holme La Bradford BD4 .... 75 F1
Glusburn BD20 .... 16 D6
Halton East BD23 .... 1 D8
Holmfirth HD7 .... 189 E7
Slaithwaite HD7 .... 151 E1
Sutton in C BD20 .... 16 D6
Wakefield WF2 .... 142 B3
Holme Leas Dr WF5 .... 140 C7
Holme Middle Sch BD4 .... 75 D3
Holme Mill La BD22 .... 34 F6
Holme Pk LS29 .... 21 F7
Holme Pl Hebden Bridge HX7 .... 89 A4
Huddersfield HD1 .... 153 D7
Holme Rd HX2 .... 112 B6
Holme St Bradford BD5 .... 74 D4
Brighouse HX3 .... 115 A7
Hebden Bridge HX7 .... 89 A3
Liversedge WF15 .... 117 B4
Oxenhope BD22 .... 51 C2
Todmorden OL14 .... 107 E7
Holme Styes La HD7 .... 199 A8
Holme Terr OL15 .... 129 D1
Holme Top La BD5 .... 74 D4
Holme Top St BD5 .... 74 D4
Holme Valley Bsns Ctr HD4 .... 171 E8
Holme Valley Memorial Hospl HD7 .... 189 A7
Holme Valley Sports Ctr HD7 .... 189 C8
Holme View LS21 .... 25 C6
Holme View Ave HD7 .... 188 D5
Holme View Dr HD7 .... 188 D5
Holme View Pk HD7 .... 188 E5
Holme Villas HD7 .... 169 C6
Holme Way WF5 .... 140 C7
Holme Well Rd LS10 .... 99 E5
Holme Wood Rd
Bradford BD4 .... 75 D3
Keighley BD22 .... 34 F6
Holme Woods La HD7 .... 197 F6
Holme's Terr HX2 .... 202 A4
Holmebank Mews HD7 .... 172 C2
Holmefield First Sch BD4 .... 75 E4
Holmefield Rd HD3 .... 152 E6
Holmefield View BD4 .... 75 F4
Holmes Rd HX6 .... 112 C4
Holmes St Bradford BD1 .... 74 D8
Leeds LS11 .... 211 F2
Holmeside Cl HD4 .... 171 F8
Holmfield HD8 .... 175 F2
Holmfield Ave
Clayton West HD8 .... 175 F2
Wakefield WF2 .... 142 B3
Holmfield Chase WF3 .... 122 B6
Holmfield Cl
Clayton West HD8 .... 175 F2
Pontefract WF8 .... 125 F4
Holmfield Cotts LS26 .... 102 E3
Holmfield Dr
Huddersfield HD7 .... 152 F5
Leeds LS8 .... 44 A1
Holmfield Gdns HX2 .... 92 A5
Holmfield Gr WF2 .... 142 B3
Holmfield Ind Est HX2 .... 92 A7
Holmfield La
Castleford WF11, WF8 .... 125 F5
Wakefield WF2 .... 142 B3
Holmfield Rd
Clayton West HD8 .... 175 F2
Sutton in C BD20 .... 16 D5
Holmfield St BD1 .... 201 A3
Holmfield Terr HD8 .... 175 F2
Holmfirth High Sch HD7 .... 189 C8
Holmfirth Junior & Infants Sch HD7 .... 189 A4
Holmfirth Rd Diggle OL3 .... 185 D1
Holmfirth HD7 .... 189 E7
Meltham HD7 .... 170 E1
Holmroyd Ave BD20 .... 16 D6
Holmsley Ave WF9 .... 182 A2
Holmsley Crest LS26 .... 101 A6
Holmsley Field Ct LS26 .... 101 C6
Holmsley Field La LS26 .... 101 C6
Holmsley Garth LS26 .... 101 B7
Holmsley Gr WF9 .... 182 A2
Holmsley La Rothwell LS26 .... 101 B6
South Kirkby WF9 .... 181 F2
Holmsley Mount WF9 .... 182 A2
Holmsley Wlk LS26 .... 101 B6
Holmwood Ave LS6 .... 59 E8
Holmwood Cl LS6 .... 59 F8
Holmwood Cres LS6 .... 59 F8
Holmwood Dr LS6 .... 59 F8
Holmwood Gr LS6 .... 59 F8
Holmwood Mount LS6 .... 59 F8
Holmwood View LS6 .... 59 E8
Holroyd Hill BD6 .... 74 C1
Holroyd Mill La BD16 .... 36 E8
Holroyd Sq HX4 .... 133 F4
Holroyd St LS7 .... 207 D2
Holsworthy Rd BD4 .... 75 E3
Holt Ave Huddersfield HD2 .... 136 C4
Leeds LS16 .... 42 C5
Holt Cl LS16 .... 42 C4
Holt Cres LS16 .... 41 F5
Holt Dr LS16 .... 42 A5
Holt Farm Cl LS16 .... 42 A5
Holt Farm Rise LS16 .... 41 F5
Holt Garth LS16 .... 42 A5
Holt Gdns Bradford BD10 .... 55 F8
Leeds LS16 .... 42 C5
Holt Head Rd HD7 .... 170 B6
Holt La Holmfirth HD7 .... 188 F6
Leeds LS16 .... 42 A5
Holt Lane Ct LS16 .... 42 B4
Holt Park App LS16 .... 42 A5
Holt Park Ave LS16 .... 42 A5
Holt Park Cl LS16 .... 42 A5
Holt Park District Ctr LS16 .... 41 F5
Holt Park Dr LS16 .... 42 A5
Holt Park Gate LS16 .... 42 A5
Holt Park Gdns LS16 .... 42 A5
Holt Park Gn LS16 .... 42 A5
Holt Park Gr LS16 .... 41 F5
Holt Park Grange LS16 .... 42 A5
Holt Park La LS16 .... 42 A5
Holt Park Rd LS16 .... 42 A5
Holt Park Rise LS16 .... 42 A5
Holt Park Vale LS16 .... 42 A5
Holt Park Way LS16 .... 42 A5
Holt Rd LS16 .... 42 A5
Holt Rise LS16 .... 42 A5
Holt St OL15 .... 129 D2
Holt The BD18 .... 55 C8
Holt Vale LS16 .... 42 A5
Holt View LS16 .... 41 F5
Holt Way LS16 .... 42 A5
Holt Wlk LS16 .... 42 A5
Holtby Gr HX3 .... 115 A7
Holtdale App LS16 .... 41 F5
Holtdale Ave LS16 .... 41 F5
Holtdale Cl LS16 .... 41 F5
Holtdale Croft LS16 .... 41 F5
Holtdale Dr LS16 .... 41 F5
Holtdale Fold LS16 .... 41 F5
Holtdale Garth LS16 .... 41 F5
Holtdale Gdns LS16 .... 41 F5
Holtdale Gn LS16 .... 41 F5
Holtdale Gr LS16 .... 41 F5
Holtdale Lawn LS16 .... 41 F5
Holtdale Pl LS16 .... 41 F5
Holtdale Rd LS16 .... 41 F5
Holtdale View LS16 .... 41 F5
Holtdale Way LS16 .... 41 F5
Holts La BD14 .... 73 B5
Holts Terr HX3 .... 113 D4
Holy Family RC Sch LS12 .... 210 A3
Holy Family Sch The BD20 .... 18 B1
Holy Family & St Michaels RC Jun & Inf Sch WF8 .... 126 A1
Holy Name Prim Sch LS16 .... 42 A3
Holy Rood La LS25 .... 104 E8
Holy Rosary & St Anne's RC Prim Sch LS7 .... 207 D3
Holy Trinity C of E First Sch BD16 .... 37 A2
Holy Trinity C of E Jun & Inf Sch WF5 .... 140 D6
Holy Trinity CE Infants Sch HX1 .... 203 D2
Holy Trinity CE Senior Sch HX2 .... 92 A6
Holy Trinity Junior Sch HX1 .... 203 D2
Holy Trinity Primary Sch LS16 .... 41 D5
Holybrook Ave BD10 .... 56 D6
Holycroft First Sch BD21 .... 35 B6
Holycroft St BD21 .... 35 B6
Holyoake Ave Batley WF17 .... 118 A5
Bingley BD16 .... 36 F1
Holyoake St OL14 .... 86 A1
Holyoake Terr
Horbury WF4 .... 140 E1
Slaithwaite HD7 .... 152 D1
Holyrood Cres WF6 .... 122 F4
Holywell Ash La BD8 .... 55 D1
Holywell Dene WF10 .... 125 A6
Holywell Gdns WF10 .... 125 A6
Holywell Gr WF10 .... 125 A6
Holywell Green Junior & Infant Schs HX4 .... 134 B4
Holywell Halt BD23 .... 1 B7
Holywell La
Castleford WF10 .... 125 B6
Thorner LS17 .... 44 D5
Holywell Mount WF10 .... 125 B6
Home Farm Ct DN5 .... 195 D5
Home Lea LS26 .... 100 D7
Home Lea Dr LS26 .... 100 D6
Home View Terr BD8 .... 55 B1
Homefield Ave LS27 .... 98 A2
Homepaddock House LS22 .... 13 F6
Homes The HD2 .... 136 F3
Homestead Dr WF2 .... 141 F6
Homestead The WF16 .... 117 E4
Honey Hole Cl OL14 .... 108 B4
Honey Hole Rd OL14 .... 108 B4
Honey Holme La BB10 .... 85 A7
Honeysuckle Cl WF2 .... 141 E7
Honeysuckle Dr WF12 .... 139 D3
Honley C of E (Controlled) Infant Sch HD7 .... 171 F5
Honley C of E (Controlled) Junior Sch HD7 .... 171 F4
Honley High Sch & Coll HD7 .... 172 A5
Honley Rd HD4 .... 172 D6
Honley Sq WF4 .... 141 A1
Honley Sta HD7 .... 172 B5
Honoria St HD1 .... 136 A1
Hood St Huddersfield HD4 .... 171 F8
South Elmsall WF9 .... 182 E1
Hooton Cres WF4 .... 162 A1
Hooton Pagnell C of E Sch DN5 .... 195 C5
Hooton Rd DN5 .... 195 F4
Hoowood La HD7 .... 187 E3
Hopbine Ave BD5 .... 74 E2
Hopbine Rd BD5 .... 74 E2
Hope Ave Bradford BD5 .... 74 C2
Shipley BD18 .... 55 D8
Hope Bldgs 11 OL14 .... 108 C5
Hope Hall St HX1 .... 203 E2
Hope Hall Terr 6 HX1 .... 203 E2
Hope Hill View BD16 .... 54 A7
Hope La BD17 .... 38 B3
Hope Pl BD21 .... 35 B5
Hope Rd LS9 .... 212 A4
Hope St Castleford WF10 .... 104 C2
Dewsbury WF13 .... 118 C1
Halifax HX1 .... 203 D3
21 Hebden Bridge HX7 .... 89 A3
Huddersfield HD3 .... 153 B5
Huddersfield, Folly Hall HD3 .... 154 A4
manton WF6 .... 144 A8
Mapplewell S75 .... 178 C1
Morley LS27 .... 98 A4
Ossett WF5 .... 140 F3
Ryhill WF4 .... 180 C8
Sowerby Bridge HX6 .... 112 C3
Wakefield WF1 .... 216 B3
Hope St E 10 WF10 .... 124 D8
Hope St W WF10 .... 124 C7
Hope Terr HD7 .... 152 D3
Hope View BD18 .... 55 D7
Hopefield Chase LS26 .... 100 B4
Hopefield Cl LS26 .... 100 B4
Hopefield Cres LS26 .... 100 B4
Hopefield Ct
East Ardsley WF3 .... 120 C7
Rothwell LS26 .... 100 B4
Hopefield Dr LS26 .... 100 B4
Hopefield Gdns LS26 .... 100 B4
Hopefield Gn LS26 .... 100 B4
Hopefield Gr LS26 .... 100 B4

Hopefield Mews LS26 .... 100 B4
Hopefield Pl LS26 .... 100 B4
Hopefield View LS26 .... 100 B4
Hopefield Way Bradford BD5 75 B1
Rothwell LS26 .... 100 B4
Hopefield Wlk LS26 .... 100 B4
Hopes Farm Mount 3 LS10 99 F7
Hopes Farm Rd LS10 .... 99 F7
Hopes Farm View LS10 ..... 100 A7
Hopetown Wlk WF6 .... 123 C3
Hopewell Pl 12 LS6 .... 205 E2
Hopewell St WF17 .... 118 B6
Hopewell Terr LS25 .... 83 B1
Hopewell View LS10 .... 99 D5
Hopewell Way WF4 .... 159 E5
Hopkin St BD4 .... 75 E1
Hopkinson Dr BD4 .... 95 C8
Hopkinson Rd HD2 .... 136 B4
Hopkinson St HX3 .... 91 F3
Hopkinsons Bldgs HX3 .... 91 F3
Hopps's Rd BD20 .... 16 C7
Hopton Ave Bradford BD4 ..... 75 B1
Mirfield WF14 .... 137 E2
Hopton Dr WF14 .... 137 E2
Hopton Hall La WF14 .... 137 F1
Hopton Jun & Inf Sch
WF14 .... 137 F4
Hopton La WF14 .... 137 F2
Hopton Mews LS12 .... 209 E3
Hopton New Rd WF14 .... 138 A3
Hopwood Bank LS18 .... 41 C2
Hopwood Cl LS18 .... 41 C2
Hopwood Gr WF10 .... 125 B7
Hopwood La HX1 .... 202 C2
Hopwood Rd LS18 .... 41 C2
Horace Waller VC Par
WF12 .... 119 A2
Horbury Bridge C of E
Jun & Inf Sch WF4 .... 140 E1
Horbury Jun & Inf Sch
WF4 .... 141 C1
Horbury Mews WF4 .... 140 F2
Horbury Rd Ossett WF5 .... 140 E3
Wakefield WF2 .... 141 E3
Horbury Sch WF4 .... 141 C1
Horley Green La HX3 .... 92 E2
Horley Green Rd HX3 .... 113 E8
Horn Cote La HD7 .... 190 A6
Horn Croft S75 .... 193 F5
Horn La Holmfirth HD7 .... 190 A6
Ingbirchworth S36 .... 191 B1
Silsden BD20 .... 5 C4
Hornbeam Ave WF2 .... 142 A8
Hornbeam Cl BD15 .... 53 F4
Hornbeam Gn WF8 .... 125 F1
Hornbeam Way LS14 .... 62 C8
Hornby St HX1 .... 202 B1
Hornby Terr HX1 .... 202 B1
Horncastle St 2 BD19 .... 116 E7
Horncastle View WF4 .... 162 D2
Horne St Halifax HX1 .... 203 D3
Wakefield WF2 .... 142 C4
Horner Ave WF17 .... 117 F6
Horner Cres WF17 .... 117 F6
Hornes La S75 .... 178 C1
Hornsea Dr BD15 .... 53 C4
Horse Bank Dr HD4 .... 153 E3
Horse Croft La HD8 .... 174 B3
Horse Fair WF8 .... 125 D1
Horse Fair Flats WF8 .... 125 D1
Horse Pond La HD3 .... 152 A7
Horsefair LS22 .... 13 E5
Horsehold La HX7 .... 88 E2
Horsehold Rd HX7 .... 88 E2
Horsfall St Halifax HX1 .... 202 C1
Morley LS27 .... 97 F6
Todmorden OL14 .... 108 E6
Horsforth Featherbank
Infants Sch LS18 .... 58 B7
Horsforth Golf Course
LS18 .... 40 F5
Horsforth New Rd LS13 .... 57 E6
Horsforth Sch & Further
Education Ctr LS18 .... 41 B1
Horsforth St Margaret's
C of E Primary Sch LS18 .. 41 B1
Horsforth Sta LS18 .... 41 C3
Horsham Ct BD22 .... 34 E5
Horsham Rd BD4 .... 75 E2
Horsley St 5 BD6 .... 74 C1
Horsman St BD4 .... 75 E1
Horton Bank Ctry Pk
BD7 .... 73 D2
Horton Bank Top First Sch
BD7 .... 73 E2
Horton Cl LS13 .... 57 F4
Horton Garth LS13 .... 57 F4
Horton Grange Rd BD7 .... 74 B5
Horton Hall Cl BD5 .... 74 D5
Horton Park Ave BD5, BD7 ... 74 C5
Horton Pl HX2 .... 91 F8
Horton Rise LS13 .... 57 F4
Horton St Batley WF16 .... 117 D3
Halifax HX1 .... 203 F2
Ossett WF5 .... 140 C6
Hospital La LS16 .... 41 F3
Hospital Rd BD20 .... 19 A1
Hostingley La WF12 .... 140 B2
Hothfield St BD20 .... 5 D1
Hothfield Street Junior Sch
BD20 .... 5 D1
Hough HX3 .... 93 A1
Hough End Ave LS13 .... 58 D1
Hough End Cl LS13 .... 58 D1
Hough End Cres LS13 .... 58 C1
Hough End Ct 1 LS13 .... 58 D1
Hough End Garth LS13 .... 58 C1
Hough End Gdns 2 LS13 .... 58 D1
Hough End La LS13 .... 58 C1
Hough Gr 16 LS13 .... 58 C2
Hough La LS13 .... 58 C2
Hough Side Cl LS28 .... 77 B7
Hough Side High Sch
LS13 .... 77 B8
Hough Side La LS28 .... 77 A7
Hough Side Rd LS28 .... 77 A7
Hough Terr 17 LS13 .... 58 C2
Hough Top LS13 .... 77 B8
Hough Tree Rd LS13 .... 77 C8
Hough Tree Terr LS13 .... 77 C8
Houghley Ave LS12 .... 58 F2
Houghley Cl LS13 .... 58 E2
Houghley Cres LS12 .... 58 F3
Houghley La LS12, LS13 .... 58 E1
Houghley Pl LS12 .... 58 F2
Houghley Rd LS12 .... 58 F2
Houghley Sq LS12 .... 58 F2
Houghton Ave WF11 .... 126 B5
Houghton Pl BD1 .... 201 A4
Houghton Rd S72 .... 194 A1
Houghton St HD6 .... 115 B3
Houghton Twrs 10 HX6 .... 112 B4
Houghton's Almshouses 1
HD5 .... 154 F3
Houldsworth Ave WF16 .... 117 E7
Hoults La HX4 .... 134 C8
Houndhill La WF7 .... 145 F5
House Grove Dr HD8 .... 175 E2
Hovingham Ave LS8 .... 208 A4
Hovingham Gr LS8 .... 208 A4
Hovingham Mount LS8 .... 208 A4
Hovingham Primary Sch
LS8 .... 208 A4
Hovingham Terr LS8 .... 208 A4
Howard Ave
Huddersfield HD3 .... 153 C7
Leeds LS15 .... 80 F7
Howard CE Jun & Inf Sch
WF7 .... 164 B7
Howard Cres WF4 .... 159 E6
Howard Ct LS15 .... 80 F7
Howard Pk BD19 .... 116 E7
Howard Pl WF17 .... 118 C3
Howard Rd HD3 .... 153 C7
Howard St Batley WF17 .... 118 C3
Bradford BD5 .... 201 A2
Halifax HX1 .... 202 C4
Ossett WF5 .... 140 D7
Wakefield WF1 .... 216 B3
Howard Villas BD19 .... 116 E7
Howard Way
Littleborough OL15 .... 129 C1
Meltham HD7 .... 170 E1
Howards Dean BD22 .... 51 D8
Howarth Ave BD2 .... 56 A5
Howarth Cres BD2 .... 56 A5
Howarth La HD1 .... 153 E3
Howarth Pl LS7 .... 206 C1
Howbeck Ave BD20 .... 19 A1
Howbeck Dr BD20 .... 36 A8
Howcans La HX3 .... 92 B5
Howden Ave
Adwick Le S DN6 .... 184 E1
Keighley BD20 .... 18 A2
Howden Cl Bradford BD4 .... 75 F1
Huddersfield HD4 .... 152 F2
Mapplewell S75 .... 177 F1
Howden Clough High Sch
WF17 .... 97 B1
Howden Clough Ind Est
WF17 .... 97 C3
Howden Clough Rd LS27 .... 97 D3
Howden Gdns LS6 .... 205 E2
Howden Pl LS6 .... 205 E2
Howden Rd BD20 .... 5 F1
Howden Way WF1 .... 142 E6
Howdenbrook HX3 .... 93 E7
Howell La DN5 .... 194 A4
Howell Wood Country Pk
WF9, DN5 .... 194 A7
Howes La HX3 .... 92 F2
Howgate BD10 .... 56 C8
Howgate Rd HD7 .... 169 F8
Howgill Gn BD6 .... 94 A6
Howlett Cross LS26 .... 100 B4
Howley Hall Golf Course
LS27 .... 118 F8
Howley Mill La WF17 .... 118 D7
Howley Park Cl LS27 .... 97 F2
Howley Park Rd LS27 .... 97 F2
Howley Park Rd E LS27 .... 98 A1
Howley Park Trad Est
LS27 .... 97 F2
Howley St WF17 .... 118 D6
Howley Wlk WF17 .... 118 E6
Howroyd La
Dewsbury WF12 .... 156 E7
Ripponden HX4 .... 133 B4
Howroyd's Yd WF5 .... 119 C1
Howson Cl LS20 .... 22 F1
Hoxton Mount LS11 .... 213 F3
Hoxton St BD8 .... 74 A8
Hoylake Ave HD2 .... 135 F3
Hoyland Rd WF2 .... 160 B5
Hoyland Terr WF9 .... 182 A2
Hoyle Court Ave BD17 .... 38 E3
Hoyle Court Dr BD17 .... 38 E3
Hoyle Court First Sch
BD17 .... 38 E2
Hoyle Court Rd BD17 .... 38 E3
Hoyle Fold BD22 .... 34 F5
Hoyle House Fold HD7 .... 152 D1
Hoyle Ing HD7 .... 152 D1
Hoyle Ing Rd BD13 .... 72 F6
Hoyle Mill Rd WF9 .... 163 D2
Hubberton Green Rd HX6 .... 111 C2
Hubert St Bradford BD3 .... 75 B6
Halifax HX2 .... 112 D7
Huddersfield HD3 .... 134 E1
Hud Hill HX3 .... 93 B4
Huddersfield Gram Sch
HD3 .... 153 C6
Huddersfield New Coll
HD3 .... 152 F7
Huddersfield Rd
Batley WF17 .... 117 E8
Bradford BD12 .... 94 C4
Brighouse HD6 .... 136 B7
Denshaw OL3 .... 167 A4
Dewsbury, Ravensthorpe
WF13 .... 138 D4
Dewsbury, West Town
WF13 .... 139 B7
Elland HX5 .... 135 A4
Halifax HX3 .... 113 C4
Holmfirth HD7 .... 189 A6
Holmfirth, New Mill HD7 .... 189 E7
Honley HD7 .... 172 A5
Huddersfield HD3 .... 135 A4
Ingbirchworth S30 .... 191 E1
Kirkburton HD8 .... 174 A4
Meltham HD7 .... 171 A5
Shepley HD8 .... 174 A4
Skelmanthorpe HD8 .... 174 D2
West Bretton WF4 .... 177 A6
Huddersfield Royal Infmy
HD3 .... 153 C8
Huddersfield Sta HD1 .... 154 A6
Huddersfield Tech Coll
Huddersfield HD4 .... 153 F2
Huddersfield Tech Coll
(Annexe) HD1 .... 153 F7
Huddersfield Tech Coll
(Brunel Ho) HD2 .... 136 E2
Huddersfield Tech Coll
HD1 .... 154 A6
Huddleston Ct WF12 .... 139 F8
Hudroyd HD5 .... 154 F3
Hudson Ave Bradford BD7 .... 74 B3
Notton WF4 .... 179 B6
Hudson Cl 1 Bradford BD7 ... 74 B3
Wetherby LS22 .... 13 E5
Hudson Cres BD7 .... 74 B3
Hudson Gdns BD7 .... 74 B4
Hudson Gr LS9 .... 208 A1
Hudson Mews LS23 .... 30 E7
Hudson Mill Rd HX7 .... 88 C5
Hudson Pl LS9 .... 208 A1
Hudson Rd LS9 .... 208 A1
Hudson St Bradford BD3 .... 75 D7
Leeds LS9 .... 208 A1
2 Pudsey LS28 .... 57 D1
Todmorden OL14 .... 86 C1
Hudson The BD12 .... 94 C3
Hudson's Terr 4 LS19 .... 40 C7
Hudswell Rd LS10 .... 215 D4
Hudswell St WF1 .... 142 E3
Huggan Row 5 LS28 .... 76 F7
Hugh Gaitskell Middle Sch
LS11 .... 213 F2
Hugh St WF10 .... 124 D7
Hughenden View LS27 .... 98 A6
Hughendon Dr BD13 .... 73 A6
Hughendon Wlk BD13 .... 73 A6
Hugill St BD13 .... 72 D6
Hulbert Croft HD5 .... 154 F4
Hulbert St BD16 .... 37 A2
Hull St LS27 .... 98 B4
Hullen Rd HX5 .... 134 D6
Hullenedge Gdns HX5 .... 134 D6
Hullenedge La HX5 .... 134 D6
Hullenedge Rd HX5 .... 134 E6
Hullett Cl HX7 .... 89 F1
Hullett Dr HX7 .... 89 F1
Hulme Sq WF10 .... 104 D1
Hulme St HX6 .... 112 B3
Humber Cl Castleford WF10 .... 125 B8
Slaithwaite HD7 .... 152 D1
Humboldt St BD1 .... 201 D3
Hume Crest 7 WF17 .... 118 C5
Humley Rd WF2 .... 160 B5
Hundhill La WF8 .... 146 D2
Hungate La LS26 .... 122 E8
Hunger Hill Halifax HX1 .... 203 E2
Ilkley LS29 .... 8 C7
Morley LS27 .... 98 A3
Hunger Hills Ave LS18 .... 41 A1
Hunger Hills Dr LS18 .... 41 A1
Hungerford Rd HD3 .... 153 D8
Hunslet Bsns Pk LS10 .... 212 B1
Hunslet Carr Primary Sch
LS10 .... 215 E2
Hunslet Green Ret Ctr
LS10 .... 215 D3
Hunslet Green Way LS10 .. 215 D4
Hunslet Hall Rd LS11 .... 214 B4
Hunslet Hall Sh Ctr LS11 .... 214 B4
Hunslet La LS10 .... 211 F2
Hunslet Moor Primary Sch
LS11 .... 214 C3
Hunslet Rd Leeds LS10 .... 211 F2
Leeds, Pottery Field LS10 .... 212 A1
Hunslet St Joseph's
Primary Sch LS10 .... 215 E4
Hunslet St Mary's CE
Primary Sch LS10 .... 215 E3
Hunslet Trad Est LS10 .... 215 F3
Hunston Ave HD3 .... 153 B7
Hunsworth La
Birkenshaw BD19, BD4 .... 95 E4
Cleckheaton BD19 .... 95 E4
Hunt Ct WF2 .... 141 E6
Hunt St Castleford WF10 .... 124 B8
Castleford, Castleford Ings
WF10 .... 103 D1
Hunt Yd 3 BD7 .... 74 A4
Hunter Hill Rd HX2 .... 91 A5
Hunters Ct BD9 .... 54 C4
Hunters Gn BD13 .... 52 E7
Hunters La OL14 .... 107 F6
Hunters Meadow BD20 .... 5 E2
Hunters Park Ave BD14 .... 73 E5
Hunters Wlk LS22 .... 13 E7
Huntingdon Ave HD2 .... 136 F4
Huntingdon Rd HD6 .... 115 C1
Huntock Pl HD6 .... 114 F5
Huntsman Fold WF2 .... 141 D6
Huntsman's Cl HD4 .... 171 D8
Huntsman's Way WF9 .... 164 E2
Huntsmans Cl Bingley BD16 .. 37 C5
Keighley BD20 .... 35 A8
Huntwick Ave WF7 .... 145 C4
Huntwick Cres WF7 .... 145 B4
Huntwick Dr WF7 .... 145 B4
Huntwick La
Featherstone WF7 .... 145 A5
West Hardwick WF7 .... 144 F3
Huntwick Rd WF7 .... 145 C4
Hurst Knowle HD5 .... 155 A4
Hurst La WF14 .... 138 B4
Hurst Rd HX7 .... 89 A4
Hurstville Ave BD4 .... 95 F6
Hurstwood HD2 .... 136 E4
Husler Gr LS7 .... 207 D3
Husler Pl LS7 .... 207 D3
Hustings The 3 WF15 .... 117 A4
Hustler St BD3 .... 56 A1
Hustler's Row LS6 .... 59 D8
Hustlergate BD1 .... 201 B3
Hutchinson La 1 HD6 .... 115 B2
Hutchinson's Pl LS5 .... 59 A3
Hutson St BD5 .... 74 D4
Hutton Dr Batley WF16 .... 117 E4
South Elmsall WF9 .... 183 A4
Hutton Middle Sch BD2 .... 56 C5
Hutton Rd BD5 .... 74 C2
Hutton Terr Bradford BD2 .... 56 D5
Pudsey LS28 .... 76 E7
Huxley Mount BD2 .... 56 C5
Hydale Ct Bradford BD12 .... 94 C6
Keighley BD21 .... 35 E5
Hyde Park Cl LS6 .... 205 F2
Hyde Park Cnr LS6 .... 205 F3
Hyde Park Pl LS6 .... 205 F3
Hyde Park Rd Halifax HX1 .. 202 C1
Leeds LS6 .... 205 F2
Hyde Park St HX1 .... 202 C1
Hyde Park Terr LS6 .... 205 F3
Hyde Pk Halifax HX1 .... 202 C2
Wakefield WF1 .... 142 E6
Hyde Pl LS2 .... 206 A1
Hyde St Bradford BD10 .... 39 B1
Leeds LS2 .... 206 A1
Hyde Terr LS2 .... 206 A1
Hydro Cl LS29 .... 8 F3
Hyman Wlk WF9 .... 183 A4
Hyne Ave BD4 .... 75 C1
Hyrst Garth WF17 .... 118 B2
Hyrst Wlk WF17 .... 118 C3
Hyrstlands Rd WF17 .... 118 C3
Hyrstmount Junior Sch
WF17 .... 118 C3

Ibbetson Cl LS27 .... 98 A7
Ibbetson Croft LS27 .... 98 A7
Ibbetson Ct LS27 .... 98 A7
Ibbetson Dr LS27 .... 98 A7
Ibbetson Oval LS27 .... 98 A7
Ibbetson Rd LS27 .... 98 A7
Ibbetson Rise LS27 .... 98 A7
Ibbotroyd Ave OL14 .... 108 A7
Ibbotson Flats 6 HD1 .... 154 B6
Ibbottson St WF1 .... 142 F3
Ida & Robert Arthington
Hospl LS16 .... 41 F2
Ida St Bradford BD5 .... 74 C3
Leeds LS10 .... 80 A2
Iddesleigh St BD4 .... 75 D6
Ideal L Ctr BD5 .... 74 D1
Idle CE First Sch BD10 .... 39 B1
Idle Rd BD2 .... 56 B3
Idlecroft Rd BD10 .... 56 B8
Idlethorp Way BD10 .... 56 C7
Ilbert Ave BD4 .... 75 C1
Ilford St LS27 .... 98 B4
Ilkley Golf Course LS29 .... 7 D6
Ilkley Grammar Sch LS29 .... 8 C3
Ilkley Hall Mews LS29 .... 8 B3
Ilkley Hall Pk LS29 .... 8 B3
Ilkley Middle Sch LS29 .... 8 E4
Ilkley Rd Addingham LS29 .... 7 B6
Burley in W LS29 .... 9 D3
Keighley BD20 .... 19 C5
Otley LS21 .... 22 F7
Ilkley Sta LS29 .... 8 B4
Illingworth Ave Halifax HX2 .. 91 E7
Normanton WF6 .... 122 E3
Illingworth Cl Halifax HX2 .... 91 E7
Yeadon LS19 .... 40 C5
Illingworth Cres HX2 .... 91 E7
Illingworth Dr HX2 .... 91 E7
Illingworth Gdns HX2 .... 91 E7
Illingworth Gr HX2 .... 91 E7
Illingworth Rd
Bradford BD12 .... 94 F4
Halifax HX2 .... 91 E7
Illingworth St WF5 .... 140 D5
Illingworth Way HX2 .... 91 E7
Imperial Arc 23 HD1 .... 154 A6
Imperial Ave WF2 .... 120 F2
Imperial Rd HD1, HD3 .... 153 D7
Inchfield Rd OL14 .... 129 A8
Incline The HX3 .... 113 E8
Independent St BD5 .... 74 C3
Industrial Ave WF17 .... 96 D1
Industrial Rd HX6 .... 112 B4
Industrial St Bacup OL13 .... 106 A2
Bingley BD16 .... 36 F3
Brighouse HD6 .... 115 B3
13 Brighouse, Scholes
BD19 .... 115 F8
Horbury WF4 .... 159 C8
Huddersfield HD4 .... 154 A4
Keighley BD22 .... 35 A6
Leeds LS9 .... 207 F1
Liversedge WF15 .... 116 E4
Todmorden OL14 .... 108 C5
Wakefield WF1 .... 216 B3
Industrial Terr Halifax HX1 .... 203 D1
Huddersfield HD5 .... 155 A5
Industry St
3 Thornton BD13 .... 72 E6
Todmorden OL14 .... 108 A1
Infirmary Rd WF13 .... 118 B1
Infirmary St Bradford BD1 .. 201 A3
Leeds LS1 .... 211 E4
Ing Field BD12 .... 95 A4
Ing Head HD7 .... 151 E1
Ing Head La HD4 .... 173 A2
Ing Head Terr HX3 .... 93 B4
Ing La HD4 .... 154 A3
Ing St BD3 .... 75 D7
Ingdale Dr HD7 .... 189 B6
Ingfield Ave
Huddersfield HD5 .... 154 D6
Ossett WF5 .... 140 E6
Ingham Cl Halifax HX2 .... 91 F8
Mirfield WF14 .... 138 C4
Ingham Croft WF14 .... 138 C4
Ingham Garth WF14 .... 138 C5
Ingham La HX2 .... 71 E1
Ingham Rd WF12 .... 139 D3
Ingham St LS10 .... 212 A1
Ingham's Ave LS28 .... 76 B8
Ingham's View LS28 .... 76 B8
Inghams Ct 23 HX3 .... 92 A1
Inghams Terr LS28 .... 76 B8
Inghead Gdns HX3 .... 93 B4
Ingle Ave LS27 .... 97 F6
Ingle Cres LS27 .... 98 A5
Ingle Ct LS27 .... 97 F6
Ingle Dean HX7 .... 88 D2
Ingle Gr LS27 .... 98 A5
Ingle Row LS7 .... 204 A2
Ingleborough Dr LS27 .... 98 C3
Inglebrook Prep Sch
WF8 .... 125 D1
Ingleby Pl BD7 .... 74 A6
Ingleby Rd BD7, BD8 .... 74 A7
Ingleby St BD7 .... 74 A7
Ingleby Way LS10 .... 99 E7
Ingledew Cres LS8 .... 44 B2
Ingledew Ct LS17 .... 43 D4
Ingledew Dr LS8 .... 44 B2
Ingleton Cl 6 LS11 .... 214 B3
Ingleton Dr LS15 .... 80 E7
Ingleton Gr 14 LS11 .... 214 B3
Ingleton Pl LS11 .... 214 B3
Ingleton Rd HD4 .... 154 B2
Ingleton St LS11 .... 214 B3
Inglewood S75 .... 178 A1
Inglewood App LS14 .... 62 B3
Inglewood Ave HD2 .... 135 C1
Inglewood Dr Leeds LS14 .... 62 B3
Otley LS21 .... 22 F7
Inglewood Pl LS14 .... 62 B3
Ingram Cl LS11 .... 210 C1
Ingram Cres
Knottingley WF11 .... 126 D3
Leeds LS11 .... 213 F4
Ingram Ct 1 LS11 .... 211 D1
Ingram Gdns LS11 .... 210 C1
Ingram Par LS26 .... 100 E5
Ingram Rd LS11 .... 210 C1
Ingram Road Primary Sch
LS11 .... 210 C1
Ingram Row LS11 .... 211 E2
Ingram Sq 18 HX1 .... 202 C1
Ingram St Halifax HX1 .... 202 C1
Keighley BD21 .... 35 B3
Leeds LS11 .... 211 E2
Ingram View LS11 .... 210 C1
Ingrow First Sch BD21 .... 35 A4
Ingrow La BD21, BD22 .... 35 A4
Ingrow West Sta BD21 .... 35 B4
Ings Ave LS20 .... 22 D2
Ings Cl Ryhill WF4 .... 162 C1
South Kirkby WF9 .... 182 D3
Ings Cres Dewsbury WF12 .... 139 C2
Guiseley LS20 .... 22 C1
Leeds LS9 .... 80 B7
Liversedge WF15 .... 117 B4
Ings Croft HX3 .... 93 C6
Ings Ct LS20 .... 22 C1
Ings Dr Low Bradley BD20 .... 4 C5
Mickletown LS26 .... 102 E3
Ings Holt WF9 .... 182 D4
Ings La Castleford WF10 .... 103 F2
Cononley BD20 .... 4 A4
Dewsbury WF12 .... 139 C2
Guiseley LS20 .... 22 C2
Ledston WF10 .... 103 E4
Low Bradley BD20 .... 4 C5
Thorp Arch LS23 .... 31 A8
Wighill LS24 .... 31 F8
Ings Mere Ct WF11 .... 105 A4
Ings Mill Ave HD8 .... 175 F3

Ings Mill Dr HD8 175 F2
Ings Mill Yd WF16 117 D4
Ings Rd Batley WF17 118 A6
Batley, Heckmondwike WF16 117 D4
Dewsbury WF13 118 E1
Hemsworth WF9 163 B1
Huddersfield HD5 155 A4
Leeds LS9 80 B8
Liversedge WF15 117 B5
Steeton BD20 17 B7
Wakefield WF1 216 B1
Ings The Brighouse HX3 115 A6
Clayton West HD8 175 F2
Ings View Castleford WF10 125 B8
Mickletown LS26 102 E3
Ings Villa WF15 117 C2
Ings Way Bradford BD8 73 E8
Ingbirchworth S36 191 D1
Lepton HD8 155 F3
Silsden BD20 17 F8
Ings Way W HD8 155 E3
Ings Wlk WF9 182 D3
Ingswell Ave WF4 179 A7
Ingswell Dr WF4 178 F7
Ingwell Ct 3 WF1 216 C2
Ingwell St WF1 216 C2
Ingwell Terr BD19 116 E7
Inholmes La LS24 15 C4
Inkerman Ct HD8 192 A5
Inkerman St
6 Bacup OL13 106 A2
Bradford, Cutler Heights BD4 75 D4
Bradford, Ravenscliffe BD2 56 D4
Inkerman Way HD8 191 F5
Inner Hey HD7 169 A4
Inner Hey Yd HD7 169 A4
Inner Ring Rd LS1, LS2 206 C1
Innings The BD10 56 A8
Institute Rd BD2 56 C5
Institute St BD20 16 C6
Intake HD7 152 E5
Intake Cl WF3 121 F5
Intake Gr BD2 56 C2
Intake High Sch LS13 58 A4
Intake La
Lofthouse Gate WF3 121 F5
Meltham HD4 170 F7
Middleton LS10 99 C3
Ossett WF5 140 E5
Pudsey LS13 57 F3
Slaithwaite HD7 169 F4
Steeton BD20 17 B4
Thorner LS14 45 D3
Woolley WF4 177 E8
Yeadon LS19 40 D3
Intake Mount LS10 99 C4
Intake Rd Bradford BD2 56 C2
Pudsey LS28 77 A8
Slaithwaite HD7 151 C2
Intake Sq LS10 99 C3
Intake Terr BD2 56 C2
Intake The LS25 83 B1
Intake View LS10 99 C3
Intercity Way LS13 58 A1
Invargarry Cl LS25 83 B8
Inverness Rd LS25 83 B7
Invertrees Ave LS19 40 C4
Iona Pl 8 HX3 92 B2
Iona St HX3 92 C1
Ireland Cres LS16 41 F3
Ireland St BD16 36 E3
Ireland Terr BD16 36 E3
Ireland Wood Primary Sch LS16 42 A4
Ireton St BD7 74 B6
Iron Row LS29 9 F1
Iron St BD19 116 C7
Ironwood App LS14 62 A3
Ironwood Cres LS14 62 A3
Ironwood View LS14 62 A4
Irvin Terr WF10 124 C7
Irving St HX1 202 B1
Irving Terr BD14 73 C3
Irwell St BD4 75 A5
Irwin App LS15 80 F7
Irwin Ave WF1 142 F7
Irwin Cres WF1 142 E7
Irwin St LS28 57 D2
Isaac St BD8 74 B8
Island The WF11 127 A5
Island View WF12 139 B6
Isles St BD8 73 F8
Ivanhoe Rd BD7 74 B5
Ive House La HX2 111 E8
Ivegate Bradford BD1 201 B3
Yeadon LS19 40 B7
Iver Way BD18 55 A7
Ives St BD17 55 B8
Iveson App LS16 41 F2
Iveson Cl LS16 41 F2
Iveson Cres LS16 41 F2
Iveson Ct LS16 41 F2
Iveson Dr LS16 41 F2
Iveson Garth LS16 42 A2
Iveson Gdns LS16 41 F2
Iveson Gn LS16 41 F2
Iveson Gr LS16 41 F2
Iveson Lawn LS16 42 A2
Iveson Primary Sch LS16 42 A2
Iveson Rd LS16 41 F2
Iveson Rise LS16 42 A2
Ivory St LS10 211 F1
Ivy Ave LS9 80 B8
Ivy Bank Ct 1 BD17 38 D2
Ivy Bank La BD22 51 C6
Ivy Chase LS28 77 B7
Ivy Cl WF1 142 E8
Ivy Cotts S71 179 D4
Ivy Cres Brighouse HX3 114 E7
Leeds LS9 80 A7
10 Leeds LS9 80 A8
Ivy Ct LS7 204 A2
Ivy Farm Cl S71 179 D1
Ivy Garth LS7 204 A2
Ivy Gdns WF10 125 D5
Ivy Gr Leeds LS9 80 B8
Shipley BD18 54 E7
Wakefield WF1 142 E8
Ivy House Rd BD5 74 E1
Ivy La Boston Spa LS23 30 C7
Bradford BD15 54 A1
Halifax HX2 91 D6
Wakefield WF1 142 E8
Ivy Mount Leeds LS9 80 A8
Slaithwaite HD7 151 F1
Ivy Pl Glusburn BD20 16 D7
Leeds LS13 58 D4
Ivy Rd Keighley BD21 35 E6
Leeds LS9 80 B8
Shipley BD18 54 E7
Ivy St Brighouse HD6 114 F3
Featherstone WF7 145 D6
Halifax HX1 202 C1
Huddersfield, Moldgreen HD4, HD5 154 C5
Huddersfield, Paddock HD4 153 C4
Keighley BD21 35 B8
Leeds LS9 80 A8
Ivy St S Halifax HX1 202 C1
Keighley BD21 35 B3
Ivy Terr Brighouse HD6 114 F3
Brighouse, Lydgate HX3 114 E7
Keighley BD21 35 F6
South Elmsall WF9 183 A3
Ivy View 8 LS9 80 A8
Jacinth Ct HD2 136 C2
Jack Bridge HX7 88 A5
Jack Close Orch S71 179 C4
Jack Field La BD20 16 A4
Jack Hill HD2 136 A1
Jack La Batley WF17 118 D2
Leeds, Mint LS11 211 E1
Leeds, Pottery Field LS10, LS11 212 A1
Jack Royd HX3 91 F2
Jackdaw La LS23 30 C8
Jackie Smart Ct LS7 207 E3
Jackie Smart Rd 1 BD5 74 E4
Jackman Dr LS18 58 D7
Jackroyd La
Huddersfield HD4 154 B2
Mirfield WF14 137 E2
Jackson Ave LS8 204 C3
Jackson Hill La BD13 92 F7
Jackson House WF9 181 D6
Jackson La HX4 133 A5
Jackson Meadows HX4 133 A5
Jackson Pl BD20 16 D4
Jackson Rd LS7 206 C3
Jackson St Bradford BD3 75 A6
Sutton in C BD20 16 D5
Jackson's La
Darrington WF8 165 E7
Dewsbury WF13 139 A1
Low Bradley BD20 4 E5
Jacky La BD22 51 C6
Jacob Kramer Coll LS2 206 B2
Jacob Kramer Coll (Art) LS2 206 B1
Jacob St Bradford BD5 74 D4
Leeds LS2 206 C1
Jacob's Row HD4 153 F3
Jacob's Well BD1 201 B2
Jacob's Well La WF1 216 C3
Jacques Gr BD20 5 F1
Jade Pl HD2 136 C2
Jaggar La HD7 171 F4
Jagger Green Dean HX4 134 B3
Jagger La Emley HD8 174 E7
Huddersfield HD5 155 A8
Jail Rd WF17 117 F5
Jail Yd LS26 100 F5
Jakeman Cl WF3 119 E8
Jakeman Ct WF3 119 E8
Jakeman Dr WF3 119 E8
James Ave Leeds LS8 204 C4
Steeton BD20 17 A5
James Cl LS25 83 A7
James Ct LS22 29 B8
James Duggan Ave WF7 145 D6
James Gate BD1 201 B3
James Gibbs Cl WF7 145 D6
James La HD7 171 A6
James St Batley WF17 118 B4
Birkenshaw BD11 96 A6
Bradford BD15 54 C1
Bradford BD1 201 B3
Brighouse HD6 115 A4
Castleford WF10 103 D1
Dewsbury WF13 118 B1
Elland HX5 135 A6
Elland, Holywell Green HX4 134 B4
Glusburn BD20 16 D7
Huddersfield HD7 152 D4
8 Liversedge WF15 117 A4
Mirfield WF14 138 A7
Oakworth BD22 34 B2
Slaithwaite HD7 152 A1
South Hiendley S72 180 F6
Thornton BD13 72 D6
Yeadon LS19 40 B4
James St E 8 BD21 35 C6
Jamie Ct BD10 56 D6
Jane Hills BD17 55 A8
Jane St Denholme BD13 52 D1
Shipley BD18 54 F8
Janesway LS25 82 F2
Janet St 5 BD22 51 E8
Jaques Cl LS6 59 B4
Jardine Ave WF7 145 D6
Jardine Rd 10 BD16 37 A3
Jarratt St BD8 55 B1
Jarratt St E BD8 55 B1
Jarrom Cl BD4 75 D4
Jarvis House 4 BD6 93 E8
Jarvis Sq WF3 100 A3
Jarvis Wlk WF3 100 A3
Jasmin Terr BD8 74 C8
Jason Terr WF17 97 A2
Jasper St Bradford BD10 56 B8
Halifax HX1 202 B3
Javelin Cl BD10 56 B6
Jay House La HD6 115 D5
Jay St BD22 51 D6
JB Priestley Liby BD7 74 C6
Jean Ave LS15 81 A7
Jebb La Cawthorne S75 176 E3
High Hoyland S75 176 F3
Jenkin Dr WF4 140 F1
Jenkin La WF4 140 F1
Jenkin Rd WF4 141 A1
Jenkinson Cl LS11 211 D1
Jenkinson Lawn LS11 211 D1
Jenkinson St WF17 118 C2
Jenkinsons Pl LS10 99 D8
Jenkyn La HD8 190 D8
Jennetts Cres LS21 22 F7
Jennings Cl BD20 17 F8
Jennings Pl BD7 74 A4
Jennings St 7 BD7 74 A4
Jenny La Baildon BD17 38 D4
Mirfield WF14 138 B7
Jensen Ave WF13 117 F3
Jepson La HX5 134 F6
Jer Gr BD7 73 E2
Jer La BD7 73 E2
Jeremy La WF16 117 D4
Jermyn St BD1 201 C3
Jerry Clay Dr WF2 120 E2
Jerry Clay La WF2 120 D2
Jerry Clay La Junior & Infants Sch WF2 120 E2
Jerry Fields Rd HX2 111 D6
Jerry La Silsden BD20 6 F1
Sowerby Bridge HX6 112 A3
Jersey Cl WF12 118 F2
Jerusalem La HX2 90 D4
Jerusalem Rd HD7 170 B7
Jerusalem Sq HX3 114 B4
Jervaulx Cl LS23 30 C7
Jervaulx Cres BD8 74 D8
Jerwood Hill Cl HX3 92 D1
Jerwood Hill Rd HX3 92 D1
Jesmond Ave S71 179 C3
Jesmond Gr Bradford BD9 54 F2
Dewsbury WF13 118 B1
Jessamine Ave LS11 213 F2
Jessamine Pl BD20 16 E6
Jessamine St WF13 138 D5
Jesse St BD8 73 D7
Jessop Ave HD5 155 A3
Jessop Fold HD7 171 F5
Jessop St Castleford WF10 124 D8
Wakefield WF2 142 C4
Jester Pl BD13 72 C2
Jew La BD22 51 C1
Jewitt La LS22 29 C7
Jill La WF14 138 D8
Jilley Royd La HD2 136 A4
Jim Allen La HX2 90 C1
Jim La HD1 153 D6
Jin Whin Ct WF10 124 A8
Jin-Whin Hill WF10 124 A8
Jinnah Ct BD8 74 D8
Jinny Moor La LS26 101 E8
Joan Royd WF16 117 D6
Joba Ave BD3 75 B7
Joffre Ave WF10 124 E6
John Baker St OL14 107 E8
John Booth Cl WF15 116 F2
John Carr Ave WF4 141 A2
John Escritt Rd BD16 37 A2
John Haigh Rd HD7 170 A8
John Jamieson Sch LS8 61 C5
John Naylor La HX2 111 E5
John Nelson Cl 9 WF17 96 F1
John O'Gaunts Wlk LS26 100 F6
John Ormsby V C Way WF12 119 A2
John Smeaton Com High Sch LS15 62 E3
John Smeaton Middle Sch LS15 62 E3
John Smeaton Sports Ctr LS15 62 E3
John St Baildon BD17 38 C1
5 Batley, Birstall WF17 96 E1
9 Batley, Heckmondwike WF16 117 D3
Bradford BD1 201 B3
Bradford, Clayton BD14 73 C4
Bradford, Tong Street BD4 75 E1
Brighouse HD6 115 A3
Castleford WF10 124 C6
Cullingworth BD13 52 D6
Denholme BD13 52 D1
Dewsbury WF13 118 C2
2 Dewsbury, Eastborough WF13 118 E1
Dewsbury, Ravensthorpe WF13 138 E5
Elland HX5 134 F6
John St continued
Elland, Lindwell HX4 134 C7
Halifax HX1 203 E3
Huddersfield HD3 153 B4
Leeds LS6 205 E3
Oakworth BD22 34 D2
Shipley BD18 55 A8
South Elmsall WF9 182 F2
Thornton BD13 72 D6
4 Todmorden OL14 108 B5
Wakefield WF1 216 C2
Yeadon LS19 40 B4
John St W 2 HX6 112 B4
John Street Mkt BD1 201 B3
John William St
3 Cleckheaton BD19 116 D8
13 Elland HX5 134 F6
Huddersfield HD1 154 A6
1 Liversedge WF15 117 B3
Liversedge, Mill Bridge WF15 117 C4
John's Cres WF2 120 E2
Johnny La LS21 23 A6
Johns Ave WF3 121 C6
Johns La HX5 134 F4
Johnson St Bingley BD16 36 F3
Bradford BD3 75 D7
Mirfield WF14 138 A3
Johnson Terr 1 LS27 98 B4
Johnston St Leeds LS6 206 B4
Wakefield WF1 216 C2
Jonathan Garth LS29 6 E8
Jons Ave WF9 182 A2
Jos La HD8 190 E8
Jos Way HD8 190 E8
Joseph Ave HX3 93 A2
Joseph Crossley's Almhouses HX1 202 C2
Joseph Priestley Coll LS26 101 B7
Joseph Priestly Coll LS27 98 B4
Joseph Priestly Institute of Further Education LS27 98 B2
Joseph St Bradford BD3 201 D3
Bradford, Tong Street BD4 75 E1
Leeds LS10 215 E4
Joseph Wright Ct BD10 39 A1
Josephine Rd HD4 153 A3
Joshua St 7 OL14 108 B6
Jowett House La S75 193 B4
Jowett Park Cres BD10 39 A2
Jowett St BD1 74 C7
Jowett Terr 7 LS27 98 A2
Jowett's La BD20 5 D8
Jubilee Ave
Lofthouse Gate WF1 121 C4
Normanton WF6 144 A8
Shepley HD8 174 A2
Jubilee Bglws WF11 126 E4
Jubilee Cl WF9 181 F6
Jubilee Cres
Birkenshaw BD11 97 A7
Crofton WF4 144 B3
Lofthouse Gate WF1 121 C4
Jubilee Croft BD11 96 F7
Jubilee Ct WF9 163 A4
Jubilee Dr 3 BD21 35 A5
Jubilee La HD4 153 A3
Jubilee Mount HD6 114 F2
Jubilee Pl 5 LS27 98 B4
Jubilee Rd Crofton WF4 144 B3
Halifax HX3 113 D3
Jubilee St Bradford BD1 55 D1
Crigglestone WF4 159 F3
Halifax HX3 203 F2
9 Hebden Bridge HX7 89 E1
6 Morley LS27 98 B4
Jubilee St N HX3 92 A3
Jubilee Terr
4 Halifax HX3 203 F2
4 Morley LS27 98 B4
Ripponden HX6 132 E6
Jubilee Trees LS29 21 C7
Jubilee Way
Pontefract WF8 146 C8
Shipley BD18 55 D8
Judy Haigh La WF12 157 D8
Judy La HD2 136 B3
Julian Dr BD13 73 C2
Julian St HD5 154 E5
Julie Ave WF4 159 E5
Jumb Beck Cl LS29 21 F8
Jumble Dyke HD6 135 F8
Jumble Hole Rd OL14, HX7 88 B1
Jumble Wood HD8 155 D3
Jumbles Ct WF3 100 C1
Jumbles La WF3 100 C1
Jumples HX2 91 D4
Jumples Cl HX2 91 D4
Jumples Crag HX2 91 D4
Jumples Ct HX2 91 D4
Jumps La
Hebden Bridge HX7 88 F1
Todmorden OL14 107 E8
Jumps Rd OL14 107 E8
Junction 1 Ret Pk LS11 213 D2
Junction Houses WF10 103 C1
Junction La WF5 141 A4
Junction Rd 3
Dewsbury WF13 139 B7
Shipley BD17 55 C8
Junction Row BD2 56 B4
Junction St LS10 211 F2
Junction Terr BD2 56 B4
June St 4 BD21 35 C8
Juniper Cl BD8 74 B8
Juniper Gr HD4 171 D6
Juniper Grove Mews HD4 171 D6
Juniper Pl LS9 208 B1
Justin Way HD4 153 A1
Kaffir Rd HD2 153 D8
Karnac Rd LS8 207 F4
Karon Dr WF4 141 B1
Kateholm OL13 106 A7
Katherine St 10 BD18 54 F8
Katrina Gr WF7 145 D4
Kay Cl LS27 97 F7
Kay St Shipley BD18 55 C5
Wakefield WF1 216 C2
Kaycell St BD4 75 B2
Kaye Hill BD13 52 D6
Kaye La Huddersfield HD5 154 E2
Huddersfield, Linthwaite HD7 152 E3
Kaye St Batley WF16 117 D3
Dewsbury WF12 139 D6
Kaye's First Sch HD8 175 F2
Kearsley Terr LS10 215 E2
Keat St HD4 153 E4
Keats Ave OL14 108 D6
Keats Cl WF8 125 D2
Keats Dr WF16 117 E2
Keats Gr WF3 121 E6
Kebble Ct BD19 117 B7
Keble Garth LS25 83 C2
Kebroyd Ave HX6 132 E7
Kebroyd La HX6 132 E7
Kebroyd Mount HX6 132 E6
Kebs Rd OL14 86 E3
Kedleston Rd LS8 43 F3
Keeble House BD2 56 D2
Keel Moorings LS13 57 F5
Keeldar Cl BD7 74 B3
Keelham First Sch BD13 71 F5
Keelham La Keighley BD20 18 A2
Todmorden OL14 87 D1
Keenan Ave WF9 182 E1
Keeper La Birkenshaw BD4 76 E2
Notton WF4 178 D5
Keeton St LS9 212 C4
Keighley Cl HX2 91 E6
Keighley Coll (Annex) BD21 35 D7
Keighley Dr HX2 91 E4
Keighley Golf Course BD20 18 A4
Keighley Ind Pk BD21 18 C1
Keighley Pl 6 LS28 57 E2
Keighley Preparatory Sch BD21 18 C1
Keighley Rd Bingley BD16 36 E5
Bradford BD8 55 C3
Cullingworth BD13 52 C7
Denholme BD13 52 D2
Glusburn BD20 16 E6
Halifax HX2 91 E5
Harden BD16 36 A2
Haworth BD22 34 E3
Hebden Bridge HX7 89 A4
Ilkley LS29 7 F2
Low Bradley BD20 4 B5
Oxenhope BD22 51 D3
Shipley BD9 55 C3
Silsden BD20 17 D8
Skipton BD23 4 A8
Steeton BD20 17 E5
Wadsworth Moor HX7 89 B8
Keighley Rd (Lidget) BD22 34 D2
Keighley Ret Pk BD21 18 C1
Keighley Sta BD21 35 D7
Keighley & Worth Valley Rly BD22 34 E1
Keir Hardy Cl WF16 117 C4
Kelburn Gr BD22 34 B3
Kelcliffe Ave LS20 22 E1
Kelcliffe Gr LS20 22 E1
Kelcliffe La LS20 22 E2
Keldholme Cl LS13 57 F5
Keldholme Rd 2 LS13 57 F5
Keldregate HD2 136 E4
Kell Beck LS21 10 F2
Kell La Halifax HX2 90 E6
Northowram HX3 92 F2
Kell St 6 BD16 37 A3
Kellett Ave LS12 78 C4
Kellett Cres LS12 78 C4
Kellett Dr LS12 78 C4
Kellett Gr LS12 78 C4
Kellett La LS12 209 E1
Kellett Mount 2 LS12 78 C4
Kellett Pl 3 LS12 78 C4
Kellett Rd LS12 209 E1
Kellett Terr 1 LS12 78 C4
Kellett Wlk LS12 78 C4
Kelloe St BD19 95 D1
Kelmore Gr BD6 93 E7
Kelmscott Ave LS15 62 D3
Kelmscott Cres LS15 62 D3
Kelmscott Garth LS15 62 E4
Kelmscott Gdns LS15 62 E3
Kelmscott Gn LS15 62 D3
Kelmscott Gr LS15 62 D3
Kelmscott La LS15 62 D3
Kelsall Ave LS6 205 E2
Kelsall Gr LS6 205 E2
Kelsall Pl LS6 205 E2
Kelsall Rd LS6 205 E2
Kelsall Terr LS6 205 E2
Kelsey St HX1 202 B4
Kelso Ct LS3 205 F1
Kelso Gdns LS2 205 F1

Kelso Gr HD5 155 A6
Kelso Hts LS6 205 F2
Kelso Pl LS2 205 F2
Kelso Rd LS2 205 F2
Kelso St LS2 205 F1
Keltus Ave BD20 16 D7
Kelvin Ave Halifax HX2 112 D6
Huddersfield HD5 154 E6
Kelvin Cres HX2 112 D6
Kelvin Rd HX5 134 E6
Kelvin Way BD2 56 C2
Kemp's Bridge WF2 142 A6
Kemps Way HD7 189 E3
Kempton Rd LS25 83 A2
Kemsing Wlk LS15 62 F2
Ken Churchill Dr WF4 141 A3
Kendal Bank LS3 205 F1
Kendal Carr LS3 206 A1
Kendal Cl Castleford WF10 125 E7
Leeds LS3 205 F1
Kendal Croft WF10 125 E7
Kendal Dr Castleford WF10 125 D8
Crofton WF4 143 C2
Leeds LS15 80 E7
Kendal Garth WF10 125 E7
Kendal Gdns WF10 125 E7
Kendal Gr LS3 206 A1
Kendal La LS3 206 A1
Kendal Rd 2 LS3 206 A1
Kendal Rise Crofton WF4 143 C2
Walton WF2 161 A6
Kendal St BD21 35 D6
Kendal Wlk LS3 210 C4
Kendall Ave BD18 54 E8
Kendall Mellor Ct 11 BD21 35 B7
Kendell St LS10 211 F3
Kenilworth Ave LS27 97 D6
Kenilworth Cl WF14 137 F6
Kenilworth Dr HX3 115 A6
Kenilworth Gdns LS27 97 D7
Kenilworth House 5 BD15 73 B8
Kenilworth Rd LS12 209 F1
Kenilworth St BD4 75 B4
Kenley Ave BD6 74 A2
Kenley Mount BD6 74 A2
Kenley Par BD6, BD7 73 F2
Kenmore Ave BD19 116 C8
Kenmore Cl BD19 116 C8
Kenmore Cres Bradford BD6 74 A2
Cleckheaton BD19 116 C8
Kenmore Dr Bradford BD6 74 A2
Cleckheaton BD19 116 C8
Kenmore Gr Bradford BD6 74 A2
Cleckheaton BD19 116 C8
Kenmore Rd Bradford BD6 74 A2
Cleckheaton BD19 116 C8
Lofthouse Gate WF2 120 F5
Kenmore View BD19 116 C8
Kenmore Way BD19 116 C8
Kenmore Wlk BD6 74 A2
Kennedy Ave HD2 136 A5
Kennedy Cl WF12 118 F3
Kennel La Oxenhope BD22 50 E2
Sowerby Bridge HX6 132 A8
Kennels La LS14 46 B8
Kennerleigh Ave LS15 62 D1
Kennerleigh Cres LS15 62 D1
Kennerleigh Dr LS15 62 C1
Kennerleigh Garth LS15 62 D1
Kennerleigh Glen 2 LS15 62 C1
Kennerleigh Gr LS15 62 D1
Kennerleigh Rise 3 LS15 62 C1
Kennerleigh Wlk LS15 62 C1
Kennet La LS25 83 A6
Kenneth St LS11 210 C1
Kennion St BD5 74 D5
Kensington Ave LS14 46 A6
Kensington Cl Batley WF17 118 B4
Halifax HX3 113 A4
Kensington Ct LS6 205 F3
Kensington Gdns HX5 134 E6
Kensington Rd Halifax HX3 113 A3
Wakefield WF1 216 A4
Kensington St Bradford BD8 55 A1
12 Keighley BD21 35 B6
Kensington Terr
Garforth LS25 82 E7
Leeds LS6 205 F3
Kenstone Cres BD10 56 A7
Kent Ave Pudsey LS28 77 A7
Silsden BD20 5 D1
Kent Cl LS28 77 A7
Kent Cres LS28 77 A7
Kent Dr LS28 77 A7
Kent Mews BD16 37 B2
Kent Rd Bingley BD16 37 B2
Pudsey LS28 76 F6
Kent St Bradford BD1 201 B2
Halifax HX1 203 D2
Kent Wlk 3 WF13 139 B8
Kentmere App LS14 61 F5
Kentmere Ave
Brighouse BD12 94 E1
Garforth LS25 83 B6
Leeds LS14 61 F7
Kentmere Cl LS14 62 A5
Kentmere Cres LS14 61 F6
Kentmere Gate LS14 61 F7
Kentmere Gdns LS14 61 F6
Kentmere Gn LS14 61 F6
Kentmere Rise LS14 62 A5
Kenton Dr WF4 160 A8
Kenton Way BD4 75 D4
Kenworthy Cl LS16 42 A5
Kenworthy Garth LS16 42 A5
Kenworthy Gate LS16 42 A5
Kenworthy Gdns LS16 42 A5
Kenworthy La HX6 132 E6
Kenworthy Rise LS16 42 A5
Kenworthy Vale LS16 42 A5
Kenya Mount BD21 34 F8
Kenyon La HX2 112 D7
Kenyon St WF9 183 A3
Kepler Gr LS8 207 E2
Kepler Mount LS8 207 E2
Kepler Terr LS8 207 E2
Kepstorn Cl LS5 59 A5
Kepstorn Rd LS16 59 B7
Kepstorn Rise 1 LS5 59 A5
Keren Gr WF2 120 E2
Kerr Mackie Primary Sch
LS8 61 A7
Kerry Garth LS18 41 B1
Kerry Hill Horsforth LS18 41 C1
Horsforth LS18 58 B8
Kerry St LS18 41 B1
Kershaw Ave WF10 125 B7
Kershaw Cres HX2 111 D7
Kershaw Ct HX2 111 D8
Kershaw Dr HX2 111 D8
Kershaw La WF11 126 E3
Kershaw Rd OL14 108 A1
Kershaw St BD3 75 D7
Kertland St WF12 139 C7
Kester Rd WF17 117 F5
Kesteven Cl BD4 75 F2
Kesteven Ct BD4 75 F2
Kesteven Rd BD4 75 F2
Kestrel Bank HD4 171 E7
Kestrel Cl LS17 43 F4
Kestrel Dr Bradford BD2 56 A4
Wakefield WF2 160 D5
Kestrel Garth 2 LS27 98 D4
Kestrel Gr LS17 43 F4
Kestrel Mount BD2 56 A4
Kestrel View HD8 173 F3
Keswick Ave HD3 135 A1
Keswick Cl Halifax HX3 113 E4
Todmorden OL14 107 F7
Keswick Dr Castleford WF10 104 E2
Wakefield WF2 141 E7
Keswick Grange LS17 28 C5
Keswick La LS17 28 C4
Keswick Rd S75 178 A3
Keswick St BD4 75 D5
Keswick View LS17 28 E5
Kettle La HD7 169 B6
Kettlethorpe Hall Dr WF2 160 C6
Kettlethorpe High Sch
WF2 160 C6
Kettlethorpe Rd WF2 160 C5
Kettlewell Dr BD5 74 B3
Kew Hill HD3 134 F3
Kew Hill Bottom HD3 134 F3
Key Hill La S72 180 F3
Key Syke La OL14 108 C5
Khaliq Ct BD3 75 B8
Khus Wlk BD21 35 C4
Kidacre St LS10 211 F1
Kiddal La LS15 46 E3
Kidroyd HD5 154 D4
Kidroyd La HD5 154 E4
Kilburn Cl HD5 154 D5
Kilburn La WF13 118 C1
Kilburn Rd LS12 209 F3
Kilby St WF1 216 A3
Kildare Cres BD15 54 A1
Kildare Terr LS12 210 B2
Kildwick CE Sch BD20 16 E8
Killingbeck Bridge LS14 61 E1
Killingbeck Dr LS14 61 E2
Killingbeck Hospl LS14 61 E2
Killingbeck Ret Pk LS14 61 E2
Killinghall Ave BD2 56 B1
Killinghall Dr BD2 56 B1
Killinghall Fst Sch BD3 56 C1
Killinghall Gr BD2 56 B1
Killinghall Rd BD2, BD3 75 D8
Kiln Bent Rd HD7 198 A6
Kiln Brow HD7 152 E4
Kiln Ct HD3 134 E1
Kiln Fold HD6 115 D3
Kiln Hill HD7 170 A8
Kiln Hill La BD20 5 B5
Kiln La Emley HD8 175 F5
Wadsworth Moor HX7 68 D3
Kilncroft HX4 133 F3
Kilner Bank HD5 154 C7
Kilner House BD2 56 D2
Kilner Rd BD6 74 A1
Kilnhouse Bank La HD7 188 B1
Kilnhurst Ave 13 OL14 108 C5
Kilnhurst La OL14 108 D4
Kilnhurst Mount OL14 108 D5
Kilnhurst Rd OL14 108 C5
Kilnsea Mount BD4 75 E3
Kilnsey Fold BD20 5 D2
Kilnsey Gr WF1 142 E8
Kilnsey Hill WF17 118 D2
Kilnsey Mews BD17 38 B3
Kilnsey Rd Bradford BD3 75 B6
Wakefield WF1 142 E8
Kilnshaw La HX7 109 F7
Kilpin Hill La WF13 117 F3
Kilroyd Ave BD19 95 D2
Kilroyd Dr BD19 95 E2
Kimberley Pl Halifax HX3 92 A4
Leeds LS9 208 B2
Kimberley Rd LS9 208 B2
Kimberley St Bradford BD4 75 C6
Brighouse HD6 115 B3
Dewsbury WF12 139 B4
Featherstone WF7 145 C6
Kimberley St continued
Halifax HX3 92 A4
Ilkley LS29 8 C5
Wakefield WF1 142 D3
Kimberley View LS9 208 B1
Kimberly Cl WF8 165 B5
Kinder Ave HD4 152 F2
Kineholme Dr LS21 22 D6
Kineton Ave OL14 108 C6
King Alfred's Dr LS6 43 A1
King Alfred's Gn LS6 43 A1
King Alfred's Way LS6 43 A1
King Alfred's Wlk LS6 43 A1
King Charles St Leeds LS1 211 F4
1 Leeds LS1 211 F4
King Charles Wlk 3 LS1 211 F4
King Cl LS17 43 A4
King Cliff Rd HD1, HD2 136 A1
King Cliffe Flats 3 HD1 154 A8
King Cross Rd HX1 202 B1
King Cross St HX1 203 D2
King Dr LS17 42 F5
King Edward Ave
Horsforth LS18 41 C1
Kippax WF10 102 F6
King Edward Cres LS18 41 C1
King Edward Rd 2 BD13 72 D6
King Edward St
Dewsbury WF12 139 B3
Halifax HX1 203 E3
Hemsworth WF9 181 E6
Leeds LS1 211 F4
Normanton WF6 123 A2
Sutton in C BD20 16 D5
King Edward Terr 1 BD13 72 D6
King Edwin's Ct LS8 61 A5
King George Ave
Horsforth LS18 41 C1
Leeds LS7 204 A2
Morley LS27 98 B6
King George Croft LS27 98 B5
King George Gdns LS7 204 A3
King George Rd LS18 41 C1
King George St WF1 121 B3
King George V
Playing Fields BD21 35 F8
King James's Sch HD4 155 A2
King La Leeds LS17 42 E6
Leeds LS17 43 B3
King Royd La WF7 163 C6
King St Batley WF16 117 D4
Birkenshaw BD11 96 F6
Bradford BD2 56 C5
Brighouse HD6 115 B2
Castleford WF10 124 E5
Cleckheaton BD19 116 E8
Elland HX5 135 A6
Halifax HX1 203 F3
Hebden Bridge HX7 110 E8
Hebden Bridge, Mytholm HX7 88 E3
Hemsworth WF9 163 B1
Horbury WF4 140 E1
Huddersfield HD1 154 B6
Huddersfield, Oakes HD3 153 C8
Keighley BD21 35 B6
Leeds LS1 211 E3
Mirfield WF14 138 A4
Morley LS27 98 A3
Normanton WF6 123 A1
Normanton, Altofts WF6 122 F4
Ossett WF5 140 E4
Pontefract WF8 146 C8
Pudsey LS28 57 E1
Silsden BD20 5 E1
Skelmanthorpe HD8 175 A2
Sowerby Bridge HX6 111 E3
Todmorden OL14 108 D6
Wakefield WF1 216 B2
Yeadon LS19 40 C7
Yeadon, Little London LS19 40 A4
King's Ave LS6 205 E2
King's Bridge Rd HD4 154 B4
King's Cres WF8 146 E7
King's Croft Gdns LS17 43 D1
King's Ct LS17 43 C1
King's Dr Batley WF17 96 E2
Bradford BD2 55 F6
King's Gate BD1 55 E1
King's Mead WF8 146 B7
King's Mill La HD1 154 B5
King's Mount
Knottingley WF11 126 B5
Leeds LS17 60 C8
King's Pl LS6 205 D4
King's Rd Bingley BD16 36 E6
Bradford BD2 55 F4
Cudworth S72 180 C1
Leeds LS6 205 E2
King's Sq 4 LS6 59 F6
Kingfield LS20 22 F2
Kingfisher Cl
Crigglestone WF4 159 F7
Leeds LS17 43 F4
Kingfisher Gr Bradford BD8 73 C7
Huddersfield HD4 171 E7
Wakefield WF2 160 D5
Kingfisher Mews LS27 98 C3
Kingfisher Way LS17 43 F4
Kings App LS13 58 E2
Kings Ave Castleford WF10 125 A7
Ilkley LS29 8 A4
Normanton WF6 122 F5
Kings Chase LS26 100 F6
Kings Cl Ackworth M T WF7 163 D5
Ilkley LS29 7 E4
Ossett WF5 140 C7
Otley LS21 23 C7
Pontefract WF8 146 C7
Kings Croft Garforth LS25 82 D6
Ossett WF5 140 C8
South Kirkby WF9 182 B3
Kings Ct Batley WF17 96 E1
Hemsworth WF9 163 B1
Sutton in C BD20 16 D4
Kings Dr Bramhope LS16 25 A1
Normanton WF6 122 F5
Kings Gr BD16 37 A4
Kings Head Dr 2 WF14 137 F6
Kings Head Rd WF14 137 F6
Kings High Sch The WF8 146 C7
Kings Lea Batley WF15 117 C2
Halifax HX3 113 B2
Ossett WF5 140 C8
Kings Mead LS26 101 A6
Kings Meadow WF5 140 C7
Kings Meadow Cl LS22 13 D7
Kings Meadow Dr LS22 13 D7
Kings Meadow Gr LS22 13 D7
Kings Meadow Mews LS22 13 D7
Kings Meadow View LS22 13 D7
Kings Mount HX4 132 F3
Kings Paddock WF5 140 C7
Kings Rd Bramhope LS16 25 B1
Bramhope LS16 25 B1
Ilkley LS29 7 F4
Normanton WF6 122 E6
Kings View HX3 114 A4
Kingsbury Pl HX1 202 B3
Kingsdale Ave
Birkenshaw BD11 96 E6
Bradford BD2 56 A3
Kingsdale Cres BD2 56 A3
Kingsdale Ct LS14 61 E6
Kingsdale Dr BD2 56 A3
Kingsdale Gdns BD11 96 E6
Kingsdale Gr BD2 55 F3
Kingsfield LS26 100 B5
Kingsland Ct S71 179 D4
Kingsley Ave
Birkenshaw BD11 96 B4
Bradford BD2 55 E3
Crofton WF4 143 E2
Featherstone WF7 145 D8
Huddersfield HD1 153 E4
Knottingley WF11 126 C5
Leeds LS16 42 B5
Lofthouse Gate WF1 121 B5
Sowerby Bridge HX6 111 F3
Wakefield WF2 160 D6
Kingsley Cl
Birkenshaw BD11 96 B4
Crofton WF4 143 E2
Lofthouse Gate WF1 121 B5
Wakefield WF2 160 C6
Kingsley Cres Baildon BD17 38 C2
Birkenshaw BD11 96 B4
Kingsley Croft BD20 16 E7
Kingsley Dr Birkenshaw BD11 96 B4
Leeds LS16 42 B5
Kingsley Garth WF1 121 B5
Kingsley Pl HX1 202 C2
Kingsley Rd LS16 42 B5
Kingsmead Leeds LS14 62 A8
Ossett WF5 140 C8
Kingsmead Dr LS14 44 F1
Kingsmill Cl LS27 97 F5
Kingston Ave HD5 154 E6
Kingston Cl Halifax HX1 202 B2
Wilsden BD15 53 C5
Kingston Ct HX1 202 B2
Kingston Dr Halifax HX1 202 B2
Normanton WF6 123 C1
Kingston Gdns LS15 62 B2
Kingston Gr BD10 39 B1
Kingston Rd BD10 39 B1
Kingston St HX1 202 B2
Kingston Terr Halifax HX1 202 B2
Leeds LS2 206 B2
Kingsway Batley WF17 96 E2
Bingley BD16 37 A2
Birkenshaw BD11 96 F6
Bradford BD2 55 F6
1 Dewsbury WF12 139 D8
Garforth LS25 82 D6
Keighley BD20 19 A1
Leeds LS15 81 C8
Lofthouse Gate WF3 121 F2
Mapplewell S75 178 A1
Normanton WF6 144 A8
Ossett WF5 140 C6
Pontefract WF8 125 D3
Kingsway Cl WF5 140 C7
Kingsway Ct Leeds LS17 43 D1
Ossett WF5 140 C7
Kingsway Dr LS29 8 A4
Kingsway Garth LS25 82 D6
Kingswear Cl LS15 62 D1
Kingswear Cres LS15 62 D1
Kingswear Garth LS15 62 D1
Kingswear Glen LS15 62 D1
Kingswear Gr LS15 62 D1
Kingswear Par LS15 62 D1
Kingswear Rise 4 LS15 62 D1
Kingswear View LS15 62 D1
Kingswell Ave WF1 121 C4
Kingswood Ave LS8 44 A3
Kingswood Cres LS8 43 F3
Kingswood Dr LS8 43 F3
Kingswood Gdns LS8 43 F3
Kingswood Gn HX3 92 F1
Kingswood Gr LS8 44 A3
Kingswood Pl 8 BD7 74 A4
Kingswood St BD7 74 A4
Kingswood Terr 9 BD7 74 A4
Kinnaird Cl Batley WF17 118 F5
Halifax HX5 134 F8
Kinsley House Cres WF9 163 A2
Kinsley Jun & Inf Sch
WF9 163 B2
Kinsley St WF9 163 B1
Kipling Cl HD4 153 D3
Kipling Ct BD10 56 D7
Kipling Gr WF8 125 D3
Kippax Ashtree Prim Sch
LS25 83 B1
Kippax Greenfield
Primary Sch LS25 83 A2
Kippax Mount LS9 212 C3
Kippax North Junior
& Infants Sch LS25 82 F4
Kippax Pl LS9 212 C2
Kipping La BD13 72 D6
Kipping Pl 6 BD13 72 D6
Kirby Cote La HX7 110 D3
Kirby Row HD5 137 C1
Kirby St BD21 18 D1
Kirk Beeston Cl LS11 213 F2
Kirk Bridge La HD7 189 D7
Kirk Cl WF12 140 B8
Kirk Cross Cres S71 179 C2
Kirk Dr BD17 38 D4
Kirk Hills LS14 46 A5
Kirk La Brighouse HX3 114 C8
Yeadon LS19 40 A7
Kirk La Mills LS19 40 A7
Kirk Lea Cres HD3 135 C1
Kirk Smeaton C of E
Prim Sch WF8 166 D6
Kirkbourne Gr BD17 38 E2
Kirkbridge Way WF9 182 F3
Kirkburn Pl BD7 74 B6
Kirkburton C of E Fst Sch
HD8 173 F6
Kirkburton Middle Sch
HD8 174 A7
Kirkby Ave LS25 83 A5
Kirkby Cl WF9 182 C3
Kirkby La Emley HD8, WF4 175 B8
Sicklinghall LS22 12 A5
Kirkby Leas HX1 203 E2
Kirkby Rd WF9 181 E6
Kirkbygate WF9 181 E5
Kirkdale WF10 125 C8
Kirkdale Ave LS12 78 B4
Kirkdale Cres LS12 78 B3
Kirkdale Dr
Crigglestone WF4 159 D6
Leeds LS12 78 B4
Kirkdale Gdns LS12 78 B4
Kirkdale Gr LS12 78 A4
Kirkdale Mount LS12 78 B4
Kirkdale Terr LS12 78 B3
Kirkdale View LS12 78 B4
Kirkfield Ave LS14 46 A6
Kirkfield Cl S75 193 F4
Kirkfield Cres LS14 46 A6
Kirkfield Dr LS15 81 D7
Kirkfield Gdns LS15 81 D7
Kirkfield La LS14 46 A5
Kirkfield View LS15 81 D7
Kirkfield Way S71 179 C2
Kirkfields BD17 38 E3
Kirkgate Batley, Birstall
WF17 96 D1
Batley, Hanging Heaton
WF17 118 F3
Bradford BD1 201 B3
Farnhill BD20 16 E8
Huddersfield HD1 154 B6
Leeds LS1, LS2 211 F3
Otley LS21 23 A7
Shipley BD18 55 A8
Silsden BD20 5 E1
Wakefield WF1 216 C2
Kirkgate Arc LS21 23 A7
Kirkgate Bsns Ctr WF1 216 C1
Kirkgate Ctr BD1 201 B3
Kirkgate La S72 180 C6
Kirkgate Sta WF1 216 C1
Kirkham Ave WF2 120 B3
Kirkham Rd BD7 74 B5
Kirkham St LS13 57 F5
Kirkhamgate Junior
& Infants Sch WF2 120 B2
Kirkhaw La WF11 126 B6
Kirkheaton Jun & Inf Sch
HD5 137 B1
Kirklands Holmfirth HD7 189 D7
Liversedge WF15 117 A4
Thorner LS14 45 F5
Kirklands Ave BD17 38 E3
Kirklands Cl Baildon BD17 38 E2
Menston LS29 22 A4
Yeadon LS19 40 A8
Kirklands Ct BD17 38 E3
Kirklands Gdns BD17 38 E3
Kirklands La BD17 38 E3
Kirklands Rd BD17 38 E3
Kirklea HD8 174 C3
Kirklees Cl LS28 57 E4
Kirklees Croft LS28 57 D4
Kirklees Dr LS28 57 D4
Kirklees Garth LS28 57 D4
Kirklees Light Rly HD8 175 D3
Kirklees Rd BD15 73 B7
Kirklees Rise LS28 57 D4
Kirkley Ave BD12 94 C1
Kirkroyds Infants Sch
HD7 189 D7
Kirkroyds La HD7 189 D7
Kirkstall Abbey LS5 58 F5
Kirkstall Ave LS5 58 F3
Kirkstall Gr BD8 73 D7
Kirkstall Hill LS4, LS5 59 B3

Kirkstall Ind Pk LS4 205 D1
Kirkstall La LS5, LS6 59 B4
Kirkstall Mount LS5 58 F3
Kirkstall Rd LS4 59 C2
Kirkstall St Stephen's C of E Primary Sch LS6 59 A4
Kirkstall Valley Primary Sch LS4 59 C2
Kirkstone Ave HD5 154 C6
Kirkstone Dr
Cleckheaton BD19 117 B8
Halifax HX2 112 C8
Kirkthorpe La WF1 143 C6
Kirkwall Ave 3 LS9 80 B7
Kirkwall Dr BD4 75 E3
Kirkwood Ave LS16 41 D4
Kirkwood Cl LS16 41 D4
Kirkwood Cres LS16 41 E5
Kirkwood Dr
Huddersfield HD3 153 B8
Leeds LS16 41 E5
Kirkwood Gdns LS16 41 E5
Kirkwood Gn HD3 153 B8
Kirkwood Gr
East Ardsley WF3 119 F8
Leeds LS16 41 D4
Kirkwood La LS16 41 D5
Kirkwood Rise LS16 41 E5
Kirkwood View LS16 41 E5
Kirkwood Way LS16 41 E5
Kismet Gdns BD3 75 C8
Kistyaen Gdns HD7 170 C3
Kit La BD20 5 C6
Kit Wood Cl BD4 75 F2
Kitchen Fold HD7 170 A8
Kitchener Ave LS9 208 B1
Kitchener Gr LS9 208 B2
Kitchener Mount LS9 208 B1
Kitchener Pl LS9 208 B1
Kitchener St Bradford BD12 95 A5
Leeds LS9 208 B1
5 Rothwell LS26 101 C6
Kitson Cl LS12 209 F2
Kitson Gdns LS12 209 F2
Kitson Hill Cres WF14 137 F6
Kitson Hill Rd WF14 137 F7
Kitson La HX6 112 D1
Kitson Rd LS10 212 A1
Kitson St East Ardsley WF3 98 D1
Leeds LS9 212 C3
Shipley BD18 55 C7
Kitson Wood Rd OL14 107 E8
Kliffen Pl HX3 113 D4
Knaresborough Dr HD2 136 A2
Knavesmire LS26 100 B5
Knight St Halifax HX1 202 B2
Huddersfield HD1 154 B7
Knight's Fold BD7 74 A4
Knights Croft LS22 13 F7
Knightsbridge Wlk BD4 95 B8
Knightsclose LS15 81 C8
Knightscroft Ave LS26 100 E6
Knightscroft Dr LS26 100 E6
Knightscroft Par WF9 183 A2
Knightshill LS15 81 D8
Knightsway Garforth LS25 82 E6
Leeds LS15 81 C8
Rothwell WF3 100 B2
Wakefield WF2 160 C6
Knoll Cl WF5 140 E7
Knoll Gdns BD17 38 B1
Knoll La HD7 188 D8
Knoll Park Dr BD17 38 B1
Knoll Pk WF3 120 D7
Knoll View BD17 38 B2
Knoll Wood Pk LS18 58 D8
Knott La Steeton BD20 16 F5
Yeadon LS19 40 E1
Knottingley C of E (C) Primary Sch WF11 127 A4
Knottingley Cty Jun & Inf Sch WF11 127 A3
Knottingley High Sch WF11 127 A3
Knottingley Rd WF8 126 B2
Knottingley Sta WF11 126 E4
Knotts Rd OL14 107 D8
Knotty La HD8 156 A3
Knowl Gr WF14 138 A5
Knowl Rd Holme HD7 187 E4
Huddersfield HD7 152 E4
Mirfield WF14 138 A5
Knowl The 9 WF14 137 F5
Knowl Top HX7 88 C6
Knowle Ave
Huddersfield HD5 154 E5
Leeds LS4 205 D3
Knowle Gr 10 LS4 205 D3
Knowle La Bradford BD12 94 D2
Meltham HD7 171 A2
Knowle Mount LS4 205 D3
Knowle Park Ave HD8 190 F8
Knowle Pl 11 LS4 205 D3
Knowle Rd Leeds LS4 205 D3
Slaithwaite HD7 152 A1
Knowle Sch WF14 138 A6
Knowle Spring Rd 1 BD21 35 B5
Knowle Terr LS4 205 D3
Knowle The HD8 190 F8
Knowle Top Dr HX3 114 E8
Knowle Top Rd HX3 114 E8
Knowler Cl WF15 117 A5
Knowler Hill WF15 117 A5
Knowler Way WF15 117 A5
Knowles Ave BD4 75 D2
Knowles Croft 8 WF13 117 F2
Knowles Hill 6 WF13 117 F2
Knowles Hill Rd WF13 117 F1
Knowles La Batley WF17 118 B4
Bradford BD4 75 D2
Cleckheaton BD19 96 B2
Knowles Rd Batley WF17 118 B4
Brighouse HD6 136 B8
Knowles St Bradford BD4 75 C2
Denholme BD13 71 D8
Knowles View BD4 75 D2
Knowlwood Rd OL14 108 A3
Knowsley Ave 14 OL14 108 A1
Knowsley St BD3 75 A6
Knowsthorpe Cres LS9 212 C1
Knowsthorpe Gate LS9 80 B5
Knowsthorpe La Leeds LS9 80 E2
Leeds, Cross Green LS9 80 B4
Knowsthorpe Rd LS9 80 C4
Knowsthorpe Way LS9 80 B4
Knox St LS13 57 D5
Knutsford Gr BD4 75 E2
Komla Cl BD1 201 C3
Krives La HD7 169 E5
Kyffin Ave LS15 80 E8
Kyffin Pl BD4 75 E5

Laburnum Cl WF3 120 C7
Laburnum Ct
Castleford WF10 124 E6
Horbury WF4 140 F1
Laburnum Dr BD17 38 D4
Laburnum Gr
Brighouse HX3 115 A6
Cleckheaton BD19 96 A1
Haworth BD22 51 E8
Horbury WF4 140 F1
Huddersfield HD7 152 F5
Skelmanthorpe HD8 175 A1
Laburnum Pl Bradford BD8 55 C1
Bradford, Apperley Bridge BD10 56 E8
Laburnum Rd Batley WF13 117 E2
Shipley BD18 55 D5
Wakefield WF1 216 A3
Laburnum St Bradford BD8 55 C1
Pudsey LS28 57 D1
Pudsey, Owlcotes Hill LS28 76 C8
Laburnum Terr HD1 154 B8
Lacey St Dewsbury WF13 139 B8
Horbury WF4 141 C2
Lacy Ave OL14 108 A1
Lacy Gr LS22 13 F4
Lacy St WF9 181 C7
Lacy Way HX5 135 A8
Ladbroke Gr BD4 75 E1
Ladderbanks La BD17 38 D4
Ladderbanks Middle Sch BD17 38 E4
Ladstone Towers HX6 112 B4
Lady Ann Rd WF17 118 E5
Lady Anne Bsns Pk WF17 118 E6
Lady Balk La WF8 125 D3
Lady Beck Cl LS2 212 A4
Lady Cl WF5 140 C8
Lady Elizabeth Hastings C of E Sch LS22 13 A1
Lady Elizabeth Hastings CE Sch LS23 14 E1
Lady Elizabeth Hastings PrimSch WF10 103 E6
Lady Heton Ave WF14 137 F6
Lady Heton Dr WF14 137 E6
Lady Heton Gr WF14 137 E6
Lady Hetton Cl WF14 137 E6
Lady House La HD4 172 A8
Lady La Bingley BD16 37 A5
Leeds LS2 212 A4
Wakefield WF2 216 A1
Lady Lane Park Sch BD16 37 A5
Lady Park Ave BD16 37 A5
Lady Pit La LS11 214 B3
Lady Wood Rd LS8 61 B6
Ladybower Ave HD4 152 F2
Ladyroyd Dr BD4 95 E6
Ladysmith Rd BD13 92 C8
Ladywell Cl BD5 74 E3
Ladywell La WF15 116 B3
Ladywood Grange LS8 61 D6
Ladywood Mead LS8 61 D6
Ladywood Terr HX1 202 C4
Ladywood Way WF13 138 E4
Lafflands La WF4 162 B1
Lairum Rise LS23 30 D5
Laisterdyke BD4 75 D6
Laisterdyke Middle Sch BD3 75 D7
Laisteridge La BD5, BD7 74 C5
Laith Cl LS16 41 F3
Laith Garth LS16 41 F3
Laith Gdns LS16 42 A3
Laith Gn LS16 41 F3
Laith Rd LS16 41 F3
Laith Staid La LS25 65 F1
Laithe Ave HD7 188 C2
Laithe Bank Dr HD7 188 C2
Laithe Cl BD20 5 E2
Laithe Field HX4 133 D5
Laithe Gr BD6 74 B1
Laithe Rd BD6 74 B1
Laithecroft Rd WF17 118 E5
Laithes Chase WF2 141 F7
Laithes Cl WF2 141 F7
Laithes Cres WF2 141 F7
Laithes Croft WF12 139 E7
Laithes Ct WF2 141 F7
Laithes Dr WF2 141 D7
Laithes Fold WF2 141 F7
Laithes View WF2 141 D7
Lake Lock Dr WF3 122 A6
Lake Lock Gr WF3 122 A5
Lake Lock Rd WF3 122 A5
Lake Row BD4 75 B5
Lake St Bradford BD4 75 B5
Keighley BD21 18 E1
Leeds LS10 215 D2
Lake Terr LS10 215 D2
Lake View
Criggleston WF2 160 C4
Halifax HX3 203 D4
Huddersfield HD4 171 E8
Pontefract WF8 125 C3
Lake Yd WF3 122 A5
Lakeland Cres LS17 43 A6
Lakeland Ct LS15 80 D6
Lakeland Dr LS17 43 B6
Lakeland Way WF2 161 A6
Lakeside Keighley BD20 19 E2
Marsden HD7 169 A4
Lakeside Chase LS19 40 C4
Lakeside Cl LS29 8 B5
Lakeside Ct
Huddersfield HD3 153 B8
Leeds LS10 215 D2
Lakeside Est WF4 162 B2
Lakeside Gdns LS19 40 C4
Lakeside Ind Est LS12 77 E7
Lakeside Mdws WF8 125 D3
Lakeside Rd LS12 77 E6
Lakeside Terr LS19 40 C4
Lakeside View LS19 40 C4
Lakeside Wlk LS19 40 C4
Lakeview Ct LS8 61 C8
Lamb Cote Rd HD2 136 D6
Lamb Hall Rd HD3 152 E8
Lamb Inn Rd WF11 127 A4
Lambe Flatt S75 177 C1
Lambert Ave LS8 204 C2
Lambert Cl HX4 134 D7
Lambert Dr LS8 204 C2
Lambert Pl BD2 56 B2
Lambert St 2 HX4 134 D7
Lambert Terr LS18 41 E1
Lambourne Ave BD10 56 E5
Lambrigg Cres LS14 62 A4
Lambton Gr LS8 207 F4
Lambton Pl LS8 207 F4
Lambton St LS8 207 F4
Lambton Terr LS8 207 F4
Lambton View LS8 207 F4
Lamma Well Rd HD7 189 A2
Lampards Cl BD15 54 A2
Lamplands WF17 118 D6
Lanark Dr LS18 41 B4
Lanark Rise WF4 162 A8
Lancaster Cl WF8 146 D6
Lancaster Cres HD5 154 F4
Lancaster Ct 9 BD21 35 B5
Lancaster La HD7 172 C1
Lancaster St
Castleford WF10 104 D1
Dearne S63 194 E1
Lancastre Ave LS5 58 F3
Lancastre Gr LS5 58 F3
Land St LS28 57 D3
Land's Bldgs WF5 140 D7
Landmark Ct LS11 213 F3
Landor St BD21 35 D8
Lands Beck Way WF15 116 F4
Lands Head La HX3 93 A4
Lands La Bradford BD10 56 C5
Guiseley LS20 22 E1
Leeds LS1 211 F4
Landscove Ave BD4 75 F2
Landsdown Ave WF9 182 A1
Landseer Ave
East Ardsley WF3 119 E8
Leeds LS13 58 E3
Landseer Cl LS13 58 D3
Landseer Cres LS13 58 E3
Landseer Dr LS13 58 E3
Landseer Gdns LS13 58 E3
Landseer Gn LS13 58 D3
Landseer Gr LS13 58 E3
Landseer Mount LS13 58 E3
Landseer Rd LS13 58 E3
Landseer Rise LS13 58 D3
Landseer Terr LS13 58 E3
Landseer View LS13 58 E3
Landseer Way LS13 58 D3
Landseer Wlk LS13 58 D3
Landsholme Ct BD4 75 F2
Landsmoor Gr BD16 37 C5
Lane Bottom HX7 87 F4
Lane Cotts S71 179 C3
Lane Court No 1 6 HD6 115 B3
Lane Court No 2 7 HD6 115 B3
Lane & Dowry Rd HD7 169 F7
Lane End Baildon BD17 38 C3
Pudsey LS28 76 F8
Thornton BD13 72 D6
Lane End Croft LS17 42 F5
Lane End Ct LS17 42 F5
Lane End Fold LS28 76 F8
Lane End La 2 OL13 106 A1
Lane End Mount LS28 76 F8
Lane End Pl LS11 211 E1
Lane End Rd OL13 106 A1
Lane Ends HX2, HX3 91 E2
Lane Ends Cl Bradford BD8 73 F8
Hemsworth WF9 163 A4
Lane Ends Gn HX3 114 C8
Lane Ends La HX7 89 C4
Lane Ends Terr HX3 114 C8
Lane Ends View WF3 121 E5
Lane Fox Ct 7 LS19 40 B6
Lane Hackings HD8 191 E7
Lane Hackings Gn HD8 191 E7
Lane Head HX7 88 E5
Lane Head Cl S75 178 A2
Lane Head La Halifax HX2 91 D8
Kirkburton HD8 173 F6
Lane Head Rd
Cawthorne S75 193 D3
Ripponden HX6 132 C5
Shepley HD8 190 E7
Lane Head Rise S75 178 A2
Lane House Gr HX2 111 E8
Lane Ings HD7 169 A4
Lane Side Bacup OL13 106 A4
Queensbury BD13 72 D3
Wilsden BD15 53 C4
Lane Side Cl BD12 94 C4
Lane Side La HD5 155 D7
Lane The Leeds LS9 212 B3
Leeds, Alwoodley LS17 42 F5
Lane Top Denholme BD13 52 D2
Huddersfield HD7 152 E1
Lanes The LS28 76 F8
Laneside Elland HX4 134 A4
Kirkburton HD8 174 A6
Morley LS27 98 B7
Laneside Cl LS27 98 B7
Laneside Fold 11 LS27 98 B7
Laneside Gdns LS27 98 B7
Laneside St OL14 108 A4
Lang Kirk Cl BD20 4 E1
Lang La BD2 55 D5
Langbar App LS14 62 D6
Langbar Ave BD9 54 D3
Langbar Cl LS14 62 D6
Langbar Garth LS14 62 D6
Langbar Gdns 2 LS14 62 D5
Langbar Gn LS14 62 D6
Langbar Gr LS14 62 D5
Langbar Grange 14 LS14 62 D5
Langbar Pl LS14 62 D6
Langbar Rd Ilkley LS29 8 A6
Leeds LS14 62 D5
Langbar Sq 1 LS14 62 D5
Langbar Towers 3 LS14 62 D5
Langbar View LS14 62 D6
Langcliffe Cl S75 178 A2
Langdale Ave Bradford BD8 73 E8
Brighouse BD12 94 E1
Leeds LS6 59 C4
Lofthouse Gate WF1 121 D5
Normanton WF6 123 A4
Langdale Cl
Castleford WF10 104 E2
Wetherby LS22 13 D6
Langdale Cres HX2 91 E1
Langdale Ct BD16 37 A4
Langdale Dr
Ackworth M T WF7 164 C7
Huddersfield HD5 154 D7
Normanton WF6 123 A4
2 Queensbury BD13 72 D1
Wakefield WF2 141 F6
Langdale Gdns LS6 59 C4
Langdale Mews WF6 123 A4
Langdale Mount WF2 161 A6
Langdale Prim Sch LS26 101 B7
Langdale Rd Batley WF12 118 F2
Bradford BD10 56 E4
Rothwell LS26 101 B6
Langdale Sq WF2 141 F6
Langdale St HX5 134 F6
Langdale Terr LS6 59 C4
Langford Cl LS29 9 E1
Langford Ct LS29 9 E1
Langford La LS29 9 F1
Langford Mews LS29 9 E1
Langford Rd LS29 9 E1
Langford Ride LS29 9 F1
Langlands Rd BD16 54 A7
Langlea Terr HX3 114 C8
Langley Ave Bingley BD16 37 A4
Bradford BD4 75 C1
Leeds LS13 58 A4
Langley Cl LS13 58 A4
Langley Cres Baildon BD17 38 E3
Leeds LS13 58 B4
Langley Garth LS13 58 A4
Langley Gr BD16 37 A4
Langley La Baildon BD17 38 E4
Clayton West HD8 175 E2
Clayton West HD8 175 E4
Langley Mount LS13 58 B4
Langley Pl 3 LS13 58 A4
Langley Rd Bingley BD16 37 A4
Leeds LS13 58 B4
Langley Terr HD3 153 A8
Langport Cl BD13 72 F1
Langsett Croft HD2 136 E5
Langsett Rd WF2 160 B5
Langthorne Cres LS27 98 C2
Langthwaite Grange Ind Est South Kirby WF9 182 D2
Langthwaite La WF9 182 E2
Langthwaite Rd WF9 182 D2
Langton Ave BD4 75 C1
Langton Cl BD19 96 A2
Langton St HX6 112 B5
Langwith Ave LS22 29 A8
Langwith Dr LS22 28 E8
Langwith Mews LS22 29 A8
Langwith Valley Rd LS22 28 E8
Lansdale Ct BD4 75 F2
Lansdowne Ave WF10 124 F7
Lansdowne Cl Baildon BD17 38 F3
Batley WF17 118 C6
Lansdowne Pl BD5 201 A2
Lansdowne St LS12 209 F2
Lanshaw Bank BD23 3 B6
Lanshaw Cl LS10 99 E6
Lanshaw Cres LS10 99 E5
Lanshaw Pl LS10 99 E6
Lanshaw Rd LS10 99 E6
Lanshaw Terr LS10 99 E6
Lanshaw View LS10 99 E6
Lapage Middle Sch BD3 75 C8
Lapage St BD3 75 C7
Lapage Terr BD3 75 C6
Lapwing Cl BD8 73 B7
Larch Ave HD7 189 C8
Larch Cl Batley WF17 97 A2
Kirkheaton HD5 137 B1
Liversedge WF15 117 C3
Normanton WF6 144 B8
Oakworth BD22 34 D2
Larch Ct WF10 124 E6
Larch Dale HD2 136 A4
Larch Dr BD6 94 D7
Larch Gr BD16 36 F5
Larch Hill BD6 94 D7
Larch Hill Cres BD6 94 D8
Larch La LS25 83 B6
Larch Rd HD1 153 D5
Larch St BD21 35 B4
Larch Wood LS14 45 C7
Larchfield Rd LS10 212 B1
Larchmont BD14 73 C4
Larchmont First Sch BD14 73 C4
Lark Hill WF17 118 A8
Lark Hill Ave BD19 116 B6
Lark Hill Cl BD19 116 B6
Lark Hill Dr BD19 116 B6
Lark St Bingley BD16 36 F3
Haworth BD22 51 D7
Keighley BD21 35 B7
Oakworth BD22 34 D2
Larkfield Ave LS19 40 C4
Larkfield Cres LS19 40 C4
Larkfield Dr LS19 40 C4
Larkfield Mount LS19 40 C4
Larkfield Rd Pudsey LS28 76 E8
Yeadon LS19 40 C4
Larkfield Terr BD21 35 E6
Larkhill Cl LS8 204 B4
Larkhill Gn LS8 43 E1
Larkhill Rd LS8 43 E1
Larkhill View LS8 204 B4
Larkhill Way LS8 43 E1
Larkhill Wlk LS8 43 E1
Larks Hill WF8 146 B6
Larkshill Jun & Inf Sch WF8 146 B6
Larkspur Way WF2 141 E7
Larwood Ave BD10 56 E4
Lascelles Hall Rd HD5 155 C6
Lascelles Mount 4 LS8 207 F3
Lascelles Pl 2 LS8 207 F3
Lascelles Rd WF16 117 E3
Lascelles Rd E LS8 207 F3
Lascelles Rd W LS8 207 F3
Lascelles St LS8 207 F3
Lascelles Terr LS8 207 F3
Lascelles View 3 LS8 207 F3
Lastingham Gn BD6 73 E1
Lastingham Rd LS13 57 F5
Latchmere Ave LS16 58 F8
Latchmere Cl LS16 59 A8
Latchmere Crest 4 LS16 58 F8
Latchmere Cross 3 LS16 58 F8
Latchmere Dr LS16 58 F8
Latchmere Gdns LS16 59 A8
Latchmere Gn 5 LS16 58 F8
Latchmere Rd LS16 58 F8
Latchmere View LS16 58 F8
Latchmere Wlk 4 LS16 59 A8
Latchmore Rd LS12 213 E4
Latchmore Road Ind Est LS12 213 E4
Latham Ct BD19 96 B2
Latham La BD19 96 A2
Latham Lea BD19 96 A2
Latimer St BD3 75 D6
Launceston Dr BD4 75 E2
Laund Rd Huddersfield HD3 134 E1
Marsden HD7 151 C3
Slaithwaite HD7 151 C3
Launton Way BD5 74 D4
Laura St 8 Brighouse HD6 115 A1
5 Halifax HX3 92 C1
Leeds LS12 210 C2
Laurel Bank
Brighouse BD12 115 C8
11 Halifax HX1 202 C1
Laurel Bank Cl HX2 92 A6
Laurel Bank Ct LS6 59 C4
Laurel Cl East Keswick LS17 28 C5
Elland HX5 134 E6
Shelf HX3 93 C6
Laurel Cres Halifax HX2 91 F3
Keighley BD21 35 B8
Laurel Ct WF5 140 C6
Laurel Dr WF17 118 A7
Laurel Fold 9 LS12 209 F3
Laurel Gr Batley WF17 117 F7
Bingley BD16 36 E5
Keighley BD21 35 B8
7 Leeds LS12 209 F3
Silsden BD20 5 D1
Laurel Hill Ave LS15 81 D7
Laurel Hill Croft LS15 81 D7
Laurel Hill Gdns LS15 81 D7
Laurel Hill Gr LS15 81 D7
Laurel Hill View LS15 81 D7
Laurel Hill Way LS15 81 D6
Laurel House 4 WF10 124 E7

Laurel Mount Batley WF16 . 117 D4
14 Halifax HX1 ..... 202 C1
Leeds LS7 ..... 204 A1
Pudsey LS28 ..... 76 E8
Laurel Pk BD15 ..... 53 C4
Laurel Pl Leeds LS12 ..... 209 F3
Middleton LS10 ..... 99 B3
Laurel St Bradford BD3 ..... 75 C6
Halifax HX1 ..... 202 C1
10 Leeds LS12 ..... 209 F3
Laurel Terr Elland HX4 ..... 133 F4
Leeds LS12 ..... 209 F3
Pudsey LS28 ..... 76 E8
Laurels The Bingley BD16 ..... 37 B3
Dewsbury WF12 ..... 139 F7
Leeds LS8 ..... 204 C3
Laurence Ct LS26 ..... 101 D7
Lavender Croft WF16 ..... 117 E4
Lavender Ct HD4 ..... 171 D6
Lavender Hill BD10 ..... 56 C5
Lavender Wlk LS9 ..... 212 C3
Lavenham Pl DN6 ..... 184 E2
Laverack Field 6 BD12 ..... 94 C3
Laverhills WF15 ..... 116 D5
Laverock Cres HD6 ..... 114 F5
Laverock La HD6 ..... 114 F5
Laverock Pl HD6 ..... 114 F5
Laverton Rd BD4 ..... 75 B4
Lavinia Terr BD14 ..... 73 D4
Law Cl LS22 ..... 13 F6
Law Common Rd
Carlecotes HD7 ..... 199 E5
Dunford Bridge HD7 ..... 199 E5
Law La HX3 ..... 114 A5
Law Slack Rd HD7 ..... 199 D6
Law St Batley WF17 ..... 117 F8
Bradford BD4 ..... 75 C2
Cleckheaton BD19 ..... 116 D8
Todmorden OL14 ..... 129 B7
Todmorden, Cornholme OL14 . 86 B1
Lawcliffe Cres BD22 ..... 51 D8
Lawefield Ave LS26 ..... 100 C6
Lawefield Gr WF2 ..... 142 A5
Lawefield Inf Sch WF2 ..... 142 A5
Lawefield Jun Sch WF2 ..... 142 A5
Lawefield La WF2 ..... 142 A5
Lawkholme Cres 4 BD21 ..... 35 C7
Lawkholme La BD21 ..... 35 C8
Lawn Ave LS29 ..... 9 F1
Lawn Rd LS29 ..... 9 F1
Lawn's La LS10 ..... 215 E3
Lawndale DN6 ..... 184 F2
Lawndale Fold S75 ..... 177 F1
Lawns Ave LS12 ..... 77 D3
Lawns Cl Gildersome LS12 ..... 77 D3
Normanton WF6 ..... 122 E4
Lawns Cres LS12 ..... 77 D3
Lawns Croft LS12 ..... 77 D3
Lawns Dene LS12 ..... 77 D3
Lawns Dr LS12 ..... 77 D3
Lawns Gn LS12 ..... 77 D3
Lawns Hall Cl LS16 ..... 42 B3
Lawns La Gildersome LS12 ..... 77 D4
Leeds LS12 ..... 77 D4
Lofthouse Gate WF2 ..... 120 E6
Lawns Mount LS12 ..... 77 D3
Lawns Park Primary Sch LS12 ..... 77 E5
Lawns Sq LS12 ..... 77 D3
Lawns Terr
East Ardsley WF3 ..... 120 D7
Gildersome LS12 ..... 77 D3
Lawns The Batley WF16 ..... 117 E4
Ilkley LS29 ..... 8 A4
Netherton WF4 ..... 158 A6
Lawns View WF6 ..... 122 E4
Lawnswood Gdns LS16 ..... 42 B2
Lawnswood Rd BD21 ..... 35 A5
Lawnswood Sch LS16 ..... 59 B8
Lawrence Ave Leeds LS8 ..... 208 C4
Pontefract WF8 ..... 146 B7
Lawrence Cres
Batley WF16 ..... 117 D6
Leeds LS8 ..... 61 C5
Lawrence Dr BD7 ..... 73 E2
Lawrence Gdns LS8 ..... 61 C5
Lawrence Rd Halifax HX3 ..... 113 B3
Huddersfield HD1 ..... 153 E6
Leeds LS8 ..... 208 C4
Lawrence St 14 HX3 ..... 92 A1
Lawrence Wlk LS8 ..... 208 C4
Lawson House 6 BD6 ..... 93 E8
Lawson Rd HD6 ..... 115 B2
Lawson St Bradford BD3 ..... 201 C4
Leeds LS12 ..... 209 E3
Lawton St HD4 ..... 154 A3
Lay Garth LS26 ..... 100 E5
Lay Garth Cl LS26 ..... 100 E5
Lay Garth Gdns LS26 ..... 100 E4
Lay Garth Gn LS26 ..... 100 E4
Lay Garth Mead LS26 ..... 100 E4
Lay Garth Pl LS26 ..... 100 E4
Lay Garth Sq LS26 ..... 100 E4
Laycock First Sch BD22 ..... 34 C7
Laycock La BD22 ..... 34 C7
Laycock Pl LS7 ..... 207 D3
Laygarth Dr HD5 ..... 155 C6
Laythorp Terr BD20 ..... 19 D1
Laythorpe Ct WF8 ..... 147 A7
Layton Ave LS19 ..... 40 E3
Layton Cl LS19 ..... 40 E2
Layton Cres LS19 ..... 40 D3
Layton Dr LS19 ..... 40 E3
Layton La LS19 ..... 40 E2
Layton Mount LS19 ..... 40 D3
Layton Park Ave LS19 ..... 40 E2
Layton Park Cl LS19 ..... 40 D3
Layton Park Croft LS19 ..... 40 E2
Layton Park Dr LS19 ..... 40 E3
Layton Rd LS18, LS19 ..... 40 E3
Layton Rise LS18 ..... 40 F3
Lazenby Dr LS22 ..... 13 D6
Lazenby Fold LS22 ..... 13 D6
Le Marchant Ave HD3 ..... 153 C8
Lea Ave HX3 ..... 113 C3
Lea Cl HD6 ..... 115 A4
Lea Croft Boston Spa LS23 ..... 30 D5
Otley LS21 ..... 23 A7
Lea Ct BD7 ..... 73 E2
Lea Dr HD8 ..... 190 F8
Lea Farm Cres LS5 ..... 58 F6
Lea Farm Dr LS5 ..... 58 F6
Lea Farm Gr LS5 ..... 58 F6
Lea Farm Mount LS5 ..... 58 F7
Lea Farm Pl LS5 ..... 58 F6
Lea Farm Rd LS5 ..... 58 F7
Lea Farm Row LS5 ..... 58 F6
Lea Farm Wlk LS5 ..... 58 F7
Lea Gdns HD7 ..... 189 E4
Lea La Featherstone WF7 ..... 145 E4
Huddersfield HD4 ..... 171 C6
Lea Mill Park Cl LS19 ..... 40 A7
Lea Mill Park Dr LS19 ..... 40 A7
Lea Park Cl LS10 ..... 99 F7
Lea Park Croft LS10 ..... 100 A7
Lea Park Dr LS10 ..... 99 F7
Lea Park Garth 2 LS10 ..... 99 F7
Lea Park Gdns 1 LS10 ..... 99 F7
Lea Park Gr LS10 ..... 99 F7
Lea Park Vale LS10 ..... 100 A7
Lea Rd WF17 ..... 117 F8
Lea Rise HD7 ..... 171 F3
Lea Side Gdns HD3 ..... 152 E7
Lea St Huddersfield HD1 ..... 154 A8
Huddersfield, Fartown HD1 . 136 A1
Huddersfield, Prince Royd HD3 ..... 135 C1
Lea The LS25 ..... 82 F5
Lea View WF17 ..... 117 F8
Leabank Ave LS25 ..... 83 A5
Leach Cres BD20 ..... 18 E2
Leach Rd BD20 ..... 18 D2
Leach Rise BD20 ..... 18 E2
Leach Way BD20 ..... 18 E2
Leadenhall St 10 HX1 ..... 202 B1
Leadwell La LS26 ..... 100 C4
Leaf St Castleford WF10 ..... 124 C7
4 Haworth BD22 ..... 51 E8
Leafield Ave Bradford BD2 ..... 56 C3
Huddersfield HD3 ..... 152 E6
Leafield Bank HD3 ..... 152 E6
Leafield Cl
Huddersfield HD2 ..... 136 D4
Leeds LS17 ..... 43 B2
Leafield Cres BD2 ..... 56 B3
Leafield Dr Bradford BD2 ..... 56 C4
Leeds LS17 ..... 43 B2
2 Pudsey LS28 ..... 76 F5
Leafield Gr BD2 ..... 56 C3
Leafield Grange LS17 ..... 43 B2
Leafield Pl LS19 ..... 39 F7
Leafield Terr BD2 ..... 56 C3
Leafield Way BD2 ..... 56 C3
Leafland St HX1 ..... 202 C3
Leafsway BD6 ..... 93 F6
Leah Pl LS12 ..... 210 C2
Leak Hall La HD8 ..... 192 A6
Leak Hall Rd HD8 ..... 191 F6
Leake St WF10 ..... 124 E7
Leamington Dr BD10 ..... 56 C8
Leamington Rd LS29 ..... 8 C5
Leamington St BD9 ..... 55 B2
Leamington Terr
Dewsbury WF12 ..... 139 D6
Ilkley LS29 ..... 8 C5
Learoyd St HD1 ..... 154 B7
Leas Ave HD7 ..... 188 F7
Leaside Dr BD13 ..... 72 D7
Leasowe Ave LS10 ..... 215 E2
Leasowe Cl LS10 ..... 215 E2
Leasowe Ct 9 LS10 ..... 215 E2
Leasowe Garth LS10 ..... 215 E2
Leasowe Gdns LS10 ..... 215 F2
Leasowe Rd LS10 ..... 215 E2
Leatham Ave WF7 ..... 145 E4
Leatham Cres WF7 ..... 145 F4
Leatham Dr WF7 ..... 145 F4
Leatham Park Rd WF7 ..... 145 F4
Leather Bank LS29 ..... 9 E3
Leathley Ave LS29 ..... 22 B4
Leathley Cres LS29 ..... 22 B4
Leathley La Leathley LS21 ..... 24 B8
Menston LS29 ..... 22 B4
Leathley Rd Leeds LS10 ..... 212 A1
Menston LS29 ..... 22 B4
Leathley St LS10 ..... 212 A1
Leavens The BD10 ..... 56 D8
Leaventhorpe Ave BD8 ..... 73 D7
Leaventhorpe Cl BD8 ..... 73 D7
Leaventhorpe Gr BD13 ..... 73 C6
Leaventhorpe La BD13, BD8 73 C6
Leaventhorpe Middle Sch BD15 ..... 73 B7
Leaventhorpe Way BD8 ..... 73 D7
Leaverholme Cl BB10 ..... 85 A7
Leavington Cl BD6 ..... 94 B6
Leconfield Ct LS22 ..... 13 C6
Leconfield House BD10 ..... 56 C7
Ledbury Ave LS10 ..... 99 F4
Ledbury Cl 4 LS10 ..... 99 F4
Ledbury Croft 3 LS10 ..... 99 F4
Ledbury Dr LS10 ..... 99 F4
Ledbury Gn 1 LS10 ..... 99 F4
Ledbury Gr 2 LS10 ..... 99 F4
Ledgard Bridge Mills Ind Units WF14 ..... 138 A3
Ledgard Dr WF4 ..... 159 F7
Ledgard Way LS12 ..... 209 F4
Ledgate La LS25 ..... 105 E4
Ledger La
Lofthouse Gate WF1 ..... 121 B4
Rothwell WF3 ..... 100 C1
Ledger Lane Junior & Infants Sch WF1 ..... 121 B4
Ledger Pl WF1 ..... 121 B4
Ledston Ave LS25 ..... 83 A5
Ledston Luck Cotts LS25 ..... 83 E2
Ledston Luck Enterprise Pk LS25 ..... 83 D2
Ledston Luck Villas LS25 ..... 83 D2
Ledston Mill La
Ledston WF10 ..... 103 E4
Ledston WF10 ..... 103 E7
Lee Bank HX3 ..... 92 B1
Lee Beck Gr WF3 ..... 121 E8
Lee Bottom Rd OL14 ..... 109 A5
Lee Bridge HX3 ..... 203 D4
Lee Brig WF6 ..... 122 F3
Lee Brigg First Sch WF6 ..... 122 E3
Lee Cl BD15 ..... 53 C6
Lee Clough Dr HX7 ..... 89 F1
Lee Ct Keighley BD21 ..... 35 F6
10 Liversedge WF15 ..... 117 A5
Ossett WF5 ..... 140 F4
Lee Gn WF14 ..... 138 A6
Lee Hall Rd HD3 ..... 135 C1
Lee Head HD2 ..... 153 F8
Lee La Ackworth M T WF7 ..... 164 B8
Halifax HX3 ..... 92 D3
Horsforth LS18 ..... 41 B2
Kirkburton HD8 ..... 173 E6
Mapplewell S71 ..... 178 E2
Royston S71 ..... 178 E2
Todmorden OL14 ..... 108 F3
Whitley Common S36 ..... 200 F4
Wilsden BD16 ..... 53 E6
Lee La E LS18 ..... 41 B2
Lee La W LS18 ..... 41 A2
Lee Mill Rd HX7 ..... 89 A5
Lee Mills Ind Est HX3 ..... 203 D4
Lee Moor La WF3 ..... 121 E8
Lee Moor Rd WF3 ..... 121 F6
Lee Mount Gdns 5 HX3 ..... 92 A1
Lee Mount Junior & Infants Sch HX3 ..... 92 A1
Lee Mount Rd HX3 ..... 92 A1
Lee Orchards LS23 ..... 30 E8
Lee Rd WF13 ..... 138 D5
Lee St Bradford BD1 ..... 201 B2
Brighouse HD6 ..... 115 A4
Dewsbury WF13 ..... 138 E6
Liversedge WF15 ..... 117 A5
3 Queensbury BD13 ..... 92 D8
Wakefield WF1 ..... 216 B2
Lee Way HD8 ..... 173 E7
Lee Wood Rd HX7 ..... 88 F5
Leech La BD13 ..... 53 A8
Leeches Hill HD3 ..... 134 C1
Leeds 27 Ind Est LS27 ..... 97 E5
Leeds, Bradford International Airport LS19 ..... 40 F7
Leeds & Bradford Rd LS13 .. 58 C4
Leeds Bsns Pk LS27 ..... 97 E4
Leeds City Art Gal LS1 ..... 211 E4
Leeds City Mus LS1 ..... 211 E4
Leeds City Office Pk LS11 . 211 F2
Leeds Coll of Building LS2 ..... 207 D1
Leeds Coll of Tech LS11 ..... 99 B8
Leeds Coll of Technology LS2 ..... 206 B1
Leeds General Infirmary LS1 ..... 206 B1
Leeds General Infirmary, Clarendon Wing LS2 ..... 206 A1
Leeds Girls' High Sch LS6 . 205 F4
Leeds Golf Ctr LS17 ..... 44 B8
Leeds Grammar Sch (Junior) LS3 ..... 205 F1
Leeds La LS26 ..... 82 B4
Leeds Met Univ LS16 ..... 42 E4
Leeds Metropolitan Univ
Leeds LS6 ..... 59 B6
Leeds LS1 ..... 206 B1
Leeds Montessori Sch LS8 ..... 61 D7
Leeds Old Rd Batley WF16 . 117 D6
Bradford BD3 ..... 75 E8
Leeds Polytechnic LS2 ..... 206 C1
Leeds Rd Barwick in E LS15 ..... 63 B6
Batley WF17 ..... 97 B2
Bradford BD2 ..... 56 B3
Bradford, Fagley BD2 ..... 56 C2
Bradford, Laisterdyke BD1, BD3 ..... 75 C6
Bradford, Thackley BD10 ..... 39 B2
Bramhope LS16 ..... 24 D4
Brighouse HX3 ..... 114 E8
Castleford WF10 ..... 124 D5
Collingham LS22 ..... 29 A8
Dewsbury WF12 ..... 118 E1
East Ardsley WF12 ..... 119 B5
Guiseley LS20 ..... 39 E8
Huddersfield HD2 ..... 136 F2
Ilkley LS29 ..... 8 D5
Kippax LS25 ..... 83 A2
Kippax, Allerton Bywater WF10 ..... 103 A5
Liversedge WF16 ..... 117 C5
Lofthouse Gate WF1 ..... 121 C5
Leeds Rd continued
Mickletown LS26 ..... 102 B3
Northowram HX3 ..... 114 A8
Ossett, Chickenley WF5 ..... 140 C8
Ossett, Gawthorpe WF5 ..... 119 C1
Otley LS21 ..... 23 D6
Pool LS16 ..... 24 D4
Rothwell LS26 ..... 100 F7
Rothwell, Robin Hood LS26, WF3 ..... 100 B2
Shipley BD18 ..... 55 D8
Wakefield WF1 ..... 216 A4
Yeadon LS19 ..... 40 D3
Leeds Road Hospl BD3 ..... 75 B7
Leeds St BD21 ..... 35 B7
Leeds Sta LS1 ..... 211 E3
Leeds Univ LS2 ..... 206 A2
Leef St 6 HD5 ..... 154 D6
Leefield Rd WF17 ..... 117 E6
Leeke Ave WF4 ..... 141 A2
Leeming St BD1 ..... 201 C4
Lees Ave WF12 ..... 139 C4
Lees Bank Ave BD22 ..... 51 E8
Lees Bank Dr BD22 ..... 51 E8
Lees Bank Hill BD22 ..... 51 E8
Lees Bank Rd BD22 ..... 51 E8
Lees Bldgs HX3 ..... 114 C7
Lees Cl Cullingworth BD13 ..... 52 C6
Huddersfield HD5 ..... 154 F7
Lees Cres WF4 ..... 159 F7
Lees Dr WF12 ..... 139 C4
Lees First Sch BD22 ..... 51 E8
Lees Hall Rd WF12 ..... 139 C3
Lees Holm WF12 ..... 139 C4
Lees House Rd WF12 ..... 139 C5
Lees La Haworth BD22 ..... 51 D8
Pudsey LS28 ..... 57 D4
Lees Mill La HD7 ..... 152 B1
Lees Moor Rd BD13 ..... 52 C6
Lees Rd 6 HX7 ..... 89 A4
Lees The BB10 ..... 85 A7
Lees Yd 15 HX7 ..... 89 A3
Leeside Ave HD2 ..... 136 C4
Leeside Prim Sch WF16 ..... 117 E6
Leeside Rd WF16 ..... 117 E6
Leesworth Ct 7 BD22 ..... 51 E8
Legrams Ave BD7 ..... 73 F5
Legrams La BD7 ..... 74 A6
Legrams Mill La BD7 ..... 74 A6
Legrams St BD7 ..... 74 C7
Legrams Terr BD7 ..... 74 C7
Leicester Cl LS7 ..... 206 B2
Leicester Gr LS7 ..... 206 B2
Leicester Pl LS2 ..... 206 B2
Leicester St BD4 ..... 75 A4
Leicester Terr 9 HX3 ..... 113 B4
Leigh Ave WF3 ..... 120 A8
Leigh Rd WF3 ..... 120 A8
Leigh St Ackworth M T WF7 . 163 D5
Sowerby Bridge HX6 ..... 112 C5
Leigh View WF3 ..... 120 A8
Leighton La 4 LS1 ..... 211 D4
Leighton Pl 1 LS1 ..... 211 E4
Leighton St LS1 ..... 211 D4
Leisure La HD8 ..... 175 E8
Leith Ct WF12 ..... 139 E1
Leith St BD21 ..... 35 B8
Lemans Dr WF13 ..... 117 F3
Lemington Ave HX1 ..... 202 C2
Lemon St Bradford BD5 ..... 74 C3
Halifax HX1 ..... 202 B3
Lemon Tree Cl WF8 ..... 146 B6
Lenacre La WF4 ..... 156 D1
Lenham Cl 1 LS27 ..... 98 A2
Lennie St BD21 ..... 35 B6
Lennon Dr BD8 ..... 74 B8
Lennox Dr WF2 ..... 141 D3
Lennox Rd Leeds LS4 ..... 205 D1
Todmorden, Cornholme OL14 ..... 86 A1
Todmorden, Portsmouth OL14 ..... 85 F1
Lenny Balk DN5 ..... 195 E7
Lens Dr BD17 ..... 38 C4
Lentilfield St HX3 ..... 92 A2
Lentilfield Terr 6 HX3 ..... 92 A2
Lenton Dr LS11 ..... 214 C2
Lenton Villas BD10 ..... 39 B1
Leodis Ct LS11 ..... 211 E2
Leonard St Bingley BD16 ..... 37 A2
Bradford BD12 ..... 94 D3
Huddersfield HD2 ..... 136 B1
Leonard's Pl 4 BD16 ..... 37 A2
Leopold Gdns LS7 ..... 207 E3
Leopold Gr LS7 ..... 207 D3
Leopold Primary Sch LS7 .. 207 E3
Leopold St Leeds LS7 ..... 207 E3
Ossett WF5 ..... 141 A4
Lepton CE Jun & Inf Sch HD8 ..... 155 D3
Lepton Jun & Inf Sch HD8 ..... 155 E2
Lepton La HD8 ..... 174 A8
Lepton Pl LS27 ..... 97 D7
Lesley Way HD4 ..... 153 A1
Leslie Ave LS19 ..... 40 C8
Leslie St HD2 ..... 136 A1
Leslie Terr 5 LS6 ..... 206 A3
Lesmere Gr BD7 ..... 73 F2
Lessarna Ct BD4 ..... 75 C5
Leven Gdns LS22 ..... 13 D7
Levens Bvd LS15 ..... 80 E6
Levens Cl LS15 ..... 80 E6
Levens Gdns LS15 ..... 80 E6
Levens Pl LS15 ..... 80 E6
Leventhorpe Cotts LS26 ..... 101 E8
Leventhorpe Ct 1 LS26 ..... 101 C5
Leventhorpe Way LS26 ..... 101 C5
Lever St 5 Bradford BD6 ..... 74 A1
Todmorden OL14 ..... 108 B5
Levita Gr BD4 ..... 75 D4
Levita Pl Bradford BD4 ..... 75 E5
4 Leeds LS15 ..... 80 F8
Lewin Gr WF10 ..... 125 D8
Lewis Cl 19 BD13 ..... 72 E1
Lewis St HX1 ..... 203 D4
Lewisham Ct LS27 ..... 98 B4
Lewisham Gr LS27 ..... 98 B4
Lewisham Rd HD7 ..... 152 A1
Lewisham St LS27 ..... 97 E3
Lexington Cl BD4 ..... 95 B8
Ley Fleaks Rd BD10 ..... 56 B7
Ley La LS12 ..... 210 A4
Ley Top First Sch BD15 ..... 73 B8
Ley Top La BD15 ..... 73 C8
Leybrook Croft WF9 ..... 181 E7
Leyburn Ave Batley WF16 ..... 117 E6
Brighouse HX3 ..... 114 E8
Leyburn Gr
2 Bingley BD16 ..... 37 A4
Shipley BD18 ..... 55 A7
Leyburn Rd DN6 ..... 184 F2
Leyburne St BD8 ..... 55 C1
Leyden Rise BD15 ..... 73 B8
Leyfield BD17 ..... 38 B3
Leyfield Bank HD7 ..... 189 C7
Leygards La HD7 ..... 170 C1
Leyland Croft HD2 ..... 136 E6
Leyland Rd Batley WF17 ..... 96 E1
Castleford WF10 ..... 125 D8
Leylands Ave BD9 ..... 54 F3
Leylands Gr BD9 ..... 54 F3
Leylands La Bradford BD9 ..... 54 F3
Keighley BD21 ..... 35 D6
Leylands Rd LS2 ..... 207 D1
Leylands Terr BD9 ..... 54 F3
Leymoor Rd HD7 ..... 152 E5
Leys Cl BD10 ..... 39 A1
Leys La Boston Spa LS23 ..... 14 C2
Emley HD8 ..... 175 B6
Hampole DN6 ..... 184 C2
Kirk Smeaton WF8 ..... 166 C7
Knottingley WF11 ..... 126 F1
Leys Rd WF8 ..... 147 E6
Leys The WF9 ..... 182 C1
Leysholme Cres LS12 ..... 209 D2
Leysholme Dr LS12 ..... 209 E2
Leysholme Terr LS12 ..... 209 E2
Leysholme View LS12 ..... 209 E2
Leyside Dr BD15 ..... 54 B1
Leyton Cres BD10 ..... 56 B7
Leyton Dr BD10 ..... 56 B7
Leyton Gr BD10 ..... 56 B7
Leyton Terr BD10 ..... 56 B7
Libbey St BD8 ..... 55 C1
Lichen Cl BD7 ..... 74 A3
Lichfield Mount BD2 ..... 55 F4
Lichfield Rd WF12 ..... 139 F8
Lickless Ave LS18 ..... 41 D1
Lickless Dr LS18 ..... 41 D1
Lickless Gdns LS18 ..... 41 D1
Lickless Terr LS18 ..... 41 D1
Lidgate Cl WF13 ..... 118 C2
Lidgate Cres WF9 ..... 182 E2
Lidgate Gdns WF13 ..... 118 C2
Lidgate La Dewsbury WF13 118 C2
Shafton S72 ..... 180 B3
Lidget Ave BD7 ..... 73 F5
Lidget Green First Sch BD7 ..... 73 F6
Lidget Green Middle Sch BD7 ..... 73 F6
Lidget Hill LS28 ..... 76 E7
Lidget La WF4 ..... 144 D1
Lidget Pl BD7 ..... 74 A5
Lidget Rd BD20 ..... 4 C5
Lidget St HD3 ..... 135 B1
Lidget Terr Bradford BD14 ..... 73 D4
Bradford, Scholemoor BD7 ..... 73 F5
Lidgett Ave LS8 ..... 204 C3
Lidgett Cres LS8 ..... 204 C4
Lidgett Ct Garforth LS25 ..... 82 E6
Leeds LS8 ..... 204 C4
Lidgett Gr LS8 ..... 204 C3
Lidgett Hill LS8 ..... 204 C3
Lidgett La Garforth LS25 ..... 82 E6
Leeds LS8 ..... 204 C3
Skelmanthorpe HD8 ..... 174 F1
Lidgett Mount LS8 ..... 43 F1
Lidgett Park Ave LS8 ..... 44 A1
Lidgett Park Ct LS8 ..... 43 F1
Lidgett Park Gdns LS8 ..... 204 C4
Lidgett Park Gr LS8 ..... 204 C4
Lidgett Park Mews LS8 ..... 44 A1
Lidgett Park Rd LS8 ..... 44 A1
Lidgett Park View LS8 ..... 43 F1
Lidgett Pl LS8 ..... 204 C4
Lidgett Rise HD8 ..... 174 F1
Lidgett Towers LS8 ..... 43 E1
Lidgett Wlk LS8 ..... 204 C3
Lifton Pl LS2 ..... 206 A2
Light Bank La BD20 ..... 6 C3
Light La WF2 ..... 141 E8
Lightcliffe CE Prim Sch HX3 ..... 114 E8
Lightcliffe Golf Course HX3 ..... 114 E8
Lightcliffe Preparatory Sch HX3 ..... 114 D7
Lightcliffe Rd
Brighouse HD6 ..... 115 A4
Huddersfield HD4 ..... 153 D4
Lightcliffe Royd La HX4 ..... 133 C6
Lightenfield La HD4 ..... 171 D7
Lightfoot Ave WF10 ..... 124 E6
Lightfoot Cl WF10 ..... 124 D6

Lighthazles Chapel Rd
HX6 132 A6
Lighthazles Rd HX6 132 B6
Lighthouse OL15 129 C1
Lightowler Cl 10 HX1 202 C3
Lightowler Rd HX1 202 C3
Lightowler St 10 BD6 74 C1
Lightridge Cl HD2 136 A4
Lightridge Rd HD2 135 F5
Lilac Ave Knottingley WF11 126 E2
Wakefield WF2 142 C3
Lilac Cl Addingham LS29 7 A8
Brighouse HD6 115 C3
Lilac Gr Bradford BD4 75 D6
Cleckheaton BD19 96 A1
Shipley BD18 55 D5
Lilac St HX3 92 A1
Lilac Wlk HD7 152 E5
Lilacs The Guiseley LS20 22 E1
Royston S71 179 E4
Liley La Kirkheaton WF14 155 F8
Lepton WF14 156 C6
Lilian St BD4 75 C3
Lillands Ave HD6 114 F2
Lillands La HD6 114 F2
Lillands Terr HD6 114 F2
Lilley St WF9 181 D6
Lilley Terr WF9 182 B2
Lilly La HX3 203 F2
Lilly St HX6 112 B3
Lily Croft BD8 55 B1
Lily St Bradford BD8 55 B1
Todmorden OL14 107 E8
Lilycroft First Sch BD9 55 B2
Lilycroft Rd BD9 55 B2
Lilycroft Wlk BD9 55 A2
Lilythorne Ave BD10 56 C8
Lime Ave Hebden Bridge HX7 88 F3
Holmfirth HD7 189 C8
Todmorden OL14 108 A6
Lime Cl BD20 18 A1
Lime Cres
South Elmsall WF9 182 E1
Wakefield WF2 142 F1
Lime Ct BD16 36 E6
Lime Gr Huddersfield HD7 152 E5
Royston S71 179 C1
South Elmsall WF9 182 E1
Yeadon LS19 40 A4
Lime Pit La WF3 121 F4
Lime St Bingley BD16 36 F3
Bradford BD7 74 B4
Cleckheaton BD19 116 C7
Haworth BD22 51 C6
Huddersfield HD1 153 E4
Keighley BD21 35 B7
Ossett WF5 140 E4
Todmorden OL14 108 A6
Lime Tree Ave Batley WF17 118 A4
Boston Spa LS23 30 D8
Elland HX5 135 A6
Leeds LS17 43 E2
Pontefract WF8 146 B8
Lime Tree Ct WF9 181 C6
Lime Tree Gdns LS23 30 E7
Lime Tree Gr BD11 96 A7
Lime Tree Sq BD18 54 D8
Lime-Tree Cres LS25 83 C1
Limers Gate OL14 106 E4
Limes Ave Halifax HX3 113 C4
Mapplewell S75 178 C2
Limes Cl S75 178 C2
Limetrees WF8 126 A4
Limewood App LS14 62 A7
Limewood Rd LS14 62 A6
Linburn Cl S71 179 A4
Lincoln Ave Batley WF16 117 D5
Liversedge WF15 116 F2
Lincoln Cl BD8 55 C1
Lincoln Cres WF9 183 A4
Lincoln Ct HD5 155 A7
Lincoln Dr WF15 117 A2
Lincoln Gr
Huddersfield HD5 155 A4
Liversedge WF15 116 F2
Lincoln Green Rd LS9 207 E1
Lincoln Rd Bradford BD8 74 C8
Dewsbury WF12 118 F1
Leeds LS9 207 E1
Lincoln St Bradford BD15 73 C8
Castleford WF10 124 E8
Huddersfield HD1 154 C6
Todmorden OL14 86 B1
Wakefield WF2 142 A7
Lincoln Towers LS9 207 E1
Lincoln Way 6 HX3 92 B1
Lincoln Wlk LS25 83 C2
Lincombe Bank LS8 204 B4
Lincombe Dr LS8 204 B4
Lincombe Mount LS8 204 B4
Lincombe Rise LS8 204 B4
Lincroft Ave HD5 154 E5
Lincroft Cres LS13 58 E3
Lincs Wold WF15 116 B4
Lindale Ave WF7 164 C7
Lindale Cl LS10 99 D7
Lindale Garth WF2 120 C2
Lindale Gr WF2 120 D1
Lindale La WF2 120 C2
Lindale Mount WF2 120 D1
Linden Ave Bradford BD3 75 E8
Leeds LS11 214 B3
Todmorden OL14 108 A6
Linden Cl Bardsey LS17 28 D4
Brighouse HD6 115 C3
Castleford WF10 125 D6
Dewsbury WF12 140 B7
Knottingley WF11 126 C4
Linden Ct LS16 59 D7
Linden Gdns 5 LS11 214 C3
Linden Gr LS11 214 C3
Linden Mount LS11 214 B3
Linden Pl
11 Hebden Bridge HX7 89 A4
3 Leeds LS11 214 C3
Linden Rd Elland HX5 134 E6
Halifax HX3 113 C4
Hebden Bridge HX7 89 A4
Hebden Bridge, Hawks Clough
HX7 89 D1
Huddersfield HD2 135 F1
Leeds LS11 214 C3
Linden Rise BD21 35 E5
Linden St LS11 214 C3
Linden Terr
Ackworth M T WF7 163 D5
Leeds LS11 214 C3
Pontefract WF8 146 C8
Linden Way LS22 13 D7
Lindholm Gdns 10 BD15 73 B8
Lindisfarne Rd BD18 54 F7
Lindley Ave HD3 135 A2
Lindley Dr BD7 73 F2
Lindley Lodge HD3 135 B1
Lindley Moor Rd HD3 134 E2
Lindley Rd Bradford BD5 74 D3
Elland HX5 134 F4
Lindley St HD3 153 A5
Lindon St 12 BD22 51 C6
Lindrick Cl Cudworth S72 180 C1
Normanton WF6 123 D1
Lindrick Gr HX2 91 F7
Lindrick Way HX2 91 F7
Lindrick Wlk HX2 91 F7
Lindsay Acre WF3 120 A8
Lindsay Ave WF2 141 C5
Lindsay Rd LS25 82 F6
Lindsey Ct LS9 207 E1
Lindsey Gdns LS9 207 E1
Lindsey Mount LS9 207 E1
Lindsey Rd LS9 207 E1
Lindwell Ave 5 HX4 134 C7
Lindwell Gr 2 HX4 134 C7
Lindwell Pl 1 HX4 134 C7
Linefield Rd WF17 118 D5
Lineham Ct WF15 117 A2
Lineholme Ave OL14 107 E7
Linfit Fold HD7 170 A8
Linfit La Kirkburton HD8 174 B8
Lepton HD8 156 C1
Slaithwaite HD7 170 B8
Ling Bob HX2 112 D8
Ling Bob Croft HX2 91 D1
Ling Bob Junior
& Infant Sch HX2 112 D8
Ling Croft LS23 30 B8
Ling La LS14 45 B7
Ling Park App BD15 53 C4
Ling Park Ave BD15 53 C4
Ling Royd Ave HX2 112 D8
Lingamore Leys S63 194 D1
Lingard St BD1 201 C4
Lingards Rd HD7 169 E7
Lingards Terr HD7 169 C6
Lingdale Rd BD6 94 B5
Lingfield App LS17 43 B3
Lingfield Bank LS17 43 B3
Lingfield Cl LS17 43 C3
Lingfield Cres
Bradford BD13 73 C2
Leeds LS17 43 B3
Lingfield Dr
Cullingworth BD22 35 A1
Leeds LS17 43 C3
Lingfield Gate LS17 43 B3
Lingfield Gdns LS17 43 B3
Lingfield Gn LS17 43 B3
Lingfield Gr Leeds LS17 43 C3
Wilsden BD15 53 D5
Lingfield Hill LS17 43 B3
Lingfield Mount LS17 43 C3
Lingfield Rd Leeds LS17 43 C3
Wilsden BD15 53 C5
Lingfield Terr BD13 73 C2
Lingfield View LS17 43 B3
Lingfield Wlk LS17 43 B3
Lings La DN6 184 A8
Lingwell App 4 LS10 99 C4
Lingwell Ave LS10 99 C5
Lingwell Chase WF3 121 C6
Lingwell Cres LS10 99 C5
Lingwell Ct
Lofthouse Gate WF3 121 A5
Middleton LS10 99 C4
Lingwell Gate Cres WF1 121 B5
Lingwell Gate Dr WF1 121 B5
Lingwell Gate La
East Ardsley WF3 120 F8
Lofthouse Gate WF1 121 A6
Middleton WF3 99 F2
Lingwell Gdns 3 LS10 99 C4
Lingwell Gn 6 LS10 99 C4
Lingwell Gr LS10 99 C4
Lingwell Mews 1 LS10 99 C4
Lingwell Nook La
Lofthouse Gate WF3 121 C6
Lofthouse Gate, Lingwell Gate
WF3 121 A8
Lingwell Park Ct LS10 99 C5
Lingwell Rd LS10 99 C4
Lingwell View 2 LS10 99 C4
Lingwell Wlk 5 LS10 99 C4
Lingwood Ave BD8 54 F1
Lingwood Ct HD7 189 D7
Lingwood Rd BD8 73 F8
Lingwood Terr 1 BD8 73 F8
Link Rd Dewsbury WF12 139 D7
Huddersfield HD1 153 D6
Wakefield WF1 216 A4
Link The Pontefract WF8 146 C6
Swillington LS26 81 F1
Links Ave BD19 95 D2
Links The WF7 124 D1
Links View S75 178 B2
Linkway BD16 54 A7
Linnburn Mews LS29 8 B3
Linnet Cl Bradford BD8 73 C7
Mirfield WF14 138 A8
Linnet Ct LS27 98 D3
Linnet Gr WF2 160 D5
Linnet St BD21 35 C8
Linnhe Ave BD6 93 F6
Linshaws Rd HD7 198 E5
Linthwaite Ardron
Meml CE Jun & Inf Sch
HD7 152 E1
Linthwaite Bsns Ctr HD7 152 D1
Linthwaite Junior
& Infant Sch HD7 152 D1
Linton Ave Batley WF17 118 A5
Leeds LS17 43 F4
Silsden BD20 5 E2
Wetherby LS22 13 D6
Linton Cl Leeds LS17 43 E4
Liversedge WF15 116 F5
Linton Comm LS22 13 A1
Linton Cres LS17 43 F4
Linton Croft 3 LS16 59 A8
Linton Dr LS17 43 E4
Linton Gr Batley WF16 117 E3
Brighouse HD6 135 E8
Leeds LS17 43 F4
Linton Hills Rd LS22 13 C4
Linton La Collingham LS22 13 C4
Spofforth LS22 13 A7
Linton Meadows LS22 13 C5
Linton Rd Collingham LS22 13 B1
Leeds LS17 43 E4
Wakefield WF1 142 F6
Wetherby LS22 13 D5
Linton Rise Leeds LS17 43 E4
Normanton WF6 123 D1
Linton St BD4 74 F4
Linton View LS17 43 E5
Lion Cott S75 193 E4
Lion St OL14 108 A3
Lionel St WF5 140 E4
Liphill Bank Rd HD7 188 D4
Lippersley La LS29 6 B6
Lipscomb St HD3 153 B5
Liquorice Way WF8 146 C8
Lisbon Sq 9 LS1 211 D4
Lisbon St LS1 211 D4
Lisheen Ave WF10 124 E6
Lishen Gr WF10 124 E7
Lisker Ave LS21 23 B7
Lisker Dr LS21 23 B7
Lismore Rd BD20 35 B8
Lister Ave BD4 75 B3
Lister Cl WF7 145 C5
Lister Ct HX1 203 E3
Lister Hill LS18 41 C2
Lister La Bradford BD2 56 A3
Halifax HX1 202 C3
Lister Lane Sch BD2 56 A3
Lister Rd WF7 145 C5
Lister St
Bradford, Dudley Hill BD4 75 C2
Bradford, Tong Street BD4 75 E1
Brighouse HD6 115 A3
Castleford WF10 124 C8
Halifax HX1 203 E3
Huddersfield HD5 154 E5
Ilkley LS29 8 A4
Keighley BD21 35 B6
Lister View BD8 55 C1
Lister Ville BD15 53 C5
Lister Wlk LS27 97 F6
Lister's Rd Halifax HX3 113 E8
Huddersfield HD2 136 B3
Listerdale WF15 117 B5
Listerhills Ind Est BD7 74 C7
Listerhills Rd BD7 74 C7
Listers Ct LS29 8 A4
Listing Ave WF15 117 B5
Listing Ct WF15 117 B5
Listing Dr WF15 117 B5
Listing La BD19, WF15 117 B6
Litell Royd WF7 144 D5
Litherop La HD8 176 C5
Litherop Rd S75 176 D3
Little Baines St HX1 202 C3
Little Bradley HX4 134 C6
Little Brunswick St 6
HD1 154 A7
Little Cake HD7 189 C2
Little Church La LS26 102 C2
Little Cote BD10 39 A1
Little Cross St 1 BD5 74 E2
Little Fountain St LS27 98 A3
Little Green La WF16 117 C5
Little Hemsworth WF9 181 E6
Little Horton Gn BD5 74 D5
Little Horton La
Bradford BD5 201 B2
Bradford, Holme Top BD5 74 D4
Little King St LS1 211 E3
Little La Bradford BD9 54 F1
Featherstone WF7 145 E4
Holmfirth HD7 188 F5
Holmfirth, Wooldale HD7 189 C6
Ilkley LS29 8 C4
Keighley BD20 19 E1
7 Morley LS27 98 C8
Little La continued
Rothwell WF3 100 E3
South Elmsall WF9 183 B3
South Elmsall, Moorthorpe
WF9 182 F3
Upton WF9 183 B7
Wadsworth Moor HX7 69 B6
Little Lane Ct 8 LS27 98 C8
Little London HX3 92 F4
Little Moor Pl LS12 209 E3
Little Neville St LS1 211 E3
Little Pk BD10 39 F1
Little Queen St LS1 211 D4
Little St BD22 51 C8
Little Wood Dr BD19 95 D2
Little Woodhouse HD6 115 A2
Little Woodhouse St LS2 206 A1
Littlebeck Dr BD16 37 C3
Littlefield Gr WF5 140 E6
Littlefield Rd WF5 140 E5
Littlefield Wlk BD6 94 B8
Littleholme St OL14 108 A3
Littlelands BD16 54 A7
Littlemoor Cres LS28 76 E5
Littlemoor Cres S LS28 76 E5
Littlemoor Gdns Halifax HX2 91 E6
Pudsey LS28 76 E5
Littlemoor Gr WF14 137 F5
Littlemoor La LS14 45 F5
Littlemoor Rd Halifax HX2 91 E6
2 Mirfield WF14 137 F5
Pudsey LS28 76 F6
Littlemoor View LS28 76 F6
Littlethorpe Hill WF15 116 D1
Littlethorpe Rd WF15 116 D2
Littletown Jun & Inf Sch
WF15 117 A6
Littleway LS17 43 C1
Littlewood Cl BD6 94 C7
Littlewood Croft HD4 154 A2
Litton Croft WF1 142 F7
Litton Rd BD22 35 A6
Litton Way LS14 62 B8
Littondale Cl BD17 38 E4
Liversedge Hall La WF15 117 A3
Livingston House BD10 56 C6
Livingstone Cl BD2 55 F6
Livingstone Rd Bradford BD2 55 F5
Shipley BD2 55 D4
Livingstone St 11 HX3 92 A1
Livingstone St N HX2 92 A5
Livinia Gr LS7 206 C2
Lloyd St OL14 108 B6
Lloyds Dr BD12 94 E6
Lobley St WF16 117 E4
Locarno Ave BD9 54 E2
Locherbie Gn BD15 54 B1
Lochy Rd BD6 93 F6
Lock La Castleford WF10 103 D1
Normanton WF6 122 F6
Lock St Dewsbury WF12 139 D4
Halifax HX3 203 F2
Todmorden OL14 108 A3
Lock View BD16 36 E4
Lock Way WF13 138 E4
Lockbridge Way HD3 153 B4
Locks The BD16 36 F4
Locksley Rd HD6 115 D1
Lockwood Ave WF14 138 B7
Lockwood Cl LS11 214 C1
Lockwood Ct LS11 214 C1
Lockwood Pk LS11 214 C1
Lockwood Rd HD1 153 F3
Lockwood Scar HD4 154 A2
Lockwood St
Bradford, Brownroyd Hill
BD6 74 C1
Bradford, Raw Nook BD12 94 E5
5 Shipley BD18 54 F8
Lockwood Sta HD1 153 E3
Lockwood Way LS11 214 C1
Lockwood's Yd 21 HD1 154 A6
Lode Pit La BD16 37 D4
Lodge Ave
Castleford WF10 125 C7
Elland HX5 135 C7
Lodge Cl HD4 153 E1
Lodge Dr Elland HX5 135 C7
Mirfield WF14 138 C4
Lodge Farm Cl WF12 139 D4
Lodge Farm Gdns WF6 122 F3
Lodge Gate BD13 52 E1
Lodge Gate Cl BD13 52 E1
Lodge Hill BD17 37 F3
Lodge Hill Cl LS12 77 E3
Lodge Hill Rd WF5 140 D8
Lodge Hill Wlk LS12 77 E3
Lodge La Crofton WF4 143 E2
Leeds LS11 214 B3
Liversedge WF15 117 C2
Wakefield WF2 160 E4
Lodge Pl HX5 135 C7
Lodge Rd LS28 76 D8
Lodge St Cullingworth BD13 52 D6
Glusburn BD20 16 B6
Haworth BD22 51 C7
Hemsworth WF9 181 D8
Leeds LS2 206 B1
Skelmanthorpe HD8 175 A2
Lodge Terr 13 LS11 214 B2
Lodge The HD7 152 E2
Lodges Cl WF4 162 C2
Lodore Ave BD2 56 B3
Lodore Pl BD2 56 B3
Lodore Rd BD2 56 A3
Loft St BD8 73 F8
Lofthouse Gate Junior
& Infants Sch WF1 121 D6
Lofthouse Pl LS2 206 B2
Lofthouse Terr LS2 206 C2
Logwood St HD1 154 A4
Lombard St Halifax HX1 202 B1
Leeds LS15 80 F7
Yeadon LS19 40 A4
Lombardi Ct WF5 140 F4
Lombardy Cl HD7 171 F3
Lombardy Garth WF2 142 A8
Lomond Ave LS18 41 B4
Londesboro Gr LS9 80 A7
Londesboro Terr LS9 80 A7
London La LS19 40 A4
London Rd Slaithwaite HD7 152 A1
Sowerby Bridge HX6 112 E3
Todmorden OL14 109 C6
London Spring Rd HX6 132 A4
London St LS19 40 A4
Long Cl BD12 94 B4
Long Close La
Holmfirth HD8 190 C7
Leeds LS9 212 C3
South Elmsall WF9 183 C6
Long Crest WF8 146 E6
Long Croft S75 178 B1
Long Croft St HD7 152 E4
Long Cswy Denholme BD13 71 C8
Dewsbury WF12 139 D3
Halton East BD23 1 D7
Leeds LS9 212 C1
Leeds, Adel LS16 42 D3
Lofthouse Gate WF3 121 F5
Ripponden HX6 131 F1
Todmorden OL14 108 F3
Wakefield WF1 216 C4
Long Cswy The
Blackshaw Head HX7 87 E4
Hebden Bridge HX2 111 A6
Holme Chapel BB10 85 D7
Sowerby Bridge HX2 111 A6
Long Dam La WF4 162 B3
Long Edge Low Rd HX6 111 B2
Long Edge Rd HX6 111 A3
Long Fallas Cres HD6 136 B8
Long Gate Haworth BD20 33 B8
Ripponden HX6 150 A8
Sutton in C BD20 33 B8
Long Grove Ave HD5 154 E6
Long Hey La OL14 108 C3
Long Heys HX4 134 C6
Long Hill End BD22 32 D8
Long Hill Rd HD2 136 C4
Long House Rd HX2 91 C6
Long Ing Rd HD7 199 A7
Long La Ackworth M T WF7 146 B1
Barwick in E LS15 63 E5
Bradford BD15 53 D1
Clayton West HD8 175 F3
Dewsbury WF12 139 F6
Flockton WF4 156 E1
Halifax, Bank Top HX3 113 F6
Halifax, Wheatley HX2, HX3 91 E2
Harden BD16 36 A1
Hebden Bridge HX7 88 E1
Hebden Bridge HX7 109 D3
Huddersfield HD5 154 E7
Kirk Smeaton WF8 166 D3
Pontefract WF7, WF8 146 F7
Queensbury BD13 92 E7
Shepley HD8 173 E2
Shipley BD9 54 E5
Sowerby Bridge HX6 112 A2
Long Lee First Sch BD21 35 F5
Long Lee La BD21 35 E5
Long Lover La HX1 202 B4
Long Mdws LS29 9 F2
Long Meadow Ct LS25 83 A5
Long Meadow Gate LS25 82 F5
Long Meadows
Bradford BD2 55 E4
Bramhope LS16 24 E2
Garforth LS25 82 F5
Long Moor La HD8 174 B1
Long Preston Chase BD10 56 D7
Long Reach HX2 91 A3
Long Riddings LS29 2 E1
Long Ridge HD6 136 A7
Long Row Bradford BD12 94 D5
Crofton WF4 144 A5
Horsforth LS18 41 C2
Thornton BD13 72 C7
Long Row Ct 2 BD5 74 E3
Long Royd Dr BD17 38 E4
Long Royd La HD8 191 B8
Long Royd Rd HX6 111 C2
Long Shaw La OL14 108 F4
Long St BD4 75 B5
Long Thorpe La WF3 100 B1
Long Tongue Scrog La
Kirkheaton HD5 155 E7
Lepton HD5 155 F6
Long Wall HX5 134 E6
Longacre WF10 124 D6
Longacre La BD22 51 E8
Longacres BD22 51 E8
Longbottom Ave
Silsden BD20 5 F1
Sowerby Bridge HX6 111 E3
Longbottom Terr HX3 113 D4
Longcauseway WF12 139 D8
Longclose Ind Est LS9 207 E2
Longcroft Huddersfield HD5 154 F2
Keighley BD21 35 C6
Longcroft Link 3 BD1 74 D7
Longcroft Pl BD1 201 A3

Longcroft Rd LS29 8 E3
Longdale Dr WF9 182 E4
Longden Ave HD4 153 D2
Longdike Ct [3] LS25 83 B1
Longdike La LS25 103 C8
Longdon Ave HD8 155 E3
Longdon Wlk HD8 155 E3
Longfellow Gr WF3 121 E6
Longfield Elland HX4 134 B4
  Heptonstall HX7 88 F4
Longfield Ave
  Huddersfield, Grove Place HD5 154 D7
  Huddersfield, Leymoor HD7 152 E5
  Northowram HX3 93 A1
  [3] Pudsey LS28 76 F7
Longfield Cl
  Huddersfield HD5 154 D7
  Todmorden OL14 108 B4
Longfield Ct WF16 117 E4
Longfield Dr
  Ackworth M T WF7 164 C7
  Bradford BD4 75 C3
  Leeds LS13 81 A8
  Mapplewell S75 178 B1
  Pudsey LS13 57 F5
Longfield Garth [3] LS13 57 F5
Longfield Gr
  [2] Pudsey LS28 76 F7
  Todmorden OL14 108 B4
Longfield La OL14 108 B3
Longfield Mount [1] LS28 76 F7
Longfield Rd Batley WF16 117 D4
  Pudsey LS28 76 E7
  Todmorden OL14 108 B5
Longfield Rise OL14 108 B4
Longfield Terr Pudsey LS28 76 E7
  Todmorden OL14 108 B4
  Wakefield WF2 141 F7
Longfield Way OL14 108 B4
Longford Terr BD7 73 F5
Longhouse Dr BD13 71 D8
Longhouse La BD13 71 D8
Longlands Ave
  Denholme BD13 52 D1
  Slaithwaite HD7 151 E1
Longlands Bank HD7 189 B8
Longlands Cl WF5 140 E6
Longlands Dr
  Haworth BD22 51 D8
  Mapplewell S75 178 B1
Longlands La LS22 12 D4
Longlands Rd Batley WF13 118 A2
  Ossett WF5 140 E6
  Slaithwaite HD7 151 E1
Longlands St BD1 201 A3
Longlands Trad Est WF5 140 E6
Longley Edge La HD7 189 B1
Longley Edge Rd HD7 189 B1
Longley La Holmfirth HD7 189 A1
  Huddersfield HD4 154 D2
  Sowerby Bridge HX6 111 F1
Longley Park Golf Course HD1, HD5 154 C4
Longley Rd HD5 154 D4
Longmeadow HX4 133 A5
Longroyd BD10 55 F8
Longroyd Ave LS11 214 C3
Longroyd Cres Leeds LS11 214 C3
  Slaithwaite HD7 151 E1
Longroyd Cres N LS11 214 C3
Longroyd Farm WF4 158 B7
Longroyd Gr LS11 214 C3
Longroyd La HD1 153 F5
Longroyd Pl
  Huddersfield HD1 153 E5
  Leeds LS11 214 C3
Longroyd St LS11 214 C3
Longroyd St N LS11 214 C3
Longroyd Terr LS11 214 C3
Longroyd View LS11 214 C3
Longroyde Cl HD6 114 F1
Longroyde Gr HD6 135 F8
Longroyde Junior Sch HD6 114 F1
Longroyde Rd [3] HD6 115 A1
Longside La BD7 74 C6
Longsight Rd S75 178 A1
Longsight Terr WF9 163 B1
Longwood Ave BD16 36 E5
Longwood Cl
  East Ardsley WF3 119 D8
  Leeds LS17 44 B5
Longwood Cres LS17 44 B5
Longwood Ct WF3 119 E8
Longwood Edge Rd HD3 152 E7
Longwood Fold WF3 119 E8
Longwood Garth WF3 119 E8
Longwood Gate HD3 152 F6
Longwood House Rd HD2 136 A3
Longwood Rd
  East Ardsley WF3 119 E8
  Huddersfield HD3 153 C5
Longwood Vale WF3 119 E8
Longwood View BD16 36 E5
Longwood Way LS17 44 B5
Longwoods Wlk WF11 127 A5
Lonsbrough Ave WF16 117 D5
Lonsbrough Flats [7] HD1 154 B6
Lonsbrough Way WF9 183 A4
Lonsdale Ave [3] WF17 117 F7
Lonsdale Cl LS10 215 D1
Lonsdale Meadows LS23 30 D7
Lonsdale Rd WF1 216 A4
Lonsdale Rise WF3 119 E8
Lonsdale St BD3 75 B8
Lord La BD22 51 B8
Lord St Batley WF13 117 F4
  Dewsbury WF12 140 B7
  Halifax HX1 203 E3
  [12] Haworth BD22 51 D7
  Huddersfield HD1 154 B6
  Keighley BD21 35 C7
  Leeds LS12 210 C2
  Slaithwaite HD7 151 F1
  Sowerby Bridge HX6 112 C5
  Todmorden OL14 108 A1
  Wakefield WF1 142 F3
Lord Terr LS12 210 C2
Lord's Bldgs [6] LS27 98 A2
Lord's La HD6 115 B1
Lordsfield Pl BD4 75 D1
Loris St BD4 75 D1
Lorne First Sch BD4 75 B4
Lorne St Bradford BD4 75 B3
  [2] Haworth BD22 51 F8
  Keighley BD21 35 E8
Lorry Bank LS7 206 C4
Loscoe Cl WF6 123 E3
Loscoe La
  Featherstone WF6, WF7 124 A1
  Normanton WF6 123 E2
Lothersdale Rd BD20 16 A7
Lotherton Hall LS25 65 B5
Lotherton La Aberford LS25 65 A6
  Aberford LS25 65 B5
Lotherton Way LS25 83 A8
Loughrigg St BD5 74 E3
Loughrigg Wlk WF7 163 E6
Louis Ave BD5 74 C4
Louis Ct LS7 207 D3
Louis Gr LS7 207 E3
Louis Le Prince Ct LS8 207 F3
Louis St LS7 207 E3
Louisa St Bradford BD10 56 B8
  Castleford WF10 124 C8
Lound La DN5 195 F5
Lovaine Gr WF2 142 D1
Love La Castleford WF10 124 C6
  Halifax HX1 203 D1
  Ossett WF5 140 C6
  Pontefract WF8 146 B8
  Rothwell LS26 100 E5
  Wakefield WF2 216 A2
Love Lane Terr WF8 146 C8
Lovell Park Cl LS7 207 D1
Lovell Park Ct LS7 206 C1
Lovell Park Gate LS7 206 C1
Lovell Park Grange LS7 207 D1
Lovell Park Hill LS7 207 D1
Lovell Park Hts LS7 207 D1
Lovell Park Mews LS7 207 D1
Lovell Park Rd LS2, LS7 206 C1
Lovell Park Towers LS7 206 C1
Lovell Park View LS7 207 D1
Lovell View WF4 162 A8
Low Ash Ave BD18 55 D7
Low Ash Cres BD18 55 D7
Low Ash Dr BD18 55 D7
Low Ash First Sch BD18 55 D6
Low Ash Gr BD18 55 D7
Low Ash Rd BD18 55 E7
Low Bank Dr BD22 34 B3
Low Bank La BD22 34 B2
Low Bank St LS28 57 D3
Low Cl Bingley BD16 37 B2
  Ilkley LS29 8 B5
Low Cliff Wlk WF16 117 E2
Low Close St LS2 206 A3
Low Cross Ct WF11 127 A5
Low Farm LS26 102 E8
Low Farm La WF7 164 A6
Low Fields Ave LS11 213 E4
Low Fields Rd LS12 213 E4
Low Fields Way LS11 213 E4
Low Fold Baildon BD17 38 C4
  Bradford BD2 55 F2
  Brighouse BD19 115 F8
  Denholme BD13 52 D2
  Leeds LS9 212 B2
  Steeton BD20 17 D5
  Yeadon LS19 40 B4
Low Gate Kirkburton HD8 173 F6
  South Elmsall WF9 183 A3
Low Gate La OL3 167 A1
Low Gipton Cres LS8 61 D3
Low Gn Ackworth M T WF7 164 B7
  Knottingley WF11 127 B4
  Yeadon LS19 40 C3
Low Grange Cres LS10 215 E1
Low Grange Rd S63 194 C1
Low Grange View LS10 99 E8
Low Green [4] BD7 74 A3
Low Green Terr BD7 74 B3
Low Hall Cl LS29 22 A4
Low Hall Pl LS11 211 D2
Low Hall Rd Menston LS29 22 B4
  Yeadon LS18 57 E8
Low Hill BD17 38 C6
Low Hills La HD3 135 A1
Low House Dr BD20 17 E8
Low House Fold WF15 116 F4
Low La Batley WF17 96 E1
  Bradford BD14 73 A5
  Brighouse HD6 115 C6
  Draughton BD23 1 E6
  Halton East BD23 1 B8
  Halton East BD23 1 B8
  Horsforth LS18 41 D1
  Netherton WF4 158 B8
  Queensbury BD13 72 C3
  Silsden BD20 18 A6
  Silsden, Silsden Moor BD20 5 C5
Low La continued
  Thornton BD14 73 A5
  Wadsworth Moor HX2 90 A7
Low Laithes Golf Course WF5 141 B7
Low Mill La
  Addingham LS29 7 B8
  Dewsbury WF13 138 E4
  Keighley BD21 35 D7
Low Mill Rd WF5 140 C3
Low Mills Rd LS12 78 B4
Low Moor CE First Sch BD12 94 E6
Low Moor Cres WF4 159 F3
Low Moor La WF4 159 E1
Low Moor Side LS12 77 D3
Low Moor Side La LS12 77 C2
Low Moor St BD12 94 D6
Low Moor Terr HX2 112 D7
Low Moorside Cl LS12 77 E3
Low Moorside Ct LS12 77 D3
Low Park Rd LS29 9 B5
Low Platt La HD3 151 B5
Low Rd
  Dewsbury, Dewsbury Moor WF13 138 F8
  Dewsbury, Earlsheaton WF12 139 E7
  Dewsbury, Overthorpe WF13 139 C1
  Huddersfield HD4 171 F8
  Leeds LS10 215 F3
Low Road Primary Sch LS10 215 E3
Low Row S75 177 E3
Low Shops La LS26 100 C6
Low Spring Rd BD21 35 F6
Low St Brotherton WF11 126 C7
  Dewsbury WF13 118 C1
  East Ardsley WF3 98 F1
  Keighley BD21 35 C7
Low Town HD8 173 F6
Low Way Boston Spa LS23 30 D6
  Bramham LS23 30 D2
Low Well Rd [4] BD5 74 D3
Low Whitehouse Row LS10 212 A1
Low Wood BD15 53 D4
Low Wood Ct BD20 18 B3
Low Wood Rise LS29 8 F3
Lowcroft LS22 29 A8
Lowdale WF12 118 E2
Lowell Ave BD7 73 F5
Lowell Gr LS13 77 A8
Lowell Pl LS13 77 A8
Lower Ashgrove BD5 74 D6
Lower Back La HX7 87 F4
Lower Bank House HX4 133 D4
Lower Bankhouse LS28 76 D4
Lower Basinghall St LS1 211 E3
Lower Bentley Royd HX6 112 A4
Lower Bower La [1] WF13 117 F2
Lower Brockwell La HX6 111 F2
Lower Brunswick St LS2 207 D1
Lower Calderbrook OL15 129 C1
Lower Cambridge St WF10 124 E8
Lower Clay Pits HX1 202 B4
Lower Clifton St HX6 112 C4
Lower Clyde St HX6 112 B3
Lower Common La HD8 175 E1
Lower Constable Rd LS29 8 D3
Lower Cross St
  [1] Dewsbury WF13 118 C1
  Halifax HX1 203 F3
Lower Crow Nest Dr HX3 115 B7
Lower Denby La HD8 192 B4
Lower Edge Rd
  Brighouse HD6 135 D7
  Elland HX5 135 D7
Lower Exley HX3 113 D1
Lower Fields Middle Sch BD4 75 C4
Lower Finkil St HD6 114 F5
Lower Fitzwilliam St [4] HD1 154 B7
Lower Fold Brighouse HD6 135 F6
  Halifax HX1 203 E3
  Honley HD7 171 F5
Lower Furney Lee OL14 108 A6
Lower Gate HD3 153 C5
Lower George St
  [5] Bradford BD6 74 B1
  [5] Todmorden OL14 108 C5
Lower Globe St BD8 74 C8
Lower Grange HD2 136 E6
Lower Grange Cl BD8 73 C7
Lower Grattan Rd [6] BD1 74 D7
Lower Greave Rd HD7 188 B8
Lower Green BD17 38 B2
Lower Green Ave [11] BD19 115 F8
Lower Hagg HD7 172 B1
Lower Hall Cl WF15 116 F4
Lower Hall Cres HD5 155 C6
Lower Hall Dr WF15 116 F4
Lower Hall La WF15 116 F4
Lower Hall Mount WF15 116 F4
Lower Hall Rd HD5 155 C6
Lower Haughs HD7 152 B5
Lower Heights Rd BD13 72 C8
Lower Hey HD7 170 D2
Lower Highfield HX2 91 B3
Lower Holme Baildon BD17 38 C1
  Slaithwaite HD7 169 D8
Lower House Cl BD10 55 F8
Lower House La HD8 156 B2
Lower Kipping La [10] BD13 72 D6
Lower Kirkgate HX1 203 F3
Lower La Birkenshaw BD4 95 D5
  Blackshaw Head HX7 87 E3
  Bradford BD4 75 C4
  Cleckheaton BD19 117 B7
  Honley HD7 171 E4
Lower Laith Ave OL14 108 C5
Lower Langwith LS22 29 A8
Lower Lark Hill BD19 116 B7
Lower Maythorn La HD7 200 D8
Lower Meadows HD7 188 D5
Lower Mickletown LS26 102 F3
Lower Mill Bank Rd HX6 132 D7
Lower Newlands HD6 115 B1
Lower North St WF17 118 B4
Lower Northcroft WF9 183 A3
Lower Northfield La WF9 182 C3
Lower Oxford St WF10 124 D7
Lower Park Gn BD20 5 C1
Lower Park Royd Dr HX6 132 E6
Lower Peel St WF13 118 C1
Lower Putting Mill HD8 192 B7
Lower Quarry Rd HD2, HD5 137 A6
Lower Range [9] HX3 92 C1
Lower Rayleigh St BD4 75 A5
Lower Rd HX4 150 F5
Lower Reins HD7 172 A6
Lower Rushton Rd BD3 75 E7
Lower Sandhills LS14 45 E3
Lower Scholes BD22 50 F8
Lower School St
  Bradford BD12 94 C6
  [3] Shipley BD18 54 F8
Lower Skircoat Gn HX3 113 C2
Lower Smithy HX7 88 A5
Lower Station Rd WF6 123 A2
Lower Swift Pl HX6 132 B2
Lower Taythes La WF8 126 A1
Lower Top of Hill HX4 150 F6
Lower Town End Rd HD7 189 C7
Lower Town St LS13 58 D2
Lower Viaduct St [2] HD1 154 B7
Lower Warrengate WF1 216 C2
Lower Wellgate [3] HX4 134 C7
Lower Wellhouse Rd HD7 152 D3
Lower Wellington Rd LS29 8 B4
Lower Westfield Rd BD9 55 A1
Lower Wheat Royd HD5 154 F2
Lower Whitegate Rd HD4 154 B3
Lower Wormald HX6 131 F1
Lower Wortley Primary Sch LS12 78 B4
Lower Wortley Rd LS12 209 E1
Lower Wyke Gn BD12 115 B8
Lower Wyke La BD12 115 C8
Lower York St WF1 216 B3
Lowerhouses HD7 152 E2
Lowerhouses C of E Infants Sch HD5 154 D3
Lowerhouses La HD5 154 D3
Lowerhouses Rd HD3 153 B6
Lowertown BD22 51 C2
Lowestwood La HD7 152 D2
Loweswater Ave BD6 93 F6
Loweswater Rd WF11 126 E2
Lowfield Cl BD12 94 E5
Lowfield Cres
  Hemsworth WF9 181 E7
  Silsden BD20 17 F8
Lowfield La BD23 3 A4
Lowfield Rd WF13 138 F8
Lowfields Bsns Pk HX5 135 A8
Lowfields Cl HX5 135 A8
Lowfields Rd LS11 213 E4
Lowfields Way HX5 135 A8
Lowlands Rd WF14 138 B4
Lowood La WF17 96 F3
Lowry Rd WF3 119 E8
Lowry View [6] BD21 35 C6
Lowther Ave LS25 82 E6
Lowther Cres LS26 82 A2
Lowther Dr LS25 82 E6
Lowther Gr LS25 82 E6
Lowther Rd LS25 82 E6
Lowther St Bradford BD2 56 B2
  Leeds LS8 207 F4
Lowther Terr LS15 82 A6
Lowtown LS28 76 F8
Lowtown Junior & Infants Sch LS28 76 F7
Loxley Gr LS22 13 D8
Loxley St WF17 118 A7
Lucas Ct LS6 206 C3
Lucas Pl LS6 206 A4
Lucas St LS6 206 A4
Luck La HD1, HD3 153 D6
Lucy Ave LS15 80 E8
Lucy Hall Dr BD17 37 F3
Lucy La HD8 155 E5
Lucy St HX3 203 F4
Luddenden Dene CE Jun & Inf Sch HX2 111 D8
Luddenden La HX2 111 D7
Luddendenfoot Junior & Infants Sch HX2 111 E5
Luddendon Pl [3] BD13 72 C2
Luddite House [8] WF15 117 A5
Ludgate Hill LS2 211 F4
Ludhill La HD4 172 D5
Ludlam St BD5 201 B1
Ludlow Ave LS25 83 B7
Ludolf Dr LS17 44 E4
Ludwell Cl WF12 139 F1
Ludwood Cl HD7 172 B5
Luke La Holmfirth HD7 172 C1
  Honley HD7 172 C1
Luke Rd BD5 74 C4
Lulworth Ave LS15 81 D8
Lulworth Cl [1] LS15 62 D1
Lulworth Cres LS15 62 D1
Lulworth Dr LS15 81 D8
Lulworth Garth LS15 81 D8
Lulworth Gr BD4 75 D2
Lulworth View LS15 81 D8
Lulworth Wlk LS15 62 D1
Lumb Bottom BD11 96 F7
Lumb Foot BD22 50 E7
Lumb Gill La LS29 7 B6
Lumb Hole Waterfall HX7 69 A3
Lumb La Bradford BD8 74 D8
  Halifax, Boothtown HX3 92 B2
  Halifax, Wainstalls HX2 90 F6
  Huddersfield HD4 172 D8
  Liversedge WF15 116 F2
  Sowerby Bridge HX6 132 C7
Lumb Rd HX7 88 D5
Lumb Terr HX2 90 F6
Lumbfoot Rd BD22 50 F7
Lumbrook HX3 93 C2
Lumbrook Cl HX3 93 C3
Lumbutts La OL14 108 F4
Lumbutts Rd OL14 108 C3
Lumby Cl LS28 76 F5
Lumby La East Keswick LS17 28 B6
  Pudsey LS28 76 F6
Lumby Leys La LS25 105 A8
Lumby St BD10 56 B8
Lumley Ave
  Castleford WF10 124 A7
  Leeds LS4 205 D3
Lumley Gr LS4 205 D3
Lumley Hill WF10 124 A7
Lumley Mount
  Castleford WF10 124 A6
  Leeds LS4 205 D3
Lumley Mount Bglws WF10 124 A6
Lumley Pl LS4 205 D3
Lumley Rd Batley WF12 118 E2
  Leeds LS4 205 D3
Lumley St Castleford WF10 124 B7
  Leeds LS4 205 D3
Lumley Terr LS4 205 D3
Lumley View LS4 205 D3
Lumley Wlk LS4 205 D3
Lunan Pl LS8 207 F4
Lunan Terr LS8 207 F4
Lund Dr WF16 117 E3
Lund Hill La Royston S71 179 F5
  Ryhill S71 179 F5
Lund La BD22 34 B6
Lund St Bingley BD16 36 F3
  Bradford BD8 73 E7
  Keighley BD21 35 C8
Lunnfields La LS25, WF11 105 C4
Lupset Cres WF2 141 E3
Lupton Ave LS9 208 B1
Lupton St Bradford BD8 55 E1
  Leeds LS10 215 E3
Lupton's Bldgs LS12 209 E3
Lustre St BD21 35 A7
Luther Pl HD2 153 E8
Luther St LS13 57 E5
Luther Way BD2 55 F3
Luton St Halifax HX1 202 B3
  Huddersfield HD4 152 F3
  Keighley BD21 35 B7
Luttrell Cl LS16 42 A2
Luttrell Cres LS16 42 A2
Luttrell Gdns LS16 42 A2
Luttrell Pl LS16 42 A2
Luttrell Rd LS16 42 A2
Lutyens The LS29 7 F4
Luxor Ave LS8 207 F4
Luxor Rd LS8 207 F4
Luxor St LS8 207 F4
Luxor View LS8 207 F4
Lydbrook Pk HX3 113 A2
Lyddon Terr LS2 206 A2
Lydford Ho [7] BD5 201 B1
Lydgate Leeds LS9 207 F1
  Lepton HD8 156 A3
  Northowram HX3 93 A3
Lydgate Cl HD7 189 E6
Lydgate Dr Holmfirth HD7 189 D7
  Lepton HD8 156 A3
Lydgate Jun & Inf Sch WF17 118 F5
Lydgate Pk HX3 114 E7
Lydgate Pl LS28 57 A7
Lydgate Rd Batley WF17 118 F5
  Shepley HD8 190 F8
Lydgate Sch HD7 189 D7
Lydgate St LS28 57 A7
Lydget Ct BD20 18 A2
Lydgetts HD7 188 D5
Lydia St LS2 212 A4
Lyme Chase LS14 61 F2
Lyme Terr DN6 184 E1
Lymington Dr BD4 75 E4
Lynch Ave [1] BD7 73 F3
Lyncroft BD2 55 F4
Lynda Gr WF5 141 A4
Lyndale LS25 103 A8
Lyndale Cres WF16 117 E4
Lyndale Dr Shipley BD18 55 F7
  Wakefield WF2 120 E2
Lyndale Gr WF6 123 C1
Lyndale Mews WF13 117 F3
Lyndale Rd BD16 37 C5
Lyndean Gdns BD10 56 A7
Lynden Ave BD18 55 E8
Lynden Ct BD6 94 A7
Lyndhurst BD20 16 C5
Lyndhurst Ave HD6 136 A7

Lyndhurst Cl LS15 62 F7
Lyndhurst Cres LS15 62 F7
Lyndhurst Gr BD15 54 C1
Lyndhurst Grove Rd HD6 136 A7
Lyndhurst Rd
Barwick in E LS15 62 F6
Brighouse HD6 136 A8
Huddersfield HD3 153 B8
Lyndhurst View LS15 62 F6
Lyndon Ave Bramham LS23 30 C3
Garforth LS25 82 E7
Lyndon Cl LS23 30 C3
Lyndon Cres LS23 30 C3
Lyndon Rd LS23 30 C3
Lyndon Sq LS23 30 C3
Lyndon Terr 3 BD16 37 A3
Lyndon Way LS23 30 C3
Lyndum Gr LS25 83 A2
Lynfield Dr Bradford BD9 54 C3
Cleckheaton WF15 116 B5
Lynfield Mount BD18 55 E8
Lynfield Mount Hosp BD9 54 D2
Lynndale Ave
Glusburn BD20 16 D7
Huddersfield HD2 135 F1
Lynnfield Gdns LS15 62 F6
Lynnwood Gdns LS28 76 C7
Lynsey Gdns BD4 95 B7
Lynthorne Rd BD9 55 C4
Lynton Ave Boston Spa LS23 30 D8
Bradford BD9 54 F2
Huddersfield HD1 153 F6
Middleton WF3 99 E2
Lynton Dr Bradford BD9 54 F2
Keighley BD20 18 F1
Shipley BD18 55 A7
Lynton Gr Bradford BD9 54 F2
Halifax HX2 71 F1
Lynton Terr 5 BD19 116 D8
Lynton Villas BD9 54 F2
Lynwood Ave Leeds LS12 209 F1
Rothwell LS26 101 D6
Shipley BD18 55 E8
Lynwood Cl
Birkenshaw BD11 96 B4
Featherstone WF7 144 E4
Knottingley WF11 127 A5
Lynwood Cres Halifax HX1 202 B1
Hemsworth WF9 163 A4
Leeds LS12 209 F1
Pontefract WF8 146 D6
Rothwell LS26 101 D6
Lynwood Ct Bradford BD10 56 A7
Keighley BD22 34 E5
Lynwood Dr Royston S71 179 C2
Wakefield WF2 160 C6
Lynwood Garth LS12 209 F1
Lynwood Gr LS12 78 C4
Lynwood La S71 179 C2
Lynwood Mews BD4 75 F2
Lynwood Mount LS12 209 F1
Lynwood Rise LS12 209 F1
Lynwood View LS12 209 F1
Lyon Rd Pontefract WF8 146 D6
Steeton BD20 16 F6
Lyon St Queensbury BD13 72 F1
Thornton BD13 72 D7
Lytham Cl WF6 123 D1
Lytham Dr BD13 73 B2
Lytham Gr LS12 78 A4
Lytham Pl 13 LS12 78 A4
Lytham St HX1 202 B3
Lytham Way HD3 153 B8
Lytton Rd BD8 73 F8
Lytton St LS10 215 D3

Mabel Royd BD7 73 F5
Mabel St HX7 89 E1
Mabgate LS9 212 A4
Mabgate Gn LS9 212 A4
Mabgate Mills Ind Ctr LS9 207 E1
Macaulay Rd HD2 135 F1
Macaulay St LS9 207 E1
Macham St HD1 153 F4
Mackey Cres S72 180 F3
Mackie Hill Cl WF4 159 D4
Mackie Hill Jun & Inf Sch WF4 159 D4
Mackingstone Dr BD22 34 B3
Mackingstone La BD22 34 B4
Mackinnon Ave WF6 123 C3
Mackintosh Memorial Homes The HX3 113 A4
Macturk Gr BD8 55 A1
Maddocks St BD18 55 A8
Madeley Rd WF4 162 C1
Madeley Sq WF10 104 C1
Madgin La HD7 171 A6
Madison Ave BD4 75 E1
Madni Cl HX1 203 D3
Madri Muslim Girls Sch WF12 139 D6
Mafeking Ave LS11 214 A1
Mafeking Gr LS11 214 A1
Mafeking Mount LS11 214 A1
Magdalen Rd HD7 187 C6
Magdalene Cl LS16 42 A3
Magdalene Fields WF6 144 D8
Magdalene Rd WF2 141 D5
Magna Gr WF2 142 E1
Magnolia Cl S72 180 D2
Magnolia Dr BD15 53 F4
Magnolia House 11 WF10 124 E7
Magpie La LS27 98 C3
Maidstone St BD3 75 C7
Mail Cl LS15 62 E3
Main Ave HD4 152 F3
Main Gate HD7 189 E2
Main Rd Denholme BD13 71 D8
Farnhill BD20 16 E8
Keighley BD20 36 D8
Steeton BD20 16 F6
Main St Aberford LS25 64 E7
Addingham LS29 6 E8
Badsworth WF9 164 E2
Barwick in E LS15 63 D7
Barwick in E, Scholes LS15 62 F6
Bingley BD16 36 F3
2 Bradford, Carr House Gate BD12 94 C4
Bradford, Wesley Place BD12 94 E6
Burley in W LS29 9 F1
Burton Salmon LS25 105 E3
Collingham LS22 29 B8
Collingham, Linton LS22 13 C2
Cononley BD20 4 A2
East Ardsley WF3 120 D7
East Keswick LS17 28 C5
Farnhill BD20 4 D2
Garforth LS25 82 E7
Guiseley, Esholt BD17 39 C5
Guiseley, Hawksworth LS20 38 F8
Hampole DN6 184 B1
Haworth BD22 51 C7
Haworth, Stanbury BD22 50 D7
Kippax WF10 103 B4
Kirk Smeaton WF8 166 D6
Ledston WF10 103 E6
Low Bradley BD20 4 C5
Menston LS29 22 A4
Mickletown LS26 102 D3
Monk Fryston LS25 105 F8
Pool LS21 24 C7
Rothwell WF3 100 D3
Shipley BD16 54 B6
Sicklinghall LS22 12 C5
South Hiendley S72 180 D6
Sutton in C BD20 16 D5
Tadcaster LS24 31 E7
Thorner LS14 45 F5
Thorner, Shadwell LS17 44 E4
Thorp Arch LS23 15 A4
Upton WF9 183 D8
Wilsden BD15 53 C5
Mainspring Rd BD15 53 C5
Maister Pl BD22 34 B3
Maitland Cl Bradford BD15 73 B7
Todmorden OL14 129 A8
Maitland Pl LS11 214 A4
Maitland St OL14 129 A8
Maize St 5 BD21 35 A4
Maizebrook WF16 117 F1
Major St Todmorden OL14 108 C5
Wakefield WF2 142 B3
Makin St WF2 142 A5
Malais La BD20 16 A5
Malham Ave Bradford BD9 54 C3
Brighouse HD6 135 E8
Malham Cl Leeds LS14 62 A4
Shafton S72 180 C3
Malham Dr Batley WF17 118 A5
Liversedge WF15 116 F1
Malham Rd Brighouse HD6 135 E7
Wakefield WF1 142 F7
Malham Sq WF1 142 F7
Malin Rd WF12 118 F3
Mallard Ave WF2 160 C5
Mallard Cl Bradford BD10 56 C5
Middleton LS10 99 F7
Mallard Ct 1 BD8 73 C7
Mallard Rd WF10 124 C6
Mallard View BD22 51 C2
Mallard Way
3 Morley LS27 98 D4
Slaithwaite HD7 169 F8
Mallards The BD20 5 E1
Mallinson St WF13 118 A1
Mallory Cl BD7 73 F6
Malmesbury Cl
Bradford BD4 75 E1
Leeds LS12 209 F2
Malmesbury Gr LS12 209 F2
Malmesbury Pl LS12 209 F2
Malmesbury St LS12 209 F2
Malmesbury Terr LS12 209 F2
Malsis Cres BD21 35 A6
Malsis Rd BD21 35 B5
Malt Kiln Croft WF2 142 E1
Malt Kiln La
2 Kippax LS25 83 B1
Thornton BD13 72 C5
Malt St 8 BD22 35 A4
Maltby Ct LS15 81 D7
Malthouse Cl LS14 45 C8
Malting Cl WF3 100 B3
Malting Rise WF3 100 B3
Maltings Ct LS11 214 C4
Maltings Rd Halifax HX2 91 D2
Leeds LS11 214 C3
Maltings The
Cleckheaton BD19 116 C8
Leeds LS6 205 E2
Mirfield WF14 137 F5
Pontefract WF8 125 D1
Rothwell WF3 100 B3
Maltkiln Dr WF4 176 F8
Maltkiln La WF10 124 E8
Malton Rd WF9 183 D8
Malton St
Halifax, Woodlands HX3 92 C2
7 Sowerby Bridge HX6 112 B5
Malvern Brow BD9 54 D2
Malvern Cl WF10 123 F5
Malvern Cres BD20 18 E3
Malvern Gr Bradford BD9 54 D1
Leeds LS11 214 B4
Malvern Rd Bradford BD9 54 D2
Dewsbury WF12 118 F1
Huddersfield HD4 154 B4
Knottingley WF11 126 E4
Leeds LS11 214 A4
Malvern Rise
Huddersfield HD4 154 B3
Leeds LS11 214 A4
Malvern St LS11 214 A4
Malvern View LS11 214 A4
Manchester Rd
Bradford BD5 74 D3
Huddersfield HD4 153 C4
Marsden HD7 168 B3
Manchester Rd Marsden HD7 168 E4
Manchester Rd (Slaithwaite) HD7 170 A8
Manchester Road Clough Head HD7 168 C4
Manchester Road (Linthwaite) HD7 152 D1
Manchester Sq LS21 23 A8
Mandale Gr BD6 93 D8
Mandale Middle Sch BD6 93 D8
Mandale Rd BD6 73 D1
Mandarin Way LS10 99 F7
Mandela Ct LS7 204 A1
Mandeville Cres BD6 93 F8
Mangrill La LS14 46 E6
Manitoba Pl LS7 204 B2
Mankinholes Bank OL14 108 F3
Manley Ct LS25 82 F5
Manley Dr LS22 13 C6
Manley Gr LS29 8 D4
Manley Rd LS29 8 E4
Manley Rise LS29 8 D3
Manley St HD6 115 A3
Mann's Bldgs WF17 97 B2
Mannheim Rd BD9 55 A2
Manningham La BD1, BD8 55 D1
Manningham Middle Sch BD8 55 D1
Mannville Gr BD22 35 A6
Mannville Pl 16 BD22 35 A6
Mannville Rd BD22 35 A6
Mannville St 13 BD22 35 A6
Mannville Terr BD7 74 D6
Mannville Way 14 BD22 35 A6
Mannville Wlk 15 BD22 35 A6
Manor Ave Leeds LS6 205 E4
Ossett WF5 140 F3
Manor Cl
Badsworth WF9 164 E2
Birkenshaw BD11 96 E7
Bradford BD8 73 D8
Bramhope LS16 24 D3
Halifax HX3 113 B4
Kirk Smeaton WF8 166 D5
Notton WF4 178 F7
Ossett WF5 140 F3
Rothwell LS26 100 E6
Yeadon LS19 40 B7
Manor Cres Pool LS21 24 C7
Rothwell LS26 100 D5
Wakefield WF2 141 E4
Walton WF2 161 A8
Manor Croft
Hebden Bridge HX7 89 B3
Leeds LS15 81 C7
South Hiendley S72 180 D6
Manor Ct Fairburn WF11 105 A4
Ossett WF5 140 F3
Otley LS21 23 A8
3 Shipley BD16 54 A7
Thorner LS17 44 F4
Manor Dr Crofton WF4 162 A7
Featherstone WF7 124 C1
Flockton WF4 157 D3
Halifax HX3 113 B4
Hebden Bridge HX7 89 B3
Leeds LS6 205 E4
Mirfield WF14 137 D7
Ossett WF5 140 F3
Royston S71 179 B3
Shipley BD16 54 B7
Skelmanthorpe HD8 175 A1
South Hiendley S72 180 D6
Manor Farm WF9 164 E2
Manor Farm Cl
Middleton LS10 99 D6
Shipley BD16 54 B6
Manor Farm Cres LS27 98 C8
Manor Farm Ct WF4 159 E4
Manor Farm Dr
Batley WF17 118 F5
Middleton LS10 99 D6
Morley LS27 98 C8
Manor Farm Est WF9 183 A3
Manor Farm Gdns LS10 99 C6
Manor Farm Gn LS10 99 C6
Manor Farm Gr LS10 99 C6
Manor Farm Rd
Crigglestone WF4 159 E4
Middleton LS10 99 D6
Manor Farm Rise LS10 99 D6
Manor Farm Way LS10 99 C5
Manor Farm Wlk LS10 99 D6
Manor Fold 4 BD16 54 B6
Manor Garth
Ledsham LS25 104 D8
Leeds LS15 81 C7
Walton WF2 161 A8
Manor Garth Rd
Dewsbury WF12 139 F7
Kippax LS25 83 B2
Manor Gdns Batley WF12 119 A2
Cullingworth BD13 52 D5
Pool LS21 24 C7
Thorner LS14 46 A6
Manor Gr Castleford WF10 124 E5
Keighley BD20 36 A8
Leeds LS7 204 A2
Ossett WF5 140 F3
Royston S71 179 B3
South Kirkby WF9 182 A1
Manor Haigh Rd WF2 141 E4
Manor Heath Rd HX3 113 B4
Manor House 2 WF1 216 C2
Manor House Bglws WF11 126 F5
Manor House Croft LS16 42 D3
Manor House La LS17 43 F7
Manor House Mus & Art Gal LS29 8 B4
Manor House Rd BD15 53 C6
Manor House St 5 LS28 76 E7
Manor Houses HD7 170 F2
Manor La Ossett WF5 140 F3
Shipley BD18 55 B7
Manor Mill La LS11 213 E1
Manor Occupation Rd S71 179 B4
Manor Park Ave
Kippax WF10 103 B5
Pontefract WF8 125 F3
Manor Park Gdns BD19 96 B3
Manor Park Rise WF8 147 D4
Manor Park Way HD8 155 D2
Manor Pk Batley WF12 119 B3
Bradford BD8 73 D8
Darrington WF8 147 D5
Ledston WF10 103 E6
Mirfield WF14 137 C7
Oakworth BD22 34 C2
Scarcroft LS14 45 C7
Manor Pl 1 WF4 141 A1
Manor Rd Batley WF17 118 F5
Beal DN14 127 F7
Clayton West HD8 176 A4
Dearne S63 194 C1
Dewsbury WF13 139 B7
Horbury WF4 141 A1
Horsforth LS18 58 A8
Huddersfield HD7 152 D4
Keighley BD20 18 A2
Kirkburton HD4 172 F6
Leeds LS11 211 E2
Morley LS27 98 C8
Ossett WF5 140 F4
Rothwell LS26 100 D6
Shipley BD16 54 B7
Wakefield WF2 141 F5
Walton WF2 161 A7
Manor Rise
Huddersfield HD4 154 B4
Ilkley LS29 8 D4
Skelmanthorpe HD8 175 A1
Walton WF2 161 A8
Manor Row Bradford BD12 94 C7
Bradford BD1 201 B3
Manor (Sports Ctr) The LS19 40 B7
Manor Sq Otley LS21 23 A8
5 Yeadon LS19 40 B7
Manor St Bradford BD2 56 B3
Brighouse BD19 115 F6
Dewsbury WF12 139 D8
Huddersfield HD4 154 B4
Leeds LS7 207 D2
Otley LS21 23 A8
Manor Street Ind Est LS7 207 E2
Manor Terr Bradford BD2 56 B3
Kippax LS25 83 B1
Leeds LS6 205 E4
Manor View
Castleford WF10 124 E5
Leeds LS6 205 E4
Pudsey LS28 76 E7
Shafton S72 180 C2
Manor Way Batley WF17 118 A4
Sutton in C BD20 16 C4
Manorcroft WF6 123 B2
Manorfield LS11 213 F3
Manorfield Dr WF4 141 A2
Manorfield Inf Sch WF17 118 A4
Manorfields Ave WF4 162 A8
Manorfields Ct WF4 162 A8
Manorley La BD6 93 E6
Manorstead HD8 175 A1
Manscombe Rd BD15 54 C1
Manse Cres LS29 9 E1
Manse Dr HD4 153 A3
Manse Rd LS29 9 E1
Manse St BD3 75 C7
Manse Way BD20 16 D6
Mansel Mews BD4 75 E2
Mansfield Ave BD16 37 C5
Mansfield Pl LS6 59 D6
Mansfield Rd Bradford BD8 55 C2
Burley in W LS29 9 E1
Mansion Gdns HD4 153 F1
Mansion La LS8 44 B1
Manston App LS15 62 C3
Manston Ave LS15 62 C3
Manston Cres LS15 62 C2
Manston Dr LS15 62 C3
Manston Gdns LS15 62 D3
Manston Gr LS15 62 C3
Manston La LS15 62 E2
Manston Rise LS15 62 C3
Manston Terr 5 LS15 62 D3
Manston Towers 3 LS14 62 D4
Manston Way LS15 62 C3
Manygates Ave WF1 142 D3
Manygates Cres WF1 142 D3
Manygates Ct WF1 142 D3
Manygates La WF1, WF2 142 D2
Manygates Pk WF1 142 D3
Manywells Brow BD13 52 C4
Manywells Cres BD13 52 D5
Manywells La BD13 52 B5
Maple Ave Bradford BD3 75 E8
Huddersfield HD7 152 F5
Oakworth BD22 34 D2
Pontefract WF8 146 C5
Maple Cl Castleford WF10 124 B5
Kirkheaton HD5 137 C1
Maple Croft
Leeds, Farnley LS12 77 D5
Leeds, Moortown LS17 43 E3
Maple Ct Leeds LS11 213 F2
Ossett WF5 140 E3
Maple Dr Leeds LS12 77 D5
Pontefract WF8 146 D6
Wetherby LS22 13 E7
Maple Fold LS12 77 D5
Maple Gr Cleckheaton BD19 96 A1
Gildersome LS12 77 D5
Huddersfield HD2 136 A5
Keighley BD20 18 A1
Normanton WF6 144 A7
Pontefract WF8 146 C5
Maple Rd Dewsbury WF12 140 B7
Mapplewell S75 178 A1
Maple Rise LS26 100 F4
Maple St 7 Halifax HX1 202 B1
Huddersfield HD5 154 C5
Todmorden OL14 129 A7
Wakefield WF2 141 F8
Maple Terr LS19 39 F7
Maple Way LS14 62 C8
Maple Wlk
Dewsbury WF12 140 B7
Knottingley WF11 126 E3
Maplin Ave HD3 134 F1
Maplin Dr 1 HD3 134 F1
Mapplewell Cres WF5 140 E5
Mapplewell Dr WF5 140 E5
Mapplewell Prim Sch
Mapplewell S75 178 B1
Mapplewell S75 178 C1
Marbridge Ct BD6 74 B2
March Cote La BD16 54 A6
March St WF6 123 A1
Marchant St WF10 124 C8
Marchbank Rd BD3 75 C8
Marchwood Gr BD14 73 D5
Marcus Way HD3 134 D1
Mardale Cres LS14 62 A3
Mardale Rd WF12 118 E2
Margaret Ave LS17 28 D4
Margaret Cl LS27 98 C6
Margaret St Halifax HX1 203 D3
Keighley BD21 35 A8
Lofthouse Gate WF1 121 A4
Wakefield WF1 216 A3
Margate 2 LS26 101 C6
Margate Rd BD4 75 A4
Margate St HX6 112 A3
Margerison Cres LS29 8 E3
Margerison Rd LS29 8 E3
Margetson Rd BD11 97 A5
Margram Bsns Ctr HX1 203 D4
Maria St LS29 9 E2
Marian Gr 11 LS11 214 B3
Marian Rd LS6 206 B3
Marian Terr LS6 206 B3
Marie Cl HD5 155 C6
Marina Cres LS27 97 F3
Marina Terr HD7 152 E5
Marine Villa Rd WF11 126 F4
Marion Ave WF2 141 D8
Marion Cl WF9 182 C2
Marion Dr BD18 55 C7
Marion Gr WF2 141 D8
Marion St Bingley BD16 37 A3
Bradford BD7 74 C7
Brighouse HD6 115 A3
Marizon Gr WF1 216 C3
Mark Bottoms La HD7 188 F6
Mark Cl BD10 56 C8
Mark La Leeds LS2 211 F4
Todmorden OL14 108 A7
Mark St Bradford BD5 74 E3
Huddersfield HD1 153 E5
Liversedge WF15 117 B4
Wakefield WF1 142 C4
Market Ave 9 HD1 154 B6
Market Ct 5 BD13 72 E6
Market Pl
1 Cleckheaton BD19 116 E7
Dewsbury WF13 139 D8
Huddersfield HD1 154 A6
Keighley BD21 35 C7
Marsden HD7 168 F4
Meltham HD7 170 D2
Normanton WF6 123 A2
Otley LS21 23 A8
Pontefract WF8 146 D8
Pudsey LS28 76 E7
Slaithwaite HD7 169 F8
Wetherby LS22 13 E5
Market Shops WF6 123 A2
Market Sq
5 Batley WF17 118 C5
3 Leeds LS14 62 B5
Shipley BD18 55 B7

Market St
Batley, Birstall WF17 96 E1
Batley, Heckmondwike WF16 117 D3
Bingley BD16 36 F3
Bradford BD1 201 B2
Bradford BD1 201 B3
4 Bradford, Brownroyd Hill BD6 74 C1
Brighouse HD6 115 B2
Cleckheaton BD19 116 E7
3 Dewsbury WF13 139 D8
Featherstone WF7 145 C6
Halifax HX1 203 E3
Hebden Bridge HX7 89 A3
Hemsworth WF9 181 D7
Holmfirth HD7 189 A5
Huddersfield HD1 154 A6
Huddersfield, Milnsbridge HD3 153 B5
Huddersfield, Paddock HD1 153 E5
Keighley BD21 35 C7
Normanton WF6 123 A2
Otley LS21 23 A8
Shipley BD18 55 B7
Steeton BD20 17 D5
Thornton BD13 72 E6
Todmorden OL14 108 A3
Wakefield WF1 216 B2
Market St Arc 2 LS1 211 F3
Market Wlk HD7 168 F4
Markfield Ave BD12 94 C5
Markfield Cl BD12 94 C5
Markfield Cres BD12 94 D5
Markfield Dr BD12 94 C5
Markham Ave Leeds LS8 207 F4
Yeadon LS19 40 C5
Markham Cres LS19 40 C5
Markham Croft LS19 40 C5
Markham St Batley WF17 118 B4
Wakefield WF2 142 A6
Markington Mews LS10 99 C3
Markington Pl LS10 99 C3
Marl Pit Hill WF8 146 A6
Marland Rd BD21 35 E8
Marlbeck Cl HD7 171 F3
Marlborough Ave
Byram WF11 126 D7
7 Halifax HX3 113 B4
Marlborough Croft WF9 182 F4
Marlborough Ct LS29 22 B4
Marlborough Gdns
Dewsbury WF13 118 B2
17 Leeds LS2 206 B2
Marlborough Gr
31 Hebden Bridge HX7 89 A3
Ilkley LS29 8 D3
19 Leeds LS2 206 B2
Marlborough Grange
8 LS1 211 D4
Marlborough House
9 HX5 134 F7
Marlborough Rd
Bradford BD8 55 C1
Bradford, Fourlands BD10 56 C8
Hebden Bridge HX7 89 A3
Huddersfield HD2 136 B5
Shipley BD18 55 A7
Marlborough Sq LS29 8 D3
Marlborough St
Keighley BD21 35 D8
Leeds LS1 211 D4
Ossett WF5 140 C5
Wakefield WF2 142 A6
Marlborough Terr HX7 89 A3
Marlborough Towers 7 LS1 211 D4
Marlborough Villas LS29 22 B4
Marlbro' Terr 5 WF13 118 B2
Marldon Rd HX3 93 A1
Marley Cl BD8 73 E8
Marley Ct BD16 36 D7
Marley Gr LS11 213 F3
Marley La BD13 72 E3
Marley Pl LS11 213 F3
Marley Rd BD21 35 F8
Marley St Bradford BD3 201 D3
Keighley BD21 35 C6
Leeds LS11 213 F3
Marley Terr LS11 213 F3
Marley View Bingley BD16 36 D7
Leeds LS11 213 F3
Marling Rd HD2 135 B3
Marlo Rd WF12 119 A2
Marlott Rd BD18 55 E8
Marlow Cl HD5 154 F6
Marlow St BD21 35 E8
Marlowe Cl 3 LS28 76 F5
Marlowe Ct Garforth LS25 82 F7
Guiseley LS20 22 D1
Marlpit La WF8 147 B5
Marmion Ave BD8 73 C7
Marne Ave BD14 73 C3
Marne Cres BD10 56 B7
Marquis Ave BD12 95 B5
Marriner Rd BD21 35 C6
Marriner's Dr BD9 55 B4
Marriner's Wlk BD21 35 C5
Marriot Gr WF2 142 F1
Marsden Ave LS11 214 A2
Marsden Ct 3 LS28 57 D3
Marsden Gate HX4 151 E7
Marsden Golf Club HD7 168 E1
Marsden Gr LS11 214 A2
Marsden Infants Sch HD7 169 A4
Marsden Junior Sch HD7 169 A4
Marsden La Marsden HD7 169 A5
Marsden, Booth Naze HD7 169 B7
Marsden Mount LS11 214 A2
Marsden Pl LS11 214 A2
Marsden St HD8 175 A2
Marsden Sta HD7 168 F4
Marsden View LS11 214 A2
Marsett Way LS14 62 B8
Marsh LS28 76 C7
Marsh Croft WF11 126 C7
Marsh Delves HX3 113 F6
Marsh Delves La HX3 113 F6
Marsh End WF11 127 B5
Marsh Gdns HD7 171 F4
Marsh Gr BD5 74 C3
Marsh Grove Rd HD3 153 D8
Marsh Hall La HD4 172 F3
Marsh La Birkenshaw BD11 96 A5
Blackshaw Head HX7 88 B3
Byram WF11 126 F6
Halifax HX3 113 F6
Knottingley WF11 127 B4
Leeds LS9 212 B4
Oxenhope BD22 51 B4
Shepley HD8 190 D7
Marsh Lea Grove WF9 181 F7
Marsh Platt La HD7 172 A5
Marsh Rd Castleford WF10 124 A6
Holmfirth HD7 189 D3
Marsh Rise LS28 76 C7
Marsh St Bradford BD5 74 D3
Cleckheaton BD19 116 E6
Honley HD7 171 F4
Leeds LS6 206 A3
Rothwell LS26 100 F5
Marsh Terr LS28 76 C7
Marsh Vale 3 LS6 206 A3
Marsh Way WF1 216 C3
Marshall Ave
Crigglestone WF4 159 F3
Leeds LS15 62 D2
Marshall Cres LS27 98 B2
Marshall Dr WF9 182 F3
Marshall Mill Ct HD8 175 E1
Marshall St Keighley BD20 18 B1
Leeds LS11 211 E2
Leeds, Cross Gates LS15 62 C2
Lofthouse Gate WF3 121 F5
Mirfield WF14 138 A3
Morley LS27 98 B4
Yeadon LS19 40 B7
Marshall Terr LS15 62 C2
Marsham Gr HD3 153 C7
Marshfield First Sch BD5 74 C2
Marshfield Pl BD5 74 D3
Marshfield St BD5 74 D3
Marshway HX1 202 C4
Marsland Ave WF1 216 C2
Marsland Ct BD19 95 D2
Marsland Pl Bradford BD3 75 D7
Wakefield WF1 216 C2
Marsland St WF1 216 C2
Marsland Terr WF1 216 C2
Marston Ave LS27 98 A3
Marston Cl BD13 72 F1
Marston Ct WF10 124 A6
Marston Mount LS9 207 E1
Marston Way LS22 13 C6
Marston Wlk WF6 122 E4
Marten Dr HD4 171 D7
Marten Gr HD4 171 E7
Marten Rd BD5 74 C3
Martin Bank Wood HD5 154 D5
Martin Cl LS27 98 C4
Martin Ct LS15 81 D8
Martin Frobisher Dr WF6 122 F3
Martin Frobisher First Sch WF6 122 F4
Martin Gr WF2 160 E6
Martin Green La HX4 134 A7
Martin St Batley WF17 96 E1
Brighouse HD6 115 B3
Normanton WF6 144 A8
Martin Terr LS4 59 C2
Martindale Dr LS13 58 E1
Martingale Dr LS10 99 D3
Martlett Dr BD5 74 F2
Marton Ave WF9 181 C6
Marton Ct BD3 75 D7
Marton Heights HX6 112 A5
Marwood Rd LS13 77 E7
Mary Rose Ct WF7 145 C4
Mary St Bradford BD4 75 C5
Bradford, Carr House Gate BD12 94 C4
Brighouse HD6 115 A4
Denholme BD13 52 E1
East Ardsley WF3 120 E8
6 Oxenhope BD22 51 C2
Pudsey LS28 57 E4
Shipley BD18 54 F8
5 Thornton BD13 72 D6
Maryfield Ave LS15 62 A2
Maryfield Cl LS15 62 A2
Maryfield Cres LS15 62 B2
Maryfield Ct 5 LS15 62 B2
Maryfield Gdns LS15 62 A2
Maryfield Gn LS15 62 A2
Maryfield Mews LS15 62 A2
Maryfield Vale 1 LS15 62 A2
Marygate WF1 216 B2
Maryville Ave HD6 114 E5
Masefield Ave BD9 54 C3
Masefield St LS20 39 F8
Masham Gr LS12 210 A3
Masham Pl BD9 54 F2
Masham St LS12 210 A3
Mason Sq HX2 91 F3
Mason St HX7 89 A3
Mason's Green HX2 91 E5
Masonic St HX1 202 A2
Massey Fields BD22 51 D8
Master La HX2 112 F4
Matherville HD8 175 A1
Matheson Ho BD3 201 C4
Matlock St 9 Halifax HX3 92 A1
Huddersfield HD4 153 C4
Matterdale Cl WF12 118 E2
Matterdale Rd WF12 118 E2
Matthew Cl BD20 18 F1
Matthew Gr HD7 170 C2
Matthew La
Low Bradley BD20 4 C5
Meltham HD7 170 D2
Todmorden OL14 108 E7
Matthew Murray High Sch LS11 213 F4
Matty Marsden La WF4 140 E2
Maud Ave LS11 214 B2
Maud Pl LS11 214 B3
Maud St BD3 75 B6
Maude Ave BD17 38 C2
Maude Cres HX6 111 E3
Maude La HX6 132 D4
Maude St Elland HX4 134 D7
Halifax HX3 92 A3
Leeds LS2 212 A3
Maudsley St BD3 75 B7
Maufe Way LS29 8 B3
Maurice Ave HD6 114 F4
Mavis Ave Dewsbury WF13 139 A6
Leeds LS16 41 E6
Mavis Gr LS16 41 E6
Mavis La LS16 41 E6
Mavis Rd WF13 117 F3
Mavis St Bradford BD3 75 B7
Dewsbury WF13 139 A6
Maw St BD4 201 C1
Mawcroft Cl LS19 40 A5
Mawcroft Grange Dr LS19 40 A5
Mawson Ct BD1 201 B3
Mawson St 6 BD18 54 F8
Maxwell Ave WF17 118 C2
Maxwell Rd Bradford BD6 93 F8
Ilkley LS29 8 D3
Maxwell St WF7 145 C5
May Ave BD13 72 E6
May Bush Rd WF1 142 E3
May St Cleckheaton BD19 95 D1
Haworth BD22 51 D6
Huddersfield HD4 153 E4
Keighley BD21 35 C8
May Terr LS9 212 C2
May Tree Cl BD14 73 D5
Mayberry Dr S75 193 F1
Maybrook Ind Pk LS12 210 B4
Maybury Ave WF4 160 A7
Mayfair BD5 74 D4
Mayfair Ave HX4 133 F1
Mayfair Pl WF9 181 D7
Mayfair Way BD4 75 D5
Mayfield Ave
Bradford BD12 94 D3
Brighouse HD6 115 B8
Halifax HX1 202 C2
Huddersfield HD5 154 F6
Ilkley LS29 8 D4
Mayfield Cl Glusburn BD20 16 C6
Ilkley LS29 8 D4
Mayfield Ct WF5 140 E3
Mayfield Dr Halifax HX1 202 C2
Keighley BD20 36 C8
Mayfield Gdns Halifax HX1 202 C2
Ilkley LS29 8 D5
Ossett WF5 140 C8
Sowerby Bridge HX6 112 D5
Mayfield Gr Baildon BD17 38 D3
Brighouse HD6 115 B8
Halifax HX1 202 C2
Huddersfield HD5 154 F6
Wilsden BD15 53 B6
Mayfield Mount HX1 202 C2
Mayfield Pl BD12 94 C3
Mayfield Rd
Hebden Bridge HX7 89 A4
Ilkley LS29 8 C4
Keighley BD20 35 B8
Leeds LS15 81 B8
Mayfield Rise
Bradford BD12 94 D3
Ryhill WF4 162 A1
Mayfield St 8 HX1 202 C1
Mayfield Terr
Bradford, Lane End BD14 73 C3
1 Bradford, Upper Wyke BD12 94 D3
12 Cleckheaton BD19 116 E7
Mayfield Terr S 9 HX1 202 C1
Mayfield View BD12 94 D3
Mayfields Way WF9 182 B1
Mayflower St LS10 80 A2
Maylea Dr LS21 22 D6
Mayman Cl WF17 118 C5
Mayman La WF17 118 B5
Maynes Cl WF12 139 D2
Mayo Ave BD5 74 E2
Mayo Cl LS8 61 D6
Mayo Cres BD5 74 E1
Mayo Dr BD5 74 E1
Mayo Gr BD5 74 E1
Mayo Rd BD5 74 E1
Mayor's Walk Ave WF8 146 D7
Mayor's Wlk WF8 146 D7
Mayors Wlk WF10 125 E7
Maypole Mews LS15 63 D8
Maypole Rd HD2 136 C4
Mayster Gr HD6 135 F8
Mayster Rd HD6 135 F7
Maythorne Ave WF17 118 A4
Maythorne Cres BD14 73 D4
Maythorne Dr BD14 73 E4
Mayville Ave Keighley BD20 36 B8
Leeds LS6 205 E3
Mayville Pl 5 LS6 205 E3
Mayville Rd LS6 205 E3
Mayville St 4 LS6 205 E3
Mayville Terr LS6 205 E3
Mazebrook BD19 95 E2
Mazebrook Ave BD19 95 E2
Mazebrook Cres BD19 95 E2
McBride Way LS22 13 F5
McBurney Cl 2 HX3 92 B2
McLaren Ave WF9 183 D8
McLaren Fields 6 LS13 58 D2
McMahon Dr BD13 73 C2
Mead Gr LS15 81 E6
Mead Rd LS15 81 E6
Mead St HD1 136 A1
Mead View BD4 75 E3
Mead Way HD8 173 E7
Mead Way LS15 81 E6
Meadow Bank
Ackworth M T WF7 146 A1
Dewsbury WF13 138 F8
Holmfirth HD7 189 C6
Ryhill WF4 162 C1
Meadow Bank Cres WF14 137 E5
Meadow Bottom Rd OL14 108 B6
Meadow Brook Chase WF6 123 C1
Meadow Brook Cl WF6 123 C1
Meadow Brook Ct WF6 144 C8
Meadow Brook Gn WF6 123 C1
Meadow Cl Bardsey LS17 28 E6
Batley WF17 97 A1
Boston Spa LS23 30 C8
Cononley BD20 4 A3
Harden BD16 36 B1
Hemsworth WF9 181 C6
Liversedge WF15 116 F1
Lofthouse Gate WF1 121 D5
Shelf HX3 93 D6
Meadow Cres Halifax HX3 91 E2
Royston S71 179 D3
Meadow Croft
East Keswick LS17 28 C5
Hemsworth WF9 181 E5
Huddersfield HD2 136 F5
Keighley BD22 34 E6
Leeds LS11 211 E1
Lofthouse Gate WF1 121 C5
Shafton S72 180 C3
Meadow Croft Cl BD10 55 F8
Meadow Ct Bradford BD15 54 A4
Brighouse HD6 115 E2
Castleford WF10 125 D6
Ossett WF5 140 C7
Royston S71 179 D3
South Elmsall WF9 183 B3
Meadow Dr Halifax HX3 91 E2
Liversedge WF15 116 F1
Meadow End LS16 24 E2
Meadow Garth
Bramhope LS16 24 F1
Lofthouse Gate WF1 121 C5
Meadow Gn HD7 170 D8
Meadow La Cononley BD20 4 A2
Dewsbury WF13 118 C1
Halifax HX3 91 E2
Leeds LS11 211 F2
Liversedge WF15 116 F1
Slaithwaite HD7 151 F1
Wakefield WF2 141 F7
Meadow Lea BD20 16 C6
Meadow Park Cres LS28 57 B2
Meadow Park Dr LS28 57 B2
Meadow Pk HD5 137 B2
Meadow Rd Bradford BD10 56 E8
Castleford WF10 124 B5
Garforth LS25 83 A7
Leeds LS11 211 E1
Royston S71 179 D3
Meadow Rise WF9 181 C7
Meadow St HD1 153 D7
Meadow The WF6 144 A7
Meadow Vale
Lofthouse Gate WF1 121 D5
Netherton WF4 158 D5
Meadow Valley LS17 43 B5
Meadow View
Barwick in E LS15 63 E8
Bradford BD12 94 C1
Leeds LS6 205 E3
Oakworth BD22 34 D2
Ossett WF5 140 C7
Skelmanthorpe HD8 175 B1
Meadow Way
Ackworth M T WF7 146 A1
East Ardsley WF3 119 D7
Leeds LS17 43 B5
Meadow Wlk
Badsworth WF9 164 E3
Halifax HX3 91 E2
Leeds LS7 204 B2
Meadowbank Ave BD15 54 B1
Meadowcroft
Draughton BD23 1 D6
Honley HD7 171 E4
Menston LS29 22 A4
Meadowcroft Cl WF1 121 D5
Meadowcroft Ct WF1 121 D5
Meadowcroft La HX6 132 E5
Meadowcroft Mews LS9 212 B3
Meadowcroft Rd WF1 121 D5
Meadowcroft Rise BD4 95 C8
Meadowfield Cl WF9 163 A3
Meadowfields Cl WF4 162 A8
Meadowfields Dr WF4 162 A8
Meadowfields Rd WF4 162 A8
Meadowgate WF5 140 C7
Meadowgate Croft WF3 100 B2
Meadowgate Dr WF3 100 B1
Meadowgate Vale WF3 100 B1
Meadowhurst Gdns LS28 76 D7
Meadowlands BD19 94 E1
Meadows The Bradford BD6 74 C1
Denby Dale HD8 191 F5
Leeds LS16 42 C3
Meadowside Rd BD17 38 E4
Meadstead Dr S71 179 B3
Meadstead Junior & Infants Sch S71 179 B3
Meadway Bradford BD6 93 F6
Featherstone WF7 144 C5
Meagill Rise LS21 10 E2
Meal Hill HD7 151 F2
Meal Hill La Holmfirth HD7 189 F3
Slaithwaite HD7 151 F2
Meal Hill Rd HD7 187 F1
Mean La Haworth BD22 50 D8
Meltham HD7 170 E2
Meanwood C of E Aided Primary Sch LS6 59 E7
Meanwood Cl LS7 206 B4
Meanwood Gr LS6 42 E1
Meanwood Rd LS6, LS7 206 B4
Meanwood St LS7 206 C2
Meanwood Towers LS6 60 A8
Meanwood Valley Cl LS7 59 F6
Meanwood Valley Dr LS7 59 F6
Meanwood Valley Gn LS7 59 F6
Meanwood Valley Gr 2 LS7 59 F6
Meanwood Valley Mount LS7 59 F6
Meanwood Valley Urban Farm LS7 60 A5
Meanwood Valley Wlk LS7 59 F6
Mearclough Rd HX6 112 D4
Mearhouse Bank HD7 189 E4
Mearhouse Terr HD7 189 E4
Medeway LS28 57 C2
Medhurst Ave LS25 83 B2
Medley La HX3 92 F4
Medley St WF10 124 E7
Medlock Rd WF4 141 A1
Medway Kirkheaton HD5 137 B2
Queensbury BD13 92 F8
Medway Ave LS25 83 A5
Medwell Way BD6 94 A6
Meeting House La HD7 152 A4
Meg La HD3 153 B5
Meggison Gr BD5 74 C4
Megnaway 3 BD5 74 E4
Melba Rd BD5 74 B3
Melbourne Ave WF2 120 F3
Melbourne Gr Bradford BD3 75 E8
Leeds LS13 58 C2
Melbourne Mews WF2 120 E4
Melbourne Pl BD5 201 A1
Melbourne Rd
Todmorden OL14 108 A1
Wakefield WF1 142 A8
Melbourne St
22 Halifax HX3 92 A1
25 Hebden Bridge HX7 89 A3
Leeds LS2 207 D1
4 Liversedge WF15 117 B3
Morley LS27 98 B4
7 Pudsey LS28 57 D2
Shipley BD18 55 A8
Melbourne Terr BD5 201 B1
Melcombe Wlk BD4 75 E4
Melford Cl S75 178 B1
Melford St BD4 75 C2
Mellor Brook HD7 151 F4
Mellor La HD7 188 B5
Mellor Mill La HX4 134 B4
Mellor St Halifax HX1 202 C1
Todmorden OL14 107 E8
Mellor Terr HX1 202 C1
Mellor's Bldgs WF4 156 D8
Mellwood La WF9 182 F3
Melrose Cl HD5 155 A6
Melrose Ct HX5 134 E6
Melrose Dr LS29 9 E2
Melrose Gr LS18 58 E8
Melrose Pl Horsforth LS18 58 D8
Pudsey LS28 76 D6
Melrose St Bradford BD7 74 A4
26 Halifax HX3 92 A1
Melrose Terr
9 Bacup OL13 106 A7
Elland HX5 134 F6
Melrose Wlk LS18 58 E8
Meltham C of E (C) Junior & Infants Sch HD7 170 E1
Meltham House La HD7 189 F4
Meltham Jun & Inf Sch HD7 170 C3
Meltham Mills Ind Est HD7 170 F2
Meltham Mills Rd HD7 170 F2
Meltham Rd
Huddersfield HD1, HD4 153 F3
Marsden HD7 169 C5
Melton Ave LS10 99 F4
Melton Cl Middleton LS10 99 F4
South Elmsall WF9 183 A5
Melton Garth LS10 99 F4
Melton Rd WF2 160 A4

Melton St WF17 118 B6
Melton Terr BD10 56 E4
Melton Way WF15 116 F1
Melville Cl LS6 206 B3
Melville Gdns LS6 206 B4
Melville Gr LS29 8 E4
Melville Pl LS6 206 B4
Melville Rd LS6 206 B3
Melville St BD7 74 C7
Memorial Dr LS6 59 F7
Mendip Ave HD3 135 A1
Mendip Cl LS25 82 F5
Mendip Rd WF12 118 F1
Mendip Way BD12 94 B6
Menin Dr BD17 38 C5
Menston Dr LS29 22 A3
Menston Infants Sch LS29 21 F4
Menston Old La
Burley in W LS29 21 F7
Menston LS29 21 F7
Menston PrimSch LS29 22 A4
Menston Sta LS29 22 B5
Menstone St 6 BD8 74 C8
Mercer Cl HD4 171 C7
Merchants Ct BD4 75 A5
Mercia Way LS15 62 E3
Mercury Row LS21 23 A7
Merewood Rd WF10 123 F7
Meriden Ave LS25 82 F5
Merlin Cl LS27 98 C3
Merlin Ct Batley WF17 118 A8
Huddersfield HD4 171 E7
Merlin Gr BD8 73 C7
Merlinwood Dr BD17 38 D4
Merlyn Rees Com High Sch LS10 99 E8
Merrill Rd S63 194 C1
Merrion Cres HX3 113 E5
Merrion Ctr LS2 206 C1
Merrion Pl LS2 211 F4
Merrion St Halifax HX3 113 E5
Leeds LS1, LS2 211 F4
Merrion Way LS2 206 C1
Merrivale Rd BD15 73 A8
Merry Bent La HX6 132 A5
Merrybents St OL14 108 D5
Merrydale Rd BD4 95 A6
Mersey St 4 OL13 106 A1
Merton Ave LS28 57 D2
Merton Cl LS25 83 C2
Merton Dr LS28 57 C2
Merton Fold 6 BD5 74 E4
Merton Gdns LS28 57 C2
Merton Rd BD7 74 D5
Merton St HD1 154 A5
Merville Ave BD17 38 C5
Metcalfe St BD4 75 B4
Methley CE Infant Sch LS26 102 C2
Methley Dr LS7 204 A2
Methley Gr LS7 60 C6
Methley Junior Sch LS26 102 D3
Methley La Leeds LS7 204 A2
Rothwell LS26 101 E4
Methley Mount LS7 204 A2
Methley Park Hospl LS26 102 A3
Methley Pl LS7 60 C6
Methley Rd WF10 124 B8
Methley Terr LS7 204 A2
Methley View LS7 204 A2
Methuen Oval 2 BD12 94 C1
Metro Travel Interchange BD1 201 C2
Mettle Cote OL13 106 A1
Mews Ct WF7 145 D5
Mews The WF6 123 B3
Mexborough Ave LS7 207 D4
Mexborough Dr LS7 207 D4
Mexborough Gr LS7 207 D4
Mexborough House 3 HX5 134 F7
Mexborough Pl LS7 207 D4
Mexborough Rd Leeds LS7 207 D4
Shipley BD2 55 D5
Mexborough St LS7 207 D4
Meynell App LS11 211 D1
Meynell Ave LS26 100 E5
Meynell Ct LS15 81 D7
Meynell Hts LS11 211 D1
Meynell Mount LS26 100 F5
Meynell Rd LS15 81 D6
Meynell Sq LS11 211 D1
Meynell Wlk LS11 211 D1
Meyrick Ave LS22 14 A6
Miall St HX1 202 C4
Michael Ave WF3 121 E5
Mickledore Cl BD7 73 E3
Mickledore Ridge BD7 73 E3
Micklefield C of E Primary Sch LS25 84 A7
Micklefield Ct LS19 40 B4
Micklefield La LS19 40 B4
Micklefield Rd LS19 40 B4
Micklegate WF8 125 D1
Micklegate Sq WF8 125 D1
Micklemoss Dr BD13 72 C2
Micklethwaite Dr BD13 92 E8
Micklethwaite La BD16 36 E7
Micklethwaite Rd WF4 159 F3
Micklethwaite View LS22 13 E4
Mickletown Rd LS26 102 C3
Mickley St LS12 210 A3
Mid Yorkshire Nuffield Hosp LS18 58 E8
Middle Cl S75 177 C1
Middle Cross St LS12 210 A3
Middle Dean St 1 HX4 134 D6
Middle Field La WF4 177 F6
Middle Hall Cl WF15 116 F4
Middle La Bradford BD14 73 C5
Collingham LS22 13 C2
Crofton WF4 162 B7
Knottingley WF11 127 A3
Middle Oxford St WF10 124 C7
Middle Rd
Dewsbury WF12, WF13 139 B7
Dewsbury, Earlsheaton WF12 139 E7
Leeds LS9 80 D2
Middle St Bradford BD1 201 B3
Sowerby Bridge HX6 111 E1
Middle Way BD21 35 E7
Middlebrook Cl BD8 73 E7
Middlebrook Cres BD8 73 D6
Middlebrook Dr BD8 73 D7
Middlebrook Hill BD8 73 D7
Middlebrook Rise BD8 73 D7
Middlebrook View BD8 73 E7
Middlebrook Way BD8 73 E7
Middlebrook Wlk BD8 73 E7
Middlecliffe Dr S36 200 D5
Middlecroft Cl LS10 99 F8
Middlecroft Rd LS10 99 F8
Middlefield La WF8 166 B4
Middlegate WF17 96 E1
Middlegate Ct BD4 95 B8
Middlemoor LS14 62 B8
Middlestown Junior & Infants Sch WF4 158 B7
Middlethorne Cl LS17 44 B5
Middlethorne Ct LS17 44 A5
Middlethorne Mews LS17 44 B5
Middlethorne Rise LS17 44 B5
Middleton Ave Ilkley LS29 8 B5
Leeds LS9 207 F1
Rothwell LS26 100 A5
Middleton Cl LS27 98 C4
Middleton Cres LS11 214 B2
Middleton Ct WF15 116 E4
Middleton District Ctr LS10 99 D5
Middleton Gr Leeds LS11 214 B1
Morley LS27 98 C4
Middleton La
Middleton WF3 99 D3
Rothwell LS26 100 A5
Middleton Park Ave LS10 99 B4
Middleton Park Cir LS10 99 B5
Middleton Park Cres LS10 99 C5
Middleton Park Ct LS10 99 B4
Middleton Park Gn LS10 99 B4
Middleton Park Gr LS10 99 B4
Middleton Park High Sch LS10 99 D4
Middleton Park Mount LS10 99 B4
Middleton Park Pl LS10 99 C4
Middleton Park Rd LS10 99 B5
Middleton Park Sq LS10 99 C4
Middleton Park Sq N LS10 99 C4
Middleton Park Sq S LS10 99 C4
Middleton Park Terr LS10 99 C4
Middleton Primary Sch LS10 99 B4
Middleton Rd Ilkley LS29 8 A4
Middleton LS10 99 F8
Morley LS27 98 C4
Middleton Rly LS11 214 C1
Middleton St BD8 55 B1
Middleton St Mary's CE Prim Sch LS10 99 C5
Middleton Terr LS27 98 C4
Middleton Way
Knottingley WF11 126 F4
Middleton LS10 99 F6
Middleway BD20 5 F1
Midge Hall Cl LS29 9 E1
Midgeham Gr BD16 36 A1
Midgehole La HX7 89 A6
Midgehole Rd HX7 89 A6
Midgeley Rd BD17 38 A1
Midgley Almshouses 16 BD22 51 E8
Midgley Gdns LS6 206 A3
Midgley Junior & Infants Sch HX2 90 C1
Midgley Pl LS6 206 B3
Midgley Rd Burley in W LS29 9 E1
Hebden Bridge HX7 89 F1
Midgley Rise WF8 125 D3
Midgley Row BD4 75 B1
Midgley Terr LS6 206 B3
Midland Cl LS10 215 F3
Midland Garth LS10 215 E3
Midland Hill BD16 36 F3
Midland Pas LS6 205 F3
Midland Pl LS11 211 D2
Midland Rd Baildon BD17 38 D2
Bradford BD8 55 D1
Leeds LS10 215 E3
Leeds, Hyde Park LS6 205 F3
Pontefract WF8 125 E1
Royston S71 179 D4
Shipley BD9 55 C5
Midland St
Huddersfield HD1 154 B8
Rothwell LS26 101 C6
Midland Terr Bradford BD2 55 E3
Keighley BD21 35 C8
Shipley BD9 55 C5
Midway HD4 171 A6
Midway Ave 1 BD16 54 A7
Milan Rd LS8 207 F3
Milan St LS8 208 A3
Mildred St BD3 56 A1
Mildred Sylvester Way WF6 123 E2
Mile Cross Gdns HX1 202 A2
Mile Cross Pl HX1 202 A2
Mile Cross Rd HX1 202 A2
Mile Cross Terr HX1 202 A2
Mile End HD7 170 D2
Mile Thorn St HX1 202 B3
Miles Garth LS17 28 F6
Miles Hill Ave LS7 60 B6
Miles Hill Cres
Bradford BD4 75 C1
Leeds LS7 60 B6
Miles Hill Dr BD4 75 C1
Miles Hill Gr LS7 60 B6
Miles Hill Mount LS7 60 A7
Miles Hill Pl LS7 60 B7
Miles Hill Primary Sch LS7 60 A7
Miles Hill Rd LS7 60 B6
Miles Hill Sq LS7 60 B6
Miles Hill St LS7 60 B6
Miles Hill Terr LS7 60 B6
Miles Hill View LS7 60 B6
Milestone Ct LS28 57 F2
Milestone Sch LS28 57 F2
Milford Gr BD19 96 A3
Milford Pl Bradford BD9 55 A3
Leeds LS4 205 D1
Milford St HD1 154 A5
Milgate St S71 179 D4
Mill Ave HD5 155 A7
Mill Bank Cl HX6 132 C7
Mill Bank Rd Meltham HD7 170 F1
Sowerby Bridge HX6 132 D7
Mill Banks BD20 5 E1
Mill Carr Hill Rd BD12, BD4 95 B5
Mill Cl Ackworth M T WF7 164 A6
Meltham HD7 170 D2
South Kirkby WF9 182 A1
Mill Cotts WF7 145 B5
Mill Croft LS27 97 D7
Mill Ct 3 BD22 51 C2
Mill Dam LS23 30 E5
Mill Dam Jun & Inf Sch WF7 164 A6
Mill Dam La WF8 125 E2
Mill Farm Dr WF2 160 C4
Mill Fold Way HX6 132 E4
Mill Forest Way WF17 118 F4
Mill Garth LS27 97 D7
Mill Gn LS12 210 C2
Mill Gr HD6 114 F4
Mill Grath WF8 146 C7
Mill Green Cl LS14 62 C5
Mill Green Garth 6 LS14 62 C5
Mill Green Gdns LS14 62 C5
Mill Green Pl LS14 62 C4
Mill Green Rd LS14 62 C5
Mill Green View LS14 62 B5
Mill Hey BD22 51 D7
Mill Hill Ackworth M T WF7 164 A8
Haworth BD22 51 C7
Leeds LS1 211 F3
Normanton WF6 123 A1
Pudsey LS28 76 E5
Rothwell LS26 100 E5
Mill Hill Ave WF8 146 C6
Mill Hill Cl WF8 147 D5
Mill Hill Gn LS26 100 E5
Mill Hill La Brighouse HD6 114 F4
Liversedge HD6 115 F1
Pontefract WF8 146 C7
Mill Hill Rd WF8 146 C7
Mill Hill Sq LS26 100 E5
Mill Hill Top BD16 53 B8
Mill House La HX6 112 A2
Mill House Rise BD5 75 B1
Mill La Ackworth M T WF7 164 A6
Adwick Le S DN6 184 F2
Bardsey LS17 28 E4
Batley, Hanging Heaton WF17 118 E3
Batley, Howden Clough WF17 97 B2
Birkenshaw BD11 96 A6
Birkenshaw, Tong BD11 77 A2
Bradford BD4, BD5 201 C1
Bradford, Woodside BD6 93 E6
Brighouse HD6 115 B2
Castleford WF10 103 D1
Cleckheaton BD19 95 D3
Dewsbury WF12 140 A7
East Ardsley WF3 120 E8
Elland HX4 134 C4
Featherstone WF7 144 D6
Flockton WF4 157 D2
Gildersome LS27 97 D7
Guiseley LS20 38 D8
Halifax HX2 91 D7
Halifax, Boothtown HX3 92 B2
Huddersfield HD5 137 B5
Leeds LS13 58 A3
Low Bradley BD20 4 C6
Mapplewell S75 177 E1
Mickletown LS26 102 D3
Normanton WF6 123 D4
Notton WF4 178 D8
Oakworth BD22 34 C2
Otley LS21 23 A8
Oxenhope BD22 51 C3
Pontefract WF8 125 F3
Pool LS21 24 D7
Queensbury BD13 72 C2
Ryhill WF4 162 B1
South Elmsall WF9 183 B4
South Kirkby WF9 182 A2
Steeton BD20 17 C5
Thorp Arch LS23 30 E8
Mill Lane Jun & Inf Sch WF17 118 D3
Mill Moor Rd HD7 170 C2
Mill Pit La LS26 100 D7
Mill Rd WF13 118 C2
Mill Row BD20 16 F6
Mill Royd St HD6 115 B2
Mill Shaw La HD7 190 B1
Mill St Batley WF17 117 E8
Bradford BD1 201 C3
Bradford, Wibsey BD6 74 A1
Castleford WF10 124 B7
Cullingworth BD13 52 D6
Elland HX3 113 A1
Glusburn BD20 16 E6
Huddersfield HD4 153 E4
Leeds LS9 212 A3
Morley LS27 98 A3
South Kirkby WF9 182 A2
Sutton in C BD20 16 E5
Mill St E WF12 139 D6
Mill St W WF12 139 C7
Mill View Burley in W LS29 9 E2
Hemsworth WF9 181 C6
Knottingley WF11 126 B4
Millacre View HD7 189 C8
Millars Wlk WF9 182 C1
Millbank LS28 76 F6
Millbank Ct LS28 76 F6
Millbank Fold LS28 76 F6
Millbank View LS28 76 F6
Millbeck App LS27 98 C4
Millbeck Cl BD8 73 C6
Millbeck Dr BD16 36 A1
Millbeck Gn LS22 29 A8
Millbridge Infants Sch WF15 117 B4
Millbridge Upper Junior Mixed Sch WF15 117 B4
Millbrook Gdns WF13 118 A3
Millcroft WF3 121 E6
Millcroft Cl WF3 121 E6
Millcroft Est LS21 24 D7
Millcroft Rise WF3 121 E6
Millenium Way LS11 214 B1
Millennium Rd BD23 4 A8
Miller Ave WF2 142 D2
Miller Cl BD2 55 E5
Miller Ct WF2 160 B4
Miller Garth WF7 164 A5
Miller Hill HD8 192 A5
Miller Hill Bank HD8 192 A5
Millergate BD1 201 B3
Millers Ct WF15 117 B2
Millers Dale LS27 97 F6
Millersdale Cl BD4 95 A7
Millfield Cl HD3 153 C7
Millfield Cres WF8 146 C6
Millfield Rd WF4 159 C8
Millfields Ossett WF5 140 C5
Silsden BD20 5 D1
Millgarth Ct LS22 29 B8
Millgarth St LS2 212 A4
Millgate Ackworth M T WF7 164 A5
Bingley BD16 36 F3
Elland HX5 134 F7
Huddersfield HD4 155 B2
Huddersfield, Yews Hill HD1 153 E5
Milligan Ave BD2 56 A5
Milligan Ct BD16 36 A1
Milligans Pl BD20 16 D7
Millmoor Cl BD9 54 D2
Millshaw Leeds LS11 213 E1
Morley LS11 213 D1
Millshaw Mount LS11 98 E8
Millshaw Park Ave LS11 98 D8
Millshaw Park Cl LS11 98 D8
Millshaw Park Dr LS11 213 D1
Millshaw Park La LS11 98 D8
Millshaw Park Way LS11 213 D1
Millshaw Rd LS11 98 E7
Millside S72 180 C3
Millside Wlk Morley LS27 98 C4
Shafton S72 180 C3
Millstone Cl WF7 164 A5
Millstone Rise WF15 117 B2
Millward St WF4 162 A1
Millwater Ave WF12 139 B5
Millwood La OL14 108 D5
Millwright St LS2 207 D1
Miln Rd HD1 154 A8
Milne Ct LS15 81 D6
Milne St BD7 74 C7
Milne's Ave WF2 141 F3
Milner Bank LS21 22 D6
Milner Cl HX4 134 C7
Milner Gdns LS9 212 C2
Milner House 2 BD15 73 B7
Milner Ing BD12 94 C5
Milner La Bardsey LS14 28 F1
Elland HX4 134 C7
Rothwell WF3 100 A2
Scarcroft LS14 45 F7
Thorner LS14 45 F7
Milner Rd BD17 38 A1
Milner Royd La HX6 112 E3
Milner St Halifax HX1 203 D3
Huddersfield HD1 153 E3
Ossett WF5 119 C1
Milner Way WF5 140 E6
Milner's La WF8 147 D4
Milner's Rd LS19 39 F7
Milnes Gr WF10 125 B7
Milnes St LS12 210 B2
Milnthorpe Cl LS23 30 C3
Milnthorpe Cres WF2 160 D7
Milnthorpe Dr WF2 160 D8
Milnthorpe Garth LS23 30 C3
Milnthorpe Gdns LS23 30 C3
Milnthorpe Gn WF2 160 D7
Milnthorpe La
Bramham LS23 30 C3
Wakefield WF2 142 D2
Milnthorpe Way LS23 30 C3
Milroyd Cres WF17 97 A2
Milton Ave
Liversedge WF15 117 C3
Sowerby Bridge HX6 112 B5
Milton Cl Crigglestone WF4 159 D6
Liversedge WF15 117 C3
Milton Cres WF2 141 C4
Milton Ct WF3 121 F6
Milton Dr Barwick in E LS15 62 F7
Batley WF15 117 C2
Hemsworth WF9 163 B2
Milton Gdns WF15 117 C2
Milton Gr WF13 118 C2
Milton Pl Halifax HX1 203 D3
Ossett WF5 140 D7
Milton Rd Liversedge WF15 117 C3
Wakefield WF2 141 D4
Milton St 1 Batley WF16 117 D5
Bradford BD7 74 C7
Castleford WF10 124 C8
Denholme BD13 71 E8
19 Sowerby Bridge HX6 112 B5
Wakefield WF2 142 A5
Milton Terr
Cleckheaton BD19 116 C8
3 Halifax HX1 203 D3
Hemsworth WF9 163 A4
Leeds LS5 59 A4
Yeadon LS19 39 F7
Milton Wlk 9 WF13 139 C8
Minden Cl WF8 146 A7
Minden Way WF8 146 A8
Minerva St HD4 152 F3
Mini Market 3 HD1 154 C8
Minnie St Haworth BD22 51 C6
Keighley BD21 35 B6
Minorca Mount BD13 52 D1
Minstead Ave HD6 135 D7
Minster Cl HX4 134 B7
Minsthorpe High Sch & Com Coll WF9 183 A5
Minsthorpe La
South Elmsall WF9 182 E4
South Kirkby WF9 182 E4
Minsthorpe Vale WF9 182 F4
Mint St Bradford BD2 56 B2
Huddersfield HD1 153 D7
Miramar HD2 136 D5
Mirey Butt La WF11 126 D3
Mirey La HX6 111 C3
Mirfield Ave BD2 56 A5
Mirfield Free Grammar Sch The WF14 137 F7
Mirfield Sports Ctr WF14 137 F7
Mirfield Sta WF14 138 A3
Miriam Lord First Sch BD8 55 B1
Miry La Barwick in E LS25 46 F1
Cleckheaton WF15 116 C5
Hebden Bridge HX7 110 F6
Holmfirth, Netherthong HD7 188 F8
Holmfirth, Thongsbridge HD7 189 B8
Yeadon LS19 40 B7
Mission St HD6 115 C1
Mistral Cl BD12 94 C2
Mistral Gr WF15 116 B5
Mistress La LS12 209 F4
Mitcham Dr BD9 55 A2
Mitchell Ave
3 Dewsbury WF13 118 B2
Huddersfield HD5 155 B5
Mitchell Cl BD10 39 C1
Mitchell La Bradford BD10 39 C1
Silsden BD20 5 E1
Mitchell Sq 8 BD5 74 E4
Mitchell St Brighouse HD6 115 A3
6 Hebden Bridge HX7 89 A2
Keighley BD21 35 D8
Sowerby Bridge HX6 112 C4
Todmorden OL14 107 E8
Mitchell Terr BD16 36 F2
Mitford Pl LS12 210 A3
Mitford Rd LS12 210 A3
Mitford Terr LS12 210 A3
Mitford View LS12 210 A3
Mitre Ct BD4 75 D3
Mitre St Dewsbury WF13 139 A8
Huddersfield HD1 153 E7
Mitton St Bradford BD5 74 C3
2 Shipley BD16 54 B6
Mixenden Cl HX2 91 C5
Mixenden Ct HX2 91 D4
Mixenden Jun & Inf Sch HX2 91 A6
Mixenden La HX2 91 D6
Mixenden Rd HX2 91 C5
Mixenden Stones HX2 91 C6
Moat End LS14 45 F5
Moat Hill WF17 97 A2
Moat Hill Farm Dr WF17 97 A2
Modd La HD7 188 F4
Modder Ave LS12 209 E3
Modder Pl LS12 209 E3
Model Ave LS12 210 A3
Model Rd LS12 210 A3
Model Terr LS12 210 A3
Moderna Bsns Pk HX7 110 F8
Moderna Way HX7 110 F8

Moffat Cl BD6 ... 93 F7
Moffatt Cl HX3 ... 91 F3
Moldgreen Junior & Infants Sch HD5 ... 154 D5
Moles Head HD7 ... 152 C6
Molly Hurst La WF4 ... 177 F7
Mona St Slaithwaite HD7 ... 151 F1
Wakefield WF2 ... 141 E6
Mona's Terr 1 OL14 ... 108 A1
Monckton Dr WF10 ... 125 C6
Monckton Rd WF2 ... 142 B2
Mond Ave BD3 ... 56 D1
Monk Barn Cl 1 BD16 ... 37 A4
Monk Bridge Ave 11 LS6 ... 59 F6
Monk Bridge Dr 6 LS6 ... 59 F6
Monk Bridge Gr 2 LS6 ... 59 E6
Monk Bridge Mount 10 LS6 59 F6
Monk Bridge Pl 1 LS6 ... 59 E6
Monk Bridge Rd LS6 ... 59 E6
Monk Bridge St LS6 ... 59 F6
Monk Bridge Terr LS6 ... 59 E6
Monk Ings WF17 ... 96 D1
Monk Ings Ave WF17 ... 96 C2
Monk St Bradford BD7 ... 74 C7
Wakefield WF1 ... 216 C1
Monkfield WF14 ... 137 E6
Monkhill Ave WF8 ... 125 D2
Monkhill Dr WF8 ... 125 D2
Monkhill La WF8 ... 125 D3
Monkhill Mount WF8 ... 125 D2
Monkhill Sta WF8 ... 125 E2
Monkmans Wharf BD20 ... 5 E1
Monkswood LS5 ... 58 F6
Monkswood Ave LS14 ... 61 F8
Monkswood Bank LS14 ... 61 F8
Monkswood Cl LS14 ... 61 F8
Monkswood Dr LS14 ... 61 F8
Monkswood Gate 6 LS14 ... 62 A8
Monkswood Gn LS14 ... 61 F8
Monkswood Hill LS14 ... 61 F8
Monkswood Rise LS14 ... 61 F8
Monkswood Wlk LS14 ... 62 A8
Monkwood Rd WF1 ... 121 B5
Mons Rd OL14 ... 107 F7
Monson Ave LS28 ... 57 B6
Mont Gr 1 BD5 ... 74 D3
Montagu Ave LS8 ... 61 C5
Montagu Cres LS8 ... 61 C5
Montagu Ct LS8 ... 61 B6
Montagu Dr LS8 ... 61 B6
Montagu Gdns LS8 ... 61 B5
Montagu Gr LS8 ... 61 C5
Montagu Pl LS8 ... 61 B5
Montagu Rd LS22 ... 14 A6
Montagu Rise LS8 ... 208 C4
Montagu View LS8 ... 61 B5
Montague Cres LS25 ... 83 A7
Montague Ct LS12 ... 209 D3
Montague Pl LS25 ... 83 A7
Montague St Bradford BD5 ... 74 C3
Sowerby Bridge HX6 ... 112 A3
Wakefield WF1 ... 142 F2
Montcalm Cres Leeds LS10 215 E2
Lofthouse Gate WF3 ... 121 F3
Monterey Dr BD15 ... 54 A4
Montfort Cl LS18 ... 41 B3
Montpelier Terr 3 LS6 ... 206 A4
Montreal Ave LS7 ... 204 A2
Montreal St 9 OL14 ... 108 A1
Montreal Terr LS13 ... 77 A8
Montrose Ave S75 ... 177 F1
Montrose Pl 2 BD13 ... 72 C2
Montrose St BD2 ... 55 D4
Montserrat Rd BD4 ... 75 F1
Monument La WF8 ... 146 E7
Monument Mews WF8 ... 146 E7
Moody St BD4 ... 201 C1
Moor Allerton Ave LS17 ... 43 E2
Moor Allerton Cres LS17 ... 43 E2
Moor Allerton Ctr LS17 ... 43 B2
Moor Allerton Dr LS17 ... 43 E2
Moor Allerton Gdns LS17 ... 43 D2
Moor Allerton Hall Primary Sch LS8 ... 43 F1
Moor Allerton Way LS17 ... 43 E2
Moor Ave Boston Spa LS23 ... 30 D6
Leeds LS15 ... 80 F7
Lofthouse Gate WF3 ... 121 E6
Moor Bottom HD7 ... 171 F4
Moor Bottom La
Bingley BD16 ... 37 B3
Elland HX4 ... 134 A8
Keighley BD21 ... 35 B2
Sowerby Bridge HX2 ... 111 A5
Moor Bottom Rd Halifax HX2 91 F6
Ripponden HX4 ... 132 F5
Moor Cl Huddersfield HD4 ... 153 C1
Leeds LS10 ... 215 D2
Moor Close Ave BD13 ... 92 C8
Moor Close Farm Mews 1
BD13 ... 92 C8
Moor Close La BD13 ... 92 C8
Moor Close Par BD13 ... 72 D1
Moor Close Rd BD13 ... 92 C8
Moor Cottage Cl HD4 ... 171 D7
Moor Cres LS11 ... 214 C4
Moor Crescent Chase
LS11 ... 214 C4
Moor Crest Rd HD4 ... 153 C3
Moor Croft Bingley BD16 ... 37 B5
Leeds LS16 ... 42 D4
Moor Dr Leeds LS6 ... 59 E6
Oakworth BD22 ... 34 C3
Otley LS21 ... 23 D8
Pudsey LS28 ... 76 F5
Moor Edge High Side BD16 36 A2
Moor End Ave HX2 ... 91 C1
Moor End Gdns HX2 ... 91 D1
Moor End High Sch HD4 ... 153 D2
Moor End La Batley WF13 ... 117 F2
Sowerby Bridge HX6 ... 112 D2
Moor End Rd Halifax HX2 ... 91 B2
Huddersfield HD4 ... 153 E3
Moor Farm Gdns LS7 ... 60 C7
Moor Flatts Ave LS10 ... 99 C5
Moor Flatts Rd LS10 ... 99 C5
Moor Fold HD7 ... 189 E7
Moor Gate OL14 ... 108 C3
Moor Gr
Lofthouse Gate WF3 ... 121 E6
Pudsey LS28 ... 76 F5
Shelf HX3 ... 93 C7
Moor Grange Ct 8 LS16 ... 58 F8
Moor Grange Dr LS16 ... 59 A8
Moor Grange Rise LS16 ... 59 A8
Moor Grange View LS16 ... 59 A8
Moor Haven Ct LS17 ... 43 A3
Moor Hey La
Elland, Elland Upper Edge HD2, HX5 ... 135 C5
Elland, Sowood Green HX4 ... 133 F2
Moor Hill Rd HD3 ... 134 F1
Moor House Ct LS17 ... 44 B4
Moor Knoll Cl WF3 ... 120 D8
Moor Knoll Dr WF3 ... 120 D8
Moor Knoll La WF3 ... 120 D8
Moor La Addingham LS29 ... 2 D1
Addingham, Addingham Low Moor LS29 ... 2 B1
Askwith LS21 ... 10 B7
Birkenshaw BD11 ... 96 C3
Burley in W LS29 ... 21 D7
Cleckheaton BD19 ... 96 B2
Clifton LS21 ... 10 C4
Collingham LS22 ... 29 F7
Darrington WF8 ... 147 A2
East Keswick LS17 ... 28 A5
Guiseley LS20 ... 22 E2
Halifax HX2 ... 91 E4
Harewood LS17 ... 27 F6
Holmfirth HD7 ... 188 E8
Huddersfield HD4 ... 171 D7
Kirkburton HD8 ... 173 F7
Kirkburton, Farnley Tyas HD4 ... 172 F5
Menston LS29 ... 21 E4
Pontefract WF8 ... 146 E4
Stutton LS24 ... 48 F8
Thorp Arch LS23 ... 14 D5
Todmorden OL14 ... 108 B3
Moor Park Ave
Huddersfield HD4 ... 153 C1
Leeds LS6 ... 59 D6
Moor Park Cl
Addingham LS29 ... 6 D8
Bradford BD3 ... 75 C8
Moor Park Cres LS29 ... 6 D8
Moor Park Ct 6 WF12 ... 118 E1
Moor Park Dr
Addingham LS29 ... 6 D8
Bradford BD3 ... 75 D8
Leeds LS6 ... 59 E6
Moor Park Gdns WF12 ... 118 E1
Moor Park Gr LS29 ... 6 E8
Moor Park Mount LS6 ... 59 E6
Moor Park Rd BD3 ... 75 C8
Moor Park Villas LS6 ... 59 E6
Moor Park Way LS29 ... 6 E8
Moor Rd Bramhope LS16 ... 24 D2
Featherstone WF7 ... 145 D5
Ilkley LS29 ... 21 C7
Leeds, Far Headingley LS6 ... 59 D6
Leeds, Hunslet Carr LS10 ... 215 D2
Leeds, Hunslet Moor LS10 ... 214 C4
Littleborough OL15 ... 129 C1
Lofthouse Gate WF3 ... 121 E6
Menston LS29 ... 21 C7
Moor Royd Halifax HX3 ... 113 A4
Honley HD7 ... 171 E3
Moor Side LS23 ... 30 B7
Moor Side Cotts BD20 ... 19 B3
Moor Side La HD7 ... 151 D3
Moor St Oakworth BD22 ... 34 D3
9 Queensbury BD13 ... 72 E1
Moor Stone Pl HX3 ... 93 C5
Moor Terr BD2 ... 56 C1
Moor Top Birkenshaw BD11 ... 96 D6
Gildersome LS12 ... 77 C1
Guiseley LS20 ... 22 E4
Mirfield WF14 ... 137 E6
Otley LS21 ... 22 E4
Moor Top Ave
Ackworth M T WF7 ... 163 E5
Kirkburton HD4 ... 172 F2
Moor Top Dr WF9 ... 181 D5
Moor Top Gdns HX2 ... 91 E8
Moor Top La WF4 ... 156 D1
Moor Top Rd
Bradford BD12 ... 94 B6
Halifax HX2 ... 112 B8
Kirkheaton HD5 ... 137 C2
Moor Top Sch WF7 ... 163 F4
Moor Valley Pk LS20 ... 38 C7
Moor View Bacup OL13 ... 106 A4
Batley WF16 ... 117 E2
Crigglestone WF4 ... 159 F5
Leeds LS11 ... 211 D1
Meltham HD7 ... 170 C3
Mickletown LS26 ... 102 F3
Mirfield WF14 ... 117 A1
Moor View Ave BD18 ... 55 A8
Moor View Cl WF10 ... 124 F7
Moor View Ct BD20 ... 36 C7
Moor View Terr BD22 ... 50 D7
Moor Way BD22 ... 34 C3
Moorbank Ct LS6 ... 59 E5
Moorbottom BD19 ... 116 B7
Moorbottom Rd HD1 ... 153 E4
Moorbrow HD7 ... 189 C2
Moorcock Rd HX7 ... 87 C5
Moorcrest Rise S75 ... 178 B2
Moorcroft WF13 ... 118 A1
Moorcroft Ave Bradford BD3 56 D1
Haworth BD22 ... 34 E3
Moorcroft Avenues HD7 ... 152 D5
Moorcroft Dr Bradford BD4 ... 75 F1
Dewsbury WF13 ... 117 F1
Holmfirth HD7 ... 189 D7
Moorcroft Park Dr HD7 ... 189 E7
Moorcroft Rd Bradford BD4 .. 75 F1
Dewsbury WF13 ... 117 F1
Moorcroft Terr BD4 ... 95 F8
Moore Ave BD6, BD7 ... 74 A2
Moore St 5 BD21 ... 35 C6
Moore View BD7 ... 73 F3
Moorehouse Gr LS9 ... 207 E1
Moorend C of E First Sch BD19 ... 95 C1
Moorfield LS27 ... 97 C7
Moorfield Ave Bradford BD3 . 56 D1
Brighouse BD19 ... 115 E7
Leeds LS12 ... 209 D4
Menston LS29 ... 21 F4
Moorfield Cl LS19 ... 40 D6
Moorfield Cres
Hemsworth WF9 ... 181 C6
Leeds LS12 ... 209 D4
Pudsey LS28 ... 76 D6
Yeadon LS19 ... 40 D7
Moorfield Croft LS19 ... 40 D6
Moorfield Ct LS19 ... 40 D6
Moorfield Dr Baildon BD17 ... 38 C5
Oakworth BD22 ... 34 D3
Yeadon LS19 ... 40 D6
Moorfield First Sch BD3 ... 75 C7
Moorfield Gdns LS28 ... 76 D6
Moorfield Gr Leeds LS12 ... 209 D4
Pudsey LS28 ... 76 D6
Moorfield Pl Bradford BD10 .. 56 B8
Hemsworth WF9 ... 181 C6
Moorfield Rd
Huddersfield HD1 ... 136 B1
Ilkley LS29 ... 8 F4
Leeds LS12 ... 209 D4
Shipley BD16 ... 54 A7
Yeadon LS19 ... 40 D7
Moorfield Sch LS29 ... 8 D3
Moorfield St Halifax HX1 ... 202 C1
Leeds, Hill Top LS12 ... 209 D4
8 Leeds, Woodhouse LS2 .. 206 A3
Moorfield Terr LS19 ... 40 C7
Moorfield View WF15 ... 116 F1
Moorfield Way BD19, LS29 . 115 E7
Moorfields LS13 ... 58 C3
Moorfoot La BD20 ... 4 A3
Moorgarth Ave BD3 ... 56 D1
Moorgate BD17 ... 38 C4
Moorgate Ave Bradford BD3 . 56 D1
Kippax LS25 ... 83 A2
Moorgate Cl LS25 ... 83 A2
Moorgate Dr LS25 ... 83 B2
Moorgate Flats HD7 ... 170 D2
Moorgate Rd LS25 ... 83 A3
Moorgate Rise LS25 ... 83 A2
Moorgate St 9 HX1 ... 202 B1
Moorhead Cl HD7 ... 170 D2
Moorhead Cres BD18 ... 54 E7
Moorhead La BD18 ... 54 E7
Moorhead Terr BD18 ... 54 E7
Moorhouse Ave
Bradford BD2 ... 56 A5
Leeds LS11 ... 213 F1
Lofthouse Gate WF3 ... 122 B6
Wakefield WF2 ... 142 A6
Moorhouse Cl
Lofthouse Gate WF3 ... 122 B7
Normanton WF6 ... 123 C3
Oxenhope BD22 ... 51 C3
Moorhouse Cres WF2 ... 142 A6
Moorhouse Ct
Oxenhope BD22 ... 51 C3
South Elmsall WF9 ... 183 A1
Moorhouse Dr BD11 ... 95 F7
Moorhouse Gap DN6 ... 183 F1
Moorhouse Gr WF3 ... 122 B7
Moorhouse La
Birkenshaw BD11 ... 96 A7
Hooton Pagnell WF9 ... 183 D1
Oxenhope BD22 ... 51 C4
Ryhill WF4 ... 162 C4
Woolley S75 ... 177 C5
Moorhouse Terr WF3 ... 122 B7
Moorhouse View
Lofthouse Gate WF3 ... 122 B7
South Elmsall WF9 ... 183 B2
Moorings The
Bradford BD10 ... 56 D8
Leeds, Alwoodley Gates LS17 . 43 E5
Leeds, Stourton LS10 ... 80 B3
Moorland Ave Baildon BD17 . 38 D5
Bingley BD16 ... 37 C5
Birkenshaw BD11 ... 96 A7
Gildersome LS27 ... 97 C8
Guiseley LS20 ... 22 E1
Leeds LS6 ... 205 F2
Mapplewell S75 ... 178 B2
Moorland Cl
Gildersome LS27 ... 97 C8
Halifax HX2 ... 91 E3
Leeds LS17 ... 43 D1
Slaithwaite HD7 ... 170 E7
Moorland Cotts HX7 ... 131 C8
Moorland Cres
Baildon BD17 ... 38 D4
Gildersome LS27 ... 97 B8
Guiseley LS20 ... 22 C2
Guiseley LS20 ... 22 E2
Leeds LS17 ... 43 C1
Mapplewell S75 ... 178 B2
Menston LS29 ... 22 A5
Pudsey LS28 ... 57 A1
Moorland Dr
Birkenshaw BD11 ... 96 B6
Crigglestone WF4 ... 159 F2
Guiseley LS20 ... 22 E2
Leeds LS17 ... 43 D1
Pudsey LS28 ... 57 A1
Moorland Garth LS17 ... 43 C1
Moorland Gdns LS17 ... 43 D1
Moorland Gr Leeds LS17 ... 43 C2
Pudsey LS28 ... 76 A8
Moorland Ings LS17 ... 43 C1
Moorland Leys LS17 ... 43 C1
Moorland Mount BD19 ... 116 B6
Moorland Pl
4 Bradford BD12 ... 94 E5
Lofthouse Gate WF3 ... 121 E8
Moorland Rd
Birkenshaw BD11 ... 96 E6
Bramhope LS16 ... 24 C2
Leeds LS6 ... 205 F2
Pudsey LS28 ... 57 A1
Moorland Rise Leeds LS17 ... 43 C2
Meltham HD7 ... 170 C2
Moorland Terr
Garforth LS25 ... 82 E6
Keighley BD21 ... 35 F6
Moorland View
Bradford BD12 ... 94 E5
Clayton West HD8 ... 176 A2
Emley HD8 ... 175 A7
Leeds LS17 ... 43 C2
Leeds, Intake LS13 ... 58 B4
Sowerby Bridge HX6 ... 111 F3
Wilsden BD15 ... 53 D4
Moorland Wlk LS17 ... 43 C2
Moorlands Holmfirth HD7 ... 189 C3
Ilkley LS29 ... 8 A2
Moorlands Ave
Bradford BD3 ... 56 D1
Dewsbury WF13 ... 118 C1
Halifax HX2 ... 91 E3
Keighley BD22 ... 34 F4
1 Mirfield WF14 ... 137 F6
Ossett WF5 ... 140 C8
Yeadon LS19 ... 40 D6
Moorlands Cres
Halifax HX2 ... 91 E3
Huddersfield HD3 ... 134 D1
Moorlands Ct 3 HX4 ... 134 B8
Moorlands Dr Halifax HX3 ... 91 E2
Yeadon LS19 ... 40 D6
Moorlands Ind Ctr BD19 ... 95 D1
Moorlands Pl HX1 ... 203 D1
Moorlands Rd
Birkenshaw BD11 ... 96 A7
Dewsbury WF13 ... 139 B8
Elland HX4 ... 134 B8
Huddersfield HD3 ... 134 D1
Moorlands Sch LS16 ... 42 D1
Moorlands Terr 6 OL13 ... 106 A1
Moorlands The
Bacup OL13 ... 106 A8
Boston Spa LS23 ... 30 C8
Leeds LS17 ... 43 E4
Wetherby LS22 ... 13 F5
Moorlands View HX1 ... 203 D1
Moorlea Dr BD17 ... 38 D3
Moorleigh Cl LS25 ... 83 B2
Moorleigh Dr LS25 ... 83 B2
Moorroyd St WF5 ... 140 C8
Moors The LS29 ... 8 B4
Moorshutt Rd WF9 ... 181 C6
Moorside Baildon BD17 ... 38 C5
Bradford BD9 ... 54 E2
Cleckheaton, Hartshead Moor Side BD19 ... 116 A6
Cleckheaton, West End BD19 ... 116 C7
Kirkburton HD8 ... 173 B6
Moorside App BD11 ... 96 F5
Moorside Ave
Batley WF13 ... 117 F2
Birkenshaw BD11 ... 96 A7
Birkenshaw, Drighlington BD11 ... 96 F5
Bradford BD2 ... 56 D2
Huddersfield HD4 ... 153 D4
Steeton BD20 ... 17 A5
Moorside Cl
Birkenshaw BD11 ... 96 F5
Bradford BD2 ... 56 C3
Moorside Cres
Bacup OL13 ... 106 A4
Batley WF13 ... 117 F2
Birkenshaw BD11 ... 96 F5
Crigglestone WF4 ... 159 F2
Moorside Croft BD2 ... 56 C2
Moorside Dr
Birkenshaw BD11 ... 96 F5
Leeds LS13 ... 58 C4
Moorside End WF13 ... 117 F2
Moorside Gdns
Birkenshaw BD11 ... 96 F5
Bradford BD2 ... 56 C4
Halifax HX3 ... 91 F4
Moorside Gn BD11 ... 96 F6
Moorside Junior & Infants Sch HX2 ... 91 F4
Moorside La Addingham LS29 .. 6 E4
Askwith LS21 ... 10 A7
Bradford BD3 ... 75 D7
Oxenhope BD22 ... 50 F5
Moorside Maltings LS11 ... 214 C4
Moorside Mews BD2 ... 56 D3
Moorside Mount BD11 ... 96 E5
Moorside Paddock BD19 ... 116 B6
Moorside Par BD11 ... 96 F5
Moorside Pl Batley WF13 ... 117 F2
Bradford BD3 ... 75 D7
Moorside Rd Batley WF13 ... 117 F2
Birkenshaw BD11 ... 96 E5
Bradford BD3 ... 75 D7
Bradford, Haigh Fold BD2 ... 56 C3
Honley HD7 ... 171 E3
Kirkheaton HD5 ... 137 C1
Wilsden BD15 ... 53 C4
Moorside Rise BD19 ... 116 B7
Moorside St Bradford BD12 ... 94 B6
Leeds LS13 ... 58 C4
Moorside Terr
Birkenshaw BD11 ... 96 F5
Bradford BD2 ... 56 D2
Leeds LS13 ... 58 C4
Moorside Vale BD11 ... 96 F6
Moorside View BD11 ... 96 F5
Moorside Wlk BD11 ... 96 F5
Moorthorpe Ave BD3 ... 56 D1
Moorthorpe Sta WF9 ... 182 E3
Moortop BD11 ... 96 E6
Moortown Corner House LS17 ... 43 D2
Moortown Golf Course LS17 ... 43 B6
Moortown Primary Sch LS17 ... 43 D2
Moorview Cres BD16 ... 53 E6
Moorview Croft LS29 ... 21 F5
Moorview Ct BD10 ... 39 A1
Moorview Dr Shipley BD18 ... 55 F7
Wilsden BD16 ... 53 E6
Moorview Gr BD21 ... 35 D5
Moorville Ave BD3 ... 56 D1
Moorville Cl LS11 ... 214 B4
Moorville Ct LS11 ... 214 B4
Moorville Dr BD11 ... 96 A7
Moorville Gr LS11 ... 214 A4
Moorville Rd LS11 ... 214 B4
Moorway LS20 ... 39 C8
Moorwell Pl BD2 ... 56 C4
Moravian Pl BD5 ... 74 D4
Morefield Bank HD7 ... 189 C8
Moresby Rd BD6 ... 93 F6
Moresdale La LS14 ... 61 F3
Moreton Cres WF10 ... 124 F7
Morlands Cl WF13 ... 117 F3
Morley Ave Bradford BD3 ... 56 D1
Knottingley WF11 ... 127 A4
Morley Carr Rd BD12 ... 94 D5
Morley Cross Hall Infants Sch LS27 ... 97 F2
Morley Cross Hall Junior Sch LS27 ... 97 F3
Morley Elmfield Infant Sch LS27 ... 98 B2
Morley Fold HD8 ... 191 F5
Morley Hall La HX2 ... 111 D6
Morley High Sch LS27 ... 97 F3
Morley La HD3 ... 153 A4
Morley St BD7 ... 201 B2
Morley St Francis RC Prim Sch LS27 ... 97 F4
Morley Sta LS27 ... 98 C5
Morley Victoria Primary Sch LS27 ... 98 A5
Morley View HX3 ... 113 E3
Morning St 13 BD21 ... 35 B4
Morningside Bradford BD8 ... 55 B1
Denholme BD13 ... 52 E1
Mornington Rd
Bingley BD16 ... 37 A3
Ilkley LS29 ... 8 C4
Mornington St BD21 ... 35 B8
Mornington Villas BD8 ... 55 D1
Morpeth Pl LS9 ... 212 B3
Morpeth St Bradford BD7 ... 74 C7
Queensbury BD13 ... 72 E1
Morphet Terr LS7 ... 206 C1
Morrell Cres WF2 ... 120 F3
Morris Ave LS5 ... 59 A5
Morris Cl WF9 ... 163 B2
Morris Gr LS5 ... 59 A4
Morris La LS5 ... 59 A5
Morris Mount LS5 ... 59 A4
Morris Pl LS27 ... 97 F5
Morris View LS5 ... 59 A4
Morrison St WF10 ... 124 E7
Morrit Ave LS15 ... 62 B1
Morritt Dr LS15 ... 80 F8
Morritt Gr LS15 ... 80 F8
Mortimer Ave Batley WF17 . 117 F5
Bradford BD3 ... 56 D1
Mortimer Cl Garforth LS25 ... 82 E7
Ossett WF5 ... 140 F6
Mortimer Row
Bradford BD3 ... 75 D7
Horbury WF4 ... 140 F1
Mortimer St Batley WF17 ... 117 F5
Bradford BD8 ... 73 F8
Cleckheaton BD19 ... 116 D7
Mortimer Terr WF17 ... 117 F5
Morton Gn HD5 ... 155 A3
Morton Gr Dewsbury WF12 . 139 B3
Keighley BD20 ... 36 D8
Morton La Bingley BD16 ... 36 D7
Keighley BD16 ... 36 D7
Morton Par WF2 ... 142 A6

Morton Rd BD4 75 D5
Morton Terr LS20 22 D1
Morton Way HD3 134 E1
Morton Wood Gr HD7 189 D3
Mortons Cl HX3 113 E3
Morvern Meadows WF9 181 F7
Morwick Gr LS15 62 F6
Moselden La HX6 150 D6
Moseley Pl LS6 206 B3
Moseley Wood App LS16 41 D4
Moseley Wood Ave LS16 41 D6
Moseley Wood Bank LS16 41 D5
Moseley Wood Cl LS16 41 D4
Moseley Wood Cres LS16 41 D5
Moseley Wood Croft LS16 41 D4
Moseley Wood Dr LS16 41 D5
Moseley Wood Gdns
LS16 41 D5
Moseley Wood Gn LS16 41 D5
Moseley Wood Gr LS16 41 D5
Moseley Wood La LS16 41 E5
Moseley Wood Rise LS16 41 E5
Moseley Wood View LS16 41 E6
Moseley Wood Way LS16 41 D6
Moseley Wood Wlk LS16 41 D5
Moser Ave BD2 56 A5
Moser Cres BD2 56 A5
Moss Bridge Rd LS13 57 F5
Moss Carr Ave BD21 35 F5
Moss Carr Gr BD21 35 F5
Moss Carr Rd BD21 35 F5
Moss Dr HX2 91 E6
Moss Edge Rd HD7 188 C1
Moss Gdns LS17 43 A5
Moss Hall La HX7 87 E4
Moss La Halifax HX2 91 E6
Hebden Bridge HX7 89 A4
Moss Lea 4 LS27 98 B7
Moss Rise Holmfirth HD7 188 E5
Leeds LS17 43 A5
Moss Row BD15 53 C6
Moss Side BD9 54 E2
Moss St Castleford WF10 124 C8
Haworth BD22 51 E8
Huddersfield HD4 154 B4
Thornton BD13 72 C7
Moss Syke LS14 45 C8
Moss Valley LS17 43 A5
Mossdale Ave BD9 54 C3
Mosstree Cl BD13 72 C2
Mossy Bank Cl BD13 72 E2
Mostyn Gr BD6 94 A8
Mostyn Mount HX3 92 A3
Mostyn Wlk WF4 159 F2
Motley La LS20 22 E2
Moulson Ct 1 BD5 74 E3
Moulson Terr BD13 71 D8
Mount Ave
1 Batley WF17 118 D3
Batley, Nunroyd WF16 117 E6
Bradford BD2 56 C5
Halifax HX2 112 C7
Hemsworth WF9 181 D7
Huddersfield HD3 134 D1
Wakefield WF2 120 F3
Mount Cres
Cleckheaton BD19 116 D8
Halifax HX2 112 C7
Holme Chapel BB10 85 A8
Wakefield WF2 141 F3
Mount Dr LS17 43 B6
Mount Gdns
Cleckheaton BD19 116 D8
Leeds LS17 43 B6
Mount Gr BD2 56 B5
Mount Jun & Inf Sch The
WF2 141 F3
Mount La Brighouse HD6 135 E6
Holme Chapel BB10 85 A8
Todmorden OL14 86 C3
Mount Pellon HX2 202 B4
Mount Pellon Rd HX2 202 A4
Mount Pisgah LS21 23 A7
Mount Pl BD18 55 B8
Mount Pleasant
Ackworth M T WF7 163 F6
Addingham LS29 6 F8
1 Bradford BD6 93 F7
Brighouse HD6 135 E6
Castleford WF10 124 F6
Denholme BD13 71 D8
Dewsbury WF12 139 E7
Emley HD8 175 D7
Glusburn BD20 16 B6
Guiseley LS20 22 E2
Huddersfield HD1 153 F3
Ilkley LS29 8 C3
Keighley BD20 36 C7
4 Kippax LS25 83 B1
Kirk Smeaton WF8 166 F6
Menston LS29 21 F4
Middleton LS10 99 C5
Ripponden HX4 132 F4
Mount Pleasant Ave
Halifax HX1 203 D4
Leeds LS8 204 C1
Mount Pleasant Dr HX7 89 F1
Mount Pleasant Gdns
5 Kippax LS25 83 B1
Leeds LS8 204 C1
Mount Pleasant
Infants Sch HD1 153 F3
Mount Pleasant
Junior Sch HD1 153 F3
Mount Pleasant La HD8 155 C4
Mount Pleasant Rd LS28 76 F8
Mount Pleasant Sports Ctr
HD1 153 F3
Mount Pleasant St
Featherstone WF7 145 D6
1 Huddersfield HD5 154 D6
2 Pudsey LS28 76 F8
Queensbury BD13 72 E1
Todmorden OL14 86 A1
Mount Pleasant View 7
OL14 108 B5
Mount Preston LS2 206 A1
Mount Preston St LS2 206 A1
Mount Rd Bradford BD6 74 A1
Bradford, Eccleshill BD2 56 B5
Huddersfield HD1 153 D7
Lofthouse Gate WF3 121 F6
Marsden HD7 168 D1
Mount Rise LS17 43 B6
Mount Royd BD8 55 C2
Mount Scar View HD7 189 D4
Mount St Batley WF17 118 D3
Bradford BD3, BD4 75 B6
Bradford, Eccleshill BD2 56 B5
Cleckheaton BD19 116 D8
Halifax HX1 203 E3
Huddersfield, Milnsbridge
HD3 153 A4
Huddersfield, Rashcliffe
HD1, HD4 153 F3
Keighley BD21 35 A7
Sowerby Bridge HX6 112 B4
Mount St Mary's High Sch
LS9 212 B3
Mount St Marys
RC Primary Sch LS9 80 A8
Mount St W HX2 202 A4
Mount Tabor Rd HX2 91 A4
Mount Tabor St LS28 76 C7
Mount Terr Batley WF17 118 C3
Bradford BD2 56 B5
Mount The
Barwick in E LS15 63 D6
Batley WF17 96 E2
Castleford WF10 125 C7
Kippax LS25 83 A1
Leeds LS15 62 B1
Leeds, Alwoodley LS17 43 B6
Normanton WF6 123 B2
Pontefract WF8 146 C8
Rothwell LS26 100 F7
Todmorden OL14 108 C6
Wakefield WF2 141 F3
Wakefield, Wrenthorpe
WF2 120 D1
Mount Vernon Rd LS19 40 C4
Mount View Halifax HX2 91 A3
Oakworth BD22 34 B2
Queensbury BD13 72 D1
Mount View Rd HD7 189 E2
Mount Wlk WF10 124 D5
Mount Zion Rd HD5 154 C6
Mountain Cres WF12 139 D2
Mountain Rd WF12 139 D2
Mountain View BD18 55 D6
Mountain Way HD5 155 C7
Mountbatten Ave
Lofthouse Gate WF1 121 C5
Wakefield WF2 160 E8
Mountbatten Cres WF1 121 C5
Mountbatten Ct 4 BD5 74 E2
Mountbatten Gdns HD3 153 B7
Mountbatten Gr WF1 121 D4
Mountcliffe View LS27 98 B7
Mountfield Ave HD5 155 B4
Mountfield Rd HD5 155 B5
Mountfield Wlk WF9 182 B1
Mountfields
Brighouse HX3 114 E8
Leeds LS3 205 F1
Mountjoy Prep Sch HD1 153 F7
Mountjoy Rd HD1 153 F7
Mountleigh Cl BD4 95 A7
Mouse Hole La WF14 138 D1
Moverley Flatts WF8 146 E7
Mowat Ct WF15 116 B5
Mowbray Chase LS26 101 B7
Mowbray Cl BD13 52 C5
Mowbray Cres LS14 62 A3
Mowbray Ct LS14 62 A3
Moxon Cl WF8 146 D6
Moxon Gr WF1 121 B3
Moxon Pl WF2 141 C5
Moxon Sq WF1 216 C3
Moxon St WF1 121 C4
Moxon Way WF1 121 C4
Moynihan Cl LS8 208 B4
Mozley Dr HX2 91 F6
Mucky La HX5 134 D4
Muddy La LS22 13 B2
Muff St BD4 75 B5
Muffit La BD19 117 D8
Mug Mill La WF12 157 E8
Mugup La HD7 189 E1
Muir Ct LS6 205 D4
Muirfield Ave WF7 124 D1
Muirfield Cl S72 180 C1
Muirfield Dr WF2 142 A2
Muirfields The S75 178 A1
Muirhead Dr BD4 75 E2
Muirlands The HD2 136 E5
Mulberry Ave Leeds LS16 42 D4
Ryhill WF4 162 B1
Mulberry Ct HD7 152 E5
Mulberry Garth
Leeds LS16 42 E3
Thorp Arch LS23 14 E1
Mulberry House 12
WF10 124 E7
Mulberry Pl WF4 162 B1
Mulberry Rise LS16 42 D4
Mulberry St
Huddersfield HD5 154 C5
13 Keighley BD21 35 D8
Leeds LS10 212 A1
Pudsey LS28 76 E7
Mulberry Terr HD1 154 B8
Mulberry View LS16 42 D3
Mulcture Hall Rd HX1 203 F3
Mulehouse La HD3 134 B1
Mulgrave St BD3 75 B6
Mullberry Gdns LS26 102 B2
Mullins Ct LS9 212 C3
Mullion Ave HD7 171 E4
Mumford St BD5 74 E3
Munby St BD8 73 E7
Muncaster Rd LS25 83 B8
Munster St BD4 75 B3
Munton Cl BD6 93 E6
Murdoch St BD21 35 F8
Murdstone Cl 5 BD5 74 E3
Murgatroyd St
Bradford BD5 74 E2
Shipley BD17 55 B8
Murray Rd HD2 153 F8
Murray St 3 BD5 74 C3
Murton Cl LS14 62 A4
Museum Ct BD2 56 C2
Museum St LS9 207 F1
Musgrave Bank LS13 58 E2
Musgrave Bldgs 6 LS28 76 F8
Musgrave Ct WF2 141 D4
Musgrave Dr BD2 56 C2
Musgrave Gr BD2 56 C2
Musgrave Mount
Bradford BD2 56 C2
Leeds LS13 58 E2
Musgrave Rd BD2 56 C2
Musgrave Rise LS13 58 E2
Musgrave St 2 WF17 96 E1
Musgrave View LS13 58 E2
Mushroom St LS9 207 E1
Musselburgh St BD7 74 C7
Mutton La BD15 53 D2
Myers Ave BD2 56 A4
Myers Croft
Huddersfield HD5 154 F6
Otley LS21 23 A7
Myers La BD2 56 A4
Myrtle Ave Bingley BD16 36 F2
Dewsbury WF13 138 E5
Halifax HX2 91 E4
Myrtle Ct BD16 36 F2
Myrtle Dr Halifax HX2 91 E4
Haworth BD22 34 F1
Myrtle Gdns HX2 91 E4
Myrtle Gr Bingley BD16 36 F2
Halifax HX2 91 E4
Huddersfield HD3 153 B6
4 Queensbury BD13 92 C8
Myrtle Park First Sch
BD16 36 F2
Myrtle Pl Bingley BD16 36 F3
Halifax HX2 91 E4
11 Shipley BD18 54 F8
Myrtle Rd Dewsbury WF13 138 E5
Elland HX5 134 F6
Huddersfield HD7 152 D4
Myrtle St 11 Bingley BD16 37 A3
Bradford BD3 75 C6
1 Huddersfield HD1 154 B7
Todmorden OL14 108 B5
Myrtle View
12 Haworth BD22 51 F8
Oakworth BD22 34 D3
Myrtle Wlk BD16 36 F3
Myson Ave WF8 125 F4
Mytholm HX7 88 E3
Mytholm Cl HX7 88 F3
Mytholm Ct HX7 88 E3
Mytholmes BD22 51 C8
Mytholmes La
Haworth BD22 51 C8
Oakworth BD22 34 D1
Mytholmes Terr BD22 51 C8
Mytholmroyd Sta HX7 110 E8
Nab Cres HD7 170 C2
Nab End BD12 94 D2
Nab End La HX4 134 D7
Nab La Batley WF17 97 B2
Mirfield WF14 137 F6
Shipley BD18 54 D7
Nab The WF14 137 E6
Nab View BD20 5 F3
Nab Water La BD22 70 C6
Nab Wood Bank BD18 54 D7
Nab Wood Cl BD18 54 E7
Nab Wood Cres BD18 54 D7
Nab Wood Dr BD18 54 D6
Nab Wood Gdns BD18 54 E7
Nab Wood Gr BD18 54 D7
Nab Wood Grammar Sch
BD16 54 C7
Nab Wood Middle Sch
BD18 54 D7
Nab Wood Mount BD18 54 D7
Nab Wood Pl BD18 54 D7
Nab Wood Rd BD18 54 D6
Nab Wood Rise BD18 54 D7
Nab Wood Terr BD18 54 D7
Nabbs La HD7 151 F1
Nabcroft La HD4 153 D3
Nabcroft Rise HD4 153 D4
Naburn App LS14 62 C8
Naburn Chase LS14 62 B7
Naburn Cl LS14 62 C7
Naburn Ct 3 LS14 62 C8
Naburn Dr LS14 62 B7
Naburn Fold LS14 62 C7
Naburn Gdns LS14 62 B7
Naburn Gn LS14 62 B7
Naburn Pl LS14 62 B8
Naburn Rd LS14 62 B7
Naburn View LS14 62 C7
Naburn Wlk LS14 62 B7
Naill's Ct BD10 39 B2
Nairn Cl HD4 153 C2
Nancroft Cres LS12 209 F3
Nancroft Mount LS12 209 F3
Nancroft Terr LS12 209 F4
Nanny Goat La LS25 82 D8
Nansen Ave 9 LS13 58 C2
Nansen Gr 10 LS13 58 C2
Nansen Mount 11 LS13 58 C2
Nansen Pl 1 LS13 58 B2
Nansen St LS13 58 A2
Nansen Terr 3 LS13 58 B2
Nansen View 2 LS13 58 B2
Naomi Rd HD4 154 A2
Napier House OL14 129 A8
Napier Rd Bradford BD3 75 D7
Elland HX5 134 E6
Napier St Bradford BD3 75 D7
Keighley BD21 35 D6
2 Queensbury BD13 72 F1
Napier Terr BD3 75 D7
Naples St BD8 55 B1
Nares St 9 Haworth BD22 51 E8
Keighley BD21 35 B7
Nares St Upper BD21 35 B7
Narrow Balk DN5 195 E5
Narrow La BD16 36 B1
Narrows The BD16 36 B1
Naseby Garth LS9 207 E1
Naseby Gdns 4 LS9 212 B4
Naseby Grange 3 LS9 212 B4
Naseby Pl LS9 212 B4
Naseby Rise BD13 72 F1
Naseby Terr LS9 212 B4
Naseby View LS9 212 B4
Naseby Wlk LS9 212 B4
Nashville Rd 4 BD22 35 A6
Nashville St 2 BD22 35 A6
Nashville Terr 1 BD22 35 A6
Nassau Pl LS7 207 E4
Nat Mus of Photography
& TV BD1 201 B2
Nathan La HX6 132 C7
Nathaniel Waterhouse
Homes HX1 203 E2
National Pk LS10 215 E4
National Rd LS10 215 E4
Natty Fields Cl HX2 91 E7
Natty La HX2 91 E7
Nature Way BD6 93 E7
Navigation Gdns WF12 139 B4
Navigation Rd
Castleford WF10 103 D1
Dewsbury WF12 139 B4
Halifax HX3 203 F2
Navigation Wlk LS10 211 F3
Navvy La S71 179 D7
Naylor Ct WF13 118 D1
Naylor La HX2 90 C1
Naylor St Dewsbury WF13 118 B2
Halifax HX1 202 B3
Ossett WF5 140 C8
Naylor's Bldgs 5 BD19 115 F8
Naze View OL14 107 F3
Neal Pl LS10 212 A2
Neal St BD5 201 B2
Neale Rd HD1 153 F3
Neale St 5 HX7 89 A2
Near Bank HD8 174 B2
Near Crook BD17 38 F1
Near La HD7 170 E2
Nearcliffe Rd BD9 55 A2
Neath Gdns LS9 61 D3
Necropolis Rd BD7 73 F5
Ned Hill Rd HX2 71 F3
Ned La Bradford BD4 75 F4
Slaithwaite HD7 169 F8
Needles Inn La LS26 101 C7
Nell Gap Ave WF4 158 A7
Nell Gap Cres WF4 158 A6
Nell Gap La Netherton WF4 158 A7
Netherton, Middlestown
WF4 158 A6
Nelson Croft LS25 82 D5
Nelson Ct LS27 97 F2
Nelson Pl 1 Morley LS27 98 A5
Queensbury BD13 72 E1
Sowerby Bridge HX6 112 D4
Nelson Rd LS29 8 B4
Nelson St Batley WF17 118 A5
Batley, Birstall WF17 96 F1
Bradford BD15 54 C1
Bradford BD5 201 B1
Dewsbury WF13 139 C8
Haworth BD22 51 E8
Huddersfield HD1 153 F4
Liversedge WF15 117 B3
Normanton WF6 123 C3
Otley LS21 23 A7
8 Queensbury BD13 72 E1
South Hiendley S72 180 E5
Sowerby Bridge HX6 112 D4
Todmorden OL14 129 A8
Nene St BD5 74 C4
Nepshaw La
Gildersome LS27 97 D4
Morley LS27 97 F5
Nepshaw La N LS27 97 E5
Nepshaw La S LS27 97 E5
Neptune St LS9 212 A3
Nesfield Cl LS10 99 F6
Nesfield Cres LS10 99 F6
Nesfield Garth LS10 99 E6
Nesfield Gdns LS10 99 E6
Nesfield Rd Ilkley LS29 7 F5
Middleton LS10 99 E6
Nesfield St BD1 201 B4
Nesfield View Ilkley LS29 7 E4
Middleton LS10 99 F6
Nesfield Wlk LS10 99 E6
Nessfield Dr BD22 34 F5
Nessfield First Sch BD22 34 F5
Nessfield Gr BD22 34 F5
Nessfield Rd BD22 34 F5
Nest Est HX7 110 D8
Nest La HX7 110 D8
Nestfield Cl WF8 125 D3
Neston Way WF5 119 D1
Nether Cl HD5 154 E8
Nether Cres HD5 154 E8
Nether Hall Ave HD5 154 E8
Nether La HD7 187 C3
Nether Moor Rd HD4 171 C8
Nether Moor View 16
BD16 37 A3
Nether St LS28 57 D4
Netherby St BD3 75 B7
Nethercliffe Cres LS20 22 D2
Nethercliffe Rd LS20 22 D2
Netherdale Ct LS22 14 A6
Netherend Rd HD7 151 F1
Netherfield Ave WF4 158 D5
Netherfield Cl
Castleford WF10 123 F5
Kirkburton HD8 173 F6
Yeadon LS19 40 B7
Netherfield Cres WF4 158 D5
Netherfield Ct LS20 22 D1
Netherfield Dr
Guiseley LS20 22 D2
Holmfirth HD7 189 A7
Netherfield Ind Pk WF13 138 E5
Netherfield Pl
Cleckheaton BD19 116 E7
Netherton WF4 158 D6
Netherfield Rd
Dewsbury WF13 138 E5
Guiseley LS20 22 D2
Netherfield Rise LS20 22 D1
Netherhall Rd BD17 38 D3
Netherhouses HD7 188 D5
Netherlands Ave BD6 94 C7
Netherlands Avenue Sch
BD6 94 D7
Netherlands Sq BD12 94 D7
Netherlea Dr HD7 188 F7
Netherleigh Sch The BD9 54 F2
Netherley Dr HD7 168 E2
Netherly Brow WF5 140 E3
Netheroyd WF7 144 C5
Netheroyd Hill Rd HD2 136 A3
Netheroyd Pl WF4 144 B4
Netherthong Junior
& Infants Sch HD7 188 F8
Netherthong Rd HD7 187 F8
Netherton Fold HD4 171 C6
Netherton Hall Gdns WF4 158 E6
Netherton Infant Sch
HD4 171 D7
Netherton Junior
& Infants Sch WF4 158 E6
Netherton La WF4 158 E7
Netherton Moor Rd HD4 171 E6
Netherwood Cl HD2 136 A3
Nettle Gr HX3 92 F1
Nettleton Ave WF14 137 F5
Nettleton Chase WF5 119 C1
Nettleton Cl BD4 76 E2
Nettleton Ct LS15 81 D8
Nettleton Hill Rd HD7 152 B6
Nettleton House WF9 181 D6
Nettleton Rd
Huddersfield HD5 155 A8
Mirfield WF14 137 F5
Nettleton St
Lofthouse Gate WF3 122 B6
Ossett WF5 140 C6
Nettleton Terr HD5 155 A8
Nettleton's Almshouses 3
HD5 154 F3
Nevill Gr BD9 54 D3
Neville App LS9 80 C6
Neville Ave Bradford BD4 75 B1
Leeds LS9 80 C6
Neville Cl Leeds LS9 80 C6
South Kirkby WF9 182 C3
Neville Cres LS9 80 D8
Neville Garth LS9 80 C6
Neville Gr Huddersfield HD5 154 F4
Leeds LS9 80 C6
Swillington LS26 82 A2
Neville Mount LS9 80 C6
Neville Par LS9 80 C6
Neville Pl LS9 80 D7
Neville Rd Bradford BD4 75 B4
Leeds LS9 80 D8
Leeds LS15, LS9 80 E7
Otley LS21 23 B7
Wakefield WF2 141 C5
Neville Row LS9 80 C6
Neville Sq LS9 80 D8
Neville St Cleckheaton BD19 116 E7
12 Keighley BD21 35 D8
Leeds LS1 211 E3
Normanton WF6 123 B1
Wakefield WF1 142 F4

Neville Terr LS9 80 C6
Neville View LS9 80 C6
Neville Wlk LS9 80 C7
Nevins Rd WF13 138 D6
Nevison Ave WF8 125 E3
New Adel Ave LS16 42 A3
New Adel Gdns LS16 42 A3
New Adel La LS16 42 A3
New Augustus St BD1 201 C2
New Ave HD5 137 B1
New Bank HX3 203 F4
New Bank Rise BD4 75 D3
New Bank St LS27 98 B5
New Bond St HX1 203 D3
New Bridge Rd HD7 170 B2
New Briggate LS1, LS2 211 F4
New Brighton
Denby Dale HD8 191 B3
Shipley BD16 54 C6
New Brook St LS29 8 B4
New Brunswick St
Halifax HX1 203 D3
Wakefield WF1 216 B1
New Cl Horsforth LS18 58 B8
Marsden HD7 151 C1
Shipley BD18 54 D7
New Clayton Terr BD13 52 D5
New Close Ave BD20 5 E1
New Close La
Marsden HD7 151 C1
Norton DN6 184 E7
New Close Rd BD18 54 C7
New Clough Rd HX6 112 D1
New Coll WF8 125 B1
New Craven Gate LS11 214 C4
New Cres LS18 58 B8
New Cross St
Bradford, Lower Woodlands BD12 95 B5
Bradford, West Bowling BD5 74 F3
New Dales La BD20 4 B7
New Delight HX7 69 A1
New England Rd BD21 35 C5
New Farmers Hill LS26 101 D7
New Fold Bradford BD6 93 E7
Holmfirth HD7 189 A5
New Gate HD7 189 C1
New Grove Dr HD5 154 E7
New Hall App WF4 157 F4
New Hall Cl WF4 159 E4
New Hall La WF4 157 F4
New Hall Rd WF8 125 E3
New Hall Way WF4 157 F3
New Hey Moor Houses HD8 173 F2
New Hey Rd Bradford BD4 75 A4
Brighouse HD6 135 D5
Elland HD3 152 A8
Huddersfield HD2, HD6 135 D5
Huddersfield, Marsh HD2, HD3 153 C7
Huddersfield, Salendine Nook HD2, HD3 152 E8
Marsden HD3 150 D2
Slaithwaite HD2, HD3, HD6 151 D5
New Holme Rd BD22 51 D6
New House
Holmfirth HD7 199 D7
Slaithwaite HD7 169 F7
New House La BD13 73 B1
New House Rd HD2 136 D4
New Inn Ct LS21 23 A7
New Inn St LS12 209 D3
New John St BD1 201 B3
New Kirkgate BD18 55 B8
New La Birkenshaw BD4 76 C2
Blackshaw Head HX7 88 D3
Bradford BD3, BD4 75 D6
Burton Salmon LS25 105 D3
Castleford WF10 123 D5
Cleckheaton BD19 116 A6
Crigglestone WF4 159 E7
East Ardsley WF3 120 C8
Farnhill BD20 4 F2
Gildersome BD11 97 B8
Halifax HX3 113 D4
Halifax, Copley HX3 113 B2
Hebden Bridge HX7 110 D4
Leeds LS11 211 E2
Marsden HD3 150 D4
Middleton LS10 99 B5
Skelmanthorpe HD8 175 B1
Slaithwaite HD7 152 A3
Slaithwaite, Scapegoat Hill HD7 152 B6
Sowerby Bridge HX2 111 B5
Upton WF9 183 A7
New Laithe Cl HD4 154 C2
New Laithe Hill HD4 154 C2
New Laithe La HD7 189 B5
New Laithe Rd
3 Bradford BD6 74 A1
Haworth BD22 49 E8
Huddersfield HD4 154 C2
New Laithes Junior Sch LS18 58 A6
New Lane Cres WF9 183 A7
New Leeds LS13 58 B5
New Line BD10 56 E7
New Longley HX6 112 A1
New Longley La HX6 112 A1
New Market LS21 23 A7
New Market Pl BD1 201 B3
New Market St LS1 211 F3
New Mill La LS23 30 E5
New Mill Rd Holmfirth HD7 189 B7
Holmfirth, Brockholes HD7 172 C3
Honley HD7 172 C3
New North Par HD1 154 A6
New North Rd
Huddersfield HD1 153 F7
Liversedge WF16 117 C5
Slaithwaite HD7 152 A2
New Occupation La LS28 76 C6
New Otley Rd BD3 201 D4
New Park Ave LS28 57 E3
New Park Cl LS28 57 E3
New Park Croft LS28 57 E3
New Park La WF2 141 B7
New Park Pl LS28 57 E3
New Park Rd BD13 72 D1
New Park St LS27 97 F3
New Park Vale LS28 57 E3
New Park View LS28 57 E2
New Park Way LS28 57 E3
New Park Wlk 4 LS28 57 D2
New Pepper Rd LS10 215 F3
New Popplewell La BD19 115 F8
New Princess St LS11 211 E1
New Rd Badsworth WF9 164 D2
Blackshaw Head HX7 87 F6
Bramham LS23 30 D3
Castleford WF11 126 A5
Cawthorne S75 193 B5
Denholme BD13 71 D8
Elland, Greetland HX4 134 B7
Elland, Old Lindley HX4 134 C2
Elland, Slack HD3 152 A8
Featherstone WF7 144 E7
Halifax HX1 203 E2
Hebden Bridge HX7 110 D1
Hebden Bridge, Hebble End HX7 88 F2
Hebden Bridge, Mytholmroyd HX7 110 E8
Holmfirth HD7 189 A7
Horbury WF4 141 B1
Kirk Smeaton WF8 166 D8
Kirkheaton HD5 137 B2
Ledsham LS25 84 D2
Mapplewell S75 178 B1
Netherton WF4 158 B7
Penistone S36 192 E1
Rothwell WF3 100 D3
Silsden BD20 5 E1
Todmorden OL14 86 C4
Todmorden OL14 108 F8
Todmorden OL14 109 A5
West Hardwick WF4 145 C1
Woolley WF4 178 B6
Yeadon LS19 39 F7
New Rd E BD19 115 F8
New Road Prim Sch HX6 112 A3
New Road Side
Horsforth LS18 58 B7
Yeadon LS19 40 B4
New Road Sq HD6 135 E6
New Row Badsworth WF9 164 E2
Bradford BD9 54 E2
Elland HX4 134 C4
Holmfirth HD7 189 A5
Pudsey LS28 57 A3
Shipley BD16 54 B8
Wakefield WF2 120 B2
New Row Cotts WF8 147 C5
New Scarbro' Rd 1 LS13 58 D2
New St Ackworth M T WF7 163 F5
Batley WF17 118 C5
Batley, Hanging Heaton WF17 118 E3
Bingley BD16 36 E7
Bradford, Bierley BD4 95 B8
Bradford, Idle BD10 56 B8
Bradford, Lower Woodlands BD12 95 B5
Brighouse, Bailiff Bridge HD6 115 B7
Brighouse, Clifton HD6 115 D2
Castleford WF10 103 E1
Clayton West HD8 175 D1
Denholme BD13 71 D8
Dewsbury WF12 139 F7
Elland HX4 133 F3
Halifax, Pellon HX2 202 A4
Halifax, Southowram HX3 114 A4
Haworth BD22 51 C6
Hemsworth WF9 163 C1
Honley HD7 171 F4
Horbury WF4 141 B1
Horsforth LS18 58 B8
Huddersfield HD1 154 A5
Huddersfield, Leymoor HD7 152 E4
Huddersfield, Milnsbridge HD3 153 A4
Huddersfield, Netherton HD4 171 C7
Huddersfield, Paddock HD1 153 E5
Kippax LS25 83 B1
Kirkheaton HD5 155 C8
Liversedge BD19 116 F6
Mapplewell S75 178 B1
Meltham HD7 170 D2
Oakworth BD22 34 D2
Ossett WF5 140 E5
Pudsey LS28 76 E6
Pudsey, Farsley LS28 57 D2
Royston S71 179 C3
Skelmanthorpe HD8 175 A2
Slaithwaite HD7 152 A1
South Elmsall WF9 182 E3
South Hiendley S72 180 D6
New Station St LS1 211 E3
New Street Cl LS28 76 E6
New Street Gdns LS28 76 E6
New Street Gr LS28 76 E6
New Sturton La LS25 83 B7
New Tanhouse 6 WF14 137 F5
New Temple Gate LS15 81 A7
New Toftshaw BD4 95 D8
New Town Ct 15 BD21 35 A7
New Way Batley WF17 118 C5
Guiseley LS20 22 C1
New Wellgate WF10 124 F6
New Wells WF1 216 B1
New Windsor Dr LS26 100 F6
New Wlk LS8 44 B1
New Works Rd BD12 94 D5
New York La LS19 40 D2
New York Rd LS2, LS9 212 A4
New York St 1 LS2 212 A3
Newall Ave LS21 10 F1
Newall Carr Rd Clifton LS21 10 F2
Otley LS21 10 F2
Newall Cl Menston LS29 22 B5
Otley LS21 10 F1
Newall Cres WF9 162 F3
Newall Hall Pk LS21 11 A1
Newall Mount Otley LS21 22 F8
Otley LS21 22 F8
Newall St Bradford BD5 74 D4
Todmorden OL14 129 A8
Newark Cl S75 178 B2
Newark Rd BD16 36 E5
Newark St BD4 75 B5
Newbridge La BD23 1 D8
Newburn Rd BD7 74 B5
Newbury Dr WF9 183 A5
Newbury Rd HD6 135 F7
Newbury Wlk HD5 137 C1
Newby First Sch BD5 74 D3
Newby Garth LS17 44 B5
Newby Rd BD20 16 E8
Newby St Bradford BD5 74 E4
Glusburn BD20 16 D7
Newcastle Cl BD11 96 D5
Newcastle Farm Ct WF11 105 A4
Newcastle Ho BD1 201 C3
Newcombe St HX5 135 A6
Newfield Ave
Castleford WF10 124 E7
Normanton WF6 123 C1
Newfield Cl WF6 123 C1
Newfield Cres WF6 123 C1
Newfield Ct WF6 123 C2
Newfield Dr Garforth LS25 83 B4
Menston LS29 22 A5
Newfield La LS25 104 D8
Newforth Gr BD5 74 C2
Newgate Mirfield WF14 138 A4
Pontefract WF8 146 C8
Newgate La HD7 170 E2
Newgate St WF17 118 F3
Newhall Bank LS10 99 D5
Newhall Chase LS10 99 D6
Newhall Cl LS10 99 D6
Newhall Cres LS10 99 D6
Newhall Croft LS10 99 D7
Newhall Dr BD6 94 F8
Newhall Garth LS10 99 D5
Newhall Gate LS10 99 E7
Newhall Gdns LS10 99 D5
Newhall Gn LS10 99 D6
Newhall La WF14 138 B2
Newhall Mount
Bradford BD6 94 F8
Middleton LS10 99 D5
Newhall Rd Bradford BD4 75 B1
Middleton LS10 99 D6
Newhill WF9 182 B1
Newhold LS25 83 A8
Newhouse Pl 2 HD1 154 A7
Newill Cl BD5 75 A2
Newlaithes Cres WF6 123 D2
Newlaithes Garth LS18 58 A6
Newlaithes Gdns LS18 58 B7
Newlaithes Rd LS18 58 B6
Newland Ave HD2 135 F1
Newland Cres WF4 159 E7
Newland Ct WF1 142 E2
Newland La WF6 122 F1
Newland Rd HD5 155 B7
Newland St
Knottingley WF11 126 B5
Wakefield WF1 142 E2
Newland View WF6 122 F3
Newlands LS28 57 D2
Newlands Ave
Adwick Le S DN6 184 F2
Bradford BD3 56 D1
Clayton West HD8 175 F2
Northowram HX3 93 A3
Sowerby Bridge HX6 111 E3
Yeadon LS19 40 A7
Newlands Cl HD6 115 B1
Newlands Cres LS27 98 E4
Newlands Dr Bingley BD16 36 E6
Glusburn BD20 16 D7
Lofthouse Gate WF3 121 E5
Morley LS27 98 D4
Northowram HX3 93 A3
Newlands Gr HX3 93 A3
Newlands Junior Sch HX6 111 E3
Newlands La HD7 188 C5
Newlands Pl BD3 56 B1
Newlands Primary Sch LS27 98 D5
Newlands Rd HX2 112 B7
Newlands Rise LS19 40 A7
Newlands The HX6 111 E2
Newlands Wlk WF3 121 E5
Newlay Bridle Path 2 LS18 58 C7
Newlay Cl BD10 56 E7
Newlay Gr LS18 58 B6
Newlay La Horsforth LS18 58 B7
Leeds LS13 58 C4
Newlay Lane Pl LS13 58 C4
Newlay Wood Ave LS18 58 C7
Newlay Wood Cl LS18 58 C7
Newlay Wood Cres LS18 58 C7
Newlay Wood Dr LS18 58 C7
Newlay Wood Fold 9 LS18 58 B7
Newlay Wood Gdns 3 LS18 58 C7
Newlay Wood Rd LS18 58 B7
Newlay Wood Rise LS18 58 C7
Newley Ave WF17 117 F8
Newley Mount LS18 58 B6
Newlyn Dr WF2 142 D2
Newlyn Rd BD20 19 A1
Newman Ave S71 179 C1
Newman St BD4 75 B2
Newmarket App LS9 80 B6
Newmarket Gn LS9 80 B6
Newmarket La Leeds LS9 80 B6
Lofthouse Gate WF3 122 D8
Newmillerdam Ctry Pk WF2 160 D2
Newport Ave LS13 58 A2
Newport Cres LS6 205 D3
Newport Gdns LS6 205 D3
Newport Mount LS6 205 D3
Newport Pl BD8 55 C1
Newport Rd Bradford BD8 55 C1
Leeds LS6 205 D3
Newport St WF8 125 C1
Newport View LS6 205 D3
Newroyd Rd BD5 74 E2
Newsam Ct LS15 81 A7
Newsam Dr LS15 80 E6
Newsam Green Rd LS26 81 E1
Newsholme La WF4 159 F7
Newsholme New Rd BD22 34 B4
Newsome Ave HD4 154 A2
Newsome High Sch HD4 153 F1
Newsome Junior Sch HD4 154 A1
Newsome Rd HD4 154 B3
Newsome Rd S HD4 154 A1
Newsome St WF13 118 B1
Newstead Ave Halifax HX1 202 A3
Hemsworth WF9 163 A3
Lofthouse Gate WF1 121 A5
Newstead Cres WF9 163 A4
Newstead Dr WF9 163 A3
Newstead Gdns HX1 202 A3
Newstead Gr Halifax HX1 202 A3
Hemsworth WF9 163 A3
Newstead Heath HX1 202 A3
Newstead La WF4, WF9 162 F3
Newstead Mount WF9 163 A3
Newstead Pl HX1 202 A3
Newstead Rd Barnsley S71 178 E1
Otley LS21 23 B7
Wakefield WF1 216 A3
Newstead Terr Halifax HX1 202 A3
Hemsworth WF9 163 A3
Newstead View WF9 163 A3
Newstead Wlk BD5 74 D4
Newton Ave WF1 121 B2
Newton Cl
Lofthouse Gate WF1 121 B1
Rothwell LS26 100 B4
Newton Ct Leeds LS8 61 C6
Lofthouse Gate WF1 121 B4
Rothwell LS26 100 B4
Silsden BD20 5 D2
Newton Dr Castleford WF10 125 B7
Holme Chapel BB10 85 A7
Lofthouse Gate WF1 121 C3
Newton Garth LS7 204 B1
Newton Gn WF1 121 B1
Newton Gr LS7 207 E4
Newton Hill Jun & Inf Sch WF1 121 C2
Newton Hill Rd LS7 204 A1
Newton La Fairburn WF11 104 C4
Ledsham WF10 104 C4
Ledston WF10 103 E4
Lofthouse Gate WF1 121 B4
Newton Lodge Cl LS7 60 C5
Newton Lodge Dr LS7 60 C5
Newton Par LS7 204 A1
Newton Park Ct LS7 204 B1
Newton Park Dr LS7 204 B1
Newton Park Mans LS7 204 A1
Newton Park View LS7 207 E4
Newton Pk HD6 114 F6
Newton Pl BD5 74 E4
Newton Rd LS7 204 B1
Newton Sq LS12 77 D3
Newton St Bradford BD5 74 E3
9 Sowerby Bridge HX6 112 B4
Newton View LS7 204 A1
Newton Way BD17 38 C4
Newton Wlk LS7 207 E4
Newtown Ave S71 179 B4
Nibshaw La BD19 117 A8
Nibshaw Rd BD19 117 A8
Nice Ave LS8 207 F4
Nice St LS8 208 A4
Nice View LS8 207 F4
Nicholas Cl BD7 73 F7
Nichols Cl LS22 13 C5
Nichols Way LS22 13 C5
Nicholson Cl BD16 37 A6
Nicholson St WF10 124 C7
Nickleby Rd LS9 80 A8
Nicola Cl 10 OL13 106 A7
Nicolsons Pl BD20 5 E1
Nidd App LS22 13 D8
Nidd Ct BD20 5 E1
Nidd Dr WF10 125 B8
Nidd St BD3 75 B6
Nidderdale Cl LS25 83 B5
Nidderdale Wlk BD17 38 E4
Nields Rd HD7 169 F8
Nightingale Crest WF2 141 C4
Nightingale St 3 BD21 35 D8
Nile Cres BD22 34 F6
Nile Rd LS29 8 B4
Nile St Haworth BD22 51 E8
Huddersfield HD1 153 F5
Keighley BD22 34 F6
Leeds LS2 212 A4
Nina Rd BD7 73 F3
Ninelands La LS25 83 A6
Ninelands Primary Sch LS25 83 A6
Ninelands Spur LS25 83 A6
Ninelands View LS25 83 A7
Ninevah La
Badsworth WF9 164 E3
Kippax WF10 102 F5
Nineveh Gdns LS11 211 D1
Nineveh Par LS11 211 D1
Nineveh Rd LS11 211 D1
Ninth Ave WF15 116 B5
Nippet La LS9 212 B4
Nixon Ave LS9 80 B7
Nixon Cl WF12 139 F1
Noble Ct HD4 171 D6
Noble St BD7 74 B5
Nog La BD9 55 A4
Nook Gdns LS15 62 F8
Nook Gn WF12 139 D2
Nook La
Sowerby Bridge HX6 131 F8
Wadsworth Moor HX7 89 D4
Nook Rd LS15 62 F8
Nook The
Cleckheaton BD19 116 E8
Cullingworth BD13 52 D6
East Ardsley WF3 119 E6
Leeds LS17 43 D5
Nook Wlk WF13 138 F8
Nooking The WF2 120 B3
Nooks The LS27 97 D6
Noon Cl WF3 121 E5
Nopper Rd
Huddersfield HD4 170 F8
Meltham HD4 170 F8
Nor Wood Rd WF9 181 D5
Nora Pl LS13 58 A3
Nora Rd LS13 58 A3
Nora Terr LS13 58 A3
Norbeck Dr BD22 51 E8
Norbury Rd BD10 56 E4
Norcliffe La
Brighouse HX3 114 A7
Halifax HX3 114 A7
Norcroft Brow BD7 74 D6
Norcroft Ind Est BD7 74 C7
Norcroft La S75 193 F3
Norcroft St BD1, BD7 74 C7
Norcross Ave HD3 153 B7
Norfield HD2 136 A4
Norfolk Ave WF17 118 B3
Norfolk Cl
Brotherton WF11 126 C8
Leeds LS7 204 A3
Littleborough OL15 129 C1
Rothwell LS26 101 D5
Norfolk Dr LS26 101 D5
Norfolk Gdns
Bradford BD1 201 B2
Leeds LS7 204 A3
Norfolk Gn LS7 204 A3
Norfolk House WF1 142 F3
Norfolk Mount LS7 204 A3
Norfolk Pl Halifax HX1 202 C2
Leeds LS7 204 A3
Norfolk St Batley WF17 118 B4
4 Bingley BD16 37 A3
3 Hebden Bridge HX7 89 A2
Norfolk Terr LS7 204 A3
Norfolk View LS7 204 A3
Norfolk Wlk
5 Dewsbury WF13 139 B8
Leeds LS7 204 A3
Norgarth Cl WF17 118 F5
Norham Gr BD12 94 D2
Norland CE (Controlled) Jun & Inf Sch HX6 112 D2
Norland Rd
Sowerby Bridge HX6 112 C3
Sowerby Bridge, Upper Greetland HX6 133 D8
Norland St BD7 73 F3
Norland Town Rd HX6 112 D2
Norland View
6 Halifax HX2 113 A4
Sowerby Bridge HX6 112 D4
Norman Ave Bradford BD2 56 B5
Elland HX5 135 A6
Norman Cres BD2 56 B5
Norman Dr WF14 137 F6
Norman Gr Bradford BD2 56 B5
Elland HX5 135 A6
Leeds LS5 59 A4
Norman La BD2 56 B5
Norman Mount
Bradford BD2 56 B5
Leeds LS5 59 A4
Norman Pl 6 Horbury WF4 141 B1
Leeds LS8 44 A2
Norman Rae Playing Fields BD9 54 F6

Norman Rd Denby Dale HD8 191 F5
Huddersfield HD2 136 A1
Mirfield WF14 137 F6
Norman Row LS5 59 A4
Norman St Bingley BD16 37 A3
Elland HX5 135 A6
Halifax HX1 202 B1
14 Haworth BD22 51 D7
Leeds LS5 59 A4
Shipley BD18 55 D7
Norman Terr Bradford BD2 56 B5
Elland HX5 135 A6
Leeds LS8 44 A2
Norman View LS5 59 A4
Normanon Pl LS11 214 A4
Normans Way WF2 142 F1
Normanton C E (Aided) First Sch WF6 123 B2
Normanton Common First Sch WF6 123 D3
Normanton Cross St WF4 159 C8
Normanton Gr LS11 214 A4
Normanton Ind Est WF6 123 D3
Normanton St WF4 159 C8
Normanton Town Mid Sch WF6 123 A1
Normanton Woodhouse First Sch WF6 123 A1
Norr Green Terr BD15 53 D6
Norridge Bottom HD7 189 A5
Norris Cl HD5 155 A4
Norristhorpe Ave WF15 117 A2
Norristhorpe La WF15 117 B2
Norristhorpe Sch WF15 117 B2
Nortech Cl LS7 207 D2
North App LS24 48 A5
North Ave Bradford BD8 55 D2
Castleford WF10 123 F7
Horbury WF4 141 C1
Otley LS21 23 A8
Pontefract WF8 146 B7
South Elmsall WF9 182 F2
Sutton in C BD20 16 D4
Wakefield WF1 216 B4
North Baileygate WF8 125 E1
North Bank Rd
Batley WF17 118 A6
Huddersfield HD2 135 F1
Shipley BD16 54 B5
North Bolton HX2 91 E7
North Bridge HX1 203 E4
North Bridge L Ctr HX3 203 E4
North Bridge St HX1 203 E4
North Broadgate La LS18 41 C1
North Brook St BD1, BD3 201 C4
North Byland HX2 91 E7
North Carr HD5 154 E7
North Carr Croft HD5 154 E7
North Cl Featherstone WF7 124 C1
Leeds LS8 61 D6
Royston S71 179 C3
North Cliffe HX6 112 B3
North Cliffe Ave BD13 72 F6
North Cliffe Cl 7 BD13 72 E6
North Cliffe Dr BD13 72 E6
North Cliffe Gr 8 BD13 72 E6
North Cliffe La BD13 72 F6
North Cres WF9 183 B4
North Croft Grove Rd LS29 8 A4
North Cross Rd HD2 135 F2
North Ct LS2 211 F4
North Cut HD6 114 F2
North Dean Ave BD22 34 E7
North Dean Bsns Pk HX3 113 D1
North Dean Rd Elland HX4 113 A1
Keighley BD22 34 F7
North Dene Rd BD20 5 E2
North Dr Bramhope LS16 24 F2
Garforth LS25 83 B4
Huddersfield HD7 152 E4
North Farm Rd LS8, LS9 208 C3
North Field La HD8 175 A2
North Field Rd DN5 195 D7
North Fold BD10 56 B8
North Gate WF14 137 E3
North Grange Mews LS6 205 F4
North Grange Mount LS6 59 F5
North Grange Rd LS6 205 F4
North Grove App LS22 13 E7
North Grove Ave LS22 13 E7
North Grove Cl LS8 61 D6
North Grove Cres LS22 13 E7
North Grove Ct LS22 13 E6
North Grove Dr Leeds LS8 61 D6
Wetherby LS22 13 F7
North Grove Mount LS22 13 E6
North Grove Rd LS22 13 E7
North Grove Rise LS8 61 D6
North Grove Way LS22 13 F6
North Halifax Grammar Sch HX2 91 F6
North Hall Ave BD10 39 A2
North Hill LS14 28 D1
North Hill Cl LS8 61 C6
North Hill Ct LS6 59 F5
North Hill Dr HD5 155 C8
North Hill Rd LS6 205 F4
North Holme St BD1 201 B4
North Ives BD22 51 C4
North John St 3 BD13 72 E1
North King St WF17 118 D4
North La Cawthorne S75 193 A2
Leeds, Headingley LS6 59 D5
Leeds, Oakwood LS8 61 C6
Rothwell LS26 101 C6
Slaithwaite HD7 151 D1
North Lingwell Rd LS10 99 C5
North Lodge Fold WF13 117 F3
North Lodge La WF8 147 F4
North Mead LS16 24 F2
North Moor La HD5 137 C2
North Ossett High Sch WF5 119 D1
North Par Bradford BD15 54 A2
Bradford BD1 201 B3
Burley in W LS29 9 E2
Halifax HX1 203 E3
Ilkley LS29 8 C4
Leeds LS16 59 A8
Otley LS21 23 A8
North Park Ave LS8 44 A1
North Park Gr LS8 44 A1
North Park Par LS8 204 C4
North Park Rd Bradford BD9 55 B3
Leeds LS8 61 A8
North Park St WF13 118 A1
North Park Terr BD9 55 C2
North Parkway LS14 62 A6
North Pl BD20 16 C5
North Queen St 1 BD21 35 C7
North Rd Bradford BD6 74 B1
Dewsbury WF13 138 E6
Fairburn WF11 105 A4
Horsforth LS18 41 B3
Kirkburton HD8 173 E7
Leeds LS9 80 D3
Leeds, Cross Gates LS15 62 C2
Royston S71 179 D4
Sutton in C BD20 16 C5
North Rise HD2 136 C2
North Road Terr WF1 216 A3
North Row Shepley HD8 190 D8
Sutton in C BD20 16 C5
North Royd HX4 133 B5
North Selby HX2 91 D7
North St Addingham LS29 7 A8
Batley WF17 118 B6
Batley, Heckmondwike WF16 117 D3
Bradford BD1 201 C3
Bradford, Oakenshaw BD12 95 A4
Bradford, Thackley BD10 39 B2
Castleford WF10 124 C8
Castleford, New Fryston WF10 104 C3
Dewsbury WF13 118 C1
Elland, Holywell Green HX4 134 B4
4 Elland, West Vale HX4 134 D7
Glusburn BD20 16 D7
Haworth BD22 51 B7
Huddersfield, Paddock HD1 153 D5
Huddersfield, Rashcliffe HD1 153 E3
Keighley BD21 35 C7
Leeds LS2, LS7 207 D1
Mirfield WF14 137 F4
Normanton WF6 144 A8
Otley LS21 23 A8
9 Pudsey LS28 76 E8
Silsden BD20 5 E2
South Kirkby WF9 182 B3
Sutton in C BD20 16 D5
Wetherby LS22 13 E5
Yeadon LS19 40 B4
North Terr Batley WF17 96 F1
3 Leeds LS15 62 C2
Yeadon LS19 40 B7
North View Bradford BD15 54 A1
Burley in W LS29 9 F1
Dewsbury WF12 139 D6
Hemsworth WF9 163 A4
Knottingley WF11 126 E4
Menston LS29 22 A3
Steeton BD20 16 F6
Sutton in C BD20 16 D5
Wilsden BD15 53 C5
North View Rd
Birkenshaw BD4 96 A7
Bradford BD3 55 F2
North View St
N Keighley BD20 18 C1
Pudsey LS28 57 E2
North View Terr
2 Dewsbury WF13 118 B2
7 Dewsbury, Chapel Fold WF13 117 F2
Haworth BD22 51 C8
5 Pudsey LS28 57 E2
North Way
Huddersfield HD2 136 E4
Leeds LS8 61 D6
North West Rd LS6 206 B3
North Wing BD3 201 C4
North Wlk Harden BD16 36 A1
Hemsworth WF9 181 D8
North's Pl WF14 138 A7
Northallerton Rd BD3 55 F1
Northampton St BD3 55 F1
Northbrook Croft 1 LS7 204 A3
Northbrook Pl LS7 204 A3
Northbrook St LS7 204 A3
Northcliffe Golf Course BD9 54 E6
Northcliffe Rd BD18 55 B6
Northcote WF5 119 C1
Northcote Cres LS11 214 B4
Northcote Dr LS11 214 B4
Northcote Fold LS22 13 B2
Northcote Gn LS11 214 B4
Northcote Rd BD2 56 B2
Northcote St LS28 57 D2
Northcote Terr BD2 56 B1
Northcroft WF9 183 A3
Northcroft Ave WF9 183 A4
Northcroft Rise BD8 54 E1
Northdale Ave BD5 74 C2
Northdale Cres BD5 74 C2
Northdale Mount BD5 74 C2
Northdale Rd BD9 55 B5
Northedge La HX3 93 D1
Northedge Meadow BD10 56 B6
Northedge Pk HX3 93 D1
Northern Sch of Contemporary Dance LS7 207 D3
Northern Cl BD7 73 F2
Northern St LS1 211 D3
Northfield Ave
Huddersfield HD1 153 E4
Knottingley WF11 126 F3
Ossett WF5 140 D6
Rothwell LS26 100 C4
South Kirkby WF9 182 C3
Wetherby LS22 13 E6
Northfield Cl 1 HX5 134 F6
Northfield Cres BD16 54 A7
Northfield Dr WF8 125 F1
Northfield Gdns BD6 74 C1
Northfield Gr Bradford BD6 74 C1
Huddersfield HD1 153 F3
South Kirkby WF9 182 C3
Northfield Jun & Inf Sch WF9 182 C3
Northfield La Horbury WF4 141 C1
Kirkburton HD8 173 E8
South Kirkby WF9 182 C3
Northfield Pl Bradford BD8 55 C1
Dewsbury WF13 118 C1
Rothwell LS26 100 B4
Wetherby LS22 13 E6
Northfield Rd Bradford BD6 74 B1
Crofton WF4 144 B3
Dewsbury WF13 118 B1
Knottingley WF11 126 F3
Ossett WF5 140 D7
Northfield St
Dewsbury WF13 118 C1
South Kirkby WF9 182 B3
Northfield Terr
Queensbury BD13 73 A1
Slaithwaite HD7 152 A2
Northfields LS23 15 A3
Northgate Baildon BD17 38 C4
Bradford BD1 201 B3
Cleckheaton BD19 116 D7
Dewsbury WF13 139 D8
Elland HX5 134 F7
Elland, Holywell Green HX4 134 B4
Halifax HX1 203 E4
Heptonstall HX7 88 F5
Honley HD7 172 B6
Horbury WF4 141 A1
Huddersfield HD1 154 B7
Huddersfield, Almondbury HD1, HD5 154 F3
Liversedge WF16 117 C4
Pontefract WF8 125 D1
1 Rothwell LS26 101 C6
South Hiendley S72 180 E6
Wakefield WF1 216 B2
Wakefield WF1 216 B3
Northgate Cl WF8 125 D1
Northgate La LS22 13 A3
Northgate Lodge WF8 125 D1
Northgate Rise LS22 13 B2
Northgates LS22 13 E5
Northlands S71 179 C4
Northlea Ave BD10 39 B1
Northolme Ave LS16 59 B7
Northolme Cres LS16 59 B7
Northorpe Ct WF14 138 C6
Northorpe La WF14 138 C7
Northowram Gn HX3 93 A3
Northowram Primary Sch HX3 93 A3
Northrop Cl BD8 55 A1
Northside Ave BD7 74 A6
Northside Bsns Pk LS7 207 D2
Northside Rd BD7 74 A6
Northside Terr BD7 73 F6
Northstead WF13 138 D7
Northumberland St 1 HD1 154 B6
Northway WF14 137 F7
Northway Cres WF14 137 F7
Northway Gdns WF14 137 F7
Northways Sch LS23 30 D5
Northwell Gate LS21 10 E2
Northwest Bsns Pk LS6 206 B3
Northwood Cl Pudsey LS28 76 F5
Rothwell LS26 101 C7
Northwood Cres BD10 56 C6
Northwood Falls LS26 101 C7
Northwood Gdns LS15 81 E7
Northwood Mount LS28 76 F5
Northwood Pk
Kirkburton HD8 173 E7
Rothwell LS26 101 C7
Northwood View LS28 76 F5
Norton Cl Elland HX5 134 F5
Halifax HX2 112 B7
Norton Dr HX2 112 B7
Norton & Kirk Smeaton Rd WF8 166 E4
Norton Rd Leeds LS8 44 A3
Wakefield WF1 216 C3
Norton St Elland HX5 134 F6
Silsden BD20 5 D1
Wakefield WF1 142 E4
Norton Terr HD4 173 C2
Norton Way LS27 98 A6
Nortonthorpe Hall Sch HD8 175 D1
Nortonthorpe Ind Est HD8 175 D1
Norville Terr LS6 205 E4
Norwich Ave LS10 215 D2
Norwood WF8 147 A5
Norwood Ave
Birkenshaw BD11 96 B4
Burley in W LS29 9 F1
Shipley BD18 55 B6
Norwood Cl LS29 9 F1
Norwood Cres
Birkenshaw BD11 96 B4
Pudsey LS28 57 F2
Norwood Croft LS28 57 F2
Norwood Dr Batley WF17 117 F8
Birkenshaw BD11 96 B4
Brierley S72 181 A3
Norwood Gr
Birkenshaw BD11 96 B4
Leeds LS6 205 E3
Norwood Green Hill HX3 93 F2
Norwood Mount LS6 205 E3
Norwood Pk HD2 135 D1
Norwood Pl Leeds LS6 205 E3
Shipley BD18 55 B6
Norwood Rd
Huddersfield HD2 135 E2
Leeds LS6 205 E3
Shipley BD18 55 B6
Norwood St Bradford BD5 74 D2
Normanton WF6 123 D4
Shipley BD18 55 B6
Norwood Terr
Brighouse HX3 94 A2
Burley in W LS29 9 F1
Leeds LS6 205 E3
Shipley BD18 55 B6
Norwood View LS6 205 E3
Nostell Cl BD8 74 D8
Nostell La WF4 162 B2
Nostell Priory WF4 162 E8
Noster Gr LS11 213 F3
Noster Hill LS11 213 F3
Noster Pl LS11 213 F3
Noster Rd LS11 213 F3
Noster St LS11 213 F3
Noster Terr LS11 214 A3
Noster View LS11 213 F3
Notre Dame Sixth Form Coll LS2 206 B3
Nottingham Cl WF3 100 A3
Nottingham St BD3 75 E7
Notton La WF4 179 B6
Nova La WF17 96 D2
Nowell App LS9 208 B1
Nowell Ave LS9 208 B1
Nowell Cl LS9 208 B1
Nowell Cres LS9 208 B1
Nowell Ct LS9 208 B1
Nowell End Row LS9 208 B1
Nowell Gdns LS9 208 B1
Nowell Gr LS9 208 B1
Nowell La LS9 208 B1
Nowell Mount LS9 208 B1
Nowell Par LS9 208 B1
Nowell Pl Huddersfield HD5 154 F4
Leeds LS9 208 B1
Nowell St Dewsbury WF13 118 B1
Leeds LS9 208 B1
Nowell Terr LS9 208 B1
Nowell View LS9 208 B1
Nowell Wlk LS9 208 B1
Nowell's Yd WF13 139 B8
Nuffield Hospl HD2 135 E1
Nunburnholme Wlk BD10 56 C6
Nunington Ave 2 LS12 209 F4
Nunington St LS12 210 A4
Nunington Terr 3 LS12 209 F4
Nunington View 4 LS12 59 C1
Nunlea Royd HX3 115 A6
Nunn's Cl WF7 145 D4
Nunn's Croft WF7 145 D4
Nunn's Gn WF7 145 D4
Nunn's La WF7 145 D4
Nunnery La HD6 135 D7
Nunns Ave WF7 145 D3
Nunns Ct WF7 145 C3
Nunns View WF7 145 C3
Nunroyd WF16 117 D5
Nunroyd Ave Guiseley LS20 39 F8
Leeds LS17 43 D1
Nunroyd Gr LS17 43 D1
Nunroyd Lawn LS17 43 E1
Nunroyd Rd LS17 43 D1
Nunroyd St LS17 43 D1
Nunroyd Terr LS17 43 D1
Nunthorpe Rd LS13 57 F5
Nurser La BD5 74 C4
Nurser Pl BD5 74 C4
Nursery Ave HX3 91 F3
Nursery Cl Baildon BD17 37 E2
Halifax HX3 91 F2
Keighley BD20 18 A3
Leeds LS17 43 C4
Nursery Garth LS22 13 F6
Nursery Gr Halifax HX3 91 F3
Leeds LS17 43 A4
Nursery La Addingham LS29 7 A8
Halifax HX3 91 F3
Leeds LS17 43 C4
Ripponden HX6 132 B3
Nursery Mount LS10 215 E1
Nursery Mount Rd LS10 215 E2
Nursery Rd
12 Bradford, Clayton BD14 73 B4
Bradford, Pickles Hill BD7 73 F2
Guiseley LS20 22 D3
Nursery St
Dewsbury WF12 139 C4
Huddersfield HD2 136 A1
Nursery Way
Boston Spa LS23 30 B8
Boston Spa, Clifford LS23 30 D5
Nursery Wood Rd WF17 118 D3
Nussey Ave WF17 96 E2
Nutclough Rd HX7 89 B4
Nutfield St 6 OL14 108 B6
Nuttall Rd BD3 201 D4
Nuttall St 1 OL13 106 B3
Nutter La WF17 96 C2
Nutter Pl BD1 201 B3
Nutter St BD19 116 C7
Nutting Grove Terr LS12 77 E5
Nutwood Wlk BD6 93 F6

O'Cot La HD3 151 B4
O'Grady Sq 4 LS9 212 C3
Oak Ave Bingley BD16 36 F2
Bradford BD8 55 D2
Burley in W LS29 21 F8
Garforth LS25 82 F7
Huddersfield HD5 154 E5
Huddersfield, Leymoor HD7 152 E5
Lofthouse Gate WF3 121 F4
Meltham HD7 170 C3
Morley LS27 98 B3
Normanton WF6 144 A8
Sowerby Bridge HX6 112 B5
Todmorden OL14 108 A7
Oak Bank 7 Bingley BD16 37 A2
Shipley BD18 55 D5
Oak Cl LS29 21 F8
Oak Cres Garforth LS25 82 F7
Leeds LS15 80 F7
Oak Dr Garforth LS25 82 F7
Slaithwaite HD7 152 D3
Oak Gr Garforth LS25 83 A7
Keighley BD21 35 A4
Morley LS27 98 C3
Oak Hall Pk WF4 159 C4
Oak Head Terr BD20 16 D8
Oak Hill HX6 132 E8
Oak Hill Rd HD6 115 B3
Oak House 9 WF10 124 E7
Oak La Bradford BD9 55 C2
4 Halifax HX1 202 C3
Sowerby Bridge HX6 132 E8
Oak Leigh S75 193 E4
Oak Mount Bradford BD8 55 D2
Todmorden OL14 108 B6
Oak Pl Baildon BD17 38 F4
Garforth LS25 82 E7
Halifax HX1 202 C3
10 Sowerby Bridge HX6 112 B5
Oak Rd Garforth LS25 82 E7
Huddersfield HD2 137 A5
Leeds, Halton LS15 80 F7
Leeds, New Wortley LS12 210 B3
Leeds, Potternewton LS7 204 A1
Morley LS27 97 F3
Shafton S72 180 D2
Oak Ridge LS22 13 C5
Oak Rise BD19 95 D2
Oak Royd LS25 82 F7
Oak Scar La HD7 189 D3
Oak St Batley WF16 117 D4
Bradford BD14 73 B4
Crofton WF4 162 A7
Elland HX5 134 F6
Haworth BD22 51 D7
9 Hebden Bridge HX7 89 A4
Lofthouse Gate WF1 121 C4
Morley LS27 98 B7
Oxenhope BD22 51 C3
Pudsey LS28 76 C8
South Elmsall WF9 182 F1
18 Sowerby Bridge HX6 112 B5
Todmorden OL14 108 A4
Oak Terr 2 Elland HX4 134 A4
2 Halifax HX1 202 C3
Huddersfield HD2 136 B2
1 Leeds LS15 62 D3
Oak Tree Ave
Holmfirth HD7 189 D3
Lepton HD8 155 D3
Oak Tree Bsns Pk LS14 62 A7
Oak Tree Cl LS9 208 C3
Oak Tree Cres LS9 208 C3
Oak Tree Ct Leeds LS9 208 C3
Silsden BD20 5 D2
Oak Tree Dr LS8 208 C3
Oak Tree Gr
Hemsworth WF9 181 F6
Leeds LS9 208 C3
Oak Tree Meadow WF2 161 A6
Oak Tree Mount LS9 208 C3
Oak Tree Pl LS9 208 C3
Oak Tree Rd HD8 155 D3
Oak Tree Sch WF7 164 A5
Oak Tree Terr HD8 155 D3
Oak Tree Wlk LS9 208 C3
Oak View BD20 5 E2
Oak View Terr 4 WF17 117 F8
Oak Villas BD8 55 D2
Oak Wood Rd LS22 13 D7
Oakbank Ave BD22 34 F5
Oakbank Broadway BD22 34 F4
Oakbank Cres BD22 34 F4
Oakbank Ct BD22 34 F4
Oakbank Dr BD22 34 F5
Oakbank Gr BD22 34 F5
Oakbank La BD22 34 F4
Oakbank Mount BD22 34 F4
Oakbank Recn Ctr BD22 34 F4
Oakbank Sch BD22 34 F4

Oakburn Rd LS29 8 A3
Oakdale BD16 37 A5
Oakdale Ave Bradford BD6 74 B1
Shipley BD18 55 D6
Oakdale Cl Bradford BD10 56 E3
Halifax HX3 92 A2
Lofthouse Gate WF3 121 B6
Oakdale Cres Bradford BD6 74 B1
Huddersfield HD3 153 A8
Oakdale Dr Bradford BD10 56 E3
Shipley BD18 55 E6
Oakdale First Sch BD18 55 E6
Oakdale Garth LS14 45 B1
Oakdale Gr BD18 55 E6
Oakdale Meadow LS14 45 B1
Oakdale Pk LS21 24 D6
Oakdale Rd BD18 55 E6
Oakdale Terr BD6 74 B1
Oakdean HD2 136 A4
Oakdene Cl LS28 76 F5
Oakdene Ct LS17 44 A4
Oakdene Dr LS17 44 A4
Oakdene Gdns LS17 44 A4
Oakdene Vale LS17 44 A4
Oakdene Way LS17 44 A4
Oaken Bank Cres HD5 154 C4
Oaken Cl OL13 106 B3
Oakenclough Rd OL13 106 B3
Oakenshaw Ct BD12 94 C2
Oakenshaw La
Bradford BD19 95 A3
Crofton WF4 143 A2
Walton WF4, WF2 161 A8
Oakenshaw St WF1 142 F3
Oakes Ave HD7 172 C2
Oakes Fold HD8 156 A3
Oakes La HD7 172 C2
Oakes Rd HD3 153 B8
Oakes Rd S HD3 153 B7
Oakes St WF2 141 D6
Oakfield LS6 205 E4
Oakfield Ave Bingley BD16 37 C2
Rothwell LS26 100 E6
Oakfield Cl Elland HX5 134 E6
Garforth LS25 82 F6
Menston LS29 22 A6
Oakfield Cres WF11 126 F3
Oakfield Ct S75 178 A1
Oakfield Dr Baildon BD17 38 D2
Mirfield WF14 137 F3
Oakfield Gr Bradford BD9 55 C2
Skelmanthorpe HD8 175 A1
Oakfield Pk WF8 165 B4
Oakfield Rd
Huddersfield HD2 135 E1
Keighley BD21 35 B4
Oakfield Terr
4 Horsforth LS18 58 E8
Shipley BD18 55 D7
Oakhall Pk BD13 72 D7
Oakhampton Ct LS8 61 C8
Oakhill Rd WF17 118 A7
Oakhurst Ave 5 LS11 214 A1
Oakhurst Gr LS11 213 F1
Oakhurst Mount LS11 213 F1
Oakhurst Rd LS11 214 A1
Oakhurst St LS11 214 A1
Oakland Ct HD8 173 F7
Oakland Dr WF4 158 D5
Oakland Rd
Netherton WF4 158 D5
Wakefield WF1 142 E3
Oakland St BD20 5 D1
Oaklands Bradford BD10 56 A8
Brighouse HD6 114 F1
Ilkley LS29 8 A3
Rothwell WF3 100 A3
Shipley BD18 54 D7
Oaklands Ave Leeds LS16 42 D3
Northowram HX3 93 B3
Pudsey LS13 57 E5
Oaklands Cl Holmfirth HD7 189 A7
Leeds LS16 42 D3
Oaklands Croft WF2 161 B6
Oaklands Dr Batley WF17 118 F5
Huddersfield HD5 154 F5
Leeds LS16 42 D3
Oaklands Fold LS16 42 D3
Oaklands Gr Leeds LS16 42 D3
Pudsey LS13 57 E5
Oaklands Rd LS13 57 E5
Oaklea Cl S75 178 B2
Oaklea Gdns LS16 42 D2
Oaklea Hall Cl LS16 42 D2
Oaklea Rd LS15 62 F6
Oakleigh Ave
Bradford BD14 73 B3
Halifax HX3 113 C3
Wakefield WF2 141 E5
Oakleigh Cl Bradford BD14 73 B4
Crofton WF4 144 C4
Oakleigh Gdns BD14 73 B3
Oakleigh Gr BD14 73 B3
Oakleigh Mews BD22 34 C2
Oakleigh Rd BD14 73 B4
Oakleigh Terr
Bradford BD14 73 B4
8 Todmorden OL14 86 B1
Oakleigh View BD17 38 B3
Oakley Gr LS11 214 C2
Oakley St WF3 99 E1
Oakley Terr LS11 214 C2
Oakley View LS11 214 C2
Oakridge Ave LS29 22 B4
Oakridge Ct BD16 37 A4
Oakroyd LS26 100 F4
Oakroyd Ave BD6 74 C1
Oakroyd Cl Birkenshaw BD11 96 A5
Brighouse HD6 115 B5
Oakroyd Dr Birkenshaw BD11 96 A4
Brighouse HD6 115 B5
Oakroyd Fold LS27 98 C8
Oakroyd Mount LS28 76 E8
Oakroyd Rd
12 Bradford, Brownroyd Oak BD6 74 C1
10 Bradford, Wibsey BD6 74 B1
Oakroyd Terr
3 Baildon BD17 38 D2
Bradford BD8 55 D2
Morley LS27 98 C8
8 Pudsey LS28 76 E8
Oakroyd Villas BD8 55 D2
Oaks Dr BD15 73 C8
Oaks Farm Cl S75 177 F1
Oaks Farm Dr S75 177 F1
Oaks Fold BD5 74 E3
Oaks Green Mount HD6 135 F7
Oaks La Boston Spa LS23 30 D8
Bradford BD15, BD8 73 D8
Oaks Rd WF17 118 E4
Oaks The Crofton WF4 144 B4
Guiseley LS20 22 E2
Morley LS27 98 B7
Oaks Wood Dr S75 178 A1
Oaksfield LS26 102 D2
Oaktree La WF7 164 C5
Oakville Rd HX7 88 D2
Oakway BD11 96 B4
Oakwell Ave Batley WF17 117 F6
Leeds LS12 210 A3
Leeds, Gledhow LS8 61 A6
Pontefract WF8 146 C6
Oakwell Cl
Birkenshaw BD11 97 A5
Bradford BD7 74 B3
Hemsworth WF9 163 A2
Oakwell Cres LS8 61 A6
Oakwell Dr LS8 61 A6
Oakwell Gdns LS8 61 A6
Oakwell Gr LS13 58 C3
Oakwell Hall WF17 96 D3
Oakwell Hall Country Pk WF17 96 D3
Oakwell Ind Pk WF17 97 A4
Oakwell Mount LS8 61 A6
Oakwell Oval LS8 61 A6
Oakwell Rd BD11 97 A5
Oakwell Terr 2 LS28 57 D3
Oakwell Way WF17 97 A3
Oakwood WF2 141 D3
Oakwood Ave
Birkenshaw BD11 96 A4
Leeds LS8 61 B6
Royston S71 179 C4
Shipley BD2 55 D4
Wakefield WF2 141 D6
Oakwood Boundary Rd LS8 61 B6
Oakwood Cl WF6 122 F4
Oakwood Cres S71 179 B4
Oakwood Ct Bradford BD8 74 C8
Leeds LS8 61 C6
Oakwood Dr Bingley BD16 37 A5
Hemsworth WF9 181 E6
Leeds LS8 61 B6
Normanton WF6 122 F4
Rothwell LS26 100 D7
Oakwood Garth LS8 61 C6
Oakwood Gdns WF4 159 D6
Oakwood Gn LS8 61 C6
Oakwood Gr Bradford BD8 55 A1
Horbury WF4 141 C2
Leeds LS8 61 B6
Oakwood Grange LS8 61 C6
Oakwood Grange La LS8 61 C6
Oakwood La LS8, LS9 61 C5
Oakwood Mount LS8 61 B6
Oakwood Nook LS8 61 B6
Oakwood Pk LS8 61 C6
Oakwood Pl LS8 61 B6
Oakwood Primary Sch LS8 208 C3
Oakwood Rd Batley WF17 118 E5
Royston S71 179 B4
Oakwood Rise LS8 61 C6
Oakwood Terr LS28 76 E6
Oakwood View LS8 61 C6
Oakwood Wlk LS8 61 C6
Oakworth First Sch BD22 34 D2
Oakworth Hall BD22 34 C2
Oakworth Rd BD21, BD22 35 A6
Oakworth Sta BD22 34 D1
Oakworth Terr BD22 34 D2
Oasby Croft BD4 75 E1
Oast House Croft WF3 100 B3
Oastler Ave HD1 153 F6
Oastler Pl BD12 94 D6
Oastler Rd Pudsey LS28 57 B6
Shipley BD18 54 F8
Oastler St WF13 139 B8
Oates St WF13 139 C8
Oatland Cl LS7 206 C2
Oatland Ct LS7 206 C2
Oatland Dr LS7 206 C2
Oatland Gdns LS7 207 D2
Oatland Gn LS7 206 C2
Oatland Hts LS7 207 D2
Oatland La LS7 206 C2
Oatland Pl LS7 206 C3
Oatland Rd LS7 206 C2
Oatland Towers LS7 206 C2
Oatlands Dr LS21 11 A1
Oats St BD22 35 A4
Oban Cl WF3 98 D1
Oban Pl 5 LS12 209 E4
Oban St LS12 209 E4
Oban Terr 6 LS12 209 E4
Occupation La
Aberford LS24 47 D4
Batley WF13 117 F3
Bramhope LS16 24 B2
Halifax HX2 91 F6
Holmfirth HD7 189 E8
Honley HD7 172 D1
Keighley BD22 34 E4
Pudsey LS28 76 C7
Occupation Rd
Huddersfield HD2, HD3 153 C8
Huddersfield, Sheepridge HD2 136 C3
Ochrewell Ave HD2 136 E3
Octagon Terr HX2 112 E4
Odda La LS20 21 E1
Oddfellow St LS27 98 A4
Oddfellows Club Houses WF7 163 D5
Oddfellows' Ct BD1 201 B3
Oddfellows St
3 Brighouse HD6 115 B4
Brighouse, Scholes BD19 115 F8
Mirfield WF14 138 A5
Oddy Pl 6 Bradford BD6 74 B1
4 Leeds LS6 59 D6
Oddy St BD4 75 E1
Oddy's Fold LS6 59 E8
Odsal Pl 9 BD6 94 D8
Odsal Rd BD6 94 D8
Offley La WF4 163 B6
Ogden Cres BD13 52 D2
Ogden La Brighouse HD6 135 F8
Denholme BD13 52 D2
Halifax HX2 71 D2
Ogden View Cl HX2 91 D7
Ogilby Ct LS26 101 B7
Ogilby Mews LS26 101 B7
Old Allen Rd BD13 53 B2
Old Arcade The 5 HX1 203 E3
Old Bank Halifax HX3 203 F3
Ripponden HX6 132 E4
Slaithwaite HD7 169 F8
Old Bank Fold 13 HD5 154 D5
Old Bank Jun & Inf Sch WF14 138 A7
Old Bank Rd
Dewsbury WF12 139 E8
Mirfield WF14 138 A7
Old Barn Cl LS17 43 A5
Old Bell Ct HX1 203 E2
Old Boyne Hill Farm WF4 160 A3
Old Brandon La LS17 44 E4
Old Bridge Rise LS29 8 A5
Old Canal Rd BD1 201 B4
Old Cawsey HX6 112 C4
Old Church St WF5 140 D5
Old Cl LS11 98 D8
Old Cock Yd HX1 203 E3
Old Corn Mill La BD7 74 A4
Old Cross Stone Rd 17 OL14 108 C5
Old Crown Rd WF2 141 D3
Old Dalton La BD21 35 D7
Old Earth HX5 135 B7
Old Earth Junior & Infants Sch HX5 135 C7
Old Farm App LS16 58 F8
Old Farm Cl LS16 59 A8
Old Farm Cres BD4 75 B3
Old Farm Cross LS16 59 A8
Old Farm Dr LS16 59 A8
Old Farm Garth 2 LS16 59 A8
Old Farm Par LS16 59 A8
Old Farm Wlk 6 LS16 58 F8
Old Fieldhouse La HD2 136 D1
Old Fold 9 LS28 57 D3
Old Forge Mews LS16 24 D3
Old Garth Croft WF11 105 A4
Old Gate
24 Hebden Bridge HX7 89 A3
Holme HD7 197 F7
Old Godley La HX3 92 F1
Old Great North Rd
Brotherton WF11 126 D8
Knottingley WF11 126 C5
Old Ground HD7 169 A8
Old Guy Rd BD13 72 C1
Old Hall HX3 113 D4
Old Hall Cl BD20 16 B6
Old Hall Court Yd WF1 143 A5
Old Hall La HD8 175 E5
Old Hall Mews WF17 118 C7
Old Hall Rd
Adwick Le S DN6 184 F2
Batley WF17 118 C7
East Ardsley WF3 119 F8
Glusburn BD20 16 B6
Old Hall Way BD20 16 B6
Old Haworth La 6 LS19 40 B7
Old Hollings Hill LS20, BD17 39 C6
Old La Birkenshaw BD11 96 B5
Bramhope LS16 24 B3
Brighouse HD6 115 B3
Cullingworth BD13 52 D6
Gildersome BD11 97 A8
Guiseley LS20 38 E8
Halifax HX3 92 B2
Halifax, Luddenden HX2 90 E1
Haworth BD22 49 F7
Holme HD7 187 C4
Huddersfield HD2 136 D5
Old La continued
Ilkley LS29 8 D3
Leeds LS11 213 F1
Marsden HD7 169 D7
Nesfield LS29 7 C7
Pool LS16 23 F4
Slaithwaite HD7 152 C5
Todmorden OL14 108 A3
Wadsworth Moor HX7 89 B8
Old Laithe La HX7 89 C5
Old Lane Ct 2 HD6 115 B3
Old Langley La BD17 38 E4
Old Lee Bank HX3 92 B1
Old Leeds Rd HD1 154 B6
Old Lees Rd HX7 89 A4
Old Lindley Rd HD3 134 D2
Old Lodge Hill or Hardings La LS29 7 F6
Old Main St BD16 36 F3
Old Malt St 1 BD22 51 C6
Old Market HX1 203 E3
Old Marsh LS28 76 C7
Old Meadows Rd OL13 106 A4
Old Mill Bsns Pk LS10 215 F4
Old Mill Cl Burley in W LS29 9 F2
Hemsworth WF9 181 C7
Old Mill La LS10 215 E4
Old Mill The LS22 13 E5
Old Mill View WF12 139 B5
Old Mill Yd WF5 140 C3
Old Moll Rd HD7 171 E5
Old Mount Farm WF4 178 A6
Old Mount Rd HD7 168 E2
Old Oak Cl LS16 59 A7
Old Oak Dr LS16 59 A7
Old Oak Garth LS16 58 F7
Old Orch The LS21 24 C7
Old Orchard The
Hemsworth WF9 181 D7
Leeds LS13 58 B4
Old Oxenhope La BD22 51 B4
Old Park Ct BD1 201 D3
Old Park Rd Bradford BD10 56 C7
Leeds LS8 61 A8
Old Pool Bank
Bramhope LS21 24 B5
Pool LS21 24 B5
Old Popplewell La BD19 115 E8
Old Power Way HX5 135 A8
Old Railway Goods Yd The HD3 153 A5
Old Rd Bradford BD7 73 E2
Denholme BD13 71 D8
Holmfirth HD7 188 D3
Morley LS27 98 C8
Netherton WF4 157 F6
Pudsey LS28 57 D2
Thornton BD13 73 A6
Wadsworth Moor HX7 69 A2
Old Riding La HX2 90 F3
Old Robin 9 BD19 116 D7
Old Run Rd Leeds LS10 215 D1
Middleton LS10 215 D1
Old Run View LS10 99 D8
Old Sawmills The HX6 132 C2
Old School Ct WF10 124 C5
Old School Mews 4 LS27 98 C8
Old Schools Gdns 14 HX3 92 C1
Old Shaw La HX7 88 A4
Old Souls Way BD16 36 E6
Old South St HD1 154 A6
Old St Hampole DN6 183 F1
Hooton Pagnell DN5 195 F7
Old Station Cotts S71 179 D7
Old Station Way LS29 6 F8
Old Town Junior & Infants Sch HX7 89 C5
Old Town Mill La HX7 89 B5
Old Turnpike HD7 172 A4
Old Wakefield Rd 5 HD5 154 D5
Old Water Mill The HX6 132 D7
Old Well Head HX1 203 E2
Old Westgate WF13 139 C8
Old Whack House La LS19 39 F6
Old Wood La BD16, LS20 21 B2
Old Woodyard The WF4 158 C2
Old Yew La HD7 188 E2
Oldfield HD7 171 F1
Oldfield Ave LS12 209 F2
Oldfield First Sch BD22 50 C8
Oldfield Gate BD22 51 A7
Oldfield La Batley WF16 117 D3
Clayton West HD8 175 F2
Collingham LS22 13 E1
Haworth BD22 51 A7
Haworth, Oldfield BD22 50 C8
Leeds LS12 210 A2
Oldfield Rd HD7 171 F1
Oldfield St Halifax HX3 92 A3
Huddersfield HD4 153 E4
Leeds LS12 209 F2
Oldgate HD1 154 B6
Oldham Rd HX6 150 C6
Oldroyd Cres LS11 213 E2
Oldroyd Rd OL14 108 E4
Oldside Ct BD20 19 E1
Olicana Pk LS29 8 A5
Olive Gr BD8 73 E8
Olive St HD1 136 B1
Olive Terr Bingley BD16 37 A3
Marsden HD7 169 C6
Oliver Ct BD11 96 D5
Oliver Gdns WF14 137 F7
Oliver Hill LS18 58 C7
Oliver La HD7 168 F4
Oliver Mdws HX5 135 B7
Oliver Rd WF16 117 E5
Oliver St BD4 201 D1
Olivers Mount WF8 146 E8
Ollerdale Ave BD15 54 A3
Ollerdale Cl BD15 54 A2
Ollerton Rd S71 178 F1
Olney St HD7 152 A1
Olrika Ct LS7 207 D4
Oltley Rd LS29 22 B5
Olympic Ct 6 BD12 94 E5
Omar St WF16 117 C4
Onchan Dr OL13 106 B1
One St BD1 74 D7
Onslow Cres BD4 75 B2
Ontario Pl LS7 204 A2
Opal St 10 BD22 35 A4
Orange St Bradford BD3 75 C6
Halifax HX1 203 E3
Orange Terr HD1 154 B8
Orange Tree Gr WF3 120 C7
Orchard Ave WF3 121 F5
Orchard Cl
East Ardsley WF3 120 D6
Halifax HX2 112 D6
Horbury WF4 141 A2
Mapplewell S75 178 B1
Meltham HD7 170 F1
Wakefield WF2 120 F3
Orchard Croft
2 Leeds LS15 62 B2
Wakefield WF2 120 E2
Walton WF2 161 A7
Orchard Ct Bramham LS23 30 D2
Huddersfield HD3 152 F6
Orchard Dr
Ackworth M T WF7 164 A5
Collingham LS22 13 B3
Crigglestone WF4 159 F7
Fairburn WF11 105 B5
South Hiendley S72 180 D6
Orchard Gate LS21 23 A7
Orchard Gdns WF4 159 F7
Orchard Gr Bradford BD10 56 D6
Menston LS29 22 B4
Orchard Head Cres WF8 125 F4
Orchard Head Dr WF8 125 E4
Orchard Head Junior & Infants Sch WF8 125 E4
Orchard Head La WF8 125 E4
Orchard La Addingham LS29 7 A8
Darrington WF8 147 C5
Guiseley LS20 22 E1
Orchard Lees HD5 155 C8
Orchard Mount LS15 62 C2
Orchard Rd Kirkheaton HD5 155 C8
1 Leeds LS15 62 B2
Todmorden OL14 107 F7
Wakefield WF2 142 E1
Orchard Rise HX6 111 F2
Orchard Sq LS15 62 B2
Orchard St Dewsbury WF12 139 D6
Huddersfield HD4 154 A4
Otley LS21 23 B7
Orchard St W HD3 153 A5
Orchard Terr
Cawthorne S75 193 F4
Huddersfield HD4 154 B4
Orchard The Boston Spa LS23 30 D8
Crofton WF4 144 A1
Elland HX4 133 F3
Featherstone WF7 124 D1
Keighley BD21 35 F7
Mirfield WF14 138 B7
Normanton WF6 123 B2
Ossett WF5 140 D5
Pontefract WF8 146 F5
Wakefield WF2, WF4 120 F3
Orchard View
Brotherton WF11 126 C8
Darrington WF8 147 C5
Wetherby LS22 13 E8
Orchard Way
Brighouse HD6 115 A4
Guiseley LS20 22 E1
Rothwell LS26 100 F6
Orchard Wlk HX7 89 F1
Orchards The Bingley BD16 37 A5
Cleckheaton BD19 117 C8
Leeds LS15 62 C2
Mickletown LS26 102 C2
Orchid Crest WF9 183 A7
Orchid Ct WF3 100 B2
Oriental St 6 LS12 209 F3
Orion Cres LS10 99 E7
Orion Dr LS10 99 E7
Orion Gdns LS10 99 F7
Orion View LS10 99 F7
Orion Wlk LS10 99 F8
Orlando Cl WF14 137 F7
Orleans St BD6 93 F7
Ormond Rd BD6 74 B1
Ormond St BD7 74 A4
Ormonde Dr BD15 73 B8
Ormonde Pl LS7 206 C3
Ormondroyd Ave BD6 94 C8
Orville Gdns LS6 205 E4
Orwell Cl WF10 125 C5
Osborne Ave WF4 141 C2
Osborne Gr HX3 114 D7
Osborne Pl
32 Hebden Bridge HX7 89 A3
3 Todmorden OL14 108 C5
Osborne St Bradford BD5 201 A1
Halifax HX1 202 B4
14 Hebden Bridge HX7 89 A3
15 Huddersfield HD5 154 D5
Osbourne Ct LS13 58 D1
Osbourne Dr BD13 72 E1
Osmond Ho 9 BD5 201 B1
Osmondthorpe La LS9 80 C7

Osmondthorpe Primary Sch
LS9 80 D8
Osprey Cl LS17 43 F4
Osprey Ct BD8 73 C7
Osprey Dr HD4 171 E7
Osprey Gr LS17 43 F4
Osprey Meadow LS27 98 D4
Ossett High Sch WF5 140 D3
Ossett La WF12 140 A6
Ossett South Parade
Infant Sch WF5 140 F4
Osterley Gr BD10 56 E5
Oswald St BD18 55 D7
Oswaldthorpe Ave BD3 56 D1
Otley All Saints Inf Sch
LS21 23 B7
Otley Ashfield Inf Sch
LS21 10 E1
Otley Golf Course LS21 22 C6
Otley La LS19 40 B7
Otley Mount BD20 19 E1
Otley Old Rd Bramhope LS16 24 B1
East Carlton LS16 23 F3
East Carlton LS16 24 B1
Leeds LS16 41 F4
Otley Rd Baildon BD17 38 E2
Bingley BD16 20 B1
Bingley, Eldwick Beck BD16 37 D6
Burley in W LS29 22 B8
Guiseley LS20 22 D1
Harewood LS17 26 C7
Keighley BD20 19 F1
Leeds, Adel LS16 42 C5
Leeds, Far Headingley
LS6, LS16 59 D6
Shipley BD17, BD18 55 B7
Otley St Halifax HX1 202 B3
Keighley BD21 35 B6
Otley Westgate Inf Sch
LS21 22 F7
Ottawa Pl LS7 204 A2
Otterburn Cl BD5 201 B1
Otterburn Gdns LS16 42 B3
Otterburn St BD21 35 C8
Otters Holt WF4 159 F7
Otterwood Bank LS22 13 F7
Ottiwells Terr HD7 168 F3
Ouchthorpe Fold WF1 121 C4
Ouchthorpe La WF1 121 C2
Queen's Ct LS17 43 C1
Oulton Dr LS26 101 C3
Oulton Infant Sch LS26 101 B6
Oulton Junior Sch LS26 101 B6
Oulton La Rothwell LS26 100 F5
Rothwell, Woodlesford LS26 101 C6
Oulton Prim Sch LS26 101 B6
Oulton Terr BD7 74 C6
Ounsworth St BD4 75 B4
Our Lady of Good Counsel
RC Sch LS14 62 A6
Our Lady of Lourdes RC
Jun & Inf Sch HD2 136 C4
Our Lady of Victories RC
Primary Sch BD21 35 A7
Our Lady's RC Prim Sch
LS14 62 A6
Ouse Dr LS22 13 D8
Ouse St 2 BD22 51 D7
Out Gang LS13 58 D3
Out La Emley HD8 175 C7
Holmfirth HD7 188 F8
Outcote Bank HD1 154 A5
Outfield Cl WF16 117 E4
Outgang La LS13 58 E3
Outlands Rise BD10 56 D8
Outlane Jun & Inf Sch
HD3 134 D1
Outside La BD22 50 F2
Outwood Ave LS18 58 D7
Outwood Grange High Sch
WF1 121 A4
Outwood La LS18 58 D7
Outwood Park Ct WF1 121 B4
Outwood Wlk LS18 58 C7
Ouzelwell Cres WF12 139 B3
Ouzelwell La WF12 139 A3
Ouzelwell Rd WF12 139 B4
Ouzlewell Gn WF3 100 D2
Oval The Baildon BD17 38 B2
Beal DN14 127 F5
Bingley BD16 37 B2
Bradford BD8 73 E8
Cleckheaton WF15 116 C5
Oval The LS25 83 A7
Oval The Guiseley LS20 39 C8
Holmfirth HD7 188 F7
Leeds, Hunslet LS10 215 E4
Leeds, The Oval LS14 61 F2
Notton WF4 179 B6
Otley LS21 10 F1
Rothwell LS26 100 F5
Ovenden Ave HX3 92 A1
Ovenden Cl 15 HX3 92 A1
Ovenden Cres HX3 92 A2
Ovenden Gn HX3 92 A2
Ovenden Rd HX3 92 A2
Ovenden Road Terr 9
HX3 92 A2
Ovenden Terr HX3 92 A2
Ovenden Way HX3 91 F2
Ovenden Wood Rd HX2 91 D2
Over Hall Cl WF14 138 B6
Over Hall Pk WF14 138 B6
Over Hall Rd WF14 138 B6
Over La LS19 40 C3
Overburn Rd BD20 16 D4
Overdale HX6 132 E7
Overdale Ave LS17 44 A5
Overdale Cl LS22 13 D6
Overdale Dr BD10, BD18 38 F1
Overdale Mount HX6 112 C5
Overdale Terr 4 LS15 81 A8
Overend St 6 BD6 74 A1
Overland Cres BD10 56 D8
Overmoor Fold BD10 56 A7
Overthorpe Ave WF12 139 D1
Overthorpe CE Jun
& Inf Sch WF12 139 C2
Overthorpe Rd WF12 139 D3
Overton Dr BD6 73 D2
Ovington Dr BD4 75 E2
Owen Ct BD16 37 A6
Ower's Cres HD7 171 E3
Owl La Batley WF12 119 B1
Batley, Chidswell WF12 119 A3
Ossett WF5 119 B1
Owl Mews HD5 155 C6
Owl Ridge LS27 98 C3
Owl St 6 BD21 35 D8
Owlar Bars Rd HD7 170 C2
Owlcotes Ctr LS28 57 D1
Owlcotes Dr LS28 76 C8
Owlcotes Garth LS28 76 B8
Owlcotes Gdns LS28 76 C8
Owlcotes La Pudsey LS28 57 C1
Pudsey LS28 76 C8
Owlcotes Rd LS28 76 B8
Owlcotes Terr LS28 76 C8
Owler Ings Rd HD6 115 A2
Owler La WF17 96 F3
Owler Mdws WF16 117 C5
Owler Park Rd LS29 7 F6
Owler's La WF9 164 F4
Owlers Cl HD2 136 F5
Owlet Grange BD18 55 C6
Owlet Hurst La WF15 117 B2
Owlet Rd BD18 55 C7
Owlett Mead WF3 99 E1
Owlett Mead Cl WF3 99 E1
Ox Heys Meadows BD13 73 A6
Ox Lee La HD7 199 E8
Oxenhope C of E Aided
First Sch BD22 51 C3
Oxenhope Sta BD22 51 C3
Oxfield Ct HD5 155 A7
Oxford Ave LS20 22 D1
Oxford Cl Cleckheaton BD19 117 B8
Queensbury BD13 92 C8
Oxford Court Gdns WF10 124 C7
Oxford Cres Bradford BD14 73 B4
Halifax HX3 113 D4
Oxford Dr
Cleckheaton BD19 117 B8
Kippax LS25 83 A2
Oxford La HX3 113 D3
Oxford Pl Baildon BD17 38 E2
Bradford BD3 201 C4
Huddersfield HD1 153 E3
Leeds LS1 211 E4
Pudsey LS28 57 E1
Oxford Rd Batley WF17 96 E1
Bradford BD2 56 B2
Cleckheaton BD19 96 B2
Dewsbury WF13 118 B1
Guiseley LS20 22 E1
Halifax HX1 203 E2
Leeds LS7 206 C3
5 Queensbury BD13 92 C8
Wakefield WF1 216 A4
Oxford Row LS1 211 E4
Oxford St
Batley, Mount Pleasant
WF17 118 B4
Batley, Nunroyd WF16 117 D4
Bradford BD14 73 B4
East Ardsley WF3 120 E8
Featherstone WF7 145 C5
Guiseley LS20 22 E1
Hebden Bridge HX7 88 F3
Huddersfield HD1 154 B7
Keighley BD21 35 A6
Morley LS27 97 F2
Normanton WF6 123 C3
South Elmsall WF9 182 F2
Sowerby Bridge HX6 112 D4
Todmorden OL14 108 B5
Wakefield WF1 142 E3
Oxford Terr Baildon BD17 38 E2
Batley WF17 118 D4
Oxford Wlk BD19 117 B8
Oxley Gdns BD12 94 C7
Oxley Hall LS16 59 C8
Oxley Rd HD2 136 C4
Oxley St Bradford BD8 74 C8
Leeds LS9 212 C3
Oxleys Sq HD3 134 D1
Oxton Mount LS9 212 C4
Oxton Way LS9 212 C4
Oyster Cl LS27 98 C3
Oyster Park Infants Sch
WF10 125 D8
Oyster Park Junior Sch
WF10 125 D8

Pacaholme Rd WF2 141 D8
Pack Fold HD7 170 C8
Pack Horse Cl HD8 176 A4
Pack Horse Ctr 5 HD1 154 B6
Pad Cote La BD22 32 A8
Padan St HX3 113 D4
Paddock BD9 55 B4
Paddock Cl
Birkenshaw BD11 96 E5
Bradford BD12 94 C1
Garforth LS25 83 A6
Mapplewell S75 178 C1
Paddock Dr BD11 96 E5
Paddock Foot HD1 153 E5
Paddock Gn LS17 28 C5
Paddock House La LS22 12 B3
Paddock Jun & Inf Sch
HD1 153 D5
Paddock La HX2 112 C8
Paddock Rd
Kirkburton HD8 174 A7
Mapplewell S75 178 C1
Northowram HD8, S75 92 E5
Paddock The Baildon BD17 38 F4
12 Brighouse BD19 115 F8
Burton Salmon LS25 105 E3
Castleford WF10 125 C6
Cullingworth BD13 52 D6
Dewsbury WF12 139 F6
East Keswick LS17 28 C5
Kirkheaton HD5 155 C7
Knottingley WF11 126 F3
Leeds LS6 59 F7
Normanton WF6 123 B1
Rothwell LS26 100 E5
Silsden BD20 5 E1
Thorner LS14 45 F5
Woolley WF4 178 A7
Paddock View WF10 125 B6
Paddy Bridge Rd HX7 89 D1
Padgum 12 BD17 38 C4
Padma Cl BD7 74 B7
Padmans La LS23 30 D8
Padstow Ave LS10 99 A5
Padstow Gdns LS10 99 A5
Padstow Pl LS10 99 A4
Page Hill HX2 91 E2
Page St HD1 154 B5
Paget Cres HD2 135 D1
Paget St BD21 35 A7
Pagewood Ct BD10 39 A1
Painthorpe House
Country Club WF4 159 E4
Painthorpe La WF4 159 E4
Painthorpe Terr WF4 159 E4
Paisley Gr 2 LS12 209 E4
Paisley Pl 3 LS12 209 E4
Paisley Rd LS12 209 D4
Paisley St LS12 209 E4
Paisley Terr 4 LS12 209 E4
Paisley View 5 LS12 209 D4
Pakington St BD5 74 D4
Palace House Rd HX7 89 A2
Paleside La WF5 140 D7
Palesides Ave WF5 140 D8
Palestine Rd 4 HX7 89 A4
Paley Rd BD4 75 A4
Paley Terr BD4 75 A4
Palin Ave BD3 56 D1
Palm St Halifax HX3 92 B2
Huddersfield HD4 154 B4
Palma St OL14 86 B1
Palmer Rd BD3 75 B8
Palmer's Ave WF9 183 B2
Palmerston St BD2 56 B2
Pangbourne Rd S63 194 C1
Pannal Ave WF1 142 E8
Pannal St BD7 74 A3
Panorama Dr LS29 7 E3
Papyrus Villas LS24 31 C6
Parade The Batley WF17 118 A4
Bradford BD4 75 E3
Leeds LS9 212 B3
Otley LS21 10 E1
2 Shipley BD16 54 A7
Yeadon LS19 39 F6
Paradise Fields WF8 125 D1
Paradise La Halifax HX2 112 B6
Stutton LS24 48 B5
Paradise Pl 3 LS18 58 E8
Paradise Rd BD9 54 F4
Paradise St Bradford BD1 74 D7
Halifax HX1 203 D2
Pudsey LS28 57 D3
Paris Mews HD7 189 C2
Paris Rd HD7 189 D4
Parish Ghyll Dr LS29 7 F3
Parish Ghyll La LS29 7 F3
Parish Ghyll Rd LS29 8 A3
Parish Ghyll Wlk LS29 8 A3
Park Ave Bingley BD16 36 F2
Birkenshaw BD11 96 E6
Bradford BD10 39 B2
Brierley S72 181 B3
Castleford WF10 124 F7
Clayton West HD8 175 F3
Crofton WF1 143 D7
Darrington WF8 147 C5
Dewsbury WF13 139 B7
Elland HX5 134 E6
Huddersfield HD1 153 F6
Keighley BD21 35 B6
Kippax LS25 83 C1
Kippax, Allerton Bywater
WF10 103 C4
Leeds LS12 209 E4
Leeds, Lady Wood LS8 61 C7
Leeds, Manston LS15 62 D2
Liversedge WF15 117 A2
Lofthouse Gate WF3 121 C6
Lofthouse Gate, Outwood
WF1 121 A4
Mirfield WF14 138 B4
Morley LS27 97 F3
Normanton WF6 123 B2
Oakworth BD22 34 D2
Pontefract WF8 146 B8
4 Pudsey LS28 76 E7
Royston S71 179 D3
Shepley HD8 173 F3
Park Ave continued
Shipley BD18 55 A8
South Kirkby WF9 182 B2
Sutton in C BD20 16 D5
Swillington LS26 82 A1
Wakefield WF2 142 B4
Yeadon LS19 40 A7
Yeadon, Larkfield LS19 40 C4
Park Cl Batley WF17 118 B3
Bingley BD16 37 A4
Birkenshaw BD11 96 E6
Bradford BD10 56 C5
Brighouse HX3 114 E7
Darrington WF8 147 C5
Halifax HX2 91 B2
Keighley BD21 35 C5
Leeds LS13 58 C3
Normanton WF6 123 A1
Queensbury BD13 72 D1
Shepley HD8 173 F3
Park Cliffe Rd BD2 56 B2
Park Copse LS18 41 A1
Park Cotts LS8 44 B1
Park Cres Addingham LS29 7 A8
Bradford BD3 56 A2
Castleford WF10 125 C7
Gildersome LS27 97 D6
Guiseley LS20 39 C7
Halifax HX3 92 A1
Leeds LS12 209 E4
Leeds, Park Villas LS8 44 B1
Rothwell LS26 101 A6
Royston S71 179 D3
Park Crest WF9 181 D7
Park Croft Batley WF17 118 B4
Dewsbury WF13 139 A8
Park Cross St LS1 211 E4
Park Ct Bradford BD9 55 C2
Featherstone WF7 124 D1
Ossett WF5 140 F4
Pool LS21 24 D6
Park Dale Castleford WF10 104 C1
Menston LS29 22 A4
Park Dr Batley WF17 118 A7
Bingley BD16 37 B5
Horsforth LS18 58 A8
Huddersfield HD1 153 E7
Lofthouse Gate WF3 121 C7
Mirfield WF14 138 B5
Shepley HD8 173 F3
Shipley BD9 55 B4
Sutton in C BD20 16 D5
Park Dr S HD1 153 F6
Park Drive Rd BD21 35 C5
Park Edge Cl LS8 61 C7
Park Est WF9 182 C2
Park Farm Ind Est LS11 99 B8
Park Field LS29 22 A4
Park Fields HX2 91 B2
Park Gate Bradford BD1 201 C3
Huddersfield HD8 171 F8
Park Gate Cl LS18 58 B8
Park Gate Cres LS20 39 D8
Park Gate Rd HD7 169 B6
Park Gdns Ossett WF5 140 F4
Sowerby Bridge HX2 112 D5
Park Gn Normanton WF6 123 A1
Silsden BD20 5 C2
Park Gr Gildersome LS27 97 D6
Horbury WF4 140 F2
Horsforth LS18 57 F8
Huddersfield HD1 153 F6
Keighley BD21 35 C8
Mirfield WF14 138 C4
9 Queensbury BD13 72 D1
Shipley BD18 54 F8
Shipley, Frizinghall BD9 55 C4
Swillington LS26 102 B8
Yeadon LS19 40 A7
Park Grove Ct BD9 55 C4
Park Grove Rd WF2 142 A5
Park Head La
Denby Dale HD8 190 F5
Holmfirth HD7 188 E4
Park Hill Huddersfield HD2 136 F6
Kexbrough S75 177 B2
Park Hill Cl BD8 54 D1
Park Hill Dr BD8 54 D1
Park Hill Gr WF1 142 F6
Park Hill La WF1 142 E6
Park Holme LS7 207 E4
Park House BD20 17 C6
Park House Cl BD12 94 E7
Park House Cres BD12 94 E7
Park House Dr WF12 139 D4
Park House Gr BD12 94 E7
Park House Rd BD12 94 E6
Park House Wlk BD12 94 E7
Park Jun Sch The WF10 124 E7
Park La Baildon BD17 38 F4
Bradford, Holme Top BD5 74 D4
Bradford, Park Lane BD14 73 B4
Denby Dale HD8 191 B5
Elland HX4 133 F1
Emley HD8 175 A5
Guiseley LS20 39 C7
Halifax HX3 113 E2
Hebden Bridge HX7 110 C8
Huddersfield HD4 172 A7
Huddersfield, Town End
HD7 152 D4
Keighley BD21 35 C5
Kippax LS25 103 C8
Kippax, Allerton Bywater
WF10 103 C5
Ledsham LS25 104 C8
Leeds LS3 211 D4
Leeds, Roundhay LS8 44 B2
Park La continued
Meltham HD7 170 E2
Mickletown LS26 102 A1
Pontefract WF7, WF8 124 E1
Queensbury BD13 72 F1
Rothwell LS26 101 A6
Sicklinghall LS22 12 B5
Sutton in C BD20 16 D5
West Bretton WF4 176 F7
Park Lane Coll of Further
Education LS3 211 D4
Park Lane Mews LS17 44 B4
Park Lea HD2 136 F6
Park Lodge Cres WF1 142 E6
Park Lodge Ct WF1 142 E6
Park Lodge Gr WF1 216 C2
Park Lodge La WF1 142 F6
Park Mead BD10 39 B2
Park Mews LS21 24 D6
Park Mill La WF5 141 B8
Park Mill Way HD8 175 F3
Park Mount Leeds LS12 209 D4
Leeds, Kirkstall LS5 59 B4
Pool LS21 24 B5
Park Mount Ave BD17 38 E3
Park Mount Terr LS5 59 A4
Park Nook HX3 113 F2
Park Par Dewsbury WF13 139 B7
Morley LS27 97 F3
Park Pl Bradford BD10 39 B2
Halifax HX1 202 C2
Leeds LS1 211 E4
Pontefract WF8 146 B8
Park Pl E HX3 114 E7
Park Pl W HX3 114 E7
Park Rd 3 Batley WF16 117 D4
Batley, Bank Foot WF17 118 D5
Bingley BD16 37 A4
Boston Spa LS23 30 C8
Bradford BD6 94 C7
Bradford BD5 201 B1
Bradford, Greengates BD10 56 E6
Bradford, Thackley BD10 39 B2
Brierley S72 181 B3
Castleford WF10 125 A5
Clayton West HD8 175 F3
Dewsbury WF12 139 C6
Dewsbury, Earlsheaton
WF12 139 F7
Dewsbury, Ravensthorpe
WF13 138 F6
Dewsbury, Westborough
WF13 118 B1
Glusburn BD20 16 C7
Guiseley LS20 39 D8
Halifax HX1 203 D2
Huddersfield, Lockwood
HD4 153 E4
Huddersfield, Milnsbridge
HD4 153 B4
Leeds LS12 209 D4
Leeds, Colton LS15 81 D6
Leeds, Whitecote LS13 58 C3
Menston LS29 22 A4
Pontefract WF8 125 B2
Shipley BD18 55 C7
Sowerby Bridge HX6 112 D5
Todmorden OL14 108 B6
Yeadon LS19 40 A7
Yeadon LS19 40 B4
Park Rd W HD4 153 D4
Park Rise Castleford WF10 124 F7
Leeds LS13 58 C4
Park Road Jun & Inf Sch
WF17 118 D5
Park Row
6 Brighouse HD6 115 B2
Burley in W LS29 9 F2
Leeds LS1 211 E4
Otley LS21 23 B8
Pudsey LS28 57 E1
Sutton in C BD20 16 D4
Park Sch The WF2 216 A1
Park Side
Cleckheaton BD19 117 A7
Flockton WF4 157 C3
Holmfirth HD7 189 E4
Horsforth LS18 58 A8
Kirkheaton HD5 137 C1
Park Spring Gdns LS13 58 B1
Park Spring Primary Sch
LS13 77 B8
Park Spring Rise LS13 58 B1
Park Sq 1 Bradford BD6 94 A8
Lofthouse Gate WF3 121 C6
Northowram HX3 93 A2
Ossett WF5 140 F4
Pool LS21 24 D6
Park Sq E LS1 211 E4
Park Sq N LS1 211 E4
Park Sq S LS1 211 E4
Park Sq W LS1 211 E4
Park St
Batley, Brown Hill WF17 117 E8
Batley, Nunroyd WF17 117 D4
Brighouse HD6 115 B2
Cleckheaton, Gomersall
BD19 117 C8
Cleckheaton, Hartshead
Moor Side BD19 116 B6
Dewsbury WF13 118 D1
Glusburn BD20 16 D6
Haworth BD22 51 D7
Horbury WF4 141 A1
Leeds LS12 209 D4

Park St continued
Leeds LS1 211 E4
Leeds, Graveleythorpe LS15 81 B8
Morley LS27 98 C8
Ossett WF5 140 F4
Shipley BD18 55 A8
Slaithwaite HD7 152 C6
Sowerby Bridge HX6 112 D4
Wakefield WF1 216 C1
Yeadon LS19 40 A7
Park Stone Rise HX3 93 B5
Park Terr Brighouse HX3 114 D7
Halifax HX1 202 C2
Keighley, Eastwood BD21 35 D7
Keighley, Thwaites Brow BD21 35 F6
Leeds LS6 59 D6
Otley LS21 23 B8
Pool LS21 24 A5
Shipley BD18 55 A8
South Elmsall WF9 183 A2
Park The S75 193 E4
Park Top LS28 57 E1
Park Top Cotts BD16 37 B5
Park Top Rd BD22 51 A5
Park Towngate The HX3 114 A4
Park View Brierley S72 181 B3
Castleford WF10 125 B6
Cleckheaton BD19 116 C7
Elland HX4 134 A1
Halifax HX1 202 C2
Hemsworth WF9 163 B1
Holmfirth HD7 189 A5
6 Kippax LS25 83 B1
Leeds, Beeston Hill LS11 214 A3
Leeds, Bramley LS13 58 C3
Lofthouse Gate WF3 121 C6
Marsden HD7 169 A4
Mirfield WF14 138 C4
Pudsey LS28 76 E7
Royston S71 179 D3
Shafton S72 180 D2
Swillington LS26 82 A1
Wakefield WF2 141 E6
Yeadon LS19 39 F7
Park View Ave
13 Haworth BD22 51 E8
Leeds LS4 205 D3
Northowram HX3 93 A1
Yeadon LS19 40 C4
Park View Cres LS8 44 B2
Park View Gr LS4 205 D3
Park View Rd Bradford BD9 55 B3
Leeds LS4 205 D2
Mapplewell S75 178 D1
Park View Terr
Bradford BD9 55 B3
8 Leeds LS15 81 A8
Yeadon LS19 40 B4
Park Villa Ct LS8 44 A1
Park Villas LS8 44 A1
Park Villas Dr WF8 125 B1
Park W LS26 100 F5
Park Way Baildon BD17 37 F1
Menston LS29 22 A4
Pool LS21 24 D7
Park Wood Ave LS11 98 F8
Park Wood Cres LS11 98 F8
Park Wood Dr LS11 98 F8
Park Wood Rd LS11 98 F8
Parkcroft LS28 57 D2
Parkdale Dr HX6 132 E7
Parker Ave WF6 122 E4
Parker La WF14 138 B5
Parker Rd Dewsbury WF12 139 C4
Horbury WF4 141 C1
Parker St Batley WF16 117 D4
East Ardsley WF3 120 C7
Glusburn BD20 16 D7
Parker's La BD20 18 A3
Parkfield Ave
14 Elland HX5 134 F6
Leeds LS11 214 A3
Mirfield WF14 138 C4
Parkfield Cl LS25 83 B2
Parkfield Cres WF14 138 C4
Parkfield Croft WF14 138 C4
Parkfield Ct LS14 61 E3
Parkfield Dr
Boston Spa LS23 30 C8
Ossett WF5 141 A5
3 Queensbury BD13 72 D1
Sowerby Bridge HX6 112 A2
Parkfield Gr LS11 214 A3
Parkfield La
Featherstone WF7 124 C2
Sowerby Bridge HX6 112 D3
Parkfield Mount
Leeds LS11 214 A3
Pudsey LS28 76 E7
Parkfield Pl LS11 214 A3
Parkfield Rd Bradford BD8 55 D2
Leeds LS11 214 A3
Shipley BD18 54 E8
Parkfield Row LS11 214 A3
Parkfield St LS11 211 F1
Parkfield Terr
3 Pudsey LS28 76 E7
Pudsey, Stanningley LS28 57 E1
Parkfield View Leeds LS11 214 A3
Ossett WF5 141 A5
Parkfield Way Leeds LS14 61 E3
Mirfield WF14 138 B4
Parkgate WF9 182 B1
Parkgate Ave WF1 142 E6
Parkhead Cl S71 179 A4
Parkhill Cres WF1 142 F6
Parkin Hall La HX6 111 B1
Parkin La Bradford BD10 56 F8
Todmorden OL14 107 E5
Parkin Sq HD7 152 B5
Parkin St WF15 116 C5
Parkin's Almshouses 2
HD5 154 F3
Parkinson App LS25 82 F8
Parkinson Cl WF1 142 E6
Parkinson La HX1 202 B2
Parkinson Lane Junior
& Infants Sch HX1 202 C2
Parkinson Rd BD13 71 E8
Parkinson St BD5 74 D4
Parkland Ave LS27 97 E3
Parkland Cres LS6 43 A1
Parkland Dr Bradford BD10 56 C7
Leeds LS6 43 A1
Parkland Gdns LS6 60 A8
Parkland Middle
& First Schs BD10 56 D7
Parkland Terr LS6 60 A8
Parkland View LS19 40 B6
Parklands Bingley BD16 37 B5
Bramhope LS16 24 D3
Castleford WF10 124 E7
Ilkley LS29 8 D4
Ossett WF5 140 F4
Parklands Ave WF4 140 E1
Parklands Cres
Bramhope LS16 24 E3
Horbury WF4 140 E1
Parklands Ct WF4 140 E1
Parklands Dr Horbury WF4 140 E1
Sowerby Bridge HX6 111 E1
Parklands Gate LS16 24 E3
Parklands High Sch LS14 62 B4
Parklands Prim Sch LS14 62 B3
Parklands Wlk HD8 173 F3
Parklee Ct BD21 35 C6
Parkmere Cl BD4 95 B8
Parkside Bingley BD16 37 B4
Cleckheaton BD19 116 E7
10 Halifax HX3 113 B4
Parkside Ave Leeds LS6 59 F7
Queensbury BD13 72 D1
Parkside Cl Leeds LS6 59 F8
Todmorden OL14 86 B1
Parkside Cres LS6 59 F8
Parkside Ct BD22 51 E8
Parkside Gdns LS6 59 F7
Parkside Gn LS6 59 F7
Parkside Gr Bradford BD9 55 A3
Leeds LS11 214 A1
Parkside Ind Est LS11 214 C2
Parkside La Leeds LS11 214 C2
Lofthouse Gate WF3 121 E2
Parkside Middle Sch
BD13 52 E6
Parkside Mount LS11 214 A1
Parkside Par LS11 214 A1
Parkside Pl LS6 59 F8
Parkside Rd Bradford BD5 74 E2
Leeds LS16, LS6 59 E8
Pudsey LS28 57 D2
Todmorden OL14 86 B1
Parkside Row LS11 214 A1
Parkside Terr BD13 52 E6
Parkside View LS6 59 F8
Parkside Wlk LS28 57 E2
Parkstone HD2 136 F6
Parkstone Ave LS16 42 A1
Parkstone Dr BD10 56 C5
Parkstone Gn LS16 42 A1
Parkstone Gr LS16 42 A1
Parkstone Mount LS16 42 A1
Parkstone Pl LS16 42 A1
Parkview Ct Leeds LS8 44 B2
Shipley BD18 55 A7
Parkville Pl LS13 58 C3
Parkville Rd LS13 58 C3
Parkway Bradford BD5 74 F2
Crofton WF4 143 F2
Gildersome LS27 97 D6
Keighley BD21 35 C5
Queensbury BD13 72 D1
Steeton BD20 17 B5
Parkway Cl LS14 61 E4
Parkway Ct LS14 61 E3
Parkway Grange LS14 61 E3
Parkway Mews LS14 62 B5
Parkway Towers LS14 61 E4
Parkway Vale
Leeds, Brooklands LS14 61 F4
Leeds, Parklands LS14 62 A4
Parkways LS26 101 B6
Parkways Ave LS26 101 B5
Parkways Cl LS26 101 B6
Parkways Ct LS26 101 B6
Parkways Dr LS26 101 B6
Parkways Garth LS26 101 B5
Parkways Gr LS26 101 B6
Parkwood Ave LS8 61 A7
Parkwood Cl HD8 173 F3
Parkwood First Sch BD21 35 D6
Parkwood Gdns LS28 57 A6
Parkwood Rd
Huddersfield HD3, HD7 152 E6
Pudsey LS28 57 B6
Shipley BD18 54 F7
Parkwood Rise BD21 35 C6
Parkwood St BD21 35 D7
Parkwood Way LS8 61 A7
Parliament Pl LS12 210 A3
Parliament Rd LS12 210 A3
Parliament St WF2 216 A2
Parlington Ct LS15 63 E7
Parlington Dr LS25 64 E7
Parlington House LS25 64 D7
Parlington La LS25 64 C4
Parlington Meadow LS15 63 E6
Parlington Villas LS25 64 E7
Parma St BD5 201 B1
Parnaby Ave LS10 215 F1
Parnaby Rd LS10 215 F1
Parnaby St LS10 215 F1
Parnaby Terr LS10 215 F1
Parratt Row BD3 75 D7
Parrock La HX7 89 B6
Parrott St BD4 75 D1
Parry Cl BD16 36 A1
Parry La BD4 75 C5
Parson La WF4 178 A8
Parson St BD21 35 D8
Parson's La LS29 6 C8
Parsonage La HD6 115 A2
Parsonage Rd
Bradford BD5 74 E3
Bradford, Tyersal BD4 75 D5
Mickletown LS26 102 D3
Parsonage St S6 92 D1
Parsons Gn LS22 13 F5
Parsons Rd BD9 55 A4
Partons Pl WF3 121 C6
Partridge Cl 5 LS27 98 D4
Partridge Cres WF12 139 F1
Pasture Ave LS7 204 A3
Pasture Cl BD14 73 E4
Pasture Cres LS7 204 A3
Pasture Dr WF10 124 A6
Pasture Fold LS29 9 E2
Pasture Gr LS7 204 A3
Pasture La
Bradford BD14, BD7 73 D4
Leeds LS7 204 A3
Pasture Mount LS12 209 E4
Pasture Par LS7 204 A3
Pasture Pl LS7 204 A3
Pasture Rd Baildon BD17 38 D2
Leeds LS8 207 F4
Pasture Rise BD14 73 D4
Pasture Side Terr E
BD14 73 D4
Pasture Side Terr W 4
BD14 73 C4
Pasture St LS7 204 A3
Pasture Terr LS7 204 A3
Pasture View LS12 209 E4
Pasture View Rd LS26 100 E5
Pasture Way WF10 124 A6
Pasture Wlk BD14 73 C4
Pastures Way HD7 152 D5
Pateley Cres HD2 136 A2
Patent St BD9 55 B2
Paternoster La 10 BD7 74 A4
Paterson Ave WF2 142 A6
Patience La WF6 122 F3
Patterdale App LS22 13 B5
Patterdale Dr HD5 154 D6
Patterdale Rd WF12 118 E2
Patterson Ct WF2 120 F3
Pattie St BD20 18 B1
Paul La Kirkheaton HD5 137 C4
Lepton HD8 156 C2
Paul Row OL15 129 D1
Pauline Terr WF10 124 C7
Pavement La HX2 91 E8
Pavement St 15 BD19 116 E7
Pavilion Cl S72 181 A3
Pavilion Ct BD4 95 C8
Paw La BD13 92 F7
Pawson St Bradford BD4 75 D6
East Ardsley WF3 120 E8
Morley LS27 97 F3
Rothwell WF3 100 B2
Peabody St 6 HX3 92 A1
Peace Hall Dr HD8 155 C5
Peace St BD4 75 C5
Peach Tree Cl WF8 146 B6
Peach Wlk BD4 75 B4
Peacock Ave WF2 141 F7
Peacock Cl WF2 141 F7
Peacock Ct LS19 40 D6
Peacock Gn LS27 98 D3
Peacock Gr WF2 141 F7
Peak View WF13 117 F2
Pear Pl 3 OL14 86 B1
Pear St Halifax HX1 202 B2
Huddersfield HD4 153 E4
Keighley BD21 35 A3
Oxenhope BD22 51 C2
4 Todmorden OL14 86 B1
Pear Tree Acre LS23 30 E7
Pear Tree Cl WF8 146 B6
Pear Tree Ct BD20 5 E2
Pear Tree La WF9 181 D7
Pearl St Batley WF17 118 A6
12 Keighley BD22 35 A4
Pearson Ave 13 LS6 205 E3
Pearson Fold BD12 94 F4
Pearson Gr LS6 205 E3
Pearson La BD9 54 D1
Pearson Rd 11 BD6 94 D8
Pearson Rd W 4 BD6 94 D8
Pearson Row 3 BD12 94 D3
Pearson St Bradford BD3 75 C6
Cleckheaton, Hartshead Moor Side
BD19 116 A6
Cleckheaton, Marsh BD19 116 E6
Leeds LS10 212 A1
Normanton WF6 123 A5
Pudsey LS28 57 B7
Pearson Terr 14 LS6 205 E3
Pearson's La WF12 156 F7
Pearsons Bldgs LS21 23 B7
Peartree Field La WF8 165 D5
Peas Acre BD16 36 E8
Peasborough View
LS29 21 F8
Pease Cl WF8 146 D6
Peasehill Cl LS19 40 C4
Peasehill Pk LS19 40 C4
Peaseland Ave BD19 116 C7
Peaseland Cl BD19 116 D7
Peaseland Rd BD19 116 D7
Peaselands BD18 55 A7
Peat Ponds HD3 134 E1
Peckett Cl HD3 153 C7
Peckfield Bar LS25 83 D4
Peckover Dr LS28 76 A8
Peckover St BD1 201 C3
Peebles Cl HD3 135 B1
Peebles Wlk WF6 123 D1
Peel Ave WF17 118 C5
Peel Cl Bradford BD4 75 E6
Horbury WF4 141 B1
Peel Cottage Rd OL14 108 A1
Peel Cottage St 5
OL14 108 A1
Peel Ct BD2 56 A2
Peel Dr OL13 106 B1
Peel House BD16 37 B2
Peel Park Dr BD2 56 B2
Peel Park Terr BD2 56 B2
Peel Park View BD3 56 A1
Peel Pl LS29 9 E2
Peel Row BD7 74 A4
Peel St Bingley BD16 37 B3
Horbury WF4 141 B1
5 Huddersfield HD1 154 A5
Liversedge WF16 117 C4
Marsden HD7 168 F4
Morley LS27 98 B4
Queensbury BD13 72 F1
8 Sowerby Bridge HX6 112 B4
Thornton BD13 72 D6
Wilsden BD15 53 C4
Peep Green Rd WF15 116 C2
Pegholme Dr LS21 22 D6
Pelham Ct BD2 56 B3
Pelham Pl LS7 60 C7
Pelham Rd BD2 56 B3
Pell Ct HD7 189 C7
Pell La HD7 189 C7
Pellon La HX1 202 C4
Pellon New Rd HX1, HX2 202 B4
Pellon St OL14 108 A2
Pellon Terr BD10 39 B1
Pellon Wlk BD10 39 B1
Pemberton Dr BD7 74 D6
Pemberton Rd WF10 125 B8
Pembridge Ct S71 179 C4
Pembroke Cl LS27 97 F5
Pembroke Ct HD4 153 B2
Pembroke Dr Morley LS27 97 F5
5 Pudsey LS28 76 E8
Pembroke Gdns LS9 61 D2
Pembroke Rd LS28 76 E8
Pembroke Rise LS25 83 C2
Pembroke St BD5 74 E4
Pembroke Towers LS9 61 D3
Pembury Mount LS15 62 F3
Penarth Ave WF9 183 A7
Penarth Rd LS15 62 B2
Penarth Terr WF9 182 F7
Penda's Dr LS15 62 D2
Penda's Gr LS15 62 D3
Penda's Way LS15 62 E3
Penda's Wlk LS15 62 D2
Pendennis Ave WF9 182 F4
Pendil Cl LS15 81 C8
Pendle Ave OL13 106 A3
Pendle Cl OL13 106 A2
Pendle Rd BD16 37 B3
Pendragon BD2 56 A3
Pendragon La BD2 56 B3
Pendragon Terr LS20 39 D8
Penfield Gr BD14 73 C4
Penfield Rd BD11 96 F6
Pengarth BD16 37 C5
Penistone Hill Country Pk
BD22 51 A6
Penistone La HD8 190 D6
Penistone Mews BD22 51 C7
Penistone Rd
Denby Dale HD7, HD8, S36 191 C3
Holmfirth, Hade Edge HD7 199 D7
Holmfirth, Lane Head
HD7, HD8 190 C6
Huddersfield HD8 155 C3
Kirkburton HD8 173 E5
Lepton HD8 155 C3
Shepley HD8 173 E5
Shepley, Lane Head
HD7, HD8 190 C6
Penlands Cres LS15 81 D7
Penlands Lawn LS15 81 D7
Penlands Wlk LS15 81 D7
Penlington Cl WF9 181 D5
Penn Cl BD2 56 B4
Penn Dr WF15 116 D6
Penn Gr WF15 116 D6
Penn St HX1 202 C4
Pennine Cl Holmfirth HD7 188 D5
Queensbury BD13 92 D7
Wakefield WF2 141 E3
Pennine Cres HD3 152 E8
Pennine Dr HD8 175 D2
Pennine Gdns HD7 152 D1
Pennine Gr OL14 108 C6
Pennine Rd Bacup OL13 106 A2
Dewsbury WF12 139 E8
Pennine Rise HD8 175 D2
Pennine View Batley WF17 97 A2
Blackshaw Head HX7 87 F4
Kirkheaton HD5 137 C2
Mapplewell S75 178 A2
Slaithwaite HD7 152 D1
Upton WF9 183 A8
Pennine Way
Clayton West HD8 175 D2
Hebden Bridge HX7 88 D1
Hemsworth WF9 181 F7
Heptonstall HX7 88 B6
Pennington Ct 12 LS6 206 A4
Pennington Gr 14 LS6 206 A4
Pennington La LS26 101 B2
Pennington Pl 1 LS6 206 A3
Pennington St LS6 206 A4
Pennington Terr
Bradford BD5 74 C4
13 Leeds LS6 206 A4
Pennithorne Ave BD17 38 C4
Pennwell Croft 6 LS14 62 D5
Pennwell Dean LS14 62 D5
Pennwell Fold LS14 62 E5
Pennwell Garth LS14 62 D5
Pennwell Gn LS14 62 D5
Pennwell Lawn LS14 62 E5
Penny Hill Ctr The LS10 215 E4
Penny Hill Dr BD14 73 D4
Penny La HD5 155 B5
Penny Lane Way LS10 215 D4
Penny Spring HD5 154 E3
Pennyfield Sch LS6 42 F1
Pennygate BD16 37 D6
Penraevon Ave LS7 206 C3
Penraevon Ind Est LS7 206 C3
Penraevon Ind Units LS7 206 C3
Penrith Cres WF10 104 E1
Penrith Gr LS12 209 F2
Penrose Beck Dr WF7 163 F5
Penrose Dr BD7 73 F3
Penrose Pl
Crigglestone WF2 159 F5
Northowram HX3 93 A2
Penryn Ave HD5 155 C8
Pentland Ave
Bradford BD14 73 C4
Knottingley WF11 126 E4
Pentland Cl BD22 35 A6
Pentland County Infants
Sch WF12 139 D6
Pentland Dr LS25 82 F5
Pentland Gr WF2 141 E3
Pentland Rd WF12 139 D6
Pentland Way 1 LS27 98 A3
Pepper Gdns LS13 58 E4
Pepper Hill HX3 93 A6
Pepper Hills LS17 43 D4
Pepper La Leeds LS10 215 F3
Leeds, Moorside LS13 58 D4
Pepper Rd LS10 215 F2
Pepper Royd St WF13 118 D1
Per La HX2 91 D8
Percival St Bradford BD3 201 D3
Huddersfield HD3 152 F6
Leeds LS2 206 B1
Percy St Bingley BD16 37 A3
Huddersfield HD2 136 A1
Keighley BD21 35 C4
Leeds LS12 210 A2
South Kirkby WF9 182 B2
Peregrine Ave LS27 98 D4
Peregrine Ct HD4 171 E7
Peridot Fold HD2 136 C2
Permain Ct HD4 154 B4
Perry Cl BD22 35 A4
Perserverance St LS28 76 C7
Perseverance La 12 BD7 74 A4
Perseverance Rd
Halifax BD13 72 A3
Queensbury BD13 72 A3
Perseverance St
Baildon BD17 38 D4
Bradford BD12 94 C4
4 Castleford WF10 124 D8
Huddersfield HD4 154 A3
13 Sowerby Bridge HX6 112 B5
Perseverance Terr
Batley WF17 118 C3
Halifax HX1 202 C1
Rothwell LS26 100 E4
Perseverence St HD4 153 A3
Perth Ave BD2 55 E3
Perth Dr WF3 119 F8
Perth Mount LS18 41 B4
Peter Hill WF17 118 D2
Peter La Halifax HX2 112 B7
Morley LS27 98 D4
Peter Laycock Ind Est
LS7 206 C3
Peterborough Pl BD2 56 B3
Peterborough Rd BD2 56 B2
Peterborough Terr BD2 56 B3
Petergate BD1 201 C3
Peterhouse Dr LS21 23 C7
Petersfield Ave LS10 99 E7
Petersgarth 5 BD18 54 E8
Peterson Rd WF1 216 C2
Pether Hill HX4 133 F3
Petrel Way LS27 98 C3
Petrie Cres LS13 57 D5
Petrie Gr BD3 75 E7
Petrie Rd BD3 75 E7
Petrie St LS13 57 D5
Petworth Croft S71 179 B4
Peverell Cl BD4 75 E3
Peveril Mount BD2 56 C3
Pexwood Rd OL14 107 F3
Pheasant Dr WF17 97 A3

Pheasant St BD21 .... 35 D8
Phil May Ct LS12 .... 210 B2
Philip Garth WF1 .... 121 C5
Philip's Gr WF3 .... 121 C6
Philip's La WF8 .... 147 C5
Philippa Way LS12 .... 78 C3
Philips Rd OL13 .... 106 A7
Phillips St WF10 .... 124 B8
Phoebe La HX3 .... 113 D4
Phoebe Lane Ind Est
HX3 .... 113 D4
Phoenix Ave HD8 .... 175 D6
Phoenix Ct Batley WF17 .... 118 F5
Todmorden OL14 .... 108 D6
Wakefield WF2 .... 142 A6
Phoenix St Brighouse HD6 .... 115 B2
Todmorden OL14 .... 108 D6
Phoenix Way BD4 .... 75 E6
Piccadilly Bradford BD1 .... 201 B3
Wakefield WF2 .... 216 A2
Pick Hill Rd HD7 .... 170 D3
Pickard Ct LS15 .... 81 C8
Pickard La BD20 .... 5 E2
Pickard Way WF13 .... 118 B1
Picker St OL14 .... 107 E8
Pickering Ave LS25 .... 83 B8
Pickering Dr WF5 .... 119 C1
Pickering La WF5 .... 119 C1
Pickering Mount LS12 .... 210 A4
Pickering St LS12 .... 210 A4
Pickerings The BD13 .... 92 E8
Pickersgill St WF5 .... 140 C8
Pickford St HD3 .... 153 A4
Pickle Top HD7 .... 151 E2
Pickles Ct 13 OL14 .... 108 B6
Pickles Hill BD22 .... 33 F1
Pickles La Bradford BD7 .... 73 F2
Skelmanthorpe HD8 .... 175 B1
Pickles St Batley WF17 .... 118 B2
13 Keighley BD21 .... 35 B5
Picklesfield WF17 .... 118 B2
Pickthall Terr OL14 .... 108 D5
Pickwood La HX6 .... 112 E2
Picton St BD8 .... 55 D1
Picton Way HD5 .... 155 A7
Pictureville BD1 .... 201 B2
Piece Hall Mus HX1 .... 203 F3
Piece Hall Yd BD1 .... 201 B3
Piece Wood Rd LS16 .... 41 D3
Pigeon Cote Cl LS14 .... 62 A6
Pigeon Cote Rd LS14 .... 62 A6
Piggott St HD6 .... 115 A3
Pighill Top La HD7 .... 151 F2
Pike End Rd HX6 .... 150 C7
Pike Law HD7 .... 152 B5
Pike Law La HD7 .... 152 B5
Pike Law Rd HD7 .... 152 B5
Pildacre Brow WF5 .... 140 C6
Pildacre Croft WF5 .... 140 C6
Pildacre La WF5 .... 140 B6
Pilden La WF3 .... 120 C7
Pilgrim Ave WF13 .... 138 F7
Pilgrim Cres WF13 .... 138 F7
Pilgrim Dr WF13 .... 138 F7
Pilkington St WF2 .... 142 C4
Pill White La LS21 .... 11 F6
Pilling La HD8 .... 175 C2
Pilling Top La HD8 .... 174 C4
Pilmer Ct WF2 .... 141 D4
Pilot St LS9 .... 207 E1
Pin Hill La HX2 .... 90 D1
Pincheon St WF1 .... 216 C2
Pinder Ave LS12 .... 77 F4
Pinder Gr LS12 .... 77 F4
Pinder St LS12 .... 77 F4
Pinder View LS12 .... 77 F4
Pinder's Gr WF1 .... 142 E8
Pinderfields
General Hospl WF1 .... 121 D1
Pinderfields Rd WF1 .... 216 B3
Pinders Cres WF11 .... 126 C5
Pinders Garth WF11 .... 126 D5
Pinders Green Ct LS26 .... 102 C1
Pinders Green Dr LS26 .... 102 C1
Pinders Green Fold LS26 .... 102 C1
Pinders Green Wlk LS26 .... 123 C8
Pinders Prim Jun
& Inf Sch WF1 .... 216 C3
Pine Cl Castleford WF10 .... 124 E6
Wetherby LS22 .... 13 E7
Pine Court Mews HD4 .... 171 D6
Pine Croft BD20 .... 18 A1
Pine Ct Huddersfield HD4 .... 171 D6
2 Leeds LS2 .... 212 A3
Pine Gr WF17 .... 118 B3
Pine Rd OL14 .... 107 F7
Pine St 7 Bacup OL13 .... 106 A1
Bradford BD1 .... 201 C4
Halifax HX1 .... 203 E2
Haworth BD22 .... 51 C6
Huddersfield HD1 .... 154 B7
South Elmsall WF9 .... 182 E1
Pine Tree Ave
Boston Spa LS23 .... 30 E8
Pontefract WF8 .... 146 B6
Pineapple Cotts WF1 .... 143 E6
Pinedale BD16 .... 36 F5
Pinehurst Ct HD3 .... 135 B1
Pines Gdns LS29 .... 7 F3
Pinewood Ave WF2 .... 141 D6
Pinewood Cl LS29 .... 8 A3
Pinewood Gdns HX4 .... 134 B4
Pinewood Pl WF11 .... 126 E3
Pinfold Cl Dewsbury WF12 .... 139 E2
Flockton WF4 .... 157 C2
Knottingley WF11 .... 126 C5
Mirfield WF14 .... 138 B5
Ripponden HX4 .... 133 A5
Pinfold Cross WF8 .... 166 D5
Pinfold Ct LS15 .... 81 B8
Pinfold Dr WF4 .... 144 A1
Pinfold Gr Leeds LS15 .... 81 A8
Wakefield WF2 .... 142 E1
Pinfold Hill
Dewsbury WF13 .... 139 B7
Leeds LS15 .... 81 B8
Pinfold La
Brighouse HD6 .... 135 D5
Flockton WF4 .... 157 C2
Garforth LS25 .... 82 F7
Kirk Smeaton WF8 .... 166 D5
Leeds LS16 .... 41 F7
Leeds LS12 .... 209 E3
Leeds, Halton LS15 .... 81 A8
Lepton HD8 .... 156 A3
Marsden HD3 .... 151 C5
Mickletown LS26 .... 102 E2
Mirfield WF14 .... 138 C5
Royston S71 .... 179 C2
Slaithwaite HD7 .... 152 A4
Sowerby Bridge HX6 .... 111 E4
Wakefield WF2 .... 142 E1
Pinfold Mount LS15 .... 81 B7
Pinfold Rd LS15 .... 81 B7
Pinfold Rise LS25 .... 64 E8
Pinfold Sq LS15 .... 81 A8
Pingle Rise HD8 .... 192 A7
Pink St BD22 .... 51 C6
Pinnacle La HX7 .... 109 E8
Pinnar Croft HX3 .... 114 A4
Pinnar La HX3 .... 113 F5
Pioneer St Dewsbury WF12 .... 139 C4
Todmorden OL14 .... 129 A7
Pioneer Way WF10 .... 123 F4
Pipe & Nook La LS12 .... 77 F7
Piper Hill WF11 .... 105 A4
Piper La LS21 .... 22 F7
Piper Well La HD8 .... 190 E6
Pipercroft BD6 .... 93 E6
Pipet Mdw LS27 .... 98 C3
Pippins App WF6 .... 123 B3
Pippins Green Ave WF2 .... 120 B2
Pirie Cl BD2 .... 55 F3
Pit Field Rd WF3 .... 100 D2
Pit La Batley WF13 .... 117 F2
Cleckheaton BD19 .... 96 B2
Denholme BD13 .... 52 C1
Micklefield LS25 .... 83 F5
Mickletown LS26 .... 102 D4
Queensbury BD13 .... 72 C4
Thornton BD13 .... 72 C4
Pitcliffe Way BD5 .... 74 F4
Pitfall St LS1 .... 211 F3
Pits La BD19 .... 115 F6
Pitt Hill La HX4 .... 133 D2
Pitt Row LS1 .... 211 F3
Pitt St Keighley BD21 .... 35 D7
Liversedge WF15 .... 117 B2
Todmorden OL14 .... 108 D5
Pitts St BD4 .... 75 D4
Place's Rd LS9 .... 212 B3
Plaid Row LS9 .... 212 B4
Plain La HX6 .... 111 C2
Plains HD7 .... 169 A5
Plains La Halifax HX5 .... 134 F8
Marsden HD7 .... 169 A5
Plane Gn WF8 .... 125 F1
Plane St Huddersfield HD4 .... 154 B3
Todmorden OL14 .... 107 E7
Plane Tree Ave LS17 .... 43 F4
Plane Tree Cl LS17 .... 43 F4
Plane Tree Croft LS17 .... 43 F4
Plane Tree Gdns LS17 .... 43 F4
Plane Tree Gr LS19 .... 40 D6
Plane Tree Nest HX2 .... 202 A2
Plane Tree Nest La HX2 .... 202 A1
Plane Tree Rd HX6 .... 112 B5
Plane Tree Rise LS17 .... 43 F4
Plane Tree View LS17 .... 43 F4
Plane Trees Cl BD19 .... 95 D3
Planet Earth OL14 .... 106 F4
Planetrees Rd BD4 .... 75 C6
Planetrees St BD15 .... 54 A1
Plantation Ave
Leeds, Blackwood LS17 .... 44 A5
Leeds, Halton LS15 .... 81 A7
Royston S71 .... 179 D3
Plantation Dr HD4 .... 154 A1
Plantation Fold BD22 .... 34 F4
Plantation Gdns LS17 .... 44 B5
Plantation Pl BD4 .... 75 C4
Plantation Way BD17 .... 38 D3
Platt La HD7 .... 152 A1
Platt Sq 7 BD19 .... 116 D7
Playfair Rd LS10 .... 215 D2
Playground LS12 .... 77 D3
Playhouse Sq LS2 .... 212 A4
Playhouse The HX1 .... 203 D2
Pleasance The LS26 .... 82 A1
Pleasant Ct 2 LS6 .... 206 A3
Pleasant Mount LS11 .... 211 D1
Pleasant Pl LS11 .... 211 D1
Pleasant St Bradford BD7 .... 74 A4
Leeds LS11 .... 211 D1
Sowerby Bridge HX6 .... 112 C4
Pleasant Terr LS11 .... 211 D1
Pleasant View WF2 .... 120 F7
Pledwick Cres WF2 .... 160 D6
Pledwick Dr WF2 .... 160 D5
Pledwick Gr WF2 .... 160 C5
Pledwick La WF2 .... 160 D5
Pledwick Rise WF2 .... 160 D5
Plevna St LS10 .... 80 A2
Plevna Terr BD16 .... 36 F4
Plimsoll St Bradford BD4 .... 75 A4
Hemsworth WF9 .... 181 D7
Ploughcroft La HX3 .... 92 C3
Ploughmans Croft BD2 .... 55 E4
Plover Dr WF17 .... 117 F5
Plover Rd HD3 .... 153 B8
Plover St Bradford BD5 .... 74 C3
Keighley BD21 .... 35 C8
Plover Way LS27 .... 98 D3
Plum St Halifax HX1 .... 202 B2
Keighley BD21 .... 35 A3
Plum Tree Cl WF8 .... 146 B6
Plumpton Ave BD2 .... 55 F6
Plumpton Cl BD2 .... 56 A5
Plumpton Dr BD2 .... 55 F6
Plumpton End BD2 .... 56 A6
Plumpton Gdns BD2 .... 55 F6
Plumpton Lea BD2 .... 55 F6
Plumpton Mead BD2 .... 55 F6
Plumpton Pl WF2 .... 142 A6
Plumpton Rd WF2 .... 142 A6
Plumpton St Bradford BD8 .... 74 A8
Wakefield WF2 .... 142 A6
Plumpton Terr WF2 .... 142 A5
Plumpton Wlk BD2 .... 55 F6
Plymouth Gr HX1 .... 202 C4
Poet's Pl LS18 .... 41 C2
Pog Hall HD7 .... 170 C8
Pohlman St 4 HX1 .... 202 B1
Pole Gate HD7 .... 151 D4
Pole Gate Branch HD7 .... 151 D4
Pole Rd BD22 .... 33 F8
Pollard Ave Bingley BD16 .... 37 B5
Cleckheaton BD19 .... 96 B1
Pollard Cl BD19 .... 96 B1
Pollard La Bradford BD2 .... 56 B1
Leeds LS13 .... 58 C5
Pudsey LS13 .... 58 C5
Pollard Park Middle Sch
BD3 .... 75 B8
Pollard St Bradford BD4 .... 201 C1
Huddersfield HD2 .... 136 B2
Lofthouse Gate WF3 .... 121 C6
1 Shipley BD16 .... 54 B6
Todmorden OL14 .... 107 E8
Pollard St N HX3 .... 203 F4
Pollard St S HD3 .... 153 B4
Pollard Way BD19 .... 96 B1
Pollard's Fields WF11 .... 126 B5
Pollit Ave HX6 .... 111 F3
Pollums La WF11 .... 105 B6
Polperro Cl WF6 .... 123 B3
Pomfret Ct WF8 .... 147 A8
Pomfret Pl LS25 .... 83 B8
Pond Cl HD4 .... 153 F2
Pond La HD8 .... 156 A2
Pond St BD21 .... 35 C8
Ponden La BD22 .... 50 A7
Pondfields Cl LS25 .... 83 B2
Pondfields Crest LS25 .... 83 B2
Pondfields Dr LS25 .... 83 B2
Pondfields Rise LS25 .... 83 B2
Ponker La HD8 .... 174 E1
Ponker Nook La HD8 .... 174 F1
Pontefract Ave LS9 .... 212 C3
Pontefract Castle WF8 .... 125 E1
Pontefract CE Sch WF8 .... 125 D1
Pontefract General Infmy
WF8 .... 146 D8
Pontefract La LS15, LS9 .... 80 C5
Pontefract Lane Cl LS9 .... 212 C3
Pontefract Mus WF8 .... 146 D8
Pontefract Rd
Ackworth M T WF7 .... 164 A8
Castleford WF10 .... 124 E7
Crofton WF4 .... 144 A2
Cudworth S72 .... 180 C1
Featherstone WF7 .... 145 E5
Hemsworth WF9 .... 163 F2
Knottingley WF11 .... 126 B4
Knottingley, Ferrybridge Hill
WF11 .... 126 D4
Leeds LS10, LS26 .... 80 B2
Normanton WF6 .... 123 D3
Pontefract St LS9 .... 212 C3
Pontefract Terr WF9 .... 181 E6
Pontey Dr HD5 .... 155 B5
Pontey Mount HD5 .... 155 B5
Pool Bank Cl LS21 .... 24 D7
Pool Bank Ct LS21 .... 24 D6
Pool Bank New Rd
Bramhope LS21 .... 24 D5
Leathley LS21 .... 24 C5
Pool Ct BD3 .... 75 A7
Pool Hill La HD8 .... 192 D6
Pool in Wharfedale C of E
Primary Sch LS21 .... 24 D7
Pool Rd Leathley LS21 .... 24 B7
Otley LS21 .... 23 C8
Pool St BD21 .... 18 E1
Poole Cres LS15 .... 62 B1
Poole Mount LS15 .... 62 B1
Poole Rd LS15 .... 62 B1
Poole Row LS25 .... 105 E3
Poole Sq LS15 .... 62 B1
Pools La S71 .... 179 E3
Pope St Keighley BD21 .... 35 D8
Normanton WF6 .... 123 C5
Popeley Rd WF16 .... 117 C6
Poplar Ave Bradford BD7 .... 73 F2
Castleford WF10 .... 125 C7
Garforth LS25 .... 82 E6
Holmfirth HD7 .... 172 C1
Leeds LS15 .... 62 D2
Shafton S72 .... 180 C2
Shipley BD18 .... 55 C5
Sowerby Bridge HX6 .... 112 C5
Todmorden OL14 .... 108 A7
Wakefield WF2 .... 141 E5
Wetherby LS22 .... 13 E7
Poplar Cl Burley in W LS29 .... 21 F8
Leeds LS13 .... 77 F8
Poplar Court LS13 .... 77 E8
Poplar Cres Halifax HX2 .... 91 F7
Morley LS27 .... 98 C1
Shipley BD18 .... 55 C5
Poplar Croft LS13 .... 77 E8
Poplar Dr Horsforth LS18 .... 57 F8
Keighley BD20 .... 36 C7
Normanton WF6 .... 123 A5
Shipley BD18 .... 55 C5
Poplar Garth LS13 .... 77 E8
Poplar Gdns LS13 .... 77 E8
Poplar Gn Leeds LS13 .... 77 E8
Pontefract WF8 .... 125 F1
Poplar Gr Bradford BD7 .... 73 F2
Cleckheaton BD19 .... 116 C6
Harden BD16 .... 36 A1
Knottingley WF11 .... 126 E2
Pontefract WF8 .... 146 B8
Shipley BD18 .... 55 C5
Poplar House 3 WF10 .... 124 E7
Poplar Mount LS13 .... 77 E8
Poplar Rd Bradford BD7 .... 74 A2
Shipley BD18 .... 55 C6
Poplar Rise Leeds LS13 .... 58 E1
Skelmanthorpe HD8 .... 175 B1
Poplar Sq 13 LS28 .... 57 D2
Poplar St Halifax HX3 .... 203 E4
Huddersfield, Fartown
HD2 .... 136 A1
11 Huddersfield, Moldgreen
HD5 .... 154 D5
Lofthouse Gate WF3 .... 121 C6
Poplar Terr
17 Huddersfield HD5 .... 154 D5
14 Keighley BD21 .... 35 A7
Keighley, Crossflatts BD20 .... 36 D7
Royston S71 .... 179 D4
South Elmsall WF9 .... 183 A2
Poplar View Bradford BD7 .... 73 E2
Brighouse HX3 .... 115 B6
Leeds LS13 .... 77 E8
Poplar Way LS13 .... 77 E8
Poplars Farm First Sch
BD2 .... 55 E4
Poplars Park Rd BD2 .... 55 E4
Poplars The Bramhope LS16 .... 24 F2
Guiseley LS20 .... 22 E2
Knottingley WF11 .... 127 B2
Leeds LS6 .... 205 E4
Lofthouse Gate WF3 .... 121 C8
Sutton in C BD20 .... 16 C4
Poplarwood Gdns BD10 .... 56 E5
Popley Butts HD7 .... 170 C1
Popley Dr HD7 .... 170 D1
Popple Wells La HX2 .... 112 A7
Popples HX2 .... 91 F7
Popples Dr HX2 .... 91 F7
Popples Side HX7 .... 88 D6
Poppleton Ct 1 WF3 .... 98 E1
Poppleton Dr WF3 .... 98 E1
Poppleton Rd WF3 .... 98 E1
Poppleton Rise WF3 .... 119 E8
Poppleton Way WF3 .... 119 E8
Porchester House 4
HD5 .... 154 D6
Porritt St BD19 .... 95 D1
Portage Ave LS15 .... 80 F7
Portage Cres LS15 .... 80 F7
Portal Cres WF14 .... 138 A8
Portal Dr WF14 .... 138 A8
Portland Ave WF8 .... 125 B1
Portland Cl HD3 .... 153 C7
Portland Cres LS1 .... 206 B1
Portland Ct BD21 .... 35 B6
Portland Gate LS1 .... 206 B1
Portland House 14 HX5 .... 134 F7
Portland Pl Bingley BD16 .... 37 A2
Halifax HX1 .... 203 E2
Upton WF9 .... 183 A7
Portland Rd Halifax HX3 .... 203 F4
Leeds LS12 .... 209 F2
Portland St Bradford BD5 .... 201 B2
Halifax HX1 .... 203 E3
Haworth BD22 .... 51 D7
Huddersfield HD1 .... 153 F6
Leeds LS1 .... 211 E4
Pudsey LS28 .... 77 A7
Wakefield WF1 .... 142 F3
Portland Way LS1 .... 206 B1
Portman St LS28 .... 57 B6
Portobello Gr WF2 .... 142 D3
Portobello Rd WF1, WF2 .... 142 D3
Portree House 7 BD6 .... 93 E8
Portsmouth Ave BD3 .... 55 F1
Portwood St BD9 .... 54 D2
Post Hill Ct LS12 .... 77 D7
Post Office Rd
Bradford BD2 .... 56 C5
Featherstone WF7 .... 145 D5
Post Office St BD19 .... 116 F6
Postcard Mus HD7 .... 189 A5
Pot La BD20 .... 17 C6
Pothouse Rd BD6 .... 94 B8
Potovens Ct WF3 .... 121 C6
Potovens La
Lofthouse Gate WF1 .... 121 B5
Wakefield WF2 .... 120 F4
Potter Ave WF2 .... 141 E4
Potter Brow Rd BD17 .... 38 C7
Potternewton Ave LS7 .... 60 B6
Potternewton Cres LS7 .... 60 B5
Potternewton Ct LS7 .... 60 C6
Potternewton Gdns LS7 .... 60 C6
Potternewton Gr LS7 .... 60 B6
Potternewton Heights LS7 .... 60 C6
Potternewton La LS7 .... 60 B6
Potternewton Mansion
Coll of F Ed LS7 .... 204 B1
Potternewton Mount LS7 .... 60 B6
Potternewton Primary Sch
LS7 .... 60 B5
Potternewton View LS7 .... 60 B6
Potters Croft WF3 .... 121 C6
Potters Gate HD8 .... 190 E1
Potters Wlk HD7 .... 152 E4
Potterton Cl LS15 .... 63 E8
Potterton Ct LS15 .... 63 E8
Potterton La LS15 .... 46 E2
Pottery La
Knottingley WF11 .... 126 D5
Rothwell LS26 .... 101 D7
Pottery Rd LS10 .... 215 D4
Pottery St Castleford WF10 .... 124 B8
Huddersfield HD3 .... 152 E8
Potts' Terr WF6 .... 144 B8
Poulton Pl LS11 .... 214 C3
Poverty La HX6 .... 111 A1
Powell Ave BD5 .... 74 C4
Powell Rd Bingley BD16 .... 37 B2
Shipley BD18 .... 55 D5
Powell St Batley WF16 .... 117 E3
Castleford WF10 .... 124 D8
10 Halifax HX1 .... 203 E3
South Kirkby WF9 .... 182 D3
Poxton Gr WF9 .... 182 E1
Prail Cl WF8 .... 125 F1
Pratt La Mirfield WF14 .... 138 A6
Shipley BD18 .... 55 C6
Precinct The WF7 .... 145 C5
Premiere Pk LS29 .... 7 E3
Prescott St HX1 .... 203 E2
Prescott Terr BD15 .... 54 B1
Preston La Halifax HX2 .... 91 D2
Swillington LS26 .... 102 E7
Preston Par LS11 .... 214 A2
Preston Pl HX1 .... 202 C3
Preston St Batley WF17 .... 118 C4
Bradford BD7 .... 74 C7
Dewsbury WF12 .... 139 E6
Preston Terr BD16 .... 36 E5
Preston View LS26 .... 82 B1
Prestwich Dr HD2 .... 135 F3
Prestwick Cl LS21 .... 22 D6
Pretoria St
Castleford WF10 .... 124 E7
Featherstone WF7 .... 145 C6
Slaithwaite HD7 .... 151 F1
Wakefield WF1 .... 142 D3
Priest Bank Rd BD20 .... 16 E8
Priest Hill Gdns LS22 .... 13 D8
Priest La HX6 .... 132 E4
Priest Royd S75 .... 178 A1
Priesthorpe Ave LS28 .... 57 B2
Priesthorpe Ct LS28 .... 57 D4
Priesthorpe High Sch LS28 .... 57 B2
Priesthorpe La LS28 .... 57 B3
Priesthorpe Rd LS28 .... 57 B4
Priestley Ave Batley WF16 .... 117 D6
Bradford BD6 .... 94 C8
Priestley Cl LS28 .... 76 F8
Priestley Dr LS28 .... 76 F8
Priestley Gdns
Liversedge WF16 .... 117 C5
Pudsey LS28 .... 76 F8
Priestley Gn HX3 .... 93 E1
Priestley Gr HD4 .... 153 F1
Priestley Hill BD13 .... 92 C6
Priestley Pl HX6 .... 112 A3
Priestley Sq WF17 .... 96 E2
Priestley St Bradford BD1 .... 201 C4
Thornton BD13 .... 72 D6
Priestley Terr 1 BD6 .... 74 C1
Priestley View LS28 .... 76 F8
Priestley Wlk LS28 .... 76 F8
Priestly Ct LS28 .... 76 F8
Priestman Cl BD8 .... 55 C1
Priestman Middle Sch
BD5 .... 74 C2
Priestman St BD8 .... 55 C1
Priestthorpe Cl BD16 .... 37 A4
Priestthorpe First Sch
BD16 .... 37 A3
Priestthorpe La BD16 .... 37 A4
Priestthorpe Rd BD16 .... 37 A4
Priestwell St OL14 .... 108 C6
Primitive St
8 Huddersfield HD1 .... 154 B6
Rothwell WF3 .... 100 D3
Primley Gdns LS17 .... 43 C4
Primley Park Ave LS17 .... 43 D4
Primley Park Cl LS17 .... 43 D4
Primley Park Cres LS17 .... 43 C4
Primley Park Ct LS17 .... 43 C5
Primley Park Dr LS17 .... 43 D5
Primley Park Garth LS17 .... 43 D5
Primley Park Gn LS17 .... 43 D5
Primley Park Gr LS17 .... 43 C4
Primley Park La LS17 .... 43 D4
Primley Park Mount LS17 .... 43 D4
Primley Park Rd LS17 .... 43 C4
Primley Park Rise LS17 .... 43 D4
Primley Park View LS17 .... 43 D5
Primley Park Way LS17 .... 43 C5
Primley Park Wlk LS17 .... 43 D5
Primose Hill WF17 .... 118 D5
Primrose Ave 2 Leeds LS15 .... 81 A8
Swillington LS26 .... 82 B1
Primrose Bank BD16 .... 37 B2
Primrose Cl Leeds LS15 .... 81 A8
Pontefract WF8 .... 146 D7
Primrose Cres LS15 .... 62 A1

Primrose Dene WF11 126 D7
Primrose Dr Bingley BD16 37 C2
Castleford WF10 125 B6
Leeds LS15 81 A8
Primrose Garth 1 LS15 80 F8
Primrose Gdns
Batley WF17 118 E6
Leeds LS15 62 A1
Primrose Gr
Huddersfield HD4 154 A3
Keighley BD21 35 E7
Leeds LS15 62 A1
Primrose High Sch LS9 207 E1
Primrose Hill
Knottingley WF11 127 A5
5 Pudsey LS28 57 E1
Primrose Hill Cl LS26 82 B1
Primrose Hill Dr LS26 102 B8
Primrose Hill Garth LS26 102 B8
Primrose Hill Gdns LS26 82 B1
Primrose Hill Gn LS26 102 B8
Primrose Hill Gr LS26 82 B1
Primrose Hill High Sch (Annexe) LS8 207 E2
Primrose Hill Rd HD4 154 A4
Primrose House WF1 216 C1
Primrose La Bingley BD16 37 C2
Boston Spa LS23 30 C7
Crigglestone WF4 159 D6
Kirkburton HD8 173 D8
Leeds LS11 214 C3
Leeds, Halton LS15 81 A8
Liversedge WF15 116 F5
Mirfield WF14 138 C7
Shipley BD2 55 D4
Primrose Rd LS15 81 A8
Primrose Row BD17 38 F4
Primrose St
2 Bradford BD8 74 C8
Huddersfield HD4 154 A4
Keighley BD21 35 F7
Primrose Vale WF11 127 A4
Primrose Way HX3 93 D7
Primrose Wlk LS27 98 C8
Prince Edward Gr LS12 78 A4
Prince Edward Rd LS12 78 A4
Prince Henry Rd LS21 11 A1
Prince Henry's Grammar Sch LS21 11 A1
Prince St Batley WF17 118 C6
Bradford BD4 75 C2
2 Dewsbury WF13 139 D8
Haworth BD22 51 D7
Huddersfield HD4 154 B4
Kippax WF10 102 F7
Silsden BD20 5 D1
Prince William Ct WF7 145 C4
Prince Wood La HD2 135 C2
Prince's Ave LS8 61 B7
Prince's Cres BD2 55 E3
Prince's Ct LS17 43 C1
Prince's Gate HX3 113 B4
Prince's St Bradford BD6 94 B8
4 Bradford, Buttershaw BD6 93 E7
Prince's Way BD1 201 B2
Princeroyd Way BD7 74 A7
Princes St WF16 117 E4
Princess Alexandra Wlk 10 HD1 154 B6
Princess Ave
Dewsbury WF12 140 A8
South Elmsall WF9 182 F2
Princess Cl WF12 140 A8
Princess Cres WF12 140 A7
Princess Ct Leeds LS17 43 D3
Normanton WF6 123 C1
Princess Gdns 9 WF13 139 B8
Princess La WF12 140 A8
Princess of Wales Prec The 4 WF13 139 D8
Princess Rd
Dewsbury WF12 140 A7
Ilkley LS29 8 A3
Princess St
Batley WF17 118 C6
Brighouse HD6 115 B2
Castleford WF10 103 F1
Cudworth S72 180 C1
Dewsbury WF12 140 B8
3 Elland HX4 134 D7
Halifax HX1 203 E3
3 Huddersfield HD1 154 A5
Lofthouse Gate WF1 121 B4
Mapplewell S75 178 A1
Mirfield WF14 138 A4
Normanton WF6 123 B2
Sowerby Bridge HX6 112 C4
Wakefield WF1 142 E2
Yeadon LS19 40 A4
Princeville First Sch BD7 74 B6
Princeville Rd BD7 74 B7
Princeville St BD7 74 B6
Prior St BD21 35 D8
Prior's La BD23 1 E7
Priordale Rd WF7 145 B4
Priory Cl 7 Bingley BD16 37 A4
Mirfield WF14 137 E6
Normanton WF6 122 F4
Ossett WF5 140 D4
Wetherby LS22 13 F6
Priory Croft WF5 140 D5
Priory Ct BD8 74 D8
Priory Ctr Sch WF4 143 F2
Priory Estate WF9 183 B3
Priory Gr BD16 37 A4
Priory Grange WF8 125 E2
Priory Mews WF3 121 F6
Priory Pl HD2 136 F5
Priory Rd Brighouse HD6 115 C2
Featherstone WF7 145 C4
Ossett WF5 140 D5
Priory Ridge WF4 162 A8
Priory Sq WF2 161 A7
Priory Way WF14 137 E6
Priory Wlk WF14 137 E6
Privilege St LS12 209 E3
Proctor St BD4 75 D2
Prod La BD17 37 E2
Progress Ave BD16 36 A1
Prospect Ave Halifax HX2 112 E4
Leeds LS13 58 C3
Normanton WF6 123 B3
Pudsey LS28 76 D8
Shipley BD18 55 C7
Prospect Bank LS23 30 D3
Prospect Cl Halifax HX2 112 E4
Shipley BD18 55 C7
Prospect Cotts WF9 182 E3
Prospect Cres
Keighley BD22 34 E5
Leeds LS10 215 D3
Prospect Ct HX2 112 B8
Prospect Dr BD22 34 E5
Prospect Gdns 4 LS15 81 B8
Prospect Gr Pudsey LS28 76 D8
Shipley BD18 55 C7
Prospect La BD11 96 B5
Prospect Mount
Keighley BD22 34 E5
Shipley BD18 55 C7
Prospect Pl Bradford BD9 54 F1
Bradford, Fagley BD2 56 C2
Brighouse HX3 94 A2
2 Brighouse, Waring Green HD6 115 A2
Elland HD3 151 F8
Halifax HX2 91 F3
Horsforth LS18 58 B8
Leeds LS13 58 C3
13 Queensbury BD13 72 E1
Rothwell LS26 100 F4
Rothwell, Town End WF3 100 B2
Prospect Rd
Batley WF16 117 C6
Bingley BD16 37 C5
Bradford BD3 55 F1
Burley in W LS29 21 F8
Cleckheaton BD19 116 D7
Huddersfield HD3 152 F6
Liversedge WF15 116 D2
Ossett WF5 140 D5
Prospect Row Halifax HX2 91 F3
Menston LS29 21 C6
Prospect Sq 12 LS28 57 D2
Prospect St Batley WF17 118 C6
Bradford BD4 201 D1
Bradford, Bank Top BD10 56 C5
Bradford, Woodside BD6 93 F7
11 Cleckheaton BD19 116 D8
Glusburn BD20 16 D7
Halifax HX3 203 F4
7 Haworth BD22 51 C6
Horbury WF4 159 C8
Huddersfield HD1 154 A5
Keighley BD22 34 F6
Pudsey LS28 76 C8
Pudsey, Farsley LS28 57 D3
Shipley BD18 55 C7
Thornton BD13 72 E6
Yeadon LS19 40 C3
Prospect Terr
3 Batley WF13 117 F2
Bradford BD15 54 C1
Cleckheaton BD19 116 D8
Leeds LS13 58 C3
Liversedge WF15 117 A4
Low Bradley BD20 4 C6
Micklefield LS25 84 A6
3 Pudsey, Farsley LS28 57 D2
Pudsey, Rodley LS13 57 E5
Rothwell LS26 100 F4
South Kirkby WF9 182 B2
Prospect View
Leeds LS13 58 D3
Liversedge WF15 116 E2
Prospect Villas LS22 13 E6
Prospect Wlk BD18 55 C7
Prosper St LS10 215 E4
Providence Ave
Baildon BD17 38 C4
Leeds LS6 206 A4
Providence Bldgs HX3 114 A4
Providence Cres BD22 34 C2
Providence Ct
5 Morley LS27 98 A5
Oakworth BD22 34 C2
Providence Gn WF8 125 E3
Providence La BD22 34 C1
Providence Pl
5 Bradford BD12 94 C4
Brighouse HD6 115 C1
Garforth LS25 82 E7
Kippax WF10 103 B3
Leeds LS2 206 C1
4 Pudsey LS28 57 E1
Swillington LS15 82 A6
Providence Rd LS6 206 A4
Providence Row
Baildon BD17 38 C4
Halifax HX2 91 F3
Keighley BD20 19 E2
Providence St
Batley WF17 118 C5
Bradford BD1 201 A3
Brighouse BD12 94 E1
2 Cleckheaton BD19 116 E8
Dewsbury WF12 139 F7
18 Elland HX5 134 F7
Leeds LS9 212 B3
6 Pudsey LS28 57 D2
Todmorden OL14 129 A7
Wakefield WF1 216 B3
Providence Terr
Leeds LS2 206 A3
Thornton BD13 72 D6
Prune Park La BD15 53 F2
Pudding La OL14 86 C2
Pudsey Bsns Ctr LS28 76 F7
Pudsey Crawshaw Sch LS28 76 F7
Pudsey Grangefield Sch LS28 76 E8
Pudsey Greenside Primary Sch LS28 76 D6
Pudsey Primrose Hill Primary Sch LS28 57 D1
Pudsey Rd Leeds LS12, LS13 77 E7
Pudsey LS28, S13 77 B7
Todmorden OL14 86 B2
Pudsey Tyersal Primary Sch BD4 75 F6
Pudsey Waterloo Infants Sch LS28 76 C7
Pugneys Central Sta WF2 160 B8
Pugneys Country Pk WF2 160 B8
Pugneys Lakeside Sta WF2 160 A8
Pugneys Light Rly WF4 160 A8
Pugneys Rd WF2 142 C2
Pule Green La HX3 92 C3
Pullan Ave BD2 56 C4
Pullan Dr BD2 56 C4
Pullan Gr BD2 56 C4
Pullan La BD17 39 C5
Pullan St BD5 74 D5
Pulmans Pl HX3 113 C2
Pump La Dewsbury WF13 138 F8
East Ardsley WF3 119 E5
Kirkburton HD8 174 C7
West Hardwick WF4 163 A8
Pump St HD8 191 B3
Pumphouse La WF14 138 B6
Punch Bowl Yd
Brotherton WF11 126 C8
Cleckheaton BD19 116 C7
Pundles HX2 91 E8
Purbeck Gr LS25 82 F6
Purcell Dr BD20 5 D2
Purley Wlk BD6 94 B8
Purlwell Ave WF17 118 B3
Purlwell Cres WF17 118 B3
Purlwell Hall Rd WF17 118 C4
Purlwell Inf Sch WF17 118 B3
Purlwell La WF17 118 C4
Purprise La HX7 69 A1
Purston Infants Sch WF7 145 D4
Purston La WF7 145 F1
Purston Park Ct WF7 145 D4
Pye Nest Ave HX2 202 A1
Pye Nest Dr HX2 112 E4
Pye Nest Gdns HX2 202 A1
Pye Nest Gr HX2 202 A1
Pye Nest Rd HX2 112 E4
Pye Nest Rise HX2 112 E4
Pyenot Ave BD19 116 E6
Pyenot Dr BD19 116 E6
Pyenot Gdns BD19 116 E6
Pyenot Hall La BD19 116 E6
Pym St LS10 212 A1
Pymont Ct WF3 100 C1
Pymont Dr LS26 101 B7
Pymont Gr LS26 101 B7
Pymroyd La HD4 153 B3
Pynate Rd WF17 118 A6
Pyrah Fold 6 BD12 94 C4
Pyrah Rd BD12 94 D7
Pyrah St Bradford BD12 94 D4
Dewsbury WF13 118 C1

Quail St BD21 35 D8
Quaker House 9 LS2 206 A3
Quaker La Bradford BD5 74 B3
Cleckheaton BD19 116 D6
Huddersfield HD1 153 E5
Quakers La
Ripponden HX6 132 D3
Yeadon LS19 40 B5
Quarmby Croft HD3 153 A7
Quarmby Fold HD3 153 A7
Quarmby Rd HD3 153 B6
Quarrie Dene Ct LS7 60 C6
Quarry Ave WF11 127 A3
Quarry Bank Ct LS5 58 F6
Quarry Cl HD7 172 C2
Quarry Cotts BD20 17 D5
Quarry Ct Halifax HX3 113 E7
Huddersfield HD3 152 F7
Quarry Dene Pk LS16 59 C8
Quarry Dr HD5 155 C5
Quarry Farm Rd LS21 24 B5
Quarry Gdns LS17 43 A6
Quarry Hill Horbury WF4 140 F1
Huddersfield HD5 155 B4
Rothwell LS26 101 C6
Sowerby Bridge HX6 112 B3
Quarry Hill Ind Est WF4 140 E1
Quarry Hill La LS22 13 E6
Quarry La 10 Batley WF17 96 F1
East Ardsley WF12 119 A6
Huddersfield HD4 171 C7
Kirkheaton HD5 155 C5
Morley LS27 98 B2
Upton WF9 183 A8
Quarry Mount Leeds LS6 206 A4
Ryhill WF4 162 B1
7 Yeadon LS19 40 C7
Quarry Mount Pl 7 LS6 206 A4
Quarry Mount Primary Sch LS6 206 A4
Quarry Mount St 6 LS6 206 A4
Quarry Mount Terr 8 LS6 206 A4
Quarry Pl Bradford BD2 56 B2
Leeds LS6 206 A3
Mirfield WF14 137 D6
Quarry Rd
Cleckheaton BD19 116 D7
Cleckheaton, Gomersal BD19 117 B7
Dewsbury WF13 139 B7
Halifax HX3 91 E2
Huddersfield HD4 153 B3
Huddersfield, Marsh HD1 153 E6
Liversedge WF15 117 A4
Pool LS21 24 B5
Rothwell LS26 101 D6
Quarry St
Ackworth M T WF7 163 F5
Keighley BD21 35 D7
Leeds LS6 206 A4
Shipley BD9 55 A4
Quarry The LS17 43 A6
Quarry View
Ackworth M T WF7 163 E5
Dewsbury WF13 117 F1
Quarrydene Dr WF10 125 B6
Quarryfield Terr WF3 120 D7
Quarryfields WF14 138 B8
Quarryside Rd WF14 137 F5
Quaver La BD15 54 B1
Quay St HD1 154 B6
Quayside BD17 55 B8
Quayside The BD10 56 E8
Quebec St Bradford BD1 201 B2
Elland HX5 135 A7
Keighley BD21 35 B6
Leeds LS1 211 E3
8 Todmorden OL14 108 A1
Wakefield WF2 216 A2
Queen Elizabeth Dr WF6 144 B8
Queen Elizabeth Gdns HD1 153 F6
Queen Elizabeth Gr WF1 142 E7
Queen Elizabeth Gram & Jun Gram Sch WF1 216 B3
Queen Elizabeth Rd WF1 142 E7
Queen Elizabeth St WF1 121 B4
Queen Margaret's Dr WF11 126 D8
Queen Margarets Ave WF11 126 D8
Queen Margarets Cl WF11 126 D8
Queen Sq LS2 206 C1
Queen St 5 Baildon BD17 38 C1
Bingley BD16 36 F3
3 Bradford, Buttershaw BD6 93 E7
Bradford, Greengates BD10 56 D7
Castleford WF10 124 E8
Cleckheaton BD19 96 B2
Dewsbury, Chickenley WF12 140 B7
Dewsbury, Ravensthorpe WF13 138 E6
East Ardsley WF3 120 D8
Elland HX4 134 C6
6 Haworth BD22 51 C6
Hebden Bridge HX7 110 E8
Horbury WF4 141 A1
Huddersfield HD1 154 B6
Leeds LS1 211 D4
Leeds, Stourton LS10 80 A2
Liversedge WF16 117 C3
Lofthouse Gate WF1 121 B4
Mirfield WF14 138 A4
Morley LS27 98 A5
Normanton WF6 123 A2
Ossett WF5 140 D5
Pontefract WF8 146 C8
Rothwell WF3 100 D3
Silsden BD20 5 E1
Skelmanthorpe HD8 175 A2
South Elmsall WF9 182 F2
Sowerby Bridge HX6 111 E3
Steeton BD20 17 C5
Swillington LS26 102 E6
Todmorden OL14 108 B5
Wakefield WF1 216 B2
Wilsden BD15 53 C4
Yeadon LS19 40 A4
Queen St S HD1 154 B5
Queen Tap Yd 24 HD1 154 A6
Queen Terr 4 WF8 146 B8
Queen Victoria Cres HX3 93 B3
Queen Victoria St LS1 211 F4
Queen's Arc LS1 211 F4
Queen's Ave Bradford BD2 55 F3
Pontefract WF8 146 A7
Queen's Cres Crofton WF4 144 C4
Ossett WF5 140 D5
Queen's Dr Cudworth S72 180 C1
Ilkley LS29 7 F3
Ossett WF5 141 A5
Shafton S72 180 B3
Queen's Drive La LS29 7 F3
Queen's Gate HX3 113 B4
Queen's Gdns Ilkley LS29 8 A3
Ossett WF5 140 D5
Queen's Gr LS27 97 F3
Queen's Park Dr WF10 125 B8
Queen's Pl LS27 98 B4
Queen's Prom LS27 98 A5
Queen's Rd Bingley BD16 36 E6
Boston Spa LS23 30 C8
Bradford BD1, BD2, BD8 55 E2
Brighouse HX3 93 F2
Cudworth S72 180 C1
Halifax HX1 202 B3
Huddersfield HD2 153 E8
Ilkley LS29 8 A3
Keighley BD21 35 B5
Leeds LS6 205 E2
Morley LS27 97 F3
Pontefract WF8 146 A7
Queen's Rise BD2 55 F3
Queen's Road Primary Sch HX1 202 B3
Queen's Sq WF8 146 A7
Queen's Wlk Leeds LS6 59 B6
Ossett WF5 140 F5
Queens Cl Bingley BD16 37 B2
Leeds LS7 60 C8
Queens Ct Cleckheaton BD19 96 B2
4 Leeds LS14 62 B5
Queens Dr Halifax HX3 114 A4
Pudsey LS28 76 D8
Rothwell WF3 100 D3
Wakefield WF2 120 E1
Queens Dr Cl WF5 140 F5
Queens Gr BD21 35 B5
Queens Mill WF13 138 E6
Queens Mill Ind Est HD1 154 A4
Queens Mill Rd HD1, HD4 154 A4
Queens Par 2 LS14 62 B5
Queens Park Cl WF10 125 B8
Queens Pl Otley LS21 23 A7
Shipley BD18 54 F8
Queens Rd Castleford WF10 125 B7
Shipley BD18 54 F8
Queens Rd W HD4 153 B4
Queens Sq HD2 136 D1
Queens Terr
Hebden Bridge HX7 88 F3
Otley LS21 23 B7
Queens's Ct LS1 211 F3
Queensbury Ave WF1 121 C5
Queensbury Cl WF6 123 C1
Queensbury Golf Course BD13 93 A8
Queensbury Rd HX3 92 B5
Queensbury Sq 6 BD13 72 E1
Queensbury Upper Sch BD13 92 E8
Queensgate Bradford BD1 201 B3
Huddersfield HD1 154 B5
Queenshill App LS17 43 C2
Queenshill Ave LS17 43 C3
Queenshill Cl LS17 43 C2
Queenshill Cres LS17 43 C3
Queenshill Ct LS17 43 C2
Queenshill Dr LS17 43 C2
Queenshill Garth LS17 43 C2
Queenshill Gdns LS17 43 B2
Queenshill Rd LS17 43 C2
Queenshill View LS17 43 C2
Queenshill Way LS17 43 C2
Queenshill Wlk LS17 43 C2
Queensthorpe Ave LS13 77 E8
Queensthorpe Cl LS13 77 E8
Queensthorpe Rise LS13 77 D8
Queensway Bingley BD16 37 B2
Garforth LS25 82 D7
Guiseley LS20 40 A8
Halifax HX1 202 B4
7 Keighley BD21 35 C7
Kirkburton HD8 174 A5
Leeds LS15 81 C8
Morley LS27 98 A4
Normanton WF6 144 A7
Pontefract WF8 125 F3
Rothwell LS26 100 E6
Royston S71 179 C4
Yeadon LS19 40 A8
Queenswood Cl LS6 59 A6
Queenswood Ct LS6 59 B4
Queenswood Dr LS6 59 A5
Queenswood Gdns LS6 59 C4
Queenswood Gn LS6 59 A7
Queenswood Hts LS6 59 C5
Queenswood Mount LS6 59 B5
Queenswood Rd LS6 59 B5
Queenswood Rise LS6 59 B4
Quincy Cl BD2 56 C4

Raby Ave LS7 207 D3
Raby Pk LS22 13 D6
Raby St LS7 207 D3
Raby Terr LS7 207 D3
Racca Ave WF11 127 B4
Racca Gn WF11 127 A4
Race Moor La BD22 34 C3
Rachael St WF4 140 F1
Racton St HD7 151 F1
Radcliffe Ave BD2 56 A5
Radcliffe Gdns LS28 76 E6
Radcliffe Gr 2 LS28 76 E6
Radcliffe La Halifax HX2 90 C2
Pudsey LS28 76 E7
Radcliffe Pl WF1 216 B2
Radcliffe Rd
Huddersfield HD3 153 B4
Slaithwaite HD7 152 B2
Wakefield WF2 141 E4
Radcliffe St HD8 174 F2

Radcliffe Terr 1 LS28 76 E6
Radfield Rd BD6 74 E1
Radford Park Ave WF9 182 B1
Radnor St Bradford BD3 75 D7
Leeds LS12 210 B2
Radwell Dr BD5 201 B1
Rae Ct WF3 121 E5
Rae Rd BD18 55 B6
Raeburn Dr BD6 94 A7
Rafborn Ave HD3 134 E1
Rafborn Gr HD3 134 E1
Raglan Ave BD22 34 F6
Raglan Cl WF10 124 A8
Raglan Ct 8 HX1 202 C3
Raglan Rd LS2, LS6 206 A3
Raglan St Bradford BD3 75 D7
Halifax HX1 202 C3
Keighley BD22 34 F6
Queensbury BD13 72 F1
2 Todmorden OL14 108 B5
Raglan Terr BD3 75 E7
Raikes La Batley WF17 96 F2
Birkenshaw BD4 76 B2
Birkenshaw, East Bierley BD4 95 E7
Bradford BD4 76 B2
Raikes Wood Dr BD4 95 E7
Railes Cl HX2 90 D1
Railgate OL13 106 C1
Railsfield Mount LS13 58 C2
Railsfield Rise LS13 58 C2
Railsfield Way LS13 58 C2
Railway Ave WF8 125 C1
Railway Cotts
Bolton Abbey BD23 2 C7
Burton Salmon LS25 105 D4
Dunford Bridge S36 199 F2
Micklefield LS25 84 A6
South Elmsall WF9 183 E7
Railway Rd Bradford BD10 56 B8
Ilkley LS29 8 B4
Leeds LS15 62 D2
Railway St Bradford BD4 75 C2
2 Brighouse HD6 115 B1
Cleckheaton BD19 116 D7
Dewsbury WF12 139 D7
Dewsbury, Scout Hill WF13 139 A6
Huddersfield HD1 154 A6
Keighley BD20 18 C1
Leeds LS9 212 B3
Liversedge WF16 117 D3
Todmorden OL14 108 B6
Railway Terr
1 Bradford BD12 94 E5
East Ardsley WF3 99 C1
Elland HX3 113 A2
Featherstone WF7 145 D5
Hemsworth WF9 163 A3
Lofthouse Gate WF1 121 A5
Normanton WF6 123 A2
Railway View
Castleford WF10 124 B7
Lofthouse Gate WF3 121 F6
Raincliffe Gr LS9 80 A8
Raincliffe Mount 11 LS9 80 A7
Raincliffe Rd LS9 80 A7
Raincliffe St 13 LS9 80 A8
Raincliffe Terr 12 LS9 80 A7
Raines Dr BD20 4 C5
Rainsborough Ave WF11 126 C3
Raistrick Way BD18 55 D8
Rake HX7 109 F8
Rake Bank HX2 91 D3
Rake Head Barn La OL14 129 A8
Rake Head Rd HD7 197 E7
Rakehill Rd LS15 63 B7
Raleigh Gdns OL15 129 C1
Raleigh St 5 HX1 202 B1
Ralph Thoresby High Sch LS16 41 F4
Rampart Rd LS6 206 A3
Ramsden Ave BD7 73 E5
Ramsden Cl WF11 126 C8
Ramsden Ct BD7 74 A4
Ramsden La Holme HD7 198 B7
Todmorden OL14 128 F7
Ramsden Mill La HD7 152 E3
Ramsden Pl BD14 73 B5
Ramsden Rd Holme HD7 198 C7
Littleborough OL15 128 C1
Ramsden St
Castleford WF10 124 C5
Halifax HX3 91 F2
Huddersfield HD1 154 A5
Huddersfield, Leymoor HD7 152 E4
Kippax LS25 102 F8
Todmorden OL14 129 A7
Ramsden Wood Rd OL14 129 A7
Ramsey Ave OL13 106 A1
Ramsey Cres WF4 158 B7
Ramsey Rd WF4 158 A7
Ramsey St BD5 74 D3
Ramsey View WF4 158 A7
Ramsgate WF3 100 B1
Ramsgate Cres WF3 100 B1
Ramsgate St HX1 202 B3
Ramshead App LS14 62 A6
Ramshead Cl LS14 62 A7
Ramshead Cres LS14 61 F7
Ramshead Dr LS14 62 A6
Ramshead Gdns LS14 61 F7
Ramshead Gr LS14 62 A6
Ramshead Heights 1 LS14 62 A5
Ramshead Hill LS14 62 A6
Ramshead Pl LS14 62 A6
Ramshead View LS14 62 A6
Rand Pl BD7 74 C5
Rand St BD7 74 C5
Randall Pl BD9 55 A3
Randall Well St BD7 201 A2
Randolph St Bradford BD3 75 E8
Halifax HX3 203 E4
Leeds LS13 58 A2
Random Cl BD22 34 F5
Ranelagh Ave BD10 56 E5
Range Bank HX3 92 C1
Range Ct HX3 203 E4
Range Gdns HX3 92 C1
Range La HX3 92 C1
Range St HX3 92 C1
Ransdale Dr BD5 74 D3
Ransdale Gr BD5 74 D3
Ransdale Rd BD5 74 D3
Ranter's Fold WF4 141 A1
Raper View LS25 64 E8
Rapes Highway OL3 167 A5
Rashcliffe Hill Rd HD1 153 F4
Raspberry Pl BD20 16 D4
Rastrick Comm HD6 136 A8
Rastrick High Sch HD6 114 F1
Rathlin Rd WF12 118 F3
Rathmell Rd LS15 80 E7
Rathmell St BD5 74 D1
Ratten Row Rd HX6 111 C1
Raven Cl WF7 124 A1
Raven La S72 180 A6
Raven Rd LS6 205 E4
Raven Royd S71 178 F1
Raven St Bingley BD16 36 F3
Halifax HX1 202 B3
Huddersfield HD1 153 D5
Keighley BD21 35 B7
Raven Terr BD8 73 C7
Ravens Ave
Dewsbury WF13 139 A6
Huddersfield HD5 154 E5
Ravens Cres WF13 139 A6
Ravens Croft WF13 139 A6
Ravens Gr WF13 139 A6
Ravens Lodge Terr WF13 139 A6
Ravens Mount LS28 76 F7
Ravens St WF13 138 F6
Ravens Way HD7 189 E4
Ravens Wlk WF13 139 A6
Ravenscar Ave 6 LS8 61 A6
Ravenscar Mount 3 LS8 61 A6
Ravenscar Pl 2 LS8 61 A6
Ravenscar Terr 4 LS8 61 A6
Ravenscar View LS8 61 A6
Ravenscar Wlk LS8 61 A6
Ravenscliffe Ave BD10 56 E4
Ravenscliffe First Sch BD10 56 E4
Ravenscliffe High Sch HX3 113 B2
Ravenscliffe Rd LS28 56 F6
Ravenscourt HD1 153 D5
Ravensdeane HD3 153 D8
Ravensfield Rd WF13 139 A6
Ravenshall Sch WF12 139 A4
Ravenshouse Rd WF13 138 F7
Ravensknowle Rd HD5 154 E5
Ravensmead WF7 145 F5
Ravensthorpe CE Junior Sch WF13 138 E5
Ravensthorpe Infants Sch WF13 138 E6
Ravensthorpe Sta WF12 138 F4
Ravenstone Dr HX4 134 C6
Ravenstone Gdns BD20 16 E5
Ravensville BD20 16 E6
Ravenswharf Rd WF13 139 A6
Ravensworth Cl LS15 62 F3
Ravensworth Way LS15 62 F3
Raw End Rd HX2 112 A8
Raw Hill HD6 135 F8
Raw La Halifax HX2 91 D5
Hebden Bridge HX7 89 D3
Raw Nook Rd HD3 152 E8
Rawden Hill LS21 25 F6
Rawdon C of E Primary Sch LS19 40 D3
Rawdon Dr LS19 40 B3
Rawdon Golf Course LS19 40 B3
Rawdon Hall Dr LS19 40 B3
Rawdon Littlemoor Primary Sch LS19 40 C4
Rawdon Rd Haworth BD22 51 C7
Horsforth LS18 57 F8
Rawdon St BD22 35 A6
Rawfield La Fairburn WF11 105 C6
Monk Fryston LS25 105 C6
Rawfolds Ave WF17 96 F2
Rawfolds Way BD19 116 F6
Rawgate Ave WF10 124 A7
Rawling St BD21 35 B5
Rawroyds HX4 134 C5
Rawson Ave Bradford BD3 75 D8
Halifax HX3 113 B3
Rawson Junior & Infants Sch HX3 92 B2
Rawson Mkt BD1 201 B3
Rawson Pl Bradford BD1 201 B3
Sowerby Bridge HX6 112 A3
Rawson Rd BD1 201 B3
Rawson Sq Bradford BD1 201 B3
Bradford, Thackley BD10 39 B1
Rawson St Bradford BD12 94 D4
Halifax HX1 203 E3
Rawson St N HX3 92 B1
Rawson Terr LS11 214 C3
Rawson Wood HX6 111 E2
Rawthorpe C of E Infants Sch HD5 154 E8
Rawthorpe Cres HD5 154 E8
Rawthorpe High Sch HD5 154 E8
Rawthorpe Junior Sch HD5 154 D7
Rawthorpe La HD5 154 E7
Rawthorpe Terr HD5 154 E8
Rawtonstall Bank HX7 88 E4
Ray Gate Holmfirth HD7 189 D8
Huddersfield HD3 152 D8
Wadsworth Moor HX2 89 F8
Ray St HD1 154 B7
Ray Winfield Ind Est WF7 163 E5
Rayfield WF2 141 F5
Raygill Cl LS17 44 B5
Raylands Cl LS10 99 F6
Raylands Ct LS10 99 F6
Raylands Fold LS10 99 F6
Raylands Garth LS10 99 F6
Raylands La LS10 99 F6
Raylands Pl LS10 99 F6
Raylands Rd LS10 99 F6
Raylands Way LS10 99 F6
Rayleigh St BD4 75 A4
Raymond Dr BD5 74 E2
Raymond St BD5 74 E2
Raynbron Cres BD5 201 B3
Raynel App LS16 42 A3
Raynel Cl LS16 42 A4
Raynel Dr LS16 42 A4
Raynel Garth LS16 42 A3
Raynel Gdns LS16 42 A4
Raynel Gn LS16 42 A3
Raynel Mount LS16 42 A4
Raynel Way LS16 41 F4
Rayner Ave Batley WF16 117 D6
Bradford BD8 54 F1
Rayner Dr HD6 115 A4
Rayner Mount BD15 73 A8
Rayner Rd HD6 115 A4
Rayner St WF4 141 A1
Rayner Terr LS28 76 F8
Rayners Ave WF15 116 C4
Raynham Cres BD21 34 F8
Raynor Cl HD3 153 C7
Raynville App 1 LS13 58 E3
Raynville Ave LS13 58 E3
Raynville Cl LS13 58 E3
Raynville Cres LS12 58 F2
Raynville Ct 2 LS13 58 E3
Raynville Dene LS12 58 F3
Raynville Dr LS13 58 E3
Raynville Gn LS13 58 E2
Raynville Gr LS13 58 E3
Raynville Grange 3 LS13 58 E3
Raynville Mount LS13 58 E3
Raynville Pl 4 LS13 58 E3
Raynville Primary Sch LS13 58 E2
Raynville Rd LS12, LS13 58 E3
Raynville Rise LS13 58 E2
Raynville St LS13 58 E3
Raynville Terr LS13 58 E3
Raynville Wlk LS13 58 E2
Raywood Cl LS19 40 A8
Reap Hirst Rd HD2 135 D2
Rebecca St BD1 74 D7
Recreation Ave 3 LS11 214 A4
Recreation Cres LS11 213 F4
Recreation Gr LS11 214 A4
Recreation La HX5 134 E6
Recreation Mount LS11 214 A4
Recreation Pl LS11 214 A4
Recreation Rd Leeds LS11 213 F2
Sowerby Bridge HX6 112 C4
Recreation Row LS11 213 F4
Recreation St LS11 214 A4
Recreation Terr LS11 214 A4
Recreation View LS11 214 A4
Rectory Ave 2 WF10 124 D8
Rectory Cl Garforth LS25 82 F7
Marsden HD7 168 F4
Royston S71 179 D1
Rectory Dr Batley WF17 97 A1
Huddersfield HD5 155 B7
Rectory Garden HD8 175 D7
Rectory Garth WF9 181 D7
Rectory La HD8 175 D8
Rectory Row 12 BD21 35 B7
Rectory St 3
Castleford WF10 124 D8
Leeds LS9 207 E1
Rectory View WF12 139 E3
Red Beck Rd HX3 92 F1
Red Beck Vale BD18 55 A5
Red Brink La HX6 111 B2
Red Deer Park La WF4 156 E5
Red Doles Ind Est HD2 136 C1
Red Doles La HD2 136 C1
Red Doles Rd HD2 136 C2
Red Hall App LS14 45 A1
Red Hall Ave LS17 44 F1
Red Hall Chase LS14 45 A1
Red Hall Croft LS14 62 A8
Red Hall Ct LS14 45 A1
Red Hall Dr LS14 45 A1
Red Hall Garth LS14 45 A1
Red Hall Gdns LS17 44 F1
Red Hall Gn LS14 45 A1
Red Hall La Leeds LS14, LS17 45 A1
Wakefield WF1 121 A1
Red Hall View LS14 45 A1
Red Hall Way LS14 45 A1
Red Hall Wlk LS14 45 A1
Red House Gdns LS29 22 A3
Red House Mus BD19 96 B1
Red La Crofton WF4 143 E5
Featherstone WF7 144 E5
Meltham HD7 170 B2
Pudsey LS28 57 C3
Red Laithes Ct WF13 138 E6
Red Laithes La WF13 138 E6
Red Lees Rd BB10 85 A8
Red Lodge Cl LS8 61 D4
Red Vale BD19 96 B2
Redbeck Cotts LS19 57 E8
Redburn Ave BD18 55 A5
Redburn Dr BD18 55 A5
Redburn Rd BD18 55 B5
Redcar La BD20 17 C2
Redcar Rd BD10 56 E6
Redcar St HX1 202 B3
Redcliffe Ave BD21 35 A7
Redcliffe Gr BD21 35 A7
Redcliffe St BD21 35 A7
Redcote La Leeds LS4 59 C2
Leeds, Upper Armley LS12 59 B1
Reddisher Rd HD7 168 E4
Reddyshore Scout Gate OL14 129 C5
Redesdale Gdns LS16 42 B3
Redfearn Ave WF16 117 D5
Redhall Cl LS11 213 E1
Redhall Cres LS11 213 E1
Redhall Gate LS11 213 E1
Redhill Ave
Castleford WF10 125 A6
East Ardsley WF3 119 E5
Redhill Cl WF3 119 E5
Redhill Cres WF3 119 E5
Redhill Dr Castleford WF10 125 B7
East Ardsley WF3 119 E5
Redhill Gdns WF10 125 A7
Redhill Inf Sch WF10 125 C8
Redhill Jun Sch WF10 125 C8
Redhill Mount WF10 125 A7
Redhill Rd WF10 125 A7
Redhill View WF10 125 A6
Redhouse La LS7 204 B3
Redland Cres WF9 163 B2
Redland Dr HD8 173 E7
Redland Gr S75 178 B2
Redlands Cl WF14 138 A7
Redmayne Gr WF11 126 D3
Redmire Ct LS14 62 B4
Redmire Dr LS14 62 A4
Redmire St BD3 75 E7
Redmire View LS14 62 A4
Redruth Dr WF6 123 B3
Redshaw Rd LS12 210 A2
Redthorne Way S72 180 C3
Redvers Cl LS16 42 A1
Redwood Ave
East Ardsley WF3 120 A8
Royston S71 179 C3
Redwood Cl Keighley BD21 35 E5
Yeadon LS19 39 F7
Redwood Dr HD2 136 E5
Redwood Gr 5
Huddersfield HD5 154 D6
Yeadon LS19 39 F7
Redwood Way LS19 39 F7
Reed Rd LS12 209 F2
Reed St Bacup OL13 106 A3
Huddersfield HD3 153 D7
Reedling Dr LS27 98 C3
Reedsdale Ave LS27 97 C7
Reedsdale Dr LS27 97 C7
Reedsdale Gdns LS27 97 C7
Rees Way BD3 201 C4
Reeth Rd HD6 135 E8
Reevy Ave BD6 93 F8
Reevy Cres BD6 93 F8
Reevy Dr BD6 94 A8
Reevy Hill First Sch BD6 73 F1
Reevy Rd BD6 94 B8
Reevy Rd W BD6 93 E8
Reevy St BD6 74 A1
Reevylands Dr BD6 94 A8
Reform St BD19 96 B1
Regal Cl HX6 132 C1
Regal Dr HX6 132 C1
Regency Ct Bradford BD8 74 B8
Leeds LS6 205 E4
Regency Gdns WF3 120 A8
Regency Park Gr 4 LS28 76 E5
Regency Park Rd LS28 76 E5
Regency Rd WF14 138 A4
Regency View BD3 56 A2
Regent Ave LS18 58 C7
Regent Cl Brighouse HD6 135 E6
Horsforth LS18 58 C7
Regent Cres Horsforth LS18 58 C7
South Hiendley S72 180 E5
Regent Ct 10 Horsforth LS18 58 C7
Leeds LS1 211 F3
Regent House 6 HX5 134 F7
Regent Mews WF17 118 F4
Regent Park Ave LS6 205 F4
Regent Park Cross Ave LS6 205 F4
Regent Park Terr LS6 205 F4
Regent Pl Bradford BD10 39 A1
8 Hebden Bridge HX7 89 A4
17 Sowerby Bridge HX6 112 B5
Regent Rd Horsforth LS18 58 B7
Huddersfield HD1 153 E7
Ilkley LS29 8 A4
Kirkheaton HD5 137 C2
Regent St 4 Bacup OL13 106 A2
Bradford BD10 56 D7
Bradford, Thackley BD10 39 A1
Castleford WF10 124 C7
Featherstone WF7 145 C5
Halifax HX1 203 D2
13 Haworth BD22 51 D7
Hebden Bridge HX7 89 A3
Hemsworth WF9 181 C7
Horbury WF4 140 F2
Regent St continued
Leeds LS7 204 A3
Leeds, Mabgate LS2, LS7 207 D1
Liversedge WF16 117 C3
Mirfield WF14 138 A3
Normanton WF6 123 C4
Queensbury BD13 72 F1
South Elmsall WF9 182 E3
South Hiendley S72 180 E5
Todmorden OL14 108 A1
Wakefield WF1 142 E3
Regent Terr Leeds LS7 204 A3
Leeds, Burley LS6 205 F2
Regents Pk WF1 142 E6
Regina Cres Brierley S72 180 E2
Ryhill WF4 162 C1
Regina Dr LS7 204 A2
Regina House LS13 77 D8
Reginald Mount LS7 207 D4
Reginald Pl LS7 207 D4
Reginald Row LS7 207 D4
Reginald St Bradford BD5 74 D3
Leeds LS7 207 D4
Reginald Terr LS7 207 D4
Reginald View LS7 207 D4
Reid Park Ave WF4 140 E1
Reighton Croft BD10 56 E6
Rein Ct LS25 64 E8
Rein Gdns WF3 119 C8
Rein Mews WF3 119 C8
Rein Rd Horsforth LS18 58 C6
Morley LS27 98 C1
Rein St LS27 98 C1
Rein The LS14 61 F6
Reins Ave BD17 38 B1
Reins Rd HD6 135 E8
Reins Terr HD7 172 A5
Reinwood Ave
Huddersfield HD3 153 B7
Leeds LS8 61 E5
Reinwood Jun & Inf Sch HD3 153 B7
Reinwood Rd HD3 153 B6
Rembrandt Ave WF3 119 F8
Renee Cl BD4 95 C8
Renfield Gr WF6 123 D3
Renshaw St BD10 39 B1
Renton Ave LS20 22 D1
Renton Dr LS20 39 D8
Renton Lea LS20 39 D8
Reservoir Pl
Dewsbury WF13 118 A1
4 Queensbury BD13 72 C2
Reservoir Rd Batley WF17 117 F4
Halifax HX2 202 A4
Haworth BD22 50 F6
Meltham HD7 170 E6
Reservoir St WF13 118 A1
Reservoir View
Skelmanthorpe HD8 174 E2
Thornton BD13 72 D7
Restmore Ave LS20 22 D2
Retford Pl BD7 74 C5
Reuben Goldberg La BD3 75 D8
Reuben St WF15 117 A5
Reva Cl BD16 37 B4
Reva Syke Rd BD14 73 B4
Revel Garth HD8 192 A5
Revie Rd LS11 213 F3
Reydon Wlk BD6 73 F1
Reyhill Gr BD5 201 B1
Reyner Ho BD5 201 B1
Reyner House Mews BD5 201 B1
Reynolds Ave BD7 73 E5
Rhine St BD4 201 D1
Rhode's Hill La LS23 30 F3
Rhodes Ave WF16 117 D6
Rhodes Cres WF8 146 D6
Rhodes Gdns WF3 121 C6
Rhodes La LS23 30 C6
Rhodes Pl BD17 55 B8
Rhodes St Castleford WF10 124 B7
Castleford WF10 124 C8
Halifax HX1 203 D3
Liversedge WF15 117 C4
Shipley BD18 55 A8
Rhodes Terr Bradford BD2 56 B4
Leeds LS12 210 B2
Rhodesia Ave Bradford BD15 73 C8
Halifax HX3 113 C3
Rhodesia St BD20 16 D6
Rhodesway BD8 73 D8
Rhodesway Sch BD15 73 C8
Rhondda Pl HX1 202 A2
Rhum Cl BD6 93 F6
Rhyddings Ave WF7 163 F5
Rhyddings Dr WF7 163 F5
Rhyddings Gdns LS29 8 D4
Rhyl St WF7 145 D6
Rhylstone Mount BD7 73 F6
Ribble St BD21 35 E8
Ribblesdale Ave LS25 83 B6
Ribbleton Gr BD3 201 D4
Ribstone St HX7 89 E1
Riccall Nook BD10 56 D6
Rice St 1 HD1 154 B5
Rich Gate HD7 189 B2
Richard Dunn Sports Ctr The BD6 74 D1
Richard Oastler Sch LS4 205 D2
Richard Pl 4 HD6 115 A4
Richard St 3 Bacup OL13 106 A7
Bradford BD3 201 D3
Brighouse HD6 115 A4
Wakefield WF1 216 B3

Richard Thorpe Ave
WF14 ... 138 B5
Richardshaw Dr LS28 ... 57 E1
Richardshaw La LS28 ... 76 E8
Richardshaw Rd LS28 ... 57 F1
Richardson Ave BD6 ... 94 C8
Richardson Cres LS9 ... 80 C7
Richardson Rd LS9 ... 80 C7
Richardson Sq 5 HD1 ... 154 A6
Richardson St BD12 ... 95 A4
Richmond Ave
Huddersfield HD2 ... 136 A2
Knottingley WF11 ... 126 B5
Leeds LS6 ... 205 E4
Sowerby Bridge HX6 ... 111 F3
Richmond Cl Halifax HX1 ... 203 E4
Leeds LS13 ... 58 A2
3 Morley LS27 ... 98 A3
Rothwell LS26 ... 100 F6
Richmond Ct Crofton WF4 ... 162 A8
Huddersfield HD4 ... 152 F3
Leeds LS9 ... 212 C3
Pontefract WF8 ... 125 D1
Rothwell LS26 ... 100 F6
Richmond Flats 7 HD1 ... 154 B7
Richmond Garth WF5 ... 140 F4
Richmond Gdns
Pudsey LS28 ... 77 A7
Sowerby Bridge HX6 ... 111 F3
Richmond Gr BD19 ... 96 B2
Richmond Green St LS9 ... 212 B3
Richmond Hill App LS9 ... 212 B3
Richmond Hill Cl LS9 ... 212 B3
Richmond Hill
Primary Sch LS9 ... 212 C2
Richmond House Sch
LS16 ... 59 C7
Richmond Lea WF14 ... 138 A6
Richmond Mews BD18 ... 54 F8
Richmond Mount LS6 ... 205 E4
Richmond Park Ave
WF15 ... 117 A3
Richmond Pl Ilkley LS29 ... 8 C3
16 Shipley BD18 ... 54 F8
Richmond Rd Batley WF17 ... 118 D2
Batley, Nunroyd WF16 ... 117 E6
Bradford BD7 ... 74 D6
Halifax HX1 ... 203 D4
Leeds LS6 ... 205 E4
Pudsey LS28 ... 57 C2
17 Shipley BD18 ... 54 F8
Upton WF9 ... 183 A7
Wakefield WF1 ... 216 A4
Richmond St
Castleford WF10 ... 124 D7
Cleckheaton BD19 ... 116 D7
Halifax HX1 ... 203 D4
Keighley BD21 ... 35 B8
Leeds LS9 ... 212 B3
8 Todmorden OL14 ... 108 C5
Richmond Terr Otley LS21 ... 22 F7
Pudsey LS28 ... 77 A7
Richmond Way LS25 ... 82 F5
Richmondfield Ave LS15 ... 63 E6
Richmondfield Cl LS15 ... 63 E6
Richmondfield Cres LS15 ... 63 E6
Richmondfield Cross LS15 ... 63 E6
Richmondfield Dr LS15 ... 63 E6
Richmondfield Garth LS15 ... 63 E7
Richmondfield Gr LS15 ... 63 E6
Richmondfield La LS15 ... 63 E6
Richmondfield Mount LS15 ... 63 E6
Richmondfield Way LS15 ... 63 E6
Rickard St LS12 ... 210 C2
Ridding Gate LS21 ... 10 E1
Riddings Cl
Hemsworth WF9 ... 181 D5
Huddersfield HD2 ... 136 D3
Riddings Rd
Huddersfield HD2 ... 136 D3
Ilkley LS29 ... 8 B4
Riddings Rise HD2 ... 136 E3
Riddlesden C of E First Sch
BD20 ... 18 F2
Riddlesden Golf Course
BD20 ... 18 C4
Riddlesden St BD20 ... 18 F1
Rider Rd LS6 ... 206 B4
Rider St LS9 ... 212 B4
Ridge Ave WF4 ... 158 A7
Ridge Bank OL14 ... 108 B5
Ridge Cl Guiseley LS20 ... 39 C8
Huddersfield HD4 ... 154 A3
Skelmanthorpe HD8 ... 175 A1
Ridge Cres WF4 ... 158 A6
Ridge Gr LS7 ... 60 A5
Ridge Hill HD6 ... 114 E1
Ridge La BD20 ... 5 C7
Ridge Lea HD6 ... 114 F1
Ridge Mount LS6 ... 206 A4
Ridge Mount Terr LS6 ... 206 A4
Ridge Rd Kippax LS25 ... 83 D2
Leeds LS7 ... 206 B4
Netherton WF4 ... 158 A6
Todmorden OL14 ... 108 B5
Ridge St HD4 ... 154 A3
Ridge Terr LS6 ... 59 E5
Ridge The LS22 ... 13 C3
Ridge View Elland HX5 ... 135 C6
Pudsey LS13 ... 77 C8
Ridge View Dr HD2 ... 135 D2
Ridge View Gdns BD10 ... 56 C7
Ridge View Rd HD6 ... 115 A1
Ridge Way LS8 ... 204 C2
Ridgedale Mount WF8 ... 125 D4
Ridgefield St WF10 ... 124 D7
Ridgemount Rd BD20 ... 18 E2
Ridgestone Ave WF9 ... 181 E7
Ridgeway Guiseley LS20 ... 39 B8
Huddersfield HD5 ... 154 E7
Queensbury BD13 ... 92 F8
Shipley BD18 ... 55 E6
Ridgeway Cl
Huddersfield HD5 ... 154 E7
Leeds LS8 ... 204 C2
Ridgeway Cres S71 ... 179 C1
Ridgeway Dr WF17 ... 97 A1
Ridgeway Gdns HD6 ... 114 E5
Ridgeway Mount BD22 ... 34 F5
Ridgeway Sq WF11 ... 126 F3
Ridgeway The WF11 ... 126 F3
Ridgeways The HD7 ... 170 D8
Ridgewood Cl BD17 ... 38 E3
Riding Head La HX2 ... 90 E1
Riding Hill HX3 ... 93 E6
Riding La HX2 ... 91 D3
Riding St WF17 ... 117 E6
Ridings Bsns Pk HX1 ... 202 B2
Ridings Cl WF3 ... 121 B6
Ridings Croft BD5 ... 75 B1
Ridings Ct WF3 ... 121 B6
Ridings Fields HD7 ... 172 C3
Ridings Gdns WF3 ... 121 B6
Ridings La Holmfirth HD7 ... 189 C7
Huddersfield HD7 ... 152 C4
Lofthouse Gate WF3 ... 121 B6
Ridings Mews WF3 ... 121 B6
Ridings Rd WF13 ... 139 D8
Ridings Sch The HX3 ... 91 F3
Ridings Sh Ctr WF1 ... 216 B2
Ridings The BD20 ... 18 B3
Ridings Way Bradford BD6 ... 93 E8
Lofthouse Gate WF3 ... 121 B6
Ridingwood Rise HD8 ... 175 E2
Ridleys Fold LS29 ... 6 F8
Rievaulx Ave BD8 ... 74 C8
Rievaulx Cl LS23 ... 30 C7
Rifle Fields HD1 ... 153 F6
Rigg La WF7, WF8 ... 164 E7
Rightox Rd HD7 ... 172 C3
Rigton App LS9 ... 212 B4
Rigton Bank LS17 ... 28 D4
Rigton Cl LS9 ... 212 C4
Rigton Dr LS9 ... 212 B4
Rigton Gn Bardsey LS17 ... 28 E4
Leeds LS9 ... 212 B4
Rigton Lawn LS9 ... 212 B4
Rigton Mews LS9 ... 212 B4
Rigton St BD5 ... 74 D3
Riley La Halifax HX2 ... 91 F8
Kirkburton HD8 ... 173 E6
Riley Pk HD8 ... 173 F6
Riley St HD4 ... 154 B4
Rill Ct WF9 ... 181 D7
Rillbank La LS3 ... 205 F1
Rillbank St LS3 ... 205 F2
Rillington Mead BD10 ... 56 D6
Rills Mead LS21 ... 23 A7
Rillside HD8 ... 173 F1
Rilston St BD7 ... 74 B6
Rimswell Holt BD10 ... 56 E6
Ring O'Bells Yd 9 WF4 ... 141 A1
Ring Rd Adel LS16 ... 42 D2
Ring Rd Beeston LS12 ... 78 C3
Ring Rd Beeston Pk
Leeds LS11 ... 98 F7
Middleton LS10 ... 99 A6
Ring Rd Farsley LS28 ... 57 C4
Ring Rd Halton LS15 ... 62 C1
Ring Rd (Horsforth) LS18 ... 58 E8
Ring Rd Low Wortley LS12 ... 78 B4
Ring Rd Meanwood LS17 ... 42 F2
Ring Rd Middleton LS10 ... 99 F6
Ring Rd Moortown LS17 ... 43 D3
Ring Rd Seacroft LS14 ... 62 B6
Ring Rd Shadwell LS17 ... 44 D2
Ring Rd Weetwood LS16 ... 42 C1
Ring Rd West Pk LS16 ... 42 A1
Ring Road Bramley LS13 ... 77 C8
Ring Road Cross Gates
LS15 ... 62 C3
Ring Road Farnley LS12 ... 77 F7
Ringby La HX3 ... 92 B4
Ringstone HX4 ... 133 A1
Ringstone Gr S72 ... 181 B3
Ringway LS25 ... 82 D6
Ringwood Ave LS14 ... 62 A8
Ringwood Cres LS14 ... 62 A8
Ringwood Ct WF1 ... 121 D5
Ringwood Dr LS14 ... 62 A8
Ringwood Edge HX5 ... 134 D6
Ringwood Gdns LS14 ... 62 A8
Ringwood Mount 1 LS14 ... 62 A8
Ringwood Rd BD5 ... 74 C3
Ringwood Way WF9 ... 181 F7
Rink Par 5 WF17 ... 118 D3
Rink St WF17 ... 118 D3
Rink Terr 4 WF17 ... 118 D3
Ripley Cl WF6 ... 123 D2
Ripley Ct WF6 ... 144 B8
Ripley Dr WF6 ... 123 D3
Ripley La LS20 ... 22 E2
Ripley Rd Bradford BD4 ... 74 F4
Liversedge WF15 ... 116 F4
Ripley St Bradford BD15 ... 54 A2
Bradford, Ripleyville BD5 ... 74 F4
Brighouse HX3 ... 115 A7
Keighley BD20 ... 18 F1
Ripley Terr HX2 ... 111 D7
Ripon Ave HD2 ... 136 B2
Ripon House 5 HX5 ... 134 F7
Ripon Rd WF12 ... 118 F1
Ripon St HX1 ... 202 A2
Ripon Terr HX3 ... 92 B1
Ripponden Junior
& Infants Sch HX6 ... 132 E5
Ripponden New Bank
HX6 ... 132 E4
Ripponden Old Bank HX6 ... 132 E4
Ripponden Old La HX6 ... 132 B3
Rise La OL14 ... 108 A5
Rise The Brotherton WF11 ... 126 C8
Kippax LS25 ... 83 A1
Leeds LS5 ... 59 A5
Northowram HX3 ... 93 A2
Pontefract WF8 ... 146 E7
Risedale Ave WF17 ... 97 B2
Risedale Cl WF17 ... 97 B2
Rishworth Ave HD8 ... 175 D6
Rishworth Cl WF2 ... 120 E2
Rishworth Hall Cl HX6 ... 132 B1
Rishworth Mill La HX6 ... 150 D8
Rishworth New Rd HX6 ... 132 B1
Rishworth Rd
Dewsbury WF12 ... 139 D8
Ripponden HX4 ... 133 A4
Rishworth Sch HX6 ... 132 C2
Rishworth St
Dewsbury WF13 ... 139 D8
Keighley BD22 ... 34 F6
Wakefield WF1 ... 216 B3
Rishworthian Ct HX3 ... 113 A1
Rivadale View LS29 ... 8 B5
Rivelin Rd WF10 ... 124 C6
River Holme View HD7 ... 172 C2
River Pk HD7 ... 171 F5
River St Brighouse HD6 ... 115 C1
6 Haworth BD22 ... 51 D7
Keighley BD21 ... 18 E1
Todmorden OL14 ... 108 C5
River Valley View HD8 ... 192 A6
River View Boston Spa LS23 ... 30 F7
Castleford WF10 ... 124 B8
Ilkley LS29 ... 8 E5
River Wlk BD16 ... 36 F3
Riverdale LS22 ... 13 F4
Riverdale Ave WF3 ... 121 F2
Riverdale Cl WF3 ... 121 F2
Riverdale Cres WF3 ... 121 F2
Riverdale Ct LS21 ... 23 B8
Riverdale Dr WF3 ... 121 F2
Riverdale Gdns
Boston Spa LS23 ... 30 F7
Otley LS21 ... 23 B8
Riverdale Rd
Lofthouse Gate WF3 ... 121 F2
Otley LS21 ... 23 A8
Rivermead WF2 ... 142 D3
Riverside Clayton West HD8 ... 175 E3
Keighley BD21 ... 35 E7
Riverside Ave LS21 ... 11 B2
Riverside Cl LS21 ... 11 B1
Riverside Cotts BD20 ... 17 D8
Riverside Cres LS21 ... 11 B1
Riverside Ct Leeds LS1 ... 211 F3
Shipley BD17 ... 38 A1
Riverside Dr
Cleckheaton BD19 ... 95 D1
Otley LS21 ... 11 B2
Riverside Est BD17 ... 55 B8
Riverside Ind Est WF12 ... 139 C7
Riverside Junior Sch HX7 ... 89 A3
Riverside Pk LS21 ... 11 B1
Riverside Villas WF2 ... 142 D2
Riverside Way WF13 ... 138 E4
Riverside Wlk LS29 ... 7 F5
Riverwood Dr HX3 ... 113 B2
Riviera Gdns LS7 ... 60 C6
Rivock Ave Keighley BD20 ... 17 F3
Steeton BD20 ... 17 D6
Rivock Gr BD20 ... 17 F3
RM Grylls Middle Sch
WF15 ... 116 B4
Roach Grange Ave LS25 ... 83 A3
Road End 4 HX4 ... 134 C7
Road Sides WF8 ... 146 D6
Roaine Dr HD7 ... 189 B4
Roans Brae BD10 ... 56 E6
Robb Ave LS11 ... 214 A1
Robb St LS11 ... 214 A1
Robbins Terr WF7 ... 145 D6
Roberson Terr BD19 ... 117 A8
Robert Ct WF15 ... 116 F3
Robert La HD7 ... 189 C7
Robert St Bradford BD3 ... 201 D2
Halifax HX3 ... 92 A2
Haworth BD22 ... 51 F8
Robert St N 2 HX3 ... 92 C2
Robert's St BD19 ... 116 C7
Roberts Ave LS9 ... 208 B2
Roberts Ct LS9 ... 208 B2
Roberts Pl Bradford BD1 ... 201 A3
Leeds LS9 ... 208 C1
Roberts St Keighley BD22 ... 34 C6
Pudsey LS28 ... 57 E1
4 Rothwell LS26 ... 101 C6
Roberts Way WF2 ... 142 F1
Robertsgate WF3 ... 100 B1
Robertshaw Rd HX7 ... 88 F3
Robertson Ave HD6 ... 136 A8
Roberttown CE (Controlled)
Jun & Inf Sch WF15 ... 116 E2
Roberttown La WF15 ... 116 F2
Robin Chase LS28 ... 76 F7
Robin Cl Bradford BD2 ... 56 C4
Pontefract WF8 ... 125 D3
Robin Dr Bradford BD2 ... 56 C4
Steeton BD20 ... 17 B6
Robin Hill WF17 ... 118 A8
Robin Hood Ave S71 ... 179 D4
Robin Hood Cres WF2 ... 141 E4
Robin Hood Gr HD2 ... 136 C4
Robin Hood Hill HD4 ... 171 F7
Robin Hood Junior
& Infants Sch WF3 ... 100 B2
Robin Hood Rd HD2 ... 136 C4
Robin Hood St 1 WF10 ... 124 E7
Robin Hood Way HD6 ... 115 E2
Robin La Batley WF13 ... 118 B2
Batley, Heckmondwike WF13 ... 117 F3
Hemsworth WF9 ... 181 A5
Pudsey LS28 ... 76 E7
Royston S71 ... 179 D4
Robin Rocks HD7 ... 172 C2
Robin Royd Ave WF14 ... 138 A8
Robin Royd Croft WF14 ... 138 A8
Robin Royd Dr WF14 ... 138 A8
Robin Royd Garth WF14 ... 138 A8
Robin Royd Gr WF14 ... 138 A8
Robin Royd La WF14 ... 138 A8
Robin St Bradford BD5 ... 74 C4
Huddersfield HD1 ... 153 D5
Robin Wlk BD18 ... 55 D6
Robin's Gr LS26 ... 100 F5
Robinia Wlk WF2 ... 142 A8
Robins The LS29 ... 21 E8
Robinson Ct BD7 ... 73 F6
Robinson La Honley HD7 ... 172 B3
Kippax LS25 ... 83 B1
Robinson St
Huddersfield HD1 ... 154 C5
Kippax WF10 ... 103 B4
Pontefract WF8 ... 125 D1
Robinwood Ct LS8 ... 44 A1
Robson Cl WF8 ... 146 D6
Robson's Rd WF1 ... 216 A2
Rochdale Rd Bacup OL13 ... 106 A1
Elland HX4 ... 134 B7
Halifax HX2, HX6 ... 112 D5
Ripponden HX6 ... 131 C2
Slaithwaite HD7 ... 151 F4
Sowerby Bridge HX6 ... 111 F1
Todmorden OL14 ... 129 B6
Todmorden, Knowl Wood
OL14 ... 108 A3
Rocheford Cl LS10 ... 215 F3
Rocheford Ct LS10 ... 215 F3
Rocheford Gdns LS10 ... 215 F3
Rocheford Gr LS10 ... 215 F3
Rocheford Wlk LS10 ... 215 F3
Rochester Cl 2 OL13 ... 106 A7
Rochester Ct WF4 ... 141 C3
Rochester Dr WF4 ... 141 C2
Rochester Gdns LS13 ... 57 F4
Rochester House BD15 ... 54 B1
Rochester Pl 5 HX5 ... 134 F6
Rochester Rd WF17 ... 96 F3
Rochester St Bradford BD3 ... 75 C7
Shipley BD18 ... 55 C6
Rochester Terr LS6 ... 205 D4
Rochester Wynd LS17 ... 44 A4
Rock Cliffe Mount HX2 ... 111 D7
Rock Edge WF15 ... 117 A5
Rock Fold HD7 ... 152 D4
Rock Hill WF10 ... 125 A6
Rock House Dr WF13 ... 118 C2
Rock La Leeds LS13 ... 58 B4
Slaithwaite HD7 ... 152 A3
Wilsden BD13 ... 72 C8
Rock Lea 5 BD13 ... 72 F1
Rock Nook OL15 ... 129 D1
Rock Rd HD3 ... 135 B2
Rock St 15 Brighouse HD6 ... 115 A3
Huddersfield HD3 ... 152 E7
Rock Terr Brighouse HX3 ... 114 D8
Castleford WF10 ... 125 A6
Huddersfield HD3 ... 135 B1
2 Leeds LS15 ... 80 F8
Morley LS27 ... 98 B5
Thornton BD13 ... 72 D6
Todmorden OL14 ... 108 A2
Rock The HD7 ... 152 E1
Rock View Elland HX4 ... 134 C4
Marsden HD7 ... 168 F3
Rockcliffe Ave BD17 ... 38 C1
Rockery Croft LS18 ... 41 C2
Rockery Rd LS18 ... 41 C2
Rockfield Terr LS19 ... 40 C7
Rockhill Cl WF17 ... 96 F1
Rockhill La BD4 ... 95 A7
Rockingham Cl LS15 ... 62 F3
Rockingham La WF9 ... 164 E4
Rockingham Rd LS15 ... 62 F3
Rockingham St WF9 ... 163 B3
Rockingham Way LS15 ... 62 F3
Rockland Cres BD7 ... 73 E5
Rocklands Ave 2 BD17 ... 38 C4
Rocklands Pl 3 BD17 ... 38 C4
Rockley Cl HD5 ... 154 E4
Rockley Dr WF2 ... 160 B6
Rockley Grange Gdns
LS25 ... 82 D5
Rockley St WF13 ... 139 D8
Rockliffe La OL13 ... 106 A1
Rockliffe Rd OL13 ... 106 A1
Rockmill Rd HD7 ... 172 C2
Rocks La HX2 ... 71 D1
Rocks Rd HX3 ... 113 A4
Rocks View 3 HX2 ... 113 A4
Rockville Terr
15 Halifax HX1 ... 202 C1
Yeadon LS19 ... 40 C6
Rockwell La BD10 ... 56 C6
Rockwood Cl
Huddersfield HD2 ... 136 E6
Mapplewell S75 ... 177 F1
Rockwood Cres
Crigglestone WF4 ... 159 D6
Pudsey LS28 ... 57 A3
Rockwood Gr LS28 ... 57 B3
Rockwood Rd LS28 ... 57 A2
Rockwood Rise HD8 ... 192 A7
Roderick St LS12 ... 209 E3
Rodger La WF2 ... 120 F2
Rodillian Sch WF3 ... 100 B1
Rodin Ave BD8 ... 73 D7
Rodley La Emley HD8 ... 175 D7
Leeds LS13 ... 58 A4
Pudsey LS28, S13 ... 57 D6
Rodley Primary Sch LS13 ... 57 F5
Rodney Yd WF1 ... 216 B2
Rods Mills La LS27 ... 98 B3
Rods View 4 LS27 ... 98 B3
Roe House BD17 ... 38 B1
Roebuck La LS21 ... 10 F4
Roebuck Memorial Homes
HD5 ... 154 F6
Roebuck St WF17 ... 96 F1
Roebuck Terr LS21 ... 10 F4
Roeburn Cl S75 ... 178 A2
Roger Ct BD2 ... 56 B2
Roger Dr WF2 ... 142 D1
Roger Fold 1 LS25 ... 83 B1
Roger Gate HX7 ... 89 C1
Roger La HD4 ... 154 C3
Rogers Ct WF3 ... 121 F6
Rogers Pl LS28 ... 76 F8
Rogerson Sq HD6 ... 115 A3
Roils Head Rd HX2 ... 112 C7
Rokeby Gdns Bradford BD10 ... 56 E6
Leeds LS6 ... 59 C5
Roker La LS28 ... 77 A5
Roman Ave
Huddersfield HD3 ... 134 D1
Leeds LS8 ... 44 A3
Roman Cl HD3 ... 134 D1
Roman Cres LS8 ... 44 B2
Roman Dr Huddersfield HD3 ... 134 D1
Leeds LS8 ... 44 B2
Roman Gdns LS8 ... 44 A2
Roman Gr LS8 ... 44 B2
Roman Mount LS8 ... 44 B2
Roman Pl LS8 ... 44 B2
Roman Rd 5 WF17 ... 117 F8
Roman Rise WF8 ... 146 C5
Roman St S63 ... 194 E1
Roman Terr LS8 ... 44 A2
Roman View LS8 ... 44 B2
Romanby Shaw BD10 ... 56 D6
Rombald's View LS29 ... 8 D5
Rombalds Ave LS12 ... 209 F4
Rombalds Cres LS12 ... 59 C1
Rombalds Ct LS29 ... 21 F4
Rombalds Dr BD16 ... 37 B3
Rombalds Gr LS12 ... 209 F4
Rombalds La LS29 ... 8 E3
Rombalds Pl 1 LS12 ... 59 C1
Rombalds St LS12 ... 59 C1
Rombalds Terr LS12 ... 209 F4
Rombalds View Leeds LS12 ... 59 C1
Otley LS21 ... 10 D2
Romford Ave LS27 ... 98 A3
Romford Ct BD6 ... 93 F6
Romney Mount LS28 ... 77 A5
Romsey Cl HD3 ... 134 F1
Romsey Gdns BD4 ... 75 E3
Romsey Mews BD4 ... 75 D3
Ronald Dr BD7 ... 74 A7
Ronaldsway Cl OL13 ... 106 B1
Roods La HD7 ... 188 B3
Rook La BD4 ... 75 C2
Rook St Bingley BD16 ... 36 F3
Huddersfield HD1 ... 154 A7
Rook's Nest Junior
& Infants Sch WF1 ... 121 C4
Rook's Nest Rd WF1 ... 121 D4
Rookeries Junior
& Infants Sch The WF8 ... 146 E6
Rookery La HX3 ... 113 D3
Rookery The LS29 ... 6 F8
Rookes Ave BD6 ... 94 C8
Rookes La HX3 ... 94 A1
Rookhill Dr WF8 ... 146 E7
Rookhill Mount WF8 ... 146 F7
Rookhill Rd WF8 ... 146 F7
Rooks Ave BD19 ... 116 C8
Rooks Cl BD12 ... 94 D1
Rookwith Par BD10 ... 56 E6
Rookwood Ave
Kippax LS25 ... 103 A8
Leeds LS9 ... 80 D8
Rookwood Cres LS9 ... 80 C8
Rookwood Gdns LS9 ... 80 C8
Rookwood Gr LS9 ... 80 C8
Rookwood Hill LS9 ... 80 C8
Rookwood Mount LS9 ... 80 C8
Rookwood Par LS9 ... 80 C8
Rookwood Pl LS9 ... 80 C8
Rookwood Rd LS9 ... 80 C8
Rookwood Sq LS9 ... 80 D8
Rookwood St LS9 ... 80 C7
Rookwood Terr LS9 ... 80 C8
Rookwood Vale LS9 ... 80 C7
Rookwood View LS9 ... 80 C8
Rookwood Wlk LS9 ... 80 C8
Rooley Ave BD6 ... 74 E1
Rooley Banks HX6 ... 111 E3
Rooley Cl BD5 ... 74 E1
Rooley Cres BD6 ... 94 E8
Rooley Ct HX6 ... 111 D3
Rooley Hts HX6 ... 111 D3
Rooley La
Bradford BD4, BD5 ... 75 B1
Sowerby Bridge HX6 ... 111 D3
Roomfield Ct 11 OL14 ... 108 B5
Roomfield St OL14 ... 108 B5
Rooms Fold LS27 ... 98 A6

Rooms La Gildersome LS27 .... 98 A8
Morley LS27 .... 98 A6
Rope Wlk Halifax HX2 .... 90 F7
Knottingley WF11 .... 127 A4
Roper Ave LS8 .... 204 C4
Roper Gdns HX2 .... 91 D4
Roper Gn HX2 .... 91 D4
Roper Gr LS8 .... 204 C4
Roper La Halifax HX2 .... 91 F8
Queensbury BD13 .... 72 B2
Roper St BD21 .... 35 B7
Ropergate WF8 .... 146 C8
Ropergate End 4 WF8 .... 146 C8
Roscoe St LS7 .... 207 D2
Rose Ave Horsforth LS18 .... 58 B7
Huddersfield, Cowersley HD4 .... 152 F3
Huddersfield, Marsh HD3 .... 153 C6
Upton WF9 .... 183 A7
Rose Bank LS29 .... 21 E8
Rose Bank Pl BD8 .... 73 E7
Rose Bank Rd OL14 .... 108 A5
Rose Cl WF9 .... 183 A7
Rose Croft LS17 .... 28 C6
Rose Ct LS25 .... 83 A7
Rose Farm App WF6 .... 122 F4
Rose Farm Cl WF6 .... 122 F5
Rose Farm Fold WF6 .... 122 F5
Rose Farm Rise WF6 .... 122 F5
Rose Garth Crofton WF4 .... 143 F1
Menston LS29 .... 21 C7
Rose Gr
7 Hebden Bridge HX7 .... 89 A4
Hebden Bridge, Mytholmroyd HX7 .... 110 E8
Rothwell LS26 .... 100 D6
Upton WF9 .... 183 A7
Rose Grove La HX2 .... 112 A5
Rose Heath HX2 .... 91 D7
Rose Hill Dr HD2 .... 135 E1
Rose La WF7 .... 163 D4
Rose Meadows BD22 .... 34 E5
Rose Mount Bradford BD2 .... 56 A3
Huddersfield HD2 .... 135 D1
Rose Mount Pl LS12 .... 210 A2
Rose Pl HX2 .... 111 E5
Rose St Bradford BD8 .... 55 B1
Halifax HX1 .... 202 B2
Haworth BD22 .... 51 C6
Horsforth LS18 .... 58 B8
Keighley BD21 .... 35 F7
Todmorden OL14 .... 108 B5
Rose Terr Addingham LS29 .... 6 F8
3 Halifax HX1 .... 202 C3
2 Halifax, King Cross HX2 .... 113 A4
Horsforth LS18 .... 58 A7
Huddersfield HD1 .... 154 B8
Low Bradley BD20 .... 4 C5
Rosebank Cres LS3 .... 205 F2
Rosebank Gdns LS3 .... 205 F1
Rosebank Ho LS6 .... 205 F2
Rosebank Rd LS3 .... 205 F1
Rosebank Row LS3 .... 205 F1
Rosebank St WF17 .... 118 B6
Roseberry St
Oakworth BD22 .... 34 D2
Todmorden OL14 .... 86 C1
Rosebery Ave Halifax HX3 .... 113 D4
Shipley BD18 .... 55 C7
Rosebery Mount BD18 .... 55 D7
Rosebery Rd BD8 .... 55 C2
Rosebery St Elland HX5 .... 134 F6
Huddersfield HD2 .... 135 F1
Pudsey LS28 .... 76 C8
Rosebery Terr Halifax HX1 .... 202 C4
3 Pudsey LS28 .... 57 F2
Rosebud Wlk LS8 .... 207 E2
Rosecliffe Mount LS13 .... 58 C2
Rosecliffe Terr LS13 .... 58 C2
Rosedale LS26 .... 100 F6
Rosedale Ave
Bradford BD15 .... 53 F2
10 Huddersfield HD5 .... 154 D5
Liversedge WF15 .... 116 D2
Wakefield WF2 .... 160 E8
Rosedale Bank LS10 .... 215 D1
Rosedale Cl Baildon BD17 .... 38 A2
Normanton WF6 .... 123 D1
Upton WF9 .... 183 B7
Rosedale Gdns LS10 .... 215 D1
Rosedale Gn LS10 .... 215 D1
Rosedale Rise LS23 .... 30 C7
Rosedale Wlk LS10 .... 215 D1
Rosegarth Ave HD7 .... 189 C7
Rosehill Ave WF9 .... 181 C6
Rosehill Cres BD12 .... 94 C4
Roselee Cl HX3 .... 113 E3
Rosemary Ave LS12 .... 210 A3
Rosemary Cl HD6 .... 115 A1
Rosemary La Brighouse HD6 .... 115 A1
Halifax HX3 .... 113 E3
Rosemont LS16 .... 24 E3
Rosemont Ave
7 Leeds LS13 .... 58 C2
3 Pudsey LS28 .... 76 F8
Rosemont Dr LS28 .... 76 F8
Rosemont Gr 8 LS13 .... 58 C2
Rosemont La 2 BD17 .... 38 D2
Rosemont Pl LS13 .... 58 C2
Rosemont Rd LS13 .... 58 C2
Rosemont St Leeds LS13 .... 58 C2
4 Pudsey LS28 .... 76 F8
Rosemont Terr Leeds LS13 .... 58 C2
Pudsey LS28 .... 76 F8
Rosemont View LS13 .... 58 C2
Rosemont Wlk 6 LS13 .... 58 C2
Rosemount OL13 .... 106 A4
Rosemount Ave HX5 .... 135 A6
Rosemount Cl 2 BD21 .... 35 B7
Rosemount Ct BD20 .... 16 D4
Rosemount Terr HX5 .... 135 A6
Rosemount Wks HX5 .... 135 A5
Rosemount Wlk 1 BD21 .... 35 B7
Rosendale Cl 3 OL13 .... 106 B3
Rosendale Cres OL13 .... 106 B3
Roseneath Pl LS12 .... 210 A2
Roseneath St LS12 .... 210 A2
Roseneath Terr LS12 .... 210 A2
Rosetta Dr BD8 .... 73 F8
Roseville Rd LS8 .... 207 E2
Roseville St LS8 .... 207 E2
Roseville Terr
Dewsbury WF12 .... 139 F8
4 Leeds LS15 .... 62 D3
Roseville Way LS8 .... 207 E2
Rosewood Ave
Keighley BD20 .... 18 F1
Kippax LS25 .... 82 F3
Rosewood Ct LS26 .... 100 F7
Rosewood Gr BD4 .... 75 D5
Rosewood Sq BD20 .... 16 D4
Rosgill Dr LS14 .... 62 A5
Rosgill Wlk LS14 .... 61 F5
Rosley Mount BD6 .... 93 F6
Roslyn Ave HD4 .... 171 C7
Roslyn Pl BD7 .... 74 B6
Ross Gr LS13 .... 58 B4
Ross Terr LS13 .... 58 A4
Rossall Gr LS8 .... 207 F4
Rossall Rd LS8 .... 207 F4
Rosse St Bradford BD8 .... 74 A8
Shipley BD18 .... 55 B8
Rossefield App LS13 .... 58 D2
Rossefield Ave
Huddersfield HD2 .... 135 E1
Leeds LS13 .... 58 D2
Rossefield Chase LS13 .... 58 D2
Rossefield Cl 3 LS13 .... 58 D2
Rossefield Dr LS13 .... 58 D2
Rossefield Gn LS13 .... 58 D2
Rossefield Gr LS13 .... 58 D2
Rossefield Lawn LS13 .... 58 D2
Rossefield Par LS13 .... 58 D2
Rossefield Pk BD9 .... 55 B4
Rossefield Pl LS13 .... 58 D2
Rossefield Rd BD9 .... 55 A4
Rossefield Sch BD9 .... 55 A4
Rossefield Terr LS13 .... 58 D2
Rossefield View LS13 .... 58 D2
Rossefield Way LS13 .... 58 C2
Rossefield Wlk 5 LS13 .... 58 D2
Rossendale Pl BD18 .... 55 A7
Rossett Ho BD3 .... 201 C4
Rossington Gr 4 LS8 .... 207 E4
Rossington Pl 6 LS8 .... 207 E4
Rossington Rd LS8 .... 61 A5
Rossington St LS2 .... 211 E4
Rossiter Dr WF11 .... 126 D3
Rosslyn Ave WF7 .... 163 F5
Rosslyn Cl WF7 .... 163 F5
Rosslyn Ct
Ackworth M T WF7 .... 163 F5
Dewsbury WF12 .... 139 F7
Rosslyn Gr
Ackworth M T WF7 .... 163 F5
Haworth BD22 .... 51 C6
Rossmore Dr BD15 .... 54 C1
Rotcher HD7 .... 169 E8
Rotcher La HD7 .... 169 E8
Rotcher Rd HD7 .... 189 A5
Rothbury Gdns LS16 .... 42 B3
Rothesay Terr BD7 .... 74 C6
Rothwell CE Prim Sch LS26 .... 100 E6
Rothwell Dr HX1 .... 203 D1
Rothwell Infants Sch LS26 .... 100 E4
Rothwell La LS26 .... 101 B5
Rothwell Mount HX1 .... 203 D1
Rothwell Rd HX1 .... 203 D1
Rothwell Sports Ctr LS26 .... 101 C4
Rothwell St HD5 .... 154 E6
Rothwell St Mary's RC JMI Sch LS26 .... 100 F4
Rothwell West Jun Sch LS26 .... 100 E4
Rough Hall La HX2 .... 90 F5
Rough Side La OL14 .... 108 C3
Round Close Rd HD7 .... 199 B6
Round Hill Halifax HX2 .... 91 F6
Mapplewell S75 .... 178 A1
Round Hill Cl Bradford BD14 .... 73 B2
Halifax HX2 .... 91 F6
Round Hill La HD5 .... 137 B3
Round Ings Rd HD3 .... 152 A6
Round St Bradford BD5 .... 74 E3
Wakefield WF1 .... 142 E4
Round Thorn Pl BD8 .... 74 A8
Round Wood Ave HD5 .... 155 A6
Roundell Ave BD4 .... 95 B8
Roundhay Ave LS8 .... 204 C1
Roundhay Cres LS8 .... 204 C1
Roundhay Gdns LS8 .... 204 C1
Roundhay Gr LS8 .... 204 C1
Roundhay Hall Hospl LS8 .... 61 A7
Roundhay High Sch LS8 .... 61 A7
Roundhay Mount LS8 .... 204 C1
Roundhay Park LS8 .... 44 C1
Roundhay Park La LS17 .... 44 B4
Roundhay Pl LS8 .... 204 C1
Roundhay Rd LS7, LS8 .... 207 F3
Roundhay Sch LS8 .... 61 A7
Roundhay St John's C of E Primary Sch LS8 .... 61 C6
Roundhay View LS8 .... 204 C1
Roundhead Fold BD10 .... 56 E8
Roundhill Ave BD16 .... 54 B7
Roundhill Mount BD16 .... 54 B7
Roundhill Pl BD1 .... 201 A3
Roundhill Rd WF10 .... 124 D7
Roundhill St BD5 .... 74 D4
Roundthorn Sch BD5 .... 74 E3
Roundway HD7 .... 172 A3
Roundway The LS27 .... 97 F4
Roundwell Rd WF15 .... 116 C5
Roundwood BD18 .... 54 F7
Roundwood Ave
Baildon BD17 .... 38 F3
Bradford BD10 .... 56 E4
Roundwood Cres WF2 .... 141 C5
Roundwood Glen BD10 .... 56 E6
Roundwood Hill Sch WF2 .... 141 D3
Roundwood Ind Est WF5 .... 141 B5
Roundwood Rd
Baildon BD17 .... 38 E4
Ossett WF5 .... 141 A4
Roundwood Rise WF2 .... 141 D4
Roundwood View BD10 .... 56 E6
Rouse Fold BD4 .... 201 C1
Rouse Mill La WF17 .... 118 D4
Rouse St 7 WF15 .... 117 A4
Row HD7 .... 169 C8
Row Gate HD8 .... 190 D6
Row La Marsden HD7 .... 169 C8
Sowerby Bridge HX6 .... 111 D3
Row St HD4 .... 153 E4
Rowan Ave Bradford BD3 .... 75 E7
Huddersfield HD4 .... 171 D6
Normanton WF6 .... 144 A7
Rowan Avenue Mews HD4 .... 171 D6
Rowan Cl Batley WF17 .... 97 A2
Knottingley WF11 .... 126 E2
Rowan Ct Bradford BD2 .... 56 C1
Wakefield WF2 .... 141 F8
Yeadon LS19 .... 40 B5
Rowan Dr HD6 .... 115 C3
Rowan Garth BD20 .... 16 D6
Rowan Gn WF8 .... 125 F1
Rowan Pl LS25 .... 83 B6
Rowan St BD20 .... 18 A2
Rowanberry Cl BD2 .... 56 B4
Rowans The Baildon BD17 .... 37 F3
Bramhope LS16 .... 24 F2
Pudsey LS13 .... 57 F3
Wetherby LS22 .... 14 A6
Rowantree Ave BD17 .... 38 B4
Rowantree Dr BD10 .... 56 C6
Rowanwood Gdns BD10 .... 56 E5
Rowe Cl WF9 .... 183 A4
Rowgate HD8 .... 191 B6
Rowland La HX7 .... 89 C4
Rowland Pl LS11 .... 214 B3
Rowland Rd LS11 .... 214 B3
Rowland St S71 .... 179 D4
Rowland Terr 6 LS11 .... 214 C3
Rowlands Ave
Huddersfield HD5 .... 154 F6
Upton WF9 .... 183 A7
Rowlestone Rise BD10 .... 56 E6
Rowley Dr Ilkley LS29 .... 8 F3
Lepton HD8 .... 155 D3
Rowley La Lepton HD8 .... 155 E2
South Elmsall WF9 .... 183 A2
Rowsley St 1 BD21 .... 35 D7
Rowton Thorpe BD10 .... 56 E6
Roxburgh Gr BD15 .... 73 B8
Roxburghe Dale WF6 .... 123 D1
Roxby Cl LS9 .... 207 E1
Roxby St BD5 .... 74 D3
Roxholme Ave LS7 .... 204 B1
Roxholme Gr LS7 .... 204 B1
Roxholme Pl LS7 .... 204 B1
Roxholme Rd LS7 .... 204 B1
Roxholme Terr LS7 .... 204 B1
Roy Rd BD6 .... 73 D1
Roy St OL14 .... 86 A1
Royal Armouries Mus The LS10 .... 212 A2
Royal Birkdale Way WF6 .... 123 D1
Royal Cl Bradford BD7 .... 73 F3
Leeds LS10 .... 215 D2
Royal Ct Leeds LS10 .... 215 D2
Pontefract WF8 .... 146 B5
Royal Dr LS10 .... 215 D2
Royal Gdns LS10 .... 215 D2
Royal Gr LS10 .... 215 D2
Royal Halifax Infmy HX1 .... 203 D1
Royal London Ind Est The LS11 .... 213 F1
Royal Park Ave LS6 .... 205 F3
Royal Park Gr LS6 .... 205 F3
Royal Park Mount LS6 .... 205 F3
Royal Park Primary Sch LS6 .... 205 E2
Royal Park Rd LS6 .... 205 F2
Royal Park Terr LS6 .... 205 F3
Royal Park View LS6 .... 205 F3
Royal Pl LS10 .... 215 D2
Royal Terr Boston Spa LS23 .... 30 E8
Huddersfield HD3 .... 153 A5
Royd Ave Batley WF16 .... 117 D6
Bingley BD16 .... 37 C3
Holmfirth HD7 .... 189 E6
Huddersfield HD3 .... 153 A5
Huddersfield, Ainley Top HD3 .... 135 A3
Mapplewell S75 .... 178 B1
Royd Cl BD20 .... 16 D6
Royd Cres Halifax HX1 .... 202 B4
Hebden Bridge HX7 .... 89 F1
Royd Croft HD3 .... 153 B6
Royd Head Farm WF5 .... 140 C5
Royd House Gr BD21 .... 35 E5
Royd House La HD7 .... 152 D1
Royd House Rd BD21 .... 35 E5
Royd House Way BD21 .... 35 E5
Royd House Wlk BD21 .... 35 E5
Royd Ings Ave BD21 .... 18 D1
Royd La Halifax HX3 .... 92 A3
Halifax, Illingworth HX2 .... 91 E7
Holmfirth HD7 .... 188 E2
Keighley BD20 .... 18 B1
Ripponden HX6 .... 132 D4
Todmorden OL14 .... 108 B6
Royd Mill Bsns Pk HD6 .... 115 C2
Royd Moor La WF9 .... 164 C1
Royd Mount 4 Halifax HX3 .... 92 C2
Holmfirth HD7 .... 189 A5
Royd Mount Middle Sch BD13 .... 72 C6
Royd Pl HX3 .... 92 C2
Royd Rd Meltham HD7 .... 187 E8
Todmorden OL14 .... 108 B7
Royd Sq 2 HX7 .... 89 A3
Royd St 3 Bradford BD12 .... 94 C4
Huddersfield HD3 .... 153 A5
Keighley BD20 .... 18 B2
Slaithwaite HD7 .... 151 F1
Thornton BD13 .... 72 C6
Todmorden OL14 .... 108 A6
Wilsden BD15 .... 53 C5
Royd Terr
Hebden Bridge HX7 .... 89 A3
Huddersfield HD4 .... 171 E8
Royd View HX7 .... 89 E1
Royd Way BD21 .... 18 C1
Royd Wood
Cleckheaton BD19 .... 116 D6
Oxenhope BD22 .... 51 D4
Roydfield St HD2 .... 136 B2
Roydlands St HX3 .... 114 D7
Roydon Gr BD9 .... 55 A2
Royds Ave Birkenshaw BD11 .... 96 B5
Brighouse HD6 .... 115 B8
Castleford WF10 .... 125 C8
Holmfirth HD7 .... 189 D6
Huddersfield HD3 .... 153 C5
Ossett WF5 .... 140 C8
Slaithwaite HD7 .... 152 D2
Royds Cl Holmfirth HD7 .... 189 D6
Leeds LS12 .... 78 C4
Royds Cres HD6 .... 115 B7
Royds Dr HD7 .... 189 D6
Royds Farm Rd LS12 .... 78 C3
Royds Gr WF1 .... 121 C5
Royds Hall Ave BD6 .... 94 C8
Royds Hall High Sch HD3 .... 153 C6
Royds Hall La
Bradford BD12, BD6 .... 94 B5
Bradford, Moor Top BD6 .... 94 A7
Royds Hall Rd LS12 .... 78 C4
Royds La Leeds LS12 .... 78 C3
Leeds, Far Royds LS12 .... 78 C4
Rothwell LS26 .... 101 A3
Royds Park Cres BD12 .... 94 D4
Royds Pk HD8 .... 192 A6
Royds Sch LS26 .... 101 B2
Royds St HD7 .... 168 F3
Royds The
Clayton West HD8 .... 176 A3
Holmfirth HD7 .... 189 A5
Royds View HD7 .... 152 D1
Roydscliffe Dr BD9 .... 54 F4
Roydscliffe Rd BD9 .... 54 F4
Roydsdale Way BD4 .... 95 A6
Roydstone Rd BD3 .... 75 D8
Roydstone Terr BD3 .... 75 D8
Roydwood Terr BD13 .... 52 D6
Roydwood Terr (Back) BD13 .... 52 D6
Royle Fold WF16 .... 117 D4
Royles Cl WF9 .... 182 C2
Royles Head La HD3 .... 152 E6
Royston C of E Jun & Inf Sch S71 .... 179 C3
Royston Cl WF3 .... 120 D6
Royston Comp Sch S71 .... 179 C4
Royston Hill WF3 .... 120 D6
Royston La S71 .... 179 C2
Royston Midland Jun & Inf Sch S71 .... 179 C3
Royston Rd S72 .... 180 B1
Ruby St Batley WF17 .... 118 A7
13 Keighley BD22 .... 35 A4
Leeds LS9 .... 207 E1
Rud La HX7 .... 110 A3
Rudd St 11 BD7 .... 74 A4
Rudding Ave BD15 .... 54 A1
Rudding Cres BD15 .... 54 A1
Rudding Dr WF17 .... 117 F6
Rudding St HD4 .... 153 D4
Rudgate Tadcaster LS24 .... 31 D4
Thorp Arch LS23, LS24 .... 15 D5
Rudgate HM Prison LS23 .... 15 A2
Rudgate Mews LS23 .... 15 A3
Rudgate Pk LS23 .... 15 A3
Ruffield Side BD12 .... 94 C5
Rufford Ave LS19 .... 40 C6
Rufford Bank LS19 .... 40 C6
Rufford Cl LS19 .... 40 C6
Rufford Cres LS19 .... 40 C6
Rufford Dr LS19 .... 40 C6
Rufford Pl 2 HX3 .... 113 B4
Rufford Rd Elland HX5 .... 134 F6
Halifax HX3 .... 113 B4
Huddersfield HD3 .... 152 F5
Rufford Ridge LS19 .... 40 C6
Rufford Rise LS19 .... 40 B6
Rufford St Bradford BD3 .... 75 C7
Wakefield WF2 .... 141 F6
Rufford Villas 4 HX3 .... 113 B4
Rufus St Bradford BD5 .... 74 B3
6 Keighley BD21 .... 35 C8
Rugby Ave HX3 .... 91 F3
Rugby Dr HX3 .... 91 F3
Rugby Gdns HX3 .... 91 F3
Rugby Mount HX3 .... 91 F3
Rugby Pl BD7 .... 74 B6
Rugby Terr HX3 .... 91 F3
Rumble Rd WF12 .... 118 F1
Rumbold Rd HD3 .... 153 D7
Rumple Croft LS21 .... 10 E2
Runnymeade Ct BD10 .... 56 B7
Runswick Ave 1 LS11 .... 210 C1
Runswick Gr BD5 .... 74 D1
Runswick Pl LS11 .... 211 D1
Runswick St Bradford BD5 .... 74 D1
Leeds LS11 .... 211 D1
Runswick Terr
Bradford BD5 .... 74 D1
Leeds LS11 .... 211 D1
Runtlings WF5 .... 140 C5
Runtlings La WF5 .... 140 C4
Runtlings The WF5 .... 140 B5
Rupert Rd LS29 .... 8 A5
Rupert St Haworth BD22 .... 51 F8
5 Keighley BD21 .... 35 C8
Rushbearers Wlk HD5 .... 154 E3
Rushcroft Terr BD17 .... 38 C3
Rushdene Ct BD12 .... 94 C1
Rushfield Vale HD8 .... 155 C4
Rushmoor Rd BD4 .... 75 D2
Rusholme Dr LS28 .... 57 C3
Rushton Ave BD3 .... 75 E8
Rushton Hill Cl HX2 .... 91 C1
Rushton Rd BD3 .... 75 E8
Rushton St Halifax HX1 .... 202 B4
Pudsey LS28 .... 57 B6
Rushton Terr BD3 .... 75 E7
Rushworth Cl WF3 .... 121 E5
Rushworth St 16 HX3 .... 92 A1
Ruskin Ave Bradford BD9 .... 54 D3
Wakefield WF1 .... 121 A3
Ruskin Cl WF10 .... 125 B8
Ruskin Cres LS20 .... 39 F8
Ruskin Ct WF2 .... 120 F2
Ruskin Dr WF10 .... 125 B8
Ruskin Gr HD2 .... 136 D3
Ruskin Pl WF10 .... 125 B8
Ruskin St LS28 .... 57 C1
Ruskin Terr 24 HX3 .... 92 A1
Russel Ct LS17 .... 28 D3
Russell Ave
Crigglestone WF4 .... 159 F3
Queensbury BD13 .... 92 E8
Russell Cl Batley WF17 .... 118 C5
Batley, Heckmondwike WF16 .... 117 E3
Russell Gr BD11 .... 96 B5
Russell Hall First Sch BD13 .... 72 E1
Russell Hall La 15 BD13 .... 72 E1
Russell Rd BD13 .... 92 D8
Russell St Bradford BD5 .... 201 A1
Dewsbury WF13 .... 118 A1
Halifax HX1 .... 203 E3
Keighley BD21 .... 35 B7
Leeds LS1 .... 211 E4
Queensbury BD13 .... 72 E1
Shipley BD18 .... 55 C5
Todmorden OL14 .... 108 C5
Wakefield WF1 .... 142 C4
Russet Fold WF15 .... 117 A5
Russets The WF2 .... 160 E6
Russett Gr HD4 .... 154 C3
Rustic Ave HX3 .... 114 A4
Ruswarp Cres BD10 .... 56 D6
Ruth St 15 Haworth BD22 .... 51 E8
Huddersfield HD4 .... 154 A2
Ruthven View LS8 .... 208 A3
Rutland Ave Pontefract WF8 .... 146 D5
Wakefield WF2 .... 142 C2
Rutland Cl Kippax LS25 .... 83 B2
5 Rothwell LS26 .... 101 D6
Rutland Ct 3 LS28 .... 76 E8
Rutland Dr Crofton WF4 .... 143 C2
Kippax LS25 .... 83 B2
Rutland House 5 BD16 .... 37 A3
Rutland Ind Est WF1 .... 142 D4
Rutland Mount LS3 .... 210 C4
Rutland Rd Batley WF17 .... 118 D6
Flockton WF4 .... 157 C3
Huddersfield HD3 .... 153 A5
Rutland St Bradford BD4 .... 201 D1
7 Keighley BD21 .... 35 B5
Leeds LS3 .... 211 D4
Rutland Terr S18 .... 210 C4
Rutland Wlk 7 WF13 .... 139 B8
Ryan Gr BD22 .... 34 D8
Ryan Middle Sch BD5 .... 74 F3
Ryan St BD5 .... 74 D3
Ryburn Golf Course HX6 .... 112 C2
Ryburn Ho 6 HX1 .... 202 B3
Ryburn La HX6 .... 132 E5
Ryburn Pl WF2 .... 216 A1
Ryburn Rd HD3 .... 153 B7
Ryburn St HX6 .... 112 B3
Ryburn Terr Halifax HX1 .... 202 B3
Ripponden HX6 .... 132 C1
Ryburn Valley High Sch HX6 .... 111 E3
Ryburn View HX6 .... 132 C3
Rycroft Ave Pudsey LS13 .... 58 B1
Shipley BD16 .... 54 A6
Rycroft Cl LS13 .... 58 B1

Rycroft Ct 2 LS13 58 B1
Rycroft Dr LS13 58 B1
Rycroft Gdns LS13 58 B1
Rycroft Gn 1 LS13 58 B1
Rycroft Pl 3 LS13 58 B1
Rycroft St BD18 55 D5
Rycroft Towers LS13 58 A1
Rydal Ave Baildon BD17 37 E1
Garforth LS25 82 F6
Shipley BD9 55 C4
Rydal Cres Morley LS27 98 D5
Wakefield WF2 141 E7
Rydal Dr Huddersfield HD5 154 D6
Morley LS27 98 D5
Wakefield WF2 141 E7
Rydal Gr WF15 117 A1
Rydal St Castleford WF10 125 D8
Keighley BD21 35 A6
Rydale Ct WF5 140 D4
Rydall Pl LS11 210 C1
Rydall St LS11 210 C1
Rydall Terr LS11 210 C1
Ryder Cl WF8 146 B8
Ryder Gdns LS8 61 A7
Rydings Ave HD6 115 A3
Rydings Cl 11 HD6 115 A3
Rydings Dr HD6 114 F3
Rydings Wlk HD6 114 F3
Rye Close La HD7 187 E4
Rye Croft HX2 91 F6
Rye Field La HX4 150 F6
Rye Field La W HX4 150 F6
Rye Garth LS22 13 D8
Rye La HX2 91 C1
Rye Pl LS14 61 F1
Rye St 9 BD21 35 B4
Rye Way WF10 125 B8
Ryebank HD7 189 B4
Ryebread WF10 103 E1
Ryecroft BD21 35 F1
Ryecroft Ave WF4 162 C2
Ryecroft Cl WF1 121 C5
Ryecroft Cres HX2 91 D1
Ryecroft Dr HD3 135 B1
Ryecroft First Sch BD4 75 F2
Ryecroft La Brighouse HD6 136 C8
Halifax HX2 91 D1
Holmfirth HD7 189 C3
Ryecroft Middle Sch LS12 77 E6
Ryecroft Rd
Cullingworth BD21 35 E1
Glusburn BD20 16 B7
Harden BD16 36 A1
Ryecroft St WF5 140 C7
Ryecroft Terr HX2 91 D1
Ryecroft Way BD20 16 C6
Ryedale HD5 137 B2
Ryedale Ave
Knottingley WF11 126 E2
Leeds LS12 78 B4
Ryedale Cl WF6 123 A5
Ryedale Ct LS14 61 F5
Ryedale Holt LS12 209 F1
Ryedale Pk LS29 8 D3
Ryedale Pl WF6 123 A5
Ryedale Way Bradford BD15 54 A2
East Ardsley WF3 119 E7
Ryefield Ave BD14 73 B5
Ryefields HD7 189 D4
Ryefields Ave HD3 153 A7
Ryefields Rd HD7 152 E4
Ryeland St BD20 16 D7
Ryelands Gr BD9 54 D4
Ryhill Ind Est WF4 162 B1
Ryhill Pits La WF4 161 E1
Ryhill Prim Sch WF4 162 B1
Rylands Ave BD16 37 B3
Rylands Mdw 17 BD22 51 E8
Rylstone Gdns BD3 56 A1
Rylstone Gr WF1 142 F8
Rylstone Rd BD17 37 F2
Rylstone St BD21 35 D8
Ryndleside 4 HD3 134 F1
Ryshworth Ave BD16 36 D6
Ryshworth Bridge BD16 36 D6
Ryshworth Middle Sch BD16 36 E7
Ryton Dale BD10 56 E6

Sable Crest BD2 55 F4
Sackup La S75 178 A2
Sackville App LS7 206 C3
Sackville Rd BD20 5 E2
Sackville St Bradford BD1 201 B3
Dewsbury WF13 138 E6
10 Hebden Bridge HX7 89 A4
Leeds LS7 206 C3
Todmorden OL14 108 C5
Sacred Heart RC Primary Sch LS29 8 D4
Sacred Heart RC Primary Sch LS5 59 B3
Sacred Heart RC Primary Sch HX6 112 A3
Saddler St 7 BD12 94 C4
Saddler's La WF11 105 C1
Saddlers Croft
Castleford WF10 125 B6
Ilkley LS29 8 A4
Saddleworth Rd Elland HX4 134 C7
Marsden HX4, HX6 150 E5
Ripponden HX4, HX5 133 C5
Sadler Cl LS16 42 C4
Sadler Copse LS16 42 C4
Sadler Way LS16 42 C4
Sadlers Wlk LS22 13 F6
Saffron Dr BD15 73 B8
Sagar La OL14 86 D3
Sagar Pl LS6 205 D4
Sagar St WF10 124 D8
Sage St BD5 74 C4
Sahara Ct BD8 55 D2
Saint St 1 BD7 74 A4
St Abbs Cl BD6 94 C7
St Abbs Dr BD6 94 C7
St Abbs Fold BD6 94 C7
St Abbs Gate BD6 94 C7
St Abbs Way BD6 94 C7
St Abbs Wlk BD6 94 C7
St Agnes Preparatory Sch LS6 59 D6
St Aidan's CE (Aided) First Sch HD8 175 A1
St Aidan's Rd BD17 38 D2
St Aidan's Sq BD16 36 E6
St Aidans Rd LS26 102 E8
St Aiden's Wlk WF5 141 A4
St Alban App LS9 208 C1
St Alban Cl LS9 208 C1
St Alban Cres LS9 208 C1
St Alban Gr LS9 208 C1
St Alban Mount LS9 208 C1
St Alban Rd LS9 208 C1
St Alban View LS9 208 C1
St Alban's Ave Halifax HX3 113 C3
Huddersfield HD3 135 A3
St Alban's Pl LS2 206 C1
St Alban's Rd HX3 113 C3
St Albans Croft HX3 113 D4
St Andrew's Ave LS27 97 F3
St Andrew's C of E First Sch BD22 35 A7
St Andrew's C of E Infants Sch HD6 115 A4
St Andrew's CE Junior & Infants Sch BD12 95 B4
St Andrew's Cl Morley LS27 97 E3
Pudsey LS13 57 E5
St Andrew's Cres BD12 95 A4
St Andrew's Dr HD6 115 A4
St Andrew's Gr LS27 97 F3
St Andrew's Pl
Bradford BD7 74 C6
Leeds LS3 210 C4
St Andrew's RC Prim Sch LS17 43 D1
St Andrew's Rd
Castleford WF10 104 D1
Huddersfield HD1 154 C7
St Andrew's St LS3 210 C4
St Andrew's Terr BD20 16 D7
St Andrew's Villas BD7 74 C7
St Andrews C of E Junior Sch HD6 115 A3
St Andrews Cl Halifax HX2 92 A5
1 Yeadon LS19 40 C7
St Andrews Croft LS17 43 B4
St Andrews Dr
Featherstone WF7 124 D1
Kirkheaton HD5 155 C8
Knottingley WF11 126 C5
Leeds LS17 43 C4
Mapplewell S75 178 A1
St Andrews Rd LS19 40 C8
St Andrews Wlk LS17 43 C4
St Ann's Ave LS4 205 D2
St Ann's Cl LS4 59 C4
St Ann's Gdns LS4 59 C3
St Ann's La LS4 59 C3
St Ann's Mount LS4 205 D3
St Ann's Rise LS4 59 C3
St Ann's Sq Leeds LS9 212 B4
Leeds, Headingley LS4 59 C3
St Ann's Tower Mews LS6 59 C4
St Ann's Way LS4 59 C3
St Anne's Ave HD3 135 A3
St Anne's Cl WF12 139 D4
St Anne's Dr LS4 59 C4
St Anne's Gn LS4 59 C4
St Anne's Pl HX4 133 E4
St Anne's RC Cath LS2 211 E4
St Anne's RC Sch BD21 35 B8
St Anne's Rd Halifax HX3 113 C2
Leeds LS6 59 C5
St Anne's St LS2 211 E4
St Anne's St WF4 162 B1
St Annes Villas WF8 125 E2
St Anns Sq HX6 112 C4
St Anthony's Dr LS11 213 F2
St Anthony's RC Prim Sch BD14 73 D5
St Anthony's RC Prim Sch LS11 213 F2
St Anthony's Rd LS11 213 E2
St Augustine's C E First Sch BD3 56 A1
St Augustine's CE Sch HX1 202 C4
St Augustine's Terr
Bradford BD3 56 A1
Halifax HX1 202 C4
St Augustines RC Primary Sch LS8 208 B3
St Austin's Catholic Infants Sch WF1 216 C3
St Austin's RC (A) Jun & Inf Sch WF1 216 C3
St Barnabas Rd
Cleckheaton WF15 116 C5
Leeds LS11 211 E2
St Barnabas Sch BD9 55 A4
St Bartholomew's C of E Primary Sch LS12 209 F3
St Bartholomew's Cl LS12 209 F3
St Bartholomews Ct WF2 141 C4
St Bede's Grammar Sch BD9 55 A3
St Benedict's RC Prim Sch LS25 82 F7
St Bernard's Ave WF8 146 B8
St Bevan's Rd HX3 113 C3
St Blaise Ct BD5 201 B1
St Blaise RC Middle Sch BD4 75 B1
St Blaise Sq BD1 201 B3
St Blaise Way BD1 201 B3
St Boltophs Cl WF11 127 A4
St Brendan's RC Sch BD10 56 D6
St Catherine's Cres LS13 58 D4
St Catherine's Dr LS13 58 D4
St Catherine's Gn LS13 58 D4
St Catherine's Hill LS13 58 D4
St Catherine's St WF1 142 F3
St Catherine's Villas WF1 142 F3
St Catherine's Wlk LS8 61 A6
St Chad's Ave
Brighouse HD6 114 E5
Leeds LS6 59 D6
St Chad's C of E Primary Sch LS16 59 B7
St Chad's CE (Aided) Jun & Inf Sch HD6 114 E5
St Chad's Dr LS6 59 C6
St Chad's Gr LS6 59 C6
St Chad's Rd Bradford BD8 55 B1
Leeds LS16 59 D6
St Chad's Rise LS6 59 C6
St Chad's View LS6 59 C6
St Christopher's Ave LS26 100 F5
St Christophers Dr LS29 6 F8
St Clair Gn WF2 141 D8
St Clair Rd LS21 23 B7
St Clair St Otley LS21 23 B8
Wakefield WF1 216 C2
St Clairs Terr LS21 23 B8
St Clare's Ave BD2 56 D2
St Clare's RC Prim Sch BD2 56 D2
St Clements Ave LS26 100 E5
St Clements Cl LS26 100 D4
St Clements Rise LS26 100 D5
St Columba's RC Prim Sch BD4 75 D2
St Cuthbert & the First Martyrs RC Sch BD9 55 A2
St Cuthbert's Ct WF7 146 A1
St Cyprians Gdns LS9 208 B2
St Davids Rd LS21 10 E2
St Edmund's Hall Prep Sch LS8 44 A1
St Edmunds Cl WF10 125 C8
St Edward's RC Primary Sch LS23 30 D7
St Edward's Terr LS23 30 D5
St Edwards Cl WF11 126 E7
St Elmo Gr 6 LS9 80 A8
St Eloi Ave BD17 38 C4
St Enoch's Rd BD6 74 B2
St Francis Gdns HD2 136 A5
St Francis of Assisi RC Primary Sch LS11 214 B3
St Francis Pl LS11 211 E2
St Francis' RC First Sch BD2 56 A4
St George's Ave
Huddersfield HD3 135 A3
Rothwell LS26 100 C7
St George's Cres LS26 100 C7
St George's Mews WF2 160 A5
St George's Pl
Bradford BD5 201 B1
Bradford, Bowling BD5 75 B4
St George's Rd Halifax HX3 92 A1
Holmfirth HD7 189 D4
Leeds LS1 206 B1
Wakefield WF2 141 D3
St George's Sq Elland HD3 152 B8
17 Hebden Bridge HX7 89 A3
18 Huddersfield HD1 154 A6
St George's St
16 Hebden Bridge HX7 89 A3
Huddersfield HD1 154 A6
St Georges Cres HX3 92 B1
St Georges Ct WF4 162 D2
St Georges Wlk WF2 160 C6
St Giles Ave WF8 146 B8
St Giles Cl HD6 114 E5
St Giles Garth LS16 24 E3
St Giles Rd HX3 114 E7
St Giles' View WF8 146 D7
St Gregory's RC Primary Sch LS14 62 D5
St Helen's Ave WF9 181 C7
St Helen's Dr LS25 83 F8
St Helen's Gate HD4 155 A2
St Helen's Gr WF2 142 F1
St Helen's La
Huddersfield HD4 155 A2
Leeds LS16 42 C3
St Helen's Pl 2 WF10 124 E7
St Helen's Way LS29 8 D4
St Helena Rd BD6 74 B1
St Helens Ave LS16 42 D3
St Helens C of E Jun N & Inf Sch WF9 181 C6
St Helens Cl LS16 42 D3
St Helens Croft LS16 42 C3
St Helens Gdns LS16 42 C3
St Helens Gr LS16 42 C3
St Helens St LS10 212 A1
St Helens Way LS16 42 D3
St Helier Gr BD17 38 D4
St Hilda's Ave LS9 212 C2
St Hilda's Cres 14 LS9 212 C2
St Hilda's Gr 15 LS9 212 C2
St Hilda's Mount 13 LS9 212 C2
St Hilda's Pl LS9 212 C2
St Hilda's Rd LS9 212 C2
St Hilda's Sch WF4 141 A2
St Hilda's Terr BD3 75 E8
St Hildas Cl S63 194 E1
St Ians Croft LS29 6 F7
St Ignatius RC Junior & Infants Sch WF5 140 E3
St Ive's Gdns HX3 113 C3
St Ive's Rd HX3 113 C3
St Ives Cl WF8 125 D3
St Ives Cres WF10 125 C5
St Ives Gr Harden BD16 36 C2
Leeds LS12 209 D4
St Ives Mount LS12 209 D4
St Ives Pl BD16 36 C2
St Ives Rd BD16 36 C2
St James App LS14 62 B4
St James Ave LS18 41 D1
St James Bsns Pk BD1 201 C2
St James C of E (C) First Sch WF4 159 F6
St James C of E Sch LS22 13 F6
St James Cl LS12 77 F8
St James Cres LS28 76 B7
St James Ct Brighouse HD6 115 B3
Halifax HX1 203 E3
Ryhill WF4 162 C1
Wakefield WF2 142 B4
St James Dr LS18 41 D1
St James Manston Prim Sch LS15 62 D3
St James Pk WF2 141 C4
St James Pl BD17 38 F4
St James Rd Baildon BD17 38 F4
Halifax HX1 203 E3
St James' Rd LS29 8 A4
St James Sq HX3 93 A3
St James St Batley WF17 118 C5
Batley, Heckmondwike WF16 117 D3
Halifax HX1 203 E3
St James Terr LS18 41 D1
St James Way WF4 159 F6
St James Wlk LS18 41 D1
St James's Ct LS8 207 E2
St James's Mews LS12 77 F8
St James's Mkt BD1 201 D2
St James's Pk WF1 142 E6
St James's Rd HD1 153 D7
St James's Sq BD5 201 B1
St James's St LS22 13 E5
St James's Univ Hospl LS9 207 F2
St John Fisher RC High Sch WF13 118 B1
St John Par WF13 139 B7
St John St Brighouse HD6 115 A1
Dewsbury WF13 139 B8
St John the Evangelist Inf & Jun Sch BD6 73 E1
St John Wlk WF13 139 B8
St John's Ave Batley WF17 118 A6
Huddersfield HD4 154 A2
Kirkheaton HD5 137 C1
Leeds LS6 205 F2
Ossett WF5 141 A5
10 Pudsey LS28 57 D3
Thorner LS14 45 F5
Wakefield WF1 216 A4
St John's C of E First Sch BD4 75 D1
St John's C of E Infants Sch WF13 139 A8
St John's CE Jun & Inf Sch HX6 132 C1
St John's CE Junior & Infants Sch WF1 216 A4
St John's CE Primary Sch HD6 115 E2
St John's Chase WF1 216 A3
St John's Cl Aberford LS25 47 E1
7 Hebden Bridge HX7 89 A3
Leeds LS6 205 F2
Ossett WF5 141 A5
Ripponden HX6 132 C1
St John's Cres
Bradford BD8 73 E8
Huddersfield HD1 154 A8
Normanton WF6 144 A7
Ossett WF5 141 A5
St John's Croft WF1 216 A4
St John's Cross HX2 91 F8
St John's Ct BD17 38 E2
St John's Ct Keighley BD20 18 A2
Leeds LS7 207 D4
St John's Ct Lepton HD8 155 F3
Thorner LS14 45 F5
Wakefield WF1 216 A3
Yeadon LS19 40 A6
St John's Dr
Huddersfield HD1 154 A8
Yeadon LS19 40 A6
St John's Garth LS25 64 E8
St John's Gr Leeds LS6 205 F2
Wakefield WF1 216 B4
St John's Hospital (Almshouses) LS25 104 D8
St John's La HX1 203 E2
St John's Mews LS19 40 A6
St John's Mount WF1 216 A4
St John's N WF1 216 A3
St John's Pk LS29 21 F5
St John's Pl BD11 96 A6
St John's Pl 7 BD19 116 E7
St John's Pl HX1 203 E2
St John's RC Jun & Inf Sch WF6 123 C2
St John's Rd
Boston Spa LS23 30 D7
Huddersfield HD1 154 A8
Ilkley LS29 8 E4
Keighley BD20 18 A2
Kirkheaton HD5 137 C1
Leeds LS3 205 F1
Yeadon LS19 40 A6
St John's Residential Sch for the Deaf LS23 30 D7
St John's Sq WF1 216 A3
St John's St Cononley BD20 4 A2
Horbury WF4 140 E1
Rothwell LS26 101 C5
Silsden BD20 5 E1
St John's Terr LS6 205 F2
St John's View
Batley WF17 118 A6
Boston Spa LS23 30 C7
St John's Way LS19 40 A6
St John's Wlk S71 179 D4
St Johns Ave LS29 6 F8
St Johns CE Jun & Inf Sch HD7 152 D5
St Johns Cl
Cleckheaton BD19 116 E7
Dewsbury WF13 139 B8
St Johns Ct HD7 188 F4
St Johns Ctr LS2 211 F4
St Johns Mews WF1 216 A4
St Johns Way BD22 34 F6
St Joseph's Catholic Primary Sch LS22 13 E6
St Joseph's Coll BD9 55 C3
St Joseph's Ct LS19 40 B2
St Joseph's Jun & Inf Sch BD21 35 B5
St Joseph's Mount WF8 146 B7
St Joseph's Primary Sch WF13 118 A2
St Joseph's RC Infant Sch BD5 74 D4
St Joseph's RC Jun & Inf Sch Brighouse HD6 114 F5
Todmorden OL14 108 B6
St Joseph's RC Junior & Infants Sch WF8 146 C8
St Joseph's RC Prim Sch BD16 37 A3
St Joseph's RC Primary Sch HX3 203 F4
St Joseph's RC Prim Sch Huddersfield HD5 154 F6
Pudsey LS28 76 F8
St Josephs RC Jun & Inf Sch Castleford WF10 124 E8
South Elmsall WF9 182 E3
St Josephs RC Junior Sch LS21 23 A8
St Jude's Pl BD1 201 A4
St Jude's St Bradford BD8 74 D8
Halifax HX1 203 D1
St Julien's Mount S75 193 E4
St Julien's Way S75 193 E4
St Laurence's Cl BD2 55 E5
St Lawrence Cl LS28 76 D7
St Lawrence St LS7 204 A2
St Lawrence Terr LS28 76 E6
St Leonard's Ct 4 BD8 54 F1
St Leonard's Farm Pk BD17 39 C5
St Leonard's Gr BD8 54 F1
St Leonard's Rd BD8 54 F1
St Leonards Cl LS29 6 F7
St Lucius's Cl HD4 172 E6
St Luke's CE Prim Sch LS11 214 B4
St Luke's Cl
Boston Spa LS23 30 D5
Cleckheaton BD19 116 B7
St Luke's Cres LS11 214 A4
St Luke's Gn LS11 214 A4
St Luke's Hospl BD5 74 D4
St Luke's Hospl HD4 153 C3
St Luke's Rd LS11 214 A4
St Luke's St LS11 214 A4
St Luke's Terr BD19 116 B7
St Luke's Terr BD20 36 D8
St Luke's View 4 LS11 214 A4
St Lukes C of E First Sch BD2 56 D4
St Lukes Cl WF17 118 E4
St Malachy's RC Sch HX2 91 E3
St Margaret's Ave
Bradford BD4 75 D2
Horsforth LS18 41 B2
Leeds LS8 61 A6
Mickletown LS26 102 D3
St Margaret's Cl LS18 41 B2
St Margaret's Ct WF9 183 B6
St Margaret's Dr
Horsforth LS18 41 B2
Leeds LS8 61 A6
St Margaret's Gr LS8 61 A6
St Margaret's Hospl LS6 59 D6
St Margaret's Pl BD7 74 B5
St Margaret's Rd
Bradford BD7 74 B6
Horsforth LS18 41 B2
Mickletown LS26 102 D3

St Margaret's Terr
Bradford BD7 74 B5
Ilkley LS29 8 B3
St Margaret's View LS8 61 A6
St Mark's Ave LS2 206 A2
St Mark's Flats 7 LS2 206 A3
St Mark's Rd
Huddersfield HD3 153 A6
Leeds LS6 206 B3
St Mark's St Leeds LS2 206 A3
Wakefield WF1 216 C4
St Mark's Terr LS22 94 C5
St Marks View HD3 153 A6
St Martin's Ave LS7 204 A1
St Martin's Cres LS7 204 A1
St Martin's Dr LS7 60 C6
St Martin's Gdns LS7 204 A1
St Martin's Gr
Castleford WF10 124 B6
Leeds LS7 204 A1
St Martin's Rd LS7 204 A1
St Martin's View
7 Brighouse HD6 115 A3
Leeds LS7 204 A1
St Martins Ave
Bradford BD7 74 C7
Otley LS21 10 F2
St Martins Cl WF7 145 C4
St Mary St HX1 203 D2
St Mary's Ave Batley WF17 118 B3
Bradford BD12 94 C2
Holmfirth HD7 188 F8
Mirfield WF14 138 C6
Swillington LS26 82 A1
St Mary's C of E First Sch WF1 216 C2
St Mary's C of E Junior & Infants Sch HX6 132 C7
St Mary's Cl Bradford BD12 94 B2
East Ardsley WF3 119 D7
Garforth LS25 82 F6
Ilkley LS29 8 C4
Leeds LS12 210 A2
Leeds, Potternewton LS7 204 A1
South Elmsall WF9 183 A2
St Mary's Cres
Bradford BD12 94 B2
Holmfirth HD7 188 F8
St Mary's Ct Kippax WF10 103 B4
Leeds LS7 204 A1
Meltham HD7 188 B8
St Mary's Dr BD12 94 C2
St Mary's Fold BD4 75 D5
St Mary's Garth LS17 28 B5
St Mary's Gdns 1 BD12 94 C2
St Mary's Heights HX2 91 D5
St Mary's Hospl LS12 77 F8
St Mary's La
Kirkheaton HD5 155 C7
Leeds LS9 212 B4
St Mary's Mews HD7 171 F5
St Mary's Mount BD12 94 B2
St Mary's Park Ct 2 LS12 77 F8
St Mary's Park Gn 3 LS12 77 F8
St Mary's Pl
1 Castleford WF10 124 D8
Dewsbury WF12 139 D6
St Mary's RC Jun & Inf Schs WF17 118 B6
St Mary's RC Prim Sch BD1 201 C3
St Mary's RC Primary Sch
Bacup OL13 106 B2
Halifax HX1 203 D2
St Mary's RC Sch
Guiseley LS29 22 C3
Horsforth LS18 41 C1
St Mary's Rd
Bradford, Manningham BD8, BD9 55 C2
Bradford, Swain Green BD4 75 D5
Holmfirth HD7 188 F8
Honley HD7 171 F5
Keighley BD20 18 F2
Leeds LS7 204 A1
Normanton WF6 122 F3
St Mary's Rise HD7 188 F8
St Mary's Sq Bradford BD12 94 C2
Honley HD7 171 F5
Morley LS27 98 A4
St Mary's St Boston Spa LS23 30 D8
Leeds LS9 212 A4
St Mary's Way HD7 188 F8
St Mary's Wlk
Micklefield LS25 83 F7
Micklefield LS25 84 A7
Mirfield WF14 138 C6
St Marys Ave WF6 122 F4
St Marys CE Fst Sch BD19 117 B8
St Marys Gate 12 HX5 134 F7
St Marys Park App LS12 77 F8
St Marys Park Cres LS12 77 F8
St Matthew Rd WF13 139 B8
St Matthew's C of E Middle Sch LS7 60 C7
St Matthew's CE First Sch BD5 74 E1
St Matthew's Dr HX3 93 A3
St Matthew's RC Sch BD15 73 B8
St Matthew's Rd BD5 74 D1
St Matthew's St 2 LS11 211 D1
St Matthew's Wlk LS7 60 C8
St Matthews Cl BD15 53 B4
St Matthews Gr BD15 53 C4
St Matthias' Ct LS4 205 D2
St Matthias' Gr LS4 205 D2
St Matthias' St LS4 205 D2
St Matthias' Terr LS4 205 D2
St Michael Ct LS13 58 D3
St Michael's & All Angels Sch HX3 93 D6
St Michael's C of E Sch LS6 59 E5
St Michael's CE Prim Sch WF2 141 E5
St Michael's Cl
Castleford WF10 124 D7
Dewsbury WF12 139 E1
Emley HD8 175 D7
St Michael's Cl 6 BD16 54 B6
St Michael's Cl WF2 142 A5
St Michael's Coll LS3 205 F1
St Michael's Cres LS6 205 D4
St Michael's First Sch BD5 74 B4
St Michael's Gdns HD8 175 D7
St Michael's Gr LS6 205 D4
St Michael's House WF2 142 A5
St Michael's La LS6 205 D4
St Michael's Mount WF12 139 E1
St Michael's Rd
Bradford BD8 74 C8
Leeds LS6 205 D4
St Michael's Terr LS6 59 D5
St Michael's Villas LS6 205 D4
St Michael's Way LS29 21 F8
St Michaels Ave 1 WF8 146 B8
St Michaels Gn WF6 123 A1
St Michaels Way LS29 6 F7
St Nicholas Catholic Primary Sch LS9 61 D3
St Nicholas Rd LS29 8 A5
St Nicholas St WF10 124 D7
St Oswald Ave WF8 146 B8
St Oswald Rd WF2 141 D5
St Oswald St 6 WF10 124 D8
St Oswald's CE First Sch BD5 74 C3
St Oswalds C of E Junior Sch LS20 39 E8
St Oswalds Garth LS20 22 F1
St Oswalds Pl WF5 140 E7
St Oswalds Terr LS20 22 E1
St Patrick's First Sch BD8 74 C8
St Patrick's RC Jun & Inf Sch Batley WF17 96 E2
Huddersfield HD2 153 E8
St Patrick's RC Junior & Infants Sch HX4 134 D6
St Patricks RC Primary Sch LS9 80 A8
St Paul's Ave
Birkenshaw BD11 96 B5
Bradford BD6 94 B8
St Paul's C of E Jun & Inf Sch WF2 141 E8
St Paul's CE First Sch BD6 94 B8
St Paul's Cl WF9 183 D8
St Paul's Dr WF2 141 D8
St Paul's Gr Bradford LS29 94 B8
Ilkley LS29 8 D4
St Paul's Pl LS1 211 E4
St Paul's RC Primary Sch LS17 43 A4
St Paul's Rd
Birkenshaw BD11 96 B5
Bradford BD6 94 B8
Bradford, Manningham BD8 55 C2
Halifax HX1 202 B1
Keighley BD21 35 D6
Mirfield WF14 138 A4
Shipley BD18 55 A7
St Paul's St
Huddersfield HD1 154 B5
Leeds LS1 211 E4
1 Morley LS27 98 B3
St Paul's Terr WF14 138 A4
St Paul's Wlk WF2 141 D8
St Paulinus Cl WF13 139 B8
St Paulinus' RC Primary Sch WF13 139 A7
St Pauls Rd HD5 155 B8
St Pauls Rise LS29 6 F8
St Peg Cl BD19 116 E7
St Peg La BD19 116 E7
St Peter & St Pauls RC Primary Sch LS19 39 F6
St Peter's Ave LS26 100 F5
St Peter's Ave HX6 111 F3
St Peter's C of E Inf Sch LS27 98 B6
St Peter's C of E Jun & Inf Sch WF1 121 F5
St Peter's CE Infants Sch HX6 111 E3
St Peter's CE Primary Sch LS9 212 B4
St Peter's Cl Batley WF17 96 D1
8 Mirfield WF14 137 F5
St Peter's Cres
Lofthouse Gate WF3 122 B6
Morley LS27 98 A6
St Peter's Ct LS13 58 D3
St Peter's Garth LS14 46 A6
St Peter's Gate Dearne S63 194 C1
Todmorden OL14 129 B8
St Peter's Gdns
Dewsbury WF12 139 F7
Leeds LS13 58 C3
St Peter's Gr WF4 141 B1
St Peter's Mount LS13 58 D2
St Peter's Par WF12 139 F7
St Peter's Pl LS9 212 A4
St Peter's RC Prim Sch BD3 75 B6
St Peter's Sq LS9 212 A4
St Peter's Sq HX6 111 E3
St Peter's St
2 Huddersfield HD1 154 B6
Leeds LS2 212 A4
St Peter's Way LS29 21 F4
St Peters Cres HD5 155 B8
St Peters Ct
Addingham LS29 6 F7
Horbury WF4 141 A1
Leeds LS11 214 C4
St Peters Gate WF5 140 D7
St Philip's Ave LS10 99 B5
St Philip's Cl
Burley in W LS29 9 F1
Dewsbury WF13 118 D1
St Philip's Dr LS29 21 F8
St Philip's RC Prim Sch LS10 99 B5
St Philip's Way LS29 21 F8
St Philips Cl LS10 99 B5
St Philips Ct HD3 135 B2
St Richards Rd LS21 10 F2
St Stephen's CE First Sch BD5 74 E3
St Stephen's Ct Leeds LS9 212 C4
Steeton BD20 17 C6
St Stephen's Rd
Bradford BD5 74 E3
Huddersfield HD1 153 F4
Leeds LS9 212 C4
Pudsey LS28 57 A7
Steeton BD20 17 C5
St Stephen's St HX3 113 A2
St Stephen's Terr BD5 74 D3
St Stephens Ct HX3 113 A2
St Swithins Dr WF3 121 F2
St Swithins Gr WF3 121 F2
St Theresa's RC Prim Sch LS15 62 C4
St Thomas a Beckett Catholic Comp Sch WF2 142 E1
St Thomas C of E Jun Sch WF7 145 C5
St Thomas Rd WF7 145 D5
St Thomas' Rd HD1 153 F5
St Thomas Row LS2 207 D1
St Thomas's Rd 2 BD1 74 D7
St Thomas's Terr WF8 125 F3
St Vincent Rd LS28 76 F6
St Vincent's Sch LS23 30 D7
St Walburga's RC Prim Sch BD18 54 F7
St Walburga's RC Prim Sch BD18 55 A7
St Wilfred's St LS28 57 B7
St Wilfrid's Ave LS8 208 B4
St Wilfrid's Catholic High Sch WF7 124 C1
St Wilfrid's Cir LS8 208 B3
St Wilfrid's Cl BD7 73 F5
St Wilfrid's Cres
Bradford BD7 73 F5
Leeds LS8 208 B4
St Wilfrid's Dr LS8 208 A4
St Wilfrid's Garth LS8 208 B3
St Wilfrid's Gr LS8 208 B4
St Wilfrid's Rd BD7 73 F5
St William's RC First Sch BD8 74 B8
St Winefride's RC Sch BD6 94 B8
St Winifred's Cl HX2 91 D5
Sal Nook Cl BD12 94 E7
Sal Royd Rd BD12 94 E6
Salcombe Pl BD4 75 E2
Salem Pl Garforth LS25 82 E7
Leeds LS10 211 F2
Salem St Bradford BD1 201 B4
Hebden Bridge HX7 88 F3
Queensbury BD13 72 D1
Salendine Nook High Sch HD3 152 F7
Salford OL14 108 B4
Salford Way OL14 108 A4
Salisbury Ave Baildon BD17 38 C3
Leeds LS12 209 F4
Salisbury Cl
Dewsbury WF12 139 F8
Normanton WF6 123 B3
Salisbury Ct LS18 41 D1
Salisbury Gr LS12 209 F4
Salisbury Mews LS18 41 D1
Salisbury Pl Halifax HX3 92 B1
Pudsey LS28 57 A7
Salisbury Rd
3 Bradford BD12 94 C6
Brighouse BD19 115 F8
Keighley BD22 35 A6
Leeds LS12 209 F4
Shipley BD9 55 C5
Salisbury St Pudsey LS28 57 A6
Sowerby Bridge HX6 112 A3
Yeadon LS19 40 B4
Salisbury Terr LS12 209 F4
Salisbury View
Horsforth LS18 41 D1
Leeds LS12 209 F4
Salley St OL15 129 C2
Salmon Cres LS18 41 C1
Salt Drake HX6 132 B8
Salt Grammar Sch BD17 37 F2
Salt Horn Cl BD12 94 F5
Salt Pie Alley WF2 216 A2
Salt St Bradford BD8 55 C1
Halifax HX1 202 C4
Saltaire 4 BD22 51 F8
Saltaire First Sch BD18 54 F8
Saltaire Rd Bingley BD16 37 D5
Shipley BD18 55 A8
Saltaire Sta BD18 37 F1
Saltburn Pl BD9 54 F2
Saltburn St HX1 202 B3
Salter Rake Gate OL14 129 B8
Salter Row 1 WF8 146 D8
Salter St WF17 118 B2
Salterhebble Hill HX3 113 D3
Salterhebble Primary Sch HX3 113 D3
Salterlee Jun & Inf Sch HX3 92 F2
Saltersgate Ave WF11 126 E4
Saltonstall La HX2 90 D5
Salts Mill Rd BD17 55 B8
Sampson St WF15 117 B4
Samuel Dr WF3 121 E5
Samuel St BD21 35 C7
Sand Beds BD13 72 F1
Sand Hill La LS17 43 D3
Sand Hill Lawns LS17 43 D3
Sand Moor Golf Course LS17 43 C6
Sand St Haworth BD22 51 C6
Huddersfield HD1 154 B5
Keighley BD21 35 C8
Sandal & Agbrigg Sta WF1 142 E2
Sandal Ave WF2 142 E1
Sandal Castle WF2 142 D1
Sandal Cliff WF2 142 E1
Sandal Endowed C of E Jun Sch WF2 160 E8
Sandal First Sch BD17 38 C3
Sandal Hall Cl WF2 142 F1
Sandal Hall Mews WF2 142 E1
Sandal Magna Jun & Inf Sch WF1 142 E2
Sandal Rise WF8 165 A5
Sandal Way WF17 96 F1
Sandale Wlk 5 BD6 93 F7
Sandall Cl LS25 83 B2
Sandall Magna HX3 93 E7
Sandals Rd BD17 38 C3
Sandbeck Ind Est LS22 13 F7
Sandbeck La LS22 14 B8
Sandbeck Way LS22 13 F7
Sandbed Ct LS15 62 D3
Sandbed La LS15 62 D3
Sandbed Lawns 3 LS15 62 D3
Sandbeds HD7 171 F6
Sandbeds Cres HX2 91 E1
Sandbeds Rd HX2 91 E1
Sandbeds Terr HX2 91 E1
Sandbeds Trad Est WF5 140 E7
Sandene Ave HD4 153 C2
Sandene Dr HD4 153 C2
Sanderling Ct 7 BD8 73 C7
Sanderling Garth 5 LS10 99 D5
Sanderling Way LS10 99 D5
Sanderson Ave
Bradford BD6 74 C1
Normanton WF6 123 A1
Sanderson La
Lofthouse Gate LS26 122 B8
Rothwell LS26 101 B1
Sanderson St WF1 216 C2
Sandfield Ave LS6 59 E6
Sandfield Garth LS6 59 E6
Sandfield Rd Bacup OL13 106 A1
Bradford BD10 56 B6
Sandford Pl LS5 59 A4
Sandford Primary Sch LS13 58 E3
Sandford Rd Bradford BD3 75 C7
Leeds LS5 59 B3
South Elmsall WF9 183 A5
Sandforth Ave HX3 92 C2
Sandgate Dr LS25 83 C2
Sandgate La Kippax LS25 83 C1
Kippax LS25 83 D3
Sandgate Rise LS25 83 C2
Sandgate Terr LS25 83 C1
Sandhall Ave HX2 112 D7
Sandhall Cres 5 HX2 112 D8
Sandhall Dr HX2 112 D7
Sandhall Gn HX2 112 D7
Sandhall La HX2 112 D7
Sandhill Cl WF8 125 D4
Sandhill Cres LS17 43 E4
Sandhill Ct LS17 43 D3
Sandhill Dr LS17 43 E4
Sandhill Gr
Grimethorpe S72 181 A1
Leeds LS17 43 E5
Sandhill Lawn WF8 146 C7
Sandhill Mount
Bradford BD10 56 B6
Leeds LS17 43 E5
Sandhill Oval LS17 43 E5
Sandhill Rise WF8 125 D3
Sandholme Cres HX3 114 D7
Sandholme Dr
Bradford BD10 56 C6
Burley in W LS29 21 F8
Ossett WF5 140 D5
Sandholme Fold HX3 114 D7
Sandhurst Ave LS8 208 A3
Sandhurst Gr LS8 208 A3
Sandhurst Mount LS8 208 A4
Sandhurst Pl LS8 208 A3
Sandhurst Rd LS8 208 A3
Sandhurst St LS28 57 A7
Sandhurst Terr LS8 208 A3
Sandiford Cl LS15 62 D3
Sandiford Terr LS15 62 D3
Sandiway Bank WF12 139 D3
Sandleas Way LS15 62 F2
Sandlewood Cl LS11 211 D1
Sandlewood Gn LS11 211 E1
Sandmead Cl Bradford BD4 75 E3
Morley LS27 98 A6
Sandmead Croft LS27 98 A6
Sandmead Way 3 LS27 98 A6
Sandmoor Ave LS17 43 D6
Sandmoor Chase LS17 43 D5
Sandmoor Cl Leeds LS17 43 D5
6 Thornton BD13 72 E6
Sandmoor Ct LS17 43 D5
Sandmoor Dr LS17 43 D5
Sandmoor Garth BD10 39 B1
Sandmoor Gdns HX3 93 B5
Sandmoor Gn LS17 43 C6
Sandmoor La LS17 43 D5
Sandmoor Mews LS17 43 D5
Sandon Gr LS10 215 E2
Sandon Mount LS10 215 E2
Sandon Pl LS10 215 E2
Sandown Ave Crofton WF4 143 F1
Halifax HX2 91 E4
Sandown Rd HX2 91 E4
Sandpiper App LS27 98 C3
Sandpiper Mews 5 BD8 73 C7
Sandringham App LS17 43 E3
Sandringham Ave
Knottingley WF11 126 C4
4 Pudsey LS28 76 E6
Sandringham Cl
Bradford BD14 73 D5
Morley LS27 98 C5
Pontefract WF8 146 C5
Sandringham Cres LS17 43 E3
Sandringham Ct
Bradford BD14 73 D5
Huddersfield HD2 136 E5
Sandringham Dr LS17 43 D3
Sandringham Fold LS27 98 C5
Sandringham Gdns LS17 43 D3
Sandringham Gn LS17 43 E4
Sandringham Mount LS17 43 E3
Sandringham Rd
Bradford BD14 73 D5
Byram WF11 126 D7
Wetherby LS22 13 E6
Sandringham Way LS17 43 D3
Sandrock Rd WF8 125 E2
Sands House La HD4 153 B1
Sands La Dewsbury WF12 139 E7
Lepton HD5, HD8 155 F6
Mirfield WF14 138 D3
Sands Rd WF12 139 E6
Sandsend Cl BD9 54 D3
Sandside Cl BD5 201 B4
Sandstone Cl HD7 171 F3
Sandway LS15 62 B2
Sandway Gdns LS15 62 B2
Sandway Gr LS15 62 B2
Sandwell St HD7 151 F1
Sandwich Cres HD2 135 F3
Sandy Bank Ave LS26 100 F6
Sandy Banks BD16 53 B8
Sandy Beck BD15 54 A3
Sandy Dyke La HX6 132 E8
Sandy Gate Harewood LS17 26 E7
Hebden Bridge HX7 89 B4
Holmfirth HX7 189 C4
Keighley BD20 35 A8
Sandy Gate La
Ackworth M T WF7 146 C3
Wadsworth Moor HX7 89 C4
Sandy Gr LS26 100 F6
Sandy La Huddersfield HD4 171 A7
Netherton WF4 158 C7
Sandy Lane First Sch BD15 54 A4
Sandy Lobby LS21 24 C6
Sandy Way 1 LS19 40 B7
Sandy Wlk Bramhope LS16 24 F2
Wakefield WF1 216 A3
Sandyacres LS26 100 F6
Sandyacres Cres LS26 100 F6
Sandyacres Dr LS26 100 F6
Sandybridge La S72 180 B4
Sandyfield Terr WF17 118 B6
Sandyfoot HX4 133 B4
Sandygate La WF9 181 C7
Sandygate Terr BD4 75 D5
Sandylands Glusburn BD20 16 D7
Huddersfield HD4 171 D6
Sandymoor BD15 54 A4
Sandywood Ct LS18 58 C7
Sandywood St BD21 35 C8
Sangster Way BD5 75 A1
Sanquah Terr WF6 123 C3
Santa Monica Cres BD10 56 A7
Santa Monica Gr BD10 56 A7
Santa Monica Rd BD10 56 A7
Santingley La WF4 162 A6
Sanworth St 2 OL14 108 C5
Sapgate La BD13 72 E6
Saplin St BD8 55 B1
Sapphire Ct WF17 118 A6
Sarah St WF3 120 D8
Sardinia St LS10 212 A1
Saunders Cl HD3 153 C7
Saunters Way WF6 123 A4
Savile Ave Bradford BD10 56 C6
Leeds LS7 207 D4
Savile Bsns Ctr WF12 139 D7
Savile Cl HD6 115 D3
Savile Cres HX1 203 D2
Savile Ct WF14 138 A6

Savile Dr Halifax HX1 203 D2
Horbury WF4 141 A2
Leeds LS7 207 D3
Savile Glen HX1 203 D2
Savile Gn HX1 203 E2
Savile Gr WF12 139 C7
Savile House 7 HX5 134 F7
Savile La HD6 115 D3
Savile Lea HX1 203 D2
Savile Mews WF12 139 C5
Savile Mount LS7 207 D3
Savile Par HX1 203 D1
Savile Park Gdns HX1 203 D1
Savile Park Jun & Inf Sch HX1 202 C1
Savile Park Rd
Cleckheaton BD19 95 D3
Halifax HX1 203 D1
Savile Park St HX1 202 C1
Savile Park Terr 17 HX1 202 C1
Savile Pit La WF12 140 A8
Savile Pk Halifax HX3 113 B4
Halifax, King Cross HX1 202 C1
Savile Pl Leeds LS7 207 D3
Mirfield WF14 138 A7
Savile Prec WF10 124 C8
Savile Rd Castleford WF10 124 C8
Dewsbury WF12 139 C6
Elland HX5 134 F6
Halifax HX1 203 D2
Hebden Bridge HX7 88 E3
Huddersfield HD3 153 C8
Leeds LS7 207 D3
Mickletown LS26 102 D3
Savile Royd HX1 203 D1
Savile Sq WF14 138 A5
Savile St Batley WF17 118 D2
Cleckheaton BD19 95 D1
Huddersfield HD3 153 A5
Savile Town CE Inf Sch WF12 139 D6
Savile Way HX5 135 A8
Savile Wlk Brierley S72 181 B3
6 Dewsbury WF13 139 C8
Saville Ave HD8 175 D7
Saville Cl WF3 100 C1
Saville Ct LS21 22 F7
Saville Gn LS9 212 C4
Saville Pk WF5 140 F4
Saville Rd HD8 175 A2
Saville St Clayton West HD8 175 D1
Emley HD8 175 D7
Ossett WF5 140 F4
Wakefield WF1 216 B3
Saw Mill HX6 132 E8
Saw Mill St LS11 211 E2
Saw Yd WF1 216 B2
Sawley Cl WF1 142 E8
Sawley St BD21 35 B6
Sawood La BD22 70 F8
Sawrey Pl BD5 201 A2
Sawyers Garth LS29 7 A8
Saxon Ave WF9 181 F2
Saxon Cl Emley HD8 175 C6
Upton WF9 183 E7
Saxon Ct LS17 43 B3
Saxon Gate LS17 43 B2
Saxon Gn LS17 43 A2
Saxon Gr Leeds LS17 43 A2
South Kirkby WF9 182 A1
Saxon Mount Leeds LS17 43 A3
South Kirkby WF9 181 F1
Saxon Rd LS17 43 A2
Saxon St Bradford BD8 74 C8
Halifax HX1 202 B4
10 Todmorden OL14 108 A1
Saxon Way WF10 125 A8
Saxton Ave BD6 73 F1
Saxton Ct LS25 82 F8
Saxton House LS19 40 B6
Saxton La LS9 212 B3
Saxton Pl HD5 155 A4
Saxton St WF15 117 C5
Sayers Cl LS5 59 B4
Sayle Ave BD4 75 B1
Sayner La LS10 212 B1
Sayner Rd LS10 212 A2
Scaitcliffe View OL14 107 F7
Scale Hill HD2 136 A2
Scalebor Park Hospl LS29 21 D8
Scaley St BD3 75 D7
Scaly Gate Holmfirth HD7 190 A2
Holmfirth HD7 190 A5
Scammonden Rd HX4 133 B3
Scape View HD7 152 E4
Scapegoat Hill Junior & Infant Sch HD7 152 B6
Scar Bottom La HX4 133 F7
Scar Gr HD4 153 F2
Scar Head Rd HX6 112 B3
Scar Hill Cotts HX4 133 E4
Scar Hole La HD7 190 A3
Scar La HD3, HD7 152 F4
Scar Top HD7 152 E4
Scar Top Cotts BD22 50 B7
Scar Top La HD4 171 D6
Scar Top Rd BD22 50 A7
Scarboro Mdws WF14 138 A5
Scarborough Gr BD18 55 A7
Scarborough La WF3 99 C3
Scarborough Rd Otley LS21 22 F7
Shipley BD18 55 A7
Scarborough St
Dewsbury WF12 139 D6
East Ardsley WF3 119 D8
Scarborough Terr WF12 139 D6
Scarbro' Junc LS13 58 D1
Scarbro Terr HX5 134 F6
Scarcroft Ct LS14 45 D8
Scarfold HD7 189 A5
Scargill Cl LS9 207 F1
Scargill Grange LS9 212 C4
Scarhouse La HD7 152 E4
Scarlet Hts BD13 72 F1
Scarr Bottom HX2 112 F4
Scarr End La Batley WF13 117 F2
Dewsbury WF12 139 F5
Scarr End View WF13 117 F2
Scarr Green Cl HD7 170 E2
Scarsdale La LS17 28 E6
Scarsdale Ridge LS17 28 E6
Scarth Ave LS9 208 A2
Scarth Terr WF3 122 B6
Scarwood Cl 8 BD16 37 A4
Scatcherd Gr LS27 97 F4
Scatcherd La LS27 97 F4
Scatcherd Park Ave LS27 98 A5
Scawthorpe Cl WF8 125 F1
Sceptone Gr S72 180 C3
Schofield La HD5 154 D6
Schofield St OL15 129 D2
Scholars Wlk BD2 56 B3
Scholebrook La BD4 76 C4
Scholemoor Ave BD7 73 E5
Scholemoor La BD7 73 E5
Scholemoor Rd BD7 73 F5
Scholes (Elmete) Prim Sch LS15 62 F6
Scholes First Sch BD19 115 E8
Scholes Junior & Infants Sch HD7 189 D3
Scholes La Barwick in E LS15 62 E8
Brighouse BD19 115 F7
Elland HX4 113 A1
Haworth BD22 33 F1
Scholes Moor Rd HD7 189 C2
Scholes Rd
Castleford WF10 104 D1
Holmfirth HD2, HD7, WF10 189 E3
Huddersfield HD2 136 A2
Scholes St BD5 74 D2
Scholey Ave HD6 136 A8
Scholey Head La BB10 85 A8
Scholey Rd HD6 136 A8
Scholfield St 11 OL14 108 B6
School Ave WF13 117 F1
School Cl Crofton WF4 144 B4
Gildersome LS12 77 D3
Halifax HX2 91 F7
Ripponden HX6 132 E4
School Cote Brow HX3 92 B6
School Cote Terr HX3 92 B6
School Cres
Dewsbury WF13 117 F1
Halifax HX2 91 F7
Wakefield WF2 141 D4
School Croft
Brotherton WF11 126 C8
Rothwell LS26 100 E6
School Dr WF11 126 C5
School Fold BD12 94 B6
School Gn Bramhope LS16 24 E2
Brighouse HD6 136 A8
Thornton BD13 73 A6
School Gr WF13 117 F1
School Green Ave BD13 72 F6
School Hill
Crigglestone WF2 160 B4
Huddersfield HD4 171 A7
Kirkburton HD8 173 F6
School La Aberford LS25 64 E7
8 Bradford BD6 74 B1
Castleford WF10 124 F6
Collingham LS22 29 B8
Denby Dale HD8 192 A6
Dewsbury WF13 117 F1
East Keswick LS17 28 C5
Emley HD8 175 D7
Halifax, Illingworth HX2 91 F7
Halifax, Southowram HX3 114 A3
Harewood LS17 44 C8
Holmfirth HD7 189 B4
Horbury WF4 141 A1
Huddersfield HD4 171 F8
Huddersfield, Hill Side HD5 155 B7
Huddersfield, Paddock HD1 153 E5
Leeds, Chapel Allerton LS7 60 C6
Leeds, Halton LS15 81 A8
Leeds, Meanwood LS6 59 E6
Leeds, Whitkirk Lane End LS15 81 E7
Liversedge WF15 116 D2
Marsden HD7 169 C6
Ryhill WF4 162 B1
Slaithwaite HD7 152 B6
Thorp Arch LS23 14 F4
9 Todmorden OL14 108 B5
Wakefield WF2 120 E2
Walton WF2 161 A7
School Land La HX7 87 F6
School Pl 16 BD12 94 C4
School Rd Keighley BD22 34 F7
Pontefract WF8 146 F7
Slaithwaite HD7 152 B6
Wakefield WF2 141 D4
Wetherby LS22 13 F6
School St 7 Batley WF17 96 F1
Bradford BD12 94 C6
Bradford BD1 201 B3
Bradford, Bierley BD4 95 B8
Bradford, Clayton BD14 73 B4
Bradford, Dudley Hill BD4 75 C3
Bradford, Oakenshaw BD12 95 A4
School St continued
Castleford WF10 124 C8
Castleford, Castleford Ings WF10 103 E1
Cleckheaton BD19 116 B7
Cullingworth BD13 52 D6
Dearne S63 194 D1
Denholme BD13 52 E1
Denholme BD13 71 E8
Dewsbury WF13 139 D8
Dewsbury, Chickenley WF12 140 B8
Dewsbury, Ravensthorpe WF13 138 E5
East Ardsley WF12 119 D5
Elland HX4 134 B7
Halifax HX1 203 F2
13 Hebden Bridge HX7 89 A3
Holmfirth HD7 189 A5
Honley HD7 171 F5
Huddersfield HD5 154 D5
Keighley BD20 18 A2
Liversedge WF15 116 F2
Liversedge, Norristhorpe WF15 117 B2
Mapplewell S75 178 C1
Mapplewell, Darton S75 177 E1
Morley, Churwell LS27 98 C8
Morley, City LS27 98 B4
Ossett WF5 119 C1
Pudsey LS28 76 D6
Pudsey, Farsley LS28 57 D3
Shipley BD16 54 B7
Steeton BD20 17 C5
Upton WF9 183 D8
Wilsden BD15 53 C5
School St W HD3 153 B8
School Terr Fairburn WF11 105 A4
Shepley HD8 174 A3
School View LS6 205 E3
School Wlk BD22 34 F7
School Yard View 17 HX3 92 C1
Schoolgate LS15 63 E7
Schreiber Bsns Pk WF1 142 D4
Scissett First Sch HD8 175 D2
Scissett Middle Sch HD8 175 D2
Sconce La BD16 38 B7
Scopsley Gn WF12 156 E8
Scopsley La WF12 156 E8
Scorcher Hills La DN6 184 E5
Score Croft HD8 175 A2
Score Hill Northowram HX3 93 A4
Shelf HX3 93 A4
Scoresby St BD1 201 C3
Scotch Park Trad Est LS12 210 A4
Scotchman Cl LS27 97 F2
Scotchman La LS27 97 E1
Scotchman Middle Sch BD9 55 A2
Scotchman Rd BD9 55 A2
Scotgate Rd HD7 171 E4
Scotland Cl LS18 41 B4
Scotland La LS18 41 B5
Scotland Mill La LS16 42 F1
Scotland St WF17 96 C2
Scotland Way LS18 41 B4
Scotland Wood Rd LS17 42 F2
Scott Ave WF16 117 D6
Scott Cl Sutton in C BD20 16 D5
Swillington LS26 82 A1
Scott Dr WF4 162 A8
Scott Gn LS27 97 B8
Scott Green Cres LS27 97 C8
Scott Green Dr LS27 97 C8
Scott Green Gr LS27 97 C8
Scott Green Mount LS27 97 B8
Scott Green View LS27 97 C8
Scott Hall Ave LS7 206 C4
Scott Hall Cres LS7 60 B6
Scott Hall Dr LS7 206 C4
Scott Hall Gn LS7 60 C5
Scott Hall Gr LS7 60 C5
Scott Hall Pl LS7 60 C5
Scott Hall Rd LS7, LS17 60 B6
Scott Hall Row LS7 207 D4
Scott Hall Sports Ctr LS7 60 B6
Scott Hall Sq LS7 60 C5
Scott Hall St LS7 206 C4
Scott Hall Terr LS7 60 C5
Scott Hall Way LS7 60 C6
Scott Hall Wlk LS7 206 C4
Scott Hill HD8 175 F3
Scott House OL14 129 A8
Scott La Cleckheaton BD19 116 E8
Cleckheaton, Gomersal BD19 96 B1
Keighley BD20 18 E2
Morley LS27 97 E3
Wetherby LS22 13 E5
Scott La W BD20 18 E2
Scott Mews LS22 13 E5
Scott St 3 Bradford BD6 94 D8
Keighley BD21 35 C7
Pudsey LS28 76 F6
Todmorden OL14 129 A8
Scott Vale HD2 136 D3
Scott Wood La LS7 206 C4
Scotts Hill Cl LS14 45 F5
Scotty Bank 7 HD6 115 A2
Scotty Croft La HD6 115 A1
Scout Bottom La HX7 110 F8
Scout Cl HX7 110 F8
Scout Hill Rd WF13 139 A6
Scout Hill Terr 2 WF13 139 A6
Scout Hill View 1 WF13 139 A6
Scout La HD7 151 B1
Scout Rd HX7 110 F8
Scout Road Junior, Middle & Infants Sch HX7 110 F8
Scrapers La OL14 108 B8
Sculptor Pl 14 HD6 115 A3
Seacroft Arc 5 LS14 62 B5
Seacroft Ave LS14 62 B5
Seacroft Chase 6 LS14 62 B5
Seacroft Cl LS14 62 B5
Seacroft Cres LS14 62 B5
Seacroft Gate 9 LS14 62 B5
Seacroft Grange County Primary Sch LS14 61 F3
Seacroft Hospl LS14 62 A1
Seacroft Ind Est LS14 62 B7
Seacroft Park Middle Sch LS14 62 B3
Seaforth Ave LS9 208 A3
Seaforth Gr LS9 208 A3
Seaforth Mount LS9 208 A3
Seaforth Pl LS9 208 A3
Seaforth Rd LS9 208 B3
Seaforth Terr LS9 208 A3
Seagrave Rd HD4 153 C3
Seaton St BD3 75 B7
Seckar La WF4 178 B8
Secker St WF2 142 B3
Second Ave Bardsey LS17 28 E5
Bradford BD3 56 C1
Cleckheaton WF15 116 B4
6 Halifax HX3 113 B4
Hemsworth WF9 163 A4
Horbury WF4 140 F1
Huddersfield HD7 152 D4
Huddersfield, Dalton HD5 154 F7
2 Keighley BD21 35 B6
Kirkheaton HD5 137 C1
Leeds LS12 210 B3
Lofthouse Gate WF1 121 B2
Rothwell LS26 100 F7
South Kirkby WF9 181 F1
Upton WF9 183 A8
Wetherby LS22 13 F5
Yeadon LS19 40 C5
Second St BD12 94 E6
Sedan St 5 HX1 203 E2
Sedbergh Cl LS15 80 D7
Sedbergh Dr LS29 8 C3
Sedbergh Pk LS29 8 B3
Sedburgh Rd HX3 203 F1
Sedge Gr BD22 51 C8
Sedgewick St 3 WF17 96 E1
Sedgfield Terr 1 BD1 74 D7
Sedgwick Cl BD8 74 D8
Seed Hill Terr Halifax HX2 91 C6
Steeton BD20 17 C5
Seed Row BD4 95 B8
Seed St BD12 94 D6
Sefton Ave Brighouse HD6 114 F5
Leeds LS11 214 A3
Sefton Cres HD6 114 F5
Sefton Dr Brighouse HD6 114 F5
Ilkley LS29 8 B3
Sefton Gr BD2 56 B3
Sefton La HD7 170 D2
Sefton Pl BD21 35 C8
Sefton Rise WF12 139 D4
Sefton St Halifax HX1 202 C4
Keighley BD21 35 C8
Leeds LS11 214 B3
Sefton Terr Halifax HX1 202 C4
Leeds LS11 214 A3
Selborne Gr Bradford BD9 55 B2
Keighley BD21 35 B5
Selborne Mount BD9 55 C2
Selborne Terr
Bradford BD9 55 B2
Shipley BD18 55 B6
Selborne Villas BD9 55 B3
Selbourne Ave WF12 139 C5
Selbourne Dr WF12 139 C5
Selbourne Rd WF12 139 C5
Selbourne Villas BD14 73 C3
Selby HX2 91 D6
Selby Ave LS9 80 E8
Selby Rd Garforth LS25 83 C4
Ledsham LS25 84 B4
Ledston LS25 83 C4
Leeds LS15, LS25, LS9 81 C8
South Milford LS25 84 B4
Swillington LS15, LS25 82 B6
Selby St WF1 216 C3
Seldon St BD5 74 B3
Selene Cl BD19 96 C2
Sellars Fold 6 BD7 74 A4
Sellerdale Ave BD12 94 D1
Sellerdale Dr BD12 94 D2
Sellerdale Rise BD12 94 D1
Sellerdale Way BD12 94 D1
Selso Rd WF12 118 F1
Seminary St LS2 206 A1
Semon Ave BD2 55 F5
Senior St Dewsbury WF13 139 B7
Huddersfield HD5 154 E5
Senior Way BD5 201 B2
Sentry HD7 171 F5
Sergeantson St 14 HD1 154 A6
Serpentine Rd BD19 116 D7
Servia Dr LS7 206 C3
Servia Gdns LS7 206 C3
Servia Hill LS6, LS7 206 B3
Servia Rd LS7 206 B3
Service Rd LS9 80 D3
Sessions House Yd WF8 125 C1
Seven Hills Primary Sch LS27 98 B4
Sevenoaks Mead BD15 54 B1
Seventh Ave
Cleckheaton WF15 116 B5
Rothwell LS26 101 A7
Severn Dr LS25 83 B6
Severn Rd Bradford BD2 56 A3
Leeds LS10 215 F3
Severn Way LS10 215 F3
Sewage Works Rd LS9 80 C3
Sewell Rd BD3 75 B6
Sewerbridge La WF7 145 A8
Seymour St Bradford BD3 75 A6
Wakefield WF2 142 C4
Seymour Wlk HD7 170 E2
Shackleton St OL14 86 C1
Shackleton Terr BD16 36 A1
Shade Junior & Infants Sch OL14 108 A3
Shade St OL14 108 A3
Shadwell La Leeds LS17 43 D2
Thorner LS17 44 B5
Shadwell Park Ave LS17 44 C5
Shadwell Park Cl LS17 44 C5
Shadwell Park Ct LS17 44 C4
Shadwell Park Dr LS17 44 C4
Shadwell Park Gdns LS17 44 C5
Shadwell Park Gr LS17 44 C4
Shadwell Primary Sch LS17 44 F4
Shadwell Wlk LS17 43 E3
Shady La BD20 4 A3
Shaftesbury Ave
Beal DN14 127 F5
Bradford BD9 54 D1
Brighouse HD6 136 B7
Leeds LS8 44 A2
Shipley BD18 55 C7
Shaftesbury Ct BD9 54 D1
Shaftesbury Rd LS8 44 A2
Shafton Hall Dr S72 180 B3
Shafton La LS11 210 C1
Shafton Pl LS11 210 C1
Shafton St LS11 211 D1
Shafton Two Gates Jun & Inf Sch S72 180 C2
Shafton View LS11 210 C1
Shakespeare App LS9 207 F1
Shakespeare Ave
Leeds LS9 207 F1
Normanton WF6 144 A7
Todmorden OL14 108 D6
Shakespeare Bldgs HD1 153 D6
Shakespeare Cl
Guiseley LS20 39 F8
Leeds LS9 207 F1
Littleborough OL15 129 C1
Shakespeare Cres WF10 125 D5
Shakespeare Ct LS9 207 F1
Shakespeare Gdns LS9 207 F1
Shakespeare Grange LS9 207 F1
Shakespeare Lawn LS9 207 F1
Shakespeare Primary Sch LS9 207 F1
Shakespeare Rd LS20 39 F8
Shakespeare St
Halifax HX1 203 E3
Leeds LS9 207 F2
Shakespeare Towers LS9 207 F1
Shalimar St HX1 202 B3
Shambles The
11 Huddersfield HD1 154 B6
Wetherby LS22 13 E5
Shann Ave BD21 34 F8
Shann Cres BD21 34 F8
Shann La BD20 17 F1
Shann St BD2 55 D4
Shannon Cl Brighouse HD6 135 E7
Ilkley LS29 7 F3
Shannon Dr HD3 134 D1
Shannon Rd
Brighouse HD6 135 E7
Leeds LS9 212 B4
Shannon St LS9 212 B4
Shapla Cl BD22 35 A6
Share Hill HD7 152 C3
Sharehill HD7 152 C4
Sharlston Junior & Infant Sch WF4 144 B4
Sharnaley Ct WF8 147 A8
Sharneyford Primary Sch OL13 106 C5
Sharon Cotts WF5 140 D7
Sharp Ave BD6 94 C8
Sharp House Rd LS10 99 F4
Sharp La
Huddersfield HD4, HD5 154 F2
Middleton LS10, WF3 99 F4
Sharp Lane Prim Sch LS10 99 E5
Sharp Royd HD5 155 A4
Sharp St 11 Bradford BD6 74 C1
Dewsbury WF13 118 D1
Sharp's Row LS28 76 E6
Sharpe St Batley WF16 117 D3
Bradford BD5 201 B2
Shaw Ave WF6 123 C2
Shaw Barn Croft LS22 13 C5
Shaw Barn La LS22 13 C5
Shaw Booth La HX2 90 F4
Shaw Cl Elland HX4 134 C4
Guiseley LS20 39 F8
Normanton WF6 123 C2
South Elmsall WF9 183 A4
Shaw Cross Bsns Pk WF12 119 A2
Shaw Cross Infants Sch WF12 119 A3
Shaw Fields HD7 169 C8
Shaw Fields La HD7 169 C8
Shaw Fold WF2 142 E1
Shaw Gate HD7 169 F6
Shaw Hill HX1 203 E1
Shaw Hill La HX3 203 F1

Shaw La Cudworth S71 179 E1
Elland HX5 135 C8
Elland, Holywell Green HX4 134 B4
Guiseley LS20 22 F1
Halifax HX4 203 F1
Holmfirth HD7 188 D4
Huddersfield HD7 153 B4
Keighley BD21 35 D3
Leeds LS6 59 D6
Mapplewell S75 178 C2
Marsden HD7 169 A8
Oxenhope BD22 51 B2
Ripponden HX6 132 C2
Royston S71 179 E1
Shelf HX3 92 F6
Slaithwaite HD7 152 C8
Sowerby Bridge HX6 112 C1
Todmorden OL14 86 C3
Shaw Lane Gdns LS20 22 F1
Shaw Leys LS19 40 A8
Shaw Lodge HX3 203 F1
Shaw Rise WF6 123 C2
Shaw Royd LS19 40 A8
Shaw St 4 Bradford BD12 94 B6
Cleckheaton BD19 116 B7
Elland HX4 134 C4
Mirfield WF14 138 A5
Shaw Wood Ave OL14 109 A6
Shaw's Terr HD7 168 F4
Shawfield Ave HD7 188 D4
Shawmount HX2 111 E8
Shaws La Barwick in E LS15 63 C6
Sowerby Bridge HX6 111 A2
Shay Cl BD9 54 F4
Shay Cres BD9 54 E4
Shay Ct Bradford BD9 54 E4
Crofton WF4 143 E1
Shay Dr BD9 54 E4
Shay Fold BD9 54 E4
Shay Gap Rd BD22 34 C7
Shay Gate BD15 53 E4
Shay Gr BD9 54 F4
Shay La Bradford BD9 54 F4
Crofton WF4 143 E1
Halifax HX2, HX3 92 A4
Holme HD7 187 E3
Walton WF2 161 C7
Wilsden BD15 53 D4
Shay Lane Prim Sch WF4 143 E1
Shay St LS6 206 B3
Shay Syke HX1 203 F1
Shay The (Halifax Town FC) HX1 203 E1
Shayfield La WF3 100 D3
Sheaf St LS10 212 A2
Shearbridge Pl BD7 74 C6
Shearbridge Rd BD7 74 C6
Shearbridge Terr BD7 74 C6
Sheardale HD7 171 E4
Shearing Cross Gdns 1 HD1 154 B8
Shed St BD21 35 C7
Sheep Hill La BD13 73 B2
Sheepridge Gr HD2 136 C3
Sheepridge Rd HD2 136 C3
Sheepscar Gr LS7 207 D1
Sheepscar Row LS7 207 D2
Sheepscar St N LS7 207 D3
Sheepscar St S LS7 207 D1
Sheepscar Way LS7 207 D3
Sheepwalk La
Castleford WF10 125 D6
Upton WF9 183 E8
Sheerien Cl S71 178 E1
Sheffield Rd HD7 189 E3
Sheila Terr WF16 117 C3
Sheldrake Ave BD8 73 C7
Sheldrake Rd WF10 124 D6
Shelf Hall La HX3 93 C5
Shelf Junior & Infants Sch HX3 93 B5
Shelf Moor HX3 93 C7
Shelf Moor Rd HX3 93 C6
Shelf Rd HX7 88 F3
Shell La LS28 57 B5
Shelldrake Dr LS10 99 D5
Shelley Ave WF16 117 E2
Shelley Cl LS26 101 C3
Shelley Cres LS26 101 C3
Shelley Ct WF4 141 C2
Shelley Dr WF11 126 B4
Shelley First Sch HD8 174 A3
Shelley Gr BD8 73 E8
Shelley High Sch HD8 174 E2
Shelley La HD8 174 A5
Shelley Sta HD8 174 B1
Shelley Wlk WF3 121 E6
Shelley Woodhouse La
Shepley HD8 174 D1
Skelmanthorpe HD8 174 D1
Shelwith Wlk LS14 62 A2
Shepcote Cl LS16 41 F3
Shepcote Cres LS16 41 F3
Shepherd St 1 BD7 74 B4
Shepherd's Gr LS7 207 E4
Shepherd's La LS7, LS8 207 F4
Shepherd's Pl LS8 207 F4
Shepherds Gr HD2 136 E3
Shepherds Thorn La HD2 136 C6
Shepley First Sch HD8 190 E8
Shepley Mount WF14 138 B7
Shepley Rd HD4 173 C2
Shepley St WF1 142 E7
Shepley Sta HD8 173 F1
Shepstye Rd WF4 141 A1
Shepton Ho 12 BD5 201 B1
Sherborne Dr BD22 34 E5
Sherborne Rd Bradford BD7 74 D6
Bradford, Thackley BD10 39 B1
Sherbrooke Ave LS15 80 F7
Sherburn App LS14 62 C6
Sherburn Cl
Adwick Le S DN6 184 E2
Birkenshaw BD11 96 B6
6 Leeds LS14 62 C6
Sherburn Ct 3 LS14 62 C6
Sherburn Gr BD11 96 B6
Sherburn Pl LS14 62 C6
Sherburn Rd
Brighouse HD6 135 E8
Leeds LS14 62 C6
Sherburn Rd N LS14 62 B7
Sherburn Row 4 LS14 62 C6
Sherburn Sq 7 LS14 62 C6
Sherburn Wlk 5 LS14 62 C6
Sheridan Cl LS28 76 F6
Sheridan Ct LS28 76 F6
Sheridan St Bradford BD4 75 B4
Lofthouse Gate WF1 121 C5
Sheridan Way LS28 76 F6
Sheriff La BD16 37 D4
Sherwell Gr BD15 54 C1
Sherwell Rise BD15 54 C1
Sherwood Ave
Cleckheaton BD19 117 B8
Huddersfield HD2 136 F5
Sherwood Cl Batley WF13 117 F3
Bingley BD16 37 C5
Cleckheaton BD19 117 B8
Sherwood Dr
Adwick Le S DN6 184 E2
Crigglestone WF2 159 F5
Huddersfield HD4 171 C7
Sherwood Gn WF3 100 A3
Sherwood Gr Shipley BD18 54 E8
Wakefield WF2 141 E4
Sherwood Ind Est WF3 100 B3
Sherwood Pl BD2 56 B2
Sherwood Rd HD6 115 C2
Sherwood Way S72 180 A1
Shetcliffe La BD4 95 C8
Shetcliffe Rd BD4 95 B8
Shetland Cl BD2 55 F4
Shibden Dr WF17 117 F6
Shibden Garth HX3 114 A8
Shibden Grange Dr HX3 92 F1
Shibden Hall HX3 113 F8
Shibden Hall Croft HX3 114 A8
Shibden Hall Rd
Brighouse HX3 114 A8
Halifax HX3 113 F8
Shibden Head First Sch BD13 92 C7
Shibden Head La BD13 92 D7
Shibden Head Mews BD13 92 C7
Shibden View BD13 92 D7
Shield Cl LS15 62 E3
Shield Hall La HX6 111 C4
Shill Bank Ave WF14 138 D6
Shill Bank La WF14 138 C6
Shillbank View WF14 138 C6
Shilling St WF1 216 C4
Shillinghill La WF8 126 B1
Shinwell Dr WF9 183 D8
Ship St HD6 115 B2
Ship Yd WF1 216 C1
Shipley Airedale Rd BD1, BD3 201 C3
Shipley CE First Sch BD18 55 B6
Shipley Coll of Further Education BD18 55 A8
Shipley College Mill Annexe BD18 37 F1
Shipley Fields Rd BD18 55 C5
Shipley Glen Cable Rly BD17 37 F2
Shipley Golf Course BD16 36 E1
Shipley Sta BD18 55 C7
Shipley Wycliffe CE Middle Sch BD18 55 A8
Shipton Mews LS27 98 B3
Shire Cl BD6 93 F7
Shire Oak Rd LS6 59 E5
Shire Oak St LS6 59 D5
Shires Gr WF3 121 F5
Shires Hill HD1 153 E5
Shirley Ave Batley WF17 96 E2
Bradford BD12 94 C1
Cleckheaton BD19 117 B8
Shirley Cl LS21 23 B7
Shirley Cres BD12 94 C1
Shirley Dr LS13 58 C4
Shirley Gr Brighouse HX3 115 A7
Cleckheaton BD19 117 B8
Shirley Manor First Sch BD12 94 C1
Shirley Mount BD19 117 B8
Shirley Par BD19 117 A8
Shirley Pl Bradford BD12 94 C1
Cleckheaton BD19 117 B8
Shirley Rd
Bradford, Shearbridge BD7 74 B6
Bradford, Tong Street BD4 75 D1
Cleckheaton BD19 117 B8
Shirley Sq BD19 117 B8
Shirley St Denholme BD13 52 E1
3 Haworth BD22 51 B7
Shipley BD18 54 F8
Shirley Terr BD19 117 B8
Shirley Wlk BD19 117 B8
Shoe Market 4 WF8 146 D8
Shoebridge Ave BD20 16 F6
Shoebroad La OL14 108 B4
Sholebroke Ave LS7 207 D4
Sholebroke Ct LS7 207 D4
Sholebroke Mount LS7 206 C4
Sholebroke Pl LS7 207 D4
Sholebroke St LS7 207 D4
Sholebroke Terr LS7 204 A1
Sholebroke View LS7 207 D4
Shoolaboards La 3 WF8 146 F8
Shop La Kirkheaton HD5 155 C8
Lofthouse Gate WF3 121 B8
Shore End La HX2 90 A7
Shore Gn OL14 86 C2
Shore New Rd OL14 86 B1
Shoreham Rd LS12 209 F2
Short Cl BD12 94 B5
Short La LS7 60 C7
Short St Dewsbury WF12 140 A7
Featherstone WF7 145 C5
5 Todmorden OL14 108 B5
Shortway Pudsey LS28 57 A1
Thornton BD13 73 A6
Shortwood La DN5 194 B4
Shroggs Rd HX3 202 C4
Shroggs St HX1 202 C4
Shroggs Vue Terr HX1 202 C4
Shutt The WF4 159 B8
Shuttleworth La BD8 73 E8
Shuttocks Cl LS25 83 A3
Shuttocks Fold LS25 83 B3
Shutts La HX3 93 E2
Sickle St BD19 116 E8
Sickleholme Ct HD2 136 E5
Sicklinghall County Primary Sch LS22 12 B5
Sicklinghall Rd LS22 13 B5
Siddal Gr HX3 113 D4
Siddal La HX3 113 E3
Siddal New Rd HX3 203 F1
Siddal Prim Sch HX3 113 E3
Siddal St HX3 113 E3
Siddal Top La HX3 113 E3
Siddall St LS11 211 E2
Siddel View HX3 113 E4
Siddon Dr HD5 155 A3
Side Copse LS21 23 B8
Side La HD3 152 F6
Sidings Cl BD2 55 D3
Sidings The Guiseley LS20 22 D1
Shipley BD18 55 C8
Sidney St LS2 211 F4
Siegen Cl LS27 98 A4
Sigget La OL14 107 F6
Sigott St HD3 152 F6
Sike Cl S75 177 D1
Sike La Holmfirth HD7 189 D5
Walton WF2 161 B5
Sikes Cl HD5 154 F4
Silcoates Ave WF2 120 E1
Silcoates Ct WF2 141 E8
Silcoates Dr WF2 120 E1
Silcoates La WF2 120 E1
Silcoates Sch WF2 120 E1
Silcoates St WF2 142 A7
Silk Mill App LS16 41 E2
Silk Mill Ave LS16 41 E3
Silk Mill Bank LS16 41 D2
Silk Mill Cl LS16 41 D3
Silk Mill Dr Keighley BD20 19 E1
Leeds LS16 41 E2
Silk Mill Gdns LS16 41 D2
Silk Mill Gn LS16 41 E2
Silk Mill Mews LS16 41 F2
Silk Mill Rd LS16 41 D2
Silk Mill Way LS16 41 E2
Silk St BD9 55 A2
Silkstone Cres WF2 160 C6
Silkstone Crest WF6 122 F4
Silkstone Ct 6 LS15 62 C1
Silkstone La S75 193 F3
Silkstone Rd BD3 75 B8
Silkstone Way LS15 62 C1
Silsbridge St 4 BD1 74 D7
Silsden Golf Course BD20 18 A8
Silsden Rd Addingham LS29 6 C7
Keighley BD20 18 E4
Low Bradley BD20 4 D5
Silson La BD17 38 E4
Silver Birch Ave BD12 94 D2
Silver Birch Cl BD12 94 D2
Silver Birch Dr BD12 94 D2
Silver Birch Gr BD12 94 D2
Silver Court Ind Est HD5 154 C5
Silver Ct LS28 57 F1
Silver La LS19 40 B7
Silver Mill Hill LS21 23 B6
Silver Royd Ave LS12 77 F6
Silver Royd Cl LS12 77 F6
Silver Royd Dr LS12 77 F6
Silver Royd Garth LS12 77 F6
Silver Royd Gr LS12 77 F6
Silver Royd Hill LS12 77 F6
Silver Royd Pl LS12 77 F6
Silver Royd Rd LS12 77 F6
Silver Royd St LS12 77 F6
Silver Royd Terr LS12 77 F6
Silver St Bradford BD8 55 B1
Fairburn WF11 105 A4
Halifax HX1 203 E3
Huddersfield HD5 154 C6
Leeds LS11 211 D2
Lofthouse Gate WF1 121 B3
Todmorden OL14 129 A7
Wakefield WF1 216 B2
Silver St E HD5 154 C5
Silver St W HD5 154 C5
Silverdale Ave Guiseley LS20 39 E8
Keighley BD20 18 E1
Leeds LS17 44 B5
Silverdale Cl LS20 39 E7
Silverdale Cres LS20 39 E8
Silverdale Dr LS20 39 E7
Silverdale Gr LS20 39 D8
Silverdale Grange LS20 39 E7
Silverdale Mount LS20 39 E7
Silverdale Rd Bradford BD5 74 E2
Guiseley LS20 39 D8
Silverdale Terr HX4 134 A6
Silverhill Ave BD3 56 D1
Silverhill Dr BD3 56 D1
Silverhill Rd BD3 56 C1
Silverwood Ave HX2 91 C1
Silverwood Wlk HX2 91 C1
Silwood Dr BD2 56 C3
Sim Royd La HD8 192 D4
Simeon St OL14 129 A8
Simes St BD1 201 A3
Simm Carr La HX3 92 D4
Simmonds La HX3 203 F1
Simmons Ct LS9 212 C2
Simmons Way LS8 208 B4
Simms Dene BD15 54 A4
Simon Cl BD4 75 F2
Simon Green Rd HD7 152 B3
Simpson Gr Bradford BD10 39 C1
Leeds LS12 210 A3
Simpson Rd
Hebden Bridge HX7 110 D8
South Elmsall WF9 183 B4
Simpson St
East Ardsley WF3 120 E8
5 Halifax HX3 92 B2
Keighley BD21 35 A7
Simpson's Lane Junior & Infants Sch WF11 126 D3
Simpsons La WF11 126 D3
Sinclair Garth WF2 160 E8
Sinclair Rd BD2 55 F5
Sinden Mews BD10 39 B2
Singleton St BD1 55 E1
Sion Hill HX3 113 E3
Sir Francis Crossley's Almhouses HX1 203 D3
Sir George Martin Dr LS16 42 D4
Sir Isaac Holden Pl BD7 74 C7
Sir Karl Cohen Sq LS12 209 E3
Sir Wilfred Pl BD10 56 B8
Sisley La OL14 109 A4
Sissons Ave LS10 99 B4
Sissons Cres LS10 99 B3
Sissons Dr LS10 99 B4
Sissons Gn LS10 99 B4
Sissons Gr LS10 99 B4
Sissons La LS10 99 B4
Sissons Mount LS10 99 A3
Sissons Pl LS10 99 B4
Sissons Rd LS10 99 A3
Sissons Row LS10 99 B4
Sissons St LS10 99 B4
Sissons Terr LS10 99 B3
Sissons View LS10 99 B3
Sitka Cl S71 179 B2
Siward St WF9 163 A4
Six Heights HX6 132 E3
Sixrood La DN6 184 F5
Sixth Ave Bradford BD3 56 C1
Cleckheaton WF15 116 B5
Rothwell LS26 101 A6
Sizers Ct LS19 40 A5
Skelbrooke Dr WF8 146 D5
Skelda Rise LS29 8 B3
Skellow Rd DN6 184 F1
Skelmanthorpe Bsns Pk HD8 175 A2
Skelmanthorpe First Sch HD8 175 B2
Skelmanthorpe Sta HD8 175 A3
Skelton Ave Leeds LS9 80 B8
Mapplewell S75 178 B1
Skelton Cres
Huddersfield HD4 153 B3
Leeds LS9 80 B8
Skelton Grange Rd LS10 80 B8
Skelton Mount LS9 80 B8
Skelton Pl LS9 80 B8
Skelton Rd LS9 80 B8
Skelton St LS9 80 B8
Skelton Terr LS9 80 B8
Skelton Wlk BD10 56 D7
Skeltons La LS14 45 C1
Skelwith App LS14 62 A2
Skinner La Bradford BD8 55 C2
Leeds LS7 207 D1
Pontefract WF8 125 D2
Skinner St LS1 211 D4
Skippon Terr LS14 45 F6
Skipton Ave HD2 136 B2
Skipton Rd Addingham LS29 2 D1
Farnhill BD20 4 C1
Glusburn BD20 16 E6
Ilkley LS29 7 E4
Keighley BD20 18 B2
Low Bradley BD20 4 B6
Silsden BD20 5 C2
Steeton BD20 17 B5
Skipton Rise LS25 83 B7
Skipton St WF17 118 C2
Skircoat Gn HX3 113 C2
Skircoat Green Rd HX3 113 C3
Skircoat Moor Cl HX3 113 A4
Skircoat Moor Rd HX3 113 A4
Skircoat Rd HX1 203 E1
Skirrow St BD16 54 B6
Skye Rd BD9 55 A3
Slack HD3 152 A7
Slack Bottom HX7 88 E6
Slack Bottom Rd BD6 94 A8
Slack House La HX7 89 B7
Slack La Crofton WF4 144 A1
Elland HD3 152 A8
Halifax HX2 90 B4
Holmfirth HD7 189 B4
Oakworth BD22 34 B3
Ripponden HX6 131 F5
Ripponden, Barkisland HX4 133 A3
South Hiendley S72 180 B5
Wakefield WF2 160 C5
Slack Top HX7 88 D6
Slack Top La HD7 190 C1
Slacks La Marsden HD7 169 A8
Slaithwaite HD7 169 E5
Sladdin Row BD13 92 C8
Slade Cl LS23 30 D7
Slade House BD2 56 D2
Slade La Brighouse HD6 135 F6
Keighley BD20 18 E2
Slade Wlk WF17 96 F1
Sladen Bridge BD22 50 F7
Sladen St 6 BD21 35 A7
Slades La HD7 170 E4
Slades Rd HD7 152 B4
Slaid Hill Ct LS17 44 B5
Slaithwaite CE controlled Junior & Infants Sch HD7 169 E8
Slaithwaite Nields Junior & Infants Sch HD7 169 F8
Slaithwaite Ave WF12 139 C4
Slaithwaite C of E Sch HD7 151 F1
Slaithwaite Cl WF12 139 C4
Slaithwaite Gate HD7 152 A5
Slaithwaite Rd
Dewsbury WF12 139 D4
Meltham HD7 170 B3
Slaithwaite Sta HD7 151 F1
Slant Gate
Huddersfield HD7 152 E2
Kirkburton HD8 173 E7
Slant La OL14 108 D6
Slate Quarry La BD16 37 B4
Slater Ave HX7 89 A4
Slater Ing La HX7 88 C5
Slaters Rd LS28 57 E1
Slates La LS29 8 B7
Slaymaker La BD22 34 C3
Slead Ave HD6 114 F4
Slead Cres HD6 114 F4
Slead Gr HD6 114 F4
Slead Royd HD6 114 F4
Slead View HD6 114 F4
Sledbrook Cres S36 200 C6
Sledgate La HD7 169 E5
Sledge Gate HD3 151 A4
Sledmere Croft LS14 62 C6
Sledmere Garth LS14 62 C6
Sledmere Gn 9 LS14 62 C6
Sledmere La LS14 62 C6
Sledmere Pl LS14 62 C6
Sledmere Sq 8 LS14 62 C6
Sleep Hill La Hampole DN6 184 B6
South Elmsall DN6 183 F7
Sleights La LS17 27 B6
Sleningford Gr BD18 54 E8
Sleningford Rd
Bingley BD16 36 E5
Shipley BD18 54 E8
Sleningford Rise BD16 36 F5
Sleningford Terr BD16 36 E5
Slicer's Yd BD16 36 F3
Slipper La WF14 137 E7
Slippery Ford La BD22 33 C6
Slippy La HX2 91 C5
Sloan Sq BD8 74 B8
Slutwell La WF8 146 D8
Smalewell Cl LS28 76 D6
Smalewell Dr LS28 76 C6
Smalewell Gdns LS28 76 C6
Smalewell Gn LS28 76 D6
Smalewell Rd LS28 76 C6
Small La Cawthorne S75 193 B1
Huddersfield HD7 152 D4
Small Lees Rd HX6 132 D3
Small Page Fold 7 BD13 72 E1
Small Shaw La HX7 69 A1
Smallpage Yd WF1 216 B2
Smallwood Gdns WF12 119 A3
Smallwood Rd
Batley WF12 119 A2
Batley WF12 119 A3
Smawell La WF4 179 B7
Smawthorne Ave WF10 124 D7
Smawthorne Gr WF10 124 D7
Smawthorne Infants Sch WF10 124 D6
Smawthorne La WF10 124 D7
Smeatley's La WF8 166 E7
Smeaton App LS15 62 E3
Smeaton Gr LS26 82 A2
Smeaton Ind Pk WF8 165 F7
Smeaton Rd WF9 183 E8
Smiddles La BD5 74 D2
Smiddy Hill LS23 15 A4
Smirthwaite St WF1 216 B4
Smirthwaite View WF6 123 A1
Smith Ave BD6 94 C8
Smith Cres HD6 135 E8
Smith House Ave HD6 115 A6
Smith House Cres HD6 115 A5
Smith House Gr HD6 115 A5
Smith House La HX3 115 A6
Smith La BD9 54 F2

Smith Rd Bradford BD7 74 B3
Dewsbury WF13 117 F1
Smith St Bradford BD7 74 D7
Bradford, Bierley BD4 95 B8
Castleford, Castleford Ings WF10 103 F1
Castleford, New Fryston WF10 104 C2
Keighley BD21 35 A8
Liversedge WF15 117 B3
Shipley BD16 54 B6
Smith Wlk WF9 183 A4
Smith's Terr HX3 92 A3
Smitherd's St BD21 35 C6
Smithfield Ave HX3 114 C8
Smithies La Batley WF17 96 E1
Liversedge FW16 117 D2
Smithies Moor Cl WF17 117 F7
Smithies Moor Cres WF17 117 F8
Smithies Moor La WF17 117 E7
Smithies Moor Rise WF17 117 F8
Smiths Ave HD3 153 D7
Smithson Ave WF10 125 C6
Smithson St LS26 100 F4
Smithville BD21 18 F1
Smithwell La HX7 88 E5
Smithy Carr La HD6 115 A4
Smithy Cl Crofton WF4 161 F8
Skelmanthorpe HD8 175 A1
Smithy Clough La HX6 132 B3
Smithy Greaves LS29 7 C7
Smithy Hill Bradford BD6 74 C1
Denby Dale HD8 191 F3
Denholme BD13 71 E6
Smithy La Bardsey LS17 28 C2
Burley in W LS29 21 E8
Denton LS29 9 B7
East Ardsley WF3 119 F8
Heptonstall HX7 88 A6
Holmfirth HD7 188 C2
Huddersfield HD5 154 C5
Leeds LS16 41 E6
Netherton WF4 157 F6
Ripponden HX6 150 D7
Skelmanthorpe HD8 175 A1
Wilsden BD15 53 C6
Smithy Mills La LS16 42 D2
Smithy Nook OL15 129 C1
Smithy Par WF12 139 F1
Smithy Place La HD7 172 B2
Smithy St HX1 203 F3
Smithy Wlk WF12 139 F1
Smyth St WF1 216 A2
Snail La HX7 110 B8
Snape Dr BD7 73 D2
Snape Fold HD5 154 F4
Snape St BD21 35 C4
Snapethorpe Cres WF2 141 D3
Snapethorpe Gate WF2 141 C4
Snapethorpe Jun Sch WF2 141 D4
Snapethorpe Rd WF2 141 D4
Snaygill Ind Est BD23 4 A8
Snelsins La BD19 95 C1
Snelsins Rd BD19 95 C1
Snittle Rd HD7 199 B6
Snow Hill Cl WF1 121 A1
Snow Hill Rise WF1 121 A1
Snow Hill View WF1 216 A4
Snowden App LS13 58 E3
Snowden Cl LS13 58 D2
Snowden Cres LS13 58 D2
Snowden Fold LS13 58 D2
Snowden Gn LS13 58 D2
Snowden Gr LS13 58 D2
Snowden Lawn LS13 58 D2
Snowden Rd BD18 55 D7
Snowden Royd LS13 58 D3
Snowden St BD1 201 B4
Snowden Vale LS13 58 D2
Snowden Way LS13 58 D3
Snowdens Wlk BD14 73 D4
Snowdon Ave WF11 126 C4
Snowdon St WF17 118 B4
Snowdrop Mews 8 BD15 73 B8
Snug La HD7 190 A1
Snydale Ave WF6 123 C1
Snydale Cl WF6 123 C1
Snydale Ct WF6 123 C1
Snydale Gr WF6 123 C1
Snydale Rd WF6 123 C1
Soaper House La HX3 93 D1
Soaper La Bradford BD6 93 D8
Shelf HX3 93 D8
Sod House Gn HX3 92 A3
Soho Gr WF2 142 A6
Soho St Bradford BD1 201 A3
Halifax HX1 202 B3
Solid HD4 153 F2
Solomon Hill HX2 90 D1
Solway Rd WF17 118 F5
Somerdale Cl LS13 58 D1
Somerdale Gdns LS13 58 D1
Somerdale Gr LS13 58 D1
Somerdale Wlk LS13 58 D1
Somers Pl 4 LS1 211 E4
Somers St LS1 211 D4
Somerset Ave Baildon BD17 38 D4
Brighouse HD6 136 B7
Somerset Ct WF11 126 F4
Somerset Rd
Huddersfield HD5 154 D4
Pudsey LS28 76 E8
Somerton Dr BD4 75 E2
Somerville Ave
Bradford BD6 94 B7
Leeds LS14 61 F2
Somerville Dr LS14 61 F3
Somerville Gn LS14 61 F2
Somerville Gr LS14 61 F3
Somerville Mount 2 LS14 62 A2
Somerville Pk BD6 94 B7
Somerville Terr LS21 23 C8
Somerville View LS14 61 F2
Sonning Rd BD15 73 B8
Soothill La Batley WF17 118 E5
East Ardsley WF17 119 A5
Sorbus Way HD8 155 E3
Sorrel Cl WF8 146 D7
Sorrin Cl BD10 56 A7
Sotheron Croft WF8 147 C5
Soureby Cross Way BD4 95 F7
Sourhall Cl OL14 107 D6
Sourhall Cotts OL14 107 D6
Sourhall Rd OL14 107 C5
South Accommodation Rd LS10, LS9 212 B1
South App Bramham LS14 47 C6
Stutton LS25 48 A3
South Ave Castleford WF10 123 F7
Horbury WF4 141 C1
Huddersfield, Cowlersley HD4 152 F3
Huddersfield, Sheepridge HD2 136 B2
Pontefract WF8 146 B7
South Elmsall WF9 182 F2
South Baileygate WF8 125 E1
South Bank
East Keswick LS17 28 C6
3 Queensbury BD13 72 F1
South Bank Rd WF17 118 A6
South Bolton HX2 91 E7
South Bradford Golf Course BD12 94 F7
South Brook Terr BD7 201 A2
South Cl Guiseley LS20 39 B8
Royston S71 179 C2
South Cliffe BD13 72 E6
South Clough Head HX2 112 A8
South Craven Sch BD20 16 D6
South Cres WF9 183 B4
South Croft
Denby Dale HD8 191 F3
Shafton S72 180 C3
South Croft Ave BD11 96 A6
South Croft Dr BD11 96 A7
South Croft Gate BD11 96 A6
South Cross Rd HD2 135 F2
South Crossland C of E Junior Sch HD4 171 D7
South Dr Guiseley LS20 39 B8
Pudsey LS28 57 D2
Royston S71 179 C2
Wakefield WF2 142 E1
South Edge Keighley BD20 35 A8
Shipley BD18 54 F7
South Elmsall Fst Sch WF9 182 F2
South Elmsall Sta WF9 183 A3
South End Ave LS13 58 E1
South End Gr LS13 58 E1
South End Mount 2 LS13 58 E1
South End Terr 1 LS13 58 E1
South Farm Cres LS9 208 C2
South Farm Rd LS9 61 D2
South Gr Brighouse HD6 114 E5
Shipley BD18 54 D7
South Halifax High Sch HX3 113 E2
South Hawksworth St LS29 8 B4
South Hiendley Jun & Inf Sch S72 180 D6
South Hill Cl LS10 99 F7
South Hill Croft LS10 99 F7
South Hill Dr BD16 37 C2
South Hill Gdns LS10 99 F7
South Hill Gr LS10 99 F7
South Hill Rise LS10 99 F7
South Hill Way LS10 99 F7
South La Cawthorne S75 193 C1
Elland HX5 134 F5
Elland, Blackley HX5 134 F4
Holmfirth HD7 189 A5
Netherton WF4 158 D4
Shelf HX3 93 C7
South Lane Gdns HX5 134 F5
South Lee LS18 41 B1
South Leeds Bsns Pk LS10 215 D4
South Leeds L Ctr LS11 211 E1
South Leeds Stadium LS11 99 C8
South Mead LS16 24 F2
South Mount LS17 28 B6
South Nelson St LS27 98 A5
South Ossett Infant Sch WF5 140 E4
South Par Bradford BD8 55 D1
Cleckheaton BD19 116 C7
Elland HX5 134 F5
Elland, Stainland HX4 133 F3
Halifax HX1 203 F2
Ilkley LS29 8 A4
Leeds LS1 211 E4
Leeds, Headingley LS6 59 D5
Morley LS27 98 B4
Ossett WF5 141 A4
Otley LS21 23 B7
Pudsey LS28 76 E6
Wakefield WF1 216 B2
South Parade Cl LS28 76 D6
South Parade Junior Sch WF5 140 F4
South Park Terr LS28 76 F4
South Park Way WF2 120 F4
South Parkway LS14 62 A4
South Parkway App LS14, LS9 61 E3
South Queen St LS27 98 B3
South Rd Cullingworth BD13 52 D5
Leeds LS9 80 C3
Shipley BD9 55 C4
South Ridge LS25 83 A1
South Royd Ave HX3 113 C4
South Selby HX2 91 D6
South Sq BD13 72 D6
South St Bacup OL13 106 A3
Bradford, Little Horton BD5 74 C3
Bradford, Oakenshaw BD12 95 A4
Brighouse HD6 115 A3
Denholme BD13 71 D8
Dewsbury WF13 139 C8
Dewsbury, Savile Town WF12 139 D6
Elland HX4 134 B4
Halifax HX1 203 D2
Hemsworth WF9 181 E6
Holmfirth HD7 189 C6
Huddersfield, Netherton HD4 171 D6
Huddersfield, Paddock HD1 153 D5
Keighley, East Morton BD20 36 D8
Keighley, Knowle Park BD21 35 B5
6 Liversedge WF15 117 B4
Mirfield WF14 138 A4
Morley LS27 98 B4
Normanton WF6 144 A7
Ossett WF5 140 D4
Ryhill WF4 162 D1
Thornton BD13 72 D7
Wakefield WF1 216 C1
Yeadon LS19 40 B4
South Terr Dewsbury WF12 139 E6
Ossett WF5 140 E3
South View 1 Batley WF17 96 F1
Bradford BD10 56 D7
Castleford WF10 124 E5
Castleford, New Fryston WF10 104 C2
Collingham LS22 28 F8
Crigglestone WF4 159 D4
Dewsbury WF12 139 D6
East Ardsley WF12 119 D5
Farnhill BD20 4 D1
Featherstone WF7 145 D6
Glusburn BD20 16 D6
Guiseley LS20 22 E1
Halifax, Snydal HX3 113 E4
Halifax, Southowram HX3 114 A4
Haworth BD22 51 C7
Holmfirth HD7 189 F3
Horsforth LS18 58 C7
Huddersfield HD1 153 D5
Keighley BD20 19 C1
Keighley, Braithwaite BD22 34 E8
4 Leeds LS15 62 C2
Menston LS29 22 A3
Pudsey LS28 57 C1
Pudsey, Crimbles LS28 76 F8
Rothwell LS26 100 D6
Shipley BD9 55 C4
Sowerby Bridge HX2 111 F5
Wetherby LS22 13 E8
Yeadon LS19 39 F7
South View Cl
Birkenshaw BD4 95 E7
Yeadon LS19 39 F7
South View Cres LS19 39 F7
South View Dr BD4 95 F7
South View Gdns WF8 147 A8
South View Gr BD19 117 B7
South View Infants Sch LS19 40 B6
South View Rd
Birkenshaw BD4 95 F7
Middleton LS10 215 E1
South View Rd 9 LS19 40 B7
South View St Silsden BD20 5 D1
Todmorden OL14 86 C1
South View Terr
6 Baildon BD17 38 C4
4 Dewsbury WF13 118 B2
Dewsbury, Ravensthorpe WF13 138 E6
Flockton WF4 156 E4
Otley LS21 23 B7
Yeadon LS19 40 C6
South Way Birkenshaw BD4 95 E7
Shipley BD18 54 D7
South Wlk BD16 36 A1
Southampton St BD3 55 F1
Southcliffe Dr BD17 38 C1
Southcliffe Way BD17 38 C1
Southcote Pl BD10 56 B8
Southdale CE (Controlled) Sch WF5 140 E4
Southdale Gdns WF5 140 E5
Southdale Rd WF5 140 E5
Southdene HD5 154 E5
Southdown Cl BD9 54 E2
Southdown Rd BD17 38 B1
Southedge Cl HX3 114 C7
Southedge Terr HX3 114 C7
Southern Rd HD4 153 A3
Southfield HX7 88 F4
Southfield Ave Bradford BD6 94 C8
Featherstone WF7 145 B4
Keighley BD20 19 A2
Leeds LS17 43 E2
Southfield Cl Horbury WF4 141 B1
Wakefield WF2 120 E1
Southfield Ct HD8 173 F7
Southfield Dr Keighley BD20 19 A2
Leeds LS17 43 E2
Southfield Fold WF4 159 B8
Southfield House LS29 6 F8
Southfield La Addingham LS29 6 E8
Bradford BD5, BD7 74 B3
Horbury WF4 159 B8
Southfield Mount
Keighley BD20 18 F2
Leeds LS12 209 F3
Southfield Rd
Addingham LS29 6 F8
Bingley BD16 37 A1
Bradford BD5 74 C2
Burley in W LS29 9 E1
Crofton WF4 144 B3
Huddersfield HD5 155 A4
Knottingley WF11 126 F3
Southfield Sq BD8 55 C1
Southfield St LS12 209 F3
Southfield Terr
Addingham LS29 6 F8
Birkenshaw BD11 96 A6
Brighouse HX3 93 C1
Southfield Way BD20 19 A2
Southfields Bramhope LS16 24 F2
Huddersfield HD5 154 E5
Southfields View WF4 158 D5
Southgate Bradford BD1 201 B3
15 Dewsbury WF13 139 C8
Elland HX5 134 F6
Guiseley LS20 39 B7
Halifax HX1 203 E3
Honley HD7 171 F4
Huddersfield HD1 154 B6
Pontefract WF8 146 D8
Rothwell LS26 101 C6
South Hiendley S72 180 E6
Wakefield WF1 216 B2
Southlands Baildon BD17 38 B1
Halifax HX2 71 F1
Kirkheaton HD5 137 B1
Southlands Ave
Bingley BD16 37 A1
Bradford BD13 73 C6
Keighley BD20 19 A1
Leeds LS17 60 C8
Yeadon LS19 40 E2
Southlands Cl
Badsworth WF9 164 E2
Leeds LS17 43 C1
Southlands Cres LS17 60 C8
Southlands Dr
Huddersfield HD2 136 A3
Keighley BD20 19 A1
Leeds LS17 60 C8
Southlands Gr Bingley BD16 37 A1
Bradford BD13 73 B6
Keighley BD20 19 A1
Southlands Gr W BD20 19 A2
Southlands Mount BD20 19 A1
Southlands Rd BD20 19 A1
Southlea Ave BD22 34 E2
Southlea Cl BD12 95 A5
Southleigh Ave LS11 99 A8
Southleigh Cres LS11 99 A8
Southleigh Croft LS11 99 B8
Southleigh Dr LS11 99 A8
Southleigh Garth LS11 99 B8
Southleigh Gdns LS11 99 A8
Southleigh Gr LS11 99 A8
Southleigh Grange LS11 99 B8
Southleigh Rd LS11 99 A8
Southleigh View LS11 99 A8
Southmere Ave BD7 74 A3
Southmere Cres BD7 74 A3
Southmere Dr BD7 73 F3
Southmere First Sch BD7 74 A3
Southmere Gr 3 BD7 74 A3
Southmere Oval BD7 73 F3
Southmere Rd BD7 74 A3
Southmere Terr BD7 74 A3
Southmoor Hospl WF9 181 D6
Southmoor La WF11 127 D3
Southmoor Rd WF9 181 D3
Southolme Cl LS5 59 A6
Southowram Bank HX3 113 E6
Southroyd Pk LS28 76 E5
Southroyd Primary Sch LS28 76 E6
Southroyd Rise LS28 76 E5
Southwaite Cl LS14 61 F4
Southwaite Garth LS14 61 F4
Southwaite La LS14 61 F4
Southwaite Lawn LS14 61 F4
Southwaite Pl LS14 61 F4
Southway Bingley BD16 37 C5
Burley in W LS29 9 C3
Guiseley LS20 39 B8
Horsforth LS18 41 A3
Huddersfield HD3 135 C1
Ilkley LS29 8 D3
Mirfield WF14 137 F7
Southwell Ave HD3 153 B7
Southwood Ave HD7 172 B5
Southwood Cl LS14 62 C4
Southwood Cres LS14 62 C4
Southwood Gate LS14 62 C4
Sovereign Cl WF17 96 F1
Sovereign Gdns WF6 123 A2
Sovereign St Halifax HX1 203 D3
Leeds LS1 211 F3
Sovereign's Way WF12 139 B3
Sowden Bldgs BD2 56 B2
Sowden Grange 15 BD13 72 D6
Sowden La HX3 93 F3
Sowden Rd BD9 54 D3
Sowden St BD7 74 B3
Sowden's Yd 3 LS6 59 D6
Sowerby Bridge High Sch HX6 112 C5
Sowerby Bridge Sta HX6 112 C3
Sowerby Croft La HX6 112 C2
Sowerby La
Hebden Bridge HX2 111 C6
Sowerby Bridge HX2 111 C6
Sowerby New Rd HX6 111 F3
Sowerby St HX6 112 B3
Sowgate La
Knottingley WF11 126 B3
Pontefract WF11 126 A3
Sowood Ave WF5 140 E3
Sowood Gdns WF5 140 F3
Sowood La Flockton WF12 157 B6
Ossett WF5 140 F3
Sowood St LS4 59 C2
Sowood View WF5 140 F3
Soyland Town Rd HX6 132 D6
Spa Bottom HD8 155 C5
Spa Croft Rd WF5 141 A4
Spa Fields HD7 152 B1
Spa Fields Ind Est HD7 152 B1
Spa Fold WF3 121 F4
Spa Gr WF2 141 E3
Spa Hill WF17 118 D5
Spa La Bingley BD16 37 A5
Boston Spa LS23 30 E7
Ossett WF5 141 A4
Slaithwaite HD7 152 B1
Spa St Batley WF17 118 D5
Ossett WF5 141 B4
Spa Well Gr S72 181 A3
Spaines Rd HD2 136 A1
Spalding Towers LS9 207 E1
Sparable La WF1 142 E3
Spark House La HX6 112 C3
Spark La S75 178 B1
Spark St HD3 152 F7
Sparks Rd HD3 153 B7
Spartal La LS25 103 E8
Spartan Rd BD12 94 D5
Sparth La HD7 188 B4
Spawd Bone La WF11 126 E3
Speak Cl WF1 142 F8
Speakers Ct WF13 139 B8
Spear Fir LS17 28 A2
Spearhead Way BD21 35 C8
Speedwell Mount 6 LS6 206 B3
Speedwell Rd WF10 123 E5
Speedwell St
Huddersfield HD1 153 D5
7 Leeds LS6 206 B3
Speeton Ave BD7 73 E2
Speeton Gr BD7 73 D2
Spen App LS16 58 F7
Spen Bank
Cleckheaton BD19 116 F7
Leeds LS16 59 A7
Spen Cl BD4 95 B7
Spen Common La LS24 47 F6
Spen Cres LS16 58 F7
Spen Dr LS16 59 A8
Spen Gdns LS16 59 B8
Spen Gn LS16 58 F7
Spen La Cleckheaton BD19 117 A8
Leeds LS16, LS5, LS6 59 A7
Leeds, Ireland Wood LS16 42 A1
Spen Lawn LS16 58 F7
Spen Mews LS16 59 A7
Spen Rd LS16 59 B8
Spen Vale St WF16 117 D2
Spen Valley High Sch WF15 117 A3
Spen Valley Ind Est BD19 116 F6
Spen Valley Rd WF13 138 F6
Spen View WF16 117 F1
Spen View La BD4 95 B7
Spen Wlk LS16 58 F7
Spence La LS12 210 C2
Spenceley St Leeds LS2 206 A2
Leeds LS2 206 A3
Spencer Ave Bradford BD7 74 A5
Morley LS27 98 A2
Silsden BD20 5 E2
Spencer Cl BD20 16 E7
Spencer La HX7 89 A1
Spencer Mount LS8 207 E3
Spencer Pl LS7 207 E3
Spencer Rd BD7 74 A5
Spencer St
7 Keighley BD21 35 B7
Mirfield WF14 138 A3
Skelmanthorpe HD8 175 A2
Sutton in C BD20 16 D5
Spencer Terr HD2 136 D3
Spenfield Ct WF15 117 A2
Spennithorne Ave LS16 42 A2
Spennithorne Dr LS16 42 B1
Spennithorne Rd DN6 184 F2
Spenser Rd LS20 39 F8
Spenser Rise LS20 39 F8
Spenslea Gr LS27 98 A2
Spibey Cres LS26 100 D7
Spibey La LS26 100 D7
Spicer House La S36 191 A1
Spicer St BD5 74 C3
Spiers Garth BD6 74 D1
Spindle St HX2 92 A5
Spindles The 3 LS10 99 D8
Spink La WF8 125 D1
Spink Pl BD8 74 D8
Spink St BD8 74 D8
Spink Well La WF3 98 F1

Spinkfield Rd HD2 153 F8
Spinks Gdns LS14 62 B4
Spinkwell Rd 4 WF13 118 C1
Spinners Chase LS28 76 E7
Spinners The BD22 51 C6
Spinners Way
Brighouse BD19 115 F8
Mirfield WF14 137 F3
Spinney The
Brighouse HD6 115 A5
Draughton BD23 1 D5
Keighley BD20 36 D7
Leeds LS9 212 B3
Leeds, Moortown LS17 43 E2
Wakefield WF2 160 E7
Wetherby LS22 13 D6
Yeadon LS19 40 A2
Spinneyfield HD2 136 A3
Spinneyfield Ct LS9 212 B3
Spinning Mill Ct BD18 54 E8
Spion Kop LS14 45 F5
Spire Ct Huddersfield HD1 153 E7
Huddersfield, Marsh HD3 153 D7
Spire Hts BD16 37 D3
Spitalgap La WF8 147 C6
Spittal Hardwick La
WF10 125 C5
Spittlerush La WF8 166 F4
Spofforth Hill LS22 13 D6
Spofforth Wlk LS25 83 B7
Spout Fold WF2 141 D6
Spout Hill HD6 135 E6
Spout House La HD6 114 E6
Spring Ave Gildersome LS27 97 C8
Keighley BD21 35 E6
Spring Bank
Cullingworth BD13 52 D5
Halifax HX2 90 E1
5 Leeds LS5 59 A4
Pontefract WF8 146 D7
Spring Bank Cres LS6 205 E4
Spring Bank Croft HD7 188 D4
Spring Bank Dr WF15 117 B2
Spring Bank Pl BD8 55 D2
Spring Bank Primary Sch
LS6 205 E4
Spring Bank Rise BD21 35 C4
Spring Bank Terr LS20 22 E1
Spring Bottom OL14 128 F7
Spring Cl Bingley BD16 37 B2
Garforth LS25 83 B6
Garforth, East Garforth LS25 83 A8
Keighley BD21 35 E6
Morley LS27 98 A7
Spring Close Ave LS9 212 C2
Spring Close Gdns LS9 212 C2
Spring Close St LS9 212 B2
Spring Close Wlk LS9 212 C2
Spring Ct BD15 54 A3
Spring Dale HD7 171 F5
Spring Dr BD21 35 E6
Spring Edge HX1 113 A4
Spring Edge N HX1 202 C1
Spring Edge S HX1 202 C1
Spring Edge W HX1 202 B1
Spring End Rd WF4 141 B3
Spring Farm La BD16 36 A1
Spring Farm Mews BD15 53 C5
Spring Garden St BD13 72 E1
Spring Gardens La BD20 18 A1
Spring Gardens Mount
BD20 18 B1
Spring Gardens Rd BD9 55 A3
Spring Gdns
7 Bacup OL13 106 A3
Batley WF17 118 B5
Birkenshaw BD11 96 F6
Bradford BD1 201 B4
Burley in W LS29 9 F1
Harewood LS17 27 A7
Holmfirth HD7 188 E5
Morley LS27 98 C7
Spring Gr Halifax HX1 202 A3
Hebden Bridge HX7 89 A4
Spring Grove
Jun & Inf Sch HD1 153 F5
Spring Grove St HD1 154 A5
Spring Grove Terr 18 LS6 205 E2
Spring Grove View 15
LS6 205 E2
Spring Grove Wlk 13 LS6 205 E2
Spring Hall Cl HX3 93 B5
Spring Hall Ct HX1 202 A4
Spring Hall Dr HX2 202 A3
Spring Hall Gdns HX2 202 A3
Spring Hall Gr HX2 202 A3
Spring Hall La
Halifax HX3 113 D4
Halifax, Pellon HX1 202 A3
Spring Hall Pl HX1 202 A3
Spring Head Halifax HX2 91 E1
Shelf HX3 93 C5
Spring Head La HD7 168 F5
Spring Head Rd
Haworth BD22 51 C8
Thornton BD13 72 F6
Spring Hill Baildon BD17 37 F3
Leeds, Adel East Moor LS16 42 E4
Leeds, Buslingthorpe LS7 206 C4
Shipley BD18 55 E7
Spring Holes La BD13 72 D7
Spring La Baildon BD16 37 D6
Batley WF17 118 B7
Crofton WF4 162 B7
Elland HX4 134 A7
Holmfirth, Hinchcliffe Mill
HD7 188 D2
Holmfirth, New Mill HD7 189 E5
Spring La continued
Holmfirth, Upperthong HD7 188 E4
Mapplewell S75 178 C3
Royston S71 179 D1
Wetherby LS22 14 C5
Spring Mill Fold HX2 90 F8
Spring Mill La WF5 140 F6
Spring Mill St BD5 74 E4
Spring Mount BD21 35 E5
Spring Park Rd BD15 53 C6
Spring Pl Bradford BD7 74 C5
Keighley BD21 35 E5
Spring Ram Bsns Pk S75 177 D1
Spring Rd LS6 205 E4
Spring Rise Draughton BD23 1 D5
Keighley BD21 35 E6
Spring Row Harden BD16 36 B1
Keighley BD21 35 B6
Oxenhope BD22 51 E1
17 Queensbury BD13 72 E1
Spring Side Rise HD7 152 D5
Spring St Bradford BD10 56 B6
Brighouse HD6 115 A2
Dewsbury WF13 118 C1
3 Haworth BD22 51 F8
7 Huddersfield HD1 154 A6
Keighley BD21 35 C8
Liversedge WF15 117 B4
Marsden HD7 168 F3
Ripponden HX6 132 D4
Slaithwaite HD7 169 F8
Todmorden OL14 86 C1
Spring Terr Halifax HX3 203 F4
Keighley BD21 35 E6
South Elmsall WF9 182 F2
Spring Vale Rd WF9 182 C3
Spring Valley LS28 57 E1
Spring Valley Ave LS13 58 C1
Spring Valley Cl
Leeds LS13 58 C1
5 Liversedge WF15 117 A5
Spring Valley Cres LS13 58 C1
Spring Valley Croft LS13 58 C1
Spring Valley Ct LS13 58 C1
Spring Valley Dr LS13 58 C1
Spring Valley Sq 3
WF15 117 A5
Spring Valley St 4
WF15 117 A5
Spring Valley View LS13 58 C1
Spring Valley Wlk LS13 58 C1
Spring View
Gildersome LS27 97 C8
Holme Chapel BB10 85 A8
Ossett WF5 140 F6
Sowerby Bridge HX2 111 D6
Spring Villas 5 OL14 86 B1
Spring Way BD21 35 E6
Spring Wood Ave HX3 113 B2
Spring Wood Dr HX3 113 B2
Spring Wood Gdns BD5 74 F2
Springbank LS25 82 C6
Springbank Ave
Gildersome LS27 97 C7
Pudsey LS28 57 E3
Springbank Cl LS28 57 E3
Springbank Cres
Garforth LS25 82 C6
Gildersome LS27 97 C8
Huddersfield HD2 136 D1
Springbank Dr LS28 57 E4
Springbank Gr LS28 57 E3
Springbank Rd
Gildersome LS27 97 C8
Huddersfield HD2 136 D1
Pudsey LS28 57 E3
Springbank Rise LS28 57 E3
Springcliffe BD8 55 B1
Springcliffe St BD8 55 B1
Springdale Ave HD1 153 F4
Springdale Cres BD10 56 C7
Springdale St HD1 153 F4
Springfield Boston Spa LS23 30 D8
Boston Spa, Clifford LS23 30 D5
Elland HD3 152 B8
Queensbury BD13 72 D1
Sowerby Bridge HX6 112 A3
Springfield Ave
Bacup OL13 106 A3
Batley WF17 118 B5
Bradford BD7 73 F5
Clayton West HD8 175 E2
Hemsworth WF9 181 E6
Honley HD7 171 F3
Ilkley LS29 8 C4
Morley LS27 98 A6
Pontefract WF8 125 F1
Slaithwaite HD7 169 E7
Springfield Cl
Clayton West HD8 175 E2
Horsforth LS18 41 E1
Leeds LS10 80 A2
Springfield Cres
Morley LS27 98 A6
Norton WF8 166 E5
Springfield Ct
Keighley BD20 35 A8
Yeadon LS19 40 B8
Springfield Dr
Cleckheaton WF15 116 C5
Denby Dale HD8 191 A4
Springfield Farm
(Riding School) BD21 52 A7
Springfield Gdns
Horsforth LS18 41 D1
Keighley BD20 35 A8
Pudsey LS28 76 F6
Springfield Gn LS10 215 E2
Springfield Gr
Bingley BD16 36 F3
Brighouse HD6 115 A5
Springfield Grange WF2 141 D6
Springfield House 3
BD19 116 E7
Springfield La
Birkenshaw BD4 76 F2
Cleckheaton FW15 116 E5
Kirkburton HD8 173 E7
Morley LS27 98 A6
Springfield Mount
Addingham LS29 2 F1
Horsforth LS18 41 D1
Leeds, Armley LS12 209 D4
Leeds, Woodhouse LS2 206 A1
South Elmsall WF9 182 E1
Springfield Pk WF14 138 B5
Springfield Pl
Bradford BD1 201 A4
Bradford, Springfield BD10 56 B6
Guiseley LS20 22 E1
Leeds LS10 215 E2
Otley LS21 22 F7
Springfield Rd Baildon BD17 38 B4
Elland HX5 135 B7
Guiseley LS20 22 E1
Keighley BD20 35 A8
Morley LS27 98 A6
Springfield Rise
Horsforth LS18 41 D1
Rothwell LS26 100 F4
Springfield St Bradford BD8 74 C8
Rothwell LS26 100 F4
Thornton BD13 72 E6
Springfield Terr
Bradford BD8 74 C8
Brighouse BD19 94 F1
Brighouse, Hipperholme
HX3 114 C8
Cullingworth BD13 52 E5
Dewsbury WF13 118 C1
Elland HD3 134 B1
Emley HD8 175 A7
Guiseley LS20 39 E8
Halifax HX2 90 C1
4 Pudsey LS28 57 D1
Springfield View WF7 145 A8
Springfield Wlk LS18 41 D1
Springfields WF11 127 B3
Springfields Ave WF11 127 B4
Springhead BD22 51 C8
Springhead Park Sch
LS26 101 A6
Springhead Rd LS26 101 A6
Springhill Ave WF4 162 A8
Springhill Cl WF1 121 A5
Springhill Dr WF4 144 A1
Springhill Gr WF4 144 A1
Springhill Mount WF4 162 A8
Springhurst Rd BD18 55 A7
Springlodge Pl BD8 55 D1
Springmead Dr LS25 82 F6
Springroyd Terr BD8 73 F8
Springs La Bickerton LS23 14 F6
Ilkley LS29 8 C4
Thorp Arch LS23 14 F6
Springs Rd Guiseley LS19 39 E6
Holme HD7 187 B4
Springs The WF1 216 B2
Springstone Ave
Hemsworth WF9 181 E7
Ossett WF5 140 D7
Springswood Ave BD18 55 A7
Springswood Pl BD18 55 A7
Springswood Rd BD18 55 A7
Springvale Rise WF9 181 D8
Springville Gdns WF9 183 B7
Springville Terr BD10 56 B7
Springwell Ave LS26 82 A1
Springwell Cl 1 LS19 40 C6
Springwell Ct
East Ardsley WF3 98 E1
Leeds LS12 210 C2
Springwell Dr BD5 74 E4
Springwell Rd Leeds LS11 211 D2
Ossett WF5 140 E5
Swillington LS26 82 A1
Springwell St LS12 210 C2
Springwell Terr 2 LS19 40 C6
Springwell View
4 Batley WF17 96 F1
Leeds LS11 211 D2
Springwood Ave
Bradford BD5 74 F3
Huddersfield HD1 153 F5
Springwood Gdns HX3 113 B2
Springwood Gr LS8 61 C6
Springwood Hall Cl HD1 153 E6
Springwood Hall Gdns
HD1 153 F6
Springwood Rd
Holmfirth HD7 189 C8
Leeds LS8 61 C6
Yeadon LS19 40 A3
Springwood Sq 6 HD1 154 A6
Springwood St 10 HD1 154 A6
Springwood Terr BD2 55 E2
Sprinkwell Cl BD3 55 F1
Spruce Ave S71 179 B3
Spruce Dr HD4 171 D6
Spruce Drive Mews HD4 171 D6
Spruce St 14 BD21 35 D8
Spruce Wlk OL14 129 A8
Sprutts La HX7 89 B8
Spry La S63 194 B3
Spur Dr LS15 62 E3
Spur St WF17 118 D4
Spurr Gr WF2 161 B6
Spurrier's Ave WF11 126 C3
Square HX1 203 E3
Square Rd Halifax HX1 203 F3
Todmorden OL14 129 A8
Square St BD4 75 A5
Square The Batley WF17 117 F6
Boston Spa LS23 30 E7
2 Bradford BD8 73 C7
Castleford WF10 125 C7
Farnley LS21 11 D4
Harewood LS17 27 A7
Keighley BD20 19 D1
Kippax LS25 83 A1
Knottingley WF11 126 C5
Shepley HD8 190 E8
Square View OL14 129 B8
Squire Gn BD8 54 F1
Squire La BD8, BD9 54 F1
Squirrel Cl WF13 118 A3
Squirrel Ct HD2 135 C2
Squirrel Ditch HD4 154 C3
Squirrel End WF13 118 A2
Squirrel Hall Dr WF13 117 F3
Squirrel La BD13 72 B5
Squirrel Wlk WF13 118 A3
Squirrels Drey WF4 159 F7
Stable Ct HD7 152 A1
Stable Fold BD12 94 D2
Stable La HX3 92 B1
Stablers Wlk WF6 123 A4
Stables La LS23 30 E7
Stables The WF2 161 A7
Stackgarth HD6 136 A8
Stackhills Rd OL14 108 C5
Stacks La HX7 110 F5
Stadium Rd BD6 94 D8
Stadium Way
Huddersfield HD1 154 C7
Leeds LS11 213 E3
South Elmsall WF9 183 B5
Stafford Ave HX3 113 C4
Stafford Hill La HD5 155 C8
Stafford Par HX3 113 C3
Stafford Pl HX3 113 C4
Stafford Rd HX3 113 C3
Stafford Sq HX3 113 D3
Stafford St Bradford BD4 75 B4
Castleford WF10 124 C8
Leeds LS10 215 E4
Morley LS27 97 F2
Stafford Terr WF2 141 F6
Stainbeck Ave LS7 59 F6
Stainbeck Gdns
Bradford BD6 93 D8
Leeds LS7 60 B7
Stainbeck La LS7 60 B7
Stainbeck Preparatory Sch
LS7 60 B7
Stainbeck Rd Leeds LS7 60 A7
Leeds, Chapel Allerton LS7 60 C8
Stainbeck Wlk LS7 60 B7
Stainburn Ave
Castleford WF10 125 A5
Leeds LS17 43 E1
Stainburn Cres LS17 43 E1
Stainburn Dr LS17 43 D1
Stainburn Gdns LS17 43 E1
Stainburn Mount LS17 204 B4
Stainburn Rd LS17 204 A4
Stainburn Terr LS17 204 A4
Stainburn View LS17 43 E1
Staincliffe CE Jun Sch
WF17 118 A3
Staincliffe Cl 7 WF13 118 A1
Staincliffe Cres 4 WF13 117 F2
Staincliffe Ct BD20 5 D1
Staincliffe Hall Rd WF17 118 A4
Staincliffe Rd WF13 118 A1
Staincross Comm S75 178 B2
Stainecross Ave HD4 153 C2
Staines Croft HD5 154 E6
Stainland Dean HX4 133 D2
Stainland Rd Elland HX4 134 C6
Halifax HX4 113 D1
Ripponden HX4 133 B4
Stainmore Cl LS14 62 A3
Stainmore Pl LS14 62 A3
Stainton Cl BD6 93 E8
Stainton La WF3 100 D3
Stair Foot La LS16 42 E5
Staircase La LS16, LS21 24 D5
Stairfoot Cl LS16 42 D5
Stairfoot View LS16 42 D5
Stairfoot Wlk LS16 42 D5
Staithe Ave LS10 99 D5
Staithe Cl LS10 99 D5
Staithe Gdns 2 LS10 99 D5
Staithgate La BD6 94 D7
Stake La HX7 110 F7
Stake Lane Bank HD7 189 C4
Stakes Fold WF16 117 E4
Stallabrass St 4 BD8 74 C8
Stalley Royd La HD7 189 F3
Stamford Ave WF10 124 A6
Stamford St BD4 75 B5
Stamford Way S75 178 B2
Stammergate La LS22 13 C2
Stamp Hill Cl LS29 6 D8
Stan Valley WF8 166 E6
Stanacre Pl BD3 201 C4
Stanage La HX3 93 C7
Stanally St OL14 107 E8
Stanbury First Sch BD22 50 D6
Stancliffe Way HD5 137 B1
Stand Bridge Garth WF4 159 F5
Standale Ave LS28 76 D8
Standale Cres LS28 76 D8
Standale Rise LS28 76 D8
Standard Dr HD4 153 B2
Standard Ind Est BD2 56 C3
Standbridge Cl WF2 160 A5
Standbridge
Jun & Fst Sch WF2 160 A5
Standbridge La
Wakefield, Kettlethorpe WF2 160 B6
Wakefield, Stand Bridge
WF2 160 C7
Standiforth La HD5 154 F6
Standiforth Pl HD5 154 F6
Standiforth Rd HD5 154 D6
Standish Cres WF9 182 C4
Stanhall Ave 3 LS28 57 D1
Stanhope Ave
Cawthorne S75 193 F5
Horsforth LS18 41 C2
Stanhope Cl LS18 41 C2
Stanhope Dr LS18 58 C8
Stanhope Gdns WF3 99 E1
Stanhope Gr WF3 99 E1
Stanhope Rd WF3 99 E1
Stanhope St HD8 175 D1
Stanks App 1 LS14 62 D4
Stanks Ave LS14 62 D4
Stanks Cl LS14 62 E4
Stanks Cross LS14 62 E4
Stanks Dr LS14 62 D5
Stanks Garth LS14 62 E4
Stanks Gdns LS14 62 D5
Stanks Gn LS14 62 E4
Stanks Gr LS14 62 D4
Stanks La N LS14 62 C5
Stanks La S LS14 62 D4
Stanks Par LS14 62 D4
Stanks Rd LS14 62 D4
Stanks Rise LS14 62 E5
Stanks Way LS14 62 D4
Stanley Ave LS9 207 F2
Stanley Cotts WF6 123 A2
Stanley Ct HX1 202 B3
Stanley Dr LS8 44 B2
Stanley Gr LS20 39 E8
Stanley Grove Junior &
Infants Sch WF3 121 F3
Stanley La Elland HX4 134 A3
Liversedge WF15 117 A5
Lofthouse Gate WF1 121 D4
Stanley Marsh
Nature Reserve WF3 121 E4
Stanley Pl Batley WF17 118 D5
Huddersfield HD7 152 D4
Leeds LS9 208 A2
Stanley Rd Bradford BD2 55 D4
Halifax HX1 202 B1
Huddersfield HD3 135 C1
Huddersfield, Ainley Top
HD3 135 A3
Keighley BD22 35 A4
Leeds LS9 208 A2
Leeds, Chapeltown LS7 207 D3
Liversedge WF15 117 A2
Shipley BD2 55 D4
Wakefield WF1 216 C3
Stanley Royd Hospl WF1 216 C4
Stanley St Bingley BD16 37 A3
Bradford, Greengates BD10 56 D7
Bradford, Idle BD10 56 B8
Brighouse HD6 115 B3
Castleford WF10 124 E8
Cleckheaton BD19 116 D8
Featherstone WF7 145 D7
Haworth BD22 51 E8
Huddersfield HD1 153 E3
Keighley BD21 35 B8
Shipley BD18 55 C5
Sowerby Bridge HX6 112 C4
Wakefield WF1 216 C2
Stanley St N HX2 92 A5
Stanley Terr Leeds LS9 208 A2
Leeds, Armley LS12 209 F3
Stanley View LS12 209 F3
Stanmoor Dr WF3 121 E6
Stanmore Ave LS4 59 C3
Stanmore Cres LS4 59 C3
Stanmore Gr LS4 59 C3
Stanmore Hill LS4 205 D3
Stanmore Mount LS4 59 C3
Stanmore Pl Bradford BD7 74 A5
Leeds LS4 59 C3
Stanmore Rd LS4 59 C3
Stanmore St LS4 59 C3
Stanmore Terr LS4 59 C3
Stanmore View LS4 59 C3
Stannard Well Dr WF4 141 B2
Stannard Well La WF4 141 C2
Stannary Pl HX1 203 D4
Stannery End La HX7 110 F7
Stanningley Ave HX2 91 C5
Stanningley By-Pass
Leeds LS13 58 D1
Pudsey LS13 58 B1
Stanningley Ct 4 LS28 57 F2
Stanningley Dr HX2 91 C5
Stanningley Field Cl LS13 58 A1
Stanningley Gr 7 WF16 117 D3
Stanningley Primary Sch
LS28 57 F2
Stanningley Rd Halifax HX2 91 C5
Leeds LS12, LS13 58 D1
Pudsey LS28 57 F2
Stansfield Cl
Castleford WF10 125 B8
Halifax HX1 202 C3

Stansfield Ct HX6 112 B3
Stansfield Dr WF10 125 C8
Stansfield Grange HX6 111 E1
Stansfield Hall OL15 129 C1
Stansfield Hall Rd OL14 108 C6
Stansfield Mill La HX6 111 F1
Stansfield Pl BD10 39 B1
Stansfield Rd
Castleford WF10 125 B8
Todmorden OL14 108 B5
Stansfield St 8 OL14 108 B6
Stansfield Terr 6 OL14 86 B1
Stanwell Ave HD2 135 D1
Stanwick House BD2 55 D4
Stapleford Ct HD2 135 D2
Stapleton House BD2 55 D4
Stapper Gn BD15 53 B6
Star St BD5 74 C3
Starbeck Rd WF1 142 E8
Starkey La BD20 4 E1
Starkie St BD21 35 B6
Starling House WF9 181 D6
Starting Post BD10 55 F7
Starwort Cl WF8 146 D7
Station App
Burley in W LS29 21 E8
Honley HD7 172 B5
Todmorden OL14 108 B5
Station Ave LS13 58 C2
Station Cl LS25 82 F7
Station Cotts LS24 31 C6
Station Cres LS12 209 E3
Station Ct LS25 82 F8
Station Fields LS25 82 F7
Station Forecourt BD1 201 B3
Station Gdns LS22 13 D5
Station Gr Glusburn BD20 16 D7
12 Leeds LS13 58 C2
Station Ind Est HX2 111 D7
Station La Birkenshaw BD11 96 B6
Collingham LS22 29 B8
East Ardsley WF3 98 E2
East Ardsley, Thorpe on the Hill WF3 99 D1
East Ardsley, Tingley WF3 98 E1
Featherstone WF7 145 C5
Huddersfield HD4 171 F8
Huddersfield, Wellhouse HD7 152 D3
Liversedge WF16 117 D3
Pontefract WF8 146 E8
Rothwell LS26 101 D7
Shepley HD8 173 F1
Thorner LS14 45 F6
Station Mount LS13 58 C2
Station Par Leeds LS5 59 B4
Todmorden OL14 85 F1
Station Pl LS13 58 C2
Station Plaza LS29 8 B4
Station Rd
Ackworth M T WF7 164 C7
Arthington LS21 24 F6
Baildon BD17 38 D3
Barwick in E LS15 62 F6
Batley WF17 118 D4
Birkenshaw BD11 96 E6
Bradford BD1 55 E2
Bradford, Clayton BD14 73 C4
5 Bradford, Raw Nook BD12 94 E5
Bradford, Wyke BD12 94 B2
Brighouse HD6 115 C2
Brighouse, Hipperholme HX3 114 C7
Brighouse, Wyke BD12 94 B2
Burley in W LS29 9 E1
Castleford WF10 124 D8
Cullingworth BD13 52 D6
Denholme BD13 71 E8
Dewsbury WF12 139 C5
Dewsbury, Earlsheaton WF12 139 F6
Elland HX4 134 C4
Garforth LS25 82 F8
Glusburn BD20 16 D7
Guiseley LS20 22 D1
Guiseley, Esholt BD17 39 C6
Halifax, Holmfield HX3 92 A5
Halifax, Luddenden Foot HX2 111 D7
Haworth BD22 51 D7
Hebden Bridge HX7 89 B2
Hemsworth WF9 181 E7
Holmfirth HD7 189 A5
Honley HD7 172 A5
Horsforth LS18 41 C3
Huddersfield, Bradley HD2 137 A5
Huddersfield, Wellhouse HD7 152 E3
Ilkley LS29 8 B4
Kippax WF10 103 C4
Kirkburton HD4 173 C2
Knottingley WF11 126 C5
Leeds LS12 209 E3
Leeds, Cross Gates LS15 62 C1
Lepton HD8 155 D3
Liversedge WF16 117 D3
Mapplewell S75 177 E1
Marsden HD7 168 F4
Menston LS29 22 B4
Mickletown LS26 102 B3
Mirfield WF14 138 A4
Morley LS27 98 B5
Normanton WF6 122 F3
Oakworth BD22 34 D1
Ossett WF5 140 E4
Station Rd continued
Otley LS21 23 A7
Oxenhope BD22 51 C2
Queensbury BD13 72 F2
Royston S71 179 B4
Ryhill WF4 162 A1
Shipley BD18 55 B7
Skelmanthorpe HD8 175 A2
Slaithwaite HD7 152 A1
South Elmsall WF9 183 A3
Sowerby Bridge HX6 112 C3
Steeton BD20 17 D6
Todmorden OL14 86 C1
Wilsden BD13 53 A4
Station St
Huddersfield HD1 154 A6
Meltham HD7 170 D2
Pudsey LS28 76 D6
Wakefield WF1 142 E2
Station Terr Kippax WF10 103 C4
Leeds LS13 58 C2
Royston S71 179 E4
Station View Leeds LS15 62 C1
Oxenhope BD22 51 C3
Steeton BD20 17 D5
Station Way LS12 209 E3
Station Works Ind Pk BD21 35 E7
Staups La
Blackshaw Head OL14 88 A2
Northowram HX3 92 F1
Staveley Ct BD16 36 F4
Staveley Dr BD18 54 D7
Staveley Gr BD22 35 A3
Staveley Rd Bingley BD16 37 A4
Bradford BD7 74 B6
Keighley BD22 35 A4
Shipley BD18 54 D8
Staveley Way BD22 35 A4
Stavely Mews 5 BD16 37 A4
Staverton St HX2 202 A3
Staybrite Ave BD16 54 A7
Staygate Gn BD6 74 E1
Staynton Cres HD2 136 F5
Stead Gate HD8 174 D2
Stead Hill Way BD17 38 F1
Stead La Ilkley LS29 21 B8
Kirkheaton HD5 155 B8
Ripponden HX6 132 C2
Thorner LS14 45 F5
Stead Rd BD4 95 E8
Stead St Halifax HX1 203 D3
Shipley BD17 55 B8
Stead's Yd LS18 41 C2
Steadman St BD3 75 B6
Steadman Terr BD3 75 B6
Steanard La WF14 138 C3
Steander LS9 212 A3
Steele La HX4 133 C1
Steep La HX6 111 B4
Steep Riding HD7 172 C3
Steeplands HD2 136 F6
Steeple Ave WF4 156 E4
Steeton Gr BD20 17 C6
Steeton Hall Gdns BD20 17 D6
Steeton Primary Sch BD20 17 D5
Steeton & Silsden Sta BD20 17 D6
Stell Hill BD22 34 D5
Stella Gdns WF8 125 F2
Stephen Cl HX3 93 A1
Stephen Cres BD2 55 E3
Stephen Rd BD6 73 F2
Stephen Row HX3 93 A2
Stephen St 10 HX7 89 A3
Stephenson Cl WF12 118 E1
Stephenson Dr LS12 77 E3
Stephenson Rd BD15 53 D2
Stephenson St 2 BD7 74 B3
Stephenson Way LS12 77 D3
Stephensons Way LS29 8 B4
Stepping Stones BD20 19 E1
Steps La HX6 112 C5
Sterling Ind Pk WF10 124 F5
Stevenson Ave WF10 125 C5
Stewart Cl BD2 56 C5
Stewart Pl 8 LS11 214 B3
Stewart St BD22 51 E8
Sticker La BD4 75 C4
Stile Common Infants Sch HD4 154 A3
Stile Common Junior Sch HD4 154 A3
Stile Common Rd HD4 154 B3
Stile Hill Way LS15 81 E6
Stile Rd OL14 108 A7
Stilemoor Rise OL14 108 A7
Stillington House BD2 55 D4
Stillwell Dr WF2 160 E8
Stillwell Garth WF2 160 E8
Stillwell Gr WF2 160 E8
Stirley Hill HD4 172 B7
Stirling Cres Bradford BD4 75 E3
Horsforth LS18 41 B4
Stirling Rd LS29 9 D1
Stirling St Halifax HX1 203 D2
Silsden BD20 5 E2
Stirling Way LS25 83 B7
Stirrup Gr BD2 55 F4
Stirton St 3 BD5 74 D3
Stithy St WF5 140 C8
Stock Hey La OL14 109 C6
Stock La HX2 112 C7
Stockeld La LS22 12 D6
Stockeld Rd LS29 8 A4
Stockeld Way LS29 8 A5
Stockerhead La HD7 170 A8
Stockheld La LS15 45 F1
Stockhill Fold BD10 56 D7
Stockhill Rd BD10 56 D7
Stockhill St WF13 139 A8
Stocking La Aberford LS25 65 A7
Knottingley WF11 127 C4
Stockingate WF9 182 B2
Stockingate Mill Primary Sch WF9 182 A1
Stockinger La LS29 6 F8
Stocks App LS14 62 B4
Stocks Ave HX7 110 D8
Stocks Bank Rd WF14 137 E6
Stocks Cres HX7 110 D8
Stocks Dr HD8 190 E8
Stocks Gdns HX7 110 D8
Stocks Hill
Leeds, Armley LS12 209 F4
Leeds, Bramley LS13 58 D3
Leeds, Holbeck LS11 211 D1
Menston LS29 21 F4
Stocks Hill Cl
Keighley BD20 19 D1
Royston S71 179 C1
Stocks La Batley WF17 118 C5
Bradford BD13 73 B1
Halifax HX2 90 E2
Hebden Bridge HX7 110 D8
Kirkburton HD4 173 B1
Sowerby Bridge HX6 111 E3
Stocks Lane First Sch BD13 73 B1
Stocks Moor Rd HD4 173 B2
Stocks Rd LS14 62 C4
Stocks Rise LS14 62 B4
Stocks St LS7 206 C3
Stocks Way HD8 190 D8
Stocks Wlk HD5 154 F3
Stocksbank Dr WF14 137 D6
Stocksmoor Rd WF4 158 C2
Stocksmoor Sta HD4 173 C2
Stockwell Dr WF17 118 D6
Stockwell Hill HD4 171 F8
Stockwell Vale HD4 171 F8
Stod Fold HX2 91 C8
Stogoen Hill BD13 73 B1
Stone Acre Ct 3 BD5 74 E2
Stone Acre Hts HD7 170 F1
Stone Brig Gn LS26 100 D4
Stone Brig La LS26 100 D4
Stone Cliffe 1 HX3 113 A4
Stone Ct Keighley BD20 36 D8
South Hiendley S72 180 E5
Stone Dene BD16 37 A6
Stone Dene Pk LS22 13 F6
Stone Fold HD7 171 F4
Stone Gr BD20 17 C6
Stone Hall Rd BD2 56 B4
Stone Hill BD16 37 B5
Stone La BD22 51 B2
Stone Pits La LS27 97 D5
Stone St Baildon BD17 38 E2
Bradford BD1 201 B3
Bradford, Sandy Lane BD15 54 A3
Cleckheaton BD19 116 C7
3 Haworth BD22 51 C6
Stone Wood La HD4, HD8 173 D1
Stonebridge BD10 56 B8
Stonebridge App LS12 77 E6
Stonebridge Ave LS12 77 F6
Stonebridge Gr LS12 77 E6
Stonebridge La
Leeds, Farnley LS12 77 E6
Leeds, Swallow Hill LS12 77 F6
Stonebridge Wlk HD8 173 F1
Stonechat Rise LS27 98 C4
Stonecliffe Bank LS12 77 E6
Stonecliffe Cl LS12 77 E6
Stonecliffe Cres LS12 77 E6
Stonecliffe Dr Leeds LS12 77 E6
Netherton WF4 158 B7
Stonecliffe Garth LS12 77 E6
Stonecliffe Gdns LS12 77 E6
Stonecliffe Gn LS12 77 E6
Stonecliffe Gr LS12 77 E6
Stonecliffe Lawn LS12 77 E6
Stonecliffe Mount LS12 77 E6
Stonecliffe Pl LS12 77 E6
Stonecliffe Terr LS12 77 E6
Stonecliffe View LS12 77 E6
Stonecliffe Way LS12 77 E5
Stonecliffe Wlk LS12 77 E5
Stonecroft Bradford BD2 56 C4
Lofthouse Gate WF3 121 E5
Stonecroft Gdns HD8 190 F8
Stonedale Cl LS21 24 E6
Stonedene Ct WF16 117 E3
Stonefield LS14 45 D8
Stonefield Ave HD4 153 B3
Stonefield Cl BD2 56 B5
Stonefield Pl WF17 96 F1
Stonefield Rd HD4 153 B3
Stonefield St
Cleckheaton BD19 116 A6
Dewsbury WF13 118 C1
Stonefield Terr LS27 98 C8
Stonegate Bingley BD16 37 A5
Leeds LS7 206 C3
Ossett WF5 140 F3
Stonegate App LS7 59 F6
Stonegate Chase LS7 59 F7
Stonegate Cl LS17 43 D3
Stonegate Cres LS7 60 A7
Stonegate Dr Leeds LS7 60 A7
Pontefract WF8 146 C6
Stonegate Edge LS7 60 A7
Stonegate Farm Cl LS7 59 F7
Stonegate Gdns LS7 59 F7
Stonegate Gn LS7 59 F6
Stonegate Gr LS7 60 A7
Stonegate La
Ackworth M T WF7 163 E5
Leeds LS7 59 F7
Stonegate Mews LS7 59 F6
Stonegate Pl LS7 59 F6
Stonegate Rd Bradford BD10 56 C6
Leeds LS17 43 C2
Stonegate Sch LS7 60 A8
Stonegate View LS7 59 F7
Stonegate Wlk LS7 60 A6
Stonehaven Ct BD21 35 E5
Stonehurst LS14 62 D4
Stonehurst Rd WF14 138 A6
Stonehyrst Ave WF13 118 D1
Stonelea HX4 133 A5
Stonelea Ct Leeds LS7 60 A7
Leeds, Far Headingley LS6 59 D5
Stoneleigh 4 BD13 72 F1
Stoneleigh Ct HD8 174 A3
Stoneleigh Gr WF5 140 D5
Stonely Dr OL14 129 A7
Stones Bank HX6 132 C2
Stones Dr HX6 132 B2
Stones La Huddersfield HD7 152 D3
Slaithwaite HD7 170 C8
Todmorden OL14 107 E4
Stones Rd OL14 107 F4
Stones Terr OL14 108 A2
Stoney Back La HD4 153 E2
Stoney Bank La HD7 189 D8
Stoney Bank St WF13 139 A6
Stoney Battery HD1 203 E4
Stoney Battery Rd HD1 153 D4
Stoney Butts La HX4 133 B5
Stoney Croft BD19 117 B7
Stoney Cross St HD4 153 F2
Stoney Ford La HD5 137 B1
Stoney Garth WF4 159 F3
Stoney Hill HD6 115 A2
Stoney La Batley WF17 118 D6
Brighouse HX3 115 A6
Crigglestone WF4 159 F2
Halifax HX3 92 A3
Horsforth LS18 58 B8
Huddersfield, Blue Bell Hill HD4 153 F2
Huddersfield, Longwood HD3 152 F6
Lofthouse Gate WF2 120 D5
Menston LS29 21 D6
Thorner LS14 45 B5
Stoney Lee Middle Sch BD16 54 B6
Stoney Ridge Ave BD9 54 B4
Stoney Ridge Hospl BD16 54 C5
Stoney Ridge Rd BD16 54 C5
Stoney Rise LS18 58 B8
Stoney Rock Ct LS9 207 F1
Stoney Rock Gr LS9 207 F1
Stoney Rock La LS9 207 F1
Stoney Royd S71 178 F1
Stoney Royd La OL14 107 F7
Stoney Royd Terr HX3 113 D4
Stoney St BD20 18 B2
Stoneybrook Cl WF4 176 F8
Stoneycroft 3 LS18 58 B8
Stoneycroft La BD20 18 B2
Stoneyhurst Sq BD4 75 E3
Stoneys Fold BD15 53 B6
Stoneythorpe 2 LS18 58 B8
Stonlea Dr HD6 135 F7
Stony Croft La HX4 133 B5
Stony Gate HD7 188 E2
Stony La
Blackshaw Head HX7 88 D2
Bradford BD15 53 F2
Bradford, Eccleshill BD2 56 C5
Brighouse HX3 114 C4
Elland HX4 134 A8
Honley BD2 171 F3
Ripponden HX6 132 D5
Todmorden OL14 86 E2
Stony Royd LS28 57 C3
Stony Royd La HX7 110 A4
Stoodley Cl OL14 109 A5
Stoodley Glen OL14 109 A7
Stoodley Grange OL14 109 B5
Stoodley La OL14 109 B7
Stoodley Pike Mon OL14 109 C5
Stoodley Terr HX2 202 A1
Stopford Ave WF2 160 E8
Stopford Garth WF2 160 E8
Storey Pl LS14 61 E1
Storie Cres WF2 141 E4
Storiths Ct LS29 6 F7
Storiths La BD23 3 B8
Stormer Hill La HX6 112 D1
Storr Hill BD12 94 D4
Storrs Hill Rd WF5 140 E2
Storth Ave HD4 152 F3
Storth Pl HD2 135 F1
Storthes Hall La HD8 173 C6
Storths Rd HD2 135 F1
Stotfold Rd DN5 194 E3
Stott Hill BD1 201 C3
Stott Rd LS6 205 E3
Stott St LS12 210 A3
Stott Terr BD2 56 D4
Stourton Rd LS29 7 F5
Stowe Gr LS9 80 C8
Stowell Mill St BD5 74 D4
Stradmore Rd BD13 71 E8
Strafford Way BD10 56 E8
Straight La Addingham LS29 6 D5
Halifax HX2 91 D5
Hampole DN6 184 B4
Straightacres La BD10 56 D5
Straits 7 BD17 38 C4
Stralau St WF17 118 C6
Strands Ct WF4 158 E6
Strangford Ct BD10 56 D8
Stranglands La WF11 126 B5
Stratford Ave LS11 214 A3
Stratford Cl HD7 152 E5
Stratford Rd BD7 74 B5
Stratford St LS11 214 B3
Stratford Terr LS11 214 B3
Strathallan Dr BD17 38 D3
Stratheden Rd WF2 142 A7
Strathmore Ave LS9 208 A3
Strathmore Cl BD2 56 B3
Strathmore Dr Baildon BD17 38 B4
Leeds LS9 208 A3
Strathmore Gdns WF9 183 B4
Strathmore Rd LS29 8 E4
Strathmore St LS9 208 B2
Strathmore Terr LS9 208 A3
Strathmore View LS9 208 A2
Stratton Pk HD6 115 B1
Stratton Rd HD6 115 C1
Stratton View BD4 75 E4
Stratton Wlk BD15 73 A8
Strawberry Ave
Garforth LS25 82 E6
Liversedge WF15 117 A3
Strawberry Bank WF15 117 A4
Strawberry Fields 8 BD21 35 C8
Strawberry Gdns S71 179 D4
Strawberry La LS12 209 F3
Strawberry Rd LS12 209 F3
Strawberry Sq 2 WF16 117 D3
Strawberry St
Keighley BD21 35 C8
Silsden BD20 5 D1
Stray The BD10 56 A6
Stream Head Rd BD13 53 B2
Streamside LS6 59 E6
Streamside Cl HX7 110 E8
Street 1 LS23 31 A8
Street 2 LS23 31 B8
Street 3 LS23 15 B1
Street 5 LS23 15 B2
Street 6 LS23 15 B3
Street 7 LS23 15 C2
Street 8 LS23 15 D2
Street Furlong La WF8 147 B7
Street Head La BD22 50 E8
Street La Gildersome LS27 97 C6
Hooton Pagnell DN5 195 F3
Keighley BD20 19 C2
Leeds LS17 43 E2
Street The LS29 6 D8
Streethouse First Sch WF7 144 C5
Streethouse Sta WF7 144 D5
Strensall Gn 11 BD6 93 E8
Stretch Gate HD8 173 F2
Stretchgate La HX2 202 A4
Stretton Cl WF7 124 A1
Strickland Ave LS17 45 A4
Strickland Cl LS17 44 F4
Strickland Cres LS17 44 F4
Strickland Rd WF9 183 D8
Strike La HD8 174 F3
Strikes La BD20 16 E3
Strines Moor Rd HD7 199 C8
Strines St OL14 129 A7
Stringer Cl BD4 95 C8
Stringer House La HD8 175 A7
Stringer La 4 WF4 141 B1
Strong Close Gr BD21 35 E7
Strong Close Rd BD21 35 E7
Strong Close Way BD21 35 E7
Stuart Gr Normanton WF6 123 A4
Slaithwaite HD7 170 A8
Stuart Pl HD2 136 F5
Stuart Rd WF8 125 C1
Stuart St Castleford WF10 124 E8
Pontefract WF8 125 C1
Stubbin La Denby Dale HD8 192 B6
Holmfirth HD7 188 C3
Stubbin Rd HD7 169 B5
Stubbing Brink HX7 88 E3
Stubbing Dr HX7 88 E3
Stubbing Holme Rd HX7 88 F3
Stubbing La Elland HX4 133 E5
Sowerby Bridge HX6 132 E8
Stubbing Way BD18 55 C6
Stubbings Cl HX7 110 E8
Stubbings Infant Sch HX7 89 A3
Stubbings Rd BD17 37 F2
Stubbings St HX7 110 E8
Stubbins HX6 132 E8
Stubbs La WF3 120 E7
Stubham Rise LS29 8 A5
Stubley Farm Rd WF16 117 D6
Stubley Holme OL14 86 A1
Stubley La OL14 86 B1
Stubley Rd WF16 117 C6
Stubley St WF1 216 A2
Stubs Beck La BD19 95 D2
Studdley Cres BD16 37 B3
Studfold View LS14 62 A2
Studio Rd LS3 205 E1
Studleigh Terr HD6 114 E5
Studley Ave BD6 94 B7
Studley Cl BD20 19 D1
Studley Rd BD3 55 F2
Stumpcross Cl WF8 125 F3
Stumpcross Ct WF8 125 F3
Stumpcross La WF8 125 F3
Stumpcross Way WF8 125 F3
Stunsteds Rd BD19 116 D8
Sturges Gr BD2 56 B1
Sturton Ave LS25 83 A7
Sturton Gr HX2 91 E6
Sturton Grange La LS25 83 C7

Sturton La Garforth LS25 83 A8
Halifax HX2 91 E7
Stutely Gr HD2 136 E5
Sty La BD16 36 F6
Styebank La LS26 100 F6
Styes La HX6 111 D4
Styveton Way BD20 17 B6
Sude Hill HD7 189 F6
Sude Hill Terr HD7 189 F6
Sudforth La DN14 127 F5
Suffolk Ave WF17 118 B3
Suffolk Cl WF5 140 C4
Suffolk Ct LS19 40 B7
Suffolk House WF1 142 F3
Suffolk Pl BD2 55 F4
Suffolk St WF17 118 B4
Sufton St HD2 135 F1
Sugar Hill LS29 6 F8
Sugar Hill Cl LS26 101 C3
Sugar La Dewsbury WF12 139 E8
Wakefield WF1 142 E3
Sugar Well App LS7 60 A5
Sugar Well Mount LS7 60 A5
Sugar Well Rd LS7 60 A5
Sugarwell Ct LS7 206 B4
Sugden Cl HD6 136 A8
Sugden St Bradford BD12 94 F4
Bradford, Lister Hills BD1 74 C7
Sugden's Almshouses
BD22 34 E3
Sulby Gr BD10 56 E7
Sullivan Cl HD4 153 D3
Sullivan Gr WF9 182 B1
Summer Fields
Jun & Inf Sch S71 179 A4
Summer Hall Ing BD12 94 C4
Summer Hill Rd LS26 102 D2
Summer Hill St BD7 74 A5
Summer La Emley HD8 175 D6
Royston S71 179 B4
Summer Lea BD10 56 A8
Summer Meadow WF8 146 C7
Summer Rd S71 179 B4
Summer St Halifax HX1 202 B1
Huddersfield, Netherton
HD4 171 D7
Huddersfield, Rashcliffe
HD1, HD4 153 F4
Summerbridge Cl WF17 118 A6
Summerbridge Cres
Bradford BD10 56 D5
Cleckheaton BD19 96 C2
Summerbridge Dr BD10 56 D5
Summerdale BD19 96 B2
Summerfield Ave
Brighouse HD6 115 B6
Leeds LS13 58 A3
Summerfield Cl
Baildon BD17 38 B3
Byram WF11 126 E8
Summerfield Ct HX2 92 A5
Summerfield Dr
Baildon BD17 38 B3
Byram WF11 126 E8
Leeds LS13 58 A3
Summerfield Gdns LS13 58 A3
Summerfield Gn
Baildon BD17 38 B3
Leeds LS13 58 A3
Summerfield Gr
Baildon BD17 38 B3
Lepton HD8 155 D2
Summerfield Pk BD17 38 B3
Summerfield Pl LS13 58 A3
Summerfield Primary Sch
LS13 57 F3
Summerfield Rd
Bradford BD10 56 C6
Leeds LS13 58 A3
Todmorden OL14 108 D5
Summerfield Rd W OL14 108 C5
Summergate Pl HX1 202 B2
Summergate St HX1 202 B2
Summerhill Ave BD20 17 D6
Summerhill Dr BD20 17 D6
Summerhill Gdns LS8 44 B2
Summerhill Gr LS25 82 D6
Summerhill La BD20 17 D6
Summerhill Pl LS8 44 B3
Summerhill Rd LS25 82 D6
Summerlands Gr BD5 75 A2
Summerscale St HX1 202 C4
Summerseat Pl BD7 74 C5
Summervale HD7 189 A6
Summerville Rd
Bradford BD7 74 C6
Pudsey LS28 57 C2
Summit St BD21 35 B8
Sun Ct WF7 145 C8
Sun Field LS28 57 D1
Sun Fold HX1 203 F2
Sun Hill Dr BD17 37 E3
Sun La Burley in W LS29 9 E2
Haworth BD22 50 E7
Wakefield WF1 216 C2
Sun St Bradford BD1 201 C4
Haworth BD22 51 C6
Keighley BD21 35 C6
Keighley, East Morton BD20 19 E1
Pudsey LS28 57 E1
Steeton BD20 17 A5
Yeadon LS19 40 C7
Sun Terr OL14 86 B1
Sun Vale Ave OL14 129 B7
Sun Way HX3 113 F5
Sun Wood Ave HX3 93 B4
Sunbeam Ave LS11 214 B3
Sunbeam Gr 7 LS11 214 B3
Sunbeam Pl LS11 214 B3
Sunbeam Terr LS11 214 B3
Sunbridge Rd BD1 74 D7
Sunbury Gr HD5 154 E6
Sunderland Ct 6 HD6 115 A3
Sunderland Rd
Bradford BD9 55 C2
Low Bradley BD20 4 D5
Sunderland St
5 Halifax HX1 203 D3
Haworth BD22 51 F8
Keighley BD21 35 B6
Sundown Ave BD7 73 E4
Sunfield Cl LS28 57 D2
Sunfield Dr LS28 57 D2
Sunfield Gdns LS28 57 D2
Sunfield Pl LS28 57 D2
Sunfield Terr 11 BD19 116 E7
Sunhurst Cl BD22 34 C2
Sunhurst Dr BD22 34 C2
Sunningdale Bradford BD8 73 D8
Micklefield LS25 83 F8
Sunningdale Ave
Leeds LS17 43 A4
Mapplewell S75 178 A1
Sunningdale Cl LS17 43 A4
Sunningdale Cres BD13 52 E5
Sunningdale Ct HD2 135 F3
Sunningdale Dr
Cudworth S72 180 C1
Leeds LS17 43 A4
Sunningdale Gn LS17 43 A4
Sunningdale Rd HD4 153 D3
Sunningdale Way LS17 43 A4
Sunningdale Wlk LS17 43 A4
Sunningdales WF6 123 D1
Sunny Ave
South Elmsall WF9 183 B2
Upton WF9 183 A7
Sunny Bank Bradford BD9 54 D2
Hebden Bridge HX7 89 F1
Hemsworth WF9 163 A3
Knottingley WF11 127 A4
Leeds LS8 204 C1
Normanton WF6 144 B7
Ryhill WF4 162 A1
Shipley BD18 55 B7
Sunny Bank Ave
Bradford BD5 74 D1
Mirfield WF14 138 A8
Sunny Bank Dr
Mirfield WF14 137 F8
Sowerby Bridge HX6 112 C4
Sunny Bank Gr Leeds LS8 204 C1
Mirfield WF14 138 A7
Sunny Bank La
Batley WF17 118 D7
Brighouse HX3 114 B6
Hebden Bridge HX7 110 C4
Sunny Bank Par WF14 137 F8
Sunny Bank Rd
Batley WF17 118 D6
Bradford BD5 74 D1
Brighouse HD6 115 A2
Glusburn BD20 16 C6
Halifax HX2 91 C5
Meltham HD7 170 C2
Mirfield WF14 138 A8
Slaithwaite HD7 152 B3
Wadsworth Moor HX7 69 A3
Sunny Bank St HX6 112 C4
Sunny Bank Terr
4 Halifax HX3 92 C1
9 Todmorden OL14 86 B1
Sunny Bank View LS8 204 C1
Sunny Bank Wlk WF14 138 A7
Sunny Brow HD4 171 F8
Sunny Brow La BD9 54 D2
Sunny Dale BD13 52 D2
Sunny Gr 5 LS27 98 C8
Sunny Heys Rd HD7 170 D3
Sunny Heys W HD7 170 D2
Sunny Hill WF2 120 E1
Sunny Hill Ave BD21 34 F5
Sunny Hill Cl WF2 120 E2
Sunny Hill Gr BD21 34 F5
Sunny Hill House Sch
WF2 120 E1
Sunny Mead HD5 155 A6
Sunny Mount
Brighouse HX3 114 C7
Harden BD16 36 B1
Keighley BD21 35 B8
Keighley, Braithwaite BD22 34 E8
Keighley, Crossflatts BD20 36 C7
Sunny Side St 1 HX3 92 C1
Sunny Vale Country Club
HX3 114 C6
Sunny View Cres HD2 136 D3
Sunny View Terr 3 BD13 92 C8
Sunnybank Denby Dale HD8 191 F5
Micklefield LS25 84 B6
Sunnybank Ave
Bradford BD3 56 F1
4 Horsforth LS18 58 B7
Sunnybank Cl BD19 115 F7
Sunnybank Cres Elland HX4 134 B7
Yeadon LS19 40 D7
Sunnybank Ct LS19 40 D7
Sunnybank Dr HX4 134 B7
Sunnybank Gr BD3 56 F1
Sunnybank Grange 1
HD6 115 A2
Sunnybank La Bradford BD3 56 F1
Elland HX4 134 B7
Sunnybank Rd Elland HX4 134 B7
6 Horsforth LS18 58 B7
Huddersfield HD3 153 D8
Sunnybank St WF5 140 D5
Sunnybank Terr HD6 115 A3
Sunnybrae Cres BD16 37 B2
Sunnycliffe BD20 36 D8
Sunnydale Ave HD6 136 A8
Sunnydale Cres LS21 22 D6
Sunnydale Croft WF5 140 E4
Sunnydale Gr BD21 35 F6
Sunnydale Pk
Keighley BD20 19 E2
Ossett WF5 140 E5
Sunnydale Rd WF5 140 F5
Sunnydale Ridge LS21 22 D6
Sunnydale Terr WF5 140 E5
Sunnydene LS14 61 F1
Sunnyfield WF3 120 C7
Sunnyfield Ave BB10 85 A8
Sunnyfield Dr WF9 163 A3
Sunnyhill Cres WF2 120 D1
Sunnyhill Croft WF2 120 E2
Sunnylea HD7 169 A4
Sunnymead HD8 175 E2
Sunnymount Terr 5 WF17 96 F1
Sunnyridge Ave LS28 76 B8
Sunnyside Batley WF16 117 D3
Brighouse HD6 136 D8
Elland HX4 134 A1
Huddersfield HD2 153 E8
Todmorden OL14 108 A5
Sunnyside Ave
East Ardsley WF3 119 D8
Liversedge WF15 116 F2
Sunnyside La BD3 55 F1
Sunnyside Rd LS13 58 B1
Sunnyvale Mount WF9 182 E3
Sunnyview WF3 120 C6
Sunnyview Ave LS11 213 F3
Sunnyview Gdns LS11 213 F3
Sunnyview Terr LS11 213 F3
Sunroyd Ave WF4 141 B2
Sunroyd Hill WF4 141 B2
Sunset Ave LS6 59 E8
Sunset Dr Ilkley LS29 8 D5
6 Leeds LS6 59 E7
Sunset Hilltop LS6 59 E8
Sunset Mount 5 LS6 59 E7
Sunset Rd LS6 59 E7
Sunset Rise LS6 59 E8
Sunset Terr LS29 8 E5
Sunset View LS6 59 E8
Surat Rd HD7 151 F3
Suresnes Rd BD21 35 B7
Surgery St BD22 51 D6
Surrey Gr Bradford BD5 74 E4
Pudsey LS28 76 E8
Surrey Rd 4 LS28 76 E8
Surrey St Batley WF17 118 D5
Halifax HX1 202 B2
Keighley BD21 35 E8
Todmorden OL14 108 B6
Sussex App LS10 215 F3
Sussex Ave Horsforth LS18 41 C3
Leeds LS10 215 F3
Sussex Cl WF9 181 D8
Sussex Cres WF10 125 E8
Sussex Gdns LS10 215 F3
Sussex Gn LS10 215 F3
Sussex Pl LS10 215 F3
Sussex St Batley WF17 118 D5
Keighley BD21 35 E8
Leeds LS9 212 C3
Sussex Wlk 2 WF13 139 B8
Sutcliffe Pl 6 BD6 94 D8
Sutcliffe St HX2 202 A4
Sutcliffe Wood La HX3 114 C6
Sutherland Ave LS8 44 A2
Sutherland Cres LS8 44 A2
Sutherland Dr HD4 153 C2
Sutherland Mount LS9 208 A2
Sutherland Rd
Brighouse HX3 114 E8
Leeds LS9 208 A2
Sutherland St LS12 210 B2
Sutherland Terr LS9 208 A2
Sutton App LS14 61 E1
Sutton Ave Bradford BD2 56 A4
Huddersfield HD5 155 A7
Sutton Cres Bradford BD4 75 E5
Leeds LS14 61 E1
Sutton Dr Cullingworth BD13 52 D5
Huddersfield HD5 155 A8
Sutton Fields BD20 16 C6
Sutton Gr Bradford BD4 75 E5
2 Morley LS27 98 A3
Sutton La Byram WF11 126 E7
Sutton in C BD20 16 E5
Sutton Rd BD4 75 E5
Sutton St LS12 210 C2
Sutton-in-Craven
C of E Primary Sch BD20 16 D5
Sutton-in-Craven County
Primary Sch BD20 16 D5
Suzanne Cres WF9 182 E3
Swain House Cres BD2 56 A5
Swain House
First & Middle Schs BD2 56 A5
Swain House Rd BD2 56 A5
Swain Mount BD2 56 A5
Swaine Hill Cres LS19 40 A7
Swaine Hill St LS19 40 A7
Swaine Hill Terr LS19 40 A7
Swale Cres LS25 83 B6
Swale Ct BD20 17 E8
Swale Dr WF10 125 B8
Swale Rise LS22 13 D8
Swales Moor Rd HX3 92 C4
Swales' Yd 2 WF8 146 C8
Swallow Ave LS12 209 D2
Swallow Cl Leeds LS17 43 F4
Pool LS21 24 D6
Swallow Cres LS12 209 D2
Swallow Dr Leeds LS17 44 A4
Morley LS27 98 D4
Pool LS21 24 D6
Swallow Fold BD8 73 C7
Swallow Garth WF2 160 D5
Swallow Gr HD4 171 E6
Swallow Hill WF17 118 A8
Swallow La
Huddersfield HD7 152 C5
Slaithwaite HD7 152 C5
Swallow Mount LS12 209 D2
Swallow St
1 Huddersfield HD1 154 A5
5 Keighley BD21 35 D8
Liversedge WF16 117 D3
Swan Bank La Halifax HX3 203 F1
Holmfirth HD7 189 A4
Swan La Elland HD3 134 B1
Huddersfield HD1 153 E3
Swan St Bradford BD5 201 B2
Leeds LS1 211 F4
Swanhill La WF8 146 D7
Swarcliffe App LS14 62 C4
Swarcliffe Ave LS14 62 D5
Swarcliffe Bank LS14 62 C5
Swarcliffe Dr LS14 62 C4
Swarcliffe Drive E 2 LS14 62 D4
Swarcliffe Gn LS14 62 D4
Swarcliffe Par LS14 62 C4
Swarcliffe Prim Sch LS15 62 C5
Swarcliffe Rd LS14 62 C5
Swarcliffe Towers 9 LS14 62 D5
Swardale Gn LS14 62 C4
Swardale Rd LS14 62 C4
Swarland Gr BD5 201 B1
Swartha La BD20 6 A2
Swastika Stone LS29 7 D2
Sweep La HD7 189 B3
Sweet St LS11 211 E2
Sweet St W LS11 211 D2
Swift Pl HX6 132 B2
Swift Way WF2 160 D5
Swift's Fold HD7 171 F5
Swillington La LS26 82 A4
Swillington Primary Sch
LS26 82 A2
Swincar Ave LS19 40 B7
Swincliffe Cl BD19 96 A4
Swincliffe Cres BD19 96 B3
Swincroft WF5 140 E5
Swindon Rd WF13 139 C8
Swine La Keighley BD20 36 B8
West Hardwick WF4 162 D5
Swine Market La HX7 110 A3
Swinegate LS1 211 F3
Swineshead La OL14 108 B3
Swineshead Rd OL14 108 A3
Swinnow Ave LS13 58 A1
Swinnow Cl LS13 58 A1
Swinnow Cres LS28 58 A2
Swinnow Dr LS13 58 A1
Swinnow Garth LS13 58 A1
Swinnow Gdns LS13 58 A1
Swinnow Gn LS28 77 A8
Swinnow Gr LS13 58 A1
Swinnow La Leeds LS13 58 A1
Pudsey LS13 77 B8
Swinnow Middle Sch LS13 77 A8
Swinnow Pl LS13 58 A2
Swinnow Prim Sch LS13 77 A8
Swinnow Rd LS13 58 B1
Swinnow View LS13 58 A1
Swinnow Wlk LS13 58 A1
Swinton Pl BD7 74 B5
Swinton Terr HX1 202 B1
Swire Smith Middle Sch
BD21 35 E6
Swires Rd Bradford BD2 56 C1
Halifax HX1 203 D2
Swires Terr HX1 203 D2
Swiss St WF10 103 E1
Swithen Hill S75 177 B3
Swithen's La LS26 100 F4
Swithen's St LS26 100 F4
Swithenbank Ave WF5 140 D8
Swithenbank St WF5 119 C1
Swithens Ct LS26 100 F4
Swithens Dr LS26 100 E4
Swithens Gr LS26 100 E4
Sycamore Ave Bingley BD16 36 F2
Bradford BD7 73 F6
Huddersfield HD3, HD7 152 F5
Kippax LS25 82 F2
Knottingley WF11 126 D3
Leeds, Halton LS15 81 A8
Leeds, Potternewton LS8 204 C1
Meltham HD7 170 D1
Todmorden OL14 108 A7
Wakefield, Brag Lane End
WF2 120 F3
Wakefield, Flanshaw WF2 141 F7
Sycamore Chase LS28 76 F7
Sycamore Cl Batley WF12 118 F2
Bradford BD3 201 D4
Bramhope LS16 24 F1
Knottingley WF11 126 D2
Leeds LS6 206 A4
Leeds, Meanwood LS6 59 F7
Lepton HD8 155 F3
Sycamore Copse WF2 141 F5
Sycamore Croft LS11 214 B3
Sycamore Ct Bradford BD3 201 D4
Huddersfield HD8 152 F5
Ilkley LS29 8 A5
Kirkburton HD8 173 F7
Sycamore Dr
Addingham LS29 7 A8
Brighouse HX3 115 A6
Cleckheaton BD19 116 B7
Elland HX5 134 D6
Royston S71 179 A3
Sycamore Fold LS11 214 B3
Sycamore Gn WF8 125 F1
Sycamore Gr
Normanton WF6 144 A8
Steeton BD20 16 F5
Wakefield WF2 141 F7
Sycamore House 5 WF10 124 E7
Sycamore Ind Est WF16 117 D2
Sycamore La WF4 176 F8
Sycamore Rd WF9 181 C6
Sycamore Rise HD7 189 D7
Sycamore Row LS13 58 A4
Sycamore St WF1 142 E4
Sycamore Terr Honley HD7 171 E3
Horbury WF4 159 C8
Sycamore View BD22 34 F6
Sycamore Way
Batley WF17 96 F1
Featherstone WF7 145 D6
Sycamore Wlk Dearne S63 194 D1
Pudsey LS28 57 D2
Sycamores The
Bramhope LS16 24 F1
Dewsbury WF13 118 B2
Guiseley LS20 22 E2
Horbury WF4 141 C1
Sydenham Pl BD3 56 A2
Sydenham Rd LS11 210 C2
Sydenham St LS11 210 C2
Sydney Gdns OL15 129 C1
Sydney St 12 Bingley BD16 37 A3
Liversedge WF15 117 B3
Pudsey LS28 57 D2
Rothwell LS26 101 D6
Syke Ave Dewsbury WF12 139 F8
East Ardsley WF3 119 D7
Syke Cl WF3 119 C7
Syke Gdns WF3 119 D7
Syke Gn LS14 45 C8
Syke Gr WF12 139 F8
Syke House La HX4 133 F7
Syke Ing Cl WF12 140 A7
Syke Ing Terr WF12 140 A7
Syke La Brighouse HX3 93 E1
Dewsbury WF12 139 F7
Halifax HX2 71 E2
Queensbury BD13 92 F7
Scarcroft LS14 45 B8
Sowerby Bridge HX6 112 B3
Syke Rd Dewsbury WF12 139 F8
East Ardsley WF3 119 D7
Wetherby LS22 14 A5
Syke Side BD20 18 B2
Syke St WF12 139 F7
Syke Terr WF3 119 C7
Syke View WF12 139 F8
Sykes Ave Batley WF16 117 E5
Mirfield WF14 138 C6
Sykes Cl Ackworth M T WF7 163 D5
Batley WF17 118 E6
Sykes Fold BD22 51 E1
Sykes Gate HX7 131 C7
Sykes La Batley WF12 119 A4
Bradford BD12 95 A4
Oakworth BD22 34 D2
Sykes Rd WF17 118 E6
Sykes St
9 Castleford WF10 124 D8
Cleckheaton BD19 116 D7
Sylhet Cl BD1 74 D8
Sylvan Ave BD13 92 D8
Sylvester Ave WF6 144 A7
Symons St WF2 216 A1
Syringa Ave BD15 54 A4
Syringa St HD1 153 D7

Tabbs Ct BD19 94 F1
Tabbs La BD19 94 F1
Tadcaster Grammar Sch
LS24 31 D2
Tadman St WF1 142 C4
Tagore Ct BD3 75 D6
Talbot Ave
Huddersfield HD3 135 C1
Leeds, Burley LS4 59 C3
Leeds, Lidgett Park LS17, LS8 43 F2
Talbot Cres LS8 43 F2
Talbot & Falcon Yd WF1 216 B2
Talbot Gdns LS8 43 F2
Talbot Gr LS8 43 F2
Talbot House 2 HX5 134 F6
Talbot Mount LS4 59 C3
Talbot Primary Sch LS8 43 F2
Talbot Rd LS8 43 F1
Talbot Rise LS17 43 F2
Talbot Row WF17 118 D5
Talbot St Batley WF17 118 C4
Bradford BD7 74 C7
4 Keighley BD21 35 A7
Normanton WF6 123 A2
Talbot Terr Leeds LS4 59 C3
Rothwell LS26 100 E4
Talbot View Leeds LS4 59 C3
Mirfield WF14 138 A6
Tall Trees Dr WF7 145 D8
Tamar St BD5 74 C4
Tammy Hall St 1 WF1 216 B2
Tamworth St BD4 75 E6
Tan House Ct BD4 95 B7

Tan House La
Ackworth M T WF7 ... 164 B7
Shelf HX3 ... 93 A5
Wilsden BD15 ... 53 B6
Tan La BD4 ... 95 B6
Tan Pit Cl DN5 ... 194 D4
Tan Pit La DN5 ... 194 D4
Tandem Ind Est HD5 ... 155 B6
Tandem Way HD5 ... 155 B6
Tandy Trad Est The LS12 .. 205 D1
Tanfield Cl S71 ... 179 A4
Tanfield Dr LS29 ... 9 E2
Tanfield Rd HD1 ... 153 F8
Tanglewood Ct 2 BD6 ... 74 A1
Tanhouse Hill
Brighouse HX3 ... 114 C7
2 Horsforth LS18 ... 58 E8
Tanhouse La WF14 ... 156 B7
Tanhouse Pk HX3 ... 114 C7
Tanhouse St WF13 ... 138 F6
Tanner Hill Rd BD7 ... 73 E3
Tanner St WF15 ... 116 B5
Tannerbrook Cl BD14 ... 73 D4
Tanners HD7 ... 169 F7
Tannery Ct Bradford BD10 ... 56 D8
Mirfield WF14 ... 137 E6
Tannett Gn BD5 ... 74 F2
Tanpits 23 HX7 ... 89 A3
Tanshelf Dr WF8 ... 146 C8
Tanshelf Ind Est WF8 ... 125 C1
Tanshelf Sta WF8 ... 125 C1
Tansy End BD22 ... 51 E2
Tanton Cres BD14 ... 73 D4
Tanton Wlk BD14 ... 73 D4
Tanyard Ave HD3 ... 153 A7
Tanyard Fold WF4 ... 160 A3
Tanyard Rd
Huddersfield, Milnsbridge
HD3 ... 153 B4
Huddersfield, Quarmby HD3 153 A7
Tarn Cl WF10 ... 104 E1
Tarn Ct Keighley BD20 ... 34 F8
Lofthouse Gate WF1 ... 121 B3
Tarn Hows Wlk WF7 ... 163 F6
Tarn La Bardsey LS17 ... 44 E7
Harewood LS17 ... 44 E7
Keighley BD22 ... 34 B8
Tarn Rd WF7 ... 145 E4
Tarn View Rd LS19 ... 40 D7
Tarnhill Mews BD5 ... 74 E4
Tarnside Dr LS14 ... 62 A3
Tate Naylor St WF13 ... 118 B2
Tatefield Gr LS25 ... 83 A1
Tatefield Pl LS25 ... 83 A1
Tateley Cl WF5 ... 119 D1
Tateley La WF5 ... 119 C1
Tatham Way LS8 ... 61 C6
Tatton St WF1 ... 142 F3
Taunton Ho 11 BD5 ... 201 B1
Taunton St BD18 ... 55 A8
Tavern St WF1 ... 216 C2
Taverngate LS20 ... 38 E8
Tavistock Way WF2 ... 160 A5
Tavora St WF1 ... 216 B3
Tawny Cl 1 LS27 ... 98 D4
Tay Ct BD2 ... 56 D5
Taylor Ave BD20 ... 5 D1
Taylor Cl WF5 ... 140 F4
Taylor Cres WF5 ... 140 F4
Taylor Dr WF5 ... 140 F4
Taylor Gr LS26 ... 102 E3
Taylor Hall La WF14 ... 137 F8
Taylor Hill Rd HD4 ... 153 E1
Taylor La Barwick in E LS15 ... 63 B5
Halifax BD13 ... 72 A3
Slaithwaite HD7 ... 152 B5
Taylor Rd 10 BD6 ... 94 D8
Taylor St Batley WF17 ... 118 C4
Cleckheaton BD19 ... 116 C7
Huddersfield HD7 ... 152 E4
Taylor Wood Cotts WF4 ... 163 B6
Taylor's Bldgs HD4 ... 154 A2
Taylors Cl LS14 ... 62 B4
Teal Cl WF10 ... 124 D6
Teal Ct BD20 ... 17 B6
Teal Dr LS27 ... 98 D4
Teal Mews LS10 ... 99 D5
Tealbeck App LS21 ... 23 B7
Tealbeck House LS21 ... 23 B7
Tealby Cl LS16 ... 41 E2
Teall Ct WF5 ... 141 A5
Teall St Ossett WF5 ... 141 A5
Wakefield WF1 ... 216 B2
Teapot Cnr DN5 ... 194 D4
Teasdale St BD4 ... 75 B3
Teasel Cl BD12 ... 95 A4
Technology Dr WF17 ... 118 E4
Teddington Ave HD5 ... 154 F6
Tees Cl WF10 ... 125 B8
Tees St BD5 ... 74 C3
Teesdale Pl WF11 ... 126 E2
Telephone Pl LS9 ... 207 D1
Telford Cl Castleford WF10 .. 124 B7
Leeds LS10 ... 215 E2
Silsden BD20 ... 17 F8
Telford Ct BD7 ... 74 B6
Telford Gdns 2 LS10 ... 215 E2
Telford Pl LS10 ... 215 E2
Telford St 7 LS10 ... 215 E2
Telford Terr LS10 ... 215 E2
Telford Way WF2 ... 120 F5
Telford Wlk 3 LS10 ... 215 E2
Telscombe Dr BD4 ... 75 D2
Temperance Field BD12 ... 94 D3
Temperance Fields BD19 .. 115 F8
Temperance St 1 LS28 ... 57 E1
Tempest Pl LS11 ... 214 A3
Tempest Rd Leeds LS11 ... 214 B2
South Kirkby WF9 ... 182 C4
Templar Dr HD5 ... 154 D5
Templar Gdns LS22 ... 13 F7
Templar La Leeds LS2 ... 212 A4
Leeds, Stanks LS15 ... 62 D4
Templar Pl LS2 ... 212 A4
Templar St Leeds LS2 ... 212 A4
Wakefield WF1 ... 142 F3
Templar's Way BD8 ... 73 E8
Templars Cl HX4 ... 134 A7
Templars Way LS25 ... 82 F6
Temple Ave Leeds LS15 ... 81 A6
Rothwell LS26 ... 100 F7
Temple Bank Specl Sch
BD9 ... 54 E2
Temple Cl
16 Huddersfield HD1 ... 154 A6
Leeds LS15 ... 81 A6
Temple Cres LS11 ... 214 A3
Temple Ct Leeds LS15 ... 80 F7
Rothwell LS26 ... 100 F7
Temple Gate LS15 ... 81 B7
Temple Gate Dr LS15 ... 81 A7
Temple Gdns WF6 ... 122 F4
Temple Gn LS26 ... 101 A7
Temple Gr LS15 ... 81 A7
Temple La Leeds LS15 ... 81 B7
Littleborough OL15 ... 129 D1
Temple Lawn LS26 ... 101 A7
Temple Lea LS15 ... 81 B7
Temple Moor High Sch
LS15 ... 81 B7
Temple Newsam Park
Golf Course LS15 ... 80 F5
Temple Newsam Pk LS15 ... 81 A5
Temple Park Cl LS15 ... 81 A7
Temple Park Gdns LS15 ... 81 A7
Temple Park Gn LS15 ... 81 A7
Temple Rd WF13 ... 139 A7
Temple Rhydding Dr BD17 . 38 C2
Temple Rise LS15 ... 81 A6
Temple Row
9 Keighley BD21 ... 35 B7
Leeds LS15 ... 81 E6
Temple Row Cl LS15 ... 81 E6
Temple St Bradford BD9 ... 55 B2
Castleford WF10 ... 124 C7
Huddersfield HD3 ... 135 B1
10 Keighley BD21 ... 35 B7
Temple View WF3 ... 100 C1
Temple View Gr LS9 ... 80 A7
Temple View Pl LS9 ... 212 C3
Temple View Rd LS9 ... 212 C3
Temple View Terr LS9 ... 212 C3
Temple Wlk LS15 ... 81 B8
Templegate Ave LS15 ... 81 B6
Templegate Cl LS15 ... 81 C7
Templegate Cres LS15 ... 81 B6
Templegate Gn LS15 ... 81 B7
Templegate Rd LS15 ... 81 B6
Templegate Rise LS15 ... 81 A6
Templegate View LS15 ... 81 B6
Templegate Way LS15 ... 81 B6
Templegate Wlk LS15 ... 81 B7
Templenewsam Halton
Primary Sch LS15 ... 81 A8
Templenewsam Rd LS15 ... 81 A5
Templenewsam View LS15 . 80 F6
Templestowe Cres LS15 ... 62 C1
Templestowe Dr 3 LS15 ... 81 C8
Templestowe Gdns 5 LS15 81 B8
Templestowe Hill 1 LS15 ... 62 B1
Ten Lands La WF4 ... 180 A7
Ten Row HD8 ... 191 A4
Ten Yards La BD13 ... 72 A8
Tenbury Fold BD4 ... 75 E3
Tennants Ct WF11 ... 127 A4
Tennis Ave BD4 ... 75 E1
Tennis Way BD17 ... 38 A1
Tennyson Ave
Lofthouse Gate WF3 ... 121 E6
Sowerby Bridge HX6 ... 111 F3
Todmorden OL14 ... 108 D6
Tennyson Cl
Knottingley WF11 ... 126 B4
Pudsey LS28 ... 76 F6
Tennyson Pl Bradford BD3 ... 75 B8
Brighouse HX3 ... 114 C8
4 Cleckheaton BD19 ... 116 D8
Tennyson Rd BD6 ... 94 B8
Tennyson St Guiseley LS20 ... 39 F8
12 Halifax HX3 ... 92 A1
6 Keighley BD21 ... 35 B5
Morley LS27 ... 98 B4
Pudsey LS28 ... 76 F6
8 Pudsey, Farsley LS28 ... 57 D2
Tennyson Terr LS27 ... 98 B4
Tennyson Way WF8 ... 125 D2
Tenter Cl HD8 ... 175 A2
Tenter Croft 5 BD17 ... 38 C4
Tenter Hill Bradford BD14 ... 73 B4
Bramham LS23 ... 30 C2
Holmfirth HD7 ... 189 F4
Tenter Hill La HD2 ... 136 D4
Tentercroft Ct WF13 ... 118 D1
Tenterden Way LS15 ... 62 F2
Tenterfield Rd WF5 ... 140 E5
Tenterfield Rise HX3 ... 93 A1
Tenterfield Terr OL14 ... 108 E6
Tenterfields Bradford BD10 ... 56 E8
Halifax HX2 ... 111 E5
Tenterfields Bsns Pk HX2 . 111 E5
Tenters Cl WF11 ... 126 D5
Tenters Gr HD2 ... 136 C3
Tenth Ave WF15 ... 116 C5
Tern St BD5 ... 74 C3
Ternhill Gr BD5 ... 201 B1
Terrace Gdns HX3 ... 92 B1
Terrace The
Boston Spa LS23 ... 30 E7
Honley HD7 ... 171 E3
Pudsey LS28 ... 76 E4
Terrington Crest BD14 ... 73 D4
Terry Rd 2 BD12 ... 94 E5
Tetley Dr BD11 ... 96 B4
Tetley La HX3 ... 93 A2
Tetley Pl BD2 ... 55 F3
Tetley St BD1 ... 201 A3
Teville Ct BD4 ... 75 E1
Tew St WF2 ... 142 C4
Tewit Cl HX2 ... 91 F7
Tewit Gdns HX2 ... 91 F7
Tewit Gn HX2 ... 91 F7
Tewit Hall Gdns HX2 ... 91 F6
Tewit Hall Rd BD3 ... 75 C8
Tewit La HX2 ... 91 F7
Tewitt Cl BD20 ... 17 B6
Tewitt La Bingley BD16 ... 37 B6
Wilsden BD13 ... 53 A2
Texas St LS27 ... 98 B2
Thacker Gate Rd HX6 ... 111 B4
Thackeray Gr HD4 ... 153 D3
Thackeray Rd BD10 ... 56 D4
Thackeray Wlk WF11 ... 126 B4
Thackley Ave BD10 ... 39 A2
Thackley Ct BD18 ... 55 C8
Thackley First Sch BD10 ... 39 B1
Thackley Old Rd BD18 ... 55 D8
Thackley Rd BD10 ... 39 A2
Thackley View BD10 ... 39 A2
Thackray Ave WF16 ... 117 E5
Thackray La WF8 ... 125 E1
Thackray St Halifax HX2 ... 112 D7
Morley LS27 ... 98 A3
Thames Dr LS25 ... 83 B6
Thane Way LS15 ... 62 E3
Thanes Cl HD2 ... 135 E1
Thanet Garth BD20 ... 17 E8
Thatchers Way BD19 ... 96 B1
Theaker La LS12 ... 209 E4
Theakston Mead BD14 ... 73 C4
Thealby Cl LS9 ... 212 B4
Thealby Lawn LS9 ... 207 E1
Thealby Pl 1 LS9 ... 212 B4
Thearne Gn BD14 ... 73 D4
Theatre Wlk 2 LS1 ... 211 F4
Theodore St LS11 ... 214 A2
Thewlis La HD4 ... 153 B1
Thick Hollins HD7 ... 170 F1
Thick Hollins Dr HD7 ... 170 F1
Thick Hollins Rd
Holmfirth HD7 ... 188 A7
Meltham HD7 ... 187 F8
Third Ave Bradford BD3 ... 56 C1
Cleckheaton WF15 ... 116 B5
Halifax HX3 ... 113 B4
Huddersfield HD7 ... 152 D4
1 Keighley BD21 ... 35 B6
Kirkheaton HD5 ... 137 C1
Leeds LS12 ... 210 A2
Lofthouse Gate WF1 ... 121 C2
Rothwell LS26 ... 101 A7
Upton WF9 ... 183 A8
Wetherby LS22 ... 13 F5
Third St 2 BD12 ... 94 E6
Thirkhill Ct 4 BD5 ... 74 E4
Thirkleby Royd BD14 ... 73 C4
Thirlmere Ave
Brighouse BD12 ... 94 E1
Elland HX5 ... 135 B7
Thirlmere Cl LS11 ... 98 E8
Thirlmere Dr
Castleford WF10 ... 125 D7
East Ardsley WF3 ... 120 A8
Wetherby LS22 ... 13 B6
Thirlmere Gdns
Bradford BD2 ... 56 B2
Leeds LS11 ... 98 E8
Thirlmere Gr BD17 ... 37 E1
Thirlmere Pl WF11 ... 126 E2
Thirlmere Rd Batley WF12 .. 118 F2
Wakefield WF2 ... 141 E6
Thirsk Cl HD2 ... 136 B2
Thirsk Dr LS25 ... 83 A2
Thirsk Grange BD14 ... 73 D4
Thirsk Row LS1 ... 211 E3
Thirstin Rd HD7 ... 171 F5
Thirteenth Ave WF15 ... 116 B5
Thistle Cl HD2 ... 135 E2
Thistle Dr WF9 ... 182 F7
Thistle Hill Ave HD5 ... 155 C5
Thistle St HD1 ... 154 B8
Thistle Way LS27 ... 97 D5
Thistlewood Rd WF1 ... 121 E5
Thomas Chippendale
Prim Sch LS21 ... 10 F2
Thomas Ct BD6 ... 74 C1
Thomas Danby Coll LS7 ... 207 D2
Thomas St Batley WF17 ... 118 B6
Batley, Heckmondwike WF16 117 D3
Brighouse HD6 ... 115 A1
Castleford WF10 ... 103 E1
Elland HX5 ... 135 A6
Elland, Holywell Green HX4 .. 134 B4
Glusburn BD20 ... 16 D7
Halifax HX1 ... 203 E3
Haworth BD22 ... 51 D6
Hemsworth WF9 ... 181 E6
Huddersfield, Lindley HD3 . 135 B1
Huddersfield, Yews Hill HD1 . 153 E4
Leeds LS6 ... 206 A3
9 Liversedge WF15 ... 117 A4
Todmorden OL14 ... 86 C1
Thomas St S HX1 ... 202 C2
Thomas St W HX1 ... 202 C1
Thomas Way WF9 ... 183 A4
Thompson Ave
Bradford BD2 ... 55 F5
Castleford WF10 ... 125 E6
Thompson Dr WF2 ... 120 F3
Thompson Gn BD17 ... 38 A2
Thompson La BD17 ... 38 A1
Thompson St Halifax HX1 ... 203 D3
Normanton WF6 ... 123 A2
Shipley BD18 ... 55 A8
Thompson's Yd WF1 ... 216 A2
Thong La HD7 ... 189 A8
Thoresby Dr BD19 ... 117 B8
Thoresby Gr BD7 ... 73 E3
Thoresby Pl LS2 ... 206 B1
Thorn Ave Bradford BD9 ... 54 D4
Dewsbury WF12 ... 139 C2
Thorn Bank OL13 ... 106 A2
Thorn Cl 8 Bacup OL13 ... 106 A2
Leeds LS8 ... 208 B3
Shipley BD18 ... 55 E6
Thorn Cres 7 Bacup OL13 . 106 A2
Leeds LS8 ... 208 B3
Thorn Cross LS8 ... 208 C4
Thorn Dr Bacup OL13 ... 106 A2
Bradford BD9 ... 54 D4
Leeds LS8 ... 208 B3
Queensbury BD13 ... 92 C7
Thorn Garth
Cleckheaton BD19 ... 116 C6
Keighley BD20 ... 18 A1
Thorn Gdns OL13 ... 106 A2
Thorn Gr Bradford BD9 ... 54 D4
Leeds LS8 ... 208 B3
Thorn Hill HX4 ... 133 F2
Thorn La Bradford BD9 ... 54 D4
Leeds LS8 ... 204 C2
Thorn Mount LS8 ... 208 C4
Thorn Park Sch
for the Deaf BD9 ... 54 D4
Thorn Rd WF12 ... 139 C1
Thorn Royd Dr BD4 ... 75 F2
Thorn St Bacup OL13 ... 106 A2
Batley WF17 ... 96 E1
Bradford BD8 ... 55 A1
3 Haworth BD22 ... 51 E8
Thorn Terr LS8 ... 208 C4
Thorn Tree St HX1 ... 202 B1
Thorn View Elland HX5 ... 135 A6
5 Halifax HX3 ... 92 C2
Hebden Bridge HX7 ... 110 E8
Leeds LS8 ... 208 B3
Thorn Wlk LS8 ... 208 C3
Thornaby Dr BD14 ... 73 C4
Thornacre Cres BD18 ... 55 E7
Thornacre Rd BD18 ... 55 E7
Thornberry Dr WF15 ... 116 B5
Thornbridge Mews BD2 ... 56 B4
Thornbury Ave BD3 ... 75 D8
Thornbury Cres BD3 ... 75 D8
Thornbury Dr BD3 ... 75 D8
Thornbury First Sch BD3 ... 75 E8
Thornbury Gr BD3 ... 75 D8
Thornbury Middle Sch
BD3 ... 75 E8
Thornbury Pk WF2 ... 141 F4
Thornbury Rd Bradford BD3 . 75 D7
Wakefield WF2 ... 141 F4
Thornbury St BD3 ... 75 D7
Thorncliff Green Rd HD8 .. 174 C7
Thorncliff La HD8 ... 174 C7
Thorncliffe Est WF17 ... 118 A3
Thorncliffe La HD8 ... 175 D7
Thorncliffe Rd Batley WF17 118 B3
Bradford BD8 ... 55 D1
Keighley BD22 ... 34 F6
Thorncliffe St HD3 ... 135 B1
Thorncroft Rd BD6 ... 74 A1
Thorndale Rise BD2 ... 55 F4
Thorndene Way BD4 ... 96 A7
Thorne Cl Normanton WF6 .. 123 C1
Pudsey LS28 ... 76 B8
Thorne End Rd S75 ... 178 B2
Thorne Gr LS26 ... 101 A6
Thorne Rd HD1 ... 153 E4
Thorne St 1 HX4 ... 134 A4
Thornefield Cres WF3 ... 119 D8
Thorner CE Primary Sch
LS14 ... 46 A6
Thorner Gr BD20 ... 5 E2
Thorner La Bardsey LS23 ... 29 D2
Barwick in E LS14 ... 45 E1
Scarcroft LS14 ... 45 E8
Thorner Rd Bardsey LS23 ... 29 E1
Barwick in E LS14 ... 46 D8
Bramham LS23 ... 30 B2
Thornes Ind Est WF1 ... 142 C4
Thornes La WF1, WF2 ... 142 C4
Thornes Lane Wharf WF1 ... 142 D4
Thornes Moor Ave WF2 ... 142 A3
Thornes Moor Cl WF2 ... 142 A3
Thornes Moor Dr WF2 ... 142 A3
Thornes Moor Rd WF2 ... 142 A3
Thornes Office Pk WF2 ... 142 B3
Thornes Park Ct WF2 ... 142 B3
Thornes Pk Brighouse HD6 . 115 A1
Shipley BD18 ... 55 D5
Thornes Rd WF2 ... 142 A3
Thorney La HX2 ... 90 D2
Thornfield Bingley BD16 ... 36 E4
Dewsbury WF12 ... 139 D6
9 Haworth BD22 ... 51 D7
Thornfield Ave
Bradford BD6 ... 94 D8
Huddersfield HD4 ... 153 E3
Pudsey LS28 ... 57 C3
Thornfield Ct 4 LS15 ... 62 B2
Thornfield Dr 3 LS15 ... 62 B2
Thornfield Hall 4 4 BD13 ... 72 E6
Thornfield Mews
Bingley BD16 ... 36 E7
Leeds LS15 ... 62 B2
Thornfield Mount WF17 ... 97 A1
Thornfield Pl BD2 ... 56 C3
Thornfield Rd
Huddersfield HD4 ... 153 E3
Leeds LS16 ... 59 B8
Thornfield Rise 2 HX4 ... 134 B7
Thornfield St 1 HX4 ... 134 B7
Thornfield Terr BD15 ... 53 B4
Thornfield Way LS15 ... 62 B2
Thornhill Ave
Haworth BD22 ... 34 E3
Huddersfield HD3 ... 153 C7
Shipley BD18 ... 55 D5
Thornhill Bridge La HD6 ... 115 A3
Thornhill Cl Netherton WF4 158 B7
Pudsey LS28 ... 57 B7
Walton WF2 ... 161 A6
Thornhill Croft Leeds LS12 . 209 E2
Walton WF2 ... 161 A7
Thornhill Dr Pudsey LS28 ... 57 B8
Shipley BD18 ... 55 D5
Walton WF2 ... 161 A7
Thornhill Gr Pudsey LS28 ... 57 B7
Shipley BD18 ... 55 D5
Steeton BD20 ... 17 B6
Thornhill Hey HX4 ... 133 F2
Thornhill High Sch WF12 .. 139 E1
Thornhill Jun & Inf Sch
WF12 ... 139 E1
Thornhill Lees C of E
Infants Sch WF12 ... 139 C4
Thornhill Park Ave WF12 . 139 D4
Thornhill Pl Bradford BD3 ... 75 E8
1 Brighouse HD6 ... 115 A1
Leeds LS12 ... 209 E2
Thornhill Rd Brighouse HD6 115 A1
Castleford WF10 ... 124 E6
Dewsbury WF12 ... 139 C5
Dewsbury, West Town
WF12, WF13 ... 139 B7
Huddersfield HD3 ... 153 A6
Huddersfield, Edgerton HD3 153 D8
Leeds LS12 ... 209 F2
Netherton WF4 ... 158 A8
Steeton BD20 ... 17 B6
Thornhill St
Dewsbury WF12 ... 139 D6
Leeds LS12 ... 209 E3
Pudsey LS28 ... 57 B6
Wakefield WF1 ... 216 B1
Thornhill Street Bglws
WF1 ... 216 B1
Thornhill Terr BD3 ... 75 D8
Thornhills Beck La HD6 ... 115 B4
Thornhills La HD6 ... 115 C4
Thornie View WF12 ... 139 C4
Thornlea Cl LS19 ... 39 F5
Thornleigh WF12 ... 139 D6
Thornleigh Ave WF2 ... 142 C3
Thornleigh Cres WF2 ... 142 C3
Thornleigh Croft WF2 ... 142 C4
Thornleigh Dr
Liversedge WF15 ... 117 B5
Wakefield WF2 ... 142 C4
Thornleigh Garth WF2 ... 142 C3
Thornleigh Gdns LS9 ... 212 C2
Thornleigh Gr 1 Leeds LS9 212 C2
Wakefield WF2 ... 142 C3
Thornleigh Mount 3 LS9 . 212 C2
Thornleigh Rd
Huddersfield HD4 ... 153 C3
Wakefield WF2 ... 142 C4
Thornleigh St 4 LS9 ... 212 C2
Thornleigh View 2 LS9 ... 212 C2
Thornmead Rd BD17 ... 38 D2
Thornsgill Ave BD4 ... 75 C3
Thornton Ave LS12 ... 209 D3
Thornton Cl Batley WF17 ... 96 F3
Hemsworth WF9 ... 181 D5
Thornton Ct 11 BD8 ... 73 F8
Thornton First Sch BD13 ... 72 D6
Thornton Gdns LS12 ... 209 D3
Thornton Gr LS12 ... 209 D3
Thornton La BD5 ... 74 C3
Thornton Lodge Hall HD1 . 153 E4
Thornton Lodge Rd HD1 ... 153 F4
Thornton Moor Rd
Denholme BD13 ... 71 B7
Oxenhope BD13 ... 71 B7
Thornton Old Rd BD8 ... 73 E7
Thornton Rd
Bradford BD1, BD13, BD8 ... 73 C7
Brighouse HD6 ... 135 E8
Denholme BD13 ... 71 F5
Dewsbury WF12 ... 139 C4
Thornton BD13 ... 72 C6
Thornton Sch BD13 ... 73 B6
Thornton St Bradford BD1 ... 74 C7
Burley in W LS29 ... 9 E2
Cleckheaton,
Hartshead Moor Side BD19 . 116 A6
Cleckheaton, Marsh BD19 ... 116 F6
Dewsbury WF13 ... 139 B8
Halifax HX1 ... 202 B1
Thornton Terr 2 HX1 ... 202 B1
Thornton View Rd BD14 ... 73 C3
Thornton's Arc LS1 ... 211 F4
Thorntons Dale LS18 ... 58 B6
Thorntonville BD19 ... 116 F6
Thorntree Ave WF4 ... 143 E1
Thorntree Cl WF8 ... 147 D4
Thorntree Ct WF4 ... 143 E1

Thornville 5 LS27 98 B7
Thornville Ave 8 LS6 205 E2
Thornville Cres 11 LS6 205 E3
Thornville Ct BD8 55 D2
Thornville Gr 6 LS6 205 E2
Thornville Mount
3 Dewsbury WF13 139 A6
5 Leeds LS6 205 E2
Thornville Pl
Dewsbury WF13 139 A6
Leeds LS6 205 E2
Thornville Rd LS6 205 E2
Thornville Row LS6 205 E2
Thornville St
Dewsbury WF13 139 A6
Leeds LS6 205 E2
Thornville Terr
Dewsbury WF13 139 B6
7 Leeds LS6 205 E2
Thornville View LS6 205 E2
Thornville Wlk WF13 139 A6
Thorp Arch HM Prison LS23 15 A2
Thorp Arch Trad Est LS23 15 B2
Thorp Ave HD7 189 B4
Thorp Garth BD10 56 B8
Thorp Pyn Croft HD5 154 E7
Thorpe Ave BD13 73 A6
Thorpe Cl LS20 39 B8
Thorpe Cres LS10 99 C3
Thorpe Ct LS10 99 C3
Thorpe Dr LS20 22 C1
Thorpe Garth LS10 99 B3
Thorpe Gate Est WF9 165 A4
Thorpe Gdns LS10 99 C3
Thorpe Gr Middleton LS10 99 C4
Thornton BD13 73 A6
Thorpe Green Dr HD7 152 E6
Thorpe La East Ardsley WF3 98 F1
Guiseley LS20 22 B1
Huddersfield HD5 155 A4
Middleton WF3 99 A2
Thorpe Audlin WF8 165 A4
Thorpe Lower La
Middleton WF3 99 F2
Rothwell WF3 100 A3
Thorpe Middle Sch BD10 56 B8
Thorpe Mount LS10 99 B3
Thorpe Pl HX6 111 C2
Thorpe Prim Sch WF3 99 E2
Thorpe Rd
East Ardsley WF3 120 C7
Middleton LS10 99 C4
Pudsey LS28 76 E8
Thornton BD13 73 A6
Thorpe Sq LS10 99 D4
Thorpe St Halifax HX3 92 B2
Keighley BD21 35 C8
Leeds LS15 81 A8
Middleton LS10 99 C3
Thorpe View Middleton LS10 99 C3
Ossett WF5 140 D8
Wakefield WF2 141 F6
Thorpes Ave HD8 192 A7
Thorpes Cres HD8 175 A1
Thorverton Dr BD4 95 E8
Thorverton Gr BD4 95 E8
Threadneedle St HD1 154 A6
Threap Croft HX2 91 F6
Three Lane Ends WF10 124 A8
Three Nooked Mews BD10 56 D8
Three Nooks S72 180 B1
Three Nooks La S72 180 B1
Three Sisters Sq 1 HD1 154 A8
Threshfield BD17 38 C3
Threshfield Cres BD11 96 A6
Thrift Way BD16 36 F2
Throstle Ave LS10 99 B3
Throstle Bank HX1 202 B1
Throstle Crest WF7 145 A8
Throstle Dr LS10 99 A3
Throstle Farm Jun & Inf Sch WF11 126 E2
Throstle Hill LS10 99 B3
Throstle La LS10 99 C3
Throstle Mount
Middleton LS10 99 B3
Sowerby Bridge HX2 111 F5
Throstle Nest WF17 118 A4
Throstle Nest Cl LS21 10 D2
Throstle Nest Rd BD20 5 D2
Throstle Nest View 4 LS18 58 C7
Throstle Par LS10 99 B3
Throstle Pl LS10 99 B3
Throstle Rd Middleton LS10 99 C3
Middleton LS10 99 E5
Throstle Row LS10 99 B3
Throstle Sq LS10 99 D3
Throstle St Middleton LS10 99 B3
Todmorden OL14 129 B6
Throstle Terr LS10 99 C3
Throstle View LS10 99 D3
Throstle Way WF11 126 E2
Throstle Wlk LS10 99 B3
Throxenby Way BD14 73 C4
Thrum Hall Cl HX1 202 B3
Thrum Hall Dr HX1 202 B3
Thrum Hall La HX1 202 B3
Thrumpton Rd S71 178 F1
Thrush Hill Rd 4 HX7 89 E1
Thrush St BD21 35 D8
Thryberg St BD3 75 A7
Thunder Bridge La HD8 173 D4
Thunderton La HX6 111 C2
Thurgory Gate HD8 155 E3
Thurgory La HD8 155 E4
Thurley Dr BD4 75 B2
Thurley Rd BD4 75 B2
Thurnscoe Gooseacre Jun & Mid Sch S63 194 C1
Thurnscoe La S72 194 A1
Thurnscoe Rd BD1 201 A4
Thurrish La HX7 69 B6
Thursby St BD3 75 B7
Thurstonland Bank Rd HD7 172 D1
Thurstonland Endowed Sch HD4 172 F2
Thurstonland Rd HD4 172 E5
Thwaite Gate LS10 215 F3
Thwaite La LS10 80 A3
Thwaite Mills (Mus) LS10 80 B3
Thwaites Ave LS29 8 C5
Thwaites Bridge BD21 35 F7
Thwaites Brow Rd BD21 35 F6
Thwaites La BD21 35 E7
Tichborne Rd 4 BD5 74 E3
Tichborne Rd W BD5 74 E3
Tichborne St FW15 116 E4
Tichbourne St WF17 117 F4
Tickhill St BD3 75 B6
Tiding Field La HD7 151 D2
Tidswell St WF16 117 E4
Tilbury Ave 7 LS11 213 F4
Tilbury Gr 5 LS11 213 F4
Tilbury Mount LS11 213 F4
Tilbury Par 6 LS11 213 F4
Tilbury Rd LS11 213 F4
Tilbury Row LS11 213 F4
Tilbury Terr LS11 213 F4
Tilbury View 8 LS11 213 F4
Tile La LS16 42 D3
Tile St BD8 55 B1
Tile Terr HD6 115 A1
Tiley Sq 5 BD5 74 E4
Till Carr La HX3 115 A8
Tillotson Ave HX6 112 A3
Tillotson St BD20 5 D2
Tillotson's Ct BD20 4 A2
Tim La BD22 34 B1
Timber St 3 Elland HX5 134 F6
3 Keighley BD21 35 E8
Timbercliffe OL15 129 D1
Timberwood HD8 173 D4
Timble Dr BD16 37 B4
Timmey La HX2 112 A5
Timothy La WF17 118 D7
Tinderley Gr HD5 154 F4
Tingley Ave WF3 98 E1
Tingley Comm
East Ardsley LS27 98 C1
Morley LS27 98 C1
Tingley Cres WF3 98 C1
Tinker La Lepton HD8 156 B2
Meltham HD7 170 D1
Tinkingfield La LS24 15 C8
Tinkler Stile BD10 55 F8
Tinsel Rd WF12 118 F1
Tinshill Ave LS16 41 E3
Tinshill Cl LS16 41 E3
Tinshill Cres LS16 41 E4
Tinshill Dr LS16 41 E5
Tinshill Garth LS16 41 E4
Tinshill Gr LS16 41 F4
Tinshill La LS16 41 E3
Tinshill Mount LS16 41 E4
Tinshill Primary Sch LS16 41 E3
Tinshill Rd LS16 41 D4
Tinshill View LS16 41 E4
Tinshill Wlk LS16 41 E4
Tinsworth Rd WF2 160 A4
Tintagel Ct WF6 123 B3
Tintern Ave Bradford BD8 73 D7
Huddersfield HD3 152 F5
Tippaty La WF11 127 A7
Tipping La HD8 175 D7
Tisma Dr BD4 95 C8
Titan District Ctr BD12 94 C2
Tithe Barn Fold LS15 63 D7
Tithe Barn La LS17 28 C2
Tithe Barn Rd WF11 127 A4
Tithe Barn St
Dewsbury WF13 139 D8
Horbury WF4 141 A1
Tithe House Way HD2 136 E6
Titus La HD8 174 D6
Titus St BD18 54 F8
Tiverton Ho 4 BD5 201 B1
Tiverton Wlk BD4 75 E2
Tivoli Pl Bradford BD5 74 C4
Ilkley LS29 8 C3
Tivy Dale S75 193 E4
Tivy Dale Cl S75 193 E4
Tivy Dale Dr S75 193 E4
Toby La BD7 74 A5
Toby Wood La HD8 191 D5
Todd Terr 2 BD7 74 B4
Todley Hall Rd BD22 34 A6
Todmorden High Sch OL14 107 F6
Todmorden Old Rd OL13 106 B5
Todmorden Rd
Bacup OL13 106 B4
Littleborough OL15 129 D2
Todmorden Sta OL14 108 A5
Todwell La BD5 74 C3
Toft La HD4 172 F6
Toft St LS12 210 A2
Tofts Ave BD12 94 C2
Tofts Gr HD6 135 F7
Tofts Grove Gdns HD6 135 F7
Tofts House Cl LS28 76 E7
Tofts Rd Cleckheaton BD19 116 D7
Pudsey LS28 76 D7
Pudsey LS28 76 E7
Toftshaw Fold BD4 95 D8
Toftshaw La BD4 95 E8
Toftshaw New Rd BD4 95 D8
Toll Bar La WF2 120 D1
Toll Bar Rd WF10 123 F7
Toller Dr BD9 54 E3
Toller Gr BD9 54 F3
Toller La BD8, BD9 55 A1
Toller Pk BD9 54 F3
Tolson Cres HD5 154 F7
Tolson Grange HD5 154 F5
Tolson Memorial Mus HD5 154 E6
Tolson St Dewsbury WF13 118 C1
Ossett WF5 140 B8
Tolson's Yd 12 HD5 154 D5
Tolworth Fold 1 BD15 73 B8
Tom Dando Cl WF6 123 E2
Tom La HD4 153 B3
Tom Wood Ash La WF9 183 E7
Tombridge Cres WF9 163 B1
Tomling Cote La BD20 18 B8
Tommy La HD7 152 E1
Tonbridge Cl BD6 93 F8
Tonbridge St LS1 206 A1
Tong App LS12 77 D6
Tong Dr LS12 77 D7
Tong Gate LS12 77 D7
Tong Gn LS12 77 D6
Tong Hall Bsns Ctr BD4 76 D2
Tong La Bacup OL13 106 B2
Birkenshaw BD4 76 E2
Tong Park First Sch BD17 38 F4
Tong Rd LS12 77 C6
Tong Recn Ctr BD4 96 A8
Tong Sch BD4 96 A8
Tong St Birkenshaw BD4 95 F8
Bradford BD4 75 D1
Tong Way LS12 77 D7
Tong Wlk LS12 77 D7
Tongue La LS6 42 F1
Toot Hill La HX6 111 B2
Total St WF1 216 C1
Toothill Ave HD6 136 A7
Toothill Bank HD6 136 A7
Toothill La HD6 136 A7
Toothill La S HD6 135 F6
Top Farm (Mus) WF4 145 B1
Top Fold WF11 105 A4
Top Headlands WF5 140 C5
Top House Farm Mews WF11 105 A4
Top La Clayton DN5 194 C5
West Bretton WF4 158 D1
Top Meadow WF14 137 F2
Top Moor Side LS11 211 D1
Top O' Th' Bank HD7 172 E1
Top o' Th' Close Rd OL14 129 C6
Top o' Th' Hill Rd OL14 108 A1
Top o' th' Moor HD4 173 C2
Top o' The Hill HD7 169 E7
Top of Carr 1 WF17 118 B2
Top of the Hill HD7 172 E1
Top Orch WF4 162 B1
Top Rd HD8 191 E7
Top Row S75 177 E3
Top St Hemsworth WF9 181 C7
Todmorden OL14 128 F7
Top Stone Cl LS25 105 E3
Topaz Cl HD2 136 C2
Topcliffe Ave LS27 98 D4
Topcliffe Ct 8 LS27 98 D4
Topcliffe Fold LS27 98 C2
Topcliffe Gn 7 LS27 98 D4
Topcliffe Gr LS27 98 C2
Topcliffe La
Morley, Tingley Common LS27 98 D2
Morley, Topcliffe LS27 98 C2
Topcliffe Mead 6 LS27 98 D4
Topcliffe Mews 9 LS27 98 D4
Tor Ave BD12 94 C1
Tor View HD7 172 C2
Torcote Cres HD2 136 C5
Tordoff Ave BD7 73 E5
Tordoff Gn 4 BD6 94 B8
Tordoff Pl LS5 59 A4
Tordoff Rd 5 BD12 94 E6
Tordoff Terr LS5 59 A4
Toronto Pl LS7 204 A2
Torre Cl LS9 80 A8
Torre Cres BD6 73 D1
Torre Dr LS9 208 A1
Torre Gdns LS9 212 C4
Torre Gn LS9 212 C4
Torre Gr Bradford BD6 73 D1
Leeds LS9 208 A1
Torre Hill LS9 208 B1
Torre La LS9 80 B8
Torre Mount LS9 208 A1
Torre Pl LS9 80 A8
Torre Rd Bradford BD6 73 D1
Leeds LS9 80 A8
Torre Sq LS9 208 B1
Torre View LS9 208 B1
Torre Wlk LS9 208 B1
Torridon Cres BD6 93 E6
Torridon Rd WF12 118 E2
Totties La HD7 189 D5
Toulston La LS23 30 F2
Tower Ave WF9 183 A8
Tower Bldgs 1 WF16 117 D3
Tower Cswy OL14 107 B7
Tower Dr The LS21 24 E6
Tower Gdns 2 HX2 112 F4
Tower Gr LS12 209 D4
Tower Hill HX6 112 B4
Tower House St LS2 206 C1
Tower La Leeds LS12 77 F8
Leeds, Hill Top LS12 209 D4
Tower Pl 6 LS12 77 F8
Tower Rd BD18 54 E8
Tower St Bradford BD2 56 B2
Todmorden OL14 86 A1
Towers Cl WF4 162 A8
Towers La WF4 144 B1
Towers Paddock WF10 125 A7
Towers Sq LS6 60 A8
Towers Way LS6 60 A8
Towlerton La WF2 120 E2
Town Ave HD1 154 C8
Town Cl LS18 41 B1
Town Cres HD1 154 C8
Town End Bradford BD7 74 A4
Garforth LS25 82 E8
Gildersome LS27 97 D7
Huddersfield, Almondbury HD5 154 F4
Huddersfield, Town End HD7 152 D4
Ossett WF5 140 D5
Town End Ave
Ackworth M T WF7 164 C7
Holmfirth HD7 189 C6
Town End Cl Glusburn BD20 16 D6
Leeds LS13 58 E1
Town End Cres HD7 189 C7
Town End La HD8 156 A3
Town End Rd Bradford BD14 73 B5
Holmfirth HD7 189 B7
Town Fields Rd HX5 134 E6
Town Gate
Bradford, Idle BD10 56 B8
Bradford, Wyke BD12 94 C3
Brighouse BD19 115 F8
Guiseley LS20 22 E1
Hebden Bridge HX2 90 B1
Heptonstall HX7 88 F5
Holmfirth HD7 189 A5
Holmfirth, Hepworth HD7 189 E2
Holmfirth, Netherthong HD7 188 F8
Holmfirth, Upperthong HD7 188 D5
Kirkburton HD8 173 E8
Lepton HD8 156 A4
Marsden HD7 168 F4
Northowram HX3 93 A2
Pudsey LS28 57 B6
Sowerby Bridge HX6 111 E3
Town Gate Cl LS20 22 F1
Town Gn WF12 139 E7
Town Hall Bldgs HX5 135 A6
Town Hall Sq 4 LS19 40 B7
Town Hall St 4 Elland HX5 134 F6
Holmfirth HD7 189 A5
Keighley BD21 35 C7
Mirfield WF14 138 A4
Sowerby Bridge HX6 112 B4
Town Hall St E 2 HX1 203 E3
Town Hall Way WF12 139 D8
Town Head HD7 171 F5
Town Hill LS23 30 D2
Town Hill St BD16 54 B6
Town La BD10 39 B1
Town Moor HD4 172 F2
Town Pl HD1 154 C8
Town Rd HD5 137 C1
Town St Batley WF17 118 C2
Birkenshaw BD11 96 A6
Dewsbury WF12 139 F7
Gildersome LS27 97 D7
Guiseley LS20 22 E1
Hemsworth WF9 181 C7
Horsforth LS18 41 B1
Leeds LS7 204 A3
Leeds, Beeston LS11 213 E2
Leeds, Moor Top LS12 209 E3
Middleton LS10 99 C5
Pudsey, Farsley LS28 57 D3
Pudsey, Rodley LS13 57 F5
Pudsey, Stanningley LS28 57 E2
Rothwell WF3 100 D2
Yeadon LS19 40 B7
Yeadon, Rawdon LS19 40 D3
Town Street Mews LS7 204 A3
Town Street Wlk 8 LS7 204 A3
Town Terr HD1 154 C8
Town The WF12 139 D2
Town Top HD5 137 C1
Town Wells Dr LS28 57 B6
Townend Pl Glusburn BD20 16 C6
8 Pudsey LS28 76 F8
Townend Rd LS12 209 E1
Townfield BD15 53 C5
Townfield La HX7 88 F5
Townfold WF5 140 E6
Towngate 8 Baildon BD17 38 C4
Brighouse, Clifton HD6 115 E2
Brighouse, Hipperholme HX3 114 C8
Halifax HX3 114 A4
Huddersfield HD4 154 A2
Keighley BD21 35 C7
Mapplewell S75 178 B1
Mirfield WF14 138 B6
Ossett WF5 140 F6
Shipley BD18 55 D7
Towngate Ave HD6 115 D3
Towngate Gr WF14 138 B5
Towngate House 1 HX5 134 F7
Towngate Junior & Infants Sch WF5 140 F6
Towngate Rd WF17 118 A5
Townhead Fold LS29 6 E8
Townley Ave HX3 114 A4
Townley Rd WF2 141 D4
Towton Dr WF10 124 A6
Track Mount WF17 118 B2
Track Rd WF17 118 B3
Trafalgar Cl HD2 136 B4
Trafalgar Rd
Dewsbury WF13 118 B1
Ilkley LS29 8 B4
Trafalgar Sq 2 HX1 202 C1
Trafalgar St Batley WF17 118 A4
Bradford BD1 201 B4
3 Halifax HX1 202 C1
Leeds LS2 212 A4
Trafford Ave LS9 208 B2
Trafford Gr LS9 208 B3
Trafford Terr LS9 208 B2
Tramways BD12 94 F5
Tranbeck Rd LS20 22 B1
Tranfield Ave LS20 22 C1
Tranfield Cl LS20 22 C1
Tranfield Ct LS20 22 C1
Tranfield Gdns LS20 22 C1
Tranmere Ct LS20 22 C1
Tranmere Dr LS20 22 C1
Tranquility LS15 62 C2
Tranquility Ave LS15 62 C2
Tranquility Ct 2 LS15 62 C2
Tranquility Wlk 1 LS15 62 C2
Transperience Mus BD12 94 F5
Transperience Way BD12, BD4 94 F6
Transvaal Terr WF17 118 B7
Tranter Gr BD4 75 E5
Tranter Pl LS15 80 E8
Travis House OL14 129 A7
Travis Lacey Terr 8 WF13 139 B8
Tredgold Ave LS16 24 F2
Tredgold Cl LS16 24 E2
Tredgold Cres LS16 24 E2
Tredgold Garth LS16 24 E3
Tree La HX2 90 F5
Tree Top View BD13 72 C2
Treefield Ind Est LS27 97 D6
Trees St BD8 55 C1
Trelawn Ave LS6 59 D5
Trelawn Cres 11 LS6 59 D5
Trelawn Pl LS6 59 D5
Trelawn St LS6 59 D5
Trelawn Terr LS6 59 D5
Tremont Gdns LS10 215 E2
Trenam Park Dr BD10 39 A2
Trenance Dr BD18 54 F7
Trenance Gdns HX4 134 A7
Trenholme Ave BD6 94 B6
Trenic Cres LS6 205 D3
Trenic Dr LS6 205 D3
Trent Ave Garforth LS25 83 B6
Normanton WF6 123 A4
Trent Rd LS9 208 A1
Trent St LS11 211 E1
Trentham Ave 8 LS11 214 B2
Trentham Gr 7 LS11 214 B2
Trentham Pl 9 LS11 214 B2
Trentham Row 6 LS11 214 B2
Trentham St LS11 214 B2
Trentham Terr 23 LS11 214 B3
Trenton Dr BD8 55 C1
Trenton Rd WF17 118 F3
Trescoe Ave LS13 58 E1
Tresham Ct WF12 118 F2
Trevelyan Sq LS1 211 F3
Trevelyan St
Brighouse HD6 115 A5
9 Huddersfield HD5 154 D5
Trevor Terr WF2 120 E6
Triangle Bsns Pk WF17 97 A3
Triangle C of E Infant & Junior Sch HX6 111 E1
Triangle The HD1 153 E5
Triath Ct WF17 117 E6
Trilby St WF1 216 C3
Trimmingham La HX2 202 A2
Trimmingham Rd HX2 202 A2
Trimmingham Villas HX2 202 A2
Trinity & All Saints' Coll LS18 41 A3
Trinity Bsns Ctr WF1 216 C1
Trinity Church Gate WF1 216 C2
Trinity Ct HD7 171 F4
Trinity Dr HD8 191 F5
Trinity Gr 2 HD6 115 A4
Trinity House 1 WF1 216 C2
Trinity Pl Bingley BD16 37 A2
Halifax HX1 203 E2
Trinity Rd Bradford BD5 74 D5
Halifax HX1 203 E2
Trinity Rise LS21 23 B7
Trinity St Batley WF17 118 C2
Halifax HX1 203 E2
Hebden Bridge HX7 88 F3
Huddersfield HD1 153 F7
Keighley BD21 35 C8
Leeds LS1 211 F4
Mirfield WF14 138 A4
Pontefract WF8 125 D1
Wakefield WF1 142 F3
Trinity Street Arc LS1 211 F3
Trinity View Bradford BD12 94 E7
Halifax HX3 203 F2
Ossett WF5 140 D7
Trinity Wlk Bradford BD12 94 E7
South Elmsall WF9 183 A4
Trip Garth LS22 13 B2
Trip La LS22 13 A2
Tristram Ave BD5 75 A2
Tristram Ctr The LS12 213 E4
Triumph Cl LS11, LS12 211 D2

Troon Dr HD2 135 F3
Troon Way WF2 142 A2
Trooper La HX3 113 E5
Trooper Terr HX3 203 F2
Trough La
Cullingworth BD13 52 A3
Denholme BD13 52 A3
South Elmsall WF9 183 C3
Trough Well La WF2 120 E3
Troughton Pl LS28 76 F5
Troughton St LS28 76 F5
Troutbeck Ave BD17 37 E1
Troy Hill LS27 98 A5
Troy Rd Horsforth LS18 41 C2
Morley LS27 98 A5
Troy Rise LS27 98 B5
Troydale Gdns LS28 77 B5
Troydale Gr LS28 77 B5
Troydale La LS28 77 B5
Trueman Ave WF16 117 E5
Trueman Ct BD12 94 E6
Trueman Way WF9 183 A4
Truncliffe BD5 74 D1
Trundles La WF11 127 B4
Truro Dr WF6 123 B3
Truro St LS12 209 F4
Truro Wlk WF6 123 B3
Trust Fold LS25 105 E3
Tubby La HD2 136 B1
Tudor Barn Ct BD18 55 D7
Tudor Cl WF8 146 C5
Tudor Croft HD2 136 F5
Tudor Ct 17 Bradford BD5 201 B1
Pudsey LS28 57 C2
Tudor Gdns LS11 213 E2
Tudor House 4 WF1 216 B2
Tudor Lawns Leeds LS8 61 C7
Lofthouse Gate WF2 120 E5
Tudor St Bradford BD5 74 D4
Slaithwaite HD7 170 A8
Tudor Way Castleford WF10 125 B8
Dewsbury WF12 139 B3
Tuel La HX6 112 B4
Tuel Lane Infant Sch HX6 112 B4
Tufton St BD20 5 E1
Tulip Ret Pk LS10 215 D3
Tulip St Haworth BD22 51 C5
Leeds LS10 215 D3
Tumbling Cl WF5 140 E6
Tumbling Hill WF8 147 A5
Tumbling Hill St BD7 74 D6
Tun La S72 180 D7
Tunnacliffe Rd HD4 154 B3
Tunnel St Denholme BD13 71 D8
Huddersfield HD4 171 C7
Tunnicliffe Pl BD20 5 D1
Tunstall Gn BD4 75 E3
Tunstall Rd LS11 214 C3
Tunwell La BD2 56 C4
Tunwell St BD2 56 C4
Tup La WF4 180 C8
Turbary Ave 2 LS28 57 E2
Turbid La HD4 171 A6
Turbury La Elland HX4 133 E8
Sowerby Bridge HX4 133 E8
Turf Ct BD13 52 C5
Turf La BD13 52 C5
Turgate La HX6 111 A1
Turkey Hill LS28 76 F6
Turley Cote La HX4 134 C2
Turn o The Nook WF5 140 C6
Turnberry Ave LS17 43 B4
Turnberry Cl
East Ardsley WF3 119 D8
Leeds LS17 43 B4
Turnberry Ct Keighley BD20 18 A3
Normanton WF6 123 D1
Turnberry Dr
East Ardsley WF3 119 D8
Leeds LS17 43 B4
Turnberry Gdns WF3 119 D8
Turnberry Gr Cudworth S72 180 C1
Leeds LS17 43 B4
Turnberry Pl LS17 43 B4
Turnberry Rise LS17 43 B4
Turnberry View LS17 43 B4
Turnbridge Rd HD1 154 C6
Turnbull Ct LS8 61 D5
Turner Ave Batley WF17 118 C5
Bradford BD7 73 F5
Turner Ave N HX2 91 D5
Turner Ave S HX2 91 E4
Turner Cl WF3 119 E8
Turner Cres LS21 11 B1
Turner Dr WF3 119 E8
Turner La Addingham LS29 6 C6
Addingham LS29 6 D8
Halifax HX3 92 D1
Turner Pl Bradford BD7 74 B5
Halifax HX2 91 E5
Turner St 5 LS28 57 D3
Turner's Ct 1 HX3 92 B2
Turners Yd LS28 57 D3
Turney St HX3 92 A2
Turnip La WF12 139 D2
Turnkey Park LS12 78 C4
Turnpike St HX5 135 A7
Turnshaw Rd Haworth BD22 33 F2
Kirkburton HD8 174 A6
Turnshaws Ave HD8 174 A7
Turnshaws Cl HD8 174 A7
Turnshaws Special Sch
HD8 174 A7
Turnsteads Ave BD19 116 B8
Turnsteads Cl BD19 116 C8
Turnsteads Cres BD19 116 C8
Turnsteads Dr BD19 116 C8
Turnsteads Mount BD19 116 C8
Turnstone Ct 3 LS10 99 D5
Turnways The LS6 59 C4
Turret Hall Rd HX7 88 C2
Turret Royd Rd HX7 88 D2
Turton Gn LS27 97 D7
Turton St WF1 216 C2
Turton Vale LS27 97 D6
Turver's La WF11 127 F3
Turvin Rd
Littleborough OL15 130 D2
Ripponden OL15 130 D2
Twain Cres WF10 125 C6
Tweed Cl WF17 97 A1
Tweedale Gdns WF13 139 B8
Tweedale St 1 WF13 139 B8
Tweedy St BD15 53 C5
Twelfth Ave WF15 116 B5
Twickenham Ct BD8 55 D2
Twitch Hill WF4 141 B1
Twivey St WF10 124 C7
Two Gates HD7 151 E1
Two Laws Rd BD22 49 D8
Tyas Gr LS9 80 B7
Tyas La HD7 151 B2
Tyburn La HD8 175 C6
Tyersal Ave BD4 75 F6
Tyersal Cl BD4 75 F6
Tyersal Cres BD4 75 F6
Tyersal Ct BD4 75 F6
Tyersal Dr BD4 75 F6
Tyersal First Sch BD4 75 D5
Tyersal Garth BD4 75 F6
Tyersal Gn BD4 75 F6
Tyersal Gr BD4 75 F6
Tyersal La Bradford BD4 75 F4
Pudsey BD4, LS28 76 A5
Tyersal Pk BD4 75 F6
Tyersal Rd BD4 75 F6
Tyersal Terr BD4 75 F6
Tyersal View BD4 75 E6
Tyersal Wlk BD4 75 F6
Tyler Cl WF6 123 E2
Tyndale Ave WF4 141 C2
Tyndale Wlk WF16 117 E5
Tyne St Bradford BD3 201 C4
1 Haworth BD22 51 D7
Keighley BD21 35 D7
Tynedale Ct LS7 60 A6
Tynwald Cl LS17 43 A2
Tynwald Dr LS17 43 A2
Tynwald Gdns LS17 43 A2
Tynwald Gn LS17 43 A3
Tynwald Hill LS17 43 A2
Tynwald Mount LS17 43 A2
Tynwald Rd LS17 43 A2
Tynwald Wlk LS17 43 A3
Tyrrel St BD1 201 B3
Tyrrell Ct WF2 141 D7
Tyson St Bradford BD1 201 A4
Halifax HX1 202 A2

Ullswater Ave WF12 118 E3
Ullswater Cl Batley WF12 118 E2
Knottingley WF11 126 E1
Ullswater Cres Leeds LS15 80 E7
Rothwell LS26 101 C6
Ullswater Dr Bradford BD6 93 F6
Wetherby LS22 13 C6
Ullswater Rd WF12 118 E3
Ullswater Rise LS22 13 C5
Una Pl HD2 153 E8
Underbank Ave HX7 88 C1
Underbank Old Rd HD7 189 B4
Undercliffe First Sch BD2 56 B1
Undercliffe La BD3 56 A1
Undercliffe Mid Sch
Bradford BD3 55 F1
Bradford BD2 56 B1
Undercliffe Old Rd BD2 56 B1
Undercliffe Pl HX3 114 B7
Undercliffe Rd BD2 56 B3
Undercliffe Rise LS29 8 E2
Undercliffe St BD3 56 B1
Undercliffe Terr 1 HX2 112 F4
Underwood Dr LS19 40 C1
Underwood Ho BD3 201 C4
Union Cross Yd HX1 203 E3
Union Gr WF15 117 B3
Union House La BD13 73 C2
Union La HX2 71 D1
Union Pl LS11 211 E2
Union Rd Bradford BD12 94 C7
Bradford, Great Horton BD7 74 B5
Liversedge WF15 117 B3
Union Sq WF1 216 C2
Union St Baildon BD17 38 E2
8 Batley WF17 96 F1
Bingley BD16 36 E7
Castleford WF10 124 B7
Dewsbury WF13 139 D8
6 Elland HX4 134 D7
Halifax HX1 203 E2
Hemsworth WF9 181 E6
6 Huddersfield HD1 154 B7
Huddersfield, Oakes HD3 153 B8
Leeds LS2 212 A4
Liversedge WF16 117 C3
1 Morley LS27 98 C8
Ossett WF5 140 D6
Otley LS21 22 F7
11 Queensbury BD13 72 E1
Slaithwaite HD7 151 F1
Sowerby Bridge HX6 111 E1
Sowerby Bridge HX6 112 C4
Wakefield WF1 216 B3
Union St S OL14 108 B5
Union Terr LS7 60 C6
Union Yd BD10 56 B8
Unity Cl LS6 206 B4
Unity Ct WF13 139 B8
Unity Hall Ct WF3 119 F7
Unity St Hebden Bridge HX7 89 A4
Keighley BD20 18 F2
Rothwell WF3 100 D3
Todmorden OL14 129 A8
Unity St N BD16 36 F2
Unity St S BD16 36 F2
Unity Terr HX1 202 A2
Univ of Bradford
Bradford, Little Horton Green
BD5 74 C5
Bradford, Shearbridge BD7 74 D6
Univ of Bradford
Management Ctr BD9 55 B4
Univ of Huddersfield HD1 154 B5
University Rd LS2 206 A2
University St WF10 124 D7
Unna Way HD1 154 A7
Unwin Pl BD9 54 E2
Upland Cres LS8 61 A5
Upland Gdns LS8 208 A4
Upland Rd LS8 208 A4
Uplands BD20 18 A1
Uplands Ave BD13 73 B2
Uplands Cl BD13 73 B2
Uplands Cres BD13 73 B2
Uplands Dr WF14 138 A6
Uplands Gr BD13 73 B2
Uplands The WF8 146 C7
Upper Accommodation Rd
LS9 212 B3
Upper Ada St 8 BD18 54 F8
Upper Addison St BD4 201 C1
Upper Allerton La BD13 72 E8
Upper Armley C of E Sch
LS12 209 E4
Upper Ash Gr WF9 183 B3
Upper Ashley La BD17 55 B8
Upper Bank End Rd HD7 189 B3
Upper Bank Hey Bottom
HX6 132 E3
Upper Barker St WF15 117 A4
Upper Basinghall St LS1 211 E4
Upper Batley La WF17 118 B8
Upper Batley Low La
WF17 118 C8
Upper Battye St WF16 117 D4
Upper Bell Croft HX3 114 A4
Upper Bell Hall HX1 202 C1
Upper Bolton Brow HX6 112 D4
Upper Bonegate HD6 115 B3
Upper Brig Royd HX6 132 E4
Upper Brockholes HX2 91 D8
Upper Brow Rd HD1 153 D5
Upper Butts BD19 116 D7
Upper Calton St BD21 35 B5
Upper Camroyd St WF13 118 D1
Upper Carr La LS28 57 A6
Upper Carr St WF15 117 A5
Upper Castle St BD5 74 F4
Upper Chelsea St BD21 35 B5
Upper Clough Rd HD7 170 D7
Upper Commercial St
WF17 118 C5
Upper Common La HD8 192 F8
Upper Croft Rd WF17 118 B4
Upper Cross St 2 WF13 118 C1
Upper Ellistones Ct HX4 134 A7
Upper Exley HX3 113 E1
Upper Ferndown Gn BD15 54 A1
Upper Field House La HX6 111 D2
Upper Field La
High Hoyland S75 176 E1
Kexbrough S75 176 E1
Upper Fountain St HX6 112 B4
Upper Fountaine St LS2 211 F4
Upper Fyfe La BD17 38 E3
Upper Gate HD7 189 E2
Upper George St
Batley WF16 117 D4
4 Bradford BD6 74 B1
3 Huddersfield HD1 154 A6
Upper Grange Ave 3 BD15 73 B8
Upper Green Baildon BD17 38 B2
1 Bradford BD7 74 A3
Upper Green Ave
10 Brighouse BD19 115 F8
East Ardsley WF3 119 D7
Upper Green La HD6 114 E5
Upper Green Way WF3 119 D7
Upper Hagg Rd
Holmfirth HD7 172 B2
Honley HD7 172 B2
Upper Hall View HX3 92 F4
Upper Hatfield Pl WF4 162 D2
Upper Haugh Shaw 10
HX1 202 C1
Upper Heaton La HD5 137 B2
Upper Heights Rd BD13 72 C8
Upper Hird St BD21 35 A5
Upper Hirst HD3 152 D8
Upper Holme HD7 169 D8
Upper House La WF15 116 C4
Upper House Rd HD7 199 C8
Upper House St BD4 75 B5
Upper Kirkgate HX1 203 F3
Upper La Cleckheaton BD19 117 B7
Emley HD8 175 D6
Netherton WF4 158 D4
Northowram HX3 92 F3
Todmorden OL14 87 D1
Upper Langwith LS22 28 E8
Upper Lombard St LS19 40 A4
Upper Lumb La HX7 110 C4
Upper Marsh HX3 113 F5
Upper Marsh La BD22 51 A5
Upper Martin Gn HX4 134 A7
Upper Mary St 9 BD18 54 F8
Upper Maythorn La HD7 200 D8
Upper Meadows
Holmfirth HD7 188 D5
Queensbury BD13 92 E8
Upper Mill Row BD20 19 E2
Upper Millergate BD1 201 B3
Upper Mosscar St BD3 201 D3
Upper Mount HD7 170 F1
Upper Mount St
Batley WF17 118 C3
Huddersfield HD1 153 F4
Upper Nidd St BD3 75 B6
Upper Norcroft S75 193 F3
Upper North St
Batley WF17 118 B4
Leeds LS2 206 B1
Upper Parish Ghyll La
LS29 7 F3
Upper Park Gate BD1 201 C3
Upper Peel St 1 WF13 118 D1
Upper Piccadilly BD1 201 B3
Upper Quarry Rd HD2 137 A6
Upper Raglan St OL14 108 B6
Upper Rd WF17 118 B2
Upper Reins HD7 172 A5
Upper Rushton Rd BD3 56 D1
Upper Seymour St BD3 75 B7
Upper South St WF13 118 C1
Upper Station Rd WF17 118 D4
Upper Sutherland Rd HX3 114 E8
Upper Swain Royd Mews
BD15 53 E4
Upper Town BD22 51 C2
Upper Town St LS13 58 C3
Upper Warrengate WF1 216 C2
Upper Washer La HX2 202 B1
Upper Wellhouse Rd HD7 152 C3
Upper West St WF17 118 E5
Upper Westlock Ave LS9 208 A1
Upper Whitley
Jun & Inf Sch WF4 156 E5
Upper Willow Hall HX2 112 D6
Upper Woodlands Rd BD8 55 A1
Upper Woodview Pl 16
LS11 214 B2
Upper Wortley Dr LS12 209 E3
Upper Wortley
Primary Sch LS12 209 E2
Upper Wortley Rd LS12 209 E3
Upper Wortley Recn Ctr
LS12 77 F7
Upper York St WF1 216 B3
Upperfield Dr HD7 152 C4
Upperhead Row 11 HD1 154 A6
Uppermoor LS28 76 D7
Uppermoor Cl LS28 76 D6
Upperthong Junior &
Infants Sch HD7 188 E4
Upperthong La HD7 188 E5
Upton Jun & Inf Sch WF9 183 C8
Upton St WF17 118 B6
Upton Wlk 4 BD15 73 B8
Upwood La BD20 19 D2
Upwood Pk BD22 51 E3
Urban Terr WF4 156 E5
Ure Cres BD8 74 D8
Ure Gr LS22 13 D8
Usher St BD4 201 D1
Usher Street First Sch
BD4 201 D1
Utley First Sch BD20 18 A2
Uttley St 4 HX3 92 B2

Vale Ave Knottingley WF11 126 D4
Leeds LS8 44 A3
Vale Cl HD5 154 F3
Vale Cres WF11 126 D4
Vale Crest WF11 126 D4
Vale Gr Queensbury BD13 72 F1
Silsden BD20 5 D1
Vale Head Gr WF11 126 D4
Vale Head Mount WF11 126 D4
Vale Junior & Infants Sch
WF11 126 D4
Vale Mill La BD22 34 D1
Vale Rd WF9 163 B1
Vale St Bacup OL13 106 A3
Brighouse HD6 115 A3
Keighley BD21 18 E1
Todmorden OL14 108 B5
Vale Terr WF11 126 D5
Vale The Collingham LS22 29 A8
Leeds LS6 59 F5
Vale View WF7 164 B7
Valentine Ct BD13 72 E7
Valestone Ave WF9 181 E7
Valley Ave Brighouse HX3 115 A8
South Elmsall WF9 183 B3
Valley Cl LS17 43 A5
Valley Cres WF2 120 F2
Valley Ct Bradford BD1 55 E1
Castleford WF10 124 A5
Leeds LS17 204 A4
Liversedge WF15 117 B5
Valley Dr Dewsbury WF12 139 E1
Ilkley LS29 8 E4
Leeds LS15 62 B1
Swillington LS26 102 E8
Wakefield WF2 120 F2
Valley Farm Rd
Middleton LS10 215 F1
Rothwell LS10 80 A1
Valley Farm Way LS10 80 A1
Valley Fold BD13 92 E8
Valley Gdns LS7 60 C8
Valley Gn LS28 76 F6
Valley Gr Halifax HX2 91 F7
Pudsey LS28 76 F6
Valley Head HD2 135 C2
Valley Mills Ind Est BD10 56 E8
Valley Mount Kippax LS25 83 A2
Pudsey LS13 77 A8
Valley Par BD8 55 D1
Valley Parade Football Gd
BD8 55 D1
Valley Pl BD1 55 E1
Valley Rd Bradford BD1 201 B4
Cleckheaton BD19 116 E8
Darrington WF8 147 E4
Dewsbury WF12 139 F1
6 Hebden Bridge HX7 89 A3
Ilkley LS29 8 D5
Keighley BD21 35 F7
Kippax LS25 83 A2
Leeds LS13 58 C5
Liversedge WF15 117 B4
Mapplewell S75 178 A1
Morley LS27 98 C5
Ossett WF5 140 D4
5 Pontefract WF8 146 D8
Pudsey LS28 76 F6
Shipley BD18 55 C6
Valley Ridge Kippax LS25 82 F2
Kippax, Kippax Common LS25 82 F3
Valley Rise LS13 58 C5
Valley Sq LS28 76 F6
Valley St WF9 182 F2
Valley Terr LS17 43 F3
Valley The LS17 43 A5
Valley View Baildon BD17 38 B1
Glusburn BD20 16 C7
Halifax HX5 134 F8
Halifax, Illingworth HX2 91 F7
Harden BD16 36 A1
South Elmsall WF9 183 B3
Valley View Cl BD22 34 E3
Valley View Gdns 12 BD22 51 E8
Valley View Gr BD2 56 A2
Valley View Rd
Heptonstall HX7 88 F4
Ossett WF5 140 D4
Valley Way HX2 91 F7
Vancouver Pl LS7 204 B2
Varley Rd HD7 169 F7
Varley St LS28 57 D1
Vaughan St Bradford BD1 74 D7
1 Halifax HX1 202 B1
Vegal Cres HX3 91 F2
Venn St HD1 154 B6
Ventnor Cl
Cleckheaton BD19 96 B2
Ossett WF5 140 D5
Ventnor Dr WF5 140 D5
Ventnor St BD3 75 A7
Ventnor Terr HX3 113 B4
Ventnor Way WF5 140 D5
Vento Cl BD6 94 B8
Venture St OL13 106 A3
Verdun Rd BD6 94 A8
Vere Sq 7 BD5 74 E4
Verity Spur LS9 80 E8
Verity St BD4 95 F7
Verity View LS9 61 E1
Vermont St LS13 58 A2
Verner St WF7 145 C4
Vernon Ave HD1 153 F7
Vernon Cl HD1 153 F7
Vernon Ct BD20 35 B8
Vernon Pl Bradford BD2 56 B2
Pudsey LS28 57 E1
Queensbury BD13 92 C7
Wakefield WF2 142 B3
Vernon Rd Leeds LS1 206 B1
Liversedge WF15 117 C4
Vernon St Haworth BD22 51 F8
Leeds LS2 206 B1
Todmorden OL14 108 A3
Vesper Cl LS5 58 F6
Vesper Ct LS5 58 E6
Vesper Gate Cres LS5 58 F6
Vesper Gate Dr LS5 58 E5
Vesper Gate Mount LS5 58 F6
Vesper Gdns LS5 58 F5
Vesper Gr 2 LS5 59 A4
Vesper La LS5 58 F5
Vesper Mount LS5 59 A4
Vesper Pl 4 LS5 59 A4
Vesper Rd LS5 58 E6
Vesper Rise LS5 58 E6
Vesper Terr 3 LS5 59 A4
Vesper Way LS5 58 E6
Vesper Wlk LS5 58 E6
Vestry St BD4 75 B3
Viaduct Rd LS4 205 D1
Viaduct St
Huddersfield HD1 154 A7
Pudsey LS28 57 D1
Slaithwaite HD7 152 A1
Vicar La Bradford BD1 201 C2
Leeds LS1, LS2 211 F4
Ossett WF5 140 E3
Vicar Park Dr HX2 112 B8
Vicar Park Rd HX2 112 B8
Vicar St 11 WF15 117 A5
Vicarage Ave
Gildersome LS27 97 C6
Leeds LS5 59 B4
Vicarage Cl Bradford BD12 94 C2
Lofthouse Gate WF1 121 C5
South Kirkby WF9 182 C3
Vicarage Dr LS28 76 D7

Vicarage Gdns
Birkenshaw BD11 96 A5
Brighouse HD6 135 F8
Featherstone WF7 145 D8
Vicarage La Bramham LS23 30 D3
Featherstone WF7 145 D5
Royston S71 179 C3
Vicarage Meadows WF14 138 C5
Vicarage Pl LS5 59 B4
Vicarage Rd
Dewsbury WF12 139 C5
Dewsbury WF12 139 D8
Huddersfield HD3 153 B6
Leeds LS6 205 F2
Shipley BD18 55 E8
Vicarage St LS5 59 B4
Vicarage St N WF1 216 C3
Vicarage St S WF1 216 C2
Vicarage Terr Batley WF17 118 A7
Leeds LS5 59 B4
Vicarage View LS5 59 B4
Vicars Rd LS8 207 F4
Vicars Terr Kippax WF10 103 B4
Leeds LS8 207 F4
Vickerman Cres HD4 153 F1
Vickerman St HX1 202 B2
Vickers Ave Leeds LS5 58 F3
South Elmsall WF9 182 E1
Vickers St Castleford WF10 124 D7
Morley LS27 97 F2
Morley LS27 97 F3
Vickersdale LS28 57 E2
Victor Dr LS20 39 E8
Victor Rd Bradford BD9 55 B2
South Kirkby WF9 182 C2
Victor St Batley WF17 118 D5
Bradford, Bradford Moor BD3 75 E7
Bradford, Manningham BD9 55 B2
Castleford WF10 124 C5
South Elmsall WF9 182 F2
Victor Terr Bradford BD9 55 B2
Halifax HX1 202 C4
Victoria App WF1 121 B3
Victoria Ave Batley WF17 118 C4
Bradford BD2 56 D4
Brighouse HD6 115 C3
Cleckheaton BD19 116 D7
Elland HX5 134 E6
Halifax HX1 202 B2
Haworth BD22 51 C8
Horsforth LS18 58 A7
Ilkley LS29 7 F4
7 Keighley BD21 35 C8
Leeds LS9 80 B7
Menston LS29 22 A5
Morley LS27 98 A5
Rothwell LS26 100 E4
Shipley BD18 54 F8
Sowerby Bridge HX6 112 C5
Wakefield WF2 142 A6
Yeadon LS19 40 D8
Victoria Bldgs
5 Dewsbury WF12 118 E1
Hebden Bridge HX7 110 C2
Victoria Cl Horsforth LS18 58 A7
Ilkley LS29 8 A4
Kippax WF10 103 B4
Yeadon LS19 40 D7
Victoria Cotts LS25 105 D4
Victoria Cres
Dewsbury WF13 118 A2
Elland HX5 134 F6
Horsforth LS18 58 A7
Pudsey LS28 76 C7
Victoria Ct Batley WF17 96 F1
Castleford WF10 124 D6
Keighley BD21 35 B8
18 Shipley BD18 54 F8
Upton WF9 183 A7
Victoria Dr Bradford BD2 56 D4
Dewsbury WF12 139 C4
Horsforth LS18 58 A7
Ilkley LS29 7 F4
Morley LS27 98 B6
Northowram HX3 93 B3
Victoria Gdns
Horsforth LS18 58 B7
Ilkley LS29 7 F4
Pudsey LS28 76 C7
Victoria Gr Horsforth LS18 58 A6
Ilkley LS29 7 F4
Leeds LS9 80 B8
Pudsey LS28 76 C7
Wakefield WF2 141 D3
Victoria Grange Dr LS27 98 A5
Victoria Grange Way 4 LS27 98 A5
Victoria House 6 LS5 59 A4
Victoria Ind Est BD2 56 C4
Victoria Jun Sch LS26 100 D6
Victoria La
Huddersfield HD1 154 B6
Huddersfield, Town End HD7 152 C4
Victoria Mews
Horsforth LS18 58 A7
Keighley BD21 35 B7
6 Morley LS27 98 A5
Victoria Mills WF17 118 B6
Victoria Mills Units HD1 154 B7
Victoria Mount LS18 58 A7
Victoria Park Ave LS13, LS5 58 F3
Victoria Park Gr LS13, LS5 58 E3
Victoria Park Sch LS13 58 E3
Victoria Park St 7 BD21 35 D8
Victoria Park View BD21 35 D8
Victoria Pk Halifax HX1 202 C3
Shipley BD18 54 F7
Victoria Pl Boston Spa LS23 30 D4
Brighouse HD6 115 B1
Castleford WF10 124 E8
Halifax HX1 202 B3
Honley HD7 171 F4
Huddersfield HD4 153 A1
6 Huddersfield, Moldgreen HD5 154 D5
5 Mirfield WF14 137 F5
Yeadon LS19 40 A7
Victoria Primary Sch LS9 80 B8
Victoria Quarter LS1 211 F4
Victoria Rd
Bradford, Eccleshill BD2 56 C4
Bradford, Wibsey Slack BD6 94 A8
Brighouse, Bailiff Bridge HD6 115 B7
Brighouse, Hipperholme HX3 114 D7
Burley in W LS29 9 E2
Cleckheaton BD19 117 C8
Dewsbury WF13 118 C1
Dewsbury, Thornhill Lees WF12 139 C4
Elland HX5 134 E6
Glusburn BD20 16 D6
Guiseley LS20 39 D8
Halifax HX1 202 C3
Haworth BD22 51 D7
Hebden Bridge HX7 89 A4
Huddersfield HD1 153 F4
Ilkley LS29 7 F4
Keighley BD21 35 B5
Leeds LS6 205 E3
Leeds, Camp Field LS11 211 E2
Leeds, Kirkstall LS5 59 A4
Liversedge WF15 117 A3
Meltham HD7 170 D2
Morley LS27 98 A6
Oakworth BD22 34 D2
Pudsey LS28 76 C7
Pudsey, Farsley LS28 57 D2
Rothwell LS26 100 D6
Royston S71 179 D4
Shipley BD18 54 F8
Sowerby Bridge HX6 112 B3
10 Todmorden OL14 108 B6
Victoria Rise LS28 76 C7
Victoria Sh Ctr BD8 74 A8
Victoria Springs HD7 188 E4
Victoria Sq Holmfirth HD7 189 A5
Leeds LS1 211 E4
Ripponden HX6 132 D4
Victoria St
Ackworth M T WF7 163 D5
3 Baildon BD17 38 C1
Batley, Birstall WF17 96 F1
Batley, Carlinghow WF17 118 B6
Batley, Nunroyd WF16 117 D4
Bingley BD16 36 E7
Bradford BD1 201 A4
9 Bradford, Clayton BD14 73 B4
Bradford, Fagley BD2 56 D2
Bradford, Sandy Lane BD15 54 A3
Bradford, Thackley BD10 39 B2
Brighouse HD6 115 B1
Brighouse, Clifton HD6 115 C2
Castleford WF10 124 B8
Clayton West HD8 175 E2
Cleckheaton BD19 116 D8
Cullingworth BD13 52 E6
Dewsbury WF13 138 E6
Elland HX4 134 D7
Featherstone WF7 145 D5
Halifax HX1 203 E3
Hemsworth WF9 181 E6
Holmfirth HD7 189 A5
Horbury WF4 140 F1
Huddersfield HD3 153 C8
Huddersfield, Deighton HD2 136 E3
Huddersfield, Folly Hall HD1 154 A4
Huddersfield, Moldgreen HD5 154 D5
Kippax WF10 103 B4
Leeds LS2 205 F1
Leeds, Chapel Allerton LS7 204 A3
Leeds, Pottery Field LS10 212 A2
Lofthouse Gate WF1 121 B4
Marsden HD7 168 F4
Morley, Churwell LS27 98 C7
Morley, Morley Hole LS27 97 F5
Oakworth BD22 34 D2
Pontefract WF8 125 D3
Pudsey LS28 57 B6
Queensbury BD13 72 F1
Shipley BD17 55 B8
Sowerby Bridge HX6 112 B3
Sutton in C BD20 16 D5
Todmorden OL14 86 C1
Wakefield WF2 142 A7
Wetherby LS22 13 F5
Wilsden BD15 53 C4
Victoria Terr
Addingham LS29 6 F8
Brighouse HX3 114 D7
Clayton West HD8 175 F2
Guiseley LS20 22 E1
Halifax HX1 202 C2
4 Halifax, King Cross HX2 113 A4
Halifax, Luddenden Foot HX2 111 E5
5 Keighley BD21 35 D7
Leeds LS3 205 F1
Low Bradley BD20 4 C5
1 Pudsey LS28 57 F2
Todmorden OL14 109 A7
Yeadon LS19 40 D7
Victoria Theatre The HX1 203 E2
Victoria Way WF1 121 B3
Victoria Wlk Horsforth LS18 58 A7
4 Leeds LS1 211 F4
Victory Ave HD3 153 C5
Victory La WF3 122 A2
Victory Rd LS29 8 B4
View Croft Rd BD17 55 C8
View Rd BD20 35 A8
View St HD5 154 D5
View The Leeds LS8 61 A8
Leeds, Alwoodley Park LS17 43 A6
Viewlands HD2 136 B4
Viewlands Cres LS29 22 D5
Viewlands Mount LS29 22 D5
Viewlands Rise LS29 22 D5
Vignola Terr BD14 73 C5
Viking Ave HD8 175 D6
Viking Rd WF8 146 E8
Villa Cl WF7 164 B8
Villa Gr BD16 37 A4
Villa Mount BD12 94 C1
Villa Rd BD16 37 A4
Villa St HX6 112 C4
Village Ave LS4 205 D3
Village Gdns LS15 81 D6
Village Mews BD15 53 C5
Village Pl LS4 205 D2
Village Rd LS16 25 F1
Village St HX3 94 A2
Village St The LS4 205 D2
Village Terr LS4 205 D3
Village The
Kirkburton, Farnley Tyas HD4 172 F6
Kirkburton, Thurstonland HD4 172 F1
Thorp Arch LS23 14 E1
Vincent Ave BD20 17 A5
Vincent St Bradford BD1 201 A3
Halifax HX1 202 B2
Vine Ave BD19 116 C8
Vine Cl HD6 115 D2
Vine Cres BD19 116 D8
Vine Ct Brighouse HD6 115 D2
Guiseley LS20 39 E8
Vine Garth HD6 115 D3
Vine Gr HD6 115 D2
Vine St Bradford BD7 74 B4
Cleckheaton BD19 116 D8
Huddersfield HD1 154 C8
Vine Terr Halifax HX1 203 D2
3 Thornton BD13 72 D6
Vine Terr E BD8 73 E8
Vine Terr W BD8 73 E7
Vinery Ave LS9 80 A8
Vinery Cl HD8 175 F2
Vinery Gr 3 LS9 80 A8
Vinery Mount LS9 80 A7
Vinery Pl LS9 80 A7
Vinery Rd LS4 205 D2
Vinery St 4 LS9 80 A8
Vinery Terr LS9 80 A7
Vinery View LS9 80 A7
Vineyard HD7 152 D5
Violet St Halifax HX1 202 C3
Haworth BD22 51 C6
Violet St N HX1 202 C4
Virginia Cl WF2 121 A6
Virginia Ct WF2 121 A6
Virginia Dr WF2 121 A6
Virginia Gdns WF2 121 A6
Virginia Rd HD3 153 C7
Virginia St BD14 73 C3
Virginia Terr LS14 45 F5
Vissett Cl WF9 181 B6
Vissitt La WF9 181 B6
Vivian Pl BD7 74 A3
Vivien Rd BD8 73 C8
Vulcan Cl WF13 139 C8
Vulcan Gdns WF13 139 C8
Vulcan Rd WF13 139 C8
Vulcan St Bradford BD4 75 D1
Brighouse HD6 115 C1
11 Todmorden OL14 108 A1

Waddilove's Hospl BD8 55 D2
Waddington St 1 BD21 35 C6
Wade House Ave HX3 93 C6
Wade House Rd HX3 93 C6
Wade St Bradford BD1 201 B2
Halifax HX1 203 F3
Pudsey LS28 57 D3
Wadhouse La WF4 160 A8
Wadlands Cl LS28 57 D4
Wadlands Dr LS28 57 C4
Wadlands Gr LS28 57 C4
Wadlands Rise LS28 57 C3
Wadman Rd HD7 189 D3
Wadsworth Ave OL14 108 A4
Wadsworth Ct HX1 202 C4
Wadsworth La HX7 89 C3
Wadsworth St HX1 202 B4
Waggon La WF9 183 C8
Wagon La BD16 37 A1
Wain Brow HD4 171 F8
Wain Ct HD4 171 F8
Wain Pk HD4 171 F8
Waincliffe Cres LS11 213 F1
Waincliffe Dr LS11 98 F8
Waincliffe Garth LS11 213 F1
Waincliffe Mount LS11 98 F8
Waincliffe Pl LS11 213 F1
Waincliffe Sq LS11 213 F1
Waincliffe Terr LS11 98 F8
Waindale Cl HX2 91 A3
Waindale Cres HX2 91 A3
Waindike Cl WF6 123 C3
Waindyke Way WF6 123 D2
Waingate HD4 171 F8
Waingate Pk HD7 152 D1
Wainhouse Rd HX1 202 B1
Wainhouse Terr HX2 202 B1
Wainman Sq 2 BD12 94 C3
Wainman St Baildon BD17 38 D4
1 Bradford BD12 94 C3
Halifax HX1 202 B3
Shipley BD17 55 B8
Wainscott Cl HX7 89 B6
Wainsgate HX7 89 B6
Wainsgate La HX7 89 B6
Wainstalls HX2 90 F5
Wainstalls La HX2 90 F5
Wainstalls Lodge La HX2 90 E5
Wainstalls Primary Sch HX2 90 F5
Wainstalls Rd HX2 90 F5
Waite St WF2 141 E6
Waites Croft WF2 120 B2
Waites Terr LS21 23 B7
Wakefield 41 Ind Pk WF2 120 F5
Wakefield Ave LS14 61 F1
Wakefield Cathedral CE Sch WF2 142 A3
Wakefield City High Sch WF1 142 F7
Wakefield Coll
Hemsworth WF9 181 E7
Wakefield WF1 216 A3
Wakefield, Thornes Park WF2 142 A4
Wakefield Coll Whitwood Ctr WF10 124 A6
Wakefield Cres WF12 139 F8
Wakefield Eastmoor First Sch WF1 216 C3
Wakefield Gate HX3 112 F4
Wakefield Girls High Sch WF1 216 A3
Wakefield Independent Sch WF4 162 F6
Wakefield (Lupset) Municipal Golf Course WF2 141 E2
Wakefield Meth Jun & Inf Sch WF2 142 C3
Wakefield Mus WF1 216 B2
Wakefield Old Rd 6 WF12 139 D8
Wakefield Rd
Ackworth M T WF7 163 E5
Birkenshaw BD11 97 A5
Bradford BD4 75 B4
4 Brighouse HD6 115 B2
Brighouse HD6 115 D1
Brighouse, Lydgate HD6, HX3 114 E7
Clayton West HD8 175 E2
Denby Dale HD8 192 B7
Dewsbury WF12 139 E8
Featherstone WF7 145 B5
Flockton WF4 157 C4
Garforth LS25 82 C4
Gildersome LS27 97 D5
Halifax HX3 113 B2
Hemsworth WF9 163 B2
Horbury WF4 141 C2
Huddersfield HD1, HD5 154 D5
Leeds LS10 215 F2
Lepton HD8 155 D3
Liversedge HD6 137 A7
Liversedge, Mill Bridge WF15 117 B4
Mapplewell S75 178 C2
Ossett WF5 140 F7
Pontefract WF8 146 B7
Rothwell LS26 100 B6
Rothwell, Royds Green LS26 101 C2
Swillington LS26 82 C4
Wakefield WF5, WF2 141 B6
Walden Dr BD9 54 C3
Walden Howe Cl WF7 145 C8
Walden St WF10 124 D7
Waldorf Way WF2 216 B1
Waldron Ho 8 BD5 201 B1
Walesby Ct LS16 41 E2
Walford Ave LS9 80 A8
Walford Gr LS9 80 A8
Walford Mount LS9 80 A8
Walford Rd LS9 80 A8
Walford Terr LS9 80 A8
Walk Royd Hill S75 177 B2
Walk The Keighley BD21 35 C6
Pudsey LS28 57 C2
Walker Ave Bradford BD7 73 E5
Wakefield WF2 141 F7
Walker Cl BD20 16 B6
Walker Dr BD8 74 B8
Walker Gn WF12 139 E2
Walker La Horbury WF4 141 B1
Sowerby Bridge HX6 112 D4
Wadsworth Moor HX7 89 C5
Walker Pl 7 Morley LS27 98 B7
Shipley BD18 55 D8
Walker Rd Bradford BD12 94 F4
Horsforth LS18 41 B1
Menston LS29 21 F4
Walker St Bradford BD4 95 B8
3 Brighouse BD19 115 F8
Cleckheaton BD19 116 D8
Dewsbury, Earlsheaton WF12 139 F6
Dewsbury, Ravensthorpe WF13 138 D4
Dewsbury, Thornhill Lees WF12 139 D3
Walker Terr Bradford BD4 75 B4
Cullingworth BD13 52 D5
Walker Wood BD17 37 F2
Walker's La Leeds LS12 78 C4
Silsden BD20 5 D7
Walker's Pl BD20 17 E8
Walker's Rd LS6 59 F5
Walker's Terr WF1 216 A2
Walkergate Otley LS21 23 A8
Pontefract WF8 125 E1
Walkers Gn LS12 78 C4
Walkers Mount WF17 118 C3
Walkers Row LS19 40 A7
Walkley Ave WF16 117 D3
Walkley Gr 10 WF16 117 D3
Walkley La WF16 117 D2
Walkley Terr WF16 117 E2
Walkley Villas WF16 117 E2
Wall Nook La HD8 190 D6
Wall St BD22 34 F6
Wallace Gdns WF3 121 B6
Wallace St HX1 202 B2
Wallbank Dr BD18 55 C6
Walled Garden The WF4 178 A7
Waller Clough Rd HD7 151 F4
Wallingford Mount BD15 73 B7
Wallis St
Bradford, Brown Royd BD8 74 A7
Bradford, Green Side BD8 73 F7
Sowerby Bridge HX6 112 B4
Wallroyds HD8 191 F5
Walmer Gr LS28 76 F5
Walmer Villas BD8 55 D1
Walmsley Dr WF9 183 B7
Walmsley Rd LS6 205 E3
Walnut Ave
Dewsbury WF12 140 B7
Wakefield WF2 141 F7
Walnut Cl Dewsbury WF12 140 A6
Leeds LS14 62 C8
Walnut Cres
Dewsbury WF12 140 A6
Wakefield WF2 141 F7
Walnut Dr Dewsbury WF12 140 B7
Normanton WF6 144 A7
Pontefract WF8 146 C6
Walnut Gr WF12 140 B7
Walnut La WF12 140 A7
Walnut Pl WF12 140 A7
Walnut Rd WF12 140 B7
Walnut St Bradford BD3 75 C6
Halifax HX1 202 C3
15 Keighley BD21 35 B4
South Elmsall WF9 182 F1
Walpole Rd HD4 153 D3
Walsden CE Infant Sch OL14 108 B1
Walsden Est OL14 129 B7
Walsden Junior Sch OL14 108 A1
Walsden Sta OL14 108 A1
Walsh La Bingley BD16 37 A7
Gildersome LS12 77 D2
Halifax HX3 92 B1
Walsh St HX1 202 B3
Walsh's Sq 19 HX1 202 C1
Walsham Dr HD3 134 F1
Walshaw La HX7 68 C3
Walshaw St 2 BD7 74 A4
Walter Clough La HX3 114 C5
Walter Cres LS9 212 C3
Walter St Bradford BD10 56 B8
Leeds LS4 205 D1
Shipley BD2 55 D4
Waltham Dr DN6 184 E2
Waltin Rd HD7 188 F1
Walton Cl OL13 106 A1
Walton Croft HD5 154 E6
Walton Dr BD11 96 F5
Walton Fold 2 OL14 108 D6
Walton Garth BD11 96 F5
Walton Grove Infants Sch WF2 161 B6
Walton Junior Sch WF2 161 A7
Walton La Brighouse BD19 115 F6
Wakefield WF2 160 F8
Walton Rd Thorp Arch LS23 14 C4
Upton WF9 183 D8
Walton LS23 15 A3
Wetherby LS22, LS23 14 C4
Walton St Bradford BD4 201 C1
Leeds, Holbeck LS11 211 E2
Leeds, Hunslet LS10 215 E4
Sowerby Bridge HX6 112 B4
Walton Station La WF2 160 F7
Walton View WF4 161 F8
Waltroyd Rd BD19 116 C7
Wansford Cl BD4 75 E2
Wanstead Cres BD15 73 B8
Wapping First Sch BD3 201 C4
Wapping Nick La HX4 134 E3
Wapping Rd BD3 201 C4
Warburton Pl 9 BD6 74 C1
Warburton Rd HD8 175 D6
Warcock La OL13 106 B3
Ward Bank Rd HD7 189 A4
Ward Ct HD6 135 F7
Ward Fall WF4 159 F3
Ward La Leeds LS10 215 D1
Lofthouse Gate WF3 122 A2
Ward Place La HD7 188 F3
Ward Sq 26 HD1 154 A6
Ward St Bradford BD7 74 A3
Dewsbury WF13 118 D1
4 Keighley BD21 35 B6
Leeds LS10 212 A1
Ward's End HX1 203 E2
Wardman St BD21 18 E1

Wards Hill WF17 118 C5
Wards Hill Ct 10 WF17 118 C5
Wareham Cnr BD4 75 E2
Warehouse Hill Rd HD7 169 A4
Warehouse St WF17 118 D4
Warhurst Rd HX5 135 A8
Waring Way WF12 118 E1
Warlands End Gate OL14 129 D5
Warlbeck LS29 7 F4
Warley Ave BD3 75 D8
Warley Dene HX2 112 B6
Warley Dr BD3 75 D8
Warley Edge La HX2 112 C7
Warley Gr Bradford BD3 75 D8
Halifax HX2 112 D7
Warley Rd HX1, HX2 202 A2
Warley Road Junior & Infant Sch HX1 202 A2
Warley St HX1 202 C2
Warley Town County Primary Sch HX2 112 B6
Warley Town La HX2 112 A6
Warley View HX2 112 D7
Warley Wood Ave HX2 111 F5
Warley Wood La HX2 111 F5
Warm La LS19 40 A5
Warmfield La WF1 143 E7
Warmfield View WF1 142 F7
Warmliegh Pk BD13 72 B1
Warneford Ave WF5 140 D7
Warneford Rd HD4 153 A3
Warneford Rise HD4 153 A3
Warnford Gr BD4 75 D3
Warrel's Ave 4 LS13 58 C3
Warrel's Ct LS13 58 C2
Warrel's Gr LS13 58 C2
Warrel's Mount LS13 58 C2
Warrel's Pl LS13 58 C3
Warrel's Rd LS13 58 C3
Warrel's Row 4 LS13 58 C2
Warrel's St LS13 58 C2
Warrel's Terr 19 LS13 58 C2
Warren Ave Bingley BD16 37 B5
Knottingley WF11 126 D3
Wakefield WF2 142 D2
Warren Cl
Liversedge WF15 117 B2
Royston S71 179 D5
Warren Ct WF1 216 C2
Warren Dr Bingley BD16 37 B4
Featherstone WF7 145 A8
Warren House WF1 216 B2
Warren House La
East Carlton LS19 23 D1
Huddersfield HD3 135 A3
Warren La Arthington LS21 25 A7
Bingley BD16 37 B4
Bramham LS24 31 B1
Mapplewell S75 178 C4
Woolley S75 178 C4
Warren Park Cl HD6 114 E5
Warren Pk HD6 114 E6
Warren Rd WF7 145 B6
Warren St WF12 139 D6
Warrens La
Birkenshaw WF17 96 D5
Cleckheaton WF17 96 D3
Warrenside
Huddersfield, Deighton HD2 136 E4
Huddersfield, Riddings HD2 136 D3
Warrenton Pl BD7 74 A5
Warrington Terr HD7 168 E4
Warsop Rd S71 178 E1
Warton Ave BD4 75 B1
Warwick Ave HD7 152 E5
Warwick Cl Bradford BD4 75 B4
1 Halifax HX3 113 B4
Warwick Ct 1 LS18 58 C7
Warwick Dr BD4 75 B4
Warwick Rd Batley WF17 118 D3
Bradford BD4 75 B4
Warwick Road Jun & Inf Sch WF17 118 C3
Warwick St WF1 142 F3
Wasdale Cres WF2 141 E7
Wasdale Rd WF2 141 E7
Washburn Ct Silsden BD20 5 E1
Wetherby LS22 13 D8
Washburn Dr BD20 16 C7
Washer La HX2 112 E4
Washer Lane Ind Est HX2 112 F4
Washfold Rd HX7 131 B7
Washington Pl LS13 77 A8
Washington St
Bradford BD8 54 F1
20 Halifax HX3 92 A1
Leeds LS12 210 B4
Pudsey LS13 77 A8
Washington Terr LS13 77 A8
Washpit New Rd HD7 189 B3
Wasp Nest Rd HD1 136 A1
Waste La Huddersfield HD5 154 E4
Mirfield WF14 137 F3
Mirfield, Lower Hopton WF14 138 A3
Wadsworth Moor HX7 69 A5
Waste The WF14 137 F3
Wastwater Dr BD6 93 F6
Watchit Hole La WF8 165 C4
Watchley La DN5 195 B3
Water Gn HX6 132 A6
Water Green La HX6 132 A6
Water Hill La HX2 112 A5
Water La Bradford BD1 74 D7
Darrington WF8 146 D2
Dewsbury, Chickenley WF12 140 A7
Dewsbury, Scout Hill WF12 139 B6
Halifax HX3 203 F2
Keighley BD21 35 B6
Kirk Smeaton WF8 166 E6
Leeds LS11 211 F3
Leeds, Camp Field LS11 211 D2
Leeds, Gamble Hill LS12 77 D7
Lofthouse Gate WF3 121 F4
Netherton WF4 158 D8
Pontefract WF8 125 F3
Pudsey LS28 57 D3
Shepley HD8 174 A3
South Kirkby WF9 181 F4
Woolley WF4 178 A8
Yeadon LS18 40 F1
Water Lane Cl WF4 158 D8
Water Row HD7 189 E6
Water Royd Ave WF14 138 A6
Water Royd Cres WF14 138 A6
Water Royd Dr WF14 138 A6
Water Royd La WF14 138 A6
Water Side La HD7 188 D2
Water St Brighouse HD6 115 B3
Clayton West HD8 175 D1
Holmfirth HD7 188 D3
Huddersfield HD1 153 F5
Huddersfield, Rashcliffe HD1, HD4 153 F3
Sowerby Bridge HX6 112 B3
Todmorden OL14 108 B5
Water Stalls Rd HX7 110 F2
Watercock St BD4 201 D1
Watercroft HD5 154 F3
Waterfall Cotts HD7 168 D5
Waterfront Mews BD10 56 E8
Watergate Brighouse HX3 114 C7
Huddersfield HD1 154 B6
Mickletown LS26 102 B1
Pontefract WF8 125 C1
Watergate Rd WF12 139 B7
Waterhouse Ct 8 LS18 58 B7
Waterhouse Dr WF3 120 B7
Waterhouse Gr WF2 142 A6
Waterhouse St
Halifax HX1 203 E3
8 Keighley BD21 35 B7
Waterloo Cl WF10 123 F5
Waterloo Cres
Bradford BD10 56 F8
Leeds LS13 58 D4
Waterloo Fold 2 BD12 94 D2
Waterloo Gr LS28 76 B7
Waterloo Junior Sch LS28 76 C7
Waterloo La LS13 58 D3
Waterloo Mount LS28 76 B8
Waterloo Rd Bingley BD16 36 F3
Brighouse HD6 115 A3
Huddersfield HD5 155 B6
Pudsey LS28 76 B7
Waterloo Rise HD5 155 A5
Waterloo St Leeds LS10 211 F3
Wakefield WF1 142 D4
Waterloo Terr HX6 112 C6
Waterloo Way LS13 58 D3
Waters Rd HD7 168 D5
Waterside Bingley BD16 36 D5
Halifax HX3 203 F2
Huddersfield HD1 153 F5
Huddersfield, Salford HD1 153 F2
Oxenhope BD22 51 C2
Silsden BD20 17 F8
Waterside Fold HX7 89 A4
Waterside Ind Pk LS10 80 B2
Waterside Mill BD22 51 E1
Waterside Rd
Bradford BD8 74 A8
Leeds LS10 80 B3
Waterside Wlk WF14 137 D5
Watersole La LS23 14 B4
Waterton Cl
South Kirkby WF9 182 D3
Walton WF2 161 A6
Waterton Gr WF2 141 F5
Waterton Jun & Inf Sch WF2 141 D4
Waterton Rd WF2 141 E4
Waterton St WF10 124 B7
Waterwood Cl WF3 119 F7
Waterworks Rd WF17 117 F4
Watery La HD7 197 F8
Watford Ave HX3 93 F3
Watkin Ave BD13 72 F6
Watkinson Ave HX2 91 F4
Watkinson Bglws HX2 91 E3
Watkinson Dr HX2 91 F4
Watkinson Rd HX2 91 F4
Watling Rd WF10 104 E1
Watmough St 2 BD7 74 A3
Watroyd La HD7 152 B2
Watson Ave WF12 140 B8
Watson Cl BD22 51 C2
Watson Cres WF1 142 E7
Watson Mill La HX6 112 B2
Watson Rd LS14 61 F1
Watson St Morley LS27 97 F3
Normanton WF6 123 A2
Watson's La LS24 31 D5
Watt St BD4 75 D6
Wattlesyke LS22 29 E8
Watts St BD14 73 B4
Watty Hall Ave BD6 74 A2
Watty Hall La BD6 74 B2
Watty Hall Rd BD6 74 A2
Watty La OL14 107 F3
Watty Terr OL14 107 F3
Wauchope St WF2 216 A1
Wauds Gates BD17 38 C1
Waulkmill Cl WF9 183 A7
Wavell Garth WF2 160 F7
Wavell Gr WF2 160 F7
Waveney Rd LS12 209 F1
Waverley Ave Bradford BD7 74 B5
Keighley BD20 36 B8
Waverley Cres HX3 114 C7
Waverley Garth LS11 214 B4
Waverley Middle Sch BD7 74 B5
Waverley Pl BD7 74 B5
Waverley Rd Bradford BD7 74 B5
Elland HX5 134 F5
Huddersfield HD1 153 F7
Waverley St
Dewsbury WF12 139 C7
Slaithwaite HD7 151 F1
Waverley Terr
Bradford BD7 74 B5
Brighouse HX3 114 C7
Huddersfield HD1 153 D7
Waverton Gn BD6 93 F7
Wavertree Park Gdns 12 BD12 94 C4
Wayland App LS16 42 D4
Wayland Croft LS16 42 D4
Wayland Ct LS16 42 D4
Wayland Dr LS16 42 D4
Wayne Cl WF17 118 C6
Wayside Ave LS14 28 D1
Wayside Cres Bardsey LS14 28 D1
Bradford BD2 56 B5
Wayside Ct BD20 18 A2
Wayside Mount LS14 28 D1
Weardale Cl BD4 75 C1
Weardley La LS17 26 B6
Weather Hill La
Hebden Bridge HX7 110 E4
Holme HD7 198 E8
Weather Hill Rd HD3 135 A2
Weatherall Pl DN6 184 F2
Weatherhead Pl BD20 5 F1
Weatherhill Cres HD3 135 A2
Weatherhouse Terr HX2 91 D1
Weaver Ct BD10 56 B8
Weaver Gdns LS27 98 D3
Weaver St LS4 205 D1
Weavers Cotts 1 BD22 51 C2
Weavers Croft
Bradford BD10 39 B2
Pudsey LS28 76 F6
Weavers Ct Leeds LS12 209 E3
Meltham HD7 170 F2
1 Pudsey LS28 76 F5
Weavers Grange LS20 22 E2
Weavers Hill BD22 51 C6
Weavers Rd WF8 125 E1
Weavers Wlk
Denby Dale HD8 192 B7
Silsden BD20 5 E2
Weaverthorpe Rd BD4 75 E1
Webb Dr BD2 56 A2
Webb's Terr HX3 203 F4
Weber Ct BD3 75 C7
Webster Hill WF13 139 C8
Webster Pl Bradford BD3 75 B7
Normanton WF6 123 A2
Webster Row LS12 209 E2
Webster St Bradford BD3 75 B7
Dewsbury WF13 139 C8
Wedgemoor Cl 14 BD12 94 C4
Wedgewood Ct LS8 44 A1
Wedgewood Dr LS8 44 A1
Wedgewood Gr LS8 44 A1
Wedgewood Sch BD4 75 F2
Weeland Ave WF4 144 B3
Weeland Cres WF4 144 C4
Weeland Ct WF11 127 A4
Weeland Dr WF4 144 C3
Weeland Rd Beal DN14 127 D4
Crofton WF4 144 C3
Knottingley WF11 127 D4
Weet Shaw La S72 180 B1
Weetlands Cl LS25 83 B2
Weetwood Ave LS16 59 D7
Weetwood County Primary Sch LS16 59 D7
Weetwood Cres LS16 59 D8
Weetwood Ct LS16 59 C8
Weetwood Grange Gr LS16 59 B8
Weetwood House Ct LS16 59 B8
Weetwood La LS16 59 D7
Weetwood Mill La LS16 59 D8
Weetwood Park Dr LS16 59 B8
Weetwood Rd
Bradford BD8 74 A8
Leeds LS16 59 B8
Weetwood Wlk LS16 59 C8
Weetworth Ave WF10 124 F6
Weetworth Pk WF10 124 E6
Weir La OL13 106 A7
Weir Side HD7 168 F4
Weir St OL14 108 A3
Welbeck Dr BD7 73 E4
Welbeck La WF1 143 B8
Welbeck Rd Batley WF17 96 F2
Leeds LS9 80 A7
Welbeck Rise BD7 73 E4
Welbeck St
Castleford WF10 124 D8
Wakefield WF1 142 D3
Welburn Ave
Brighouse HX3 114 D7
Leeds LS16 59 B7
Welburn Cl WF2 142 F1
Welburn Dr LS16 59 B7
Welburn Gr LS16 59 B7
Welburn Mount BD6 93 E8
Welbury Dr BD8 55 C2
Weldon Ct BD4 75 E4
Weldon Dr HD3 152 A8
Welfare Ave LS15 63 E7
Welham Wlk BD3 56 A1
Well Bank Rd BD4 75 D3
Well Cl Swillington LS26 102 E8
Yeadon LS19 40 C3
Well Close Rise LS7 206 C2
Well Close St HD6 115 B3
Well Croft BD18 55 B7
Well Garth LS15 62 C2
Well Garth Bank LS13 58 B4
Well Garth Mount LS15 62 C2
Well Garth View LS13 58 C4
Well Gr HD2 136 C3
Well Green La HD6 114 F5
Well Head Dr HX1 203 E2
Well Head La Halifax HX1 203 E2
Sowerby Bridge HX6 111 C3
Well Heads BD13 72 A6
Well Hill Honley HD7 171 F4
Otley LS21 22 F7
Yeadon LS19 40 B7
Well Hill Gr S71 179 C4
Well Holme Mead LS12 77 E3
Well House Ave LS8 61 A5
Well House Cres LS8 61 A5
Well House Dr LS8 61 A5
Well House Gdns LS8 61 A5
Well House Rd LS8 61 A5
Well La Batley WF17 118 D5
Brighouse HD6 115 E2
Dewsbury WF13 138 F8
Guiseley LS20 22 E1
Halifax HX1 203 F3
Holmfirth HD7 189 B4
Kippax LS25 83 A1
Leeds LS7 204 A3
Todmorden OL14 108 B5
Yeadon LS19 40 B7
Yeadon, Rawdon LS19 40 C3
Well Royd Ave HX2 112 C7
Well Royd Cl HX2 112 D7
Well St Bradford BD1 201 C3
Denholme BD13 71 D8
3 Dewsbury WF12 118 E1
2 Elland HX4 134 B4
Guiseley LS20 22 E1
Huddersfield HD1 153 F5
Keighley BD21 35 B7
Liversedge WF15 117 A5
Pudsey LS28 57 D3
Sutton in C BD20 16 E5
Todmorden OL14 108 B4
Wilsden BD15 53 C5
Well Terr LS20 22 E1
Well View LS20 22 E1
Welland Dr LS25 83 B6
Wellands Gn BD19 116 B7
Wellands La BD19 116 A7
Wellands Terr BD3 75 C7
Wellcroft LS21 23 B7
Wellcroft Gr WF3 119 F7
Wellesley Gn WF2 141 E7
Wellesley St BD1 201 C3
Wellfield Ave WF4 156 E5
Wellfield Bank HD4 153 D2
Wellfield Cl Flockton WF4 156 E5
Huddersfield HD7 152 E2
Wellfield Gdns BD13 72 D3
Wellfield Rd HD3 153 C7
Wellfield Terr OL14 108 B4
Wellgarth Bradford BD6 93 F7
Halifax HX1 203 D1
Wellgarth Rd WF7 145 E4
Wellgate Castleford WF10 124 F6
Elland HX4 134 C8
Mapplewell S75 178 B1
Slaithwaite HD7 152 B3
Wellhead Cl LS16 24 E4
Wellhead Mews WF4 159 F4
Wellholme HD6 115 B3
Wellhouse WF14 138 B7
Wellhouse Ave WF14 138 B7
Wellhouse Cl WF14 138 A7
Wellhouse Jun & Inf Sch HD7 152 D3
Wellhouse La
Huddersfield HD5 137 A1
Mirfield WF14 138 B7
Wellington Arc 7 HD6 115 B2
Wellington Bridge St
Leeds LS12 210 C4
Leeds LS12 211 D3
Wellington Bsns Ctr HX5 135 A7
Wellington Cres BD18 55 A7
Wellington Ct
Birkenshaw BD11 96 A6
Halifax HX2 202 A4
Wellington First Sch BD2 56 B3
Wellington Garth 3 LS13 58 D4
Wellington Gdns LS13 58 D4
Wellington Gr
Bradford BD2 56 B2
Leeds LS13 58 D4
Pudsey LS28 76 C7
Wellington Hill LS14 45 A3
Wellington Middle Sch BD2 56 B3
Wellington Mount LS13 58 D4
Wellington Pl
2 Halifax HX1 203 F2
Knottingley WF11 126 D4
Wellington Rd
Bradford BD2 56 B3
Dewsbury WF13 139 C8
Ilkley LS29 8 B4
Keighley BD21 35 C7
Leeds LS12, LS3 210 C3
Leeds, New Wortley LS12, LS3 210 B2
Todmorden OL14 108 B6
Wilsden BD15 53 C4
Wellington Rd E 10 WF13 139 C8
Wellington Rd Ind Est LS12 210 C3
Wellington Sq 4 BD21 35 C6
Wellington St Batley WF17 118 C4
Bingley BD16 36 F3
Bradford BD15 54 C1
Bradford BD1 201 C3
Bradford, Haigh Fold BD2 56 B3
Bradford, Idle BD10 56 B7
Bradford, Swain Green BD4 75 D6
Castleford WF10 124 B8
11 Dewsbury WF13 139 C8
Huddersfield HD3 153 B8
Leeds LS1 211 D3
3 Liversedge WF15 117 B3
Morley LS27 98 A4
Queensbury BD13 72 F1
Wakefield WF2 141 E7
Wilsden BD15 53 C4
Wellington St S HX1 203 F2
Wellington St W HX1 203 D2
Wellington Terr Leeds LS13 58 D4
Marsden HD7 169 A4
Wellington Wlk 8 WF13 139 C8
Wells Croft LS6 59 E7
Wells Ct Halifax HX3 92 B1
Ossett WF5 140 C5
Wells Gr LS20 22 E1
Wells Green Gdns HD7 188 F7
Wells Mount
Denby Dale HD8 191 A6
Guiseley LS20 22 E1
Wells Prom LS29 8 B3
Wells Rd Dewsbury WF12 139 E2
Guiseley LS20 22 E1
Ilkley LS29 8 B3
Wells Terr HX3 94 A2
Wells The HX2 112 D7
Wells Wlk LS29 8 B3
Wellstone Ave LS13 77 B8
Wellstone Dr LS13 58 B1
Wellstone Garth LS13 77 C8
Wellstone Gdns LS13 77 B8
Wellstone Gn LS13 58 B1
Wellstone Rd LS13 77 B8
Wellstone Rise LS13 77 B8
Wellstone Way LS13 77 B8
Wellthorne Ave S30 191 E1
Wellthorne La S36 191 D1
Welton Gr LS6 205 E3
Welton Mount LS6 205 E3
Welton Pl LS6 205 E3
Welton Rd LS6 205 E3
Welwyn Ave Batley WF17 117 F6
Shipley BD18 55 F7
Welwyn Dr Baildon BD17 38 C2
Shipley BD18 55 F7
Welwyn Rd WF12 118 F3
Wembly Ave BD13 72 F6
Wenborough La BD4 75 F3
Wendel Ave LS15 63 D7
Wendron Cl WF15 116 F1
Wendron Way BD10 56 B7
Wenlock St BD3 201 D2
Wenning St BD21 35 E8
Wensley Ave Leeds LS7 60 C7
Shipley BD18 55 A7
Wensley Bank BD13 72 C6
Wensley Bank Terr BD13 72 C6
Wensley Bank W BD13 72 C6
Wensley Cres LS7 60 C7
Wensley Dr Leeds LS7 60 C7
Pontefract WF8 146 E6
Wensley Gdns LS7 60 B8
Wensley Gn LS7 60 B7
Wensley Gr Brighouse HD6 135 E8
Leeds LS7 60 C7
Wensley Rd LS7 60 B8
Wensley St 5 WF4 141 A1
Wensley St E 6 WF4 141 A1
Wensley View LS7 60 C7
Wensleydale Ave LS12 58 F2
Wensleydale Cl 2 LS12 58 F2
Wensleydale Cres LS12 58 F2
Wensleydale Ct LS7 60 C7
Wensleydale Dr LS12 58 F2
Wensleydale Mews 1 LS12 58 F2
Wensleydale Par 2 WF17 117 F8
Wensleydale Rd BD3 75 E7
Wensleydale Rise
Baildon BD17 38 E4
3 Leeds LS12 58 F2
Went Ave WF7 145 C3
Went Croft WF8 146 D5
Went Edge Rd
Kirk Smeaton WF8 165 F6
Thorpe Audlin WF8 165 F6
Went Fold WF8 146 D5
Went Garth WF8 146 D5
Went Gr WF7 145 C3
Went Hill Cl WF7 164 A8
Went La Featherstone WF4 145 D2
West Hardwick WF4 163 C7
Went View WF8 165 A5
Went-Dale Rd WF8 146 D5
Wentbridge La WF8 165 C6
Wentbridge Rd WF7 145 E4

Wentcliffe Rd WF11 126 B4
Wentdale WF8 166 E6
Wentwell Rd WF7 144 D5
Wentworth Ave
Emley HD8 175 C6
Leeds LS17 43 C4
Wentworth Cl
Menston LS29 22 A4
Woolley WF4 177 F7
Wentworth Cres LS17 43 C4
Wentworth Ct HD6 135 F7
Wentworth Dr
Crofton WF4 162 A8
Emley HD8 175 C6
Halifax HX2 91 F7
South Kirkby WF9 182 C3
Wentworth Gate LS22 13 B6
Wentworth Gr HX2 91 F7
Wentworth Park Rise WF8 147 D5
Wentworth Rd WF7 145 B4
Wentworth St
Huddersfield HD1 153 F7
Wakefield WF1 216 A3
Wentworth Terr
Hemsworth WF9 163 B3
Wakefield WF1 216 A3
Yeadon LS19 40 D3
Wentworth Way Leeds LS17 43 C4
Wakefield WF2 142 E1
Wepener Mount LS9 208 B1
Wepener Pl LS9 208 B1
Wesley App LS11 213 F2
Wesley Ave Bradford BD12 94 E7
4 Leeds LS12 209 F3
Wesley Ave S 3 BD12 94 E6
Wesley Cl Batley WF17 96 E1
Leeds LS11 213 F3
Wesley Croft LS11 213 F3
Wesley Ct 3 Halifax HX1 203 E3
Leeds, Beeston LS11 213 F2
Leeds, Woodhouse LS6 206 A3
Ossett WF5 140 C6
Yeadon LS19 39 F7
Wesley Dr BD12 94 E7
Wesley Garth LS11 213 F3
Wesley Gn LS11 213 F2
Wesley Gr BD10 39 C1
Wesley Hall Ct WF3 121 F2
Wesley House LS11 213 F3
Wesley Pl Dewsbury WF13 139 C8
Featherstone WF7 145 D4
Keighley BD21 35 B3
Leeds LS9 212 B3
5 Leeds, Armley LS12 209 F3
Silsden BD20 5 E1
Wesley Rd Leeds LS12 209 F3
Pudsey LS28 57 C2
Wesley Row 10 LS28 76 E8
Wesley Sq 6 LS28 76 E7
Wesley St
7 Castleford WF10 124 D8
Castleford, Cutsyke WF10 124 C5
Cleckheaton BD19 116 D8
Dewsbury WF13 139 C8
Leeds LS11 213 F3
Morley LS27 98 A4
Ossett WF5 140 D6
Otley LS21 23 A8
Pudsey, Farsley LS28 57 D3
Pudsey, Rodley LS13 57 F5
Pudsey, Stanningley LS28 57 D1
South Elmsall WF9 182 E2
Wakefield WF1 142 E3
Wesley Terr
1 Bacup OL13 106 A7
Denby Dale HD8 191 F6
Leeds LS13 58 D3
Pudsey LS28 76 E8
Pudsey, Rodley LS13 57 F5
Wesley View Pudsey LS28 76 E7
1 Pudsey, Rodley LS13 57 F5
Wesleyan Terr BD4 75 C3
Wessenden Head Rd HD7 170 D1
Wessenden Rd HD7 169 A1
West Acre Dr WF17 118 E5
West Acres WF11 126 D7
West Ave Baildon BD17 38 C3
Boston Spa LS23 14 C1
Bradford BD15 53 F3
Brighouse HX3 115 A7
Halifax HX3 113 B4
Honley HD7 171 F4
Horbury WF4 141 C1
Huddersfield HD3 135 C1
Leeds LS8 61 C8
Pontefract WF8 146 A8
Royston S71 179 D4
South Elmsall WF9 183 B4
West Bank Bradford BD9 54 F4
Halifax HX2 91 D4
Keighley BD22 34 F8
West Bank Cl BD22 34 F8
West Bank Gr BD20 18 E2
West Bank Rd BD20 18 D2
West Bank Rise BD22 34 F8
West Bolton HX2 91 D7
West Bowling Golf Course BD5 75 A1
West Bradford Golf Course BD9 54 C2
West Bretton Junior & Infants Sch WF4 176 F8
West Busk La LS21 22 D6
West Byland HX2 91 D7
West Carr La HD3 150 E2
West Chevin Rd
Menston LS29 22 E5
Otley LS21 22 E5

West Cl Huddersfield HD2 136 B2
Normanton WF6 123 A3
Pontefract WF8 146 E5
West Cliffe HX3 113 E6
West Croft Addingham LS29 6 F8
Bradford BD12 94 C2
Sutton in C BD20 16 D4
West Ct
6 Leeds, Bramley LS13 58 C1
Leeds, Roundhay LS8 61 C8
West Dale LS23 14 C1
West Dene Leeds LS17 43 F6
Silsden BD20 5 E2
West Dr Oxenhope BD22 51 C3
Pontefract WF8 146 E7
West End Boston Spa LS23 14 C1
Gildersome LS27 97 C7
Gildersome, New Farnley LS12 77 D3
Hebden Bridge HX7 89 A3
Queensbury BD13 92 D8
West End App LS27 97 E3
West End Ave
Featherstone WF7 145 A8
Holmfirth HD7 189 C6
Royston S71 179 A3
West End Cl LS18 40 F1
West End Cres S71 179 A3
West End Dr
Cleckheaton BD19 116 C6
Horsforth LS18 41 A1
West End Golf Course HX2 112 C8
West End Gr LS18 40 F1
West End Junior & Infants Sch LS18 40 F1
West End La LS18 40 F2
West End Middle Sch BD19 116 C7
West End Prim (Jun & Inf) Sch WF9 181 C7
West End Rd Halifax HX1 202 A2
Huddersfield HD7 152 C4
Pudsey LS28 57 B6
West End Rise LS18 40 F1
West End Terr Bradford BD2 56 B5
Guiseley LS20 22 C1
5 Hebden Bridge HX7 89 E1
Shipley BD18 55 A8
West Farm Ave LS10 99 B5
West Field LS14 45 E4
West Field La HD7 189 C6
West Garforth Junior Sch LS25 82 E6
West Gate Holme HD7 198 F8
Holmfirth HD7 188 F1
Wetherby LS22 13 E5
West Gr 11 Baildon BD17 38 C4
Royston S71 179 A4
West Grange Cl LS10 215 D1
West Grange Dr LS10 215 D1
West Grange Fold LS10 215 D1
West Grange Garth LS10 215 D1
West Grange Gdns LS10 215 D1
West Grange Gn LS10 215 D1
West Grange Rd LS10 215 D1
West Grange Wlk LS10 215 D1
West Grove Ave HD5 154 D6
West Grove St 10 LS28 57 D1
West Grove Terr HX1 203 D3
West Hall La LS29 3 A1
West Hall Sch WF3 122 B6
West Hill Ave LS7 60 C7
West Hill St HX1 203 D3
West House 2 HX5 134 F7
West Ings Cl WF11 127 B5
West Ings Cres WF11 127 B5
West Ings Ct WF11 127 B5
West Ings La WF11 127 B5
West Ings Mews WF11 127 B5
West Ings Way WF11 127 B5
West La Askwith LS21 9 E5
Baildon BD17 38 B3
Boston Spa LS23 14 C1
Cleckheaton BD19 95 B1
Crofton WF4 144 B2
Halifax HX3 113 F3
Haworth BD22 51 B7
Keighley BD21, BD22 35 A7
Low Bradley BD20 4 C5
Sutton in C BD20 16 C4
Thornton BD13 72 D6
West Lea Cl LS17 43 B1
West Lea Cres
East Ardsley WF3 119 D7
Yeadon LS19 39 F6
West Lea Dr
East Ardsley WF3 119 D6
Leeds LS17 43 B1
West Lea Garth LS17 43 B1
West Lea Gdns LS17 43 B1
West Lea Gr LS19 39 F6
West Leeds Boys High Sch LS12 209 D3
West Leeds Girls High Sch LS12 209 D3
West Leeds High Sch LS12 209 D3
West Leeds St BD21 35 A7
West Lodge Cres HD2 135 B4
West Lodge Gdns LS7 60 C6
West Mead WF10 125 A7
West Moor Rd WF9 163 A2
West Moor View HD7 171 E4
West Moorlands Ave
WF13 118 B1
West Mount Pl HX1 202 C4
West Mount St LS11 214 A3
West Oaks Special Sch LS23 30 D7

West Par Guiseley LS20 22 E1
Halifax HX1 203 D2
Ilkley LS29 8 C4
Leeds LS16 59 A8
Rothwell LS26 100 F5
Sowerby Bridge HX6 112 D4
Wakefield WF1 216 B2
West Parade Ct WF1 216 B1
West Parade Flats 2 HX1 203 D2
West Parade St WF1 216 B1
West Park Ave LS8 44 B3
West Park Chase LS8 44 A3
West Park Cl LS8 44 A3
West Park Cres LS8 44 B2
West Park Dr
Darrington WF8 147 D2
Leeds LS16 59 A8
West Park Dr E LS8 44 B3
West Park Drive (W) LS8 43 F3
West Park Gdns LS8 44 B2
West Park Gr Batley WF17 118 A5
Leeds LS8 44 B2
West Park Pl LS8 44 B2
West Park Rd Batley WF17 117 F4
Bradford BD8 73 F8
Leeds LS8 44 B2
West Park St
8 Brighouse HD6 115 B2
Dewsbury WF13 118 B1
West Park Terr
Batley WF17 118 A5
8 Bradford BD8 73 F8
West Parks LS28 76 D7
West Pasture Cl LS18 40 F1
West Pinfold S71 179 C2
West Pk LS20 22 C2
West Pl HD5 154 D6
West Primley Park Dr LS17 43 D5
West Rd LS9 80 C3
West Rd (N) LS9 80 D3
West Royd BD15 53 C4
West Royd Ave
Bradford BD2 56 B4
Halifax HX1 202 C2
Mirfield WF14 138 A6
Shipley BD18 55 E8
West Royd Cl Halifax HX1 202 C1
Shipley BD18 55 D8
West Royd Cres BD18 55 E8
West Royd Dr
Mirfield WF14 138 A6
Shipley BD18 55 E8
West Royd Gr
Mirfield WF14 138 A6
Shipley BD18 55 E8
West Royd Mount BD18 55 E8
West Royd Pk WF14 138 A6
West Royd Rd BD18 55 E8
West Royd Terr BD18 55 E8
West Royd Villas 1 HX1 202 C1
West Royd Wlk BD18 55 E8
West Scausby Pk HX2 91 E7
West Shaw La BD22 51 A3
West Side Ret Pk LS20 39 F7
West Slaithwaite Rd HD7 169 C7
West St Baildon BD17 38 C4
Batley WF17 118 D5
2 Batley, Heckmondwike WF16 117 C4
Batley, Lower Soothill WF17 118 E5
Birkenshaw BD11 96 E5
Bradford BD2 56 B3
Bradford, Eastbrook BD1 201 C2
Brighouse, Bailiff Bridge HD6 115 B7
2 Brighouse, Waring Green HD6 115 A3
Castleford WF10 124 C8
Cleckheaton BD19 116 D7
Cleckheaton, Gomersal BD19 96 B1
Dewsbury WF12 139 C7
Elland HX4 134 B4
Halifax HX1 202 C3
Huddersfield HD3 135 B1
Ilkley LS29 8 B4
Leeds LS3 210 C4
Lofthouse Gate WF3 121 F2
Morley LS27 98 B3
Normanton WF6 123 A2
Pudsey LS28 76 E8
Royston S71 179 D4
Ryhill WF4 162 C1
Shelf HX3 93 B4
South Elmsall WF9 183 B4
South Hiendley S72 180 E5
South Kirkby WF9 182 A2
Sowerby Bridge HX6 112 B3
Todmorden OL14 108 A6
Wakefield WF2 141 F5
West Terrace St 9 LS28 57 D1
West Vale Dewsbury WF12 139 B6
Leeds LS12 210 B1
West Vale Junior & Infants Sch HX4 134 D7
West View
Ackworth M T WF7 163 D5
Arthington LS21 24 F6
Batley WF17 118 B2
Bradford BD4 75 A4
Brighouse BD19 94 F1
Crigglestone WF4 159 E4
Elland HX4 134 A4
Halifax HX1 202 B2
Halifax, Boothtown HX3 92 B2
Holme Chapel BB10 85 A8
Huddersfield HD1 153 D5

West View continued
Ilkley LS29 8 B3
Kippax LS25 83 B2
Leeds LS11 214 A4
Micklefield LS25 84 B6
Otley LS21 23 B8
15 Pudsey LS28 57 D2
Rothwell LS26 101 C5
Silsden BD20 5 E2
Wakefield WF2 120 B2
Yeadon LS19 39 F7
West View Ave
Burley in W LS29 9 E1
Castleford WF10 125 A7
Halifax HX2 202 A3
Shipley BD18 55 E7
West View Cl BD18 55 E7
West View Cres HX2 202 A3
West View Ct LS19 39 F7
West View Dr HX2 202 A3
West View Rd
Burley in W LS29 9 E1
Halifax HX3 92 B2
West View Rise HD1 153 D5
West View St 8 BD22 51 F8
West View Terr HX2 202 A4
West Villa Rd LS20 22 E1
West Way Leeds LS1 211 D4
Shipley BD18 54 D7
West Wells Cres WF5 140 C5
West Wells Rd WF5 140 D5
West Winds LS29 21 E5
West Wood Ct LS10 99 A5
West Wood Rd LS10 98 F4
West Yorks Transport Mus BD1 201 B1
West Yorkshire Ind Est BD4 95 E8
West Yorkshire Playhouse The LS2 212 A4
Westacres HD6 136 B8
Westborough Dr HX2 112 D7
Westborough High Sch WF13 139 A8
Westbourne Ave
Garforth LS25 82 D6
Leeds LS11 214 B3
1 Pontefract WF8 146 C7
Westbourne Cl Otley LS21 22 E7
Wakefield WF2 160 C6
Westbourne Cres
Garforth LS25 82 D6
Halifax HX3 113 D3
Pontefract WF8 146 B7
Westbourne Dr
Garforth LS25 82 D6
Guiseley LS20 22 C1
Menston LS29 22 A5
Westbourne First Sch BD8 55 B2
Westbourne Gdns LS25 82 D6
Westbourne Gr
Garforth LS25 82 D6
Halifax HX3 113 D3
Otley LS21 22 E7
Westbourne Mount
16 Leeds LS11 214 B3
2 Pontefract WF8 146 C7
Westbourne Pl
15 Leeds LS11 214 B3
Pudsey LS28 57 D1
Westbourne Rd
Bradford BD8 55 B2
Huddersfield HD1 153 D7
Pontefract WF8 146 C7
Westbourne St LS11 214 B3
Westbourne Terr
Garforth LS25 82 D6
Halifax HX3 113 D3
Westbrook Cl LS18 41 B2
Westbrook Ct HX3 203 D4
Westbrook Dr HD5 155 B6
Westbrook La LS18 41 B2
Westbrook Lane Primary Sch LS18 41 B3
Westbrook St BD7 74 D6
Westbrook Terr WF17 118 B6
Westburn Ave BD22 34 F5
Westburn Cres BD22 34 F5
Westburn Gr BD22 34 F5
Westburn Way BD22 34 F5
Westbury Cl BD4 75 D5
Westbury Gr LS10 215 F2
Westbury Mount LS10 215 F1
Westbury Pl HX1 202 A2
Westbury Pl N LS10 215 F2
Westbury Pl S LS10 215 F1
Westbury Rd BD6 73 D1
Westbury St Bradford BD4 75 D5
Elland HX5 135 A7
Middleton LS10 215 F1
Westbury Terr Halifax HX1 202 A2
Middleton LS10 215 F1
Westcliffe Ave BD17 38 B3
Westcliffe Dr HX2 112 D7
Westcliffe Rd
Cleckheaton BD19 116 C7
Shipley BD18 55 B7
Westcliffe Rise BD19 116 C7
Westcombe Ave LS8 44 A2
Westcombe Ct 13 BD12 94 C4
Westcroft HD7 171 E4
Westcroft Ave HX3 93 B4
Westcroft Dr WF5 119 C1
Westcroft Rd Bradford BD7 74 A4
Hemsworth WF9 181 D7
Westdale Dr LS28 76 D8
Westdale Gdns LS28 76 D8
Westdale Gr LS28 76 D8

Westdale Rd LS28 76 D8
Westdale Rise LS28 76 D8
Westend St BD1 74 D7
Westercroft La HX3 93 B3
Westercroft View HX3 93 B3
Westerley Cl HD8 174 A3
Westerley Cres BD20 5 C1
Westerley La HD8 174 A3
Westerly Croft LS12 209 F4
Westerly Rise LS12 209 F4
Westerly Way HD8 174 A3
Westerman Cl WF7 145 D6
Westerman St WF1 142 E3
Western Ave Batley WF17 97 A1
Keighley BD20 18 D3
Pontefract WF8 125 F1
Western Ct WF8 125 F1
Western Gales Way WF6 123 D1
Western Gr LS12 209 E1
Western Mount LS12 209 E1
Western Pl BD13 73 B1
Western Rd
Huddersfield HD4 153 A4
Leeds LS12 209 E1
Western St LS12 209 E1
Western Way BD6 94 A7
Westerton Cl WF3 120 B8
Westerton Ct BD12 95 B5
Westerton Prim Sch WF3 119 D7
Westerton Rd WF3 119 E7
Westerton Wlk WF3 120 B8
Westfell Cl BD22 34 F6
Westfell Rd BD22 34 F6
Westfell Way BD22 34 F6
Westfield Brighouse HX3 114 D7
Pudsey LS28 57 D1
Thornton BD13 73 A6
Westfield Ave
Brighouse HX3 114 D7
Castleford WF10 124 C5
Dewsbury WF12 140 A8
Huddersfield HD3 153 B7
Kippax LS25 83 A1
Kippax, Allerton Bywater WF10 103 A5
Knottingley WF11 126 F3
5 Leeds LS12 77 F8
Meltham HD7 170 C3
Pontefract WF8 146 C6
Skelmanthorpe HD8 174 F1
Yeadon LS19 39 F6
Westfield Bungalows WF9 183 A2
Westfield Cl Batley WF16 117 C5
Rothwell LS26 100 C4
Yeadon LS19 39 F6
Westfield Cotts WF8 146 C5
Westfield Cres
Bradford BD2 56 B1
Dearne S63 194 C1
Keighley BD20 18 F2
Leeds LS3 205 F1
Ossett WF5 140 C5
Ryhill WF4 162 A1
Shipley BD18 55 E6
Wakefield WF2 120 B2
Westfield Ct Horbury WF4 140 F2
Leeds LS3 205 F1
Mirfield WF14 138 A5
Rothwell LS26 100 C4
Westfield Dr
Brighouse HX3 114 D7
Keighley BD20 18 F1
Ossett WF5 140 C5
Skelmanthorpe HD8 174 F1
Yeadon LS19 39 F6
Westfield Farm WF5 140 C6
Westfield Gdns
Brighouse HX3 114 D7
Kippax LS25 82 F2
Westfield Gn BD4 75 E4
Westfield Gr
Ackworth M T WF7 164 C8
Bradford BD10 56 A8
Castleford WF10 124 C5
Dewsbury WF13 138 F8
Ingbirchworth S36 191 D1
Kippax WF10 103 A5
Shipley BD18 55 E6
Wakefield WF1 216 B4
Yeadon LS19 39 F6
Westfield Ind Est LS19 40 A7
Westfield La Bradford BD10 56 A8
Brighouse BD12, BD19 94 D1
Darrington WF8 147 C3
Emley HD8 174 F8
Kippax LS25 83 A1
Norton WF8 166 F3
Shipley BD18 55 F7
South Elmsall WF9 182 F2
South Milford LS25 84 F2
Thorner LS14 45 E4
Westfield Mount LS19 39 F6
Westfield Oval LS19 39 E6
Westfield Pk WF1 216 B4
Westfield Pl
Brighouse BD19 94 E1
Halifax HX1 202 C2
Wakefield WF2 120 B2
Westfield Rd Batley WF16 117 D5
Bradford, Clayton BD14 73 B4
Bradford, Girlington BD9 55 A2
Hemsworth WF9 181 D7
Horbury WF4 140 F2

Westfield Rd continued
Keighley BD20 18 F1
Knottingley WF11 126 F3
Leeds LS3 205 F1
Morley LS27 98 A4
Rothwell LS26 100 C3
Wakefield WF1 216 B4
Westfield St Batley WF16 117 C5
Halifax HX1 203 D2
Ossett WF5 140 C5
Westfield Terr
Baildon BD17 38 C4
Bradford BD2 56 B1
2 Bradford, Clayton BD14 73 B4
Halifax HX1 202 C4
2 Hebden Bridge HX7 89 E1
4 Horbury WF4 141 A1
Kippax WF10 103 A5
Leeds LS3 205 F1
Leeds, Chapel Allerton LS7 60 C7
Wakefield WF1 216 B4
Westfield View WF1 216 B4
Westfield Villas WF4 140 F1
Westfields
Castleford WF10 124 C5
Royston S71 179 A4
Westfields Ave WF14 138 B5
Westfields Rd WF14 138 A5
Westgarth LS22 13 B3
Westgate Baildon BD17 38 C4
Bradford BD1 74 D7
Bradford, Eccleshill BD2 56 C4
Brighouse HD6 115 E2
Cleckheaton BD19 116 D7
Dewsbury WF13 139 D8
Elland HX5 134 F7
Guiseley LS20 39 B8
Halifax HX1 203 E3
Hemsworth WF9 181 C6
Honley HD7 171 F4
Huddersfield HD1 154 A6
Huddersfield, Almondbury HD5 154 F2
Leeds LS1 211 D4
Liversedge WF16 117 C4
Meltham HD7 170 D2
Otley LS21 22 F7
Shipley BD18 55 B8
Wakefield WF1, WF2 216 B2
Westgate Cl WF3 121 C8
Westgate Ct WF3 121 C8
Westgate End WF2 142 A5
Westgate Gr WF3 121 C8
Westgate Hill First Sch BD4 96 A8
Westgate Hill St BD4 96 B8
Westgate La WF3 121 C8
Westgate Market HX1 203 E3
Westgate Ret & L Pk WF2 216 A1
Westgate Sta WF2 216 A2
Westgate Terr
Birkenshaw BD4 96 A8
13 Dewsbury WF13 139 C8
Westgrove Ct BD19 116 C8
Westhill Ave BD13 52 E5
Westholme Rd HX1 202 B2
Westholme St BD1 201 A2
Westland Cl BD20 16 E6
Westland Ct LS11 99 B8
Westland Rd LS11 214 B1
Westland Sq LS11 99 B8
Westlands Dr BD15 54 C1
Westlands Gr BD15 54 C1
Westlea Ave BD20 18 F1
Westleigh 3 BD16 37 A4
Westleigh Cl BD17 38 A2
Westleigh Dr BD17 38 A2
Westleigh Rd BD17 38 A2
Westleigh Way BD17 38 A2
Westley Ave HD7 188 F8
Westlock Ave LS9 208 A1
Westmead LS28 57 A1
Westminster Ave BD14 73 A4
Westminster Cl LS13 57 F4
Westminster Cres
Bradford BD14 73 A4
Leeds LS15 80 E7
Westminster Croft LS13 57 F4
Westminster Dr
Bradford BD14 73 A4
Pudsey LS13 57 F4
Westminster Gdns BD14 73 A4
Westminster Pl BD3 55 F1
Westminster Rd BD3 55 F1
Westminster Terr BD3 55 F1
Westmoor Ave BD17 38 B4
Westmoor Cl BD17 38 B4
Westmoor County Sch WF13 117 F1
Westmoor Pl LS13 58 B3
Westmoor Rd LS13 58 B3
Westmoor Rise LS13 58 B3
Westmoor St LS13 58 B3
Westmoreland Mount 1 LS13 58 D4
Westmorland House 3 WF1 216 B2
Westmorland St WF1 216 B2
Westmount St 11 WF8 146 C8
Westoff La S72 180 D7
Weston Ave BD13 92 D8
Weston Cres LS21 10 F1
Weston Dr LS21 10 E1
Weston La LS21 10 E1
Weston Moor Rd LS21 10 D8
Weston Park View LS21 10 D1
Weston Rd LS29 8 B4
Weston Ridge LS21 10 E1
Weston St BD22 34 F5
Weston Vale Rd BD13 92 D8
Westover Ave 6 LS13 58 C3
Westover Gdns LS28 76 C7
Westover Gn LS13 58 C3
Westover Gr 3 LS13 58 C3
Westover Mount 10 LS13 58 C3
Westover Rd LS13 58 C3
Westover St 2 LS13 58 C3
Westover Terr 1 LS13 58 C3
Westover View 5 LS13 58 C3
Westridge Dr HD4 153 C1
Westroyd Clifton LS21 11 A3
Pudsey LS28 76 C6
Westroyd Ave
Cleckheaton BD19 95 D2
Pudsey LS28 76 C6
Westroyd Cres LS28 76 C6
Westroyd Gdns LS28 76 C6
Westroyd Infant Sch LS28 57 D2
Westvale Mews LS13 58 E1
Westview Ave BD20 35 B8
Westview Cl BD20 4 C5
Westview Ct BD20 35 A8
Westview Gr BD20 35 A8
Westview Way BD20 35 B8
Westville Ave LS29 8 A4
Westville Cl LS29 8 A4
Westville Rd LS29 8 A4
Westville Way BD13 72 D6
Westward Croft HD3 135 C2
Westward Ho Halifax HX3 92 A4
16 Queensbury BD13 72 E1
Westway Batley WF17 118 F3
Bingley BD16 37 B5
Bradford BD9 54 C2
Garforth LS25 82 D6
Guiseley LS20 39 B8
Keighley BD20 17 F1
Mirfield WF14 137 F7
Pudsey LS28 57 C3
Westways WF2 120 F2
Westways Cl WF2 120 F2
Westways Dr LS8 61 C7
Westways Rise WF2 120 F2
Westwinn Garth LS14 45 C1
Westwinn View LS14 45 C1
Westwood Ave
Bradford BD2 56 B5
Honley HD7 172 C5
Westwood Cl
Featherstone WF7 145 D7
Morley LS27 98 B6
Westwood Cres BD16 54 A8
Westwood Dr LS29 7 F2
Westwood Edge Rd HD7 152 A3
Westwood Fold HD7 152 B2
Westwood Gr BD2 56 B5
Westwood Primary Sch LS11 99 A4
Westwood Rd
Castleford WF10 124 B5
Ossett WF5 140 F5
Westwood Rise Ilkley LS29 7 F2
Morley LS27 98 B6
Westwood Side LS27 98 B7
Westwood St HD5 137 A6
Westwood Way LS23 30 D8
Wetherby Bsns Pk LS22 13 F6
Wetherby County Primary Sch LS22 13 E5
Wetherby Gr 8 LS4 59 C2
Wetherby High Sch LS22 13 F5
Wetherby Pl LS4 205 D2
Wetherby Race Course LS22 14 B6
Wetherby Rd Bardsey LS17 28 E4
Bramham LS23 30 C3
Collingham LS22 13 D3
Kirk Deighton LS22 13 E8
Leeds LS8 61 D7
Scarcroft LS14 45 C6
Sicklinghall LS22 12 D5
Thorner LS14 45 C6
Thorp Arch LS23 14 F4
Wetherby LS22 13 D3
Wetherby Terr 6 LS4 59 C2
Wetherhill St WF17 118 B5
Wetherill Terr 4 WF13 117 F3
Wetlands Rd HD7 170 E1
Wetton Ct BD3 75 D7
Weydale Ave HD3 153 A8
Weyhill Dr BD15 73 B8
Weymouth Ave
Bradford BD15 73 A8
Huddersfield HD3 153 B7
Weymouth St HX1 203 E3
Whack House Cl LS19 40 A6
Whack House La LS19 40 A7
Whalley La BD13 52 E2
Whams Rd S36 200 F2
Wharf St Bradford BD3 201 C4
Brighouse HD6 115 B2
Dewsbury WF12 139 D7
Leeds LS2 212 A3
Shipley BD17 55 B8
Sowerby Bridge HX6 112 C4
12 Todmorden OL14 108 A1
Wharfdale View LS29 22 A4
Wharfe Bank LS22 28 E8
Wharfe Cl LS16 42 D4
Wharfe Cres LS21 24 D7
Wharfe Gr LS22 13 D5
Wharfe Grange Hospl LS22 13 D5
Wharfe Mews LS29 22 B4
Wharfe Pk LS29 7 A8
Wharfe Rein LS22 28 E8
Wharfe St LS21 23 B8
Wharfe View Pool LS21 24 C7
Wetherby LS22 13 D5
Wharfe View Rd LS29 8 B4
Wharfe Way WF10 125 B8
Wharfedale Ave LS7 206 B4
Wharfedale Cres
Garforth LS25 82 F6
Skelmanthorpe HD8 175 B1
Wharfedale Ct Leeds LS14 61 F5
Otley LS21 23 A8
Wharfedale Dr Ilkley LS29 8 C4
Normanton WF6 123 A4
Wharfedale Gdns BD17 38 E4
Wharfedale General Hospl LS21 10 F2
Wharfedale Gr LS7 206 B4
Wharfedale Mews LS21 23 A8
Wharfedale Mount
Leeds LS7 206 B4
Shelf HX3 93 B5
Wharfedale Pl LS7 206 B4
Wharfedale Rd BD4 95 A7
Wharfedale Rise
Bradford BD9 54 C2
East Ardsley WF3 119 D7
Wharfedale St LS7 206 B4
Wharfedale View
Addingham LS29 6 E8
Leeds LS7 206 B4
Wharfeside La LS29 8 C5
Wharncliffe Cres BD2 56 D4
Wharncliffe Dr BD2 56 D4
Wharncliffe Gr
Bradford BD2 56 D4
Shipley BD18 55 B6
Wharncliffe Rd
Shipley BD18 55 B6
Wakefield WF2 160 A4
Wharton St 4 WF15 117 B4
Wharton Terr 3 WF16 117 D3
Whartons Prim Sch The LS21 11 A2
Whartons The LS21 11 A2
Wheat Cl WF13 138 F8
Wheat Field Ave HD3 153 A8
Wheat Head Cres BD22 34 E5
Wheat Head Dr BD22 34 F5
Wheat Head La BD22 34 E5
Wheat St BD22 35 A4
Wheatcroft WF10 125 B7
Wheatcroft Ave WF17 118 C4
Wheater House WF1 216 B2
Wheater Rd BD7 74 A5
Wheatfield Ct LS28 76 D6
Wheathouse Rd HD2 135 F1
Wheathouse Terr HD2 135 F1
Wheatings The WF5 140 F5
Wheatlands Ilkley LS29 8 C4
Pudsey LS28 57 C2
Wheatlands Ave
Bradford BD9 54 E2
Glusburn BD20 16 C7
Wheatlands Cres BD9 54 E2
Wheatlands Dr
Bradford BD9 54 E2
Liversedge WF15 116 F2
Wheatlands Gr BD9 54 E2
Wheatlands La BD20 16 C7
Wheatlands Sq BD9 54 E2
Wheatley Ave Ilkley LS29 8 E4
Normanton WF6 123 B1
Wheatley Cl 3 HX3 92 A1
Wheatley Ct HX2 91 D4
Wheatley Dr WF14 138 A3
Wheatley Gdns LS29 8 E3
Wheatley Gr LS29 8 F3
Wheatley Hill La HD8 192 E8
Wheatley La LS29 8 F4
Wheatley Lane Ends HX3 91 E2
Wheatley Rd Halifax HX3 91 F2
Ilkley LS29 8 C3
Wheatley Rise Ilkley LS29 8 E3
Mapplewell S75 178 B2
Wheaton Ave LS15 81 B8
Wheaton Ct 9 LS15 81 A8
Wheatroyd Cres WF5 140 E2
Wheatroyd La HD5 154 E2
Wheelright Coll WF13 139 B7
Wheelwright Ave LS12 209 D1
Wheelwright Cl LS12 209 D1
Wheelwright Dr WF13 118 B2
Wheelwright St 12 WF13 139 C8
Wheldale La WF10 104 E2
Wheldon Rd WF10 104 B2
Whernside Mount BD7 73 E2
Whernside Way HX2 91 A3
Wherwell Rd HD6 136 C8
Whetley Cl BD8 74 C8
Whetley First Sch BD8 74 A8
Whetley Gr BD8 55 A1
Whetley Hill BD8 74 C8
Whetley La BD8 74 A8
Whetley Middle Sch BD8 74 A8
Whetley Terr 1 BD8 74 C8
Whewell St 4 WF17 96 E1
Whimbrel Cl 4 BD8 73 C7
Whimbrel Mews LS27 98 C3
Whin Cl WF9 181 D5
Whin Gdns S63 194 D1
Whin Knoll Ave BD21 34 F8
Whin Mount WF6 144 C8
Whin St BD21 35 A7
Whin View Ct WF4 162 C1
Whinberry Pl WF17 96 F3
Whinbrook Cres LS17 43 C1
Whinbrook Ct LS17 43 C1
Whinbrook Gdns LS17 43 C1
Whinbrook Gr LS17 43 C1
Whinburn Sch BD20 17 F2
Whincop Ave WF10 124 A7
Whincover Cl LS12 77 F5
Whincover Cross LS12 77 F5
Whincover Dr LS12 77 F5
Whincover Gdns LS12 77 F5
Whincover Gr LS12 77 F5
Whincover Grange LS12 77 F5
Whincover Hill LS12 77 F5
Whincover Mount LS12 77 F5
Whincover Rd LS12 77 F5
Whincover View LS12 77 F5
Whincup Gdns 4 LS10 215 E2
Whinfield LS16 42 B4
Whinfield Ave BD22 34 E7
Whinfield Cl BD22 34 F8
Whinfield Dr BD22 34 E8
Whinfield Pl WF5 141 B4
Whingate LS12 209 D3
Whingate Ave LS12 209 D3
Whingate Bsns Pk LS12 209 E3
Whingate Cl LS12 209 D3
Whingate Gn LS12 209 D3
Whingate Gr LS12 209 D3
Whingate Primary Sch LS12 209 D3
Whingate Rd LS12 209 D3
Whingrove Ave HD7 170 D1
Whinmoor Cl S75 193 F1
Whinmoor Cres LS14 45 A1
Whinmoor Ct Leeds LS14 45 A1
Silkstone S75 193 F1
Whinmoor Dr S75 193 F1
Whinmoor Gdns LS14 45 A1
Whinmoor La LS17 44 F3
Whinmoor View S75 193 F1
Whinmoor Way Leeds LS14 62 D5
Silkstone S75 193 F1
Whinmore Gdns BD19 117 C7
Whinney Cl WF7 144 D5
Whinney Field HX3 113 C4
Whinney Hill Pk HD6 115 B5
Whinney Moor Ave WF2 141 E4
Whinney Royd La HX3 93 A5
Whinny La WF7 144 D5
Whins La Spofforth HG3 12 C8
Thorp Arch LS23 14 F1
Whins The BD21 35 A2
Whinside Cres S63 194 C1
Whirlaw Ave OL14 108 A7
Whirlaw La OL14 108 B8
Whiskers La HX3 92 E4
Whisperwood Cl WF1 121 D5
Whisperwood Rd WF1 121 D5
Whitacre Cl HD2 136 E3
Whitacre St HD2 136 E3
Whitaker Ave BD2 56 C3
Whitaker Cl BD2 56 C3
Whitaker St Batley WF17 118 D4
Pudsey LS28 57 D2
Whitburn Way 7 BD15 73 B8
Whitby Ave HD2 136 B2
Whitby Cres WF12 139 F8
Whitby Rd BD8 55 A1
Whitby Terr BD8 55 A1
Whitcliffe Mount Sch BD19 116 B8
Whitcliffe Rd BD19 116 D8
Whitcliffe Road First Sch BD19 116 D8
Whitcliffe Sq BD19 116 D8
White Abbey Rd BD8 74 C8
White Apron St WF9 182 B2
White Birch Terr HX3 91 F2
White Castle Ct BD13 72 B2
White Cross HD2 136 E5
White Cross Gdns S72 180 D6
White Cross Rd WF12 118 E2
White Ct WF4 162 A8
White Field La HX7 110 C8
White Gate Halifax HX2 91 D7
Honley HD7 171 F5
White Gate Rd
Holme HD7 198 D7
Holmfirth HD7 188 D1
White Gr LS8 61 A8
White Hart Dr HD4 154 A2
White Hart Fold
South Elmsall WF9 183 B6
8 Todmorden OL14 108 B5
White Hill HD7 169 C7
White Horse Cl WF17 97 B2
White Horse Fold WF10 103 E6
White Horse Yd WF1 216 B2
White House Bglws WF2 142 B3
White La Bradford BD6 74 D1
Haworth BD22 33 F3
Hooton Pagnell DN5 195 E4
White Laith Ave LS14 62 B8
White Laith Primary Sch LS14 62 C7
White Laithe App 2 LS14 62 B8
White Laithe Cl LS14 62 B8
White Laithe Croft LS14 62 B8
White Laithe Gdns LS14 62 C8
White Laithe Gn LS14 62 C8
White Laithe Gr LS14 62 C8
White Laithe Rd LS14 62 C8
White Laithe Wlk 4 LS14 62 C8
White Lands LS19 40 A4
White Lane Top 1 BD6 94 D8
White Lee Cl WF16 117 E6
White Lee Croft HX7 89 F1
White Lee Gdns HX7 89 F1
White Lee Rd WF16 117 E6
White Lee Side WF16 117 E6
White Ley Bank HD7 190 A7
White Ley Rd WF8 166 E1
White Rose Ave
Garforth LS25 83 A8
Huddersfield HD5 154 F6
White Rose Ctr LS11 98 E7
White Rose Way LS25 83 A7
White Slack Gate OL14 129 A6
White St 7 LS26 101 C6
White Walls La HD7 187 F3
White Wells LS29 8 B2
White Wells Gdns HD7 189 D3
White Wells Rd HD7 189 D3
White's Cl BD9 54 D3
White's Rd WF1 216 C2
White's Terr BD8 55 B1
White's View BD8 74 B8
Whiteacre St HD2 136 F3
Whitebeam Gn WF8 125 F1
Whitebeam La 6 LS10 99 D8
Whitebeam Pk HD2 135 D2
Whitebeam Wlk BD2 56 B5
Whitebridge Ave LS9 80 E8
Whitebridge Primary Sch LS15 80 E7
Whitebridge Spur LS9 61 E1
Whitebridge View LS9 61 E1
Whitechapel Cl LS8 61 C6
Whitechapel Gr BD19 95 A1
Whitechapel Middle Sch BD19 116 C8
Whitechapel Rd
Brighouse BD19 116 A8
Cleckheaton BD19 116 C8
Whitechapel Way LS8 61 B6
Whitecliffe Cres LS26 82 A2
Whitecliffe Dr LS26 82 A2
Whitecliffe Rise LS26 82 A2
Whitecoat Primary Sch LS13 58 D4
Whitecote Gdns LS13 58 B4
Whitecote Hill LS13 58 B4
Whitecote La Leeds LS13 58 B4
South Milford LS25 84 F4
Whitecote Rise LS13 58 B4
Whitefield Pl BD8 74 A8
Whitegate
East Keswick LS17 28 C6
Halifax HX3 113 D4
Whitegate Dr HX3 113 D4
Whitegate Hill WF8 164 E8
Whitegate La WF8 164 E8
Whitegate Rd Halifax HX3 113 D4
Huddersfield HD4 154 B4
Whitegate Terr HX3 113 D4
Whitegate Top HX3 113 E5
Whitegates Cl WF1 121 A1
Whitegates Gr HD8 155 D2
Whitehall Ave
Bradford BD12 94 C1
Mirfield WF14 138 A7
Wakefield WF1 121 A1
Whitehall Cres WF1 121 A1
Whitehall Croft LS26 100 F5
Whitehall Ct 1 WF4 141 B1
Whitehall Gr
Birkenshaw BD11 96 B5
Birkenshaw, Drighlington BD11 96 D6
Whitehall Quay LS1 211 E3
Whitehall Rd
Birkenshaw BD11 96 E6
Bradford BD12 94 C1
Brighouse BD12 94 C1
Whitehall Rd BD19 95 D2
Whitehall Rd
Gildersome LS12 77 D2
Gildersome LS12 77 D2
Leeds LS1, LS12 211 D3
Slaithwaite HD7 170 C8
Whitehall Rd E BD11 96 B5
Whitehall Rd W
Birkenshaw BD11 96 A4
Cleckheaton BD19 95 E3
Whitehall Rise WF1 142 A8
Whitehall St
Brighouse HX3 114 D8
Wakefield WF2 141 F5
Whitehall Trad Est LS12 77 F4
Whitehall Way WF13 139 D8
Whitehaven Cl BD6 93 F7
Whitehead Gr BD2 56 C1
Whitehead La
Huddersfield HD4 154 A3
Meltham HD4, HD7 170 F6
Whitehead Pl BD2 56 C1
Whitehead St BD3 75 B6
Whitehead's Terr 1 HX1 202 B3
Whitehill Cres HX2 91 E6
Whitehill Dr HX2 91 E6
Whitehill Gn HX2 91 F6
Whitehill Prim Schs HX2 91 E6
Whitehill Rd Halifax HX2 91 E6
Haworth BD22 33 D5
Whitehouse Ave LS26 102 D8
Whitehouse Cres LS26 102 E8
Whitehouse Dr LS26 102 D8
Whitehouse La
Swillington LS26 82 C2
Yeadon LS19 40 F8
Whitehouse St LS10 212 A1
Whitelands 1 LS28 76 F8
Whitelands Cres BD17 38 D3
Whitelands Rd BD17 38 D3
Whiteley Ave HX6 111 F3
Whiteley Croft LS21 23 A7

Whiteley Croft Cl LS21 23 A7
Whiteley Croft Garth LS21 22 F7
Whiteley Croft Rd LS21 23 A7
Whiteley Croft Rise LS21 23 A7
Whiteley St
Featherstone WF7 145 C5
Huddersfield HD3 153 B4
Whiteley Terr HX6 132 C2
Whitelock St LS7 207 D1
Whiteplatts St 12 OL14 108 B6
Whiterose Mead LS25 83 A7
Whiteshaw Mews BD13 52 D2
Whitestone Cres LS19 40 B7
Whitestone La 2 HD1 154 B8
Whiteways BD2 55 E3
Whitewood Cl S71 179 B3
Whitfield Ave LS10 215 E4
Whitfield Gdns LS10 215 E4
Whitfield Pl LS10 215 E4
Whitfield Sq LS10 215 E4
Whitfield St
9 Cleckheaton BD19 116 D8
Leeds LS8 207 F3
Whitfield Way LS10 215 E4
Whitford Freight Ctr WF10 123 D5
Whitham Cl LS23 30 D8
Whitkirk Cl LS15 81 E8
Whitkirk La LS15 81 D8
Whitkirk Primary Sch LS15 81 C7
Whitlam St BD18 54 F8
Whitley Gdns LS8 207 E3
Whitley Grange Hospl WF12 138 F1
Whitley La HX3 114 A5
Whitley Pl WF10 103 B4
Whitley Rd Dewsbury WF12 139 B1
Keighley BD21 35 A5
Whitley Common S36 200 E7
Whitley Spring Cres WF5 140 F6
Whitley Spring Rd WF5 140 F6
Whitley St Bingley BD16 36 F3
Bradford BD3 201 D3
Halifax HX1 203 D2
Whitley Terr S36 200 D5
Whitley Way WF4 156 E5
Whitteron Cl HD3 135 B1
Whittle Cres BD14 73 B5
Whitton Croft Rd LS29 8 B4
Whitty La HX2 112 B6
Whitwell Ave HX5 135 B7
Whitwell Dr HX5 135 B7
Whitwell Gr HX5 135 B7
Whitwell Green La HX5 135 B6
Whitwell St BD4 201 D1
Whitwood Common La WF10 123 E5
Whitwood Enterprise Pk WF6 123 B3
Whitwood La
Brighouse HD6 115 D7
Castleford WF10 123 E6
Whitwood Terr WF10 123 E5
Whitworth Rd 1 WF13 139 B7
Wholestone Gate HD7 152 B5
Whytecote End BD12 94 C4
Wibsey Bank BD6 74 D1
Wibsey First Sch BD6 74 B1
Wibsey Middle Sch BD6 74 B1
Wibsey Park Ave BD6 94 A8
Wicken Cl BD10 56 C6
Wicken La BD13 72 D7
Wicket LS28 57 B7
Wickets Cl BD6 94 D8
Wickets The Leeds LS6 59 F7
Leeds, Whitkirk Lane End LS15 81 E7
Wickham Ave
Boston Spa LS23 30 C8
Bradford BD6 94 C8
Wickham Cl LS23 30 C8
Wickham St Brighouse BD19 94 F1
Leeds LS11 214 A3
Wicking La HX6 132 A8
Wickins La HD7 188 D6
Wickleden Gate HD7 189 D3
Widdop Rd HX7 88 D6
Wide La Morley LS27 98 C3
Morley, Bantam Grove LS27 98 D4
Oakworth BD22 34 B3
Wigan St BD1 74 D7
Wigeon App LS27 98 C4
Wiggan La HD2 136 D4
Wiggin Cross HD7 152 E1
Wighill La Thorp Arch LS23 15 C2
Wighill LS24 15 C2
Wighill St BD20 16 D5
Wightman St BD3 56 A1
Wignall St BD20 18 B2
Wigton Chase LS17 44 A5
Wigton Gate LS17 43 E6
Wigton Gn LS17 43 F6
Wigton Gr LS17 43 E6
Wigton Moor Primary Sch LS17 43 F5
Wigton Park Cl LS17 43 F6
Wike La LS17 28 B3
Wike Ridge Ave LS17 44 B6
Wike Ridge Cl LS17 44 A6
Wike Ridge Ct LS17 44 B6
Wike Ridge Fold LS17 44 A6
Wike Ridge Gr LS17 44 B5
Wike Ridge La
Harewood LS17 44 C7
Leeds LS17 44 C7
Wike Ridge Mews LS17 44 B5
Wike Ridge Mount LS17 44 B5
Wike Ridge View LS17 44 A5
Wilberlee Jun & Inf Sch HD7 151 D2
Wilby St BD19 116 D7
Wilcock La BD20 4 F5
Wild Gr LS28 76 A7
Wild's Yd WF1 216 C1
Wilday Cl BD16 36 E6
Wildspur Gr HD7 189 E4
Wilford Rd S71 178 E1
Wilfred Ave LS15 81 B8
Wilfred St Bradford BD14 73 D4
2 Leeds LS15 81 B8
Wilfrid Terr LS12 78 A4
Wilkin St BD21 35 B7
Wilkinson Fold 9 BD12 94 C3
Wilkinson Terr BD7 73 F6
Wilkinson Way LS21 10 E1
Willan's Rd WF13 118 C1
Willans Ave LS26 100 E7
Willerton Cl WF12 119 B3
Willgutter La BD22 33 F1
William Ave 2 LS15 80 E8
William Henry Smith Sch The HD6 135 E8
William Henry St
1 Brighouse HD6 115 A3
2 Shipley BD18 54 F8
William Hey Ct LS9 208 B2
William Horsfall St HD4 153 C3
William Prince Gr WF1 142 E4
William Rise LS15 80 E8
William St Batley WF13 117 F3
Bradford BD5 201 B2
Bradford, Buttershaw BD6 93 F7
Bradford, Swain Green BD4 75 D5
Bradford, Tong Street BD4 75 D1
10 Brighouse HD6 115 A1
Castleford WF10 103 D1
Castleford, New Fryston WF10 104 C2
Denholme BD13 52 D1
Dewsbury WF12 139 E8
Dewsbury, Ravensthorpe WF13 138 E5
Elland HX4 134 D6
3 Huddersfield HD1 154 B7
Huddersfield, Paddock Brow HD4 153 C4
Leeds LS6 205 E3
2 Liversedge WF15 117 B4
Morley LS27 98 C8
Pudsey LS28 57 F2
8 Pudsey, Stanningley LS28 57 D1
William View LS15 80 E8
Williams Dr BD20 17 B5
Williams Rd BD20 17 B5
Williamson St HX1 202 C4
Willis St LS9 212 B3
Willoughby Terr LS11 210 C1
Willow App LS4 205 E1
Willow Ave Boston Spa LS23 30 D6
Bradford BD2 56 A6
Leeds LS4 205 E1
Willow Bank Halifax HX1 202 C1
Todmorden OL14 108 B6
Willow Bank Dr WF8 125 E3
Willow Beck WF4 179 A6
Willow Cl Bradford BD6 94 C7
Burley in W LS29 9 E1
Cleckheaton BD19 117 B7
Guiseley LS20 22 E1
Halifax HX2 112 D6
Leeds LS4 205 E1
Willow Clough HX6 132 D2
Willow Cres
Boston Spa LS23 30 D6
Bradford BD2 56 A6
Leeds LS15 80 F7
Normanton WF6 144 A8
Sowerby Bridge HX6 112 C5
Willow Croft
Cleckheaton BD19 116 C7
Menston LS29 22 A4
Willow Ct Castleford WF10 124 E6
Featherstone WF7 124 C1
Garforth LS25 82 E7
Pool LS21 24 D6
Wakefield WF2 141 D7
Willow Dene Ave HX2 112 D5
Willow Dr Bradford BD6 94 C7
Halifax HX2 112 D6
Hemsworth WF9 181 D5
Wakefield WF1 142 E3
Willow Field HD8 156 A3
Willow Fold WF2 141 F7
Willow Garth
Crigglestone WF4 159 F6
Featherstone WF7 124 C1
Leeds LS4 205 E1
South Elmsall WF9 183 B2
Willow Garth Ave
Glusburn BD20 16 D7
Leeds LS14 62 B8
Willow Garth Cl LS14 62 B8
Willow Gdns Bradford BD2 56 A6
Castleford WF10 125 D5
Guiseley LS20 22 E1
Wakefield WF2 141 D7
Willow Glade LS23 30 D5
Willow Gn WF1 121 B3
Willow Gr Boston Spa LS23 30 D6
Bradford BD2 56 A6
Huddersfield HD7 152 E5
Keighley BD21 35 A3
Kippax LS25 82 F3
Ossett WF5 140 E3
Wakefield WF1 142 E3
Willow Hall Dr HX6 112 D5
Willow Hall La HX6 112 D5
Willow La
Boston Spa LS23 30 D5
Crofton WF1 143 D7
Featherstone WF7 124 C1
Huddersfield HD1 154 A8
Wakefield WF2 141 D7
Willow La E
Featherstone WF7 124 C1
Huddersfield HD1 154 B8
Willow Mews WF2 141 F7
Willow Mount WF2 141 F7
Willow Park Dr HX3 93 D6
Willow Park Junior Sch WF8 146 F8
Willow Pk
Lofthouse Gate WF1 121 B2
Pontefract WF8 146 F8
Willow Rd Batley WF17 118 E4
Castleford WF10 124 D6
Dearne S63 194 D1
Knottingley WF11 127 A5
Leeds LS4 205 E1
Pudsey LS28 57 D2
Wakefield WF2 141 D7
Willow Rise Halifax HX2 112 D6
Skelmanthorpe HD8 175 A1
Willow Sq 3 LS26 101 C5
Willow St Bradford BD8 74 A8
Cleckheaton BD19 95 D1
Halifax HX1 202 C2
Sowerby Bridge HX6 112 D4
Willow Terr
Batley WF17 118 E4
Sowerby Bridge HX6 112 C5
Willow Terrace Rd LS1 206 B1
Willow Tree Cl BD21 35 D5
Willow Tree Gdns
Bingley BD16 37 C5
Burley in W LS29 9 F2
Willow Vale LS22 13 E7
Willow View
Sowerby Bridge HX6 112 C5
Wakefield WF2 141 F7
Willow Villas BD2 56 A6
Willow Way BD20 16 C4
Willow Well Rd LS15 80 F8
Willow Wlk WF15 117 A3
Willowbank Gr HD5 137 B1
Willowbridge La WF10 124 A6
Willowbridge Rd WF8 166 F5
Willowbrook DN6 184 F2
Willowdene La WF8 125 D3
Willowfield Ave HX2 112 D5
Willowfield Cl HX2 112 D6
Willowfield Cres
Bradford BD2 56 A6
Halifax HX2 112 D6
Willowfield Dr HX2 112 D5
Willowfield Rd HX2 112 D6
Willowfield St BD7 74 B6
Willowfield Terr HX2 202 A1
Willowfield View HX2 112 D6
Willowgarth Cl WF4 180 A8
Willowgarth High Sch S72 181 A1
Willows The
Crigglestone WF4 159 F5
Halifax HX2 91 E7
Harden BD16 36 B1
Horbury WF4 141 A1
Leeds LS17 43 C2
Wills Gill LS20 22 F1
Willwood Ave HD3 153 B7
Wilman Dr WF5 140 C6
Wilman Hill 3 BD6 74 B1
Wilman Post WF5 140 C6
Wilmar Dr HD3 134 E1
Wilmer Dr
Shipley, Frizinghall BD18 55 A5
Shipley, Heaton BD9 55 A4
Wilmer Rd BD9 55 A3
Wilmington Gr LS7 206 C2
Wilmington St LS7 207 D2
Wilmington Terr LS7 206 C2
Wilmot Rd LS29 8 C4
Wilmur Mount HX2 111 D6
Wilsden First Sch BD15 53 C5
Wilsden Hill Rd BD15 53 B5
Wilsden Old Rd BD16 36 B1
Wilsden Rd Bradford BD15 53 F3
Harden BD16 36 B1
Wilshaw Mill Rd HD7 188 B7
Wilshaw Rd HD7 188 B8
Wilson Ave
Mirfield WF14 137 F5
Ossett WF5 141 A4
Steeton BD20 17 B6
Wilson Ct WF1 121 C4
Wilson Dr WF1 121 B4
Wilson Gdns HD3 153 A4
Wilson Rd Bingley BD16 36 F4
Bradford BD12 94 E4
Halifax HX1 202 B1
Mirfield WF14 137 F5
Wilson St Bradford BD8 55 C1
Castleford WF10 124 C8
Featherstone WF7 145 C5
Glusburn BD20 16 D7
Pontefract WF8 125 D1
Sutton in C BD20 16 E5
Wilson Terr WF14 137 F5
Wilson Wood St WF17 118 C2
Wilson's Row LS26 102 F3
Wilsons Yd 6 LS28 57 D1
Wilton Ave HD2 136 E5
Wilton Gr LS6 59 E6
Wilton Rd LS29 8 A3
Wilton St Bradford BD5 201 B2
Brighouse HD6 114 F3
Dewsbury WF12 139 D7
Wilton Terr BD19 116 D7
Wimborne Dr
Bradford BD15 54 C1
Keighley BD21 34 F8
Winbrooke Terr BD6 74 A1
Winburg Rd BD7 74 A5
Winchester St LS12 210 A3
Winchester Way WF9 183 A4
Winden Cl
Crigglestone WF4 159 D6
Lofthouse Gate WF3 121 C5
Winden Gr WF3 121 B5
Windermere Ave LS29 22 A6
Windermere Dr
Garforth LS25 82 F6
Knottingley WF11 126 E1
Leeds LS17 42 F6
Windermere Rd
Bacup OL13 106 A3
Baildon BD17 37 F1
Batley WF12 118 E2
Bradford BD7 73 E3
Castleford WF10 125 D7
Meltham HD7 170 E1
Wakefield WF2 141 F7
Windermere Terr 3 BD7 73 E3
Winders Dale 2 LS27 98 A6
Windgate BD20 17 F8
Windhill Ave S75 178 A3
Windhill CE First Sch BD18 55 E8
Windhill Cres
Mapplewell S75 178 A3
Wakefield WF1 142 E8
Windhill Ct WF1 142 F8
Windhill Dr S75 178 A3
Windhill La S75 178 A3
Windhill Mount S75 178 A3
Windhill Old Rd BD10, BD18 38 F1
Windhill Rd WF1 142 F8
Winding Rd HX1 203 E3
Winding Way LS17 43 B5
Windle Edge S36 199 D1
Windle La BD20 4 A2
Windle Royd La HX2 112 C7
Windmill App LS10 99 E8
Windmill Ave S72 181 A1
Windmill Chase LS26 100 E4
Windmill Cl LS10 99 E7
Windmill Cres
Northowram HX3 93 A2
Skelmanthorpe HD8 175 B1
Windmill Ct LS14 62 B6
Windmill Dr HX3 93 A2
Windmill Field Rd LS26 100 E4
Windmill Gn LS26 100 E4
Windmill Gr BD19 117 B6
Windmill Hill Bradford BD6 74 B1
Pudsey LS28 76 C6
Windmill Hill La
Emley HD8 174 F8
Flockton WF4 156 F1
Windmill La Batley WF17 97 A1
Bradford BD6 74 C1
Guiseley LS20 22 D4
Rothwell LS26 100 E4
Whitley Common HD7 190 D3
Yeadon LS19 40 C6
Windmill Primary Sch LS10 99 E8
Windmill Rd Bramham LS23 30 E4
Middleton LS10 99 E8
Windmill Rise LS25 64 E6
Windmill View
Holmfirth HD7 189 C2
Wakefield WF1 216 C4
Windrose Cl WF6 123 A4
Windsor Ave
Ackworth M T WF7 164 C7
Leeds LS15 81 B8
Silsden BD20 5 D1
Windsor Cl Batley WF12 119 B2
Kippax LS25 83 A2
Normanton WF6 123 C1
Windsor Cres Halifax HX2 91 E1
Oakworth BD22 34 B2
Rothwell LS26 100 E6
Wakefield WF1 121 A1
Windsor Ct
16 Bradford BD5 201 B1
Leeds LS17 43 E2
Morley LS27 98 A4
Windsor Dr
Huddersfield HD5 155 A6
Knottingley WF11 126 B5
Liversedge WF15 117 B2
Skelmanthorpe HD8 175 B1
Windsor Gdns WF12 119 B2
Windsor Gn LS25 83 B7
Windsor Gr Oakworth BD22 34 B2
Thornton BD13 72 D6
Windsor Mount LS15 81 B8
Windsor Pl HD2 136 E5
Windsor Rd
Batley, Chidswell WF17 119 B2
Batley, Copley Hill WF17 97 B2
Hebden Bridge HX7 89 A4
Hemsworth WF9 181 F6
Huddersfield HD4 152 F3
Oakworth BD22 34 B2
Shipley BD18 55 B7
Todmorden OL14 108 A6
Wakefield WF2 120 F1
Windsor Rise WF8 146 B5
Windsor St Bradford BD4 201 D1
Halifax HX1 203 E2
South Elmsall WF9 183 A2
Windsor View
Batley WF12 119 B2
1 Hebden Bridge HX7 89 A4
Windsor Wlk Batley WF17 97 B2
Brighouse HX3 115 A6
Windy Bank La
Cleckheaton WF15 116 B4
Liversedge WF15 116 B4
Queensbury BD13 92 B6
Windy Gr BD15 53 D4
Windy Harbour La OL14 87 B1
Windyridge St WF4 140 F2
Wine St LS1 211 E4
Wine Tavern La HX6 111 B3
Wine Tavern Rd HX6 111 B3
Winfield Dr HD3 152 F8
Winfield Gr 4 LS2 206 B2
Winfield Pl 1 LS2 206 B2
Winfield Rd BD4 95 E6
Winfield Terr 2 LS2 206 B2
Wingate Ave BD22 34 F6
Wingate Croft WF2 160 F8
Wingate Ct LS12 209 E3
Wingate Gr WF2 160 F8
Wingate Way BD22 34 F6
Winget Ave HD4 152 F3
Wingfield Ct BD16 37 A4
Wingfield Mount BD3 75 B8
Wingfield St BD3 75 B8
Winmarith Ct S71 179 B3
Winney Bank La HD7 189 C5
Winnipeg Pl LS7 204 A2
Winnow La LS23 30 B7
Winrose App LS10 99 E7
Winrose Ave LS10 215 D1
Winrose Cl BD12 94 C4
Winrose Cres LS10 99 E8
Winrose Dr LS10 99 D8
Winrose Garth LS10 99 E8
Winrose Gr LS10 99 E8
Winrose Hill LS10 215 E1
Winsford Dr HD5 155 B7
Winslow Rd BD10 56 E4
Winston Ave BD20 16 E7
Winston Gdns 2 LS6 59 C5
Winston Mount LS6 59 C5
Winston Terr BD7 74 A5
Winter Ct BD15 54 A3
Winter Hill Elland HD3 152 A7
Halifax HX3 114 A3
Winter St HX1 202 B1
Winter's Cotts HX7 88 C2
Winter's La HX7 88 C2
Winterbourne Ave LS27 98 B6
Winterburn La HX2 112 A6
Winterburn St 3 BD21 35 C8
Winterbutlee Gr 16 OL14 108 A1
Winterbutlee Rd OL14 108 A1
Winterneb HX2 111 E5
Wintersett La WF4 162 A5
Winterton Dr BD12 94 C5
Winthorpe Ave WF3 99 D2
Winthorpe Cres WF3 99 D2
Winthorpe St LS6 59 F6
Winthorpe View WF3 99 E2
Winton Gn 2 BD6 94 B6
Winton St HD1 153 E3
Wintoun St LS7 207 D1
Wistons La HX5 135 A7
Witchfield Hill HX3 93 D6
Witham Rd BD18 54 E8
Witham Way LS25 83 B6
Withens Ct S75 178 A1
Withens End La HX4 150 E7
Withens Hill Croft HX2 91 D7
Withens La
Hebden Bridge HX7 109 F3
Ripponden HX4 150 F8
Withens New Rd
Halifax HX2 71 B2
Hebden Bridge HX7 109 E3
Withens Rd Batley WF17 96 E2
Halifax HX2 91 A7
Within Fields HX3 114 A4
Within Fields Prim Sch HX3 114 A5
Withins Cl BD5 74 B3
Withyside HD8 192 A6
Witmore St WF9 183 A3
Witton St WF1 216 C3
Woburn Dr HD5 155 B6
Woburn Terr 1 BD14 73 B4
Wold Cl BD13 72 D6
Wolfstones Rd HD7 188 D6
Wolley Ave LS12 77 D3
Wolley Ct LS12 77 D3
Wolley Dr LS12 77 D3
Wolley Gdns LS12 77 D3
Wolseley Rd LS4 205 D2
Wolseley St BD14 73 C5
Wolsey Ave 2 WF8 146 B8
Wolsley Terr 1 HX1 202 C3
Wolston Cl BD4 75 E2
Womersley Pl 4 LS28 76 D6
Womersley Rd WF11 127 B2
Womersley St HX1 202 B3
Wonder St WF1 216 C1
Wood Ave WF16 117 D5
Wood Bank Sch HX2 111 E8
Wood Bottom La HD6 114 E4
Wood Bottom Rd HD4 171 C5

Wood Cl Baildon BD17 38 B2
Hemsworth WF9 163 A2
Leeds LS7 60 C7
Low Bradley BD20 4 C5
Normanton WF6 122 E3
Rothwell LS26 100 D6
Wood Cres LS26 100 C6
Wood Croft Brighouse HD6 114 F1
Sowerby Bridge HX6 111 E3
Wood Dr LS26 100 C6
Wood End HD4 153 F3
Wood End Cl HX3 113 B3
Wood End Cotts WF14 137 F3
Wood End Cres BD18 55 D8
Wood End La
Ripponden HX4 133 D6
Shepley HD8 190 C7
Wood End Rd HD4 171 E8
Wood Farm La HD7 172 C2
Wood Gn WF10 123 F5
Wood Gr Leeds LS12 77 D7
Ossett WF5 140 D8
Wood Hey La HX7 89 B1
Wood Hill LS26 100 D6
Wood Hill Cres LS16 41 C3
Wood Hill Ct LS16 41 D4
Wood Hill Garth LS16 41 D4
Wood Hill Gdns LS16 41 D4
Wood Hill Gr LS16 41 D3
Wood Hill Rd LS16 41 D4
Wood Hill Rise LS16 41 D4
Wood La Bardsey LS17 28 E3
Barwick in E LS15 62 E6
Batley WF17 118 D3
Bradford BD2 55 F5
Brighouse HX3 114 D2
Brighouse, Hipperholme HX3 114 B8
Castleford WF10 123 F5
Crigglestone WF4 160 B3
Denby Dale HD8 191 E6
Dewsbury WF13 118 D1
Gildersome LS12 77 E2
Halifax HX2, HX3 91 E2
Holmfirth HD7 189 A6
Horsforth LS18 58 C8
Huddersfield HD4 154 C3
Kirkburton HD8 173 C4
Kirkheaton WF14 137 E4
Leeds LS6 59 E5
Leeds LS12 78 A3
Leeds, Chapel Allerton LS7 60 C7
Leeds, Farnley LS12 77 D7
Leeds, Whitecote LS13 58 C4
Mapplewell S71 178 E2
Netherton WF4 157 E7
Northowram HX3 93 B1
Pudsey LS28 57 B7
Rothwell LS26 100 D6
Royston S71 179 C1
Slaithwaite HD7 169 F5
Sowerby Bridge HX6 111 E4
Swillington LS26 102 E7
Thorp Arch LS23 14 E3
Wadsworth Moor HX2 90 B5
Wood Land Ct LS6 59 E5
Wood Lea Byram WF11 126 D8
Todmorden OL14 107 E8
Wood Moor Rd WF9 181 F7
Wood Mount
Netherton WF4 157 F6
Rothwell LS26 100 C6
Wood Nook La Honley HD4 171 C2
Sowerby Bridge HX6 112 C5
Wood Nook Terr LS28 57 C1
Wood Pl Bradford BD8 74 C8
3 Leeds LS11 214 A3
Wood Rd Bradford BD5 74 E4
Shipley BD9 55 C4
Wood Row LS26 102 B3
Wood Royd Hill La HD7 200 B8
Wood Sq HX3 92 B2
Wood St 4 Baildon BD17 38 C1
Batley WF17 118 C5
Bingley BD16 36 E6
Bradford BD15 54 C1
Bradford, Lister Hills BD8 74 C8
Brighouse HD6 115 B2
Castleford WF10 124 C8
Clayton West HD8 175 D1
Cleckheaton BD19 116 C7
Crofton WF4 144 B3
Dewsbury WF13 118 D1
East Ardsley WF3 120 D8
Elland HX5 135 A6
4 Haworth BD22 51 C6
Horsforth LS18 41 C2
Huddersfield HD1 154 A6
Huddersfield, Longwood HD3 153 A5
Huddersfield, Moldgreen HD5 154 D6
Keighley BD21 35 C6
Morley LS27 97 F5
Ossett WF5 140 D8
Skelmanthorpe HD8 174 F2
Slaithwaite HD7 151 F1
South Hiendley S72 180 F6
Steeton BD20 17 C5
Todmorden OL14 108 B6
Wakefield WF1 216 B2
Wood St N HX3 92 B2
Wood Terr HD4 154 A3
Wood Top Brighouse HD6 114 E5
Marsden HD7 168 F3
Wood Top Rd HX7 89 B2
Wood View Baildon BD17 38 A2
Denholme BD13 52 C3
Huddersfield HD2 135 D1
Morley LS27 98 C8
Wood View Ave WF10 124 A7
Wood View Bglws WF10 124 A7
Wood View Cl WF10 124 A7
Wood View Cres WF10 124 A7
Wood View Dr BD2 56 D2
Wood View Gr HD6 114 F4
Wood Villas HX7 88 C1
Wood Vine Rd LS28 57 C1
Wood Yard Cotts WF2 161 B8
Wood's Row LS28 57 E1
Woodacre Cres LS17 28 C3
Woodacre Gn LS17 28 C4
Woodacre La LS17 28 C4
Woodale Ave BD9 54 D3
Woodbine Ave 5 WF8 146 C8
Woodbine Gr BD10 56 B7
Woodbine Rd HD1 136 B1
Woodbine St
Bradford BD1 201 D3
6 Halifax HX1 202 C1
Ossett WF5 140 D7
Woodbine Terr
Bradford BD10 56 B7
Clayton West HD8 175 F3
7 Halifax HX1 202 C1
9 Horsforth LS18 58 C7
Leeds, Bramley LS13 58 C3
Leeds, Headingley LS6 59 E6
Todmorden OL14 86 B1
Woodbourne LS8 61 C7
Woodbourne Ave LS17 43 C1
Woodbridge Cl Leeds LS6 59 B5
Wakefield WF1 142 E6
Woodbridge Cres LS6 59 A6
Woodbridge Fold 2 LS6 59 A5
Woodbridge Garth LS6 59 B5
Woodbridge Gdns LS6 59 A5
Woodbridge Gn LS6 59 B5
Woodbridge Lawn LS6 59 A5
Woodbridge Pl LS6 59 A5
Woodbridge Rd LS6 59 A5
Woodbrook Ave HX2 91 C5
Woodbrook Cl HX2 91 C5
Woodbrook Pl HX2 91 C5
Woodbrook Rd HX2 91 C5
Woodburn Ave WF12 139 F6
Woodbury Rd BD8 55 B2
Woodchurch View HD7 189 B8
Woodcliffe Ct LS7 60 C7
Woodcock St WF1 142 D3
Woodcock Way WF9 183 A4
Woodcot Ave BD17 38 D2
Woodcroft WF2 142 E1
Woodcross LS27 98 A6
Woodcross End LS27 98 A7
Woodcross Fold LS27 98 A6
Woodcross Garth LS27 98 A7
Woodcross Gdns LS27 98 A6
Woodedge Ave HD5 155 A6
Woodend WF10 102 F6
Woodend Cres WF10 102 F5
Woodend Ct BD5 74 F2
Woodend Middle Sch BD18 55 D8
Woodend Rd WF14 137 F4
Woodfield Ave
Batley WF17 118 A4
Elland HX4 134 B7
Woodfield Ct HD2 153 F8
Woodfield Dr Elland HX4 134 C6
Low Bradley BD20 4 C5
Woodfield Pk WF2 161 A6
Woodfield Rd
Cullingworth BD13 52 E7
Norton DN6 184 E8
Woodfield Terr LS28 76 F6
Woodford Ave HX3 113 D4
Woodford Cl BD15 73 A8
Woodford Dr HD5 155 B7
Woodgarth Gdns BD4 75 F3
Woodhall Ave Bradford BD3 56 E1
Leeds LS5 58 E6
Woodhall Cl
Crigglestone WF4 159 F6
Netherton WF4 158 A6
Pudsey LS28 57 A2
Woodhall Cres HX3 113 A3
Woodhall Croft LS28 57 A2
Woodhall Ct Leeds LS15 81 D6
Pudsey LS28 57 A5
Woodhall Dr
Ackworth M T WF7 163 F6
Batley WF17 118 A4
Leeds LS5 58 E6
Woodhall Gr LS26 102 D3
Woodhall La LS28 57 A2
Woodhall Park Ave LS28 57 B2
Woodhall Park Cres E LS28 57 B1
Woodhall Park Cres W LS28 57 A1
Woodhall Park Croft LS28 57 B1
Woodhall Park Dr LS28 57 B1
Woodhall Park Gr LS28 57 A2
Woodhall Park Mount LS28 57 A2
Woodhall Pl BD3 56 E1
Woodhall Rd Bradford BD3 56 E2
Pudsey, Calverley LS28 57 A5
Pudsey, Upper Fagley LS28 56 E2
Woodhall Terr BD3 56 E1
Woodhall View BD3 56 F1
Woodhead Cl HD2 136 C3
Woodhead La
Brighouse HD6 115 E2
Gildersome LS27 97 C7
Woodhead Rd Batley WF17 97 B4
Bradford BD7 74 B6
Holmfirth, Brockholes HD7 172 B3
Holmfirth, Hinchcliffe Mill HD7 188 D3
Honley HD7 172 B3
Huddersfield HD4 153 E2
Woodhead St
14 Cleckheaton BD19 116 E7
Halifax HX2 202 A4
Woodhill Rise BD10 56 E8
Woodhill View LS22 13 E6
Woodhouse Ave
Huddersfield HD2 136 C2
Keighley BD21 35 C5
Woodhouse CE(A) Infant Sch HD2 136 C3
Woodhouse Cl
East Ardsley WF3 120 B6
Keighley BD21 35 C5
Woodhouse Cliff LS6 206 A4
Woodhouse Cotts HD3 151 D5
Woodhouse Cres WF6 144 B8
Woodhouse Dr BD21 35 C5
Woodhouse First Sch WF6 144 A8
Woodhouse Flats LS2 206 A2
Woodhouse Gdns HD6 136 C8
Woodhouse Gr
Huddersfield HD2 136 C2
Keighley BD21 35 C5
Todmorden OL14 108 D5
Woodhouse Grove Sch BD10 39 F1
Woodhouse Hall Rd HD2 136 C2
Woodhouse Hill HD2 136 C2
Woodhouse Hill Ave LS10 215 E2
Woodhouse Hill Gr 8 LS10 215 E2
Woodhouse Hill Pl LS10 215 E2
Woodhouse Hill Rd LS10 215 E2
Woodhouse Hill Terr 5 LS10 215 E2
Woodhouse La
Brighouse HD6 136 B8
East Ardsley WF3 120 B5
Emley HD8 176 A7
Halifax HX3 113 A3
Holmfirth HD7 188 D1
Leeds LS2 206 A2
Woolley WF4, S75 178 B5
Woodhouse Mount WF6 144 A8
Woodhouse Prim Sch HD6 136 B8
Woodhouse Rd
Keighley BD21 35 C4
Todmorden OL14 108 E6
Wakefield WF1 142 E7
Woodhouse Sq 7 LS3 206 A1
Woodhouse St LS6 206 A3
Woodhouse Terr 12 BD6 94 D8
Woodhouse Way BD21 35 C5
Woodhouse Wlk BD21 35 C5
Woodkirk Ave WF3 119 D8
Woodkirk Gdns WF12 119 B6
Woodkirk Gr Bradford BD12 94 C1
East Ardsley WF3 119 D8
Woodkirk High Sch WF3 119 C8
Woodland Ave
Crofton WF1 143 C7
Swillington LS26 82 A1
Woodland Cl Bradford BD9 54 C4
Crigglestone WF4 159 F2
Leeds LS15 81 C8
Woodland Cres
Rothwell LS26 100 D6
Shipley BD9 54 C4
Swillington LS26 82 A1
Woodland Croft LS18 41 C2
Woodland Ct BD16 36 E5
Woodland Dr
Brighouse HD6 114 F3
Halifax HX2 112 D5
Leeds LS7 204 A3
Skelmanthorpe HD8 175 B1
Swillington LS26 81 F1
Wakefield WF2 160 D6
Woodland Gr
Ackworth M T WF7 146 A1
Dewsbury WF13 138 F8
Leeds LS7 207 E4
Shipley BD9 54 C5
Swillington LS26 82 A1
Woodland Hall HX7 88 A4
Woodland Hill LS15 81 B8
Woodland La LS7 204 A3
Woodland Meadow HD8 173 F7
Woodland Mount 1 LS7 207 E4
Woodland Park Rd LS6 59 E5
Woodland Pk LS26 101 C5
Woodland Rd
Huddersfield HD2 136 F2
Leeds LS15 81 B8
Wakefield WF2 141 D5
Woodland Rise Leeds LS15 81 C8
Wakefield WF2 141 D6
Woodland Sq
Brighouse HD6 115 C1
1 Leeds LS12 77 F8
Woodland Terr LS7 60 A7
Woodland View
Blackshaw Head HX7 88 C2
Leeds LS7 204 A3
Pontefract WF8 146 E6
Pudsey LS28 57 A7
Woodlands Crofton WF4 143 F1
East Ardsley WF3 120 C7
Horbury WF4 141 C2
Ilkley LS29 8 D4
Leeds LS17 43 E2
Ossett WF5 140 D7
Sowerby Bridge HX6 111 F2
Woodlands Ave
Castleford WF10 125 C6
Cleckheaton BD19 96 A1
Halifax HX3 92 C1
Holmfirth HD7 189 C8
Lepton HD8 155 E3
Pudsey LS28 57 C1
Todmorden OL14 108 B6
Woodlands CE First Sch BD12 95 A4
Woodlands Cl
Denby Dale HD8 192 A6
East Ardsley WF3 120 C7
Huddersfield HD2 137 A6
Ilkley LS29 7 E4
Pudsey BD10 39 F1
Scarcroft LS14 45 C8
Woodlands Cres
Cleckheaton BD19 96 A1
Hemsworth WF9 181 E8
Woodlands Croft LS25 103 B8
Woodlands Ct LS16 42 B1
Woodlands Dr
Cleckheaton BD19 96 A1
East Ardsley WF3 120 C7
Garforth LS25 83 B6
Lepton HD8 155 E2
Morley LS27 97 F6
Pudsey BD10 39 F1
Yeadon LS19 40 C2
Woodlands End HD8 155 E3
Woodlands Fold BD11 96 B5
Woodlands Gr Baildon BD17 37 F2
Bradford BD13 73 B1
Halifax HX3 92 C1
Ilkley LS29 7 E4
Kippax LS25 103 C8
Pudsey LS28 57 C1
Shipley BD16 54 B7
Woodlands La WF13 138 F8
Woodlands Middle Sch WF6 144 A8
Woodlands Mount HX3 92 C2
Woodlands Park Gr LS28 76 D5
Woodlands Park Rd LS28 76 D5
Woodlands Pk LS14 45 C8
Woodlands Prim Sch LS9 208 B3
Woodlands Rd
Batley WF17 118 A8
Bingley BD16 37 C4
Bradford, Girlington BD8 55 A1
Bradford, Little Moor BD13 73 A1
Cleckheaton BD19 96 A1
Halifax HX5 134 F8
Halifax, Woodlands HX3 92 C1
Lepton HD8 155 E3
Woodlands Rd E HD8 155 D3
Woodlands Rise
Haworth BD22 51 C6
Ilkley LS29 7 E4
Woodlands St BD8 74 C8
Woodlands Terr
Bradford, Girlington BD8 55 A1
Bradford, Lower Woodlands BD12 95 B5
Pudsey LS28 57 C1
Woodlands The
Hebden Bridge HX7 89 A2
Pontefract WF8 146 E6
Woodlands View
8 Halifax HX3 92 C1
Kippax LS25 103 C8
Scarcroft LS14 45 C7
Woodlands Way HD8 155 E2
Woodlea Boston Spa LS23 30 D8
6 South Elmsall WF9 182 F2
Woodlea App Leeds LS6 42 F1
Yeadon LS19 39 F6
Woodlea Ave HD3 153 C6
Woodlea Chase LS6 59 F8
Woodlea Cl LS19 39 F5
Woodlea Croft LS6 42 F1
Woodlea Ct
Leeds, Blackwood LS17 44 B4
Leeds, Meanwood LS6 59 F8
Woodlea Dr Leeds LS6 42 F1
Yeadon LS19 39 F5
Woodlea Garth LS6 42 F1
Woodlea Gdns LS6 42 F1
Woodlea Gr
1 Leeds, Beeston LS11 213 F3
Leeds, Meanwood LS6 59 F8
Yeadon LS19 39 F6
Woodlea Lawn LS6 42 F1
Woodlea Mount
Leeds LS11 214 A3
Yeadon LS19 39 F6
Woodlea Pk LS6 59 F8
Woodlea Pl
Leeds, Beeston Hill LS11 214 A3
Leeds, Meanwood LS6 42 F1
Woodlea Rd LS19 39 F5
Woodlea St LS11 213 F3
Woodlea View LS19 39 F5
Woodleigh Ave
Bradford BD5 74 E1
Garforth LS25 82 E7
Woodleigh Cres WF7 163 F6
Woodlesford Cres HX2 91 B2
Woodlesford Junior & Infants Sch LS26 101 C7
Woodlesford Prim Sch LS26 101 D7
Woodlesford Sta LS26 101 D7
Woodliegh Gr HD4 153 C1
Woodliffe Cres LS7 60 C7
Woodliffe Dr LS7 60 C7
Woodman Ave Elland HX5 134 F5
Huddersfield HD2 137 A5
Woodman Ct BD6 93 E6
Woodman St LS15 81 A8
Woodmoor Cl WF4 159 E4
Woodmoor Dr WF4 159 E4
Woodmoor Rd WF2 160 B5
Woodmoor Rise WF4 159 E5
Woodnook Cl LS16 41 D2
Woodnook Dr LS16 41 D3
Woodnook Garth LS16 41 D3
Woodnook Rd LS16 41 D3
Woodrow Cres LS26 102 A3
Woodrow Dr BD12 94 E6
Woodroyd HD7 152 C5
Woodroyd Ave
Bradford BD5 74 F2
Honley HD7 172 B5
Royston S71 179 C1
Woodroyd Cl S71 179 C1
Woodroyd Dr HX3 91 F2
Woodroyd Gdns Ilkley LS29 8 F3
Sowerby Bridge HX2 111 F5
Woodroyd Middle Sch BD5 74 E2
Woodroyd Rd Bradford BD5 74 E3
Bradford, Marshfields BD5 74 E2
Woodroyd Terr BD5 74 F2
Woods Ave HD7 169 B4
Woods Mews LS29 8 C4
Woods Mount HD7 169 B4
Woods Terr HD7 169 B4
Woodside Castleford WF10 125 C8
Denby Dale HD8 192 A6
Keighley BD20 18 A1
Shipley BD18 55 D8
Wakefield WF2 120 E2
Woodside Ave
Crofton WF4 144 C3
Leeds LS6 59 F7
Leeds, Burley LS4 59 C2
Shipley, Cottingley BD16 53 F7
2 Shipley, Saltaire BD18 54 E8
Wakefield WF2 120 E2
Woodside CE Infant Sch LS18 41 D1
Woodside Cl LS27 98 A6
Woodside Cres
Batley WF17 118 A4
Crofton WF4 144 C4
Halifax HX3 92 B1
Shipley BD16 53 F7
Woodside Ct
Cullingworth BD13 52 D6
Horsforth LS18 58 E8
Woodside Dr Morley LS27 98 A7
Shipley BD16 53 F7
Wakefield WF2 120 E2
Woodside Gdns LS27 98 A7
Woodside Gr Elland HX4 134 D6
Halifax HX3 92 C1
Kippax WF10 102 F6
Woodside Hill Cl LS18 58 E8
Woodside La
Huddersfield HD2 136 B4
Morley LS27 98 A7
Woodside Lawn LS12 77 D7
Woodside Mews LS6 59 F7
Woodside Middle & First Schs BD6 94 A6
Woodside Mount HX3 203 D4
Woodside Park Ave LS18 58 D8
Woodside Park Dr LS18 58 D8
Woodside Pl Halifax HX3 92 B1
Leeds LS4 59 C2
Woodside Rd
Boston Spa LS23 30 B7
Bradford BD12 94 C4
Halifax HX3 203 D4
Huddersfield HD4 153 D2
Silsden BD20 5 C1
Woodside St WF10 102 F6
Woodside Terr
6 Elland HX4 134 D6
Halifax HX3 92 C1
7 Leeds LS4 59 C2
Woodside Veiw HD4 152 F3
Woodside View
Elland HX4 134 D6
Halifax HX3 92 B1
Holmfirth HD7 188 E4
Leeds LS4 59 C2
Shipley BD16 54 A7
Woodsley Gn LS6 205 F2
Woodsley Rd
Bradford BD10 56 A6
Leeds LS2, LS3, LS6 205 F2
Woodsley Terr LS2 206 A1
Woodsome Ave WF14 137 E6
Woodsome Dr Lepton HD8 155 D2
Mirfield WF14 137 F6
Woodsome Est WF17 118 B4
Woodsome Hall Golf Course HD8 155 B1
Woodsome Hall La HD8 173 C8
Woodsome Lees La HD8 173 D7
Woodsome Pk HD8 155 D2
Woodsome Rd HD4 155 B2
Woodstock Cl LS16 42 D3
Woodstock Cres HD3 153 B8
Woodstock Wlk BD5 201 B1
Woodthorne Croft LS17 44 A4

Woodthorpe Cl WF2 ... 160 E7
Woodthorpe Dr WF2 ... 160 E7
Woodthorpe Glades WF2 .. 160 E7
Woodthorpe La WF2 ... 160 E6
Woodthorpe Park Dr
WF2 ... 160 E7
Woodthorpe Terr HD1 ... 153 F5
Woodvale Cl BD4 ... 75 E5
Woodvale Cres BD16 ... 37 A5
Woodvale Gr BD7 ... 73 E5
Woodvale Rd HD6 ... 115 B3
Woodvale Way BD7 ... 73 E5
Woodview Birkenshaw BD11 . 96 D7
Bradford BD8 ... 55 D3
Woodview Ave BD17 ... 38 F4
Woodview Cl LS18 ... 41 C2
Woodview Gr LS11 ... 214 B2
Woodview Mount LS11 ... 214 B2
Woodview Pl LS11 ... 214 B2
Woodview Rd
Keighley BD22 ... 34 F4
Leeds LS11 ... 214 B2
Woodview St LS11 ... 214 B2
Woodview Terr
Bradford BD8 ... 55 D3
10 Keighley BD21 ... 35 B4
Leeds LS11 ... 214 B2
Woodville Ave
2 Horsforth LS18 ... 58 D8
Huddersfield HD7 ... 152 E4
Woodville Cres 4 LS18 ... 58 D8
Woodville Ct Leeds LS8 ... 44 B1
Wakefield WF2 ... 142 C2
Woodville Gr
9 Haworth BD22 ... 51 F8
1 Horsforth LS18 ... 58 D8
Middleton LS10 ... 215 E1
Woodville Pl Bradford BD9 ... 54 F4
6 Horsforth LS18 ... 58 E8
Huddersfield HD2 ... 136 E6
Woodville Rd
Dewsbury WF12 ... 139 D8
Keighley BD20 ... 35 B8
Woodville Sq LS10 ... 215 E1
Woodville St 25 Halifax HX3 . 92 A1
5 Horsforth LS18 ... 58 E8
Shipley BD18 ... 55 D8
Woodville Terr
Bradford BD5 ... 201 A1
10 Haworth BD22 ... 51 F8
3 Horsforth LS18 ... 58 D8
Woodward Ct WF14 ... 138 B7
Woodway Horsforth LS18 ... 58 C7
Shipley BD16 ... 53 F7
Woodway Dr LS18 ... 58 C7
Woodworth Gr BD21 ... 35 B3
Wool Row La HD8 ... 174 C5
Wool St WF16 ... 117 D3
Woolcomb Ct BD9 ... 55 B2
Woolcroft Dr HD7 ... 189 C6
Wooldale Junior Sch
HD7 ... 189 D6
Wooldale Rd HD7 ... 189 C6
Wooler Ave LS11 ... 214 A2
Wooler Dr LS11 ... 214 A2
Wooler Gr LS11 ... 214 A2
Wooler Pl LS11 ... 213 F2
Wooler Rd LS11 ... 213 F2
Wooler St LS11 ... 213 F2
Woolford Way WF3 ... 121 D6
Woolgreaves Ave WF2 ... 160 D6
Woolgreaves Cl WF2 ... 160 D6
Woolgreaves Croft WF2 .. 160 D6
Woolgreaves Dr WF2 ... 160 D7
Woolgreaves Garth WF2 .. 160 D6
Wooller Rd BD12 ... 94 D5
Woolley Colliery Rd S75 ... 177 E2
Woolley Edge La WF4 ... 177 E6
Woolley Hall Coll WF4 ... 178 B7
Woolley Low Moor La
WF4 ... 159 D2
Woolley Park Gdns WF4 ... 178 A7
Woolley View WF4 ... 159 F2
Woollin Ave WF3 ... 119 E6
Woollin Cres WF3 ... 119 E6
Woolmarket 6 WF8 ... 146 D8
Woolpack HX1 ... 203 E3
Woolpack's Yd WF1 ... 216 A2
Woolrow La HD6 ... 115 C6
Woolshops HX1 ... 203 E3
Woolstocks La S75 ... 193 E3
Wootton St BD5 ... 74 E4
Worcester Ave LS10 ... 99 F4
Worcester Cl WF3 ... 99 C1
Worcester Dr LS10 ... 99 F4
Worcester Gr HD4 ... 154 B3
Worcester Pl BD4 ... 75 A4
Worden Gr BD7 ... 73 E4
Wordsworth App WF8 ... 125 D2
Wordsworth Ct LS26 ... 101 C3
Wordsworth Dr WF11 ... 126 B4
Wordsworth Gr WF3 ... 121 F5
Wordsworth Way BD16 ... 37 A5
Workhouse La Elland HX4 .. 134 D6
Halifax HX2 ... 112 A7
Wormald Row LS2 ... 211 F4
Wormald St
Dewsbury WF13 ... 139 C8
Huddersfield HD5 ... 154 F3
Liversedge WF15 ... 117 C3
Worrall Rd WF2 ... 160 A4
Worrall St LS27 ... 97 F3
Worsley Pl DN6 ... 184 F2
Worsnop Bldgs 15 BD12 ... 94 C4
Worsnop St BD12 ... 94 D6
Worstead Rd BD22 ... 51 F8
Worth Ave BD21 ... 18 E1
Worth Bridge Rd BD21 ... 35 E8
Worth Valley Middle Sch
BD22 ... 35 A3
Worth Way BD21 ... 35 C6
Worthing Head Cl 2 BD12 . 94 D3
Worthing Head Rd BD12 ... 94 D3
Worthing St BD12 ... 94 D3
Worthinghead First Sch
BD12 ... 94 D3
Worthington St BD8 ... 74 C8
Worthville Cl BD21 ... 35 C5
Wortley Heights LS12 ... 210 A2
Wortley High Sch LS12 ... 209 D2
Wortley La LS12 ... 210 C2
Wortley Moor La LS12 ... 209 E2
Wortley Moor Rd LS12 ... 209 D3
Wortley Pk LS12 ... 210 B2
Wortley Pl WF9 ... 181 C7
Wortley Rd LS12 ... 209 E3
Wortley St BD16 ... 37 B3
Wortley Twrs LS12 ... 210 B2
Worts Hill La HD3 ... 151 B4
Worts Hill Side HD7 ... 151 C4
Wrangbrook La WF9 ... 183 D7
Wrangbrook Rd WF9 ... 183 D8
Wranghorn Ave LS6 ... 205 F3
Wranghorn Pl LS6 ... 205 F3
Wranghorn Terr LS6 ... 205 F3
Wray's Bldgs WF4 ... 141 A1
Wrelton Cl S71 ... 179 B3
Wren Ave BD7 ... 73 E5
Wren Croft WF8 ... 125 D3
Wren Dr LS27 ... 98 D3
Wren Garth WF2 ... 160 D5
Wren Hill WF17 ... 118 A8
Wren Nest Rd HX6 ... 132 A4
Wren St 17 Haworth BD22 ... 51 D7
Huddersfield HD1 ... 153 D5
Keighley BD21 ... 35 C8
Wrenbeck Ave LS21 ... 11 B2
Wrenbeck Cl LS21 ... 11 B2
Wrenbeck Dr LS21 ... 11 B2
Wrenbury Ave LS16 ... 41 D5
Wrenbury Cres LS16 ... 41 E5
Wrenbury Gr LS16 ... 41 E5
Wrenthorpe La
Wakefield WF2 ... 120 D1
Wakefield, Wrenthorpe WF2 120 E1
Wrenthorpe Primary Sch
WF2 ... 120 F2
Wrenthorpe Rd WF2 ... 120 E2
Wrexhall Rd WF12 ... 118 E2
Wrexham Rd LS29 ... 9 D2
Wright Ave BD22 ... 34 D3
Wright St 5 Bacup OL13 ... 106 A7
Oakworth BD22 ... 34 D2
Sutton in C BD20 ... 16 D5
Wrigley Ave BD4 ... 75 B1
Wrigley Hill HX2 ... 91 E5
Wroe Cres BD12 ... 94 C3
Wroe Pl BD12 ... 94 C3
Wroe St WF13 ... 117 F1
Wroe Terr BD12 ... 94 C3
Wrose Ave Bradford BD2 ... 56 A5
Shipley BD18 ... 55 D6
Wrose Brow Rd BD18 ... 55 D8
Wrose Dr BD18 ... 55 D6
Wrose Gr BD18 ... 55 D6
Wrose Hill Pl BD2 ... 55 D5
Wrose Mount BD18 ... 55 E6
Wrose Rd Bradford BD2 ... 56 A6
Shipley BD18 ... 55 E6
Wrose View Baildon BD17 ... 38 C3
Shipley BD18 ... 55 D6
Wrosecliffe Gr BD10 ... 55 F8
Wycliffe Cl LS13 ... 57 D5
Wycliffe Dr LS17 ... 43 D2
Wycliffe Gdns BD18 ... 55 A8
Wycliffe Rd Pudsey LS13 ... 57 D5
Shipley BD18 ... 55 A8
Wycliffe St WF5 ... 140 D7
Wycoller Rd BD12 ... 94 C4
Wycombe Gn BD4 ... 75 E3
Wyebeck Ave LS9 ... 80 D7
Wyke Cres BD12 ... 94 D2
Wyke La BD12 ... 94 E3
Wyke Manor Sch BD12 ... 94 D3
Wyke Middle Sch BD12 ... 94 C3
Wyke Old La HD6 ... 115 B7
Wykebeck Ave LS9 ... 80 D8
Wykebeck Cres LS9 ... 80 D8
Wykebeck Gdns LS9 ... 80 D8
Wykebeck Gr LS9 ... 80 D8
Wykebeck Mount LS9 ... 80 D8
Wykebeck Pl LS9 ... 80 E8
Wykebeck Primary Sch
LS9 ... 61 D2
Wykebeck Rd LS9 ... 80 D8
Wykebeck Sq LS9 ... 80 D8
Wykebeck St LS9 ... 80 D8
Wykebeck Terr LS9 ... 80 D8
Wykebeck Valley Rd LS9 ... 61 D2
Wykebeck View LS9 ... 80 D8
Wykelea Cl BD12 ... 94 D3
Wyncliffe Gdns LS17 ... 43 D2
Wyncroft Gr LS16 ... 24 F2
Wyncroft Rise BD18 ... 55 D5
Wyndham Ave BD2 ... 55 F3
Wyndy Ridge BD13 ... 72 C7
Wynford Ave LS16 ... 42 B1
Wynford Dr WF9 ... 183 A3
Wynford Gr LS16 ... 42 B1
Wynford Mount LS16 ... 42 A1
Wynford Rise LS16 ... 42 B1
Wynford Terr LS16 ... 42 A1
Wynford Way BD12 ... 94 E7
Wynmore Ave LS16 ... 24 F2
Wynmore Cres LS16 ... 24 F2
Wynmore Dr Bramhope LS16 24 F2
Huddersfield HD3 ... 134 F1
Wynne St BD1 ... 74 D8
Wynthorpe Rd WF4 ... 141 B1
Wynyard Dr LS27 ... 97 F4
Wyther Ave 2 LS5 ... 58 F3
Wyther Dr LS5 ... 59 A3
Wyther Gn LS5 ... 59 A3
Wyther La LS5 ... 58 F3
Wyther Lane Ind Est LS5 ... 58 F3
Wyther Park Ave LS12 ... 58 F1
Wyther Park Cl 1 LS12 ... 58 F1
Wyther Park County
Primary Sch LS5 ... 58 F3
Wyther Park Cres LS12 ... 58 F2
Wyther Park Gr LS12 ... 58 F2
Wyther Park Hill LS12 ... 58 F2
Wyther Park Mount LS12 ... 58 F1
Wyther Park Pl LS12 ... 58 F2
Wyther Park Rd LS12 ... 58 F1
Wyther Park Sq LS12 ... 58 E1
Wyther Park St LS12 ... 58 F1
Wyther Park Terr LS12 ... 58 F1
Wyther Park View LS12 ... 58 F2
Wyvern Ave HD3 ... 153 C6
Wyvern Cl Batley WF17 ... 118 C6
Bradford BD7 ... 73 F5
Wyvern Pl HX2 ... 202 A4
Wyvern Terr HX2 ... 202 A4
Wyverne Rd HD7 ... 152 E4
Wyvil Cres LS29 ... 8 E5
Wyvil Rd LS29 ... 8 E5

Yarborough Croft HX3 ... 93 A4
Yard No 1 WF17 ... 118 A3
Yard No 2 WF17 ... 118 A3
Yard No 4 1 WF17 ... 117 F8
Yardley Way BD12 ... 94 E6
Yarn St LS10 ... 215 E4
Yarwood Gr 2 BD7 ... 73 E3
Yate La BD22 ... 51 C3
Yates Flat BD18 ... 55 D6
Yates La HD3 ... 153 B4
Ye Farre Cl 3 HD6 ... 115 A4
Yeadon Dr HX3 ... 114 A4
Yeadon House BD20 ... 16 C5
Yeadon Moor Rd
Yeadon LS19 ... 40 E6
Yeadon LS18 ... 41 A8
Yeadon Westfield
Infant Sch LS19 ... 39 F6
Yeadon Westfield
Junior Sch LS19 ... 39 F6
Yew Gr HD4 ... 152 F3
Yew Green Ave HD4 ... 153 E3
Yew Green Rd HD4 ... 153 E3
Yew La LS25 ... 83 B6
Yew Pk HD6 ... 114 E5
Yew St HD2 ... 136 A1
Yew Tree HD7 ... 169 F7
Yew Tree Ave BD8 ... 54 D1
Yew Tree Cl
Low Bradley BD20 ... 4 C6
Shipley BD18 ... 55 D6
Yew Tree Cres BD8 ... 54 E1
Yew Tree Ct
6 Liversedge WF15 ... 117 A5
Todmorden OL14 ... 129 A8
Yew Tree Gr BD8 ... 54 E1
Yew Tree La Bradford BD13 .. 72 E8
Holmfirth HD7 ... 188 C3
Huddersfield HD4, HD7 ... 152 F3
Leeds LS15 ... 81 E6
Slaithwaite HD7 ... 169 F7
Yew Tree Rd
Huddersfield HD2, HD3 ... 135 B3
Shepley HD8 ... 173 F1
Yew Tree St WF1 ... 142 E4
Yew Tree Wlk WF11 ... 126 E2
Yew Trees Ave HX3 ... 93 A3
Yew Trees Croft HX2 ... 90 C1
Yewbank Cl LS29 ... 8 A4
Yewbank Terr LS29 ... 8 A4
Yewdall Rd LS13 ... 57 E5
Yewdall Way BD10 ... 56 C6
Yews Hill Rd HD1, HD4 ... 153 E4
Yews Mount HD1 ... 153 F4
York Ave HD2 ... 136 A2
York Cl WF9 ... 183 A4
York Cres 1 BD16 ... 37 A2
York Dr
Batley, Bank Foot WF17 ... 118 D6
Batley, Nunroyd WF16 ... 117 D6
York Gate LS21 ... 23 C4
York Gr Batley WF17 ... 118 D6
4 Mirfield WF14 ... 137 F5
York House Bradford BD10 ... 56 C7
4 Elland HX5 ... 134 F7
York Pl Ackworth M T WF7 ... 164 B7
8 Cleckheaton BD19 ... 116 D8
Leeds LS1 ... 211 E4
14 Todmorden OL14 ... 108 B5
Wetherby LS22 ... 13 F6
York Rd Batley WF17 ... 118 C6
Bickerton LS22 ... 14 D7
Burley in W LS29 ... 9 F1
Dewsbury WF12 ... 139 F8
Leeds, Killingbeck LS14, LS9 ... 61 E1
Leeds, Whinmoor
LS14, LS15 ... 62 C6
Mirfield WF14 ... 137 F5
Wetherby LS22 ... 14 D7
York Road Ind Est LS22 ... 13 F6
York St Bingley BD16 ... 37 A2
Bradford BD8 ... 73 E7
Brighouse HD6 ... 115 A1
Castleford WF10 ... 124 E8
Dearne S63 ... 194 F1
Glusburn BD20 ... 16 D7
Halifax HX1 ... 203 D2
2 Hebden Bridge HX7 ... 89 A2
Hemsworth WF9 ... 181 E5
Leeds LS9 ... 212 A3
Normanton WF6 ... 122 F3
Queensbury BD13 ... 72 E1
Todmorden OL14 ... 108 B6
York Terr HX3 ... 92 B1
York Villas WF6 ... 123 B2
Yorkshire Martyrs
Collegiate Sch BD4 ... 96 A8
Yorkshire Mining Mus
WF4 ... 157 E6
Yorkshire Sculpture Pk
WF4 ... 176 E7
Yorkshire Television
Studios LS3 ... 205 E1
Yorkshire Way BD7 ... 74 B3
Young St BD8 ... 73 F8
Young's Ct LS25 ... 64 E6

Zakaria High Sch WF17 ... 118 D4
Zealand St BD4 ... 75 D4
Zermatt Gr LS7 ... 60 C6
Zermatt Mount LS7 ... 60 C6
Zermatt St LS7 ... 204 A2
Zermatt Terr LS7 ... 204 A2
Zetland Pl LS8 ... 207 F3
Zetland St
12 Huddersfield HD1 ... 154 B6
Wakefield WF1 ... 216 B2
Zion Cl HD3 ... 135 B1
Zion Dr S75 ... 178 B1
Zion St Bacup OL13 ... 106 A3
Hebden Bridge HX7 ... 89 E1
Leeds LS9 ... 212 B2
Ossett WF5 ... 119 C1
Zoar St LS27 ... 98 A4

Notes

Addresses

Name and Address	Telephone	Page	Grid Reference

Name and Address	Telephone	Page	Grid Reference

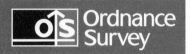

Ordnance Survey

STREET ATLASES

ORDER FORM

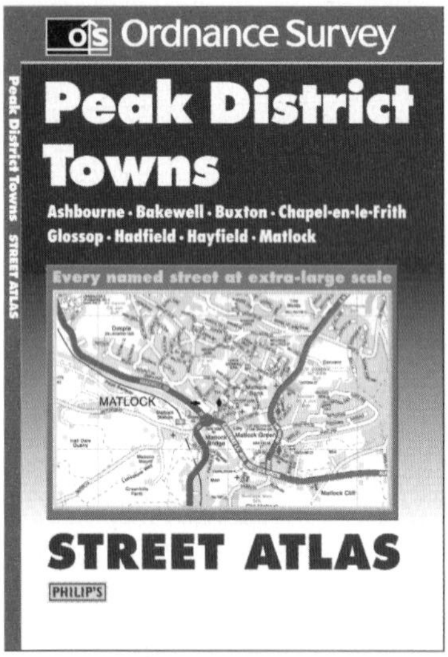

PHILIP'S

The Street Atlases are available from all good bookshops or by mail order direct from the publisher. Orders can be made in the following ways. **By phone** Ring our special Credit Card Hotline on **01933 443863** during office hours (9am to 5pm) or leave a message on the answering machine, quoting your full credit card number plus expiry date and your full name and address. **By post or fax** Fill out the order form below (you may photocopy it) and post it to: **Philip's Direct, 27 Sanders Road, Wellingborough, Northants NN8 4NL** or fax it to: **01933 443849**. Before placing an order by post, by fax or on the answering machine, please telephone to check availability and prices.

COLOUR LOCAL ATLASES

	PAPERBACK	
	Quantity @ £3.50 each	£ Total
CANNOCK, LICHFIELD, RUGELEY	☐ 0 540 07625 2	➤ ☐
DERBY AND BELPER	☐ 0 540 07608 2	➤ ☐
NORTHWICH, WINSFORD, MIDDLEWICH	☐ 0 540 07589 2	➤ ☐
PEAK DISTRICT TOWNS	☐ 0 540 07609 0	➤ ☐
STAFFORD, STONE, UTTOXETER	☐ 0 540 07626 0	➤ ☐
WARRINGTON, WIDNES, RUNCORN	☐ 0 540 07588 4	➤ ☐

COLOUR REGIONAL ATLASES

	HARDBACK	SPIRAL	POCKET	
	Quantity @ £10.99 each	Quantity @ £8.99 each	Quantity @ £5.99 each	£ Total
BERKSHIRE	☐ 0 540 06170 0	☐ 0 540 06172 7	☐ 0 540 06173 5	➤ ☐
	Quantity @ £10.99 each	Quantity @ £8.99 each	Quantity @ £4.99 each	£ Total
MERSEYSIDE	☐ 0 540 06480 7	☐ 0 540 06481 5	☐ 0 540 06482 3	➤ ☐
	Quantity @ £12.99 each	Quantity @ £9.99 each	Quantity @ £4.99 each	£ Total
DURHAM	☐ 0 540 06365 7	☐ 0 540 06366 5	☐ 0 540 06367 3	➤ ☐
EAST KENT	☐ 0 540 07483 7	☐ 0 540 07276 1	☐ 0 540 07287 7	➤ ☐
WEST KENT	☐ 0 540 07366 0	☐ 0 540 07367 9	☐ 0 540 07369 5	➤ ☐
	Quantity @ £12.99 each	Quantity @ £9.99 each	Quantity @ £5.50 each	£ Total
GREATER MANCHESTER	☐ 0 540 06485 8	☐ 0 540 06486 6	☐ 0 540 06487 4	➤ ☐
TYNE AND WEAR	☐ 0 540 06370 3	☐ 0 540 06371 1	☐ 0 540 06372 X	➤ ☐
	Quantity @ £12.99 each	Quantity @ £9.99 each	Quantity @ £5.99 each	£ Total
BIRMINGHAM & WEST MIDLANDS	☐ 0 540 07603 1	☐ 0 540 07604 X	☐ 0 540 07605 8	➤ ☐
BUCKINGHAMSHIRE	☐ 0 540 07466 7	☐ 0 540 07467 5	☐ 0 540 07468 3	➤ ☐
CHESHIRE	☐ 0 540 07507 8	☐ 0 540 07508 6	☐ 0 540 07509 4	➤ ☐
DERBYSHIRE	☐ 0 540 07531 0	☐ 0 540 07532 9	☐ 0 540 07533 7	➤ ☐
EDINBURGH & East Central Scotland	☐ 0 540 07653 8	☐ 0 540 07654 6	☐ 0 540 07656 2	➤ ☐
GLASGOW & West Central Scotland	☐ 0 540 07648 1	☐ 0 540 07649 X	☐ 0 540 07651 1	➤ ☐

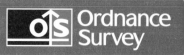

Ordnance Survey

STREET ATLASES ORDER FORM

COLOUR REGIONAL ATLASES

	HARDBACK	SPIRAL	POCKET	
	Quantity @ £12.99 each	Quantity @ £9.99 each	Quantity @ £5.99 each	£ Total
NORTH HAMPSHIRE	☐ 0 540 07471 3	☐ 0 540 07472 1	☐ 0 540 07473 X	➤ ☐
SOUTH HAMPSHIRE	☐ 0 540 07476 4	☐ 0 540 07477 2	☐ 0 540 07478 0	➤ ☐
HERTFORDSHIRE	☐ 0 540 06174 3	☐ 0 540 06175 1	☐ 0 540 06176 X	➤ ☐
OXFORDSHIRE	☐ 0 540 07512 4	☐ 0 540 07513 2	☐ 0 540 07514 0	➤ ☐
SURREY	☐ 0 540 06435 1	☐ 0 540 06436 X	☐ 0 540 06438 6	➤ ☐
EAST SUSSEX	☐ 0 540 07306 7	☐ 0 540 07307 5	☐ 0 540 07312 1	➤ ☐
WEST SUSSEX	☐ 0 540 07319 9	☐ 0 540 07323 7	☐ 0 540 07327 X	➤ ☐
WARWICKSHIRE	☐ 0 540 07560 4	☐ 0 540 07561 2	☐ 0 540 07562 0	➤ ☐
SOUTH YORKSHIRE	—	☐ 0 540 07667 8	☐ 0 540 07669 4	➤ ☐
WEST YORKSHIRE	☐ 0 540 07671 6	☐ 0 540 07672 4	☐ 0 540 07674 0	➤ ☐
	Quantity @ £14.99 each	Quantity @ £9.99 each	Quantity @ £5.99 each	£ Total
LANCASHIRE	☐ 0 540 06440 8	☐ 0 540 06441 6	☐ 0 540 06443 2	➤ ☐
NOTTINGHAMSHIRE	☐ 0 540 07541 8	☐ 0 540 07542 6	☐ 0 540 07543 4	➤ ☐
STAFFORDSHIRE	☐ 0 540 07549 3	☐ 0 540 07550 7	☐ 0 540 07551 5	➤ ☐

BLACK AND WHITE REGIONAL ATLASES

	HARDBACK	SOFTBACK	POCKET	
	Quantity @ £11.99 each	Quantity @ £8.99 each	Quantity @ £3.99 each	£ Total
BRISTOL AND AVON	☐ 0 540 06140 9	☐ 0 540 06141 7	☐ 0 540 06142 5	➤ ☐
	Quantity @ £12.99 each	Quantity @ £9.99 each	Quantity @ £4.99 each	£ Total
CARDIFF, SWANSEA & GLAMORGAN	☐ 0 540 06186 7	☐ 0 540 06187 5	☐ 0 540 06207 3	➤ ☐
EAST ESSEX	☐ 0 540 05848 3	☐ 0 540 05866 1	☐ 0 540 05850 5	➤ ☐
WEST ESSEX	☐ 0 540 05849 1	☐ 0 540 05867 X	☐ 0 540 05851 3	➤ ☐

Post to: Philip's Direct,
27 Sanders Road, Wellingborough,
Northants NN8 4NL

◆ Free postage and packing

◆ All available titles will normally be dispatched within 5 working days of receipt of order but please allow up to 28 days for delivery

☐ Please tick this box if you do not wish your name to be used by other carefully selected organisations that may wish to send you information about other products and services

Registered Office: 2-4 Heron Quays, London E14 4JP

Registered in England number: 3597451

I enclose a cheque / postal order, for a **total** of ☐

made payable to *Octopus Publishing Group Ltd*, or please debit my

☐ MasterCard ☐ American Express ☐ Visa

account by ☐

Account no ☐☐☐☐ ☐☐☐☐ ☐☐☐☐ ☐☐☐☐

Expiry date ☐☐ ☐☐

Signature..

Name..

Address...

....

....

....POSTCODE

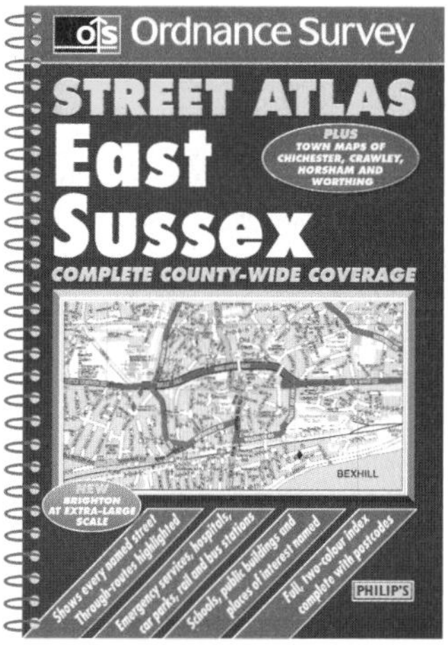

PHILIP'S

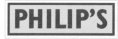